PSYCHOLOGY

PSYCHOLOGY

Richard M. Lerner Pennsylvania State University

Philip C. Kendall Temple University

Dale T. Miller Simon Fraser University

David F. Hultsch University of Victoria

Robert A. Jensen Southern Illinois University

MACMILLAN PUBLISHING COMPANY
NEW YORK

Copyright © 1986, Macmillan Publishing Company,
a division of Macmillan, Inc.

Printed in the United States of America

All rights reserved. No part of this book may be reproduced or transmitted in any form or by any means, electronic or mechanical, including photocopying, recording, or any information storage and retrieval system, without permission in writing from the publisher.

Macmillan Publishing Company
866 Third Avenue, New York, New York 10022

Collier Macmillan Canada, Inc.

Library of Congress Cataloging in Publication Data

Main entry under title:

Psychology.

    Bibliography: p. 655
    Includes index.
    1. Psychology.   I. Lerner, Richard M.
BF81.P7 1986   150   85-7123
ISBN 0-02-369880-2

Printing: 1 2 3 4 5 6 7 8   Year: 6 7 8 9 0 1 2 3

CREDITS

Page 1 photo, Owen Franken/Stock, Boston. Pages 18–19, Highlight 1.2 from American Psychological Association (1973), *Ethical principles in the conduct of research with human participants.* Copyright 1973 by the American Psychological Association. Used by permission of the publisher. Page 23 photo, Arthur Tress/Photo Researchers, Inc. Page 68, Figure 3.2 (see color insert No. 1), courtesy of Richmond Products, Boca Raton, Fla. Page 76, Figure 3.9 and page 77, Figure 3.10 redrawn from Figure 6-6, p. 160 in S. Coren, C. Porac, and L. M. Ward (1984), *Sensation and perception,* 2d ed., (Orlando, Fla.: Academic Press). Used by permission of Academic Press, Inc. Page 82, "Focus on the Psychologist," selection from autobiographical essay by David H. Hubel reprinted by permission of the Nobel Foundation, Stockholm. Copyright © The Nobel Foundation 1982. Page 85, Highlight 3.2 from Coren, Porac, and Ward, *op. cit.*, Box 6-6, p. 174 by permission of Academic Press, Inc. Page 96, Figure 3.28 based on S. Weinstein, Figure 10-2, p. 200 in D. R. Kenshalo, ed. (1968), *The skin senses* (Springfield, Ill.: Charles C Thomas), courtesy of Charles C Thomas, Springfield, Illinois. Page 98, Table 3.2 from J. E. Amoore, J. W. Johnston, Jr., and M. Rubin (1964), The stereochemical theory of odor, *Scientific American* 210:2:42. Copyright © 1964 by Scientific American, Inc. All rights reserved. Page 112, Table 4.3 from F. A. Geldard (1962), *Fundamentals of psychology* (New York: Wiley), p. 93. Copyright © 1962 by John Wiley & Sons, Inc. Used by permission of John Wiley & Sons, Inc. Page 113, Highlight 4.2 from Box 9-3, p. 267 in Coren, Porac, and Ward, *op. cit.* Reprinted by permission of Academic Press, Inc. Page 122, Figure 4.13 from Figure 9-9, page 288 in Coren, Porac, and Ward, *op. cit.* Reprinted by permission of Academic Press, Inc. Page 128, Figure 4.25 (see color insert No. 1) redrawn from color plate number 4, in Coren, Porac, and Ward, *op. cit.* Reprinted by permission of Academic Press, Inc. Page 131, Figure 4.29 based on Walk, Sheperd, and Miller (1978) in M. R. Rosenzweig and A. L. Leiman (1982), *Physiological psychology* (Lexington, Mass.: D. C. Heath). Copyright © 1982 by D. C. Heath and Company. Reprinted by permission of the publisher. Page 158, Table 5.1 from R. M. Julien (1981), *A primer of drug action*, 3d ed. (San Francisco: W. H. Freeman). Used by permission of W. H. Freeman and Company. Page 163, Table 5.2 from p. 207 of J. Witters and W. L. Witters (1983), *Drugs and society* (Monterey, Cal.: Wadsworth). Copyright © 1983 by Wadsworth, Inc. Reprinted by permission of Wadsworth Health Sciences Division, Monterey, California 93940.

ISBN 0-02-369880-2

CREDITS

Page 170, Highlight 5.3, selection translated from laboratory notes of Dr. Albert Hoffman in K. Liska (1981), *Drugs and the human body with implications for society* (New York: Macmillan). Used by permission of Macmillan Publishing Company. Page 177 photo, Peter Simon/Stock, Boston. Page 201, Figure 6.10 based on E. C. Tolman and C. H. Honzik, Introduction and removal of reward, and maze performance in rats. *University of California Publications in Psychology,* 4 (1930), 257–275, (Berkeley: University of California Press). Used by permission of the University of California Press. Page 214, Figure 7.3 and page 215, Figure 7.4 based on G. Sperling (1960), The information available in brief visual presentations, *Psychological Monographs* 74, No. 498. Copyright 1960 by the American Psychological Association. Used by permission of the author. Page 216, Figure 7.5 from L. R. Peterson and M. J. Peterson (1959), Short-term retention of individual verb items, *J. Exp. Psychology* 58, 193–198. Copyright 1959 by the American Psychological Association. Used by permission of the author. Page 218, Figure 7.6 from S. Sternberg, High-speed scanning in human memory, *Science* 153 (3 August 1966), 652–654. Copyright 1966 by the American Association for the Advancement of Science. Used by permission of the author and the AAAS. Page 224, Figure 7.8 from D. Rundus and R. C. Atkinson (1970), Rehearsal procedures in free recall: a procedure for direct observation, *J. Verbal Learning and Verbal Behavior* 9:99–105. Used by permission of the author and Academic Press, Orlando, FL. Page 229, Figure 7.9 based on G. Mandler (167), Organization and memory, in D. W. Spence and J. T. Spence, eds., *The psychology of learning and motivation,* Vol. I (New York: Academic Press). Used by permission of the author and Academic Press, Inc. Page 225, Figure 7.10 based on G. A. Bower, M. C. Clark, A. M. Lesgold, and D. Winzenz (1969), Hierarchical retrieval schemes in recall of categorized work lists, *J. Verbal Learning and Verbal Behavior* 8, 323–343. Used by permission of Gordon Bower and Academic Press, Inc. Page 232, Figure 7.14 based on B. Murdock (1962), The serial position effect of free recall, *J. Exp. Psychol.* 64: 482–488. Copyright 1962 by the American Psychological Association. Used by permission of the author. Page 232 bottom, Figure 7.15 based on M. Glanzer and A. R. Cunitz (1966), Two storage mechanisms in free recall, *J. Verbal Learning and Verbal Behavior* 5:351–360. Used by permission of the author and Academic Press, Inc. Page 240, Figure 7.16 based on A. M. Collins and M. R. Quillian (1969), Retrieval time from semantic memory, *J. Verbal Learning and Verbal Behavior* 8:240–247. Used by permission of Allan M. Collins and Academic Press, Inc. Page 241, Figure 7.17 based on A. M. Collins and E. F. Loftus (1975), A spreading-activation theory of semantic processing, *Psych. Review* 82:407–428. Copyright 1975 by the American Psychological Association. Used by permission of the author. Page 251, Figure 8.5 based on N. Johnson (1965), The psychological reality of phrase structure rules, *J. Verbal Learning and Verbal Behavior* 4:469–475. Used by permission of the author and Academic Press, Inc. Page 258, Figure 8.6 based on D. V. Howard (1983), *Cognitive psychology: memory, language, and thought* (New York: Macmillan). Used by permission of the author. Page 258 bottom, Table 8.1 from A. S. Luchins (1942), Mechanization in problem solving, *Psych. Monographs* 54, whole No. 248. Copyright 1942 by the American Psychological Association. Used by permission of the author. Page 259, Figure 8.7 based on K. Duncker (1945), On problem solving, *Psych. Monographs* 58, whole No. 270. Copyright 1945 by the American Psychological Association. Used by permission of the author. Page 262, Table 8.2 from H. C. Ellis and R. R. Hunt (1983), *Fundamentals of human memory and cognition,* 3d ed. (Dubuque, IA: William C. Brown Co.) Used by permission of the author. Pages 270–271, Figure 8-12 from J. W. French, R. B. Ekstrom, and L. A. Price (1963), *Kit of reference tests for cognitive factors* and from R. B. Ekstrom, J. W. French, H. H. Harman, and D. Dermen (1976), *Manual for kit factor-referenced cognitive tests,* (both, Princeton, NJ: Educational Testing Service). Used by permission of Educational Testing Service. Page 287, Figure 9.3 after R. E. Nisbett (1968), Taste, deprivation and weight determinants of eating behavior, *J. Personality and Social Psychology* 10(2):107–116. Used by permission of the author. Page 300, Figure 9.4 from R. Plutchik (1980), A language for emotions, *Psychology Today* 13(February), 68-78. Reprinted by permission from *Psychology Today* Magazine. Copyright © 1980 by the American Psychological Association. Page 303, photo, Erika Stone/Photo Researchers, Inc. Page 314, Figure 10.1 redrawn from C. M. Jackson (1929), Some aspects of form and growth, in W. J. Robbins, S. Brody, A. F. Hogan, C. M. Jackson, and C. W. Green, eds., *Growth* (New Haven: Yale University Press). Used by permission of Yale University Press. Page 340, Figure 11.1 from J. M. Tanner (1973), Growing up, *Scientific American* 229:34–43. Used by permission of the author and W. H. Freeman and Company, Publishers. Page 348, Figure 11.3 after N. W. Shock (1972), Energy metabolism, caloric intake, and physical activity of the aging, in L. A. Carlson, ed., *Nutrition in old age* (a symposium of the Swedish Nutrition Foundation) (Uppsala, Sweden: Almquist & Wiksell). Used by permission of the author. Page 354, Figure 11.5 after D. F. Hultsch (1971), Adult age differences in free classification and free recall, *Developmental Psychology* 4:338–342. Copyright 1971 by the American Psychological Association. Used by permission of the author. Page 356, Figure 11.7 based on J. L. Horn and G. Donaldson (1980), Cognitive development: II. Adulthood and development of human abilities, in O. G. Brim, Jr., and J. Kagan, eds., *Constancy and change in human development: a volume of review essays* (Cambridge, MA: Harvard University Press). Used by permission of the author and Harvard University Press. Page 358, Figure 11.8, based on J. L. Horn and R. B. Cattell (1966), Age differences in primary mental ability factors, *J. Gerontology* 21:210–220. Used by permission of the author and the Gerontological Society of America. Page 359, Figure 11.9 after K. W. Schaie and G. Labouvie-Vief (1974), Generational versus ontogenic components of change in adult cognitive behavior: a 14-year cross-sectional study, *Developmental Psychology* 10:3 305–320. Copyright 1974 by the American Psychological Association. Adapted by permission of the author. Page 364, Figure 11.10 after D. J. Levinson (1978), *The Seasons of a Man's Life,* p. 57 (New York: Alfred A. Knopf). Copyright © 1978 by Daniel Levinson. Used by permission of the author and Alfred A. Knopf, Inc. Page 371, photo Baron Wolman/Woodfin Camp & Associates. Page 383, Tables 12.4 and 12.5 reproduced by permission from the Wechsler Adult Intelligence Scale-Revised.

CREDITS

Copyright © 1981 by The Psychological Corporation. All rights reserved. Page 385, Table 12.7, R. B. Cattell and A. K. S. Cattell, Four example items adapted from the Culture Fair Intelligence Test, Scale 2, Form A test booklet, Tests 1, 2, 3, and 4, copyright 1949, 1960 by the Institute for Personality and Ability Testing, Inc. All rights reserved. Reproduced by permission of the copyright owner. Page 385, Table 12.7 reproduced from J. C. Raven (1958), *Standard progressive matrices* (U.K.: Psychological Corporation). Used by permission of J. C. Raven Limited. Page 391, Table 12.8, sample items from the Minnesota Multiphasic Personality Inventory (MMPI) used by permission of the author and the publisher. Pages 392-393, Figure 12.1 reproduced from N. J. Butcher, *MMPI Report*, by permission of the author. Page 394, Table 12.10 from J. B. Rotter, *Locus of control scale*, by permission of the author. Page 395, Table 12.11 from C. Spielberger et al. (1968), *The state trait anxiety inventory* (Palo Alto, CA: Consulting Psychologists Press, Inc.). Reproduced by special permission from Consulting Psychologists Press, Inc., Palo Alto, CA 94306. Page 433 photo, © Arthur Tress 1982/Woodfin Camp & Associates. Page 439, Figure 14.3 from M. Frankenhaeuser (1980), Psychoneuroendocrine approaches to the study of stressful person-environment transation, in H. Selye, ed., *Selye's guide to stress research*, Vol. I (New York: Van Nostrand Reinhold). Used by permission of the author. Page 443, Figure 14.5 from M. S. Nomikos, E. Opton, Jr., J. R. Averill, and R. S. Lazarus (1968), Surprise versus suspense in the production of stress reaction, *J. Pers. Soc. Psychol.* 8:204–208. Used by permission of Richard Lazarus. Page 444, Figure 14.6 from S. Epstein (1962), The measurement of drive and conflict in humans: theory and experiment, in M. R. Jones, ed., *Nebraska symposium on motivation* (Lincoln, NE: University of Nebraska Press). Used by permission of the author and the University of Nebraska Press. Copyright © 1962 by the University of Nebraska Press. Page 445, Figure 14.7 from W. D. Fenz and S. Epstein (1967), Gradients of physiological arousal in parachutists as a function of an approaching jump, *Psychosomatic Medicine* 29:33–51. Used by permission of the author. Page 448, Figure 14.8 from M. Frankenhaeuser, B. Nordheden, A. L. Myrsten, and B. Post (1971), Psychophysiological reactions to understimulation and overstimulation, *Acta Psychologica* 35:298–308. Used by permission of M. Frankenhaeuser and North-Holland Publishing Company. Page 450, Figure 14.9 from J. R. Kaplan et al. (1983), Social stress and atherosclerosis in hormocholesterolemic monkeys, *Science* 220:733–735, Figures 1 and 13. Copyright 1983 by the American Association for the Advancement of Science. Used by permission of the author and the AAAS. Page 451, Table 14.2 based on M. F. Lowenthal, M. Thurnher, and D. Chiriboga (1975), *Four stages of life*, pp. 157–165 (San Francisco: Jossey-Bass). Used by permission of Dr. Marjorie Fiske, Human Development Program, University of California, and Jossey-Bass, Inc. Page 459, Tables 14.3 and 14.4 from S. Gore (1978), The effect of social support in moderating health consequences of unemployment, *J. Health and Social Behavior* 19:157–165. Used by permission of the author and the American Sociological Association. Page 465, Figure 14.11 from S. M. Miller (1980), When is a little information a dangerous thing? Coping with stressful events by monitoring versus blunting, in S. Levine and H. Ursin, eds., *Coping and Health* (New York: Plenum Publishing Corporation). Used by permission of Plenum Publishing Corporation. Pages 477–479, Table 15.2 from American Psychiatric Association (1980), *Diagnostic and statistical manual of mental disorders*, Third Edition (*DSM-III*) (Washington, D.C.: American Psychiatric Association). Used by permission of the American Psychiatric Association. Page 479 bottom, Table 15.3, data adapted from J. C. Coleman, J. N. Butcher, and R. C. Carson (1980), *Abnormal psychology and modern life*, 6th ed. (Glenview, Ill: Scott, Foresman). Used by permission of Scott, Foresman and Company. Page 483, Table 15.4 adapted from D. Rosenthal (1970), *Genetic theory and abnormal behavior*, New York: McGraw-Hill. Used by permission of McGraw-Hill Book Company. Pages 512–513, Transcript 1 from I. B. Weiner (1975), *Principles of Psychotherapy* (New York: Wiley). Used by permission of the author and John Wiley & Sons, Inc., Publishers. Page 514–515, Transcript 2 from C. R. Rogers (1961), *On becoming a person*, in D. Wedding and R. J. Corsini, eds., *Great cases in psychotherapy*. Itasca, Ill: Peacock. Used by permission of Houghton Mifflin Company, Boston. Pages 518–519, Transcript 3 from M. R. Goldfried and G. C. Davison (1976), *Clinical behavior therapy* (New York: Holt. Copyright © 1976 by Holt, Rinehart and Winston. Used by permission of Marvin R. Goldfried and CBS College Publishing. Pages 525–527, Transcript 4 from A. Ellis, Rational-emotive therapy, in R. Corsini, ed., *Current psychotherapies*, 2d ed. (1979) (Itasca, Ill: Peacock). Used by permission of the author and F. E. Peacock Publishers, Inc. Page 529, Transcript 5 from A. T. Beck, A. J. Rush, B. F. Shaw, and G. D. Emery (1979), *Cognitive therapy of depression*, New York: Guilford Press. Used by permission of the author and the Center for Cognitive Therapy. Copyright © 1978 by Aaron T. Beck, M.D. Further information about this scale and/or permission to use and reproduce the scale may be obtained from the Center for Cognitive Therapy, Room 602, 133 South 36th St., Philadelphia, Pa. 19104. Page 545 photo from Stock, Boston. Page 559, Figure 17.2 from P. Ekman and W. V. Friesen (1975), *Unmasking the face:* A guide to recognizing emotions from facial clues (Englewood Cliffs, NJ: Prentice-Hall). Used by permission of Paul Ekman. Page 567, Figure 17.3 from M. R. Lepper, D. Greene, and R. E. Nisbett (1973), Undermining children's intrinsic interest with extrinsic reward: A test of the "overjustification" hypothesis, *J. Personality and Social Psych.* 28:129–137. Copyright 1973 by the American Psychological Association. Used by permission of the author, M. R. Lepper. Page 575, Figures 18.1 and 18.2 from S. E. Asch (1946), Forming impressions of personality, *J. Abnormal and Social Psych.* 41:258–290 (table, p. 263). Copyright 1946 by the American Psychological Association. Used by permission of the author.

*To the
Center for Advanced Study in the
Behavioral Sciences—
its concept and its spirit*

Preface

We have approached the writing of *Psychology* as a serious task of scholarship and pedagogy. Guided by a commitment to the field and to teaching others about it, we have sought to bring both the students and their instructors a scholarly—yet readable—coverage of the contemporary challenges and advances within psychology.

Introductory psychology may be the student's only opportunity to become acquainted with the principles and findings of a science that is important for individuals and for society, or it may be the foundation for a college major and a career. To instructors in the discipline, introductory psychology represents the premier teaching challenge. They must convey the substance, excitement, and promise of psychology, so that students will think intelligently about the field, will understand its contributions and limitations, and will appreciate its future problems and promises. For these reasons, writing an introductory psychology text is a significant and exciting endeavor.

Moreover, the horizons of psychology have so expanded that it is difficult for a single author to capture all areas of the discipline. Our approach was to enlist five authors, each with published and recognized expertise in a different area of psychology—developmental, clinical, social, cognitive, and physiological. Beyond this individual and collective expertise was a collaborative enterprise: At least two of the authors worked on each chapter, and all helped to revise the final manuscript. The end result, we believe, is an interwoven and cohesive text that is accurate in its content, current in its topical coverage, and fair in its analysis of controversy. It is a text written to help the instructor to teach psychology and to enable the student to enjoy learning about it.

The proper gestation period for a comprehensive text is at least five years. For us, this book began six years ago, when three of us were Fellows at the Center for Advanced Study in the Behavioral Sciences. Since then we have expanded our team of authors and met the challenges of writing a text that is both intellectually sound and useful for students and their instructors. Students may be interested to know that we often had to search for classic but hard to find references, to respond to comments and rewrite the drafts of our manuscript, and to struggle to discover how to help the student use the text in the best possible way. Features such as the chapter highlights, the chapter summaries, the key terms and annotated references at the end of each chapter, and the glossary and reference list at the end of the book are part of our effort to make this book an effective tool for mastering introductory psychology. In particular, we believe that each chapter's "Focus on the Psychologist" will allow students to appreciate the motivations and creative energies involved in shaping the work of some of the leading contributors to the science of psychology. Finally, we have provided an additional study aid for students—a *Study Guide* by Charles Meliska and William M. Hastings of Monmouth College, Illinois—and two teaching resources for instructors—an *Instructor's Manual* by Lawrence Guzy of SUNY, Oneonta, and a *Test Item File* by Roy F. Baumeister of Case Western Reserve and David Zehr of Beloit College. These will make studying and teaching from *Psychology* more stimulating for both students and instructors.

ACKNOWLEDGMENTS

The authors of a text are not its only parents. We are particularly grateful to two sets of our colleagues. First, we wish to thank all of the scholars who provided autobiographical contributions to the "Focus on the Psychologist" section:

Virginia S. Sexton, *St. John's University*
Carl W. Cotman, *University of California—Irvine*
David H. Hubel, *Harvard University*
Colin Blakemore, *Oxford University*
James L. McGaugh, *University of California—Irvine*
Martin E. P. Seligman, *University of Pennsylvania*
Fergus I. M. Craik, *University of Toronto*
John Horn, *University of Denver*
Judith Rodin, *Yale University*
Jerome Kagan, *Harvard University*
Paul B. Baltes, *Max Planck Institute (Berlin)*
Anne Anastasi, *Fordham University*
Edward E. Jones, *Princeton University*
Richard S. Lazarus, *University of California—Berkeley*
Paul E. Meehl, *University of Minnesota*
G. Terrence Wilson, *Rutgers University*
Ellen S. Berscheid, *University of Minnesota*
Robert B. Cialdini, *Arizona State University*
E. Mavis Hetherington, *University of Virginia*

Second, we are extremely grateful for the positive and critical comments provided by numerous colleagues who served as reviewers. Their advice, guidance, and efforts on our behalf helped to shape and improve this text. The following especially deserve our thanks:

Robert C. Beck, *Wake Forest University*
William H. Calhoun, *University of Tennessee*
Chris Cozby, *California State University—Fullerton*
David Edwards, *Iowa State University*
David Gerbing, *Baylor University*
Alan L. Gilchrist, *Rutgers University—Newark*
J. Barnard Gilmore, *University of Toronto*
Joseph Grosslight, *Florida State University*
Carl Gustavson, *North Dakota State University*
Lawrence T. Guzy, *SUNY—Oneonta*

PREFACE

Charles LaBounty, *Hamline University*
Ellen Lenney, *University of Maine*
Richard Lippa, *California State University—Fullerton*
Charles Meliska, *Monmouth College*
Ralph R. Miller, *SUNY—Binghamton*
Harry R. Murray, *University of Western Ontario*
Nora Newcombe, *Temple University*
William H. Overman, *University of North Carolina—Wilmington*
Samuel Roll, *University of New Mexico*
Timothy Schallert, *University of Texas*
Jonathon Segal, *Trinity College*
Virginia Sexton, *St. John's University*
David Zehr, *Beloit College*

We are grateful also to our editors, James D. Anker and Gerald Lombardi, and to the production staff at Macmillan who helped to turn our manuscript into a finished book. In addition, we thank Elizabeth Parkes, Patricia L. East, and Laura E. Hess for their assistance in organizing the book's backmatter, and we are grateful to Joy Barger, Teresa Charmbury, and Kathleen Hooven for their expert and professional secretarial skills. Richard M. Lerner is grateful for support provided by the John D. and Catherine T. McArthur Foundation and by the William T. Grant Foundation during the writing of this book.

Finally, we wish to thank all the "significant others" in our lives. Their love and support were vital to us throughout our work. We thank: Cindy, Amy, David, and Debby Hultsch; Otto and Dorothy Jensen; M. Sue, Mark, and Reed Kendall; Jacqueline, Blair, and Justin Lerner; and Carol and Josh Miller.

R.M.L.
P.C.K.
D.T.M.
D.F.H.
R.A.J.

Author Biographies

Richard M. Lerner is Professor of Child and Adolescent Development and Director of the Center for the Study of Child and Adolescent Development at The Pennsylvania State University. He received his Ph.D. in Psychology in 1971 from the City University of New York. He is the author or editor of ten books and over 100 articles and chapters. Dr. Lerner is on the editorial board of *Child Development,* is the associate editor of the *International Journal of Behavioral Development,* and is co-editor of the annual series *Life-Span Development and Behavior.* Dr. Lerner was a 1980–1981 Fellow at the Center for Advanced Study in the Behavioral Sciences and is a Fellow of the American Psychological Association and the American Association for the Advancement of Science. Dr. Lerner has written extensively about philosophical and theoretical issues in human development and is noted for his research on children's and adolescents' personality and social development. His current research involves a longitudinal study of early adolescent development.

Philip C. Kendall, Ph.D., was recently appointed Head of the Division of Clinical Psychology at Temple University. He has taught in the Department of Psychology, as Professor of Psychology, at the University of Minnesota from 1977 to 1984. The author of numerous monographs and research articles, Dr. Kendall has also authored *Clinical Psychology: Scientific and Professional Dimensions* (with J. Ford) and is one of the co-authors of the *Annual Review of Behavior Therapy.* Dr. Kendall serves as associate editor of *Cognitive Therapy and Research,* editor of *Advances in Cognitive-Behavioral Research and Therapy,* and in 1977 and from 1980–1981 was a Fellow at the Center for Advanced Study in the Behavioral Sciences, Stanford, California. Dr. Kendall is noted for his work in the area of cognitive-behavioral assessment and therapy, specifically with children, and has lectured throughout the United States and Canada and in Europe and South America.

Dale T. Miller is Professor of Psychology at Simon Fraser University in British Columbia, Canada. He received his Ph.D. in Psychology in 1975 from the University of Waterloo. He has taught psychology at the University of Western Ontario, University of British Columbia, University of Michigan, and Princeton University. Professor Miller's research interests focus on social perception and prosocial behavior. His articles have appeared in many journals, including *Psychological Bulletin, Journal of Experimental Social Psychology,* and *Child Development.* He is currently a member of the editorial board of *Journal of Personality* and *Social Psychology.*

David F. Hultsch is Lansdowne Professor of Psychology at the University of Victoria. He received his Ph.D. degree in Psychology in 1968 from Syracuse University. Dr. Hultsch is a Fellow of the American Psychological Association and the Gerontological Society of America. He is on the editorial board of *Psychology and Aging*. Dr. Hultsch has done extensive research on memory and cognitive development in adulthood and aging. His current work is focused on older adults' knowledge, beliefs, and feelings about their own memory functioning. He has co-authored two other textbooks on psychology.

Robert A. Jensen is an associate professor in the Developmental Biopsychology Program at Southern Illinois University in Carbondale, Illinois. He received his Ph.D. in biopsychology from Northern Illinois University in 1976 and was the recipient of a U.S. Public Health Service Fellowship to do postdoctoral studies at the University of California, Irvine. He is an author or editor of five books and over 50 research articles and chapters. He is a member of the editorial board of *Behavioral and Neural Biology* and has served as a managing editor of that journal. His research centers around studies of brain processes that modulate learning and memory in rats and mice and of the role that neuropeptides play in directing behavior. Currently, he is working on research investigating how opiate-like substances in the brain, which are released in response to some kinds of stress, may change immune system functioning and alter susceptibility to illness.

Brief Contents

PART ONE   Introduction
- **1** Psychology: An Introduction   3

PART TWO   Biology, Sensation, Perception, and Consciousness
- **2** Biology and Behavior   25
- **3** Sensory Processes   65
- **4** Perception   102
- **5** Consciousness   136

PART THREE   Learning, Cognition, Motivation, and Emotion
- **6** Learning   179
- **7** Cognitive Processes: Remembering and Forgetting   208
- **8** Cognitive Processes: Language, Thought, and Intelligence   245
- **9** Motivation and Emotion   277

PART FOUR   Development Over the Lifespan
- **10** Development: Infancy and Childhood   305
- **11** Development: Adolescence, Adulthood, and Aging   334

PART FIVE   Personality and Individuality
- **12** Tests and Measures   373
- **13** Personality   407

PART SIX — Conflict, Adjustment, and Mental Health

14 Stress and Coping — 435
15 Abnormal Behavior — 468
16 Therapies for Behavior Problems — 509

PART SEVEN — Social Behavior

17 Attitudes and Social Perception — 547
18 Social Influence and Group Behavior — 570
19 Psychology and Contemporary Society — 592

APPENDICES

A Statistical Appendix: Description and Generalization — 615
B The Psychology Journal Article — 629

GLOSSARY — 637

REFERENCES — 655

NAME INDEX — 683

SUBJECT INDEX — 691

Detailed Contents

PART ONE
Introduction

1 Psychology: An Introduction   3
PSYCHOLOGY: THE SCIENTIFIC STUDY OF MENTAL AND BEHAVIORAL FUNCTIONING   4   /   *Psychology Is a Science*   5   *Psychology Studies Mental and Behavioral Functioning*   5
HISTORY OF PSYCHOLOGY   5
PSYCHOLOGY AND THE SCIENTIFIC METHOD   10   /   *Naturalistic Observation*   10   *Controlled Observation*   12   *The Controlled Experiment*   12   *Questionnaires and Interviews*   15
THE ETHICS OF PSYCHOLOGICAL RESEARCH   17
PLAN OF THE BOOK   19
SUMMARY   21
KEY TERMS   21
SUGGESTED READINGS   21

PART TWO
Biology, Sensation, Perception, and Consciousness

2 Biology and Behavior   25
INTRODUCING THE NERVOUS SYSTEM   26   /   *The Central Nervous System*   27   *The Peripheral Nervous System*   28   *The Neuroendocrine System*   30
TASKS THAT THE NERVOUS SYSTEM PERFORMS   30   /   *The Nervous System Monitors the World Outside the Body*   30   *The Nervous System Takes Care of Its Partner in Life, the Body*   31   *The Nervous System Stores and Retrieves Memories*   31   *The Nervous System Directs Behavior*   32   *The Nervous System Produces Thinking and Creativity*   32   *The Nervous System Generates Personality*   32
THE NEURON: THE BASIC UNIT OF THE NERVOUS SYSTEM   33   /   *What Neurons Are and Where They Are Found*   33   *The Structure of Neurons*   36
NEURONAL SIGNALING   38   /   *The Resting Potential*   38   *The Action Potential*   40   *Synaptic Transmission*   44
PUTTING IT ALL TOGETHER: GENERATING BEHAVIOR—A SIMPLE REFLEX   48
THE ANATOMY OF THE CENTRAL NERVOUS SYSTEM   49   /   *The Spinal Cord*   49   *The Brain Stem*   50   *The Cerebellum*   51   *The Midbrain*   51   *The Hypothalamus*   52   *The Thalamus*   53   *The Cerebral Hemispheres*   53
CORTICAL LOCALIZATION OF FUNCTION   54   /   *Sensory Projection Areas*   54   *Motor Areas*   56   *Frontal Lobes*   57   *Temporal Lobes*   58   *Parietal Lobes*   59
LATERALIZATION IN THE BRAIN   59   /   *Hemispheric Specialization*   59   *Split-Brain Research*   60
SUMMARY   61
KEY TERMS   63
SUGGESTED READINGS   63

3 Sensory Processes   65
WHAT DO OUR SENSES TELL US?   65   /   *An Adequate Stimulus*   66
SENSORY QUALITIES: DISTINGUISHING BETWEEN STIMULI   67   /   *The Nature of the Stimulus Versus the Sensory Response*   67   *The Doctrine of Specific Nerve Energies*   67
THE VISUAL SYSTEM   68   /   *The Electromagnetic Spectrum and Visible Light*   68   *The Structure of the Eye*   69   *Receptor Cells in the Retina*   72   *Transduction in the Retina*   74   *Visual Pathways from Eye to Cortex*   78   *Feature Detectors in the Cortex*   81   *Color Vision*   84

xvii

THE AUDITORY SYSTEM 87 / *The Nature of Sound* 87 *The Transduction of Sound* 90 *The Perception of Auditory Space* 94
THE BODILY SENSES 94 / *The Sense of Touch* 95 *The Position Senses* 95 *The Senses of Taste and Smell* 97
SUMMARY 99
KEY TERMS 101
SUGGESTED READINGS 101

4 Perception 102
PERCEPTION: WHAT IS IT? 102 / *Sensation and Perception* 102 *Perceptual Constancies* 104
SENSORY THRESHOLDS 106 / *Absolute Thresholds* 106 *Signal-Detection Theory* 107 *Difference Thresholds* 111 *Adaptation of Sensory Systems* 112
PRINCIPALS OF VISUAL PERCEPTUAL ORGANIZATION 114 / *Extracting a Meaningful Visual Image* 114 *Some Gestalt Principles of Perceptual Organization* 115
THE PERCEPTION OF MOVEMENT 117 / *Cues for the Perception of Movement* 117 *Stroboscopic Movement* 118 *Movement Perception and the Frame of Reference* 118
THE PERCEPTION OF VISUAL THREE-DIMENSIONAL SPACE 118 / *Binocular Vision* 119 *Monocular Depth Cues* 121
VISUAL ILLUSIONS 123
THE PERCEPTION OF COLOR 126
THE DEVELOPMENT AND MODIFICATION OF PERCEPTION 128
EXTRASENSORY PERCEPTION 131 / *Parapsychology* 132 *Studies of Telepathy and Clairvoyance* 132 *Difficulties with ESP Research* 133
SUMMARY 133
KEY TERMS 135
SUGGESTED READINGS 135

5 Consciousness 136
BODILY RHYTHMS 136 / *Circadian Rhythms* 137
SLEEP 138
A TYPICAL NIGHT'S SLEEP 139 / *Techniques of Sleep Research* 139 *Stages of Sleep* 140 *REM Sleep (Active Sleep)* 142 *Sleep Patterns from Infancy Through Adulthood* 143 *How Much Sleep Is Normal* 145
SLEEP AND DREAMING 145 / *Who Dreams and When* 146 *Eye Movements and Dreams* 146 *Other Aspects of REM Sleep* 147 *Nightmares and Other Bad Dreams* 148

PATHOLOGIES OF SLEEP 149 / *Insomnia* 149 *Sleeping Pills* 150 *Narcolepsy* 151 *Sleepwalking* 153
HYPNOSIS 153 / *Entering the Hypnotic State* 154 *Characteristics of Hypnosis* 154 *Clinical Uses of Hypnosis* 155
DRUGS 156 / *Who Takes Drugs* 156 *Types of Psychoactive Drugs* 157 *Sedative-Hypnotic Drugs (CNS Depressants)* 160 *Behavioral Stimulants* 163 *Opiates and Narcotics* 167 *Psychedelics and Hallucinogens* 169 *Marijuana* 171
MEDITATION 172
SUMMARY 173
KEY TERMS 175
SUGGESTED READINGS 176

PART THREE
Learning, Cognition, Motivation, and Emotion

6 Learning 179
CLASSICAL CONDITIONING 181 / *Principal Features of Classical Conditioning* 183 *Conditioned Emotional Responses* 184
INSTRUMENTAL LEARNING OR OPERANT CONDITIONING 184 / *The Research of Thorndike* 185 *The Law of Effect* 186 *Operant Conditioning* 187 *Shaping and the Method of Successive Approximations* 188
MAJOR FEATURES OF ASSOCIATIVE LEARNING 189 / *Acquisition* 189 *Extinction* 190 *Spontaneous Recovery* 190 *Generalization* 191 *Discrimination* 191 *Primary and Secondary Reinforcement* 191 *Positive and Negative Reinforcement* 192 *Schedules of Reinforcement* 194
COGNITIVE LEARNING 197 / *Insight* 199 *Cognitive Maps and Latent Learning* 200 *The Learning of Higher-Order Concepts* 201 *Observational Learning: Modeling and Imitation* 204
SUMMARY 205
KEY TERMS 206
SUGGESTED READINGS 207

7 Cognitive Processes: Remembering and Forgetting 208
APPROACHES TO HUMAN MEMORY 209 / *Early Ideas about Memory* 209 *The Information-Processing Approach* 210

DETAILED CONTENTS

THE BASIC MEMORY SYSTEM 212 / *Sensory Memory* 213 *Short-Term Memory* 215 *Long-Term Memory* 218
THE RELATIONSHIP AMONG TYPES OF MEMORY 231 / *Multistore Models* 231 *Levels of Processing* 234
THE ROLE OF PRIOR KNOWLEDGE IN MEMORY 234 / *Constructive Memory* 235 *Reconstructive Memory* 236
THE ORGANIZATION OF KNOWLEDGE 239 / *Semantic Versus Episodic Memory* 239 *Network Models* 239 *Schema Theory* 242
SUMMARY 243
KEY TERMS 244
SUGGESTED READINGS 244

8 Cognitive Processes: Language, Thought, and Intelligence 245

LANGUAGE 245 / *The Structure of Language* 246 *Competence Versus Performance* 251 *Language Comprehension and Production* 252 *The Acquisition of Language* 253
THOUGHT 256 / *Problem Solving* 257 *Concept Formation* 260 *Reasoning* 263
INTELLIGENCE 266 / *The Structure of Abilities* 266 *The Content of Abilities* 269 *Creativity and Intelligence* 271 *Heredity, Environment, and Intelligence* 272 *Improving Intelligence* 273
SUMMARY 274
KEY TERMS 276
SUGGESTED READINGS 276

9 Motivation and Emotion 277

BASIC DRIVES 278 / *Homeostasis* 278 *Regulatory Systems* 279
HUNGER 279 / *Signals for Eating* 280 *Signals for Satiety* 282 *The Hypothalamus and Eating Behavior* 283 *Obesity* 284
THIRST 287 / *Signals for Drinking* 287
HUMAN MOTIVATION 288 / *Theories of Human Motivation* 288 *Motivational Factors in Aggression* 291
EMOTION 295 / *The Nature of Emotions* 295 *Emotional Expression* 298 *The Structure of Emotions* 300
SUMMARY 301
KEY TERMS 301
SUGGESTED READINGS 301

PART FOUR
Development Over the Lifespan

10 Infancy and Childhood 305

THE BEGINNING OF DEVELOPMENT: GENES AND HEREDITY MECHANISMS 306 / *Genes* 307 *Heredity-Environment Interaction* 307
FEATURES OF PRENATAL DEVELOPMENT 309 / *The Period of the Ovum (Zygote)* 309 *The Period of the Embryo* 310 *The Period of the Fetus* 310 *Influences on Prenatal Development* 311 *The Birth Experience* 313
DEVELOPMENT DURING INFANCY 314 / *Physical Growth* 314 *Sensory and Perceptual Changes* 315 *Infant Reflexes and Motor Development* 315 *Complex Behavioral Sequences and Infant States* 316 *Emotions in Infancy* 316 *Cognitive Changes During Infancy* 317 *Social Development in Infancy* 322
DEVELOPMENT IN CHILDHOOD 325 / *Stability and Change in Psychometric Intelligence During Childhood* 325 *Language Development* 326 *The Social World of the Child* 328 *The Role of Play in Child Development* 330 *Influences of Television on Child Development* 331
SUMMARY 332
KEY TERMS 333
SUGGESTED READINGS 333

11 Development: Adolescence, Adulthood, and Aging 334

ADOLESCENCE 335 / *A Definition of Adolescence* 336 *Storm and Stress in Adolescence: Fact or Fiction?* 337 *Physical and Physiological Changes* 338 *Cognitive Changes* 341 *Identity Development* 342 *Sexuality* 343
ADULTHOOD AND AGING 345 / *Biological Changes* 345 *Cognitive Functioning* 352 *Personality Development* 359 *Stages of Adult Development* 362 *Dying, Death, and Grief* 365
SUMMARY 368
KEY TERMS 369
SUGGESTED READINGS 369

PART FIVE
Personality and Individuality

12 Tests and Measures 373

REQUIREMENTS OF TESTS 376 / *Reliability* 376 *Validity* 378

MEASUREMENTS OF INTELLECTUAL
   ABILITY 379 / *The Stanford-Binet Intelligence
   Scale 380   The Wechsler Intelligence Tests 382
   Are Intelligence Tests Fair? 384*
TESTS OF APTITUDE AND ACHIEVEMENT 387
MEASURES OF DEVIANT AND NORMAL
   PERSONALITY 389 / *Objective Measures 389
   Projective Methods 396*
BEHAVIORAL ASSESSMENT 402 / *Naturalistic
   Observation 402   Self-monitoring 403
   Analogue Assessments 404*
THE GOAL OF PSYCHOLOGICAL
   MEASUREMENT 404
SUMMARY 405
KEY TERMS 406
SUGGESTED READINGS 406

13 Personality 407
THE STUDY OF PERSONALITY 407
FREUD'S PSYCHOANALYTIC THEORY OF
   PERSONALITY 408 / *The Structures of
   Personality 410   Stages of Psychosexual
   Development 411   Neo-Freudians 412*
TYPES AND TRAITS 414 / *Sheldon's Constitutional
   Psychology 414   Personality Traits and Factor
   Analysis 416*
SELF-THEORIES 418 / *Rogers' Self-Theory 418*
LEARNING AND SOCIAL LEARNING
   THEORIES 419 / *Learning Theory and
   Personality 420   Social Learning and Personality
   422*
THE COGNITIVE SIDE OF PERSONALITY 425 /
   Schemata 426   Attributional Processes 426
THE SOURCE OF BEHAVIOR: PERSONALITY
   TRAITS VERSUS SITUATIONAL
   INFLUENCES 427
SUMMARY 431
KEY TERMS 432
SUGGESTED READINGS 432

PART SIX
Conflict, Adjustment, and Mental Health

14 Stress and Coping 435
THE NATURE OF STRESS 436 / *The General
   Adaptation Syndrome 436   Psychological Stress 439*
SOURCES OF PSYCHOLOGICAL STRESS 440 /
   *Harm 440   Threat 441   Conflict 442
   Overload and Underload 444*

PSYCHOLOGICAL STRESS AND HEALTH 446 /
   *From Life Events to Daily Hassles 446   Causality
   and Process in the Stress-Health Relationship 449*
APPRAISING STRESS 451 / *Primary
   Appraisal 452   Secondary Appraisal 452*
COPING WITH STRESS 453 / *Coping
   Resources 454   Coping Responses 460*
SUMMARY 465
KEY TERMS 466
SUGGESTED READINGS 467

15 Abnormal Behavior 468
A BRIEF HISTORY OF THOUGHT ABOUT
   ABNORMAL BEHAVIOR 470
DEFINING ABNORMAL BEHAVIOR 472
MODELS OF ABNORMAL BEHAVIOR 473 /
   *Learning Model 473   Psychodynamic Model 474
   Systems Model 475   Medical Model 476*
CLASSIFYING ABNORMAL BEHAVIOR 477 /
   *DSM III System 479   Pros and Cons of
   Classification 480*
SCHIZOPHRENIA 481 / *Genetics and
   Schizophrenia 483   Stress and Schizophrenia 484
   Subtypes of Schizophrenia 486*
AFFECTIVE DISORDERS 490 / *Bipolar
   Disorder 490   Major Depression 491
   Cyclothymic Disorder 492   Understanding the
   Causes of Depression 492*
ANXIETY DISORDERS 494 / *Generalized Anxiety
   Disorder 495   Phobic Disorder 496   Obsessive-
   Compulsive Disorder 497*
SOMATOFORM DISORDERS 498
PERSONALITY DISORDERS 499 / *Narcissistic
   Personality Disorder 499   Dependent Personality
   Disorder 500   Antisocial Personality Disorder 500
   Paranoid Personality Disorder 500*
PSYCHOSEXUAL DISORDERS 501 / *Sexual
   Dysfunction 501   Sexual Preferences 502*
ADDICTIVE DISORDERS 502
ABNORMAL BEHAVIOR IN CHILDHOOD 505 /
   Attention Deficit Disorder 505   Autism 505
SUMMARY 506
KEY TERMS 507
SUGGESTED READINGS 507

16 Therapies for Behavior Problems 509
PSYCHOANALYTIC THERAPY: THE FREUDIAN
   APPROACH 511
PSYCHOANALYSIS: DOES IT WORK? 513
CLIENT-CENTERED THERAPY: THE ROGERIAN
   APPROACH 514 / *The Effects of Client-Centered
   Therapy 515*

DETAILED CONTENTS

BEHAVIOR THERAPY 516 / *Systematic Desensitization 518   Operant Procedures 520   Modeling 522*
COGNITIVE-BEHAVIORAL THERAPY 524 / *Rational Emotive Therapy 525   Cognitive-Behavioral Treatment of Depression 528   Cognitive-Behavioral Therapy with Children 530*
OTHER PSYCHOLOGICAL THERAPIES 530 / *Reality Therapy 530   Gestalt Therapy 531   Transactional Analysis 531   Existential Therapy 532*
GROUP THERAPY 532 / *Family Therapy 534*
COMMUNITY INTERVENTIONS 535
THE EFFECTS OF PSYCHOLOGICAL THERAPY 536 / *Negative Effects of Therapy 538*
MEDICAL APPROACHES TO THE TREATMENT OF PSYCHOLOGICAL PROBLEMS 539 / *Drugs 540   Psychosurgery 541   Electroconvulsive Therapy 542*
SUMMARY 543
KEY TERMS 544
SUGGESTED READINGS 544

PART SEVEN
Social Behavior

17 Attitudes and Social Perception 547
ATTITUDES 547 / *The Nature of Attitudes 547   Attitude Formation 548   Attitude Change 549   Attitudes and Behavior 552   Attraction: The Case of Interpersonal Attitudes 554*
SOCIAL PERCEPTION 558 / *Inferring Emotions 558   Inferring Personality Traits 559   Biases in Social Perception 561   Implicit Theories of Personality 563   The Survival of False Beliefs 564*
SELF-PERCEPTION 566 / *Perceiving Our Emotions 566   Inferring our Attitudes 567*
SUMMARY 568
KEY TERMS 569
SUGGESTED READINGS 569

18 Social Influence and Group Behavior 570
SOCIAL INFLUENCE 571 / *Social Comparison 571   Conformity 574   Compliance 576*
GROUP DYNAMICS 581 / *Group Influences in Individual Performance 581   Group Problem Solving 583   Social Roles 585   Crowding and Personal Space 588*

SUMMARY 590
KEY TERMS 591
SUGGESTED READINGS 591

19 Psychology and Contemporary Society 592
SOCIAL POLICY AND SCIENCE 593 / *Social Problems: Understanding, Remediation, Prevention, and Enhancement 594   Conclusion: The Role of Psychology in Social Policy 595*
FEATURES OF CONTEMPORARY SOCIETY 595
THE FAMILY IN CONTEMPORARY CONTEXT 595 / *Divorce 596   Maternal Employment 598   Child Abuse 601*
PSYCHOLOGY AND THE LAW 604 / *The Jury 604   Judges Versus Juries 606*
PSYCHOLOGY AND MEDICINE: 1. THE SAMPLE CASE OF BEHAVIORAL MEDICINE 607 / *Lifestyle Change 608   Medical Compliance 609*
PSYCHOLOGY AND MEDICINE: 2. THE SAMPLE CASE OF COGNITIVE PSYCHOLOGY AND THE DIAGNOSIS AND TREATMENT OF ALZHEIMER'S DISEASE 610
SUMMARY 613
KEY TERMS 613
SUGGESTED READINGS 613

APPENDICES

A Statistical Appendix: Description and Generalization 615
DESCRIPTIVE STATISTICS 615 / *Frequency Distributions 616   Measures of Central Tendency 616   Measures of Variability 618   The Normal Frequency Distribution 619   Correlation 620*
INFERENTIAL STATISTICS 623 / *Populations and Samples 624   The Significance of a Difference 624*
SUMMARY 627
KEY TERMS 627
SUGGESTED READINGS 628

B The Psychology Journal Article 629
SCIENTIFIC COMMUNICATION 629
THE RESEARCH REPORT 630 / *Title 630   Author and Institution 630   Abstract 631   Introduction 631   Method 631   Results 632   Discussion 632   References 633*
PSYCHOLOGY JOURNALS 634

GLOSSARY	637	NAME INDEX	683
REFERENCES	655	SUBJECT INDEX	691

Focus on the Psychologist

Virginis S. Sexton, St. John's University	20
Carl W. Cotman, University of California—Irvine	29
David H. Hubel, Harvard University	82
Colin Blakemore, Oxford University	120
James L. McGaugh, University of California—Irvine	144
Martin E. P. Seligman, University of Pennsylvania	195
Fergus I. M. Craik, University of Toronto	222
John Horn, University of Denver	268
Judith Rodin, Yale University	286
Jerome Kagan, Harvard University	312
Paul B. Baltes, Max Planck Institute (Berlin)	357
Anne Anastasi, Fordham University	388
Edward E. Jones, Princeton University	428
Richard S. Lazarus, University of California—Berkeley	461
Paul E. Meehl, University of Minnesota	487
G. Terrence Wilson, Rutgers University	517
Ellen S. Berscheid, University of Minnesota	557
Robert B. Cialdini, Arizona State University	580
E. Mavis Hetherington, University of Virginia	597

PART ONE

Introduction

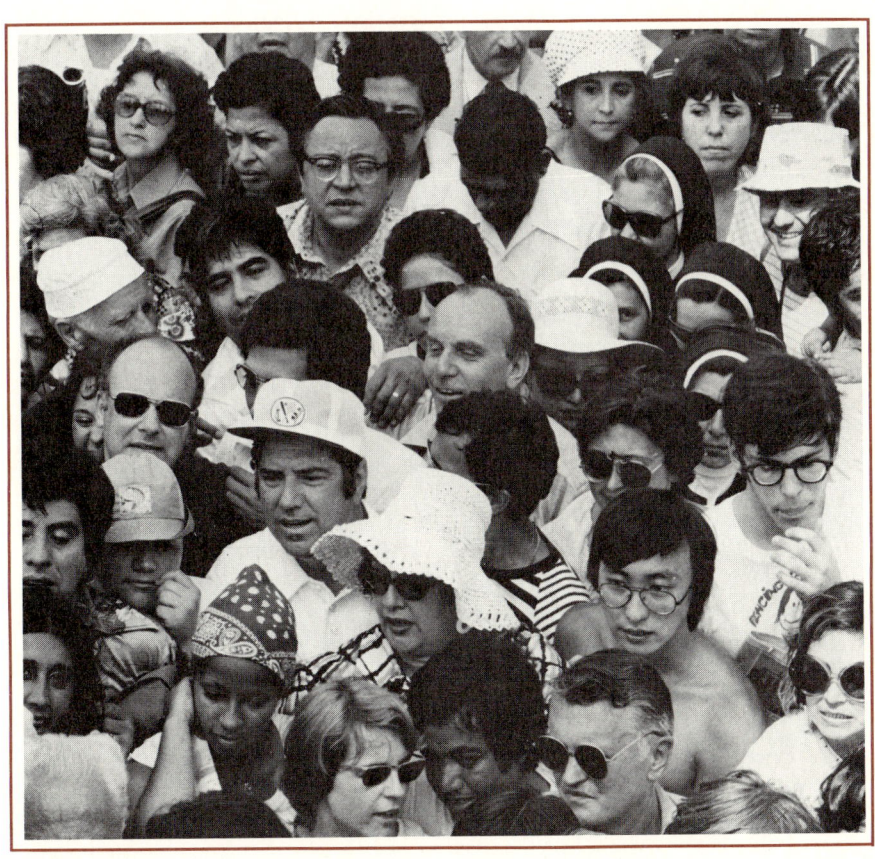

1
Psychology: An Introduction

PSYCHOLOGY: THE
   SCIENTIFIC STUDY
   OF MENTAL AND
   BEHAVIORAL
   FUNCTIONING
  Psychology Is a Science
  Psychology Studies Mental
   and Behavioral Functioning
HISTORY OF PSYCHOLOGY
PSYCHOLOGY AND THE
   SCIENTIFIC METHOD
  Naturalistic Observation
  Controlled Observation
  The Controlled Experiment
  Questionnaires and Interviews
THE ETHICS OF
   PSYCHOLOGICAL
   RESEARCH
PLAN OF THE BOOK
SUMMARY
KEY TERMS
SUGGESTED READINGS

Have you ever seen someone act in a way you thought was odd or strange? Did you wonder what made the person act as he or she did? Have you ever wondered why you yourself did, said, or thought something?

The answer to these questions is probably yes. Most people are interested in their own and others' behaviors and thoughts, and many people often wonder what makes themselves or others "tick." In other words, people often try to understand behavior and thought.

Psychology is a science devoted to such understanding. Its subject matter pertains to topics (e.g., your own behaviors) about which you probably have many opinions and beliefs. However, you may find as you read this book that your beliefs about the bases of behavior are not always accurate. You may discover that you had some misconceptions. Misconceptions are, in fact, common about psychology.

To illustrate, look at the 20 statements listed in Table 1.1. Write down whether you think each statement is true or is false. Then turn to the end of this chapter for the correct answers. If you are surprised by your score on this pretest, you may take comfort in knowing that most students at the start of introductory psychology are also surprised by their scores.

People usually begin to study psychology with preconceived but usually erroneous notions about what psychology is and about what is known of psychological functioning. Perhaps the major goal of this book is to rid you of your misconceptions about psychology and provide you with a solid

TABLE 1.1
A pretest for introductory psychology: which of the twenty statements related to psychology are true and which are false?

1. To change people's behavior toward members of ethnic minority groups, we must first change their attitudes.
2. Children's IQ scores have very little relationship to how well they do in school.
3. Women are more likely than men to say that they are lonely.
4. People who are weak in some academic subjects are usually good in others.
5. The best way to ensure that a desired behavior will persist after training is completed is to reward the behavior every time it occurs throughout training.
6. Under hypnosis, people can perform feats of physical strength which they could never do otherwise.
7. Boys and girls exhibit no behavioral differences until environmental influences begin to produce such differences.
8. Fortunately for babies, human beings have a strong maternal instinct.
9. Memory can be likened to a storage chest in the brain into which we deposit material and from which we can withdraw it later if needed. Occasionally, something gets lost and we forget.
10. The weight of evidence suggests that the major factor in forgetting is the decay of memory traces with time.
11. Unlike men, the lower animals are motivated only by bodily needs—hunger, sex, thirst, and so on.
12. The human being has five senses (vision, hearing, taste, smell, and touch).
13. Blind people have unusually sensitive organs of touch.
14. Genius is closely akin to insanity.
15. The more you memorize by rote, the better you will become at memorizing.
16. The basis of the baby's love for his mother is the fact that she fills his physiological needs.
17. Children memorize much more easily than adults.
18. The more highly motivated you are, the better you will do at solving a complex problem.
19. A psychosis is an extreme form of neurosis.
20. Biologists study the body; psychologists study the mind.

Source: Statements derived from L. T. Brown (1983) and Gardner and Hund (1983).

grounding in what we have come to know about thought and behavior. We shall explain what the field is and what is known about such topics as the brain and behavior, personality, child development, learning, memory, psychotherapy, attitudes, and motivation—to name just a few.

PSYCHOLOGY: THE SCIENTIFIC STUDY OF MENTAL AND BEHAVIORAL FUNCTIONING

Psychology is the scientific study of mental and behavioral functioning. This means that, first, *psychology is a science,* and second, that its subject matter—the topic psychology studies—is both the *mental* (the internal) and the *behavioral* (the external) aspects of an individual's functioning. Psychologists study such mental, or internal, phenomena as consciousness, perception, learning, memory, intelligence, and motivation. In addition, psychologists study how people behave in group situations, what behaviors people use to cope with stressful events in their lives, the behaviors shown by infants versus children versus adolescents, and what behaviors can be said to mark the disordered behavioral patterns of schizophrenia or manic-depression. All these topics are studied scientifically.

PSYCHOLOGY IS A SCIENCE

Some people think only of physics, chemistry, or biology when they think of a science. Although these fields are different from psychology, they share at least one important characteristic: They all use the "scientific method" to study their subject matter.

The scientific method is really not just one way of studying such things as electricity, atoms, plants, or people's behavior. The term *scientific method* refers (1) to *assumptions* about how best to understand the world, and (2) to many different techniques of *observation,* ways of viewing the subject matters of the different branches of science. The key assumptions of the scientific method pertain to the belief that the world may be known through observation. This pursuit of knowledge through observation is called *empiricism,* and the methods of science are sets of procedures used to observe (make empirical) the phenomena of the world. Later in the chapter we define exactly what scientific methods of observation are. But we should understand here that to be a science any branch of knowledge must follow the rules of scientific method. As long as we observe the subject matter of our science according to the rules of the scientific method, we are doing scientific work.

Psychology, then, is a science because, like chemistry and physics, it makes the assumptions and follows procedures involved in scientific methods of observation. Psychology observes its subject matter through the scientific method, *and* it has all the general characteristics of any science. For instance, it makes observations systematically and purposefully (Kaufmann, 1968). Yet there is an important difference between such branches of science as physics and chemistry, on the one hand, and psychology on the other. This difference refers to the *subject matter* of psychology.

PSYCHOLOGY STUDIES MENTAL AND BEHAVIORAL FUNCTIONING

Behavior refers to actions or movements. Behavior exists and may be studied in any and all living organisms, from flys and earthworms to chimpanzees and human beings. Internal mental and/or cognitive functions of organisms may also be studied.

Psychology's concern with behavioral and mental functioning is focused on individuals. Other social sciences focus more on the group, society, or culture. Of course, not every psychologist is concerned with the same aspects of individual behavior or mental functioning. That is, different types of psychologists have different interests. Highlight 1.1 describes several types of psychologists.

HISTORY OF PSYCHOLOGY

In the 1870s psychology as it is recognized today did not exist. It was then called *mental philosophy* and was a branch of philosophy. Things began to change in 1875 when William James opened up the first psychological laboratory in the United States, at Harvard University. However, this laboratory was designed only for demonstration, not for experimentation.

HIGHLIGHT 1.1
Types of Psychologists

Most psychologists in the United States belong to the American Psychological Association. Founded in 1892 with about 20 members, it is today an organization of over 60,000 people arranged in 40 divisions. Each division reflects a different area of interest to psychologists. The presence of so many divisions reflects the many different types of psychologists. Some of these are:

BIOPSYCHOLOGISTS

Biopsychologists study the biological and physiological bases of mental and behavioral functioning. For instance, they focus on how the nervous system (e.g., parts of the brain and the spinal cord) and the body's system of ductless glands—the endocrine glands—influence behavior and thought.

LEARNING PSYCHOLOGISTS

These psychologists study changes in behavior which occur through the association of stimulation and responses to stimulation *and/or* through the functioning of one's mental processes (e.g., one's memory).

SENSORY AND PERCEPTUAL PSYCHOLOGISTS

Psychologists who study sensation and perception are interested in discovering how our sensory systems (e.g., our visual and auditory systems) function and how people come to make particular associations to their sensory stimulation (i.e., how people perceive).

COGNITIVE PSYCHOLOGISTS

Cognition refers to knowing. Cognitive psychologists study the means by which people come to know, how knowledge is organized, and how knowledge is used. Some of the major topics studied by cognitive psychologists are thinking, remembering, forgetting, concept formation, language, and intelligence.

MOTIVATIONAL PSYCHOLOGISTS

A motive is the force that provokes or impels an animal to behave; it is the reason for behavior. Psychologists who study motivation are interested in discovering what motives exist for people, and how they act to influence behavioral and mental (e.g., cognitive) functioning. For instance, are people motivated to forget events that made them feel sad? Are people impelled to change their memories such that pleasant experiences are most easily recalled?

COMPARATIVE PSYCHOLOGISTS

How do various species of animals differ? Are there any similarities among animals as different as fish, rats, monkeys, and human beings? Comparative psychologists study similarities and differences in behavior among different species. For example, comparative psychologists may be concerned with whether learning is the same for rats and human beings, or they may be interested in discovering whether sensation and perception are the same among insects, fish, monkeys and human beings.

DEVELOPMENTAL PSYCHOLOGISTS

Developmental psychologists are interested in discovering similarities and differences in mental and behavioral functioning that exist at different age levels. For instance, how are the thinking abilities of a 2-year-old child different from or similar to those of a 7-year-old, a 17-year-old, and a 70-year-old? What motivates a child's behavior, and how does this contrast with the main reasons for the behavior of a teenager, an adult, and an aged person?

PERSONALITY PSYCHOLOGISTS

Psychologists interested in the study of personality are concerned with which characteristics make a person unique, that define that person as an individual. Personality psychologists tend to agree that all people possess some characteristics which are common to all people, some characteristics which are shared by only some other people, and some characteristics which are special for a given person only.

SOCIAL PSYCHOLOGISTS

Social psychologists try to study the influence of groups—of the social setting—on an individual's behavior and, also how individuals behave in groups that have partic-

Developmental psychologists with young children. Developmental psychologists are interested in discovering the similarities in mental and behavioral functioning that exist at different ages in a person's development. (Mimi Forsyth/Monkmeyer)

ular characteristics. For example, is a person more likely to help another if no one else is present to help, if one other potential helper is present, or if two other potential helpers are present?

MEASUREMENT PSYCHOLOGISTS

These psychologists are often termed psychometricians. "Psycho" here refers to mind or mental, and "metric" to measurement, and thus such psychologists are really "mental measurers." What sort of things do these psychologists measure, however? Psychologists often need a means by which they can determine how much knowledge a person has achieved, how much intelligence a person has, or what characteristics of personality a person possesses. To measure such mental and behavioral characteristics psychometricians construct *tests* (devices used to measure a specific characteristic of functioning).

CLINICAL AND COUNSELING PSYCHOLOGISTS

The largest number of psychologists are those who are concerned with assessing and treating maladaptive behavioral problems. Clinical psychologists are typically concerned with assessing and treating undesired or problematic emotions and behaviors. Psychoanalysis, client-centered therapy, behavior therapy, and cognitive-behavior therapy are some of the therapeutic strategies in the repertoire of current clinical psychologists. Counseling psychologists are similar, although they may not typically deal with people having major behavioral problems. Instead, they may emphasize helping basically healthy people find ways to enhance their lives.

EDUCATIONAL PSYCHOLOGISTS

How can we improve children's learning, reading ability, and mathematical skills? Educational psychologists apply knowledge of basic cognitive, learning, and behavioral functioning to the school. These steps are taken to improve students' achievement and to avoid and/or eliminate learning and school behavior problems.

INDUSTRIAL/ORGANIZATIONAL PSYCHOLOGISTS

Machines are often run by human beings. People fly planes, drive cars, operate computers, and despite increasing automation, run much of the equipment that is associated with the production of goods. People work in large companies and other large organizations (e.g., universities). Industrial/organizational psychologists study the *human factors* that make human operation of machines efficient; they study also how individual behavior influences the functioning of organizations. They work to improve the structure of organizations and the performance of the people who populate them.

VOCATIONAL PSYCHOLOGISTS

All of us have or want careers. Work occupies most of our lives, and the choice of a career is very important. But how do we choose our life's work? How can we be sure that our skills and interests can be matched with the right career? Are there particular personality or motivational characteristics that lead to success in particular types of work? How do we discover if we have such characteristics? These questions are among those asked and answered by vocational psychologists. Such psychologists have as their goal the matching of people with careers, so that the person is satisfied with his or her life.

William James (1842–1910), called the "father of American psychology," was the major intellectual force responsible for separating psychology from philosophy in the United States. (Mary Evans Picture Library/Photo Researchers, Inc.)

Wilhelm Wundt (1832–1920) opened the first psychological laboratory designed for experimentation in Germany in 1879. (Bettmann Archive)

James is said to be the "father of American psychology" (Boring, 1950) because he was the major intellectual force responsible for separating psychology from philosophy. In 1890, James had his appointment at Harvard changed from Professor of Philosophy to Professor of Psychology. In the same year he published *The Principles of Psychology* (James, 1890). Soon afterward he brought a European researcher (Hugo Münsterberg) to change Harvard's demonstration laboratory to one in which actual experiments were conducted. James succeeded in launching psychology as a science. By 1900 there were about 40 psychological laboratories in the United States.

The first psychological laboratory designed for experimentation had been founded in 1879 in Leipzig, Germany, by Wilhelm Wundt. Wundt is generally regarded as the father of scientific psychology (and 1879 is usually cited as the birth year of the discipline). He labeled his approach physiological psychology, but his student, E. B. Tichener, termed it *structuralism*. Within this approach the purpose of psychology is to analyze the component elements—the structures—of the mind, which are defined as sensations, images, and feelings. To analyze the structures of the mind a technique termed *introspection* was used: One looked into one's own mind to report on its structure.

American psychologists, however, argued that introspection was too subjective: No one could check to see if the reports were accurate. American psychologists were also more concerned with the *function* (the use) of behavior than with its structure.

The focus on functionalism arose as a consequence of American psychology's interest in the ideas of Charles Darwin (1859), who proposed a theory of evolution based on the ideas of natural selection and the survival of the fittest: Those animals whose physical *and behavioral* characteristics allow them to meet the demands of the environment—to fit their natural settings—will survive and reproduce. In Darwin's view, then, the most important aspect of behavior is not its structure but its function, that is, whether the behavior allowed the animal to fit its setting and survive.

G. Stanley Hall, a major promotor of the new science of psychology in the United States, was a strong follower of Darwin and thought of himself as the "Darwin of the mind" (S. H. White, 1968). Hall founded the American Psychological Association (APA) in 1892 and became its first president. Hall also proposed the first scientific theory of human development, one based on a "translation" of Darwin's evolutionary theory into a theory of human development.

An interest in the function of behavior and a distrust of subjectivism led psychology to seek a means by which it could be objective. Such a means was supplied by John B. Watson, who founded an approach to psychology labeled *behaviorism*. To be truly scientific, Watson (1913, 1918) argued, one must focus on measurable behavior, which is a response (R) to an objectively definable stimulus (S). By studying S-R connections, how stimuli in the environment control an animal's responses, psychology could take its place alongside the other natural sciences, such as physics and chemistry. Behaviorism was readily adopted by virtually all psychologists in colleges and universities, and several predominantly behaviorist theories eventually arose.

In the 1930s, as World War II approached, many European psychologists came to the United States to escape the Nazis, and began to teach in American universities. They brought with them views which differed from American, behavioristic views. For instance, the theory of Sigmund Freud, termed *psychoanalysis,* was increasingly introduced in universities at this time through, for example, the teaching of Erik Erikson. In addition, a group of

PSYCHOLOGY: AN INTRODUCTION

Charles Darwin (1809–1882). His emphasis on the importance of the *function* of an animal's behavior was a major influence in American psychology. (Bettmann Archive)

G. Stanley Hall (1846–1924) founded the American Psychological Association (APA) in 1892. (Granger Collection)

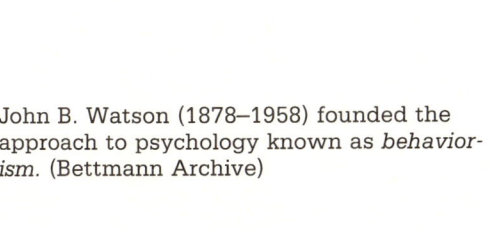

John B. Watson (1878–1958) founded the approach to psychology known as *behaviorism*. (Bettmann Archive)

German psychologists, including Max Wertheimer, Wolfgang Köhler, Kurt Koffka, and Kurt Lewin, believed that one should not try to analyze mental or behavioral functioning into parts made up of stimulus-response units. They argued that when parts combine into a whole, the whole often has characteristics not present in any of the parts. For example, hydrogen and oxygen are gases that do not have the characteristic of "liquidness," but combined, they constitute water, a liquid. Wertheimer, Köhler, Koffka, and Lewin argued that the mind worked in the same way: "The whole is more than the sum of its parts." Thus one should study the sum, the whole, the total, not the constituent parts (e.g., the S-R connections). These psychologists were termed *Gestalt* (meaning "totality") *psychologists* because of their stress on the need to focus on the whole (the total) mind.

Thus one consequence of World War II was the introduction into American psychology of different theoretical views about psychological functioning. However, the war also brought other, less theoretical changes in psychology. Many servicemen and women returned from the war with physical and emotional problems that needed to be treated. Their needs stimulated the development of several areas of psychology. Tests were needed to determine what was wrong with the veterans, as were psychometricians and psychological examiners. The need to treat undesired behavioral and/or emotional problems so stimulated the growth of clinical and counseling psychology that today more psychologists specialize in these areas than in any other.

In sum, from World War II through the 1980s, psychology has become more diverse in both its theoretical views and in the areas that interest psychologists. Throughout this period, both the topics studied by psychologists and the types of applications of psychological knowledge have multiplied.

PSYCHOLOGY AND THE SCIENTIFIC METHOD

Typically, one thinks of a scientist as a person in a white lab coat, toiling over test tubes and charts and "experimenting." Certainly, some scientists do these things; and some of them are psychologists. Yet the science of psychology is by no means limited to this technique. Indeed, because of their diverse interests, psychologists study mental and/or behavioral phenomena in many ways.

The scientific method is not one method, but a set of methods. Each method allows systematic, purposeful observations to be made in a different way. Psychologists use different methods of scientific observation to pursue their interests because there are many different ways in which behavior occurs and can be best studied. In fact, we may say that four major types of scientific method of observation are used in psychology: naturalistic observation, controlled observation, experimental observation, and observation through the use of questionnaires and/or interviews. We will consider the characteristics, advantages, and disadvantages of each of these methods.

NATURALISTIC OBSERVATION

In this type of observation, the psychologist attempts to see things as they exist naturally; that is, the psychologist tries to observe things uninterrupted as they are actually happening in a real-life setting. For example, suppose that a psychologist was interested in the "aggressive" behavior shown by 5-year-olds in play. Such behavior might be defined as hitting, pushing, and throwing things at others. The psychologist might want to know if such behavior is shown by 5-year-olds, and if so, how often and in what manner. Naturalistic observation might be chosen as a way of making the observations necessary to find out these things.

The psychologist would find a group of 5-year-old children at play, for example, in a kindergarten class or a day-care center. After the children got used to the psychologist's presence, he or she would simply observe and record the behavior of the children. The psychologist would in no way interfere with the children's behavior. Rather, their behavior, as it naturally occurred in the real-play situation, would be observed and recorded.

Such naturalistic observation has real-world, or *ecological, validity* because it is *actually* an observation of behavior as it exists in its true ecology. If we want to see how aggressive behavior exists among 5-year-olds when they are playing, a good way to find this out is to observe 5-year-olds at play!

On the other hand, naturalistic observation also has its disadvantages. Although we see behavior as it actually occurs in the real world, all we can do is describe how the behavior looks and when we saw it appear. We cannot be certain *why* the behavior happened as it did.

Because the psychologist neither controls the situation, nor *manipulates* (i.e., attempts to influence) the behavior, it is not known what caused or affected it. There are many reasons for the inability to know causes. One is that many things may be happening at once. The psychologist, even with the help of cameras, may be unable to observe everything. And even if many things are observed, the psychologist does not know that what has been chosen for observation is really important or relevant to the reason for the

Psychologists observing a child at play. In controlled observation, psychologists attempt to observe behavior as it happens in a controlled setting. (Stock Boston)

behavior's occurrence. Thus incomplete or biased observations may be obtained.

It may also be difficult to see the behavior of interest. In other words, there is no way to *ensure* that the behavior of interest (e.g., aggression) will be seen often enough to assure systematic observations of it. The behavior of interest may be so infrequent that no systematic or repeatable observations can be communicated, and naturalistic observations of infrequent behaviors can produce misleading conclusions. Because of these disadvantages, other methods of observation are also used in psychology.

CONTROLLED OBSERVATION

Rather than studying behavior based on observations of its occurrence in the real world, the methods of controlled observation can be employed to increase the likelihood of observing the behavior of interest. This goal is sought by controlling the situation in which the behavior will take place. If a psychologist believes that aggression in 5-year-olds does not occur very frequently and yet wants to study this behavior, he or she might see the advantage of controlled observation. Suppose that two 5-year-olds are placed in a room with a very attractive toy which can be used by only one child at a time. After putting the children in this situation for a very short time we would certainly expect to see some aggression as we defined it.

Controlled observation allows the psychologist to influence the observations because he or she controls and manipulates the situation. Situations are chosen on the basis of their likelihood of "producing" the behavior of interest. Yet this technique also has a disadvantage: By itself it allows the psychologist directly to manipulate the situation alone, not the behavior of the people in the study. One knows that a certain type of behavior may be expected to occur in this standard, controlled situation with some certain degree of regularity; but one may not know what in the situation influenced the behavior to take the form that it took.

Yet controlled observation can provide *normative* information; that is, by having people respond in standard, controlled situations, we learn what behavior to expect in such situations. A *norm* is behavior that we may typically expect from certain people in specific situations. In fact, in a later chapter we will see that when psychologists use a special type of controlled observation technique—known as *a psychological test*—important normative information about such aspects of functioning as intelligence and personality may be discovered.

THE CONTROLLED EXPERIMENT

This is the observational technique that gives the psychologist the best understanding of the basis of people's behavior in a particular situation. In a controlled *experiment* the psychologist actually attempts to manipulate events which he or she believes will influence the person's behavior. That is, besides controlling a situation, the psychologist also controls exactly what happens to the person in the situation. Such control is used to see what will result when people are exposed to certain, specific events. The goal is to establish a cause-effect relationship, and the psychologist hopes to find evidence that "a change in X will cause (have the effect of) a change in Y." In an experiment the psychologist tries to control the important influencing factors that act on the subjects of the study; of course, what the subjects do *depends* on them.

To illustrate, a psychologist might conduct an experiment to determine whether students learn better when everything is quiet versus when music is playing. The psychologist might ask: How will different subjects learn if one-half are stimulated with (or distracted by) contemporary music while trying to study, while the other half are not stimulated (or distracted) by sound at all? The psychologist would then expose subjects to different events—either the "music" or the "quiet" stimulation—and the psychologist would be interested in observing if differences in learning resulted between subjects exposed to one condition as opposed to the other. In an experiment, then, the psychologist tries to see if the subjects' behavior can be affected, or changed, as a consequence of the different conditions that the psychologist manipulates.

The Independent Variable. The condition that the psychologist chooses to vary, that is, the various events with which the psychologist stimulates the subjects, is called the *independent variable*. A *variable* may be defined as anything that can change. Noise (or sound level), age, height, intelligence, amount of tenseness, and years in college are all variables. Anything that can change (or vary) in terms of how much of it exists is a variable. An independent variable is something which the psychologist chooses to vary through intentional manipulation in an experimental study of behavior. This variable is "independent" of the subject's behavior. It is what the psychologist chooses to manipulate.

The Dependent Variable. Although the independent variables, or the stimulus conditions, are chosen by the psychologist for manipulation and are thus independent of the subjects, their effects on the subjects' behaviors are not independent of the subjects. How the subjects behave in response to the different stimulations they receive *depends* on the subjects, and in an experiment the behavior shown in response to an independent variable's stimulation is termed the *dependent variable*.

In an experiment the psychologist alters a specific stimulus—the independent variable—to see its effect on the dependent variable (i.e., the subjects' *responses* to the various stimuli). As in our example, the psychologist manipulates the background sound stimulus (sound or quiet) to see what effect this change will have on the subjects' learning. In this illustrative experiment, then, the level of background sound is the independent variable, and the resulting degrees of subject learning constitutes the dependent variable. In Figure 1.1 we see some hypothetical results of such an experimental manipulation. On the baseline of the graph, the *x axis*, we see listed the two levels of the independent variable. Along the line perpendicular to the baseline, the *y axis*, we see some of the possible levels of learning responses, represented as "percentage learned." Here, then, a high percentage learned corresponds to better learning, and a low percentage learned corresponds to poorer learning. We see then that the group that studied with quiet had about 75% of their learning scored correct; the group that studied with music had only about 50% correct learning. In subsequent chapters we will often see the results of various studies of behavior graphed in this way: the inde-

Figure 1.1
Results of an imaginary experiment concerned with the effects on learning of studying with either quiet or music.

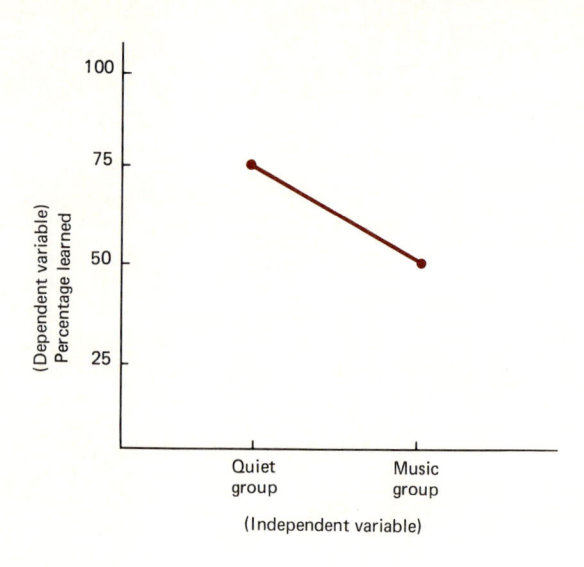

pendent variable along the baseline and the dependent variable along the perpendicular *y* axis.

Controls. Controlling the independent variable to which subjects are exposed is important, but the psychologist also has to control many other variables. In fact, in an ideal experiment the only thing that can be different between the two groups of people is that one studies with music playing and the other studies in a quiet environment. Any other stimulus which, if varied, could have some effect on the subjects' responses (on the dependent variable) must not be allowed to vary. Only through *control* will the psychologist be sure that any changes in the subjects' learning are due *only* to the changes in the independent (stimulus) variable.

Thus the psychologist would want to make sure that such things as age, intelligence, and educational background of the two groups were not different before the study was conducted. If the psychologist found differences in how well people learned when stimulated with music versus quiet, the psychologist would want to be sure that such differences were due to this different stimulation between the two groups and did not arise because one group was composed of, say, 5-year-olds while the other group was composed of, say, 20-year-olds, or because one group consisted of very bright people while the other group contained people of average intelligence. If such differences existed between the two groups, the psychologist could not be sure that the differences found in the dependent variable were, after all, really due only to the variations introduced by the independent variable. Unless an experiment is properly controlled, the differences could just as easily have been due to age, intelligence, or educational differences. When an experiment is properly controlled, the psychologist can make sound determinations of what caused the variations in the dependent variable.

Controlled experimental observations have an advantage not found with either naturalistic observation or controlled observation. When the psychologist observes how changes in the independent variable affect the subjects' behavioral responses, he or she may state that the difference in the subjects' behaviors was the result of the different conditions to which they were exposed. In other words, experimental observation allows the psychologist to discover a basis of a particular behavior within the specific situation used for study.

Suppose that the results seen in Figure 1.1 were actually found; that is, the group that studied with quiet learned better than the group that studied with music. Given all the proper controls, the psychologist examining this difference could now say that the basis of the different levels of learning seen in the situation used in the experiment was the different sound stimulation given the two groups. Hence experimental observations allow the psychologist to discover bases of studied behaviors within a controlled experimental setting.

The controlled experiment also has disadvantages, however. The results of an experiment tell us only the effect of a specific stimulus on a certain behavior in one specific situation. We cannot necessarily apply these results to a different situation, where perhaps other stimuli may be used and/or other things may or may not be controlled. Thus we cannot easily apply results of one experiment to other experimental situations *unless* everything about the two situations is identical. Moreover, in the real world everything is not as controlled as it is in an experiment. Things vary naturally, and since many variables stimulate a person at the same time (instead of one at a time), each of these variables may affect behavior singularly or in combination. While experimental observations give us important information about a basis for behavior in a specific siutation, that situation is rarely identical to events in the real world. Hence we must apply or "generalize" the results of controlled experimental observations cautiously to the real world.

A disadvantage of experimental observation—that it may not have real-world validity—is an advantage of naturalistic observation. On the other hand, the disadvantage of naturalistic observation—that it cannot easily discover a basis of a behavior—is an advantage of the controlled experiment. Ideally, a psychologist interested in discovering the most accurate information about behavior should try to move back and forth between these two methods of scientific observation, observing reality in the natural world but testing hypotheses carefully under controlled conditions. Actually, psychologists tend to use one or the other of the foregoing types of observation; *or,* because of the disadvantages associated with each technique, they may choose yet another type of method of observation.

QUESTIONNAIRES AND INTERVIEWS

Rather than try to observe all the possible variables that may influence behavior in all possible naturalistic situations, and/or try to study each variable separately in one experiment after another, many psychologists choose merely to ask people about themselves. That is, psychologists often ask people they are interested in studying a series of questions about behavior. The questions may pertain to just about anything—for example, beliefs about politics, religion, sex, or drug use; typical reactions to events; what experiences are recalled from childhood; and many, many more. How the questions are both asked and answered can also take many forms. A printed series of questions may be given to subjects, or the same questions may be asked in an oral interview. Subjects, on the other hand, may respond to such questions through writing, speaking, or both.

Such techniques have obvious disadvantages. People may lie; they may try to answer in a way that they think is favorable to them, and/or they may

Psychologists have long used interviews, as with the client pictured here, because these face-to-face encounters allow psychologists to obtain considerable information about a person's behavior. (Ken Roberts/Stock Boston)

respond with answers they think the psychologist wants to hear. For example, when asked whether they have ever "engaged in illegal drug use," people may respond "no" because they think this makes them look better rather than because "no" is the truth. Similarly, when asked if they think people of one religion are inferior to people of another religion, subjects may also respond "no" because they think that is the "socially correct" response or because they think psychologists want to discover a lack of prejudice in people.

Another potential disadvantage is that what people say about their behavior may differ from how they behave. We may not be intentionally lying when we say that we behave in certain ways; yet we may be too involved with ourselves to describe our behavior accurately. Hence we may unintentionally be distorting the facts of our behavior, or we may be forgetting and/ or not remembering certain things accurately. For instance, we may report that we *always* obey traffic laws, and yet, a bit later, we may speed home to dinner.

Finally, psychologists may include questions which make certain answers more likely than others, or their behavior may bias the subjects' answers to questions. For instance, a researcher who establishes a warm rapport with a subject may elicit answers which differ from those elicited by a cold and/or hostile interviewer.

Despite these disadvantages, questionnaires and interviews do have important advantages. They allow psychologists to obtain considerable information about behavior quickly. If a questionnaire has both written questions and answers, for instance, one psychologist may obtain information from several hundred people at the same time. Moreover, some aspects of behavior may not be ethical or easy to investigate except through questionnaires or interviews. For instance, whereas few people would allow their sexual behavior to be observed daily, more people might provide anonymous information on a questionnaire about their sexuality.

PSYCHOLOGY: AN INTRODUCTION

Psychologists have long favored questionnaires and interviews and have sought to overcome the disadvantages of such techniques (R. B. Cattell, 1973). For instance, techniques have been developed to measure people's tendency to lie on questionnaires, and psychologists have attempted to devise ways to "screen" the actual purpose of the questions from the subject, or at least make it hard to guess. A final point in regard to measurement is important to note here. *Correlational statistics* typically are used to measure the association among responses on questionnaires. As is explained in greater detail in the Statistical Appendix, a *correlation coefficient* is a statistic which describes whether one measure is or is not related to another.

THE ETHICS OF PSYCHOLOGICAL RESEARCH

Few people would object to a chemist putting a gas in a jar to see how changes in temperature would affect it. Yet, many people—*including psychologists*—would object to putting a young child alone in a dark room for several hours to see the effects that certain sudden loud noises have on the child's behavior. It would be wrong to stress the child in this way, even though it might be scientifically important. Thus there are often *ethical reasons* which prevent a psychologist from making particular scientific observations.

As we consider the various areas of psychology, we shall see that psychologists always confront ethical considerations when they study behavior and/or apply their knowledge to the real world. The psychologist who studies nonhuman animal behavior has to decide if it is ethical to sacrifice an ani-

Many psychological experiments involve animal subjects. This pigeon is about to participate in an experiment in conditioning. (Van Bucher/Photo Researchers)

mal's life to study a particular behavior problem; even if a decision is made to sacrifice the animal, it is nevertheless the psychologist's ethical responsibility to act humanely. In turn, the psychologist who attempts to apply scientific knowledge to treat a person's emotional problems has to decide if a technique which *may* seem to hurt in the short term should be used for the long-range goal of helping. Hence psychologists must always consider whether it is ethically correct to study behavior in the way they want. The American Psychological Association has published a set of ethical principles for psychologists to follow in both their applied and research endeavors (1981). The APA has also published (1973) a list of ethical principles for research with human participants. These principles help the researcher decide if ethical considerations are being followed in an investigation. These principles are summarized in Highlight 1.2.

HIGHLIGHT 1.2
Ethical Principles in the Conduct of Research with Human Participants

The American Psychological Association (1973) has formulated ten ethical principles to be followed by psychologists conducting research with humans. These are the following:

PRINCIPLE 1

In planning a study the investigator has the personal responsibility to make a careful evaluation of its ethical acceptability, taking into account these Principles for research with human beings. To the extent that this appraisal, weighing scientific and humane value, suggests a deviation from any Principle, the investigator incurs an increasingly serious obligation to seek ethical advice and to observe more stringent safeguards to protect the rights of the human research participants.

PRINCIPLE 2

Responsibility for the establishment and maintenance of acceptable ethical practice in research always remains with the individual investigator. The investigator is also responsible for the ethical treatment of research participants by collaborators, assistants, students, and employees, all of whom, however, incur parallel obligations.

PRINCIPLE 3

Ethical practice requires the investigator to inform the participant of all features of the research that reasonably might be expected to influence willingness to participate, and to explain all other aspects of the research about which the participant inquires. Failure to make full disclosure gives added emphasis to the investigator's responsibility to protect the welfare and dignity of the research participant.

PRINCIPLE 4

Openness and honesty are essential characteristics of the relationship between investigator and research participant. When the methodological requirements of a study necessitate concealment or deception, the investigator is required to ensure the participant's understanding of the reasons for this action and to restore the quality of the relationship with the investigator.

PLAN OF THE BOOK

To fully appreciate the scope of modern psychology, and to be introduced to the diversity of the problems and topics studied by each of these subareas of the science, we will have to consider the major topics studied in each of the major areas of contemporary psychology. In succeeding chapters we will study the areas of interest of the different types of psychologists, such as those described earlier in this chapter (in Highlight 1.1)—biopsychology, sensation and perception, motivation and emotion, learning, development, cognition, personality, abnormal psychology, psychotherapy, psychological tests and measurement, and social psychology. We will also describe several of the relatively new areas of major concern to psychologists—both in highlights

PRINCIPLE 5

Ethical research practice requires the investigator to respect the individual's freedom to decline to participate in research or to discontinue participation at any time. The obligation to protect this freedom requires special vigilance when the investigator is in a position of power over the participant. The decision to limit this freedom increases the investigator's responsibility to protect the participant's dignity and welfare.

PRINCIPLE 6

Ethically acceptable research begins with the establishment of a clear and fair agreement between the investigator and the research participant that clarifies the responsibilities of each. The investigator has the obligation to honor all promises and commitments included in that agreement.

PRINCIPLE 7

The ethical investigator protects participants from physical and mental discomfort, harm and danger. If the risk of such consequences exists, the investigator is required to inform the participant of that fact, secure consent before proceeding, and take all possible measures to minimize distress. A research procedure may not be used if it is likely to cause serious and lasting harm to participants.

PRINCIPLE 8

After the data are collected, ethical practice requires the investigator to provide the participant with a full clarification of the nature of the study and to remove any misconceptions that may have arisen. Where scientific or humane values justify delaying or withholding information, the investigator acquires a special responsibility to assure that there are no damaging consequences for the participant.

PRINCIPLE 9

Where research procedures may result in undesirable consequences for the participant, the investigator has the responsibility to detect and remove or correct these consequences, including, where relevant, long-term aftereffects.

PRINCIPLE 10

Information obtained about the research participants during the course of an investigation is confidential. When the possibility exists that others may obtain access to such information, ethical research practice requires that this possibility, together with the plans for protecting confidentiality, be explained to the participants as a part of the procedure for obtaining informed consent.

From American Psychological Association (1973).

FOCUS ON THE PSYCHOLOGIST

Virginia S. Sexton

VIRGINIA STAUDT SEXTON Ph.D., Fordham University, is professor of psychology at St. John's University, and former president of the International Council of Psychologists, the Eastern Psychological Association, and the New York State Psychological Association. She is currently Vice President of Psi Chi, Eastern Region. Her principal research interests are history of American psychology, psychology of women, international psychology, and professional and ethical issues. She is author of 100 articles and co-author/editor of five books (with Henryk Misiak) including *History of Psychology: An Overview; Phenomenological, Existential, and Humanistic Psychologies;* and *Psychology Around the World.*

From earliest times, humans have been interested in observing and analyzing other humans' behavior and in speculating about their motivation. Today psychologists, as specialists in behavior, apply scientific methods to its study. Early in my career as a psychologist, I became interested in the history of psychology, specifically in the behavior and motivation of those men and women who created and developed the science of psychology. This interest led me to participate in a collaboration with Henryk Misiak, a colleague who shared my interests in the history of psychology, and with whom I was to co-author four books and edit still another.

As I pursued the study of psychology's history, I soon realized the wisdom of Ralph Waldo Emerson's dictum, "There is no History; only Biography." For example, my interest in psychology's history led me to write biographical essays about such major contributors to the field as Floyd Allport, Kurt Koffka, Ivan Pavlov, Max Wertheimer, Herman Witkin, and Wilhelm Wundt. In particular, I found it especially rewarding to study the lives of theorists like Sigmund Freud, Alfred Adler, and Karen Horney—not simply their theories. As I did, I learned how much their own life experiences and circumstances influenced the kinds of theories they developed.

In fact, the contributions to psychology, made by the great men and women of the past, no matter what their native lands, were largely influenced by their lives and careers, their struggles, problems, failures, and successes. This realization was reflected in a book I wrote with Professor Misiak in 1976, *Psychology Around the World,* and by papers I authored regarding the history of women's accomplishments in psychology. In addition, as I pursued this scholarship and, as well, participated in such organizations as the International Council of Psychologists, the Interamerican Society of Psychology, the International Association of Applied Psychology, the Association for Women in Psychology, and the Association for Women in Science, I have come to believe that perhaps the greatest contribution to us made by the men and women whose lives forged our history is that they serve as models and inspirations to us, their intellectual and scientific heirs.

and in the chapters themselves. In fact, Chapter 19 deals with psychology and contemporary society, and discusses such topics as psychology and the law; the effects of day care, maternal employment, and divorce on child development; and the nature of intellectual and personality functioning in the aged.

SUMMARY

1. Psychology is defined as the scientific study of mental and behavioral functioning. Psychology is a science because of its adherence to the assumptions and procedures involved in the scientific method. The subject matter of psychology is the mental and the behavioral characteristics of the individual.

2. There are many different topics which psychologists study. These range from studying the physiological bases of behavior to studying the effects of social situations on a person's behavior.

3. Psychology was not always a science. Originally a branch of philosophy, psychology became a separate discipline with the establishment of the first laboratory devoted to psychological experimentation. This laboratory was founded by Wilhelm Wundt, in Leipzig, Germany, in 1879, and was associated with an approach to psychology termed structuralism, an approach which used introspection to analyze the mind into its component elements.

4. In the United States William James was the first major promoter of scientific psychology. American psychology, promoted by James and other early contributors (e.g., Hall and Watson) was focused more on the function of behavior than on its structure.

5. The scientific methods used by psychology include (a) naturalistic observation; (b) controlled observation; (c) experimental observation; and (d) observation through the use of questionnaires and interviews. Each of these methods of scientific observation have their own unique set of observational characteristics, as well as their advantages and disadvantages.

6. Psychologists cannot just choose a method with which to study a problem. Such choices must be made in respect to ethical standards of conduct. Psychologists adhere to a set of published standards of ethical behavior; these are rules which guide psychologists' professional and research activities.

KEY TERMS

Scientific method
Empiricism
Structuralism
Introspection
Behaviorism
Gestalt
Naturalistic observation
Controlled observation
Experiment
Independent variable
Dependent variable
Ethics

SUGGESTED READINGS

American Psychological Association. Ethical principles of psychologists. *American Psychologist,* 1981, *36,* 633–638. This article summarizes the professional and research principles of ethics to which psychologists adhere. Ethical principles about the practice of psychology, and about the use of both human beings and animals as research subjects, are presented.

BORING, E. G. *A history of experimental psychology* (2nd ed.). New York: Appleton-Century-Crofts, 1950. A classic, scholarly, and thorough presentation of the history of psychology, focusing on the early contributions to establishing psychology as an experimental science.

CAMPBELL, D.T., & STANLEY, J. C. Experimental and quasi-experimental designs for research on teaching. In N. L. Gage (Ed.), *Handbook of research on teaching.* Chicago: Rand McNally, 1963. A classic authoritative statement about the features of experiments and of the problems that may be encountered on trying to design a sound experimental study.

KAUFMANN, H. *Introduction to the study of human behavior.* Philadelphia: Saunders, 1968. A short but thorough presentation of the key assumptions and characteristics of science in general and of psychology in particular.

MISIAK, H., & SEXTON, V.S. *History of psychology in overview.* New York: Grune & Stratton, 1966. An excellent presentation of the history of psychology, one encompassing events in the United States, Europe, and in countries outside the North American and European continents.

Answers to: A Pretest for Introductory Psychology (Table 1.1, page 4): All 20 statements in Table 1.1 are false.

PART TWO

Biology, Sensation, Perception, and Consciousness

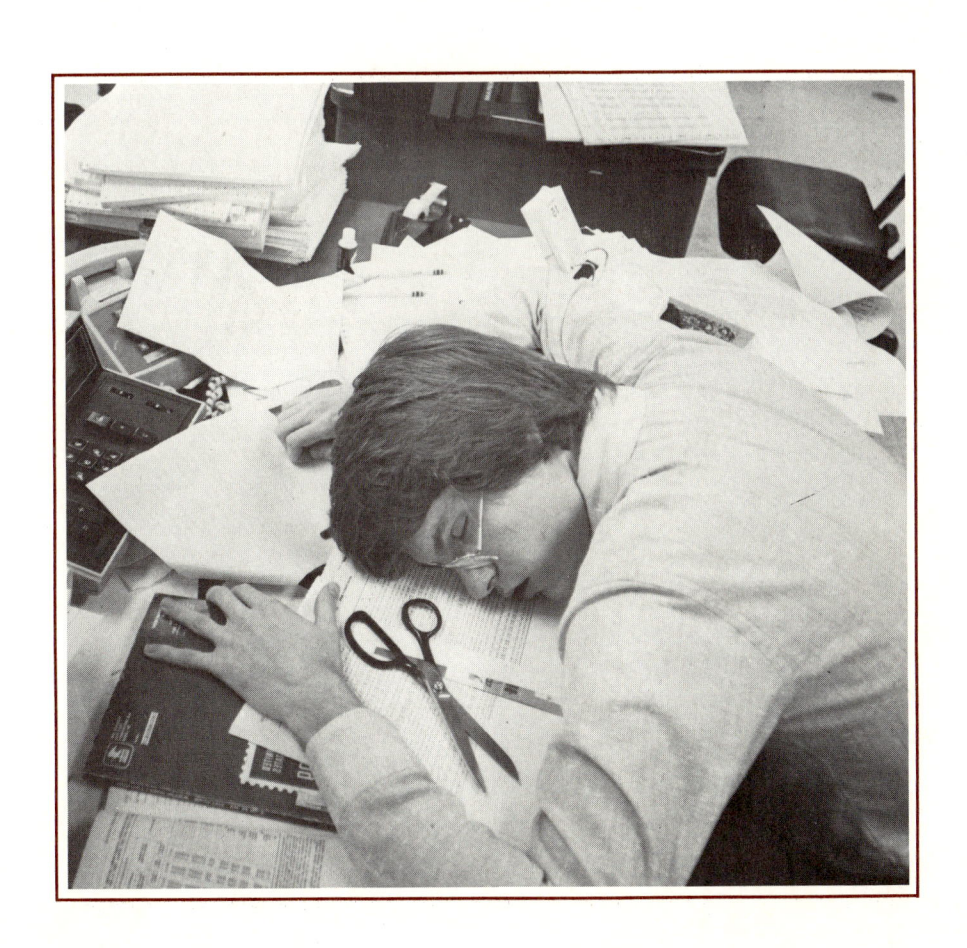

2

Biology and Behavior

INTRODUCING THE NERVOUS
  SYSTEM
  The Central Nervous System
  The Peripheral Nervous
    System
  The Neuroendocrine System
TASKS THAT THE NERVOUS
  SYSTEM PERFORMS
  The Nervous System Monitors
    the World Outside the Body
  The Nervous System Takes
    Care of Its Partner in Life,
    the Body
  The Nervous System Stores
    and Retrieves Memories
  The Nervous System Directs
    Behavior
  The Nervous System Produces
    Thinking and Creativity
  The Nervous System Generates
    Personality
THE NEURON: THE BASIC
  UNIT OF THE NERVOUS
  SYSTEM
  What Neurons Are and Where
    They Are Found
  The Structure of Neurons
NEURONAL SIGNALING
  The Resting Potential
  The Action Potential

  Synaptic Transmission
PUTTING IT ALL TOGETHER:
  GENERATING
  BEHAVIOR—A SIMPLE
  REFLEX
THE ANATOMY OF THE
  CENTRAL NERVOUS
  SYSTEM
  The Spinal Cord
  The Brain Stem
  The Cerebellum
  The Midbrain
  The Hypothalamus
  The Thalamus
  The Cerebral Hemispheres
CORTICAL LOCALIZATION OF
  FUNCTION
  Sensory Projection Areas
  Motor Areas
  Frontal Lobes
  Temporal Lobes
  Parietal Lobes
LATERALIZATION IN THE
  BRAIN
  Hemispheric Specialization
  Split-Brain Research
SUMMARY
KEY TERMS
SUGGESTED READINGS

INTRODUCING THE NERVOUS SYSTEM

Inside your head is an immensely complex information-processing system that directs your perceptions, thoughts, memories, feelings, and actions. This system is composed of billions upon billions of nerve cells packed into a space not much larger than a standard desk telephone. Yet within this system lies the very essence of one's being. If this system should be altered in some way, say by drugs or injury, one's behavior, thoughts, and perceptions would also be altered. This is so because each of these processes is a direct result of the workings of the nervous system. In fact, we can say that all human behavior results from the direction of bodily actions by the nervous system.

It is therefore clearly important for those with an interest in psychology to understand a little about how the nervous system is constructed and something about the basic principles that underlie its operations. In this chapter we first introduce the basic parts of the nervous system and then discuss some of the tasks that the nervous system performs. Later in the chapter after learning how individual cells in the nervous system function, we conclude with a discussion of various parts of the brain and their different jobs. (For a more detailed discussion of the nervous system and how it is put together, you may wish to consult one of the several basic physiological psychology and neuroanatomy texts listed at the end of this chapter.)

The nervous system can be divided into two major parts: the *central nervous system* (CNS) and the *peripheral nervous system* (PNS). The central nervous system has only two components, the *brain* and the *spinal cord;* all the rest of the nervous system is considered to be part of the peripheral nervous system.

HIGHLIGHT 2.1
Early Ideas About the Relative Importance of the Brain

The brain is the central control region for most behavior. Although this fact may seem obvious to us today, it is actually a fairly new idea. Ancient cultures had a far different conception of the importance of the brain. When the ancient Egyptians mummified a body, they preserved most of the internal organs, such as the stomach and liver, but discarded the brain, which they considered unimportant for the afterlife. Although some ancient Greek philosophers, such as Hippocrates, believed that the brain was the seat of thought and learning, Aristotle, noting that the head gives off a good deal of body heat, concluded that the principal function of the brain is to cool overheated blood. The writers of the Old and New Testaments never mention the brain at all, although the heart is spoken of many times as the source of human feelings, and the bowels are often referred to as the seat of courage, passion, and even piety. Today the heritage of these beliefs is reflected in many ways. We say that someone has "a broken heart"; that one is "kindhearted" or perhaps "heartless"; that a courageous person has a lot of "guts"; and we give paper hearts (rather than little paper brains) on Valentine's Day.

THE CENTRAL NERVOUS SYSTEM

A photograph of a human brain is shown in Figure 2.1. Note the wrinkled surface of the cerebral cortex, which forms the surface of the two cerebral hemispheres and the cerebellum, which looks something like a small sub-brain attached to the back side of the larger cerebral hemispheres.

The two cerebral hemispheres are not identical, but are a symmetrical pair in the same way that your right and left hands are symmetrical mirror images of each other. The hemispheres of the brain are similar in function, although as we will see later, each also has certain jobs that it performs better than the other hemisphere. The two sides of the brain are connected by several large bands of nerve fibers that allow the two sides of the brain to communicate with each other. This permits the two halves of the brain to function as a unified whole. Later we shall discuss what happens when one of the major connections between the two hemispheres is severed.

The spinal cord is the other part of the central nervous system. Messages from the brain destined to activate various muscles or regulate the activity of internal organs travel down the spinal cord, leave it through the ventral roots of the cord (see Figure 2.2), and continue to their destinations via the many nerve pathways of the peripheral nervous system.

Traveling in the opposite direction, messages from sensory receptors in all parts of the body are carried to the spinal cord by the sensory nerves of the peripheral nervous system. These messages enter the spinal cord through the dorsal roots. Some of these sensory messages will be relayed to the brain by the spinal cord, while others will elicit reflexive responses which are generated in the spinal cord itself without involving the brain at all. *Reflexes* mediated by the spinal cord are very important and include those that maintain muscle tone, posture, and some aspects of coordinated movement, such as walking, running, or grasping.

Figure 2.1
The human brain provides the basis for consciousness, thinking, and behavior. In this specimen, the outer membranes have been removed, revealing the deeply grooved surface of the cerebral cortex and cerebellum. Some of the many blood vessels that supply the brain with oxygen and nutrients can also be seen in this photograph. (Walter Dawn)

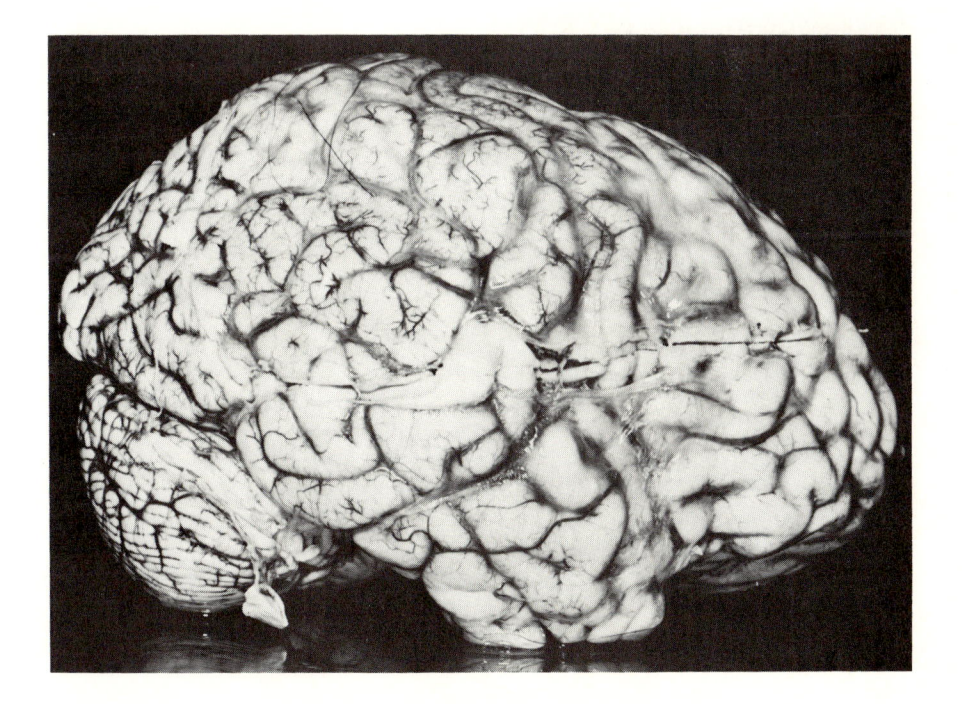

Figure 2.2
The spinal cord and associated pathways. On the left is a drawing showing the general location of the spinal cord. It extends only about two-thirds of the way down the spinal column. At each level of the spinal cord a pair of spinal nerves is formed that innervate specific regions of the body. The lower right-hand portion of this figure shows how the spinal cord is encased in the bones of the spinal column and is surrounded by the dura mater. Each vertebra of the spinal column has openings for the spinal nerves to pass through. In the upper right is a cross section through the spinal cord. Sensory information enters the spinal cord through the dorsal roots, while messages directing the actions of muscles and glands leave the spinal cord through the ventral roots. The white matter of the spinal cord is made up of axons that extend up and down the spinal cord; the gray matter is where cell bodies and synapses are found.

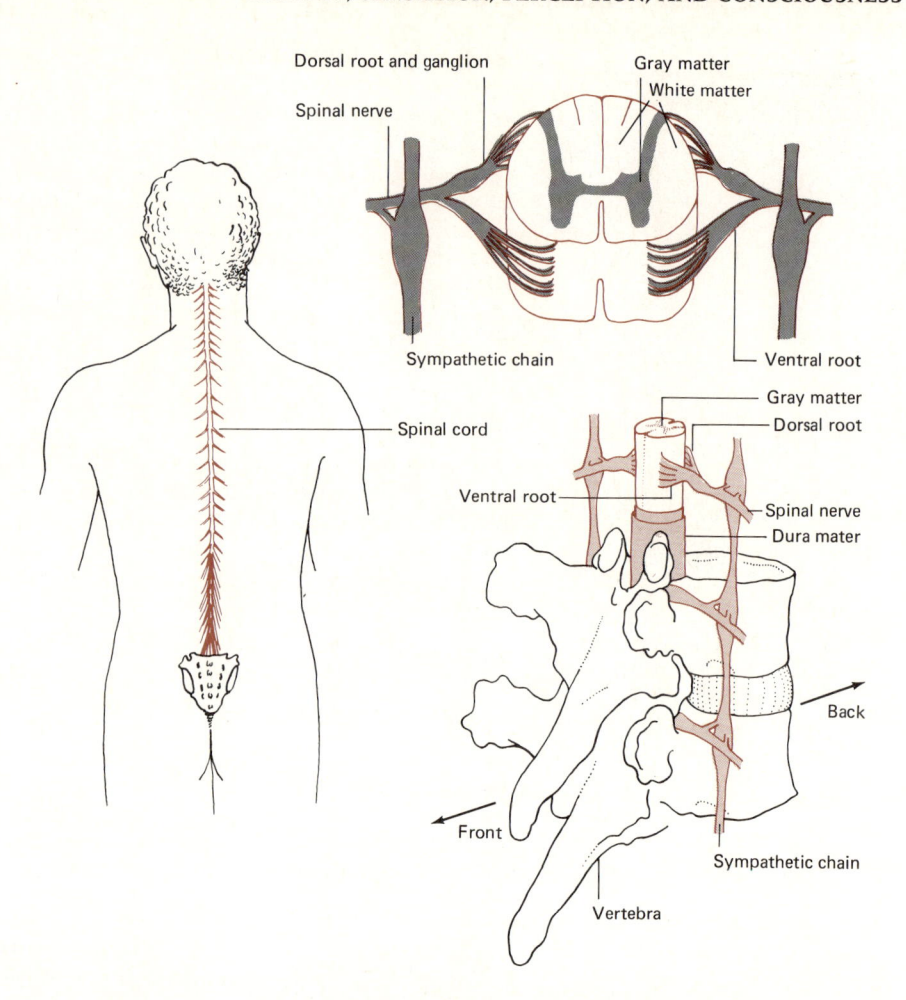

The spinal cord is not simply a passive transmitter of sensory and motor information. Besides mediating reflexive responses, it also processes sensory information so that the messages coming from receptors in the body are sharpened and made more distinct before they are relayed to the brain (see Angevine & Cotman, 1981).

THE PERIPHERAL NERVOUS SYSTEM

The peripheral nervous system is composed of two major parts, the somatic system and the autonomic system. The *somatic system* has two primary functions: It transmits information from the sense organs to the central nervous system, and other messages from the central nervous system to the skeletal muscles. Therefore, the somatic system can be subdivided into sensory and motor divisions. The sensory part of the somatic division of the peripheral nervous system tells the brain what is going on in the environment and throughout the body, so that it can decide what behaviors to initiate next. The motor portion of the somatic system then carries the resultant information from the brain to the muscles, which then contract in patterned ways to generate behavior.

FOCUS ON THE PSYCHOLOGIST

Carl W. Cotman

CARL W. COTMAN is a professor in the Department of Psychobiology at the University of California, Irvine. He received his Ph.D from Indiana University in 1968.

I am fascinated by the plastic properties of synapses in the mature brain and have devoted several years to the study of synaptic plasticity. Synaptic plasticity is a special type of *behavioral plasticity,* a term introduced by William James to describe any meaningful change in behavior. We now know that while the basic circuitry of the CNS is laid down during development, CNS circuits remain plastic or modifiable throughout life. This represents a major change in our thinking about brain function from several years ago when brain circuitry was considered fixed once it formed.

I suppose some people always knew the type of career they would pursue. I am certainly not one of the these, although the past events point more clearly toward my eventual career goals than I perhaps realized at the time. I have been interested in science since high school and can recall doing several independent projects because of my curiosity about chemistry and biology. I recently discovered a blueprint I did in high school for a mechanical drawing class for which the assignment was to draw my ideal house. The one I drew had a lab but no bedroom! I attended a small liberal arts college in Ohio, Wooster College. I felt that since I was interested in more than simply science, a broad liberal arts background would be appropriate. I majored in chemistry out of natural interest and because it was an outstanding department. I became "hooked" on research through an undergraduate research program. Wooster had an outstanding program, and I think this type of "hands-on" experience has launched many careers. I decided that I did not want to pursue pure chemistry but became interested in an emerging discipline—the study of the chemistry of the brain. I thought that the prospects of discovering molecular mechanisms for brain function and for neurological disorders were the most exciting application of chemistry. Today we are much closer to understanding the chemical events underlying synaptic plasticity and the treatment of neurological disorders. It has indeed been exciting to contribute to the development of this field.

What are the ultimate capabilities of the mature brain to modify its connections during normal maturation and to grow and repair itself after injury? How can such plasticity be promoted to gain greater adaptability and greater recovery of function after injury?

Much research is now focused on discovering the molecular events that underlie plasticity in the mature and aged brain. It is now clear that the mature brain contains growth factors that can support sprouting and transplantation and in general appear to participate in the maintenance and repair of the brain. We have shown that these factors, called *neurotrophic factors,* increase in response to injury. The activity of neurotrophic factors appears to increase over several days and participates in brain regrowth and healing processes after injury. Recently, several molecules have been identified (e.g., those that enhance cell survival, stimulate sprouting, and promote cellular differentiation). These agents may eventually be useful for stimulating regeneration and the growth of neural circuits after injury. They also may play a role in the maintenance and plasticity of circuitry in the healthy brain. I believe that the time is right to make major advances toward developing therapeutic approaches to enhance synaptic plasticity and the regeneration of neural circuits after injury. Most, if not all, of the molecular and cellular events necessary for reconstruction of the injured CNS can take place in the adult, can be induced, or are accessible to intervention. It is an exciting time to be working in the area.

The second major part of the peripheral nervous system, the *autonomic nervous system* (ANS), modulates the activities of many internal organs that carry out basic life-maintenance processes of the body. The actions of the blood circulatory system, digestive system, respiratory system, and reproductive system, among others, are all modulated by the ANS. The autonomic nervous system is called "autonomic" because it is under relatively little conscious control and therefore seems to operate almost automatically. Most of us would find it difficult to consciously alter autonomic functions that would increase the rate of stomach contractions or alter blood flow, for example. Yet the ANS is not completely automatic, and one can gain some control over its functions by using techniques popularly known as biofeedback or through some of the meditative exercises associated with Eastern cultures.

THE NEUROENDOCRINE SYSTEM

Working together with the central nervous system and the peripheral nervous system are the various chemicals or hormones released by the various organs and glands in the body. Collectively, these hormonal systems are referred to as the *neuroendocrine system,* and the chemicals released by this system are another way that the brain can influence behavior. Tiny amounts of some of these chemicals can change our mood and attentiveness, alter feeding or drinking, and influence reproductive behaviors. Some hormones released early in life determine whether a person will have a male or a female body and may even influence some behavioral characteristics, such as aggressiveness, that become evident only at maturity. The brain is clearly an organ which can be strongly influenced by hormones released from other parts of the body (McEwen, 1976).

TASKS THAT THE NERVOUS SYSTEM PERFORMS

THE NERVOUS SYSTEM MONITORS THE WORLD OUTSIDE THE BODY

To respond appropriately to changing conditions in one's environment, the nervous system must have rapid access to a wide variety of sensory information and be able to interpret it accurately. The nervous system does this very well in a three-part sequence. First, it takes in sensory information using specialized cells called receptors, which respond to various kinds of environmental stimuli. For example, some receptors respond to light reflected from the things we see, others respond to specific chemical characteristics in the foods we eat, and still others respond to certain chemicals suspended in the air or to vibrations of air molecules.

Since all of these receptor systems send messages to the brain, the second task of the nervous system is to make sense out of all the sensory messages that are continually bombarding it. It must put incoming stimuli into perspective and attend to those events that are most immediately important while ignoring most of the others. Then the brain must decode and interpret these messages.

The final task of the nervous system, and the ultimate goal of processing sensory information, is to direct behavior in a way that is appropriate and meaningful to the world around it. Some behaviors may be simple reflexes such as an eye blink or a change in posture, others may result in storage of a memory, while still others may lead to complex patterns of behavior such as flying an airplane, painting a picture, or writing a term paper.

THE NERVOUS SYSTEM TAKES CARE OF ITS PARTNER IN LIFE, THE BODY

The nervous system uses the body as its connection to the outside world. The body carries the nervous system from place to place, responds to various objects and events in the environment, and provides sensory information; in short, it does the behaving. The body also provides oxygen, food energy, environmental stability, and protection for the nervous system. To do all this effectively, the body must be in good condition, so many nervous system functions are directed toward keeping it healthy. There must be enough food to provide energy for behavior, appropriate water balances, adequate blood pressure, just enough stomach acidity, a fairly constant internal temperature, and a host of other things. Each of these bodily processes is directly or indirectly controlled by the nervous system.

The nervous system carries out these bodily maintenance functions for us with very little conscious effort on our part. If we consider the regulation of body temperature as an example of nervous system control of bodily processes, we can get some idea of just how well the nervous system does this. A person maintains a body temperature of 37 degrees Celsius (°C) [98.6 degrees Fahrenheit (°F)] with amazing accuracy; a variation of a degree or two is enough to make you think that you might be getting sick. This internal temperature is held constant in spite of many different conditions—in winter and summer, on ski slopes, and at the beach. Metabolism speeds up to generate more heat when body temperature drops, while mechanisms such as perspiration cool you when temperature rises (see Heller, Cranshaw, & Hammel, 1978).

The nervous system directs behaviors that help to maintain body temperature. If you are too cold, you put on more clothes and go to warmer places; if you are too hot, then jackets and hats are taken off, and you move into the shade or a cool building.

The nervous system protects itself and the body from injury. When there is either psychological or physical stress, the nervous system initiates the release of hormones and directly activates other systems that help the body cope with stress. For example, pain is the body's signal to the nervous system that something very bad is happening and that behavior should be changed immediately to relieve the distress. Some of these protective nervous system responses are so important that they do not even involve the brain. If you touch a very sharp object, the spinal cord will begin the withdrawal response before the message of pain even reaches the brain.

THE NERVOUS SYSTEM STORES AND RETRIEVES MEMORIES

One of the most important functions of the nervous system is learning and remembering. It is our enormous capacity to store memories that makes human beings so different from other animals. As a result of our memory processes, we can learn how to cope with new situations, to perform complex tasks (such as learning the fundamentals of psychology), to relate to friends and associates, and how to use spoken and written language to communicate ideas and feelings to someone else. Each of these kinds of tasks depends critically on the capacity of the nervous system to store and retrieve memories.

Although psychologists and neurobiologists know a great deal about principles of learning and also about what chemicals enhance memories and what treatments worsen them, you may be surprised to learn that the key to how memories are stored in the brain is still lacking. Clearly, each time you learn new information, something in your brain has to change when the information is stored; otherwise, the information could never be retrieved. However, no one yet knows just what this change in the brain is.

THE NERVOUS SYSTEM DIRECTS BEHAVIOR

The end point of all neural activity is, of course, the generation of behavior. On the basis of incoming sensory information, already stored memories, and complex cognitive processes, the nervous system sends messages to the muscles of the body, ordering them to move in certain ways. Although this seems simplistic, very few people ever think of their behavior as being the direct result of nervous system activity.

Movements can be both simple and complex behavioral responses. Some patterns of movement are as uncomplicated as the reflexive withdrawal from a hot object. Other behaviors, such as walking or swimming, involve complex patterns of muscle contractions. Still others, including the extraordinarily complicated and very exact movements required to play a piano concerto, dance a ballet, or fly a jet fighter, demonstrate the incredible adaptability, speed, and precision of which the nervous system is capable.

THE NERVOUS SYSTEM PRODUCES THINKING AND CREATIVITY

Conscious thought and creativity are also the result of nervous system actions. The brain generates thoughts and ideas, solves problems, and creates new things. When one writes a short story, performs mathematical calculations, carves a sculpture, or just doodles on a pad of paper, the brain is directing creative behavior. Our understanding of how the brain does these complex tasks is rudimentary, but we do know that all behavior is the result of CNS activity (Granit, 1977). No magic is involved.

THE NERVOUS SYSTEM GENERATES PERSONALITY

Although the complexities of personality are best described by global behavioral concepts such as superego, extroversion, or depression, we must remember that these are also the result of brain function. Concepts such as ego, defense mechanisms, gender identity, and temperament are all descriptions of behaviors directed by the nervous system. Many emotional responses are the result of cognitive processes interacting with internal bodily arousal, and some of the characteristic behaviors and problems of adolescence are caused by changes in the concentrations of certain hormones circulating through the body. The nervous system, interacting with memories of previous experiences and our current environment, determines who we are (Eccles, 1966; Popper & Eccles, 1977).

There is an important corollary to this idea: When the brain malfunctions or is injured, thoughts and behavior will change; they may become pathological or disturbed. Many forms of mental illness result from malfunctions of the CNS, and when drug therapies such as antipsychotic medications or antidepressants are given, persons with disturbed behavior often show improvement. Similarly, drugs that upset normal neural function, such as alcohol, cocaine, and LSD, also alter behavior.

THE NEURON: THE BASIC UNIT OF THE NERVOUS SYSTEM

WHAT NEURONS ARE AND WHERE THEY ARE FOUND

All bodily tissues are made up of many individual cells. Each of these cells is specialized to do a particular job. Cells of the kidneys, liver, and muscles each do specific tasks, and the cells of the nervous system are no exception to this pattern. These cells, called *neurons,* act together to carry out the many and varied functions of the nervous system that were just described.

It may seem difficult to understand how aspects of behavior such as imagination, thought, and creative ability can be produced by means of cells such as neurons. Yet this is undeniably the case. When considered only as a collection of individual cells, the brain seems to be very simple, but this simplicity is more than offset by the extraordinary number of neurons in the brain. Current estimates put the number of neurons in the average human nervous system at around 100 billion. Some suggest there may be far more (Kandel, 1981). If you consider that each of these billions and billions of cells may be interconnected with a few hundred to several thousand other neurons, some idea of the astronomical number of patterns of interaction possible in such a system begins to emerge.

There are not only enormous numbers, but also many different kinds of neurons in the nervous system, each with a specific job to do. Neurons come in many different sizes, shapes, and structures. In fact, well over 1,000 different types of neurons are found in the human brain, a far greater variety of kinds of cells than in any other organ of the body (Palay & Chan-Palay, 1977).

So many different types of neurons exist because neurons perform many different tasks. Some neurons transmit information from one place to another; others integrate the inputs originating from many other neurons; still others modulate the activity of whole neural systems or release hormones into the bloodstream. It appears, however, that most neurons act as complex information processors, integrating signals that come from a variety of sources.

How can sense be made out of a system composed of so many individual units and so many different cell types? One way is to examine different parts of the neurons for similarities and differences that relate to the jobs they do.

We find that most neurons have the same basic parts: a *cell body,* where genetic information is stored and much of the metabolism of the cell occurs; *dendrites,* many branching arms that extend from the cell body and usually receive information from other cells; and an *axon,* a long single thread that transmits information from one place in the nervous system to another. Not

BIOLOGY, SENSATION, PERCEPTION, AND CONSCIOUSNESS

all neurons have clearly distinguishable dendrites and axons, though, and the existence differences in the axons and dendrites is one way that allow us to classify neurons. See Figure 2.3 for some typical neurons.

Neurons can also be classified by size and the type of job they do. Neurons that carry messages from one part of the body or nervous system to another are typically called *projection neurons*. They have relatively large cell bodies, which are needed to nourish their long dendritic and axonal processes.

Figure 2.3
Neurons come in many different sizes and shapes. Each has a specialized function, which results in wide differences in their appearance.

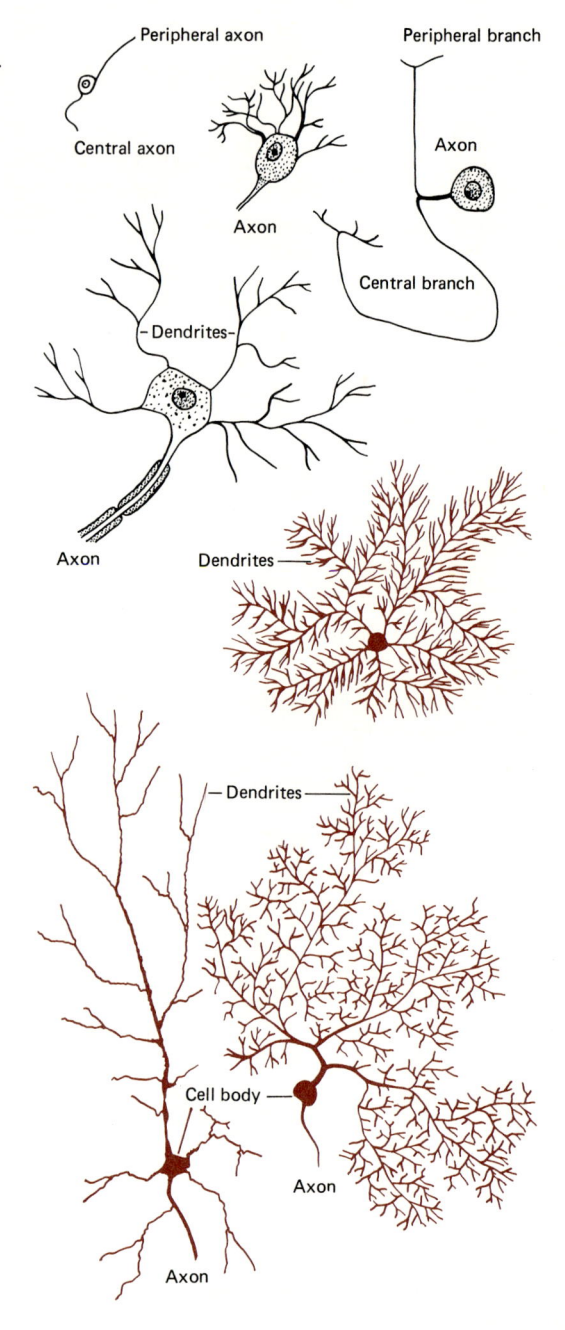

BIOLOGY AND BEHAVIOR

Most neurons, however, tend to have cell bodies that are, compared to most projection neurons, quite small, and most of their connections are with other neurons close by and within the same general functional unit. These small neurons, found only in the central nervous system, are called *local-circuit neurons.* They are the cells that make possible all the complex operations of the nervous system. Projection neurons carry information to and from the cells of the central nervous system, but the billions of local-circuit neurons act on those messages and generate new messages that ultimately result in behavior. In some brain regions, 95% of the neurons are local-circuit neurons (Angevine & Cotman, 1981). The more complex the function of a particular region of the central nervous system, the greater the ratio between the number of local-circuit neurons and the number of projection neurons.

Figure 2.4
Schematic drawings of three different kinds of neurons that transmit information from one place to another in the nervous system. The unipolar neuron has just one extension from the cell body that divides into branches—one that goes to receptors in the body, and one that projects into the central nervous system. The bipolar cell has two arms extending from the body. The multipolar cell has many dendrites and a distinct axon.

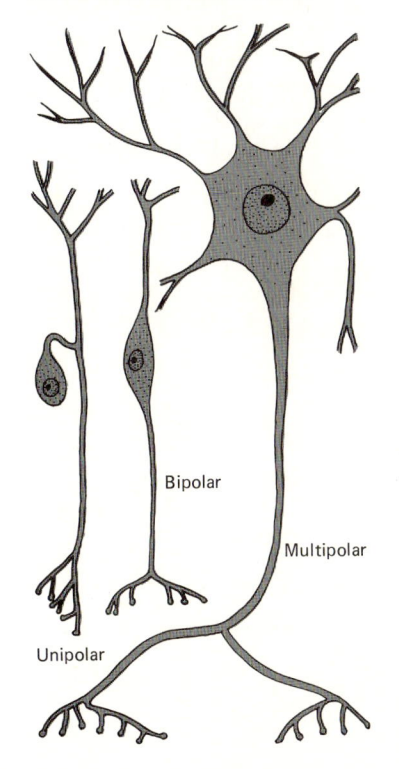

Neurons of the Peripheral Nervous System. In general, neurons of the peripheral nervous system (Figure 2.4) send their axons from the spinal cord to various muscles, internal organs, and sensory receptors throughout the body. These important components of the peripheral nervous system have two basic jobs to do. One is to carry information from the central nervous system to the many different structures of the body that actually do the work. The other is to carry sensory messages from all regions of the body to the CNS.

Each time you move, electrochemical messages travel from the central nervous system along the axons of the peripheral nervous system neurons to the appropriate skeletal muscles, causing the muscles to contract and thus generating movement. In the same way, heart rate, breathing, and some glandular secretions are modulated by messages transmitted from the central nervous system along the long peripheral nervous system neurons. Neurons that send information from the central nervous system to the various targets in the periphery are called *motor neurons.*

Other neurons of the peripheral nervous system have a different job to do. They carry sensory information from receptors located all over the body to the central nervous system, so that it can stay informed about what is going on, both inside the body and in the outside world. Each receptor is connected to a *sensory neuron* linking the periphery to the central nervous system. Some receptors have their own sensory neurons, whereas others may share a single sensory neuron. When many receptors are connected to one sensory neuron, the capacity to make fine discriminations between stimuli is not very good, but if the ratio of receptors to sensory neurons approaches one to one, the capacity to make precise sensory distinctions is excellent. We explore this idea in more detail in Chapter 3.

Neurons of the Central Nervous System. Like cells of the peripheral nervous system, neurons of the central nervous system each do particular jobs. Some CNS neurons receive and process sensory information carried to them by peripheral sensory neurons. Sometimes only a very few neurons in the brain or spinal cord act on the sensory information and a simple reflexive response results. More often, incoming sensory information alters the activity of many millions of neurons, and complex responses, such as a change in conscious thought patterns, a feeling of emotion, or perhaps the encoding of a memory, result. It is the interaction of billions upon billions of central nervous system neurons that produces what we know as thought and the sensation of consciousness (see Hoyle, 1983).

THE STRUCTURE OF NEURONS

Now we will look more closely at these remarkable cells that make up the brain, spinal cord, and peripheral nervous system, to see how they are constructed. Looking at a section of brain under the microscope, you would generally see only the outside surface of the neurons. This view, though, clearly shows that these cells, although they do very important jobs and are very numerous, are very, very small; their sizes are typically described in microns (μm; a micron is a millionth of a meter; a thousandth of a millimeter). Cell bodies of neurons range in size from about 4 μm in diameter to about 100 μm (Carpenter, 1976). Although some neurons may possess axons that project for more than a meter in humans and for several meters in animals such as the giraffe or whale, the cell body is still very small and the axon is very thin, usually only a few microns in diameter in most mammals.

The Neuron Membrane. Each neuron is covered by a thin skin called the *cell membrane*. It defines the boundary of the cell and is a very complex structure. Suspended in the membrane are many complex *protein molecules* which are responsible for the many functions that make the membrane an active participant in the operations of the cell. For example, complex protein molecules in the membrane actively remove some substances from inside the cell. Other molecules in the membrane transport many of the substances needed by the cell to the inside. The membrane also generates an electrical charge within the cell, a charge which is critical in the transmission of information along the axon.

The Cell Body. Inside the cell body are many tiny structures called *organelles*, each doing a specific job. One can liken the inside of a neuron to a tiny corporation with each division carrying out its separate function. Note the *cell nucleus* in Figure 2.5. It can be thought of as the executive suite of the cellular corporation, where central planning and engineering take place and where the important blue prints for cell function are stored. The DNA (deoxyribonucleic acid), found only in the nucleus, directs the functioning of the cell.

Also prominent within the cell are tiny beadlike organelles called *mitochondria*. The mitochondria serve as power plants for the cell; many important steps in extracting energy from the metabolism of glucose take place in them. Those cells or cell regions that need a lot of energy have many mitochondria; those with only a small demand for energy have few.

Within each neuron is a very convoluted structure that looks somewhat like a crumpled sheet of newspaper. Called the *endoplasmic reticulum*, it can be thought of as the assembly line of the cellular corporation. It divides the interior of the cell into various regions, moves substances around inside the cell, and provides a support structure for the molecules which actually synthesize proteins.

The *Golgi apparatus*, also in the cell body, can be conceived of as the cell's shipping room because it provides many of the products made in the cell body with a protective covering before they are transported to other regions of the neuron or secreted from the cell.

Finally, there are the *lysosomes*, which act as the cellular janitorial staff. These important organelles clean up the waste products that result from the various metabolic activities of the cell. Without lysosomes, these substances would soon build up to toxic levels which would seriously affect the functioning of the neurons. Lysosomes contain enzymes that digest proteins, fats,

BIOLOGY AND BEHAVIOR

Figure 2.5
Structures within the cell body of a typical neuron. Each plays an important role in the functioning of the cell so that it can do its assigned tasks.

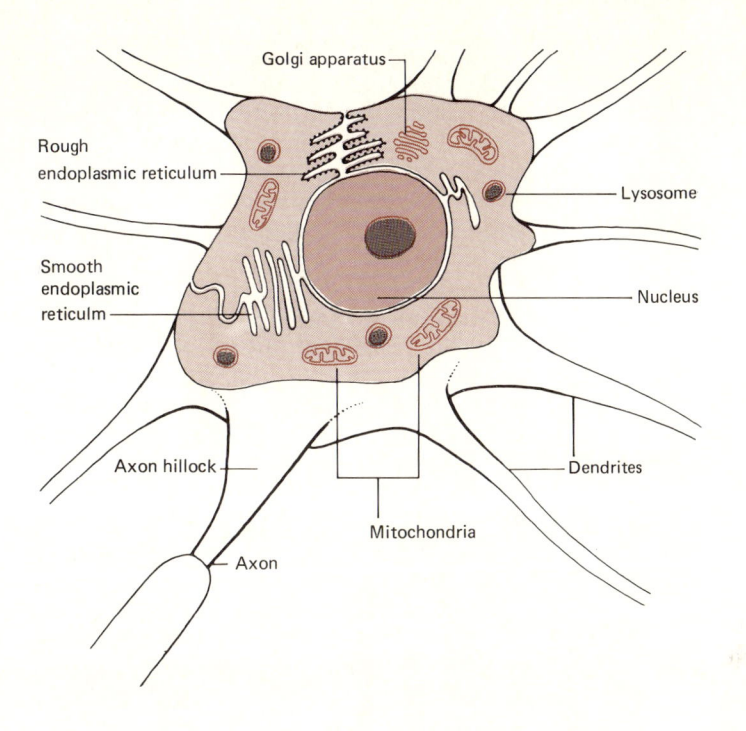

[Diagram of neuron cell body with labels: Golgi apparatus, Rough endoplasmic reticulum, Smooth endoplasmic reticulm, Axon hillock, Axon, Mitochondria, Dendrites, Nucleus, Lysosome]

and other substances. Should a genetic disorder cause a deficiency in one or more of these enzymes, an illness results. Those affected with Tay-Sachs disease, for example, cannot produce an enzyme that breaks down a certain kind of fat (Okada & O'Brien, 1969). This substance builds up in the cells and eventually leads to serious mental retardation, deterioration of brain function, and death.

Input and Output Structures: Dendrites and Axons. DENDRITES. As we saw earlier, dendrites are branches that extend from the cell body and spread out in complex and often elaborate ways. The arrangement of the dendritic branches is often a clue to the particular function of a cell in the nervous system, for it is through the dendrites that neurons receive much of their information through *synaptic connections* from other neurons.

Chemical messages are used at most synaptic connections to send information from one neuron to another. Cells with many elaborate and branching dendrites receive information from many other cells, while those with relatively uncomplicated arrangement of dendrites receive inputs from comparatively few cells. In addition, some cells make synaptic connections on the cell body or even on axons, rather than on the dendrites.

When the synaptic connections are made on the dendrites, they occur both on the branches of the dendrites and on tiny bumps on the dendrites known as *dendritic spines*. Some cells have huge numbers of spines on their dendrites, and some cells in the cerebellum have as many as 100,000 spine synapses (Fox, Hillman, Siegesmund, & Duta, 1967).

Communication at most synapses is a one-way process. The cell sending information releases a chemical that influences the activity of the receiving cell. Information passes from synaptic terminals to the dendrites or cell body, but does not go the other way. Later in the chapter, we discuss in some detail how synaptic connections operate.

AXONS. The *axon*, the major output pathway of most neurons, is a long, thin, tubelike structure that carries information from the cell body to other cells. The conduction of information down the axon is electrochemical and not like the conduction of electricity in wires at all.

The axon joins the cell body at a region called the *axon hillock* and extends away from the cell for some distance. This distance varies considerably among different types of neurons. In some neurons the axon is only a few microns long, whereas in other types of neurons, the axons may be a meter or even much more in length. To get some idea of the relationships in size between the cell body and a long axon, visualize a hose attached to a basketball; the hose represents the axon and the basketball represents the cell body. In this case, the hose might stretch the length of Manhattan, about 14 miles (Carlson, 1981). In many animals the axon is covered with a sheath made of a fatty substance called *myelin* that helps to speed conduction of impulses down the axon. Most neurons have only one axon, but an axon may divide into many branches, especially near its end. At the end of each branch are the terminals, which make synaptic connections between the axon and the target cell.

Synaptic Terminals. The synaptic terminal found at the end of each branch of an axon is a small swelling which contains the chemicals that transmit a message across the synaptic connection to the receiving cell. When a message that has traveled from the cell body along the axon arrives at a synaptic terminal, it causes the release of a chemical into the gap between the terminal and the target cell. The chemicals released by synaptic terminals are called *neurotransmitter substances*. There are well over 20 substances released by different cells in the nervous system that act as neurotransmitters (Schwartz, 1981). Some of these neurotransmitters have generally excitatory effects, whereas others tend to be inhibitory. Still others seem to have modulatory effects which alter the long-term responsiveness of the target cells.

There are many different kinds of chemicals that serve as neurotransmitters. Many of them are important in directing behavior, producing consciousness, and maintaining rational thought processes. Interference with a neurotransmitter called acetylcholine produces paralysis. Additionally, aspects of schizophrenia are thought to be related to changes in synapses in the brain that use dopamine as a neurotransmitter, while substances that affect receptors for the neurotransmitter serotonin produce hallucinations. Neurotransmitters are certainly among the most important chemicals in your body.

NEURONAL SIGNALING

THE RESTING POTENTIAL

So far we have described the tasks performed by the nervous system and the different kinds of cells that do these tasks, but we have not yet discussed the way in which these cells transmit information from one place to another. In this section we see how an electrical potential is developed in neurons and how this potential transmits impulses along the length of the axon so that information can be carried from one region of the nervous system to another.

During the late eighteenth century, scientists begin to speculate that the brain might communicate with the rest of the body through electrical signals. Galvani (1737–1798) demonstrated that electrical stimulation of the nerves in a frog's leg could produce contractions in some of the muscles of the leg.

He hypothesized that nerve conduction might resemble electrical conduction in a wire. Later, a French researcher named du Bois-Reymond (1818–1896) demonstrated that there is a difference in electrical charge between the outside and inside of an isolated nerve fiber and that electrical impulses appeared to be occurring in the nerve. It has only been comparatively recently, however, that researchers discovered the mechanisms that underlie nerve conduction.

One of the problems they faced is the small size of most vertebrate axons. Their microscopic diameter made the study of their properties very difficult. However, in 1938 the zoologist J. Z. Young reported that squids have some neurons with axons almost a half a millimeter in diameter, and that these giant axons are ideal for studying the physiology of nerve conduction. The squid's giant axon is so large that electrodes can easily be inserted inside it to record the electrical events occurring across the cell membrane (see Figure 2.6).

Once techniques of studying the giant axon of the squid had been developed, researchers quickly observed that the inside of the axon is negatively charged in relation to its outside and that this charge is important in the conduction of impulses along the length of the axon. The difference in electrical potential across the axon membrane, that is, between the inside of the cell and the outside, is called the *resting potential.* The resting potential charges up the neuron and gets it ready to act. How is this charged developed?

To understand the resting potential, we must first understand a little about neuron membranes. Recall that the membrane surrounding each neuron is a complex structure with many protein molecules embedded in it. Some of these protein molecules serve as channels for substances to pass through the membrane from outside to inside, and vice versa. These membrane channels allow some substances to move with relative freedom through the membrane while blocking the passage of others. One can say that the membrane is *selectively permeable* to certain substances.

The substances we are concerned with now are called *ions;* they are molecules or atoms that have either gained or lost electrons, thus giving them either a negative or positive charge. The neuron membrane restricts the passage of some ions while allowing others to move back and forth through ion channels in the membrane with relative freedom (see C. F. Stevens, 1979).

The selectively permeable neuron membrane allows potassium ions to move quite freely across it while almost completely restricting the movement of sodium ions as well as some large negatively charged ions. Further, since

Figure 2.6
The squid in neurobiology. Important advances in our understanding of how axons conduct information were made by examining the workings of the giant neurons of the squid nervous system. The mantle nerve cells have very large axons, which can be removed and studied. In this diagram, an electrode has been inserted into the inside of a giant axon, and a resting potential of −70 millivolts is being measured. If the axon were to be stimulated to threshold, an action potential could be recorded using the voltmeter. (Photo by Marineland)

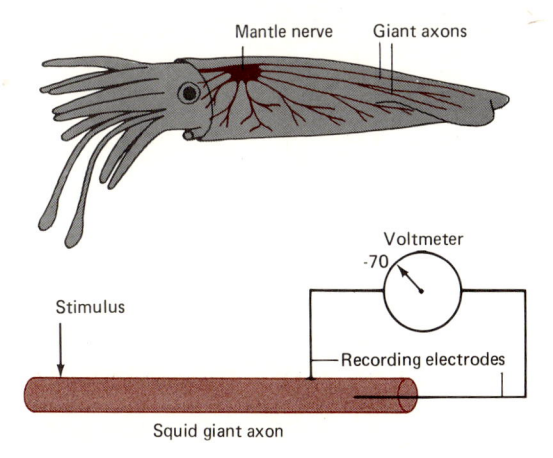

there is a much higher concentration of positively charged potassium ions inside the axon than outside it, some potassium ions will tend to move from a region of higher concentration (inside) to a region of lower concentration (outside). As each potassium ion moves to the outside, it carries with it a positive charge. This loss of positive charges from the inside of the cell causes the inside to become negatively charged in relation to the outside of the cell.

This process leads to the establishment of a resting potential that is about −70 millivolts (mV; a millivolt is one thousandths of a volt) in relation to the outside of the cell (see Koester, 1981). Another way of putting it is to say that as a result of the movement of ions across the cell membrane, the outside and the inside of the cell become like poles of a very tiny battery, with the inside being negatively charged while the outside is positive.

The resting potential is found in every neuron of all living creatures with a nervous system. Each of the billions of neurons in the human brain has a resting potential which allows it to function. The charge across the membrane is not very large compared to the 1.5 V of a standard flashlight battery, but consider that most neurons in the mammalian nervous system are very small. When viewed in that way, the 70-mV resting potential seems large indeed.

THE ACTION POTENTIAL

Neuronal Conduction. How does the establishment of a resting potential enable neurons to transmit information? To understand neural conduction, let us set up a hypothetical experiment using the giant axon of the squid. The arrangement can be seen in Fig. 2.7. If we stimulate the axon with a very small electric shock, nothing much is recorded by the electrodes at the other end of the axon. However, if we stimulate the axon with a sufficiently strong depolarizing electric shock, that is, a stimulus that decreases the difference in potential across the membrane to *threshold,* an impulse or action potential is generated that travels the full length of the axon without any decrease in its strength. What is the basis of this rather remarkable event?

If the charge across the membrane is decreased to threshold (depolarization), sodium channels in the membrane which were closed when the cell was at rest now open up, and for a brief instant [less than 1 millisecond (ms)] the membrane becomes freely permeable to sodium ions. These positively charged sodium ions, which are in high concentration on the outside of the membrane, rush across the membrane to the inside of the cell. Enough of them move across the membrane to make the inside of the axon positive in relation to the outside. When this has occurred, the sodium channels in the membrane close down once more and potassium ions move from the inside of the axon, across the membrane, to the outside. The movement of potassium ions is propelled by two different kinds of forces. Since the inside of the membrane is now positively charged due to the influx of the sodium ions, the positively charged potassium ions are forced out (like charges repel). The potassium ions are also moving from a region of high concentration to a region of lower concentration. The movement of positively charged potassium ions to the outside of the membrane results in the restoration of the negative resting potential inside the cell (see Keynes, 1979). This entire sequence of events called the *action potential,* takes only a couple of milliseconds. It is shown in Figure 2.8.

How does this sequence of ionic movements cause an impulse to be transmitted along the axon? Depolarization of one region of the axon to threshold also causes adjacent regions of the axon to be depolarized. The movement

BIOLOGY AND BEHAVIOR 41

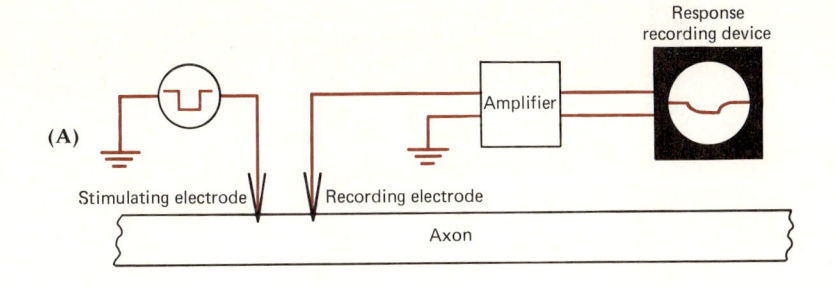

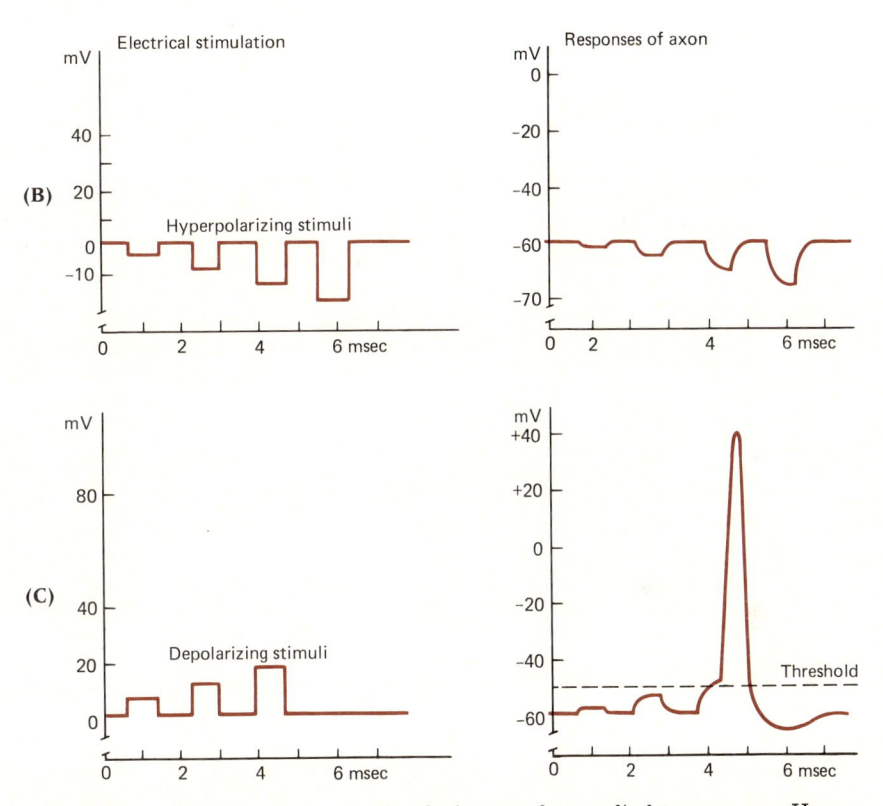

Figure 2.7 Different kinds of stimulation can be applied to an axon. Hyperpolarizing stimulation makes larger the difference in electrical charge between the inside and the outside of the cell membrane, while depolarizing stimulation decreases this electrical potential. In the upper portion of this figure is a schematic diagram of a typical laboratory setup for studying the effects of stimulation of an axon. The stimulating electrode, shown on the left, delivers electrical pulses that either hyperpolarize or depolarize the axon. Responses of the axon to this stimulation are recorded with the electrode on the right, amplified, and are displayed on a recording device. Hyperpolarizing pulses cause the potential across the membrane to be briefly increased (from −60 mV to around −65 or −70 mV). The resting potential then recovers when each stimulation pulse is terminated. Depolarizing stimuli, on the other hand, decrease the difference in electrical charge across the membrane. Small amounts of depolarization have little effect, but when the membrane is depolarized to threshold, then an action potential, or nerve impulse, is produced which is propagated throughout the entire length of the axon. (Based on Rosenzweig & Leiman, 1982)

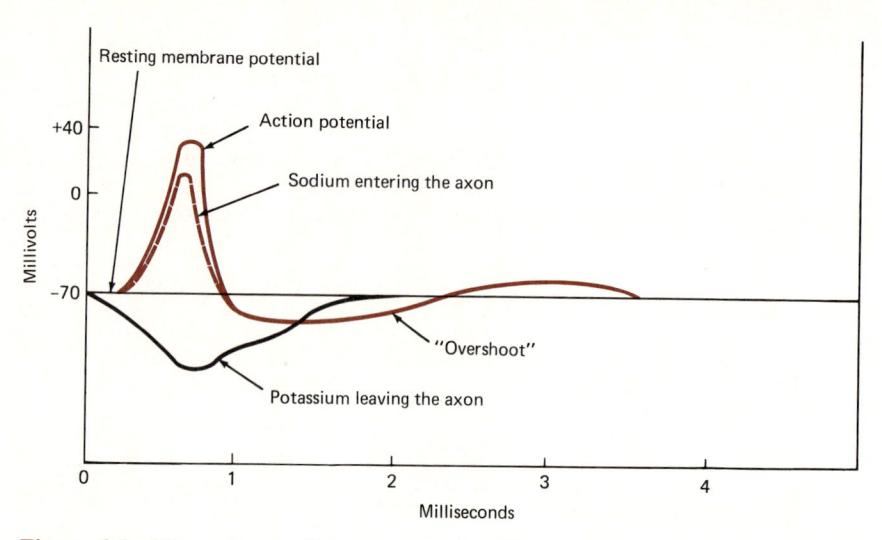

Figure 2.8 The pattern of movement of sodium and potassium ions during the generation of an action potential. As the membrane becomes depolarized, potassium ions begin to leave the cell. When threshold is reached, positively charged sodium ions rush into the axon, causing the inside of the axon to become positively charged. When the peak of the action potential is reached, sodium ions stop coming in, but potassium ions continue to leave. Since the potassium ions are also positively charged, their exit causes the inside of the cell to become more negative, and the resting potential is restored. The "overshoot" is caused by a continued movement of potassium ions to the outside of the cell after the resting potential has been restored and by a decreased leakage of sodium ions into the axon. (Based on D. N. Robinson, *The Enlightened Machine*, Encino, CA: Dickinson, 1973)

of sodium ions to the inside in one region depolarizes that part of the membrane which is nearby, so that sodium ions also start to come in there. The action potential travels along the axon the way a flame travels along a burning fuse. Once the fuse is lit (heating it to threshold), the flame travels the full length of the fuse, with each portion igniting the region next to it.

This sequence can happen many times before the axon begins to fill up with sodium ions, but since it will fill up eventually, there must be a mechanism to put the extra sodium ions back outside the membrane while also ensuring that enough potassium ions are inside to maintain the resting potential. The sodium-potassium pump mechanism does this job. The sodium-potassium pump mechanism requires a good deal of metabolic energy, but it is the only phase of the action potential that uses much energy. All the rest occurs as a result of a change in the characteristics of the membrane and the resultant movement of ions across it. Clearly, this is a very efficient way of carrying information along axons that are some distance from the cell body, the source of most nutrients (Hodgkin, 1964).

The All-or-None Law. An important implication of all that we have discussed so far is that the strength of the action potential is unaffected by the strength of the depolarizing stimulus. Once threshold is reached, the sodium channels open up and the action potential occurs. Increasing the strength of the stimulus cannot change the amplitude of the action potential, since that is a function of the resting potential and the characteristics of the sodium channels. Nor can it increase the speed of conduction along the length of the axon, since that is a function of how quickly depolarization of one region of the axon can affect adjacent regions. Taken together, these observations are called the *all-or-none law* of nerve conduction. As with a length of burning fuse, the speed of burning and the heat that is generated depend on the characteristics of the fuse, not whether it was lit with a match or a blow torch. All that is necessary is that ignition occur; from then on, the fuse burns or it does not. There is no other option.

Coding of Information in the Nervous System. Since the action potential occurs in an all-or-none fashion and since the intensity of the stimulus has no effect on the amplitude of the action potentials once the cell has been depolarized to threshold, how does the nervous system encode information about stimuli of different intensities? The sound level in a rock music club, for example, is much louder than the sound level in a library, yet the auditory system has no difficulty transmitting that information to the brain. How does this fit in with the all-or-none law?

One way that the nervous system encodes the intensity of a stimulus is by increasing the rate of generation of action potentials in sensory neurons as the stimulus becomes more intense. A very mild stimulus might cause the neuron to send only two or three action potentials per second down the axon toward the central nervous system, while a more intense stimulus might cause the neuron to fire as fast 100 times or more a second. The amplitude of each action potential spike remains constant; what changes is the *rate* at which action potentials are generated. This frequency code (Figure 2.9) is

Figure 2.9 The relationship between stimulus intensity and the rate of generation of action potentials. These oscilloscope traces show the responses of an axon to three different levels of stimulation. Because the time scale is so slow, each individual action potential looks like a straight vertical line. In the upper tracing, the axon responds to a low level of stimulation with just a few action potentials per second. However, as the stimulus is increased in intensity, as seen in the lower two traces, the rate of production of action potentials increases proportionately. It is important to note that increasing the intensity of stimulation has no effect at all on the height of the individual action potentials (the all-or-none law). (Based on Eccles, 1973)

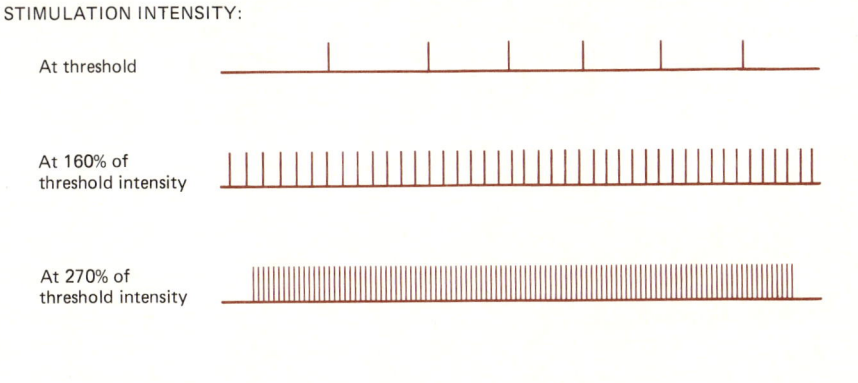

just one of several different ways that the nervous system encodes information (Bullock, 1973).

Conduction Velocity. Speed of conduction along an axon is determined by two factors: the size of the axon and whether it has a *myelin sheath*. In general, the larger an axon, the faster it will conduct. Some small unmyelinated axons conduct at speeds of less than 2 meters per second (m/s); large unmyelinated axons, such as those found in the squid or other invertebrates, may conduct impulses as fast as 15 or 20 m/s. However, this is still slow compared to what myelinated axons can do.

As can be seen in Figure 2.10, the myelin sheath is a fatty coating that is wrapped around an axon and is made up of many distinct units, each separated by a small gap called a *node of Ranvier*. In myelinated axons, the action potential occurs only at these breaks in the myelin sheath. Between the nodes of Ranvier the impulse travels by electrical conduction. Thus the action potential seems to jump from node to node down the length of the axon, much as a stone may skip across the surface of a pond. This enhances the conduction of neural messages considerably because it is much more efficient to generate an action potential at just a few points rather than along the entire length of the axon. Conduction velocities in some myelinated axons can approach speeds of 120 m/s, even though the combined diameter of the cell and its myelin sheath may be only one-fiftieth of the diameter of a squid giant axon that does not conduct nearly as fast (Carpenter, 1976). It is easy to see that the evolution of complex and efficient nervous systems depended on the development of the myelin sheath.

SYNAPTIC TRANSMISSION

Now that we have discussed how nerve cells carry impulses, we need to explore in more detail how neurons communicate with one another. Once an action potential reaches the axon terminals, what happens there that

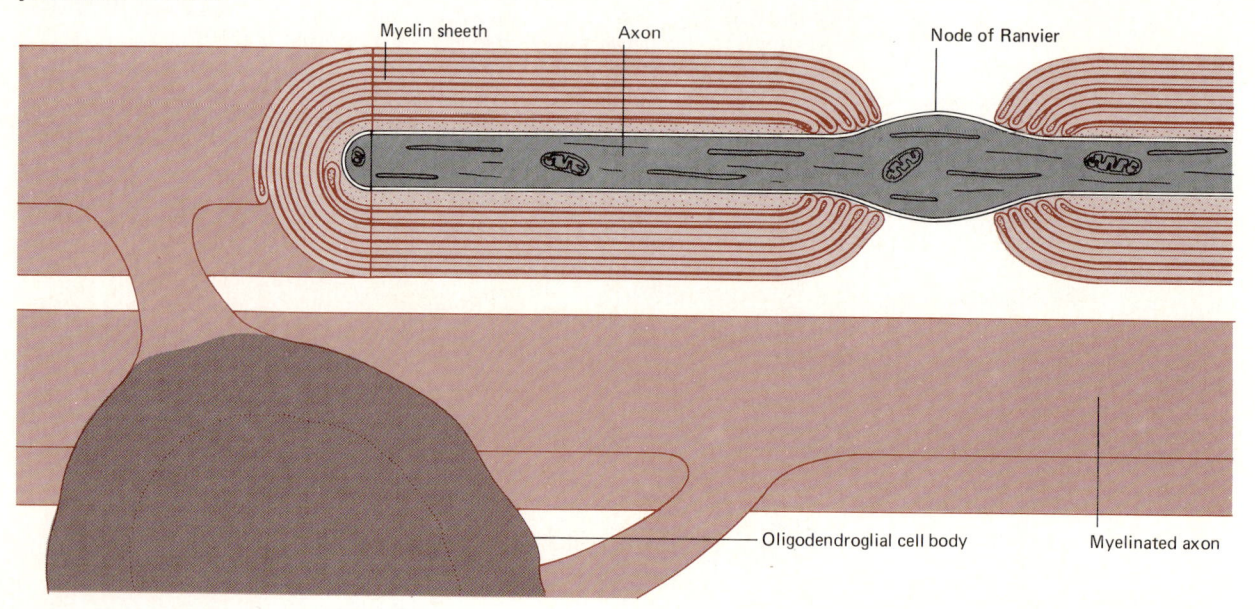

Figure 2.10
The myelin sheath. Myelin is a fatty coating that is wound tightly around the axons of many neurons. In the central nervous system, myelin is produced by specialized cells known as *oligodendroglia*. A single oligodendroglial cell may provide myelin sheaths for several axons. Gaps in the myelin sheath are known as *nodes of Ranvier*, and they provide a location for action potentials to occur.

BIOLOGY AND BEHAVIOR

permits the action potential to influence its target cell? Communication between neurons and between neurons and other kinds of cells occurs at synaptic junctions. The term *synapse,* meaning "to join," connotes a junction between two things. For years the question of whether the communication at synapses is electrical or chemical caused heated debate among neuroscientists. Some held that synaptic transmission involves the release of some chemical that stimulates the target cell; others maintained that the electrical impulse of the action potential is somehow passed to the postsynaptic cell. In fact, both ideas are essentially correct. There are both chemical synapses and electrical synapses. However, electrical synapses have only limited importance in the human nervous system. They are more common in invertebrate nervous systems (Bennett, 1977), but that does not concern us here.

The electron microscope is a particularly important tool in the study of synaptic processes because it enables researchers to see synaptic terminals that are so small that even the most powerful light microscopes cannot reveal them. A typical synapse of an axon onto a dendrite (Figure 2.11) shows a number of important structural features. The axon terminal, often referred to as the *presynaptic element,* is a swelling at the end of the axon that is close to but does not actually touch the dendrite, or *postsynaptic element.* The tiny gap between them is called the *synaptic cleft.* Inside the presynaptic axon terminal are many spherical objects that are called *synaptic vesicles.* These vesicles contain a chemical *neurotransmitter* which stimulates the target cell when released into the synaptic cleft.

Now let's follow the chain of events in chemical synaptic transmission. An action potential travels down an axon toward the synaptic terminals. All along the length of the axon, positively charged sodium ions are rushing in

Figure 2.11
Axons making synaptic connections on dendritic spines. Each dendrite of a neuron may receive inputs from hundreds of other neurons, some from great distances away.

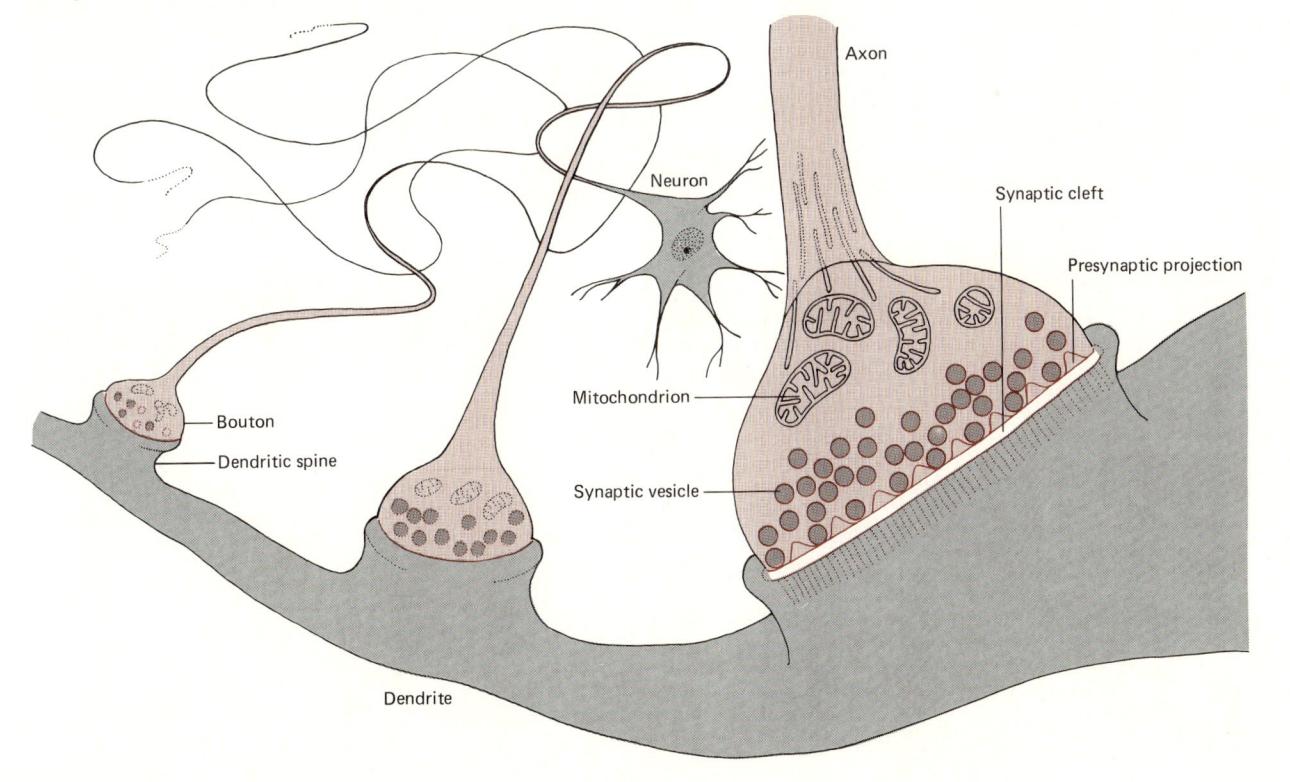

BIOLOGY, SENSATION, PERCEPTION, AND CONSCIOUSNESS

to cause a depolarization, and potassium ions are moving back out restoring the resting potential. When the action potential reaches the synaptic terminal, different positively charged ions, in this case calcium ions, move into the presynaptic terminal.

This movement of calcium ions into the terminal causes some of the synaptic vesicles to move toward the presynaptic membrane, fuse with it, and release their contents of neurotransmitter substance into the synaptic cleft. The neurotransmitter released from the vesicles diffuses across the synpatic cleft and activates receptors on the postsynaptic element (see Martin, 1977). This process is shown in Figure 2.12.

A neurotransmitter can affect the target cell in three ways. First, it can stimulate it by causing it to become depolarized, that is, move the resting potential closer to the threshold for the generation of an action potential. Second, a neurotransmitter can inhibit the postsynaptic cell by hyperpolar-

Figure 2.12
Above: a single synaptic terminal is shown connecting to the dendrite of another neuron, the postsynaptic cell. Located inside the synaptic terminal are vesicles containing a neurotransmitter. *Below:* When an action potential arrives at the terminal an influx of calcium ions causes some of the vesicles to fuse with the inside of the presynaptic membrane and release their contents into the synaptic cleft. The molecules of neurotransmitter then diffuse across the cleft and activate receptors on the dendrite to modify the activity of that cell.

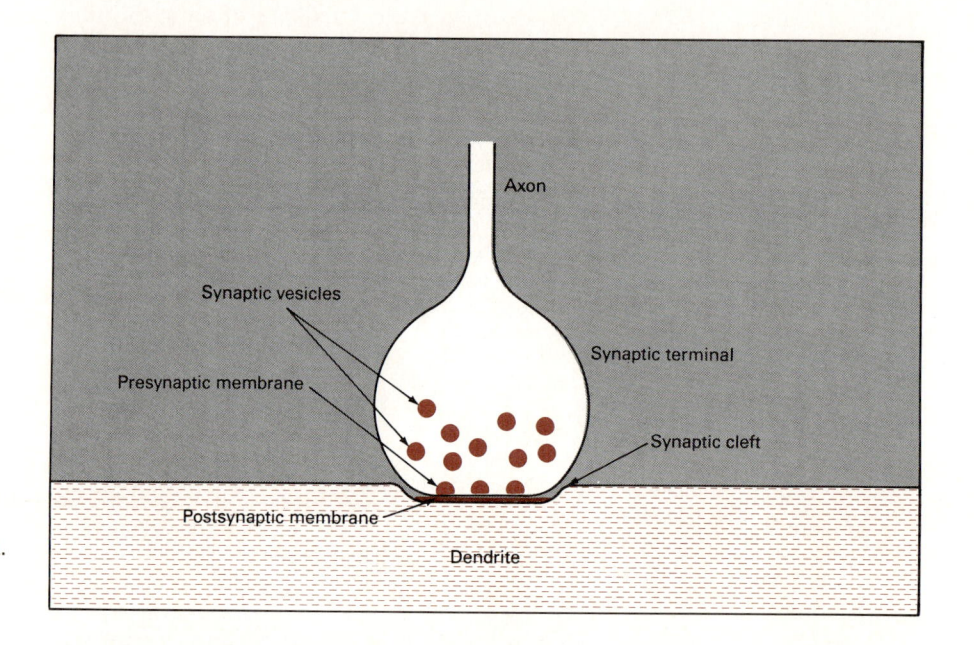

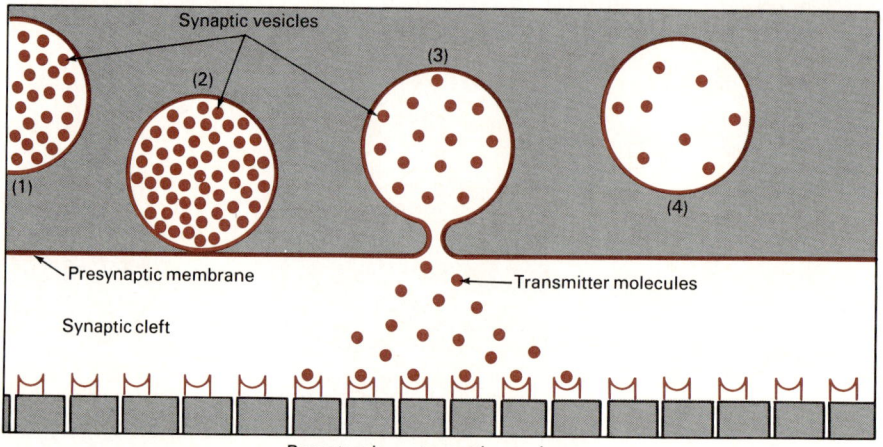

Figure 2.13
Synaptic terminals on a neuron. Most neurons receive a large number of synaptic connections from many other neurons. Here, a neuron is receiving synaptic connections both on the cell body and on the dendrites. These inputs, some excitatory and others inhibitory, are integrated together; their combined effects determine whether or not an action potential will be initiated.

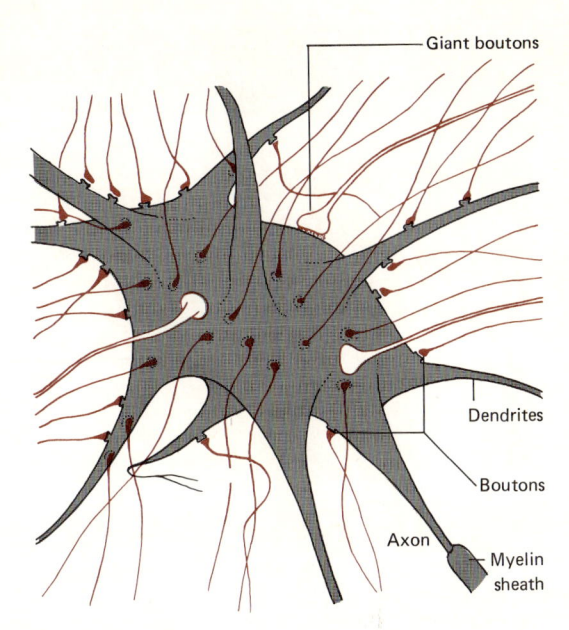

izing it, that is, making the difference in electrical charge between the outside and inside of the cell greater, so that the resting potential is moved farther from threshold. Third, it can activate receptors on the postsynaptic membrane that cause some internal chemical change to occur within the target cell.

Let's explore the first two of these actions. As shown in Figure 2.13, each neuron has literally hundreds of synaptic terminals attached to its dendrites and cell body. Some excite, others inhibit; that is, some of them will depolarize the postsynaptic cell, whereas others will tend to hyperpolarize it.

The influence of each synaptic input can be likened to voters in an election. Some vote to generate an action potential by releasing a chemical neurotransmitter that produces a depolarization; others vote with a hyperpolarizing chemical influence that there shall be no action potential. The outcome of this election depends on the total relative strength of the excitatory depolarizing inputs versus the inhibitory hyperpolarizing inputs. If the excitatory influences win out, the cell body will be depolarized to threshold and an action potential will be initiated at the axon hillock, the region where the axon joins to the cell body. If the inhibitory influences prevail, the postsynaptic cell will remain silent.

What happens to the molecules of neurotransmitter in the synaptic cleft after they stimulate receptors on the target cell? Clearly, there must be some means of shutting synaptic activity down. Inactivation of neurotransmitters typically happens in one of two ways, by enzymatic inactivation or by reuptake. In enzymatic inactivation, the neurotransmitter is attached by enzyme molecules located in the synaptic cleft. The enzyme destroys the neurotransmitter molecules that were released from the presynaptic terminal, either by breaking them down or by adding some new atoms to each molecule. Either of these mechanisms inactivates the neurotransmitter by altering its chemical structure so that it no longer reacts with the postsynaptic receptors. At other types of synapses, inactivation is through reuptake of the transmitter back into the presynaptic terminal, where it is repackaged into new vesicles for release at a later time.

PUTTING IT ALL TOGETHER: GENERATING BEHAVIOR—A SIMPLE REFLEX

We now have at our disposal all the basic principles we need to understand a simple form of behavior, a reflex. As an example we will use the simplest reflex in the body, the knee-jerk reflex, a reflex that uses only a single kind of central nervous system synapse. We are all aware that when one taps on the tendon located just below the kneecap, the lower leg and foot rise slightly if they are free to do so, yet few people understand how this response actually happens.

A tap to the tendon causes those muscles of the thigh that are attached to the tendon to be stretched a little (see Figure 2.14). Embedded in these muscles, and indeed in every muscle, are tiny little receptors, called *muscle spindles*, that respond to being lengthened or stretched. When the knee is tapped, the muscle is slightly stretched, as are the muscle spindle receptors. Lengthening the muscle spindle receptors causes them to depolarize the sensory neurons connected to them. If these sensory neurons are sufficiently depolarized so that threshold is reached, action potentials are generated that travel up the leg to the spinal cord. The action potentials enter the spinal cord through the dorsal roots and synapse with motor neurons in the gray matter of the spinal cord.

Figure 2.14 A simple reflex arc. Stimulation of the knee (represented by the small hammer) results in a stretching of the tendon attached to a muscle of the upper leg. This causes the muscle to be lengthened slightly, causing the muscle spindle receptors embedded in the muscle to be lengthened also. Lengthening the spindle receptors causes them to activate the sensory neurons attached to them, resulting in action potentials. The action potentials travel along the sensory neurons and into the spinal cord. These messages then stimulate motor neurons, and a message travels out along their axons back to the muscle. The muscle then contracts, causing an upward movement of the lower part of the leg. In the right portion of the figure, it can be seen that all sensory information enters the spinal cord via the dorsal roots and that all motor information leaves the spinal cord via the ventral roots. In addition, sensory information travels down the cord from the brain to activate spinal motor neurons, while sensory information ascends to the brain from sensory neurons.

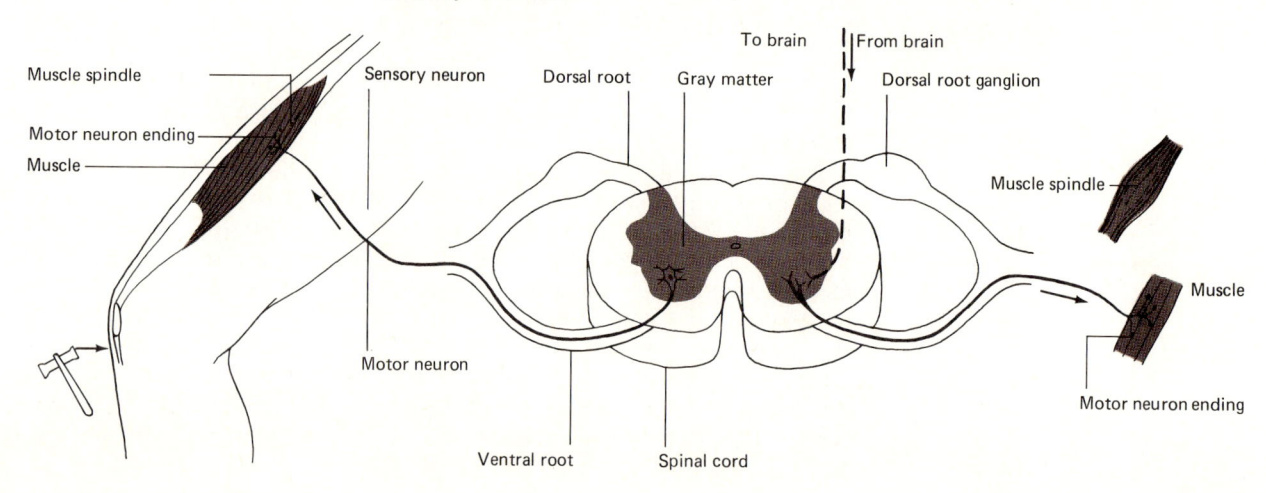

At the spinal cord synapses, the arrival of action potentials causes calcium to enter the presynaptic terminals, which triggers the release of neurotransmitter. The neurotransmitter crosses the synaptic cleft, depolarizes the postsynaptic motor neurons, and if enough synapses are activated, the motor neurons will be depolarized to threshold. Then action potentials travel out of the spinal cord via the ventral roots, down the leg, and to the muscles of the thigh.

When the action potentials reach the motor neuron terminals, a neurotransmitter known as acetylcholine is released onto the muscle fibers. The acetylcholine from the motor neuron terminals depolarizes the muscle fibers, causing them to contract. This contraction produces the leg-lift response. The acetylcholine is then broken down by an enzyme that is specialized for the job, and the whole system is ready to respond again.

In this simple reflex, we have all the basics of a behavior: a stimulus and a response. The stimulus caused action potentials to travel to the central nervous system, where release of a neurotransmitter caused motor neurons to be activated. Action potentials then traveled to the muscle, where through release of another neurotransmitter, a simple behavior was generated. In most reflexive responses, the chain of neurons is longer, with many small interneurons or local-circuit neurons interposed between the sensory input and the motor output. More complex motor behaviors, such as walking, involve millions of neurons.

THE ANATOMY OF THE CENTRAL NERVOUS SYSTEM

Up to this point we have studied the major subdivisions of the nervous system's structure: the central nervous system (brain and spinal cord) and the peripheral nervous system (somatic system and autonomic nervous system). We have also seen how neurons transmit information from one place in the nervous system to another and how they communicate with each other. Now we will introduce some of the neuroanatomical features of the nervous system and try to see how the organization and form of various brain regions are related to the jobs that these regions perform. We will start at the bottom or tail end of the central nervous system and work our way up and forward until we reach the cerebral cortex, the most advanced portion of the brain.

THE SPINAL CORD

The *spinal cord* is the primary pathway that the brain uses to communicate with the rest of the body. It is a relatively large bundle of nerve fibers and cell bodies that extends from the base of the skull about two-thirds down the spine. Recall that action potentials carrying sensory information enter the spinal cord through the *dorsal roots* (see Figure 2.14) and that some of those sensory messages may elicit a reflexive response through interactions with spinal cord neurons. Most sensory information, though, travels up the spinal cord to the brain, where it influences the activities of millions and even billions of neurons.

In contrast to sensory messages traveling up the cord, output from the brain travels down the spinal cord and then activates motor neurons in the spinal cord. Action potentials then travel along the axons of these motor neurons and out of the spinal cord via the *ventral roots* to various target organs in the body.

Many fairly complex response patterns are mediated by neurons in the gray matter of the spinal cord. Besides reflexive withdrawal and extension, such behaviors as posture, patterns of walking, and scratching are also mediated by spinal cord neurons.

THE BRAIN STEM

The *brain stem* forms the junction between the spinal cord and the rest of the central nervous system. In addition, it contains a number of collections of neurons which are important in the regulation of bodily processes. The brain stem is made up of two component parts: the medulla and the pons (see Figure 2.15).

The Medulla. The *medulla*, sometimes called the medulla oblongata, joins directly to the spinal cord. Within the medulla are several neural structures that control vital internal functions, such as regulation of the cardiovascular system, control of respiration, and the maintenance of muscle tone. Some of the cranial nerves, which innervate the mouth and face, and a cranial nerve providing much of the control for one division of the autonomic nervous system originate in the medulla.

The Pons. The *pons* is a large bulge in the brain stem that lies next to the medulla and directly underneath the cerebellum. The pons contains major pathways that lead to and from the cerebellum. Neurons in the pons are important in controlling sleep and waking. Several cranial nerves serving the

Figure 2.15
A view of the underside of the brain. Clearly visible here is the brain stem consisting of the medulla and pons. The medulla and pons lie underneath the cerebellum, and they contain the beginnings of many important cranial nerves. Also shown here are the olfactory bulbs and the optic nerve.

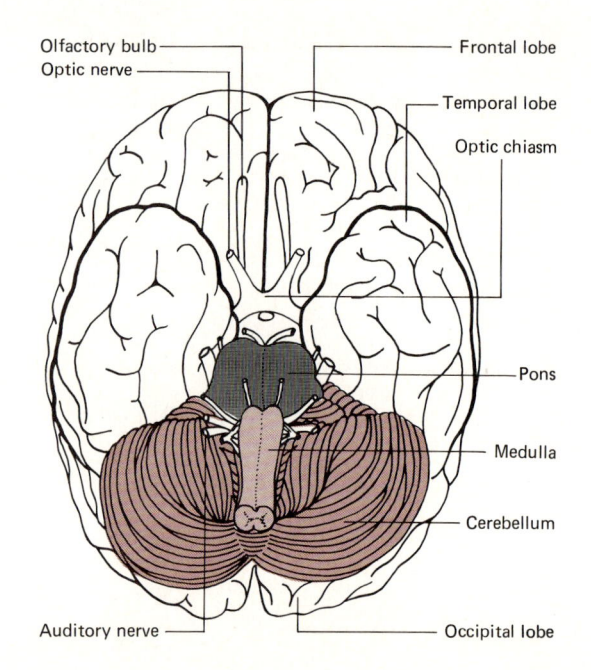

BIOLOGY AND BEHAVIOR

head and face, as well as those that mediate balance and hearing, also originate in the pons.

THE CEREBELLUM

The *cerebellum* looks like a miniature brain attached to the back of the main brain (see Figure 2.15). It is covered by a deeply wrinkled cerebellar cortex, which gives it a distinctive appearance. The cerebellum is very important in the modulation and control of movement. Without a cerebellum it would be impossible to walk, purposefully grasp an object, or even stand still. The cerebellum receives information from many different sensory systems about such things as limb position, balance, sight, and sound. It then puts all this information together and modulates motor output. The result is smoothly coordinated patterns of motion.

THE MIDBRAIN

Just above the pons lies a group of fairly small neural structures that together are called the midbrain (see Figure 2.16). The *midbrain* is composed of two components, one called the *tectum* (which means "roof") and the other called the *tegmentum* (which means "floor").

The tectum is easily identified because it is made up of four small bumps called *colliculi* (from the Latin for "little hills"). The upper two colliculi are called the *superior colliculi;* their principal function is to mediate visual reflexes and visual attention. Without them, visual processes would be much less efficient. The lower two bumps, called the *inferior colliculi,* are important in processing auditory information as it travels from the ears into the central nervous system.

Figure 2.16
A midline view of the brain. In this drawing, the left hemisphere has been removed showing a medial view of the right half of the brain. The midbrain consists of two parts. The upper portion contains the superior colliculi (important in visual reflexes) and the inferior colliculi (important in auditory information processing). The thalamus serves as a relay station for messages in all sensory systems except the sense of smell. The hypothalamus, located beneath the thalamus, modulates many motivated behaviors and most internal bodily processes. The corpus callosum is a large band of myelinated axons that connects the two hemispheres.

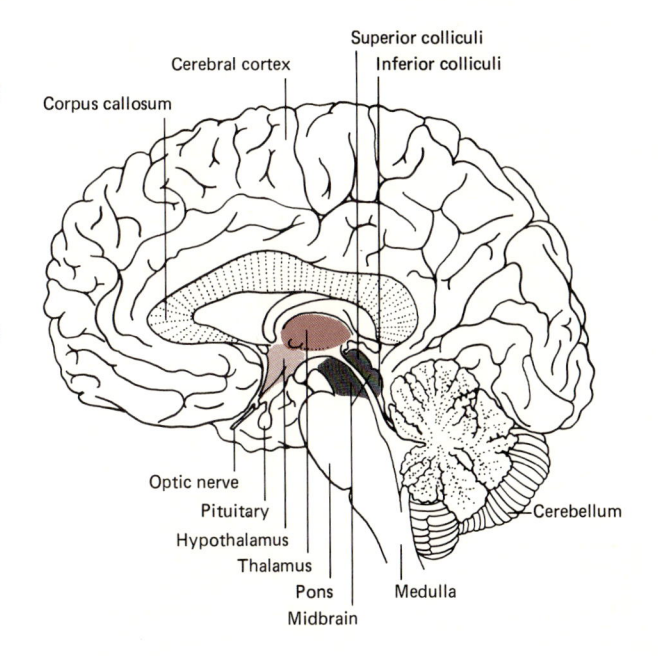

The tegmentum contains several structures important in the control of eye movements as well as other kinds of movement. One of these structures in the tegmentum is known as the *substantia nigra,* and when neurons in this brain region die, Parkinson's disease results (see Highlight 2.2).

THE HYPOTHALAMUS

At the base of the brain (see Figure 2.16) is the *hypothalamus,* which is connected to the pituitary gland by a small stalk. The hypothalamus is relatively small compared to some other brain structures, but its size (around 1% of the brain) belies its great importance. The hypothalamus modulates food intake, helps maintain water balance, and controls many of the body's hormone systems through its actions on the pituitary gland. The hypothalamus also controls the autonomic nervous system and directs behaviors important to individual and species survival. A number of these hypothalamic functions are discussed in subsequent chapters.

HIGHLIGHT 2.2
Parkinson's Disease

One way to see how the principles that we have introduced influence one's everyday life is to look at behavior when something goes wrong in the brain. A good example is the condition known as Parkinson's disease, a progressive degenerative disease that causes severe disturbances in motor behavior. There is rigidity of the limbs, tremor, and difficulty in beginning a movement, and all movements are slowed down. In advanced cases, almost no movement is possible except eye blinks. What is going on here?

The basal ganglia are subcortical brain areas that work together with neurons of the motor cortex to control the skeletal muscles. Damage to the basal ganglia due to some sort of injury to the brain produces severe impairment in motor control. The interesting thing about Parkinson's disease is that the problem does not lie directly in the basal ganglia but in another brain structure located back in the midbrain, called the substantia nigra. This brain region sends axons up to the basal ganglia to modulate the activity of neurons located there. In Parkinson's disease, cells of the substantia nigra degenerate slowly and cannot release their neurotransmitter, which is called dopamine, onto cells of the basal ganglia. As a result, the basal ganglia cells do not function properly, and the tremor, rigidity, and other characteristics of Parkinson's disease appear.

What can be done to help people afflicted with this condition? One effective treatment is to administer a substance that when metabolized produces the same neurotransmitter that would have been released from the axon terminals of the substantia nigra cells. This substance, known as L-dopa, is converted in the brain to dopamine. The presence of this additional dopamine helps alleviate many of the symptoms of Parkinson's disease.

Administration of L-dopa is a useful therapy for Parkinson's disease, but many problems remain unsolved. This treatment has both limitations and serious side effects in some people. Administration of L-dopa can produce a behavioral disturbance similar to schizophrenia. It can also result in uncontrollable movements of the muscles of the face and arms. The need for further basic research cannot be overemphasized. As our understanding of the neurobiological basis of behavior increases, new treatments based on this improved understanding will continue to be developed. There is great hope, but much remains to be done.

THE THALAMUS

Above the hypothalamus (not surprisingly, since "hypo" means "beneath") is the *thalamus* (Figure 2.16). It is composed of two egg-shaped segments each deeply embedded in its respective hemisphere. Incoming neural fibers from all senses, except smell, pass to the thalamus, where they make a synaptic connection before going on to other brain regions. For all senses (except smell), the thalamus functions like a big telephone switching network directing incoming messages to their appropriate destinations. Beyond its function as a sensory relay station, the thalamus also processes and integrates sensory information.

THE CEREBRAL HEMISPHERES

In relation to the rest of the human brain, the cerebral hemispheres are huge and completely cover many of the other brain structures. The outer covering of the hemispheres is called the *cerebral cortex.* Underneath the cortex is white matter, made up of axons running to and from the cortex and several groups of subcortical brain structures.

Subcortical Brain Regions. One group of these subcortical structures is called the *basal ganglia,* and these are large collections of cell bodies and synapses which are concerned with the control of skeletal muscles. They are also thought to be involved in the encoding of memories of learned procedures and methods.

Another major group of subcortical brain structures is known as the limbic system. The *limbic system* is a set of interconnected brain components involved in motivation and emotional behavior. Some parts of the limbic system are also involved in the storage of memories of specific units of information. Such memories are probably not actually stored in the limbic system, but it is clear that these brain regions are very important in controlling and directing the storage of memories.

Cerebral Cortex. Cortex in Latin means "bark," and the *cerebral cortex*, a wrinkled collection of billions of neurons, covers the surface of the cerebral hemispheres in much the way that bark covers a tree. The surface features of the cortex are called *Sulci,* meaning "small grooves," and *gyri,* which are the raised regions between the sulci. The presence of sulci and gyri greatly enlarges the surface area of the cortex and allows more cortex to be compressed into a smaller space, just as a crumpled piece of paper has the same surface area as a flat sheet but occupies less space on a table. The amount of cortical surface area in relation to brain and body size is generally related to evolutionary development. More advanced animals generally have more cortex in relation to their body size (Riddell, 1979; Rosenzweig, 1979).

As shown in Figure 2.17, the cortical surface can be divided into five regions on the basis of the sulci and gyri. These regions are referred to as *lobes.* Figure 2.17A is a view of the lateral surface of the brain; we can see the frontal, temporal, and parietal lobes and a little bit of the occipital lobe. Figure 2.17B, a view of one hemisphere separated down the middle from the other, shows the rest of the occipital lobe and part of the limbic lobe.

The two hemispheres are joined by a broad band of myelinated axons known as the *corpus callosum,* which allows the two hemispheres to interact

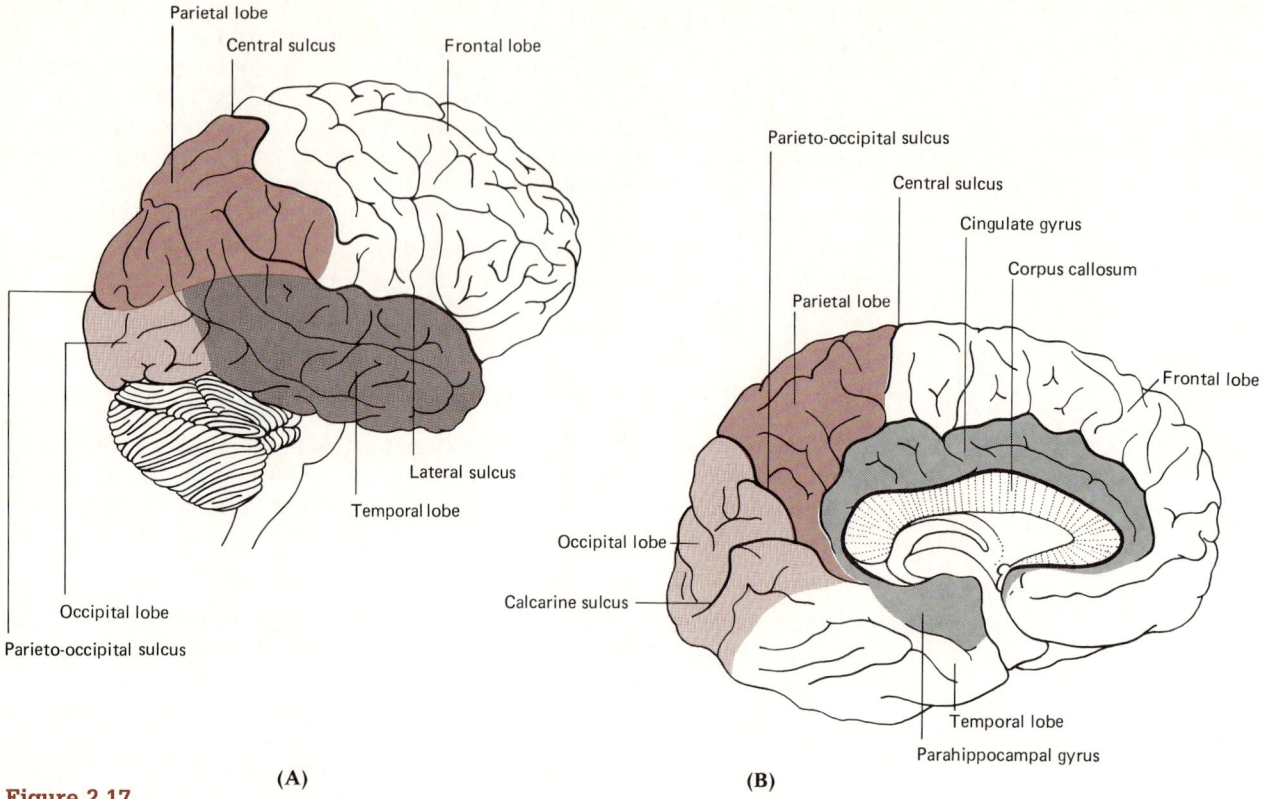

Figure 2.17
The lobes of the cortex as seen from a lateral and medial perspective.

with each other. Should the corpus callosum be cut, an operation that has been performed to treat severe epilepsy, the two hemispheres of the brain cannot communicate. Under some experimental conditions such persons behave as if they have two independent brains.

CORTICAL LOCALIZATION OF FUNCTION

As noted earlier, the cortex seems to be particularly well suited to advanced intellectual function. It is the region of the brain that is most highly developed in human beings and other intelligent animals, such as chimpanzees, dogs, and bottlenose dolphins. Researchers do not completely understand how the cortex does its job. However, much is known about some aspects of cortical function and the tasks different cortical regions seem specialized to perform. In the following sections we explore some features of cortical function and indicate, at least in some cases, in which parts of the cortex these operations appear to take place.

SENSORY PROJECTION AREAS

One of the earliest discoveries about the localization of different brain functions in the cortex was that messages from various kinds of sensory receptors

BIOLOGY AND BEHAVIOR

project to different regions of the cortex. Some kinds of stimuli seem to activate one cortical region, whereas others activate a different one.

Pioneering researchers found that auditory information projects from a relay nucleus in the thalamus to a region of cortex that is on the uppermost part of the temporal lobe. The area of cortex receiving sensory information from the thalamus is called the *auditory projection area,* or simply the auditory area (see Figure 2.18). These projections are arranged systematically, and researchers have found that sounds of low frequency or pitch activate different cortical neurons than sounds of higher frequency. Specificity of projections such as this is typical of most sensory systems and is explored in depth in Chapter 3.

Action potentials carrying visual information from the eyes are also relayed through synaptic connections in the thalamus, and then the action potentials from the thalamic neurons activate cortical neurons in the occipital lobe at the very back of the brain. In the occipital lobe these patterns of action potentials are interpreted and the sensation of vision is generated (Williams and Warwick, 1975). Much of the visual cortex is located on the medial surface of the cortex along a cortical groove known as the *calcarine* (pronounced "kal-ka-rine") *sulcus* (Figure 2.19).

The bodily senses are also mapped on the surface of the cortex. These senses, including touch, pressure, and skin temperature, are usually grouped together under one heading, the *somatosensory system.* Neural pathways carrying somatosensory information from each part of the body project to the thalamus and then to particular regions of the cortex that are devoted to processing information about the bodily senses from that particular region of the body. These regions are called the *somatosensory areas* and are found primarily in the parietal lobe just behind the *central sulcus.* Also, some somatosensory information is projected to cells in front of the central sulcus.

Sensory projections from the body form a representation on the surface of the cortex that is often referred to as a *homunculus,* or "little man." The *sensory homunculus* shown in Figure 2.20 is a graphical representation of how these projections are arranged. The sensory homunculus is distorted, the result of the distortion being that some regions of the body are more sensitive than others to touch stimulation. Those areas of the body where fine sensory discriminations can be made have proportionately more cortex devoted to them than do those regions that are less capable (Carpenter, 1976). The hands, lips, and tongue have much more somatosensory cortex devoted to

Figure 2.18
Auditory projection area near the lateral sulcus.

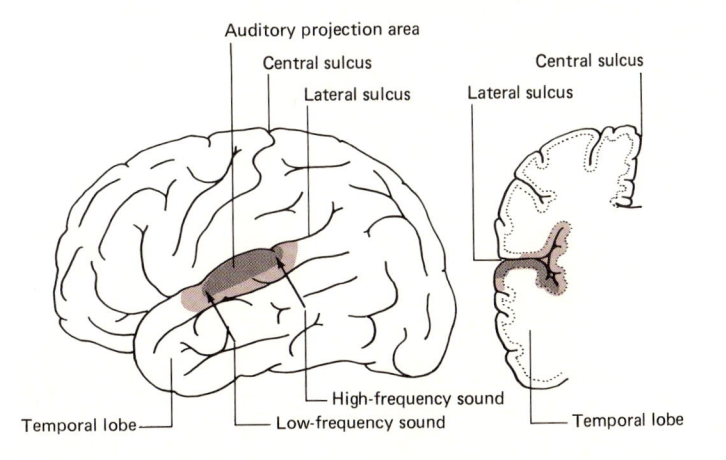

Figure 2.19
The visual pathways from the eyes to the occipital lobe. The occipital lobe contains specialized interconnections of neurons that interpret the patterns of action potentials generated by the cells of the retina in response to visual stimulation.

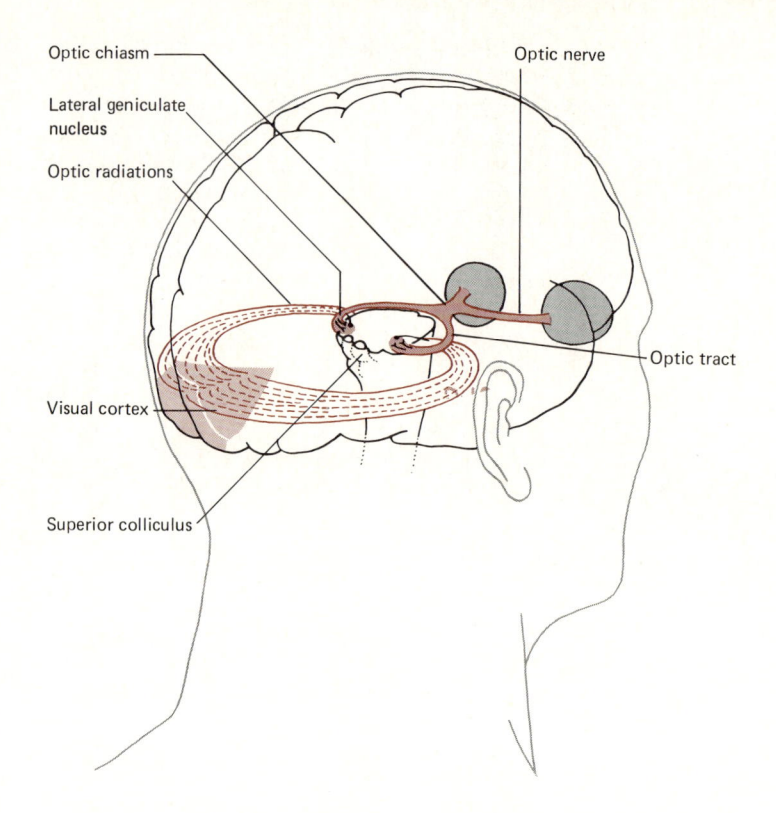

them than do the back, arms, or legs. Perhaps this is why we like to hold hands and kiss rather than rub knees or elbows.

Neural pathways carrying somatosensory information cross over from one side of the body to the other on their way to the brain, so that they end up in the somatosensory cortex on the opposite side of the body. Thus stimulation of receptors in the left leg will activate cortical neurons on the upper part of the somatosensory cortex in the right hemisphere; stimulation of the right thumb will activate neurons in the middle regions of the somatosensory cortex in the left hemisphere.

MOTOR AREAS

Cortical areas devoted to motor control lie in large part just in front of the central sulcus, and as with sensory areas, specific parts of the cortex are connected to specific parts of the body. Again, equal areas of the body do not have equal amounts of cortex controlling their muscles. A graphical representation of this arrangement of the cortex is called a *motor homunculus* (shown in Figure 2.20). Those parts of the body that can move rapidly and precisely, such as the lips, tongue, thumb, and fingers, have much more cortical area devoted to them than do those brain regions that control parts of the body less able to make precise movements, such as the legs and shoulders.

Working as partners with the cortex in the control of movement are the basal ganglia discussed earlier. In primitive animals with little if any cortex, the basal ganglia control all movement. But in more advanced animals, such as ourselves, the partnership between the basal ganglia and the motor cortex

BIOLOGY AND BEHAVIOR   57

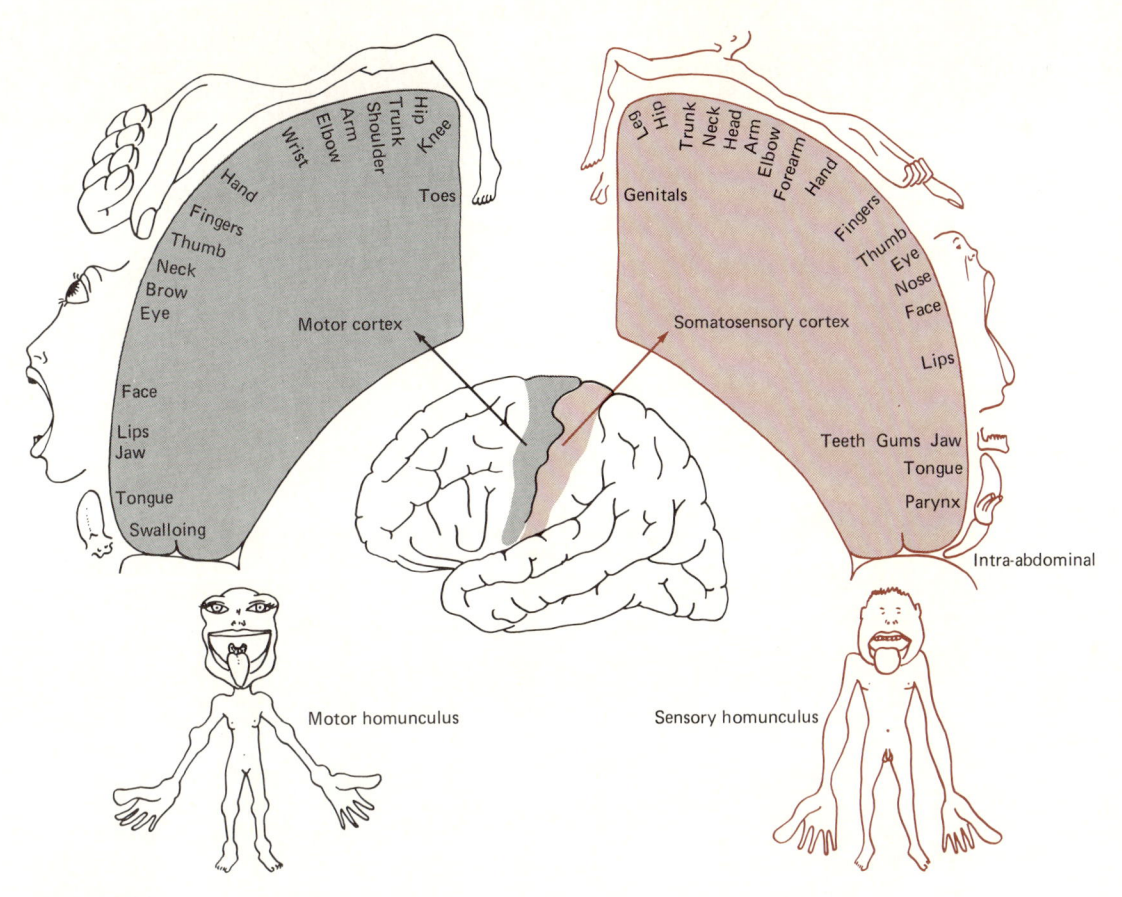

Figure 2.20
On the right is a representation of the surface of the body in the primary somatosensory areas of the cortex. This kind of representation is sometimes called a homunculus, and it depicts the body surface with each area drawn in proportion to the amount of cortex receiving sensory inputs from that portion of the body. On the left is a motor homunculus, a representation of how much cortex is devoted to the control of the skeletal muscles in each portion of the body. (Based on Penfield and Rasmussen, 1950)

permits us to learn, relatively easily, a full range of rapid and accurate motor responses (see Cote, 1981).

The cortex does much more than merely respond to sensory stimuli and generate patterns of motor response. It is the highly developed functions of the cortex that make human beings unique among all living things. The cortex produces that incredible blend of responses to stimuli, retrieval of memories, and individual creativity that make us such extraordinary creatures. In the following sections we explore some complex human behaviors and their relationships to the cerebral cortex.

Much of what we know about the various functions of cortical regions comes from studies of the behavior of persons who have suffered some cortical damage. For this reason, the conclusions that can be drawn are necessarily quite limited, but a general picture does emerge. Let's look at it.

FRONTAL LOBES

The frontal lobes of the cortex are particularly well developed in human beings. Their great size and huge number of interconnections with other parts of the central nervous system make the frontal lobes perhaps the most uniquely human of all brain regions. For example, there is one cortical region, known as *Broca's area,* which is very important in the production of speech. It is located in the lower part of the frontal lobe and usually in the left hemisphere

Figure 2.21
Cortical areas associated with language. Notice how the auditory projection area and the cortical areas devoted to the control of the mouth, tongue, and throat lie between Broca's area and Wernicke's area.

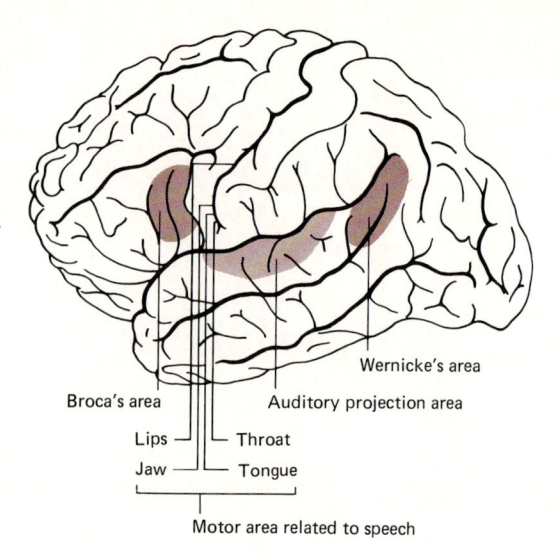

in most people. Broca's area is adjacent to those cortical motor areas devoted to the control of the mouth, tongue, and muscles of the throat (Figure 2.21). When this small brain area is injured, the affected person has great difficulty speaking.

This condition, known as *Broca's aphasia,* is very debilitating. There is no paralysis of the muscles used in speech, however; they still work perfectly. What is impaired is the capacity to bring together rapidly the neural commands for the individual muscle movements that are needed to form one word after another in a meaningful way (Geschwind, 1979). Often, people with Broca's aphasia can still read, write, and understand spoken words without difficulty. But they lack the executive control over the production of speech that seems to be a function of this small region of the frontal lobe.

Other regions of the frontal lobes are also important, although their functions are not as specific as that of Broca's area. One major loss often seen after extensive injury to the frontal lobes is a decrease in anxiety and loss of concern for the consequences of one's actions. There is also a loss of capacity to plan for the future, a decline in the quality of judgments, and the appearance of socially inappropriate behaviors as well as flattened emotional responses. There is also little concern for the past or future.

Although patients with substantial frontal lobe damage show only slight decreases in measures of general intelligence, their ability to function effectively in day-to-day life is seriously impaired. For example, a person with frontal lobe damage may persist in some meaningless repetitive activity for a very long time and show almost no capacity to work toward a future goal.

In summary, besides their importance in generating speech, the frontal lobes seem to provide the capacity to adapt to changing conditions and to plan for the future on the basis of experience. These brain regions also seem to mediate some types of emotional responses as well as those feelings associated with concern and responsibility.

TEMPORAL LOBES

We have already seen that the auditory cortex occupies part of the temporal lobes. What other functions are found there? Areas of the temporal lobe are involved in integrating neural information from the senses of smell, vision, taste, hearing, and other sensory experiences. This integration is done in a very elaborate and complex manner, so that sensory input can be processed as whole experiences and not merely as isolated sensations (J. W. Brown, 1972). The temporal lobes are also very important in the storage and retrieval of some kinds of memories, especially of bits of arbitrary information.

In most people, the left temporal lobe also contains a brain area that is important in language perception. Known as *Wernicke's area* (Figure 2.21), it seems to mediate the reception of spoken language. Damage to this region produces a severe reduction in language comprehension which is referred to as receptive aphasia or *Wernicke's aphasia*. Damage to this region causes problems in both speech comprehension and speech production (Luria, 1970). The speech of those affected with Wernicke's aphasia is often fluent and has an appropriate rhythm. The problem is that these people do not make sense. Many have little comprehension of either written or spoken language (J. W. Brown, 1972).

PARIETAL LOBE

Damage to the parietal lobe produces various losses depending on the location of the injury. For example, after parietal lobe damage one side of the body may be almost totally neglected and even denied as being part of one's self. Affected persons may comb their hair on only one side of their head or shave just one side of their face. In other people with parietal lobe damage, there may be losses in the use of language or in sensory processing. Sometimes the faces of friends and even close relatives cannot be identified from photographs (J. W. Brown, 1972).

These different kinds of losses indicate that the parietal lobe is involved in many kinds of operations. It maps the body and produces an awareness of spatial relationships. As a result, when the parietal lobe of one hemisphere is damaged, one can lose acceptance and even awareness of an entire half of one's body and its surroundings. These decreases in self-awareness and inability to make identifications are referred to as *agnosias* (from the Greek meaning "not knowing"). There are a number of different types of agnosias that generally involve losing the ability to localize sensations or to recognize sensory stimuli.

LATERALIZATION IN THE BRAIN

HEMISPHERIC SPECIALIZATION

We noted earlier that in most people, Broca's area and Wernicke's area are located in the left hemisphere. Indeed, it has been known for over a century that the two cerebral hemispheres are not equivalent in language function and that a person whose left hemisphere was injured is much more likely to show problems with language than one who suffered a similar injury to the right hemisphere. Until the last 15 years or so, psychologists usually referred to the language hemisphere as the dominant hemisphere. Today, however, the idea that one hemisphere is dominant over the other is losing favor to the idea that neither is dominant and that each cerebral hemisphere is specialized for different functions.

This idea, called *lateralization of function,* is not particularly novel or surprising if you recall that most parts of the body are lateralized to some degree. For example, the liver is located on the right side of the body, and the heart is on the left. There are even slight differences in the size of the feet: the right foot is usually slightly larger than the left.

SPLIT-BRAIN RESEARCH

Until fairly recently it was very difficult to observe lateralization of function in the brain because of the extensive interconnections between various brain areas. All that most psychologists would accept was that most people's language functions are found in the left hemisphere. Recent advances in neurosurgery, however, have led to some patients having the major connection between the two hemispheres, the corpus callosum, severed to treat severe epilepsy. In some of these people, it has been possible for researchers to observe that the two hemispheres are indeed specialized for some functions (Sperry, 1982).

In this research, visual stimuli are presented either to the left or right hemisphere and the responses are noted (see Figure 2.22). This can be done because the retina of each eye is functionally divided into left and right visual fields. Almost all information presented to the right visual field is transmitted to the visual cortex of the left hemisphere, and virtually all information presented to the left visual field goes to the right hemisphere. Since the corpus callosum has been cut, information presented to the right hemisphere cannot be transferred over to the left hemisphere. So if different visual information is presented to each visual field, each hemisphere will be unaware of what the other half of the brain saw.

If words are projected on a screen to the right visual field, the neural message will travel to the left hemisphere and the person will easily be able to read the words and respond verbally. When the same stimuli are presented to the right hemisphere, only limited language capacity is evident. The right hemisphere cannot generate very adequate verbal responses in this kind of task. But the right hemisphere is not at all retarded. While the left may show superiority in tasks that involve verbal processes or systematic and analytic thought, the right is superior on tests of spatial relations and in performing tasks related to the arts, music, and holistic thought.

Why should there be this kind of hemispheric specialization? No one knows for sure, but researchers have some good theories. Neurobiologists have long noted that the sensitivity and precision of sensory systems are reduced along the midline of the body, yet it is midline structures, tongue, lips, and throat that are involved in speech. Further, the midline of the body receives motor projections from both hemispheres. Perhaps speech developed better when one hemisphere gained complete control of this function rather than having to compete or coordinate activities with the other hemisphere.

There are still other advantages to hemispheric specialization. Lateralization lets the brain do two kinds of thought at once. If the left hemisphere is somewhat more logical and analytic and the right hemisphere is more general in its functions, a problem can be attacked in both ways simultaneously. When the answer is attained by reasoned logic, the left hemisphere approach was probably more successful; an intuitive answer may be taken as evidence of the right hemisphere at work. To refer to "intuitive thought"

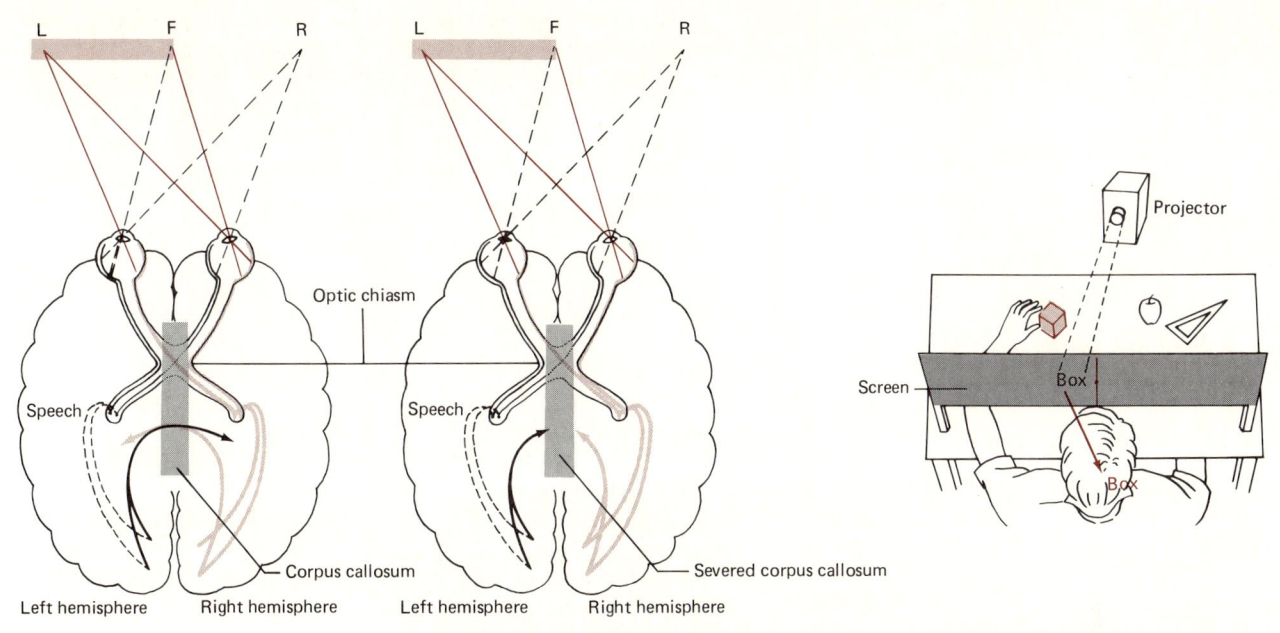

Figure 2.22 The effects of severing the corpus callosum. In the left part of the figure is a representation of a normal brain. Information from the left visual field is projected to the right hemisphere. From there it is transmitted across the corpus callosum so that the left hemisphere can be informed about the visual message. If the corpus callosum is cut, then information from the left visual field is restricted just to the right hemisphere. On the right, we see a person whose corpus callosum was cut in the course of treatment of severe epilepsy. He is fixating on a spot on a screen so that when the word "BOX" is flashed on the screen it will be only in his left visual field. As a result, this message will be transmitted along the visual pathways just to his right hemisphere. In responses to the stimulus, he will be able to correctly select the box on the table from the other objects with his left hand but not his right hand. Furthermore, because of the limited language capacity of the right hemisphere, he may not be able to say what word it was that he saw projected on the screen even though he can correctly pick out the box. (Based on Gazzaniga, 1967)

is probably not very accurate because if the right hemisphere had better verbal ability, it could probably outline the thought processes that it used to arrive at an answer.

However, the preceding discussion should not make us forget that all parts of the brain function in an integrated and harmonious way to generate our thoughts and behavior. The study of the brain holds many undreamed of mysteries and challenges. Although we are only beginning to understand some aspects of brain function, these modest advances have revolutionized our view of ourselves and of our relationship with the world.

SUMMARY

1. The nervous system can be divided into two major parts: the central nervous system (CNS), composed of the brain and spinal cord, and the peripheral nervous system (PNS), comprising the somatic system and autonomic system.

2. The brain is made up of two symmetrical cerebral hemispheres connected by large bands of nerve fibers. It also contains the cerebellum, midbrain, and brain stem. The spinal cord carries messages to and from the brain and also mediates a wide variety of reflexive responses.

3. The somatic system, part of the peripheral nervous system, transmits sensory information from sensory receptors to the CNS. It also transmits messages from the CNS to the skeletal muscles. The autonomic system modulates the activities of many of the internal organs that carry out the life-maintenance processes of the body.

4. The various parts of the nervous system perform many tasks: The nervous system monitors the world outside the body; carries out bodily maintenance functions; stores and retrieves memories; directs behavior; produces thinking and creativity; and generates complex behaviors such as personality.

5. The basic unit of the nervous system is the neuron. There may be well over 100 billion of these specialized cells in a human brain, each interconnected with hundreds or thousands of other neurons. Neurons integrate signals from many sources and then transmit signals to other cells in the nervous system.

6. In general, neurons have tiny bodies, but some neurons may have axonal processes that extend for several meters. Each neuron is covered by a thin membrane that allows only selected substances to enter the cell. The cell body contains a variety of tiny structures that ensure the proper functioning of the neuron. The dendrites are treelike branches extending from the cell body that receive information coming from other neurons, while the axon transmits information away from the cell body to other cells. Synaptic terminals found at the ends of axons send information to other cells through the release of specific chemical transmitter substances.

7. Each neuron has an electrical charge called the resting potential that is the result of the outward movement of positively charged potassium ions across the membrane from the inside of the cell, where they are concentrated, to the fluids outside the cell. This leaves some negative charges behind, causing the inside of the cell to be negatively charged.

8. During the action potential sodium ions move across the membrane into the axon, causing a reversal in electrical charge in the region where the action potential is occurring. Movement of potassium ions to the outside restores the resting potential. This activity stimulates an adjacent region of the axon, a progression that continues without decreasing in strength down the entire length of the axon. Some axons are covered with a sheath of myelin, which speeds conduction by permitting action potentials to occur only at breaks in the sheath called nodes of Ranvier.

9. Axons terminate at synaptic connections with other cells. The synaptic terminals contain chemical neurotransmiters, which, when released, influence the activity of target cells. These chemical influences can be either excitatory or inhibitory, and the relative strengths of these influences determine the effect on a target cell.

10. The spinal cord is the primary pathway that the brain uses to send and receive information from the body. The medulla, which joins directly with the spinal cord, mediates reflexes related to bodily functions. The pons contains a number of important cell groups and neural pathways. The cerebellum integrates and modulates motor responses and learned reflexes. The midbrain mediates visual reflexes, processes auditory information, and participates in the control of movements. The hypothalamus modulates food intake, controls water balances, and regulates the secretion of many different kinds of hormones. The thalamus processes sensory information and relays it to the cortex. The limbic system modulates motivation emotional behaviors, and the storage of memories.

11. Different regions of the cerebral cortex appear to mediate specific functions. Most sensory systems project to the cortex: the auditory pathways terminate in the temporal lobe, while visual information is projected to the occipital lobe. Somatosensory messages are mostly directed to the parietal lobe just posterior to the central sulcus, while motor control is mediated by cortical areas just in front of the central sulcus. Regions of the left hemisphere in the frontal and temporal lobes are important in most people for the production and comprehension of speech.

12. Although the functional differences between the hemispheres are not clear cut, in most people the left hemisphere seems to have greater language capacity and tends to mediate logical thought, while the right hemisphere is often more general in its functions.

KEY TERMS

Central nervous system
Peripheral nervous system
Brain
Spinal cord
Reflex
Autonomic nervous system
Neuroendocrine system
Cell body
Dendrites
Axon
Projection neurons
Local-circuit neurons
Cell nucleus
Mitochondria
Lysomes

Neurotransmitter
Resting potential
Threshold
Action potential
All-or-none law
Myelin sheath
Synapse
Synaptic cleft
Synaptic vesicles
Dorsal roots
Ventral roots
Brain stem
Medulla
Pons
Cerebellum
Midbrain
Hypothalamus

Thalamus
Cerebral cortex
Basal ganglia
Limbic system
Corpus callosum
Somatosensory system
Central sulcus
Sensory homunculus
Motor homunculus
Broca's area
Broca's aphasia
Wernicke's area
Wernicke's aphasia
Agnosia
Lateralization of function

SUGGESTED READINGS

BLAKEMORE, C. *Mechanics of the mind.* Cambridge: Cambridge University Press, 1977. This book was originally prepared as a series of lectures for the BBC. It is very readable and beautifully illustrated.

BRAZIER, M. A. B. The historical development of neurophysiology. In J. Field, H. Magoun, & V. Hall (Eds.) *Handbook of physiology,* Vol. 1, Sect. 1: *Neurophysiology* (pp. 1–58). Washington D.C.: American Physiological Society, 1959. This outstanding chapter covers the beginnings of the sciences that we know today as physiological psychology and neuroscience. Although technical, a serious student should find it fascinating.

CALVIN, W. H. *The throwing madonna.* New York: McGraw-Hill, 1983. Clearly written essays by an eminent neurobiologist relating art, literature, and poetry to neurobiology. The title essay raises the question of why most of us throw with our right hand, and the author wonders if it might be because mothers usually hold their babies with their left arm.

CARLSON, N. R. *Physiology of behavior* (2nd ed.) Boston: Allyn and Bacon, 1981. One of the best textbooks on physiological psychology. The material is clearly written and up to date.

FEARING, F. *Reflex action: A study in the history of physiological psychology.* Cambridge, Mass.: MIT Press, 1970. An excellent paperback on the development of physiological psychology and the part that the early study of reflexes played in the shaping of contemporary brain research.

PENFIELD, W. *The mystery of the mind.* Princeton, N.J.: Princeton University Press, 1975. An exciting account of early research into localization of function in the cerebral cortex by an eminent pioneer in that field.

PETERS, A., PALAY, S. L., & WEBSTER, H. DE F. *The fine structure of the nervous system.* Philadelphia: Saunders, 1976. This book contains a series of electron micrographs of the internal components of neurons and other cells of the nervous system. It provides a marvelous look into a tiny world and gives a good idea how neurons go about their jobs.

Scientific American, September 1979. Reprinted as a book entitled *The brain.* San Francisco: W. H. Freeman, 1980. An excellent overview of contemporary neuroscience.

SPRINGER, S. P., & DEUTSCH, G. *Left brain, right brain.* San Francisco: W. H. Freeman 1981. A good survey of recent research into the differences and similarities in function of the two cerebral hemispheres. The book is fairly easy to read and very interesting.

3

Sensory Processes

WHAT DO OUR SENSES TELL US?
   An Adequate Stimulus
SENSORY QUALITIES: DISTINGUISHING BETWEEN STIMULI
   The Nature of the Stimulus Versus the Sensory Response
   The Doctrine of Specific Nerve Energies
THE VISUAL SYSTEM
   The Electromagnetic Spectrum and Visible Light
   The Structure of the Eye
   Receptor Cells in the Retina
   Transduction in the Retina
   Visual Pathways from Eye to Cortex
   Feature Detectors in the Cortex
   Color Vision
THE AUDITORY SYSTEM
   The Nature of Sound
   The Transduction of Sound
   The Perception of Auditory Space
THE BODILY SENSES
   The Sense of Touch
   The Position Senses
   The Senses of Taste and Smell
SUMMARY
KEY TERMS
SUGGESTED READINGS

WHAT DO OUR SENSES TELL US?

To discuss sensation and perception is to approach from a scientific point of view one of the great philosophical questions of all time: From where does human knowledge come? Is some of our knowledge built in—that is, are we as human beings preprogrammed to know certain things—or is all knowledge the result of information obtained through the senses? The answer is both straightforward and quite complex. By studying the mechanisms of sensation and perception and examining how they develop and are modified, psychologists have come to some surprising conclusions about the origins of knowledge.

   The English philosopher John Locke (1632–1704) and others of the British Empiricist school of thought maintained that all knowledge originates with information obtained through the bodily senses. The empiricists argued that the mind of a newborn can be likened to an empty book or a blank tablet (a *tabula rasa*) and that everything a person is and knows must arise from personal experience. Therefore, the British Empiricists concluded that most differences between individuals are determined by differences in their environments and life events.

Clearly though, sensation, perception, and the origins of knowledge are more complex than this. The very nature of the human organism largely determines what sorts of information are taken in and how we respond to it. The German philosopher Immanuel Kant (1724–1804) maintained that the human mind processes information in certain predetermined ways—that there are preexisting categories that help to organize sensory information. Kant argued that human beings can perceive the world only through categories such as "time," "causality," and "space." These innate categories, according to Kant, shape our perceptions of the world.

Neither of Locke's nor Kant's approach in its pure form adequately explains how we learn about the world and construct our own particular version of reality. They do point out, however, that both our unique nature as human beings and our capacity to learn interact to determine our perceptions of the world. In this chapter we discuss how some stimuli and events in our environment activate our senses. We also explore the central nervous system mechanisms that underlie sensory function. In Chapter 4 we explore how sensory information is processed by the nervous system to generate conscious experience.

AN ADEQUATE STIMULUS

Have you ever blown a whistle that emits a tone so high that your dog can hear it but you cannot? Have you ever been puzzled by the ability of some animals to get around in the dark while you keep bumping into things, or been amazed by the capacity of a hawk to spot a mouse from over 100 ft in the air?

There are many sensory events in the world that we simply cannot respond to. This is because the receptors of human sensory systems respond to a relatively limited range of sensory stimuli. Thus our eyes respond to light energy of only certain specific wavelengths and intensities; our ears detect vibrations of the air within a limited range of frequencies; our senses of smell and taste alert us to the presence of molecules with only certain shapes or chemical properties. Moreover, each of our receptor systems can respond to only specific kinds of inputs. Those receptors that respond to light energy cannot respond to sound energy, and receptors that respond to touch or pressure cannot respond to tastes or odors. A stimulus to which a particular receptor can normally respond is referred to as an *adequate stimulus* for that receptor.

As illustrated earlier, an adequate stimulus for the auditory system of a dog or cat can be quite different from an adequate stimulus for the human auditory system. Although dogs and cats respond to the same sounds that we hear, they can also hear sounds that are an octave or more above the highest tones within our sensory range. There are many other examples of adequate stimuli for the receptors of certain animals that cannot be perceived by other animals or by human beings. For example, the receptors in the eye of a bee can detect light that is in the ultraviolet range—light to which the human eye is blind. Some birds can even respond to cues provided by the magnetic field of the earth. Just because our human receptors cannot pick

SENSORY PROCESSES

up certain kinds of sensory information does not mean that those stimuli are of no consequence in the world; it means only that some sensory information does not provide an adequate stimulus for human receptor systems.

In short, there are many different kinds of receptor systems, each with its own particular characteristics that permit activation by only certain types and ranges of stimuli. The activation of a receptor system by an adequate stimulus causes sensory messages to be sent to the CNS so that the brain can be informed about what is occurring in the world around it.

SENSORY QUALITIES: DISTINGUISHING BETWEEN STIMULI

THE NATURE OF THE STIMULUS VERSUS THE SENSORY RESPONSE

To get a good idea of how sensory systems work and of the interactions between the processes of sensation and perception, try this simple experiment on yourself. Take a reasonably sharp pencil in your right hand and hold it vertically with the point down over the back of your left hand, as shown in Figure 3.1. Then touch it down gently in several different locations on the back of your left hand. When you do this, pay particular attention to the nature of what you feel when the pencil point touches your skin. At some places the pencil point will feel as if it were cold. However, at other locations on your hand you experience the sensation of pressure or perhaps itchiness. Try to find a spot that elicits the sensation of cold and another that creates the sensation of pressure. What is going on? Clearly the pencil point did not change its properties when different sensations were felt. The explanation for the different sensations must be found somewhere in the neural systems which are responding to pressure from the pencil point.

As you just demonstrated, there are several different regions on the back of your hand, each producing specific sensations when they were stimulated. Receptors in these regions send their messages to the brain where they are interpreted as cold, pressure, or pain. When, for example, a receptor that normally responds to cold is stimulated by the pencil point, action potentials (see Chapter 2) are sent to the brain. These neural impulses are interpreted by the brain as the sensation of "cold" even though the stimulus was actually pressure. The brain responds this way because that particular nerve pathway usually carries messages of cold.

There are many illustrations of this phenomenon. For example, most of us have, after rubbing our eyes in a dark room, experienced a sensation of light flashes, rings, or stars. There was of course no light there, but pressure on the eyes caused the stimulation of neural elements in the eye, which in turn generated action potential impulses that traveled along the visual pathways to the brain, where they were interpreted as light.

THE DOCTRINE OF SPECIFIC NERVE ENERGIES

It was evidence of this sort that led the German physiologist Johannes Mueller (1801–1858) to propose what has come to be called the *doctrine of specific nerve energies*. Mueller proposed that the nature of a perceived sensation is

Figure 3.1
Touch different parts of the back of your hand gently with the tip of your pencil. Does the pencil point feel different in some areas than in others? Why does this happen?

the result of which particular neural systems are being activated by a stimulus, rather than the actual nature of the stimulus itself. In other words, the nature of a perceived sensation is determined by which nerve pathways are activated, not by the event that activates the pathways. Mueller maintained that we cannot be directly aware of objects or events in the world, only of the activity of nerves carrying sensory messages; that is, receptors and neural pathways act as the intermediaries between events in the world and consciousness. Further, he suggested that these neural-receptor systems impose some of their own characteristics on what is perceived by the mind. Essentially, this means that the most important aspect of sensation centers on which neural pathways are activated rather than on the nature of the stimulus. Although revolutionary in Mueller's time, the idea that sensation and perception are the result of neural events that impose their own characteristics on stimuli is widely accepted today and much of this chapter and Chapter 4 is devoted to exploring extensions of this concept.

Surprisingly vivid sensations can be produced by electrically stimulating certain brain areas. In such experiments, the investigator applies a mild electric current to a region of the brain. If that brain area mediates some sensory process, the person will report a vivid sensation such as a taste, touch to the hand, a light flash, or a sound, even though no sensory event occurred. What happened? Simply, the electric current delivered to the brain activated many of the same neurons that would normally be activated by a stimulus originating outside the body (Calvin & Ojemann, 1980).

THE VISUAL SYSTEM

Human beings are visual animals. We gain most of our information about the world around us through vision: We see objects and events, we view visual media such as the movies or television, and we read. Vision is our dominant sense. Although our sense of hearing is very important, especially in social situations, it ranks second to vision in human sensory priorities. The expression "I won't believe it until I've seen it with my own eyes" illustrates the trust that most of us place in the accuracy and reliability of our visual system. Because of the special place that vision holds in our lives, it has been widely studied by psychologists and neurobiologists. As a result, it is probably the most thoroughly understood of the major sensory systems.

THE ELECTROMAGNETIC SPECTRUM AND VISIBLE LIGHT

Light is part of what is called the *electromagnetic spectrum*. The term expresses the relationship that exists between various kinds of radiant energy, ranging from magnetic fields through radio waves, visible light, x-rays, gamma rays, and beyond. Figure 3.2 (see color insert) illustrates the electromagnetic spectrum, showing the many different kinds of radiant energy and their associated wavelengths. We call the small portion of this spectrum that we can detect with the receptors in our eyes *visible light*.

But just what is electromagnetic energy? Sir Isaac Newton (1642–1727) discovered that sunlight or other white light can be broken down by a glass prism into light of many colors. Newton suggested that light acts as if it were a stream of particles of energy (called *photons*) that travel in a straight line unless bent by a lens or prism. A glass prism causes the paths of different kinds of photons to separate, revealing light or different colors.

While light often acts as if it were composed of beams of particles of energy or photons, under other conditions it acts as if it were made up of waves. The Scottish physicist James Clerk Maxwell (1831–1879) suggested that in this case light could be thought of as a change in the electromagnetic field surrounding a beam of photons. The wavelength of the electromagnetic energy would then be defined as the distance between the peaks of the photon waves.

Electromagnetic waves can vary enormously in length. For example, the wavelength of the electromagnetic energy produced by electric house current, which oscillates 60 times a second [a frequency of 60 hertz (Hz)] is sometimes over 3,000 miles long, while the wavelengths of the electromagnetic energy used in AM radio broadcasts are several hundred meters long. This is because the frequency of the oscillations is much faster. Radar and other types of microwaves oscillate billions of times a second and may have wavelengths of only a few centimeters.

Rapidly vibrating molecules, vibrations caused for instance by heating an object, produce radiation of still shorter wavelengths. Heating a piece of iron, for example, will cause it to emit electromagnetic energy known as heat waves or *infrared radiation*. Adding more heat will increase the frequency of this radiation until some of it reaches the lowest ranges of visible light. We now say that the metal is "red hot." Heating it to still higher temperatures (adding more energy) will cause it to become "white hot" and emit electromagnetic energy of still shorter wavelengths. As you can see from Figure 3.2, the longest wavelengths of visible light are what we call red light, while the shortest wavelengths give rise to the sensation of violet light.

If the frequency of the radiation is increased still more, that is, above violet, we enter the range of radiation called *ultraviolet light*. Our photoreceptors cannot respond to radiation of these wavelengths, although some insects, notably honeybees, see quite well with ultraviolet light. Still shorter wavelengths yield x-rays, gamma rays, and cosmic rays. The range of wavelengths to which our eyes respond is really quite limited considering the extent of the electromagnetic spectrum.

We experience different wavelengths of light in the visible range of the electromagnetic spectrum as different colors. Thus the sensation of red light is produced by radiation of about 700 nanometers (nm; a billionth of a meter) in wavelength. Violet light is radiation of about 400 nm. The various colors of the visible spectrum and their associated wavelengths are shown in Figure 3.2.

THE STRUCTURE OF THE EYE

Now that we have some idea of what light is, we can learn how our eyes convert the energy of light into action potentials or neural energy. The action potentials produced by cells in the eye travel back to the brain, where they are interpreted. The result of this interpretation is the sensation of vision.

The eye is often compared to a camera, and the analogy is quite useful. Since both have similar functions, it is not surprising that eyes and cameras

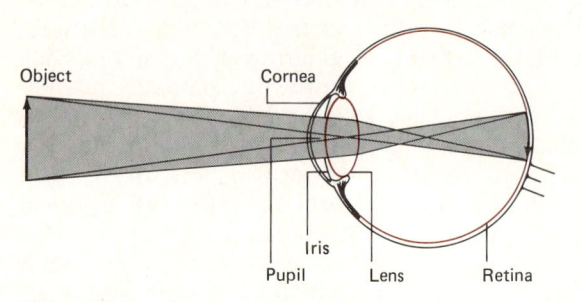

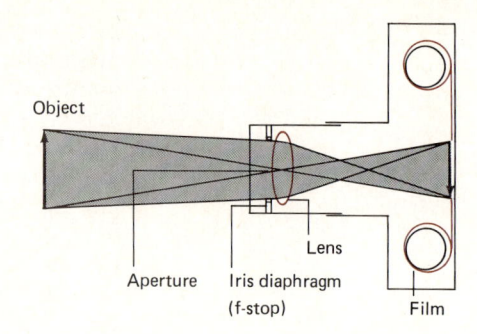

BIOLOGY, SENSATION, PERCEPTION, AND CONSCIOUSNESS

Figure 3.3
The eye and the camera. Both have similar features that enable them to respond to or record visual images.

have several features in common (see Figure 3.3). For example, both have a lens which bends the rays of light so that an image is focused on a light-sensitive surface. In cameras, the lens is a complex structure composed of several carefully shaped pieces of glass, while the light-sensitive surface is made up of special chemicals coated onto the film.

In the eye, the image is focused by two elements, the *cornea* (see Figure 3.4), which actually does most of the light bending involved in focusing, and the *lens*, which takes care of fine focusing. The light-sensitive surface in the eye is made up of the receptor cells of the retina, located at the back of the eye.

Both the eye and most reasonably sophisticated cameras can alter their point of focus so that the image of near or distant objects will be sharp and clear. In the camera the lens moves back and forth—closer to the film when focusing on a distant object, farther away from the film when taking a close-up picture. In the eye, a series of small muscles alter the shape of the lens,

Figure 3.4
A section through a human eye. The cornea and the lens together focus a tiny inverted image onto an incredibly dense array of receptor cells in the retina. These receptor cells, together with other cells of the retina, convert patterns of light energy into patterns of action potentials that travel along the optic nerve to the brain, where they are decoded and generate the sensation of vision. (Photo copyright © by Dr. D. W. Fawcett/Mizoguti)

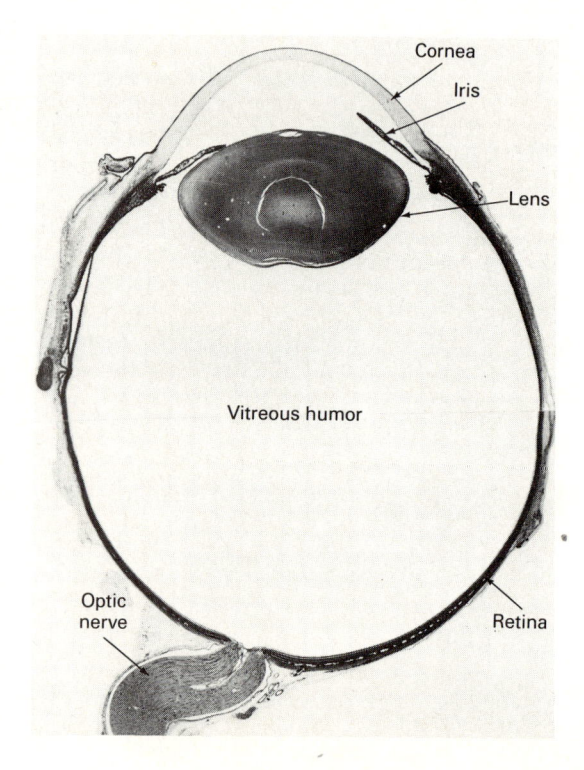

increasing its focusing power by making it rounder for looking at near objects, and decreasing its focusing power by making it flatter for looking at distant objects This process of changing the shape of the lens to focus the image is known as *accommodation*.

Both a camera and the eye also have ways to control the amount of light that enters. In the camera this is accomplished by an adjustable metal diaphragm, and in the eye by the *iris,* two small circular muscles that reflexively open or close the pupillary opening as the amount of light decreases or increases.

The large chamber of the eye between the lens and the retina is filled with a thick liquid known as *vitreous humor*. This almost jellylike liquid, containing many layers of strands that help it keep its shape, is generally clear, but sometimes it contains small bits of floating cellular debris. These "floaters" cast shadows on the retina, seen under some conditions, such as when you are staring at a clear sky or some other featureless background. Usually, such floaters are very difficult to see clearly because they move with the eye and therefore are hard to fix on.

The *retina* is the structure that changes light energy into neural responses, that is, action potentials. This process is known as *transduction* and is seen in one form or another in all sensory systems. The retina is made up primarily of neural tissue and is about as thick as a sheet of heavy paper. It is composed of several layers of cells, shown in a micrograph in Figure 3.5 and schematically in Figure 3.6 (Dowling & Boycott, 1966).

As light travels through the retina it passes first through the layer of ganglion cells. The axons of these cells form the optic nerve, which carries the visual message from the eye to the brain. The middle layer of the retina is made up of several types of cells, including the bipolar cells that connect the ganglion cells to the receptor cells, which are found in the third layer (see Gregory, 1978).

Figure 3.5
A view through a microscope of some of the cells of the retina. The rods and cones are seen as shadowy parallel lines near the top third of the picture. Below them are the nuclei of the rods and cones. Below them are the bodies of horizontal cells and bipolar cells, and near the bottom of the micrograph are bodies of the ganglion cells, cells whose axons form the optic nerve. Light, which is coming from the bottom in this figure, passes through the lens and has to pass through all of these cells before it reaches the rod and cone receptor cells. (Photo copyright © Biophoto Associates)

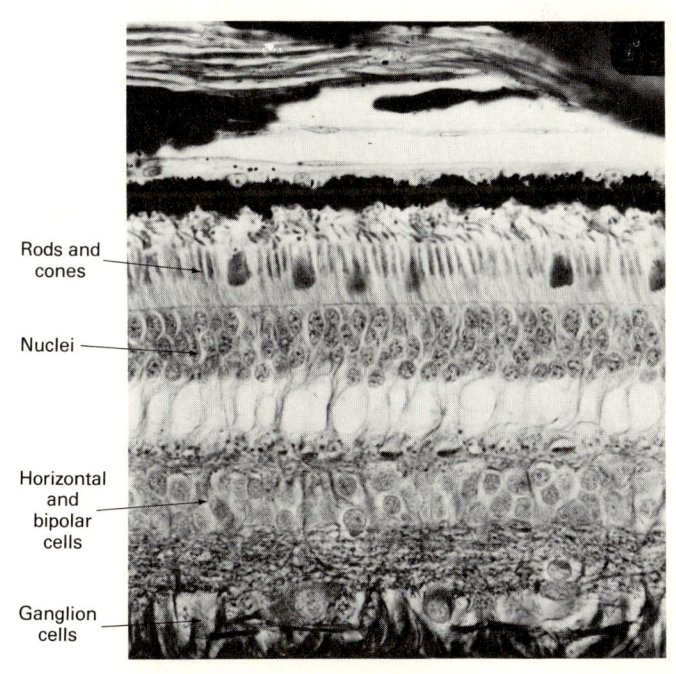

Figure 3.6
A schematic drawing of the connections of the cells in the periphery of the retina. Light passes by many cells of the retina on its way to stimulate the rod and cones. Stimulation of these receptors causes the activation of bipolar cells which, in turn, activate the ganglion cells which send action potential messages back to the brain. Note that the inputs from several receptor cells converge on just a few ganglion cells. The horizontal cells and amacrine cells produce lateral inhibition which enhances contrast in the neural message. If this had been a drawing of cells in the fovea, there would have been only cone receptors and there would have been about equal numbers of cones, bipolar cells, and ganglion cells.

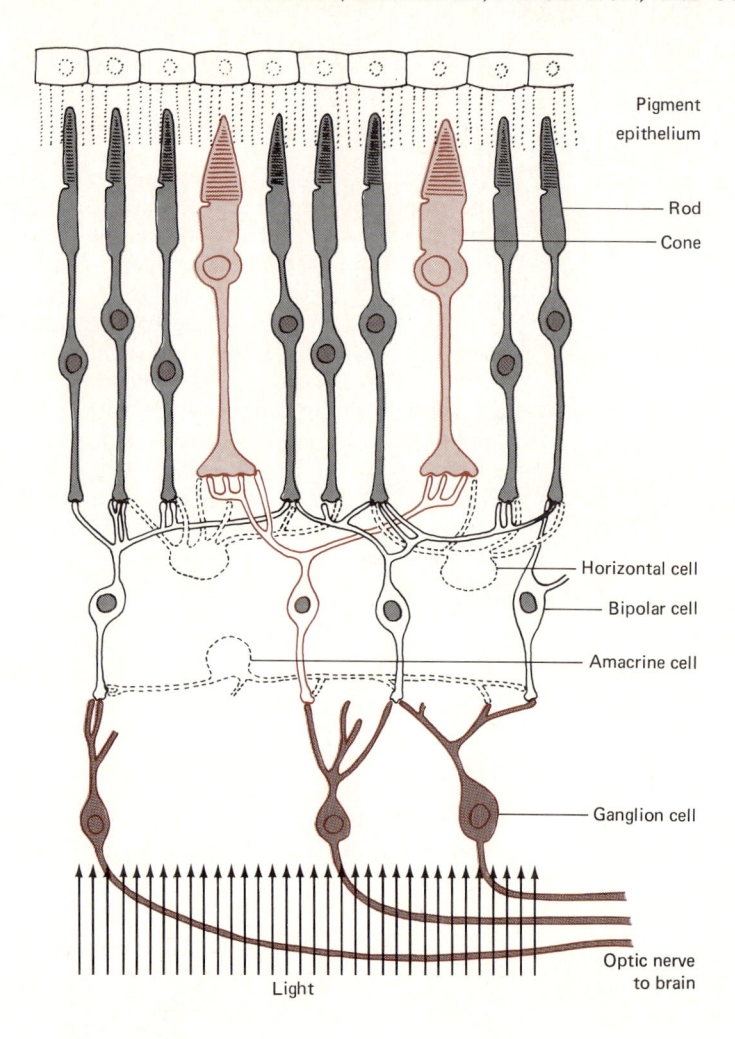

RECEPTOR CELLS IN THE RETINA

At the back of each of our eyes there are about 130 million receptor cells that detect the presence of light. These cells convert light energy into neural activity. There are two types of retinal receptor cells and they can be distinguished by their characteristic shapes, from which they also derive their names. The *rod receptor cells* are long, thin, tube-shaped cells, while the *cone receptor cells* are shorter and more tapered.

The rod and cone receptor cells are connected to bipolar cells, which, in turn, pass neural information to cells called ganglion cells. The *ganglion cells* are the cells that send their axons, carrying the neural messages of vision, back to the brain.

There are two other types of cells in the retina, which have connections perpendicular to the connections of the rods, cones, and bipolar cells. These laterally conducting cells are called *horizontal cells* and *amacrine cells*. These cells are responsible for some of the neural interactions that occur in the retina, resulting in a sharper visual image being sent to the brain.

Light has to negotiate a path through all these cells before it reaches the

SENSORY PROCESSES

light-sensitive portions of the rods and cones located at their far ends. That light energy which passes through the system and does not stimulate the receptors is absorbed by the *pigment epithelium* at the very back side of the retina. This dark pigment reduces the amount of reflected and scattered light, which might otherwise blur a clear image.

In some nocturnal animals, which are required to get along in very low levels of light, the pigment epithelium is replaced by a shiny reflective surface known as the *tapetum*. This reflective material lets the light pass through the retina twice, once as it enters and again as it is reflected out. This gives the receptors twice the opportunity to be stimulated by each photon that enters the eye. The presence of the tapetum explains why cats, raccoons, and other nocturnal animals have eyes that reflect an automobile headlight beam or light from a flashlight so brightly that they appear to glow in the dark.

As noted above, the message that light has stimulated a receptor cell is relayed to the ganglion cells by the bipolar cells and then to the brain by the axons of the ganglion cells. In the periphery of the retina, several receptor cells typically converge on a single bipolar cell, and then several bipolar cells converge on a single ganglion cell. In the central part of the retina, however, each bipolar cell responds to only one cone receptor, and most ganglion cells are connected to a single bipolar cell. This central region is called the *fovea* in human beings and the area centralis in other animals. It is a small depression or dimple in the surface of the retina containing a very high density of receptor cells. Because of the nearly 1:1 ratio between receptors and ganglion cells, the fovea can make extremely fine visual discriminations and it is the area where most of the "seeing" of fine detail takes place. When you "look" at some object, you orient your eyes in such a way that the image of that object is projected on the fovea.

There is another important distinction between different regions of the retina. Cone cells are concentrated in the fovea and decrease in density as one moves outward from the center of the retina, while rod cells are found in more peripheral regions. In fact, the fovea contains no rods at all, only cone receptors. The distribution of rods and cones in the human retina is shown in Figure 3.7.

The presence of two distinct types of receptors in the retina suggests that they must also have different functions, as indeed they do. Rods are active in very dim light—they are our receptors for night vision. Cones need more light to function and are used in daylight.

Figure 3.7
Distribution of receptors in the eye. The cone receptors are concentrated in the fovea, while the rod receptors are more densely distributed 20 to 40 degrees away from the fovea. There are no receptors at all where the optic nerve leaves the retina (the blind spot).

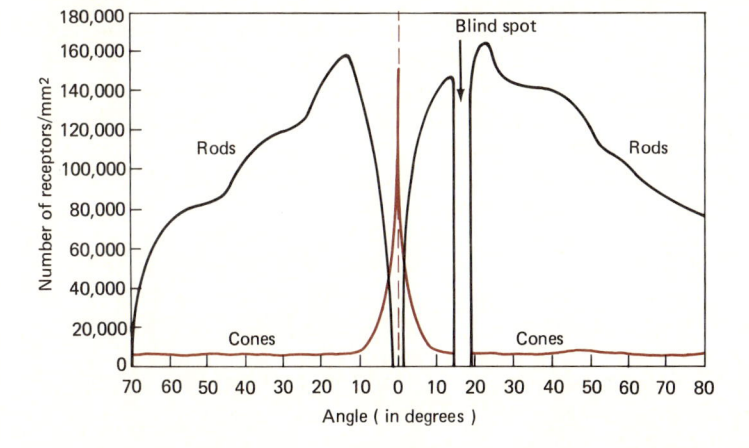

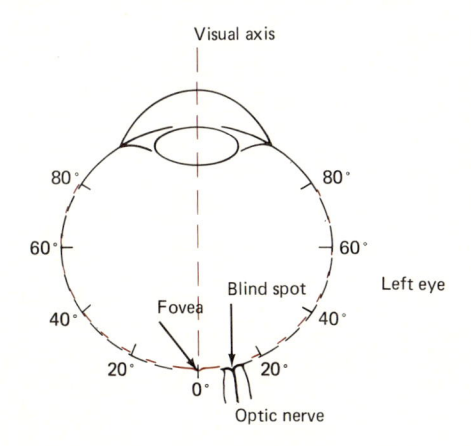

Vision in low light levels using the rod receptors is called *scotopic vision;* vision in brighter light is called *photopic.* Photopic vision sees in color; with scotopic vision there is no sensation of color.

The idea of seeing only in black and white when the lighting is very dim seems strange to some people, but to convince yourself, think about your visual sensations when you are out for a walk at night. The trees do not look green, nor can you tell the color of a passing car. Remember how difficult it is to match colors in a dark closet? If you shine a flashlight you can see color, because it provides enough light to activate the cone receptors and produce photopic vision.

The biological advantage of having both scotopic and photopic vision is obvious. We must be able to respond efficiently over a wide range of illumination. The difference in light intensity between the dimmest light we can detect and a quick glance at the noonday sun is about 100 billion to 1. Having two systems to take care of the higher and lower portions of this range is a good way of getting around the problem of seeing during both day and night. Animals that are active only during one part of the day do not need two types of receptors. Those that are predominantly nocturnal, such as owls or mice, have retinas that contain only rod receptors, while those active during the day, such as chipmunks, some turtles, and many birds, have retinas that contain only cone receptors.

Recall how difficult it is to find an unoccupied seat when you go from the brightly lit outdoors into a darkened movie theater. Yet, later, it was quite easy to see your surroundings. The increase in sensitivity of the receptors of the visual system as you remain in the dark is called *dark adaptation.* Both cones and rods show substantial increases in sensitivity during dark adaptation, but they do it a different rates. The cones adapt rapidly, showing substantial increases in sensitivity in just 2 or 3 minutes. After about 10 minutes in the dark the cones reach their maximum sensitivity and do not show further increases. The rods take somewhat longer, showing maximum sensitivity after about 25 minutes in the dark. Although much slower to adapt, the rods are much more sensitive to low levels of illumination.

TRANSDUCTION IN THE RETINA

As noted earlier, the task of the retina is to convert the energy contained in photons of light into action potentials. This process is called *transduction* and the question that we will address now is how retinal cells accomplish this conversion. The process of transduction involves several complex chemical reactions, and although they are not completely understood, neurobiologists have a good idea of the major events taking place. The process begins with the absorption of photons by pigments in the receptor cells. Any substance that absorbs photons is called a *pigment,* and both rods and cones possess a region containing substances known as visual pigments. Figure 3.8 shows this region where the transduction process begins.

In the rods, the visual pigment is called *rhodopsin* (which means visual red). When a molecule of rhodopsin in a rod receptor cell absorbs a photon of light, it changes its shape and then rapidly undergoes several chemical reactions. These light-induced chemical reactions cause a change in the polarity of the rod receptor, which, in turn, causes activation of the bipolar cell connected to the rod receptor. The bipolar cell then stimulates a ganglion cell, the next cell in the chain.

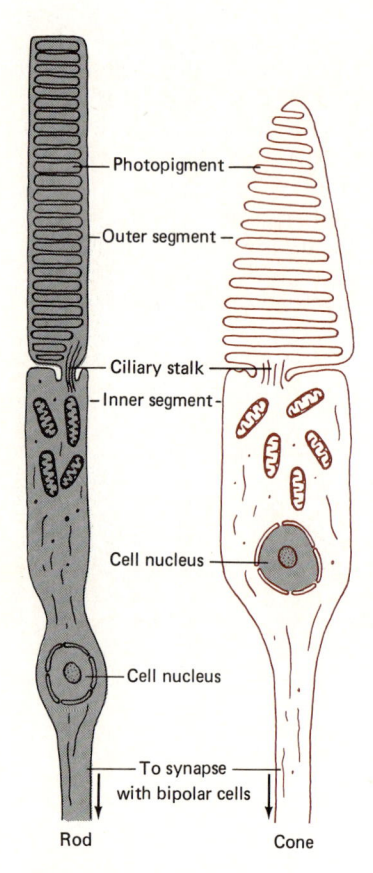

Figure 3.8
Rod and cone receptors. Rod receptors are used when there is little light. Cone receptors are active when there is a fairly high level of illumination. Cone cells have different kinds of photopigments so that they respond differently to light of different wavelengths, generating the sensation of color vision.

SENSORY PROCESSES

In the cones visual transduction is a more complex process and is less well understood. However, neuroscientists believe that a pigment called *iodopsin* (visual purple) is the important photochemical in these cells. The absorption of photons of light by iodopsin eventually activates bipolar cells and subsequently depolarizes ganglion cells to such a degree that action potentials are generated.

Axons of ganglion cells from all over the retina join together in one place to form the *optic nerve*, which extends from the back of each eye into the brain. Since the bodies of the ganglion cells are located on the outer surface of the retina, their axons must penetrate the retina at the point where they join to form the optic nerve. Hence there are no rods or cones in this region of the retina and it is, not surprisingly, called the *blind spot*.

What about the other cells in the retina, the horizontal cells and the amacrine cells? What is their function? These cells help sharpen the neural message going back to the brain by accentuating the differences between visual stimuli projected onto adjacent regions of the retina. Indeed, the retina is not a passive responder to photons of light as is film in a camera—the retina actively interacts with the visual stimuli, often resulting in a neural message that is not an exact representation of the visual stimulus. A good example of active processing by the retina can be seen in the ways the visual system accentuates borders through contrast effects.

HIGHLIGHT 3.1
Spot Your Blind Spot

Since there are no visual receptors where the optic nerve punches through the retina on its way to the brain, we should have a "hole" in our vision, yet we are usually not aware that it is there. Is there really a blind spot, and why don't we notice it?

You can demonstrate the presence of your blind spot by using the figure below. Close your left eye or place your hand over it so that you are looking at the X in the figure only with your right eye. Now, keeping your eye fixed on the X, move the page toward and away from you. At some point, when the book is about 30 centimeters (30 cm = 1 ft) away from your eye, the small figure on the bicycle will disappear. At this point, the lens of your eye is projecting the image of that figure onto your blind spot.

Note that not only does the figure seem to disappear, but the line appears to run completely through where the figure was. This indicates that the brain fills in the missing information by generating visual messages on the basis of information that is projected onto adjacent regions of the retina. This phenomenon explains why you are not normally aware of your blind spot. Indeed, some people who have suffered extensive damage to parts of their visual system have large "holes" in their vision and yet are quite unaware of them until tests similar in principle to this demonstration are performed.

Figure 3.9
The middle part of the upper portion of this figure changes uniformly from very dark gray to light gray. This transition in stimulus intensity is shown in part (B) of the figure. However, the transition does not appear to be uniform. There appears to be a dark band near region 1 and a bright band near region 2. These are called Mach bands and are a result of lateral inhibition in the retina. To explain the production of Mach bands, a few retinal cells, which are illuminated by the Mach band-producing stimulus at the top of the figure, are shown schematically in part (C). Cells a, b, c, and d are all receiving the same amount of illumination. However, there is a difference in their responses. Cell b, for example, is stimulated by the bright light, but it is also strongly inhibited by the activity of cells a and c, which are adjacent to it. Cell d, is receiving the same amount of light as b, but it is receiving less lateral inhibition. Although it is strongly inhibited by cell c, it is less inhibited by cell e, which is not receiving as much light. Therefore cell d responds more vigorously; see part (D) of the figure, than cell b, even though both are receiving the same intensity of stimulation. The result is a bright band near region 2. Now, look at the other side of the figure. Cells g, h, i, and j are all receiving the same intensity of stimulation. Cell i is only weakly inhibited by cells j and h, but cell g, adjacent to cell f, which is receiving more light, is more strongly inhibited. Therefore its response intensity will be decreased, producing the sensation of a dark band. (Redrawn from Coren, Porac, & Ward, 1984, after Cornsweet, 1970)

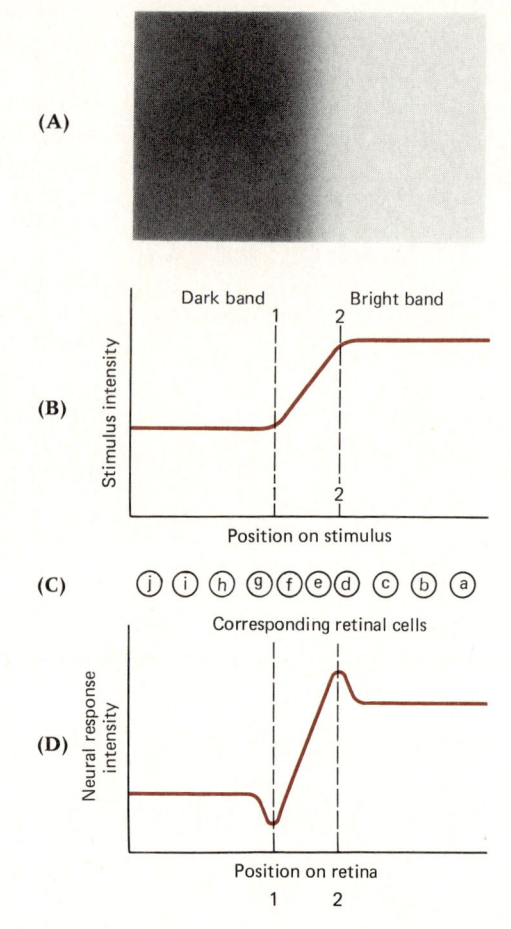

In Figure 3.9 a dark region gradually and uniformly changes into a lighter region. But this is not what we see. Instead, we see two fuzzy lines at points A and B on the figure. There seems to be a darker region at A and a lighter region at B. These are called *Mach bands* and their presence shows that the visual system is actively striving to increase the contrast between the dark regions of the figure and the lighter ones, even though the actual transition is uniform.

This can be further illustrated by using staircase brightness pattern. In Figure 3.10 we can see a series of stripes. Each stripe is uniform in its brightness but the right side of each seems to be darker than the left. This is a result of the enhancement of a border by the visual system. The actual brightness of each stripe is shown in portion B of the figure, but the apparent brightness is shown in part C. The edges closer to their lighter or darker neighbors are subject to contrast effects. As a result, the junction between each stripe is enhanced (Cornsweet, 1970).

An understanding of the neurobiological basis of this phenomenon had to await the development of modern electrophysiological techniques. Recent experiments have demonstrated that retinal cells, as well as other neurons located in the brain, are interconnected so that they can mutually inhibit the responses of adjacent cells. In the retina this is accomplished largely through the influence of the horizontal cells and amacrine cells.

SENSORY PROCESSES

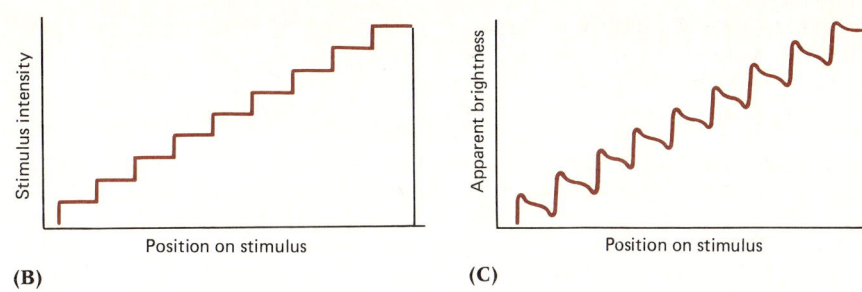

Figure 3.10 The stripes in this figure do not appear to be uniformly bright. The left edge of each stripe appears somewhat lighter, and the right edge appears to be a little darker. The actual changes in stimulus intensity are diagrammed in part (B) of the figure, but how they actually appear is shown in part (C). The brighter regions are acting through lateral inhibition in the retina to inhibit adjacent areas more strongly than do the darker regions of the figure.

Figure 3.11 illustrates the basic principles of *lateral inhibition* and how it works to produce contrast effects. Lateral inhibition is inhibition exerted in a sideways direction. In this simplified system receptor cells A and B are both being illuminated by a visual stimulus. Cell B is receiving more intense illumination than cell A. The activation of cell A stimulates the next neuron in the chain (cell D), which transmits the information toward the brain. However, the activity of cell D is inhibited by the more intense activation of cell B. It exerts an inhibitory effect on cell D through the activation of laterally oriented inhibitory cell C. As a result, cell D fires at a reduced rate. Excitatory effects are shown as dark arrows. This laterally acting inhibition exaggerates the contrast in the message that is passed to the brain via the ganglion cell axons.

This explanation highlights the importance of the concept of receptive fields in the visual system. The *receptive field* of a given neuron (e.g., a ganglion cell or some cell in the brain) is that region of the retina which, when stimulated, alters the activity of that neuron. Each ganglion cell or neuron in the visual system in the brain can be activated or inhibited by light striking some particular region of the retina, that is, its receptive field. The receptive fields of some cell in the visual cortex, for example, may be quite large and encompass several thousand rod and cone receptor cells. A receptive field is usually determined using single-cell recording techniques, and such experiments are typically performed in anesthetized cats. The results of such studies generalize well to many different species of animals, including human beings (Werblin, 1973).

In experiments that study the neurobiological mechanisms operating in the visual system, a microelectrode is typically placed somewhere in the

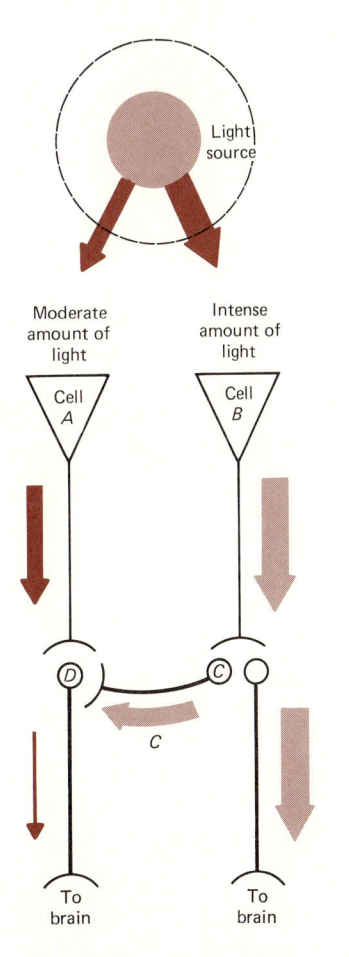

Figure 3.11 Contrast effects produced by lateral inhibition. Receptor cells A and B are both being illuminated by a visual stimulus. Cell B is receiving more intense illumination than cell A. The activation of cell A stimulates the next neuron in the chain (cell D), which transmits the information toward the brain. However, the activity of cell D is inhibited by the more intense activation of cell B. It exerts an inhibitory effect on cell D through the activation of laterally oriented inhibitory cell C. As a result, cell D fires at a reduced rate. Excitatory effects are shown as dark arrows.

Figure 3.12
A simplied drawing of how neural responses are recorded from the visual system of a cat.

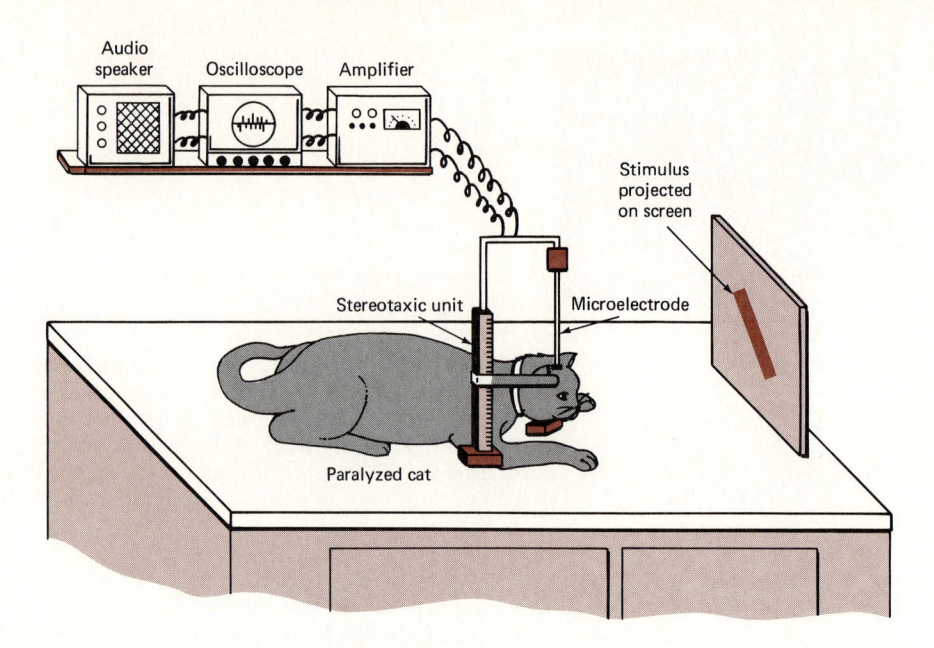

visual system and this type of electrode is so small that it can record activity from only one single cell at a time. For example, microelectrodes can be placed in the retina, optic nerve, or in parts of the brain that mediate the sense of vision. Spots of light (the visual stimulus) are then projected on a screen which is located in front of an experimental animal, such as a cat. See Figure 3.12 for a schematic diagram of such a recording setup. Hubel and Wiesel pioneered this research strategy and together were awarded a Nobel prize for their work in 1981. Much of what we know about the ways that the nervous system processes visual information comes from their work and that of their associates.

Let us suppose that the electrode is placed in the optic nerve. It is therefore recording the action potentials produced by a single ganglion cell in the retina. (Recall that the optic nerve is composed of the axons of retinal ganglion cells.) Researchers find that somewhere on the retina there is a very small region that when stimulated by light will cause the ganglion cell being studied to increase its firing rate, that is, its production of action potentials. Immediately adjacent to that excitatory region of the retina for that particular ganglion cell is another area, which has just the opposite effect. Stimulation of the adjacent area by light causes the ganglion cell to decrease its firing rate. The area of the retina in which light affects that cell's firing rate (either increasing it or decreasing it) is called the *receptive field* of that cell. In the example shown in Figure 3.13A, the receptive field of the cell being studied has an excitatory center and an inhibitory surround.

VISUAL PATHWAYS FROM EYE TO CORTEX

From the retina onward to the brain, the sensation of vision is an entirely neural event. The receptor cells convert the presence or absence of light to changes in voltage across each receptor cell membrane. This change in membrane potential causes an alteration in the release of neurotransmitters by the receptor cells. The bipolar cells of the retina respond to these neurotrans-

SENSORY PROCESSES

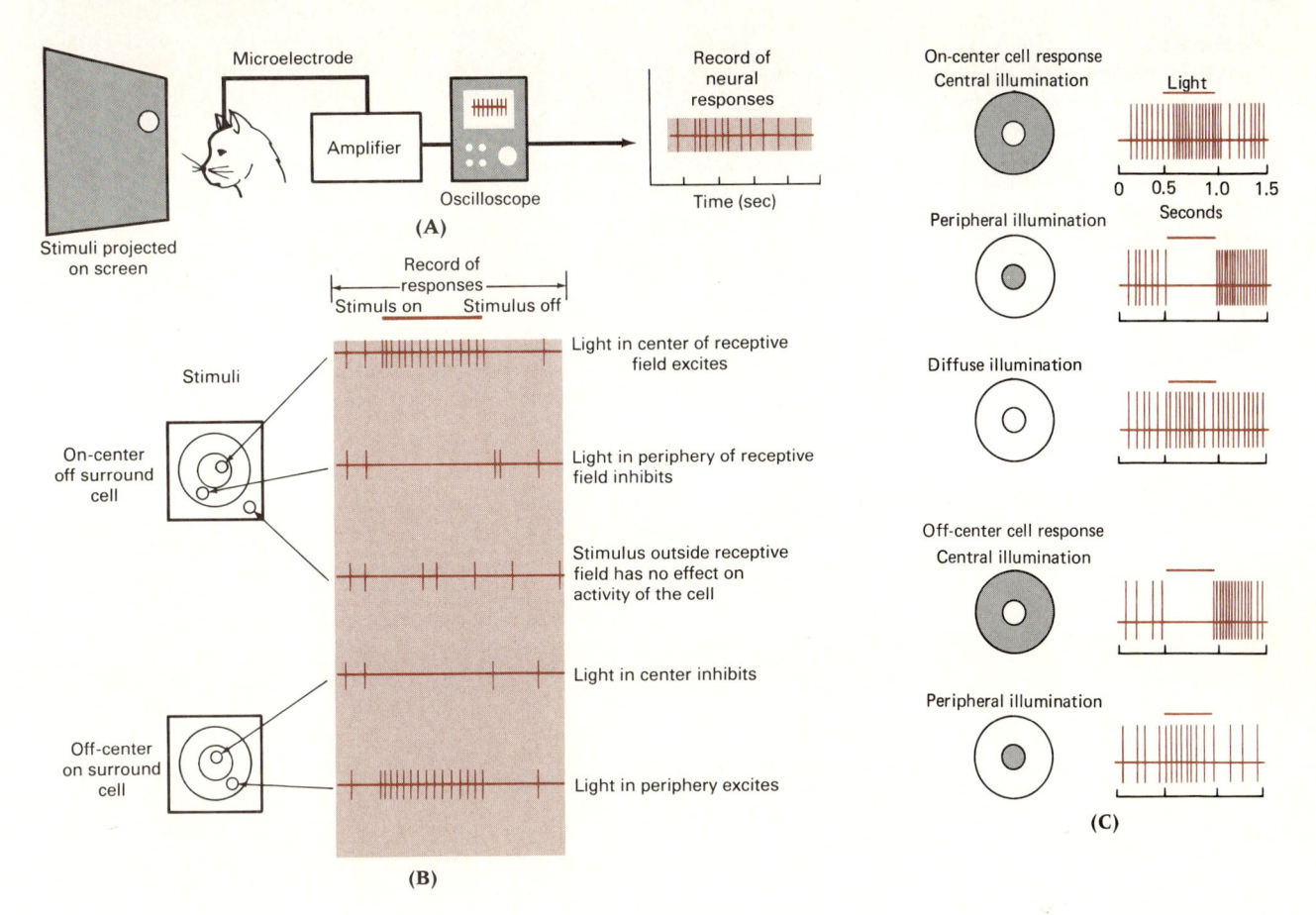

Figure 3.13 (A) The receptive field of any neuron in the visual system is that specific region of the retina which, when stimulated by light, causes a change in the firing of that neuron. In this illustration, visual stimuli are projected on the screen. Since the cat's head and eyes are stationary, projecting the stimuli onto different places on the screen causes different regions of the retina to be stimulated. This illustration shows the procedures used to study the characteristics of the receptive fields of retinal ganglion cells, cells whose axons comprise the optic nerve. Changes in the position and type of stimulus causes different patterns of responding in the retinal ganglion cells. (B) Retinal ganglion cells generally have circular receptive fields. Some cells are excited by illumination of the central part of the receptive field and show inhibition of firing when the area surrounding the center of the receptive field is illuminated. These cells are called *on-center cells*. (C) Other cells show a decrease in firing when light illuminates the central part of their receptive field and an increase in firing rate when the surrounding area is illuminated. These cells are called *off-center cells*. Neither kind of cell responds well to diffuse illumination of the entire receptive field. (Based on Kuffler & Nicholls, 1976).

Figure 3.14
The visual pathways. Neural messages from the medial half of each eye cross over at the optic chiasm to the other side of the nervous system. Those from the temporal half of the retina do not. The only synapses in the visual pathway between the retina and cortex are found in the lateral geniculate nucleus of the thalamus.

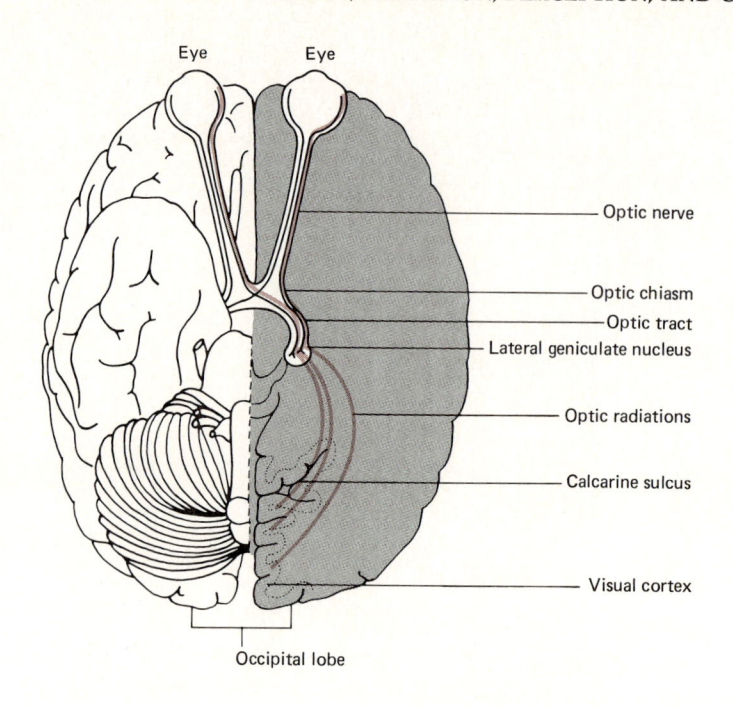

mitters and, as a result, stimulate the ganglion cells. The ganglion cells generate patterns of action potentials that travel via the optic nerve toward the brain. The pathway from the retina to the visual cortex is shown in Figure 3.14.

The first thing that is apparent from Figure 3.14 is that the retina of each eye is functionally divided in half and that the optic nerve from each half projects to different parts of the brain. The more medial half of the retina is referred to as the *nasal half* because it is close to the nose. The outer half of each retina is called the *temporal half* because it lies close to the temple. The axons from ganglion cells in the nasal half of each retina cross over to the opposite side of the nervous system at a structure called the *optic chiasm.* Axons extending from ganglion cells in the temporal half of each retina do not cross over but project to the side of the brain on which the eye is.

The next stage in the visual pathway is in a portion of the thalamus known as the *lateral geniculate nucleus.* It is called the lateral geniculate because it is on the side of the thalamus (lateral), and the layers of cells have a kneelike bend in them (*genu* in Latin means "knee"). Each axon coming from a ganglion cell in the retina synapses in the lateral geniculate nucleus. This is the only place where synapses occur in the pathway from the retina to the visual cortex. Relatively little processing of the neural message takes place in the lateral geniculate and it appears to serve primarily as a relay station for the messages from the eye on their way to the cortex.

From the retina to the optic chiasm the visual pathway is known as the *optic nerve.* From the optic chiasm to the lateral geniculate, it is termed the *optic tract,* and from the lateral geniculate to the cortex it is called the *optic radiations* because the fibers fan out to innervate a wide area of cortex.

The portion of the cortex that processes visual information is located at the back of the brain in the *occipital lobe.* (The visual areas of the cortex are shown in Figure 2.20.) Much of the visual area is on the medial half of each hemisphere and surrounding a sulcus known as the *calcarine sulcus* (pronounced "kal-ka-rine"). The axons forming the optic radiations terminate in the region just adjacent to the calcarine fissure. Visual processing takes place near this area as well as in other regions of the cortex. In the visual cortex the action potential code that was generated by the ganglion cells of the retina is interpreted and what we know as the sensation of vision is produced.

FEATURE DETECTORS IN THE CORTEX

Now we are faced with the task of understanding just how the cortex interprets the action potential messages that come to it via the visual pathway to produce a perceptual experience. As noted earlier, Hubel and Wiesel made major advances in our understanding of the cortical processes that underlie vision. They studied the responses of cells in the visual cortex of cats when various kinds of visual stimuli were presented. What they found was quite extraordinary. Some cells in the cortex respond best to very specific kinds of stimuli. For example, some cells were activated by lines or bars of light in a particular position and at a particular orientation in the visual field, while others required movement of the visual stimulus before they would respond. Indeed, some cells required movement of a stimulus of a distinct size and shape in a particular direction at a certain speed (Hubel & Wiesel, 1962, 1965, 1979).

Hubel and Wiesel categorized cortical cells according to the type of visual stimulus needed to produce the greatest rate of generation of action potentials. *Simple cortical cells* respond best to an edge or a bar of light at a particular location and set at a particular orientation in the visual field. A simple cell might react with a burst of action potentials when a certain region of the retina is stimulated with a thin bar of light oriented 60 degrees from the horizontal. Another simple cell might respond best to a vertical bar of light. This kind of response to a bar of light is shown schematically in Figure 3.15.

Hubel and Wiesel found that other cortical cells showed a similar preference for stimuli of a given orientation, but not in a particular region of the retina. They called these cells *complex cortical cells* because they show a higher degree of perceptual abstraction than that of simple cells. That is, they are, to some degree, indifferent to the specific location of stimulation on the retina, but the angle of orientation of the stimulus is still very important.

Still other cells are classed as *hypercomplex cortical cells*. These cells seem to show a still higher degree of abstraction in that they respond best to the conjunction of several different kinds of stimuli at the same time. One hypercomplex cell might react to a bar of light of only a particular length, whereas another might react best to two lines of light coming together at a particular angle (Hubel & Wiesel, 1979).

These findings led to the development of a number of new theories of vision. Some researchers suggested that the visual system might be organized in a hierarchical fashion; that is, more complex neural events (those with a higher degree of abstraction) might be built on the inputs from simpler ones. This would suggest that there might be specialized cells that respond to each kind of visual experience. Further studies suggested that such hierarchical models are probably not completely correct.

Fortunately, about the time that difficulties with the hierarchical model of visual perception were being discovered, another model of visual processing, the *spatial frequency filter model* was being developed. To understand it, we must become acquainted with an entirely different way of regarding spatial vision (Campbell & Robson, 1968).

FOCUS ON THE PSYCHOLOGIST

David H. Hubel

DAVID H. HUBEL is John Franklin Enders University Professor in the Department of Neurobiology at Harvard University. A Member of the National Academy of Science and of the Royal Society, London, he was awarded the Nobel Prize for Physiology or Medicine in 1981.

I was born in 1926 in Windsor, Ontario, and attended McGill University in Montreal where I did honors mathematics and physics, partly to find out why nothing worked in electronics, but mainly because it was more fun to do problems than to learn facts. I still much prefer to do science than to read about it. I graduated in 1947 and, almost on the toss of a coin, despite never having taken a course in biology (even in high school, where it was considered a subject only for those who could not do Latin or mathematics) I applied to Medical School at McGill. Rather to my horror I was accepted. At first I found it very difficult, given my total ignorance of biology and the need to memorize every muscular insertion in the body. I spent summers at the Montreal Neurological Institute doing electronics, and there I became fascinated by the nervous system.

To my surprise I also found I enjoyed clinical medicine: it took three years of hospital training after graduation, (a year of internship and two of residency in neurology) before that interest finally wore off. The years of hospital training were interrupted by a year of clinical neurophysiology under Herbert Jasper, who was unequalled for his breadth and clarity of thinking in brain science.

On setting foot into the United States in 1954 for the Neurology year at Johns Hopkins I was promptly drafted by the army as a doctor, but was lucky enough to be assigned to the Walter Reed Army Institute of Research, Neuropsychiatry Division, and there, at the age of 29, I finally began to do research.

Scientifically, I could hardly have chosen a better place than Walter Reed. As in Montreal, the focus was on the entire nervous system, not on a subdivision of biological subject matter based on methods. I worked under the supervision of M.G.F. Fuortes. We began by collaborating for six months on a spinal cord project, my only apprenticeship in experimental neurophysiology. I also learned and benefited much from a most able and helpful research assistant, Calvin Henson. My main project while at Walter Reed was a comparison of the spontaneous firing of single cortical cells in sleeping and waking cats. I began by recording from the visual cortex: it seemed most sensible to look at a primary sensory area, and the visual was easiest, there being less muscle between that part of the brain and the outside world. It was first necessary to devise a method for recording from freely moving cats and to develop a tungsten microelectrode tough enough to penetrate the dura. That took over a year, but in the end it was exciting to be able to record from a single cell in the cortex of a cat that was looking around and purring.

In 1958 I moved to the Wilmer Institute, Johns Hopkins Hospital, to the laboratory of Stephen Kuffler, and there I began collaboration with Torsten Wiesel. A year later Kuffler's entire laboratory (nine families) moved to Harvard Medical School in Boston, at first as part of the Department of Pharmacology under Otto Krayer, who was largely responsible for bringing Kuffler to Harvard. Five years later, in a move unprecedented for Harvard, we became the new Department of Neurobiology.

SENSORY PROCESSES

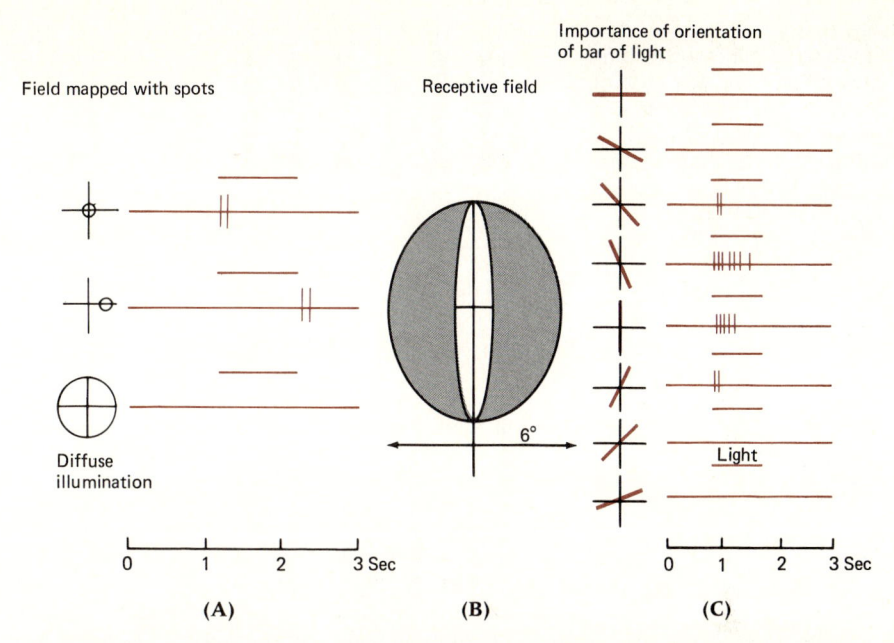

Figure 3.15 Responses of a simple cell in the visual regions of the cortex of a cat. At the left (A) the receptive field is mapped with spots of light. Illumination of the center of the receptive field, as shown by a horizontal line, produces a small burst of action potentials. Illumination of a region away from the center produces an "off response," that is, a burst of action potentials when the light is turned off. Diffuse illumination causes no response at all. The receptive field of this particular cortical cell (B) has an elongated shape. It has a narrow central "on" area surrounded by a larger "off" region. The best kind of stimulus for this cell (C) is a near-vertical bar of light projected at the center of the receptive field (fourth record from the top in part C in this figure). (Based on Kuffler & Nicholls, 1976)

The *spatial frequency* of a visual stimulus means the number of light-dark cycles that it shows per degree of visual space. In Figure 3.16 the dark bars have different numbers of light-dark cycles in the same visual space and hence have different spatial frequencies.

If the transition from light to dark varies more gradually visual patterns like the ones shown in Figure 3.17 are produced. These patterns can be expressed mathematically as sine waves of different sizes and frequencies. Indeed, very complex patterns can be expressed by using a series of a few sine waves and their harmonics. This kind of expression is called a *Fourier analysis*. It permits scientists to express extremely complex waveforms as the combination of several sine waves (DeValois & DeValois, 1980).

There is evidence that the visual system may perform a kind of Fourier analysis of visual stimuli. That is, the visual system may break down a scene

Figure 3.16
Two different spatial frequencies. The left figure has twice the spatial frequency as the right figure. This is because twice as many bars occur in the same space.

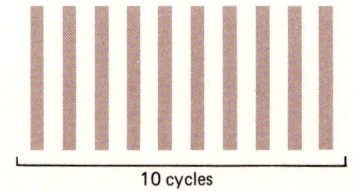

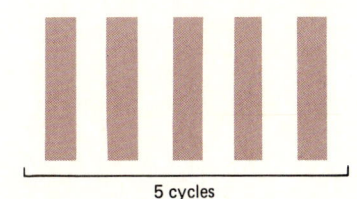

Figure 3.17
Two visual grids with different kinds of changes in light intensity. On the left is a high-contrast spatial grid in which there are large changes in light intensity, which occur abruptly, as shown in the graph below. On the right is a visual grid with lower contrast—that is, the transition occurs less abruptly and is less strongly modulated.

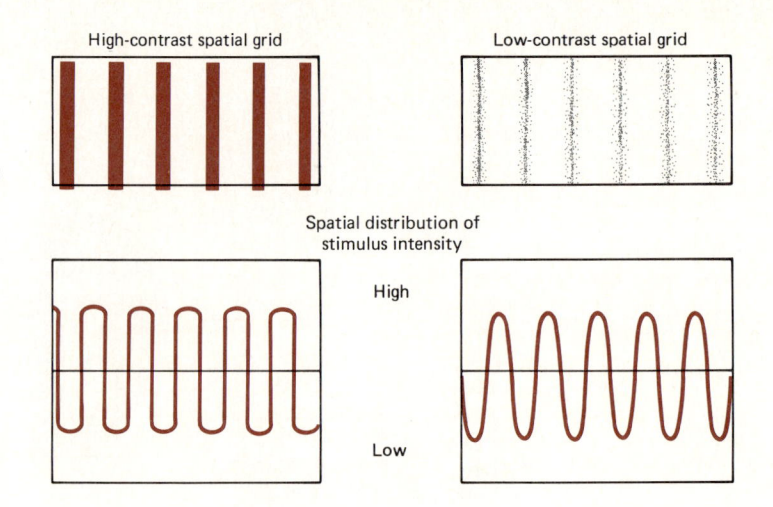

(e.g., a landscape) into a neural representation of a series of sine waves at different frequencies and angles of orientation. Many cortical cells are sensitive to patterns of specific spatial frequencies; some appear to respond best to higher spatial frequencies, whereas others respond best to lower spatial frequencies. Today, there is strong evidence that spatial frequency analysis by the visual system plays a very important role in visual processing (DeValois & DeValois, 1980; Ginsburg & Campbell, 1977).

COLOR VISION

As we noted earlier, the human eye responds to light of wavelengths that lie roughly between 400 and 750 nm. We give names to light of different wavelengths and call them colors. But colored light does not exist. What does exist is electromagnetic energy of different wavelengths. The visual system responds to light of different wavelengths by producing the sensation of color. If the human visual system were not constructed in the way it is, there would be no sensation of color or it would be different.

Now we must understand the neurobiological mechanisms underlying color vision. There are two types of mechanisms. First, cells of the retina react differently to light of various wavelengths; that is, red light (700 nm), for example, causes a different message to be sent out along the ganglion cell axons than that caused by green light (520 nm). Second, there are mechanisms in the brain that convert these messages from the retina into the psychological experience of color vision.

Since color vision depends on cone receptors, we shall start with them to understand color vision. Research shows that there are three types of cone receptors. Each type is differentially sensitive to light of different wavelengths. Each responds to a broad range of wavelengths within the visible-light spectrum, but each type of cone is most sensitive to light of a certain wavelength. The differential responsiveness of cone receptors of light of different wavelengths can be expressed by *spectral sensitivity curves* such as those shown in Figure 3.18. These patterns of response are produced by differences in the pigment found in each type of receptor. Pigments in cone cells preferentially absorb light from certain regions of the spectrum. One kind of pigment absorbs light of rather short wavelengths, and therefore receptors containing this pigment are more sensitive to light in the blue-violet range. The two

HIGHLIGHT 3.2
Responses to Spatial Frequencies

You can demonstrate the presence of neural systems that respond to particular spatial frequencies by performing the following experiment. The patterns below represent three different spatial frequencies. The upper pattern on the left is of a high spatial frequency; the one below it is of a lower spatial frequency. The two patterns on the right are identical and their spatial frequency lies between the two on the left. Hold your book so that the page is about 40 cm (16 in.) away and look at the small bar between the two gratings on the left for about 15 to 20 seconds. Keep your eyes fixed on the bar. As you do, those parts of your visual system attuned to high and low spatial frequencies will become fatigued. Those attuned to high spatial frequencies will become fatigued in the upper part of your visual field, while those attuned to lower spatial frequencies will become fatigued in the lower portion of your visual field.

Now, look at the dot between the gratings on the right side of the page. The upper and lower gratings seem different even though you know they are the same. The upper grating appears to be more widely spaced than the lower grating.

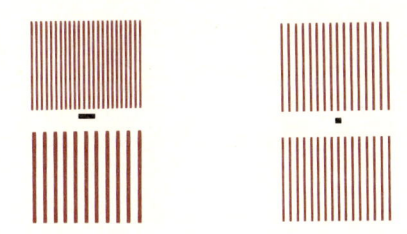

This illusion occurred because the fatigued neural systems are not functioning optimally, and thus the perceived spacing of the grids is shifted away from the fatigued neural systems. That such a perceptual change can occur following fatigue demonstrates the existence of neural systems that respond to gratings of specific spatial frequencies. This exercise was suggested by a demonstration in S. Coren, C. Porac, and L. M. Ward *Sensation and Perception* (2nd edition). Orlando, Fla.: Academic Press, 1984.

---

other types of cone receptors have pigments that absorb light of longer wavelengths, and these receptors are more sensitive to green and red light.

One rather surprising thing about these spectral sensitivity curves is that they overlap so much. Many wavelengths of light will activate at least two types of receptors, and some wavelengths, around 475 nm, will activate all three. How then do we manage to make precise color discriminations with such broad-band receptors? We discriminate between different hues because each receptor type responds in a characteristic fashion to the wavelength of the light that is stimulating it. If the light is of long wavelengths, say about 575 nm, both the "red" and "green" cone receptors will be activated, but

Figure 3.18
The curves shown here represent the absorption of light by the visual pigments in three different kinds of cone cells in the human eye. Each has its own particular characteristics of absorption of light, which in turn determines the responsiveness of that kind of cone receptor to light of different wavelengths.

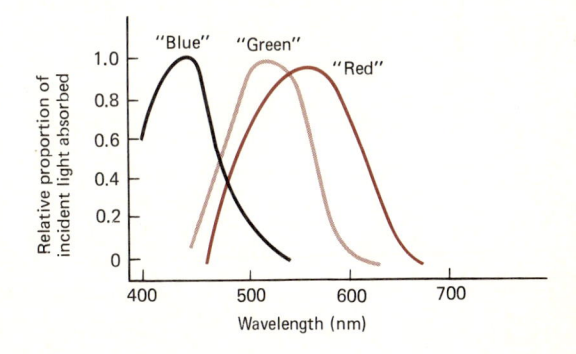

85

not equally. Similarly, light from the middle- and short-wavelength parts of the spectrum elicit different patterns of receptor activation and neural messages, which will be interpreted by the brain as yellow, blue, or violet, for example.

Each different wavelength of light energy causes a different and characteristic ratio of response among the outputs from the three types of receptors. To tell what wavelength of light is being projected onto the retina, the nervous system must simply note the intensity of the message that is being sent from each of the three receptor types. This explanation of our ability to see color is called the *trichromatic theory of color vision*.

But the trichromatic explanation does not fit all the data. Human beings behave as if there are four, not three, primary colors. When subjects in such experiments are presented with many color samples and asked to pick out those that appear to be pure colors, they tend to identify four unique colors. Besides blue, green, and red, predicted by the trichromatic theory of color vision, subjects include yellow. The perception of yellow as a pure color is not predicted by trichromatic theory because there are no receptors that respond best to light of wavelengths in the "yellow" region of the spectrum.

To explain the inclusion of yellow as a pure or primary color, psychophysiologists currently favor an explanation known as the *opponent-process theory* (Hering, 1878/1964; Hurvich, 1981; Hurvich & Jameson, 1974). This theory suggests that there are four primary color qualities (red, yellow, green, and blue) and two brightness qualities (black and white). These qualities are organized into opposing pairs: red with green, blue with yellow, and black with white. Members of these pairs are thought to act as antagonists, so that neural activation of one member of the pair automatically inhibits the other. This explains why some color combinations, such as greenish red and bluish yellow, are never reported by observers and, indeed, are difficult even to imagine.

The experience of color, then, is the result of how the red-green and yellow-blue opponent-process pairs are activated. Because these pairs oppose one another, their activities can be likened to weights on a balance beam. If activation of red decreases, the other side of the balance (green) must necessarily increase. The same holds true of yellow and blue. Now, if the red-green balance is weighted toward red and the yellow-blue balance is weighted toward yellow, the combination will be perceived as orange (red plus yellow).

It follows that if each of the opponent-process systems are equally weighted, they should cancel each other and there would be no sensation of color. Then the stimulus should be perceived as being without color. This does happen with white light. Further, in laboratory experiments when color wheels painted with color spectrally opposed are rotated so that the colors combine, the colors cancel each other and the net result is the sensation of gray (DeValois & DeValois, 1975).

Some people with defects in their color vision have provided important verification of these theories. Those with very limited ability to discriminate color stimuli are often called *color blind*, although very few people are actually totally incapable of seeing any colors at all. Problems in color vision take many forms. The most drastic (and fortunately rare) is seen in people with no functioning cone receptors. They have only scotopic vision, with no capacity to discriminate colors. As one would expect, they also have great difficulty with very bright light and are quite uncomfortable in daylight.

In most cases, defects in color vision are due to a missing visual pigment in one class of cone cell or to a defective opponent process. The most common defect of color vision is difficulty in distinguishing red from green, due to

SENSORY PROCESSES

problems in perceiving either red or green. A test for red-green color blindness is shown in Figure 3.19 (see color insert). People who have problems perceiving blue are very rare, as are those with yellow-blue color blindness. Note, however, that the forms of color blindness follow the pattern that would be predicted by opponent-process theories of color vision.

THE AUDITORY SYSTEM

Sounds surround us whether we live in noisy cities or quiet rural areas. Sounds are such a pervasive part of our existence that we take them very much for granted, yet they enrich our lives and add an important dimension to our experiences. We seek them out: buy records, make music, go to concerts, even whistle to ourselves when there seem to be no other pleasing sounds. In conversations with others, we carefully study sounds, noting subtle changes in tone and pitch. We then interpret these sounds and respond appropriately to them.

In this section we will learn how sounds are extracted from the environment and are translated into patterns of action potentials, the only language that the brain understands. First, however, we need to know something about the physical nature of sound itself.

THE NATURE OF SOUND

The stimulus for hearing is the movement of molecules. Unlike light, which travels easily through a vacuum, sound waves require a medium for transmission—molecules of some substance to move or vibrate. Air molecules are the usual medium for sound transmission, but sounds can also travel through liquids (whales communicate by sound) and solids (many apartment walls are excellent conductors of sound).

Sound, as usually perceived, is a series of fairly rapid changes in air pressure produced by a mechanical movement. When you play a piano, hit a piece of lumber with a hammer, or speak, mechanical movements cause the surrounding air to move. Sound is the result. Suppose that you beat on a drum. Striking the drumhead causes it to vibrate rapidly back and forth (see Figure 3.20). When the drumhead moves, adjacent air molecules move with

Figure 3.20
When a drum-head is struck, it moves rapidly back and forth. Each outward movement of the drum-head pushes against the air, compressing it, while each inward movement produces a small decrease in the pressure of the air adjacent to it, a rarefaction. These compressions and rarefactions move away from the drum at the speed of sound.

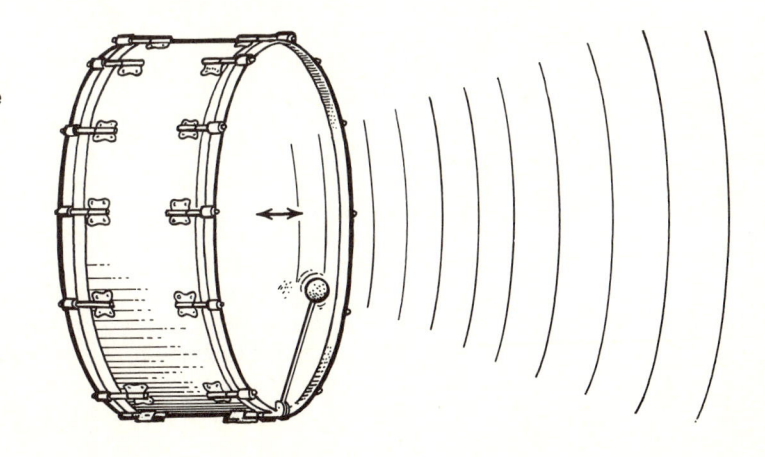

it. As the drumhead moves outward, it pushes some air ahead of it, increasing the air pressure slightly and producing what is called a *compression*. As the drumhead moves back, it leaves a small partial vacuum where it had been. This region of slightly lower air pressure is called a *rarefaction*. The rapid movement of the drumhead back and forth creates a series of brief increases and decreases in air pressure which move outward at around 340 meters per second (760 miles per hour), the speed of sound.

Now, suppose that you press a key on a piano. Movement of the key causes a small hammer to strike a piano string, causing it to vibrate. The vibrations of the string (with help from the sounding board of the piano) cause compressions and rarefactions to be produced as the string collides with air molecules and then rapidly moves away from them. If the key you pressed is near the right-hand side of the piano, the string is "tuned" to vibrate several thousand times a second. The distance between each compression and rarefaction will be quite short, and many of them will pass a given point in a second. This produces what is sensed as a high-frequency tone. On the left side of the piano are the large, long strings, which vibrate much more slowly and, as a result, compressions and rarefactions follow each other less often. These strings produce low-frequency tones.

The *frequency* of a sound is defined as the number of complete cycles of compression and rarefaction that occur in 1 second. Frequency is the physical equivalent of the psychological sensation of *pitch*. In general, as frequency increases, so does the perceived pitch of the sound.

Sound frequency is commonly measured in units called *hertz* (Hz). As with our sense of vision, the human auditory system can respond to only a limited range of frequencies. Human beings are said to hear sounds that lie in a frequency range between 15 and 20,000 Hz. However, this figure is for young adults; beyond our mid-twenties, our sensitivity to sounds at the extremes of this frequency range declines. This is especially true for sounds at the high end of the frequency range. One of the ironies of modern life is that when you can finally afford to purchase a high-fidelity music system that faithfully reproduces all the frequencies in the entire human hearing range, you can no longer hear them.

Animals such as rodents, bats, and some dogs and cats can hear sounds of much higher frequencies. Indeed, some species of bats can hear sounds over 100,000 Hz. In contrast, other animals, such as whales, may be able to hear sounds as low as 2 or 3 Hz, sounds far out of the human hearing range. The human auditory system is most sensitive to sounds in the middle of our frequency range, about 1,000 to 5,000 Hz, and our sensitivity declines for sounds that are beyond either end of that range (Newby, 1979). Speech sounds (usually about 200 to 800 Hz), generally the most important sounds in our daily lives, are somewhat below the range of maximum sensitivity, but we still have very good sensitivity for them. Our reduced sensitivity to sounds at the extreme ends of the range probably prevents us from being distracted by irrelevant sounds.

Sounds can also vary in their intensity or amplitude. The greater the *amplitude* (intensity) of a series of sound waves, the greater is the difference in pressure between the compression and rarefaction phases of each sound wave. The amplitude of a sound is the physical dimension on which the psychological dimension of *loudness* is based. Those sounds that are perceived as being very loud have a large difference in pressure between each compression and rarefaction. Conversely, sounds that are so soft that they can barely be heard result from very small pressure changes.

The auditory system can respond to an enormous range of sound intensities. To express this range conveniently, a special scale was developed years ago by Alexander Graham Bell (1847–1922). The units of this scale are called *decibels* (dB). *Deci* signifies tenths and *bel* commemorates Mr. Bell. It is a logarithmic scale, so the numbers increase much less rapidly than does the corresponding sound energy. As a general rule, the perceived loudness of a sound doubles each time the physical energy of the sound increases by 10 dB.

The upper limit for sound intensity is that level of loudness that produces pain. Interestingly, the noise blood makes when it passes through the arteries and veins of the interior portions of the ear determines the lowest intensities of sound that we can hear. At the most sensitive part of our hearing (1,000 to 5,000 Hz), sounds with an intensity range of about 140 to 150 dB can be perceived. A range of 150 dB means that from the weakest sounds to the loudest sounds (when the sound produces pain) there is about a 7.5 million-fold difference in sound energy (Coren, Porac, & Ward, 1984). No wonder the decibel scale is logarithmic. Intensity levels of various sounds are given in Table 3.1.

Most sounds that we encounter are composed of many different frequencies all occurring at the same time. Their cycles of compression and rarefaction are very complex, owing to the interactions of waves of different frequencies. Such interactions produce the characteristic *timbre* of a sound, enabling us to distinguish between a piano, a violin, and a clarinet, for example, all playing the same musical note. Although the fundamental pitch is the same for each, their waveforms differ substantially and therefore so does their subjective quality of timbre.

An important feature of the auditory system is its capacity to analyze complex sounds into their component parts. To demonstrate this capability, you will need a musical instrument that can play several notes at the same time such as a guitar or a piano. First play a fairly low note, then play one that is somewhat higher in pitch. You will have no trouble telling them apart. Now sound both notes at once. The chord that you hear is a complex sound, but you can still easily hear that it is composed of two distinct tones. Now try it with three notes. This is a little harder to discriminate, but if you listen carefully, each note still has its individual identity. As the number of notes is increased, a limit is reached and the auditory system can no longer analyze the sound. Further, if these sound waves are unrelated, the auditory system perceives them as *noise*.

Our ability to analyze a complex sound into its component parts is called *Ohm's acoustical law* after its discoverer, Georg S. Ohm (1787–1854), who is also remembered for his research on the principles of electrical conduction.

TABLE 3.1
Sound energy levels of various sounds

Source	Sound Level (dB)
Space shuttle launch (from 50 m)	180
Pain threshold (approximate)	140
Loud thunder; average rock band (5 m)	120
Heavy auto traffic; noisy subway	100
Noisy automobile	80
Normal conversation (at about 1 m)	60
Quiet library	40
Whisper	20
Still forest	10
Threshold of hearing	0

THE TRANSDUCTION OF SOUND

The first step in the perception of auditory information is the conversion of compressions and rarefactions of air into neural signals. This process of transduction is accomplished in a very efficient fashion through that immensely complex yet completely practical example of biological engineering known as the ear. The *outer ear* (see Figure 3.21) serves to channel sound waves into the auditory canal, where they cause the eardrum to move back and forth. Compressions push it in, while rarefactions cause it to move outward.

Attached to the eardrum is a chain of three tiny bones, each about the size of a grain of rice, known collectively as the *ossicles* (see Figure 3.21). These tiny bones form a bridge between the eardrum and the *cochlea*, a fluid-filled, spiral-shaped structure embedded in the bones of the skull which contains the actual receptors for hearing. The ossicles are joined together by fine flexible ligaments that permit them to move back and forth with the eardrum. This system allows the movements of the eardrum to be transmitted through the three ossicles, from the malleus to the incus to the stapes, and then through the oval window of the cochlea to the cochlear fluid, thereby setting up waves in this fluid.

Why such a complex arrangement? Why not just join the ear drum to the oval window? These connections through the ossicles are necessary because fluids, such as the fluid in the cochlea, have more inertia than air and are therefore much more difficult to set vibrating. To solve this problem there must be some way of amplifying the air movements. This is accomplished in two ways. First, there is a large difference in surface area between the eardrum and the oval window. In human beings the eardrum has about 22 times more surface area than does the oval window. Because of this, a slight force exerted by the air becomes concentrated, and therefore stronger, at the oval window. Second, the lever action of the ossicles adds a further degree of amplification in the conversion of air movements into fluid movements. The result is a very efficient transfer of vibrations in the air to the fluid of the cochlea.

In some ways the cochlea looks like a snail. In human beings it has 2½ turns from its base to the apex and is divided lengthwise into sections by several membranes. In Figure 3.23 we see a representation of the cochlea, showing it in cross section and how it would look if it were unrolled.

Figure 3.21
The auditory apparatus of the ear (shown in more detail in figure at right). Air movements cause the ear drum to vibrate, causing the ossicles to vibrate also. Vibrations of the stapes bone in the oval window causes movement of the fluids of the cochlea, which in turn cause traveling waves to be produced along the length of the basilar membrane.

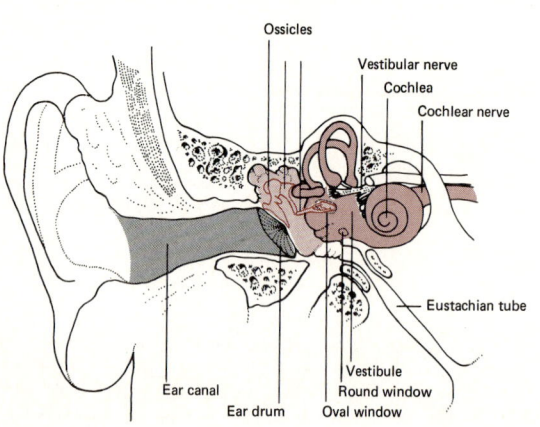

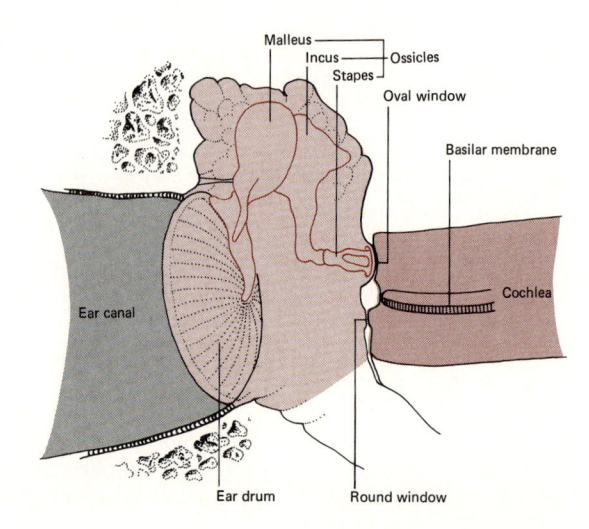

SENSORY PROCESSES 91

Figure 3.22 The eardrum. This photograph was taken using a scanning electron microscope. The eardrum moves rapidly back and forth in response to tiny changes in air pressure. (Dr. G. Bredberg)

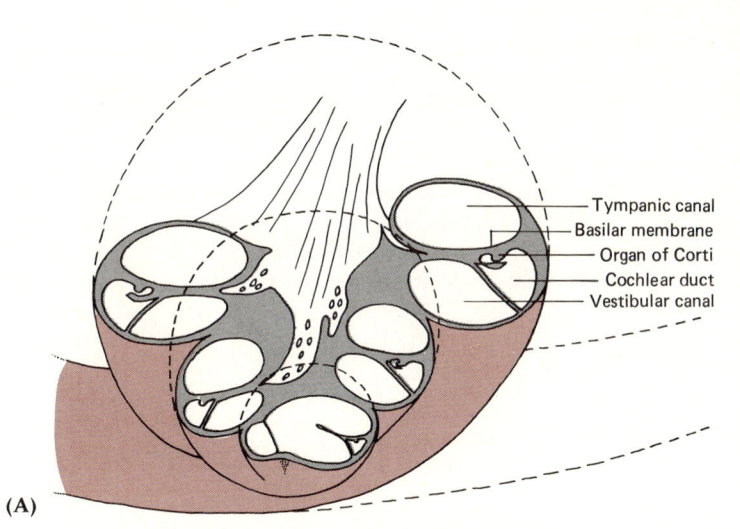

Figure 3.23 Section through the cochlea. The cochlea is a snail-like structure embedded in the bones of the skull. This drawing shows how the basilar membrane and the organ of Corti extend the length of the cochlea turning around two and one-half times. (B) The hair cells of the organ of Corti are also shown greatly enlarged. They extend from the organ of Corti, which rests on the basilar membrane to the tectorial membrane. When the basilar membrane moves, the organ of Corti moves with it, causing the hair cells to be bent. This causes the hair cells to depolarize the neurons attached to them and to generate action potentials that travel down the auditory nerve to the brain.

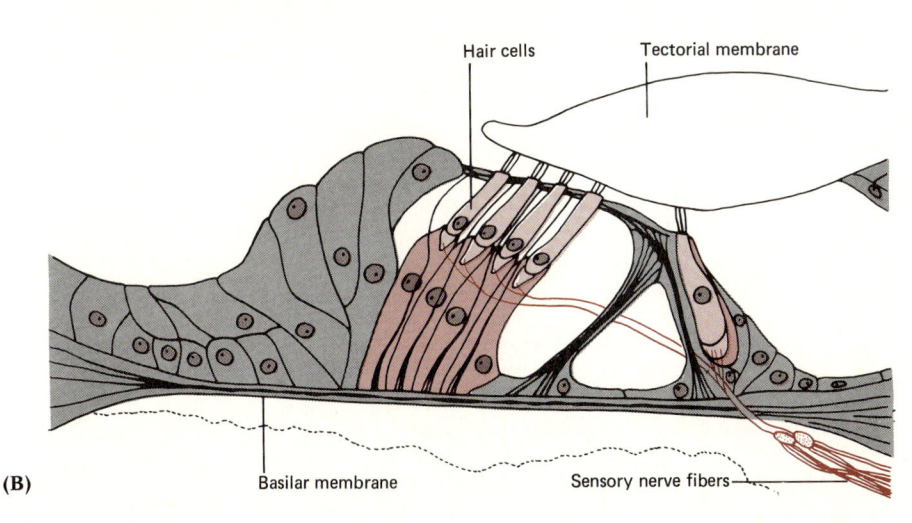

(A) Tympanic canal, Basilar membrane, Organ of Corti, Cochlear duct, Vestibular canal

(B) Hair cells, Tectorial membrane, Basilar membrane, Sensory nerve fibers

We owe much of our understanding of the principles of cochlear function to Georg von Békésy (1899–1972), who was awarded a Nobel prize for his work in 1961. He noted that movement of the stapes bone at the oval window sets up waves in the cochlear fluid that produce movements all along the length of the basilar membrane in the cochlea. These movements of the basilar membrane take the form of a *traveling wave*. The traveling wave, shown in Figure 3.24, moves along the basilar membrane, becoming smaller on each side of a main peak (von Békésy, 1957, 1960).

Resting on the basilar membrane are the actual auditory receptors themselves—the *hair cells*. These tiny hair cells extend across to another membrane, called the *tectorial membrane*. This whole system is arranged so that the hair cells are twisted or bent when the basilar membrane moves relative to the tectorial membrane. Bending a hair cell depolarizes a sensory neuron connected to that cell. This generates an action potential which travels to the brain through the auditory nerve.

Sound waves of different frequencies cause the basilar membrane to be bent by the traveling wave in different places along its length. Sounds of low frequency cause the basilar membrane to be most bent near its end, that is, at the apex of the cochlea. Sounds of medium frequency cause it to be most bent somewhere near the middle, while high-frequency sounds cause it to be most bent near the oval window, at the base of the basilar membrane (von Békésy, 1960).

This leads to an ideal mechanism for the transduction of sounds of different frequencies. Particular frequencies of sound cause maximum movements of specific regions of the basilar membrane. This movement activates only certain hair cell receptors, which are connected to specific fibers of the auditory nerve. The brain interprets the activity of a specific set of auditory nerve fibers as an indication that a sound of a particular pitch was heard. The *place theory of hearing,* a mechanism first proposed over 100 years ago

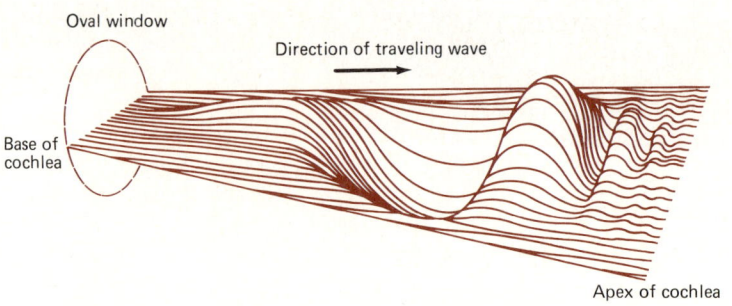

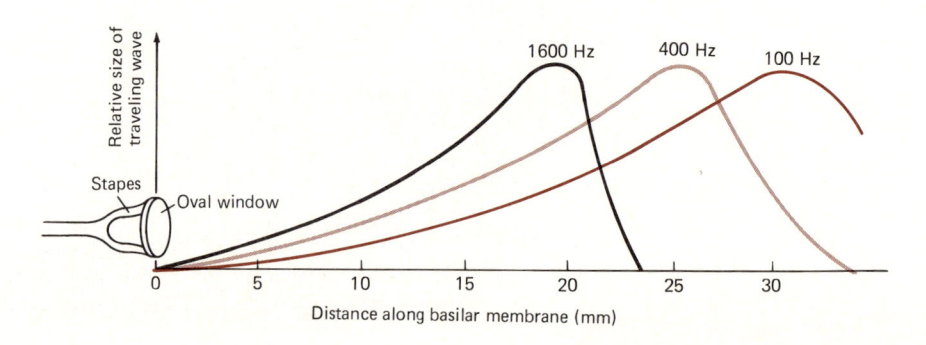

Figure 3.24
The upper part of this figure is a representation of a traveling wave on the basilar membrane of the cochlea. The lower part of the figure shows a graph of the relative sizes of traveling waves on the basilar membrane for tones of three different frequencies. As frequency increases, the waves become sharper, and their peaks move closer to the base of the cochlea.

SENSORY PROCESSES

Figure 3.25
A traveling wave on the basilar membrane. In this drawing the traveling wave is depicted next to a piano keyboard to illustrate the principle that the transduction of sounds of particular frequencies occurs at specific regions along the basilar membrane. High frequencies are coded near the oval window (the upper right-hand portion of the figure), while lower frequencies are coded by maximum bending of the basilar membrane near the apex (lower left). The inset shows how the basilar membrane bends at three successive times as a traveling wave moves down the length of the membrane.

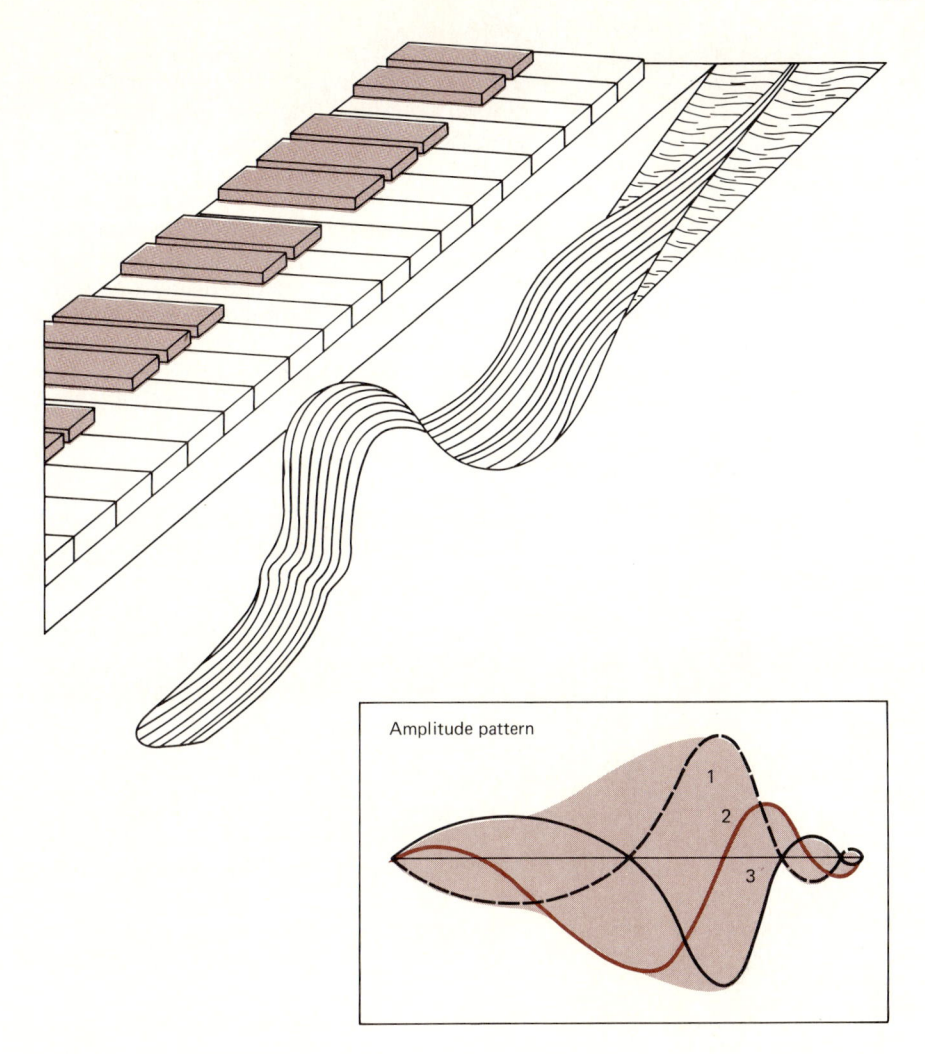

by Hermann L. Helmholtz (1821–1894), describes the way the cochlea transduces sounds of different frequencies into different neural messages.

There are some difficulties with place theory, though. One difficulty is that it cannot explain the perception of sounds below about 400 Hz. Below this frequency such large portions of the basilar membrane are bent by the movement of cochlear fluids that most of the hair cells appear to be about equally stimulated. Since we can easily discriminate between different sounds below 400 Hz, some mechanism other than place of maximal bending on the basilar membrane is needed to explain the perception of low-frequency sounds.

A second mechanism, called *frequency theory* (see Figure 3.26), suggests that the sense of pitch for lower frequencies is a function of the rate of firing of fibers in the auditory nerve (Miller & Taylor, 1948). For sounds of low frequencies, the auditory nerve fires at exactly the same frequency as the sound. The higher the pitch, the faster the nerve fires. However, here we have a problem. Neurons, even the fastest, can fire only 100 or 200 times a second, a relatively slow rate compared to many sound frequencies. So frequency theory incorporates a second hypothesized mechanism called *volley*

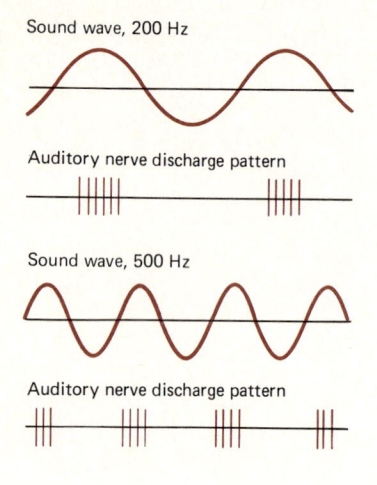

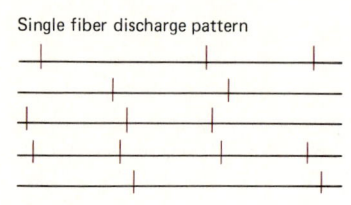

Figure 3.26
Illustration of coding in auditory nerve neurons. The pattern of discharges in the auditory nerve is locked to the frequency of the sound wave. The pattern of action potentials at 200 Hz has a longer interval between bursts than at 500 Hz. The bursts of action potentials is made up of the firing of a number of single axons in the auditory nerve (see lower portion of the figure).

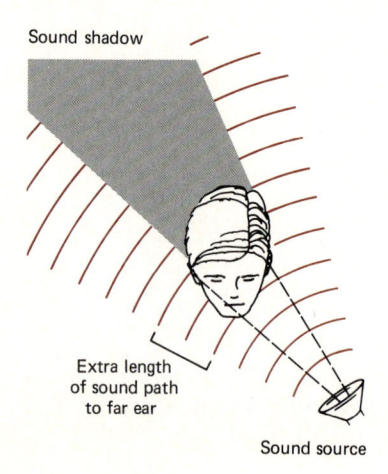

theory which proposes that a pattern of neural activity is produced in the auditory nerve, a pattern which mirrors the sound frequency. In volley theory several neurons firing one after another cooperate to generate a high rate of generation of action potentials in the auditory nerve. Research evidence suggests that a volley mechanism may work for sounds as high as 4,000 Hz (Wever, 1970).

Taken together, these findings indicate that for high-pitched sounds place coding is used to send information about the frequency of a sound to the brain, while a frequency of firing code is used for lower-pitched sounds. Both are probably used to some degree for sounds between 250 and 4,000 Hz.

Action potentials also code sound amplitude or loudness. This is accomplished both through the discharge rate of individual cells in the auditory nerve and by the number of cells firing at any given time. Both pitch cues and loudness cues are important in extracting meaning from an auditory stimulus.

THE PERCEPTION OF AUDITORY SPACE

Why did you buy a stereo set? Why not a unit with a single amplifier and one speaker rather than two channels? The reason is simple—stereo reproduction sounds more natural and realistic than monaural sound. This is because the auditory system, besides being able to distinguish pitch and loudness, can determine just where a sound originated in three-dimensional space. To do this, the auditory system uses information about differences in sound intensity heard at each ear and also, incredible as it may seem, differences in the time of arrival of a sound at each ear.

When a sound originates straight ahead, it reaches both ears at exactly the same time and at the same intensity. Because there is no difference between the inputs to the two ears, the brain perceives the sound as coming from straight ahead. However, if the head is turned only slightly, about 3 degrees or so, a difference in arrival time of the sound at each ear occurs. This difference can be as small as 30 microseconds (μs; a microsecond is a millionth of a second), yet it is all that is needed for the sound to be perceived as originating from one side.

A second clue to sound localization utilizes the sound shadow cast by the head. The ear farther from the sound source is partially shielded by the head and is thus in a sound shadow; hence there is an intensity difference in the sound received at each ear. This cue works best with sounds of fairly high frequency and is less important for low-frequency sounds since they tend to "bend" around the head and cause little or no sound shadow. A sound shadow is shown schematically in Figure 3.27.

Thus, arrival times of the sound or parts of a sound wave are important

Figure 3.27
Cues for the perception of the location of sounds in three-dimensional space. Each ear receives somewhat different information when the source of a sound is to one side of the observer's midline. With sounds of greater frequency than 1,000 Hz, the head blocks some of the sound, producing a sound shadow and resulting in differences in sound intensity reaching the two ears. Furthermore, sounds take longer to reach the more distant ear, resulting in differences in time of arrival of the sound at each ear. Both intensity differences and differences in time of arrival are important cues in the localization of sounds in space.

for locating the origin of low-frequency sounds. For high-frequency sounds, however, intensity differences are more important in locating the source of these kinds of sounds (see Lindsay & Norman, 1977).

THE BODILY SENSES

THE SENSE OF TOUCH

Although classically one of the "five senses," the sense of touch actually encompasses several different sensory mechanisms, all with receptors located in the skin. These receptors mediate the *skin senses,* informing the brain about events occurring next to the body. We also use the skin senses to explore new objects. How much more satisfying to pick up and hold an object in a store than just to look at it. Further, much of the sex act involves the skin senses. Indeed, during sex, many people strive to keep auditory and visual stimulation to a minimum, so that there is little competition with tactile sensations for their attention.

At least four different types of sensations can arise from the skin: pressure, warmth, cold, and pain. Although they are distinct sensations, separate receptor systems for them have not been identified, and many researchers are investigating how different skin senses are transduced.

The sense of touch varies considerably in sensitivity from one part of the body to another. The most sensitive areas are those such as the feet, hands, lips, and tongue, areas of the body used to learn about objects in our environment. Psychologists can measure the sensitivity of different regions of the body to tactile stimulation by determining the *two-point threshold*. If two fairly sharp points, such as the points of a drawing compass, are gently pressed close enough together on the skin, they will be perceived as one point. If they are separated somewhat more, they will then be perceived as two points. The two-point threshold test measures how far apart two points must be before they are felt as two distinct touches. A summary of two-point threshold data is shown in Figure 3.28. These values (the distance between the two points) reflect both the concentration of receptors on the skin surface and the amount of somatosensory cortex in the brain devoted to the representation of each bodily region (see Chapter 2). Recall that a relatively large amount of cortex is devoted to the sensory representation of the mouth, tongue, hands, and feet, while a much smaller percentage of cortex receives messages from the legs and torso.

THE POSITION SENSES

One group of senses helps us to know about our own movements and where our arms and legs are at any given moment. Movements of the limbs are sensed through a group of processes called *kinesthesis*. These kinesthetic senses get their information from receptors in the joints, tendons, and muscles. Receptors in the joints inform the brain about the relative position of various body parts, while the receptors in the tendons and muscles send information about the amount of tension on the system and the length of the muscles. Together these receptor systems provide the brain with detailed and precise information about the relative location of each part of the body. To dem-

Figure 3.28
Two-point discrimination thresholds at different places on the surface of the body. These measures are obtained using a device something like a drawing compass with two points. The points are adjusted closer or farther apart until the subject can just distinguish the sensation of a single point from the sensation of stimulating the skin with two points. As seen in this drawing, the fingers, nose, and upper lip are quite sensitive, responding with a two-point discrimination when the points are separated by less than 10 mm. On the other hand, the upper arm, thigh, and calf all are relatively insensitive, requiring the stimuli to be separated by at least 40 mm before a discrimination can be reliably made. (Based on S. Weinstein, in D. R. Kenshalo, ed., *The Skin Senses,* Springfield, IL: Charles C Thomas, 1968)

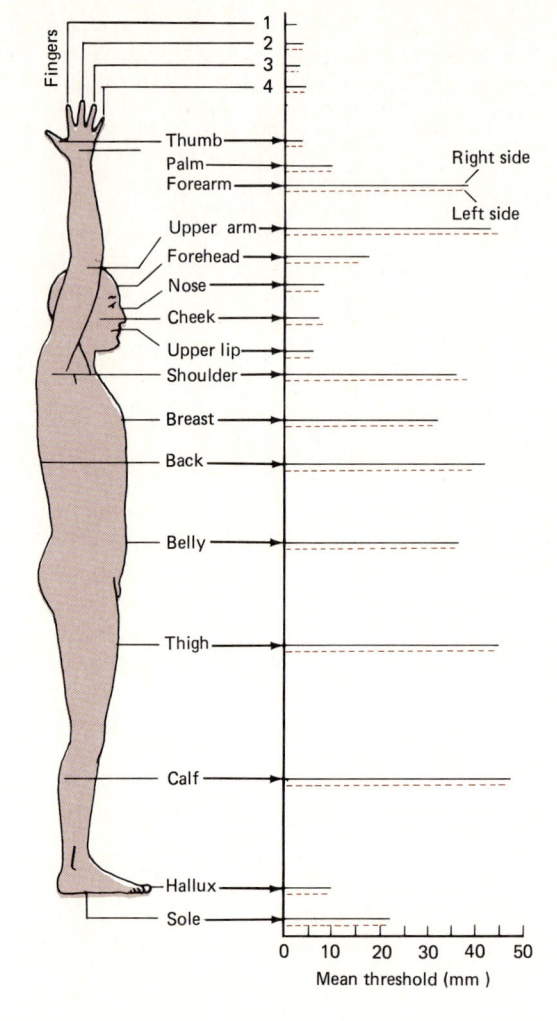

onstrate to yourself how accurate this system is and how well your nervous system is keeping track of the position of each limb, close your eyes and touch your right kneecap; then still without opening your eyes, touch the heel of your left foot. Easy, wasn't it? But that task would be next to impossible without a properly functioning kinesthetic system.

The kinesthetic system signals position relative to other parts of the body, but the *vestibular system* (see Figure 3.29) signals the body's position in space. Receptors of the vestibular system respond to the force of gravity and to movements of the head. The receptors for the vestibular system are associated with the cochlea and are located in the bones of the skull just behind each ear. There are two main components to the vestibular system, and each does a specific job.

The *vestibular sacs* provide information about the precise orientation of the head when it is not moving. It is a very simple system. At the bottom of each fluid-filled vestibular sac are some small crystals that stimulate hair cells lining the walls of the sac. As the head assumes different positions, the crystals roll to the lowest part of the sac and bend different hair cells, which respond by generating action potentials. These action potentials are decoded by the brain as indicating head position.

SENSORY PROCESSES

Figure 3.29
The various components of the vestibular system serve different functions. The three fluid-filled semi-circular canals are oriented in three different planes at right angles to each other. Near the base of each canal is an enlargement called an *ampulla*. When the head is rotated in one of these planes (nodding "Yes," from side to side, or around as in indicating "no"), the fluid moves, stimulating hair cells in the ampulla and generating messages that inform the brain of head movements. The utricle and saccule help to sense acceleration of the head either forward or backward.

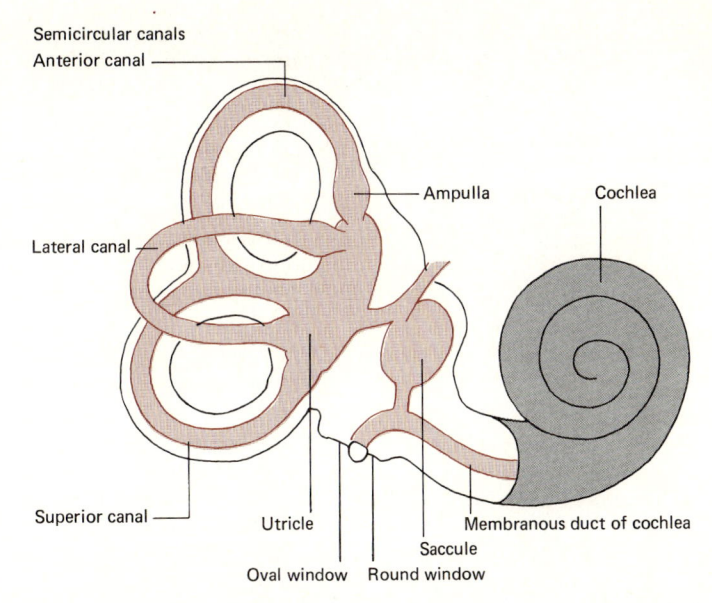

The second receptor system, called the *semicircular canals*, responds to movement of the head. There are three canal systems set perpendicular to one another, so that whatever direction the head moves in, one or more of them can respond. Each semicircular canal is filled with fluid which moves as the head moves. The movement of fluid results in the bending of hair cells and the generation of neural action potentials. If you rotate your head to one side or the other, receptors are activated in the semicircular canals which are set in the horizontal plane. If you nod your head up and down, receptors set in one vertical plane are stimulated, and if you rock your head from side to side, the third set of receptors is activated. Thus any complex head movement can be accurately tracked by the brain.

The vestibular system is particularly important in the control of vision. As you move through daily life, your head is in constant motion. The vestibular system sends messages that help produce steady vision despite all your head movements. As the head moves one way, the vestibular system sends messages to the muscles of the eyes, causing them to move the eyes in the opposite direction. This system enables us to view the world from a steady frame of reference.

THE SENSES OF TASTE AND SMELL

The stimuli for the senses of taste and smell are molecules of certain chemicals that react with specific receptors. Both of these senses require an agent or medium to carry the stimulating molecules to the receptors. For taste, these molecules are generally dissolved in water and carried to the receptors in the foods that we eat and drink. Molecules that stimulate the sense of smell must be suspended in the air as gases.

The senses of smell and taste typically work together, and distinctive tastes usually have an important odor component. For example, most of us would have no difficulty telling the difference between the tastes of strawberries and peaches. However, most of that difference is actually based on the sense of

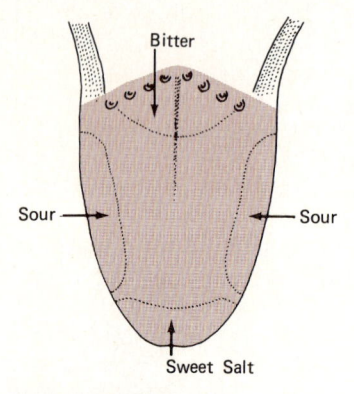

Figure 3.30
Maximum sensitivity to the four basic tastes—sweet, sour, salty, and bitter—is distributed unevenly over the surface of the tongue. Salty and sweet are detected most easily at the tip of the tongue, sour is most readily detected by receptors at the sides, and bitter is best detected at the back of the tongue.

TABLE 3.2
The seven primary odors with familiar examples

Primary Odor[a]	Familiar Example
Camphoraceous	Moth repellent
Musky	Angelica root oil
Floral	Roses
Pepperminty	Mint candy
Ethereal	Dry-cleaning fluid
Pungent	Vinegar
Putrid	Rotten eggs

[a] Each of the primary odors is detected by a different receptor in the nose. Most odors are composed of several of these primaries combined in various proportions.
Source: Amoore, Johnston and Rubin (1964).

smell, not taste. Remember how bland and flat foods tasted the last time your nose was stopped up because of a cold?

There appear to be just four *basic tastes: sweet, sour, salty,* and *bitter.* It is their chemical properties that make substances taste as they do. For example, acidic compounds often taste sour, whereas those that have a metal ion, such as sodium or potassium, may taste salty. However, the exact relationship between chemical structure and taste is complex and not fully understood. It is not yet clear why sugar, saccharin, and aspartame, for example, each with a very different chemical structure, should all taste sweet.

The receptors for the sense of taste are called *taste buds* and are located in small infoldings on the tongue. The taste buds for different tastes are located in separate regions of the tongue (Figure 3.30). Sweet and salty tastes are detected best by taste buds located on the tip of the tongue, while sour tastes are detected by receptors located at the sides of the tongue. The receptors that respond best to substances that taste bitter are located near the back of the tongue.

If a region of the tongue is stimulated continuously with a specific taste for around 10 seconds or more, sensitivity to that taste will quickly decline. This process is called *adaptation,* and as we have already seen, it can be observed in all sensory systems. Following continuous exposure to salty tastes, the threshold to this taste declines until it can hardly be detected. This explains why some people salt and resalt their food. As they eat the salty food, they adapt to the salty taste, and therefore they need a higher concentration of salt to achieve the same taste. To avoid this problem, you should eat something that is not salty between bites of salty food. This is especially important for those who must restrict their intake of salts to control high blood pressure. The same principles of adaptation hold for other tastes as well.

Adaptation to one flavor can affect how other tastes are perceived. This is called *cross adaptation.* For example, exposure to one form of sour food will make the system less sensitive to other sour tastes. Exposure to one taste may also make another flavor seem more intense. This is called *taste potentiation.* For example, exposure to a bitter taste will make the taste system more sensitive to sweet. You can demonstrate this to yourself by swishing a mouthful of strong, bitter, caffeinated coffee around in your mouth for about 30 seconds. Spit it out and then take a sip of water. The normally tasteless water will taste quite sweet after exposure to the bitter coffee.

The mechanisms that mediate the sensation and perception of odors are somewhat more complex than those for the sense of taste. This is because odors, unlike tastes, do not fit into a few simple classes. Odors seem to be difficult to describe precisely. However, researchers have tried to identify primary odors and have developed several useful classifications, one of which is shown in Table 3.2.

Research into the physiological basis of the sense of smell suggests that the structural shape of the molecules stimulating the receptors largely determines which specific odor is perceived. This idea is called the *stereochemical theory of odor.* Substances that smell camphoraceous have large spherical molecules, while those that smell musky tend to have molecules that are flat and more disklike.

The transduction of smell occurs in the olfactory epithelium. The receptor cells located there have an unbranched dendrite on one end of the cell body that reaches out to the surface of the olfactory epithelium. There it expands into a terminal with a number of tiny hairlike processes called *cilia.* The cilia have special receptor sites where the different-shaped odor molecules that are carried to these receptors can become attached and stimulate the cell. Many aspects of this process are not understood, and there are still many puzzling questions. For example, a single camphor molecule is much larger than one of the cilia on an olfactory receptor cell. How can such molecules become attached to receptor sites so much smaller than they are?

The sense of smell is certainly one of our less important senses, but many other animals depend on it for survival and social communication. To a dog, smells are an important way of finding food and are critical for defining territory and for social interactions. If a dog had written this chapter, the relative amounts of space devoted to the senses of smell and vision might well have been reversed.

Odors that are secreted by a member of one species and which serve as messengers or produce particular reactions in other members of that species are called *pheromones*. Some pheromones influence reproductive behavior. For example, the female of many species secretes a chemical odor cue, often in the urine, that signals that she is sexually receptive. Other pheromones serve to signal alarm or that danger is present. Further, infant rats respond to odors emitted from the mother rat and use them to locate the nest.

Human beings may also respond to pheromones. Mature women are more sensitive to certain musklike odors than are men and sexually immature girls. Further, this sensitivity changes with the menstrual cycle and correlates well with periods of fertility. If this is the case, it follows that there might be a male pheromone in human beings. To date, no such odor has been identified, but such a phermone may be part of our evolutionary heritage that is masked by frequent bathing and the use of deodorants.

SUMMARY

1. All sensory information is obtained through receptor systems which respond to events and energy in the surrounding environment. A stimulus which has the capacity to activate a particular receptor and which is of a type to which the receptor normally responds is termed an adequate stimulus.

2. The nature of a perceived sensation is the result of what particular neural systems are being activated rather than the actual nature of the stimulus itself. We are not directly aware of a stimulus but of the activity of the nerves carrying sensory messages from the receptors.

3. Visible light is a small portion of the electromagnetic spectrum, which comprises energy forms such as magnetism, radio waves, light, x-rays, and cosmic rays. The wavelengths of visible light range about 700 nm (red) to approximately 400 nm (violet).

4. The cornea and lens of the eye focus light reflected from objects being viewed onto the retina, which contains receptors that convert the light energy into neural events, a process known as transduction. The rod receptors are active only when illumination is quite low (scotopic vision). Cone receptors are used when there is more light (photopic vision) and they mediate color vision. Cone receptors are concentrated in the fovea, which is the region of the retina which produces the sharpest sensation of vision.

5. Other cells in the retina use lateral inhibition to enhance contrast in the neural message sent from the eyes to the brain. Many cells in the visual system have receptive fields that have excitatory and inhibitory regions. Ganglion cells of the retina, whose axons comprise the optic nerve, and cells of the lateral geniculate nucleus, whose axons project to visual cortex, have circular receptive fields.

6. The retina is functionally divided in half with messages from the nasal half of each retina crossing over to the opposite side of the nervous system at the optic chiasm, while neural messages from the temporal half do not cross. The axons then extend as the optic tract to the lateral geniculate nucleus of the thalamus, where they synapse. The geniculate neurons project their axons via the optic radiations to visual cortex in the occipital lobe at the back of the brain.

7. Some cells of the visual cortex respond best when very specific kinds of visual stimuli are projected onto the retina. Simple cells in the visual cortex respond best to an edge or bar of light of a specific orientation projected onto a particular region of the retina. Complex cells show a higher degree of perceptual abstraction and respond best to a stimulus of particular orientation, but the criterion of specific location on the retina is relaxed. Hypercomplex cells show still more abstraction and respond best to a conjunction of several different kinds of stimuli.

8. The visual system also acts as a spatial frequency analyzer, expressing the visual stimulus as the neural representation of a series of sine waves and their harmonics.

9. Each wavelength of light energy causes a different and characteristic ratio of response among the outputs from the three types of cone receptors. There are four primary color qualities (red, yellow, green, and blue) and two brightness qualities (black and white) organized into opposing pairs. When one pair is activated, the other is inhibited and the experience of color is the result of how the red-green and yellow-blue opponent-process pairs are activated.

10. Sounds result from the movement of air molecules in alternating patterns of compression and rarefaction. Human beings are generally thought to hear sounds in the range 15 to 20,000 Hz. The difference in pressure between the compressions and rarefactions determines the amplitude of a sound.

11. Sound waves cause the movement of the eardrum, which moves a chain of tiny bones known as the ossicles. This movement sets up movement of the fluids in the cochlea, which sets up traveling waves along the length of the basilar membrane, which is located inside the cochlea. Sounds of different frequencies cause the basilar membrane to be maximally displaced at different places along its length. Hair cell receptors on the basilar membrane are bent by the traveling waves and generate action potentials which convey information about the location of maximal displacement of the basilar membrane. Low-frequency sounds are probably coded through the generation of patterns of action potentials that closely mirror the frequency of the sound.

12. The location of sounds in three-dimensional space is accomplished by the perception of differences in the amplitude of the sound as it reaches each ear and differences in time of arrival of the sound at each ear.

13. At least four different types of sensations can arise from receptors in the skin: pressure, warmth, cold, and pain. Different regions of the body have different capacities to discriminate between tactile stimuli depending on the density of receptors. Kinesthetic senses help us to know about the consequences of our movements and where our limbs are at any moment. These senses are mediated by receptors in the joints, muscles, and tendons. The vestibular system monitors the body's position in space. Static head position is monitored by the vestibular sacs, while movement of the head is monitored by the semicircular canals.

14. There are four basic tastes: sweet, sour, salty, and bitter. Although taste receptors on the tongue can respond to several different tastes, most seem to respond preferentially to a single taste. Much of the sense of taste is actually mediated by the olfactory system.

15. The receptors for the sense of smell are located in the olfactory epithelium, and they respond to the chemical properties and shapes of molecules suspended in the air.

KEY TERMS

Tabula rasa
Adequate stimulus
Doctrine of specific nerve energies
Electromagnetic spectrum
Photons
Cornea
Lens
Accommodation
Iris
Vitreous humor
Retina
Transduction
Rod receptor cells
Cone receptor cells
Ganglion cells
Fovea
Scotopic vision
Photopic vision
Pigment
Rhodopsin
Iodopsin
Optic nerve
Blind spot
Mach bands
Lateral inhibition
Receptive field
Nasal half of the retina
Temporal half of the retina
Optic chiasm
Lateral geniculate nucleus
Optic tract
Optic radiations
Occipital lobe
Calcarine sulcus
Simple cortical cells
Complex cortical cells
Hypercomplex cortical cells
Spatial frequency filter model
Spatial frequency
Fourier analysis
Spectral sensitivity curves
Trichromatic theory of color vision
Opponent-process theory of color vision
Color blind
Compression
Rarefaction
Frequency
Pitch
Hertz
Amplitude
Loudness
Decibel
Timbre
Ohm's acoustical law
Outer ear
Ossicles
Cochlea
Malleus
Incus
Stapes
Traveling wave
Hair cells
Tectorial membrane
Place theory of hearing
Frequency theory of hearing
Volley theory of hearing
Skin senses
Two-point threshold
Vestibular system
Vestibular sacs
Semicircular canals
Basic tastes: sweet, sour, salty, bitter
Taste buds
Adaptation of sensory systems
Cross adaptation
Taste potentiation
Stereochemical theory of odor
Pheromone

SUGGESTED READINGS

COREN, S., PORAC, C., & WARD, L. M. *Sensation and perception* (2nd ed.). Orlando, Fla.: Academic Press, 1984. An excellent comprehensive textbook that deals with most aspects of sensory processes. There are many demonstrations outlined in this book that the reader can perform to illustrate a wide variety of principles of sensation and perception.

GREGORY, R. L. *Eye and brain* (2nd ed.). New York: McGraw-Hill, 1973. This is a brilliantly conceived and executed introductory discussion of the psychology of vision. Well written and fairly easy to understand, this book is almost required reading for anyone interested in visual processes.

LINDSAY, P. H., & NORMAN, D. A. *Human information processing* (2nd ed.). New York: Academic Press, 1977. An excellent general textbook covering the whole field of sensory processes, perception, and information processing.

LUDEL, J. *Introduction to sensory processes.* San Francisco: W. H. Freeman, 1978. A well-produced and illustrated survey of sensory processes. It is nicely organized and written in a style that assumes the reader has little or no background in the field.

SCHMIDT, R. F. *Fundamentals of sensory physiology.* New York: Springer-Verlag, 1978. An advanced look at the mechanisms underlying sensory systems. The information contained in this book should answer any questions an introductory psychology student might have about how sensory systems operate.

4

Perception

PERCEPTION: WHAT IS IT?
  Sensation and Perception
  Perceptual Constancies
SENSORY THRESHOLDS
  Absolute Thresholds
  Signal-Detection Theory
  Difference Thresholds
  Adaptation of Sensory Systems
PRINCIPLES OF VISUAL
  PERCEPTUAL
  ORGANIZATION
  Extracting a Meaningful Visual
    Image
  Some Gestalt Principles of
    Perceptual Organization
THE PERCEPTION OF
  MOVEMENT
  Cues for the Perception of
    Movement
  Stroboscopic Movement

  Movement Perception and the
    Frame of Reference
THE PERCEPTION OF VISUAL
  THREE-DIMENSIONAL
  SPACE
  Binocular Vision
  Monocular Depth Cues
VISUAL ILLUSIONS
THE PERCEPTION OF COLOR
THE DEVELOPMENT AND
  MODIFICATION OF
  PERCEPTION
EXTRASENSORY PERCEPTION
  Parapsychology
  Studies of Telepathy and
    Clairvoyance
  Difficulties with ESP Research
SUMMARY
SUGGESTED READINGS

PERCEPTION: WHAT IS IT?

SENSATION AND PERCEPTION

In Chapter 3 we discussed the ways in which an incoming sensory message is converted to neural messages in several different sensory systems. These neural messages, resulting from the activation of receptors, are then conveyed to the brain, where they are interpreted and given meaning. It was easy to see from Chapter 3 that the ear is not merely a microphone responding passively to sounds; and neither is the eye merely a recorder of visual stimuli in the same way that a camera is. Even at the level of receptors, sensory systems actively organize and process sensory information, extracting meaningful messages and sending them on to the brain. In this chapter we explore other aspects of sensory information processing. We will try to understand how we experience objects and events: that is, how we apprehend or "know" through our senses. How, for example, do we "see" a tree against a blue sky and not simply a mass of green against a larger area of blue.

Why is a tree seen as an object with a kind of reality and independent existence when all that stimulates the visual system is a small, inverted image projected onto the retina of the eye? Whether the tree is viewed from afar, presenting a very tiny image to be projected onto the retina, or from so close up that only a small portion of the tree's bark can be contained on the retina at any one time, the perceptual response is the same, "I see a tree." Therefore, one central question of perception is this: How do we perceive a constant object despite many variations in the nature of the stimulus?

At one time, psychologists believed that what we call "sensation" arises from innate physiological mechanisms, while "perception" is determined by our previous experiences and the ways that we have learned to interpret and catalog certain kinds of sensory events. However, as we learn more about sensory systems and perceptual phenomena, it is becoming increasingly apparent that there is no clear-cut distinction between those processes classified as sensation and those thought of as perception. Indeed, as we have already seen, a surprisingly large amount of information processing takes place at the level of receptor systems such as those of the ear or eye.

A distinction between sensation and perception can be useful in some cases. When psychologists speak of *sensation,* they are referring to the neurobiological operation of sensory systems. A physiological psychologist investigating principles of sensation is interested in learning how events in the environment activate neural systems and how those systems operate at the cellular level. For example, a physiological psychologist might be performing research on how certain types of molecules carried in the air interact with cells located in the head behind the nose to generate what we know as the sense of smell.

In contrast, a psychologist interested in *perception* wants to know how sensory stimuli interact with cognitive processes. He or she might concentrate on how individuals detect, interpret, and make use of sensory information. Psychologists who study perception know that it does not precisely mirror external reality. There are a number of reasons for this.

First, as we have already noted, there are many aspects of our surroundings to which we simply cannot respond: Sounds that are too high or too low, electromagnetic energy of wavelengths our receptors cannot detect, odors for which we have no receptors, and so on.

Second, we sometimes perceive things that are not actually present. For example, when we go to the movies, a series of still pictures presented one after another causes us to perceive motion. Drugs, illness, and some behavior disorders can cause people to perceive stimuli and events that are not there at all.

Third, our expectations, past experiences, and desires can all influence how a given sensory stimulus is interpreted. A classic example of how expectation can influence perception is shown in Figure 4.1A. You probably read those two words as "THE CAT" yet the middle letter in each word is the same. You didn't read "TAE CHT" or something like that, because there are no such words in your vocabulary. Your expectancy influenced your perception.

Similarly, Figure 4.1B is confusing, too. It does not fit what we have learned about form and perspective. We try to organize such an image according to previous experiences with two-dimensional drawings that repre-

TAE CAT
(A)

Figure 4.1
(A) Expectancies influence your perceptions. The figure in the middle of each word is the same, but in one case it is seen as an "H" and in the other as an "A." (B) M. C. Escher's *Other World* (January 1947). (Collection, The Museum of Modern Art, New York)

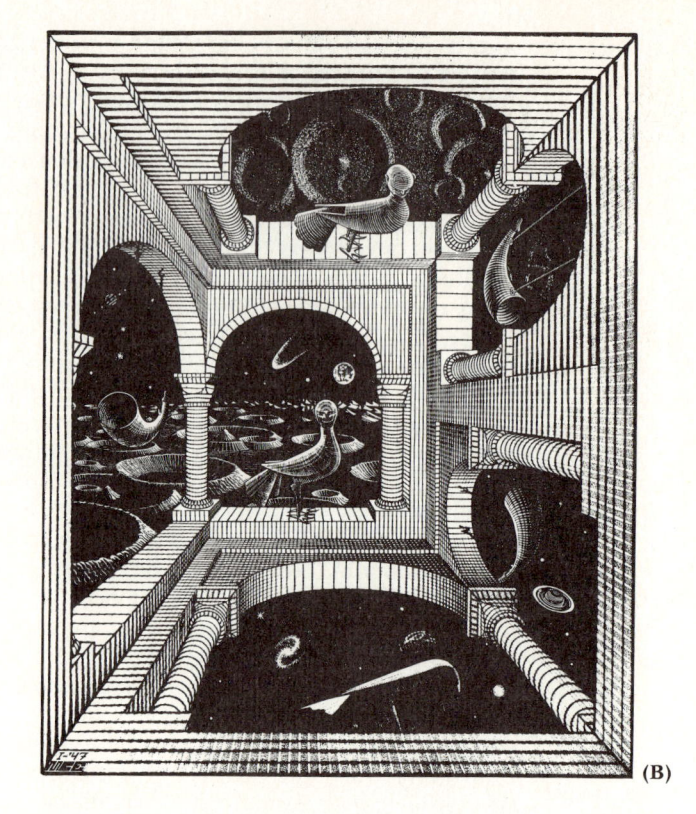

(B)

sent three-dimensional figures, but we fail. Perception is much more than the simple registration of sensory information; it is complex, high-level cognitive activity.

PERCEPTUAL CONSTANCIES

Take a coin, say a dime, in your hand. Hold it up. Look at the face of the coin. The image projected on your retina is fairly circular. What shape is the dime? Circular, of course, Now slowly turn the coin until you are looking at the edge. The image on your retina underwent a transition from being circular, to oval, to a straight line. Yet, in spite of these changes, you did not change your opinion about the shape of dimes. You still perceived the dime as being circular even though the image projected on your retina changed. Your perceptual systems compensated for the changes in orientation of the coin and provided a perception which was constant.

This is because we have learned that we live in a reasonably stable world and would regard it as highly unlikely that the dime was actually changing shape. Therefore, it is not surprising that perceptual mechanisms make use of constancies in the interpretation of stimuli. Although constancies are a general feature of almost all perceptual systems, psychologists generally refer to four basic kinds of perceptual constancies: shape, size, location, and color.

With the dime illustration we introduced the idea *shape constancy*, a perceptual process which interprets changing patterns of retinal stimulation in terms of the unchanging shapes that produced them. A rectangular door remains rectangular in perception as one approaches it from the front, opens

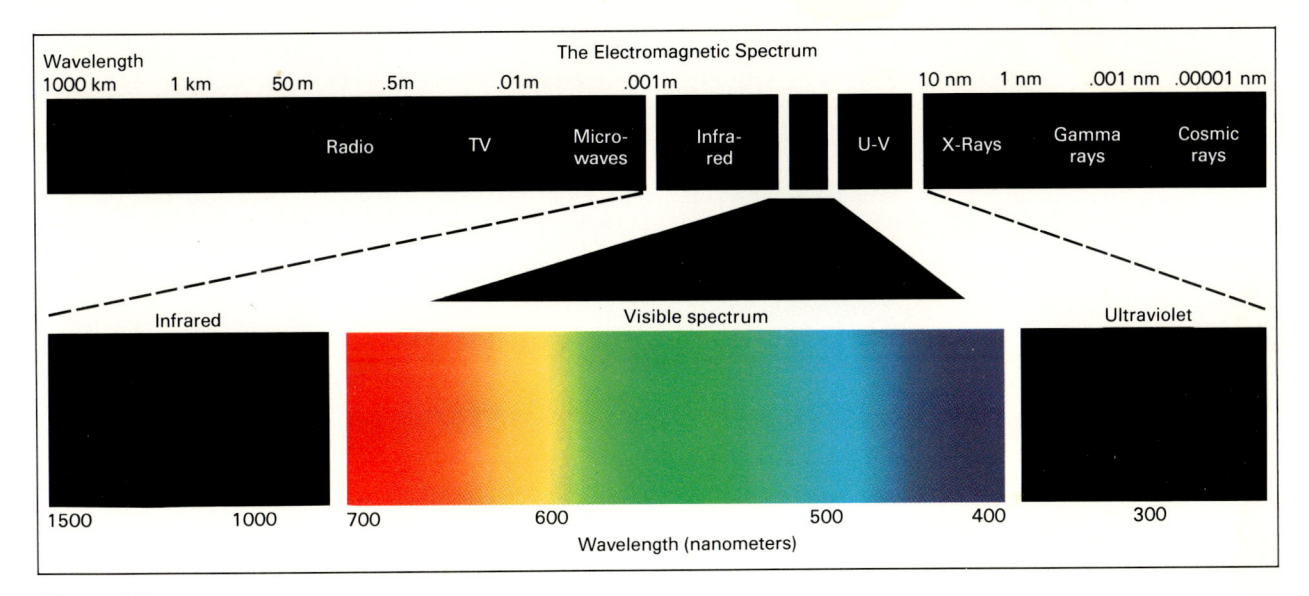

Figure 3.2
The electromagnetic spectrum. Electromagnetic radiations vary greatly in wavelength from the very long-wave radiations produced by alternating currents that have wavelengths of thousands of kilometers to the extraordinarily short wavelengths (0.00001 nm) of high-energy cosmic rays. Within this range is a small band of energy to which receptors in our eyes have the capacity to respond. We call this band of electromagnetic energy visible light, and it ranges in wavelength from around 750 to 400 nanometers.

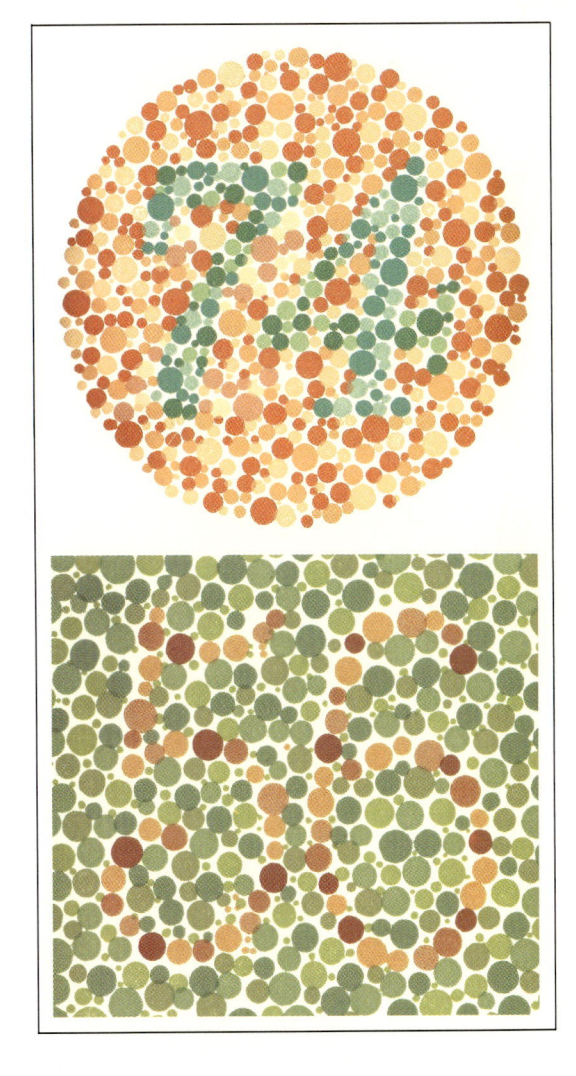

Figure 3.19
Dvorine Pseudo-Isochromatic Plates. These images are commonly used to test for color blindness. A person who is color blind cannot pick out the numbers made up of many colored dots from the background colored dots. (Courtesy Richmond Products.)

Figure 4.20
The color circle. The relationship between hues can be seen by arranging them in a circle according to their perceptual similarity rather than by wavelength. The four unique colors are equally spaced 90 degrees from each other in this representation.

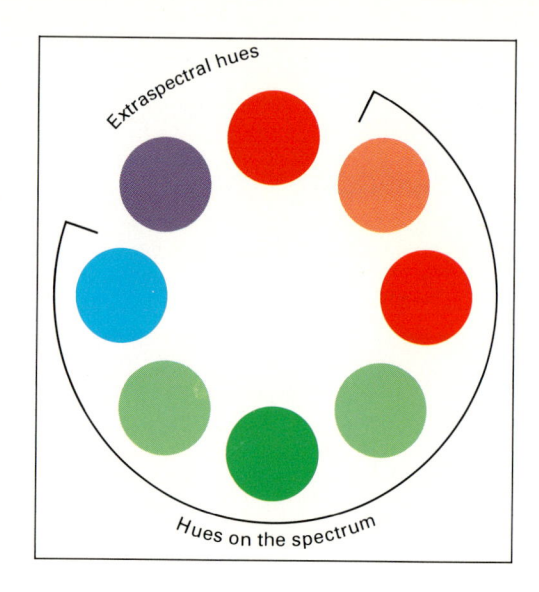

Figure 4.23
The color solid. This representation combines the dimensions of hue, saturation, and brightness. Hue is shown on the circumference, and saturation is shown on the interior. If one sliced through the color solid at the middle, a color circle like that shown in Figure 4.21 would result. The less saturated reds—crimson and pink—are shown on the red axis. The dimension of brightness is represented vertically in the color solid. Maroon, a dark red, is shown on the color solid, still on the red axis, but toward the dark end of the color solid. It is important to realize that for maximum saturation, brightness has to be at the intermediate value. This is why the color solid is largest at the middle, with intermediate values on the brightness scale. (Photo by Munsell.)

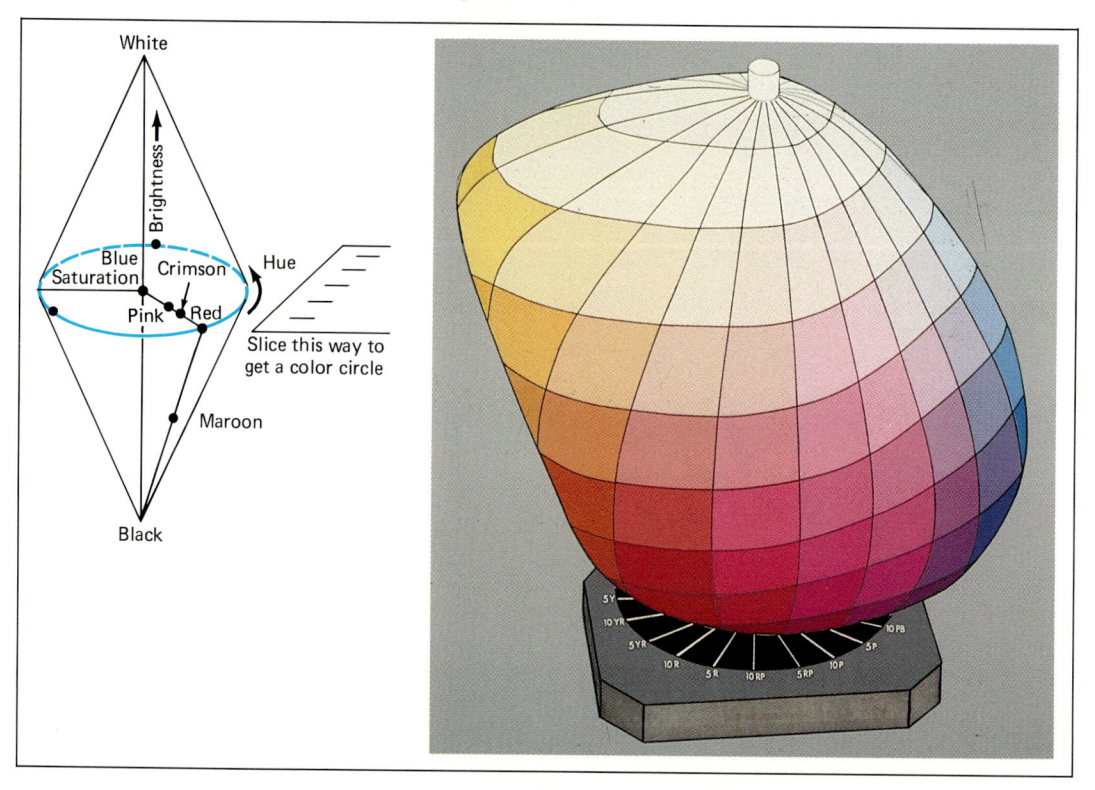

Figure 4.24
Subtractive color mixtures. Each of the three pigments printed on this page absorbs light of some wavelengths while it reflects a rather broad range of others. When they are combined, some wavelengths are subtracted out and new colors are generated.

Color afterimages. Hold your book upright, and stare at the dot in the center of the flag for around a minute. Then, without looking up, move your vision over to the blank white area to the right of the flag. Rather than a green, black, and yellow flag, you should see a faint image of a flag in the traditional red, white, and blue. Staring at the colors for a period of time causes some of the sensory systems to become fatigued so that their complementary colors (green—red; black—white; yellow—blue) are seen.

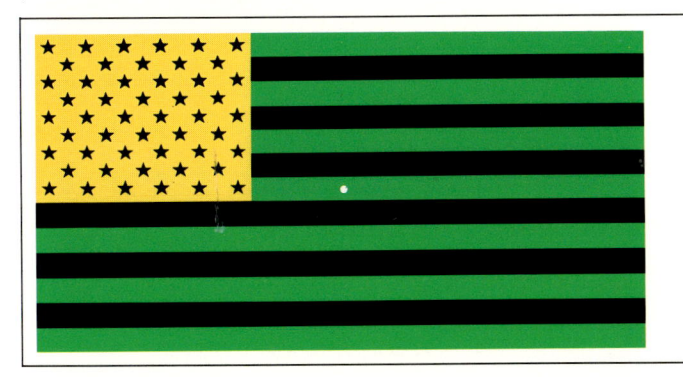

Figure 4.25
Additive color mixtures. The top part of this figure shows a checkerboard of small red and green squares. On the bottom is a solid yellow (mustard) disk. Prop up your book so that you can see it as you back up across the room. If you have backed up far enough so that you cannot see the individual squares of the checkerboard, the two disks should look much the same. The light reflected from the individual squares gets blurred on the retina, giving the color mixture effect. Just for reference, the two original colors are shown as bars to the left of the upper disk. A color television produces a variety of colors from tiny red, green, and blue dots in much the same way. (Based on Coren, Porac, and Ward, 1984.)

A

B

it so that it is viewed obliquely from the side, and finally as seen from the edge just before one passes through.

There is also an automatic perceptual assumption that objects remain the same size despite changes in the size of the retinal image. As you walk to class you might encounter one of your professors coming toward you. At first, he or she may produce only a small retinal image, but as the two of you approach each other, the retinal image of your professor becomes larger and larger; clothing colors become more distinct, details become sharper. Yet you do not perceive your professor as growing larger, changing colors, and developing details right before your eyes.

This phenomenon is called *size constancy* and it is related in some ways to the perception of distance. For example, if a tree 300 ft away casts a retinal image that is about one-half the size of the retinal image of a tree 150 ft away, the two trees will be perceived as being approximately the same size. If, however, it is difficult to judge distance accurately, errors in size constancy may occur. When you view people and cars from the top of a very tall building, they often look extremely tiny, like toys, even though we consciously know they are not. The failure of size constancy when viewing objects from above probably occurs because most of us are inexperienced at judging distances from that perspective.

Look up from your book and turn your head from side to side. The entire visual field of the room you are in just swept across the retina of your eyes but yet, the room did not appear to move. Under most conditions we are able to maintain *location constancy* quite easily. This illustrates how changes in sensory stimulation (the image on the retina) is not necessarily reproduced in your final perceptual experience. Often our knowledge about the environment (in this case about the general stability of rooms) is a better predictor of the perceptual experience than the sensory events which theoretically provide our link with the external world.

The final kind of perceptual constancy we will discuss is color constancy. Have you ever taken color photographs indoors without the aid of flash? When they were developed, did they look reddish or orange? The room did not seem to look that way at all at the time you took the pictures—the colors looked perfectly normal. What happened? As it turns out, light from ordinary incandescent light bulbs is not well balanced. It contains a large proportion of long-wavelength radiation, reds and oranges, and relatively less blue and violet. Your visual system compensates for this difference in the quality of illumination and colors are perceived normally. This is because our perceptual processes include an expectation of light sources being similar to sunlight, so we tend to interpret colors accordingly. However, your camera film cannot make such a compensation, and therefore the pictures accurately reproduce the lighting conditions in which they were taken and look orange. Our ability to perceive objects as being uniformly of one color despite differences in the amount or color of the light illuminating them is called *color constancy*.

These and other kinds of constancies arise from tendencies to perceive our surroundings in terms of stability and predictability. Our capacity to use perceptual constancies allows us to interpret changing and sometimes ambiguous sensory inputs, accurately and rapidly. The perceptual constancies depend to some degree on our previous experiences with similar perceptual situations, and when we have not had such experiences, they often work poorly. For example, you might mistake the colors of a friend's clothes under the colored lights of a party but correctly perceive the colors of your own.

In this chapter we first discuss some questions related to the detection of sensory events and then explore some of the many ways that sensory stimuli are interpreted by the brain to yield meaningful perceptions.

SENSORY THRESHOLDS

ABSOLUTE THRESHOLDS

The basic task of any sensory system is to detect energy changes in the environment. Such energy changes can take many forms, such as the movements of air molecules (as in the case of sound energy), pressure on the skin, differences in temperature or light levels, or even the presence of certain chemicals. How strong does a stimulus need to be for a person to sense it? Some sounds are just too faint for us to hear, and some odors are simply not strong enough to be detected, even though dogs might easily respond to both.

The minimal amount of stimulus energy that can be detected is called the *absolute threshold.* This idea was first introduced into psychology by Johann Friedrich Herbart (1776–1841), who defined what he called the "threshold of consciousness." He thought of this threshold as the intensity of stimulation at which the detection of an event passes from a level of unawareness into consciousness or, as he put it, to the state of a real idea in the mind. The essential idea here is that below some critical level of stimulus intensity, one cannot detect the occurrence of an event, but when this critical intensity or threshold value is exceeded, one can expect an observer to detect its presence.

How is an absolute threshold determined? As we shall see, it is quite a bit more complicated than might be imagined (see Baird & Noma, 1978). One way of determining an absolute threshold is by using a technique called *the method of limits,* a technique which can be used for determining many different kinds of thresholds (Guilford, 1954). Let us describe a typical experiment using the method of limits to determine the absolute threshold for a visual stimulus. The observer in this experiment sits in a totally dark room and the experimenter presents a spot of light starting with a very faint, undetectable light flash. The experimenter then flashes additional spots of light, gradually increasing their brightness until the observer reliably reports seeing them. Now the experimenter begins with a clearly visible spot of light, and over the next series of trials gradually decreases their brightness until the observer reports that the light flashes can no longer be seen. After several series of stimulus presentations, an average intensity value for detection can be calculated and an absolute threshold determined. This technique was given its name, the method of limits, by Kraepelin in 1891 because the stimulus series is stopped when the observer reliably and consistently changes his or her judgments, that is, reaches a limit.

Another way of determining an absolute threshold is through the *method of constant stimuli.* Using this technique, an experimenter will take a set of stimuli that range in intensity from totally imperceptible to clearly perceptible and present them to an observer, one at a time, in a mixed or random order. The observer has to respond with a "yes" when the stimulus is detected and a "no" when it is not. When each stimulus intensity has been presented a number of times, an absolute threshold can be calculated. In this case the absolute threshold for a stimulus is defined as that intensity which can be accurately detected 50% of the time. The rule of 50% is, of course, arbitrary, but psychologists consider it to be a logical and reasonable standard.

HIGHLIGHT 4.1

Using the Method of Limits to Determine Your Hearing Threshold

For this demonstration you will need a very quiet room, a small travel alarm clock that ticks fairly loudly, and 10 coins. Place the clock at one end of the room and then walk to the other end of the room. The distance should be such that you cannot hear the clock ticking. Then, slowly walk forward approaching the ticking clock. When you can just hear it, place a coin on the floor to mark the spot. Now move close to the clock and slowly back up until you can no longer hear the ticking and place a second coin on the floor to mark that spot. It will probably be in a different place than the first coin. Repeat this procedure moving toward and then away from the clock until you have placed all 10 coins on the floor. As you place the coins on the floor, try not to look at the locations of previously placed coins, as that information could bias your results. When you have finished, the 10 coins will have formed a loose cluster. The center of this cluster is the distance away from the sound source that results in a sound intensity that is at your absolute threshold for hearing that particular sound as determined by the method of limits.

Why didn't all the coins end up in exactly the same place? There may be several reasons. First, changes in the level of background noise in the room may have masked the ticking of the clock. Further, psychological factors may also have been responsible: Your attention may have wandered or you may have anticipated the sound before it was actually heard.

Absolute thresholds have been determined for many different sensory stimuli under ideal observing conditions, and a few of them, expressed in generally understandable units of measurement, are shown in Table 4.1. These values clearly demonstrate that our senses are exquisitely sensitive and can respond to very tiny amounts of stimulation.

SIGNAL-DETECTION THEORY

Although absolute threshold experiments are still performed and continue to provide useful information, there is a general consensus among psychologists that there is no such thing as a true absolute threshold (Swets, 1961).

Thresholds are not constants; they vary with time, conditions of testing, and with the state of the observer. Suppose, for example, that one is conducting a study of auditory detection thresholds under very quiet conditions. As we noted in Chapter 3, your auditory system may be sensitive enough to

TABLE 4.1
Some absolute thresholds for common stimuli

Vision	A candle flame 30 miles away on a clear dark night
Hearing	The tick of a watch under quiet conditions at 20 ft
Taste	One teaspoon of sugar dissolved in 2 gallons of water
Smell	One drop of perfume diffused into the entire volume of a six-room apartment
Touch	The wing of a bee falling on your cheek from a distance of 1 cm

Source: E. Galanter. Contemporary psychophysics. In R. Brown, E. Galanter, E. H. Hess, and G. Mandler (Eds.), *New directions in psychology*. New York: Holt, Rinehart and Winston, 1962.

respond to the sound of blood rushing through the arteries and veins of your ear. If a very weak signal were to be presented between heart beats, it might well be detected, while if it were presented just as the noise of the rushing blood reached its peak (right after a heart beat) the stimulus might well be missed. Viewed in this way, the task of the observer is to distinguish the signal from random noise. The study of this process is called signal detection theory (Green & Swets, 1966).

According to *signal-detection theory*, every perception requires that an observer make a discrimination between the *signal* (the stimulus to be perceived) and *noise* (random background activity of the nervous system, body, and the environment). Signal-detection theory is a theoretical and mathematical system which recognizes that one is not simply a passive receiver of stimuli, but that decisions are constantly being made concerning the presence or absence of stimuli. When driving in city traffic at night, one has to decide whether that red light ahead is a traffic light (signal) or some other red light, say, on a theater marquee (noise).

Let us return to the experiment in which an observer is attempting to detect very weak sounds. The observer indicates "Yes, I heard it" by pressing a button or giving some other kind of sign. As the tones become progressively weaker, the task become more difficult and the observer becomes more and more doubtful as to whether there really was a signal or not on some of the trials. With stimuli at or near threshold, whether to respond or not becomes a real problem. "Did I hear it, or was it just my imagination?"

If no other factors entered in, we might expect that at threshold, an observer would correctly identify the stimulus about 50% of the time. But other factors usually do enter in. Such factors might be the motives and expectations of the subject. These and other factors contribute to what is known as *response bias*. For example, a very cautious person might be likely to show a higher threshold for detecting stimuli than would a person who wished to impress the experimenter with his or her sensitivity. Psychologists deal with such problems by deliberately manipulating such biases and then observing the results of these manipulations on the responses of their subjects.

To understand how the manipulation of response bias is done, we need to look at each of the possible outcomes in a signal detection experiment and give them names. In such an experiment a signal is presented on some trials and is not presented on other trials. Therefore, there are four possible outcomes using such a procedure. They are shown in Table 4.2.

An "event present" is a trial in which the experimenter actually delivers the target stimulus (occurring in the presence of whatever noise there may be). An "event absent" trial occurs when no signal is delivered and the observer perceives only noise. There are only two possible responses that a subject can make: "yes" or "no." A "yes" response indicates that he or she detected the stimulus on that particular trial, while a "no" indicates that the subject judged that the signal was not delivered. When a signal is actually delivered and the observer responds "yes," the observer scores a "hit." If the observer responds with a "no," that would be a "miss." If the observer responds with a "yes" but no signal was actually presented on that trial (event absent), a "false alarm" is scored, and if the observer responds "no" and there indeed was no signal presented, a "correct negative" is scored. These categories depend not only on the nature of the stimulus, but also on the decisions made by the observer. Hits and correct negatives are correct responses, while misses and false alarms are incorrect responses.

Suppose that you are a subject in an experiment similar to the one described above and that your ability to detect the presence of a very faint tone

TABLE 4.2
Possible outcomes in a signal detection experiment

	Response	
	Yes	No
Event present	Hit	Miss
Event absent	False alarm	Correct negative

is being measured. After a ready signal you will respond by pushing one button to indicate "yes," you heard the tone, and a different button "no," indicating that you did not hear it. Now, on some trials you might not be completely sure whether you heard the tone or not, and so occasionally you would respond with "no" when the tone was actually present and therefore score a miss; on others a false alarm would be scored when you pressed the "yes" button when no tone was sounded. If the tone was present on half (50%) of the trials, you would soon develop some expectancies about the experimental conditions.

Now suppose that the tone were present on 90% of the trials; then your expectancies would be quite different and you would probably respond "yes" to even the faintest of sensations, perhaps even to random noise. This is reasonable behavior. Because the stimulus occurs so frequently, your chances of being correct are quite high. This strategy would cause you to get many hits, but a lot of false alarms too.

If the experimental conditions were such that the stimulus is actually presented only on 10% of the trials, what would happen then? It is likely that you would not respond to ambiguous sensations and that you would wait until a signal was clearly perceived. In this case your response pattern would change with your expectations and you would probably score many correct negatives and many misses but relatively few hits. Expectancies, determined by the probability of signal presentation, changed your behavior in this signal detection task.

What does all this have to do with the determination of sensitivity to a particular stimulus? We need to separate our sensitivity from our decision strategy. If the strength of the signal (loudness of the tone in this case) is held constant, but the probability of occurrence of the signal varies, a curve may be plotted describing the relationship between the proportion of hits and false alarms as the probability of signal occurrence is varied. The resulting curve, shown in Figure 4.2, is known as a *receiver operating characteristic curve* (ROC curve). The name is derived from its original use at Bell Laboratories to measure the intelligibility of speech transmitted through different types of telephone equipment.

In this kind of curve, the probability of a false alarm when a signal was not actually presented (event absent) is plotted against the probability of a hit when a signal was presented. In the case with a probability of 70% that an event will actually be present, the observed proportion of hits might be

Figure 4.2
A receiver-operating characteristic curve (roc). In this case, the observer's response bias is varied by varying the probability that a signal is actually going to be presented on a given trial. These probabilities are shown as points along the curve. When the probability that a signal will be presented is fairly low, 0.3 for example, the subject's expectation leads to a response pattern in which there are few "yes" responses. As a result, the proportion of "false alarms" is lower than the proportion of hits. The zero sensitivity line represents chance performance with a signal below threshold.

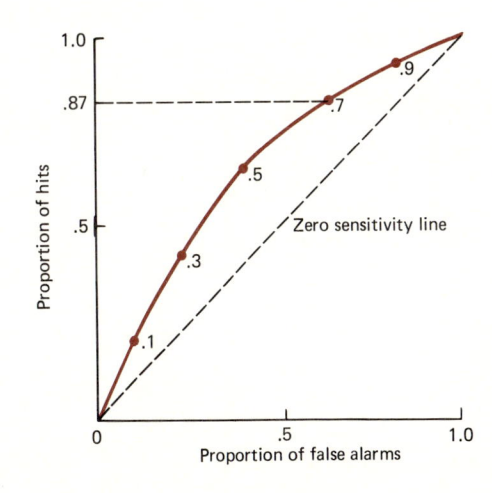

.87 and the proportion of false alarms around .58. Why did the subject incorrectly report detecting the signal 58% of the time when there was no signal actually there? This is because event present trials occurred with a frequency of 70% and event absent trials occurred only 30% of the time. It was reasonable to respond "yes" even when doubtful.

The ROC curve in Figure 4.2 shows that when the signal is infrequently presented, that is, when there are lots of event absent trials, the observer usually responds "no." This can be seen in the lower-left portion of the curve. The subject's expectation, built up over a large number of trials, that there will be large numbers of event absent trials inhibits making "yes" responses, a pattern of behavior leading to a decrease in the proportion of hits and false alarms. At the other end of the curve, when the signal is presented very frequently, the observer typically responds "yes" even on those trials when there is no signal or event there. Therefore, as you can see, a ROC curve depicts an observer's response pattern for one signal strength when the probability of presenting an event varies.

If we were to change the intensity of the signal (e.g., make the tone louder), the curve would become more angular, as shown by curve A in Figure 4.3. However, if the strength of the signal is lowered, the line becomes more flattened (curve B). A signal that is below threshold produces a straight line (zero sensitivity), reflecting chance performance. Therefore, the amount of bow in the curve can be used as a measure of the detectability of the signal to a particular subject. The measure used to describe the degree of bowedness in a ROC curve is called d'. When d' is equal to zero, an undetectable stimulus, the ROC curve is a straight line. As the signal becomes more intense, its detectability increases, the curve becomes more bowed, and d' increases.

As can be seen, the response pattern of a subject can be altered by varying the detectability of the stimulus, or the probability of occurrence of the stimulus. When this is done, the proportions will always fall somewhere on a ROC curve defined by some value of d'. Response patterns can be changed by any of a variety of factors, and signal-detection theory allows researchers to separate out these factors and arrive at relatively pure assessments of sensory capacities (Egan, 1975). The measure, d', represents the sensory capabilities of a subject which is independent of other factors. Thus a d' value of 1 might represent the threshold intensity of a particular stimulus.

Signal-detection methods appear to be the most accurate ways of determining a person's sensitivity to a particular stimulus. With these experimental

Figure 4.3
Two receiver-operating characteristic curves with signals of different intensities. The curve shown as A represents the curve obtained with a signal that is strong enough to detect fairly easily. The proportion of hits is high relative to the proportion of false alarms. As signal intensity decreases, the curve flattens out (curve B) and finally becomes a straight line (zero sensitivity). The detectability of a given signal, therefore, is reflected by the amount of bowedness in the curve.

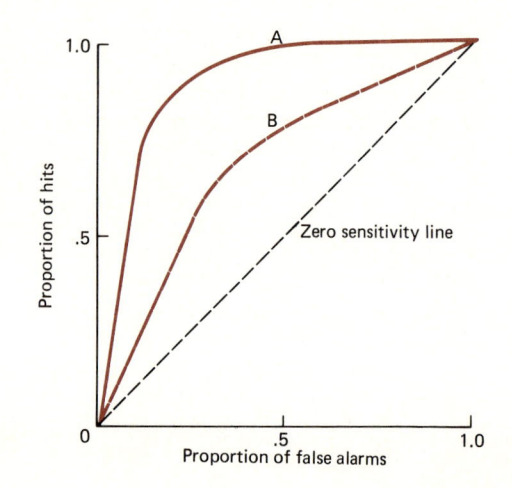

PERCEPTION

techniques, the subject decides whether or not the stimulus was perceived. Further, the subject's response biases can be adjusted by varying the probabilities of stimulus occurrence or the consequences of making a miss or false alarm. Signal-detection theory makes use of the fact that perception is much more than simply the activation of sensory receptors; it also involves interpretation of the stimulus, that is, cognitive processes. In deciding whether a stimulus was present or not, there is always the possibility that the sensory experience was produced by internal random noise and not by the stimulus. It is for the subject to decide which actually occurred.

DIFFERENCE THRESHOLDS

Thresholds for detection are not fixed. They depend importantly on the conditions of testing. In the experiment described in the box several pages back, you would expect the coins to cluster much closer to the clock if a fan were running in the room. Further, if a stereo set were playing in the next room, you probably would be unable to tell if the clock were ticking at all. Clearly, the conditions accompanying a stimulus, the stimulus background, determine its detectability. Lighting a single candle produces a large change in the illumination of a darkened room. But lighting the same candle while sunlight streams through the windows produces no perceptible change in room illumination. The amount of stimulus change relative to background stimulation seems to be an important variable in perceiving an event.

This suggests another question that you might ask about how we perceive stimuli: How much of a change in the intensity of a stimulus does it take before we notice that a change in intensity has occurred, and how do the background conditions influence this value? The just detectable amount of change is called a *difference threshold,* and it is defined as the smallest degree of change in a stimulus that can be detected 50% of the time. This quantity is called a *just noticeable difference* (JND).

Clearly, measuring a JND is going to be more complicated than determining an absolute threshold because so much depends on the conditions under which the measurement is taken. It is going to take a lot more light to produce a just noticeable increase in the amount of light in a room with many windows on a bright sunny day than it will in a dimly lit restaurant. Gustav Theodor Fechner (1801–1887), who developed the concept of the JND, recognized this problem and worked at developing a general law that would relate stimulus intensity to sensory magnitude.

Fechner used the formulations of the physiologist Ernst Heinrich Weber (1795–1878), who noted that the size of the difference threshold is proportional to the intensity of the stimulus. Weber observed that if a stimulus is very intense (bright light, heavy weight, strong pressure), a correspondingly large change in that stimulus must occur before any difference can be detected.

This relationship is called *Weber's law* and can be expressed algebraically as

$$\frac{\Delta I}{I} = K$$

where ΔI is the size of the JND at a given stimulus intensity of I, and K is the resultant constant of proportionality for that particular type of stimulus. The fraction $\Delta I/I$ is called the *Weber fraction*. Table 4.3 lists a few typical middle range values for the Weber fraction for several sensations. The con-

Gustav Theodor Fechner (1801–1887) developed the concept of the just noticeable difference (J.N.D.), which is the smallest degree of change in a stimulus that can be detected 50 per cent of the time. (Bettmann Archive)

Ernst Heinrich von Weber (1795–1878). Weber's Law states that the size of the difference threshold is proportional to the intensity of the stimulus. (Bettmann Archive)

TABLE 4.3
Some Weber fraction values ($\Delta I/I$) for different senses

Vision (brightness, white light)	1/60
Kinesthesis (lifted weights)	1/50
Pain (heat on the skin)	1/30
Hearing (tones of medium pitch and loudness)	1/10
Pressure (on the skin)	1/7
Smell (odor of india rubber)	1/4
Taste (table salt)	1/3

Source: F. A. Geldard. *Fundamentals of Psychology.* New York: Wiley, 1962, p. 93.

stant of proportionality varies among the different senses but holds quite well, except at extreme ranges, within any given sensation.

To see how the Weber fraction works, imagine that you are judging the difference between two weights, and both objects weigh about 100 grams (g). Since the Weber fraction for lifted weights or kinesthesis is 1/50, and 1/50 of 100 g is 2 g, we would expect, by the Weber fraction for kinesthesis, to be able to distinguish between a weight of 100 g and a weight of 102 g. If we were to use heavier weights, Weber's law tells us that the difference would have to be larger to be perceptible: 4 g if the weights were about 200 g; 8 g if the weights were about 400 g.

Fechner extended Weber's finding to express a general relationship between the physical intensity of a stimulus and its sensory consequences. This relationship, known as *Fechner's law,* states that the strength of a perceived sensation increases as the logarithm of the intensity of a stimulus:

$$S = K \log I$$

where S stands for the perceived magnitude of the sensation, K is a constant, and I represents the intensity of the stimulus. Although recent research has suggested that there are a number of difficulties with this formulation, such a relationship does make good adaptive sense. Because we, and other animals, must respond to such a wide range of intensities of stimulation, the nervous system must be able to compress this range into one that is more comprehensible. A logarithmic scale is ideally suited for this (S. S. Stevens, 1975).

ADAPTATION OF SENSORY SYSTEMS

While you are sitting reading this book you are probably not aware of the pressure of your clothes on your body or the sensations inside your mouth—until right now. Listen carefully. Do you hear anything (traffic noise, furnace fan, voices) of which you had not been aware? There is a whole sensory world occurring all around us that we typically screen out. This screening is called *sensory adaptation* and it is a change in the sensitivity of sensory systems as a result of continued stimulation (see Helson, 1964). It is as if the sensory system gets used to a stimulus and stops responding to it. But it is not quite that simple, because if there is a change in the stimulus—either an increase or a decrease—you will notice it. Recall how you notice the sound of a ventilator fan in a room just as it turns off.

Many sensory systems respond best to changes in stimuli. Think of what it is like to jump into a cool swimming pool. At first the water feels really cold, but after a few minutes, you hardly notice the temperature. The cool water is perceived as less uncomfortable. Why does this occur? Sensations

PERCEPTION

of warmth and cold are generally caused by changes in the particular skin temperature to which you have adapted. For example, an object feels cold when pressed to the skin, because it causes the skin temperature to drop from the perceptual neutral point to which it had previously adapted. Temperature receptors in the skin can adapt to temperatures that range from about 18 to 40°C.

Adaptation is also seen in other sensory systems, such as the olfactory system. Continued exposure to a particular odor results in a rapid decline in our sensitivity to that smell. Depending on the nature of the odor and its concentration, exposure to that odor can cause the perception of even a very strong smell to disappear completely. When one enters a kitchen, the cooking odors may be quite noticeable, but after a few minutes these smells can hardly be detected. Although the effects of adaptation are greatest on the particular odor which is actually present, adaptation to one odor will often affect detection thresholds to other similar odors—cross adaptation. Exposure to pure air (an absence of odors) quickly results in a restoration of olfactory sensitivity.

HIGHLIGHT 4.2
Demonstrating Sensory Adaptation

TEMPERATURE ADAPTATION

To do this demonstration you will need an assistant and three bowls large enough for you to submerge your hands at least up to the wrist. The water in one bowl should be approximately 30°C (2 cups of hot tap water and 4 cups of cold) and should feel slightly cool to the touch. The second bowl should contain water that feels fairly warm (try 4 cups of hot water to 2 cups of cold). Now place your right hand in one of these containers and your left hand in the other for 3 minutes. During this time have your assistant prepare a third container with water that is intermediate in temperature between the first two (3 cups of cold and 3 cups of hot water).

After your hands have been in the warm and cool water for 3 minutes, each hand should have adapted to that water temperature and you should feel very little, if any, thermal sensation. Now take your hands out and put them both into the container of water of an intermediate temperature. The hand that was in the cool water should feel as if it is in warm water, while the other hand should feel as if it is in cool water. Since the water temperature is actually the same for both hands, the perception of temperatures must be caused by the change in temperature relative to the temperature to which the skin of each hand had adapted.

TOUCH ADAPTATION

To do this demonstration you will need a stopwatch or a watch with a sweep second hand, two circles cut from cardboard with diameters of about 2.5 cm and 5 cm, a nickel, and a willing friend. Have your friend take off his or her shirt and lie face down on a bed or the floor. Now place one of the cardboard circles on the skin of your friend's back and measure the time that passes before he or she reports that it can no longer be felt. Do the same with the other cardboard circle. Now do the experiment again, but this time place the nickel on the cardboard circles so that the pressure is slightly increased. When you look at your data, you should note that the lighter touches (those without the nickel) and those with the larger surface area of stimulation (less pressure on the skin per square centimeter) disappear faster from perceptibility; that is, they show more rapid sensory adaptation.

These demonstrations are based on material in S. Coren, C. Porac, and L. M. Ward. *Sensation and perception* (2nd ed.). Orlando, Fla.: Academic Press, 1984.

PRINCIPLES OF VISUAL PERCEPTUAL ORGANIZATION

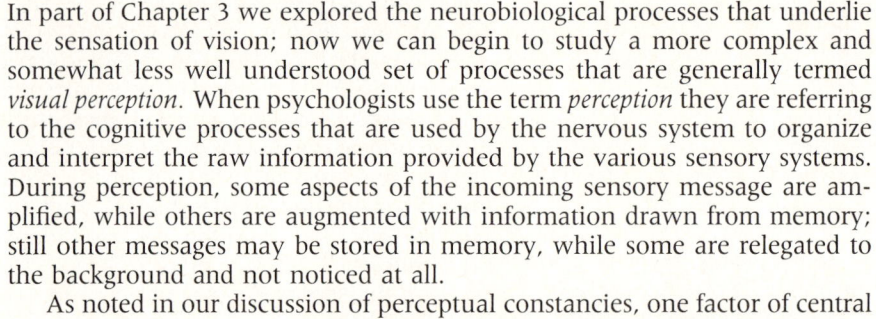

In part of Chapter 3 we explored the neurobiological processes that underlie the sensation of vision; now we can begin to study a more complex and somewhat less well understood set of processes that are generally termed *visual perception*. When psychologists use the term *perception* they are referring to the cognitive processes that are used by the nervous system to organize and interpret the raw information provided by the various sensory systems. During perception, some aspects of the incoming sensory message are amplified, while others are augmented with information drawn from memory; still other messages may be stored in memory, while some are relegated to the background and not noticed at all.

As noted in our discussion of perceptual constancies, one factor of central importance in perception is our past experience. We use it to help us interpret new stimuli. When we encounter an ambiguous visual stimulus we make guesses about it on the basis of similar objects or events we have previously seen. Indeed, a major part of the perceptual process involves relating new stimuli to past experiences and trying to answer such questions as: "Have I ever seen something like this before?" or "What kind of thing is it?" or "What is it doing?" or "Where is it going?"

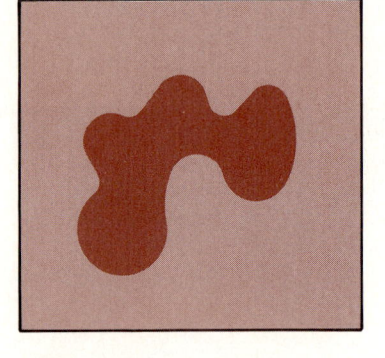

EXTRACTING A MEANINGFUL VISUAL IMAGE

Distinguishing Figure from Ground. A basic principle of visual perceptual organization is that we tend to see "things." We interpret the visual message transmitted from the retina to the brain as objects against a background. A ship stands out against the background of sea and sky, a camel stands out against a background of desert sand, the figure of a person stands out against a background of hills and trees. This interpretative process is called the separation of *figure* from *ground* and it can be seen in all sensory systems. In Figure 4.4, the dark form is perceived to be a figure, while the white field tends to be interpreted as the ground or background. The figure appears to extend forward from the page, while the ground appears to recede into the distance behind it.

The separation of figure from ground is a function of our perceptual systems, which impose meaning onto the raw visual sensation. This process becomes more apparent in the classic reversible figure-ground pattern seen in Figure 4.5. What is it? A pair of faces or a vase? Either can be seen. Two figure-ground organizations are possible and the perceptual system seems to shift back and forth between them, not allowing them to exist simultaneously and yet unable to decide between them. At any moment, which is figure (the vase or the faces) and which is ground is a direct result of the interpretations applied to the stimulus by your perceptual system as it attempts to extract a meaningful visual image from an ambiguous stimulus.

Grouping Elements in a Visual Stimulus. The perceptual system uses other principles besides the establishment of figure-ground relationships to process a visual stimuli into interpretable messages. Look for a few seconds at the array of equally spaced dots in Figure 4.6. The image before you is not static. It appears to be a continually changing pattern of rows, diagonals, and possibly large and small squares. You know that the printed page is not changing

Figure 4.4
The separation of figure from ground. The dark form is seen as an object extending forward from the page; the lighter area recedes into the background.

Figure 4.5
A reversible figure–ground pattern. Two organizations of figure and ground are possible: two faces or a vase.

PERCEPTION   115

Figure 4.6
This array of equally spaced dots does not appear to be static; rather, it seems to be continually changing pattern as the visual system organizes and groups the dots in various ways.

in this way, yet you perceive constantly shifting patterns. The changes in the pattern of dots that you see are a result of your visual system trying various ways to organize and group the elements of this ambiguous visual stimulus.

Psychologists have carefully studied the principles of organization that the visual system uses to interpret visual stimuli. This research has resulted in some very interesting conclusions about how we see our world and led to the establishment of general principles of perceptual organization.

SOME GESTALT PRINCIPLES OF PERCEPTUAL ORGANIZATION

In the early part of this century a branch of psychology known as *Gestalt psychology* developed in Germany. *Gestalt* is a German word that is difficult to translate into English, but terms such as "pattern," "form," "whole," and "configuration" convey the general idea. The Gestalt psychologists, led by Koffka (1935), Köhler (1959), and Wertheimer (1959), emphasized studies of basic principles of perception in their quest for a better understanding of how the mind works.

The Gestalt psychologists maintained that one of the major tasks perceptual processes must perform is the recognition of shapes or form. They noted that we tend to perceive whole objects even when we are looking at only a part or some component of that object. The Gestalt psychologists argued that the perception of an object is more than just the sum of the parts; the mind adds and fills in missing parts to assemble a whole perceptual experience. To explain these perceptual processes, the Gestalt psychologists developed a number of principles of perceptual organization that apply best to vision, but they also apply to other kinds of perception as well. Among these principles is one that we have already discussed, the separation of figure from ground.

Another Gestalt perceptual organizing principle is called *closure*. It is the process of mentally filling in the missing pieces of a stimulus so that we perceive a complete representation rather than a collection of isolated components. Look at the pictures in Figure 4.7. What do you see? The process of closure assembles a rather abstract collection of irregular black shapes into a meaningful image of a dog and a horse and rider. As with most Gestalt principles of perception, closure extends to other sensory modes besides vi-

Figure 4.7
The Gestalt principle of closure. What do you see here? The visual system assembles these irregular shapes into meaningful images, supplying, in a way, some of the missing information.

sion. Most of us can recognize a familiar tune by hearing only small parts of it. Similarly, we can often obtain useful information from only brief snatches of a conversation.

Continuity, another Gestalt principle of perceptual organization, is closely related to closure, and it is the tendency to perceive visual elements as continuing smoothly along their original course. The upper part of Figure 4.8(a) looks like a sine wave oscillating along a horizontal axis. These two components are shown in Figure 4.8(b). Because of the principle of continuity, we do not perceive it as being composed of the elements shown in Figure 4.8(c).

When objects are close to one another in space or time they are generally perceived as belonging together. This is the Gestalt principle of *proximity,* and it operates in a variety of ways. For example, when we see several people standing near one another we perceive them as a group. Perhaps they are waiting for a bus, or standing in line to buy tickets, perhaps there is no common purpose at all. But we think of the people who are close together as being parts of a unit, separate and distinct from those people who may be walking or riding past. Suppose that we listen to a series of drum beats in which there are three taps on the drum followed by a pause, three more taps followed by another pause, and so on. We do not think of them as separate drum beats but as groups of three: rat tat tat, —, rat tat tat, —, rat tat tat.

The final Gestalt principle of perceptual organization that we shall discuss here is *similarity*. We tend to group objects, persons, and events according to their similarity in color, shape, and other factors. If among the guests at a party there are visitors from a nation where the characteristic style of dress

Figure 4.8
The Gestalt principle of continuity. The visual system tends to interpret the figure shown in the upper part of this figure as being composed of a sine wave and straight line rather than the equally possible interpretation shown in the lower part of the figure.

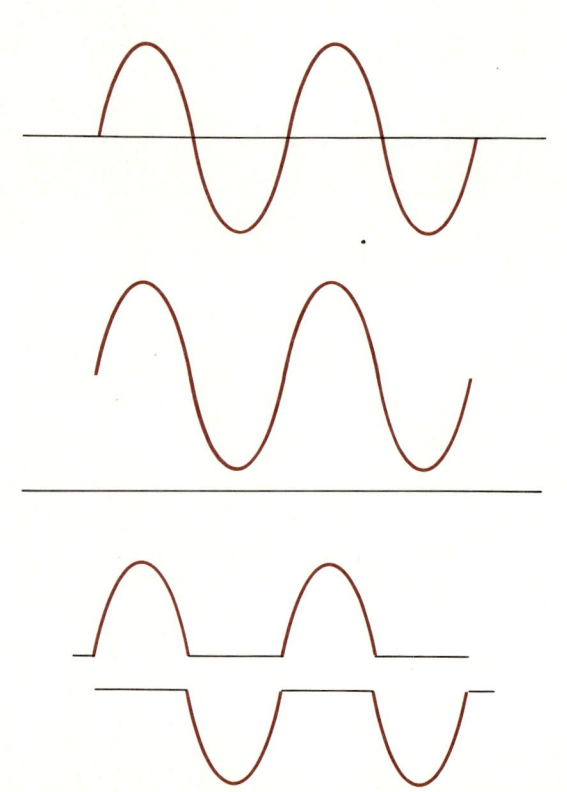

Figure 4.9
These two arrays of dots are perceptually organized on the basis of similarity, one as rows and one as columns.

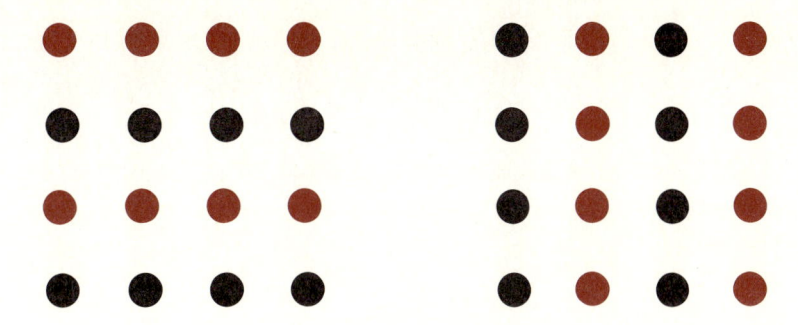

is substantially different from ours, those people will tend to be grouped separately from the other guests. The left part of Figure 4.9 is perceived as dots organized as rows, while the right portion is perceived as dots organized into columns. This discrimination is made by grouping dots on the basis of similar color.

THE PERCEPTION OF MOVEMENT

When you look at a moving object, how do you know that it is moving? At first glance this might seem like a relatively easy question to answer. You might answer that the image projected onto the retina by the moving object is constantly changing, and therefore it is successively stimulating different receptors. But your eyes are constantly in motion, too. How can we tell the difference between an object that moves when our eyes are still and one that is stationary when our eyes move? Further, why is it that you can perceive motion from a series of still pictures when you watch television or go to a movie? These and other questions have been the focus of extensive study by psychologists and we will deal with some of them here.

CUES FOR THE PERCEPTION OF MOVEMENT

Some of the cues for motion are to be found in the visual environment itself. When an object moves in front of a stationary background, it covers and then uncovers various parts of that background. In addition, when an object moves, we see it from different perspectives and even see new portions, while other parts of it may disappear entirely from view. The object appears to change in shape as it moves. In this case it does not matter whether or not our eyes move or not as the object is watched; we perceive motion. Changes in the parts of the background that are visible coupled with changes in the apparent shape of the moving object provide quite enough information to produce the perception of movement (J. J. Gibson, 1968).

But these cues cannot explain how one can perceive the movement of a light in a darkened room or the perception of movement of a flying airplane viewed against a cloudless sky. The movements of your eyes as you track the moving object against a featureless background also provide cues to the perceptual system. In this case, even though the image may remain quite steady on the retina, eye movements as they follow the stimulus produce the information needed for the perception of movement.

STROBOSCOPIC MOVEMENT

No doubt you have watched an animated neon sign in which a series of flashing lights generated the perception of movement. This perceived movement when there is no real movement is called *stroboscopic movement* or *apparent movement*. Imagine that you are in a darkened room and are watching two lights that are alternately turned on and off. If the distance between the two lights is appropriate and the timing just right, one light will seem to move from one point to the other, back and forth. The effect can be quite strong and is indistinguishable from a light that actually does move back and forth. This perception of movement is called the *phi phenomenon* and it has many applications, including advertising signs and video displays.

When we watch a movie, we are actually looking at a series of still photographs being projected onto the screen at the rate of 24 distinct images per second. Each picture is slightly different from the preceding one, but because they are presented so rapidly, they blend together to produce the perception of stroboscopic motion. With the help of those perceptual processes which generate apparent motion, a movie or television image appears to be in continuous motion even though the images actually change incrementally many times each second.

MOVEMENT PERCEPTION AND THE FRAME OF REFERENCE

How do you know that something is moving? When a friend of yours rolls a bowling ball down a bowling alley, you perceive that the ball is moving and that the alley remains stationary. However, it could be just the reverse. The alley could be moving and the ball stationary. The effect would be the same: The ball would come into contact with the pins. How does the perceptual system decide which alternative is the correct one?

Certainly learning and the principles of location constancy play some role; you have learned that bowling alleys are firmly fixed in place. However, an important general principle of perception is illustrated here. We generally perceive the moving object as being the object which is enclosed in a frame of reference. The dimensions of the bowling alley provide a frame of reference for the perception of the moving ball. When there is some ambiguity, the perceptual systems regard the larger object as stationary and the smaller object as moving. When we view the moon through a thin layer of moving clouds, the moon appears to be rushing through stationary clouds. This is because the whole sky (including the clouds) becomes the perceptual frame of reference. Astronauts orbiting the earth at tens of thousands of kilometers per hour have no sensation of movement at all because there is no frame of reference.

THE PERCEPTION OF VISUAL THREE-DIMENSIONAL SPACE

Our world has three dimensions, up-down, left-right, and front-back, but the image that is projected on the retina has only two dimensions, up-down and left-right. How, then, does the visual system generate the sensation of depth? As we shall see, this is a *tour de force* of neural processing.

BINOCULAR VISION

To perceive three dimensions, a visual stimulus must be viewed with both eyes. Since our eyes are separated by about 6 to 8 cm, each eye views a three-dimensional scene from a slightly different perspective. Therefore, a slightly different version of the scene is projected onto the retina of each eye. Whatever difference there is between the two views is called *binocular disparity*, and it forms an important basis for depth perception (Figure 4.10).

To demonstrate binocular disparity for yourself, point the index finger of your right hand at your nose and hold it about 15 or 20 cm from the tip of your nose. Close one eye and then the other and note the difference in the view of your hand and finger provided by each eye. With both eyes open, the view is three-dimensional. Each eye alone sees a two-dimensional view, but the views are different. Binocular disparity is greatest when objects are relatively close to the observer, as in this case. The disparity becomes progressively smaller the farther away an object is, and the difference in the image seen by each eye becomes undetectably small when objects are much more than 10 m from an observer.

A variety of optical devices use binocular disparity to generate the impression of three-dimensionality from two-dimensional stimuli. These include the techniques used in "3-D" movies, stereoscopes, View Masters, and the vision-testing devices used in some driving exams.

But how can the brain detect tiny differences between two views of the world taken only 7 cm apart? Recall from Chapter 3 that because axons from the nasal half of each retina cross over at the optic chiasm, visual information from the right visual field of each eye goes to the left hemisphere, and visual information from the left visual field of each eye goes to the right hemisphere.

Figure 4.10
Binocular disparity as a cue for depth perception. The dark and light-colored pegs are different distances away from the eyes; therefore, different images are projected onto each retina. This is because each eye views the world from a slightly different direction. The difference between the two images is interpreted by the brain, and it helps to generate the sensation of depth in a visual scene.

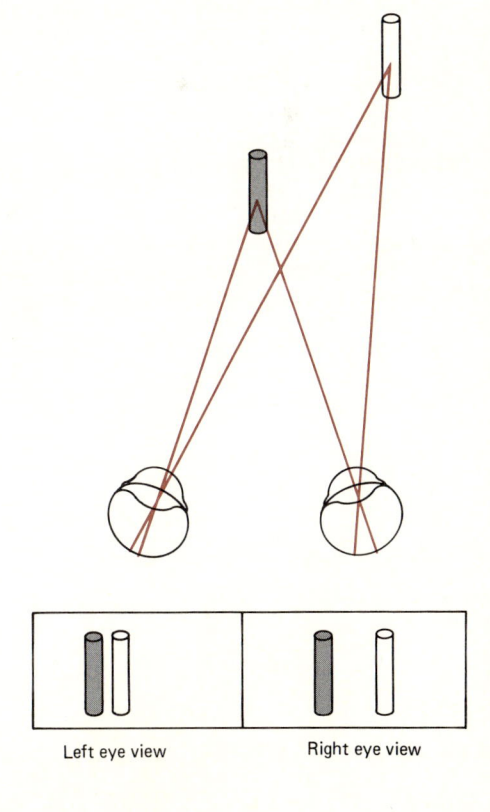

Left eye view   Right eye view

FOCUS ON THE PSYCHOLOGIST

Colin Blakemore

COLIN BLAKEMORE (Ph.D., University of California, Berkeley) is Waynflete Professor of Physiology and Chairman of the Physiology Department, University of Oxford. He is currently a fellow of Magdalen College, Oxford, and has formerly been a Royal Society Locke Research Fellow and Director of Medical Studies for Downing College, Cambridge. He has taught at the University of Cambridge, New York University, and MIT. His principle research interest is the neurophysiological interpretation of perception, and he has recently been concentrating on the development of the primate visual system.

In the early 1960s, when I was a medical undergraduate, the studies of David Hubel and Torsten Wiesel from Harvard Medical School were starting to appear in the journals. Their discovery that neurons in the visual cortex were usually selectively sensitive for the orientation of a bar or edge in the visual field had an immediate and extensive impact amongst psychologists as well as neurophysiologists. It pointed the way towards a neurophysiological explanation of perception, and it is that general question that has fascinated me ever since.

I became especially interested in binocular vision—how we can combine information from our two eyes into a single perceptual image and can use the tiny differences between the two retinal images to generate a sensation of three-dimensional depth (stereoscopic vision), unless they are so different that "rivalry" occurs. It seemed to me that Hubel and Wiesel's discovery that most visual cortical cells can be stimulated by a similar line or edge shown to either eye held the key to the explanation of rivalry and stereoscopic fusion.

We found that many of the binocular cells in the cat visual cortex are selectively sensitive to the retinal disparity of stimuli and the preferred disparity *varies* from cell to cell, thus providing a neural mechanism for binocular depth discrimination. I went on to examine how cortical cells with similar properties are clustered together locally. I also did work on the mechanisms of binocular vision in the very center of the visual field, where the projection of nerve fibers from the two halves of each retina to different sides of the brain poses particular problems for the combination of information from the two eyes in stereoscopic vision.

Parallel with these interests, I had started work in the late 1960s on the development of the visual system. I thought that it might be possible to reveal the "columns" of orientation-selective neurons in the striate cortex, described by Hubel and Wiesel, by rearing kittens so that they would see only lines of a single orientation. My expectation was that those columns of cells that had not been properly stimulated early in life might undergo cell shrinkage or other degenerative changes that could be seen through the microscope. So, I kept kittens in the dark except for daily periods of exposure in a striped environment, where they could see only lines of one orientation. And to our amazement, we found that the population of cortical neurons had become highly biased as a result of this unusual visual experience, so that very few cells responded to orientations that the animal had not seen when it was young.

For the past few years, I have been concentrating on the development of the primate visual system, partly working in collaboration with François Vital-Durand. Our latest work has concentrated on the neural mechanisms for spatial resolution (visual acuity). We have shown that these mechanisms take a long time (up to two years in the monkey) to mature after birth. Interference with the normal use of the two eyes, for instance through deprivation of vision in one eye, can lead to a failure of normal development of visual acuity in that eye. We have shown that this defect is due specifically to a failure of development in the input of information to the visual cortex.

I think that the study of development is fascinating and important for several reasons. First, it obviously has its own inherent interest; second, it gives insight into clinical problems of development in human beings; and finally the study of how a biological system develops may help us to understand how it functions in its adult form.

PERCEPTION   **121**

Because distant objects produce a smaller image on the retina than do objects that are closer, skyscrapers in the background appear to be farther away than the monuments in this cemetery. (Marc P. Andersen)

This allows the brain to search easily for differences between the visual information coming from each eye and to use those differences to generate the sensation of depth.

Two eyes are necessary for true depth perception, yet we can easily perceive depth with one eye closed, and, of course, artists can paint pictures on a flat canvas that produce a surprising sensation of depth. Therefore, there must be cues for depth perception other than binocular disparity. There are several such cues and they are generally called *monocular depth cues*.

MONOCULAR DEPTH CUES

The first of these cues, called *relative size,* is based on the fact that distant objects produce a smaller image on the retina than do objects that are closer. We use change in relative size to judge depth. Closely related to the idea of relative size are the familiar converging lines of railroad tracks or other parallel lines extending to the horizon. Although the tracks stay the same distance apart, they appear to converge, and this apparent convergence yields a perception of great distance. This is known as a *perspective cue* for depth perception.

The use of perspective cues and relative size cues to produce the sensation of three dimensions from a two-dimensional picture is shown in Figure 4.11. The three men appear to be different sizes; what misleads us is that the room has a tilted floor. The men are actually about the same height.

Other important monocular depth cues are the *texture gradients* that are seen when we look at near and far objects. Suppose that you are looking across a large expanse of grass in a park. In the part of the lawn that is close

Figure 4.11
An Ames Room. The men in this photograph are all about equal height. However, this room has been designed to produce erroneous perspective cues. The back wall of the room on the left is much farther away than it is on the right. Further, the floor is tilted. As a result, the man on the right is standing much closer to the camera than the other two, hence he appears to be much taller. With normal perspective cues, the man on the left would simply appear to be farther away than the smaller. (William Vandivert)

Figure 4.12 Texture gradients produce the sensation of depth. The people in the lower part of the picture appear to be much larger and detailed than those farther up. We interpret this difference in texture as indicating that the larger ones are closer and the smaller ones are far away. (Marc. P. Andersen)

to you, each blade of grass is visible. Farther away, only a general impression of blades of grass can be seen; still farther, the lawn is simply varying shades of smooth green. Changes in texture gradients as cues for depth are shown in Figure 4.12. In Figure 4.13 we can see how an abrupt change in texture can produce the sensation of a corner or even a cliff.

Figure 4.13
Changes in texture of the visual scene can produce the sensation of depth. On the right is the change in texture that might be produced by the intersection of two surfaces at right angles, such as a floor and wall. In the lower part of the figure is the change in texture that might be produced by viewing the edge of a cliff. (Adapted from Coren, Porac, & Ward, 1984)

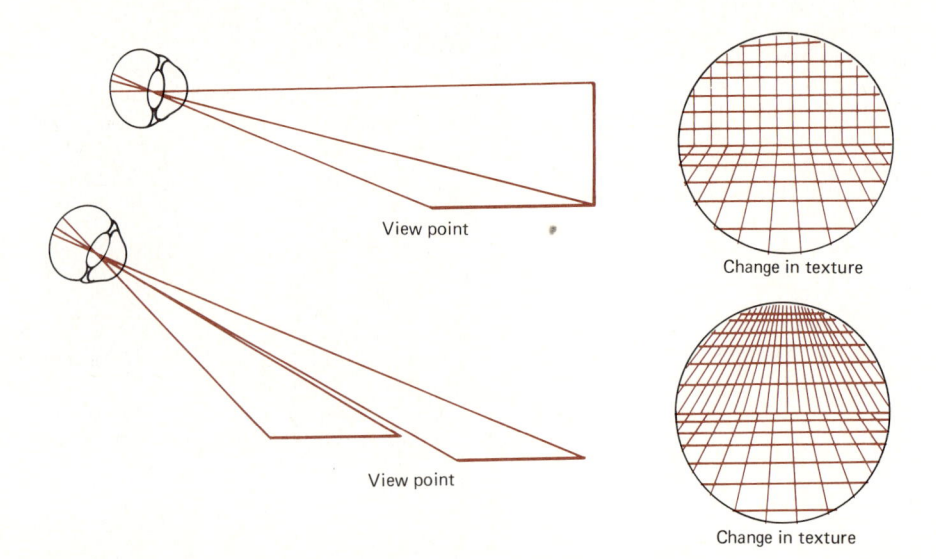

VISUAL ILLUSIONS

The principles of perception that we have illustrated so far are used to form an accurate representation of the external world from the neural messages generated by sensory stimuli. Occasionally, however, our perceptual systems will draw erroneous conclusions from sensory messages. When such an error occurs we refer to the mistaken perception as an *illusion*. Often illusions occur because of the inappropriate application of perceptual principles. We already saw that the moon viewed through a frame of moving clouds appears to be moving across the heavens. This is because the moving clouds are perceived as being a stationary frame of reference.

The same sort of error occurs in the well-known Ponzo illusion shown in Figure 4.14. In this case the upper of the two horizontal bars appears to be longer than the lower one. However, if you measure them you will find that they are exactly the same length. Why should one appear to be longer than the other? The illusion results from the frame of reference provided by the two converging lines at the side. The converging lines are interpreted as perspective cues, and therefore they make the upper bar appear farther away, so that it is perceived as being larger.

A good illustration of how the Ponzo illusion works can be seen in the photograph in Figure 4.15. The converging handrails provide a perspective cue of distance because we know from experience that they are always the same distance apart. Therefore, the bar superimposed between the handrails in the lower part of the picture will be perceived as being smaller than one of the same length superimposed on the upper part of the photograph. Indeed, if the bars were real objects lying between the handrails, we would be correct in judging the upper one to be larger.

Other illusions are produced by similar inappropriate applications of perceptual principles. You may have noticed that when the moon or sun is rising

Figure 4.14
The Ponzo illusion. The two horizontal bars, which are actually of equal length, seem to be of unequal size with the upper one appearing to be longer than the lower one. This effect is produced by perspective cues, which make the top bar appear to be farther away than the lower one and therefore larger.

Figure 4.15
Although bars A and B are actually the same size, B appears to be much bigger because of the context in which it is seen. This interpretation of perspective cues provides an explanation of the Ponzo illusion seen in Figure 4.14. (Photo courtesy James D. Anker)

or setting, that is, near the horizon, it appears to be much larger than when it is high in the sky. People have attributed this effect to magnification by the earth's atmosphere and to differences in head position when viewing the sun or moon. Actually, their images as projected on the retina never vary in size. Then why do the sun and the moon look so much larger at the horizon?

The answer is not completely straightforward, but the main reason seems to be that the horizon is erroneously perceived as being much farther away than is the sky directly overhead. In other words, the sky looks like a flattened dome. The perceptual system, however, compensates for differences in apparent distance, and therefore the moon or the sun is perceived as being much larger when it is near the horizon because it is perceived as being farther away. In experimental tests of this hypothesis (Kaufman & Rock, 1962), subjects observed an artificial moon through optical devices that controlled the appearance of a horizon. These subjects reported that the moon appeared to be larger when the horizon appeared to be farther away.

Other illusions result when perspective cues are ambiguous, such as the impossible figure shown in Figure 4.17 and the *reversible figures* shown in Figure 4.18. In Figure 4.19 you can see how context can influence the perception of length and alter the appearance of parallel lines.

What are we to conclude? Is seeing really believing? How many of our impressions of the world are illusory, and how many are accurate? Illusions occur in all sensory systems (remember that the pencil point felt cold in some places when you touched the back of your hand with it when you were reading Chapter 3), and when they occur they remind us of just how complex and automatic our perceptual processes really are. Far from being examples of abnormal perception, illusions provide information about the principles that underlie normal, accurate perceptual processes. They demonstrate that perception is the result of many kinds of information and several different organizing principles all acting together to try to present an accurate picture of the outside world to the consciousness.

Figure 4.16 The moon illusion. In the drawing at the left, the moon is near the horizon, and the depth cues indicate to the visual system that the moon is far away. The perceptual system takes this into account, and as a result, the moon appears to be large. On the right, the moon has risen and is more overhead, depth cues are less prominent, and the apparent distance away seems to be less. Therefore the moon is perceived as being smaller.

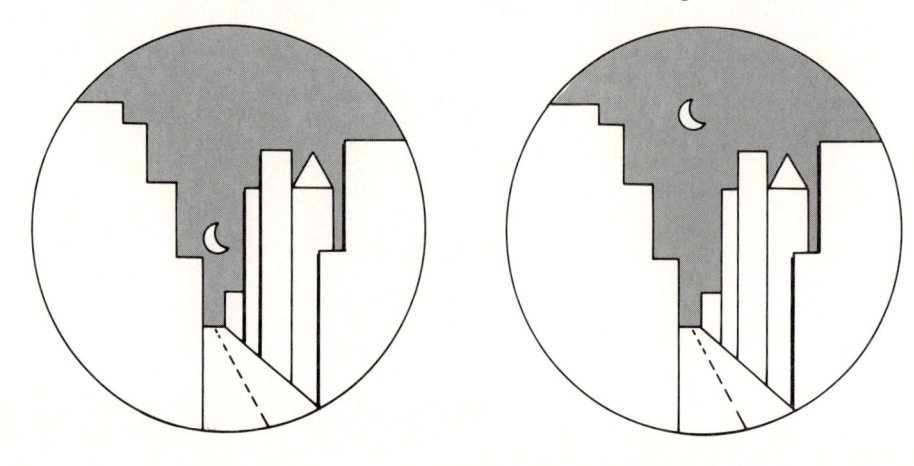

PERCEPTION   **125**

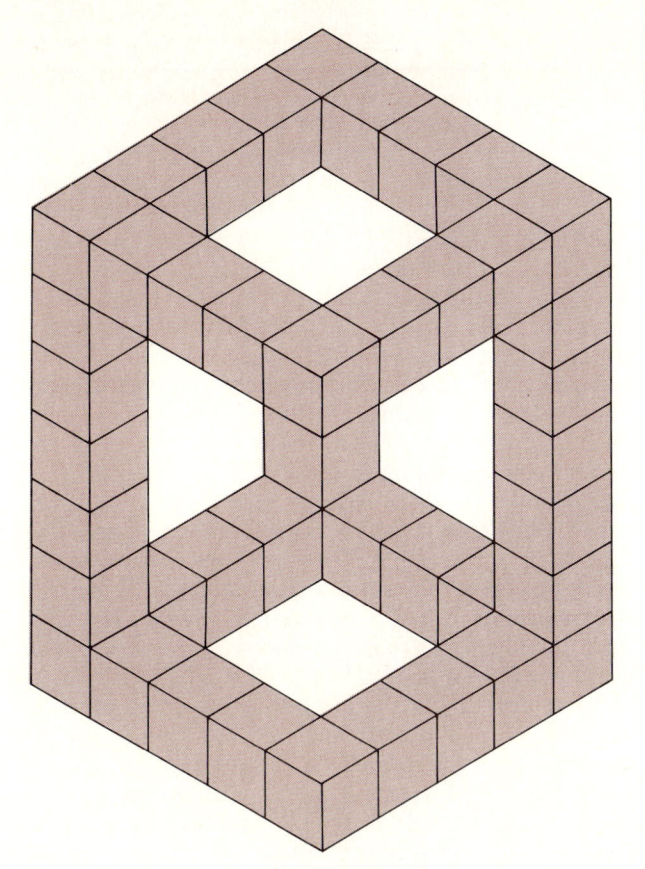

Figure 4.17 On the left an impossible figure. This drawing is difficult to interpret because the perspective cues conflict with one another. The top half of the figure and the bottom half are correct by themselves, but when combined, they produce confusion.

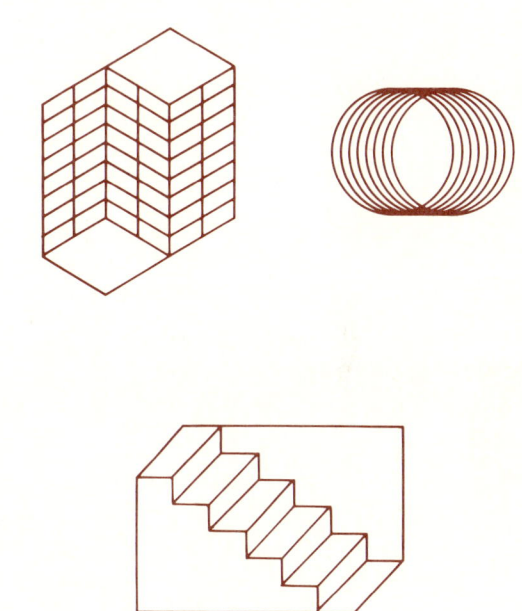

Figure 4.18
A series of reversible figures. Each of these drawings uses perspective cues ambiguously so that the figures can be viewed in two different ways. The figures appear to shift from one configuration to the other, and it is difficult to see both at the same time.

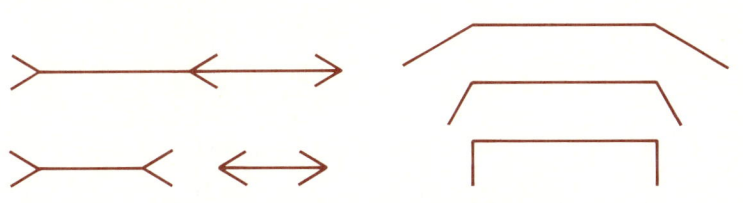

The Müller-Lyer illusion   Angles affect the apparent length of lines

Figure 4.19 Influences on the apparent length of lines. The left portion of this figure shows the famous Müller-Lyer illusion. The horizontal lines on the left appear to be considerably longer than their counterparts on the right. In the right portion of the figure, there are three lines of equal length, but the greater the angle, the greater the apparent elongation of the horizontal lines.

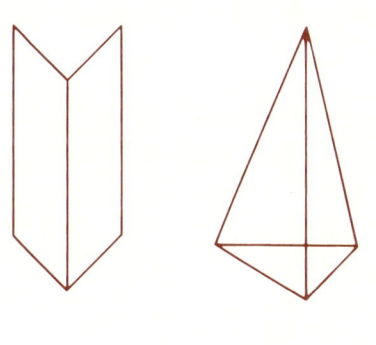

THE PERCEPTION OF COLOR

As we noted earlier, the human eye responds to light of wavelengths that lie roughly between 400 and 750 nm. We give names to light of different wavelengths or frequencies. We call them colors, but colors do not exist as actual entities. What does exist is electromagnetic energy of different wavelengths. When light of a certain wavelength, say 730 nm, strikes the retina, the visual system responds by interpreting that stimulus as "red."

If you have ever looked at the little color chips that display the array of colors available in a paint shop, you can begin to appreciate the complexity and diversity inherent in the perception of color. Because of this complexity we need special terms that allow us to describe precisely the sensation of color. We can classify colors according to three distinct characteristics: hue, brightness, and saturation. All the thousands and thousands of different colors that we can perceive can be scaled according to these three dimensions.

Hue is the psychological term for the dimension of color that most closely corresponds to differences in wavelength. Hue is not a property of the *achromatic colors,* that is, white, gray, and black, but is characteristic of *chromatic colors* such as orange, green, or yellow. Pure monochromatic colors are the sensations produced by light of only a single wavelength. Such colors are similar to those found in a spectrum of colors produced by passing white light through a prism or in light from a laser.

Unique yellow, that is, a yellow that does not appear to contain any red or green, is light with a wavelength of approximately 580 nm. Unique green, which does not seem to contain any blue or yellow, is light of 515 nm, and unique blue, which contains no red or green, has a wavelength of around 475 nm. Interestingly, unique red, a shade of red that does not appear to contain any yellow or blue, is actually a mixture of light of several different wavelengths.

In the color circle shown in Figure 4.20 (see color insert), the four unique colors, red, yellow, green, and blue, are spaced 90 degrees apart with unique red at the top. Some colors are perceived to be more similar than others, so the color circle is organized in that way. For example, orange seems to lie somewhere between red and yellow, while green seems to be more like blue and yellow than red. Further, we cannot generate all the different hues simply with monochromatic light of different frequencies. The sensation of the hue of purple, for example, requires the presence of light with both blue and red wavelengths.

A second dimension of color is called *saturation.* This term refers to the purity of a color, or how much of a given hue is present. Pure colors of a single wavelength are highly saturated, but as other wavelengths are added, the color will appear to be more and more washed out. As white light, which contains many different wavelengths, is added to a given hue, the hue becomes less saturated. The dimension of the degree of saturation of a color can be added to our color circle (see Figure 4.21) so that both hue and saturation can be visualized. Taking the hue of red as an example, we can start with white light at the center of the color circle and see that pink is simply a relatively unsaturated red; that is, pink contains a good deal of white light in addition to light of the frequencies that we know as red. The color crimson is somewhat more saturated than the color pink, so crimson is shown farther from white and nearer the color red on the color circle.

The third and final dimension of color is *brightness:* the impression we

PERCEPTION

Figure 4.21
A color circle. The various hues are shown on the outside of the circle, and the dimension of saturation is shown on the red axis. At the edge of the color circle is pure or saturated red. As one moves inward toward the center, some white (which consists of all wavelengths) is added to red, and the color crimson results. Still more white added to crimson yields pink. The degree that a spectral hue is diluted by white light determines the saturation of that color.

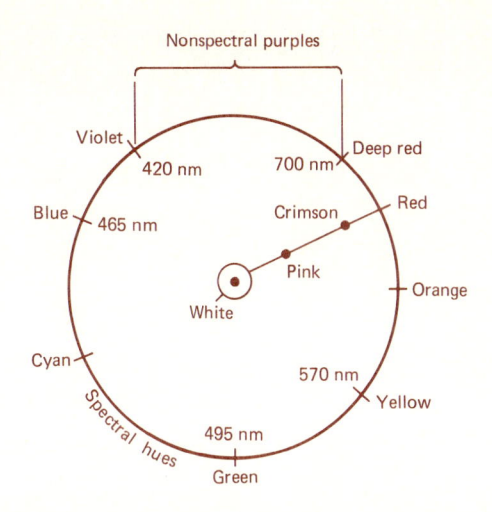

have of the intensity of a visual stimulus. For example, light green appears to be brighter than forest green, maroon darker than red, and some grays appear brighter than others. Indeed, the dimension of brightness is best understood using achromatic stimuli, stimuli that do not have the dimension of hue. These achromatic stimuli differ only in brightness. Black has no brightness, dark gray has some, lighter grays have even more, and white is maximally bright. This dimension of the visual experience is illustrated in Figure 4.22. The same principles hold true for colors. Gold is seen as a darker color than yellow, and sky blue is seen as a brighter color than navy blue.

To represent all three dimensions of color—hue, saturation, and brightness—using the scheme of the color circle, one would need to construct a three-dimensional *color solid* (see Figure 4.23). The tapered shape of this solid becomes evident if we consider the fact that at very high or very low levels of brightness, colors appear to be weak, meaning that they are of low saturation. Hence at extremes of brightness, the saturation dimension will become smaller, causing the diameter of the color circle to shrink. Therefore, our color solid will have the appearance of two cones placed with their bases in contact. If we mentally slice through the color solid at any level of brightness, we would get a color circle with the totally saturated colors represented along the perimeter and achromatic colors (totally unsaturated) represented along the central core. This is shown in Figure 4.23 (see color insert).

This is not all there is to color. Some colors are mixtures of several different hues. We saw in Chapter 3 that a prism can separate white light into a spectrum of colors; in fact, that is a definition of white light: the presence of electromagnetic energy of all wavelengths in the visible range. Then why, when you color a piece of paper with all the crayons in the box, does the resultant mess appear to be black rather than white? To answer this question, we must first consider what makes a given object appear to be of a given color, and then we must distinguish between additive color mixtures and subtractive color mixtures.

Why does a red car sitting in the sunlight appear red? It looks red because different wavelengths which make up the white sunlight are selectively absorbed and reflected by the pigments in the paint. In this case, the paint absorbs light of all wavelengths except those of red, which it reflects. Hence the light that reaches the eye is of long wavelengths (the shorter wavelengths of light have been absorbed) and the car is perceived as red.

Figure 4.22
The dimension of brightness. Colors can also be classified according to their brightness. The dimension of brightness can be most clearly seen in a series of grays. Gray is hueless and varies from white to black only on the dimension of brightness.

Now suppose that we are mixing paints using a pigment that absorbs light of all wavelengths except those in a fairly wide blue range (400 to 550 nm). Light of these wavelengths are reflected by the paint. Therefore, any object coated with this paint will appear to be blue. Now we mix in a second pigment. This pigment by itself reflects light in the range 500 to 600 nm; all other wavelengths are absorbed. Because of these absorbent and reflective characteristics, paint made with this pigment will appear to be yellow. When the two pigment are mixed together, light of almost all wavelengths will be absorbed, and only light of a very limited range of wavelengths (500 to 550 nm) will be reflected. We know that these wavelengths are green. Thus an object painted with a mixture of these two pigments appears to be green because light of all other wavelengths has been subtracted out. This is called a *subtractive color mixture* and is shown diagrammatically in Figure 4.24 (see color insert). If we were to mix in a third pigment that absorbs green light, the resultant mixture will appear to be black. This is what happens when one colors paper with all the crayons in the box.

In a subtractive color mixture, the wavelength of the color stimulus is determined before light reaches the eye. In *additive color mixtures,* several different wavelengths of light stimulate the eye simultaneously. Look at the colored checkerboard pattern in Figure 4.25 (see color insert). The red squares reflect light of a longer wavelength than that reflected by the green squares. Now prop up your book and walk back across the room until you can no longer see the individual squares. What appeared to be an array of red and green squares now appears to be yellow. Note that this additive color mixture matches the color in the square to the right.

What happens in this demonstration is that the images of the individual squares of the checkerboard can no longer be resolved. The image is blurred across the retina yielding a mixture of wavelengths that are interpreted as yellow. A color television set works in a similar way. If you take a magnifying glass and look at the screen, you will see that there are many tiny dots of red, green, and blue. When you sit at a normal viewing distance you can no longer see the individual dots, and mixtures of these colors yield the wide variety of colors that you see on your screen.

In so very many ways, the perception of color adds a meaningful and important aesthetic quality to our lives. Interesting and distinctive people or events are thought of as "colorful." Colors influence our moods and feelings. Some colors seem to make us feel calm and relaxed, whereas others cause us to feel tense and irritable. Colors also seem to cross into other sensory domains, such as temperature. Some colors, those of the longer wavelengths, are thought of as warm colors, while the shorter wavelength greens and blues are typically seen as being somehow cooler. The important message of this section on color vision is that the perception of color is the result of psychological processes, not the result of an intrinsic property of colorful objects.

THE DEVELOPMENT AND MODIFICATION OF PERCEPTION

Now that we have explored a few principles of perception, we need to address a question that has concerned psychologists for many years: Are these principles inborn, or are they learned through experience? Experiments address-

PERCEPTION

Figure 4.26
The visual cliff. This youngster is investigating a visual cliff. Even though there is a strong sheet of glass extending from the cliff, he stays back from the edge, indicating that even at a young age, perspective cues for depth are understood and utilized.

ing this question are difficult because the number of responses that a very young child can make is very limited. Nevertheless, researchers have developed ingenious methods for measuring whether infants as young as 6 months of age can respond to depth cues.

The *visual cliff* apparatus (Figure 4.26) is one effective way to do this. The drop-off, which is covered by a sheet of clear glass, is perceived by adults because of the change of texture, perspective, and binocular disparity. The question to be answered through experiments with the visual cliff was whether infants would respond to these cues. When the experiments were performed, the evidence was quite clear. Very few infants crawled onto the sheet of glass over the cliff even when called to by their mothers. Indeed, most young animals, including lambs, rats, gerbils, and day-old chicks, stay on the "shallow side" of the visual cliff. These results suggest that the use of depth cues is probaby innate and does not have to be learned.

Even in children only a few days old, the visual system seems to be working to extract features from the environment. Although their eyes cannot alter focus and can form a sharp image only for objects about $\frac{1}{2}$ m away, newborns show a preference for forms that resemble a human face rather than those that are a random jumble of features (see Figure 4.27).

Further, in studies of eye movements, when an infant is presented with sample forms, its eyes orient toward various features of the pattern rather than moving randomly across the visual field. Again, this suggests that the visual system, even in very young infants, is actively processing visual information and attempting to extract some sort of meaning from sensation.

Now suppose that an infant or an experimental animal were not allowed any visual stimulation during early life and then after some years or, in the case of laboratory animals, months, vision was permitted. Would normal vision develop? In studies of human beings who have had years of blindness from birth and then had sight restored, the evidence is inconclusive. Some people show fairly effective visual perception, whereas others have great difficulty recognizing forms through vision alone.

In experimental animals the results are more clear cut. Visual experience in which the animal attends to stimuli is essential for development of normal visual perception. In one classic study, pairs of kittens were raised in the dark for 8 weeks and were then allowed daily 3-hour periods of exposure to visual stimuli. One kitten in each pair was placed in a small gondola, part of a sort of kitty carousel, which was mechanically connected to a harness placed around the other kitten, as shown in Figure 4.28. In this way one of the kittens in each experimental group could walk around freely within the visual field and learn how its movements affected the visual input, while the other kitten received essentially the same visual stimulation but did not actively interact with the visual environment.

Figure 4.27
Two arrangements of the components of a face. Stimuli similar to these were used to test the reactions of infants to faces. Newborn children showed a distinct preference for stimuli that resemble human faces. This indicates that even at a very young age the visual system attempts to identify features in visual stimuli (Fantz, 1961).

Figure 4.28
The effect of active and passive movements were compared in this sort of apparatus. One kitten was allowed to walk about more or less freely so that it could learn to relate visual events to behavior. The passive kitten was carried in a small gondola. Linkage provided by the chain and bar enabled the passive kitten to receive essentially the same visual stimulation as the active kitten. The passive kitten did not have the opportunity to associate its behavior with vision. When the kittens were tested, researchers found that the kittens that rode passively in the apparatus failed to develop normal sensory–motor coordination compared to the active kittens. (Based on "Plasticity in Sensory-Motor Systems" by R. Held. *Scientific American*, November 1965. Copyright ©1965 by Scientific American, Inc. All rights reserved.)

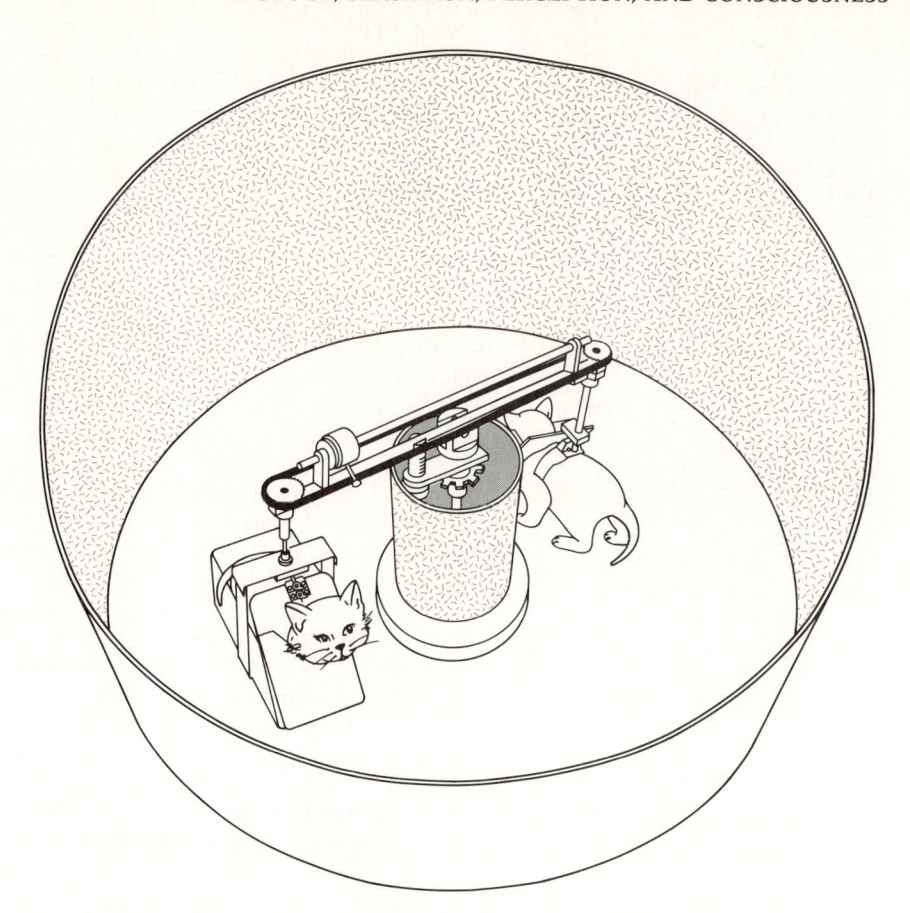

The kittens spent 30 hours in the carousel over 10 days, and this was their only visual experience. Those kittens who had the opportunity to move about freely showed the development of depth discrimination with normal behavior in a visual cliff test, whereas the passive kittens who did not have an opportunity to behave in response to visual stimulation were quite retarded. Held and Hein (1963) concluded that "self-produced movement with its concurrent visual feedback is necessary for the development of visually guided behavior."

However, more recent work suggests that attention rather than self-produced movement may be the critical factor. In an experiment conducted by Walk, Sheperd, and Miller (1978), kittens raised in the dark were placed in the situation shown in Figure 4.29. The only visual experiences they had was watching small cars speed around a track. The kittens were not allowed to move about and learn about the visual consequences of their own movements, yet their performance on tests of visual discrimination was as good as that of kittens given visual stimulation under the active locomotive conditions described above. These results indicate that attention to visual stimuli rather than self-induced movement may be the critical factor in the development of visual perception.

Just how modifiable are the processes of visual perception? Can adult human beings learn to adapt to an altered perceptual world? George Stratton (1865–1957) tried such an experiment over 80 years ago. He developed and wore for more than a week a set of optical prisms fashioned into glasses that

PERCEPTION

Figure 4.29
Attention influences the development of perception. In this study, the kittens watched toy automobiles move around a track. This experience, which generated a good deal of attention, promoted fairly normal perceptual development compared to kittens that did not receive such exposure. (Based on Walk, Shepherd, and Miller, 1978)

turned his entire visual scene upside down and inverted it left to right. When he first put on the prisms he had serious difficulties getting about or even performing simple tasks. He would reach down to get an object that was up and turn right when he should have turned left. But after 8 days he had adjusted to his turned-about world to such an extent that he no longer had any difficulty with motor tasks and further, the world as he looked at it did not appear to be upside down. Indeed, when he removed the prisms, he suffered aftereffects from having successfully adapted to an inverted world. Normal vision seemed strange, and he had to relearn how to perform some motor tasks.

Stratton adapted to an altered visual world, but it is unclear whether he came to see it as normal. However, the change produced by the prisms that he wore was very large. Research with optical devices that produce less severe changes in the visual stimulus than complete inversion suggests that at least some effects are truly perceptual and that the optically altered world is seen as normal. Subjects wearing glasses that cause the visual field to be tilted approximately 20 degrees adapt so completely to the tilt after several hours that they do not notice it at all. Indeed, when the prisms are removed, these subjects behave as if the normal world were tilted 20 degrees in a direction opposite to that produced by the prisms.

EXTRASENSORY PERCEPTION

Do you believe that perceptions can occur without the involvement of sensory systems, or through sensory systems not yet discovered by physiologists and psychologists? Do you think that people can transmit their thoughts or cause events to occur simply through mind power? Many people do believe in just such ideas. But is there evidence that supports the existence of such phenomena as telepathy, precognition, or psychokinesis?

PARAPSYCHOLOGY

The term used to describe organized research into paranormal or psychic phenomena is *parapsychology*. This kind of research is typically divided into two major divisions. The first is the study of perceptions or cognitions that seem to occur independent of any known sensory receptor systems. Known as *extrasensory perception* (ESP), these perceptions generally include three kinds of phenomena. The first is known as *clairvoyance* or "second sight." In clairvoyance, a person obtains information about another person, event, or even some object with no apparent sensory means of getting that information. Related to clairvoyance is *telepathy*, in which a person learns about the thoughts of another person, again with no apparent means of communication other than "mind reading." A third major kind of ESP is called *precognition*. In this case, a person is said to have knowledge about events yet to take place, that is, knowledge about the future.

Research into ESP is generally viewed by the scientific community as being disreputable. Too often, scientists investigating these phenomena have been duped or misled by clever charlatans. Further, much parapsychological research has been conducted without adequate or appropriate controls and analyzed with dubious statistical procedures. Yet belief in the paranormal and in ESP persist. Let us examine some of the research evidence.

STUDIES OF TELEPATHY AND CLAIRVOYANCE

Many early scientific studies of ESP were performed by Rhine and his associates using a card-guessing procedure (Rhine, 1942). A deck of 25 cards imprinted with five different symbols was used. In a typical experiment, the cards are shuffled and arranged so that their faces are not visible to the subject. In a telepathy study, the experimenter then looks at each card one at a time and tries to transmit a message about the identity of the card to the subject. In a clairvoyance experiment, the experimenter does not look at the cards and attempt to transmit a message. The subject is required to guess which of the five symbols is on each card. Simply by chance, a subject should guess about 5 cards out of the 25 correctly, and this is what happens with most subjects. However, some subjects do seem to be able to score better than chance. One woman who was studied over a number of years with a large number of tests averaged 6.8 correct guesses per 25 cards (Soal & Bateman, 1954). Although an average of 6.8 correct out of 25 does not seem to be particularly impressive, this finding is statistically highly significant; that is, such an outcome is very unlikely to be due to chance factors alone. Other studies in which subjects are asked to guess which of four lights, which are turned on in random order, will be illuminated next have produced similar results in some subjects. In one study, over 5,000 trials were given to each of two subjects; one subject scored 1.3% above chance level and the other about 2.2% above chance (Schmidt, 1969).

DIFFICULTIES WITH ESP RESEARCH

Findings such as these are not strong enough to convince many skeptics. They point out that the idea of chance expectations is frequently misunderstood. On the average when you flip a coin you will expect that it will land about 50% of the time heads and about 50% of the time tails. That is the chance expectation. Does this mean that if you flip the coin six times you will always get three heads and three tails? No. This will simply be the most frequent outcomes. Rarely, but inevitably, if you flip the coin enough times, you will get six heads in a row and also six tails. The huge number of trials that have been used in some parapsychological research in order to achieve statistical significance limits the effectiveness of these studies in convincing the scientific community of the validity of the findings. In one study, a very "sensitive" subject was given 1,600 trials and was correct on 917 of them, when the chance level of performance was 800 (Pratt & Blom, 1964). Is this sufficiently strong evidence to demonstrate conclusively the reality of ESP phenomena? Many do not think so.

Further compounding the difficulties with ESP research is a general realization that it is often difficult to reproduce the results. To be accepted scientifically, a phenomenon should be reproducible in any laboratory when the same experimental methods are used. However, very often parapsychological researchers have great difficulty in replicating experiments in their own laboratories, let alone in other labs. Further, many claims of ESP and other psychic phenomena have been shown to be fraudulent, while some experiments have had serious methodological flaws. These problems—namely, the apparent inability of ESP researchers to generate consistent and reliable data—lead many scientists to reject the whole area of investigation.

The question of the existence of ESP does not go away, though. There are researchers in the field of parapsychology who are convinced that we are on the threshold of learning about unknown properties of the mind and consciousness and that important advances are soon to come. Others remain skeptical, although willing to listen to new evidence. In any case, parapsychology and ESP research are currently disciplines without a mechanism to explain an elusive phenomenon. The effects are highly implausible, and until better evidence is found that systematically relates paranormal phenomena to accepted biological and psychological mechanisms, we must remain doubtful (Hansel, 1980; Marks & Kammann, 1980).

SUMMARY

1. When psychologists use the term "sensation," they are referring to the neurobiological operation of sensory systems. The term "perception," on the other hand, refers to the relationship between sensory stimuli and the cognitive processes that organize and interpret them. Perception is much more than the registration of sensory events; it is a complex, high-level cognitive activity.

2. One task of perceptual systems is to maintain the perception of a stable world in the face of changing stimulation. Shape and size constancies are perceptual processes that allow objects to be perceived as remaining the same despite differing retinal images. Location constancy helps us keep the objects we see in their appropriate locations despite movements on the retina. Color constancy is the process by which objects are seen to be of one color despite differences in illumination.

3. The minimal amount of stimulus energy that can be detected is called the absolute threshold for that kind of sensory event. The method of limits or the method of constant stimuli are sometimes used to determine absolute thresholds. Thresholds, however, vary with testing conditions and signal-detection theory suggests that observers must make distinctions between a stimulus to be detected (the signal) and random background activity (noise). Using the principles of signal-detection theory, researchers can control for such factors as expectancy and response biases, and these methods are currently among the most accurate ways of determining a person's sensitivity to a particular stimulus.

4. A difference threshold is the smallest amount of change in a stimulus that can be detected 50% of the time—a just noticeable difference. In general, the size of a difference threshold is proportional to the intensity of the stimulus, a principle known as Weber's law. Further, the strength of a perceived sensation increases as the logarithm of the intensity of a stimulus (Fechner's law). The use of logarithmic rather than linear scales by sensory systems enables the nervous system to respond to a wider range of intensities of stimulation.

5. Most sensory systems respond best to changes in stimuli and stop responding (adaptation) when stimuli are constant.

6. There are a number of interpretative process that help us understand sensory stimuli. Past experience helps us interpret ambiguous stimuli. The separation of figure from ground helps us impose meaning on a visual sensation, as does the grouping of elements in a visual stimulus.

7. The Gestalt principles of perceptual organization also help add meaning to sensory events. The Gestalt principle of closure is the process of mentally filling in missing pieces of a stimulus. Continuity is the tendency to perceive stimulus elements as continuing on their course. The principle of proximity refers to our tendency to perceive objects that are close together in some way as belonging together, and the principle of similarity is our tendency to group stimuli that are alike on one or more dimensions.

8. Some of the cues for the perception of movement come from changes in the shape, form, and perspective of the moving object as well as changes in the relationship between the object and a stationary background. The apparent movement of the images on a motion picture screen are the result of stroboscopic movement.

9. The perception of depth by the visual system is a result of the slight difference in the view received by each eye (binocular disparity), and monocular depth cues such as relative size, perspective cues, and texture gradients. Together these cues are used by the central nervous system to produce the sensation of three-dimensional space.

10. Hue is the psychological term for the dimension of color that closely corresponds to the physical dimension of wavelength of light. Saturation refers to the purity of a given color, and brightness is the impression of intensity of a color. These three dimensions of color can be visualized using a color solid.

11. An object appears to be of a certain color because its pigments absorb some wavelengths and reflect others. The reflected wavelengths determine the perceived color of the object; the others are absorbed, that is, subtracted out. In additive color mixtures several different wavelengths of light stimulate the eye simultaneously, yielding a mixture of wavelengths that are perceived as being of a certain color.

12. The question of whether perceptual mechanisms are innate or learned can be studied using techniques such as the visual cliff. These studies indicate that the use of depth cues is probably innate, as is the preference for forms that resemble faces. Research using experimental animals suggests that visual experience is important for the proper maturation of the visual system.

13. Although many people believe in the phenomena of extrasensory perception, such as clairvoyance, telepathy, and precognition, there is very little scientific evidence for their existence.

KEY TERMS

Sensation
Perception
Absolute threshold
Method of limits
Method of constant stimuli
Signal-detection theory
Signal
Noise
Response bias
Receiver operating characteristic curve
Difference threshold
Just noticeable difference
Weber's law
Weber fraction

Fechner's law
Sensory adaptation
Figure
Ground
Reversible figure
Gestalt psychology
Closure
Continuity
Proximity
Similarity
Stroboscopic movement
Apparent movement
Phi phenomenon
Frame of reference
Binocular disparity
Monocular depth cues
Relative size

Perspective
Texture gradient
Hue
Achromatic color
Chromatic color
Saturation
Brightness
Color solid
Subtractive color mixture
Additive color mixture
Visual cliff
Parapsychology
Clairvoyance
Telepathy
Precognition

SUGGESTED READINGS

COREN, S., PORAC, C., & WARD, L. M. *Sensation and perception* (2nd ed.). Orlando, Fla.: Academic Press, 1984. An excellent comprehensive textbook that deals with many aspects of perception. The many demonstrations that illustrate important perceptual principles make this book both valuable and interesting.

CORNSWEET, T. N. *Sensation and perception.* Belmont, Calif.: Wadsworth, 1980. A more technical treatment of the field of perception written by one of the leading researchers in the field. Visual processes are emphasized.

LINDSAY, P. H., & NORMAN, D. A. *Human information processing.* New York: Academic Press, 1977. Although this book has some of the features of an introductory psychology textbook, its major emphasis is perception and the cognitive processing of sensory and verbal information. In many ways a definitive book.

LUCKIESH, M. *Visual illusions.* New York: Dover, 1965. Originally published in 1922 this book has become a classic of sorts. It is still one of the very best introductions to the field of visual illusions. Although clearly a product of its times, this book is well worth looking into.

SPOEHR, K. T., & LEHMKUHLE, S. W. *Visual information processing.* San Francisco: W. H. Freeman, 1982. A clear, readable introduction to the view that perception is a cognitive process. A wide range of topics is covered that are not usually discussed in more conventional perception books.

5

Consciousness

BODILY RHYTHMS
   Circadian Rhythms
SLEEP
A TYPICAL NIGHT'S SLEEP
   Techniques of Sleep Research
   States of Sleep
   REM Sleep (Active Sleep)
   Sleep Patterns from Infancy
      Through Adulthood
   How Much Sleep Is Normal
SLEEP AND DREAMING
   Who Dreams and When
   Eye Movements and Dreams
   Other Aspects of REM Sleep
   Nightmares and Other Bad
      Dreams
PATHOLOGIES OF SLEEP
   Insomnia
   Sleeping Pills
   Narcolepsy

   Sleepwalking
HYPNOSIS
   Entering the Hypnotic State
   Characteristics of Hypnosis
   Clinical Uses of Hypnosis
DRUGS
   Who Takes Drugs
   Types of Psychoactive Drugs
   Sedative-Hypnotic Drugs and
      CNS Depressants
   Behavioral Stimulants
   Opiates and Narcotics
   Psychedelics and
      Hallucinogens
   Marijuana
MEDITATION
SUMMARY
KEY TERMS
SUGGESTED READINGS

BODILY RHYTHMS

Our world is constantly changing, and many of these changes are cyclical; there are rhythms of change affecting the earth as well as living organisms. Many changes occur in predictable cycles, although some cycles of change are very slow and difficult to detect, except through geological evidence, such as the rise and fall of continental ice sheets during periods of glaciation. More rapid cycles include the changes of the seasons due to the rotation of the earth around the sun. Still faster are the day-night cycles, the ebb and flow of the tides, and the regular vibrations of crystals and atomic particles.

   Our bodies and behavior also show rhythms and predictable cycles. Some rhythms are quite long, such as the monthly hormonal cycles in females. Others are daily and best exemplified by patterns of waking and sleeping. Breathing and heartbeat are also rhythmic processes.

Within most living organisms, including human beings, biological clocks regulate many internal and behavioral functions, ranging from reproductive patterns, through sleep and waking cycles, to heart rate, gastrointestinal contractions, and a host of other processes.

Changes in the activity of some sea creatures are linked to the rhythms of the tides. These changes continue to occur with the tidal cycles even if the animal is placed in an aquarium, indicating that these rhythms are internally generated and not a direct response to changes in water level.

CIRCADIAN RHYTHMS

Of particular interest to psychologists are the rhythmic changes that recur on a daily basis. Changes that occur on a 24-hour cycle are called *circadian rhythms*, from the Latin for "around the day." Circadian rhythms take many forms besides waking and sleeping. Blood sugar levels, hormone concentrations, body temperature, states of awareness, and changes in mood all show circadian cycles.

As with many other rhythms, circadian rhythms are internally generated and can be independent of day-night cycles. Laboratory animals housed in constant environments or human beings who spend long periods in artificial environments with no periodic changes in illumination still show bodily rhythms, most of which have a period between 24 and 25 hours. These daily rhythms even persist in experiments in which researchers spend several months deep in a cave, where external influences are held to a minimum (Kleitman, 1963). Evidence from studies such as these indicates that circadian rhythms are caused by the nervous system and that they do not occur solely in response to environmental changes. Circadian rhythms do, however, become linked to changes in the external environment. When there are changes in the environment, such as traveling to a different time zone or taking a job on the night shift, circadian rhythms tend to persist in the old patterns for a week or more, and because they are out of phase with patterns of living, substantial discomfort often occurs.

Indeed, our resistance to disruption of circadian rhythms is seen especially vividly in cases of *jet lag*. When you travel from one time zone to another,

American tourists suffering from jet lag in Europe. When we travel from one time zone to another, our bodily rhythms tend to remain in phase with old time. (Posterfield–Chickering)

your bodily rhythms tend to remain in phase with the old time. They change slowly, and only gradually over days do they become entrained or linked to the new light-dark cycle (Webb, Agnew, & Williams, 1971). A good example of this is the sight of newly arrived Europeans wandering through the lobbies of New York hotels at 5 o'clock in the morning, waiting for the restaurants to open for breakfast. Their circadian rhythms are still linked to Paris time or perhaps Eastern European time zones, which are 5 or more hours ahead of New York time.

Generally, one can adjust to a new time zone at the rate of about ½ to 1 hour per day. So if you travel to a place with a 3-hour time differential from your home, you can expect that it will take about 4 to 6 days to get your hormonal cycles, body-temperature rhythms, and sleep patterns completely adjusted to the new time (Klein, Wegmann, & Hunt, 1972; Kleitman, 1963).

SLEEP

Sleep and waking are among the most noticeable of our circadian rhythms. All mammals sleep as do many other kinds of creatures. Fish become immobile at certain times of the day, birds find a safe perch and sleep, other animals retire to their burrows. Some sleep during the daylight hours, others sleep at night. Some sleep for many hours, others for only a few. The human need to sleep is as strong as the needs for food and water. We simply cannot go without sleep for long, without experiencing discomfort. Without sleep, performance on many kinds of tasks is impaired, behavior becomes radically disturbed.

Yet the question of why we sleep has puzzled scientists and other thinkers since ancient times. Why must 1 hour of unconsciousness be spent for every 2 hours of consciousness? By the time you are 21 years old, over 7 years of your life has been spent in sleep, and over a normal lifetime we can expect to spend something like 23 years asleep. Clearly, if the amount of time spent in an activity is any indication of its importance, sleep must be an important enterprise indeed (Hartmann, 1973).

The ancient Greek philosopher and mathematician Pythagoras felt that sleep has a restorative function. He suggested that since being awake generally demands an upright posture for most of the day, this might cause the blood to drain out of the head and into body cavities. Therefore, he proposed, we must spend some portion of each day lying down so that the blood can flow back into the head. Although this idea has received no experimental support whatsoever, it was the forerunner of a whole series of theories that focus on the restorative functions of sleep.

Following in this tradition, some have suggested that being awake may deplete some important metabolic substance or perhaps produce some toxic by-product and that sleeping restores the body to normal. However, no depletion or toxic by-products of consciousness have yet been identified.

Others have suggested that after a day of conscious activity, the brain may need to rest for a while. This idea is attractive, but again, it does not seem to be correct. Although the pattern of metabolic activity in the brain during sleep differs from that seen when a person is awake (Greenberg, 1980), the overall rate of cerebral oxygen consumption during sleep is very similar to that observed when awake (Mangold, Sokoloff, Conner, Kleinerman, Therman, & Kety, 1955). Indeed, as we will see shortly, the brain is quite active during some stages of sleep.

Some psychologists have focused on the behavioral adaptiveness of sleep and have suggested that sleep may serve a protective function, helping animals avoid predators, and keeping them from needlessly expending energy or engaging in behaviors that may get them into trouble. Once bodily needs are met, this theory suggests, it would be efficient to "tune out" and go to sleep until more demands are made and behavioral responses are called for (Webb, 1975).

Other psychologists, such as James L. McGaugh, have suggested that we should really be asking, "Why awaken?" Could it be that sleep is the natural state of life, from which we awaken to care for such survival processes as feeding, cleansing, and reproducing? When these functions are accomplished, one can go back to the natural state of sleep.

These ideas have some support. Lions and other cats, which are very efficient at obtaining the essentials of life, may spend over 70% of each day asleep. Shrews, which are small mouselike creatures, have a very high level of metabolism and a correspondingly large need for food. Not surprisingly, shrews sleep for only a few hours each day.

Research into the biological basis of sleep is continuing. Recent progress suggests that the brain produces sleep-inducing substances that may be small proteins (Schoenenberger & Monnier, 1977). It is possible that these substances are released in a circadian rhythm and that they may initiate sleep (Nagasaki, Kitahama, Valatx, & Jouvet, 1980; Pappenheimer, Miller, & Goodrich, 1967). This research, if successful, may lead to more effective and much safer sleep-inducing medicines. But even if researchers find that the brain really does produce sleep-inducing substances, the question of why it does may remain unanswered.

A TYPICAL NIGHT'S SLEEP

Sleep is not simply an extended period of unconsciousness. Rather, there are different stages of sleep that one passes through several times each night (Aserinsky & Kleitman, 1953). The identification of the various stages is rather recent advance in our knowledge about sleep, having occurred during the last three decades or so. As with many other advances in science, a better understanding of sleep became possible with the development of new research instrumentation, in this case, the development of the modern polygraph. This technical advance made it possible for psychologists to define objectively various aspects of sleep and to study these aspects systematically in the laboratory.

TECHNIQUES OF SLEEP RESEARCH

The development of techniques to record an *electroencephalogram* (EEG) opened up the study of sleep to scientific investigation. To record an EEG, electrodes are attached to the subject's scalp. These electrodes pick up electrical signals that reflect the synaptic activities of literally millions of neurons in the brain located beneath each electrode. Because these electrical signals are so very tiny, they must be amplified several thousand times before they can be recorded.

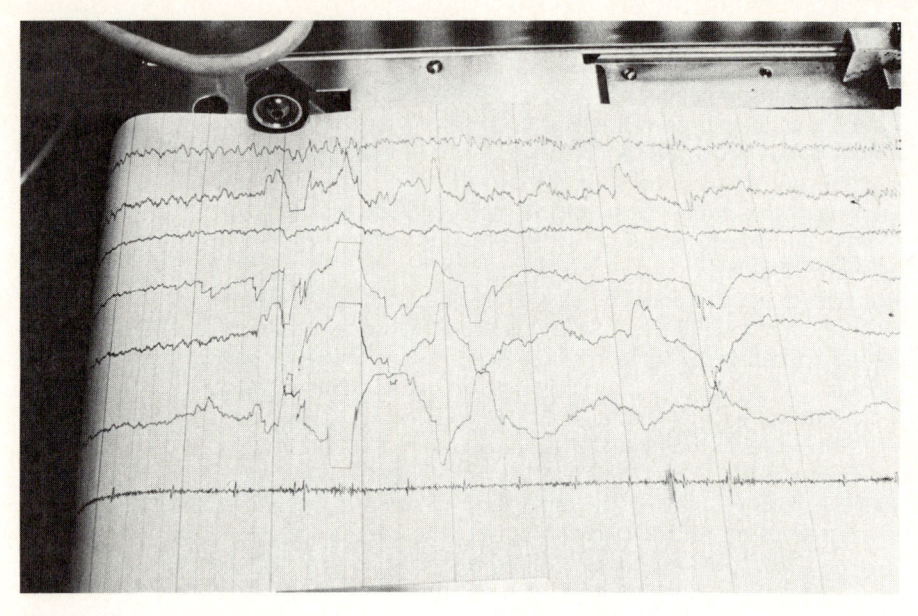

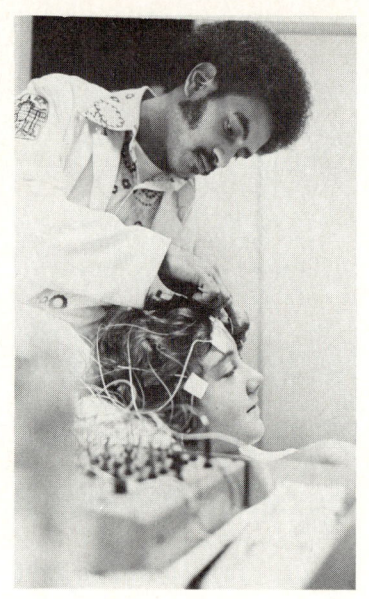

140   BIOLOGY, SENSATION, PERCEPTION, AND CONSCIOUSNESS

To record an EEG, electrodes attached to the subject's scalp pick up electrical signals from millions of neurons in the brain. (Robert Goldstein/The Sleep–Wake Disorders Center, Montefiore Medical Center, Bronx, N.Y. and Mimi Forsyth/Monkmeyer)

Figure 5.1
Typical EEG records. The upper trace shows a short sample of beta activity. The frequency is fairly rapid and the amplitude low. Alpha activity, in contrast, is slower, with a substantially higher amplitude.

To do this, researchers typically use a device called a *polygraph* (meaning literally, a machine that makes many charts or graphs). The polygraph amplifies the tiny electrical signals from the brain, as well as signals from other parts of the body, and passes them to a series of motors that drive the polygraph pens which trace a record of the pattern of electrical activity on a long strip of paper.

In sleep research, EEG activity from the brain, together with measures of muscle tone, eye movements, heart beat, and breathing, are often recorded on the same sheet of paper. Through these polygraph recordings, wakefulness and sleep can be objectively defined and the various phases of sleep distinguished.

STAGES OF SLEEP

Although many variables can affect the onset, pattern, and duration of sleep, studies conducted over the past 30 years have revealed a pattern of sleep which is characteristic of most adults. In the following paragraphs we describe the patterns of sleep that an average young adult subject in a sleep laboratory might show (Dement, 1978).

An awake and alert person with eyes open will show an EEG record that is of low amplitude and fairly high frequently (15 to 25 Hz). This kind of activity is known as beta activity and it appears to be quite random (see Figure 5.1).

When the subject becomes pleasantly relaxed and the eyes are closed, a distinctive EEG pattern appears; it consists of fairly regular voltage changes that occur at a rate of 9 to 12 Hz. This EEG pattern is known as *alpha rhythm*.

As the subject becomes drowsy the amplitude of the alpha rhythm decreases and is replaced by lower-amplitude irregular activity such as that shown in Figure 5.2. The transition to sleep is fairly rapid and clear-cut when observed in the EEG record. The subject is now asleep and experiencing what researchers call *stage 1 sleep*. If awakened at this time, it is likely that the subject would deny having been asleep, even though he or she had not been

CONSCIOUSNESS

Figure 5.2
Stages of sleep. The first trace, stage W, indicates drowsy wakefulness with a large amount of alpha activity. The lines below the traces for stage 3 and stage 4 sleep indicate periods when delta activity was present. (Based on A. Rechtschaffen and A. Kales, *A Manual of Standardized Terminology, Techniques, and Scoring System for Sleep Stages of Human Subjects*, Washington, D.C.: U.S. Government Printing Office, 1968)

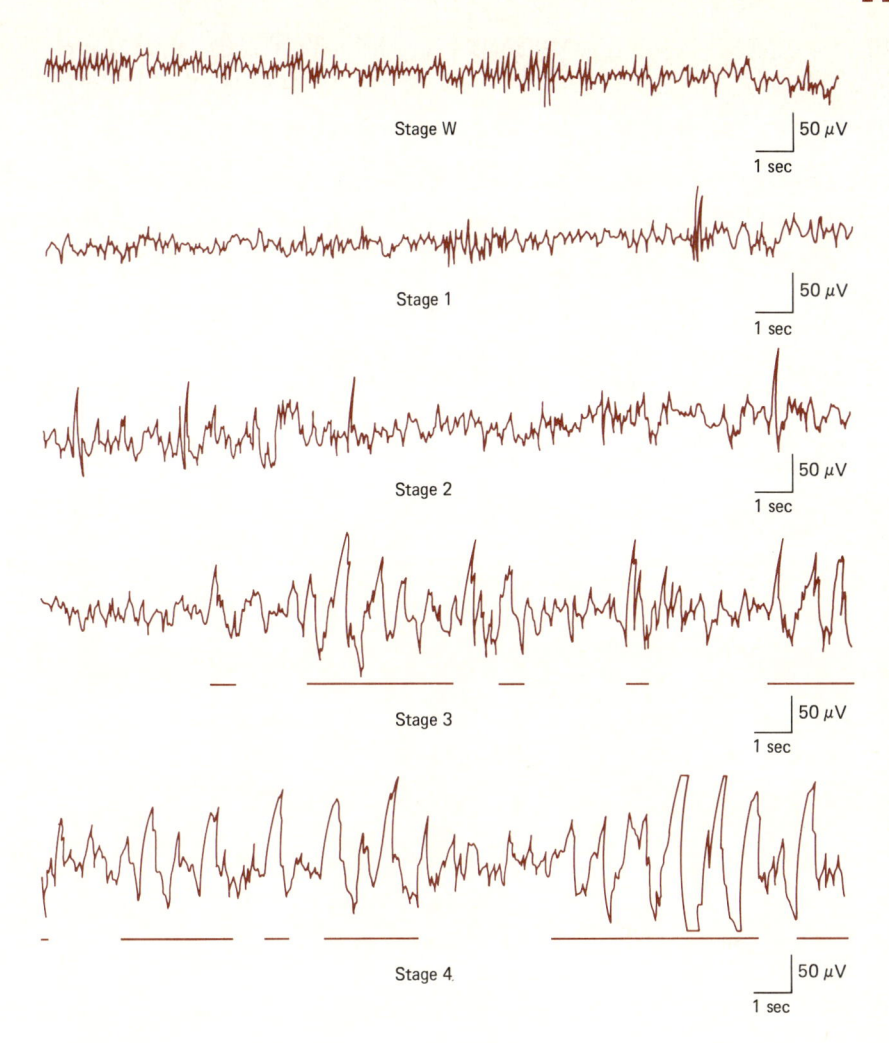

responding to external stimuli for several minutes. This is an illustration of the fact that we have only a limited awareness of our sleep processes and that most people have difficulty accurately monitoring their own sleep processes, a finding that all sleep researchers are keenly aware of. Stage 1 sleep usually lasts somewhat less than 10 minutes, during which there is a general slowing of heart rate and some reduction in muscle tone.

Stage 2 sleep is characterized by short bursts of faster activity in the EEG record called *sleep spindles*. These spindles are made up of regular 14- to 18-Hz waves that for a second or two, progressively increase and then decrease in amplitude. Also during stage 2 sleep, the electrodes monitoring eye movement show that the subject's eyes are rolling slowly around beneath the eyelids in an uncoordinated fashion.

In *stage 3 sleep*, high-amplitude, low-frequency waves appear, accompanied by sleep spindles. These large slow waves are called *delta waves* and range in frequency from about 4 Hz to less than 1 Hz. During stage 3 sleep, heart rate and breathing both decline and the muscles continue to relax. In *stage 4 sleep* spindle activity disappears, leaving just the big delta waves in the EEG record. During the first 3 to 4 hours after one falls asleep, stage 2 sleep will usually lead to stage 3 and stage 4 sleep, although in the last half of a night's sleep, stages 3 and 4 may not be attained. The four stages of sleep that we have just discussed are all classified under the heading of *quiet sleep*.

REM SLEEP (ACTIVE SLEEP)

From 1 hour to 90 minutes after the subject has fallen asleep, a very curious phenomenon occurs. The delta waves disappear from the EEG record, there is a short return to stage 2 sleep, and the EEG begins to show fast, low-amplitude activity, very much like that seen when a person is awake and alert. But paradoxically, the person is still very much asleep and will require a fairly strong stimulus to awaken. Because of this, early sleep researchers referred to this stage of sleep as *paradoxical sleep* (Aserinsky & Kleitman, 1955). During this stage of sleep breathing becomes faster and less regular, heart rate increases, muscle tone in the neck and chin decreases to almost zero, and the electrodes recording eye movement show that the eyes are darting rapidly back and forth beneath the closed eyelids. These eye movements gave this stage of sleep the name *rapid-eye-movement* (REM) *sleep*. Many sleep researchers, however, prefer the term *active sleep* to REM sleep because it does not call attention to just one aspect of this stage of sleep.

If awakened at this time, our subject would probably report that he or she had just been dreaming. Although dreams do occur during other sleep stages, REM sleep nearly always seems to coincide with dreaming.

Following an episode of REM sleep, EEG patterns associated with stage 2 sleep reappear, followed by stage 3, and possibly stage 4 sleep. In normal adults episodes of REM sleep alternating with periods of quiet sleep occur throughout the night at about 90-minute intervals. This pattern is shown graphically in Figure 5.3 (Hartmann, 1973). During a typical night, about 45% to 50% of sleep time is spent in stage 2 sleep, while active sleep or REM sleep accounts for about 25%. Sleep that occurs early in the night is char-

Figure 5.3 The course of a night's sleep in a young adult subject. There were two periods of awakening during the night and four episodes of REM sleep. The episodes of REM sleep occurred at approximately 90-minute intervals. Note that each period of REM sleep was preceded by stage 2 sleep. (Based on A. Kales and J. Kales, "Evaluation, diagnosis and treatment of clinical conditions related to sleep," *Journal of the American Medical Association*, 213, 1970, 2229–2235)

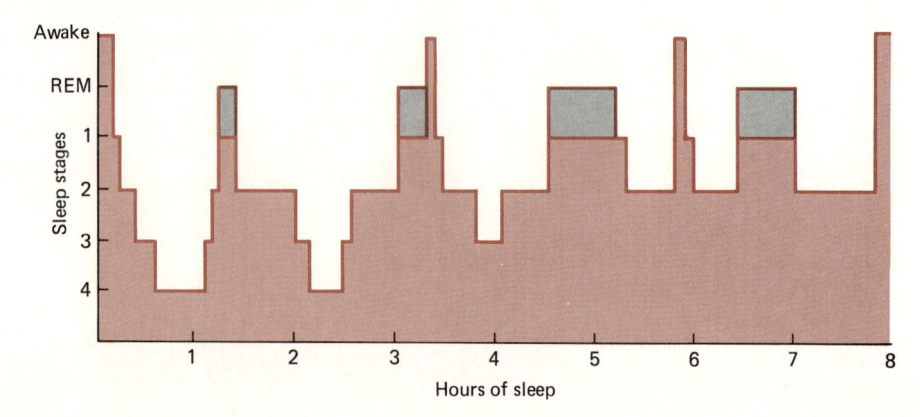

CONSCIOUSNESS

acterized by more stage 3 and stage 4 sleep than sleep that occurs more toward morning. In contrast, there is much more REM sleep in the latter half of a night's sleep.

SLEEP PATTERNS FROM INFANCY THROUGH ADULTHOOD

As we develop from infancy through adulthood and into old age, our sleep-waking cycles also change. These changes are especially pronounced during early life, although sleep patterns also change in the aged. These changes in sleep patterns with age are shown in Figure 5.4. As can be seen, infants sleep much more than do adults, and much of that sleep time is spent in REM sleep. Indeed, during the first 2 to 3 weeks of life, an average infant will spend almost 50% of its sleep time in REM sleep (Roffwarg, Muzio, & Dement, 1966).

In infants, a regular cycle of waking and sleeping takes several weeks to become established, often much to the distress of the new parents, and a clear 24-hour circadian cycle may not appear until an infant is about 3 to 4 months old (Kleitman & Englemann, 1953). At about 2 months of age, sleep is polyphasic, with several sleep-waking cycles each day. A 4- to 5-year old child shows a well-developed circadian cycle, with a biphasic sleep pattern that consists of a long night's sleep and an afternoon nap.

As one moves into adulthood, the total number of hours spent asleep decreases, as does the percentage of REM sleep. The average adult gets a little less than 8 hours of sleep a day, 20% of which is REM sleep. By age 70, this has decreased to fewer than 6 hours and about 14% REM sleep, with a number of periods of arousal during the night (Hartmann, 1973; Roffwarg et al., 1966).

Figure 5.4
Changes with age in total amounts of daily sleep, daily REM sleep, and percentage of REM sleep. Note that the amount of REM sleep falls from around 8 hours at birth to less than 1 hour in old age. The amount of nonREM sleep remains more constant, falling from around 8 hours to around 5 hours. (Based on Roffwarg, Muzio, & Dement, 1966)

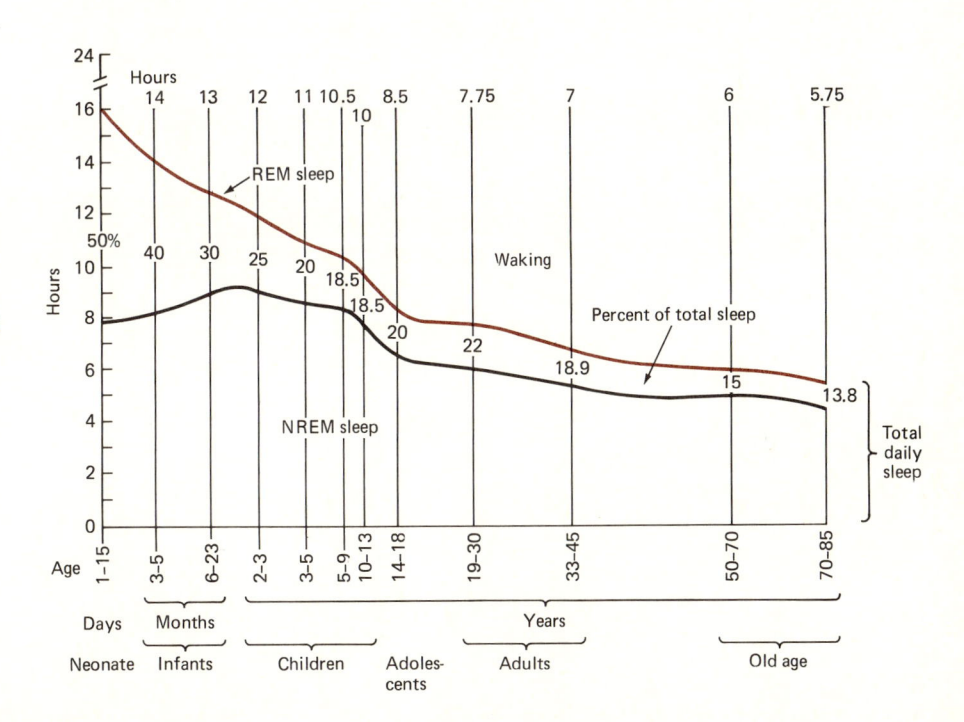

FOCUS ON THE PSYCHOLOGIST

James L. McGaugh

DR. JAMES L. MCGAUGH is Director of the Center for the Neurobiology of Learning and Memory and Professor of Psychobiology at the University of California, Irvine. He did his graduate study at the University of California, Berkeley. He taught at San Jose State and the University of Oregon before joining the faculty at Irvine as founding chair of the Department of Psychobiology. He received the Distinguished Scientific Contribution Award from the A.P.A. for his research on memory modulation.

Why can't we remember all our experiences? Some memories are readily formed while others require effort. And, some memories are clearly more lasting than others. This is both curious and highly important since most of what we do is based on memory. The importance of memory is clearly revealed by those with severe memory disorders such as Alzheimer's disease, whose victims eventually lose the ability to cope with life.

My research on this problem is guided by the assumption that the physiological states of the brain during and after learning influences the storage of memories. It has long been known that memory is impaired if the brain is injured shortly after learning. Often, only events experienced just prior to the injury are forgotten—older memories are intact. This phenomenon, *retrograde amnesia*, suggested that these injuries may interfere with the formation of memory. The evidence also suggested that other brain states might be optimal for storing newly-acquired information. In experiments, I found that stimulant drugs improved animal memory retention.

There is now extensive evidence that retention can be enhanced by drugs, electrical stimulation of the brain, and hormones if the treatments occur shortly after training. The findings strongly suggest that the treatments enhance memory by producing brain states favorable for storing information. Humans and other animals release hormones, including epinephrine (adrenalin) and ACTH into the blood and brain when they are aroused. Recent findings indicate that these hormones may act on the brain to influence memory. Clearly, we learn and remember better when we are aroused and motivated. Differences in the strengths of memories may be due to the hormonal consequences of experiences.

Studies indicate that memory is also influenced by states of sleep. Retention is best if subjects remain asleep between learning and retention testing. The findings also strongly suggest that the brain state associated with REM sleep is favorable for storing newly acquired information and that drugs used to induce sleep (including benzodiazapines and scopolomine) can impair memory.

There are three important implications of this research. First, by being alert and attentive, we can produce brain states optimal for learning and memory. Second, memory impairment might be a major side effect of sleep-inducing drugs. Third, it may be possible to treat some memory disorders.

HOW MUCH SLEEP IS NORMAL?

Some people seem to require about twice as much sleep each night as others. Some persons sleep 10 or more hours each night, whereas others seem to get along just fine sleeping 4 to 5 hours. Clearly, these are both substantial deviations from the average. The popular media often report stories of people who sleep very little, and some of these cases have been carefully studied. There have, for example, been cases, verified by EEG recordings, of perfectly healthy persons who sleep only 1 to 3 hours each night (Dement, 1978; Meddis, 1979). However, this does not mean that the rest of us can get by comfortably on this little sleep.

Aspects of personality may be related to the amount of sleep that is needed. Hartmann (1978) studied people who told him that they were either short sleepers or long sleepers. When he tested these subjects in the laboratory, he found that the principal difference between the people who said that they were short or long sleepers was that the "short sleepers" showed only about half as much REM sleep as did the "long sleepers." There were few differences in the total amount of time members of each group spent in quiet sleep. These subjects were also interviewed and given psychological tests. Taken together, these measures suggested to Hartmann that short sleepers are generally more energetic, sociable, confident, and optimistic about life. In contrast, the group composed of long sleepers contained more persons who were suffering from some sort of personal stress or who were mildly depressed. Hartmann suggested that people with problems generating concern and worry may require more REM sleep to deal with those problems.

How much sleep is needed seems to depend on individual factors. The average in young adults is about 7½ hours, but if you generally sleep less or more than that, it is probably not a matter of concern as long as you awaken feeling rested and refreshed.

SLEEP AND DREAMING

Throughout human history dreams have been viewed in many different ways. Some cultures consider dreams important predictors of the future, or as a way that higher spiritual powers communicate with mortals. The Old and New Testaments contain many references to messages communicated during dreams, and dreams figure prominently in the religious texts of many other faiths throughout the world. "Prophetic" dreams have altered human history: They have influenced kings and other rulers to act in certain ways and, on occasion, altered the tactics and even the outcomes of military campaigns.

Do dreams really allow one to see into the future? No, although they certainly do seem to have that kind of power in some cases. Freemon (1972) classified prophetic dreams into three general groups. First, there are after-the-fact dreams, in which the "prophet" selects a dream to fit the current situation from a large group of previously dreamt prophetic dreams. The content of the selected dream is revealed only *after* the critical events have occurred. Second, there are statistical dreams. These dreams are remembered only if the predicted event comes true and are forgotten (perhaps conveniently) if it does not. Third, there are dreams based on inner knowledge, the knowledge of things that one knows to be true, but is consciously and unconsciously ignoring. These dreams can sometimes help a therapist get at the roots of a client's problem.

Today there is general agreement that there is nothing magic about dreams. They do not actually enable one to look into the future. Rather, dreams seem to reflect the brain's aroused state during REM sleep. The cortex is active, but essentially cut off from sensory input. Therefore, it is not constrained by facts of the real world, and dream content can, in essence, wander off in any direction, recombining information stored in memory in novel and sometimes bizarre ways. Memories of recent important events often provide much of the raw material for dreams, especially those dreamt during the first two or three episodes of REM sleep. During sleep, the result of this mental activity is perceived as being very real, since the accuracy of the dream cannot be judged against any external standard. Once one awakens, the dream may seem quite absurd, even though the experience seemed to be absolutely real during the time that the dream was occurring. No wonder that through the ages dreams have been thought to have special meaning. In the following sections we explore some aspects of contemporary thinking about the nature of dreams.

WHO DREAMS AND WHEN

Researchers have studied dream reports of subjects who were awakened during different stages of sleep. When subjects are awakened during REM sleep, they can recount a dream they had just been having 70% to 90% of the time. Dreams occur during other sleep stages much less frequently. These dreams seem to be different from REM sleep dreams in their form and content and are remembered less well (Herman, Ellman, & Roffwarg, 1978).

The dreams that occur during REM sleep are characterized by vivid imagery and by a feeling of acting out a play on stage. These dreams have a story line, and one seems to experience the sights, sounds, and acts of the dream. When they are occurring, REM sleep dreams seem to be very real. In contrast, the dream reports from other stages of sleep seem to be characterized more by single ideas, thoughts, or feelings. In these dreams subjects report thinking about problems or experiencing particular emotions; the development of a story with action and physical sensations is generally absent. The frequency of dreaming is also much lower in these stages of sleep. When awakened during slow-wave sleep, subjects report dreams only 10% to 15% of the time (Webb & Cartwright, 1978).

Previously, we noted that REM sleep occurs at intervals of about every 90 minutes throughout a night's sleep and that when awakened during this phase of sleep, most people report that they had been dreaming. But many people say that they never dream. Do these people, too, show phases of REM sleep, and do they ever dream? The answer to both of these questions is yes. All normal persons dream and show periods of REM sleep. When those people who claim that they never dream are tested in a sleep laboratory and are awakened during REM sleep, many are quite astonished at the vividness of the dream they had just been having. Most people who claim that they never dream show normal sleep patterns that include several periods of REM sleep. The difference, then, seems to be that some people remember their dreams much better than others.

EYE MOVEMENTS AND DREAMS

As noted earlier, one characteristic of active sleep is rapid movement of the eyes from one side to the other. When discovered, this phenomenon was so striking that researchers thought that these eye movements were an attempt of the eyes to follow the action of a dream (in other words, if you were to dream that you were watching a basketball game, your eyes would "follow" the action and the ball from one end of the court to the other). We now know that the eye movements appear to be driven by bursts of electrical activity that can be recorded from the pons, lateral geniculate nucleus of the thalamus, and those brain stem nuclei that control eye movements. Further, there are many differences between the kinds of eye movements during REM sleep and the eye movements seen when one is actually viewing real-life events. At this time, the weight of the evidence suggests that the eye movements of REM sleep are unrelated to dream content, although this is still a matter of some controversy (Dement, 1978).

OTHER ASPECTS OF REM SLEEP

Some have maintained that time is compressed during dreams, and what seems to take many minutes actually occurs in just a few seconds. It is not clear how this idea first originated, but it is popular and durable. It is also incorrect. Time seems to pass at the same rate during dreams as it does when one is awake. The first experiments that established this were performed by Dement and Wolpert (1958), who gently sprayed cool water from a hypodermic syringe onto the backs of sleeping subjects who were, according to their EEG records, in REM sleep. Then they waited about 30 seconds to several minutes, and awakened the subjects to see whether the experience of being sprayed with water had been incorporated into the dream and how much time had seemed to pass. When subjects included the water in their dreams, the perception of how much time passed between wetting and awakening was quite accurate. Other investigations have generally supported the conclusion that dream stories unfold gradually.

HIGHLIGHT 5.1
How to Remember Your Dreams Better

A number of helpful techniques have been developed that may enable you to learn more about that fascinating world that your mind creates each night as you sleep. If you are interested in trying to improve your recollection of your dreams, you should start by getting a pad of paper and a pencil and placing them within easy reach beside your bed. As you go to sleep, concentrate on remembering your dreams. The next morning when you awaken, reach out and get the paper and pencil and quickly jot down what you can remember. Do this with as little movement as possible. This is important because the feelings of the warm bed, the covers, and your posture may all be cues to help you to remember.

This routine, based on one discussed by Linde and Savary (1974), will take practice, but if you keep at it, your performance will improve. You may well be surprised by how much you can remember about your dreams and how rich and vivid your dream life is.

Researchers think that dreams leave such fragile memories because little is learned during sleep and because the onset of sleep tends to induce amnesia. Those dreams that are best remembered are those followed by a short period of waking. These few minutes awake make it possible to store the memory of the dream that just occurred. For some reason, when you go to sleep concentrating on remembering your dreams, you tend to be more aroused after the dream episode and therefore more likely to store the memory of the dream.

148   BIOLOGY, SENSATION, PERCEPTION, AND CONSCIOUSNESS

In males, episodes of REM sleep are accompanied by penile erections. Are these erections related to the sexual content of dreams? Here, too, the answer is no. All periods of REM sleep seem to result in erection of the penis, whether or not the dream has any sexual content or overtones. Of course, dreams with explicit sexual content may result in an ejaculation or "nocturnal emission," but these are relatively infrequent. Normal males have erections several times each night. Female sex organs are also affected during REM sleep, showing associated fluid secretions and increased vaginal blood flow.

NIGHTMARES AND OTHER BAD DREAMS

Each of us has experienced the raw terror of a nightmare. You may have had one that was so real and so vivid that you awakened thoroughly frightened and soaked with sweat. Nightmares are surprisingly common. Most college students report having at least one nightmare a year, and young children have them much more often.

Many nightmares occur during REM sleep, and these dreams often have themes of being chased by dangerous creatures, falling, being hurt, or being unable to take action when action is needed. The latter feeling may be related to the loss of muscle tone associated with REM sleep. Only very limited movement is possible during this phase of sleep, and during a nightmare it may lead to a feeling of paralysis and helplessness. REM sleep nightmares may be continuations of otherwise normal dreams that somehow go awry and develop a frightening story content.

Some of the most terrifying nightmares occur in stage of sleep other than REM sleep, especially in stage 4 sleep. These very frightening dreams gen-

The Nightmare by Rockwell Kent. Each of us has experienced the raw terror of a nightmare. (Rare Book and Manuscript Library, Columbia University)

John Henry Fuseli's *The Nightmare* depicts the sensations of a woman having a nightmare while deep in stage 4 sleep. (Founder's Society Detroit Institute of Arts)

erally do not have a well-developed story line, but center around negative feelings and emotions. They often take the form of internally directed aggression and at other times of feelings of being crushed, choked, or suffocated. The French term for this sort of nightmare is *le cauchemar* or literally "the pressing devil," and it seems to provide a very apt description of this sort of sensation.

PATHOLOGIES OF SLEEP

Probably all of us have had difficulty going to sleep at the appropriate time. Most of us have also had difficulty staying awake, again at the appropriate time. Either of these problems, if they persist, can thoroughly disrupt one's life. Recall the frustration of not being able to sleep, how you tossed and turned cursing your fate for hours. Imagine what it would be like if that condition were chronic and happened almost every night.

The converse can also be very distressing. You have probably dozed off at some time or another when you were supposed to be awake and paying attention. Perhaps this was in church, at a social event, or even during a psychology lecture. Surely, this would be most distressing if it happened repeatedly.

Physicians in general practice report that the two most common complaints that cause people to seek medical attention are pain and problems with sleep. Estimates of the number of people who complain of sleep disturbances are difficult to determine accurately, but they range from 15% to about 50% of the population. Sleep problems clearly cannot be ignored, and those who are interested in psychology should have some understanding of them.

INSOMNIA

One major symptom of sleep disorders is excessive sleepiness during the day. This can take the form of general tiredness and a lack of alertness, and some of those most severely affected may actually drop off to sleep several times during normal waking hours. Those who attribute their excessive daytime sleepiness to poor sleep during the night are usually classified as *insomniacs*. Others, who are sleepy during the day but do not associate this feeling with disturbed sleep during the night, are termed *hypersomniacs*.

Insomnia is a chronic inability to obtain the quantity or quality of sleep needed to function efficiently during the day. There is substantial evidence that many of those who complain of insomnia may actually sleep quite normally. William Dement, a leading sleep researcher, examined 127 self-professed insomniacs in his sleep laboratory and found that the average time to go to sleep was about 15 minutes and the average time in sleep was 7 hours (Carskadon, Mitler & Dement, 1974). Yet, when awakened, even after several hours of sleep, especially during an episode of REM sleep, these persons often denied that they had been asleep at all. One explanation for this is that these unfortunate people may dream that they are awake and are having difficulty falling asleep (Dement, 1978).

The most common causes of insomnia are psychological. Depression is often associated with disturbed sleep, especially very early morning awakening. Many people who are subsequently diagnosed as depressed first seek professional attention for their sleep disturbance and not for their depression. Anxiety and worry about events in one's life can also lead to difficulty in falling asleep, further decreasing one's ability to cope with already existing problems.

SLEEPING PILLS

So many people have difficulty sleeping that more than 150 million dollars of nonprescription sleeping aids are sold each year in the United States alone. Similar huge quantities are sold in many other industrialized nations. Further, millions of prescriptions are also written annually by physicians for drugs that are supposed to help their patients sleep. In 1977, more than 25 million prescriptions for sleeping pills were written, and in that year, over 2 million people took sleeping pills each night for 2 months or longer. This was done despite good research evidence that the drugs which were being prescribed are generally ineffective, potentially habit forming, and dangerous.

Further, many people drink alcoholic beverages shortly before bedtime in an attempt to induce a better night's sleep. This practice leads to dependence on their "nightcap" and potential serious problems with alcoholism. No wonder that a panel of experts sponsored by the National Academy of Sciences identified the abuse of sleeping medications as a major public health hazard (Solomon, White, Parron, & Mendelson, 1979).

The problem of overprescription of sleeping medications is made worse because the drugs do not work very well and may lead to further problems with sleep. As William Dement (1978) has pointed out many times: "Sleeping pills cause insomnia." Sleeping medications do not induce normal sleep. Barbiturate sleeping pills suppress REM sleep for the first few nights they are taken. With continued use of barbiturates, some REM sleep does return, but it may not be quite normal. Further, after several weeks of nightly use, barbiturate sleeping pills loose their effectiveness, and a higher dose is needed to cause sleep (Dement, Guilleminault, & Zarcone, 1975; Hartmann, 1978).

After some period of regular barbiturate sleeping pill use, most people typically try to stop taking the medication. This results in difficulty in going to sleep and a large rebound in REM sleep, with frequent awakening and nightmares. After several nights of disturbed sleep, the person usually starts taking the barbiturates again, well before normal sleep patterns are reestablished. Thus a dangerous cycle continues. Some common barbiturates and their trade names are: amobarbital (Amytal), pentobarbital (Nembutal), phenobarbital (Luminal), and secobarbital (Seconal).

Because of these and other problems with barbiturate sleeping pills, many physicians are now prescribing sleeping medications that belong to the benzodizepine family of drugs. Benzodiazepines commonly used to treat sleep difficulties include diazepam (Valium), flurazepam (Dalmane), and triazolam (Halcion). These drugs also have some problems. Some, such as diazepam and flurazepam, are metabolized rather slowly, and with continued use, the drugs as well as their active metabolites accumulate in the body, resulting in difficulty in awakening and decreased alertness. These symptoms are often interpreted as an indication that the person is still not getting enough sleep, so the dosage is increased. Withdrawal from long-term use of benzodiazepine sleeping medications can also produce disturbed sleep and a subsequent return to chronic drug use.

The use of sleeping medications by the elderly is a special problem. As we discussed earlier, many people over 60 sleep fewer than 6 hours each night, with 5 hours sleep being quite common. If older people are unaware that a decrease in sleep is a normal change occurring with age, they may demand sleeping medications. This is especially hazardous because the chances of side effects of drug use are greater in the elderly, and because they have somewhat slower metabolic processes, drugs take longer to leave their bodies. This increases the chance of a dangerous overdose. Unfortunately, almost 40% of all sleeping pill prescriptions are written for persons over age 60. Still more worrisome is that over 90% of elderly residents of some nursing homes are regularly prescribed sleeping medications by staff physicians (Solomon et al., 1979).

NARCOLEPSY

The major symptom of *narcolepsy* is irresistible attacks of sleepiness that can occur without warning. Narcolepsy is a serious form of hypersomnia and it can be very debilitating. Often, those affected feel extremely sleepy and try to fight the sleepiness by moving about, opening windows, drinking coffee, and turning up the radio or television. A short nap of about 15 minutes usually causes the sleepiness to disappear, and the person may feel much better and ready to resume the day's activities.

Some persons afflicted with narcolepsy also suffer a sudden loss of muscle tone associated with the sleep attack. This is called *cataplexy*. In some, the cataplexy is simply a weakness in the muscles of the upper body, but in others, the whole body can be involved and the person may fall to the ground. This sort of cataplexy often occur during arousing experiences such as surprise, laughter, or sexual activity (Zarcone, 1973).

This muscular weakness and collapse seen in the cataplexy associated with narcolepsy provided researchers with an important clue in their search for the causes of narcolepsy. Recall that periods of REM sleep are associated

Narcolepsy leads to irresistible attacks of sleepiness that can occur without warning. (Arthur Tress)

with loss of muscle tone. It appears that many narcoleptics can go directly from the waking state into REM sleep without having to go through a regular sleep cycle. Indeed, the appearance of REM sleep shortly after the beginning of sleep is one defining characteristic of narcolepsy (Dement, Holman, & Guilleminault, 1976).

For many years some psychologists interpreted narcolepsy as an attempt by the unconscious mind to escape from unpleasant situations. In this view, the sleep attacks were escape responses that allowed one to leave the realities of life. However, this idea is now discounted as the physiological basis for the condition becomes better understood. Further, symptoms of narcolepsy can be found in all personality types: from normal persons to those suffering from a variety of serious psychopathologies.

There appears to be a strong genetic influence in narcolepsy, and symptoms can persist in families for several generations. The American Narcolepsy Association estimates that about 250,000 Americans suffer from some form of this condition, and most of them are undiagnosed as narcoleptics. These people are sometimes objects of disapproval for their apparent lazy habits. At present there is no very effective therapy for narcolepsy, although amphetamines and drugs that tend to inhibit REM sleep sometimes help somewhat.

HIGHLIGHT 5.2
Narcolepsy and Failures of Memory

Going to sleep results in amnesia for those events that occur just before going to sleep. This property of sleep would make it very difficult for a narcoleptic to encode new information while the sleep attacks are occurring. In the following case history, a man who is afflicted with narcolepsy describes some of his symptoms in this transcript of a tape-recorded interview.

Case 4 (45-year-old male): "I started to need more sleep at night 10 years ago, but daytime sleepiness was not really a problem until 5 years ago. Two years ago, I developed a new symptom: I began to be very forgetful. I misplaced objects that I use every day. I then find them in the most incredible places. I put my watch in the refrigerator and my toothbrush in the mailbox. Everybody in the family is aware of these misplacements and they are subjects of amusement. The problem is more serious at work. I have to attend numerous meetings and I do not really fall asleep but I 'blank out.' Decisions are taken that I cannot remember. I am running out of excuses such as 'I was not there' because of vacation, sick leave, etc. and I am on the verge of being fired or being forced to retire because of my complete lack of memory. I try to concentrate and give great attention to these meetings. I usually remember perfectly the beginning but progressively in the smoky room I have the feeling that I don't perceive anything any more. I completely lose the notion of time; I suddenly realize that the meeting is over; it could have lasted for 30 minutes or 3 hours; it does not make any difference—it usually seems very short. The only solution that I have found is to tape the meetings and listen to them later on, but sometimes I do not realize that the cassette tape should be turned over. The very frightening feeling is the complete absence of control of my mind, and the existence of multiple 'blanks' throughout the day." [From C. Guilleminault and W. C. Dement, *Amnesia and disorders of excessive daytime sleepiness.* In J. L. McGaugh, and R. R. Drucker-Colin, R. A. Jensen, and J. L. Martinez, Jr. (Assoc. Eds.). *Neurobiology of sleep and memory.* New York: Academic Press, 1977]

SLEEPWALKING

Sleepwalking, sometimes called *somnambulism*, is a disorder that receives a good deal of attention in sleep laboratories and the popular press. Sleepwalkers are often the focus of jokes and cartoons, and many misconceptions have been built up about sleepwalking.

Up until fairly recently, people assumed that sleepwalkers were simply acting out the dream that they are having at the time. However, this idea is false. Polygraph recordings clearly show that sleepwalking does not take place during REM stage. Somnambulism occurs during stage 4 sleep, usually early in the night's sleep and not later when REM sleep is more prominent. In any case, given the loss of muscle tone associated with REM sleep, sleepwalking would be quite impossible during REM sleep dreams.

A typical episode of sleepwalking begins when a person who has been sleeping quietly, sits up, gets out of bed, and begins to walk about, sometimes covering considerable distances. A sleepwalker's eyes are open, and he or she can avoid obstacles, but the facial expression is blank. Walking is at first unsteady, but soon the movements become coordinated and the gait more regular. There is substantial activation of the autonomic nervous system. A sleepwalker may perform purposeful acts such as sweeping or dusting the table and may even speak a few words. A sleepwalker's attention is quite difficult to attract, and if spoken to the person will usually respond with only grunts or monosyllables. Contrary to popular opinion, waking a sleepwalker will not result in a violent attack, nor are sleepwalkers protected by mysterious spiritual forces. If left alone, most sleepwalkers will, in time, return to bed quite unharmed by the experience and with little or no recollection of it the next morning.

Sleepwalking, as with some other disorders of sleep, has a genetic component. If one member of a family is a sleepwalker, the probability that other members of that family will also show this trait is considerably higher than would be expected by chance. Sleepwalking is more common in children than in adults, and it is typically outgrown by adolescence. Attempts to treat somnambulism are generally ineffective and can make the child very anxious (Dement, 1978). Patience seems to be the best treatment.

HYPNOSIS

Hyponosis has puzzled psychologists for many years. Through hypnosis, the hypnotist can exert some degree of control over another person, and trance-like states can be produced. Yet we know relatively little about its causes and consequences, although information about it is rapidly growing. Our lack of knowledge may be due in part to the fact that hypnosis has had at times a relatively unsavory reputation as a tool for charlatans and as a form of entertainment. Indeed, the performances by stage hypnotists today may lead one to conclude that hypnosis is little more than an elaborate magic trick. As we shall see, however, this is definitely not the case. Unlike ESP and other similar phenomena, hypnosis can be studied scientifically, it can be reliably induced, and recent findings have provided important insights into some of the cognitive mechanisms that mediate hypnosis (Shor, 1979).

ENTERING THE HYPNOTIC STATE

There are various ways to induce a hypnotic state, but certain principles are almost always used (Hilgard, 1968). The subject may be asked to stare at a certain point on the wall, a swinging pendulum, or the second hand of a watch. Speaking in low, well-modulated tones, the hypnotist invites the subject to enter into hypnosis. The subject is never told that he or she *must* enter hypnosis; the decision is voluntary. The subject is asked to relax and to become calm, comfortable, and drowsy. During this time, the subject is encouraged to listen only to the hypnotist's voice and to enter the hypnotic state without worries or cares. The voluntary entrance into hypnosis and the elements of relaxation and freedom from care are essential to the induction of a hypnotic state. The person who is being hypnotized must be willing to give up control and to accept the suggestions of the hypnotist. Otherwise, there can be no hypnosis. A person cannot be hypnotized against his or her will.

The focusing of attention and the hypnotist's speech together lead to the hypnotic state in many people. However, it does not succeed with everyone. About 10% of the population cannot be hypnotized at all, and only a similar percentage can be induced to enter the deepest trances. Some people may even be so resistant to giving up control to the hypnotist that the procedure, which is calming in most people, produces severe anxiety and discomfort. There seem to be many factors that influence one's susceptibility to hypnosis. Early childhood experiences seem to be one important variable. Some research has suggested that those who were raised in a strict family environment and who learned to follow orders may be more susceptible to hypnosis. So are those who are interested in seeking out new sensations and who have rich and imaginative fantasy lives (Hilgard, 1965, 1979).

Those who do enter into hypnosis describe it as a state of detachment dominated by deep relaxation and calmness. Hypnotized subjects often say that their minds are blank. The past and future seem to be relatively unimportant to a person in a hypnotic state. There seems to be a kind of relaxed willingness to accept any suggestion that the hypnotist might take without asking any questions.

These changes in attention and other cognitive variables might lead you to suspect that brain function is profoundly altered during the hypnotic state. Early researchers thought it might even be similar to brain function seen during sleep. However, this does not appear to be the case. Physiological measurements taken from hypnotized persons indicate that EEG, heart rate, blood pressure, and respiration are essentially the same as those observed when these people are in a normal waking state and quite unlike those seen when sleeping.

CHARACTERISTICS OF HYPNOSIS

A major characteristic of mild levels of hypnosis is *suggestibility*. Because the hypnotized subject is so passive and relaxed, he or she rarely does anything until told to do so by the hypnotist. Then the person typically devotes total attention to that task. Suggestibility increases dramatically during hypnosis. A hypnotist can, for example, suggest that there is a hamburger and a plate of french fries sitting on a table and invite the hypnotized subject to eat them. The person will behave as if he or she were eating the nonexistent meal, and perhaps even comment favorably on its taste.

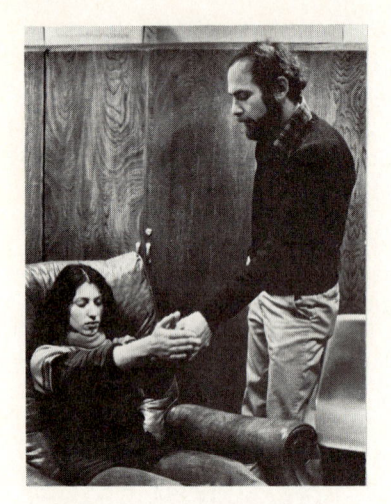

To be hypnotized, a person must be willing to give up control and to accept the suggestions of the hypnotist. (Mimi Forsyth/Monkmeyer)

Posthypnotic suggestion is related to suggestibility. In this case, subjects carry out instructions given to them while in a hypnotic state after they have been taken out of the trance. Usually, the hypnotist also suggests to the subject that he or she will not remember that the instructions were given. This procedure is called inducing *posthypnotic amnesia*. For example, the hypnotist may instruct a man to take off his shoes when given a prearranged signal, and further, not to remember anything about this instruction when he comes out of the hypnotic state. Some time later the hypnotist gives the signal, and the man immediately takes off his shoes. When asked why he did it, the man may reply with something like "My feet hurt, so I took off my shoes." This is clearly not the real reason he took his shoes off, but it satisfies the subject, if not other onlookers. Thus hypnosis seems to alter motivation, which at least in part, results from an increase in suggestibility.

What about the seemingly remarkable things that some hypnotized people do? Most of us are familiar with demonstrations of hypnosis in which a person lies suspended only by head and feet between two chairs. Although it may be difficult to believe, it you are of normal weight and strength you can do that, too, and without hypnosis. Although we do not recommend it, the feat is really not all that difficult. Audiences for stage hypnotists find the feat amazing simply because they do not question its difficulty. In this case, hypnosis simply shows what most any of us can do if properly motivated (Barber, 1979).

Hypnotic age regression has generated a great deal of controversy over the years. Deeply hypnotized subjects can be asked to go back to an earlier stage in their life, apparently behaving as if they are becoming younger and younger. Some psychologists believe that these subjects actually can experience the world as a child might and, more important, can remember long-lost memories of childhood. If a deeply hypnotized woman is told that she is now 7 years old, she will begin to behave as a 7-year-old. She may fingerpaint, print, draw, show emotional responses, and have a spoken vocabulary very much like that of a 7-year-old child. The effect is very convincing, and it is easy to accept the premise without further inquiry that the age regression is genuine. But is it?

Age-regressed behavior may look genuine to an observer unfamiliar with the person's childhood, but there are almost always major differences when compared to reports of that person's actual childhood behavior. Further, the memories that are "recalled" under these conditions are no more accurate than those remembered by nonhypnotized subjects. When there is accurate recall of childhood events, it appears that those happenings were described to the subject by parents or friends at a later date. Reports of age regression to the time of birth (or before) do not stand up to careful inquiry and seem to be generated by the subject's imagination in response to requests from the hypnotist (O'Connell, Shor, & Orne, 1970). During hypnotic age regression subjects "role-play" or try to act as though they are much younger in response to the hypnotist's suggestion. Their behavior differs significantly from that of real children (Orne, 1975).

CLINICAL USES OF HYPNOSIS

Evidence that age regression under hypnosis is probably role playing rather than genuine age regression does not mean that hypnosis cannot be a valuable technique. It can produce very strong emotional experiences which can be useful in some aspects of psychotherapy. For example, memories of events that are very painful are sometimes pushed out of consciousness, yet they still exert powerful effects. Hypnosis can bring these memories back into consciousness so that they can be dealt with directly. Hypnosis can also help change a person's motivation to enable him or her to accomplish difficult and perhaps psychologically threatening tasks. Hypnosis can also help control pain and fear. Terminally ill patients can be helped through their last weeks through hypnotic suggestion.

It is important to realize that hypnosis can be dangerous in inexperienced hands and that it is not a subject for amateur experimentation. Hypnosis can be very powerful and because of the heightened suggestibility and emotional susceptibility that occurs during hypnosis, it is possible that very unpleasant emotional feelings can occur. Therefore, if you plan on being hypnotized, check the credentials and qualifications of the hypnotist. Do not let just anyone do it. Most hypnosis is done in therapeutic situations, but it is well to remember that just because someone has learned how to hypnotize people does not qualify that person as a therapist. Hypnosis should be used only by those who have broadly based therapeutic training from recognized academic programs. People who use hypnosis as therapy should also be competent in other therapeutic strategies.

Hypnosis is a valuable technique that researchers are still trying to understand. There is nothing magical about it. Although many physiological measurements taken from hypnotized subjects are essentially the same as those observed in a normal waking state, hypnosis is clearly different from the normal waking state.

Hypnosis can also help researchers to learn much about human potentials and about the relationships between conscious thought processes and those that seem to be unconscious. Studies of hypnosis may also lead to a better understanding of mind-body interactions and how the brain modulates pain and susceptibility to disease (Hilgard, 1979).

DRUGS

WHO TAKES DRUGS

Most of us use drugs at one time or another. Many of us may even be dependent on them to some degree. We take drugs to fight disease, increase wakefulness and energy, reduce pain, alter mood, and induce sleep. The word "drug" has negative associations for many people, suggesting narcotics, pep pills, and hallucinogens. However, the definition is much broader than that. A *drug* is any substance that when taken into the body alters physical or psychological function. Included in this definition are many common, socially acceptable substances that most people, even the most conservative, regularly use. For example, millions regularly ingest the drug caffeine, which is found in coffee and many soft drinks. Many people are so dependent on caffeine that they cannot comfortably start their day, or function effectively through it, without several doses of this stimulating drug. Millions also take the drug nicotine in tobacco, and most of these people are quite heavily dependent on this drug. Still others consume alcohol with meals and at social gatherings, and all of us are aware of the addictive potential of alcohol. Most of us also occasionally take drugs such as aspirin to reduce pain and other drugs, such as sleeping pills, hay fever medicine, and cold tablets, when we feel they are needed.

We live in a drug-taking society. We are the targets of a constant stream of commercial messages urging us to solve almost all our problems—problems such as from anxiety, sinus headache, sleeplessness, and underarm wetness—through chemicals. Advertisers tell us that we can acquire social glamour or perhaps the ruggedness of a cowboy if we smoke a certain cigarette. The sellers of alcoholic beverages press home their message that alcohol consumption is an important part of most social occasions and that we *deserve* a beer at the end of a day's work. No wonder Americans spend billion of dollars each year for legal drugs that alter consciousness, mood, and attention. Similar huge amounts are spent for illicit drugs.

In this section we shall be concerned mainly with *psychoactive drugs*, that is, drugs that affect the central nervous system. These are the drugs such as alcohol, tranquilizers, and opiates that are taken to alter mood and produce changes in consciousness. Psychoactive drugs are also the primary drugs of misuse and abuse.

Drug use is hardly a new problem. It has existed from the beginnings of recorded history and probably long before (Weil & Rosen, 1983). Alcoholism is mentioned in the code of Hammurabi (ca. 2240 B.C.). Drugs were important in ancient Greece. The oracles of Delphi probably spoke under the influence of intoxicating vapors and drugs. Various drugs also figure in the writings of Homer and in later Greek plays.

There are many descriptions in the writings of ancient cultures of the use of opium, hallucinogenic mushrooms, marijuana, and other unidentified substances. Drug use has been woven into the fabric of human existence for a long time, and there is no indication that this will change. Therefore, it is important that students of psychology understand the mechanism of action of some common drugs, their effects on behavior, and their potential for being abused.

There are two terms that should be understood before we proceed further. The first, *drug tolerance,* is defined as a progressively decreasing response to a drug with continued use. When tolerance develops, a larger and larger dose of a drug is needed to produce the same effect. The second, *physical dependence,* refers to a condition in which a person needs to continue taking a drug to function normally. When a drug is withheld, a drug-dependent person will undergo withdrawl symptoms. These symptoms can be alleviated by taking further doses of the drug (Julien, 1981).

TYPES OF PSYCHOACTIVE DRUGS

There are literally thousands of different psychoactive agents. Many are natural substances, such as mushrooms and plant roots or seeds or extracts obtained from them, while others are synthetic chemicals. To be able to make some sense of this tremendous diversity, we need a classification system. We shall use the drug classification developed by Robert Julien (Julien, 1981). In this system psychoactive drugs can be placed into one of four basic groups. They are shown in Table 5.1 together with representative examples of each type of drug. In the following sections we discuss the characteristics of drugs in these categories. Antipsychotic agents, another drug category, will not be discussed here.

TABLE 5.1
Four classes of drugs that alter mood or behavior

1. Sedative-hypnotic compounds (CNS depressants)
   Barbiturates
      Long-acting: phenobarbital (*Luminal*)
      Intermediate-acting: amobarbital (*Amytal*)
      Short-acting: pentobarbital (*Nembutal*), secobarbital (*Seconal*)
      Ultrashort-acting: pentothal (*Thiopental*)
   Nonbarbiturate hypnotics
      Glutethimide (*Doriden*)
      Methyprylon (*Noludar*)
      Methaqualone (*Parest, Quaalude, Somnafac, Sopor*)
   Antianxiety agents
      Meprobamate (*Miltown, Equanil*)
      Chlordiazepoxide (*Librium*)
      Diazepam (*Valium*)
   Others
      Ethyl alcohol; bromide; paraldehyde; chloral hydrate; anesthetic gases and liquids (ether, halothane, chloroform, etc.)
2. Behavioral stimulants and convulsants
   Amphetamines: *Benzedrine; Dexedrine; Methedrine*
   Clinical antidepressants
      Monoamine oxidase (MAO) inhibitors: *Parnate*
      Tricyclic compounds: *Tofranil; Elavil*
   Cocaine
   Convulsants: strychnine; *Metrazol; Picrotoxin*
   Caffeine
   Nicotine
3. Narcotic analgesics (opiates)
   Opium; heroin; morphine; codeine; *Numorphan; Dilaudid; Percodan; Demerol*
4. Psychedelics and hallucinogens
   LSD (lysergic acid diethylamide)
   Mescaline
   Psilocybin
   Substituted amphetamines: DOM (STP); MDA; MMDA, TMA
   Tryptamine derivatives; DMT; DET; bufotenin
   Phencyclidine (*Sernyl*)
   Cannabis: marijuana; hashish; tetrahydrocannabinol

Note: Only representative agents from each class of drug are listed. Brand names are shown in italics.

SEDATIVE-HYPNOTIC DRUGS (CNS DEPRESSANTS)

Drugs in the category of sedative–hypnotic drugs are compounds that depress activity in the central nervous system. A *sedative* tends to induce calmness and lessen irritability and excitement, while a *hypnotic* promotes sleep. The difference between sedative and hypnotic effects often lies only in the size of the dose. At low doses most sedative-hypnotic drugs relieve feelings of anxiety and tension. At higher doses they can produce sleep, and at still higher doses, general anesthesia, coma, and death.

Barbiturates. All *barbiturates* are derivatives of barbituric acid, a compound first synthesized by the great German organic chemist of aspirin fame, Adolph Von Baeyer (1835–1917), in 1864. Barbiturates have substantial medical value, but because of their potential for abuse and misuse, many authorities believe that they have become a significant social hazard. Still they continue to be very popular—about 450 thousand kilograms (over a million pounds) of barbiturates are produced and consumed each year (Liska, 1981).

   The primary medical use of barbiturates is to produce sedation or drowsiness. They are also used as daytime sedatives to reduce feelings of anxiety. In addition, barbiturates such as phenobarbital are useful as anticonvulsants in some epileptics and as a treatment for the convulsions produced by poisons such as strychnine. Barbiturates such as thiopental are frequently used as anesthesia for minor surgery and as preoperative anesthetics for more major surgery (see Harvey, 1980).

There are a number of very serious problems related to barbiturate use besides those discussed earlier in the section on sleep. In large doses, or in combination with other drugs such as alcohol, barbiturates can kill. Recent estimates suggest that barbiturates are involved in about 75% of all drug-related deaths in the United States each year. Barbiturates are particularly dangerous because their respiratory-depressant effects are compounded greatly by alcohol. This is termed a *synergistic effect*, and the effect of combining the two drugs is much stronger than one would expect from the effect of each drug taken alone. All too often a person will return home from a party in a somewhat intoxicated state and take the usual number of barbiturate sleeping pills before going to sleep. The resulting respiratory depression is much more severe than twice that caused by either drug taken alone; because of this the person could easily die during sleep.

Barbiturates are also used as street drugs—"downers." When used this way they can produce a euphoria comparable to morphine and thus provide an escape from daily life (McClane & Martin, 1976). "Downers" are taken by people in all age groups and social groups. They have street names based on the color of the capsules, such as "red birds" (secobarbital), "blue devils" (amobarbital), and "yellow jackets" (pentobarbital). Barbiturates are sometimes taken to counter the effects of stimulant drugs while at other times they are taken in combination with, or as a substitute for, opiates such as heroin.

Today the risk-benefit ratio for barbiturates is shifting heavily against them, and their legitimate use is declining. Many physicians no longer prescribe them except in unusual circumstances. However, the diversion of legally manufactured drugs into illicit channels, as well as their clandestine manufacture, remains a major problem.

Nonbarbiturate Sedative-Hypnotic Drugs. One problematic sedative-hypnotic drug in this classification is *methaqualone*, which used to be sold legally under trade names such as Parest and Quaalude. Methaqualone became a drug of abuse (the tablets are sometimes referred to as "ludes") shortly after its introduction as a prescription hypnotic. Today, the drug is not legally manufactured or sold in the United States, although substantial quantities are illegally imported from South America for street sale. Methaqualone has been promoted as a "love drug" with aphrodisiac properties. In fact, its actions on the nervous system are quite similar to those of barbiturates; methaqualone actually impairs sexual performance.

Regular use of methaqualone can lead to tolerance and dependence. Life-threatening withdrawal symptoms, including major convulsions, may occur when the drug is stopped after long-term use at fairly high doses. Common side effects of methaqualone use are loss of appetite, nausea, diarrhea, fatigue, dizziness, headache, and depersonalization. Even moderate doses of the drug can cause a hangover (Harvey, 1980). For these reasons methaqualone has been banned or is strictly controlled in many countries.

Antianxiety Agents. Drugs that reduce tension and anxiety are very popular. Indeed, well over 5 billion doses of various antianxiety agents are sold each year in the United States. Sometimes called the minor tranquilizers, *antianxiety agents* reduce behavioral agitation and psychological stress and promote a general feeling of well-being. They are also used to treat muscle spasms, lower back pain, and the symptoms produced by withdrawal from alcohol or narcotics. Most antianxiety agents are mildly sedative and these drugs can generally induce sleep but not anesthesia.

There are several different classes of antianxiety agents. One type is called the *benzodiazepines*, which are grouped together because they all have a similar chemical structure. They include chlordiazepoxide (Librium), diazepam (Valium), flurazepam (Dalmane), lorazepam (Ativan), parazepam (Vestran), and triazolam (Halcion). The other general class of antianxiety agents is based on the compound *meprobamate* and includes Miltown and Equanil. Meprobamate-related drugs are not as frequently prescribed today as they were in the 1960s because they have more negative side effects than the benzodiazipines (Baldessarini, 1980).

Although psychologists themselves do not prescribe medications, they are interested in their effects. This is because antianxiety agents as a group are the most widely prescribed drugs in the United States. Millions of prescriptions are written for Valium and Librium each year. The sheer number of prescriptions raises questions about their appropriateness and potential for overuse. Some anxiety is part of normal living and it is not necessarily detrimental. Anxiety about getting a bad grade may well motivate a student to study harder for an exam. Similarly, anxiety about meeting a monthly quota may induce a person to work harder. But anxiety can become overwhelming and persistent. Then a decision must be made whether to intervene with drug therapy.

Properly used, antianxiety agents can help combat some of the stresses of life. They are also a useful adjunct to some forms of psychological therapy. But, too many people insist that their physicians prescribe tranquilizers. Further, a physician may sometimes write the prescription simply to satisfy a difficult and annoying patient even though tranquilizer use may be inappropriate. This can lead to indiscriminate drug use for months and even years. After a while, the decision to continue taking the drug is no longer in the hands of the patient—tolerance and dependence have developed—and withdrawal from the drug has become difficult. Further, when people stop taking antianxiety agents, they may still have the same problems that caused them to start taking the drug in the first place. Therefore, psychotherapy may be needed.

It is very difficult to overdose with benzodiazepines alone, but there can be synergistic effects in combination with other drugs producing potentially dangerous consequences. In a recent government publication, diazepam was listed as the most common drug leading to visits to emergency rooms. In one survey it was mentioned in over 54,000 overdose cases. Diazepam was also listed as the first or second most abused drug in 19 of 23 cities surveyed. Clearly, antianxiety agents must be treated with respect. Just because they are sometimes called minor tranquilizers does not mean that their effects are minor (Liska, 1981).

Alcohol. *Ethyl alcohol* is the most widely used psychoactive drug. It is every bit as powerful at altering consciousness as the drugs we have just discussed. Its use is so generally socially accepted that many governments obtain a substantial portion of their revenues through taxes on the sale of alcohol, and some governments even promote and subsidize its manufacture. Yet more people become dependent on, are psychologically and physically dis-

Alcohol is the most widely used and socially accepted psychoactive drug. (Hugh Rogers)

abled by, and are killed by alcohol than all other psychoactive drugs combined, including heroin, amphetamines, marijuana, and the barbiturates. In many ways, alcohol is the nation's number one drug problem.

To get some idea of the behavioral problems associated with alcohol, here are a few facts about alcohol use in the United States compiled by Liska (1981):

1. Forty percent of admissions to mental hospitals each year are related to alcohol.
2. More than 50% of all arrests each year are due to alcohol (approximately 2,000,000 arrests yearly).
3. Alcohol use accounts for 11,000,000 accidental injuries each year.
4. Alcohol plays a major role in half of the highway fatalities and about 28,000 people lose their lives each year in traffic accidents in which at least one driver had been drinking.
5. Alcoholics experience a suicide rate 58 times greater than that of nonalcoholics.
6. Alcoholism and alcohol abuse drain our economy of at least $15 billion each year because of lost work time plus health and welfare services, property damage, medical expenses, and overhead costs.
7. The life expectancy of heavy drinkers is estimated to be shorter by 10 to 12 years than that of the general public.
8. Considering the ill effects of drinking problems on just the immediate families of drinkers, some 36 million Americans can be regarded as caught in alcohol's web: unhappy marriages, broken homes, desertion, divorce, poverty, and displaced children.

Statistics such as these are the concern of all behavioral scientists. Legislating alcohol use and making it illegal proved ineffective during prohibition, and other coercive legislative solutions are also likely to fail. Solutions, when they do come, will probably arise from behavioral and neurobiological research, performed perhaps by someone who is just beginning a career in psychology by reading this text.

Alcohol is consumed in many forms, including beer, wine, brandy, whiskey, gin, and vodka. It is not *what* you drink but the concentration of alcohol in the bloodstream that determines its effect on your behavior. Blood alcohol concentration is determined by how much is consumed over time and by body weight. The percentage of ethyl alcohol differs across different drinks. For example, most domestic beers contain about 4% alcohol. If you drink a 12-oz can of beer, you will actually get about ½ oz of alcohol. Table wines contain about 12% alcohol—a typical 6-oz glass of wine will provide a little less than ¾ oz of alcohol. Hard liquors, such as whiskey origin, are about 40% alcohol (80 proof), although some are 50% alcohol (100 proof) or even more. Therefore, the 1½-oz shot of liquor in a cocktail provides about the same amount of alcohol as that in the 6-oz glass of table wine.

When consumed, alcohol is rapidly and completely absorbed into the bloodstream from the stomach and especially the upper portions of the small intestine. If the stomach is empty, absorption will be rapid. Food in the stomach will act as a sponge, taking up the alcohol and delaying absorption until the food and alcohol pass together into the small intestine.

The rate at which people metabolize alcohol is fairly constant, and larger persons metabolize it only slightly faster than do smaller or lighter people. In general, the body can metabolize the alcohol in one drink (¾ oz) in about 1 hour (Riche, 1980). Neither coffee, exercise, nor cold showers will speed up this process. Only time causes blood alcohol levels to fall and sobriety to return.

Each person has a unique reaction to alcohol, depending on the social situation, rate of emptying of the stomach, and other factors, such as previous drinking experience. However, the behavioral effects are most directly related to the concentration of alcohol circulating in the blood, which in turn depends directly on the amount drunk and body mass (Wallgren & Berry, 1970). The blood alcohol level of a 190-lb man drinking 3 oz of whiskey in an hour will be much lower than that in a 120-lb woman drinking the same amount over the same time. Thus smaller people should not attempt to "keep up" with larger people in alcohol consumption. This is because the concentration of alcohol in the bloodstream of lighter people increases much faster with a given amount drunk because they simply have less body mass in which to distribute to alcohol. Some of the behavioral effects of various blood alcohol concentrations in non-alcohol tolerant people are shown in Table 5.2.

Small amounts of alcohol produce an elevation of mood, a lessening of inhibitions, and a general sense of well-being. With somewhat larger amounts, the decrease in inhibition continues, while sedative effects begin to increase. Alcohol, as with other sedative-hypnotic drugs, is not an aphrodisiac. The alcohol-produced disinhibition may cause loss of decorum and restraint, but the depressant effects ultimately interfere with sexual activity. Shakespeare wrote of alcohol: "It provokes the desire, but it takes away the performance."

Many people believe that only the derelicts who wander city streets are alcoholics. Actually, these people account for less than 5% of all alcoholics. Most alcoholics have jobs, families, close friends, and some social position. About 70% to 80% of problem drinkers are men, but the reported incidence of alcoholism in women is rising steadily, perhaps because women are becoming more willing to seek treatment.

Before 1960, alcoholism was considered a moral and criminal issue. Drunkenness was a crime, and alcoholics were generally denied medical treatment. Then psychological and medical opinion began to view alcoholism as an illness and alcoholics as persons who cannot tolerate the effects of

TABLE 5.2
Psychological and physical effects of various blood alcohol concentration levels

Number of Drinks[a]	Blood Alcohol Concentration (percent)	Psychological and Physical Effects
1	0.02–0.03	No overt effects, slight mood elevation
2	0.05–0.06	Feeling of relaxation, warmth; slight decrease in reaction time and in fine-muscle coordination
3	0.08–0.09	Balance, speech, vision, hearing slightly impaired; feelings of euphoria, increased confidence; loss of motor coordination
	0.10	Legal intoxication in most states; some have lower limits
4	0.11–0.12	Coordination and balance becoming difficult; distinct impairment of mental faculties, judgment
5	0.14–0.15	Major impairment of mental and physical control: slurred speech, blurred vision, lack of motor skills
7	0.20	Loss of motor control—must have assistance in moving about; mental confusion
10	0.30	Severe intoxication; minimum conscious control of mind and body
14	0.40	Unconsciousness, threshold of coma
17	0.50	Deep coma
20	0.60	Death from respiratory failure

Note: For each hour elapsed since the last drink, subtract 0.015% blood alcohol concentration, or approximately one drink.
[a] One drink = one beer (4% alcohol, 12 oz) or one highball (1 oz of whiskey).
Source: P. Jones-Witters & W. L. Witters. *Drugs and Society: A Biological Perspective.* Monterey, CA: Wadsworth, 1983, p. 207.

alcohol. The difference between those who can drink in moderation and those who cannot lies in their reaction to alcohol. These differences are due to a combination of genetic, biochemical, and social factors that we are just beginning to understand.

Today the World Health Organization defines *alcohol dependence syndrome* as "a state, psychic and usually also physical, resulting from taking alcohol and characterized by behavioral and other responses that always include a compulsion to take alcohol on a continuous or periodic basis in order to experience its psychic effects and sometimes to avoid the discomfort of its absence; tolerance may or may not be present" (National Institute on Alcohol Abuse and Alcoholism, 1980).

Alcoholism can be treated. With appropriate therapy over half of treated alcoholics can recover and lead alcohol-free lives. Both inpatient therapy settings, where the alcoholic remains in a hospital-like institution for some time, and outpatient settings seem to have comparable success rates in treating alcoholism. The prognosis is best for those who have a high degree of motivation, reasonably high socioeconomic status, and social ability. The outlook is much poorer for skid-row alcoholics and those with alcohol-related psychosis. As with any other problem behavior, the sooner therapy is started, the better the chances for success.

BEHAVIORAL STIMULANTS

Amphetamines. *Amphetamines* are synthetic substances with effects similar to those of the body's own arousing substances, epinephrine (adrenalin) and norepinephrine. There are a wide variety of amphetamine-related drugs, but as their effects are typically quite similar, we shall discuss them together. At moderate doses these drugs increase general central nervous system arousal through the activation of brain stem structures and also induce sensations of euphoria and pleasure. They do this by causing an increase in the release of the neurotransmitters norepinephrine and dopamine from synaptic terminals in the brain and also by producing an increase in the release of epineprhine from the adrenal glands. Additionally, amphetamines block the reuptake of norepinephrine and dopamine back into synaptic terminals, resulting in an increased effect of these neurotransmitters because they stay in the synaptic cleft longer (Weiner, 1980).

There are only three conditions in which amphetamines are suggested as appropriate therapy because of their great potential for abuse. These three conditions are 1) narcolepsy and sometimes *petit mal* epilepsy, 2) attention deficit disorder in children, and 3) obesity (Julien, 1981).

In some cases of narcolepsy, amphetamines help the affected person stay awake. Some forms of narcolepsy do not respond well to amphetamines however, and other forms of treatment are needed.

Attention deficit disorder (called hyperkinesis by some) is a behavioral problem seen in about 4% of grade school children and early adolescents. It involves abnormally high levels of physical activity, short attention span, and aggressive as well as unpredictable behavior. The drugs commonly used to treat this disorder are amphetamine derivatives called methylphenidate (Ritalin) and pemoline (Cylert).

To some it may seem paradoxical to treat this kind of behavioral disorder with a stimulant drug; however amphetamines typically act to enhance low levels of responding and to suppress higher levels of behavior. It is thought that the effects of amphetamines on the behavior of children with attention deficit disorder is related to this characteristic, biphasic action of amphetamines. However, it must be emphasized that indiscriminate use of amphetamine derivatives in dealing with children with behavior problems is dangerous. Many children are incorrectly diagnosed each year as suffering from attention deficit disorders and are prescribed inappropriate therapies. Physicians, psychologists, and school counselors should carefully look at the child's social and family situation as well as school performance before deciding to begin drug therapy.

The use of amphetamines in weight control is controversial. There is no doubt that these drugs have powerful effects on some of the neural mechanisms that suppress appetite. However, the effect is only short-term, wearing off after 3 or 4 weeks as drug tolerance develops. To achieve further suppression of appetite, the dose must be increased. This is why the Federal Food and Drug Administration approves amphetamine use only for short-term weight reduction. Because amphetamines produce strong feelings of euphoria, their continued use leads to a very strong psychological dependence and substantial difficulty in living comfortably without regular doses of the drug. Further, because amphetamines have only short-term effectiveness in controlling appetite, probably "most of the five billion doses of diet pills made in the U.S.A. each year are actually used as euphoriants" (Myers, Jawetz, & Goldfein, 1972).

Some persons (once called "speed freaks") inject high doses of amphetamines directly into their veins. This produces intense feelings of euphoria that are sometimes referred to as an amphetamine "flash" or "rush" (Kramer, Fischman, & Littlefield, 1967). When used in this way, an amphetamine is typically taken in a cycle or "run" of intensive drug use that may last from several days to a week. The cycle starts with several days of repeated injections of amphetamine, with gradually increasing doses. Tolerance develops quickly and the person may inject several grams of amphetamine in a day, a dose that could be fatal to someone who is not drug tolerant (Jaffe, 1980).

When administered directly into the bloodstream, the effects of amphetamine on behavior are striking. At first the person will feel energetic, confident, outgoing, and capable of doing almost anything. The person does not sleep, eats very little, is very talkative, and may accomplish much during the first day or two of the run. After several days, the effects of the drug become progressively disruptive and unpleasant. Symptoms include confused and disorganized behavior, stereotyped repetition of certain acts, and teeth grinding. Often there are feelings of irritability, fear, and suspicion.

With continuing large doses, hallucinations, patterns of disordered thought, and antisocial behavior almost identical to those of paranoid schizophrenia may occur. Indeed, the similarity between the two can be so great that it is often difficult for clinicians to distinguish between a person suffering from amphetamine-induced psychosis and an acute paranoid schizophrenic episode without a urine analysis to detect the presence of the drug. This similarity, though, has provided researchers with important clues about the neurobiological basis of certain kinds of psychosis.

Cocaine. Like amphetamines, *cocaine* acts on the catecholamine systems of the brain and body. It produces its psychological effects by inhibiting the uptake of norepinephrine and dopamine back into presynaptic terminals. This increases the amount of neurotransmitter in the synaptic cleft and augments the actions of these neurotransmitters. Because of similar biochemical actions, cocaine's behavioral effects are very similar to those of amphetamine (Jaffe, 1980; Wesson & Smith, 1977). Both drugs elevate mood, induce euphoria, and produce feelings of well-being as well as limitless energy and power. Cocaine also reduces fatigue.

Although much remains to be learned about the neural actions of cocaine, it is thought that shortly after it is taken, cocaine stimulates cortical activity, and then several minutes later it activates brain stem regions of the central nervous system. A dose of cocaine may be metabolized in as little as 15 minutes, and the stimulant effects are typically gone within an hour or so (Javaid, Fischman, Schuster, Dekirmenjian, & Davis, 1978). Therefore, to maintain the effect, repeated doses of cocaine must be administered fairly frequently, an expensive process.

Cocaine is also a potent local anesthetic, and when the drug is inhaled it anesthesizes sensory nerve endings in the nose. Cocaine also relaxes the bronchi and constricts the blood vessels of the nose, which initially causes freer breathing. But when the drug wears off, the bronchi constrict and the blood vessels dilate, resulting in a stuffy nose and bleeding nasal membranes. When taken intravenously with other drugs, such as heroin, cocaine can be lethal.

The physical withdrawal symptoms following cocaine use are not severe, although some depression is often seen after the euphoric effects have diminished. Debilitating psychological dependence on the drug often occurs. Taken regularly, cocaine can disrupt eating and sleeping habits and can lead to anxiety, paranoid thinking, and difficulty in concentrating.

Caffeine. Caffeine is the most widely used stimulant drug in the world. It is found in many products, including coffee, tea, soft drinks, and chocolate. A cup of brewed coffee contains somewhere between 85 and 125 milligrams (mg) of caffeine, while a cup of instant coffee contains a little more than one-half of that amount. A 12-oz can of cola drink has between 30 and 50 mg of caffeine, and a 2-oz chocolate bar may contain 50 mg.

Many people have a *psychological dependence* on caffeine, and their morning "drug fix" is a normal part of getting going. Two cups of coffee in the morning supply sufficient caffeine to produce cortical activation, to increase the speed and clarity of thought, and to decrease feelings of fatigue. Caffeine also produces wakefulness. If taken several hours before going to bed, it may delay the onset of sleep (Rall, 1980). Excessive caffeine intake by people who drink more than 10 cups of coffee each day can disrupt behavior and metabolism. At present, there is little or no convincing evidence that dependence on caffeine is harmful, although pregnant women are probably well advised to limit their intake of this drug, as well as any other psychoactive substances that cross freely into the bloodstream of the fetus.

Nicotine. *Nicotine* is the primary drug in tobacco. Today, most cigarettes deliver less than 1 mg of nicotine, although cigarettes manufactured before the 1970s often contained three times as much nicotine as the current products. About 25% of the nicotine in cigarette smoke enters the bloodstream, reaching the brain less than 10 seconds after it is inhaled. About half the nicotine in a cigarette is metabolized in 20 to 30 minutes, and most regular cigarette smokers smoke one cigarette every 30 to 40 minutes, consuming something over a pack of 20 cigarettes each day. It appears that these people are smoking to regulate and maintain a constant level of nicotine in the bloodstream. Smokers who are given cigarettes that are lower in nicotine than their usual brand will typically smoke more cigarettes and inhale more deeply and more often; as a result, nicotine levels in the blood remain about the same as with their usual brand (Jarvik, 1979; Schacter, 1978).

Nicotine produces a mild stimulation of central nervous system activity that is considered pleasant by most smokers. It also causes an increase in epinephrine release from the adrenal glands. This, in turn, causes an increase in heart rate, blood pressure, and basal metabolic rate. Nicotine also has some appetite suppressive properties and may inhibit hunger contractions in the stomach. Further, there is a substantial amount of carbon monoxide in cigarette smoke. Molecules of carbon monoxide bind to hemoglobin in the blood, substantially reducing its oxygen-carrying capacity. This is one factor

The great difficulty that most heavy cigarette smokers have in quitting smoking argues that tobacco use is a true addiction. (Bohdan Hrynewych/Stock Boston)

which causes shortness of breath following exercise in smokers, and it also may be a factor in the lower birth weight and lower survival rate of infants born to women who smoked during pregnancy.

Nicotine is a powerful drug which rapidly produces tolerance and dependence. A person who is just beginning to smoke may consume only one or two cigarettes per day at first, but after just a few weeks or months of regular smoking, consumption often climbs to a pack a day or more. A regular smoker who consumes a pack or more of cigarettes takes in a dose of nicotine that would have caused serious discomfort and illness when that person started smoking. This indicates that substantial drug tolerance to nicotine does develop.

The symptoms of withdrawal from nicotine are quite mild, but they do exist. Regular cigarette smokers report that when their cigarette supply is cut off, they feel irritable, have headaches and stomach upset, and experience difficulty concentrating. The great difficulty that most heavy cigarette smokers have in quitting smoking argues that tobacco use is a true addiction.

Several behavior factors facilitate addiction to tobacco. Since the drug reaches the brain rapidly after each puff, there are at least 10 drug-produced rewards per cigarette, each one closely paired with the act of smoking. Second, withdrawal symptoms occur quickly, symptoms that can be relieved by lighting another cigarette. Third, smoking becomes paired with other rewarding activities, such as finishing a meal, driving, or drinking alcohol. Finally, there is strong social pressure to smoke, both from commercial advertising and from peer groups.

OPIATES AND NARCOTICS

Opiates are natural and synthetic drugs with effects similar to morphine, the major active ingredient in *opium*. The major medical uses of opiates are to relieve pain, cough, and diarrhea. Opiates are strongly addictive, causing both drug tolerance and physical dependence with repeated use. When an opiate user's supply is interrupted, withdrawal symptoms occur. These symptoms can be very severe and sometimes life-threatening in long-term users.

Opiates have had a very checkered history, sometimes praised, sometimes reviled. To many people opiates embody all that is bad and evil about drug use. Because of this, there are strong social sanctions and severe criminal penalties associated with the nonmedical use, sale and possession of opiates.

All opiates act on specific receptors in the central nervous system. Normally, these receptors are stimulated by the naturally occurring opioid substances found in the brain, known as the *enkephalins* and the *endorphins* (Snyder & Childers, 1979; Terenius, 1978). These opioids act to modulate pain and mood and probably mediate some aspects of acupuncture analgesia. When morphine, heroin, or some other opiate is administered, molecules of these substances become bound to opiate receptors and mimic the actions of the body's own painkillers. In this way they stimulate specific neural systems, producing analgesia, alterations in mood, and sedation.

Opium. Opium is a natural extract which is obtained from the juice of the seed pod of the opium poppy plant. Its properties, analgesic and sedative, as well as euphoric, have been known for thousands of years. There are references to opium in ancient Sumerian tablets written about 6,000 years ago, and the ancient Egyptians, Greeks, and Romans had a good working knowledge of its properties and uses.

In the early nineteenth century, many writers and other intellectuals experimented with opium, and some wrote eloquently about their experiences. "Thou hast the keys of Paradise, oh just, subtle, and mighty opium!" wrote Thomas De Quincey, who, with many others, believed that opium enhanced creative and intellectual forces. Charles Baudelaire, Elizabeth Barrett Browning, Samuel Taylor Coleridge, Alexander Dumas, and Edgar Allan Poe were all addicted to opium at some time in their lives.

Opium was introduced to the United States by the Chinese laborers who built many of the railroads in the West. Opiate use was further encouraged by the widespread use of the opium extract, morphine, which was administered by physicians to wounded soldiers during the Civil War. Around the turn of the century, many patent medicines contained opiates, and these medicines were taken by people in all social classes and age groups. This resulted in an estimated 1 million Americans regularly taking opiates and about 1 person in every 400 being at least somewhat opiate dependent. At the turn of the century, opiates could be purchased over the counter at neighborhood drugstores or obtained by mail order.

Heroin. In 1898 a significant event occurred in the history of drug use. In that year the Bayer Company introduced a new opiate product that crosses from the bloodstream into the CNS much more rapidly than morphine. This compound, known chemically as diacetylmorphine, was superior to codeine (another opium derivative) as a cough suppressant and far superior to morphine as a painkiller, mostly because it acted so much more quickly. Further, the Bayer Company maintained in its early advertising that this drug had less potential than morphine for causing addiction. For these reasons they named the new drug *Heroin*, because it was such a heroic drug. However, heroin's addiction properties were quickly recognized and in less than 20 years, with the passage of the Harrison Narcotics Act of 1914, it became a controlled substance. In 1924 it was outlawed, and today heroin has no generally accepted medical uses in the United States, although there are some who feel that its advantages as an analgesic warrant reconsideration of the use of this drug in some terminally ill patients who suffer from severe and chronic pain.

With the passage of the Harrison Narcotics Act, opiate use in the United States declined until around 1960, when only 1 person in 4,000 was addicted. Since then the incidence of heroin addiction has increased dramatically, until today there are between 400,000 and 600,000 heroin addicts, or about 1 person in every 500.

Heroin addiction is expensive because the drug must be taken on a regular basis to prevent withdrawal symptoms. Since heroin is available only through illicit channels, and therefore at highly inflated prices, addiction can cost hundreds of dollars a day. To obtain this much money, many heroin users turn to crime, usually burglary, robbery, and mugging, thus adding another dimension to an already serious social problem.

It is not clear what strategy is most appropriate for dealing with opiate addiction. Some favor decriminalization of heroin, arguing that dependence on heroin is much like a diabetic's dependence on insulin; the drug is needed daily to maintain normal life. Further, they argue, inexpensive availability of heroin should result in a dramatic decline in the crime rate as well as a decrease in the income of organized crime syndicates.

Others argue that decriminalization of heroin use would simply result in a huge increase in the number of drug users, with a correspondingly great cost to society in terms of disrupted lives, lost work hours, and a variety of health problems. They argue that the heroin problem can be successfully attacked only through strict enforcement of drug laws and severe punishment of drug sellers and drug users.

Both strategies have been tried in various countries and neither has been very successful. An effective approach to the problem of heroin addiction will probably come only from research into the neurobiological mechanisms that underlie opiate tolerance and dependence, coupled with behavioral studies of the psychological and social factors that promote drug use and abstinence (Jaffe, 1980).

PSYCHEDELICS AND HALLUCINOGENS

Because of the diversity of physiological and behavioral effects that psychedelic and hallucinogenic drugs produce, it is difficult to describe simply what they do. The immense variety of drug-induced effects is almost staggering. The most profound effects include altered and enhanced sensory and perceptual experiences. Because these drugs loosen a person's ties to reality, one may perceive visual, auditory, or other sensations that do not exist (*hallucinations*). Often, however, these are not true hallucinations; these drug effects are more likely to be massive changes in perception. Faces may change shape and furniture may melt, but the drug user is usually aware that these are drug-induced distortions, unlike the case with true hallucinations when that distinction cannot be made.

Users of these drugs also often report that they have mystical experiences while under the influence of the drug. The feeling of being out of one's body, of having a different existence, or of experiencing a sense of timelessness are among the many effects which have been reported. Hallucinogens do not appear to mimic the disturbed thought processes associated with psychosis. Indeed, the changes that occur during psychosis are quite unlike those seen during drug use. For this reason the term *psychedelic*, meaning mind revealing or mind manifesting, is often preferred when discussing these drugs.

Most psychedelic and hallucinogenic drugs produce their effects by altering some aspect of synaptic transmission. Some drugs, such as physostygmine and atropine, act on synapses where acetylcholine is the neurotransmitter. Others, such as mescaline, appear to act on norepinephrine synapses, and *lysergic acid diethylamide* (LSD) and psilocybin appear to cause their effects by influencing brain serotonin systems (Haigler & Aghajanian, 1977).

LSD is perhaps the prototypical psychedelic substance. Taken in doses of as little as 25 to 100 micrograms (μg; a microgram is a millionth of a gram) LSD produces heightened sensory experiences and perceptual distortions. The drug experience may be pleasurable and rewarding or extremely frightening (Freedman, 1969). At least part of this variability seems to be due to the expectations of the drug user and differences in the surroundings in which the drug is taken. Those having a "bad trip" or unpleasant LSD experience have been known to commit suicide or to physically injure themselves or others. Too often this occurs when a person is unaware that he or she has been given a dose of LSD and becomes frightened by the unexpected transformations in perception. A few people have needed psychological treatment to help them get over the effects of a frightening LSD experience. Further, some people have flashbacks to the drug state, sometimes several months after last taking LSD. These are in all likelihood some sort of reactivation of stored memories of the experience rather than an actual drug effect (Stanton, Mintz, & Franklin, 1976).

HIGHLIGHT 5.3
The World's First LSD Trips

Albert Hoffmann was a chemist who worked for the Sandoz Pharmaceutical Company. He had synthesized LSD in 1938 and after a series of psychological screening tests in laboratory animals without any substantial behavioral effects noticed, the compound was placed "on the shelf." About 5 years later, Hoffmann had occasion to handle the bottle containing LSD. Apparently, some was absorbed through the skin, because Hoffmann began to have very unusual experiences. He was a careful scientist and he carefully recorded his reactions to the drug. They are some of the most dramatic descriptions of LSD effects, probably because he had no preconceived notions as what to expect. This translation from Hoffmann's journals was prepared by Kenneth Liska (1981).

> Last Friday, the 16th of April, I was forced to interrupt my work in the laboratory in the middle of the afternoon, and to go home and seek care, since I was overcome by a remarkable uneasiness combined with a slight dizziness. At home I lay down and fell into a not unpleasant, intoxicated-like state which was characterized by an extremely exciting fantasy. In a twilight condition with closed eyes (I found the daylight to be annoyingly bright), there crowded before me without interruption, fantastic pictures of extraordinary plasticity, with an intensive, kaleidoscopic play of colors. After about two hours this condition disappeared.

Hoffmann suspected that his experience was due to the LSD. Therefore, he decided to take what he thought would be a very small dose of the drug again, but under more controlled conditions, and to record his experiences in his laboratory notebook. We now know that he took a rather heavy dose. Needless to say, the effects were very vivid and startling. He described them this way:

> Here stop the laboratory notes. The last words can be written only with great effort. I asked my lab helper to accompany me home, since I believed the process would take the same course as the disturbance on the Friday before. However, already on the bicycle ride home it was clear that all symptoms were more intense than the first time, I already had great trouble speaking clearly and my field of vision wavered and was distorted as a picture in a curved mirror. Also I had the feeling of not leaving the spot whereas my lab helper later told me we had traveled at a brisk pace.
> So far as I can remember, the following symptoms were most pronounced during the height of the crisis and before the physician came: dizziness, visual disturbance; the faces of those present appeared to me as colored grimaces; strong motor unrest alternating with paralysis; the head, the entire body and all of the limbs appeared at times heavy, as if filled with metal; cramps in the calves, hands at times numb, cold; a metallic taste on the tongue; throat dry, constricted; a feeling of suffocation; alternately stupefied, then again clearly aware of the situation, noting as though I were a neutral observer, standing outside my self, that I shouted half crazily or chattered unintelligibly.

Six hours later, Hoffmann was still showing some effects of his intoxication, although his condition had improved substantially.

> The visual disturbances were still pronounced. Everything appeared to waver, and proportions were distorted, similar to a reflection in moving water. In addition, everything was drenched in changing colors of disagreeable, predominantly poisonous green and blue hues. Colorful, very plastic and fantastic images passed before my closed eyes. It was especially noteworthy that all acoustical perceptions, perchance the noise of a passing car, were translated into optical sensations, so that through each tone and noise, a corresponding colored picture, kaleidoscopically changing in form and color was elicited.

Since the 1960s, marijuana has become popular as a recreational drug in the United States. (Peter Simon/Stock Boston)

Arguments about LSD use have generated more heat than light and much more needs to be learned about this drug. We do know that tolerance does develop when LSD is taken regularly; a person must stop taking the drug for a time before the drug effects return to full strength. Physical dependence on LSD does not seem to occur, because withdrawal symptoms have not been observed. Some psychological dependence may occur in people who become preoccupied with the drug and its effects. However, for some reason this preoccupation does not last, and most users eventually return to more traditional and perhaps predictable drugs, such as marijuana and alcohol (Jaffe, 1980).

MARIJUANA

Marijuana is derived from the crushed leaves, flowers, and sometimes stems of the hemp plant *Cannabis sativa*, which grows throughout the world in temperate through tropic regions. This plant contains the psychoactive ingredient in marijuana *delta-9-tetrahydrocannabinol* (THC). This is the same active ingredient as that in hashish, which is a concentrated resinous extract of the cannabis plant. Marijuana and hashish have been used in India for thousands of years as an aid to spiritual meditation and as an intoxicant. Since the 1960s, marijuana has become popular as a recreational drug in the United States.

During the early twentieth century marijuana use was associated with the least wealthy socioeconomic groups in society, and it was condemned by the Bureau of Narcotics as a "killer drug" that led inevitably to violent crime, heroin addiction, and ultimately to personal destruction. Marijuana use became an emotional subject, and decisions regarding it were made on the basis of few facts and often incorrect information. The result was that very harsh penalties were often imposed for the possession and sale of even small quantities of marijuana. Then, in the late 1960s, there was a dramatic increase in marijuana use among young people from middle-class backgrounds. This drug became a symbol of youth rebellion and a subject of great concern to adults. As people discovered that marijuana use did not inevitably lead to violence, or even to the use of other drugs, confidence in governmental authority was badly shaken.

The situation is quite different today. Many studies of the effects of THC have been performed, and several very comprehensive governmental reports prepared. The general consensus is that there is no scientific evidence that marijuana use causes violent or criminal behavior. Indeed, marijuana is far less likely than alcohol to produce aggressive behavior. The National Commission on Marijuana and Drug Use (1972) concluded:

Neither the marijuana user nor the drug itself can be said to constitute a danger to public safety. For, as two researchers have so cogently stated for the Commission, "whatever an individual is, in all of his cultural, social and psychological complexity, is not going to vanish in a puff of marijuana smoke!"

The primary effects of marijuana use center on an increased sense of well-being accompanied by relaxation. In social situations marijuana may induce hilarity and sociability, followed by dreamy relaxation. The National Committee on Marijuana and Drug Abuse noted that marijuana may produce

alteration of sensory perceptions including expansion of space and time; and a more vivid sense of touch, sight, smell, taste, and sound; a feeling of hunger, especially a craving for sweets; and subtle changes in thought formation and expression. To an unknowing observer, an individual in this state of consciousness would not appear noticeably different from his normal state.

There are major differences in the effects produced by the usual low social doses of marijuana and those produced by high doses of hashish, even though the active agent, THC, is the same. High doses produce sensory alterations and hallucinations not seen with lower doses (Jaffe, 1980). The biological basis of the effects of THC are not well understood at present.

Marijuana use causes a substantial impairment in the performance of airplane pilots and automobile and truck drivers in controlled studies. Further, there is some evidence that marijuana use impairs the formation of memories and the transfer of these memories into permanent long-term storage.

MEDITATION

Meditation has been a feature of many Eastern and Middle-Eastern cultures for centuries. Only recently, however, have Americans and Europeans become interested in it. In essence, meditation seeks an altered state of conscious awareness through controlled thought.

During much of each day our minds are filled with a constant stream of thoughts. Some of these thoughts may be disturbing, keeping us in a state of turmoil. The techniques of meditation try to break into this stream of conscious thought and interrupt its flow for a while. In this way, according to the proponents of meditation, one can focus one's attention on the experience of being alive and achieve tranquility and relaxation that are unknown normally.

Some researchers believe that meditation can produce alternations in consciousness and thoughts that verge on a mystical experience. (Barbara Alper/Stock Boston)

Meditation takes many forms. Some types, such as Zen meditation, require focusing attention on specific questions or thoughts called *koans*. These are riddles without logical answers, designed to free the mind from logical thought. Through intense concentration on the koans and through discipline, one is said to be able to leap into enlightenment. Other meditative techniques involve concentrating attention on some external object, such as a vase, candle flame, or an abstract symbol called a mandala. Regardless of the form of meditation, the goal is changed conscious awareness.

Transcendental meditation, a technique developed and popularized by Maharishi Mahesh Yogi, is better suited for Westerners than some other forms of meditation. It requires no long apprenticeship and training and can be mastered relatively easily by most people. It relies on the repetition of a meaningless word or sound called a *mantra*. In essence the mantra is a nondistracting sound that the meditator repeats over and over during a 15- to 30-minute meditation period each morning and evening. During this period the person sits quietly and comfortably, eyes closed, repeating the mantra. Other thoughts are ignored. Many who practice this form of meditation maintain that their thinking becomes more developed and creative in a very natural and pleasant way.

Meditation seems to differ from the relaxation produced by hypnosis. During hypnosis, EEG, and other physiological measures do not change from the waking state. In meditation, however, there is a definite slowing of some physiological processes. These changes are like those that accompany normal relaxation and reduction of anxiety. Indeed, Benson (1975) argues that the various meditation techniques are just ways of inducing a normal relaxation response and that there is nothing mysterious about meditation. It is simply a method by which people learn to become more relaxed and tranquil.

However, others feel that meditation, when practiced properly and extensively, can produce alterations in consciousness and thoughts that go far beyond mere relaxation. These people feel that meditation can cause altered perceptions that verge on a mystical experience. The nature of this experience is difficult for those who have experienced it to describe, but for some it does appear to go beyond ordinary sensations.

SUMMARY

1. Circadian rhythms are changes in bodily function or behavior that recur on a daily basis. They are internally generated but become linked to a particular day–night cycle. The patterns of sleep and waking are the most obvious of our circadian rhythms.

2. Sleep is not simply an extended period of unconsciousness but there are a number of different stages of sleep that one passes through several times each night. These different phases of sleep are best studied through electroencephalograms (EEG) recorded using a polygraph.

3. Between 60 and 90 minutes after falling asleep, the EEG record begins to appear as if one is waking up, but sleep, paradoxically, continues accompanied by rapid darting movements of the eyes. This stage of sleep, often called rapid eye movement (REM) sleep, is accompanied by an increase in heart rate and a decrease in skeletal muscle tone. Dreams with story content typically occur during this stage of sleep. In normal adults periods of REM sleep occur at about 90 minute intervals.

4. Sleep-waking cycles change as people develop from infancy through adulthood and old age. Infants sleep much more than do adults and much of that sleep time is spent in active sleep. As an individual matures, the total number of hours spent asleep decreases as does the percentage of REM sleep.

5. There are substantial differences among individuals in the amount of sleep needed each night. At least some of these differences may be related to aspects of personality with individuals having worrisome problems requiring more REM sleep.

6. Dreams reflect the aroused state of the brain during REM sleep. Memories of recent important events often influence the content of dreams, and these dreams seem very real since the accuracy of the dream cannot be judged against any external standard. Dreams that occur in stages of sleep other than REM sleep seem to be characterized by single ideas or feelings.

7. Time does not appear to be compressed during dreams and time seems to pass at the same rate during dreams as it does when one is awake. Penile erections occur during periods of REM sleep and this does not indicate dreams with sexual content.

8. Many people suffer from disturbances of sleep. Those who attribute excessive daytime sleepiness to poor sleep during the night are usually classified as insomniacs while those who are sleepy during the day but do not associate these feelings with disturbed sleep are termed hypersomniacs. Depression and anxiety are leading causes of disturbed sleep. Sleeping pills lead to a dangerous cycle of dependence on the medications and are themselves a leading cause of disturbed sleep. The major symptom of narcolepsy, a serious form of hypersomnia, is irresistible attacks of sleepiness. The muscle weakness sometimes associated with narcolepsy is called cataplexy. Attacks of narcolepsy appear to be related to the inappropriate occurrence of episodes of REM sleep.

9. Sleepwalking (somnambulism) occurs during stage 4 sleep and does not seem to be associated with dreaming. It is a genetically linked trait that is more common in children than adults.

10. The hypnotic state is very different from sleep and it is characterized by a voluntary entrance into hypnosis, deep relaxation, and heightened suggestibility. The increase in suggestibility accounts in large part for the high degree of control that the hypnotist apparently has over the subject.

11. A drug is any substance that when taken into the body alters physical or psychological function. Drugs can be commonly consumed substances such as caffeine, alcohol, nicotine, and aspirin as well as opiates, barbiturates, and other compounds more typically thought of as drugs. Drug tolerance is a progressively decreasing response to a drug with continued use. Physical dependence is a condition in which a person needs to continue taking a drug in order to function normally and prevent withdrawal symptoms.

12. A sedative is a drug that induces calmness and lessens irritability. A hypnotic drug promotes sleep. Barbiturates are sedative-hypnotic drugs that are not used as frequently as they once were because their respiratory depressant effects are greatly amplified by alcohol, because they can produce tolerance and dependence, and because they are often street-drugs of abuse. Antianxiety agents reduce behavioral agitation and psychological stress as well as reducing muscle spasms, and withdrawal symptoms from alcohol. The antianxiety agents are widely prescribed drugs and are often used inappropriately.

13. Alcohol is widely used and accepted in many societies, but it has powerful consciousness-altering effects. There many serious societal problems related to the use of alcohol. When consumed, alcohol is rapidly and completely absorbed into the bloodstream and its concentration there is a function of amount ingested and body weight. The concentration of alcohol in the bloodstream determines its behavioral effects with a level of 0.1% being the criteria for intoxication in most states. The difference between those who can drink in moderation and

14. Behavioral stimulants such as amphetamines are related to the body's own arousing substances, epinephrine and norepinephrine. Amphetamines are useful in the treatment of some cases of narcolepsy, but their use in the treatment of attention deficit disorder in children is more controversial. It is clear that these drugs can be useful in some cases. The most problematic use of amphetamines is in weight control because their appetite suppressant effect lasts for only a few weeks and then drug tolerance develops. Further, there is the potential for developing psychological dependency with continued use of amphetamines.

15. Cocaine acts by enhancing the effects of dopamine and norepinephrine and produces feelings of high energy, euphoria, and well being. Psychological dependence on cocaine often develops with repeated use. Caffeine is found in many products including soft drinks and coffee and it can produce psychological and physical dependence when taken regularly. Nicotine produces a mild stimulation of the nervous system and pleasurable sensations.

16. Opiates are strongly addictive, causing both euphoria and sedation. Their use also leads to drug tolerance and physical dependence. Opium is an extract obtained from the sap of the opium poppy while morphine is one of the active ingredients in opium. Heroin is a morphine derivative that enters the nervous system very quickly. These drugs have all become serious problems to society and effective strategies for controlling their use have yet to be developed.

17. Psychedelic and hallucinogenic drugs produce altered sensory and perceptual experiences as well as producing sensations that do not have a basis in physical reality. Many of the effects of these drugs are modulated by psychological and environmental factors. Some psychological dependence may develop to these drugs.

18. The use of marijuana is controversial. Its primary effects center on an increased sense of well being accompanied by feelings of relaxation. Marijuana can cause impairment in one's ability to operate motor vehicles or other machinery.

19. Meditation is a way of achieving increased conscious awareness and feelings of calmness and relaxation. There is a general slowing of physiological processes during meditation and there is evidence that the perceptions experienced by some people during meditation approach the qualities of a mystical experience.

KEY TERMS

Biological clocks
Circadian rhythms
Jet lag
Electroencephalogram
Polygraph
Alpha rhythm
Sleep spindles
Delta waves
Quiet sleep
Paradoxical sleep
Rapid-eye-movement sleep
Active sleep
Insomnia
Hypersomnia
Narcolepsey
Cataplexy
Sleepwalking
Somnambulism

Hypnosis
Suggestibility
Posthypnotic suggestion
Posthypnotic amnesia
Hypnotic age regression
Drug
Psychoactive drug
Drug tolerance
Physical dependence
Sedative drug
Hypnotic drug
Barbiturates
Tranquilizer
Methaqualone
Benzodiazepines
Ethyl alcohol
Amphetamines
Cocaine
Caffeine

Psychological dependence
Nicotine
Opiates
Opium
Enkephalins
Endorphins
Heroin
Hallucinations
Psychedelic drug
Lysergic acid diethylamide (LSD)
Marijuana
Cannabis sativa
Delta-9-tetrahydrocannabinol
Meditation
Transcendental meditation

SUGGESTED READINGS

DEMENT, W. C. *Some must watch while some must sleep.* New York: W. W. Norton, 1978. An excellent general introduction to the nature of sleep, disorders of sleep, and the techniques used in sleep research. This book was written by a leading sleep researcher.

DRUCKER-COLLIN, R., SHKUROVICH, M., & STERMAN, M. B. (Eds.). *The functions of sleep.* New York: Academic Press, 1979. A very technical book of readings that should provide the interested reader with detailed information about some aspects of the neurobiology of sleep.

HARTMANN, E. L. *The functions of sleep.* New Haven, Conn.: Yale University Press, 1973. A readable discussion of the biology and psychology of sleep. An excellent introduction to the field of sleep research by one of its founders.

JONES-WITTERS, P., & WITTERS, W. L. *Drugs and society: A Biological Perspective.* Monterey, Calif.: Wadsworth Health Sciences, 1983. A nicely prepared comprehensive discussion of psychoactive drugs, their history, and their effects. The book is clearly written and up to date.

JULIEN, R. M. *A primer of drug action* (3rd ed.). San Francisco: W. H. Freeman, 1981. This book contains a great deal of useful information about a wide variety of commonly used drugs. There is a good section on the chemical properties of drugs for those readers who want a more technical approach to drug effects.

LISKA, K. *Drugs and the human body.* New York: Macmillan, 1981. Although intended as a textbook, this very readable book provides a discussion of drugs, their effects, and their impact on society. A very good general introduction to the field of psychopharmacology.

WEBB, W. B. *Sleep: The gentle tyrant.* Englewood Cliffs, N.J.: Prentice-Hall, 1975. Another good general survey of the field of sleep research.

PART THREE

Learning, Cognition, Motivation, and Emotion

6
Learning

CLASSICAL CONDITIONING
   Principal Features of Classical
     Conditioning
   Conditioned Emotional
     Responses
INSTRUMENTAL LEARNING
    OR OPERANT
    CONDITIONING
   The Research of Thorndike
   The Law of Effect
   Operant Conditioning
   Shaping and the Method of
     Successive Approximations
MAJOR FEATURES OF
    ASSOCIATIVE LEARNING
   Acquisition
   Extinction
   Spontaneous Recovery
   Generalization

   Discrimination
   Primary and Secondary
     Reinforcement
   Positive and Negative
     Reinforcement
   Schedules of Reinforcement
COGNITIVE LEARNING
   Insight
   Cognitive Maps and Latent
     Learning
   The Learning of Higher-Order
     Concepts
   Observational Learning:
     Modeling and Imitation
SUMMARY
KEY TERMS
SUGGESTED READINGS

Can you imagine if human beings did not change their behavior as a consequence of experience? Babies, after first touching a hot stove, would continue to do so time and time again. Children faced with the problem of climbing onto their beds would never discover that they could boost themselves up by standing first on the bed's sideboard or a toy or a stool. Teenagers, making the transition from junior high school to high school, would never be able to find their way around the building; no matter how often they walked through the building, they would never discover how best to go from their home-room classroom to their other classroom. And you, young adults, would never be able to remember, not to mention master, the material in this book—no matter how many times you studied it.

    The ability to change behavior as a consequence of experience is, then, a very important part of human functioning. This ability to change allows us to meet the problems and challenges presented in our environment. Therefore, this ability is an *adaptive* one; that is, it is one which allows us to change our characteristics to fit our changing world. There are many adaptive processes which are involved in human functioning. However, *learning* is a major instance of human adaptation because it allows us to change in ways which may solve the problems and meet the challenges present in our lives.

Because they can learn, most babies after one or certainly just a very few experiences with a hot stove will no longer touch one. Children, before they are even 2 years of age, will solve the problem of finding a way to boost themselves onto their beds—not to mention tables, countertops, and other high and often precarious places. New high school students learn, usually within only a few days, to find their way around their new school. Most young adults can, albeit with some effort and application, learn the material in this text, as well as those assigned in their other college courses.

Thus, across our lives, learning plays an important role in virtually every arena of our functioning. Because we can learn, we can acquire the knowledge we need to succeed in school. But, in addition, we learn about ourselves—our likes and dislikes, our attitudes, and our values. We learn similar things about our friends. We also learn the rules of our society, that is, what it takes to get a job, be a good citizen, have a successful marriage, and be a good parent. In short, learning is a pervasive means by which human beings change to fit the demands of their complex and changing world.

Of course, not all changes in behavior are due to learning. Fatigue or injury can change behavior, as can the administration of a drug. However, when the effects of the injury, the drug, or fatigue dissipate or wear off, behavior can return to its previous level. Furthermore, while some biological changes, such as those associated with physical growth and maturation, can cause relatively permanent behavior changes; these changes are not attributed to learning. One cannot say appropriately that the 2-year-old child "learned" to grow 3 in., and thus can now reach a door handle to open it. Thus, at the very least, we should reserve the term *learning* for relatively permanent changes in behavior which result from specific experience.

We use the phrase "at the very least" to alert you to another important feature of learning. As you read and then study this chapter, you are certainly learning. Your knowledge about the topic of learning is changing. However, this change is not immediately evident in your behavior. Your learning may not be demonstrated until a discussion with classmates or until an examination. Learning does not merely involve changes in behavior. Rather, the *potential* for behavior is altered as a result of having learned. This change in behavior potentiality illustrates the *learning-performance distinction*: One does not observe learning directly; one observes only performance. From experience-based changes in how a person behaves (or performs), one may infer that learning has occurred. But learning may exist and not be evident until the opportunity arises to perform the changed behavior. Your instructor cannot know how much you have learned about introductory psychology until you have an opportunity to perform, for example, on a test.

As we shall see later in this chapter, psychologists who have studied learning have long known that learning may not be evident in performance until well after it has occurred. Indeed, the term *latent learning* was introduced by Tolman and Honzik (1930) to describe this situation. We shall have reason to discuss further some of the implications of the concept of latent learning later in the chapter. Here we may note that because it is so important for human functioning, many psychologists have studied learning. However, learning is such a complex topic that not all psychologists have approached it in the same way, or agree about what to study. Indeed, different types of learning have been studied by different psychologists. Two types of learning that have been studied are *associative learning*, involving relations between

LEARNING   181

stimuli and responses, which includes the topics of classical conditioning and instrumental, or operant, learning, and *cognitive learning*, which involves an organism's knowledge. In this chapter we discuss both of these types.

CLASSICAL CONDITIONING

Ivan Petrovich Pavlov (1849–1936) won the Nobel prize in 1904 for his research on digestion. Pavlov used dogs as subjects, measuring their salivation in response to the placement of food in their mouths. In his studies Pavlov (1927) noticed that stimuli other than food in the mouth evoked salivation in his subjects. The mere sight of the food, or even of the person who regularly brought the food to the dog, also elicited salivation. Pavlov began to study this phenomenon in its own right. Using the apparatus illustrated in Figure 6.1, he soon discovered that virtually any stimulus—for example, a buzzer or a bell—could be presented to the animal in such a way as eventually to elicit salivation. The way in which such stimuli come to elicit salivation involves classical conditioning.

To understand how classical conditioning occurs, we must focus on the initial associations with which the organism enters the learning situation. Some stimuli reliably (i.e., regularly) elicit strong responses. For example, food in the mouth reliably elicits salivation. No prior association, or learning, is necessary to establish this relation between the stimulus (food) and the response (salivation). We term the food stimulus an *unconditional*, or *unconditioned*, stimulus (UCS). A UCS is a stimulus that reliably elicits a response of strong magnitude without previous learning. Moreover, since no previous

The Russian biologist, Ivan Pavlov (1849–1936), shown here in his lab, discovered the phenomenon of classical conditioning. (Bettmann Archive)

Figure 6.1
The apparatus used by Pavlov to study classical conditioning.

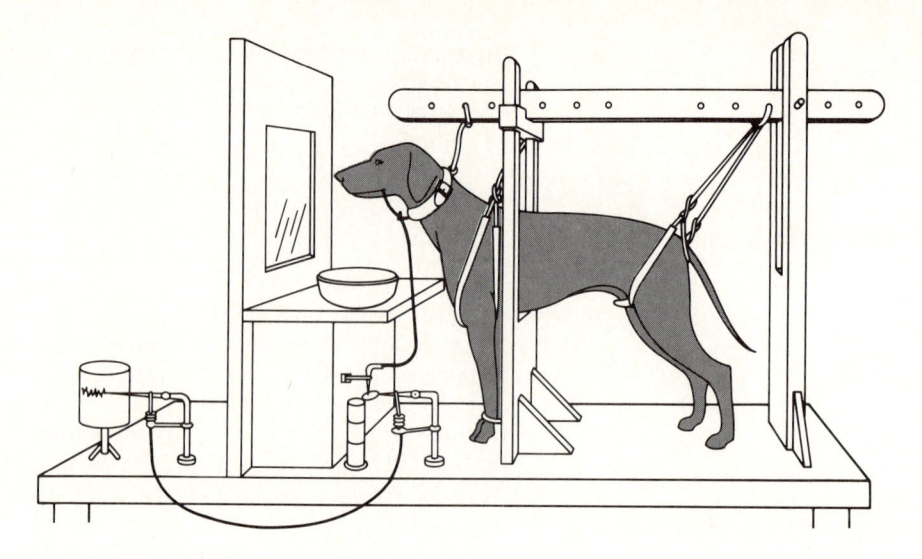

association, or learning, is necessary in order for the UCS to elicit the salivation, this salivation response is an *unconditioned response* (UCR), an unlearned response. This relationship may be represented as

UCS (food) → UCR (salivation)

Of course, there are numerous stimuli in an organism's environment which do not elicit this particular UCR. That is, they are neutral in respect to the UCS → UCR relation; such neutral stimuli do *not* elicit the UCR. However, if one takes such a neutral stimulus (e.g., a bell) and repeatedly pairs this stimulus with the UCS, a different state of affairs will come to prevail.

For instance, suppose that one rings the bell and then presents the food. At first, no salivation will occur in response to the bell. The animal *will* react to the bell, however. It will show what Pavlov termed the *orienting reflex*, a response involving the animal's attending to the new stimulus. But, as noted, the orienting reflex does not involve salivation. However, Pavlov showed that after several repeated pairings of the bell and the food, the bell will come to elicit the salivation. Because of the repeated pairings of the bell and the food, the bell begins to acquire some of the properties of the food: the bell becomes associated with the food and it, too, leads to salivation.

Thus the bell, previously a neutral stimulus, has become a *conditioned stimulus* (CS). Through repeated pairings of the bell and food, the bell comes to elicit a learned, or *conditioned, response* (CR). In this case the bell comes to elicit salivation.

Figure 6.2 illustrates the relations among stimuli and responses that exist prior to classical conditioning (Figure 6.2A), during classical conditioning (Figure 6.2B), and after it is completed (Figure 6.2C). It is important to note that the order in which the CS and the UCS are presented during classical conditioning is important in establishing a CR. Note in Figure 6.2B that the CS occurs prior to the UCS. This sequence and temporal separation (termed *forward pairing*) is important in best establishing a CR. Conditioning is less well established when the CS and UCS occur at the same time (*simultaneous pairing*); and when the CS follows the UCS (a situation termed *backward conditioning*), conditioning is least well established. Research indicates that a ½-second interval between the CS and the UCS is most effective in establishing many CRs (Kimble, Mann, & Dufort, 1955); however, the optimal

Figure 6.2
The relations among stimuli and responses in classical conditioning.

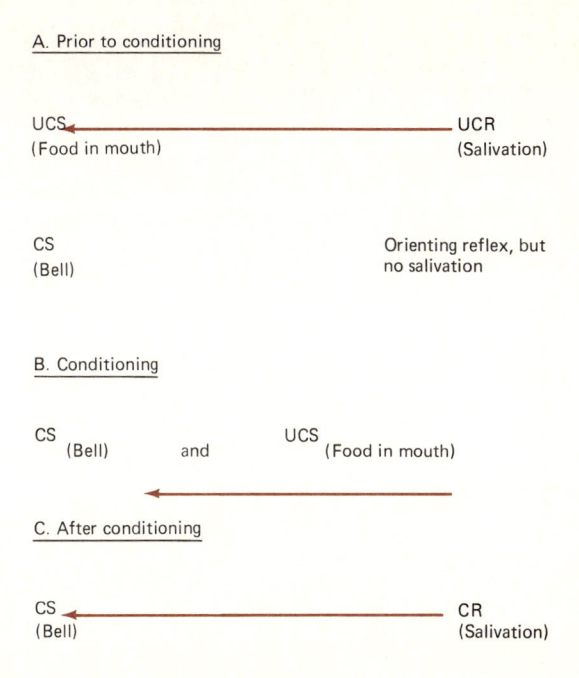

A. Prior to conditioning

UCS ←――――――――――― UCR
(Food in mouth)   (Salivation)

CS   Orienting reflex, but
(Bell)   no salivation

B. Conditioning

CS   and   UCS
(Bell)   (Food in mouth)
     ←――――――――――――

C. After conditioning

CS ←――――――――――― CR
(Bell)   (Salivation)

CS-UCS interval varies greatly as a function of the task. The temporal relationships in classical conditioning among the CS, UCS, CR, and UCR are illustrated in Figure 6.3, here in regard to forward pairing.

PRINCIPAL FEATURES OF CLASSICAL CONDITIONING

In classical conditioning the CS and the UCS are said to elicit the response. The term *elicit* suggests that classical conditioning involves responses of the body's involuntary musculature and the autonomic nervous system. Hence we have neither to learn to salivate nor to learn to blink in response to a puff of air to our eyes. Rather, such responses are reflexive in nature; they are involuntary responses—hence classical conditioning involves the conditioning of our involuntary, reflexive responses. In many cases such responses are almost literally pulled out of us by the stimulus in question (e.g., the food or the puff of air).

Moreover, the link between the CS and the UCS is a critical one in establishing classically conditioned responses. The more often the CS is paired with the UCS, the greater is the probability that the CS will evoke a CR. This occurs because the UCS, when it follows the CS, *reinforces* the association

Figure 6.3
The temporal relations among the stimuli and responses involved in classical conditioning.

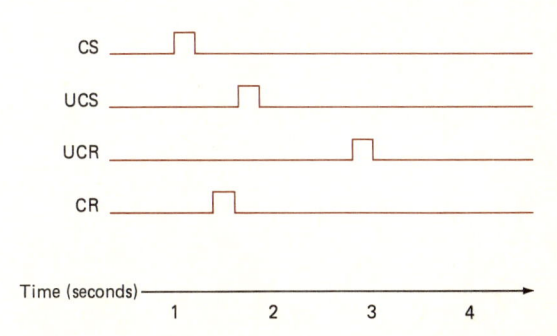

between the conditioned stimulus and the conditioned response. A reinforcer is a stimulus which produces or maintains a behavior, or, simply, which makes a behavior more probable (Kimble, 1961). In short, classical conditioning involves an association between two stimuli, the CS and the UCS. Indeed, to Pavlov, it was this association that is the principal thing learned in classical conditioning. More recent discussions of what is learned in classical conditioning have emphasized not the contiguity between the CS and UCS but rather the *contingency* among the events occurring during classical conditioning.

Contiguity means that two events occur in close proximity in both time and space. In classical conditioning there *is* contiguity between the times of occurrence of the CS and the UCS. Pavlov believed that temporal contiguity was what was learned in classical conditioning. But Rescorla and his colleagues (e.g., Rescorla & Holland, 1976, 1982; Rescorla & Wagner, 1972) have emphasized that what an animal learns in classical conditioning is how events "go together," how one event's occurrence depends on—or is contingent on—the occurrence of another event. Thus the dog in the Pavlovian classical conditioning situation does not learn that a bell and food occur together—are contiguous. Rather, the dog learns that food occurs when a bell is sounded and that food does not occur when a bell is not sounded. The dog learns that the presentation of food depends (is contingent) on the prior presentation of a bell. To Rescorla, the relations among events are what is learned in classical conditioning.

CONDITIONED EMOTIONAL RESPONSES

Some psychologists think that classical conditioning provides the basic building blocks for all associative learning. Moreover, it appears that emotional responses are particularly susceptible to this sort of conditioning. Emotional reactions such as fear, anger, and disgust involve heightened activity of organs and glands controlled by the autonomic nervous system (e.g., the heart and the respiratory and digestive systems). Reactions of these organ systems, and the emotions that accompany them, are readily learned through classical conditioning.

For example, a rat will show the unconditioned emotional response of fear when a strong electrical shock is delivered to its feet through the floor of its cage. The shock is a UCS and the emotional response is a UCR. However, if a buzzer is always sounded a short time before the shock begins, the rat will begin to act afraid in response to the buzzer even before the shock occurs. The buzzer will become a CS and the emotional response will become a CR, a *conditioned emotional response* (CER). Evidence suggests that conditioned emotional responses may persist for years.

INSTRUMENTAL LEARNING OR OPERANT CONDITIONING

Instrumental learning, or *operant conditioning*, represents the second instance of associative learning. In this type of associative learning an animal learns to emit a behavior in order to produce some outcome. In other words, an

Operant conditioning at work. The dog has learned that a certain behavior—jumping—will produce a certain outcome—a dog biscuit. (Peter Simon/Stock Boston)

animal will learn to perform, to respond, in order to produce some stimulus. For example, a dog might learn to stand on its hind legs or to lie down to gain a biscuit. In either case, the dog's response is *instrumental* in producing a stimulus. The response must *operate* on the environment in order to make a particular stimulus occur or appear. Such learning typically involves our voluntary muscles.

Thus instrumental learning involves forming an association between a response and a stimulus. As is also the case in classical conditioning, a response is strengthened as a function of the repeated occurrence of a stimulus. Furthermore, the response made in instrumental learning is strengthened because the stimulus with which it is associated is a reinforcer. However, in contrast to classical conditioning, in instrumental learning the reinforcing stimulus is contingent on the emission of a response. Thus, as in classical conditioning, a contingency is learned. However, whereas in classical conditioning the contingency which is learned is about the association between two stimuli (the CS and the UCS), in instrumental conditioning the contingency which is learned is about the association between a response and a reinforcing stimulus. Simply put, in instrumental learning, unless the response (e.g., lying down) is emitted, the reward (e.g., the dog biscuit) will not "occur."

THE RESEARCH OF THORNDIKE

Instrumental conditioning has been studied in the United States for more than 80 years, starting with the research of Edward L. Thorndike (1874–1949). Thorndike (1898, 1911) devised a research strategy involving placing animals in a situation which posed a problem for them. For instance, Thorndike placed cats, which were kept hungry, into a chamber which he termed a *puzzle box*. An illustration of this apparatus is presented in Figure 6.4. What made this box a puzzle for the cat is that escape from the box—and to a

Figure 6.4
An illustration of the Puzzle Box used in Thorndike's research.

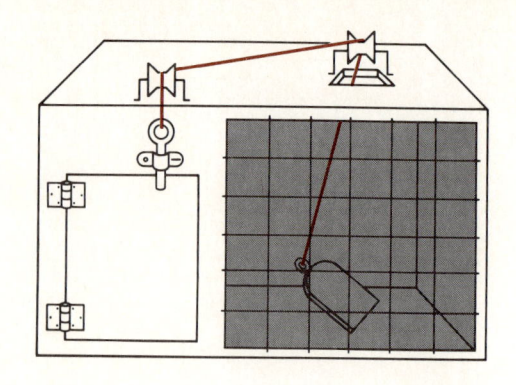

waiting small supply of food—required the performance of a specific behavior. For example, in the puzzle box shown in Figure 6.4 the cat must step on a treadle to escape from the box and attain the food. The treadle is attached to a rope which, when pulled down via a press on the treadle, opens the latch which locks the door to the box.

When a hungry cat is first placed into the puzzle box, its behavior is not focused primarily on the treadle. It may scratch on the walls of the box, push against the door, or brush against the rope attached to the treadle. Thus there occur many "errors"—behaviors which do not result in the attainment of food. However, when the cat happens to step on the treadle, the door latch is released and food can then be gotten. At this point, the cat is allowed to eat the food and the trial—of behavior and reward—is completed. The cat is then placed back in the box and another trial begins.

With each succeeding trial the amount of time that passes before the cat performs the "correct" behavior decreases. In other words, across trials fewer and fewer errors occur. The time between placement in the puzzle box and the emission of the correct response decreases across trials. This decrease in response latency is evidence for the occurrence of learning.

THE LAW OF EFFECT

Thorndike (1911) postulated the *law of effect* to account for this learning. The stimulus of being in the puzzle box was associated initially with several responses—scratching, pushing, brushing, as well as stepping on a treadle. Across trials all but the treadle-stepping response stopped occurring. Only the treadle-stepping response became—in Thorndike's (1911) terms—"stamped in." The basis for this stamping in, Thorndike reasoned, was that the consequences of the several responses differed. Only the treadle push was followed by a reward, and only it was strengthened. The other responses were not followed by rewards, and as a result, they were weakened.

The law of effect describes the process of stamping in, or strengthening, a response to a stimulus via associating that response with a reward, or reinforcer. Simply, the consequences—the effects—of a response to a stimulus determine whether that response is strengthened or weakened. If the effect is to produce a reward, the probability of that response (the treadle push in the puzzle box) being made to the stimulus is strengthened. If the consequence of a response (e.g., a cage scratch) is to produce no reward, the probability of that response being made to the stimulus is lessened.

The length of time between the performance of a response to a stimulus and the occurrence of reinforcement has been found to be an important

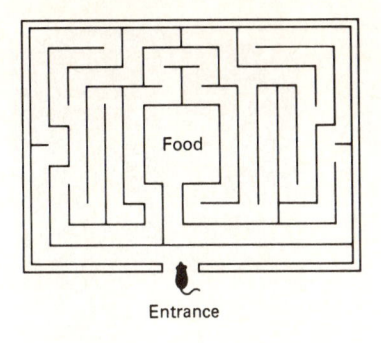

Figure 6.5
An illustration of a maze used for studying instrumental learning.

determinant of the strength of the response "stamped in." The greater the *delay of reinforcement*, the weaker the response (Hull, 1932). In turn, of course, the shorter the delay between responding and reinforcement, the stronger the response.

OPERANT CONDITIONING

Animals may learn to escape from puzzle boxes, or as illustrated in Figures 6.5 and 6.6, respectively, to run along certain paths in a maze or to press a lever or key in an "operant conditioning" chamber. Any of these responses in any of these respective types of apparatus may be used to study instrumental learning. The illustration of the operant conditioning apparatus allows us to introduce a prominent variant of the techniques used to study instrumental learning.

The operant conditioning chamber is often referred to as a "Skinner Box." This name is used because B. F. Skinner designed the original operant chamber. We have indicated already that instrumental learning or conditioning may also be termed operant conditioning. In either case, to obtain a reward, the animal must perform a behavior: it must be instrumental, or it must operate, in order to produce a reinforcing stimulus.

However, one reason it is useful to use the term *operant behavior* in addition to the term *instrumental behavior* is that the method used to study learning is somewhat different when using puzzle boxes or mazes, on the one hand, and operant chambers, on the other. With the former type of apparatus the animal is studied on a trial-by-trial basis. For instance, each time an animal reaches the end of a maze and obtains the food placed there, the trial is terminated and the animal is removed from the goal box. However, in an operant chamber the animal is not removed from the chamber after each bar press or after each reward. Instead, the animal is typically kept in

Figure 6.6
An illustration of an operant conditioning chamber used for studying instrumental learning.

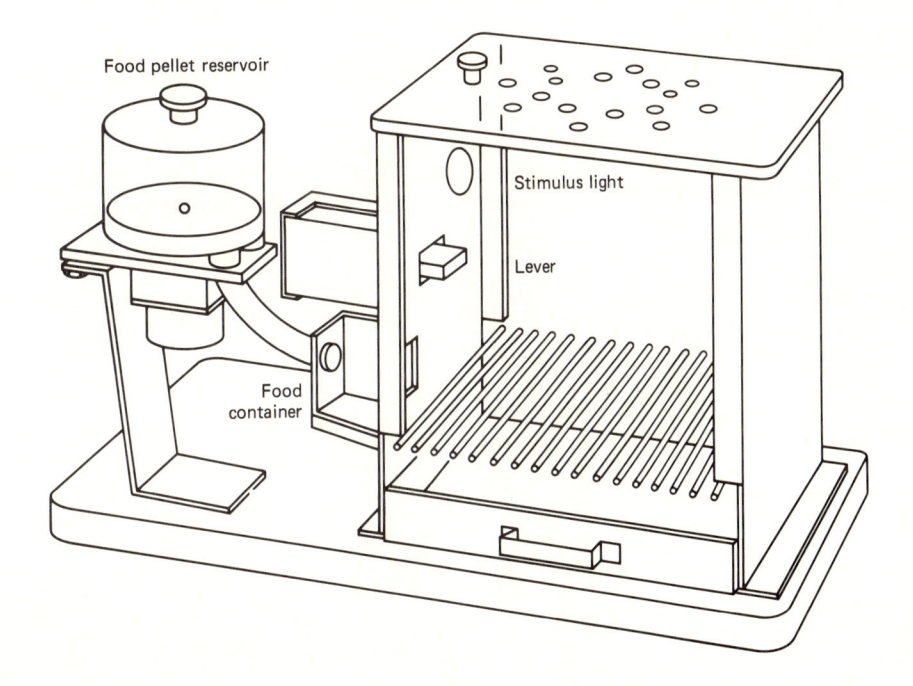

B. F. Skinner in his lab. Skinner has done some of the most influential research in operant conditioning. (Monkmeyer)

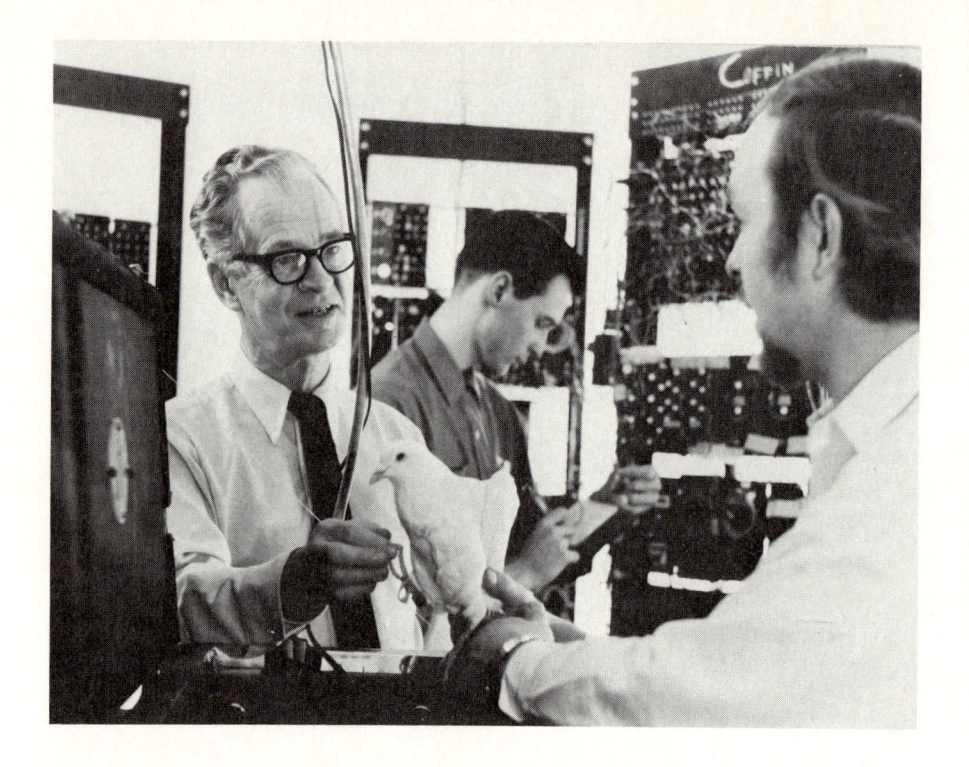

the chamber for a relatively long period of time and is free to operate the lever or key continuously during this period. Thus several rewards may be attained and there is not, therefore, the separation of behavior into a trial-by-trial series. Thus the *rate* of responding across time can be studied quite readily in an operant conditioning chamber.

SHAPING AND THE METHOD OF SUCCESSIVE APPROXIMATIONS

As with animals first placed into a puzzle box, animals placed in an operant chamber do not ordinarily operate the lever or key (which when pressed, leads to a reward) at a high rate initially. Indeed, when the lever or key is placed in particular portions of the chamber—for instance, relatively high on one wall—it may be the case that particular animals may perform the requisite response only rarely.

Nevertheless, the rate of emission of the required response may be systematically increased in the animal. Over time the animal's behavior may be altered, or *shaped*, such that the correct response occurs often. Shaping of behavior may be achieved through the *method of successive approximations*.

To illustrate, a food pellet may be delivered to the cup within the operant chamber, shown in Figure 6.6; if this is done repeatedly when the experimental animal (e.g., a rat) is near the cup, and if the rat is hungry and eats the pellets, the rat may start to stay close to the cup. Since the cup is also close to the lever present in the chamber, the rat, by being close to the cup, is also close to the lever. As the rat continues to come near the cup and the lever, a behavior a bit closer to a bar press may be then required for delivery of food into the cup. For instance, brushing the wall underneath the lever

LEARNING 189

may now be required. Next, touching the wall with the front section of its body may be required. Then a front paw touching the wall may be the behavior necessary for food delivery. Next, a touch of the lever by the paw may be required for food delivery. Finally, a complete bar press may be required. Thus, by gradually and successively approximating the requisite response, an animal's behavior may be shaped.

MAJOR FEATURES OF ASSOCIATIVE LEARNING

Both classical and operant conditioning are types of associative learning. As such, they have a number of characteristics in common. Let us discuss several of them.

ACQUISITION

Response acquisition refers to the process of learning or acquiring a response. It entails either adding a response to a *new* stimulus to the organism's repertoire of responses, as in classical conditioning (e.g., salivating in response to some CS), or *strengthening* an already existing response (e.g., bar pressing) through operant or instrumental conditioning. Acquisition involves an increase in response strength as a result of practice or experience in some situations. Each trial (pairing of CS with UCS) increases response strength in classical conditioning, as does each pairing of an operant response with reinforcement in operant conditioning, until some maximum response strength is achieved.

This rat has learned that pressing a lever in its operant chamber will produce a pellet of food. Its behavior has been shaped by the need to press harder and harder to get its reward as heavier weights are placed on the other end of the lever. (Omikron)

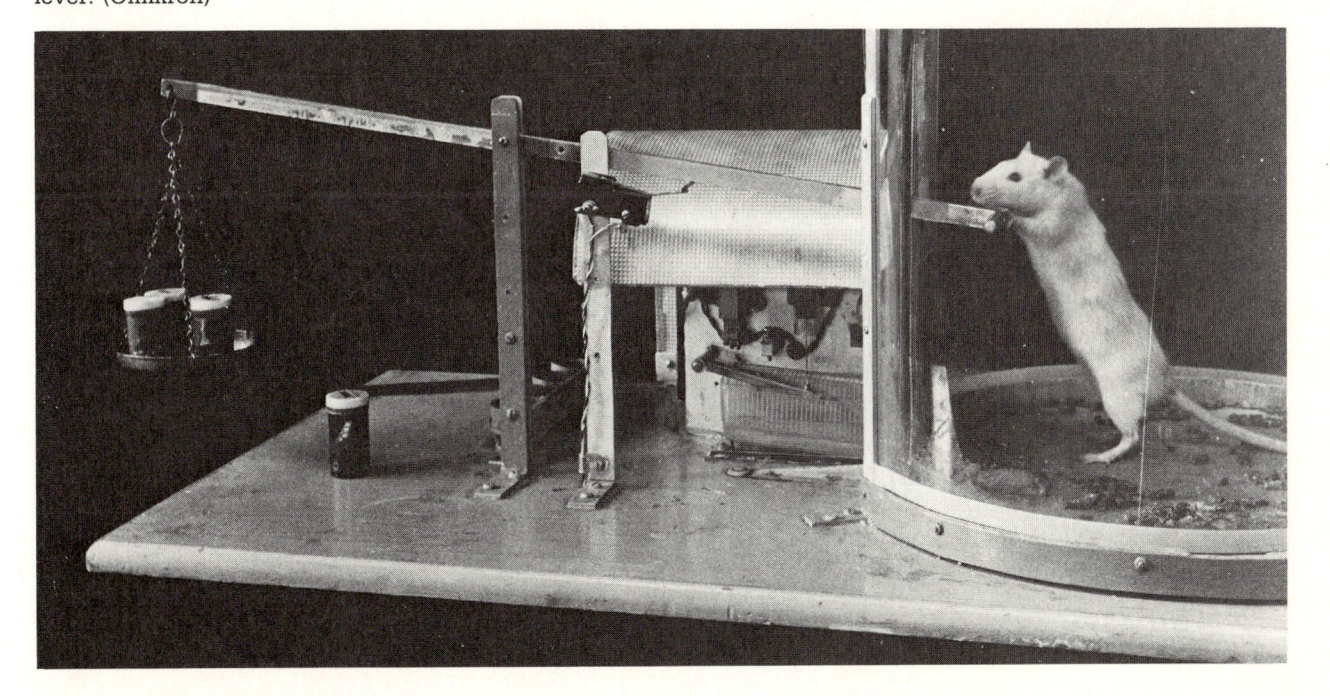

Figure 6.7
Acquisition involves a change in the behavioral (response) repertoire of an organism. (Adapted from Lerner, 1976, p. 256.)

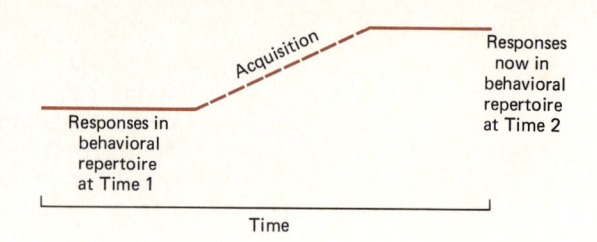

Acquisition, then, constitutes a modification of behavior. The organism has a repertoire (a set) of behaviors. When acquisition occurs, however, this repertoire is altered; more responses are added to the set. Acquisition is illustrated in Figure 6.7.

EXTINCTION

If a response is acquired as a result of a contingency, what will happen if that contingency is withdrawn, for example, if the CS is given without the UCS or the instrumental response occurs without the reinforcer? Typically, the response will slowly decrease and eventually disappear. This is called *extinction*. In other words, extinction is a decrease in response strength or likelihood as a consequence of unreinforced trials. Figure 6.8 illustrates extinction.

SPONTANEOUS RECOVERY

Suppose that a rat has been conditioned through reinforcement to emit a particular response to a specific stimulus. Let us further imagine that after the response was acquired, reinforcement was withdrawn until no further responses to the stimulus were seen, that is, until extinction occurred. Finally, imagine that after the response was extinguished the rat was removed from the test apparatus and returned to its home cage; then after some time in its home cage, it is brought back to the test apparatus and the stimulus presented again. What will happen?

Most likely, the rat will resume responding, although perhaps not fully at the conditioned rate. The phenomenon is termed *spontaneous recovery*, that is an increase in response strength after a period away (a "time-out") from extinction.

Figure 6.8
Extinction involves a decrease in response strength as a function of unreinforced trials.

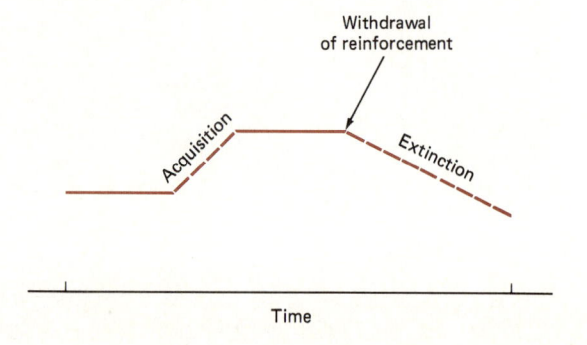

GENERALIZATION

Some stimuli are so similar to those associated with reinforcement that they will be responded to even though never actually reinforced. This is *generalization*. An example of generalization would be if a response to a tone of 500 Hz is associated with reinforcement, and then if a tone of 510 Hz is presented and is responded to.

The greater the similarity between the original stimulus and the new ones, the greater the probability of the new stimuli evoking responses; in turn, the probability of a response decreases when the similarity between the original and the new stimuli also decreases. These relations between stimulus similarity and the probability of response form what is termed the *stimulus generalization gradient*. This gradient is illustrated in Figure 6.9.

DISCRIMINATION

Not all stimuli an animal responds to will produce reinforcement. If responses to one stimulus are associated with reinforcement and responses to another stimulus are not, responses will eventually occur only in relation to the stimulus associated with reinforcement. In other words, *discrimination* is differential responding to stimuli due to differential likelihood of reinforcement. For example, if responses to a tone of 500 Hz are always reinforced but responses to a tone of 600 Hz are never reinforced, discrimination would be demonstrated when appreciably more responses were made to the first tone than to the second.

PRIMARY AND SECONDARY REINFORCEMENT

Some stimuli, such as food, may be termed *primary reinforcers*. These are stimuli which are reinforcers in and of themselves. They need no prior association with another reinforcer to produce or maintain behavior. The food which follows a bar press in operant conditioning, and the UCS (food in the

Figure 6.9
An illustration of a stimulus generalization gradient.

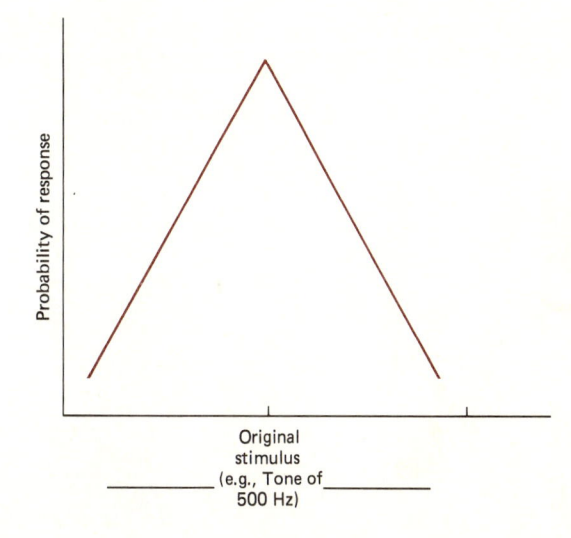

mouth, or electric shock) in classical conditioning, are examples of primary reinforcers.

However, some stimuli are reinforcers because they have been associated with another reinforcer. Such stimuli are *secondary reinforcers*. Examples exist of secondary reinforcers within both classical conditioning and operant conditioning. In classical conditioning, after the CS is repeatedly paired with the UCS, the CS also obtains reinforcing power. For instance, a bell, serving as a CS, may elicit salivation. In operant conditioning we can illustrate a secondary reinforcer by imagining a situation wherein a bar press will result in food delivery *only* when a key next to the bar is lit. If the animal presses the bar when the key is not lit, no food (no primary reinforcer) will appear. After some experience in this situation the animal will bar press only when the key is lit. The illuminated key cues the occasion for the occurrence of a primary reinforcer, and after repeated pairings with the primary reinforcer the lit key becomes also a reinforcer—but here a secondary one. This can be demonstrated by discontinuing the connection between the lit key and the delivery of food consequent to a bar press. The rat will still press the bar even though food is not being delivered.

In our everyday lives secondary reinforcers abound. For instance, we may work very hard for money. But money in and of itself cannot be eaten or drunk. It is not food or water. However, because it is associated with the availability of these stimuli, money has become a powerful secondary reinforcer of our behavior.

POSITIVE AND NEGATIVE REINFORCEMENT

Reinforcements may be either positive or negative. In the case of either a positive or negative reinforcer, however, it is still the case that behavior is produced or maintained (made more probable) by the reinforcing stimulus.

Money is one of the strongest secondary reinforcers of our behavior, because it is associated in our minds with the ability to produce food and other things that we need or desire. (F. B. Grunzweig)

But *positive-reinforcing stimuli* maintain behavior through their production. We will behave in order to produce, or increase the presence of, such stimuli as food, water, or money. However, there are also *negatively reinforcing stimuli*. We will behave in order to terminate or decrease the presence of such stimuli as a glaring light, a very loud noise, or an electric shock. For example, if we are placed in a situation in which a painful electric shock will be delivered continuously if we do not press a bar, we will soon press the bar to terminate (turn off) the electric shock. Thus responses are emitted, but in this case it is in order to terminate (escape from) a stimulus, a negative reinforcement. It is useful here to explain the distinction between escape and avoidance learning.

Escape and Avoidance. In *escape learning* we behave so as to eliminate the presence of a negative reinforcer (e.g., an aversive stimulus such as an electric shock). For instance, an animal may be placed in a shuttle box, a box which is divided in half by a low rail over which the animal is capable of jumping. If one side of the box also has a grid on the floor, through which electric shock may be delivered, the animal may escape the shock by jumping over the railing. The learning of this response would be an instance of escape learning.

In *avoidance learning* we behave so as to avoid the aversive stimulus completely. To illustrate, suppose that in the example of the shuttle box, a tone was sounded for 10 seconds prior to turning on the electric current. If the animal jumped over the railing during the time the tone was on, the shock would be avoided. Learning this response would be an example of avoidance learning.

In studying escape and avoidance learning, Seligman and his associates (e.g., Seligman, Maier, & Solomon, 1971) identified a phenomenon which they labeled *learned helplessness*. For an animal to show avoidance learning, it must be able to control its environment. For instance, it must be able to jump over the railing. But what will be learned if aversive stimuli cannot be avoided? Seligman and Maier (1967) placed one group of dogs in a hammock where, although their movement was restricted, they could escape from a shock by pushing a button. A second group of dogs was placed in a similar hammock but could not escape the shock. A third group was placed in a hammock but received no shock. After this treatment, dogs from all groups were placed in a shuttle box akin to the one described above; that is, an electrified grid was present on one side of the box and the railing dividing the box could be jumped over by the dogs. The dogs from the first group—the ones who had been able to escape from the shock when in the hammock—learned to escape to the unelectrified side of the shuttle box; similarly, the third group of dogs—which had received no shock when in the hammock—also learned to escape. But the dogs in the second group never showed escape learning in the shuttle box.

Seligman and Maier (1967) interpreted these findings as indicating that the dogs from the second group learned that their actions were not associated with a change in the situation, that is, with the elimination of the aversive stimulus. In other words, they had learned that they could not escape, that they were helpless; as such they did not try to escape in the shuttle box situation—a situation wherein escape was possible. The occurrence of such a phenomenon is what Seligman et al. (1971) term learned helplessness.

Punishment. A given response may be associated with either a positive or a negative reinforcer. When a behavior produces a positive reinforcer (e.g., food) or terminates a negative reinforcer (e.g., a bright light glaring in our eyes), that behavior is strengthened, in the sense that it becomes more likely, or probable, in the future (Bijou, 1976; Bijou & Baer, 1961). However, sometimes behavior can result in the loss of a positive reinforcer or the production or a negative reinforcer. For example, parents might take away a child's candy treats when the child behaves badly (e.g., when the child hits his or her sibling); in turn, the parents might spank the child for his or her misbehavior. Such situations constitute *punishment*; that is, there are two ways in which punishment may occur. First, punishment occurs through the loss of a positive reinforcer (e.g., candy). Second, it occurs through the administration of a negative reinforcer (e.g., spanking). Children will behave in ways to get back the candy (the positive reinforcers) and to stop the spankings (the negative reinforcers) from being administered.

SCHEDULES OF REINFORCEMENT

In our preceding discussions of the role of reinforcement in both classical conditioning and operant conditioning, we often used examples in which a reinforcement is associated with each response. We have, then, been speaking implicitly of a *continuous reinforcement schedule*. A schedule of reinforcement is the plan or system by which reinforcement is associated with a response. A continuous reinforcement schedule is a situation where there is a one-to-one relation between a response and a reinforcement (in operant conditioning) or between a CS and a UCS (in classical conditioning). However, in the real world such continuous reinforcement schedules rarely, if ever, occur. The basketball player does not put the ball in the hoop every time he or she shoots. The college student does not get a date every time he or she asks for one. The college professor does not get an acceptance from a publisher each time he or she submits a manuscript. Nevertheless, basketball players keep on shooting, college students continue trying to date, and professors continue writing and submitting manuscripts.

These behaviors are maintained because they are on a *partial reinforcement schedule*. In such a schedule there is not a one-to-one relation between a response, or a CS, and a reinforcement. Instead, behavior is reinforced only some of the time; reinforcement is intermittent.

Ferster and Skinner (1957) investigated the influence of various *schedules of reinforcement*. Their research and that of others (see Kimble, 1961) indicates that with operant conditioning, partial, or intermittent, reinforcement leads to greater responding than does a schedule of continuous reinforcement. For instance, responses acquired as a consequence of an *intermittent reinforcement schedule* will be more difficult to extinguish than will responses acquired as a consequence of a continuous reinforcement schedule. This phenomenon is labeled the *partial-reinforcement effect* (Grant, Hake, & Hornseth, 1951; Humphreys, 1939), and it helps us understand why the basketball player keeps shooting, the college student keeps trying to date, and the professor keeps writing. Because the shooting, dating, and writing behaviors were acquired as a consequence of partial reinforcement schedules, they are more resistant to extinction than behaviors reinforced continuously. For instance, if we had never missed a basket, been turned down for a date, or had a manuscript rejected for publication, the first time such an event occurred would represent quite a major, abrupt, and probably quite upsetting experience for us, one that might have more of an impact on our continuing behaviors than would

Voting in an election, which occurs regularly at the end of a set-tem, is an example of a fixed interval schedule. (Bill Anderson/Monkmeyer)

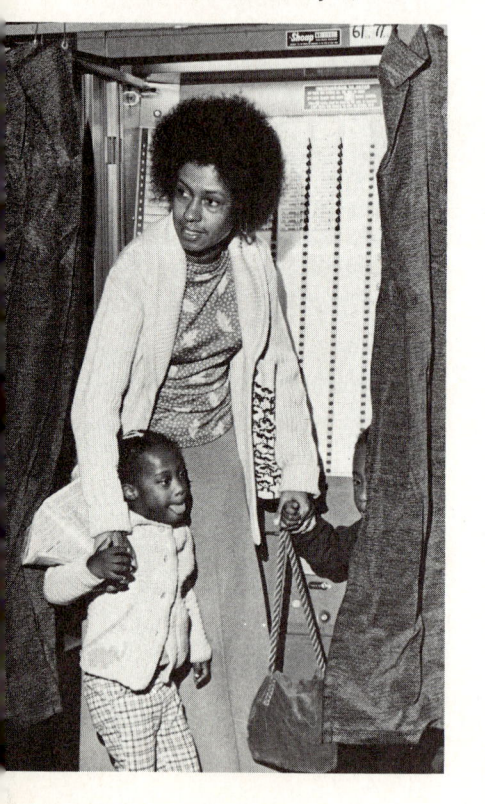

FOCUS ON THE PSYCHOLOGIST

Martin E. P. Seligman

MARTIN E. P. SELIGMAN received his Ph.D. in Experimental Psychology from the University of Pennsylvania, where he was both a Woodrow Wilson and a National Science Foundation Fellow. Dr. Seligman has taught at Cornell University and at the University of Pennsylvania, where he is now Professor of Psychology. Among his many awards and honors are the receipt in 1975 of a Guggenheim Fellowship and in 1976 of the American Psychological Association award for Distinguished Early Career Scientific Contributions.

My intellectual life began when I failed to make the eighth-grade basketball team. Cut off, thereby, from everything of value to 13-year-olds, I began to read books. Freud's *Introductory Lectures* stunned me. Could one lead a life, find a profession, pursuing such insights? Over the years, my sense of what counted as valid insight was to change, but not my sense of what counted as an important question.

At the end of my undergraduate days I visited R. L. Solomon at the University of Pennsylvania. Solomon described a phenomenon that had been stumbled across in his laboratory: a few odd dogs "looked helpless" after receiving inescapable shock (Solomon, either out of modesty or shame, now denies this). At any rate, I entered Penn in 1964. Working with Bruce Overmier and then with Steve Maier, I took seriously the passivity of dogs pretreated with inescapable trauma. Their predecessors, who had observed the phenomenon as an occasional consequence of Pavlovian conditioning, had treated it as annoyance. Having tested and found wanting conventional learning-theoretic explanations of the phenomenon, Maier and I ultimately proposed that animals could learn that outcomes were independent of their actions, that they were, in short, helpless. We also found that they could immunize dogs against helplessness by prior experience with mastery, and could reverse helplessness by "directive" therapy.

I taught at Cornell from 1967 to 1969 during the "Troubles." My fondest memories of Cornell were the joys of teaching and coming to know fine undergraduates, joys made sweeter and more intense by the intimacy of a university in crisis. Some of these undergraduates urged me to acquire clinical experience in order to calibrate and bolster my belief that psychopathology could be modeled in the learning laboratory.

I took this advice and in 1970 spent a year in the Psychiatry Department at Penn receiving clinical training. Albert Stunkard and Aaron Beck were my patrons and teachers. But it was one of the younger psychiatrists, Dean Schuyler, who taught me the most: When I asked him about his remarkable success as an active therapist, Schuyler said: "Yes, all my patients get better. The reason is that they get to know me as a person, and I'm a good person." During this year, I began to flesh out and test the hypothesis that learned helplessness models depression in man.

In 1971 I rejoined the Psychology Department at Penn as an associate professor and was promoted to professor in 1976. During those and recent years, I have been blessed with excellent students and collaborators. With them I have carried out a program of research on helplessness and depression. In addition to exploring learned helplessness in rats, we developed procedures that produce helplessness in man, parallel to the rat and dog phenomenon. Nondepressed college students made helpless by inescapable noise or unsolvable problems become passive, have difficulty learning, show distorted expectations about their skill, show lowered aggression and depressive affect—a set of deficits identical to those shown by depressed students left untreated. We have tested therapies for reversing these helplessness and depressive deficits and for testing the continuity of these deficits with more severe depression.

Today, I harbor what I consider unconventional and unpopular beliefs for a learning theorist: that animals are cognitive; that human psychopathology can be modeled in the laboratory; that the field of animal learning is justified by its benefits to human beings; and that the evolutionary function of dreaming is to carry out prepared emotional conditioning.

195

be the case if we had experienced success in these endeavors only intermittently.

There are numerous ways in which intermittent or partial reinforcement may occur. In other words, there are several types of schedules of reinforcement. A reinforcement may occur only after a specific *number* of responses have been emitted, or it may occur only after a specific period of *time* has elapsed. The former type of schedule is termed a *ratio* schedule, the latter an *interval* schedule.

The ratio or interval may be either fixed or variable. That is, if one must emit 20 responses for each reinforcement (e.g., if one must press a bar 20 times to get candy), one is on a *fixed ratio* (FR) schedule (in this case an FR 20 schedule). An example of a fixed ratio schedule from everyday life comes from factory workers who are employed on a piecework basis. Such workers get paid each time a set number of products are finished. For instance, within a quilt factory a given pieceworker might be paid each time he or she completes three quilts. Here, then, the worker is on a FR 3 schedule.

However, the number of responses required for any one reinforcement may vary from time to time, but around an average value (e.g., on the average 20 bar presses are needed to get a candy). In such a case one is on a *variable ratio* (VR) schedule (VR 20 in this case). We have already seen some examples of variable ratio schedules from everyday life. The basketball player may have a 50% shooting percentage. This does not mean, of course, that out of each 10 shots at the basket he or she always scores the first five and misses the last five. Rather, this means that—on the average—the percentage of scores is 50 in any given set of 10 shots; however, he or she may get more or less in the basket for any given set of 10 shots. Similarly, we may get a date on the average only once out of every four times we ask for one. However, being on this VR 4 schedule does not mean that we may not experience a period when we get a date each time we ask for one.

As noted, there are also interval schedules of reinforcement. If one can obtain a reinforcement only after a fixed time has elapsed (e.g., if a bar press is reinforced only once every 30 minutes), one is on a *fixed interval* (FI) schedule (in this case, an FI 30-minute schedule). The occurrence of national political conventions is an example of events happening on a fixed interval schedule. In the United States these conventions occur only once every 4 years. Moreover, voting in a presidential election is behavior which occurs on a similar 4-year fixed interval schedule.

Finally, if the time before a response will be reinforced varies around an average value, one is on a *variable interval* (VI) schedule (e.g., one could be on a VI 30-minute schedule). Fishing is an activity which is on a variable interval schedule. On some fishing trips one has to wait only a very short time between "bites" or "catches." However, at other times the intervals between bites may be quite long. Indeed, even within the same day someone may experience both short and long intervals between bites.

The various schedules of reinforcement have distinct effects on behavior. For instance, Ferster and Skinner (1957) have found that variable schedules produce more steady and consistent response rates; that is, the number of responses emitted per unit of time (e.g., the number of responses per minute) is stable. For example, responding on a FI schedule often decreases after a reinforcement, and it is not until the fixed, elapsed time approaches that response rate increases again.

In sum, reinforcement schedules, as well as the other major features of instrumental learning and classical conditioning that we have reviewed, have

HIGHLIGHT 6.1
Applications of Associative Learning

Principles and phenomena of classical conditioning and operant conditioning have a good deal of use in people's everyday lives. As discussed more fully in Chapter 16, classical conditioning has been used to treat problematic behaviors and emotions (Davidson, 1974; Wolpe, 1962). For instance, among alcoholics, the pairing of alcohol (CS) with a drug (UCS) that causes nausea and vomiting (UCR) leads eventually to feelings of nausea (CR) in connection with the alcohol itself. Such a CR reduces the probability of alcohol consumption.

Behavior problems can also be treated by the application of operant conditioning principles. For instance, children who show disruptive behavior in school or in the home can be placed on a *token economy system* (Kendall, 1981). In such a system small (usually plastic) chips (or paper stars) are given for "good" (i.e., desired) behavior; chips or stars may be lost for "bad" behavior. These chips or stars become secondary reinforcers since they may be "traded in" periodically for such things as candy or small toys. The employment of a token economy system is especially useful with young children, for example, 2- to 4-year-olds, who may not have the internal, cognitive resources necessary to control their behavior adequately in certain situations (Kendall, 1981; Lerner & Hultsch, 1983).

Associative learning principles have been also applied to education. In the 1950s Skinner developed "teaching machines," which were devices allowing students to proceed at their own pace, step by step in a lesson, and to receive immediate feedback after each response. A primary feature of the use of such a device is to *individualize instruction*. Each student proceeds at his or her own rate and receives immediate reinforcement for each response.

To use a teaching machine a student activates a device (pulling a lever, turning a knob, etc.) which presents some information to the student through a window in the machine. The student is required to answer some question about the information. He or she responds by writing the answer in a space present in another window in the machine. The student then activates another device (e.g., he or she turns another knob) and the correct answer to the question is presented. A student repeats this sequence over the course of a "lesson" and is presented with increasingly more difficult information and questions. Through this procedure the student receives *programmed instruction*. That is, information is presented to the student systematically but without the reliance of a teacher to present it.

Programmed instruction has also been presented in specially designed textbooks termed *programmed texts*. Here each bit of information is presented as a "frame," which contains a statement and a sentence-completion type of question. Answers to the questions are provided elsewhere in the book, for example, on the following page.

With the advent and increasing availability of computers, the teaching machines of the 1950s have given way to these much more technologically sophisticated tools for programming instruction. More and more, *computer-assisted learning* systems are finding their way into today's educational settings, affording a much more elaborate means to program instruction for students.

---

relevance to our everyday lives. Highlight 6.1 focuses on some of the real-world applications of associative learning phenomena. In addition to these practical uses of associative learning, there are some limits to their application. These are noted in Highlight 6.2.

COGNITIVE LEARNING

Associative learning—classical and operant conditioning—represents the most basic form of learning. But some learning involves more complex processes, such as perception (Chapter 4) and memory (Chapter 7). These processes involve "cognition" (or knowledge); psychologists who study the role of

HIGHLIGHT 6.2
Limits of Associative Learning

Despite their wide applicability, there are constraints on the use of classical and operant conditioning. Breland and Breland (1961) have found that when an operantly conditioned behavior interferes with the performance of an animal's biologically based behavior, there will occur an *instinctual drift*; that is, the animal will not perform the operant behavior—even though that behavior will be reinforced—but it will perform the instinctual behavior—even though that behavior is not reinforced. For example, Breland and Breland (1961) tried to train pigs through operant conditioning to carry a coin in their snouts and drop it into the slot of a piggy bank. But when a stimulus is placed in a pig's snout, it typically "roots it"; that is, it drops it onto the ground and pushes on it. The pigs studied by Breland and Breland (1961) showed instinctual drift; they rooted the coins instead of dropping them into the slots and receiving reinforcement.

The existence of phenomena other than instinctual drift also constitute constraints on the applicability of associative learning phenomena. For example, in experimental situations (e.g., in an operant chamber) animals sometimes acquire responses which are not related to reinforcement. This is termed *autoshaping*. For example, pigeons may peck at a lit key even though reinforcement is not contingent on a key peck response (Brown & Jenkins, 1968) and despite the fact that performance of such responses may delay or prevent reinforcement (Williams & Williams, 1969).

In addition, Seligman (1975) has pointed out that learning depends on biological response *preparedness*. Certain biological characteristics of animals make it easier for them to learn particular responses than others. For example, rats may be taught easily to press a bar to obtain food or water. However, bar pressing to escape painful electric shock is quite difficult to teach a rat since its natural reactions—its preparedness—in the face of such stimulation involves fleeing and/or fright, behaviors which are not consistent with remaining near a lever and pressing on it regularly. Similarly, different animals have distinct response orientations to particular stimuli, making some stimuli useful in training and others not useful. For instance, different animals show distinctive *taste aversions* to certain foods (Garcia, Ervin, & Koelling, 1966). Garcia et al. showed that taste aversions are much more easily learned when taste stimuli are followed by *sickness* than when followed by shock, for example. In turn, shock-induced avoidance is more easily learned when signaled by tone and/or light than by taste.

---

cognition in learning believe that cognitive structures (e.g., memories) exist which preserve information and help to organize it (Horton & Mills, 1984). In other words, rather than emphasizing that what one acquires when one learns is merely a stimulus-response association, psychologists who adopt a cognitive orientation stress that knowledge is what is acquired in learning. Thus they focus on the organization, or structure, of knowledge, and on how the cognitive structure is used.

To illustrate, memories are seen to help us retain and organize what we learn by virtue of their organization into *schemata*, for instance, mental "pictures" or images of places, events, or objects. If we all close our eyes, we can picture "in our mind's eye" an image of our bedroom. We may see our bed, a nightstand, a closet door, and a window. We may see the relative location of these objects within the room. Thus our schemata for our bedroom constitute a mental representation of objects and of the relationship among them. That is, the objects in the room are not organized randomly in our memory. Rather they are formed into a pattern—a structure—and it is this mental structure, this memory of our room, that constitutes the organization of our knowledge and allows us to retrieve from our memory information about "our bedroom."

LEARNING

For instance, we could tell someone entering the room in the dark how to find his or her way to the closet, the nightstand, or the window. The schemata of our bedroom, by virtue of their structure, allow us to retrieve our knowledge from our memory and to use it to solve a problem (e.g., telling someone how to find a book left on the nightstand without turning on the light in the room and running the risk of waking up your roommate). The role of cognition in learning can be demonstrated by reference to several lines of research.

INSIGHT

Classic studies by Wolfgang Köhler (1925) demonstrate the role of particular types of cognitive processes in chimpanzees' learning to solve complex problems. Köhler found that chimps, rather than solving problems through trial and error, often solved problems through *insight*, that is, a sudden perception of the relationship among the objects involved in a problem. To illustrate, Köhler placed one of his most "intelligent" chimps, Sultan, in a cage in which food (a banana) was just beyond the bars of the cage. Sultan's arms were not long enough to reach through the bars to get the food. However, also in the cage was a stick. Sultan quickly perceived the relationship among the objects in this situation (i.e., among the food, the stick, and his arm). He used the stick as a "rake" and pulled the food to him.

Another example of insight in Sultan's learning to solve problems occurred when neither of two sticks present in his cage was long enough to serve as a useful rake. However, while manipulating them Sultan discovered that he could join the two sticks by placing the end of one into the other. He then immediately used the joined sticks to rake in the food.

A final example of the role of insight in Sultan's learning to solve problems comes from a situation in which food placed on the ceiling of his cage was beyond his reach, even when he jumped. However, Köhler had placed in the

An example of insight: Sultan, the chimp, learning to use a stick as a rake. (Yerkes Regional Primate Research Center of Emory University)

cage several boxes. Sultan tried to stand on one of the boxes, but it was not high enough to allow him to reach the food. Before long, Sultan perceived the relationship among the objects in the situation. He piled several boxes on top of each other and climbing on them, was able to reach the food.

The role of insight in learning to solve problems is not limited to chimps or human beings. Several species of animals show such cognitive learning. Indeed, Epstein (1981) has found insight learning to be present among birds.

COGNITIVE MAPS AND LATENT LEARNING

The schemata of your bedroom (e.g., the mental representation or image you have of the objects in it and of the relationships among them) comprise a *cognitive map*: a cognitive image of the organizīon of an area or a territory in which you live. Such mental maps tell us where particular objects are located in a given territory, and thus what portions of the territory easily or directly lead to other portions. We all have several such cognitive maps "in our heads" (e.g., of our bedrooms, of our homes, of our neighborhood, of our campus, of our country).

When one learns one forms a particular type of cognition—an expectancy—simply the knowledge that one object or event will follow another. For example, in learning our way home from the grocery store, we expect that one event (turning a corner) will be followed by another (seeing our house up the street). Thus in learning a cognitive map of an area, we form expectations of what leads to what, and Tolman (1932) believed that mere experience in moving through an area will allow such cognitive learning to occur. However, it is important here to recall the concept of latent learning introduced at the beginning of the chapter in our discussion of the distinction between learning and performance. The learning of expectancies (of how objects relate to each other) may not be evident (or overt); rather, such learning may be covert, *latent*, or simply not demonstrated in behavior until there is some reason, some incentive, to make it overt or manifest.

For example, has someone at home ever asked you: "Have you seen my car keys?" And have you responded with something like: "Yes, I saw them on the kitchen table when I came in a few minutes ago." This is an example of latent learning. Your mere experience in entering the kitchen was enough for you to learn that the keys were on the table. However, you probably did not know that you were learning this. Indeed, had their owner not forgotten where the keys were, you would never have had the incentive to make this learning manifest. In other words, in latent learning we have a situation in which some incentive is necessary for you to make your knowledge manifest, but it is not necessary for you to learn it in the first place.

A classic study by Tolman and Honzik (1930) demonstrates latent learning. Three groups of rats ran through a maze for several days. One group always received a reward when completing the maze. A second group did not receive a reward for 10 days but on day 11 and thereafter did find a reward at the end of the maze. The third group never received a reward at the end of the maze (i.e., for days 1 to 10, 11, or thereafter). The results of the study are presented in Figure 6.10.

The figure indicates that for the first 10 days of the study the rewarded group outperformed the nonrewarded groups. The rewarded group made fewer errors than did the rats that received no rewards for days 1 to 10. However, even without receiving a reward, both groups of nonrewarded rats showed some improvement in running the maze; both groups made fewer

Figure 6.10
The results of the study of latent learning by Tolman and Honzik (1930).

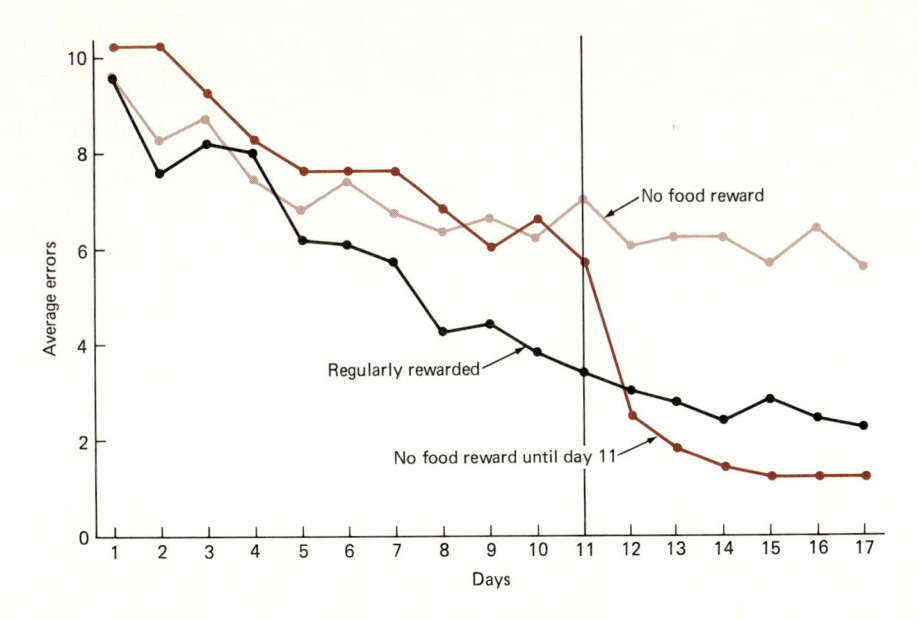

errors across the days. However, the striking findings occurred in regard to the rats which, after experiencing all the days without reward, encountered it on day 11. The introduction of the reward resulted in an immediate decrease in errors; indeed, this newly rewarded group now made fewer errors than the regularly rewarded group.

These results suggest that as in the example of the keys, the rats in the maze knew considerably more about the maze than was demonstrated overtly by their behavior. It is merely necessary to present an adequate reason for the demonstration of latent knowledge (e.g., "Have you seen my car keys" or a food reward), and the cognitive structure is made manifest. Thus, as we shall see again later in the chapter, all that may be necessary for cognitive learning (about a territory, an event, an object, or a person) to occur is mere observation (of the event, etc.). Reward, or reinforcement, may be necessary, however, for such cognition to become manifest in performance, or overt behavior.

THE LEARNING OF HIGHER-ORDER CONCEPTS

Still another area of cognitive learning involves the acquisition of knowledge about the principles, or abstract relations, involved in a problem. Earlier in the chapter we noted that a key parameter of learning was *generalization*, that is, responding similarly to two stimuli which are physically similar. However, in some animals (e.g., monkeys, chimps, and human beings) such transfer occurs not only in respect to physical similarity among stimuli, but also in response to stimuli which are linked by a common principle or concept.

Learning Sets. The research of Harlow (1959) on learning sets in monkeys demonstrates the learning of principles. Harlow exposed monkeys to two stimuli on each of numerous trials. On each trial the stimuli were different, for example, on Trial 1 a small green square on the right of the monkey and a large red circle on the left might have been presented, while on Trial 2 a large yellow triangle could have appeared on the right and a small blue

This monkey has learned to distinguish among the stimuli outside its cage. Pressing the buzzer, not pulling of the handles, will produce a reward. (University of Wisconsin Primate Laboratory)

rectangle could have been on the left. To get a reward, the animal might have to learn to choose the larger of the two stimuli, irrespective of location, or it could have had to learn to choose the stimulus on the right side, irrespective of size, or it could have had to learn to alternate sides from trial to trial. The point is that the solution cannot be achieved merely by reference to the physical characteristics of the stimuli. There is a *principle* involved in this learning. Harlow (1959) found that after several trials monkeys could learn such principles. Moreover, the animals learned to solve *successive* problems faster and faster; that is, the monkeys got better at problem solving after practice.

Reversal and Nonreversal Shifts. There are other examples of the learning of higher-order concepts, such as the principles involved in a problem. Kendler and Kendler (1962) devised a way to study problem-solving behavior in various organisms (e.g., rats and human beings), as well as in people of various ages (e.g., nursery school children and college students). In their procedure, subjects are presented with two large and two small squares. One of each type of square is painted black and one of each type is painted white. Thus there is a large black and a large white square, and a small white and a small black square. The subject's task is to learn to respond either to the color dimension (and thus ignore the size) or to the size dimension (and thus ignore the color). For example, a subject may be presented with a large black square and a small white square on one trial and then perhaps a large white square and a small black square on another trial. Now, if size is made the aspect of the stimuli that should be responded to and, further, a response toward the bigger of the two squares will always lead to a reward, the subject should choose the large stimulus in each trial, no matter what the color. In other words, the subject first learns that size is the relevant aspect of the stimuli; therefore, the subject learns to respond to the difference in size and not to respond to (ignore) differences in color of the squares.

Rats, nursery school children, and college students can all learn this first problem-solving task. The interesting thing about this type of problem solving is what happens when the rules about the relevant aspect of the stimuli are changed. In the first problem-solving task, size was the relevant dimension (the big squares were rewarded and the small squares were not). Now, without directly indicating to the subject that this rule has changed, it is possible to keep the size of the stimuli as the relevant dimension (and the color as the nonrelevant dimension), but make choice of the small squares the response that will be rewarded. Thus the same dimension of the stimuli (size) is still relevant, but there has been a reversal in which aspect of the size (from large to small) will lead to a reward. Kendler and Kendler call this type of alteration a *reversal shift*; the same stimulus dimension is still related to reward, but the positive and negative stimuli are reversed.

Another type of shift may be made, however, in the second problem-solving task. Instead of size being the reward-relevant dimension, color can be. Now response to the black squares (regardless of their size) will lead to a reward, and response to the white squares (regardless of their size) will not. This type of change involves a shift to the other dimension of the stimuli and is not within the same dimension. Hence the Kendlers termed this second type of possible change a *nonreversal shift*. Figure 6.11 illustrates the reversal and the nonreversal shifts. In all cases in this figure the stimuli toward which a response will lead to a reward are marked +, and the stimuli toward which a response will not be rewarded are marked −.

After learning the first problem (e.g., after making 10 correct responses to the large stimuli), would it then be easier to learn a reversal shift or a nonreversal shift (again using the criterion of 10 consecutive correct responses for learning)? Kendler and Kendler (1962) indicate that rats learn a nonreversal shift easier than a reversal shift. So do most nursery school children. The children reach the criterion for making a nonreversal shift faster than they reach the criterion for making a reversal shift. However, somewhat older children and college students find a reversal shift easier.

Figure 6.11
Examples of a reversal shift and a nonreversal shift. (From Kendler & Kendler, 1962.)

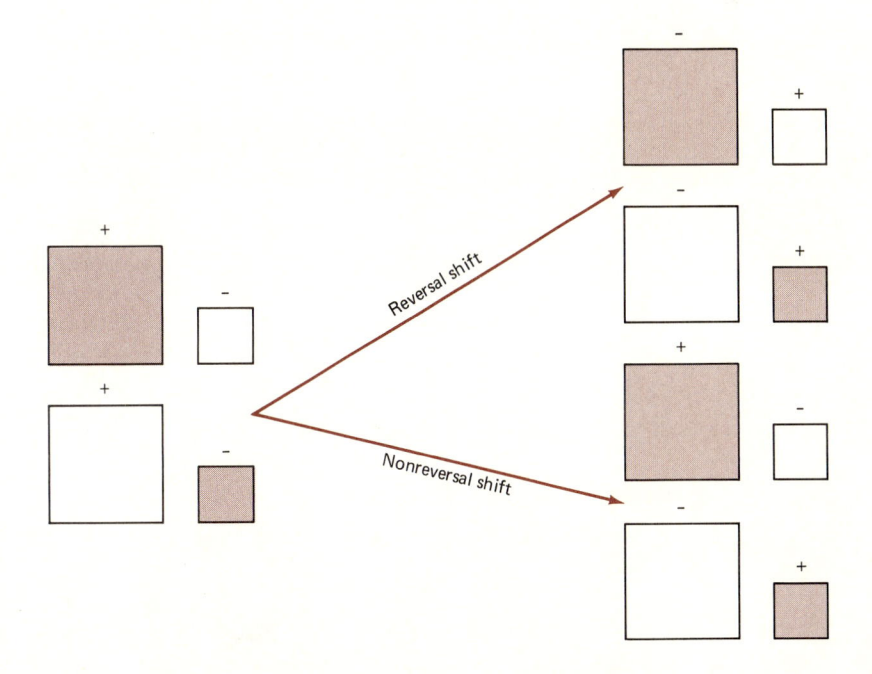

The Kendlers interpret these age changes by suggesting that a new *mental* process develops in children. This new mental process, not present at earlier ages, involves cognitive phenomena, such as efficient language processes. The presence of these cognitions are believed to alter children's problem-solving behavior, so that a reversal shift becomes easier than a nonreversal shift.

Another example may be offered of a line of research bearing on the role of cognition in learning. This line of research builds on the contributions of Tolman (1932) on the role of observation in learning; moreover, as did the research of Tolman (Tolman & Honzik, 1930), this research makes the point that whereas reinforcement may be necessary for performance, it is not necessary for learning.

OBSERVATIONAL LEARNING: MODELING AND IMITATION

As discussed by Liebert and Wicks-Nelson (1981), *observational learning* "occurs through exposure to the behaviors of others, the others being presented either live or symbolically in literature, films, television, and the like" (p. 170). As evidence that observational learning has occurred, the observer produces behaviors which are an *imitation* of what was observed. Thus this form of learning is often labeled *imitative learning*, and the actor that produced the to-be-copied or to-be-imitated learning is labeled the *model*. Because one learns from observing others in one's social milieu, this form of learning is also often termed "social learning." As argued by Bandura (1971), and earlier by Tolman (1932; Tolman & Honzik, 1930), behaviors need not receive reinforcement, or even occur, in order to be learned from a model.

A classic experiment by Bandura (1965) illustrates this view. Bandura presented a short film to nursery school children. In the film an adult was shown making a series of aggressive behaviors, for example, yelling at a large, inflated plastic doll, or hitting it with a hammer. The children watching this film were divided into three groups, each of which saw a different ending to the film. Group 1 was a "model rewarded" group. Here, at the end of the film a second adult gave the first one some candy for his "excellent" performance. Group 2 was a "model punished" one; a second adult scolded and spanked the first one. Children in group 3 saw neither reward nor punishment given to the model; here "neutral" consequences to the model were shown.

After the film ended, children in all groups were placed individually in a room having many of the same toys that had been available to the model. Hidden observers recorded each child's behavior. Children in both the "model rewarded" and the "neutral" group imitated more than did children in the "model punished" group.

However, despite these performance differences, there was evidence that children in all three groups equivalently learned the model's actions. Bandura (1965) offered children in all three groups rewards (e.g., a glass of fruit juice) if they would demonstrate what they had seen the model do in the film. This inducement canceled out the above-described performance differences, and children from all groups showed comparable amounts of imitative learning.

From these data it is possible to see why Bandura (1965) makes a distinction between learning and performance. It appears that reward or punishment influences whether children will perform observed behavior; it does

LEARNING

Social learning is accomplished by observing those around us. These children are demonstrating aggressive behavior learned from a film showing adult aggression. (Albert Bandura)

not appear to influence their learning the behavior (Shaffer, 1979). In other words, the response consequences to the model affect whether an observationally learned behavior will be imitated. However, the mere observation of the model may be sufficient for learning to occur.

In sum, observational learning processes are quite distinct from those involved in classical and operant conditioning. Moreover, their distinction is today thought to lie to a great extent in the role that cognitive processes play in observational learning (Bandura, 1978, 1980a, 1980b).

SUMMARY

1. Learning is a major instance of human adaptation. Learning involves changes which allow us to meet the challenges and solve the problems we face in our environments. More specifically, learning involves relatively permanent changes in behavior which result from experience.

2. The potential for behavior changes as a consequence of learning. Some of our learning may not be immediately evident in our behavior. Because of the latent character of some learning it is necessary, therefore, to distinguish between learning and performance.

3. Several types of learning exist. One type of learning which has been studied extensively is associative learning. Classical conditioning and instrumental learning (or operant conditioning) are examples of associative learning. A second type of learning which has been studied extensively is cognitive learning.

4. In classical conditioning an unconditioned stimulus (UCS), which elicits an unconditioned response (UCR), is paired with a neutral stimulus. After repeated associations between the UCS and this second stimulus, the second stimulus becomes a conditioned stimulus (CS). It now elicits a response markedly similar to the UCR; that is, the CS elicits a conditioned response (CR). Classical conditioning typically affects part of the autonomic nervous system and involuntary musculature involved in emotion. Hence, classical conditioning seems to be particularly important in conditioned emotional responses.

5. In instrumental learning, or operant conditioning, an animal learns to perform in order to produce a stimulus. The response made in instrumental learning is strengthened because the stimulus with which it is associated is a reinforcement. Thorndike introduced the law of effect to account for instrumental learning. This postulate is that the consequences—the effects—of a response to a stimulus determine whether that response is strengthened or weakened. If the effect is to produce a reward, the probability of that response being made to the stimulus is strengthened.

6. In operant conditioning the animal is free to perform continuously the response associated with reward. However, an animal placed into an experimental apparatus, for example, an operant conditioning chamber, may need to have its behavior shaped in order for it to perform the requisite response regularly. The method of successive approximations may be used to shape behavior.

7. There are several major features of associative learning. Among these are acquisition, extinction, spontaneous recovery, generalization, discrimination, primary and secondary reinforcement, positive and negative reinforcement, and schedules of reinforcement (involving continuous and partial, or intermittent, schedules of reinforcement).

8. There are numerous types of applications of the principles and phenomena of classical and operant conditioning. For instance, principles from these instances of associative learning may be used in the treatment of behavioral and emotional problems. However, there are constraints on the applicability of associative learning principles and on their use in accounting for all behavior. These constraints arise due to phenomena such as instinctual drift, autoshaping, preparedness, and taste aversion.

9. Cognitive learning involves the role of cognitive structures, such as memories, which help us preserve and organize information. These structures may take the form of mental images, or schemata. Several lines of research demonstrate the role of cognition in learning. This research deals with the role of insight, with cognitive maps and latent learning, and with the learning of higher-order concepts.

10. In cognitive learning there is evidence that reward may be necessary for performance but not for acquisition. In observational learning, for example, behaviors are imitated as a consequence of observing the actions of others; reinforcement appears to influence performance but not learning.

KEY TERMS

Associative learning
Classical conditioning
Instrumental learning
Operant conditioning
Law of effect
Reinforcement
Acquisition
Extinction
Spontaneous recovery
Generalization
Discrimination

Primary reinforcement
Secondary reinforcement
Escape learning
Avoidance learning
Learned helplessness
Continuous reinforcement schedule
Partial reinforcement schedule

Intermittent reinforcement schedule
Cognitive learning
Schemata
Insight
Cognitive maps
Latent learning
Higher-order concepts
Observational learning
Imitation

SUGGESTED READINGS

BANDURA, A. *Social learning theory*. Englewood Cliffs, N.J.: Prentice-Hall, 1977. A presentation of the features of the leading observational learning approach to learning.

BIJOU, S. W., & BAER, D. M. *Child development;* Vol. 1: *A systematic and empirical theory*. New York: Appleton-Century-Crofts, 1961. A concise presentation of the application of an associative learning approach to human behavior and development.

FERSTER, C. B., & SKINNER, B. F. *Schedules of reinforcement*. New York: Appleton-Century-Crofts, 1957. The classic presentation of the ways in which schedules of reinforcement influence the acquisition and maintenance of responses.

BOWER, G. H., & HILGARD, E. R. *Theories of learning* (5th ed.). Englewood Cliffs, N.J.: Prentice-Hall, 1981. A comprehensive, scholarly, and readable presentation of the past and current major theoretical approaches to learning.

KIMBLE, G. A. *Hilgard and Marquis' conditioning and learning*. New York: Appleton-Century-Crofts, 1961. Itself a classic, this is a revision of a classic compendium of research findings pertinent to parameters of the learning process.

7

Cognitive Processes: Remembering and Forgetting

APPROACHES TO HUMAN
   MEMORY
  Early Ideas About Memory
  The Information-Processing
    Approach
THE BASIC MEMORY SYSTEM
  Sensory Memory
  Short-Term Memory
  Long-Term Memory
THE RELATIONSHIP BETWEEN
   TYPES OF MEMORY
  Multistore Models
  Levels of Processing
THE ROLE OF PRIOR
   KNOWLEDGE IN
   MEMORY

  Constructive Memory
  Reconstructive Memory
THE ORGANIZATION OF
   KNOWLEDGE
  Semantic Versus Episodic
    Memory
  Network Models
  Schema Theory
SUMMARY
KEY TERMS
SUGGESTED READINGS

Imagine the following sequence of events. You wake up and see that it is past 7:30. You know that it is Monday morning and that you have a second-period history class, so you get out of bed, take a shower, and get dressed. You fix your favorite breakfast of French toast and sausages, and as you eat it, you listen to the news on the radio. After finishing breakfast, you grab your books and hurry to class so that you won't be late. The professor, who reminds you vaguely of your Uncle Harry, is unusually interesting today and you take a lot of notes. After class, you bump into your friend Jan and you decide to go to the student union for a cup of coffee. You talk to Jan about last week's party, and then go to the library to look up some material for a paper you are writing for your biology class.

    A simple story describing a morning in the life of a hypothetical college student. Yet almost none of the events described in this story would be possible without memory. Imagine what your life would be like if you could not remember. Even the simplest actions which we take for granted, such as recognizing a book, conversing with a friend, or even knowing who we are, would be impossible. In contrast, imagine what your life would be like if you were able to remember everything. In the science fiction trilogy *The Faded Sun*, C. J. Cherryh invents a race of beings, the Regul, who forget nothing—a characteristic that restricts their flexibility since they could not disregard inconsistencies in information.

APPROACHES TO HUMAN MEMORY

Memory and forgetting are integral parts of being human. How do people remember? What makes them forget? Scholars have been asking these questions since the beginning of history. Ideas about how memory works have changed dramatically over time.

EARLY IDEAS ABOUT MEMORY

An early and enduring view was rooted in the assumption that all learning and memory are based on the association of ideas or events that occur together in time. This view, introduced by Aristotle over 2,000 years ago, was elaborated on during the seventeenth and eighteenth centuries. Philosophers, including John Locke, George Berkeley, and David Hume, were impressed by the fact that sensations or events that occurred together in time were often remembered together. The concept of association was intended to account for how these sensations, events, or ideas became bound together.

The British Associationists, philosophers such as (A) John Locke (1632–1704), (B) George Berkeley (1685–1753), and (C) David Hume (1711–1776), accepted (D) Aristotle's view that learning and memory were based on the association of ideas or events that occur together in time. Their ideas were highly influential in the development of cognitive psychology. (Bettmann Archive)

(A)

(B)

(C)

(D)

These philosophers, known as the British associationists, relied on introspection as the main source of their information about memory. That is, they observed their own mental activities as they occurred. Late in the nineteenth century, Hermann Ebbinghaus, a German psychologist, provided a laboratory method for studying associations. Ebbinghaus studied associations by memorizing, and then attempting to recall, literally thousands of nonsense syllables, such as KEJ, RIF, and ZOF. He used nonsense syllables to minimize the influence of preexisting associations on his performance. Ebbinghaus's remarkable experiments resulted in the discovery of several fundamental characteristics of memory. Figure 7.1 shows two of his findings that have been replicated many times under different conditions.

Ebbinghaus's work laid the foundation for associationistic theories of memory which dominated psychology during the first half of the twentieth century. In these theories, associations were still the central elements. Learning was seen as involving the formation of stimulus-response (S-R) bonds. Stimulus and response became associated with one another as a result of contiguous exposure, with reinforcement sometimes being required for the bond to be formed. Acquisition was thought to occur as a result of increases in the number of S-R associations, or as a result of strengthening of existing associations through processes such as repetition. The act of remembering was seen as involving the emission of previously acquired responses under appropriate stimulus conditions. Forgetting was thought to be a function of the loss or weakening of associative bonds through processes such as decay or interference.

The emphasis of early theorists on associations as the basic building blocks of learning and memory was logical. Indeed, the idea that concepts in the mind are connected in various ways is still prevalent in cognitive psychology. However, the idea that memory can be explained solely on the basis of S-R associations has largely been discarded. Instead of being seen as passive recorders of associations, human beings are being seen as active information-processing systems.

THE INFORMATION-PROCESSING APPROACH

The view that human beings are complex information-processing systems developed as a result of integration of ideas from several disciplines with psychology beginning about the time of World War II. Three main influences

Figure 7.1
Results of Ebbinghaus' classic research on remembering nonsense syllables. The first panel shows that the number of repetitions necessary to learn a list increases with the length of the list. The second panel shows that the rate of forgetting is very rapid at first, but then tapers off. (Based on Ebbinghaus, 1964.)

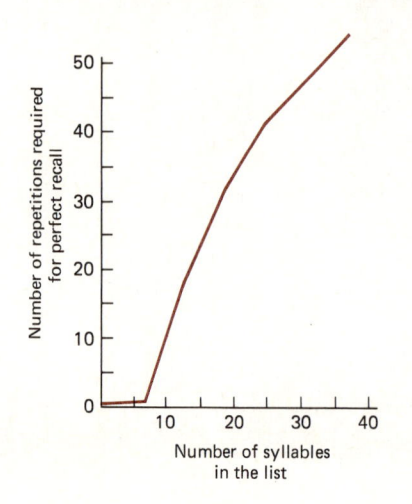

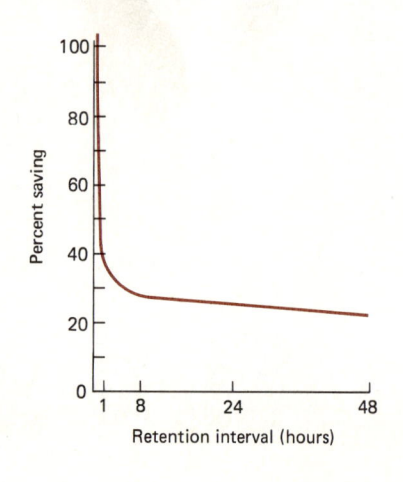

contributed to the development of modern cognitive psychology, and consequently, to current views of memory.

The first was the development of information theory within communication science. Information theory sought to describe the properties and operation of all communication systems. One of its concepts was channel capacity: the maximum number of signals that a channel (e.g., a telephone line) can carry in a fixed period of time. Psychologists such as Broadbent (1958) suggested that human beings were also communication systems. Following this analogy, psychologists discovered that there are upper limits on how many things a person can think of simultaneously, identify at a glance, or remember. Of course, psychologists had been aware of such limitations, but their significance was not appreciated until the contributions of communication science. Once psychologists grasped the importance of these limitations, they also discovered that human beings have many mechanisms for overcoming them.

Linguistics also contributed to the new perspective on cognitive behavior. In the 1950s, Chomsky (1957) began to develop a theory of the structure of language. His work suggested that language is more complex than had previously been thought, and that explanations of it based on S-R formulations could not account for these complexities. Linguists pointed out that people have never heard most of the sentences they generate. Indeed, it is agreed that the number of potential sentences in a language is infinite. Given this, it is very difficult to argue that you could have learned the meaning of sentences through past association with specific stimuli, as suggested by S-R theories of language. Rather, linguists argued that the key to understanding language was to see it as an abstract system of relations governed by rules. Linguistic's attack helped to loosen the hold of associationism on psychology. Psychologists have discovered that rules, novelty, and productivity are characteristic of memory and other cognitive processes in addition to language.

The third field to influence current conceptions of cognition was computer science. Computing machines were developed around 1950. However, it remained for Newell and Simon (1962) to conceptualize the computer and the human mind as specific instances of the same kind of system—an information-processing system. These theorists argued that the essence of an information-processing system is its ability to represent things symbolically and to manipulate these symbols. To do this, an information-processing system must be able to recognize a new instance of a symbol when it reoccurs. To do this, of course, requires memory. Thus computers take symbolic input, recode it, manipulate it, store it, and give back symbolic output. All these activities are governed by a set of rules known as a program. Newell and Simon suggested that human beings do similar things. This general view of cognition leads to several basic assumptions about the nature of the memory process.

First, memory involves multiple stages of processing. Suppose that someone asks you: "What's the capital city of Oregon?" To answer this question correctly, you have to complete all three basic stages of the memory process. The first stage is *acquisition*: You must already have been exposed to and learned the answer. The second stage is *storage*. Presumably, during learning some enduring record, a *memory trace*, is left in the nervous system. To answer the question, the memory trace must be retained for later use. The final stage is *retrieval*: You must be able to recover the appropriate memory trace from among many others. If you are unable to respond by answering "Salem," it may be because of difficulty at any one of the three stages—acquisition, storage, or retrieval.

People remember things verbatim such as telephone numbers. (Susan Wagner)

Second, memory involves the manipulation of information. Memory is not a passive process of recording information through multiple repetitions. Rather, a person actively manipulates the information through several control processes. *Control processes* are memory strategies which people use voluntarily. They include such things as altering the format of the information, organizing it, rehearsing it, and so on. The control processes the person brings to bear on the information will depend on many factors, including the nature of the task, the nature of the material, and the person's prior experience.

Third, memory is both reproductive and constructive. People remember many things verbatim—names, telephone numbers, shopping lists, and so forth. That is, much of our memory seems to reproduce the stimulus conditions at the time of acquisition. However, particularly with complex information, our memory also goes beyond the information given, and we remember information that was not actually presented but that is constructed from our knowledge of the world. For example, having seen *Star Wars*, you remember that Darth Vader was evil, even though that bit of information may never have been stated explicitly in the film. Rather, you construct that information from your knowledge and interpretation of his behavior and store it in memory together with the specific actions that you saw.

THE BASIC MEMORY SYSTEM

The information-processing approach suggests that memory involves multiple stages, manipulation of information, and reproductive and constructive activity. But is memory a single thing? Consider the following dilemma. You look up a telephone number and reach for the telephone to dial it. Just as you are ready to begin dialing, someone interrupts and asks you something.

COGNITIVE PROCESSES: REMEMBERING AND FORGETTING   213

Figure 7.2
A generalized diagram of the human memory system showing the characteristics of and relationships among sensory memory, short-term memory, and long-term memory.

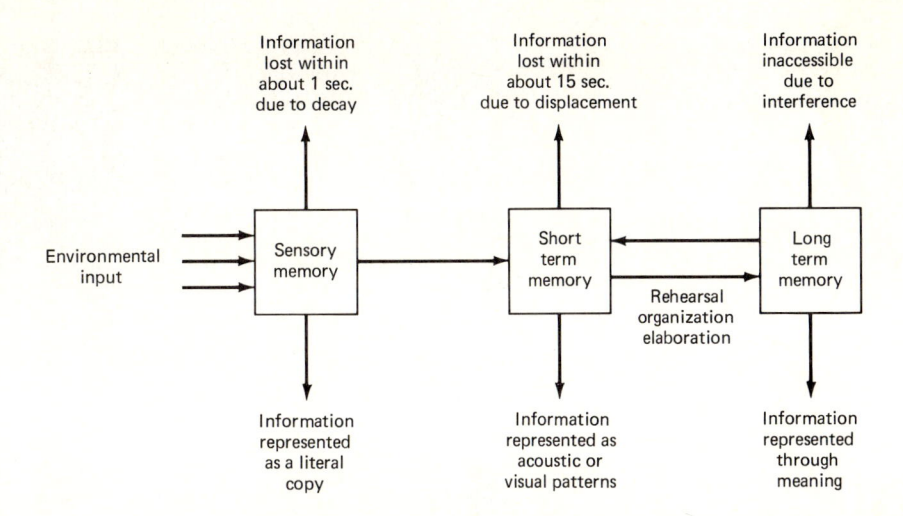

```
                    Information          Information          Information
                    lost within          lost within          inaccessible
                    about 1 sec.         about 15 sec.        due to
                    due to decay         due to displacement  interference
                         ↑                    ↑                    ↑
                    ┌─────────┐          ┌─────────┐          ┌─────────┐
   Environmental →  │ Sensory │     →    │  Short  │     →    │  Long   │
   input         →  │ memory  │          │  term   │   ←      │  term   │
                 →  │         │          │ memory  │  Rehearsal│ memory │
                    └─────────┘          └─────────┘  organization└─────┘
                                                      elaboration
                         ↓                    ↓                    ↓
                    Information          Information          Information
                    represented          represented as       represented
                    as a literal         acoustic or          through
                    copy                 visual patterns      meaning
```

You answer, and when you return your attention to the telephone number, you find that you have forgotten it. Indeed, it turns out that human beings can retain only a very limited amount of information in consciousness at a given moment. Yet we obviously remember vast amounts of information over very long periods of time. For example, you remember your own phone number, together with a lot of other pieces of information, despite interruptions.

Observations such as this led psychologists to suggest that there are different types of memory. In particular, as shown in Figure 7.2, three types of memory have been identified: sensory, short-term, and long-term. *Sensory memory* is the momentary retention of an unprocessed copy of a stimulus. It lasts for only the briefest instant. *Short-term memory* involves the conscious retention of information that has just been presented or retrieved from long-term memory. The capacity of short-term memory is very limited, and unless information is processed further, it is lost as new information enters. Finally, *long-term memory* is a permanent storage system with unlimited capacity.

SENSORY MEMORY

As shown in Figure 7.2, information enters memory through the various senses. A sensory "register" probably exists for all five sensory systems (visual, auditory, tactile, olfactory, gustatory), although only vision and audition have been studied. Information enters the sensory registers automatically if the senses are functioning properly. Moreover, it is not recognized, categorized, or otherwise processed until it has passed through the sensory registers. Thus information in the sensory registers is a literal copy of the stimulus involved. Since our senses are bombarded by many stimuli at any one instant, the capacity of the sensory registers is assumed to be relatively large. However, information is maintained in sensory memory only for a brief moment—less than 1 second. Sensory information is lost in one of two ways if it is not processed further. Either it simply dissipates with the passage of time (decay), or new information entering the senses writes over the old information (interference).

What is the function of the sensory registers? To process information, we must attend to it. To attend to it, we must sort it out. This process takes time.

Information in long-term memory is encoded in many ways, including smell and taste. (Van Bucher)

The sensory registers, then, preserve the incoming information long enough for this initial sorting process to occur. They let us select those sensory inputs we will process further.

What is the evidence for the existence of sensory memory as we have described it? Let us examine one type of sensory memory—visual sensory memory (*iconic memory*). Glance very briefly at the display of letters in Figure 7.3, then close your eyes and try to say as many of them aloud as you can. You probably could report only four or five letters, even though you feel you saw more in your brief glance. Why should this be the case? Sperling (1960) suggested that people could record a great deal of information in a brief glance, but could not report all of it because visual sensory memory faded too quickly. Although other investigators had also suggested this, Sperling developed a method for testing it. Earlier investigators had asked people to report everything they saw in a brief visual display. Sperling did this too. However, he also asked people to report only part of what they saw. Sperling showed people visual displays of 12 letters similar to those in Figure 7.3 for 50 ms. In the first part of the experiment, he asked people to report as many of the letters as they could. Using this method, he found that people could remember about four or five letters. In the second part of the experiment, Sperling asked the people for partial reports. After he presented each display of letters, he identified one of the three rows in the display by sounding a high, medium, or low tone. This was a signal to the person to report only the letters in that row. The tone was sounded after the letters were gone, and the row was chosen at random, so that the person could not anticipate which row he or she would be asked to report. With this method, Sperling found that people could correctly report almost all four letters in any of the rows (if the tone was sounded immediately after the display), suggesting that they saw the entire display. However, even the briefest of delays resulted in a loss

```
X   M   R   J
C   N   K   P
V   F   L   B
```

Figure 7.3
An example of the kind of display used to investigate visual sensory memory. The display is presented briefly, and people are asked to report either some or all of the letters it contains. (Based on Sperling, 1960.)

Figure 7.4
Results from Sperling's experiment. A display of letters was presented for a very short time. People were asked either to report all of the letters or, signaled by a tone, only one row of the letters. As the tone that signals the row to be reported is delayed, the number of items people can report declines. The solid bar shows the number of items reported when people are asked to report the whole display. (Sperling, 1960.)

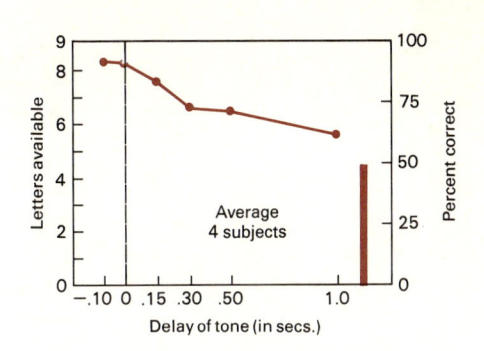

of information. If the tone was delayed just 300 ms, recall dropped to about 70%. After a delay of 1 second, recall under partial report was no different from that under full report (see Figure 7.4).

Sperling's results support the idea of a visual sensory register which stores a relatively large amount of information for a very brief time. Later research has confirmed Sperling's pioneering work, although the exact duration of visual sensory memory depends on several factors, such as the brightness of the display and the characteristics of the visual field following it. Sperling's procedures have been used to study auditory sensory memory (*echoic memory*), with similar conclusions.

SHORT-TERM MEMORY

We indicated that the purpose of the sensory registers is to preserve incoming information long enough for it to be selectively processed further in memory. This is done by attending to the information which then enters short-term memory. As you can see in Figure 7.2, information can also enter short-term memory from long-term memory. Short-term memory is sometimes called *working memory* because it is here that conscious mental processes are performed.

Encoding. Unlike the sensory registers, information is stored in short-term memory in processed form—it is *encoded* in some way. When you try to remember the telephone number you just looked up, the digits seem to be held in mind on the basis of their acoustic characteristics, that is, the way they sound. How is information coded in short-term memory? Is the code auditory, visual, or both?

Evidence suggests that verbal information is often coded acoustically in short-term memory, even when it is presented visually. For example, Conrad (1964) showed people lists of letters and then asked them to write them down in order. When Conrad carefully analyzed the recall errors people made, he found that certain sorts of errors were made more often than others. Specifically, when people made errors, they were likely to recall a letter that sounded like the presented letter. Thus, when the correct letter was B, they were more likely to err by recalling V or T than by recalling M or S. Although people are likely to confuse letters that sound alike, they rarely confuse letters that look alike, such as E and F or M and N (Conrad, 1965). Similar results occur when the materials to be remembered are words. Such findings suggest that acoustic coding is used in short-term memory. Even when the material is presented visually, material is apparently recoded to acoustic form.

Is encoding in short-term memory exclusively acoustic? Recent research has suggested that it is not. For example, visual encoding appears to be employed when one has to store items that are difficult to describe verbally. A good example of this comes from a study in which people were asked to make judgments that required the mental rotation of complex three-dimensional figures. The results of these studies suggested that people formed an image of the test stimulus and then mentally rotated it (Cooper & Shepard, 1973).

The dominance of acoustical encoding in short-term memory may reflect experience. For example, it has been demonstrated that younger children are less likely to use acoustical encoding as an aid to memory than are older children. In one study, children were shown pictures of objects and then were asked to pick out the objects they had seen from a number of alternatives. In one condition the names of the objects were acoustically similar (e.g., rat, cat, mat, hat, etc.), while in the other they were acoustically dissimilar (e.g., girl, bus, train, spoon, etc.). It was found that the older children remembered the acoustically dissimilar words better than the acoustically similar words. However, the younger children remembered both sets of objects equally well (Conrad, 1971).

Storage. Information can be maintained in short-term memory only by attending to it, rehearsing it, or otherwise manipulating it. As soon as attention is shifted away from one piece of information to another, the first item begins to decay and is lost completely within 15 to 30 seconds. A classical experiment by Peterson and Peterson (1959) demonstrated the transient nature of short-term memory. These investigators asked people to study three consonants (e.g., MVK) and then to recall them after various delay intervals up to 18 seconds. To prevent people from rehearsing the letters during the delay interval, the investigators had the people count backward by threes from a given number until they received the signal to recall the letters. As shown in Figure 7.5, recall declines rapidly, until almost all of the information is unavailable after a delay of only 18 seconds.

Since you can only attend to a relatively small amount of information at any one time, the capacity of short-term memory is relatively small. Numerous attempts to estimate the capacity of short-term memory have consistently shown that it is about seven items plus or minus two. This limit appears to hold for all kinds of stimulus materials, test procedures, and people. It is so

Figure 7.5
Results from Peterson and Peterson's experiment. People were asked to study a three-letter combination and to remember it. Immediately after seeing the letters, they were asked to count backward from a given number by threes until they received a signal to recall the letters. The longer the interval until the signal was given, the fewer items people were able to remember. (Peterson & Peterson, 1959.)

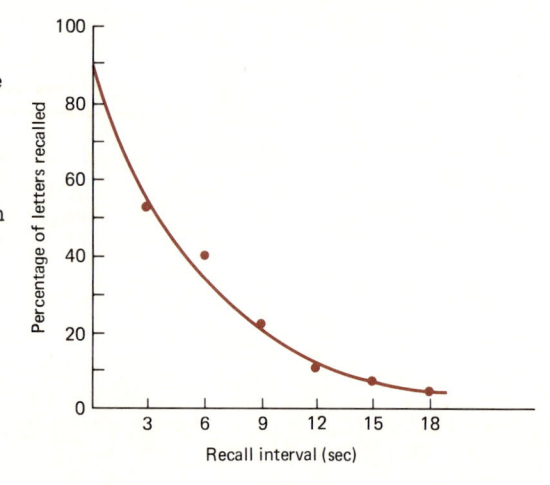

pervasive that after summarizing the extensive literature on short-term memory, G. A. Miller (1956) referred to it as the "magical number seven."

One method to demonstrate the capacity limits of short-term memory is to present people with a sequence of items (digits, letters, words) and ask them to recall them in order. Several sequences are presented to the person, beginning with a few items and gradually increasing to many. The maximum number of items that the person can recall without making any errors is his or her memory span. For adults, this is almost certainly between five and nine. You can try this procedure yourself. Arrange lists of 4, 6, 8, and 10 digits in an unsystematic order. Then read each list to another person, asking them to repeat the digits in order as soon as you finish reading them. It is very probable that they will remember the 4-digit list perfectly, but will make errors on the 10-digit list.

Note that the capacity limit of short-term memory is determined by the number of items rather than the amount of information. For example, suppose that you are asked to remember the following sequence of letters and digits: R2D2C3PO. Rather than processing this sequence as eight separate items, you may be able to process it as two items: the names of the robots in the movie *Star Wars*. G. A. Miller (1956) labeled this process of grouping items together as *chunking*. Chunking uses information already stored in long-term memory to group new information entering short-term memory. That is, you had to know about the two robots in order to form the two chunks described in the example above.

Retrieval. How is information retrieved from short-term memory? This question appears to have an intuitively simple answer. If information in short-term memory is in consciousness, it should be available without having to search for it. However, like many intuitively simple answers, this one seems to be incorrect.

S. Sternberg (1966) conducted a series of studies demonstrating the nature of retrieval in short-term memory. In his basic task, Sternberg showed people a series of one to six digits (e.g., 4371). Then after 2 seconds, he showed them a test digit. On some of the trials, the test digit had been shown before as part of the series (e.g., 3), whereas on some of the trials, it had not (e.g., 6). The person's task was to indicate, by pressing one of two buttons as rapidly as possible, whether the test digit had been part of the series for that trial. Because the length of any series did not exceed the immediate memory span, people made very few errors on this task. What is of interest, however, is their *reaction time*, that is, the time between the presentation of the test digit and the person's response of pressing the button. As shown in Figure 7.6, reaction time increases linearly with the size of the set of digits presented. For every digit added to the set, there is a fixed increase of 37 ms in reaction time.

These results suggested to Sternberg that retrieval from short-term memory is serial and exhaustive. That is, people compare the test digit to each digit in the set until all digits have been compared. Such a search process makes sense if the test digit is not in the set. However, it does not appear to make sense if the test digit is in the set (unless it is the last one compared). Yet it takes as long for people to answer "yes" (filled circles in Figure 7.6) as to answer "no" (open circles in Figure 7.6), suggesting that they evidently search all the items. Sternberg argued that high-speed exhaustive scanning is more efficient than scanning that would terminate when a match occurred.

Sternberg's results have been replicated many times. However, when the basic task is varied, different results appear. For example, if the items in the

Figure 7.6
Results of an experiment designed to assess retrieval from short-term memory. The time required to decide whether a test digit was a member of a previously presented set of digits increases linearly as the size of the set increases. Filled circles represent the time taken to say "yes" (the digit was a member of the set), whereas the open circles represent the time taken to say "no" (the digit was not a member of the set). These results led Sternberg to theorize that retrieval from short-term memory is characterized by a high-speed serial and exhaustive search. (Sternberg, 1966.)

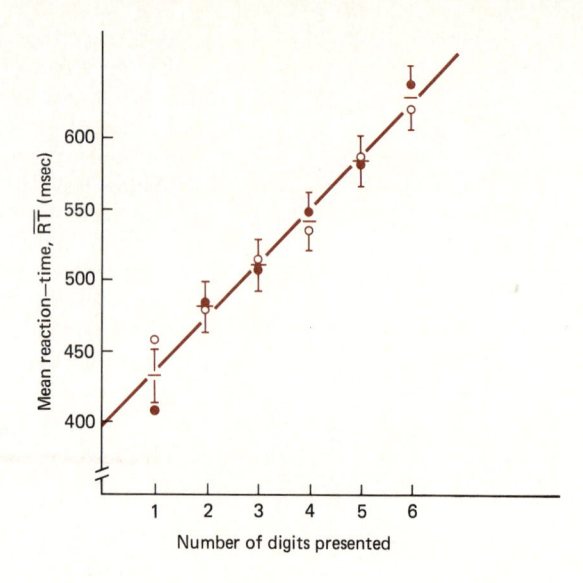

set are words from different conceptual categories, people appear to search exhaustively within categories, but stop with the category containing the item rather than searching every category in the set (Naus, Glucksburg, & Ornstein, 1972). Nevertheless, the bulk of the data suggest that a primary strategy for retrieval from short-term memory consists of a rapid, serial, exhaustive search.

LONG-TERM MEMORY

Long-term memory involves the maintenance of information no longer in consciousness. Long-term memory may endure for only a few minutes or for many years. The capacity of long-term memory is postulated to be essentially unlimited. Long-term memory, then, is like a vast warehouse of information stored until it is needed. Although this analogy is, in some ways, an oversimplification, the basic idea is correct. Long-term memory is required because we do not need to be aware of all of our knowledge all of the time. Indeed, if we were, it would probably be impossible to think. How is information encoded, stored, and retrieved from this vast warehouse?

Encoding. Information in long-term memory appears to be encoded in many ways—for example, through sound, sight, and meaning. Smells and tastes are probably also encoded in long-term memory.

PHONOLOGICAL ENCODING. Some information appears to be encoded on the basis of its sound. Such encoding probably helps us recall the words of a song or recognize a voice on the telephone. A study by Nelson and Rothbart (1972) demonstrates the involvement of phonological encoding in long-term memory. These investigators asked people to learn to associate pairs of numbers and words such as 27-tacks and 13-pray, so that they could say the word when they were shown the number alone. Four weeks after they had learned a list of 24 such pairs they were unexpectedly asked to complete a single relearning trial. Three types of pairs were involved. Some of the pairs were identical to those used in the original task (e.g., 27-tacks, 13-pray). Some of the pairs consisted of the same stimuli from the original task, paired with words that had different meanings but that sounded the same as those from the original task (e.g., 27-tax, 13-prey). Finally, some of the pairs consisted of the same stimuli from the original task paired with words that were unrelated to those used in the original task (e.g., 27-jury). As you would expect, relearning was best for those pairs that were identical to the originals. However, relearning was better for pairs that included responses that sounded like the original words than for pairs that required responses unrelated to the original words. Thus the phonological properties of the original words must have been encoded.

VISUAL ENCODING. People must encode visual information since we can recall and recognize complex scenes. One set of studies has focused on the ability to recognize pictures. People appear to be exceedingly good at this task. For example, in one series of studies, Shepard (1978) showed people various visual materials, including random geometric shapes and three-dimensional objects, and asked them to form mental images of these materials. Later, he asked the people to pick out these stimuli from among other similar representations of the materials. The identifications were made very quickly and accurately.

People appear to be able to remember very large amounts of visual information. For example, Standing (1973) found that people can examine enormous numbers of photographs and still recognize almost all of them a day and a half later. Recognition of pictures was much better than recognition of words. People could recognize about 90% of 1,000 photographs but only 62% of 1,000 words. The ability to remember visual information appears to involve a visual code rather than simply verbal recoding of visual information. Some studies have used complex stimuli which are difficult to describe verbally. For example, in one study people were asked to remember pictures of snowflakes which were very similar and which elicited similar verbal descriptions (Goldstein & Chance, 1970). Although verbal recoding may facilitate memory for pictures, it does not appear to be required.

SEMANTIC ENCODING. Coding on the basis of the meaning of materials is widespread in long-term memory. Indeed, it appears to be the preferred code for verbal materials. Evidence for this comes from several sources. For example, if people are shown a list of words and are later asked to recognize those they have seen before from a larger list, they will often err and "recognize" words they have not seen before. In such instances, people are most likely to err by naming words that are semantically related to the words presented. For example, if the word "lake" appeared on the original list, you may falsely recognize the word "pond."

A similar phenomenon occurs when people are asked to recognize sentences they have heard before. These studies suggest quite clearly that people encode sentences in terms of their meaning. For example, in one study, Bransford and Franks (1971) presented people with a set of sentences, each one of which contained a part of a complete idea. For instance, the sentence "The tall tree in the front yard shaded the man who was smoking his pipe" involves four separate ideas:

"The tree was tall."
"The tree was in the front yard."
"The tree shaded the man."
"The man was smoking his pipe."

These one-idea sentences can be combined into longer sentences as well. Examples of two-idea and three-idea sentences would be, respectively:

"The tree shaded the man who was smoking his pipe."
"The tree in the front yard shaded the man who was smoking his pipe."

During the task, people were shown enough of the possible one-, two-, and three-idea sentences to expose them to all four components of the complete idea. Four such complete ideas were represented in the set of sentences. Following presentation of the sentences, people were asked to judge whether they had heard each sentence before. This recognition set of sentences contained repetitions of the sentences actually seen, sentences that were consistent with the idea sets but which had not been seen, and sentences that were unrelated to the idea sets. Generally, people were certain that they had heard the complex sentences that described all four events. In fact, they had never heard a sentence describing all four events, or even a sentence that long. Nevertheless, the more idea units a sentence contained, the more likely it was to be recognized as having been seen before. Further, these judgments were almost the same for old and new sentences. Thus whether a sentence had actually been seen before or not had little influence on its rating as long as it was consistent with the idea. Sentences inconsistent with the idea (e.g., "The tree in the front yard shaded the old car") were not recognized as "old" sentences. In summary, people formed a precise, unified representation of the meaning of each idea set and remembered this rather than separate words and sentences.

Meaning. We have seen that a particular item or event may be encoded along multiple dimensions in long-term memory. Thus a particular word such as "squirrel" may be encoded along physical, phonological, visual, and semantic dimensions. The particular dimensions will vary with the nature of the stimulus and the context in which it is being processed. However, the nature of the encoding appears to determine what is remembered and how well it is remembered. Specifically, the more deeply the meaning of an item is processed, the better it tends to be remembered.

This conclusion is illustrated by studies that have tried to restrict how people encode information and then determine how much they can recall. Essentially, people are shown a list of words and are asked to perform a particular operation on them that will lead to a certain type of encoding. They are not told that they will be asked to remember the words later; thus this is called an *incidental learning task*.

For example, in one experiment performed by Craik and Tulving (1975), people were told that the purpose of the study was to study perception and reaction time. The people were shown a list of words, one at a time, and were asked to answer a question about each word as it was presented. The purpose of the questions was to induce the people to encode the words in particular ways. Three types of questions were used. The first was designed to induce encoding of the physical characteristics of the word. People were asked how the word was written, for example, "Is the word printed in capital letters?" The second was designed to induce encoding of the phonological characteristics of the word. People were asked about how the word sounded, for example, "Does the word rhyme with train?" Finally, the third was designed to induce encoding of the semantic characteristics of the word. People were asked whether the word fit appropriately into a sentence, for example, "Would the word fit the sentence: 'They met a _____ in the street'?" Following a series of 60 trials with questions and answers, the people were unexpectedly asked to recognize the words from among a larger list, includ-

Figure 7.7
Results of Craik and Tulving's experiments to assess the effect of different levels of encoding on retention. The more the words are processed in terms of their meaning, the better they are retained. (Based on Craik & Tulving, 1975.)

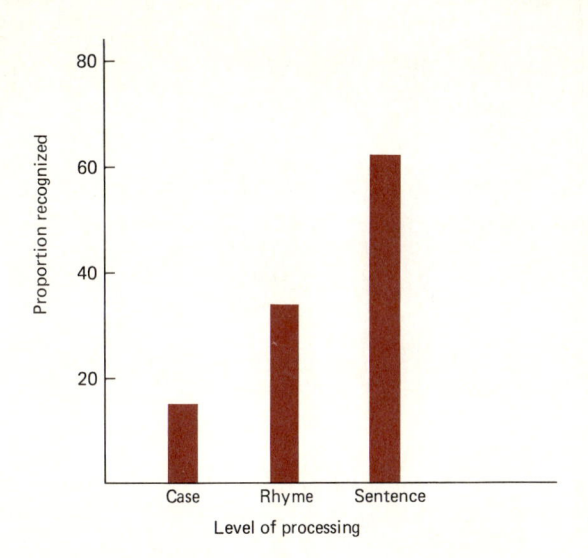

ing the original 60 words and 120 distractor words. As shown in Figure 7.7, retention was poorest for words that had been encoded on the basis of their physical characteristics, intermediate for words that had been encoded on the basis of their phonological characteristics, and best for words that had been encoded on the basis of their semantic characteristics. Thus level of retention appears to depend on how the information is processed. One may envision a continuum of levels of processing defined by the extent to which the information has been encoded in terms of its meaning. If the processing is shallow, that is, nonsemantic, retention will generally be poor. If the processing is deep, that is, semantic, retention will generally be good.

Recently, Craik (1981) has suggested that memory depends on the elaborateness as well as the depth of encoding. That is, although stimuli may be processed through a series of levels, at any particular level the stimulus may be processed more or less fully. For example, you may be able to process the words "aardvark" and "horse" in terms of their semantic meaning. However, because of differences in your knowledge of these two animals you are likely to have more elaborate encoding for "horse" than for "aardvark." One study by Craik and Tulving demonstrated the importance of elaboration. This experiment used the same basic incidental learning task described above except that all the questions were designed to induce semantic encoding. Specifically, people were asked to determine whether the word fit into a sentence. However, the sentences varied in length. It was anticipated that less elaborate semantic processing would be involved in determining whether the word fit into a simple sentence (e.g., "She cooked the _____") than into a more complex sentence (e.g., "The great bird swooped down and carried off the struggling _____"). Indeed, when people were asked to remember the words later, they recalled the words associated with the complex sentences better than those associated with the simple sentences.

REHEARSAL. What sorts of mechanisms do people use to achieve depth and elaborateness in encoding? One of the simplest ways to encode information in long-term memory is to repeat it again and again, a strategy labeled *rehearsal*. For example, when you are introduced to someone, you may repeat their name either aloud or mentally. However, not all rehearsal appears to facilitate long-term memory. For example, Craik and Watkins (1973) showed

FOCUS ON THE PSYCHOLOGIST

Fergus I. M. Craik

FERGUS CRAIK was educated at the Universities of Edinburgh and Liverpool. His first teaching post, which he held from 1965 to 1971, was at Birkbeck College—part of the University of London. In 1971 he moved to his present position at the University of Toronto, where he teaches and conducts research into various aspects of human memory.

From the start I was interested in designing and running experiments; for my undergraduate thesis project, I carried out a study on time perception as a function of the information transmitted in a complex perceptual judgement. The stimulus varied in up to five dimensions simultaneously, and the design called for 120 subjects—each tested individually. But I enjoy designing experiments and even testing subjects.

After graduating from Edinburgh, I moved to Liverpool to work in a research group studying problems of aging. In some ways the group was a successor to the extremely influential research team that had studied aging and human skill under Alan Welford at Cambridge in the 1950s. My assigned topic was age changes in decision making and judgment, but I also became interested in the effects of aging on perception, attention, memory, and skilled performance. I thus studied the relatively new topic of signal detection theory and, through several visits to Donald Broadbent's research unit in Cambridge, became very familiar with British research on reaction time, attention, and other aspects of perceptual-motor skills. When I moved to Birkbeck College, London, in 1965, I continued to work on age differences in attention and memory but was becoming progressively more interested in problems of memory as such. I carried out a number of experiments on short-term memory—a hot topic at that time—but became generally dissatisfied with the current notion that the short-term memory store was a self-contained and rather peripheral part of the input system.

I also thought that the "separate" functions of attention and memory had a lot in common. "Holding information in short-term memory" seemed remarkably similar to "continuing to pay attention" to the information. Anne Treisman at Oxford had an interesting model of attention, which proposed that stimuli could be analyzed at various levels, from early sensory analyses through to later analyses concerned with word identification and meaning. These notions might have some implications for memory, if memory could be thought of as the result of different types of processing, rather than as information held in "stores" of different sizes. When I came to Toronto in 1971, I found that one of my colleagues, an ex-Australian named Robert Lockhart, had been developing similar views. We both argued that remembering should be thought of as an active, functional *process* rather than as a fixed series of mechanisms. Quite simply, the experimental data did not bear out the idea that each memory store had constant characteristics; when the materials or the context or the instructions changed, the characteristics of capacity and trace durability also changed. This was a bit odd if the stores were fixed structures. So Lockhart and I proposed our "levels of processing" view instead, arguing that stimuli were processed essentially for perception and comprehension and that "deeper" meaningful processing resulted in a long-lasting record of the analyses carried out. It turned out that many other researchers had been unhappy with the "memory stores" view so that the levels of processing approach were generally well received.

Since the "levels" paper was published in 1972, I have carried out many experiments to support the position; such a series was published in an article with Endel Tulving in 1975. Our current work involves the relations between encoding and retrieval processes and also (perhaps stimulated by my own forgetfulness) a revived program of experiments on age changes in memory functions.

COGNITIVE PROCESSES: REMEMBERING AND FORGETTING   223

As these actors know, one of the simplest ways to achieve depth and elaborateness in encoding information in long-term memory is to rehearse it in a meaningful way. (Burt Glinn/Magnum)

people a series of word lists and told them that they would be asked to recall the last four words of each list. They were also told that if they wished to rehearse the words, they should do so aloud. People were also told whether they would be asked to recall the lists immediately after presentation or following a 15-second delay. After all the lists had been seen and recalled, the people were unexpectedly asked to recall all the words. Craik and Watkins found that people rehearsed the words more when they were told that recall would be delayed than when it was not. However, the probability of recalling a word on the final unannounced recall test (a measure of long-term memory) did not depend on the number of times a word had been rehearsed. Memory was poor in all instances.

Results such as these have led to the conclusion that there are two types of rehearsal: *maintenance rehearsal* and *elaborative rehearsal*. When people simply repeat something over and over without giving it any thought, they will maintain it in short-term memory but will not transfer it to long-term memory. This is what happens when you look up a telephone number and then repeat it over and over until you can dial it—apparently, the people in Craik and Watkin's study did the same. Because they were only asked to recall the last four words on the list, their rehearsal was simply designed to maintain these items in short-term memory. Because they were not transferred to long-term memory, they were unavailable at the final unexpected recall test.

By contrast, elaborative rehearsal does improve long-term retention. Presumably, elaborative rehearsal involves relating the information to other information from past experiences. A study by Rundus and Atkinson (1970) shows that when people know they will be asked to remember the words, rehearsal facilitates recall. In this study, people were shown lists of words and were asked to learn the list by rehearsing the words aloud, either by themselves or together with other words from the list. Following presentation of a list, the people were asked to write down as many of the words as they could in any order. As shown in Figure 7.8, there was a close relationship between the number of rehearsals and the amount of recall.

Figure 7.8
Results of Rundus and Atkinson's experiment to assess the effect of rehearsal on memory. People were shown lists of words and asked to learn them by rehearsing the words aloud. There was a close relationship between the number of rehearsals and recall for all but the last words in the lists. The more the words were rehearsed, the better they were recalled. (Rundus & Atkinson, 1970.)

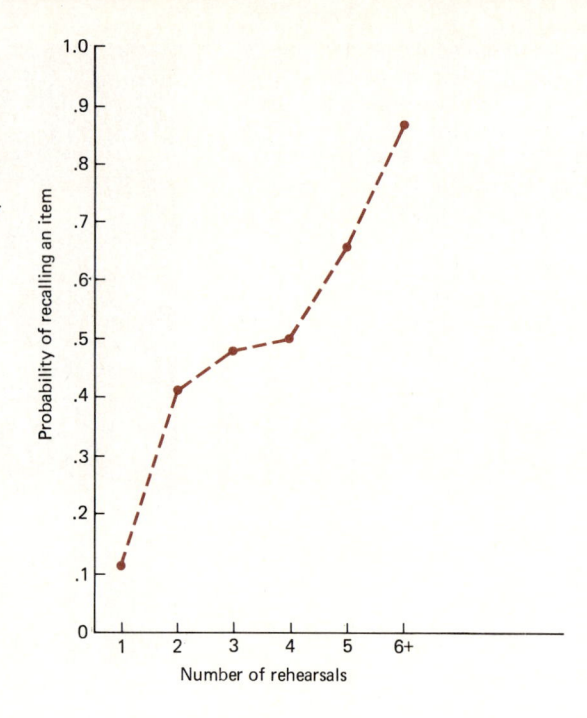

ORGANIZATION. Earlier in the chapter we saw that the capacity of short-term memory was defined in terms of "chunks" rather than the absolute number of items. Thus you would probably be able to repeat back successfully only four nonsense syllables (e.g., LOK, WUK, JAX, LOR), but would be able to repeat back successfully a 22-word sentence (e.g., "In the 1983 Superbowl, played in Pasadena, California, the Washington Redskins defeated the Miami Dolphins by a score of 22 to 17"). As you might expect, chunking is also important for long-term memory. In fact, psychologists have suggested that it is *necessary* for long-term memory (Mandler, 1967). Certainly, we can say that the process of relating, grouping, organizing, or chunking information is one major process involved in the elaboration of meaning.

The importance of *organization* was evident very early, when it was noted that people use semantic categories to organize information in memory. You have done this yourself when you make up a shopping list and group the items in various categories, such as meats, vegetables, dairy products, and so on. If you lost your list and had to shop from memory, you would tend to remember the items in clusters. The categories function as retrieval cues for the specific items.

Clustering is also observed in the laboratory. In one classical study, Bousfield (1953), showed people a list of 60 words that belonged to one of four categories (animals, vegetables, professions, and first names), and asked to recall them in any order they wished. The words were presented in random order, but people tended to recall words from the same category together, a phenomenon labeled *recall clustering*.

It is clear that people use organization to facilitate the recall of information that falls into categories. However, it has also become clear that organization is a general phenomenon that is not restricted to situations involving ready-made categories. People impose their own *subjective organization* on the material. This phenomenon is illustrated by a series of studies conducted by Mandler (1967). He asked people to sort large sets of unrelated words (up

Figure 7.9
Results of one of Mandler's experiments to assess the relationship between organization and recall. Subjects were asked to sort 52 words into from two to seven categories of their own choosing until they were able to do so consistently. They were then asked to recall the words. There is a fairly linear relationship between the number of categories used and the number of words recalled. (Based on Mandler, 1967.)

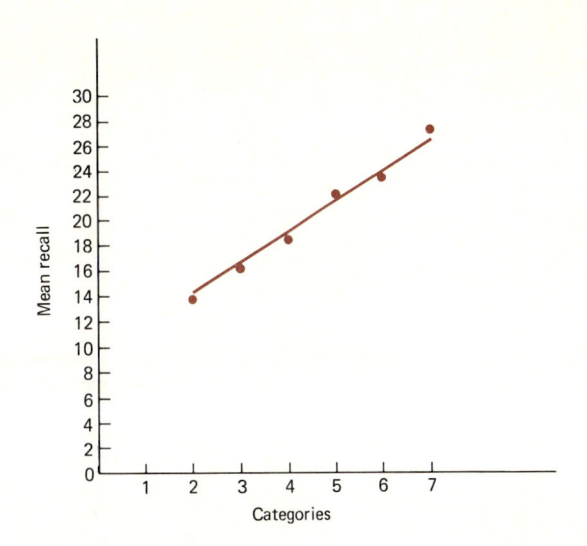

to 100) into categories of their own choosing. They continued to sort the cards until they consistently sorted the words into the same categories. Following this, free recall of the words was requested. The results showed that people tended to cluster their recall. Further, as shown in Figure 7.9, there was a strong relationship between the number of categories used during sorting and the number of words recalled. The more categories the person made, the better the recall.

Findings such as these led Mandler and others to argue that organization was central to long-term memory. According to this view, our capacity to process information is limited and we can remember large amounts of information only by organizing it into larger and larger units. Recall of the higher-order units provides access to their contents. The usefulness of such hierarchical organization for memory is illustrated by a study by Bower, Clark, Lesgold, and Winzenz (1969). These investigators asked two groups of people to learn a list of 112 words. The words belonged to one of four conceptual hierarchies, one of which is shown in Figure 7.10. Some of the people saw the words organized in their conceptual hierarchies, as in the

Figure 7.10
An example of a conceptual hierarchy used to determine the effect of organization on recall. (Based on Bower, Clark, Lesgold, & Winzenz, 1969.)

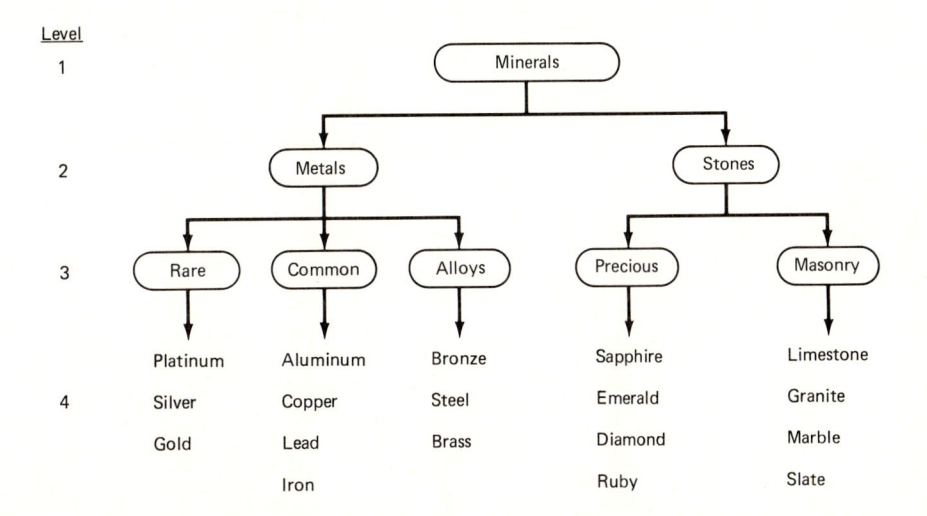

figure. Others saw the same number of words arranged in the same way, but selected at random. After only one trial, people remembered 65% of the words presented in the conceptual hierarchy, but only 18% of the words presented in the randomly arranged hierarchies. After just three trials, people remembered 100% of the words presented in the conceptual hierarchy, but only 47% of the words presented in the randomly arranged hierarchies.

IMAGERY. Think about your kitchen. Does it have a window? Where is it located? Where are the sink, range, and refrigerator located? What do the handles on the kitchen cabinets look like? You can probably answer these questions, and in doing so can "see" your kitchen or other familiar places.

Imagery has been recognized as an important strategy for long-term memory since ancient times. For example, one technique, the method of places and images (also called the method of loci), was developed by the Greeks and Romans as a remembering system for oratory. This system involves visualizing each item to be remembered in a different spatial location. During recall, each spatial location is mentally inspected and the item placed there is retrieved. This technique may appear cumbersome, but it is often used by professional mnemonists and can be very effective. For example, consider the unusual case of a Soviet newspaper reporter called S (the first letter of his name) studied for many years by Alexander Luria (1968). Luria reports that S could recall incredible amounts of information following a brief and seemingly effortless examination. He could remember long lists of digits or words even years after their presentation and even when these retention tests were performed without warning. Luria reports that S was highly skilled at applying various techniques to facilitate memory. Apparently, S relied heavily on imagery to form these memories. He reported that he automatically changed words into vivid images that he could in some cases touch, taste, or smell as well as see.

Experimental evidence also indicates that imagery facilitates the encoding of information in long-term memory. For example, Bower (1972) asked people to memorize 100 pairs of unrelated nouns (e.g., dog-bicycle), so that when the first word of the pair was presented (dog) they would be able to supply the second (bicycle). The people studied 20 pairs, one at a time, and were then given the recall test. After all 100 pairs had been studied and recalled once, a final recall test was given. Half of the people were instructed to associate the words by forming an image in which the objects were interacting in some way (e.g., the dog riding the bicycle). The others were simply given standard instructions to learn the pairs. On this final recall test the imagery groups recalled about 80% of the responses correctly, whereas the control group recalled only about 50%.

Similarly, Pavio (1971) has proposed that the ability to create images of words affects the ease with which they can be learned and remembered. To do this, Pavio first asked people to rate words on a scale to determine the ease and speed with which they evoked concrete images. This work suggested that some words, such as "alligator," "king," and "peach," were indeed easy to imagine, whereas others, such as "adage," "obsession," and "situation," were not. Pavio and his colleagues then asked people to learn to associate pairs of words in which the stimulus and response members were varied in terms of their imagery level. Different lists included high-high, high-low, low-high, and low-low pairs. The results indicated that memory for the pairs was ordered as follows: high-high, followed by high-low, followed by low-high, followed by low-low. Pavio suggested that vivid images that are easily retrieved serve as conceptual pegs to which the response words can be attached.

COGNITIVE PROCESSES: REMEMBERING AND FORGETTING

The importance of retrieval cues in our everyday lives is obvious. The sight of overflowing trash cans reminds us that it is trash collection day. (Burt Glinn/Magnum)

Storage and Retrieval (Forgetting). We have considered some of the ways in which information is encoded in long-term memory. Of course, if this information is to be useful, we must be able to retrieve it. Is forgetting due to the complete or partial erasure of memory traces, or is the information still stored in memory but is simply inaccessible? It is possible that everything that we have ever experienced is stored in our memories. Forgetting may simply be the failure to retrieve information that is stored. Indeed, this is the position accepted by many psychologists.

How often have you failed to recall the name of someone you know relatively well? The frustrating thing about this experience is that you often know you know the name. It is right on the tip of your tongue, but you cannot recall it. Usually, you would recognize the name immediately if you heard it, and you may recall it later given appropriate cues or more time. What factors determine whether we can retrieve information stored in memory?

RETRIEVAL CUES. One view suggests that whether or not forgetting occurs depends on the presence or absence of retrieval cues (Tulving, 1974). That retrieval cues are important is obvious from our everyday experience. We are reminded by the sight of the overflowing trash can that today is the day the trash collector comes and the cans must be put outside. We are reminded by the sight of a friend's new baby of our experiences with our own children years before. These everyday observations have been demonstrated in the laboratory. For example, in one study, Tulving and Pearlstone (1966) asked people to recall a list of words belonging to several conceptual categories (e.g., animals: cow, rat, etc.; weapons: e.g., bomb, cannon, etc.). At the time of recall, half of the people were given retrieval cues consisting of the category names of the specific words in the list (e.g., animals, weapons, etc.), while the other half were not. The group given the retrieval cues recalled more words. Further, following a second recall test, during which the category names were made available to both groups, both groups performed the same (Figure 7.11).

A major factor influencing the effectiveness of a retrieval cue is how congruent it is with information that was present at the time of encoding. That is, a retrieval cue is likely to be effective only if it reinstates the conditions of encoding. This has been labeled the *encoding specificity hypothesis* (Tulving

Figure 7.11
Results of an experiment by Tulving and Pearlstone demonstrating the importance of retrieval cues. People were asked to recall a list of words belonging to several conceptual categories. At the time of recall, half the people were given retrieval cues consisting of the category names of the words in the list, while the other half were not. The group given the retrieval cues recalled more words. Following a second recall test, during which the category names were made available to both groups, both groups performed the same. (Based on Tulving & Pearlstone, 1966.)

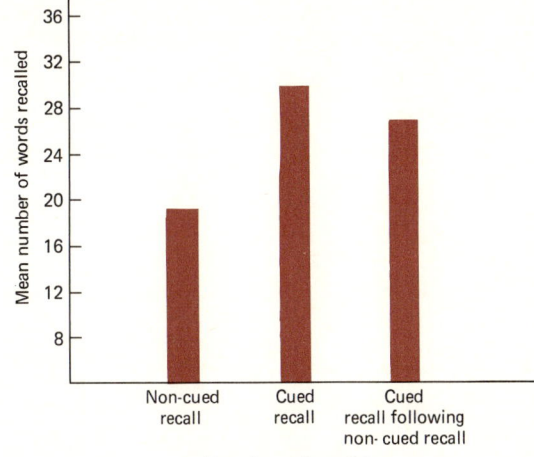

& Thompson, 1973). The importance of encoding specificity for the effectiveness of retrieval cues is illustrated by a study by Bower (1970) in which people were asked to remember nouns that could belong to multiple categories (e.g., ruby can be classified as a gem or as a color). People were shown one of two lists in which adjectives were used to specify the meanings of the nouns. On the one list, the adjectives were selected so that the nouns fell into eight categories e.g., birds: chirping *cardinal*, homing *pigeon*; foods: lamb *chop*, roast *ham*). On the other list, the adjectives were selected so that the nouns fell into many unique categories (e.g., church *cardinal*, stool *pigeon*, karate *chop*, theatrical *ham*). At recall, some of the people were given the names of the eight categories (e.g., birds, foods, etc.) as recall cues, while others were not. Bower reports that the cues enhanced recall for the list in which the adjectives had identified the noun as members of the eight categories, but actually reduced recall for the list in which the adjectives had identified the nouns as members of the unique categories. Thus "bird" appeared to be an effective retrieval cue for cardinal when the latter was encoded as chirping cardinal but not when it was encoded as church cardinal.

The importance of the similarity between the context of encoding and the context of retrieval goes beyond the semantic meaning of the to-be-remembered materials. Studies have shown that physiological and emotional states and the physical environment are important for retrieval. For example, Godden and Baddeley (1975) provided a striking demonstration of the importance of the physical environment. They asked divers to learn five lists of 36 unrelated words either on dry land or 20 ft under the water. The divers were then asked to recall the words in either the same environment they had studied them in or in a different environment. As shown in Figure 7.12, the divers clearly remembered the words better when they were asked to recall them in the same environment in which they had studied them.

Similarly, a person's state also appears to be important. For example, in one recent study, hypnotism was employed to induce specific emotional contexts (Bower, Monteiro, & Gilligan, 1978). People were asked to learn two lists. For one list, a positive emotional state was hypnotically induced by having the people review a pleasant event in their lives. For the other list, a negative emotional state was hypnotically induced by having them review a traumatic event in their lives. Positive or negative emotional states were also

Figure 7.12
Results of an experiment by Godden and Baddeley. People were asked to learn and recall lists of words either on dry land or under water. People remembered the words better when they were asked to recall them in the same environment in which they had studied them. (Based on Godden & Baddeley, 1975.)

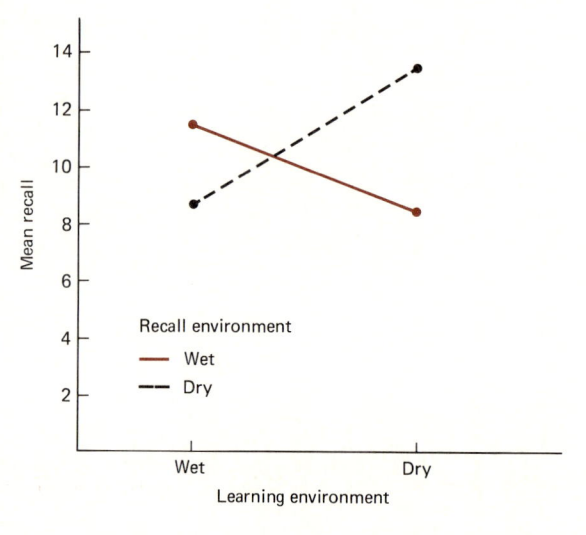

hypnotically induced at the time of the recall test. The results showed that better recall was obtained when the emotional state at recall matched the emotional state at the time of encoding than when it did not.

INTERFERENCE. We have seen that a number of factors affect the ease with which information can be retrieved from long-term memory. Some, such as the presence of effective retrieval cues or similarity of the context of retrieval to the context of encoding, facilitate remembering. But why do we forget? Forgetting could be due to many factors. For example, one early idea was that the memory trace simply decays with time. In an early attempt to test this idea, Jenkins and Dallenbach (1924) asked people to learn a list of nonsense syllables and then tested their retention after intervals of 1, 2, 4, or 8 hours. During the retention interval some of the people slept, while others went about their normal waking activities. The forgetting that occurred during the sleep condition was attributed to decay, whereas the additional forgetting that occurred during waking was attributed to interference. Forgetting increased as the retention interval increased, and although forgetting occurred in both conditions, more occurred in the waking condition than in the sleep condition. This led Jenkins and Dallenbach to conclude that forgetting is more a matter of interference than it is a matter of decay.

Recent theory continues to suggest that we cannot remember information primarily because other information acquired before or since interferes with retrieval. Interference theorists distinguish between two types of interference: retroactive and proactive. In *retroactive interference*, recently learned information interferes with one's ability to remember previously learned information. This is presumably what happened in the Jenkins and Dallenbach study. In *proactive interference*, previously learned information interferes with one's ability to remember new information.

The standard experimental designs for demonstrating these types of interference are shown in Figure 7.13. An important factor influencing the amount of interference is the amount of similarity of the information. The more the similarity between Task A and Task B, the greater the interference.

Why does interference occur? One explanation is that retrieval is more difficult when many similar bits of information are stored. This was illustrated by Tulving and Psotka (1971). They constructed several 24-word lists containing four words from each of six conceptual categories (insects, metals, types of buildings, etc.). They asked all the people to learn and remember an

Figure 7.13
Standard experimental designs for demonstrating retroactive and proactive interference.

Retroactive interference

Group	Initial learning	Retention interval	Retention test
Experimental	Learn A	Learn B	Recall A
Control	Learn A		Recall A

Proactive interference

Group	Initial learning	Retention interval	Retention test
Experimental	Learn A Learn B		Recall B
Control	Learn B		Recall B

HIGHLIGHT 7.1
Improving Memory

Most of us complain about our memories. We forget people's names, to buy milk at the store, and our appointment with the dentist. Is there anything we can do to improve our long-term memory? Indeed there is. In the previous sections we have stressed that long-term memory depends on (1) elaborating the meaning of the information to be remembered, and (2) the development of a retrieval plan which provides cues facilitating access to the information to be remembered. Numerous techniques facilitate these goals. Sometimes these are called *mnemonic techniques*, after the Greek word *mneme* meaning "memory."

1. *Rehearsal:* One of the simplest techniques to improve long-term memory is simply to rehearse the information. This assures that you pay attention to the information and facilitate its entry into long-term memory. This technique is useful when you are being introduced and you wish to remember someone's name. When you are introduced, repeat the person's name aloud, and then during the next minute or two look at the person and rehearse it silently.
2. *Interactive imagery:* Earlier we mentioned that forming unique images of objects can improve recall significantly. This technique can be applied to everyday problems such as remembering names. Essentially, you try to develop an interactive image that links some distinctive feature of the face with the person's name. Thus you may be able to remember Professor Montford's name if you visualize a shiny red Ford perched on his mountainous nose.
3. *The method of loci:* This technique, first described in Roman treatises on oratory, may be used to remember long strings of information. The first step is to select a set of familiar and easily distinguishable locations, for example, specific locations in your house, such as the stove, the dining room table, the hearth of the fireplace, and so on. Each item to be remembered is then visualized or "located" in one of these places. Thus to remember your grocery list, you might visualize the eggs hanging on the knob of the front door, the lettuce lying on the hearth of the fireplace, the cat food piled into a pyramid on the sofa. To retrieve the information, you simply go to each of the locations (take a mental walk through your house) and retrieve the item located there.
4. *Rhyming:* You probably know many rhyming mnemonics already. For example, "i before e except after c," or "Thirty days hath September, April, June, and November. All the rest have 31, except February, which has 28." The pattern of sound in the rhyme serves as an effective retrieval cue since departure from the rhyme is immediately obvious.
5. *Narrative chaining:* This technique involves making up a narrative which incorporates the information you wish to remember. The more distinctive the story, the better. For example, the following might be used to recall the main parts of a neuron. "In the city of New Ron (neuron), the nuclear (nucleus) scientist was locked up in the cell, body (cell body) and soul. He was there because he brought down his ax on (axon) the dead buttons (terminal buttons). But in d' end he was right (dendrite)."

These techniques are particularly useful for remembering lists of items. But what about remembering that great joke you heard the other day, or the main points from the chapter on motivation and emotion? The basic point remains accurate. You are likely to remember best when you process the meaning of the information and develop a retrieval plan to permit access to the material at the time of recall. For example, in the case of a chapter in one of your textbooks, there is an overall organization that may serve as a useful retrieval plan, particularly for the type of information that may be required on an essay examination.

---

initial target list. This provided a measure of original learning. Some people were then asked to learn one, two, three, four, or five additional lists. These additional lists produced retroactive interference: The average number of words recalled declined as a function of the number of additional lists learned. Following the interpolated lists, the people were asked to recall the original list. However, the investigators then asked the people to recall the original list again, this time presenting them with the category names of the words (insects, metals, etc.) as retrieval cues. When these cues were supplied, even the people who had learned five additional lists did very well at recalling the original list. These results suggest that forgetting occurred because the interpolated lists made discrimination of the retrieval cues needed for recall more difficult.

THE RELATIONSHIP BETWEEN TYPES OF MEMORY

We have described three broad types of memory. Information appears to enter the memory system through the sensory registers. Similarly, it is clear that people can consciously process only a limited amount of information at once, thus leading to the suggestion of short-term or working memory. Finally, any theory of memory must account for the preservation of the vast amounts of information that human beings appear able to retain: hence the suggestion of long-term memory. However, although there is widespread agreement about these three general functions of memory, there is also widespread disagreement about the exact relationships among these three types of memory.

MULTISTORE MODELS

One of the earliest and most influential positions suggested that sensory, short-term, and long-term memory represented separate storage structures of memory (Atkinson & Shiffrin, 1968). The stores were said to be structurally distinct because they preserved information in different formats, for different lengths of time, and lost information in different ways. Further, information was thought to flow through the three stores in serial fashion. That is, information entered through the sensory registers was transferred to the short-term store, and was finally transferred to the long-term store. But do short- and long-term memory represent distinct storage structures of memory?

Evidence on this comes from two sources. First, some studies show a sharp discontinuity in performance on certain memory tasks, suggesting that the distinction between short- and long-term memory may be justified. This evidence comes from studies using *free-recall tasks*. In this task, people are presented with a list of words, one at a time, and are asked to recall as many as possible in any order. The opportunity to recall the words in any order desired is what is "free" about a free-recall task. When one examines the percentage of words, averaged over many lists, that people recall at each of the positions of the list, an interesting pattern appears, as shown in Figure 7.14. This curve is called a *serial position curve*. As you can see, people remember the words presented at the end of the list better than those presented at any other point in the list. This is called the *recency effect*. People also remember the words presented at the beginning of the list relatively well, although not as well as those presented at the end. This is called the *primacy effect*. Recall of words presented in the middle of the list is worst. According to some psychologists, the recency effect mostly reflects recall from the short-term store. That is, these words are recalled so well because they are still in "working memory" when the person is asked to recall the words. Performance on the rest of the list mostly reflects recall from long-term memory. The words at the beginning of the list are retrieved from long-term memory

Figure 7.14
Results of Murdock's experiment showing the serial position curve. People were shown lists of 20 words, one at a time for one second. After each list, the people recalled as many words as they could in any order. The results show that the words presented at the beginning of the lists (primacy effect) and the words presented at the end of the lists (recency effect) were recalled better than those presented in the middle of the lists. (Based on Murdock, 1962.)

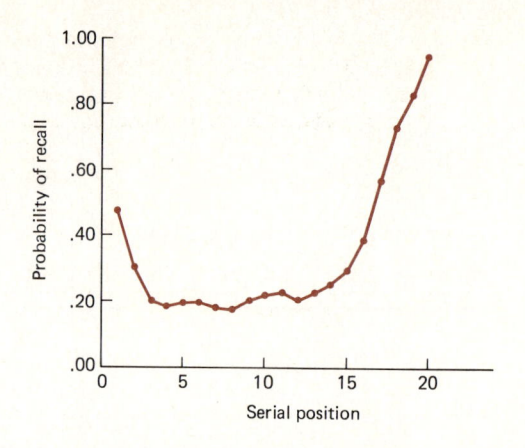

better than those in the middle of the list because the people have had more time to rehearse or otherwise think about the former than the latter.

If the words presented at the end of the list are recalled well because they are in short-term memory at the time of recall, any activity that would interfere with "working memory" should reduce the recency effect. This is exactly what happens. In one experiment, Glanzer and Cunitz (1966) asked people to recall lists of words either immediately after their presentation or after counting out loud from a given number. As shown in Figure 7.15, when there is no delay between presentation and recall, the usual serial position curve is found. However, when there is a delay of 30 seconds between presentation and recall filled with a task that prevents rehearsal, the recency effect disappears. Recall of the remainder of the list, however, is not affected. Data such as these support the distinction between short- and long-term memory.

Figure 7.15
Results of Glanzer and Cunitz experiment showing the serial position curve when free recall was tested immediately after presentation as opposed to following a 10- or 30-second delay during which rehearsal was prevented. The delay conditions interfered with the recency effect but not the primacy effect, thus suggesting that the former represents retrieval from short-term storage. (Based on Glanzer & Cunitz, 1966.)

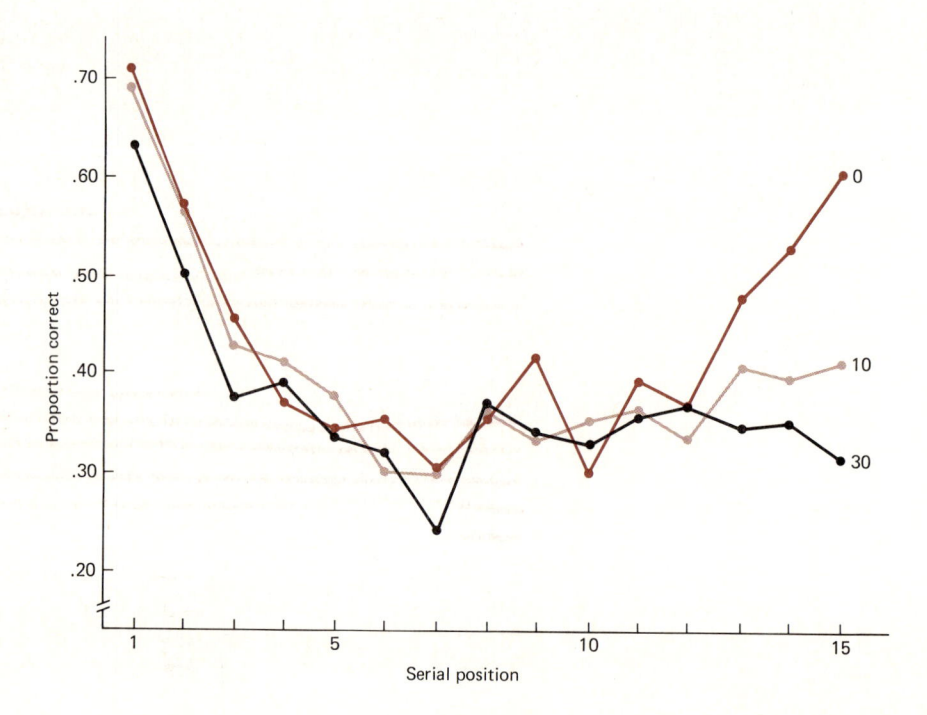

Perhaps even more compelling evidence for this distinction comes from clinical descriptions of a condition known as anterograde amnesia, which is produced by certain lesions in the temporal cortex. Patients with anterograde amnesia have difficulty remembering new events. On the other hand, they easily remember things that were learned or experienced before the onset of the condition. Anterograde amnesia may occur as the result of several conditions, including chronic alcoholism, senile dementia, or cerebral injuries. In a few instances it has been the tragic side effect of radical brain surgery. Milner (1966) describes such a case (H.M.). At age 27, H.M. had portions of both temporal lobes, including parts of the cerebral cortex, hippocampus, and amygdala, removed to relieve severe epileptic seizures. After the surgery, H.M. showed pronounced anterograde amnesia. He could not recognize anyone he had met before, no matter how many times he was introduced to them. When the family moved to a new house, he was unable to remember the new address and find his way home alone. Other abilities, however, were unimpaired. He could remember new experiences if he paid continual attention to them. Similarly, he remembered events that occurred before the surgery without difficulty. His speech, emotions, and intellectual functioning were unimpaired. The surgery, then, apparently interfered with H.M.'s ability to transfer memory from short-term to long-term memory.

Thus the representation of the memory system as involving separate structures actually fits quite well with many of the experimental facts presented in the previous sections. However, in recent years, the utility of describing memory as a set of three separate storage locations with fixed characteristics has been seriously questioned. Indeed, memory appears to be too flexible for such a rigid theoretical model.

A number of experimental findings do not fit nicely into the multistore model. For example, the multistore model proposes that information in short-term store is coded acoustically, and that only in the long-term store is information coded semantically, that is, in terms of its meaning. However, in several studies, Shulman (1970, 1972) demonstrated that semantic codes were also used in short-term memory. Shulman asked people to remember lists of 10 words. Following the presentation of the list, a "probe" word was presented and people were asked to judge if it was identical, a synonym (similar meaning), or a homonym (similar sound) of a word on the list. Recall that previous work had suggested that words recalled from the end of the list (recency effect) represented the contents of the short-term store, whereas words recalled from the beginning of the list represented the contents of the long-term store. If this were true, Shulman reasoned, the correct identification of synonyms and homonyms should vary according to the position of the original word in the list. Since the identification of synonyms requires semantic knowledge (characteristic of the long-term store), synonym probes should have been judged more accurately for words at the beginning of the list than for words at the end of the list. In contrast, because the identification of homonyms requires acoustic knowledge (characteristic of the short-term store), homonym probes should have been judged more accurately for words at the end of the list than for words at the beginning of the list. In fact, both types of probes were judged equally accurately for words at both points in the list, suggesting that both types of coding are involved in the two memory "stores."

Results such as Shulman's called into question many of the basic assumptions of the multistore theories. As a result, several of the proponents of these theories have revised them to incorporate the apparent flexibility of human memory. For example, Atkinson and Juola (1974) kept the assumption of three separate memory stores, but have placed greater emphasis on flexible processing strategies. They suggest that after entering the memory system through the sensory registers, information is coded in two ways: an uninterpreted perceptual code made up of physical features such as lines and curves, and an interpreted conceptual code made up of attributes that combine to identify the meaning of a concept. Multiple perceptual codes are linked to the same conceptual code stored in long-term memory. Thus one feature of the revised model has been to abandon the idea that the three stores have different and fixed ways of coding information.

LEVELS OF PROCESSING

The problems with the multistore theories led other investigators to reject them entirely. One of the most significant alternatives was developed by Craik and Lockhart (1972), who suggested viewing memory as a function of different *levels of processing*. In this view, information does not pass through a series of three memory stores at all. Rather, memory is determined by the operations performed on the incoming information. The operations may be perceptual, involving the sensory aspects of the information, and/or conceptual, involving the semantic aspects of the information. According to Craik and Lockhart, different operations lead to memory traces with different degrees of permanence. Perceptual operations coding the sensory aspects of the information are *shallow* and produce memory traces that are short-lived. Conceptual operations, coding the semantic aspects of the information, are *deep* and produce memory traces that are long-lived. Jacoby and Craik (1979) have suggested that perceptual and conceptual operations may occur simultaneously. Nevertheless, the more information is processed in terms of its meaning, the better it will be remembered.

Besides the depth at which information is processed, Jacoby and Craik (1979) have also suggested that the extent to which information is elaborated, regardless of its level, is also critical for memory. *Elaboration* refers to the extensiveness or richness of analysis carried out. For example, suppose that we asked people to read a story and either to underline all the words with capital letters or to proofread it for misspellings and grammatical errors. Both tasks involve mostly perceptual analysis, but the proofreading task probably requires more elaborate processing at this level. Hence memory for the story should be better following proofreading than following underlining words with capital letters. This view, then, suggests that it is the operations that are performed that determine memory. We remember information best when it is encoded deeply in terms of its semantic meaning. Further, the more the semantic meaning of the information is elaborated, the better we can remember it.

THE ROLE OF PRIOR KNOWLEDGE IN MEMORY

We have emphasized the importance of meaning in long-term memory. For example, we have stressed that in many instances memory for the form of the material erodes, while memory for its meaning persists. If you are shown a list of words, some of which are printed in capital letters and some in lower case letters, you are likely to be able to remember the words, but not the case in which they were printed. Meaning becomes even more crucial when we move from the relative simplicity of words to the complexity of sentences, stories, and events. Research with these complex materials suggests that what we remember goes well beyond the information given (Jenkins, 1974). That is, when processing sentences, texts, or complex real events, we appear to use our general knowledge of the world to construct our memory of the information or event. It is this construction, rather than a simple replica of the information, which gets stored. This construction may later be reconstructed at the time of retrieval.

CONSTRUCTIVE MEMORY

One way that previously acquired knowledge can affect memory is that people may use their knowledge to make certain assumptions or inferences at the time of input. This has been called the *constructive hypothesis* (Bransford & Franks, 1972). From this perspective, part of the process of comprehension involves the construction of meaning that goes beyond the information that is actually presented.

People make inferences about what they read and see, and this information is stored together with the information that is actually presented. For instance, Kintsch (1974) presented people with a series of short texts in which certain information was either explicitly or implicitly presented:

Explicit: "A carelessly discarded burning cigarette started a fire. The fire destroyed many acres of virgin forest."
Implicit: "A burning cigarette was carelessly discarded. The fire destroyed many acres of virgin forest" (p. 155).

After reading either the explicit or implicit versions of the paragraphs, people were asked to verify a test sentence corresponding to the implicit information (e.g., a discarded cigarette started a fire). Kintsch found that people could recognize the test sentences as true even when they were not explicitly stated. On an immediate test this judgment was rendered more quickly if the sentence was explicit rather than implicit. On a delayed test, however, verification times for the two types of sentences were the same. These results suggest that regardless of whether the test sentences were explicitly given in the text, the reader will infer the information and store it in memory.

When making such inferences, however, people make relatively fine discriminations. Consider the following short passages presented to people by Johnson, Bransford, and Solomon (1973):

"John was trying to fix the bird house. He was pounding the nail when his father came out to watch him and to help him do the work."
"John was trying to fix the bird house. He was looking for the nail when his father came out to watch him and to help him do the work."

After reading passages such as these people were asked to recognize a set of test sentences containing exactly the same words as the sentences contained in the texts presented before. Some of the test sentences explicitly stated information that might be inferred from the information contained in the passages. The crucial sentence for the passages presented above was as follows:

"John was using the hammer to fix the bird house when his father came out to watch him and to help him do the work."

People who heard the first version of the passage were much more likely to falsely recognize this test sentence than were people who heard the second version of the passage.

Our ability to make inferences and to store these in memory together with what is actually presented is essential for the comprehension of complex materials such as conversations, stories, and real events. Consider the following sentences:

"Mary heard the ice cream man coming."
"She remembered her pocket money."
"She rushed into the house."

Rumelhart and Ortony (1977) point out that these three sentences constitute a "snippet" of a story which is easily interpreted by most people. However, to do this, people must make a number of assumptions and inferences: The ice cream man is a vendor who sells ice cream; Mary wanted some ice cream; obtaining ice cream from the ice cream man requires money; Mary did not have any money in her possession; Mary was outside the house; presumably, her remembered pocket money was inside the house; the ice cream man would arrive quickly, so she had to hurry to get the money; and so on.

You can see that inferences are essential to comprehension and memory for complex materials. Imagine attempting to relate a story (even a simple one like Mary's wish to buy some ice cream) if your listener could neither make nor store inferences. Even the simplest conversations would be torturously explicit.

RECONSTRUCTIVE MEMORY

A second way that previously acquired knowledge can influence memory is suggested by the *reconstructive hypothesis*. From this perspective people remember only the gist or general outlines of what was presented and then reconstruct "what must have happened" on the basis of their general knowledge. This is illustrated in the research of Loftus and her associates. For example, in a series of experiments, people saw films of complex, fast-moving events such as automobile accidents (Loftus, 1975; Loftus & Palmer, 1974). Some time later they were asked about their memories for these events. Loftus's work shows that the wording of the questions at the time of recall had a substantial effect on the answers people gave. For example, after seeing a film of an automobile accident, some people were asked "How fast were the cars going when they hit each other?", while others were asked "How fast were the cars going when they smashed into each other?" One week later the people returned and without viewing the film again were asked several other questions about the accident. A critical question was, "Did you see any broken glass?" There was no broken glass in the accident, yet people who had been asked the earlier question using the verb "smashed" were more than twice as likely to erroneously report seeing it than people who had been asked the earlier question using the verb "hit." Studies such as this suggest that people's memories may be supplemented by information that occurs after the event.

In another study, people were shown a brief videotape of an automobile accident and then were asked questions about it. The critical question concerned the speed of a white sports car. Half of the people were asked "How fast was the white sports car going while traveling along the country road?"; the other half were asked "How fast was the white sports car going when it passed the barn while traveling along the country road?" In fact, no barn appeared in the scene. However, one week later when asked more questions about the accident, about 17% of those asked the question presupposing the barn claimed to have seen it, whereas only about 3% of those asked the question not presupposing the barn did so (Loftus, 1975).

Thus our memories can be transformed by events occurring after the information has originally been encoded. There does appear to be a limit to the extent to which this occurs, however. For example, people will tend to resist accepting information that blatantly contradicts a perceived detail in the event. Thus if people see a series of slides depicting the theft of a bright red wallet from a woman's handbag, they will resist the presupposition that the wallet was brown (Loftus, 1979).

Our memory for complex information is also influenced by knowledge of the world in the form of general abstractions. The importance was illustrated many years ago by a classical set of studies conducted by Sir Frederick Bartlett (1932). In one study, for example, Bartlett asked people to recall an unusual Indian folk tale on several occasions over a period of months. Bartlett reported a high degree of inaccuracy in the participants' recall, and that they appeared to be unaware of the extent of this inaccuracy. Further, the inaccuracy resulted not only from omission and condensation, but also from transformation of the original material. These elaborations appeared to be efforts by the Victorian-era British participants to recast the unusual tale into a form compatible with their cultural knowledge. Thus statements about "hunting seals" and "canoes" were recalled as "fishing" and "boats." These results led Bartlett to suggest that we form generalized descriptions about the nature of objects and events on the basis of past experiences. During learning, new information is integrated with existing descriptions. When the material to be remembered conflicts with these descriptions, as in the unusual folk tale used by Bartlett, recall is distorted.

Recent studies have confirmed that reconstructive processes influence memory. For example, Spiro (1977) asked people to read one of two presumably true stories dealing with an engaged couple, Bob and Margie. Both stories related Bob's strong desire not to have children and his reluctance to tell Margie about his feelings. In one version, he finally tells her and finds that she feels as he does. In the other version, he finds she is horrified by his views, since children are very important to her. Later, the experimenter casually mentioned different things to different people. Some were informed that Bob and Margie did eventually get married and were still together, while others were informed that they never married and had not seen each other since the engagement was broken. Still others were not informed about the current status of the couple. After varying intervals, the people were asked to remember the story as best they could. Reconstructive theory predicts that people who received information that was consistent will make fewer reconstructive errors than those who received information that was inconsistent.

For example, people who first heard that neither Bob nor Margie wanted children and then heard that they were happily married received consistent information. However, people who heard that Bob and Margie disagreed about having children and then heard that they were happily married received inconsistent information. Spiro found that reconstructive errors increased as the degree of conflict in the information increased. People reconstructed the story so that it "balanced." For example, faced with the information that the couple disagreed but were happily married, they may have misremembered that one of the partners later changed his or her mind, or that their disagreement was minor rather than major. Further, having reconstructed the story, the participants expressed a high degree of confidence that their memories were accurate.

HIGHLIGHT 7.2

Knowing About Dinosaurs: The Expert Child

More and better structured knowledge is one thing that is generally associated with expert status. Indeed, this characteristic is often used to explain the better memory performance of those with more skills. For example, in an interesting demonstration of this point, Chi (1978) tested the recall of good young chess players (average age 10½ years) and mediocre adult chess players. They were shown an arrangement of chess pieces on a chess board, and asked what part of the board they could remember perfectly. Chi found that the young players could remember more pieces than the adult players (an average of 9.3 versus 5.9 pieces). Further, in an untimed test, the young players were able to memorize all the pieces on the board far more rapidly than were the adult players.

Results such as these have led Chi, along with others, to argue that what differentiates the memory capacity of younger children from that of older children or adults is the amount and structure of knowledge. This notion is quite different from the traditional view that suggests that young children cannot group, relate, and abstract information in ways that facilitate superior memory performance. To show that this was not so, Chi attempted to demonstrate that when a child knew a lot about a topic, information would be represented in complex ways and that this would predict memory performance.

In one study, Chi and Koeske (1983) sought to represent one child's knowledge of dinosaurs. The 4½-year-old boy had been learning about dinosaurs for about a year and a half. Like many children of his age, he was very interested in these prehistoric creatures. He had a collection of nine books on dinosaurs from which his parents read to him an average of 3 hours a week. He also had a collection of plastic dinosaur models that he played with.

Chi selected 40 dinosaurs from the books and divided them into two groups: those the boy knew fairly well and those he knew less well. Chi then used a variety of tasks to develop a semantic map of the child's knowledge of these two groups of dinosaurs. An adult semantic map would contain clusters of complex links between the names of the dinosaurs and the properties associated with them. For example, triceratops and stegosaurus might be linked because they are both armored, eat plants, and so on. Chi found that the child's semantic map was highly structured in this fashion, with more linkages exhibited for the well-known group than for the less-well-known group.

Chi also found that a year after the initial tests, the boy could identify over five times the number of dinosaurs from the well-known group than from the less-well-known group. He could also recall more properties of the dinosaurs in the first group. In sum, the child's knowledge for well-known information appears to evidence the complex organization characteristic of adults, and the extent of this structure predicts memory performance.

THE ORGANIZATION OF KNOWLEDGE

Memory is very much a function of the relationship between current inputs and what one already knows. As a result, psychologists have become interested in how people organize their knowledge.

SEMANTIC VERSUS EPISODIC MEMORY

Tulving (1972) drew a distinction between memory for specific events and memory for general knowledge. He labeled the former episodic memory and the latter semantic memory. *Episodic memory* refers to memory for the occurrence of specific events in specific contexts. For example:

I remember that I had French toast for breakfast this morning.
I remember that I met my wife in the college bookstore in 1961.
I remember that my class meets on Tuesdays and Thursdays at 9:30 a.m.

In contrast, *semantic memory* contains a person's knowledge of symbols, words, concepts, and the rules for manipulating them. Semantic memory is not related to a specific time or place. Obviously, one learned in the past that birds fly, but one cannot recall specifically when or where this information was encoded. For example:

I know that eagles can fly.
I know that Montpelier is the capital of the state of Vermont.
I know that water freezes at 0°C.

The knowledge contained in each of these statements is divorced from the particular time and place of learning. Nevertheless, in order to "know" these things, they must have been stored in memory and retrieved. Semantic memory research represents an effort to understand how this information about the world is stored, combined, manipulated, and accessed by people. This major effort represents a relatively new direction in cognitive psychology. What are some of the conclusions?

NETWORK MODELS

One major concern has been the issue of how our world knowledge is organized and accessed. Consider the following requests:

Name a fruit that begins with *a*.
Name a dangerous fish.
Name a make of car that is made in Japan.
Name a president of the United States who served only one term.

You could probably answer these questions quickly and easily. How did you do this? You certainly did not search your knowledge randomly until you stumbled on a potential answer, such as "apple." Obviously, we have

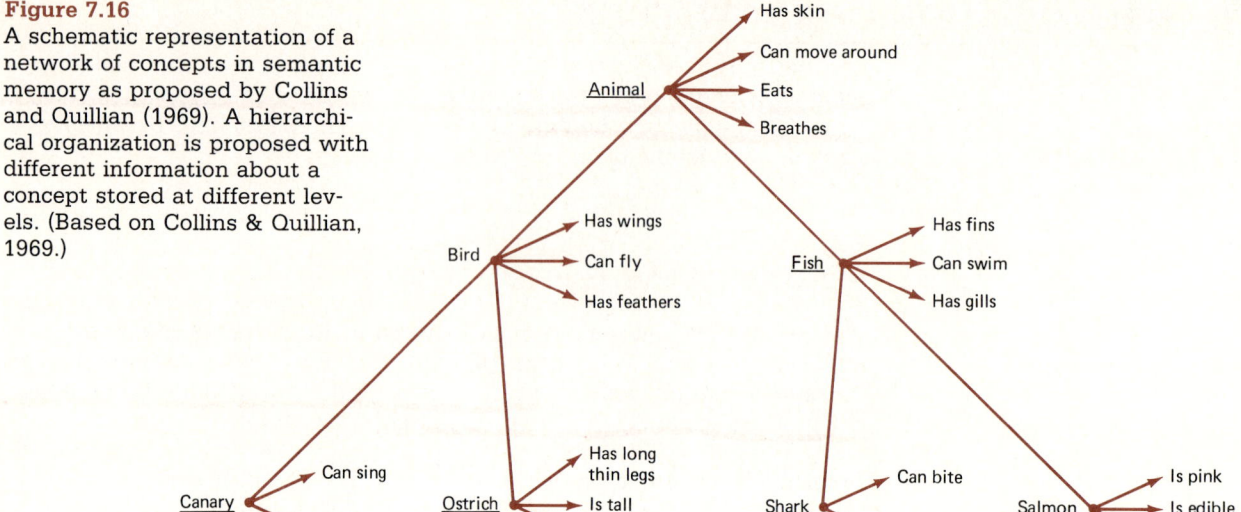

Figure 7.16
A schematic representation of a network of concepts in semantic memory as proposed by Collins and Quillian (1969). A hierarchical organization is proposed with different information about a concept stored at different levels. (Based on Collins & Quillian, 1969.)

selective access to information, which means that it must be organized in some way. How is information in semantic memory organized? One way researchers have tried to examine this question is by looking at the speed with which people are able to access information. For example, Collins and Quillian (1969) proposed that information in semantic memory is hierarchically organized as shown in Figure 7.16. According to this view, subordinate information, such as the fact that canaries are yellow, is stored under more superordinate information, such as the fact that canaries are birds, which in turn, is stored under still more superordinate information, such as the fact that canaries are animals. Thus different information about a concept was seen as being stored at only one level of the hierarchy. If information is organized in this fashion, the time needed to have access to a particular piece of information should depend on the number of levels that must be searched to develop an answer. Consider the following questions:

"Is a canary yellow?"
"Does a canary fly?"
"Does a canary have skin?"

If information about canaries is organized hierarchically, it should take less time to answer the first question than the second, and less time to answer the second question than the third. Research conducted by Collins and Quillian found this to be the case.

However, some observations do not fit the hierarchical model very well. For example, people verify the sentence "A robin is a bird" faster than the sentence "A chicken is a bird." But according to the hierarchical model, both sentences should involve the same number of levels to make the decision. In effect, people judge a robin to be a more typical bird than a chicken (Rosch, 1973), and this appears to affect access.

Problems such as this led Collins and Loftus (1975) to propose a revision of the hierarchical model described above. In the revised model, semantic

COGNITIVE PROCESSES: REMEMBERING AND FORGETTING

memory is depicted as a network of interconnected concepts that form clusters, as shown in Figure 7.17. Concepts that are closely related share short paths and many links. Note that the network is no longer hierarchically organized. Rather, accessibility is assumed to be determined by two factors. First, it takes less time to traverse a short path than a long one. Presumably, the length or strength of a path depends on how often that link is used. Second, once a person has access to a concept, adjacent concepts are activated, which in turn activate adjacent concepts, and so on. Thus access to the concept "fire engine" activates related concepts, such as "red," which in turn activates related concepts, such as "roses." Because of this feature, the model has been called the *spreading activation model*. Second, it is assumed that concepts are activated in proportion to their distance from the original concept. Thus, given the concept "fire engine," the concept "ambulance" would be activated before the concept "vehicle."

The spreading activation model does have some advantages over the hierarchical model. It can explain why people can verify the sentence "A robin is a bird" faster than a sentence "A chicken is a bird." Presumably, since robin is a more typical instance of the category bird than is chicken, robin will be located closer to bird in the network than will chicken. Nevertheless, the model has not been fully evaluated. Efforts to understand the organization of our world knowledge are just beginning.

Figure 7.17
A schematic representation of a network of concepts in semantic memory, as proposed by Collins and Loftus. The shorter the line connecting the concept, the greater the relatedness. (Based on Collins & Loftus, 1975.)

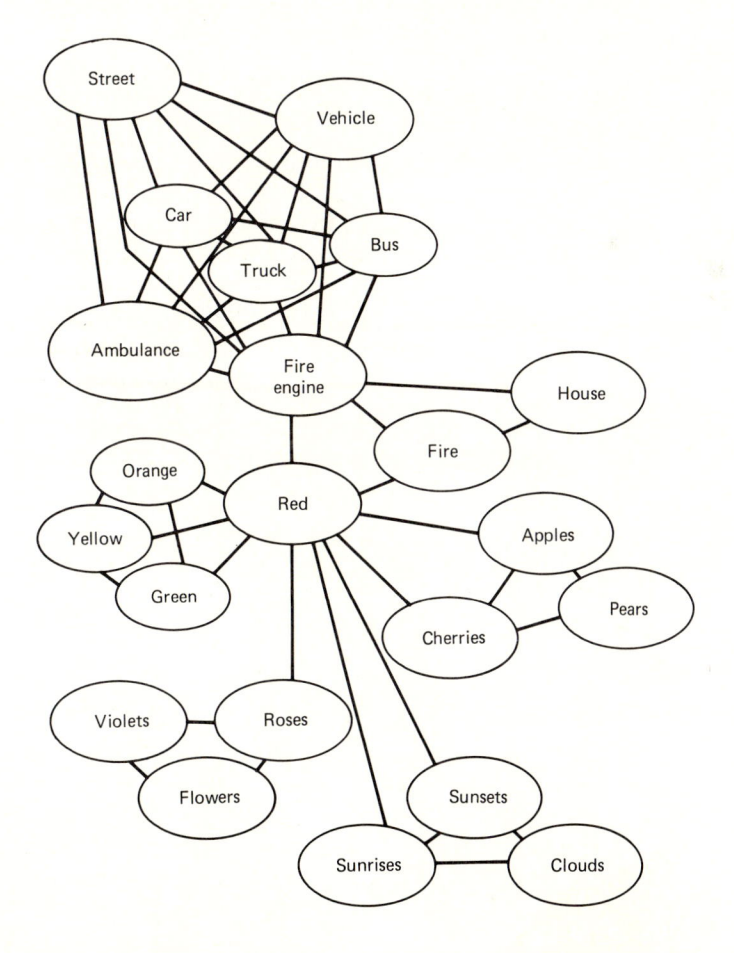

SCHEMA THEORY

There is another level on which our world knowledge appears to be organized. A *schema* (plural *schemata*) is a packet of generalized knowledge about an object or event. For example, Schank and Ableson (1977) describe the schemata of complex events which they label *scripts*. Consider the following sentences:

"John was the quarterback. As time ran down, he threw a 60-yard pass into the end zone. His team won the game."

To interpret these sentences, you must make many assumptions. Schank and Ableson suggest that our comprehension of such communications is guided by scripts that characterize sequences of events. Consider Schank and Ableson's analysis of the restaurant script. The participants may include a customer, waiters or waitresses, a chef, and a cashier. The sequence of events may involve entering the restaurant, selecting a table or being seated, ordering the food, preparing it, eating it, and then leaving. A script then contains a complex sequence of multiple concepts. Scripts must contain a great amount of information to encompass the tremendous variability that can occur in a given situation. Consider the following stories (Schank & Ableson, 1977):

"John went to a restaurant. He asked the waitress for *coq au vin*. He paid the check and left."
"John went into the restaurant. John ordered a Big Mac. He paid for it and found a nice park to eat in."

In the first script we assume that John sat at a table, looked at a menu, waited some time before receiving his food, and so on. In the second script we assume a different kind of restaurant. For example, the same story with *coq au vin* substituted would take longer to interpret.

Schema theorists suggest that we have a multiplicity of scripts for driving a car, taking a trip on an airplane, going to a class, and so on. Such schemata are important for memory. If the information we encounter conflicts with our schemata, it will be hard to comprehend and remember. For example, within the Western culture tradition, simple stories are formed as a series of episodes, each of which contains a setting, a complication, and a resolution. Typically, events are ordered temporally and related causally. Stories from some other cultural traditions, however, are based on a different schema. For example, Apache stories are based on a "principle of fours." That is, there must be four episodes, involving four actors, using four instruments, and so on (Kintsch, 1978). Kintsch (1978) has shown that a person will find a story based on a familiar schema easier to comprehend and remember than one without a familiar schema. American college students, when presented with stories from these two cultural traditions, could comprehend and summarize the Western-culture stories better than the Apache stories. This was true even though the individual sentences of the two types of stories did not differ in ratings of comprehensibility, imagery, and bizarreness. Thus, out of context, the sentences of the Apache story provided no difficulty. Without the proper schema, however, it was difficult to understand the story they told.

People also recall different things about the same information depending on the schema they adopt. For example, Pichert and Anderson (1977) asked two groups of people to read the same story about two boys and a house in which they were playing. One group was asked to read the story from the perspective of a potential home buyer, the other from the perspective of a burglar. The results showed that recall of the story was strongly influenced by the perspective taken. Those taking the perspective of a potential home buyer were likely to recall the leaky roof (a potential problem to a home buyer), but not the color television set (potential loot to a burglar).

SUMMARY

1. Early theorists viewed learning, remembering, and forgetting as based on the formation, emission, and loss of stimulus-response bonds.

2. Recent theorists view human beings as complex information-processing systems. They suggest that memory involves multiple stages (acquisition, storage, and retrieval), active manipulation of information by the person, and both reproduction and construction of information.

3. Three types of memory have been identified: sensory, short-term, and long-term.

4. Sensory memory is the momentary retention of an unprocessed copy of a stimulus.

5. Short-term or "working" memory involves the conscious retention of information that has just been presented or retrieved from long-term memory.

6. Information is encoded both acoustically and visually in short-term memory, although acoustical encoding appears to dominate.

7. Information can be maintained in short-term memory only by attending to it, rehearsing it, or otherwise manipulating it.

8. The primary strategy for retrieval from short-term memory consists of a rapid, serial, exhaustive search.

9. Long-term memory involves permanent storage of information no longer in consciousness.

10. Information is encoded phonologically, visually, and semantically in long-term memory.

11. Information is remembered best in long-term memory when it is processed deeply and elaborately in terms of its meaning.

12. Deep and elaborate processing may be achieved by several processes, including rehearsal, organization (chunking), and imagery.

13. One major reason for forgetting is the failure to retrieve information that is stored.

14. A retrieval cue is likely to be effective only if it reinstates the conditions of encoding (encoding specificity hypothesis).

15. Retrieval failure is often due to interference. In retroactive interference, recently learned information interferes with one's ability to remember previously learned information. In proactive interference, previously learned information interferes with one's ability to remember new information.

16. Early theorists suggested that sensory, short-term, and long-term memory represent separate storage structures. An alternative view (levels of processing framework) suggests that memory is determined by the operations performed on incoming information. Operations that encode and elaborate the semantic meaning of the information improve memory.

17. What people remember goes beyond the information given. People make inferences about what they read and see and store these. They also remember the general outlines of what was presented and reconstruct events on the basis of their general knowledge.

18. Episodic memory refer to memory for specific events in specific contexts. Semantic memory refers to a person's knowledge of symbols, words, and concepts.

19. Our knowledge appears to be organized as a complex network of concepts linked to each other on the basis of certain distinctive features.

20. Our knowledge is also organized through schemata, or packets of generalized knowledge about objects or events.

KEY TERMS

Acquisition
Storage
Retrieval
Sensory memory
Short-term memory
Long-term memory
Encoding

Rehearsal
Organization
  (chunking)
Imagery
Retroactive interference
Proactive interference
Serial position curve

Levels of processing
Constructive hypothesis
Reconstructive hypothesis
Episodic memory
Semantic memory
Schema

SUGGESTED READINGS

BRANSFORD, J. D. *Human cognition: Learning, understanding, and remembering.* Belmont, Calif.: Wadsworth, 1979. A selective analysis of human cognition emphasizing the active nature of learning, understanding, and remembering.

HOWARD, D. V. *Cognitive psychology: Memory, language, and thought.* New York: Macmillan, 1983. An up-to-date, basic textbook on cognitive psychology.

LACKMAN, R., LACHMAN, J., & BUTTERFIELD, E. *Cognitive psychology and information processing: An introduction.* Hillsdale, N.J.: Lawrence Erlbaum, 1979. A sophisticated review of the information-processing approach to cognition.

LOFTUS, E. F. *Memory.* Reading, Mass.: Addison-Wesley, 1980. A readable introduction to understanding and improving human memory.

LURIA, A. R. *The mind of a mnemonist* (L. Solotaroff, trans.). New York: Basic Books, 1968. A fascinating account of a person with an extraordinary memory.

8

Cognitive Processes: Language, Thought, and Intelligence

LANGUAGE
   The Structure of Language
   Competence Versus
      Performance
   Language Comprehension and
      Production
   The Acquisition of Language
THOUGHT
   Problem Solving
   Concept Formation
   Reasoning

INTELLIGENCE
   The Structure of Abilities
   The Content of Abilities
   Creativity and Intelligence
   Heredity, Environment, and
      Intelligence
   Improving Intelligence
SUMMARY
KEY TERMS
SUGGESTED READINGS

As a result of a severe head injury suffered in an automobile accident, Mark K, age 29, is unable to articulate words, a form of aphasia. He can respond to a request to pick up a pencil, for example, but cannot say the word aloud.

As a result of a genetic defect, Carol L., age 16, has the intellectual capabilities of a 4-year-old. She can perform routine self-care functions and is able to learn fairly simple concepts. However, she is unable to solve complex problems and lacks the judgment to engage in unsupervised activity away from home or at the special school she attends.

The centrality of language, thought, and intelligence for human functioning is perhaps most strikingly displayed when they are absent or impaired in some manner. These cognitive abilities are crucial to our adaptation to our environment. We must perceive relationships, form concepts, solve problems, and accumulate knowledge about the world. Let us examine the nature of these complex abilities.

LANGUAGE

Language is an impressive cognitive capability. It is the basis for much of our everyday thought and social interaction. It is a major mechanism by which we represent the world around us and manipulate these representations to solve problems that confront us. It is the primary means by which we communicate with others about our knowledge, interests, beliefs, and goals. Further, it permits the transmission of this information from one generation to another, producing social change through cultural training. Thus language forms the basis of human culture: our law, politics, religion, commerce, and technology. Indeed, some theorists have argued that it is language that makes us uniquely human (Lenneberg, 1967). In this view, human language is qualitatively different from the communication systems of other species. Regardless of whether this is true, language is a significant product of our evolutionary history. This is suggested by the fact that its acquisition is universal. All children who are physiologically intact and reared in a reasonably appropriate environment acquire language. What is more, they acquire it in a few short years without apparent effort.

THE STRUCTURE OF LANGUAGE

Language is produced through sounds (spoken language), symbols (written language), or gestures (sign language). However, not any sounds, symbols, or gestures will do. You know that "Tle ijxk pt hgtlrm qrrty" is not an acceptable communication in English. You would probably guess that it is not an acceptable communication in any language. In fact, languages are composed of a limited number of sounds combined in particular ways. Thus a primary characteristic of language is its regularity. This regularity may be described at a basic level for all human languages. Although English, German, Chinese, and Arabic seem quite different, they are all constructed from the same fundamental components, shown in Figure 8.1.

As shown in the figure, the components are organized hierarchically. Specific rules govern the formation of components at each level. At the bottom of the hierarchy are elementary speech sounds called *phonemes*. These are combined in certain ways to yield *morphemes*, the minimal units of meaning and words. In turn, morphemes and words are combined in certain ways to yield phrases and sentences which convey the complex meanings of the communication.

Phonemes. Human beings can produce a vast array of sounds. However, not all of these different sounds are important for language. Consider the word *car*. Different people will pronounce this word differently. For example, some speakers from the northeastern United States tend to roll the r sound so that the word sounds more like *cah*. Regardless, the utterance is compre-

Language is the prime example of using a symbolic representational system to express our understanding of the world. (Yvonne Freund)

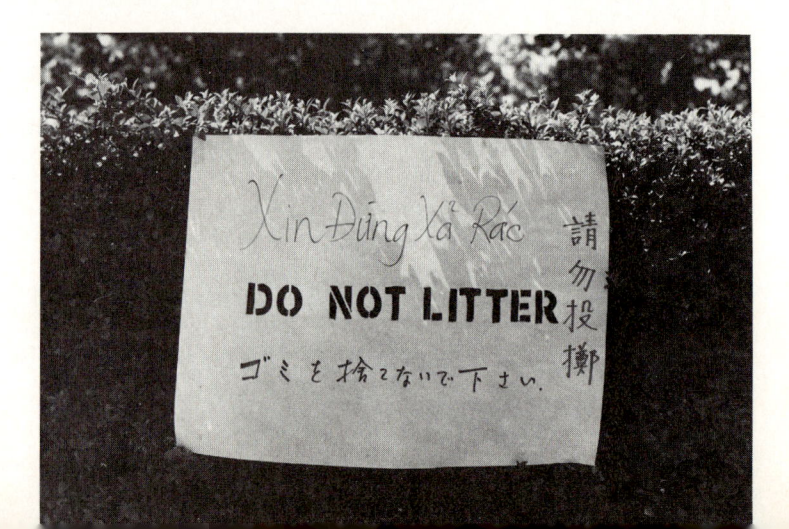

COGNITIVE PROCESSES: LANGUAGE, THOUGHT, AND INTELLIGENCE   247

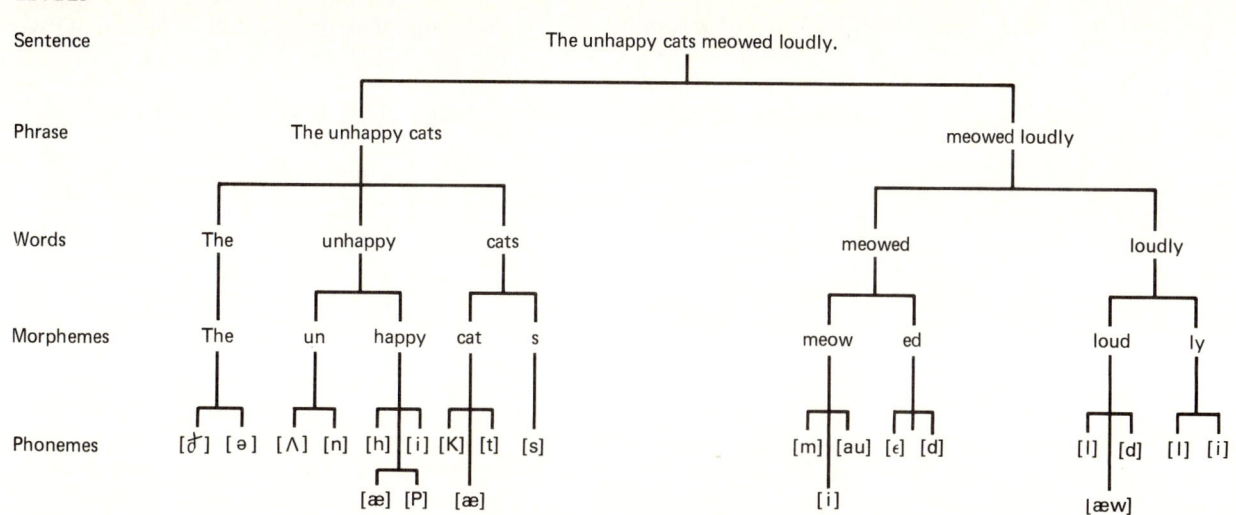

LEVELS

Figure 8.1
The structural levels of language.

hended as referring to a wheeled vehicle. However, if we change the *r* to a *t*, the meaning is quite different. Phonemes, then, are the smallest units of sound that produce a difference in the message. *Cat, rat, mat, sat, bat, hat,* and *fat* differ only by a single phoneme.

Each language has a limited number of phonemes. English uses about 40; other languages use as many as 70 (Abkhaz) or as few as 11 (Hawaiian). Thus different languages are characterized by different phonemes. This is one reason it is difficult to learn a foreign language. For example, in English, L and R are different phonemes, so *cloak* is perceived as different from *croak*. However, in Japanese, L and R belong to the same phoneme and may be substituted for one another without changing the meaning of the word.

No matter which phonemes are discriminated, all languages have rules for combining phonemes. For example, in English, combinations that begin with more than three consonants are unacceptable. Egyptian Arabic requires a consonant at the beginning of the utterance.

Morphemes. Fixed sequences of phonemes form morphemes, which define the next level of the hierarchy. Morphemes are the smallest units of language that carry meaning. Words such as *page, hat, step,* and *dog* that are both morphemes and words are called *free morphemes*. Other morphemes must be used with at least one other morpheme to form a word. These include prefixes (e.g., *anti*personnel, *de*stabilize, *un*happy) and suffixes (e.g., dog*s*, plant*ed*, runn*ing*). These are called *bound morphemes*. Just as with phonemes, bound morphemes may be combined only in certain ways. Thus *nonsense* is acceptable, whereas *sensenon* is nonsense.

Although there are rules for combining phonemes into morphemes and for the use of bound morphemes, it is important to note that there are essentially no rules for assigning meaning to words. Morphemes and words are connected to what they signify in purely conventional fashion. This is demonstrated by etymological research, which seeks to discover the origins of meaning. For example, the word *person*, which in contemporary English refers to individuality, has its roots in the Latin word *persona*, which referred to the mask worn by an actor in a play. In this context, then, it characterized a conventionalized type rather than a unique individual. There may be no connection at all between an earlier and a current meaning. For example, when asked by Captain Cook for the name of an animal, an Australian native is purported to have answered *kangaroo*, which meant "I don't know."

Phrases and Sentences. Finally, at the last level of the hierarchy, morphemes and words are combined into phrases and sentences. These units convey the complex meanings of the language. Again, certain rules govern these combinations. These rules constitute the *syntax* of the language. For example, in English, verbs usually follow nouns, whereas in other languages the reverse is true. Thus, *I am happy* is correct, whereas *Happy I am* is not. How do you know that this is the case?

To native speakers, sentences consist of distinct parts rather than a string of words. Thus linguists have found it useful to describe sentences in terms of their phrase structures. Figure 8.2 shows the phrase structure of a simple sentence. It consists of two major components, a noun phrase and a verb phrase. These, in turn, are composed of components. Linguists have formulated phrase structure rules that specify these components or phrase structures. For the sentence in Figure 8.2, the rules listed may be described as follows: For example, rule 1 specifies that the sentence can be rewritten as a noun phrase plus a verb phrase. Rule 2 specifies that the component noun phrase can be rewritten as an article plus an optional adjective plus a noun. Rule 3 specifies that the component verb phrase can be rewritten as a verb plus a noun phrase. Rule 4 rewrites articles as *the*, rule 5 rewrites noun as *quarterback*, and so on, although multiple components would be acceptable.

Thus the generation of a phrase structure grammar involves a description of the component structure of the sentence. This exercise can illustrate some interesting features of language. For example, the sentence *They are cooking apples* is ambiguous. An analysis of the phrase structure as shown in Figure 8.3 illustrates this ambiguity. Depending on the meaning, *cooking* is either part of a verb phrase (A) or a noun phrase (B).

However, the ambiguity of some sentences cannot be represented in an analysis of their phrase structures. For example, the following are ambiguous sentences whose ambiguity is not apparent in their phrase structures:

Visiting relatives can be boring.
The shooting of the hunters was awful.
The police were ordered to stop drinking.

Figure 8.2
The phrase structure rules of a sentence. The symbol → means *can be written as* following: 1. Sentence (S) → Noun Phrase (NP) + Verb Phrase (VP). 2. NP → Article (Art) + [Adjective (Adj.)] + Noun (N). 3. VP → Verb (V) + NP. 4. Art → The. 5. N → quarterback, pass. 6. Adj → strong, long. 7. V → threw.

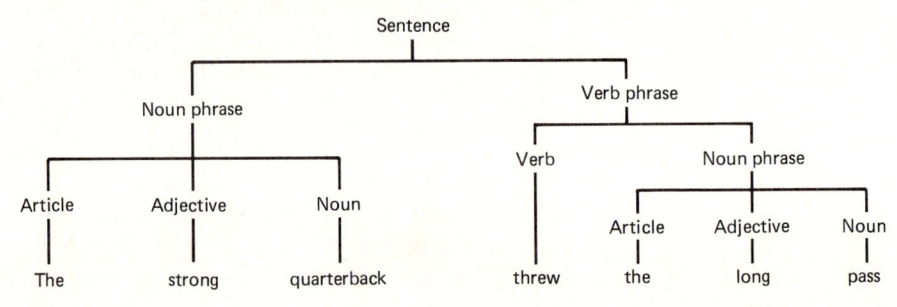

COGNITIVE PROCESSES: LANGUAGE, THOUGHT, AND INTELLIGENCE

Figure 8.3
The surface structures that illustrate the two possible meanings of the ambiguous sentence, *They are cooking apples*. (A) That those people (they) are cooking apples. (B) That those apples are for cooking.

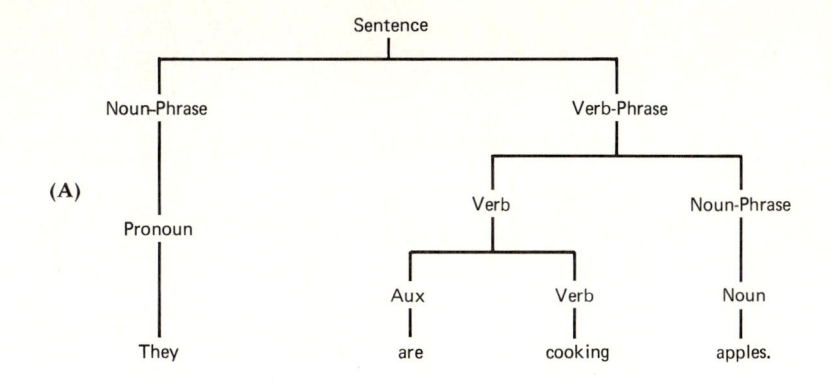

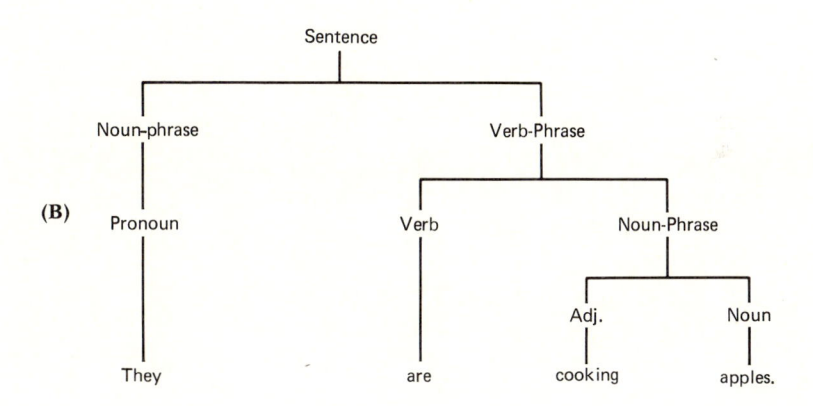

Phrase structure grammars fail to deal with another problem. Consider the following sentences:

The dog chased the cat.
The cat was chased by the dog.

These sentences mean essentially the same thing, yet their phrase structures are clearly different. Such problems prompted Chomsky (1957) and other linguists to argue that phrase-structure grammars are inadequate descriptions of natural languages.

To deal with the issue, Chomsky distinguished between the surface structure of a sentence and the deep structure of a sentence. *Surface structure* refers to the phrases in the actual sentence. *Deep structure* refers to the phrases in a hypothetical sentence that more directly reflects the meaning of the sentence. Figure 8.4 shows the surface structure (A) and deep structures for two meanings (B and C) of the sentence *Visiting relatives can be boring*. Chomsky proposed that there are transformational rules that convert different deep structures into the same surface structure, or the same deep structure into different surface structures. According to this view, deep structure and its transformational rules are central to the structure and meaning of sentences. We make sense out of what we hear by attempting to understand its deep structure.

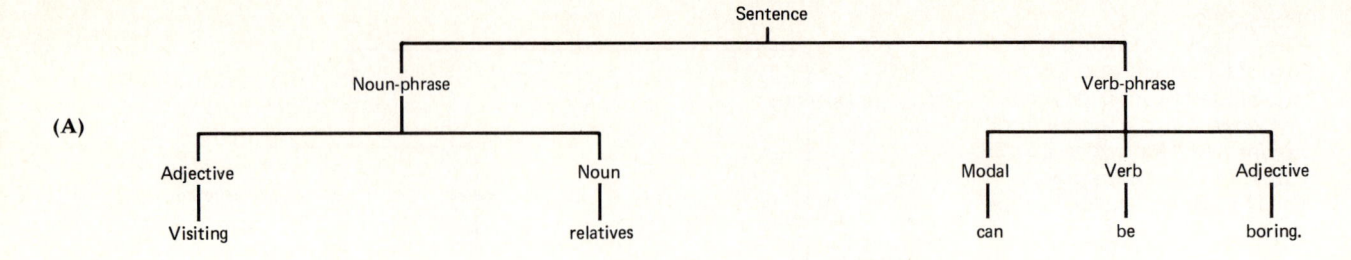

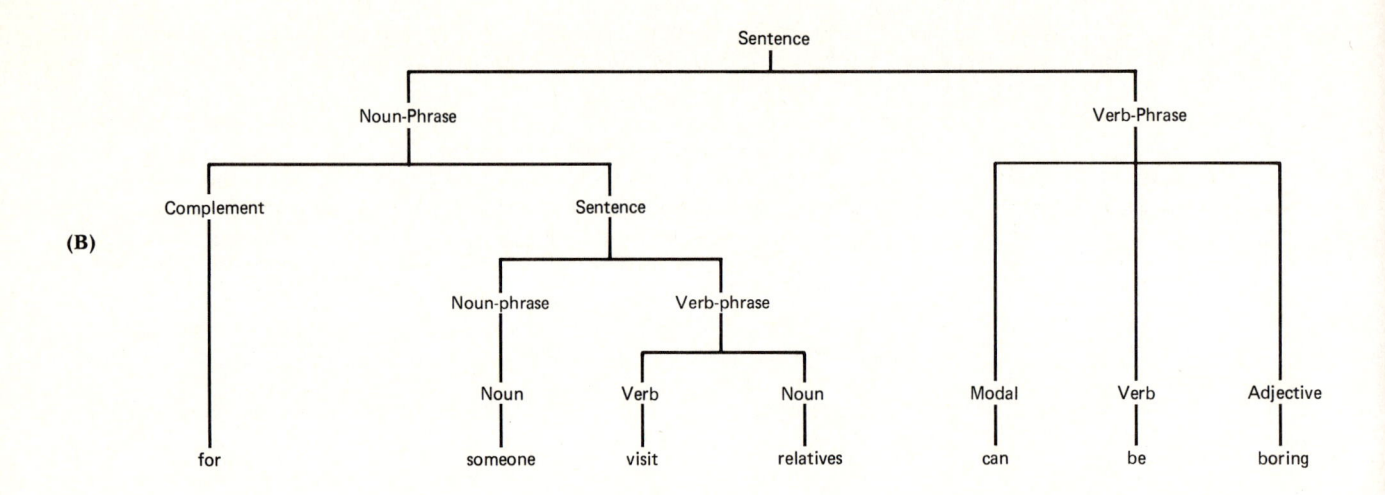

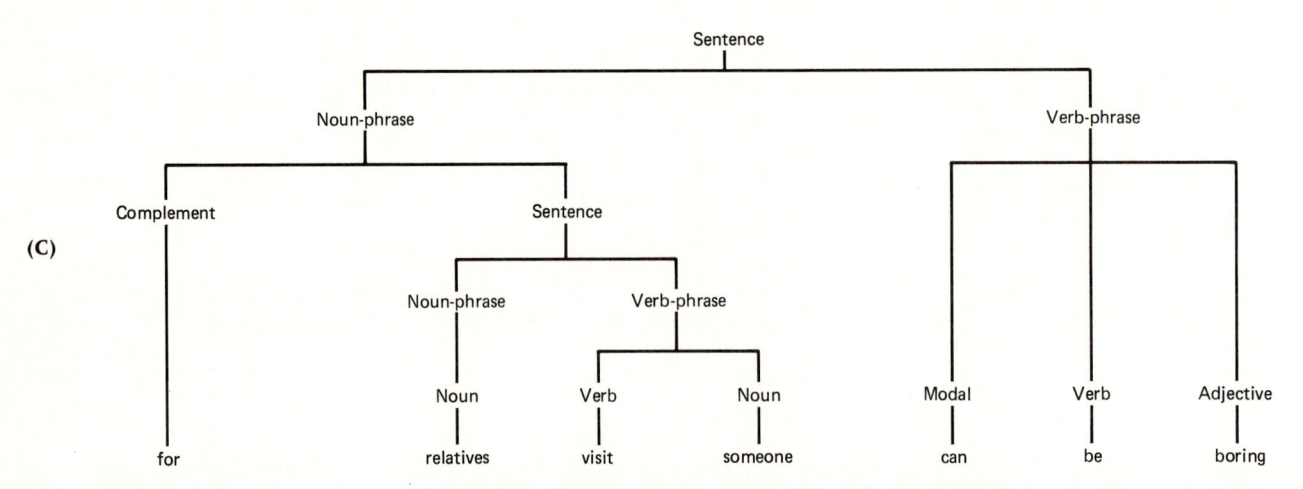

Figure 8.4 The surface structure (A) and deep structures for two meanings (B) and (C) of the ambiguous sentence, *Visiting relatives can be boring*.

COMPETENCE VERSUS PERFORMANCE

In the preceding section we focused on the structure of language rather than how it is used. Chomsky labeled this a distinction between *competence* and *performance*. He argued that competence determines performance, and some research suggests that this is true.

For example, Johnson (1965) attempted to examine the relationship between surface structure and memory. People were asked to learn to associate numbers with complete sentences such that they could repeat the sentences when shown the numbers. Figure 8.5 shows two of the sentences and their surface structures (A). Figure 8.5 also shows the probability of recalling each word in a sentence, given that the previous word has been recalled (B). That is, B shows the occurrence of errors at various transition points in the sentence. As you can see, most errors occur at the transition between phrases: for sentence one at transition 3, which is the boundary between the noun phrase and the verb phrase, and for sentence two at transitions 2 and 5.

In another study, Sachs (1967) examined the relationship between deep structure and memory. Sachs hypothesized that if deep structure was primary, memory for it should last longer than memory for surface structure. To examine this question, she asked people to read a story and then asked them to tell her whether a test sentence was exactly the same as a sentence from the story. Some of the test sentences were identical to those in the story, and others were altered. In the latter cases, the alteration affected either deep structure or surface structure. Sachs found that changes in both deep and surface structure were detected if the test sentence was presented immediately after the target sentence. However, if the test sentence was delayed, only deep-structure changes were detected with any accuracy.

Such results point to the impact of linguistic structure on performance. However, other results based on predictions derived from transformational

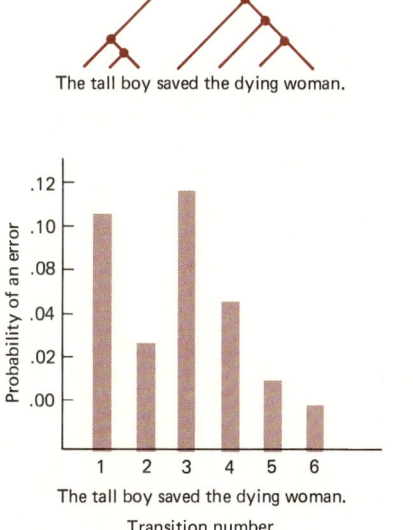

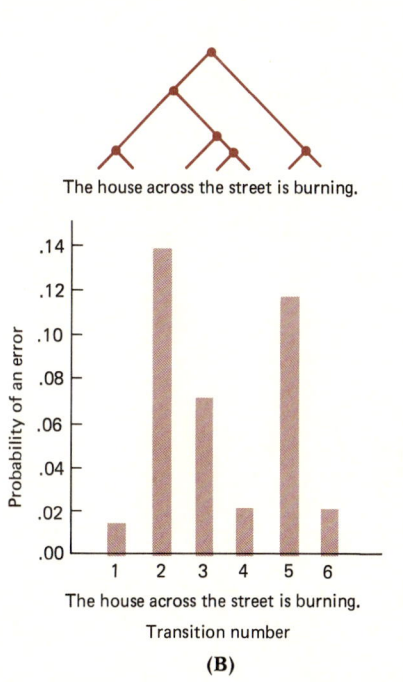

Figure 8.5
The results of an experiment to examine the relationship between sentence structure and memory. Part (A) shows two of the sentences (and their surface structures) that people were asked to remember. Part (B) shows the probability of recalling each word in the sentence given that the previous word has been recalled. Errors tend to occur at the transition between phrases suggesting the psychological importance of sentence structure. (Based on Johnson, 1956)

grammar are often inconsistent. Thus the exact relationship between competence and performance remains unclear. In addition, some psychologists believe that performance encompasses much more than what is derived from competence. In the next section we examine several elements of language performance.

LANGUAGE COMPREHENSION AND PRODUCTION

The use of language requires coordination between two distinct processes: production and comprehension (Clark & Hecht, 1983). *Production* is the generation of language, the uttering of words, sentences, paragraphs, and so on. *Comprehension* is the understanding of language. If people did not coordinate production and comprehension—if they did not use these two processes in compatible ways—a speaker could not use language to communicate meaning, and when the speaker became a listener, could not infer the meaning of another speaker. In short, part of acquiring language is attaining the ability to both produce and understand language.

Although the coordination between production and comprehension may seem obvious, such integration does not always exist. For instance, most Americans can recognize and *understand* the several regional dialects that exist in the United States. For example, many of us can understand the dialects found in the South, in New York or New England, or in the Midwest. Yet despite our ability to understand all these dialects, we do not necessarily have the ability to speak them, to produce them. In turn, many religious ceremonies involve the production of language (e.g., of Hebrew in Judaism, or as used to be the case, of Latin in Catholicism) without comprehension. That is, the participants in these religious ceremonies often say prayers—produce language—in a tongue which they do not comprehend.

Clark and Hecht (1983) believe that the absence of a necessary coordination between comprehension and production means that there exists one linguistic process for understanding and another for talking. They conclude that people must acquire, across their development, the ability to coordinate these two processes.

Studies of vocabulary use support this point. Goldin-Meadow, Seligman, and Gelman (1976) found that 1- to 2-year-olds comprehended the word "dog" just as an adult would; the children could also select a picture of a dog from an array of pictures when asked to do so. However, when asked to name the picture of the dog, the children tended to produce "wuf-wuf," *not* the word "dog." Thus these children comprehend the adult word "dog" but could only produce a "child-word," "wuf-wuf" (Clark & Hecht, 1983). These data and those of other studies (e.g., Karmiloff-Smith, 1977), suggest that young children lack complete coordination between understanding and production. Moreover, not only does it seem that children may comprehend without being able to produce, but it seems that when the two processes are not coordinated, understanding seems to occur earlier in development than production.

The process of knowing the meaning of language is central to a person's understanding of the world, because so much of our experience involves the use of symbolic, representational systems, of which language is the prime example. As early as 1953, Wittgenstein claimed that learning the meaning of a language, or even of a word, was exceedingly difficult because the meaning of a word is inherently vague and dependent on the context within which the word is used.

Some writers have proposed that a word's meaning actually exists not as a precise, dictionary definition, but as a group of procedures for deciding how to use a word in a particular context, be it one made up of other people or simply surrounding words (e.g., a sentence) (Miller, 1976). Similarly, Clark and Clark (1977) propose that while a word does have a linguistic meaning, to use and to comprehend a word one must coordinate one's knowledge of the linguistic meaning with one's knowledge of the social context.

To illustrate the need to coordinate linguistic word meaning with social context, consider how both sorts of information *must* be used to understand statements in which nouns are used as verbs in new ways:

"He *porched* the newspaper." (Danks & Glucksberg, 1980, p. 399)
"She *Nixoned* the evidence."
"The lawyers *eight-balled* the witness."

In the first sentence the act of a delivery boy throwing a newspaper on the porch of a house was conveyed by the new verb. In the second sentence, the meaning refers to the role of a former president in tampering with evidence pertinent to a crime. In the last sentence, the act involves putting a trial witness in a difficult situation.

Clark and Clark (1972) suggest that people use such novel words, and they believe that their listeners can comprehend the intended meaning because the listeners know *both* the linguistic meaning of the word and the social context. In such cases, one can see that meaning is a construction, an integration based on these two sources of information. Such meaning, because it is novel, cannot, therefore, be retrieved from semantic memory (Danks & Glucksberg, 1980).

THE ACQUISITION OF LANGUAGE

We have seen that language involves both elements of structure and process, but where does it come from? Is it learned? Is it built in? As with most psychological phenomena, several theories seek to explain the acquisition of language. Today, there seem to be three major views: (1) a *learning theory* approach, which argues that learning principles can account for language acquisition; (2) *performationism*, or a nativist view, which contends that language is innate; and (3) an *interactionist* view, held by many current theorists, recognizing the influences of both genetic and environmental factors on language development.

The Learning Theory Approach. From the beginning of life, the infant produces sounds that will later be the basis of the first words. As development progresses, new sounds appear in relatively systematic fashion. One attempt at explaining just how and why language development proceeds in this orderly fashion is through *learning theory principles*. Theorists who adhere to this view (e.g., Skinner, 1957) contend that parents *positively reinforce*, or reward, with praise and attention, any correct sounds emitted by the infant. These reinforced sounds will therefore occur more frequently in the child's speech and will eventually become an established part of his or her language. The learning theory view also argues that sounds which are incorrect will not be reinforced and will therefore eventually disappear. Other learning theorists (e.g., Bijou, 1976) stress *imitation* and contend that the child picks up words, phrases, and sentences directly through imitation and then, through reinforcement, the child learns when to use them appropriately.

Some learning theorists believe that children develop language in an orderly fashion because their parents *positively reinforce* correct sounds with praise and attention. (Erika Stone)

Learning theory accounts of language acquisition have not been well supported by research. For example, children's tendency to imitate words and phrases does not appear to facilitate the later spontaneous use of those items (Leonard, Schwartz, Folger, Newhoff, and Wilcox, 1979). Similarly, Bloom, Hood, and Lightbow (1974) found that although both imitative and spontaneous types of words exist in a child's speech, imitation of particular words and phrases decreases and the spontaneous use of those items increases with age (Bloom et al., 1974). Finally, studies of parent–child interaction reveal that mothers are *not* more likely to reward sounds that occur in their language than they are to reward random sounds (Wahler, 1969).

Despite the evidence which goes against learning theory accounts of the initial acquisition of language, learning principles have been shown to be crucial in modifying already acquired language and in overcoming language deficits in some people. So although learning principles have not been to be the sole factor in the normal acquisition of language by the young child, they can play an important and useful role later in the child's developing language.

Preformationism. Preformationist theories stress that all human beings have an innate biological predisposition for language. Preformationists view language as an abstract system of rules which cannot be learned through traditional learning principles. These theories can take several forms; for example, Chomsky (1968) argues that the human nervous system contains a structure which includes an innate concept of human language. Lenneberg (1967) holds that the ability to speak language is an inherited species-specific characteristic of human beings (but see Highlight 8.1). Lenneberg (1967) contends that the systematic fashion by which language unfolds is tied to biological maturation, just as learning to walk is maturationally determined.

Lenneberg's theory has received considerable support, in part due to evidence that human beings learn language more easily and quickly during one period of biological development (i.e., from infancy to puberty). Similarly, Lenneberg notes that particular language developments occur in a universal sequence and at about the same rate in *all* normal children, despite their native language and whatever cultural variation exists. Thus all children start babbling at about 6 months, say their first word at about 12 months, and start to use two-word combinations at about 24 months. Finally, as we have seen earlier, all appear to share some universal structural features.

However, some data do not support particular preformationist ideas. One such idea is the "critical period" hypothesis. In regard to language, this hypothesis holds that the acquisition of a first language must occur before particular brain developments (cerebral lateralization) is complete (i.e., about the age of puberty). Snow and Hoefnagel-Hohle (1978) tested one prediction derived from this hypothesis: Acquisition of a second language will be relatively fast, successful, and qualitatively similar to first-language acquisition only if it occurs before the critical period of prepuberty maturation is over. This prediction was tested by studying the naturalistic acquisition of Dutch by English speakers of different ages. The children were tested three times during their first year in Holland to assess several aspects of their second-language ability. The results were that the 12- and 15-year-old subjects and the adult subjects made the *fastest* progress during the first few months of learning Dutch. At the end of the first year the 8- to 10- and the 12- to 15-year-olds had achieved the best control of Dutch. On the other hand, 3- to 5-year-old subjects scored lowest on all the tests employed. All these results ran exactly counter to what the critical period hypothesis would lead us to expect.

HIGHLIGHT 8.1

Is Language Confined to Human Beings?

Every human society, no matter how primitive, has a language. But is language restricted to human beings? Many animal species possess the ability to communicate. For example, bees are able to communicate with one another about the direction and distance of sources of pollen and nectar by an alternating movement that is like a dance. The closer the food, the faster the dance. Direction is indicated by a wiggling motion of the abdomen (von Frisch, 1967). However, communication is broader than language. The bee's dance, for instance, is a closed system. No new types of information can be added, only direction and distance. Other communication patterns exhibited by various species of birds and mammals show the same stereotyped quality.

But are animals incapable of language, or is it simply that it does not develop spontaneously in their natural environments? Psychologists have sought to answer this question by attempting to teach animals, particularly the great apes, language. Early attempts failed (Hayes, 1951; Kellog & Kellog, 1933). For example, Hayes reared a chimp named Vicki at home as a child might be. Vicki learned to follow numerous spoken directions, but was only able to say *mama, papa,* and *cup* after extensive training.

It is now clear that such efforts failed primarily because apes' vocal apparatus is not designed to produce speech. As a result, recent investigators have taken a different approach; they have sought to capitalize on apes' manual dexterity and teach them nonverbal languages. Gardner and Gardner (1969, 1975), for example, attempted to teach a chimp named Washoe American Sign Language (Ameslan), which is used by many deaf people. With this system, Washoe eventually learned about 130 signs. More important, she was able to learn to string signs together to make primitive sentences such as *Greg tickle*. However, these were often irregular and repetitive.

In a similar effort, Patterson (1978) provided informal and intensive Ameslan training to Koko, a female gorilla. Patterson reports that by about 4 years of age, Koko exhibited a wide range of languagelike behaviors. She commonly produces over 150 signs a day. She combines signs showing consistent word order in constructions such as *tickle me*. Koko has also produced novel combinations such as *cookie rock* when she was given a stale sweet roll.

Do these studies allow the conclusion that apes can be taught a language? Psychologists disagree. The consenses appears to be that apes can learn words and possibly primitive sentences. However, many psychologists argue that this is insufficient evidence for language. So far, apes have given no evidence of the ability to develop a hierarchical structure of language that will permit them to generate complex sentences. However, research in this area is continuing.

In sum, although most theorists agree that human beings are biologically prepared for the acquisition of language, they contend that biological principles cannot account for *all* aspects of language development.

Interactionism. Most modern theorists recognize that language develops through interactions between biological capacities and learning encounters with the environment. Human beings are biologically prepared for learning language, but experience with the spoken language is also necessary for language learning. This perspective also emphasizes the *active* role the child plays by learning language, rather than the *passive* role he or she is thought to play by the learning theory approach. Furthermore, the role of others in the child's social environment in facilitating language acquisition is emphasized. Research has demonstrated that parents have a great influence on the ease with which their child develops language.

Parents and other adults modify their speech when talking to a child, and children are, in turn, more attentive to simplified speech (Nelson, 1973). By about 5 years of age, children themselves appear to have mastered this language interaction pattern, that is, to modify speech in regard to the age of

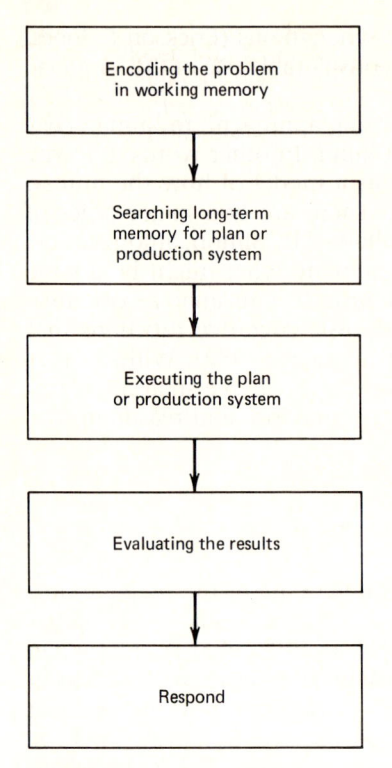

Figure 8.6
Stages of problem solving. (Based on Howard, 1983)

As shown in Figure 8.6, such a system has four stages. In the first stage, the person perceives the problem and converts it into a set of propositions in working memory. Since the capacity of working memory is limited, errors may occur because parts of a complex problem are overlooked. This may be particularly true if the person is unable to use some strategy for remembering (e.g., writing the problem down). The second stage involves searching long-term memory for a solution or for information that will help the person construct a plan or production system to arrive at a solution. Sometimes this involves retrieving a solution to a very similar problem solved in the past. On the other hand, it may be necessary to construct an entirely new solution based on inferences and recombinations of prior knowledge. The third stage consists of executing the potential solution the person has developed in stage 3. If the potential solution is simple, this stage may be carried out quickly and easily. However, if it is complex, the execution process itself may lead to errors. Finally, in the last stage, the person evaluates the results by comparing the outcome with the goal represented in memory. This permits the person to judge whether he or she has completed the task or must continue to search for a solution. If the problem has been solved, the person may focus on identifying cues that will permit retrieval of the solution at a later date. If the problem has not been solved, the evaluation process may suggest the nature of the inadequacy.

Rigidity. People often fail to see the solutions to problems. One reason for this is that they fixate on one aspect of the problem, ignoring others that are relevant for success, a difficulty labeled *rigidity*. There are several types of rigidity.

One type of rigidity involves continued use of a solution that has worked in the past, but which is inefficient or ineffective in the current situation. This is called a *response set*. Consider the problems shown in Table 8.1. The best solution to the first several problems involves the following procedure: fill pitcher B; then fill pitcher A from pitcher B and discard; next fill pitcher C from pitcher B twice and discard; the water remaining in pitcher B is the goal amount.

People generally continue to use this solution for all the problems even though the last two problems are solved more efficiently by using only pitchers A and C. If problems 6 and 7 are presented first, people notice the simpler

TABLE 8.1 An example of water-jar problems used to investigate rigidity. The goal is to measure exactly 100 units of water. The only tools you need to do this are three pitchers that hold different amounts. Describe the sequence of filling and pouring that would be necessary to measure the goal amount.

Problem	Pitcher A	Pitcher B	Pitcher C	Goal
1	21	127	3	100
2	14	46	5	22
3	18	43	10	5
4	7	42	6	23
5	20	57	4	29
6	23	49	3	20
7	15	39	3	18

Source: Luchins (1942).

COGNITIVE PROCESSES: LANGUAGE, THOUGHT, AND INTELLIGENCE

Figure 8.7
One version of problem designed to investigate functional fixedness. Figure out how to mount the candle vertically on the wall so it will act as a lamp. (Based on Duncker, 1945)

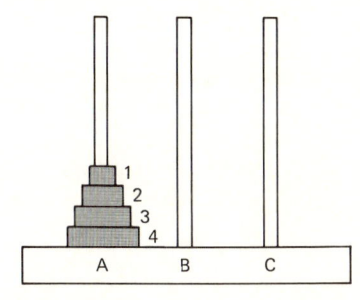

Figure 8.8
The "Tower of Hanoi" Problem. By moving only one disc at a time from the top of a stack, move the discs so they are on Peg C in the same order as they are initially on Peg A. You must always have smaller discs on top of larger ones. For instance, disc 4 can never be on top of disc 3. The task is to solve the problem in as few moves as possible.

solutions. But when they are presented last, peoples' previous experience tends to misdirect their focus to the more complex solution.

A second type of rigidity involves a tendency to perceive a problem from only one perspective, a tendency labeled *perceptual set*. Consider a classic problem developed by Duncker (1945), shown in Figure 8.7. The correct solution is to (1) empty the box containing the tacks, (2) attach the box to the wall using several of the tacks, (3) light the candle and allow some wax to drip onto the box, and (4) affix the candle to the box by embedding it in the melted wax. However, since the box is full of tacks, people often fail to see it as having any other potential uses. Duncker called this *functional fixedness*. If the box is presented empty, people generally solve the problem more easily.

Incubation and Insight. Sometimes, a rest interval between periods of work on a problem will increase the likelihood of its successful solution. Everyone has experienced the effects of such *incubation*. The name we struggled to remember suddenly seems to pop into consciousness without effort minutes or hours later. A strategy for organizing a term paper suddenly becomes clear days after one has given up in frustration. Incubation seems to occur only after the person has devoted considerable time and effort to the problem. It also seems to often be accompanied by a flash of insight—an "aha" experience characterized by a feeling of certainty that the solution is correct. We should note, however, that incubation and insight have been difficult to demonstrate precisely under controlled conditions. The evidence for these processes is largely anecdotal.

Strategies. When presented with relatively simple problems, one may use several alternative and different strategies to find a solution. For example, consider the "Tower of Hanoi" puzzle (e.g., Simon, 1975). Here the problem solver must move a pyramid of disks from one to another of three pegs (Figure 8.8). However, the rules are that only the top disk on any peg may be moved *and* a larger disk cannot be placed on a smaller one. Many different strategies may be used to solve this problem. Some useful strategies depend on perceptual cues, others on setting superordinate and subgoals, and still others on following a pattern. For example, a pattern-following strategy useful for solving the Tower of Hanoi puzzle would be to move the disks in the order 1, 2, 1, 3, 1, 2, 1, 4, 1, 2, 1, 3, 1, 2, 1, and so on. Thus problems such as the Tower of Hanoi involve *transforming* a stimulus from an initial state to a final one. As such, these problems are quite useful in exploring the strategies used in problems of *means-ends* relationships; they allow the cognitive psychologist to understand the different strategies (means) that human beings use to solve a problem (reach an end).

Expert Knowledge. Most research on problem solving has used volunteer college students as participants. The tasks used in these cases do not call for much, if any, specific prior knowledge about a given problem. However, often in life, people *specialize* in solving one or another type of problem. Some people are experts at games such as chess, for example, and many studies have been undertaken to examine problem solving by expert chess players. The questions asked in such research are: (1) What kinds of knowledge must an expert have; (2) how is that knowledge stored in long-term memory (LTM); and (3) what perceptual cues, if any, evoke this LTM? The classic work of deGroot (1965) discovered that a chess master could reconstruct the board positions of about 25 pieces after viewing the board for only 5 to 10 seconds. An ordinary player could remember only about 25% of this total after the same exposure.

Semantically Rich Domains. This area of problem solving is related to "expert knowledge." That is, experts have extensive knowledge about solving a particular type of problem, and a *semantically rich domain* is a problem area requiring extensive knowledge for solving problems. In the study of semantically rich domains there are two central research questions. First, *how much* knowledge in LTM does an expert have? Second, what is the organization of this knowledge, and how does the expert gain access to it? Besides chess masters, these questions have been studied with experts in fields as diverse as chemical engineering, thermodynamics (Bhaskar & Simon, 1977), and medical diagnosis (Davis, Buchanan, & Shortliffe, 1977).

Production Systems. How do we know that stimuli, or ideas, seemingly suddenly retrieved from long-term memory, function to change human thought? Although a final answer to this question is not possible to formulate, cognitive psychologists' study of *production systems* appears to be a step in the right direction. A *production* is simply a set of instructions. It has two parts. First, a *condition* is a sort of test. The test may be (1) a perceptual one, "asking" if a stimulus is of a particular sort (e.g., a word *or* a random arrangement of letters); or (2) a symbolic one, "asking" if a set of symbols (again, for example, a word) matches knowledge held in short-term memory (STM). If the appropriate condition is met, if the "test" is "passed," the second part of the production occurs. This is the *action*. For instance, if the perceptual test of "word" is passed, the action of "recognition" of the word will occur.

Understanding Process. Before someone can begin to solve a problem, he or she must understand its nature; that is, as Simon (1979, p. 371) reminds us, "a problem well formulated is half solved." In recent years, cognitive psychologists have begun to explore the process involved in the initial understanding of a problem. One major finding has been that skill gained in solving one form of a problem will not always transfer to comparable forms of the same problem (Greeno, 1975). Second, even minor changes in how a problem is presented—changing the tense of the instructions, for example—can considerably alter a solver's ability to deal with the problem efficiently (Hayes & Simon, 1976).

CONCEPT FORMATION

What is similar about Charles DeGaulle, Leonid Breshnev, and Lyndon Johnson? One answer to this problem is that they were all presidents of their respective countries. Another answer is that they are all deceased. If someone could solve the problem of identifying the common element among these three people-stimuli, one would have abstracted the *concept* unifying the stimuli. A concept may be defined as an "abstraction from particular instances" (Erickson & Jones, 1978, p. 73). In other words, all stimuli are instances of a common, abstract quality—presidential status in this case. In arriving at a common link among stimuli, one would have formed a concept.

Concept Identification. Although research in concept formation, or concept learning, is typically discussed as a topic separate from problem solving per se, most research on concept formation involves a type of problem solving. For example, people are presented with a set of stimuli that may differ along several separate dimensions: for example, stimuli may differ in regard to size (small or large), color (red or blue), and shape (triangular or circular). In the study of concept formation the problem the person must solve is to classify (sort or arrange) the stimuli according to some simple rule. For example, the "rule" with the above-described stimuli may be that all small stimuli go into one group, for example, a group associated with a reward, and all large stimuli go into another group, one not associated with a reward. Alternatively, all red stimuli may be instances of the target concept, while all nonred stimuli are not. Of course, more complex concepts, such as small red stimuli, may characterize the correct solution (Figure 8.9).

The identification of concepts involves at least two processes. First, the person must determine which attributes are relevant. That is, the person must determine whether the stimulus characteristics of color, size, or shape are the basis for a solution of the problem. In going about this process of attribute identification, people use various strategies. One strategy is called *conservative focusing*. Suppose the person has been informed that a small red circle is an instance of the concept. The conservative focusing strategy involves altering one feature at a time. For example, the person may now select a small red triangle. If this is still an instance of the concept, the person now knows that the shape of the stimulus is irrelevant. The person may then select a small blue circle. If this is an instance of the concept, the attribute of color is eliminated and the person knows that size is the relevant dimension.

In addition to identifying attributes, a second process involved in concept formation is *rule learning*. The issue here is identification of the rules by which attributes are combined. In investigating rule learning, people are often in-

Figure 8.9
Instances of stimuli relevant to the concept *small* and the concept *red*.

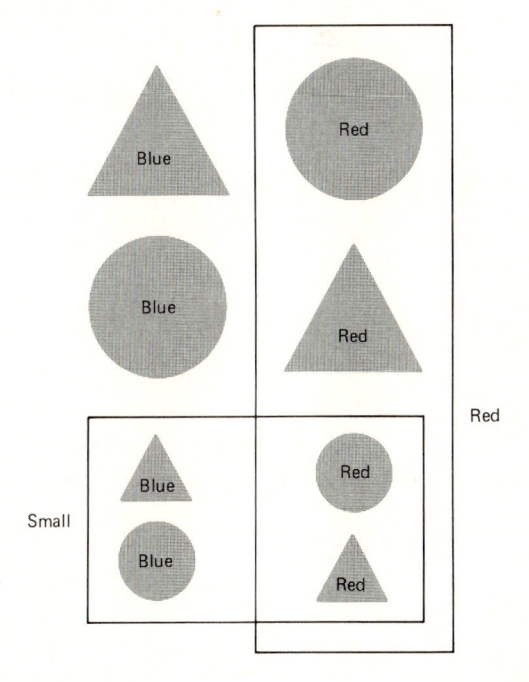

262 LEARNING, COGNITION, MOTIVATION, AND EMOTION

Placing groups of stimuli in common categories helps us to make the world less complex. (Owen Franken/Stock Boston)

formed of the relevant attributes in advance. The task, then, is to learn the particular rule that governs the correct combination. There are several types of rules, some of which are shown in Table 8.2. For example, conjunctive rules require the joint presence of two attributes. On the other hand, disjunctive rules involve the presence of *either* attribute A *or* attribute B, or both. In general, conjunctive rules are easier to learn than disjunctive rules, which, in turn, are easier to learn than conditional rules. Biconditional rules are the most difficult to learn (Bourne, 1970).

Categorization. A key topic related to concept formation is what Mervis and Rosch (1981) term *categorization*: They note that:

A category exists whenever two or more distinguishable objects or events are treated equivalently. This equivalent treatment may take any number of forms, such as labeling distinct objects or events with the same name, or performing the same action on different objects. Stimulus situations are unique, but organisms do not treat them uniquely; they respond on the basis of past learning and categorization. In this sense, categorization may be considered one of the most basic functions of living creatures (Mervis & Rosch, 1981, p. 89).

TABLE 8.2
Examples of rules involved in concept formation

Rule	Example
Attribution	All red objects are instances of the concept
Conjunction	All objects that are both red *and* triangular are instances of the concept
Inclusive disjunction	All objects that are red *or* triangular *or* both are instances of the concept
Conditional	*If* the object is red, *then* it must be triangular to be an instance of the concept
Biconditional	Red objects are instances of the concept *if and only if* they are triangles

Source: Ellis and Hunt (1983).

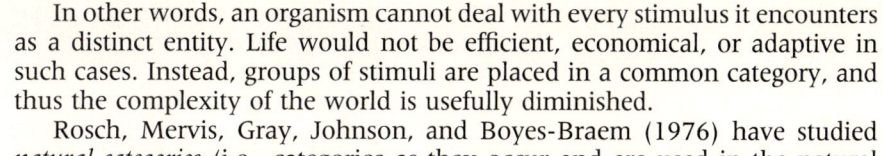

COGNITIVE PROCESSES: LANGUAGE, THOUGHT, AND INTELLIGENCE

In other words, an organism cannot deal with every stimulus it encounters as a distinct entity. Life would not be efficient, economical, or adaptive in such cases. Instead, groups of stimuli are placed in a common category, and thus the complexity of the world is usefully diminished.

Rosch, Mervis, Gray, Johnson, and Boyes-Braem (1976) have studied *natural categories* (i.e., categories as they occur and are used in the natural world) and have noted that any stimulus may be categorized at several different levels of abstraction. For instance, a robin is a bird, but it is also a vertebrate, an animal, and a living entity. Thus a hierarchy of categories (e.g., robin, bird, animal, etc.) exists for any object. Nevertheless, Rosch et al. (1976) have found that there are *basic level categories*, that is, those in which the information value to the person is most efficient. For instance, a given object in the home may be categorized as a chair, as a piece of furniture, or as a human-made stimulus. The category level "chair" has been found to be a basic level category in that it allows the information in the category to be used most efficiently, in this case for sitting. Not all pieces of furniture or human-made stimuli are suitable for sitting.

Rosch et al. (1976) have found that basic level categories are acquired before categories at other hierarchical levels. In addition, they have indicated that basic level categories involve people using similar behaviors to interact with category members, have members of the category which possess similar general shapes, and have category members which can be similarly reflected with a common mental image.

Mervis and Rosch (1981) also note that there is a *nonequivalence of category members*; in other words, not all members of a category equally represent their category. For instance, the chairs depicted in Figure 8.10 do not equally represent the basic category of chair. Mervis and Rosch (1981) indicate that category members which share the most common attributes with other members of the category, and thus have the highest "family resemblance," are good *exemplars* of the category. Indeed, such exemplars have few, if any, attributes in common with members of other, even related categories. Moreover, because the boundaries between categories are not necessarily well defined (e.g., when does a chair stop being in the category "chair" and enter the category "loveseat"?), these high family resemblance exemplars are typically rated as being most representative of a category.

In sum, concept attainment and categorization are key ways in which human beings solve the problems of dealing with a complex and changing world. But what are the mental activities that occur when a concept is being attained or a categorization is being made? Cognitive psychologists believe that various types of *reasoning* occur in the process of attaining a concept. But what is reasoning?

REASONING

Several types of reasoning exist, but in a general sense reasoning involves the cognitive manipulation of physical, pictorial, or linguistic symbols.

Inductive Reasoning. Attaining a concept involves being able to integrate the stimuli by moving cognitively from some empirical instance to the general and abstract. When one moves cognitively from the specific to the more general, one is using *inductive reasoning*. In the examples above pertaining to finding the rule by which the stimuli could be correctly categorized, concept attainment depended on the person being able to move from the specific

Figure 8.10
Different members of the category, *chair*. The various instances are nonequivalent, because they vary in the degree to which they share common attributes with other members of the category and are thus *typical* of it.

stimuli presented to him or her to the general, abstract rule governing the correctly organized. The cognitive function involved in this task was inductive reasoning.

Simon (1979) notes that the human ability to induce an order or a pattern among stimuli is a centrally important competence. It allows human beings to deal efficiently and economically with the numerous stimuli that affect them. Kotovsky and Simon (1973) have studied our abilities to discover the patterns in sequences of letters or numbers. For instance, consider the letter sequence ABBA, CDDC, E---. What letters will complete the sequence? The answer here is FFE. In turn, consider the number sequence 1221, 3443, 5---. The numbers that will complete the sequence are 665. In both instances, inductive reasoning will have been needed for a correct answer. Moreover, one can further induce that in both instances the *same* formal rule—initial item (letter or number), next item in typical original succession, repetition of this item, return to the original item—may be used for correct solution.

Deductive Reasoning. Induction is not the only form of reasoning that human beings may use to solve problems or attain concepts. *Deductive reasoning* refers to cognitive movement from the general to the specific. That is, one begins with a general idea or rule and deduces instances. In a syllogism there are typically three components: (1) a general proposition or premise is made; (2) a statement presents a fact related to the first premise; and (3) a statement, or assertion is made which represents a conclusion necessarily derived or *deduced from* the prior premise and fact. Thus the issue in a syllogism is whether the final statement is true. Is it logically, that is, necessarily, the case that given A (the premise) and B (the fact), C (the conclusion) is correct? Does C necessarily follow from A and B?

For instance, consider the following syllogism, attributed to Woody Allen:

(A) Aristotle is a man.
(B) I am a man.
(C) Therefore, I am Aristotle!

Given the premise, A, and the fact, B, may we *infer*, or deduce, that C is correct? No. Since human beings other than Aristotle fall into the category "man," the fact that B is true does not allow one logically to deduce that the person referred to in "C" is Aristotle. This is an *invalid syllogism*.

In a *valid syllogism*, however, the conclusion does follow logically from the premise. For instance, consider the following syllogism:

(A) Boats and only boats float on water.
(B) X is floating on water.
(C) Therefore, X is a boat.

This is an example of a valid syllogism, albeit one with a counterfactual premise.

J. R. Anderson (1976) has found that people's performance on syllogisms can be improved by manipulating the instructions they are given and/or by linking their performance with specific systems of rewards or "payoffs." In turn, Dickstein (1976) has found that people perform better on valid than on invalid syllogisms. Finally, Scribner (1975) has found that some people's failure at syllogistic reasoning problems derives not from an inability to make logical deductions or true inferences, but due to a tendency to treat a premise on an empirical rather than an abstract basis. For instance, consider the following valid syllogism:

(A) All the people from the town of *X* are farmers.
(B) Mr. Jones is from the town of *X*.
(C) Therefore, Mr. Jones is a farmer.

Scribner (1975) found that some people refuse to reach the conclusion stated in C, despite its correctness, because they maintain that they do not know Mr. Jones personally and therefore cannot say whether he is a farmer. In such cases the reasoner would be treating the premise more as an empirical possibility than as a necessary premise from which to make deductions or inferences.

Other Types of Reasoning. Another form of reasoning involves making *transitive inferences*. To explain this type of reasoning, suppose a group of people learned that in a series of adjacent stimuli—such as the sticks presented in part one of Figure 8.11—stick A was longer than stick B and, in turn, that stick B was longer than stick C. We could represent this knowledge as (1) A > B, and (2) B > C. After this is learned, people may then be tested by questioning them as to whether C > A, whether B > A, or whether A > C. A correct, transitive inference would be that A > C, since A is greater—longer—than another stick, B, which is known to be longer than C.

Trabasso and Riley (1975) and Riley (1976) have found that people do better on tests involving the items at the beginning and end of a series (the A and C sticks, for example) and on tests wherein the distance is of a greater rather than a lesser magnitude. For example, if there were 10 sticks in a series such as the one represented in the second part of the figure (i.e., sticks A to J), people would tend to do better on tests with a wider separation of items (e.g., B to I) than with tests having less distance between items (e.g., C to E). Moreover, they indicate that performance improves as people age from childhood to adulthood, particularly when training with verbal examples is given.

A final form of reasoning that we will mention is *conditional reasoning*. The general form of this type of reasoning is: If *P*, then *Q*: that is, *if* event *P* exists, then event *Q* must also exist. To illustrate, suppose that you were given a card with a picture of a bear on one side and a picture of a triangle on the other. You were also told that the "rule" was that if there is a bear on one side, there is a triangle on the other. Thus if bear (*P*), then triangle (*Q*). Next you are given four cards: Card one shows a bear (*P*); card two shows a lion (which we will term "not bear" and symbolize $\bar{P}$); card three shows a triangle (*Q*); and card four shows a circle ($\bar{Q}$). Now, which of these four cards would you have to turn over to see if the rule given to you were correct?

Wason and Johnson-Laird (1972) have explained that only two cards—*P* and $\bar{Q}$—need to be turned over to verify the rule. We need to turn over *P* (the bear) to see if a triangle exists, and we need to turn over $\bar{Q}$ (the circle) to verify that a bear does not exist. However, this solution is not often selected. Instead, people tend to examine either *P* alone, or perhaps both *P* and *Q*. Somewhat less often, *P*, *Q*, and $\bar{Q}$ are examined, and thus an extra and unnecessary step—*Q*—is included. Wason and Johnson-Laird (1972) note that performance tends to be better when concrete rather than abstract stimuli are used to appraise conditional reasoning.

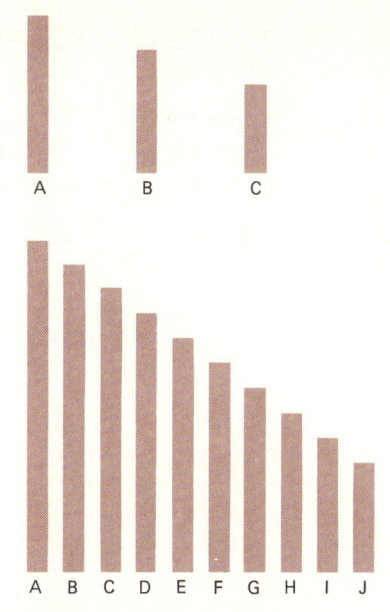

Figure 8.11
Series of stimuli that may be used to investigate transitive inferences. For example, if A is judged longer than B, and B is judged longer than C, then one can infer that A is longer than C.

INTELLIGENCE

Intelligence is a highly controversial topic. Psychologists have frequently disagreed about its definition and measurement. Major controversies have erupted over the extent to which various groups differ in intellectual ability and the degree to which genetic or environmental influences are responsible for these differences. What is the status of these issues in modern and present-day psychology?

First, it is important to distinguish the construct of intelligence from measures of intelligence. Early investigators focused on developing tests designed to discriminate between bright and dull school students, so that they could be assigned to the appropriate curriculum. For this reason, little attention was paid to questions of how abilities were organized or the nature of the processes on which they were based. Intelligence was defined as whatever it was that the test measured. This applied approach led to the development of numerous measures which proved quite useful in several contexts (the development and application of intelligence tests is discussed in Chapter 12). However, it left unanswered many crucial, theoretical questions about the nature of intelligence.

Taking a different approach, other investigators have focused on the structure and content of intellectual abilities. By *structure* we mean the way abilities are organized or related to one another. By *content* we mean the subtasks, processes, and strategies involved in complex intellectual abilities.

THE STRUCTURE OF ABILITIES

Children who achieve high scores on intelligence tests also tend to do well in school. (Suzanne Szasz)

Investigators have attempted to identify the structure of abilities by examining the relationhips among individual differences on multiple-ability tests. This has been called the *differential approach*. A basic assumption of this differential approach is that differences in performance between persons on different tests are a function of a relatively small number of underlying dimensions of intelligence. These dimensions have been identified primarily by a complex statistical technique called *factor analysis*. What are the underlying dimensions that appear to characterize human intelligence?

General Intelligence. Literally hundreds of tests have been developed to measure intelligence. Amazingly, these measures tend to correlate positively, although not highly, with one another. That is, relative to other people, someone scoring high on a test of, say, arithmetic ability will tend to score high on a test of, say, vocabulary ability, even though the tests appear to measure different things. Performance on measures of intelligence also tends to correlate positively with commonsense indicators of intellectual ability, such as school achievement. Such relationships led early investigators to postulate the existence of *general intelligence*. For example, Spearman (1927) proposed that intelligence may be characterized by two factors: general ability (g) and specific abilities (s). According to Spearman, g was involved in the performance of all mental tasks, whereas s was involved in the performance of a single task. However, Spearman proposed that g was the major determinant of intellectual performance.

Primary Mental Abilities. Although many different ability measures do correlate positively with one another, the magnitude of these relationships is often quite low. This led some investigators to discount the notion of *g*. Instead, they proposed that these are a number of separate *primary mental abilities*. Each of these presumably represents a relatively independent cognitive function based on a different set of determinants. Estimates of the number of such primary ability factors range from 7 (Thurstone & Thurstone, 1941) to 120 (Guilford, 1967). Current researchers tend to suggest that between 20 and 30 primary ability factors are sufficient to account for the bulk of the individual differences found on hundreds of tests (Horn, 1978).

Fluid-Crystallized Theory. It is easier to understand human abilities as consisting of a relatively few primary mental abilities than to consider all the possible tests or problems that could be indicative of intelligence. However, some investigators have noted that a system involving even as few as 20 to 30 abilities may be too complex (Horn, 1978). Further, they note that the primary mental abilities are not completely independent. Rather, they tend to be positively correlated, again suggesting the existence of some sort of general ability. To deal with these issues, R. B. Cattell (1971) and Horn (1970, 1978; Horn & Donaldson, 1980) sought to examine what is common to the primary mental abilities by applying the same factor analytic techniques to these factors as was originally applied to the individual tests. Such analyses generate a set of second-order abilities. Using this approach, Cattell and Horn have suggested that intelligence may be described by two basic factors: fluid and crystallized intelligence.

According to Horn (1978), both fluid and crystallized intelligence involve behaviors characteristic of the essence of human intelligence: perceiving relationships, abstracting, reasoning, forming concepts, and solving problems. However, they reflect different processes of acquisition, are influenced by different antecedents, and are reflected in different measures.

Fluid and crystallized intelligence are indexed by different types of tests, but both involve perceiving relationships, forming concepts, and solving problems. (Van Bucher)

FOCUS ON THE PSYCHOLOGIST

John Horn

JOHN HORN has been a professor at the University of Denver since 1961. He has worked on the nature of intelligence, the rebellions of youth, the ethics of research, the organization of personality, the diagnosis and treatment of alcoholism, and, in general, human life span development.

People like to think that they control the major events of their lives—that they are masters of their fates, captains of their souls. Everybody likes self-made men and women. We like to think we are self-made. Sometimes I think I have controlled the events that got me into psychology—that I am a self-made man. It may help me to believe this, but in my saner moments I know it isn't true. The truth is I drifted into my job, and there wasn't much control in the drift, not by me, and not by others.

In high school I had thought that I would become a feature writer for an important newspaper. On the side, I would write the Great American Novel and some good essays for magazines. I had a keen interest in people. I was sure I was crazy and that there were serious things wrong with me. I reckoned that others were crazy, too. I thought that if I could understand just how other people were crazy, then I could understand how I was crazy, and this would make it better. I would write about this. People would read what I wrote, understand themselves better, and therefore like my writing.

This kind of thinking, and the fact that I cut school so frequently, led me to quit high school (in my junior year) and begin bumming around the U.S.A. I tried a variety of jobs. You name an easy-to-get job, chances are I worked at it for awhile. I didn't care much about these jobs but mainly regarded them as ways of learning about life and of getting to know people.

I was bumped from this trajectory by Uncle Sam, who demanded that I help with the "police action in Korea." It had a profound influence on me. Several of my friends were killed, and I killed people. I came to realize pointedly that not only are ordinary people crazy, powerful people are too, and viciously so. I learned to distrust ideology. I also had exotically pleasant experiences. I met strangely interesting people in Korea and Japan. I came out of two years in the army with much more sense of purpose.

Using scores from tests I took in the Army, I got into Denver University. I determined to get a job that was based on learning. I took courses in psychology, but these were for fun, not because I imagined there was work I could do in psychology. However, I became aware that people were getting paid to obtain graduate educations in psychology, and one could get a job based on such education. I filled out a major in psychology in my senior year.

Then came a chance to study clinical psychology and personality in Australia. Most important, however, Sam Hammond introduced me to the work of Raymond Cattell. Then luck rolled another winner for me: Cattell invited me to come to work with him in Illinois. There began a collaboration that has extended over 25 years, and is still active.

Cattell's theory is the nearest thing to a complete theory of human functioning so far attempted, Freudian theory being a distant second. The theory is based on operational definitions and efforts to establish empirically verified scientific laws. The orientation of this theory promised to provide a comprehensive and accurate basis for understanding people. Yet that promise was far from realized. There was much to do, both in reformulating theory and in finding evidence to support or reject it. A career opened up for me.

Thus it was that I lucked into circumstances where I could pursue my interests in understanding people and even believe that I might gain some such understanding—and contribute to it. Not a very inspirational story, I'm afraid, but perhaps those who are a bit puzzled about where life is leading can take heart from it.

On the one hand, fluid intelligence reflects incidental learning processes—the degree to which a person has developed unique qualities of thinking independent of culturally based content. Fluid abilities appear to be closely related to neurological integrity. They are not "built in," but damage to the central nervous system is likely to impair them. Crystallized intelligence, on the other hand, reflects intentional learning processes—the degree to which a person has been acculturated, that is, has incorporated the knowledge of skills of the culture into thinking and actions. Crystallized abilities appear to be less sensitive to neurological impairment.

As you might expect, given this distinction between incidental and intentional processes of acquisition, fluid crystallized intelligence are indexed by different types of tests. No single measure of fluid or crystallized intelligence exists because each of these abilities is a conglomerate of several primary mental abilities, which, in turn, are indexed by different types of tests. Thus any given test may reflect both abilities, although some tests are relatively pure measures of one or the other. Regardless, fluid intelligence tends to be indexed by tests that minimize the role of cultural knowledge, whereas crystallized intelligence tends to be indexed by tests which maximize the role of such knowledge. Look at the sample items in Figure 8.12 and see how well you fare. Relatively little cultural knowledge, other than basic terms and relationships, is required to answer the fluid items. But you must have considerable knowledge about the culture in which you live to answer the crystallized items.

THE CONTENT OF ABILITIES

Recently, investigators have attempted to move beyond the groupings identified above and identify the processes involved in intellectual abilities (Carroll, 1978; Horn, 1978; R. J. Sternberg, 1979). In these views, global measures of intelligence may be better understood if we identify the specific encoding, retrieval, comparative, and other processes that support or make up the complex abilities.

For example, Horn (1978) has identified a number of second-order factors that he views as processes for organizing and retaining information in support of fluid and crystallized intelligence. These include visual processes (e.g., perceiving how things change as they move in space, keeping visual configurations in mind), auditory processes (e.g., detecting subtle sound differences, or a pattern of sound embedded within noise), short-term acquisition and retrieval (e.g., maintaining awareness of stimulus elements and retrieving them when needed), and verbal productive thinking (e.g., recalling information from one's past experience and bringing it to bear on a problem solution).

Using a different approach, R. J. Sternberg (1979) has attempted to understand complex abilities such as inductive and deductive reasoning by analyzing the information-processing components that make them up. Sternberg suggests that reasoning tasks involve five basic components: inference, application, justification, encoding, and response. Sternberg has found that the way people execute these components affects the problem solution. For example, when solving analogy problems, better reasoners tend to spend more time encoding the terms of the analogy than do poor reasoners spend encoding them.

Figure 8.12
Sample test items marking fluid and crystallized intelligence. (Based on Ekstrom, French, Harman, & Derman, 1976; and French, French, Ekstrom, & Price, 1963)

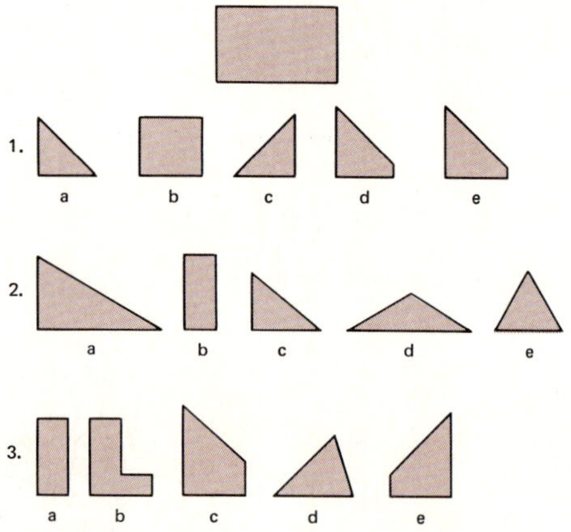

Secondary ability	Primary ability	Test item
Fluid	Induction	Each problem has five groups of letters with four letters in each group. Four of the groups of letters are alike in some way. You are to find the rule that makes these four groups alike. The fifth group is different from them and will not fit the rule.[a] 1. NOPQ DEFL ABCD HIJK UVWX 2. NLIK PLIK QLIK THIK VLIK 3. VEBT XGDV ZIFX KXVH MZXJ
Fluid	Visualization	Below is a geometric figure. Beneath the figure are several problems. Each problem consists of a row of five shaded pieces. Your task is to decide which of the five shaded pieces will make the complete figure when put together. Any number of shaded pieces from two to five may be used to make the complete figure. Each piece may be turned around to any position but it cannot be turned over.[b]
Crystallized	Verbal meaning	Choose one of the four words in the right-hand box which has the same meaning as the word in the left-hand box.[c] 1. bizarre — market, conventional, odd, imaginative 2. pecuniary — involving money, esthetic, trifling, unusual 3. germane — microbe, contagious, relevant, different

Answers: *Induction*—(1) DEFL (2) THIK (3) VEBT; *visualization*—(1) a, c, d, e (2) a, d, e (3) b, c, e; *verbal meaning*—(1) odd (2) involving money (3) relevant; *mechanical knowledge*—(1) welding (2) perfume atomizer (3) Stillson wrench.
[a] Letter Sets Test, I-1; Educational Testing Service, 1962, 1976.
[b] Form Board Test, VZ-1; Educational Testing Service, 1962, 1976.
[c] Vocabulary Test, V-5; Educational Testing Service, 1962, 1976.
Source: Adapted from Ekstrom, French, Harman, and Dermen, 1976; French, Ekstrom, and Price, 1963.

Figure 8.12 *(Continued)*

Secondary ability	Primary ability	Test item

Crystallized	Mechanical knowledge	Complete each of the statements by selecting the correct alternative or answer.[d]
		1. The process of heating two pieces of heavy metal so hot that they will fuse (melt together) is known as:
		   riveting welding
		   soldering forging
		
		2. A paint sprayer functions in exactly the same way as a:
		   centrifugal water pump
		   carbon dioxide fire extinguisher
		   perfume atomizer
		   vacuum cleaner
		
		3. The tool used to rotate a cylindrical object such as a water pipe is a:
		   Stillson wrench box end wrench
		   open end wrench socket wrench

[d] Mechanical Information Test, MK-2; Educational Testing Service, 1962 (test no longer in print).

CREATIVITY AND INTELLIGENCE

Creativity is hard to define (Barron & Harrington, 1981; Guilford, 1950; Guilford & Christensen, 1973; Wallach & Kogan, 1965). Some definitions focus on the *products* of a person's endeavors, on his or her paintings, plays, or poems, for example. Other definitions focus on the person's *processes*. For instance, some theorists (e.g., Guilford, 1950; Wallach & Kogan, 1965) believe that creative thinking is marked by the ability to think *divergently*, that is, to think in unusual or atypical ways about a topic. For example, although one might think that a *brick* can only be used for building or construction, a divergent thinker might be able to generate numerous other distinct uses for it (e.g., as a paperweight; as a weapon; when heated, as a bedwarmer; when crushed, as a dye; as a footrest, etc.).

Invoking thought processes as a component of the person that makes him or her creative raises the issue of the relation between intellectual processes or abilities and creativity. Is there a relation between intelligence and creativity? The answer is a qualified yes. Several studies have found that groups of people identified as creative adults (artists, scientists, mathematicians, and writers, for example) score very high on tests of general intelligence (Baron, 1969; Baron & Harrington, 1980). However, when one relates the quantity or quality of these people's creative achievements to their intelligence scores, relations tend to be either nonexistent or quite small. In other words, *creative people* (or, better, people judged as creative) *tend to be intelligent*, but their intelligence and the quantity or quality of their products do not seem to be related.

However, creative people tend to be perceived and rated as being more intelligent than noncreative people, even when no actual relation exists between measured intelligence and creative production (Barron & Harrington, 1980). This finding suggests that people's (raters') criteria for judging intelligence includes those that psychologists identify as being associated with creative functioning. This may indicate that nonscientists use the term "intelligence" more broadly than do many scientists (Barron & Harrington, 1980).

Creative people such as artists tend to score very high on tests of general intelligence. (Catherine Ursillo)

HEREDITY, ENVIRONMENT, AND INTELLIGENCE

One of the most fundamental and controversial questions about intelligence concerns the basis of differences among people in their scores on tests of intelligence. This question has often been couched within the controversy labeled the heredity-environment, or nature-nurture issue. Nowhere is this controversy more clearly seen than in the case of differences in the average scores of black and white Americans on intelligence tests. The mean difference between these groups is about 15 IQ points in favor of whites (Scarr-Salapatek, 1971). Where do these differences come from? Are the genes associated with differences in race associated with genetically based differences in intelligence (i.e., in nature)? Or are environment differences between blacks and whites (i.e., nurture) the basis of differences in intelligence?

Many psychologists (e.g., Kagan, 1969) have stressed the cultural disadvantages of black Americans. Such environmental disadvantages, they argued, account for the difference. However, others proposed that the differences are due to differences in the gene distributions for these two groups (Jensen, 1969). In turn, Jensen argued that intelligence is a trait showing *heritability*, the degree to which differences among people are associated with genetic differences. Jensen (1969) indicated that individual differences in intelligence are due mostly (e.g., 80%) to genetic differences between black and white Americans. Therefore, he argued that an alternative hypothesis to the one which contends that it is nurture, or environment, which accounts for the differences is the idea that the IQ differences between black and white populations are based on genetic differences between the populations.

This hypothesis provoked a great deal of controversy. This controversy dealt with several issues. First, several scholars argued that the mathematical formulas on which the calculation of heritability was based were at worst erroneous, or at best too limited to be applied appropriately to human beings (e.g., Layzer, 1974; Goldberger, 1979). Such mathematical problems mean, they argued, that it was not statistically possible to determine the relative influence of heredity and environment on intelligence.

A second issue raised by some scholars (Kamin, 1974) was that much of the data Jensen (1969) used to estimate that the heritability of intelligence was .80 was *fraudulent!* A major source of data upon which Jensen (1969) relied was the studies reported by the famous British psychologist, Sir Cyril Burt. Over the course of several years, Burt (e.g., 1955, 1958, 1966) reported that he had collected information on the IQ scores of identical (monozygotic) twins (see Chapter 10) who were separated at birth, or shortly thereafter, and reared apart. As discussed in Chapter 10, such twins come from the same fertilized egg, which splits after conception; thus these twins have the same genetic inheritance. Burt (1966) and Jensen (1969) contended that if such twins had high relations in their respective IQ scores, despite their being reared apart, evidence for the inheritance of IQ would be obtained.

Over the course of several years, Burt collected a larger and larger sample of such identical twins reared apart. In all reports he made of the relation between the twins' IQ scores, Burt reported that the relation was quite high. In fact, despite the fact that his sample size increased over the years from just a few cases to more than 50, the magnitude of the relation (expressed as a correlation coefficient) never changed in size, even when calculated to the third decimal place! Kamin (1974) was the first to notice this constancy, a constancy which is so unlikely that it must be considered equivalent to what most people would term an "impossibility." Kamin's observation led several scholars to question the authenticity of Burt's (1955, 1958, 1966) data (e.g., Goldberger, 1979; Hearnshaw, 1979). After considerable sleuthing (e.g., see Gillie, 1976), it was concluded that Burt's (1955, 1958, 1966) reports had, indeed, been fabricated.

However, even when Burt's reports are erased from the scientific literature, there are other studies (Bouchard & McGue, 1981) which indicate some genetic basis of intelligence, although perhaps not as high as Jensen claimed. This observation led to another issue. That is, many scholars pointed out that the level of heritability associated with intelligence (be it high or low) was *not* an indication of the degree to which our intelligence may change over the course of our lives (Lehrman, 1970). Simply put, high heritability does *not* mean that environment cannot influence the expression of a trait over the course of development (Hebb, 1970). This role of environment is apparent from the findings discussed in the following section.

IMPROVING INTELLIGENCE

Intelligence may be changed through environmental enrichment (intervention). For instance, although there is no evidence of major differences in intelligence among infants of different races or social classes, poor white and poor black children have, on the average, significantly lower IQ scores than do middle-class children by the time the school years begin (Mussen, Conger, Kagan, & Geiwitz, 1979, p. 192). Moreover, as these children from the lower social class continue through school, they do progressively worse and worse. However, major attempts at intervening to enhance the cognitive development of these children have occurred. Although those efforts have neither met with unequivocal success nor avoided criticism (see Jensen, 1969, 1973), the weight of current evidence indicates that intervention can succeed. However, such attempts have to involve major changes in the lives of the youths involved and are most successful if they occur early in their lives. Moreover, even in those intervention efforts wherein immediate enhancement of cognitive function is not found, there is some evidence that positive, although delayed, effects of intervention can occur. In a review of 10 long-term follow-up studies of children involved in preschool intervention projects in the 1960s, Palmer (1977) notes that when these children reach later elementary or junior high school, they score higher on various achievement tests and on IQ tests than do children who did not experience early intervention programs.

There are numerous, specific examples of successful intervention efforts. In one classic study, Skeels (1966) found that the intelligence of seriously retarded babies being reared in an orphanage could be enhanced by assigning them, before 3 years of age, to "mothers" who themselves were mentally retarded older girls living in an institutional setting. This group was compared with a matched group of infants who remained in the orphanage. The infants who were reared by the mentally retarded mothers gained an average of 32 IQ points within 2.5 years, while the comparison group showed an average loss of 21 IQ points. Twenty years after leaving their respective institutions, both groups were again studied. The mothered children were all self-supporting and had completed an average of 12 years of school. The average grade completed by the comparison group was the fourth, none was really self-supporting, and many were in state institutions.

There is evidence that enhancement programs begun after infancy can also work. Gray and her colleagues (Gray & Klaus, 1965; Klaus & Gray, 1968), in the Early Training Project of Peabody College, worked with black children about 3 years of age who came from poverty-stricken families. Children assigned to an experimental group received special training in special school sessions. Children in a control group received no such training. After training, the children in the experimental group were better than those in the control group in various verbal abilities, and follow-up studies—done after 27 months and when two years of public school had been completed—showed that the experimental-group children continued to perform better than those in the other group. Moreover, Gray, Ramsey, and Klaus (1979) report some evidence for a continuing effect of the intervention, albeit a small one, when the groups reached their late adolescent and early adulthood years.

When they reach elementary school, children who were involved in preschool intervention programs tend to score higher than other children in IQ tests. (Erika Stone)

SUMMARY

1. Language is produced through sounds, symbols, or gestures.
2. Languages are regular and are composed of the same hierarchically organized components. Specific rules govern the formation of the components at each level.
3. At the bottom of the hierarchy are phenomes, which are elementary speech sounds.
4. Phenomes are combined according to certain rules to yield morphemes (the minimal units of meaning) and words.
5. Morphemes and words are combined according to certain rules to yield phrases and sentences which convey meaning relationships.
6. Linguists distinguish between the surface structure and the deep structure of a sentence. Surface structure refers to the phrases in the actual sentence. Deep structure refers to the phrases in a hypothetical sentence that more directly reflect the meaning of the sentence.
7. In addition to the structure of language, psychologists have been interested in how people actually use language.

COGNITIVE PROCESSES: LANGUAGE, THOUGHT, AND INTELLIGENCE

8. Production refers to the generation of language, while comprehension refers to the understanding of language. Both of these processes are important, but they are not always coordinated. For example, we can comprehend certain dialects without being able to produce them.

9. Several theories have been suggested to explain the acquisition of language ability.

10. Learning theories suggest that language is acquired by exposure to a model and reinforcement of appropriate responses.

11. Preformationist theories suggest that language is an innate, biologically determined characteristic of human beings and unfolds as part of the process of maturation.

12. Interaction theories suggest that human beings are biologically prepared for learning language, but that experience with language is also necessary for language acquisition.

13. Problem solving is an activity that occurs in an unfamiliar context when a motivated person is initially unsuccessful.

14. Information-processing theorists have suggested that problem solving involves four stages: encoding the problem in working memory, searching long-term memory for a plan or solution, executing the plan or solution, and evaluating the results.

15. People often fail to see the solution to problems. This may result from response sets (continued use of solutions that have worked in the past but are ineffective in the present) or perceptual sets (tendency to perceive a problem from only one perspective).

16. Sometimes a rest interval between periods of working on a problem will improve the likelihood of its solution. This is called incubation.

17. A concept is an abstraction from particular instances.

18. The identification of concepts involves at least two processes. First, one must determine which attributes are relevant. Second, one must identify the rule by which attributes are combined.

19. Objects may be categorized at several levels of abstraction. However, there appear to be basic level categories that are most efficient. In addition, within basic level categories some members of the category are judged to be more typical than others.

20. Inductive reasoning involves moving from the specific to the more general.

21. Deductive reasoning involves moving from the general to the specific.

22. Psychologists have frequently disagreed about the definition and measurement of intelligence.

23. The differential approach has tried to identify the structure of abilities or the way abilities relate to one another. Investigators have discovered several underlying dimensions of intelligence using this approach.

24. Fluid-crystallized theory suggests that intelligence may be characterized as encompassing two basic types of intelligence.

25. Fluid abilities reflect the degree to which a person has developed unique qualities of thinking independent of culturally based content and are indexed by novel tasks.

26. Crystallized abilities reflect the degree to which a person has incorporated the knowledge and skills of the culture into thought and action and are indexed by tasks reflecting such knowledge and skills.

27. Creativity involves both producing products and the ability to think in unusual or atypical ways.//
28. There is considerable controversy over whether differences in intelligence among people are related to their heredity or to their environment. However, despite conflicting evidence regarding this issue, it is clear that intelligence can change over time.

KEY TERMS

Phonemes
Morphemes
Syntax
Competence
Performance
Production
Comprehension
Rigidity
Incubation
Concept identification
Rule learning
Categorization
Inductive reasoning
Deductive reasoning
General intelligence
Primary mental abilities
Fluid intelligence
Crystallized intelligence
Heritability

SUGGESTED READINGS

CATTELL, R. B. *Abilities: Their structure, growth, and action.* Boston: Houghton Mifflin, 1971. Theoretical analysis of intellectual abilities from a psychometric perspective.

CHOMSKY, N. *Language and mind.* New York: Harcourt Brace & World, 1968. Classical analysis of the structure of language.

CLARK, H. H., & CLARK, E. V. *Psychology and language.* New York: Harcourt Brace Jovanovich, 1977. Basic textbook review of theory and research on language.

ROSCH, E. H., & LLOYD, B. B. (Eds.). *Cognition and categorization.* Hillsdale, N.J.: Lawrence Erlbaum, 1978. An advanced examination of the importance of categorization in cognitive function.

SIMON, H. A. *Models of thought.* New Haven, Conn.: Yale University Press, 1979. Critical examination of human thought.

9
Motivation and Emotion

BASIC DRIVES
   Homeostasis
   Regulatory Systems
HUNGER
   Signals for Eating
   Signals for Satiety
   The Hypothalamus and Eating
     Behavior
   Obesity
THIRST
   Signals for Drinking

HUMAN MOTIVATION
   Theories of Human Motivation
   Motivational Factors in
     Aggression
EMOTION
   The Nature of Emotions
   Emotional Expression
   The Structure of Emotions
SUMMARY
KEY TERMS
SUGGESTED READINGS

Human and animal behavior does not occur randomly. It is directed toward or away from specific goals, objects, or events. Our behavior is directed so that we generally approach pleasant things and avoid unpleasant things. We walk toward a friend's home, reach for the peanut butter on the shelf, work toward earning money, and stay away from dark alleys at night. Similarly, we study hard (even though studying may be fairly unpleasant) to earn a degree and also to avoid the embarrassment of getting a bad grade. *Motivation* (its Latin root *motus* means "movement") refers to the direction of behavior. Motivation explains why a person or other animal makes a certain response or changes its behavior. Generally, when psychologists use the term "motivation" they mean goal-directed patterns of behavior. Thus a thirsty rat is said to be motivated when it runs a maze correctly to obtain a drink of water.

Besides directing behavior, motives also energize it. As a motive becomes more intense, it arouses us so that our goal-directed behavior is more energetic. The converse is also true. Sometimes the sight of a plate of food can be very exciting. At other times, the same plate of food will be ignored. We have not forgotten what food is, we just are not hungry all the time.

In the following sections, we will consider both the energizing and directional functions of motivation. We begin with a discussion of how the body maintains appropriate and healthy internal conditions. To do this, we discuss some simple, essentially unlearned motives that human beings share with most other animals. Two of these motives, hunger and thirst, are discussed in some detail because they are vitally important and because they illustrate

Human behavior is not random. We are drawn toward pleasant things and away from unpleasant ones. (Jean-Claude Lejeune/Stock Boston)

some basic principles of motivation. Later in the chapter we discuss several aspects of complex human motivation, focusing on aggression. Finally, we consider the nature and origin of human emotions.

BASIC DRIVES

HOMEOSTASIS

Each of the trillions of cells in our bodies has very specific needs. To carry out their assigned tasks, cells require just the right amounts of oxygen, water, glucose, and other nutrients. Cells also require that their temperature and a whole host of other variables be precisely controlled. The body's tendency to maintain a constant internal environment is termed *homeostasis*.

During our evolution, we developed many ways of controlling internal bodily conditions so that each cell has an appropriate environment. Some of these controls are automatic and occur far from conscious experience. For example, the regulation of blood oxygen content and body temperature happens without any conscious intervention. These homeostatic controls were discussed earlier, in Chapter 3.

Others, however, can involve very complex patterns of behavior. Feeding is a good example of a regulatory process that leads to goal-directed behavior. First, our central nervous system integrates information from various parts of the body to generate a message that, in essence, says we are hungry. This message (hunger) motivates other, more complex, behaviors. For example, to get food we may have to walk home, examine the contents of the refrigerator, decide what to have, prepare the meal, and then eat. Our central nervous system also signals how hungry we are, indicating how much food we need and when we have had enough and are satiated. Some time later, the whole pattern will be repeated, as food is again needed to provide the cells of the body with nutrients. The same sort of pattern occurs with the control of water intake, bodily fluids, mineral balances, sleep, and many other systems.

REGULATORY SYSTEMS

To maintain consistency in one's internal environment, regulatory systems are needed. *Regulatory systems* consist of four essential components. The first is the *system variable*, the factor to be regulated (e.g., body temperature, fluid balance, or nutrient level). Second is the *set point*, the optimum value of the system variable that the body tries to maintain (e.g., a body temperature of 98.6°F). Third, there must be a *monitor* that watches for deviations from the set point, so that fourth, a *correctional mechanism* can restore the system variable back to the set point when deviations occur.

A good example of how regulatory systems work is the control of temperature in a house through changing weather and seasons. Here, the system variable is air temperature inside the house. The monitor is the thermostat, and the correctional mechanisms are the furnace and air conditioner. The set point for this system is determined by how the thermostat is adjusted. When the temperature in the house falls below the set point for heating, the furnace turns on and runs until the temperature rises to the set level. The furnace then shuts off. When temperature rises above the set point for cooling, the air conditioner switches on and works to lower it to the vicinity of the set point. This is shown diagrammatically in Figure 9.1.

HUNGER

We shall now take a look at a particular biological motive, hunger. How do we regulate our eating behavior so that our bodies are adequately, but not excessively supplied with food? This is one of the most thoroughly studied

Figure 9.1
A negative feedback system for controlling both heating and cooling.

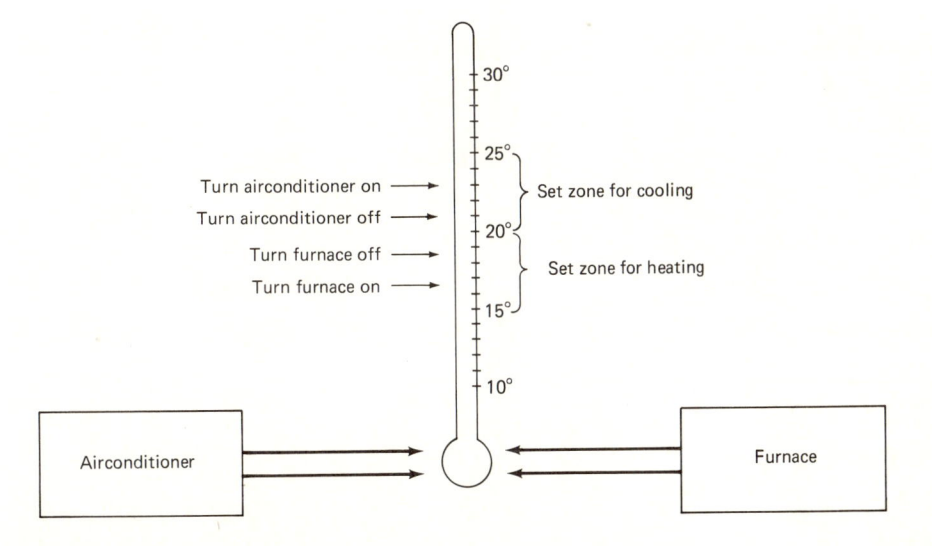

questions in physiological psychology, both because it is important as a model for understanding the regulation of other systems and because the control of obesity is a major concern to many people.

For all but the most simple animals, eating involves some sort of *goal-directed behavior*. Feeding behaviors range from grazing to foraging to hunting, but the underlying motive is the same: to get nutrients needed to feed and maintain their bodies. Physiological factors such as sensory mechanisms, patterns of motor responses, and the capacity to learn probably all evolved to provide more efficient ways of obtaining food.

Whether its eating behavior is simple or complex, each animal must respond to a variety of cues. It must eat when food is needed, select the appropriate food, engage in whatever feeding behavior is needed to eat that food, and finally stop feeding when enough has been eaten. The striking thing about the regulation of food intake is its precision. Day after day, we manage to eat just enough to meet the body's needs. When we eat more than we metabolize, the leftover food is stored as fat. An excess of just 100 calories a day (one chocolate chip cookie) will result in the gain of a pound a month. However, without much conscious effort on our part, our weight remains fairly constant over a long period. In one study, the weight of a group of males increased from 73 kilogram (kg) at age 21 to only 77 kg at age 30, where it remained fairly constant to age 60 (USHDEW Ten State Nutrition Survey, 1972). Although body composition may change somewhat with age, weight remains remarkably constant from year to year. It is as if each person has a particular set point for body weight. We may not always like it, but we maintain our weight even in the face of crash diets, irregular mealtimes, desserts, and holiday meals. In the next sections we explore some of the mechanisms that enable us to regulate our eating behavior so precisely.

SIGNALS FOR EATING

The goal of eating is to regulate the amount of nutrients available to be metabolized into energy for behavior and to build and maintain the body. What signals cause human beings and animals to start eating? What is happening when we say that we are hungry?

When we eat more than we metabolize, the leftover food is stored as fat. An excess of just over 100 calories a day will result in the gain of a pound a month. (Arthur Grace/Stock Boston)

Stomach Factors. It seems intuitively correct that feelings of an empty stomach should be important cues for hunger. However, as is so often the case, the simple explanation is not the correct one. In fact, a stomach does not even seem to be necessary for someone to experience hunger. People who have had their stomachs surgically removed still report normal feelings of hunger. Similarly, having a full stomach does not inhibit feelings of hunger. Eating a large green salad without salad dressing does not satisfy hunger. Stomach cues appear to be somewhat more important in telling us that we have had enough to eat, as we will see later in the chapter.

Glucose. Glucose is a sugar, and the primary food for the brain. Because of this, some researchers have suggested that low glucose levels in the blood might be an important cue for hunger. Since it is well known that *glucoreceptors* in the brain monitor the amount of glucose in the blood, this theory suggests that when blood glucose levels fall, a person should feel hungry. The fact that giving glucose injections to hungry rats and human beings causes them to stop eating supports this theory. This does not appear to be the whole story, however. Diabetics, who lack insulin (the hormone that allows cells of the body to absorb glucose), have very high glucose levels unless they receive this hormone. Yet untreated diabetics are almost always hungry, a finding that does not support the idea that hunger is produced by low blood glucose levels.

What may be a more important determinant of hunger than the absolute level of blood glucose is the difference between glucose levels in the arteries and those in the veins. When the difference between the levels is small, glucose metabolism is low and hunger results. This is why untreated diabetics, who metabolize little glucose, are constantly hungry.

The bulk of the research evidence today suggests that glucoreceptors by themselves are only moderately important in the regulation of food intake. Other systems seem to work along with them to regulate feeding.

Fats. Food that is eaten in excess of what is needed is converted into fat (*lipids*) and stored in fat deposits in the body. If there is insufficient food, these fat deposits are metabolized and used as a source of energy. It seems quite reasonable that the brain might regulate the amount of fat stored in the body by regulating food intake. The amount of lipids circulating in the blood might therefore serve as a cue for hunger. This hypothesis proposes that neural receptors monitor the availability of lipids in the body and in the diet. Indeed, rats and other animals do alter their food intake in response to changes in the quantity of fats in their diet (Friedman, 1978), which suggests that some mechanism, possibly a lipid detector, monitors sources of energy other than glucose.

Learning and Other Factors. Sensory characteristics of food, such as taste, smell, and temperature, are all very important in determining what and how much we eat. Many animals show strong innate preferences for certain foods, such as the human preference for sweet-tasting foods.

Most food preferences in human beings are learned, however, and can often be easily changed. Social and cultural factors play a major role in determining what we will and will not eat. Would you look forward to a meal of raw fish and seaweed? How about a snack of walrus blubber? It all depends on your background and experiences. Learning can also be important in other animals. A rat which eats a novel-tasting food is more likely to develop a preference for it if the animal was very hungry when it first tasted the new flavor.

Dislike for a novel flavor is also learned quite easily. Many animals can learn to avoid a taste that has been associated with illness. John Garcia and other researchers have extensively studied this phenomenon, known as *taste aversion learning*, in rats, birds, coyotes, and human beings. If a rat eats food with a distinctive taste and later becomes sick because a drug or other treatment has been administered with the food, the rat will refuse to eat more food with that taste, even if it is very tasty and the rat very hungry.

People also show this kind of learning. In one study, children who were receiving chemotherapy treatments for cancer were given a specially flavored ice cream shortly before they experienced the nausea produced by the treatment. Some weeks later, the children showed a conditioned aversion to the specific flavor of ice cream they ate, but not to other flavors of ice cream (Bernstein, 1978). A learned taste aversion developed in the children, even though they knew from long experience that their nausea was produced by the drugs and not by the ice cream.

Learning plays other roles in regulating feeding behavior. We learn to eat at certain times of the day. When the clock says noon, many people feel that they should eat lunch, even though they may not be particularly hungry. Even the sight of foods that we have learned are tasty can stimulate hunger and eating behavior.

SIGNALS FOR SATIETY

Stomach Factors. Earlier, we saw that an empty stomach is not the key factor in feeling hungry and that a full stomach is just one factor that signals *satiety*. How stomach factors alter hunger-motivated eating behavior is a complex question. In an experiment demonstrating the importance of stomach factors, Davis and Campbell (1973) allowed rats to eat until they were satiated. Then some of the food was removed from the stomach through a small tube. A short time later, when the rats were given access to food again, they ate almost exactly the same amount of food as had been removed. This and many other studies suggest that the stomach does inform the brain how full it is. But then, why doesn't simple bulk in the stomach, such as an inflated balloon or lettuce, lead to feelings of satiety?

In answer to this question, one researcher has suggested that some of the receptors important to satiety may respond to the concentration of various nutrients in the stomach rather than to stomach fullness (Deutsch, 1978). Because many of these receptors are deep in the folds of the stomach wall, they will be stimulated only by exposure to the nutrients when the stomach is stretched by a meal. This suggests that both the quantity and the quality of food is important in sending messages of satiety to the brain.

Liver Factors. Researchers now believe that the liver may be one of the most important control sites for eating. Injecting a sugar solution such as glucose into the abdominal cavity of an animal provides an illustration of the liver's function: (1) most of the glucose will be absorbed by the liver, and (2) eating behavior will be suppressed. However, if the same amount of glucose is injected directly into the bloodstream or the brain, no such suppression of feeding occurs (Russek, 1971). This suggests that glucose receptors in the liver may be more important than glucose receptors in the brain for controlling food intake.

THE HYPOTHALAMUS AND EATING BEHAVIOR

So far, we have discussed several of the system variables involved in eating behavior. We have seen how it is influenced by body weight, the amount of body fat, learning, and glucose concentrations in the blood. Now we will turn our attention to those brain mechanisms that are involved in feeding. Many of the control systems that regulate eating behavior are located in a tiny region of the brain known as the *hypothalamus*. The hypothalamus is a collection of neurons and fiber tracts at the base of the brain that is directly involved in the control of the *autonomic nervous system*, hormone release, and the organization of such survival-related behaviors as eating, drinking, and reproduction.

Long ago, physicians noted that tumors of the hypothalamus were often associated with extreme *obesity*, and it was speculated that some part of the hypothalamus might normally act to suppress eating. Some time later, Hetherington and Ranson (1939) reported that lesions of the ventromedial region of the hypothalamus caused overeating, or *hyperphagia*. For example, a rat with a lesion of the *ventromedial hypothalamus* (VMH) will double its weight during the weeks that follow surgery (see Figure 9.2). The lesioned animals gorge on palatable foods and become greatly obese. This phenomenon is considered to indicate that the missing VMH normally serves as a mechanism to stop eating.

Figure 9.2
A rat with a lesion on the ventromedial hypothalamus (VMH) will gorge on palatable foods and become greatly obese. (Dr. Neal E. Miller)

Lesions of the *lateral hypothalamus* (LH) produce quite the opposite effect on feeding behavior. LH lesions cause a strong suppression of eating and drinking. Feeding behavior after LH lesions goes through a series of stages. At first, there is a complete absence both of eating (*aphagia*) and drinking (*adipsia*). Even when food is placed in its mouth, the starving rat will spit it out. Generally, animals with LH lesions will die without force-fed nutrients and liquids. If an animal is kept alive by forced eating, it will eventually pass through a phase of undereating (*anorexia*), until finally it is able to regulate its body weight quite well. The basis of the LH syndrome is unclear, but the lesion may temporarily lower the animal's set point for body weight. It seems to act as if normal weight is too much.

The role of the hypothalamus in controlling eating behavior is not completely clear. However, we do know that the old idea that the hypothalamus contains the sole eating and satiety control centers is incorrect. More likely, the hypothalamus is a brain area that acts to integrate many different signals and mechanisms that influence eating and body weight.

OBESITY

Weight Regulation in the Obese. In the United States and many other developed countries, obesity is a major problem with both physical and psychological components. Overweight people spend enormous amounts of money on diet books, special foods, drugs, and other treatments to lose weight. Most of these people are unsuccessful. Often only a few pounds are lost despite intensive effort and substantial discomfort. Further, those who do lose weight almost invariably regain it. Only about 5% of dieters will lose 20 lb or more and not see those pounds return. Data from many careful studies provide strong evidence that the long-term maintenance of lowered body weight is extremely difficult, and some researchers feel that with our present state of knowledge, obesity is a nearly incurable condition (Bennett & Gurin, 1982; Grinker, 1982).

Much of this difficulty results from following advice or weight-control programs based on misconceptions about obesity. The first of these misconceptions is that overweight people lack willpower and eat much more than do thin people. Many studies show that this is generally not true—the obese usually eat only a little more, and often less, than people of normal weight (Stunkard, 1980). But if obesity is not related to excessive consumption of calorie-laden food, just what factors are involved?

The complete answer to this question is not currently available, but researchers have learned a lot about some of the variables that seem to be involved. A good way to conceptualize weight control is to think of body weight as being maintained at some *set point*, much the same way that body temperature is maintained at the set temperature of 37°C (98.6°F). It is not known whether this set point has a real physiological basis or if it is just a useful way of thinking about weight control. In any case, it appears that some people maintain their body weight at higher or lower set points than others. As noted earlier, most people and animals regulate their weight very precisely, varying little from year to year. Our internal regulatory mechanisms control weight much better than we could ever do consciously. Food intake is carefully balanced with energy expenditure so that body weight remains steady.

HIGHLIGHT 9.1
Treating Obesity

Almost invariably, overweight people are given advice such as "Eat less and exercise more." It is a simple prescription, and will work if followed long enough. Unfortunately, however, most obese people fail to control their weight. The obese person is often considered to be uncooperative or weak-willed by friends, family, and physician. But as we have already seen, many factors that regulate body weight are beyond one's conscious control, and are usually far more important than a conscious wish to eat less.

This does not mean that there is no hope for those who weigh more than they would like. Weight control and weight loss are complex problems, but most people can lose weight permanently. There are, however, no magic remedies, despite what one might read. Overweight people must remember that when they are trying to control their food intake, they are unusually responsive to those cues that initiate eating and must take steps to avoid them. They must also pay careful attention to the second part of the prescription above—exercise.

Exercise is important in any weight-loss program because it converts calories (a measure of food energy) into heat or mechanical energy: the more one exercises, the more calories are burned. Exercise also indirectly influences basal metabolic rate and may even lower the body's set point for weight. If one exercises infrequently, metabolism slows down, fewer calories are burned, and more are converted into fat and stored. The development of fat deposits, in turn, makes physical activity more difficult and unpleasant, leading to even less exercise—certainly a vicious cycle.

From Thompson, Jarvie, Lakey, & Cureton (1982).

Energy expenditure by the body depends on two factors: basal metabolic rate and general activity level (exercise). Basal metabolism accounts for about two-thirds of a normal person's energy use and is closely regulated by neural control mechanisms. When a person attempts to lose or gain weight, the central nervous system detects a change in the amount of food energy available, and alters metabolism and behavior either up or down to compensate for this change. To achieve a long-term change in body weight, one would have to work against these internal control mechanisms. This suggests that one cannot achieve long-term weight changes through acts of willpower. Many of the body's feeding mechanisms will attempt to keep the internal state constant. In studies where human volunteers or laboratory animals are either overfed or underfed and are then allowed to eat however much they want at mealtimes, body weight returns rather quickly to preexperimental levels.

Food Cues and the Obese. As noted earlier in this chapter, the taste, texture, and appearance of food are important in determining how much is eaten. One interesting research question is whether the obese respond differently to such cues than people of more normal weight. It appears that they do. In one study, obese persons ate much less ice cream which had been treated with a little quinine to make it taste bitter than did underweight subjects. On the other hand, when the ice cream was rich and tasty and not adulterated with quinine, the overweight subjects ate more of it than did the underweight participants. These results are shown in Figure 9.3. They indicate that taste factors are more important to the obese than to others.

285

FOCUS ON THE PSYCHOLOGIST

Judith Rodin

DR. JUDITH RODIN is a Philip R. Allan Professor of Psychology and also a Professor of Psychiatry. She received her Ph.D. from Columbia University in 1970. She has been elected to the Institute of Medicine of the National Academy of Sciences. Dr. Rodin has received a Distinguished Scientific Award for an Early Career Contribution to Psychology in 1977 and an Outstanding Health Psychology Contribution Award in 1980, both from the American Psychological Association. She was elected President of the Eastern Psychological Association from 1982 to 1983 and the Division of Health Psychology of APA from 1982 to 1983.

From my earliest work in psychology, my interests have focused on the interactions between mind and body. All of my research, regardless of the particular topical area at the time, has dealt with how psychological states and environmental factors affect physical health and illness, and reciprocally, the effects of these biological variables on cognitive and affective experiences. This question has led me to study obesity, aging, cancer and infectious disease, stress and coping, and the determinants of good health. In general, I believe that there is a dynamic interaction between psychological and biological variables that affects behavior, with one set of processes affecting the other in feedback loops.

When we began our work on obesity, most psychologists were focusing on the role of stress and anxiety or personality factors in promoting overeating. Stanley Schachter and his graduate students, of whom I was one, considered the hypothesis that responsiveness to compelling cues in the environment may be a major factor in promoting overeating and thus overweight. Thus, we saw overweight people as neither psychologically disturbed nor driven by internal longings and anxieties, but rather compelled to overeat because our environment is so stimulating in available food cues. Ultimately, that hypothesis was too simple, and I moved to a much more complex biopsychosocial approach in which genetic predisposition interacts with environmental responsiveness and current psychological and biological status to determine whether overeating leads to overweight. My students and I then found that being overweight led to major metabolic changes that can keep a person obese even with relatively minimal food intake. This was my first exposure to the fact that behavior may inexorably alter biological state in a way that determines the effects of subsequent behavior.

My work on aging has reflected this same underlying interest. With my students, I sought to challenge the prevalent view of inevitable biological decline with aging. Instead, we held the hypothesis that psychological and environmental changes associated with growing older may threaten a person's physical integrity and well-being, and thus lead to decline. This suggested that interventions affecting environmental and psychological changes with aging might actually alter or improve biological status. We tested and confirmed this hypothesis in numerous studies using a variety of psychological interventions and many different biological markers of improved health.

In recent years, I have made an effort to apply all of our work, in terms both of social change and clinical intervention. We are interested in the great increase in eating disorders among women, for example, because they reflect the incredible effects of social pressure toward thinness and the biological consequences of being responsive to such pressure. We have recently shown that repeated cycles of gaining and losing weight may be detrimental biologically and make weight maintenance extremely difficult. In fact, one of the reasons why purging has become so prevalent among former dieters, is that they can no longer lose weight as successfully as they once did by dieting alone. Trying to understand why women are so much more vulnerable than men to eating disorders has led us into the literature on the psychology of women, where we found, much to our amazement, virtually no research on how women (or men) view their bodies and its effects on their self-esteem. This is now becoming an exciting area of research for us as well.

Figure 9.3
Taste and obesity. The effects of food quality on the amount eaten by overweight and underweight individuals. (After Nisbett, 1968)

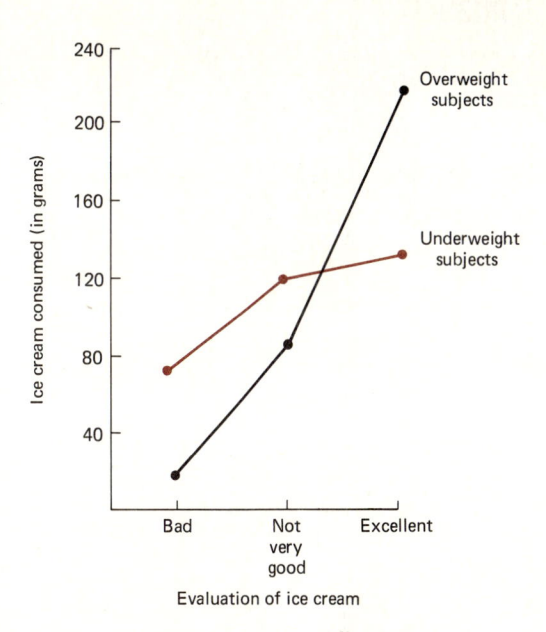

Obese people also seem to be more responsive to other kinds of cues. For example, Rodin (1981) demonstrated that a very graphic verbal description of highly delectable food prompted overweight people to eat more food than did those of normal weight who listened to the same description. Many other studies report very similar results, indicating that obese people are more responsive than others to cues associated with food.

THIRST

Most animals, including human beings, need water, and lots of it. Although most of us can go for weeks without food, no one can live for more than a few days without water. Water accounts for almost two-thirds of our body weight and is necessary for the proper functioning of most bodily processes. It is used in many chemical reactions, and to carry oxygen and other nutrients through the body. Water is also important in eliminating waste products. We literally cannot live without it.

SIGNALS FOR DRINKING

When you think of thirst, you probably think first of a dry mouth. Somewhat surprisingly, however, a dry mouth is not really very important in controlling fluid intake. People without functioning salivary glands do not drink more water, although they do drink much more frequently.

A more important factor seems to be the amount of water in the body cells. A water deficit decreases the amount of water in the fluid surrounding the cells, with a resultant increase in the concentration of salts in the fluid. This causes the water inside the cells to move across the cell membrane into the *extracellular fluid* (osmosis). As a result, the cells become dehydrated. A special class of cells called *osmoreceptors* located in the hypothalamus seem to respond to this kind of cellular dehydration. When cellular dehydration occurs, osmoreceptors react by generating the sensation of thirst. For example, when very tiny amounts of salts, sugars, or other substances that can cause cellular dehydration are injected into the area of a rat's brain where osmoreceptors are located, it will begin to drink even though it has no water deficit.

Drinking also occurs in response to a decrease in blood volume, even when there is no cellular dehydration. People who suffer injuries that cause a substantial loss of blood report being thirsty, as do many blood donors. The thirst that results from a decrease in blood volume is called *hypovolemic thirst*. The mechanisms that underlie the hypovolemic thirst system are not yet well understood. However, researchers do have some clues. They think that a decrease in blood volume is detected by *volumetric receptors* in the heart and kidneys.

The mechanisms that control the termination of drinking are not simply the reverse of the above, that is, the result of overhydration of the cellular and extracellular fluid compartments. When water is ingested, some of it is quickly absorbed into cellular compartments. This in itself reduces the urge to drink. The water also stimulates sensory systems such as those in the mouth, throat, and stomach, which monitor the amount of water taken in. As you can guess, learning is also quite important—we often just take a swallow or two of water and stop drinking long before the water has had a chance to be absorbed (Blass & Hall, 1976).

Primary drinking occurs in response to a loss of body fluids. (Anestis Diakopolous/Stock Boston)

HUMAN MOTIVATION

People are not motivated by biological drives alone. The desire to do well on an exam is not rooted in a biological need; nor is the desire to become rich, nor the desire to reduce human suffering. Motives such as these are generally termed *psychological motives* and are distinguished from *biological motives*, such as hunger and thirst. Human behavior is guided by a complex interaction of biological and psychological motives. Biological motives generally are considered to be more basic than psychological motives, but the latter can sometimes dominate the former, as in our society's preoccupation with dieting and thinness.

THEORIES OF HUMAN MOTIVATION

Most approaches to the topic of human motivation can be placed in one of three categories: instinct or biological theories, learning theories, and cognitive theories.

Instinct Theories. The belief that complex human behavior is propelled by instinct or innate factors is not widely held today, but it was at one time. For instance, McDougall (1926), one of the earliest social psychologists, identified a long list of instincts which he believed determined human social behavior. Included in this list were flight, repulsion, curiosity, pugnacity, self-abasement, self-assertion, reproduction, gregariousness, and acquisition. By the 1930s, instinct had dropped out of common usage in psychology, but the related concepts of impulse and drive were among the most widely used.

SOCIOBIOLOGY. The biological base of social behavior is once again controversial due to the new field of sociobiology. *Sociobiology* seeks to explain the biological bases of social behavior within an evolutionary framework (Barash, 1982; Wilson, 1978). It differs in significant ways from Darwin's model of evolution, however. For Darwin, the adaptiveness of behavior was judged in terms of its survival value for the individual and the species. Sociobiology, on the other hand, focuses on the adaptiveness of behavior for the individual's genes. According to Darwin, fitness was primarily a matter of surviving and reproducing. In contrast, sociobiology claims that it is not the individual but the genes that are trying to survive. Fitness is not simply a matter of self-reproduction but of gene reproduction. As a result, those behaviors that increase the survival chances of those with whom we share genes—our relatives—also assume evolutionary significance.

Altruism provides a good illustration of the old and new views of fitness and selection. For the model that emphasized group (species) selection, the existence of altruism posed a serious problem. How could altruism evolve in a species when its most altruistic members (those who risked their lives most often for others) would be the least likely to survive? Over time, altruistic genes should become increasingly less common in the gene pool, leading to the evolution of self-interest, not altruism. When we shift our focus from the group to the individual, however, we find a way out of this paradox. The tendency to show care and concern for individuals with whom the organism shares genes through common descent can be considered a special case of self-interest. If a person risks his or her life to save a relative (one with whom the person shares genes), he or she is, in fact, behaving in a self-interested fashion. Such action may result in death, but the person's genes will still be perpetuated. Moreover, the more genes that one person has in common with another, the more it is to the person's advantage (at least to his or her genes' advantage) to help the other.

Learning Theories. Why does a person expend great efforts to achieve an education or develop a skill? Is he or she biologically compelled? Most likely, the person has simply learned to achieve. People are motivated to work hard because they have been reinforced for working hard. Hard work is often instrumental in securing rewards they value, such as praise, money, and status. Other learning principles, such as observational or vicarious learning, are also relevant to human motivation. For example, observing the notoriety and attention that a daredevil receives may motivate observers to engage in dangerous behaviors themselves.

SELF-EFFICACY THEORY. One of the most recent learning theories of human motivation is Bandura's (1977a) theory of self-efficacy. *Self-efficacy* refers to the expectation that one can effectively cope with and master situations, and can bring about desired outcomes through personal efforts. Changes in motivation, according to this theory, occur through changes in one's sense of self-efficacy, or belief that "I can." To illustrate this theory, consider a person who takes up tennis. What factors will affect the person's sense of self-efficacy, and hence motivation, in this domain? One factor to which Bandura points is *past performance accomplishments*. If the person has performed well at other sports, his or her expectation of success will be high. *Vicarious experience* can also be important. Knowing that a friend of comparable athletic ability has recently become proficient will increase the person's sense of self-efficacy. *Verbal persuasion* is another factor influencing motivation. The more a person is encouraged by his or her friends, the greater will be his or her perceived self-efficacy.

People are motivated to strive or work hard because they value the reward it secures. (Tom Cheek/Stock Boston)

Cognitive Theories. Cognition involves thinking, perceiving, abstracting, synthesizing, and organizing information from the external world. Cognitive-motivational theorists believe that human beings are neither primarily propelled by biological instincts nor goaded by stimuli and environmental contingencies. Instead, they emphasize the way in which people process and construe the information in their world (Weiner, 1980).

One important cognitive capacity that influences human motivation is the ability to anticipate consequences. Anticipated consequences guide behavior in the same way as do actual consequences. We need not have experienced a car accident to be motivated to fasten our seat belts. Another important cognitive process is causal explanation (Ross & Fletcher, 1985). The impact that an event, such as a task failure, has on a person greatly depends on how that person explains the event. If he or she believes that a poor performance reflects low ability and is likely to be repeated, the person may not be motivated to try very hard in the future. On the other hand, someone who believes that the poor performance was due to low effort may be optimistic about his or her future performance and motivated to work harder. Similarly, our explanations for another's misfortune can significantly influence our motivation to help that person. If we blame a person for his or her misfortune, we tend to show the person much less sympathy than if we think the misfortune is not of his or her own making (Brickman, Rabinowitz, Karuza, Coates, Cohn & Kidder, 1982). The same stimulus event can thus produce very different levels of motivation, depending on the way the event is perceived or interpreted.

Most psychologists believe that human motivation is influenced by biology, learning, *and* cognition. To understand fully what factors control or influence social behavior, we must consider all three components. As an example, we will discuss aggression—one of the most significant and widely studied of all social behaviors.

MOTIVATIONAL FACTORS IN AGGRESSION

Human aggression is one of the most significant social problems facing contemporary society. It is impressive in both its frequency and destructiveness. Little wonder that the search for factors that motivate and control aggression has attracted such a large and diverse group of scientists. The question of why we are aggressive bears directly on the central question concerning human nature: Is it good or evil? Is aggression part of our genetic makeup, or does it reflect the influence of culture?

The Biological Component of Aggression. The argument for a strong innate basis to aggression has a long history in Western thought. One psychologist who emphasized this view was Sigmund Freud. Freud maintained that human aggressiveness stemmed from a universal *death instinct*, which he termed *thanatos*. According to Freud, the energy of the death instinct builds up in people until it pushes them toward self-destructive behavior, and ultimately suicide. To avert this fate, people tend to redirect this energy toward others. Freud was pessimistic about the possibility of eliminating human aggressiveness; he believed that the most that society could do was to provide nondestructive outlets for aggressive energy (e.g., competitive sports). Another scientist who believes that human beings, as well as other species, are innately aggressive is the Nobel-prize-winning ethologist Konrad Lorenz (1966). Unlike Freud, who did not specify where the death instinct came from, Lorenz contends that human beings are aggressive because aggression is an adaptive quality for any species. Two functions that an aggressive nature serves, Lorenz argues, are (1) to motivate members of a species to spread themselves over the available environment, thereby maximizing the use of its resources; and (2) to ensure that only the strongest and healthiest members of the species mate and reproduce. Unfortunately, there is little existing research to support the theories of Freud and Lorenz.

Konrad Lorenz. (Konrad Lorenz)

The sociobiological account of aggression is very similar to that of Lorenz. Both accounts consider aggression from an evolutionary perspective, although Lorenz focuses on group selection, whereas sociobiologists focus on gene selection. The major difference between the two positions concerns the conditions believed to evoke aggression. Lorenz believes that aggressive tension builds up in people and will explode out, regardless of the circumstances, if not routinely expressed. Sociobiologists do not share Lorenz's "steam boiler" image of human aggression, and emphasize instead its triggering by specific situations.

Human beings are probably selected for aggressive behavior under the following circumstances: when crucial resources are limited . . . ; when aggression leads to success, either in obtaining such resources or in further aggression . . . ; when experiencing pain or discomfort or frustration; when social systems are disrupted and there is opportunity for advancement or need to defend one's situation. (Dawkins, 1982, p. 352)

THE FRUSTRATION-AGGRESSION HYPOTHESIS. Another influential account of aggression is called the *frustration-aggression hypothesis* (Dollard, Doob, Miller, Mowrer & Sears, 1939). In this formulation, aggression stems from a *drive* that is aroused when a person's efforts to achieve a goal are frustrated. The tendency to aggress may or may not be biologically based, but the relationship with frustration is invariant: frustration always leads to the impulse to aggress, and aggression is always preceded by frustration. Furthermore, aggression is often *displaced* toward objects or persons other than the source of the frustration. Thus a student angry with her professor might kick a cat or insult her roommate.

Early research supported the frustration-aggression hypothesis, but it soon became clear that the link between them is far from invariant (Miller, 1941). Often when we are frustrated, we withdraw or become depressed rather than aggressing. Moreover, not everyone who aggresses is frustrated. Soldiers often attack and kill others out of patriotism or duty; public executioners and hired assassins regularly kill people whom they do not know simply because they are being paid to do it. Frustration is clearly not the only cause of aggression.

All biological and drive accounts of aggression share a pessimism about the possibility of controlling human aggression. Freud and Lorenz believe that aggression is "pushed out" of us by internal impulses, whereas drive theories, such as the frustration-aggression hypothesis, contend that aggression is "pulled out" of us by modifiable, but not totally avoidable, frustrations in day-to-day life. More optimistic are those theories which contend that aggression is a learned behavior.

The Learned Component of Aggression. Most contemporary psychologists reject the assumption that social behaviors, including aggression, are controlled by instincts or biological impulses. Our biological nature may define the range of our behaviors, but experience exercises the greatest control over our actions. Even sociobiologists (e.g., Wilson, 1978) acknowledge that the "genetic leash" on human beings is very long and permits considerable environmentally produced flexibility.

Experience controls our behavior through learning. Three types of learning have been implicated in the acquisition of aggressive behavior: (1) classical conditioning, (2) instrumental learning, and (3) vicarious learning.

CONDITIONING AND AGGRESSION. Most of the events that evoke aggressive behavior in people gain this capacity through learning rather than from genetic endowment (Berkowitz, 1980). Potent elicitors of aggression, such as

Frustration is a common cause of aggression. (Michael Hayman)

personal insults, verbal challenges, status threats, and provocative aggressive displays, do not instigate 2-year-olds to fight. Situations or people can elicit aggression through continuous association with anger or violence. Weapons are an example of a stimulus that can acquire *aggressive cue* value through their association with anger and aggression. In Berkowitz's (1968) words: "Guns not only permit violence, they stimulate it as well. The finger pulls the trigger, but the trigger may also be pulling the finger" (p. 22).

Toch's (1969, 1980) studies of chronic assaulters also illustrate how aggression elicitors are conditioned during natural social interactions. One of the violent people he interviewed reported suffering a humiliating beating as a youngster at the hands of an imposing opponent, a painful incident that determined his selection of future victims. Thereafter, he would become violent at any slight provocation by a large person. These characteristics so controlled his aggressive behavior that they overrode the potential risk of attacking powerfully built opponents.

REINFORCEMENT AND AGGRESSION. Aggressive actions are often followed by reward and thus tend to be repeated. The rewards achieved by aggression can be the elimination of some unpleasant state, such as pain or humiliation, or the acquisition of some more positive outcome. Buss (1961) has proposed three major classes of incentives that reinforce aggression in humans: gain of money, prestige, and status. Children learn the rewards of aggression very early. Patterson and Reid (1970) contend that children become aggressive because they learn that aggression enables them to control resources, such as toys and territories. Even when aggression results in punishment, such as criticism or spanking, the rewarding influence of the attention associated with these punishments may produce the stronger effect. It is sad but true that the fastest way for people to get national attention in our society is for them to commit some extreme act of aggression.

VICARIOUS LEARNING AND AGGRESSION. Albert Bandura (1983), the leading proponent of "social learning" theory, believes that we learn aggression not only by experiencing its payoffs, but also by *observing* others. Like other social behaviors, aggression can be acquired by watching others act and noting the resultant consequences. Bandura (1983) believes that in everyday life aggressive models are found most often in (1) one's family, (2) one's subculture, and (3) the mass media. There is considerable evidence for Bandura's analysis. For example, children of parents who discipline with physical aggression tend to use similar tactics when relating to others. Also, physically abusive parents tend to have been abused themselves as children (Straus & Gelles, 1980). The violent subculture of teenage gangs can also provide its junior members with numerous aggressive models (Cartwright, 1975).

The most controversial source of aggressive models is television. The average American family watches 3 to 5 hours of television a day (Nielson, 1981), and 8 to 10 programs contain violence (Gerbner, Gross, Signorelli & Morgan, 1980). Prime-time programs average 5 violent acts per hour; Saturday morning children's programs, almost 18 per hour. It is easy, therefore, to understand the widespread concern over the cumulative effect of violence on television. In one informal survey, 9 out of 10 prison convicts admitted that they learned new tricks by watching crime programs. Most startling, 4 out of 10 said that they had attempted specific crimes they had seen on television (*TV Guide*, 1977). More systematic research also indicates that watching violent television is linked to subsequent aggressiveness (Eron, 1982; Geen, 1983). The influence of violence against women in the media is a topic of particular current interest (see Highlight 9.2).

HIGHLIGHT 9.2
Aggression and Violent Pornography

A Presidential Commission on Obscenity and Pornography (1970) concluded that there was no evidence of adverse effects of pornography. More recent research suggests a less optimistic conclusion, however. Pornography, especially that depicting violence against women, *has* been shown to have negative effects. Donnerstein (1980), for example, found that exposure to violent pornography increased the amount of shock male subjects delivered to females in a laboratory situation. Repeated exposure to violent pornography has also been found to increase rape fantasies in males (Malamuth & Donnerstein, 1983).

Violent pornography can also influence people's perceptions and attitudes. The more violent pornography people are exposed to, the less disturbed they are by violent acts, such as rape (Malamuth & Check, 1980). A study reported by Malamuth and Check (1981) dramatically demonstrates the influence that viewing violent pornography can have on attitudes. These researchers showed 271 male and female college students two movies that contained numerous acts of violence against women (*Swept Away* and *The Getaway*). A week later these students were asked for their attitudes on certain issues, including several pertaining to violence against women. The attitudes expressed by these students were significantly more tolerant of violence against women than were those of students who had viewed nonviolent movies. For example, these students were more likely to *agree* that "Many women wish to be raped" than were the control group and were more likely to *disagree* that "A man is never justified in hitting his wife." These findings raise serious social and moral issues, especially since violent sexuality in the media appears to be increasing (Malamuth & Spinner, 1980).

The Cognitive Component of Aggression. The behavior of human beings is influenced more by perceptions, thoughts, attitudes, and values than is the behavior of any other species. The relevance of cognitive processes to aggression can be illustrated by considering three processes: the inference of intentionality, the anticipation of consequences, and the labeling of emotional states.

THE INFERENCE OF INTENTIONALITY. Slamming a door on another's fingers will sometimes provoke aggression from the injured person, and sometimes it will not. A major determinant of people's responses to events such as this is whether they perceive the other's actions as intentional or accidental. Unpleasant experiences produced by the "accidental" acts of others are much less likely to provoke aggression than are those resulting from intentional acts (Kulik & Brown, 1979). Our interpretation of these experiences influences our behavior more than does their objective features.

THE ANTICIPATION OF CONSEQUENCES. One determinant of whether a person behaves aggressively in a particular situation is the consequences that he or she anticipates (Bandura, 1983). A person is less likely to aggress if he or she expects retaliation or punishment. Indeed, it appears that one of the major reasons that alcohol consumption increases aggression is that it impairs people's ability to anticipate the consequences of their actions (Zillmann, 1979).

THE LABELING OF EMOTIONAL STATES. One reasonable response to the question "When do people aggress?" is "When they are angry." This analysis seems straightforward, but it suggests another question: What is anger? Probably the most common answer is that "anger is a specific emotional state produced by certain environmental conditions." Many psychologists would disagree with this statement, however. Rather than view anger as a specific emotional state, many psychologists prefer to view it as a label people apply to a general state of arousal which occurs in particular contexts (Zillmann, 1983). For example, aroused people who had just pumped an exercise bike or watched a film of a Beatles rock concert aggressed more when they were provoked than did nonaroused people (Zillmann, Katcher, & Milavsky, 1972). This research suggests that arousal produced by any means can be labeled anger and can lead to aggression if there are strong aggressive cues in the environment.

EMOTION

Emotions can activate and direct behavior in the same way that biological or psychological motives can. People will do all sorts of things to escape or avoid unpleasant emotional states as well as to obtain pleasant ones. Emotions frequently accompany motivated behavior. The failure to achieve, for example, may be accompanied by the emotion of sadness, just as success may be accompanied by the emotion of happiness or joy.

The distinction between motives and emotions is not clear. In general, we can say that an emotion arises in response to an event or aspect of the environment. Motives, on the other hand, tend to arise from internal stimuli (thirst, hunger, boredom, etc.) and are directed toward objects in the environment. This distinction is not entirely satisfactory, however. We all know that an external event, such as the presence of food, can arouse hunger in us; and anyone on a diet knows that a chronic state of hunger can give rise to emotions.

THE NATURE OF EMOTIONS

What exactly is an emotion? Two components are generally believed to make up emotional experience: physiological response and subjective feelings. When we experience an emotion, a variety of physiological changes occur, including:

1. The pupils of the eyes dilate.
2. The heart rate increases.
3. Breathing deepens and becomes more rapid.
4. The hairs on the skin become erect, causing "goose bumps."
5. Gastrointestinal movement stops as blood is redirected from the stomach and intestines toward the skeletal muscles.
6. The liver releases sugar into the bloodstream to increase energy.
7. Perspiration increases, while production of saliva decreases.

Emotional states also involve changes in subjective feelings. The English language has over 500 words used to describe emotions (Averill, 1975). Whereas there is general agreement that both physiological changes and subjective feelings are involved in emotional experience, there is considerable disagreement as to how these two components are related and how central they are to the nature of emotion.

The James-Lange Theory. Perhaps the most common understanding of emotional experience is that events in the environment (e.g., an attacking bear) trigger an emotional feeling (fear), which in turn gives rise to internal responses (perspiration, increased heart rate). Until about a century age, that was the accepted theory of emotion. At the end of the nineteenth century, however, William James, an American psychologist, and Carl Lange, a Danish physiologist, independently proposed a radically different theory of emotion. These researchers proposed that the bodily responses occurring during an emotional experience occur as a *direct* response to an environmental event or stimulus and that emotional feelings *follow* from these responses. In other words, physiological responses lead to subjective feelings rather than the other way around. According to this position, if there were no physiological changes, there would be no emotions. James (1890, pp. 449–450) states his position as follows:

> Common-sense says, we lose our fortune, are sorry and weep; we meet a bear, are frightened and run; we are insulted by a rival, are angry and strike. . . . My theory . . . is that the bodily changes follow directly the perception of the existing fact, and that our feeling of the same changes as they occur is the emotion . . . that we feel sorry because we cry, angry because we strike, afraid because we tremble, and not that we cry, or tremble, because we are sorry, angry or fearful, as the case may be.

Criticisms of the James-Lange position were swift and severe. The most compelling criticisms came from Walter Cannon (1927), a physiologist. Cannon's first criticism was that physiological patterns do not vary sufficiently to give rise to the great range of emotional experiences. The emotional experiences of ecstasy and anger, for instance, are quite distinct, yet the physiological patterns associated with each are quite similar. His second major criticism was that emotional reactions occur too quickly in most situations to be responses to physiological changes, which generally occur very gradually.

Despite the criticisms of the James-Lange theory, it still has some popularity. For one thing, with increasingly sensitive measurement techniques, researchers have recently been more successful in linking perceived emotional states to distinct physiological patterns (Fehr & Stern, 1970). Second, there is now reason to believe that the slowness of physiological reactions compared to emotional reactions may be accounted for by learning. Research indicates that the more experience people have in particular emotion-provoking situations, the faster their emotional reactions occur (Mandler, 1975).

The Facial Feedback Hypothesis. Recent evidence consistent with the James-Lange theory has also come from tests of the *facial-feedback* hypothesis (Izard, 1977). This hypothesis contends that our subjective experience of emotion comes from an awareness of our facial expressions. In other words, we are happy because we smile and sad because we frown. For example, when Laird (1974) induced college students to frown while electrodes were attached to their faces—"contract those muscles," "pull your brows together"—they reported feeling angry. Those induced to smile, on the other hand, felt happier and found cartoons more amusing. A study reported by Burns, Vaughan, and Lanzetta (1981) also confirms that people tend to experience the emotion that their faces are displaying. In this study, students observed a person receiving electric shock. Some of the observers were asked to make an expression of pain whenever the shock came on. Compared to observers not given this instruction, these grimacing students perspired more and had a faster heart rate whenever they observed the person being shocked. Acting the victim's emotion apparently enabled the observers to feel more empathy.

There is also evidence that posture affects emotion (Bull, 1951). People who are required to stoop and shuffle are inclined to feel unhappy regardless of their previous mood. It is not clear why this should be so. Perhaps posture gives rise to different physiological responses which we associate with different emotional states.

By way of summary, we can say that there is some evidence to suggest that subjective experience is influenced by visceral activity, but this is not the whole story.

The Schachter-Singer Theory. One of the studies that Cannon cited as evidence against the James-Lange theory was one conducted by Marañon (1924). Marañon first injected 210 patients with adrenaline, a drug that produces a pattern of physiological changes very much like that which occurs during strong emotion, then recorded the experience the patients reported. Seventy-one percent of the subjects reported only the immediate physiological reactions (and no emotion at all). The rest said they felt "as if" they were experiencing an intense emotion but could not identify what the emotion was. It was only when subjects were provided with emotion-provoking thoughts, such as the memory of a deceased parent, that they reported having "real" emotions.

The findings of Marañon (1924) impressed two psychologists, Schachter and Singer (1962), who proposed that emotions are a joint product of two factors: physiological arousal and cognitive appraisals regarding the source of that arousal. These researchers agreed with James that physiological arousal is a *necessary* condition for emotion, but they disagreed with James that such arousal is a *sufficient* condition. The major thrust of the Schachter and Singer formulation concerns the importance of the person's interpretation of the source of the physiological arousal. To be more specific, Schachter and Singer postulated that feedback from physiological arousal determines only the intensity of the emotion, while the cognitive appraisal of situational cues determines which, if any, emotion will be experienced. Thus precisely the same state of arousal might be experienced as joy, anger, sadness, or any variety of other emotions, depending on the kinds of cues present in the situation. If no emotional cues are present, or if the person has a nonemotional explanation for his or her state of physiological arousal, no emotion is likely to be experienced.

In an early test of their theory, Schachter and Singer (1962) manipulated physiological arousal by administering to subjects injections of either epinephrine (a hormone secreted by the adrenal gland) or a placebo (an inactive substance). Subjects were told that the injection was a vitamin supplement. Some of the subjects in the epinephrine group were provided with accurate information about the drug (e.g., they were told it would raise their heart rate or cause facial flushing); others were not given such information. All subjects were then exposed to the actions of an accomplice, who either behaved in a euphoric, playful fashion (e.g., he shot papers at a wastebasket) or demonstrated extreme anger while filling out an offensive questionnaire.

The feelings that subjects reported having were in line with Schachter and Singer's prediction. The reports of subjects who had been told of the drug's effect, and thus had a ready explanation for their arousal, were not

A general emotional state of arousal can be labeled *anger* and can lead to aggression, if there are aggressive cues in the environment. (Phyllis Greenberg)

influenced by the accomplice's behavior. In contrast, those not provided with this information appeared to rely on the confederate's behavior to help interpret their own feelings. When the confederate was euphoric, they tended to describe their own feeling as that of happiness; when the confederate was angry, they tended to describe their own feeling as that of anger. The results support the hypothesis that physiological arousal is important for the experience of emotion, but that the quality of the experience also depends on a person's appraisal of the situation.

Numerous studies support Schachter and Singer's prediction that arousal for which we have no ready explanation will be interpreted in ways consistent with external cues (see Zillmann, 1983). There appear to be some limitations, however. For one thing, it appears that people generally do not interpret unexplained arousal neutrally, but rather as feelings of unease or nervousness (Maslach, 1979). Thus it may be quite difficult to induce people to interpret unexplained arousal in positive terms, even in the presence of appropriate external cues (Marshall & Zimbardo, 1979).

EMOTIONAL EXPRESSION

Without a doubt, the most expressive part of our body is our face. But are our facial expressions controlled more by innate or cultural factors? Scientists debate the roots of emotional expression as well as the nature of emotions.

The Innate Component. Charles Darwin (1872) was one of the first scientists to contend that there is an innate basis to emotional expression. He claimed that certain expressions appeared in all human cultures. Subsequent work has supported Darwin's contentions. At least six different emotions are represented by distinct facial expressions: happiness, sadness, surprise, fear, anger, and disgust (Buck, 1983). The universality of these emotions is established in two ways (Ekman & Friesen, 1975). The first involves asking people from different cultures to imagine emotion-provoking events (a good friend has come to visit you; you find a dead animal that has been lying in the hot sun for several days), and then show by facial expression how they would feel in each case. The fact that people in different cultures respond with the same facial expression to each event supports the contention that at least certain expressions are universal. A second means of establishing the universality of emotional expression is to see if people from different cultures describe various facial expressions with the same emotional labels. Here, too, the evidence supports the universality hypothesis. A smile is interpreted as a sign of happiness, a scowl as anger, and so on, all over the world.

Additional evidence comes from the study of infants. Izard and his co-workers (Izard, Huebmer, Risser, McGinnes & Dougherty, 1980) videotaped the facial expressions shown by infants to various emotion-provoking situations (e.g., separation from their mothers, medical inoculations). The responses of adults to these videotapes indicated that even babies as young as 1 or 2 months can demonstrate discrete, recognizable emotional expressions. The fact that people who have been blind since birth display the same facial expressions as those who can see is also consistent with the innate link hypothesis (Buck, 1983).

The Learned Component. Although the case for an innate basis to emotional expression seems to be strong, learning is also important. Our biology may determine the facial expression that we adopt to demonstrate fear, but our culture is largely responsible for what makes us fearful and for how readily we express fear or any emotion. For example, in our culture it is bad manners to show disgust at being served an unappealing dish at a dinner party, whereas in other cultures such expressions are not discouraged and may even be encouraged. The *display rules* of a culture govern the when, where, what kind, how strong, and how long of emotional expression (Averill, 1980). Because of differences in *display rules*, universal tendencies in emotional expression may often be concealed.

Different emotions are represented by distinct facial expressions such as joy, sadness, and surprise. (Elizabeth Hamlin, Ellis Herwig, John Running/Stock Boston)

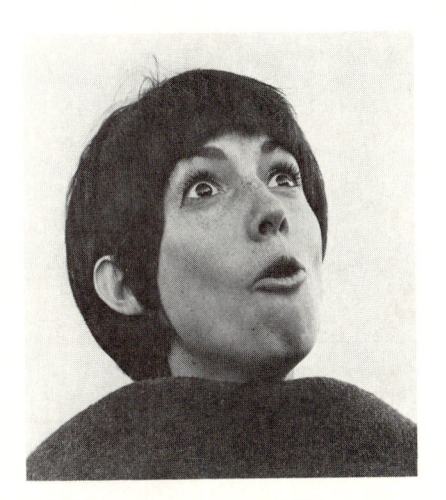

Figure 9.4
Plutchik's emotion wheel. The eight primary emotions (within wheel) combine to form eight secondary emotions (outside of wheel). (Source: Plutchik, 1980)

THE STRUCTURE OF EMOTIONS

How many emotions do we experience? How are these emotions related to one another? Debates over the structure of emotional experience have raged since the early Greek philosophers. Contemporary attempts to define the structure of emotions rely primarily on empirical procedures. The two most common ones require judgments about either facial expressions (Green & Cliff, 1975; Schlosberg, 1954) or affect-laden words (Plutchik, 1980; Russell, 1980). People's responses to these tasks provide evidence of both the number of separate emotions and of their relation to one another.

Dimensions of Emotion.   Consider sadness and elation. How are they related? Are they best described as two independent emotions, no more closely related than any others, or are they polar opposites? No clear answer has emerged. Some studies indicate that there are between six and twelve independent, *unipolar* factors of emotion, such as sadness, anxiety, anger, elation, tension, and so on (Curran & Cattell, 1975; Nowlis, 1965). Other studies indicate that emotions are better represented by between two and four *bipolar* factors (Russell, 1980; Schlosberg, 1954). Russell (1980), for example, contends that emotional states can be thought of as falling in a circular order in a two-dimensional bipolar space, the axes of which are interpreted as pleasure-displeasure and degree of arousal.

Plutchik (1980) has provided the most elaborate analysis of emotional experience. He had subjects rate 22 emotional words (*joyful, angry, frightened,* etc.) on a series of 34 adjective scales (good/bad, strong/weak, hot/cold, sweet/sour, etc.). When he plotted the responses of subjects, Plutchik found eight primary emotions (sadness, surprise, fear, disgust, anger, joy, anticipation, and acceptance) which fell in a circle (see Figure 9.4). Each primary emotion had its opposite, with disgust falling directly opposite acceptance, and sadness falling directly opposite joy. Plutchik also found that each emotion blended into the next, forming a second emotion, so that remorse turned out to be a mixture of disgust and sadness, love a mixture of joy and acceptance.

Recent work is clarifying the structure of emotional experience but controversy will continue for some time. The structure of emotional experience is important to understand because it is utilized in conceptualizing one's own state as well as the meaning of the facial expressions of others.

SUMMARY

1. Human and animal behavior does not occur randomly. It is directed toward specific goals, objects, or events. Motivation refers to the directing of behavior. Basic motives, such as hunger and thirst, are unlearned and are essential to life in both human beings and animals.

2. It is necessary for the body to maintain a constant internal environment. This state, called homeostasis, is preserved by a variety of regulatory mechanisms.

3. Hunger is the most intensively studied biological motive. A variety of cues signal the arousal and satiation of hunger. Many of the control systems that regulate feeding behavior are located in the hypothalamus.

4. Thirst is another important biological motive. We experience thirst when our body cells become dehydrated or we lose blood. Osmoreceptors located in the hypothalamus are believed to monitor cellular dehydration, while volumetric receptors located in the liver and kidneys are believed to monitor blood volume.

5. Human behavior is guided by a complex interaction of biological and psychological motives. Most psychologists believe that human motivation is influenced by biology, learning, and cognition.

6. Aggression is an example of a social behavior that is believed to have biological, learned, and cognitive components.

7. Emotions are distinct from motives or drives. They arise in response to an event or aspect of the environment. Motives, on the other hand, tend to arise from internal stimuli (e.g., hunger), and are directed toward objects in the environment (e.g., food).

8. Emotions consist of physiological changes and subjective feelings. The James-Lange theory contends that the subjective (feeling) component follows from the physiological response to an external event. The Schachter-Singer theory contends that the subjective component is dependent on both physiological changes and the individual's cognitive appraisal of the situation.

9. Research suggests that there may be an innate component to emotional expression. Happiness, surprise, sadness, fear, anger, and disgust are communicated with the same facial expressions across a wide range of cultures. Learning is also important in emotional expression, though, especially concerning display rules.

10. There is little agreement on how many distinct emotions there are. On the basis of recent research, it appears that there are between 6 and 12 independent emotions.

KEY TERMS

Motivation
Homeostasis
Regulatory systems
System variable
Set point
Correctional mechanism
Glucoreceptors
Lipids
Taste aversion learning
Satiety
Hypothalamus
Autonomic nervous system
Hyperphagia
Ventromedial hypothalamus
Lateral hypothalamus
Obesity
Aphagia
Adipsia
Anorexia
Extracellular fluid
Osmoreceptors
Hypovolemic thirst
Volumetric receptors
Psychological motive
Sociobiology
Self-efficacy theory
Frustration-aggression hypothesis
Drive
Aggressive cue
James-Lange theory
Facial feedback hypothesis
Schachter-Singer theory
Display rules

SUGGESTED READINGS

Baron, R. A. *Human aggression.* New York: Plenum Press, 1977. A highly readable and comprehensive review of the psychological research on aggression.

Buck, R. *Human motivation and emotion.* (2nd ed.). New York: Wiley, 1983. A broad introduction to the psychological literature on emotions and motivation.

Franken, R. E. *Human motivation.* Monterey, Calif.: Brooks/Cole, 1982. A discussion of the general theories of motivation as well as specific types of motivation, such as altruism and drug addiction.

Weiner, B. *Human motivation.* New York: Holt, Rinehart and Winston, 1980. A general discussion of the major theories of motivation with special emphasis on cognitive theories.

PART FOUR

Development Over the Lifespan

10

Development: Infancy and Childhood

THE BEGINNING OF
   DEVELOPMENT: GENES
   AND HEREDITY
   MECHANISMS
Genes
Heredity-Environment
   Interaction
FEATURES OF PRENATAL
   DEVELOPMENT
The Period of the Ovum
   (Zygote)
The Period of the Embryo
The Period of the Fetus
Influences on Prenatal
   Development
The Birth Experience
DEVELOPMENT DURING
   INFANCY
Physical Growth
Sensory and Perceptual
   Changes
Infant Reflexes and Motor
   Development

Complex Behavioral
   Sequences and Infant
   States
Emotions in Infancy
Cognitive Changes During
   Infancy
Social Development in
   Infancy
DEVELOPMENT IN
   CHILDHOOD
Stability and Change in
   Psychometric Intelligence
   During Childhood
Language Development
The Social World of the Child
The Role of Play in Child
   Development
Influences of Television on
   Child Development
SUMMARY
KEY TERMS
SUGGESTED READINGS

If, as William Shakespeare said, all the world is a stage and all people its players, the human life span is the drama we all enact. The drama begins when parents share the pain and the joy of the childbirth experience. The acts that follow involve the infant rolling from his or her back onto his or her stomach and beginning to crawl; the toddler making his or her first, tentative steps; the child, on the first day of school, with one eye on the new teacher and the other on the all-too-quickly departing parent; the early ado-

305

lescent spending hours gazing in the mirror wondering about complexion, about hair style, and about love; two young adults making a commitment to share their lives together; the middle-aged adult striving for success on the job and trying to find time for family, friends, and relaxation; the aged person, retired, and perhaps alone, contemplating the end of his or her life cycle.

Most people are fascinated by the changes that constitute the human life span. These changes are also of central concern to those psychologists who study *development*. *Development refers to systematic changes in a person across his or her life.* In this chapter we describe some of the major features of development from conception through the end of childhood.

THE BEGINNING OF DEVELOPMENT: GENES AND HEREDITARY MECHANISMS

Development begins at *conception*. Conception refers to the time when the reproductive or germ cell (the sperm) of the father fertilizes the germ cell (the ovum) of the mother. With this fertilization a new cell is formed—a *zygote*—from which another organism will eventually develop.

The germ cells that unite at conception are "special" in that each contains only half the chemical units—termed *chromosomes*—necessary to form a new member of the species. In human beings there are typically 46 chromosomes in every cell of the body. However, in adults capable of reproduction, each spermatozoon or ovum has only 23 chromosomes. Thus in the zygote these two sets of chromosomes pair up to form a cell that has the normal human number of chromosomes. This process, which ensures that each parent will contribute to the offspring's characteristics and future development, is termed *genetic inheritance*.

Sex determination is an important illustration of how genetic inheritance is expressed. One of each set of transmitted chromosomes is sex-linked. That

Humans typically have 46 chromosomes in each cell of their body. (J. F. Gennaro)

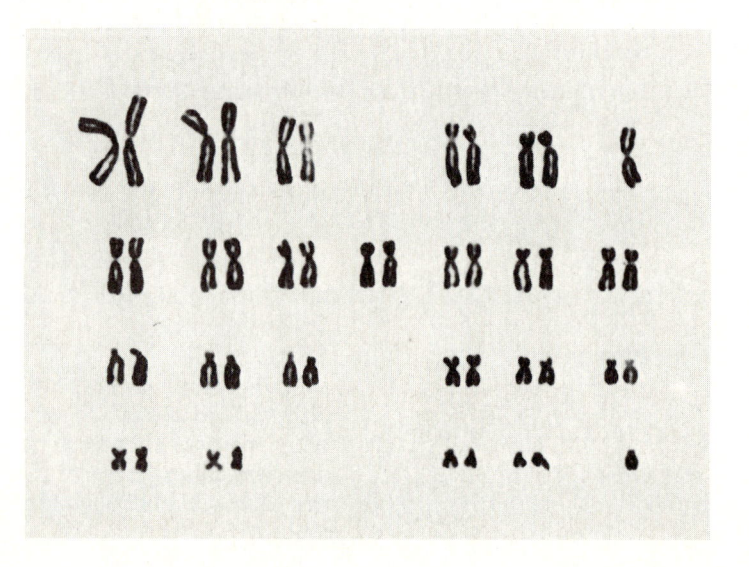

is, one of the 23 chromosomes in the male germ cells is either an X or a Y chromosome, while in the female germ cells there are only X chromosomes. Whether an X combines with a Y is largely a chance event, but if such a combination does occur, a male offspring will be produced. If the chance combination involves a match between an X from the mother and an X from the father, a female will be produced.

GENES

Chromosomes influence characteristics other than sex type. These numerous, complex influences occur through combinations involving the smaller chemical units found in each chromosome, units called *genes*. Each chromosome in a human cell is outfitted with thousands of genes, which are believed to line up along the threads of the chromosome. Scientists believe that each gene—or pair of genes or group of paired genes—carries a coded message that is responsible for a phase of development. This code is carried in the large molecules of protein, called *deoxyribonucleic acid* (DNA), that are found in the *nucleus* of every cell. Information from the DNA is transmitted from the nucleus to the rest of the cell, termed the *cytoplasm*. This transmission occurs through the influence of DNA on *ribonucleic acid* (RNA). RNA is a messenger; it carries the "code" contained in the DNA to the cytoplasm.

The vast number of combinations of genes—and the number runs into the trillions—contributes to the great diversity of the human species; indeed, the chance of any two people receiving the same combination of genes in the lottery of life and thus coming out exactly alike is less than 1 in 70 trillion (Hirsch, 1970). The only exceptions are identical, or *monozygotic*, twins—two children who come out of one fertilized egg cell (*mono* = single; *zygote* = egg) that splits into two separate ones after conception.

Often, two genes may be slightly different, although they form a pair and together handle an inherited characteristic. These genes are known as *alleles*. Since half of a child's genes come from each parent, a child has two alleles of each gene. If the alleles of both parents match, the child is *homozygotic* for that gene. If the alleles contributed by the parents are different, the child is *heterozygotic* for that gene.

Of course, all organisms have an environment within which they exist, and we may now ask: How do these two things—heredity and environment—contribute to human development?

HEREDITY-ENVIRONMENT INTERACTION

Genes interact with the environment to shape all structures and functions of the person. As discussed in a classic paper by Anastasi (1958), nature and nurture interaction may be conceptualized through reference to the concept of *norm of reaction*. We inherit from our parents a *genotype*, a set of genes. The concept of norm of reaction means that each genotype provides not one particular set of behaviors which may develop, but rather, a range of potential behavioral outcomes. What we see eventually resulting from our genotype, therefore, is the end result of a complex interaction of the environment and this range of potentials—this norm of reaction—represented by our genotype.

What we see, then, is the *phenotype*, which is defined as the outcome of our particular genotype-experience interaction. In other words, if we had had a different experiential history, another phenotype would have developed. Therefore, from any one genotype a virtually infinite number of phenotypes could develop.

To illustrate one way in which heredity (genotype) and environment interact to influence behavior development, consider processes of physical growth and maturation. Some may think that such processes are largely genetically determined. Yet growth and maturation are linked to environmental variables, especially those pertaining to nutrition. These interactions are discussed in Highlight 10.1.

To sum up, biological and environmental variables interrelate to influence development. As we have noted, such interaction occurs prior to birth and continues throughout life. But what are the features of development across life? Let us begin to answer this question by describing how the person changes before birth.

HIGHLIGHT 10.1
Nutrition and Infant and Child Development

Physical growth and maturation do not unfold independent of the environment. The nutritional adequacy of one's social context profoundly influences one's growth.

In infancy and early childhood malnutrition may lead to a disease which involves the halting of growth, tissue decay, and even death. Children in their early years may suffer from abdominal swelling, hair loss, changes in skin color, and lowered resistance to disease.

Malnutrition delays physical growth. But children have great recuperative powers, provided that the adverse conditions leading to malnutrition are not carried too far or continued too long (Harrison, Weiner, Tanner, & Barnicot, 1977). During a short period of malnutrition, the organism slows its growth and, as Harrison et al. phrase it, "waits for better times" (p. 343). When the better times come, growth takes place unusually fast, until it reaches the normative trajectory. Weight, height, and skeletal development seem to catch up at about the same rate.

Females appear to be better buffered against the effects of malnutrition or illness. They are less easily "thrown off" their normative growth trajectories than are males.

The earlier the malnutrition, the worse its effects. Relative to body size, the caloric requirements for children are higher than those of adults. Thus infants' need for food is relatively greater than that of adults; infants need to grow while adults need to maintain. A 3-week-old baby quietly sleeping much of the time has a caloric requirement per unit of body weight more than twice that for an adult engaged in moderately heavy labor (Katchadourian, 1977). During an infant's first month of life, caloric requirements are highest—from 100 to 120 calories per kilogram of body weight. (These figures decline slowly until age 16 in males and 13 or 14 in females, and more rapidly thereafter, until the adult requirement of 40 to 50 calories per kilogram is reached; Holt, 1972; Katchadourian, 1977.)

Since severe malnutrition may interfere with nervous system (e.g., the brain) development—the specific form of damage depending on the age when malnutrition occurs—nutritional deficits may interfere with intellectual development in infancy (cf. Hetherington & Parke, 1979). For example, research in Central America found that malnourished children do not develop language as early as do better nourished children (Cravioto & DeLicardie, 1975).

Impairment of intellectual development in children associated with prebirth malnutrition seems most pronounced when the mother herself has a history of poor diet, when the malnutrition has been severe and long-lasting, and when poor nutritional factors are combined with poor postbirth social and economic factors (Hetherington & Parke, 1979, p. 87). Conditions of illness which preclude proper nutritional intake can also impair learning abilities, such as short-term memory and attention (Klein, Forbes, & Nader, 1975).

FEATURES OF PRENATAL DEVELOPMENT

Developmental changes occur from the moment of conception on. However, about 280 days pass between conception and birth. This span is divided into three periods.

THE PERIOD OF THE OVUM (ZYGOTE)

Taking about 10 to 14 days, the period from fertilization until the zygote becomes attached to the uterine wall of the mother is labeled the period of the ovum, or zygote. At the end of this period, the zygote is made up of several dozen cells and has developed tendrils by which it will attach to the uterine wall. When it does so, the next period of *in utero* (within the uterus) development begins.

Maternal nutrition is extremely important for healthy prenatal development. (David S. Strickler/Monkmeyer)

Malnutrition does not affect all aspects of growth equally. Katchadourian (1977) points out that a child's size and rate of growth seem to be more affected by malnutrition than is the shape of his or her body parts. Moreover, different nutrition backgrounds do not seem to affect body proportions. For instance, Greulich (1957) reports that children of Japanese ancestry who are reared in the United States are taller at all ages than are Japanese children born and raised in Japan, but the ratio of length of leg to total height is the same in the two groups.

As with physical growth, the effects of malnutrition can be counteracted. Early malnourished Korean children, adopted and raised by American parents in American homes providing good nutrition, performed at least as well on intellectual and achievement tests, given later in life, as did their American-born peers. But those Koreans who had suffered the most extreme early malnutrition performed less well than did those who were less malnourished (Winick, Karnig, & Harris, 1975). During infancy, Lester (1975) found that well-nourished Guatemalan 1-year-olds showed an orientation response to a sound, while malnourished infants did not show this important response at all. In turn, Brody and Brody (1976) found that 1-year-olds whose mothers had received protein supplements during pregnancy showed faster habituation (a form of learning) and longer attention than did children whose mothers had either received no supplements or one consisting of calories with less protein. Lloyd-Still, Hurwitz, Wolff, and Schwachmore (1974) found that the psychological effects of severe malnutrition during the first 6 months of life can be reversed if the infant is given adequate nutrition, stimulation, and a stable socioeconomic environment. In sum, the effects of malnutrition on infant and child physical growth and intellectual development occur in relation to a complex set of factors derived from other biological factors and the interpersonal, physical, and sociocultural context of the infant and child, and these effects can be remedied if appropriate contextual variation occurs.

THE PERIOD OF THE EMBRYO

The developing prenatal organism is termed an *embryo* from about the end of the second week after conception through to the end of the tenth week. During this period many significant changes occur. Indeed, from the time of initial fertilization to the end of the embryonic period, the organism grows 2 million percent (Hetherington & Parke, 1979).

The rapidly increasing number of cells begin to differentiate in this period. Three distinct layers of cells are formed. From the outer layer, the *ectoderm*, the skin, nervous system, hair, and nails will eventually develop. The muscles, bones, circulatory, and excretory systems eventually develop from the middle layer, *mesoderm*. From the inner layer of cells, or the *endoderm*, important components of the gastrointestinal system, the liver, lungs, several glands, and adipose tissue eventually develop.

A membrane covering the developing embryo—the *amniotic sac*—develops during this period, and this sac is filled with amniotic fluid. The fluid acts as a cushion against shocks or shoves the embryo may experience when, for example, the mother may fall or bump into something.

The *umbilical cord* also forms. It is an organ connecting the embryo to the uterine wall at a site called the *placenta*. The umbilical cord is a passageway for certain chemicals from mother to infant and from infant to mother. By the third week after conception, the head and the tail of the embryo can be seen, and the heart is formed and begins to beat. By the fourth week the embryo reaches a length of 0.2 in, and the mouth, liver, and gastrointestinal tract can be seen. By the fifth week arms, legs, and the beginning of eyes can be identified. The embryo reaches a length of about 1 in. by the eighth week after conception, and the face, mouth, eyes, and ears are well formed and identifiable. The formation of sex organs begins, and fingers and toes can be identified. During the ninth and tenth weeks after conception, the muscles and cartilage develop, and organs like the pancreas, lungs, and kidneys can be seen. The liver produces red blood cells during this time.

THE PERIOD OF THE FETUS

This last period of prenatal development lasts from about the end of the second month after conception until birth. Throughout the fetal period numerous major developments occur. Further growth and differentiation of the bodily organs and systems developed in the embryonic period continue here, and these organs all begin to function. For example, the fetus shows motor (muscular) behavior; it moves its head and trunk and can even respond to tactile (touch) stimulation. Spontaneous movements of the arms and legs occur by the end of the third month.

By 2 months after conception, the reproductive system begins to develop, and during the third month after conception, the fetus reaches a length of about 3 in. and weighs about 0.75 oz. During the fourth month after conception, the fetus attains a length of about 4.5 in., and by the end of the fifth the fetus reaches a length of about 10 in. (and a weight of about 8 oz). The eyes become completely formed and taste buds appear during the sixth month of gestation. During the seventh month, the fetus is *viable*; it can live if born. During the eighth month of gestation, the typical fetus is about 18 in. long and weighs about 5.5 lb. During the ninth month, the typical fetus completes its in utero growth, reaching a length of about 20 in. and a weight of about 7.0 to 7.5 lb.

INFLUENCES ON PRENATAL DEVELOPMENT

As a consequence of certain chemicals passing through the placental wall and into the umbilical cord, events and phenomena in the environment surrounding the infant can affect its development. Delivered through the mother, these often involve chemical agents that are harmful to the infant. Such agents are termed *teratogens*, and are often associated with physical malformations and behavioral disorders. Other characteristics associated with the mother, for example, her age, can also affect the infant's prenatal development. However, it is important to note that the time at which these potential influences act, in regard to when in the in utero developmental sequence they occur, plays an important role in their effect on the developing organism.

Effects of Maternal Nutrition. Poor nutrition in mothers is associated with several negative developments, both prenatally and postnatally. Mothers with poor diets (e.g., little protein, a lot of fat) are more likely to have miscarriages, premature births, stillbirths, longer labors, birth complications such as anemia and toxemia (a disorder involving high blood pressure), and babies more likely to die in early infancy or to have serious diseases later (Hetherington & Parke, 1979; Mussen, Conger, & Kagan, 1979; Tompkins, 1948).

Alcohol and Tobacco Consumption. Estimates are that over 80% of pregnant women in the United States drink alcohol and that 57% of pregnant women smoke (Hetherington & Parke, 1979). Each of these behaviors is associated with problems, prenatally and postnatally. The rate of premature births, aborted pregnancies, and low-birth-weight babies is higher for mothers who smoke than for those who do not (Frazier, Davis, Goldstein, & Goldberg, 1961). Similar differences are found when mothers who drink are contrasted with those who do not, and even moderate maternal drinking during pregnancy has been associated with problem behavior in infants (Landesman-Dwyer, Keller, & Streissguth, 1977). Heavy drinking by the mother can result in the infant having a disorder termed *Fetal Alcohol Syndrome* (FAS), a disorder marked by physical and mental problems. When pregnant women both drink and smoke, they further increase the chance of their child's having physical and behavioral problems.

Effects of Drug Use. In the late 1950s and 1960s many women took a tranquilizing drug—*thalidomide*—during their pregnancy, and the ingestion of this drug produced gross anatomical defects in the limbs of their infants. Similarly, at about this same time many women took the drug *diethylstilbestrol* (DES) to prevent miscarriage. However, it has recently been found that daughters of women who took DES have a higher-than-average probability of developing cancer of the cervix when reaching adolescence. If these daughters become pregnant, they also have a higher-than-average probability of pregnancy or birth complications. Mothers who are addicted to heroin or to morphine have infants who are also addicted. Often these infants are of low birth weight or are premature and are much more excitable and irritable than are babies born of nonaddicted mothers (Brazelton, 1970; Strauss, Lessen-Firestone, Starr, & Ostrea, 1973).

FOCUS ON THE PSYCHOLOGIST

Jerome Kagan

JEROME KAGAN received a Ph.D. in Psychology from Yale University in 1954 and, after a teaching assignment at Ohio State University and two years in the United States Army, went to the Fels Research Institute to work on a longitudinal project from 1957 to 1964. He went to Harvard in 1964 and has remained there since. During his twenty-one years at Harvard, his research has been focused on the development of cognitive and temperamental characteristics in children.

Richard Kearsley, Philip Zelazo, and I were studying the effect of day care on young infants during the first three years of life. Our need for political protection in a working-class area of Boston prompted the Chinese-Christian Church to volunteer as our patrons. In exchange for their help, we enrolled some Chinese-American children, as well as Caucasian children, in the investigation. That decision turned out to be profitable.

The main finding of the study was that the Chinese and Caucasian children differed in their psychological reaction to the unfamiliar. The Chinese children were generally more inhibited, timid, and vigilant than the Caucasians, and, most important for our current work, the Chinese children showed a high and stable heart rate when they were attending to events that required effortful processing of information. This is important because the display of a high and stable heart rate when performing mental work is one index of higher sympathetic arousal. The robust quality of that finding led me to initiate a small cross-sectional study to check on the replicability of the phenomenon within a group of Caucasian children. When the same relation emerged, we decided to initiate a major longitudinal study of two cohorts of Caucasian children, who were selected in either the second or third years of life. We have been following these children through their sixth year. The children who had been selected to be extremely inhibited and timid, on the one hand, or fearless and sociable, on the other (about 10 per cent of the normal population fall into each group) retained their salient characteristics across the preschool years. However, because our culture values the sociable over the timid child, very few extraverts became timid and vigilant, while a small proportion of the inhibited children became more sociable as a result of gentle parental socialization pressure.

About one half of the inhibited children show physiological signs, implying that a very specific circuit in the central nervous system is under higher arousal. One might call this circuit the stress circuit, and it involves the hypothalamus, pituitary, adrenal gland, reticular activating system, and sympathetic arm of the autonomic nervous system. When an animal, child, or adult encounters unfamiliarity, stress, or challenge, hypothalamic discharge has three different consequences. First, the pituitary secretes ACTH, which in turn causes the adrenal cortex to secrete cortisol. Second, the reticular activating system of the mid-brain discharges, causing an increase in muscle tension. Finally, the sympathetic nervous system is activated, causing changes in a variety of sympathetic target organs, including a rise and stabilization of heart rate, an increase in blood pressure, and dilation of the pupil. Many more inhibited than uninhibited children show all three expected signs of the hypothalamic discharge—namely, increased cortisol secretion to stress, increased muscle tension, a higher and more stable heart rate, and a larger pupil. Our current view is that a small proportion of children are born with a lower threshold in this stress circuit. It is not yet clear whether this lower threshold is due only to genetic forces or to a combination of genetic and prenatal factors.

It is of interest that many commentators on human nature have consistently written about the differences between sympathetically and parasympathetically dominated nervous systems. Pavlov regarded this distinction as one between strong and weak nervous systems. It is obviously related to Jung's differentiation between introverts and extraverts.

Maternal Diseases. Contraction of virus-caused diseases by the pregnant woman can produce severe defects in the infant. For example, even a mild contraction of *rubella* (or German measles) in early pregnancy can result in heart defects, deafness, cataracts, blindness, or mental retardation (Illingworth, 1975). Toxemia, a disorder involving high blood pressure, retention of fluid, and rapid and high weight gain, results in the death of 13% of pregnant mothers who contract it; about 50% of the unborn infants whose mothers contract this disease die (Illingworth, 1975; Lubchenco, 1976). Children who survive have an increased likelihood of mental retardation.

Maternal Emotional States. Emotional disturbance during pregnancy is associated with prematurity, miscarriage, prolonged labor, delivery complications, and infant hyperactivity, irritability, sleep problems, and irregular eating (Despres, 1937; Sontag, 1941; Ferreira, 1969; Joffe, 1969).

Maternal Age. The age of the mother when pregnant is associated with differences in the likelihood of prenatal and postnatal problems. About 6% of first babies born to mothers under the age of 15 years die in the first year of their lives—a rate exceeding 2.5 times that for first-time mothers in their early twenties (U.S. Bureau of the Census, 1980). Mothers under 15 years of age also face more risk of dying themselves; their rate of death is 60% higher than that for mothers in their early twenties. Walters (1975) notes that if infants are born to adolescent mothers, the chances of their having birth defects are much greater than for infants born to postadolescent mothers. In turn, women who deliver their first baby when over 35 years of age have much greater likelihoods of having more problematic pregnancies, labors, and deliveries than do younger women. However, most mothers—at all ages—will have normal, uncomplicated pregnancies and deliveries.

THE BIRTH EXPERIENCE

At the end of about 280 days labor and the birth process begin, ending with the delivery of the *neonate* (meaning newborn). The neonatal period, which is considered to last for about 7 to 10 days, includes the relatively brief period surrounding birth, the *perinatal period*.

Most infants have no complications or serious impairment as a consequence of their birth. Less than 10% of all infants (the rate is slightly higher in males and lower in females) have abnormalities, and many of these eventually disappear (Hetherington & Parke, 1979). The physical and behavioral conditions of the newborn in the perinatal period can be measured by use of a system developed by pediatrician Virginia Apgar. An *Apgar score* is given an infant 1 minute and 5 minutes after birth. The attending obstetrician or nurse rates the infant in the following way: *heart rate* (0 = absent; 1 = less than 100 beats per minute; 2 = 100 to 140 beats per minute); *respiratory effort* (0 = no breathing for more than 1 minute; 1 = slow and irregular breathing; 2 = good breathing with normal crying); *muscle tone* (0 = limp and flaccid; 1 = some flexion of the extremities; 2 = good flexion, active motion); *body color* (0 = blue or pale body and extremities; 1 = body pink with blue extremeties; 2 = pink all over); and *reflex irritability* (also rated on a 0, 1, or 2 scale). As may be obvious, the higher the score, the better the physical and behavioral condition of the infant. Apgar scores of between 7 and 10 indicate a good condition, a score of 4 possible difficulties, and a score of 3 or below that the infant's survival may be threatened, and immediate intervention is required in such a situation.

DEVELOPMENT DURING INFANCY

Most developmental psychologists define infancy as the first 2 years of life. All agree that it is a period within which major developments occur in virtually every aspect of a person's functioning. We shall describe some of the most important developments that occur in this period.

PHYSICAL GROWTH

The 24 months after birth involve considerable physical changes. For example, by age 2 most boys have achieved 49.5% of what will be their final adult height and most girls have achieved 52.8% (Bayley, 1956). In fact, in the first year of life alone, boys achieve 42.4% and girls reach 44.7% of their final height (Bayley, 1956).

However, during the first 2 years and, in fact, across the life span, different parts of the body grow at different rates. Before birth the head is the fastest-growing part of the body, attaining almost three-fourths of its final adult size by the time a person is born. In the first year of life, the trunk grows more than other bodily areas; from the end of the first year of life until puberty, the legs grow the most. Figure 10.1 illustrates that at different times of life a body part, like the head, may represent a different proportion of total body size.

Figure 10.1
Across the life span, a body part represents a different proportion of total body size. (Redrawn from Jackson, 1929, by permission)

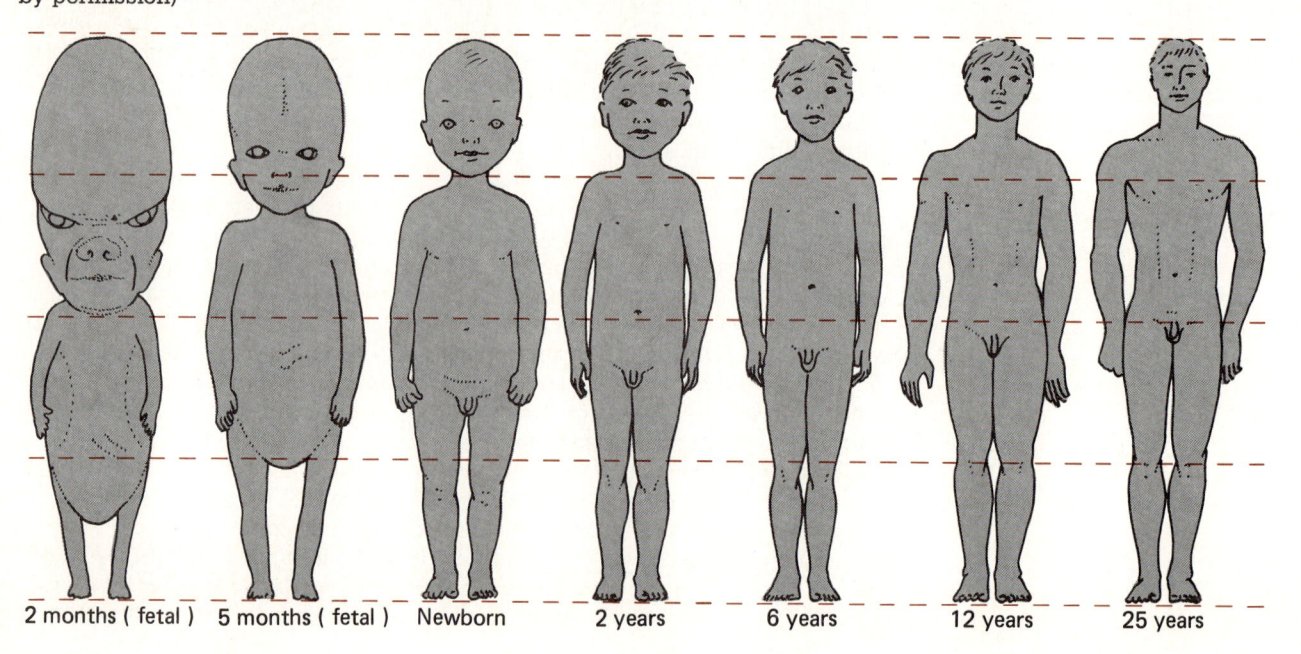

2 months (fetal)   5 months (fetal)   Newborn   2 years   6 years   12 years   25 years

SENSORY AND PERCEPTUAL CHANGES

There is a lot of sensory functioning in infancy. Moreover, as the person advances toward childhood, initial perceptual activity takes place, and this involves the role of associations acquired, for instance, through principles of associative learning (Chapter 6) and through preverbal instances of cognitive (e.g., memory) functioning (Chapters 6 and 7).

In regard to taste perception, newborns have been found to suck at different rates on a nipple in relation to whether the nipple contained glucose or sucrose (two sweet-tasting substances), or water (Engen, Lipsitt, & Peck, 1974). In fact, in one study of 1- to 3-day-old infants (Nowlis & Kessen, 1976), increases in strength of the sucking response were directly associated with increases in concentrations of these sweet-tasting substances.

Infants' hearing is well developed. Sounds can be localized, and sounds of differing loudness and duration will be responded to differently (Brackbill, 1970). For example, Muir and Field (1979) reported that most newborns turned their heads toward a continuous sound source presented 90 degrees from the midline of their heads. Similarly, at birth and at 1 month of age, infants can turn their heads to an off-centered sound (Field, Muir, Pilon, Sinclair, & Dodwell, 1980). Moreover, by 16 weeks of age, binaural cues can be detected (Bundy, 1980).

Considerable research has been conducted on vision in infancy. While newborns cannot focus their eyes well at all distances (Fantz, Ordy, & Udelf, 1962)—that is, they do not show good accommodation—they do respond differently to light and dark (Fantz et al., 1962), see color (Bornstein, Kessen, & Weiskopf, 1976; Fagan, 1974), can discriminate separations between stimuli (i.e., they show visual acuity; Fantz et al., 1962), and can follow a moving stimulus (Bower & Paterson, 1973; McKenzie & Day, 1976).

From early in their lives infants seem to respond more to stimuli that have some meaning to them; for example, they respond more to a patterned than to a nonpatterned stimulus. Moreover, infants show preferences for the more meaningful of two stimuli. Fantz (1961), for example, found that infants showed more *attention* to—as measured by length of time their eyes fixated on—a picture of a bull's-eye than to a plain red, white, or yellow stimulus. Moreover, he found that more patterned stimuli than the bull's-eye were given even greater attention by the infants. A stimulus having newspaper print was fixed on longer than the bull's eye. Most interesting in the work of Fantz (1961) and others (Hainline, 1978), a stimulus pattern that looked like a face was shown the most attention of all.

INFANT REFLEXES AND MOTOR DEVELOPMENT

The infant does more than just receive stimulation or attach meaning to stimulation. The infant can act on its world from the first moments of birth onward. The newborn has a large repertoire of *reflexes*. Reflexes are *relatively invariant motor outputs* (i.e., muscular movements) *in response to particular sensory input* (e.g., stimulation). For example, neonates blink in response to light tactile (touch) stimulation of the cheek, and they show the *rooting reflex*; that is, infants turn their heads toward the stimulation.

Of course, neonatal reflexes are not the only motor behavior shown by the infant. Considerable nonreflexive, complicated motor behavior is also seen. Table 10.1 lists norms for the attainment of particular motor behaviors (Bayley, 1935; Gesell & Amatruda, 1941; Shirley, 1933).

TABLE 10.1
Some norms of infant motor development

Motor Behavior of Infant	Normative Age (months)
Raises chin while lying on stomach	1
Raises chest while lying on stomach	2
Sits with support	4
Sits without support	7
Stands with help	8
Stands by holding furniture	9
Creeps	10
Walks when led	11
Pulls self up to stand	12
Climbs stairs	13
Stands alone	14
Walks alone	15
Goes up and down stairs without help	18
Can run and walk backward	24

Source: Adapted from Gesell and Amatruda (1941) and Shirley (1933).

COMPLEX BEHAVIORAL SEQUENCES AND INFANT STATES

The development of the infant's reflexive and motor functioning is involved in an array of more complex sequences of behavior. These behaviors are those often involved in allowing the infant's survival as a biological organism; they involve infants' sleep and waking patterns, their toileting behavior, and their eating and drinking behavior. Table 10.2 summarizes some developmental changes in these functions.

EMOTIONS IN INFANCY

Emotions are present even in newborns. For instance, smiling, screaming, or crying are behavioral signs that the newborn is experiencing emotions. The presence of different emotions is useful to infants. It helps them communicate to their caregivers. Emotions provide signs to caregivers about whether a situation or a stimulus is experienced as pleasurable or unpleasurable (e.g., painful), and therefore emotions help the infant to interact socially with caregivers. For instance, an infant's smile tends to elicit a similar reaction from a caregiver, and cries typically lead a caregiver to try to soothe an infant (Bell, 1974; Gewirtz & Gewirtz, 1968).

Human infants smile very early, within the first week of life, and smiling follows a developmental sequence. The earliest type of smiling is the spontaneous or reflex smile, evoked by stroking the infant's cheek or lips (Gewirtz, 1965). During the first several weeks of life spontaneous smiling occurs frequently when the infant is in a particular state of sleep, one wherein rapid eye movement (REM) occurs (Emde, Gaensbauer, & Harmon, 1976). Between the end of the first month of life and the end of the second, infants' smiles start to be elicited by social stimuli, for instance, the face or voice of a parent. By 4 months of age smiling is seen often with another emotion, laughter (Sroufe, 1978).

During the fifth and sixth months of life the infant begins to use the emotions of caregivers as information about how to react emotionally (Campos, 1980–81). In an ambiguous or strange situation, an infant will look to his or her caregiver. If the caregiver is smiling, the infant will also smile; if

TABLE 10.2
Changes in sleep and waking cycles, toileting, eating, and drinking behaviors in infancy

Cycle of Behavior	General Characteristics
Sleep and waking cycles	Neonatal period: sleep 80% of time per day
	6 to 7 months: sleep through the night without awakening
	12 months: sleep 50% of time per day
Toileting behaviors	Neonatal period: involuntary release of waste products
	2 months: usually two bowel movements per day
	4 months: predictable interval of time between feeding and bowel movement
Eating and drinking behaviors	Neonatal period: seven to eight feedings a day
	1 month: five to six feedings a day
	2 months: solid foods introduced
	12 months: three meals a day

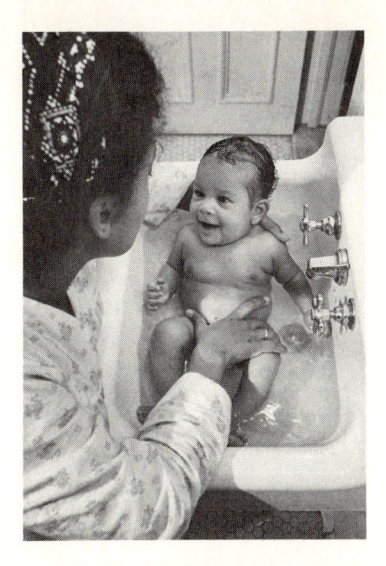

Smiling is a behavioral sign that an infant is experiencing pleasure and that tends to elicit a similar response from a caregiver. (Chester Higgins, Jr.)

the caregiver shows fear, the infant will also show fear (Campos & Stenberg, 1981; Feinman & Lewis, 1983). Campos (1980–81) labels this phenomenon as *social referencing*, that is, the use of social information by an infant in determining the infant's own emotional reactions.

In sum, infants show emotions from their first days of life onward (Sroufe, 1979). However, while you or we know typically when we are happy, sad, angry, or afraid, it is not likely that infants are actually aware of—actually know—their own emotional state until they are about 1 year old (Lewis & Brooks, 1978), that is, until they begin to develop a self-concept (Yarrow, 1979). Development of a concept of self requires, of course, cognitive development on the part of the infant. Emotions, then, not only relate to the infant's social world, and thus his or her social development, but emotions also relate to other key aspects of the infant's development; his or her cognitive development.

COGNITIVE CHANGES DURING INFANCY

During infancy, the person's intellectual, or cognitive, capacities undergo marked development. These processes have been studied in several different ways. One approach is associated with the *psychometric* (mental measurement) study of cognition. To understand this approach we have to discuss how developmental psychologists measure an infant's intelligence. A second approach is most identified with the theory and research of Jean Piaget. We shall discuss both of these means to understand intellectual functioning in early life.

Measures of Infant Intelligence. Since infants lack language, one cannot question them the way one can with other children in tests of intelligence. One can assess babies' sensory and motor behaviors—and indeed this is what most infant tests of intelligence actually do—but such measures are not very similar to those found on tests of intelligence aimed at older children (Lewis & McGurk, 1972). Understandably, scores from infant intelligence tests are not highly related to intelligence measured at subsequent child, adolescent, or adult levels (Bloom, 1964).

Nevertheless, although infant "intelligence" tests are thus best thought of as measures of sensorimotor maturity rather than of abstract mental abilities, they can indicate when extreme variations from normative sensorimotor development exist *in the infancy period*. In such cases test results may signal potential developmental problems. Several tests measure the sensorimotor status of the infant. Some of them are noted in Highlight 10.2.

The Theory of Jean Piaget (1896–1980). Piaget proposed that cognitive development progresses through phases. He cast this proposal in the form of a *stage theory* of development. Stage theory holds that all people pass through a series of qualitatively different levels of organization in an invariant sequence. Thus stages are seen as universal levels of progression which may not be skipped or reordered. The only possible individual differences are in the rate one passes through stages and in the final level of development reached. Some people's development may not proceed, for instance, because of illness or death; but *if* they had developed, they would have progressed in the specific sequence.

> **HIGHLIGHT 10.2**
>
> # Tests of Infant Sensorimotor Status ("Intelligence")
>
> There are several tests with which psychologists can measure an infant's sensorimotor abilities. Four of the most frequently used ones are:
>
> 1. *Bayley Scales of Mental and Motor Development* (Bayley, 1933, 1968): This test is one of the most often used measures of infant intelligence. Some of the items on this test are: (a) Can the infant follow a moving object with his or her eyes at about 2.5 months of age?; (b) Can the infant reach for an object with one hand at about 13 months?; (c) Can the infant put round blocks in round holes at about 17 months? Other items involve grasping objects, turning the head to follow objects, and at older ages, imitating simple actions and drinking from a cup.
> 2. *The Gesell Developmental Schedules* (Gesell & Amatruda, 1947): This test is divided into four areas of development. It covers the age range from 4 weeks to 6 years (i.e., well beyond the infancy age level). Motor behavior is assessed through items relating to such behaviors as holding the head erect, sitting, standing, creeping, and walking. Adaptive behavior is assessed by such behaviors as eye-hand coordination and problem solving. Language behaviors and social behaviors are also assessed.
> 3. *The Cattell Infant Intelligence Scale* (R. B. Cattell, 1947): This test is designed to measure children within the ages of 2 to 30 months. The test uses items from the Gesell schedules, from the Stanford-Binet, and from other tests as well. Some items involve following movement with the eyes, lifting the head, and use of the finger.
> 4. *The Brazelton Neonatal Behavioral Assessment Scale* (Brazelton, 1973): The test is used with infants in the first 10 to 14 days of their lives (i.e., during their neonatal period). The test measures on infant's responses to the environment through taking neurological and behavioral assessments. Scores are based on the infant's best performance. Items involve behaviors relating to changing responses to a rattle and to a pinprick, alertness, and motor maturity. However, behavioral capabilities believed to reflect the quality of the parent-infant relationship are the focus of the assessments (St. Clair, 1978).

Stage-Independent Conceptions of Cognitive Development. Some of what Piaget proposes are principles of cognitive development that apply to all stages of development. Cognition is always organized and is always an adaptive system. Its functioning allows the person to adapt to the environment and thus to survive. Piaget believes that the process of adaptation is divided into two *always* functioning complementary processes: *assimilation* and *accommodation.*

Cognitive assimilation involves changing one's knowledge about some object to fit one's already existing knowledge. For example, an infant may have knowledge of its mother's breast, gained through its *actions* on this external stimulus object. The infant has sucked on its mother's nipple and has thereby come to "know" the mother's breast. The person develops an internal cognitive structure from its actions on an external stimulus. Thus to Piaget the basis of knowledge lies in action. Assimilation occurs when, for instance, the infant discovers its thumb and begins to suck on it as it did the nipple.

Accommodation involves altering the subject to fit the object. Cognitive accommodation involves altering already existing cognitive structures in the person to match new, external stimulus objects. The infant could accommodate to its thumb, rather than assimilate it, by acting on the thumb not as it did on its mother's nipple, but rather by altering its actions. Such a change in action would modify the already existing cognitive structure. Rather than matching the object to his or her present cognitive structure, the infant—through making different actions—matches the object.

A person's adaptation to the environment involves a balance—an equilibrium—between the activity of the person on the environment (assimilation) and the activity of the environment on the person (accommodation). Thus assimilation and accommodation are seen as complementary processes. Piaget terms this balancing process *equilibration*, and contends that it is the moving force behind cognitive development. Whenever the person alters the environment, incorporating it into an already existing internal structure, there must also be a compensatory alteration of the person's structure to match the objects in the external environment. There must be a balance in action—and thus of all knowledge—between person and environment.

Stages of Cognitive Development. Piaget (1950, 1970) describes four stages of cognitive development. People may differ in their rate of development through a stage, but some rough age boundaries for each stage can be indicated. Although only the first stage in his theory relates to infancy, it is useful to discuss all four of the stages.

Piaget labels the first stage *sensorimotor* and suggests that it lasts from birth through about 2 years. Changes in this stage involve the development of what Piaget terms *schemes*. A scheme is an organized sensorimotor action sequence; the sequence of action involved in the scheme is always the same and cannot be reversed. It is similar to a reflex such as an eye blink, in which a puff of air always precedes and leads to an eye blink.

For much of the early portions of the sensorimotor stage, the infant's cognitive development could be described as "out of sight, out of mind." The infant interacts with objects in the external world but acts as if their existence depended on his or her sensing them (Piaget, 1950). When objects are not in the infant's immediate sensory world, the infant acts as if they do not exist. The infant is *egocentric;* there is no differentiation between the existence of an object and sensory stimulation provided by that object (Elkind, 1967).

Jean Piaget (1896–1980) proposed a stage theory of development that holds that all people progress through a series of qualitatively different levels of organization in an invariant sequence. (Anderson/Monkmeyer)

There is no knowledge that objects exist permanently independently of the subject. Thus there is no scheme of object permanency.

There are numerous instances of the infant's lack of a scheme of object permanency. For example, the child acts as if a person or object appears and disappears by virtue of going into and passing out of sight. Only as a consequence of repeated sensorimotor actions will a child develop an internalized representation of an object and come to know that it exists even though he or she is not perceiving it. When this occurs, the child has "conquered the object" (Elkind, 1967).

The second stage in Piaget's theory, the *preoperational stage*, is usually associated with ages 2 through 6 or 7. The major cognitive achievements in this stage involve the elaboration of *representational ability*. The most obvious example of the development of representational systems is language; words are used to symbolize objects, events, and feelings. Other indications of representational ability in this stage involve the emergence of *symbolic play* (as when the child uses two crossed sticks to represent a jet plane) and of *delayed imitation* (as when a child sees daddy smoking a pipe and pacing across the room and repeats the act hours later).

Cognitive development in the preoperational stage has limitations. The child in this stage is also egocentric, but here the egocentrism involves a failure to separate the symbol of the subject from the object in the real world. The child can symbolize objects with words but fails to differentiate between the words and the things to which the words refer. For example, the child believes that the word representing an object is inherent in it, that an object cannot have more than one word to symbolize it (Elkind, 1967). The child does not know that an object is independent of the word symbolizing it.

As a result, the child acts as if words carry more meaning than they really do (Elkind, 1967). One indication of this inability may be the preoperational child's failure to show *conservation,* the ability to know that one aspect of a stimulus array has remain unchanged, although other aspects have changed. To illustrate, imagine a 5-year-old with a mommy doll and a daddy doll. Six marbles are placed beside the daddy doll in positions directly corresponding to the mommy doll's marbles. The materials would look like those in Figure 10.2(a). If the 5-year-old is shown this arrangement and asked, "Which doll

Imitating a parent's behavior is one of the major achievements of the preoperational stage in children (ages two through six or seven). (Erika Stone)

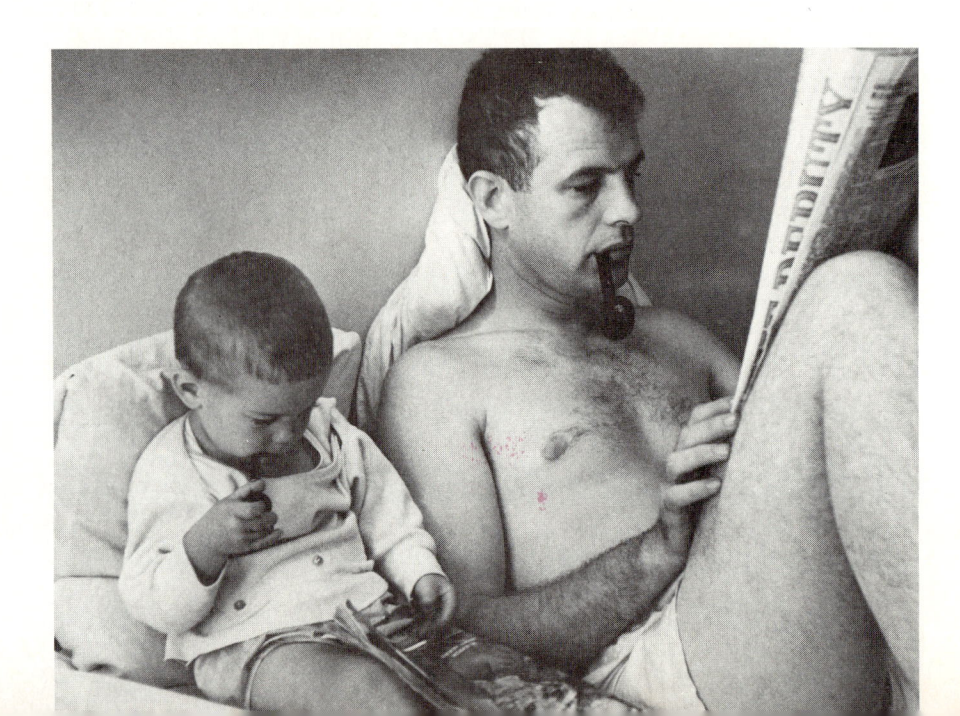

Figure 10.2
Examples of a test of number conservation.

has more marbles to play with—the mommy doll or the daddy doll, or do they both have the same?", the child would probably say that both dolls have the same. However, if the mommy doll's marbles are spread out like those in Figure 10.2(b), the preoperational 5-year-old will say that the mommy doll has more! This is an example of the inability to conserve numbers. The child does not know that one aspect of the stimulus array—the number of marbles—has remained unchanged, although another aspect of the array—the positioning of the marbles—has changed.

Until a child enters the *concrete operational stage* (from about 6 to 7 years of age through 11 or 12 years), the child's cognitive structure is composed predominantly of schemes, which cannot be used to mentally reverse various physical actions because they are reflexlike. The emergence of *operational structures* gives the child this ability. An operation is reversible. Unlike schemes, operations allow one to know that actions can be counteracted by reversing them. Moreover, operations *are* internalized actions. People in this stage do not have to see a clay sausage being rolled back into a ball to know that one can return the clay to its original shape. They can just think of this action. Their thought about concrete, physical actions does not require them actually to see these actions. They can reverse the actions in their heads and come to the same conclusion about them as if they had actually seen them happen.

Despite the accomplishments involved in the concrete operational stage, there are limitations of thought. That is, although the child can deal with objects internally, actions and objects must have a concrete, real existence. The label for this stage is *concrete operational*, meaning that thought is bound by concrete, physical reality. That is why things or events that are *counterfactual*—that are not actually present in the real world—cannot be understood by the concrete operational child.

If someone asks you to imagine that coal is white and then asks you to indicate what color coal would be when burning at its hottest, you would probably have an answer to this counterfactual question. You might think that since coal is actually black and when burning at its hottest is white, then if it were white, it would be black when burning at its hottest. The point here is *not* the particular solution, but your ability to deal with the counterfactual question. The concrete operational child cannot do this. For example, the response might be, "But coal is black!" (Elkind, 1967). In essence, a major limitation of concrete operational thought is that it is limited to thinking about concrete, real things.

The last stage of cognitive development in Piaget's theory is termed the *formal operational stage*. It begins at about 11 or 12 years of age and continues for the rest of life, according to Piaget (1972). In this stage, thought becomes hypothetical in emphasis. Now discriminating between thoughts about reality and actual reality, the child comes to recognize that his or her thoughts about reality have an element of arbitrariness about them, that they may not actually be real representations about the true nature of experience. Thus the

TABLE 10.3
Piaget's stages of cognitive development (in years)

Stage	Approximate Age Range	Major Cognitive Achievement	Major Cognitive Limitation
Sensorimotor	0–2	Scheme of object permanency	Egocentrism: lack of ability to differentiate between self and external stimulus world
Preoperational	2–6 or 7	Systems of representation; symbolic functioning (e.g., language, symbolic imitation)	Lack of conservation ability; egocentrism: lack of ability to differentiate between symbol and object
Concrete operational	6 or 7–12	Ability to show experience-independent thought (reversible, internalized actions); conservation ability	Egocentrism: lack of ability to differentiate between thoughts about reality and actual experience of reality
Formal operational	12–	Ability to think hypothetically, counterfactually, and propositionally	Egocentrism: imaginary audience, personal fable

Source: Adapted from R. M. Lerner (1976).

child's thought about reality take on a hypothetical "if . . . then" characteristic: "*If* something *were* the case, *then* something else would follow." In forming such hypotheses about the world, the child's thought can be seen to correspond to formal, scientific, logical thinking. This emergence accounts for the label applied to this stage—the formal operational stage.

Table 10.3 summarizes the main features of the four stages of cognitive development in Piaget's theory.

SOCIAL DEVELOPMENT IN INFANCY

All human beings are born into a social world. Social interaction—with mothers, fathers, siblings, grandparents, and even other infants—is a major part of an infant's life.

Infant-Caregiver Interactions. Both parents and infants can influence the others' behavior. For example, vocalizations by the infant are exchanged with parental vocalizations and perhaps also with touching. The looking behavior of an infant elicits more maternal vocalization than its touching behavior, but maternal touching and vocalization appear to evoke equal levels of infant vocalization.

Thus infants and their caregivers exist in a reciprocal social relationship. Not only is there evidence that the infant's skill in such social interactions increases throughout the infancy period, but there is also reason to believe that such development has important implications for other facets of the infant's functioning. Farran and Ramey (1980) report that those infants who have higher scores on measures of involvement with infant-mother interactions also show evidence of higher intellectual performance at 20 months of age.

Attachment in Infancy. An important means by which an infant becomes socially active is by establishing an *attachment* with his or her primary caregiver. Ainsworth (1973, p. 2) stresses that the "hallmark of attachment is *behavior* that promotes proximity to or contact with the specific figure or figures to whom the person is attached" (Ainsworth, 1973, p. 2, italics added). Actually, attachment is a very complex phenomenon. If infants are deprived of their attachment figure (e.g., their mother), they often cry or show other signs of distress. In turn, if infants have a secure attachment relation with their primary caregiver, there is evidence that the basis of healthy social development is formed.

Matas, Arend, and Sroufe (1978) studied the relation between the quality of attachment in infancy and the quality of play and problem-solving behavior at 2 years of age. When tested at 2 years of age, infants who were securely attached at 18 months of age were found to be more enthusiastic, persistent, and cooperative than were infants of the same age who were insecurely attached. Similarly, Waters, Wippman, and Sroufe (1979) found that secure attachment involves more than the absence of negative or maladaptive behavior directed toward a caregiver. In comparison to anxiously attached 18-month-old infants, securely attached ones smile more and combine this smiling with vocalizing and/or showing toys during free-play periods. Thus if infants have secure, reciprocal relations with their caregivers, healthy development will be likely. But what if infants are seriously deprived of such interaction?

Effects of Social Isolation and Deprivation. In a series of classic studies, Harry F. Harlow arranged to have rhesus monkeys reared by surrogate cloth or wire monkeys. Harlow sought to find out if the ties infants showed to mothers, for example, were due more to the food they provided or to the warmth and comfort they delivered. Two "wire monkeys" were placed in the infant monkey's cage. One wire monkey delivered food through a nipple. The other was wrapped in a soft cloth but did not deliver food. All other features of the monkeys were identical. Harlow (Harlow & Harlow, 1962; Harlow & Zimmerman, 1959) found that except when feeding, the infant clung more often to the cloth-wrapped "monkey," the one, Harlow contended, that provided "contact comfort." In times of stress the infant was also most likely to cling to the cloth mother.

As part of these investigations, Harlow had to isolate the infant monkeys from their real mothers, and thus Harlow's studies of mothering were also studies of social isolation or of deprivation of social interaction with particular members of one's species. Much of what is known about the effects of social isolation comes from these studies.

SOCIAL ISOLATION IN RHESUS MONKEYS. Human infants cannot be studied the way one studies rhesus monkeys. Thus, although we cannot necessarily generalize to human beings the results of studies done on nonhumans, at the very least, such studies provide hypotheses about the role of social interaction in humans.

There have been numerous studies of the effects of early social deprivation in rhesus monkeys (e.g., Harlow & Harlow, 1962, 1966, 1970). Monkeys socially isolated for the first 6 months or longer show extremely abnormal patterns of behavior when removed from isolation. These problems often persist into adulthood. For example, after 3 months of social deprivation, an infant monkey removed from isolation avoids all social contact and buries its head in its arms and crouches (Fuller & Clark, 1966a, 1966b). Monkeys isolated 6 months or longer develop abnormal social and sexual behavior during their adolescence and adulthood (Harlow & Harlow, 1962). Indeed, Suomi and Harlow (1972, p. 166) note that the longer monkeys are "denied the opportunity to interact with peers, the more gross are their social in-

After three months of social deprivation, an infant monkey avoids all social contact, buries its head in its arms, and crouches. (Sponholz/Monkmeyer)

adequacies." However, the effects of such social isolation are not irreversible. In fact, following on the observation of Suomi and Harlow (1972), several studies have shown that the effects of social isolation in rhesus monkeys can be revised by exposing monkeys reared in isolation to peer monkeys (Chamove, 1978).

SOCIAL ISOLATION AND DEPRIVATION IN HUMAN CHILDREN. Children in certain institutions often experience some social isolation. In the 1940s, several studies found that children who spend the first year of their life in understaffed institutions do not develop as adequately as do children reared at home by their parents (e.g., Spitz, 1945, 1946). For example, in one study by Spitz, infants growing up in a foundling home were isolated from one another by sheets hung around most of their cribs; thus they received little social or visual stimulation. The children had few toys and were generally kept in their cribs for their first year of life. A second group of infants were reared in a nursery which provided a fairly stimulating environment. Spitz found that the two groups of children became increasingly dissimilar as they aged. The foundling-home children lagged further and further behind the other children. They also developed severe behavioral and emotional problems. In fact, Spitz concluded that "while the children in 'Nursery' developed into normal healthy toddlers, a two-year observation of 'Foundling-home' showed that the emotionally starved children never learned to speak, to walk, to feed themselves. With one or two exceptions . . . those who survived were human wrecks who behaved in a manner of agitated or of apathetic idiots" (Spitz, 1949, p. 149) who "would lie or stare with wide open, expressionless eyes, frozen, immobile faces and a far away expression as if in a daze, apparently not perceiving what went on in their environment" (Spitz & Wolff, 1946, p. 314).

In a more recent study, Provence and Lipton (1962) studied physically healthy infants who were living in an institution that provided appropriate nutritional and medical care but low levels of social stimulation. By the end of the first year of life, the children came to resemble those studied by Spitz—although these institutionalized infants had not differed from normal home-reared ones in the first months of life.

Some studies show that such early social deprivation can have long-lasting effects on human beings. Goldfarb (1945, 1947) studied one group of children who left an institutional setting for a foster home during the first year of their lives and a second group of children who remained in an unstimulating orphanage for the first 3 years of their lives before leaving for foster homes. Goldfarb assessed each group when they were just over 3, 6, 8, and 12 years old. On all measures, the second group was inferior to the first. Children in the second (i.e., institutional) group had difficulty forming close personal relationships and tended to be socially withdrawn.

The Reversibility of Early Deprivation Effects. Several studies suggest that negative effects of being deprived of social interaction can be reduced. For example, in a study by Skeels (1966), mentally retarded women served as substitute mothers for a group of institutionalized infants, and the infants' social and intellectual development markedly improved. Similarly, early deprivation has been reversed in other studies (e.g., Clarke & Clarke, 1976; Kagan & Klein, 1973).

DEVELOPMENT IN CHILDHOOD

The childhood years of life involve both constancy and change. Many of the developments begun in infancy are continued through these later periods. This is continuity. But new cognitive, social, and physical characteristics also develop. This is change. In this portion of the chapter we discuss the continuities and changes that characterize childhood.

STABILITY AND CHANGE IN PSYCHOMETRIC INTELLIGENCE DURING CHILDHOOD

If you can read and understand this book, you have at least above-average intelligence. Did a correspondingly high level of intelligence exist before your present age level? Said another way, would a measure of one's cognitive ability taken in the very early school years have served as a good basis for predicting one's current intellectual level?

Bayley (1949) studied a group of people from birth to age 18 years. Using different tests of intelligence at succeeding age levels to measure subjects appropriately, Bayley related IQ scores at one age to those of other ages through use of a statistic termed the *correlation*. A correlation may vary from −1.0 to +1.0, with values closer to +1.0 indicating a strong, positive relation between two sets of scores. A positive correlation means that as scores in one set of measures increase, so do scores in the other set. A negative correlation means that as scores in one set increase, scores in the other decrease. A correlation "coefficient" of +.75 between height and weight, for example, would mean that greater height was associated with greater weight.

Bayley (1949) found that intelligence at age 1 year was not related to intelligence at age 18 years. The correlation between IQ scores from these two age levels was .0 (there was no relationship whatsoever). The correlation between IQ scores at 2 years and at 18 years was +.41; between 4 and 18 years, +.71; and between 11 and 18 years, +.92. Thus there is a rapid movement toward consistency of IQ scores across the early years of life. This movement toward consistency slows during adolescence. By age 18 years, IQ scores have become stable for a time. One reason for the low relation between early childhood intelligence and adolescent intelligence is that what is measured at age one is not akin to what is measured at age 18. At the earlier period, measures involve sensorimotor behavior, while at the later period, they involve such abilities as verbal reasoning and mathematical concepts. There is little reason to expect scores on these two types of tests to relate to each other across age, since even when such tests are administered at the same point in life (e.g., adulthood), they are not correlated (Bloom, 1964; Cronbach, 1960). However, as tests at age levels beyond 1 year come increasingly to include measures of abilities akin to those measured at age 18 years, there is a corresponding increase in the correlation; thus there seems to be an increasingly greater "overlap" (J. E. Anderson, 1939; Bloom 1964) in IQ scores.

LANGUAGE DEVELOPMENT

One of the most fascinating accomplishments for the young child is the acquisition of language. This seemingly effortless ability to acquire sounds, words, and grammatically correct sentences is a complex and creative task. In the early stages of language development, the child's speech is not simply a poor copy of adult speech; rather, it is complex and governed by rules. By about the age of 5, the child will be using a language that in many ways is almost as sophisticated as that of an adult. In Chapter 8 we discussed several theories of language acquisition. Here we focus on a description of some of the major features of language development.

Stages of Vocalization. Before uttering a first real word, the infant proceeds through a number of stages of early vocalization.

UNDIFFERENTIATED CRYING (BIRTH TO 1 MONTH). During this stage of early vocalization, the newborn signals all of his or her needs by crying. The crying is called undifferentiated because a listener cannot distinguish between the infant's cries of pain, hunger, and fear. Undifferentiated crying in the newborn is a reflexive action.

DIFFERENTIATED CRYING (2 MONTHS). During this stage of early vocalization, which develops at about 2 months of age, the crying is more distinguishable to the adult; therefore, it is termed differentiated crying. There are different patterns and pitches to signal hunger, pain, or distress, and it appears to be a better means of communication for the infant.

BABBLING (3 OR 4 TO 8 MONTHS). The next stage of early vocalization is *babbling*, which is the repetition of simple vowel and consonant sounds like "ma, ma, ma" and "da, da, da." At this stage the infant produces phonemes, the basic sound units of the language. Babbling is a universal phenomenon that occurs most often when the baby is alone and contented (Lenneberg, 1967).

LALLATION (6 TO 8 MONTHS). This stage begins around 6 to 8 months. Unlike babbling, lallation involves the imperfect or accidental imitation by babies of their own sounds and those of others, setting the stage for communication.

ECHOLALIA, OR IMITATION (9 OR 10 MONTHS). This stage of early vocalization, or the prelinguistic period, occurs when the infant consciously imitates the sounds that he or she hears. The infant now begins to respond differently to adult speech, and by the end of the first year, infants can discriminate among the basic phonemes and reproduce adult language. During these stages of prelinguistic development there is increasing evidence that the child can comprehend language, although he or she cannot produce it.

PATTERNED SPEECH (1 YEAR). This final stage of early vocalization begins at about 1 year of age, when the child consciously produces adult-like, intelligible sounds and, most important, uses them to communicate with others.

Stages of Linguistic Speech. Just like early vocalizations, once the child has acquired communicable speech, he or she proceeds to develop that speech through a series of stages.

ONE- AND TWO-WORD UTTERANCES. From ages 1 to 2, the child's speech is comprised of one-word utterances, used to communicate and to function as sentences. At about 2 years of age, they begin to combine words into two-word sentences, such as "Where Mommy" and "Allgone shoe." These two-word combinations increase slowly, and seemingly suddenly, there appear to be many of them. At this time, the child is also beginning to discover some of the simple rules of grammar.

EARLY SENTENCES. According to Roger Brown (1973), who conducted a longitudinal study of the development of language in three children, there are five stages of linguistic development. Brown and his colleagues contend that the best index of language development in the early stages is through *mean length of utterance* (MLU), which is measured in terms of *morphemes*, the smallest units of speech that have meaning. Morphemes include the words *to* and *dog* as well as parts of words that have meaning, such as *-ing*, *-ed*, *-s*, and other endings. Brown's first stage begins with the first two-word utterance, lasts until MLU = 2.0 morphemes (stage 1), and continues until MLU = 4.0 morphemes (stage 5).

Girls seem to go through these stages earlier than boys. For example, Schachter, Shore, Hodapp, Chalfin, and Bundy (1978) studied male and female young children aged about 2 to 2.5 years. The sexes were matched for age, class, and race. The girls in the youngest group were significantly advanced in both MLU and in the length of their longest utterances; similar advancements were seen among girls in the older groups.

STAGE 1 SPEECH. During stage 1, the earliest sentences are produced by the child. These sentences are sometimes termed *telegraphic* because they are abbreviated versions of adult speech. They are comprised mainly of nouns and verbs. Thus the child often leaves out small words (such as *of* or *the*) and word endings from his or her speech. For example, instead of saying "I'll give you the doll," the young child might say, "I give doll" or "give doll."

The child is following simple rules of grammar at this stage in his or her linguistic development, as evidenced by putting words in the correct position and the tendency to make errors that are consistent with the rules he or she has learned. One type of error is *overgeneralization* or *overregularization*. For example, when first learning that adding an *-s* or an *-es* pluralizes a noun, a child might say "fishes" for more than one fish or "foots" or "feets" for more than one foot. Or when the child has learned that past tenses are formed by adding *-ed*, he or she may use this rule to make a past tense out of an irregular verb (e.g., "I goed").

STAGE 2 SPEECH. According to Brown, stage 2 starts with an MLU of 2.0 and extends to 2.5. At this time the children's sentences are becoming more and more complex; they learn prepositions, a few articles, irregular verbs, some verb tense inflection, plurals, and so on. These are not acquired simultaneously, nor are they used perfectly. These *grammatical morphemes* seem to be acquired in a remarkably *invariant* order. Why this happens is still not entirely known, but there is a definite constancy with which these morphemes appear in children's speech.

STAGES 3 AND 4 SPEECH. These stages cover the range from an MLU of 2.5 to 3.5. During these stages, vocabulary increases and grammatical rules are used more consistently.

STAGE 5 SPEECH. During this last stage, with an MLU of 3.5 to 4.0, all of Brown's subjects reached a major achievement: the construction of complex sentences in which two or more sentences are joined by the conjunction *and* ("You clap and I yell") or one sentence is embedded in another ("You hope you can go"). They also began to use complex sentences containing *wh-* clauses ("When I get older, I can go there").

In sum, in a relatively few months from the appearance of the first word (at 12 months), there are rapid changes in the number of words in the child's vocabulary and in the complexity of the child's sentences. Children typically begin to use two words together at about 18 to 20 months of age. By 28 months children can use three-word sentences, and within another 10 months—by a little over the third birthday—sentences like "Why he going to have some seeds?" "The station will fix it," and "Who put dust on my hair?" are heard (Brown & Bellugi, 1964). In fact, after about 5 years of age, most children have become so expert in their native language that they can correctly differentiate between grammatical and ungrammatical sentences (e.g., deVilliers & deVilliers, 1974).

THE SOCIAL WORLD OF THE CHILD

The social word of children is made up of parents and peers. These people affect the child, who, in turn, also influences them. We focus first on one major way in which parents influence their children.

Parental Childrearing Practices. In describing three general types of parental *caregiving practices*—authoritarian, permissive, and authoritative—Baumrind (1967, 1968, 1971, 1972) has identified clusters of parenting practices that may be seen in other independent studies. In addition, by showing that these different clusters are related differentially to child behavior, she has provided demonstrations of the role of the parent on a child's functioning.

One type of parent that Baumrind identifies is the *authoritarian parent*. This type of parent tries to shape, control, and evaluate the behavior and attitudes of the child in accordance with a set, absolute standard of behavior. This parent stresses the value of obedience to his or her authority. He or she favors punitive, forceful measures to curb "self-will" whenever the child's behaviors or beliefs conflict with what the parent thinks is correct. The parent's belief in respect for authority is combined with respect for work, order, and the traditional social structure. The authoritarian parent does not encourage verbal give-and-take. Instead, he or she believes that a child should accept the word of the parent about what is correct (Baumrind, 1968, p. 261).

A second type of parent Baumrind identifies is labeled the *permissive parent*. This type of parent attempts to accept and affirm the child's behaviors, desires, and impulses. The parent consults with the child about decisions regarding family "policy" and offers the child rationales for family rules. But the permissive parent presents himself or herself to the child not as an active "agent," with the responsibility for shaping or modifying the child's present

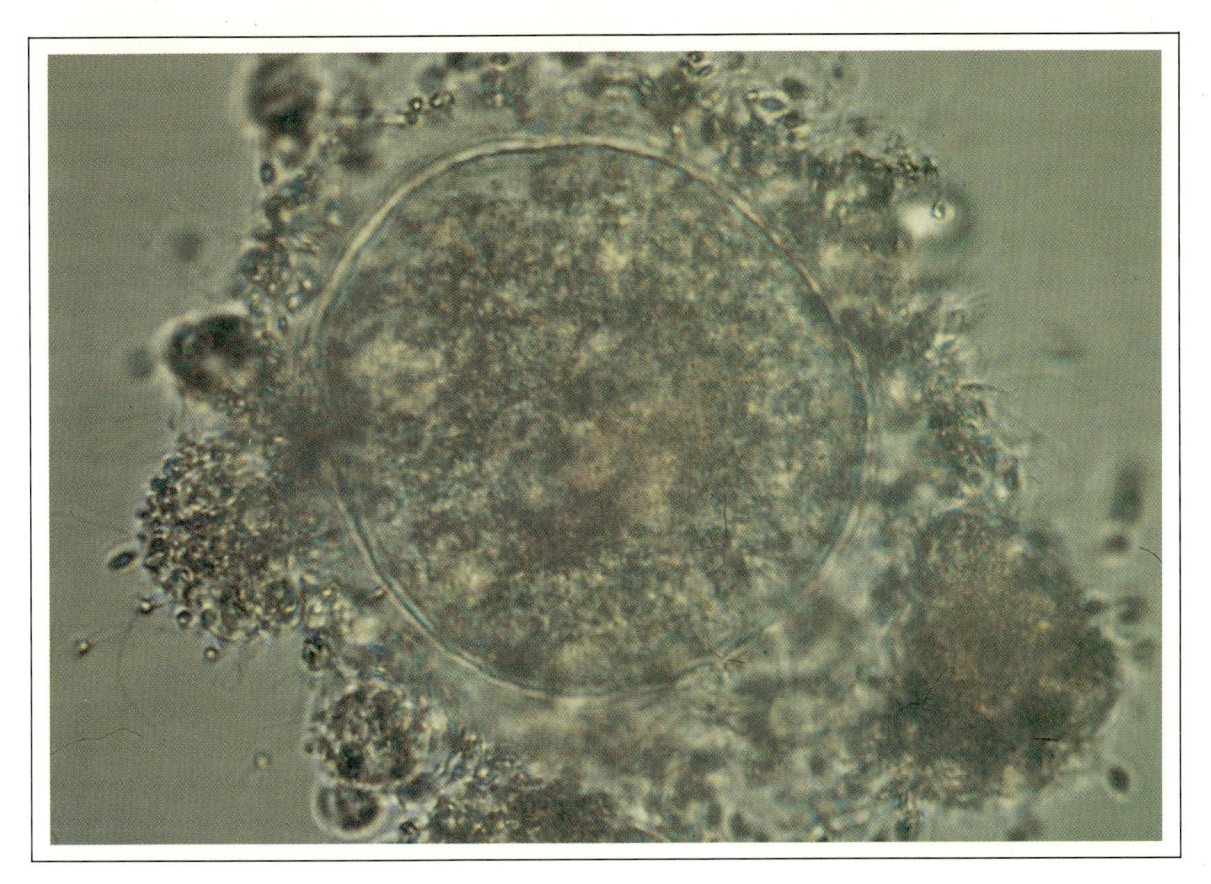

Sperm cells approaching an ovum just prior to conception. Only one of the sperms seen in the photograph will fertilize the ovum. (Alexander Tsiaras/Science Source)

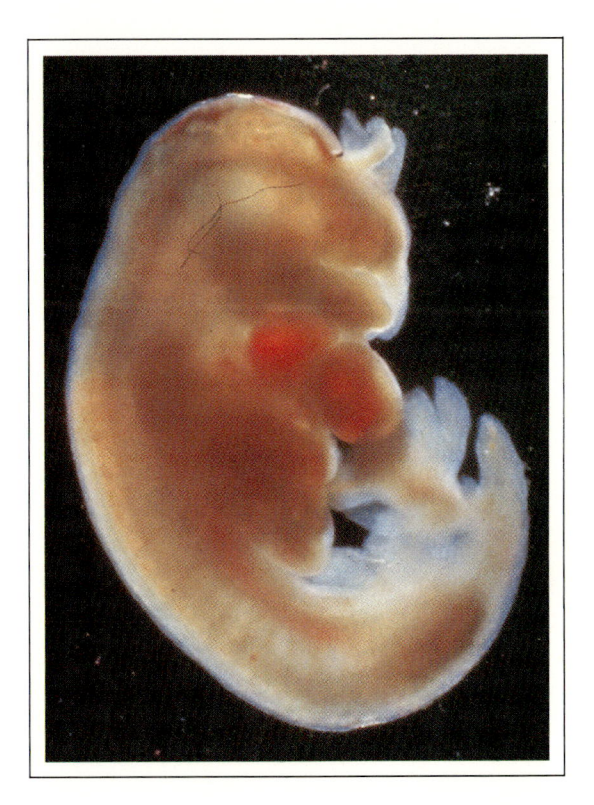

An embryo, at about six weeks post-conception. The embryo is one-sixth of an inch long. The faint oval visible at the top is the developing eye. The heart is the curved red tube-like structure in the center. (© Petit Format/Nestle/Science Source)

An embryo at about eight weeks post-conception. Although only one-half of an inch long, the arms, legs, body, and face have taken shape. (© Petit Format/Nestle/Science Source)

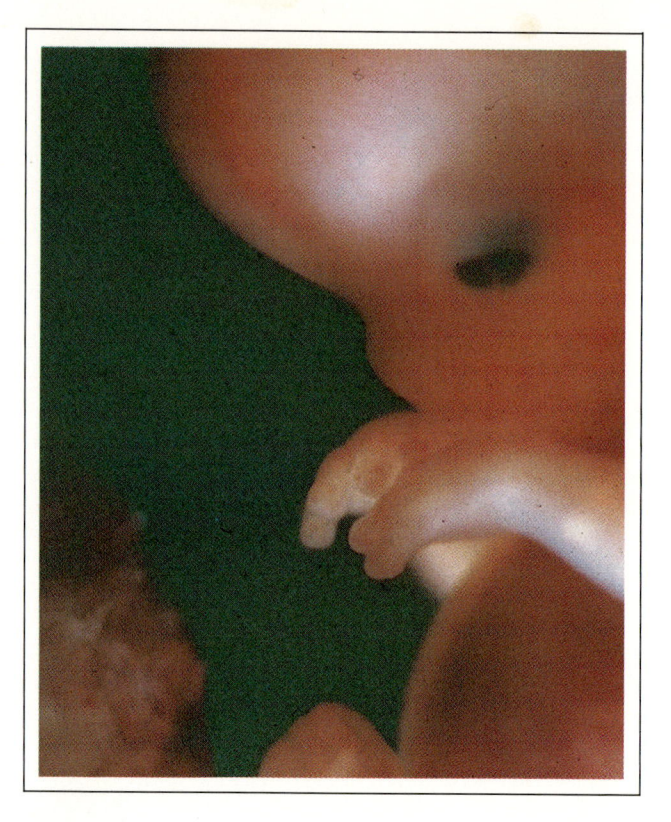

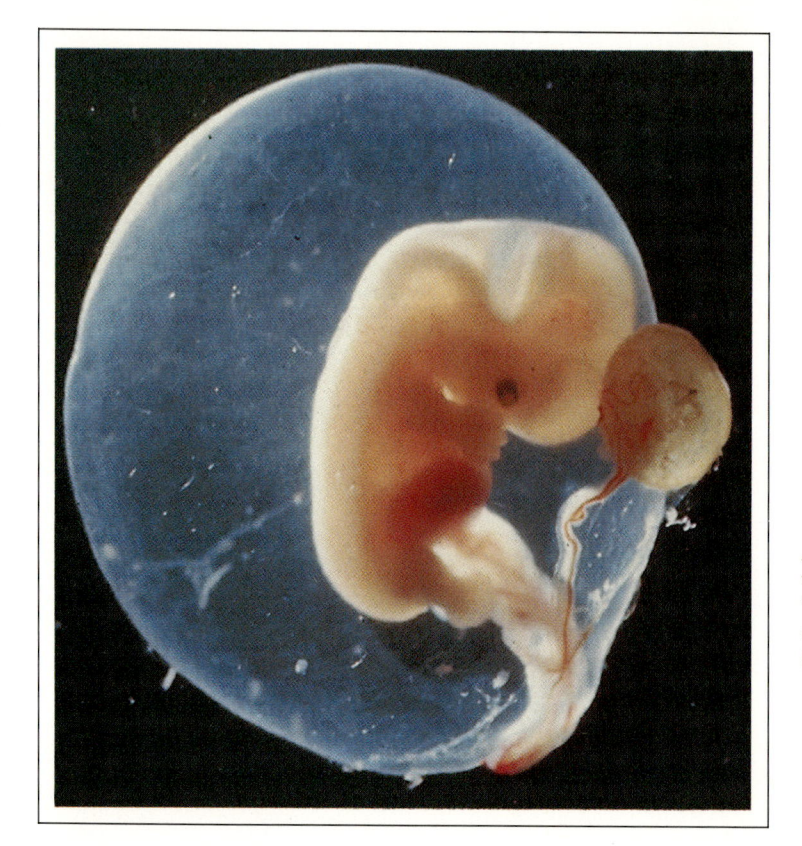

Another view of the embryo at about eight weeks. Eyes, arms, and legs are visible. The location of the embryo in the amniotic sac is seen. (© Petit Format/Nestle/Science Source)

The fetus at four months is about six inches long. The eyelids are closed. Skin is beginning to develop more fully. But blood vessels can still be seen through the thin surface covering the fetus. (© Petit Format/Nestle/Science Source)

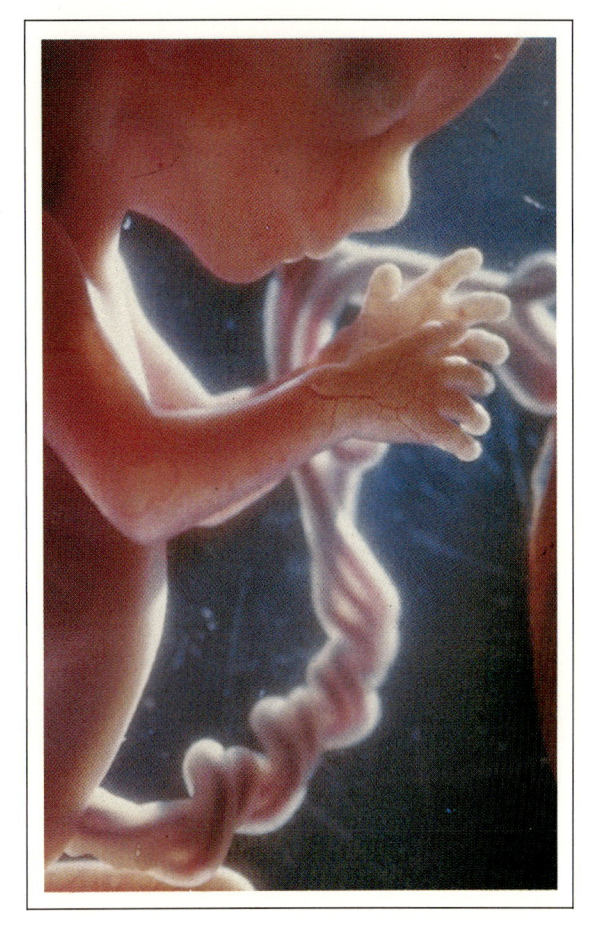

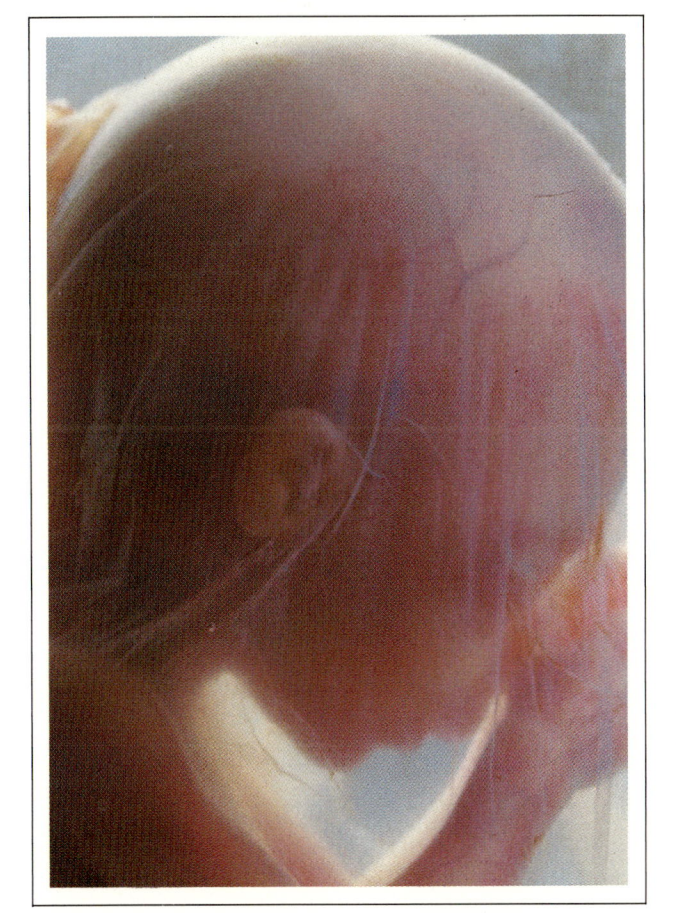

The fetus at about four and a half months. About eight inches long, thumb sucking occurs and, when not asleep, there is considerable arm and leg movement. (© Petit Format/Nestle/Science Source)

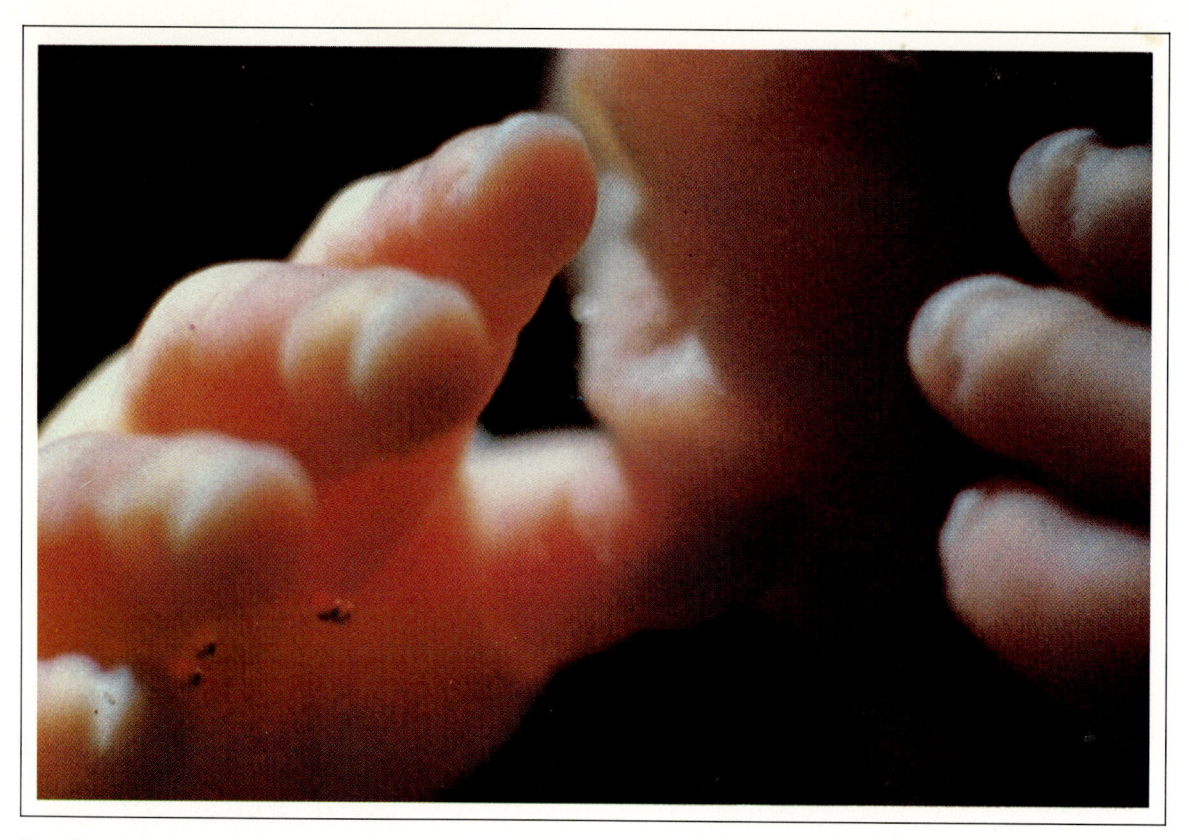

The fetus at about five and a half months. Now about one foot in length, the formation of the face's features is evident. Fingernails can be seen as well. (© Petit Format/Nestle/Science Source)

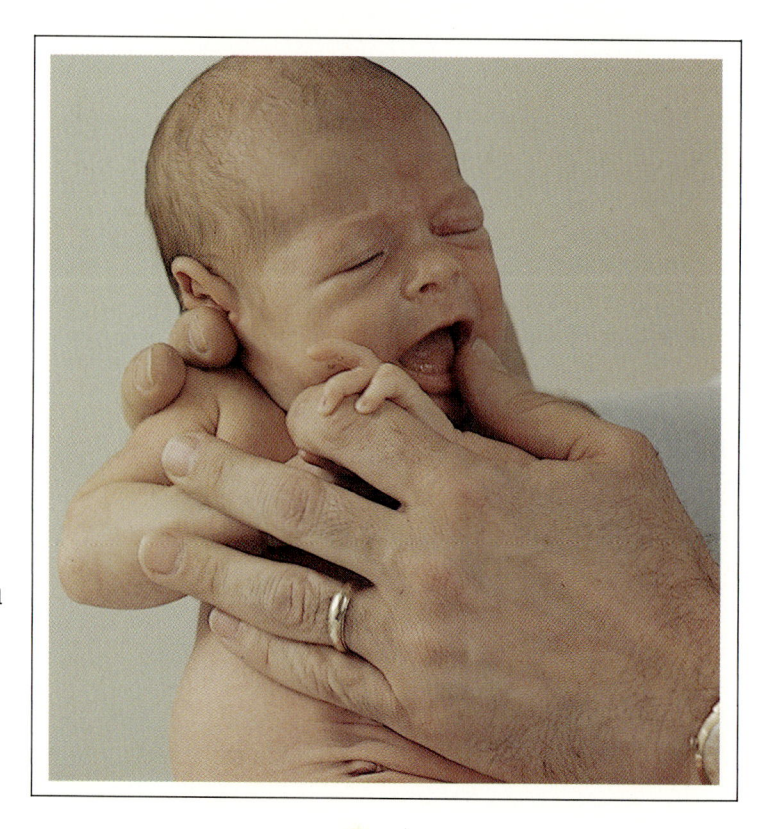

A newborn baby. (© Edward Lettau, 1976)

or future behavior, but as a family "resource," someone to be used as the child wishes. This parent largely allows the child to govern his or her own behavior. As such, the permissive parent avoids exercising control over the child and, in fact, often does not encourage the child to obey external (social) standards. Thus reason, but not overt power, is used to rear the child (Baumrind, 1968, p. 256).

The third type of parent Baumrind identifies is labeled the *authoritative parent*. This type of parent tries to direct his or her child's activities in a rational, issue-oriented style. Through explanations and reasoning the parent attempts to *induce* the desired behavior in the child. Verbal give-and-take is encouraged, because this allows the parent to share with the child the reasoning behind a policy. This parent does exercise firm control over the child, but does not overburden the child with restrictions. Rather, the child's interests, specific needs, and capabilities are taken into account. By combining power with induction, the authoritative parent attempts to rear the child with rules in which the *rights and duties of parents and children* are complementary (Baumrind, 1968, p. 261; Gardner, 1978).

In Baumrind's (1968, 1971) view, extremely authoritarian or permissive parenting have equally bad consequences for children's development because neither is as effective in leading to desired child behavior as is authoritative parenting. Most parents, whether they are authoritarian, permissive, or authoritative, want their children to be friendly, cooperative, achievement oriented, and dominant—behaviors that describe a socially competent, responsible, and independent person (Baumrind, 1972). Compared to the other two parenting types, authoritative parents are more likely to have children who score higher on measures of cooperation with adults and friendliness with children. These children are more competent in doing things necessary to succeed in their daily activities.

Child Effects on Parents. Children shape their parents' childrearing behavior, and several studies document such child effects. For example, Parke and Sawin (1975) show that the punitiveness of parental discipline is likely to be a direct consequence of the child's response to discipline. The defiant child, for example, is likely to elicit increasingly severe punishment from his or her caregiver. This suggests, of course, that the authoritarian parent whom we spoke of earlier might be more inclined to behave authoritatively if the child were inclined to cooperate with such rearing.

Peer Relations. A *peer group* can be said to exist at any age level. Such a social group is often defined as all people who are social equals or who have similar characteristics such as age or grade level (cf. Hetherington & Parke, 1975). Recent definitions of peers, however, have stressed behavioral and/or psychological similarity. Lewis and Rosenblum (1974), for example, suggest that peers are children who interact at about the same level of behavioral complexity.

Hartup (1979), who is one of the leading investigators of the role of peer interaction in child development, has noted that peers play an important role in child development. Roff, Sells, and Golden (1972) found that poor peer relations in childhood are associated with severe maladjustment in later life. Similarly, Furman and Masters (1980) report that the more disliked a child is by his or her peers, the greater his incidence of social deprivation. In turn, having exposure to peer interaction seems to aid socialization because a person learns to live by the rules of the social groups within which he or she lives. For example, in a study by Furman, Rahe, and Hartup (1979), 24

Most parents want their children to be friendly, cooperative, achievement-oriented, and dominant. (Barbara Rios)

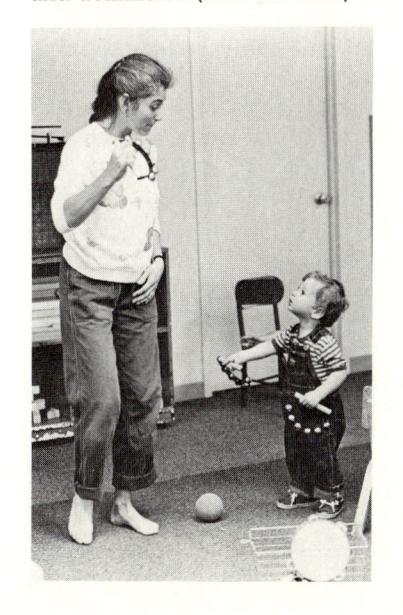

socially withdrawn, preschool children were assigned to one of three conditions: (1) socialization experience with a younger child during 10 play sessions, (2) socialization experience with an agemate during a similar series of sessions, and (3) no treatment. The socialization sessions, particularly those with the younger partner, increased the sociability of the withdrawn children in the classrooms.

Thus, playing with peers is an important part of healthy development in childhood. Let us look more directly at the importance of a child's play.

THE ROLE OF PLAY IN CHILD DEVELOPMENT

Although there is still no generally accepted definition of play, we will use Dearden's (1967): Play is nonserious and self-contained activity engaged in for the sheer satisfaction it brings.

Most social interactions of peers occur in play. Indeed, children spend more of their time, outside school, playing with friends than involved in any other activity (Hetherington & Parke, 1979). Play appears to facilitate the cognitive, social, and emotional development of children. For example, C. E. Rosen (1974) gave disadvantaged kindergarten children 40 days of instruction and practice in sociodramatic play (i.e., to act out selected social problems). Compared to children who did not experience this play training, the children whom she instructed showed improvements in problem-solving behavior (e.g., in their effectiveness in solving group problems requiring maximum cooperation and minimum competition). The trained children also improved their *role-taking* skills—another instance of advanced cognitive functioning. In turn, Rubin and Maioni (1975) found that preschoolers who engaged in more dramatic play were also the most popular.

The Development of Play. How children play changes across their development. In a classic study of 2- to 5-year-olds, Parten and Newhall (1943) discovered, first, that the number of social contacts children made and social interaction among them increased with age. The youngest children spent most of their time in *solitary play*, which involved no interaction between a child and another. Older children tended to engage in *parallel play:* Although they played side by side, often engaging in similar behaviors (e.g., putting sand into a pail), they did not really interact with each other. It was the 5-year-olds who tended to engage most often in truly interactive play—*cooperative play*. These children talked to each other and had reciprocal, coordinated exchanges.

Before age five, children engage often in parallel play. In such play, they play side by side but do not really interact. (Bettye Lane)

Peers and a child's play with them are important parts, then, of the social world of childhood; each contributes in significant ways to the child's development. Children of today, however, experience another quite significant element of their social world, one that is a major influence on them: television.

INFLUENCES OF TELEVISION ON CHILD DEVELOPMENT

No dimension of the social world other than the family may influence the development of today's children more than television. Although not all children now watch more television than in previous decades, television-viewing habits are still related to socioeconomic, intellectual, personality, and developmental variables. In general, television viewing begins at age 2, increases rapidly until age 7, and continues to rise until adolescence (Lyle & Hoffman, 1972). Fowles (1975) reports that children as young as 18 months are attentive to television and material and visual qualities. Cereal companies have learned that 2-year-olds can identify cereal boxes with the premiums on them (Choate, 1975). Between 3.5 and 4 years, children can recognize that the cereal is separate from the program.

Effects of Viewing Television Aggression. Most evidence indicates a relation between the actual viewing of televised violence and the incidence of aggressive behaviors (Stein & Friedrich, 1975). Although not applicable to all children, the recurrence of this relationship in studies assessing effects of actual viewing patterns suggests that altering the incidence of violence on television can change the probability of violent behaviors among today's youth. For instance, a 10-year longitudinal study (Eron, Lefkowitz, Huesmann, & Walder, 1972) found a positive relation between a preference for violent television programs and aggressive behavior among third-grade boys. Moreover, these preferences for violent television were also related to aggressive behavior in the same boys 10 years later. However, television-viewing preferences were not related to aggression among the girls studied.

Viewing televised violence seems to promote more aggressive behavior in boys than in girls. (David S. Strickler/Monkmeyer)

Effects of Viewing Prosocial Television. Although there have been fewer empirical studies of the effects of viewing prosocial television programs than of viewing aggressive or violent television programs, data demonstrate "that television and film programs can modify viewers' social behavior in a prosocial direction. Generosity, helping, cooperation, friendliness, adhering to rules, delaying gratification, and lack of fear can all be increased by television material" (Rushton, 1979, p. 345). In one study for example, Coates, Pusser, and Goodman (1976) observed preschool children's behavior before, during, and after 1 week of exposure to two programs: "Sesame Street" and "Mister Rogers Neighborhood." The children were observed to see how often they gave positive reinforcement and punishment to other children and to adults in the preschool. For children whose initial (previewing) scores were low, "Sesame Street" increased the giving of positive reinforcement and punishment to, and social contacts with, other children and with adults in the preschool. For children whose initial levels of giving reinforcement and punishments were high, "Sesame Street" had no effect. However, for *all* children, "Mister Rogers' Neighborhood" increased the giving of positive reinforcement to other children and adults.

SUMMARY

1. Human beings typically have 46 chromosomes in every cell in the body. However, in adults capable of reproduction, each sperm or ovum has only 23 chromosomes. When the sperm fertilizes the ovum and conception occurs, the new organism receives its genetic inheritance.

2. The contribution of heredity to development involves the gene, or unit of heredity. Each gene carries a coded message that influences development. This code is carried in deoxyribonucleic acid (DNA), a chemical found in the nucleus of every cell. Genes interact with the environment to shape all structures and functions of the person.

3. There are three periods of prenatal development. The period of the ovum begins at fertilization and lasts until the zygote becomes attached to the uterine wall. This period usually lasts from 10 to 14 days. The period of the embryo lasts from about the end of the second week after conception through to the end of the tenth week. The various bodily tissues, organs, and systems emerge and begin to develop in this period. The period of the fetus lasts from the end of the second month after conception until birth. Further growth and differentiation of the bodily organs and systems developed in the embryonic period continue here. In addition, these organs all begin to function.

4. There are several influences on prenatal development. Poor maternal nutrition, maternal alcohol and tobacco consumption, and maternal drug use can result in negative developments both prenatally and postnatally. Contraction of diseases by the mother and marked emotional stress in the mother during her pregnancy are also associated with such problems. There is some relation between maternal age and prenatal and postnatal problems.

5. Upon birth the average infant weighs 7.5 lb and is about 20 in. in length. By 2 years of age, most boys have achieved 49.5% of what will be their final adult height and most girls have achieved 52.8% of their final adult height.

6. Sensory and perceptual abilities develop in infancy. Infants can discriminate among substances of different tastes and show a preference for touching novel, as opposed to familiar, stimulus objects. Infants' hearing and vision are also well developed. Infants respond differentially to light and dark, show visual acuity, and can follow a moving stimulus.

DEVELOPMENT: INFANCY AND CHILDHOOD

7. In regard to motor functioning, there are numerous neonatal reflexes present in the newborns' behavioral repertoire. Infants show evidence of emotions (e.g., crying, smiling) in the first days of life. Emotions communicate to the infant's caregivers information about what the infant is experiencing.

8. Measures of intelligence taken at different times within the infancy period do not correlate well with each other.

9. Jean Piaget's theory of cognitive development views knowledge as developing through stages (sensorimotor, preoperational, concrete operational, and formal operational). This development involves a process of equilibration between assimilation and accommodation.

10. Considerable research supports the idea that the nature of infant-family relations is one of bidirectional socialization.

11. Social isolation and deprivation can have harmful effects. However, these effects can be altered or even reversed.

12. Language development proceeds through predictable stages; in a relatively short time the child goes from one-word utterances to complex sentences.

13. Parents use different techniques to rear their children. Baumrind has identified three techniques: authoritarian, authoritative, and permissive. These parenting styles are associated with differences in children's behavior development.

14. Peers provide a key feature of children's social context. Peer deprivation can have severe negative and emotional effects on a child's development.

15. A major activity children engage in with peers is play. Play is related to cognitive, social, and emotional development. Children often move from solitary play, to parallel play, to cooperative play.

16. Viewing television can have both positive and negative effects on a child's development. Viewing of televised aggression can increase aggression in children. In turn, prosocial behavior (e.g., helping) can be enhanced by viewing television.

KEY TERMS

Zygote
DNA
Teratogen
Apgar score
Social referencing
Assimilation

Accommodation
Equilibration
Sensorimotor stage
Preoperational stage
Concrete operational stage
Formal operational stage

Attachment
Morpheme
Overregularization
Authoritarian parenting
Permissive parenting
Authoritative parenting

SUGGESTED READINGS

BELL, R. O., & HARPER, L. V. *Child effects on adults.* Hillsdale, N.J.: Lawrence Erlbaum, 1977. This book summarizes the ways in which children influence the behavior of their caregivers. It emphasizes the reciprocal character of child-adult relationships.

LERNER, R. M., & HULTSCH, D. F. *Human development: A life-span perspective.* New York: McGraw-Hill, 1983. A comprehensive presentation of development from conception through the adult and aged years.

LEWIS, M., & ROSENBLUM, L. A. (Eds.). *The effects of the infant on its caregiver.* New York: Wiley, 1974. Presents chapters by several researchers who have documented the ways in which infants (even very young ones) can influence the behaviors of their caregivers. The reciprocal nature of these interactions is stressed.

PIAGET, J. *The psychology of intelligence.* London: Routledge & Kegan Paul, 1950. A short presentation of the major features of Piaget's developmental theory of cognitive development, written by Piaget himself.

11

Development: Adolescence, Adulthood, and Aging

ADOLESCENCE
  A Definition of Adolescence
  Storm and Stress in
    Adolescence: Fact or
    Fiction?
  Physical and Physiological
    Changes
  Cognitive Changes
  Identity Development
  Sexuality

ADULTHOOD AND AGING
  Biological Changes
  Cognitive Functioning
  Personality Development
  Stages of Adult Development
  Dying, Death, and Grief
SUMMARY
KEY TERMS
SUGGESTED READINGS

How would you answer this question: *What was the last major event in your life that, for better or worse, interrupted or changed your usual activities?* How did people of varying ages respond? Read the following excerpts.

Lisa, age 16: That's easy. The *big* (drawing out the word) move. See, 6 months ago we moved here from the East Coast. My dad was transferred. I just about died when I found out. I mean leaving my friends and all. It was really tough at first. I was pretty depressed, even though mom and dad tried to help by taking us to see the sights. But now that school's started things are better. I've made some new friends, and the boys are pretty cute. I still miss the old place, but I guess California is gonna' be OK— the weather's sure better *(laughs)*.

Jack, age 22: I guess graduation from college. No, that's not right. Do upcoming events count? Right now the biggest event in my life is one that is going to happen. I have a job interview coming up in 2 weeks with the XYZ Corporation. Since graduation, everything in my life seems to be on hold. I had two other interviews since I graduated, but the positions were only slightly related to my field. This one looks like it fits me perfectly. If I can land this job, it sure will be a major event.

Bob, age 30: That would have to be the trouble with the business. I sell and service air conditioners. I just opened the business about 4 years ago, and there were a lot of startup costs. But just as I was beginning to get on my feet, this energy thing hit for real. Sales of air conditioners have really fallen off because of the cost of electricity. Even people who already have it aren't using it. I'll tell a customer that he needs a couple of hundred bucks worth of repairs on his central system, and he'll tell me that he'll do without it this summer. Between the drop in business and interest rates, we're really getting squeezed. Besides the business loan, we owe a couple of thousand on our car. Then there's the usual credit card bills. On top of everything else our roof has started to leak, and it looks like the whole thing will have to be replaced. I'm not sure where we go from here. We've talked about trying to get another loan from the bank, but I don't know what we'll be able to get. I do know that if business doesn't pick up soon we're going to be in real trouble.

Joan, age 42: My son getting married, and then having my granddaughter. This happened a little over 2 years ago. Paul was 18 then and Suzie was only 17. They were still in high school and Suzie got pregnant. That part was very difficult. My husband passed away quite a few years ago, so Paul and I were quite close. At first, I was so afraid this was going to ruin his life; I guess I handled it badly. I tried to convince him he was making a mistake, and there were several weeks of tears and arguments. The final straw came when I told Suzie's father about their plans. You see, they had asked me not to tell him—but I thought he had a right to know. That was a mistake. He beat her up and threw her out of the house. I felt so badly that I stopped arguing with the kids, and they moved in with me. Since then, Paul has finished high school and is working in a television repair shop. He's taking courses part-time at the university, too. And, of course, there's Amy. She just had her second birthday last week, and she's as cute as she can be. I guess it was hard on all of us, but when I look at that little girl, I know it worked out for the best.

Max, age 62: Well, my heart attack, I guess. That certainly changed my activities, I used to work 16 hours and smoke three packs of cigarettes a day. Now, I only work half-days at the office, and no smoking. I guess it has been a change for the best. It was a pretty severe attack. I was in intensive care for 3 weeks, and it took almost 6 months before I could get around much. That was really frustrating. But I am beginning to get used to taking it slower. The doctors says that if I go back to my old style, I'll just do myself in. I still worry about the business, though. My partner has been doing most of the work, and I know I am going to have to make some hard decisions soon. I guess I'm just not ready to retire yet.

We all experience such events. Indeed, adolescence, adulthood, and aging may be viewed as a series of transitions defined by life events. Riegel (1975), for instance, found that when recalling both their personal and cultural pasts, people focused on periods of transition defined by critical events rather than on periods of stability. In this chapter we examine the nature of these transitions occurring during adolescence, adulthood, and aging.

ADOLESCENCE

Adolescents are always news. Scarcely a month passes without a story appearing in a magazine, in a newspaper, or on television about how today's adolescents are rebelling or conforming, are becoming more sexually liberated or showing conservative political tendencies, are engaging in some previously unheard-of fad, or are nostalgically returning to the ways of some bygone decade.

If what the popular media presents about adolescents seems contradictory, it merely reflects the contradictory attitudes people in general hold about this age group. Adolescents are no longer children, but at the same time, they are not adults. We expect much more from a 17-year-old than we do from a 10-year-old (e.g., we may expect the adolescent to hold a summer job); in turn, however, we do not fully trust the adolescent's maturity. Few parents would let their 17-year-old have the family car, for example, to take on an unsupervised vacation paid for with money earned during the summer.

Moreover, a popular stereotype exists about adolescents being as confused about themselves as society may be about them. Adolescents are believed to be unsure of who they are, ambivalent about their feelings toward their parents, and uncertain of the role they will play when they become mature adults. This alleged confusion is popularly labeled as the "storm and stress" of adolescence.

To what extent are these popular depictions of and stereotypes about adolescents correct? Does scientific evidence support these impressions? In this section we answer these questions.

A DEFINITION OF ADOLESCENCE

An adolescent is not just someone who has attained a given age, reached reproductive maturity, or moved beyond the roles of a child. An adolescent may be all of these things, or much more.

Adolescence involves changes among numerous biological, psychological, and social characteristics. These characteristics change at varying rates, some faster or slower than others. A person may have some characteristics (e.g., cognition) that are adultlike, others (e.g., emotions) which are still childish, and still others (e.g., physical makeup) which are between the two. We may define *adolescence as that period within the life span when most of a person's characteristics are changing from what is typically considered childhood to what is typically considered adulthood.*

Easily visible changes of adolescence include those involving the developing body and the styles of dress of the adolescent. Also visible is a change in the adolescent's social relationships. For example, the young teenager begins to spend more and more time with peers rather than with family members. Less visible alterations involve inner-biological changes, such as

The young teenager tends to spend more and more time with peers rather than family members. (Paul Conklin/Monkmeyer)

the release of hormones into the bloodstream, and modifications in thought or "cognitions." The adolescent's emotional characteristics are also likely to take on a different character.

STORM AND STRESS IN ADOLESCENCE: FACT OR FICTION?

With all these changes occurring, in many cases quite rapidly, the adolescent begins to wonder who he or she is, and many experience what Erikson (1959) has termed an "identity crisis." That is, to resolve the issue of identity, many adolescents ask: "Who is this person who looks so different, who feels so many different things, and who thinks so differently?" Parents, too, may begin to wonder about the person they have raised for so many years. "What kind of adult will be child be?" "Will these next few years be the same as our earlier years together?" Adolescence may be a time wherein some of the parent's dreams or aspirations about the child are realized, or it may be a time of disappointment.

These feelings and events are well known to parents, to teachers, and to the many writers who have romanticized or dramatized the adolescent experience in novels, short stories, or news articles. But does available scientific information verify the romantic, literary characterizations of adolescence? Is adolescence necessarily a stormy and stressful period? Available evidence indicates that the answers to these questions are no. For instance, many people hold that because of supposed adolescent rebelliousness and close contact with friends, parents must control their children more during this time. In contrast, Bandura (1964) observed that by adolescence most children had so thoroughly adopted parental values and standards that parental restrictions actually were reduced. Bandura also noted that although the storm-and-stress idea of adolescence implies a struggle by youth to free themselves of dependence on parents, parents begin to train their children in childhood to *be independent*. Finally, Bandura found that the adolescent's choice of friends was not a major source of friction between adolescents and parents. Adolescents tended to form friendships with those who shared similar values. As such, the peers tended to support those standards of the parents that already had been adopted by the adolescents themselves.

Bandura pointed out, however, that these observations do not mean that adolescence is stressless or problem free. He was careful to note that *no* period of life is free of crisis or adjustment problems, and any period of life may present particular adjustment problems for some people and not for others. Thus one has to be careful about attributing problems seen in one group of adolescents to all adolescents. To illustrate, in a portion of his study Bandura observed a sample of antisocial boys. Their excessive aggression did lead to their adolescence being associated with storm and stress. However, Bandura found that one could not appropriately view the problems of these boys as resulting just from adolescence. Their problem behaviors were present throughout their childhood. However, when the boys were physically smaller, the parents could control their aggressive behavior better than they could during adolescence.

From Bandura's (1964) study it may be concluded that (1) even when storm and stress is seen in adolescence, it is not necessarily the result of events in adolescence, but instead may be associated with prior developments; (2) storm and stress is not necessarily characteristic of the adolescent period—many possible types of adolescent development can occur. The existence of such different paths through adolescence is supported by the results of other studies.

Offer (1969) found three major routes through the adolescent period: continuous growth, surgent growth, and tumultuous growth. *Continuous growth* involves smooth changes in behavior. Adolescents showing such development were not in any major conflict with their parents and did not feel that parental rearing practices were inappropriate or that parental values were alien to them. Most adolescents fell into this category. Such a pattern is like the one we have seen Bandura (1964) describe. In *surgent growth* development involves an abrupt and rapid change, but is not necessarily associated with storm and stress. It was *tumultuous growth*, the third type of adolescent development, that was characterized by crisis, stress, and problems. For such adolescents, "storm and stress" aptly denotes the nature of their change.

Thus only for some people is the adolescent period one of storm and stress. Indeed, based on the Bandura (1964) and Offer (1969) studies, it may be assumed that such turmoil is experienced by only a minority of adolescents. This conclusion is bolstered by the data of Douvan and Adelson (1966). In their study, as in the studies noted previously, most adolescents shared the basic values of their parents and were satisfied with their family life and the style of treatment by their parents. Moreover, these adolescents chose friends who had values similar to those of the adolescents' parents. This means that *peer group* influences and parental influences on the adolescent would tend to be consistent. Highlight 11.1 discusses the influence of parents and peers on one key aspect of the adolescent's life: education.

Available data, then, are inconsistent with the stereotype that adolescence is a *generally* stressful and stormy period. But despite these data, the stereotype persists in several quarters (see Adelson & Doehrman, 1980). One reason that the stereotype has resisted eradication is that neither many scientists nor the public have until relatively recently paid adequate attention to what is known scientifically about adolescent development. Indeed, before the last 15 years, the study of adolescence had been characterized by "scientific neglect" (Adelson & Doehrman, 1980), that is, by a seeming belief among scientists that little development of fundamental importance to adult life occurred during this period (Lerner, 1981). However, due to (1) the theoretical interest of scientists who study life *transitions*—that is, periods, such as adolescence, wherein the person undergoes major physical, cognitive, and social changes (Lerner, 1981), and (2) the appearance of real problems in adolescence—for example, increasing rates of adolescent drug use, pregnancy, abortion, childbearing, venereal disease, and life-damaging or fatal accidents, scientists have begun to pay more attention to this period of life (Adelson, 1980; Lerner, 1981; J. P. Hill, in press). Let us consider some of the major characteristics of adolescence that have been discovered.

PHYSICAL AND PHYSIOLOGICAL CHANGES

For convenience, the physical and physiological changes of adolescence may be labeled "bodily" changes. They do not begin or end all at once; however, a general order for these changes applies to most, but certainly not all people (Katchadourian, 1977). It is convenient to speak of phases of bodily changes in adolescence in order to draw important distinctions among various degrees and types of change.

HIGHLIGHT 11.1
Parental and Peer Influences on Education

The parents and peers of adolescents influence both aspirations about and actual outcomes of the adolecents' accomplishments in school. According to information from the U.S. Bureau of the Census (1978), the college aspirations of high school seniors tend to be correlated with the educational attainment of the head of the household in which they lived. About 70% of students who were living in households in which the head had completed at least a year of college themselves had definite college plans. When the head of the household had completed high school but not any college, only 45% of students had definite college plans. Of those living in families having a head of household who had not completed high school, only 35% had definite college plans.

Sewell and Shah (1968a, 1968b) found that parents' educational attainment is highly related to their adolescent children's educational aspirations and also to the actual success of the adolescents in the school setting. High educational attainment of parents, particularly fathers, was found to predict similarly high (e.g., college) attainment by students.

Particular types of parent-adolescent interactions appear to facilitate successful school functioning. Morrow and Wilson (1961) found that compared to a group of low achievers, high-achieving adolescents tended to come from families where they were involved in decisions, where ideas and activities were shared, and where parents were likely to praise the adolescents' performance and show trust in their competence. In turn, low-achieving adolescents came from families marked by parental dominance and restrictiveness (Morrow & Wilson, 1961). Both Morrow and Wilson (1961) and Shaw and White (1965) found that high-achieving adolescents tend to identify with their parents, whereas low-achieving adolescents do not.

Still other data indicate that the type of parental behaviors found by Morrow and Wilson (1961) relate to high adolescent school achievement. Both Swift (1967) and Rehberg and Westby (1967) report that parental encouragement and rewards are associated with better adolescent school performance. Wolf (1964) reports that parent-child interactions that involve encouragement to achieve and development of language of skills are highly correlated with intelligence.

Peers also influence adolescents' aspirations and educational performance; in most cases, family and peer influences converge. Rigsby and McDill (1972), in a study of over 20,000 adolescents, found a positive relation among the proportion of peers perceived to have college plans, the actual proportion with college plans, and adolescents' own likelihood of planning for college.

Similarly, Kandel and Lesser (1969) found a great deal of correspondence between the educational aspirations of the peers and of the adolescent if adolescent peer relationships were close and intimate; however, most adolescents (57%) had educational plans that agreed with peers and parents. In turn, among those adolescents who disagreed with their parents, there was also a great likelihood (50%) that they would also disagree with peers. When there was a discrepancy between parent and peer orientations, the parental orientation tended to prevail (Kandel & Lesser, 1969).

Bodily changes involve alterations in height, weight, fat, and muscle distribution, glandular secretions, and sexual characteristics. When some of these changes have begun, but most are yet to occur, the person is in the *prepubescent* phase. When most of those bodily changes that will eventually take place have been initiated, the person is in the *pubescent* phase. Finally, when most of those bodily changes have already occurred, the person is in the *postpubescent* phase, which ends when all changes are completed.

The bodily changes of adolescence involve a period of changing physical and physiological characteristics during which the person reaches an adult level of reproductive maturity. But puberty is not synonymous with all maturational changes. In fact, some authors (e.g., Schonfeld, 1969) see puberty, the point at which the person can reproduce, as only one stage within the pubescent phase.

But this point is *not* synonymous with menarche (the first menstrual cycle) in females or with the first ejaculation in males. The initial menstrual cycles of females, for instance, typically are not accompanied by ovulation. Similarly, for males there is a gap between the first ejaculation, which usually occurs between 11 and 16 years of age (Kinsey, Pomeroy, & Martin, 1948), and the capability to fertilize.

Thus neither menarche, the first seminal emission, nor puberty itself is commensurate with all bodily changes associated with the prepubescent, pubescent, and postpubescent phases of adolescence. These changes relate to both *primary* and the *secondary* sexual characteristics. Primary sexual characteristics are present at birth and involve the internal and external genitalia (e.g., the penis in males and the vagina in females). Secondary sexual characteristics are those which emerge to represent the two sexes during the prepubescent through postpubescent phases (e.g., breast development in females and pigmented facial hair in males).

Variation in the rate of bodily change in adolescence is related to psychological and social developments. Studies indicate that early-maturing adolescent boys are better adjusted and have more favorable interactions with peers and adults than do late-maturing boys (Jones & Bayley, 1950; Mussen & Jones, 1957; Petersen, 1983). These advantages of early maturation, and the possession of a body type that has strong muscles and bones (a mesomorph), and disadvantages of late maturation, and either a plump (endomorph) or thin (ectomorph) body type, tend to continue through the middle adult years for males. For females, however, early maturation is associated with more psychosocial disadvantages than is late maturation (Petersen, 1983). These relations for female adolescent rates of physical maturation, bodily appearance, and personality and social functioning have not been determined in later adult life. Figure 11.1 depicts some of the bodily variations associated with early and late maturation in male and female adolescents that are of exactly the same age.

There are problems of physical maturation and functioning during adolescence. Often, adolescents' behavior promotes these problems. For instance, they may overeat and become obese or undereat and experience a disorder known as *anorexia nervosa*, which affects predominantly adolescent females (see Highlight 11.2).

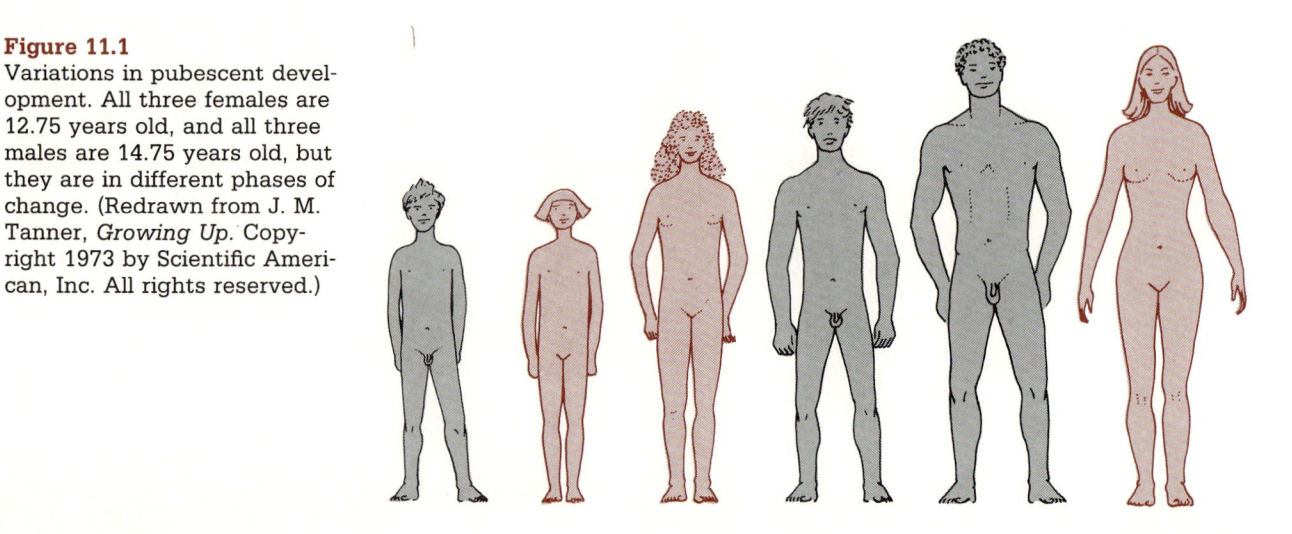

Figure 11.1
Variations in pubescent development. All three females are 12.75 years old, and all three males are 14.75 years old, but they are in different phases of change. (Redrawn from J. M. Tanner, *Growing Up*. Copyright 1973 by Scientific American, Inc. All rights reserved.)

HIGHLIGHT 11.2
Characteristics of Anorexia Nervosa

1. *Behavior directed toward losing weight:* Anorectics drastically reduce their total food intake, especially foods high in carbohydrates and fats. There are daily intakes of as little as 80 to 100 Calories, and anorectics often induce vomiting after ingestion of food and/or make extensive use of laxatives (H. Bruch, 1973; Crisp, 1970, 1974; Vigersky, 1977).
2. *Peculiar patterns of handling food:* Although limiting themselves to a few low-calorie foods, anorectics often prepare elaborate meals for others, collect recipes, and become preoccupied with thoughts of food and calories (H. Bruch, 1973, 1977; Sours, 1969). Anorectics have also been known to hoard, conceal, and crumble food.
3. *Weight loss:* Anorectics are characterized by a loss of at least 25% of original body weight, but frequently as much as 50% of original body weight is lost (H. Bruch, 1973, 1977; Crisp, 1970, 1974; Sours, 1969; Vigersky, 1977).
4. *Intense fear of gaining weight:* Anorectics fear they will become obese. This fear does not lessen with increased weight loss; indeed, they become preoccupied with the size and appearance of their body, often spending long periods of time gazing in the mirror (H. Bruch, 1973, 1977; Vigersky, 1977).
5. *Disturbance of body image:* Although preoccupied with their body, anorectics do not perceive it accurately. They misjudge body size, often believing they are overweight—despite increasing thinness—or, alternatively, believe they look quite good, despite their poor physical state (Andersen, 1977; H. Bruch, 1973, 1977; Vigersky, 1977).
6. *Other medical and psychological problems:* Since anorexia nervosa affects predominately adolescent females, problems with the menstrual cycle are a common complication of this disorder. However, this is an outcome of the anorexia, not a cause of it. Indeed, anorexia nervosa occurs when there are no known medical problems that would account for the weight loss (H. Bruch, 1973, 1977; Crisp, 1970, 1974; Sours, 1969; Vigersky, 1977). However, obesity often precedes anorexia nervosa, and some estimates are that about one-third of all anorectics have been at least slightly overweight prior to the onset of the disorder (Crisp, 1970, 1974; Sours, 1969; Vigersky, 1977).

COGNITIVE CHANGES

The physical changes of adolescence are complicated because the person is also undergoing cognitive and emotional changes. Thus Piaget (1950, 1970), Inhelder and Piaget (1958), and Elkind (1967) have noted that new thought capabilities come to characterize the adolescent. That is, before adolescence the youth's thought was tied primarily to the concrete physical reality of "what is." For example, the child with a very happy home life will think that all families are happy, whereas an abused or neglected child might think the opposite; neither child may be able to understand other possibilities. However, the adolescent can deal with hypothetical and abstract aspects of reality, and indeed begins to think primarily in a hypothetical, "what if . . . ?" manner.

Thus the adolescent no longer sees the way the world is organized as the only way it could be. That is, family life, the system of government, the adolescent's status in the peer group, and the rules imposed on him or her are no longer taken as concrete, immutable things. Rather, as the new thought capabilities that allow adolescents to think abstractly, hypothetically, and counterfactually come to predominate their styles of thought, those capabilities allow adolescents to imagine how things could be. These imaginings could relate to government, self, parents' rules, or what he or she will do in life. In short, anything and everything becomes the focus of an adolescent's hypothetical, counterfactual, and imaginary thinking.

The major focus of the adolescent's concerns becomes himself or herself. This is appropriate, given all the radical physical and physiological changes. Adolescents need to focus on themselves to try to understand what is going on. This concern with the self and with the problems of defining the self relate to the topic of *identity*. Let us focus now on this key problem of adolescence.

IDENTITY DEVELOPMENT

In adolescence the person comes to ask: "What is the nature of these changes happening to me?" "What will they do to me?" "What will I become?" "Am I the same person that I think I am?" As all these uncertainties are being introduced, another set of problems emerges. The adolescent in our society typically is asked to make a choice, a decision about what he or she is going to do when grown. Society, perhaps in the form of parents or teachers, asks the adolescent to choose a *role*, a socially prescribed set of behaviors (such as those evidenced by a teacher, lawyer, or physician). The young adolescent may be asked to choose between a college preparatory or a vocational program in school, and thus embark on a path that will affect his or her life years later.

The expectations that are placed on youth at this age are, in part, a response to the outward physical changes taking place. The young adolescent appears to be on the brink of adulthood, at least physically. The cognitive maturity that becomes gradually more visible encourages others to regard the adolescent as an adultlike figure. Thus we see that just as the adolescent is influenced by parents, peers, teachers, and society, the reverse is also true—the adolescent influences how others react to him or her. Because of this relationship between society and the adolescent, with society pressing for new behaviors as the adolescent adjusts to changes within and without, it may be very difficult for the adolescent to cope.

Precisely at the time in life when people may be least ready to make a long-term choice, they are often required to do so. For adolescents to commit themselves to a certain role in society and to adjust to the larger world, they

Adolescents in our society are asked to make a decision about what they are going to do as adults and then embark on a path that will affect their lives for years. (Mimi Forsyth/Monkmeyer)

must know their interests, attributes, skills, and capabilities. In short, adolescents have to know themselves, something that is not simple, considering the multiple changes that they are experiencing. Adolescents must first settle questions about their identity before they can make a commitment to a social role. When the answers to these questions are not clear, a feeling of crisis may emerge. As we have already mentioned, Erikson (1959) labels the search for self-definition and self-identification as the *identity crisis*. Successful resolution of this crisis may take years and does not necessarily occur before the adolescent is already following one direction in life.

To summarize, the adolescent—because of the impact of all the changes converging on him or her—may enter a state of crisis and a search for self-definition. Accordingly, the adolescent attempts to find a place—or role—in society. Such definition will provide a set of rules for beliefs, attitudes, and values (an "ideology") and a prescription for behaviors (a role) that will enable youth to know what they will "do with themselves" in the world. This search for an ideology and a set of behaviors that match the adolescent's own preferences and that also fulfill a particular role is really a search for the adolescent's "goodness of fit" with society.

Often, the adolescent's search for a place in society develops over time and involves testing various possible roles and/or belief systems. To an adult the youth may seem lost, maladjusted, or even a "victimizer" of society (Anthony, 1969). Indeed, for some adolescents the crisis of identity involves nontraditional life-styles, drugs and alcohol, or roles that neither they nor their parents believe are ultimately best suited for them. For even fewer adolescents, the identity crisis results in the adoption of a "negative identity," that is, a delinquent or an antisocial role (Erikson, 1959). However, most youth, by the time they pass through their adolescent years, have found a place in society (Lerner & Spanier, 1980); they know who they are and what they believe in; and they have begun on a career path which will allow them to make a productive contribution to their society.

Nevertheless, despite this positive outcome for most adolescents, there is one aspect of their functioning which causes concern for them and for their parents throughout this period. This aspect is sexual functioning. We shall conclude our discussion of adolescents by focusing on this feature of their lives.

SEXUALITY

Sex is one of the greatest concerns of adolescents and of adults who worry about them, and it is not difficult to imagine why. Sexuality first becomes important in adolescence. Sexual *behavior* and sexual *interaction* take on meaning as the adolescent begins to think about social events in and out of school and about love and dating.

For the typical adolescent, heterosexual activity progresses through a sequence of steps: kissing, light petting, heavy petting, and coitus. The age at which this begins and the speed at which it progresses varies greatly. Some adolescents have intercourse before they reach puberty; others never kiss anyone or have a date throughout adolescence; still others may go through the entire sequence of sexual involvement on their first date (Spanier, 1976; Zelnick & Kantner, 1977).

A recent national survey of never-married females aged 15 to 19 found that 35% were sexually experienced by the time of the interview and that 55% had sexual intercourse by age 19 (Zelnick & Kantner, 1977). Eighteen percent of American females have already had sexual intercourse by age 15, suggesting that many of the concerns about pregnancy outside marriage are justified for younger, as well as older adolescents.

Jessor, Costa, Jessor, and Donovan (1983) studied several hundred male and female adolescents from junior high school (1969–1972) through young adulthood (7 years later). They collected data on these people's personality, their perception of their environments, and their behavior, and tried to use this information to predict the time of first intercourse. Jessor et al. report that male and female adolescents who place higher value on independence and a lower value on academic achievement, and have more socially critical beliefs about society, more tolerance of deviance, and less religiosity have sexual intercourse at an earlier age than do other adolescents.

Contraceptive Use. In 1976, 25% of sexually experienced adolescent females had *never* used contraception, and another 45% had used it only sometimes. Only 30% reported that they had always used it. Although an improvement over 1971, these figures point to the serious problem of nonuse of contraceptive among adolescents. Almost two out of three adolescents reported that they had not used any form of contraception during their last sexual experience. Even by age 19, only a little more than two-thirds of the respondents reported that they used contraceptives at the last intercourse.

Zelnick and Kantner (1977) report that the older a female is at the time of first intercourse, the more likely that she will begin contraception at the same time she begins to have sex. However, there is no evidence that the gap between age at first intercourse and age at first contraceptive use has declined for females. A study of the relative influence on males and females to use contraception demonstrated that partner influence was most important, parental influence least important, with peer influence in between (Thompson & Spanier, 1978).

Reasons for Inadequate Protection. Among the reasons why adolescents have premarital intercourse without adequate contraceptive protection are ignorance of which contraceptive methods are effective and where to get them; rejection of a method prescribed by a physician because the patient thinks it unsafe; objection to contraception on religious or moral groups; denial that contraception works; irresponsibility; immaturity; willingness to take risks; availability of abortion; rebellion against society or parents; hostility toward the other sex; equation of love with self-sacrifice; a belief that intercourse is sinful and pregnancy is the punishment; a feeling that pregnancy is a gift of love; the belief that sex is for procreation only; unwillingness to deny oneself or to delay intercourse; a desire of the female to become pregnant; the feeling that "it can't or won't happen to me"; the belief that intercourse is a demonstration of love; the belief that the girl was too young to become pregnant; the belief that intercourse was too infrequent or occurred at the wrong time of the month; and difficulty in adolescent couples talking to each other about contraception (Adams & Gullotta, 1983; Lehfeldt, 1971; Sandberg & Jacobs, 1972; Scales & Beckstein, 1982; Shah, Zelnick, & Kantner, 1975).

In the future, it will be increasingly important for parents and persons working with adolescents to pay attention to education about contraception and motivation for contraceptive use. The widespread lack of contraceptive use among adolescents comes at a time when the most effective methods of protection ever known to exist are readily available, when many state laws restricting the distribution of contraception to minors have been eliminated,

Sexual interaction becomes more meaningful as adolescents begin to think about love and dating. (Mimi Forsyth/Monkmeyer)

when family planning clinics and other health services are available for virtually all American adolescent females, and when adolescent knowledge about contraception is at an all-time high (Shea, 1984; Thompson & Spanier, 1978).

ADULTHOOD AND AGING

Recognition of the significance of the changes experienced during adulthood and aging has come about only recently. Not long ago, adulthood was viewed as a time of stability when what had been developed earlier was utilized. Aging was viewed as a time of decline, when what had been developed earlier was lost. We now know that this is too simplistic. Adulthood and aging are as significant and interesting as any other period of the life cycle, and are characterized by both "growth" and "decline." Let us examine the nature of some of these changes.

BIOLOGICAL CHANGES

The biological changes associated with adulthood and aging are those associated with a lessened chance of survival. For example, at age 25, a white male in the United States can expect to live 47 more years. By age 45, this has been reduced to about 29 years, and by age 85 it is only about 6 years. A more comprehensive picture is given in Figure 11.2, which shows the mortality rates for men and women of different ages in 1976.

Biological Theories of Aging. What causes the decreasing survival potential revealed in the mortality data of Figure 11.2? Why does the human life span appear to have an upper limit (see Highlight 11.3)? All modern biological theories of aging have a genetic basis (Shock, 1977). It is assumed that the life span of a species is ultimately determined by a program built into its genes. Thus the human being has a maximum life span of about 115 years, the horse 62 years, the cat 28 years, and the mouse only 3.5 years. Support for the genetic basis of aging comes from Hayflick's (1965) work, which shows that certain cells of the body, grown under culture conditions *(in vitro)*, can divide only a limited number of times. Previous to this discovery, it had

Figure 11.2
Shows the number of persons, starting with 100,000 live births, who survive to the exact age marking the beginning of the age interval. For example, of 100,000 female babies born alive, 98,631 will complete the first year of life and enter the second; 97,868 will reach age 20; and 65,139 will reach age 75. (Source: U.S. Department of Health, Education, and Welfare, 1978)

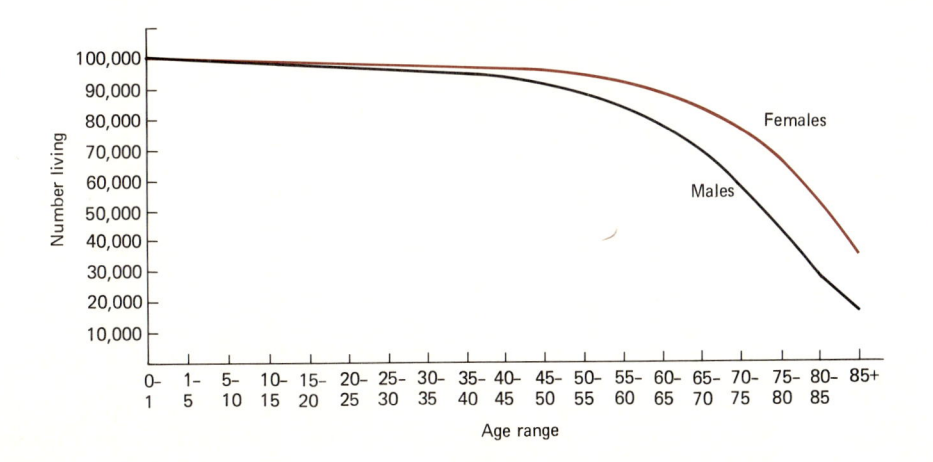

been thought that cells could divide indefinitely under culture conditions. However, Hayflick found that fibroblast cells (connective tissues cells which normally divide) taken from human embryonic tissue undergo only about 50 doublings before cell division ceases. Further, the older the person from whom the cell samples are obtained, the fewer doublings the cells will undergo. However, the cells of even a very elderly person will still divide, suggesting that people rarely live out their potential life span. Hayflick's work, then, suggests that the aging of the organism may be programmed into the cell's code.

HIGHLIGHT 11.3
Did Methuselah Really Live 969 Years?

The purported longevity of Methuselah in the Bible is undoubtedly a myth. But how long can human beings live? In examining this question it is important to distinguish between *average life expectancy* and *maximum life span*. Life expectancy refers to the average length of life. Maximum life span refers to the extreme upper limit of human life.

Life expectancy fluctuates dramatically as a function of nutrition, disease, sanitation, health care, and other environmental factors. For example, it is estimated that the average life expectancy at birth in ancient Rome may have been as low as 22 years. The life expectancy figure during the Middle Ages is estimated at 30–35 years. This figure had only risen to around 40 by 1850. The greatest gains were made during our century: life expectancy at birth in the United States increased from 47.3 years in 1900 to 72.8 years in 1976. Note, however, that increases in life expectancy at maturity and beyond are much smaller. For example, in 1900 average life expectancy at age 20 in the United States was 42.8 years. By 1976 it had increased to only 47.3 years (U.S. Department of Health, Education, and Welfare, 1978).

The dramatic increase in life expectancy at birth is largely a function of health-related advances, which, in particular, have led to a reduction of infant mortality. As a result, a greater proportion of all persons are reaching older ages. For example, in 1900 only 40.9% of the cohort born 65 years earlier were still alive; in 1976, 75.1% were still alive. The increase in life expectancy, then, has resulted largely from improved environmental conditions which have reduced the incidence of premature deaths, particularly in infancy and childhood.

A few years ago there were a number of reports in the popular press of extraordinary longevity in several parts of the world. These included the Republic of Georgia in the USSR, the Vilcabamba Valley in Ecuador, and the province of Hunza in Kashmir. These areas were purported to contain far more persons over the age of 100 than one would expect. For example, whereas about 3 centenarians per 100,000 population would be normal, regions in the Caucasus mountain area of the USSR report about 400 centenarians per 100,000 population. In these areas, reports of persons aged 100 to 120 are common, and reports of persons aged 120 to 170 are not unusual.

Although these claims make "good press," a careful examination of the evidence suggests that they are unfounded (Medvedev, 1974). Generally, the documentation is very poor. There was no birth registration, and few of the very old can produce reliable documents of other types (e.g., military, marriage, education). Usually, the reports have been substantiated by recall of significant past events and by interviews with other residents of the village. Medvedev (1974) notes that social rather than biological factors may account for the phenomenon. For example, in these regions older persons receive much honor and respect. Centenarians often hold special positions in the community and engage in special activities (e.g., chairman of local celebrations). Such positive valuing of the extremely old may result in exaggerations of chronological age.

Thus all indications point to an upper limit on the human life span of about 110 to 120 years. However, some writers speculate that this limit may be exceeded in the not too distant future as researchers discover the basic mechanisms of the aging process (Medvedev, 1975). Others disagree that such a breakthrough will occur and point out that the goal of extending human life raises a host of difficult moral, ethical, political, and economic issues. What problems do you foresee?

DEVELOPMENT: ADOLESCENCE, ADULTHOOD, AND AGING

TABLE 11.1
Classification and summary of biological theories of aging

Classification and Name	Summary
Genetic theories	
DNA damage theory	DNA damage leads to faulty enzyme production and ultimately, to cell death
Somatic mutation theory	Natural radiation of dividing cells produces chromosomal mutations and eventual cell death
Cellular error theory	Faulty transcription of RNA from the DNA results in errors in enzyme production and eventual cell death
Nongenetic theories	
Accumulation theory	Aging results from the buildup of metabolic wastes in the cells
Free-radical theory	Unstable chemical compounds (free radicals) react with cell molecules, interfering with their functioning
Cross-linkage theory	Bonds between molecules (cross-linkages) develop with time, leading to biochemical failure
Physiological theories	
Wear and tear theory	The organism's system simply wears out with time because of stress and usage
Immunological theory	The immune system deteriorates with age, resulting in increased susceptibility to disease and deterioration
Neuroendocrine theory	Homeostatic control systems deteriorate with age, resulting in the inability of multiple systems to function effectively

Source: Based on Shock (1977).

Although it is clear that aging has a genetic basis, many theories have been proposed to explain aging. Some have argued that aging is the result of complex disease processes that are unrecognized. Others have argued that aging is the result of "built-in" processes that predispose the person to disease and deterioration. Several of the theories proposed are summarized in Table 11.1. Each has had some success in explaining a part of the aging phenomenon, but none of them has won general acceptance.

We have briefly noted some of the molecular, cellular, and physiological changes that may be responsible for aging. These changes affect virtually all major systems of the human body: skeletal, muscle, skin, pulmonary, cardiovascular, neural, endocrine, reproductive, gastrointestinal, and excretory. The aging rates associated with some of these parts of the human body are illustrated in Figure 11.3. Note that although the biological changes associated with aging are inevitable and universal, they do not affect all systems equally. Figure 11.3 shows the wide variation in decline which occurs in several indices with age. But how are these changes related to behavior, the basic focus of our inquiry in this text? In the following sections, we will give several examples of how biological changes influence behavior and behavior influences biological changes.

The Eye and Visual Perception. It is clear that some biological changes that occur with age have a rather direct influence on our behavior. For example, surveys show that both blindness and the loss of visual acuity are associated with increasing age. Figure 11.4 shows the corrected visual acuity in the better eye for older adults aged 60 to 90 years. Visual acuity of 20/50 or worse indicates impairment sufficient to limit activities such as reading and

Figure 11.3
Shows average declines in several physiological functions in males. Mean values for 20- to 35-year-old subjects are taken as 100 per cent. Declines are shown as average linear projections from this point. Different functions decline at different rates. (After Shock, 1972)

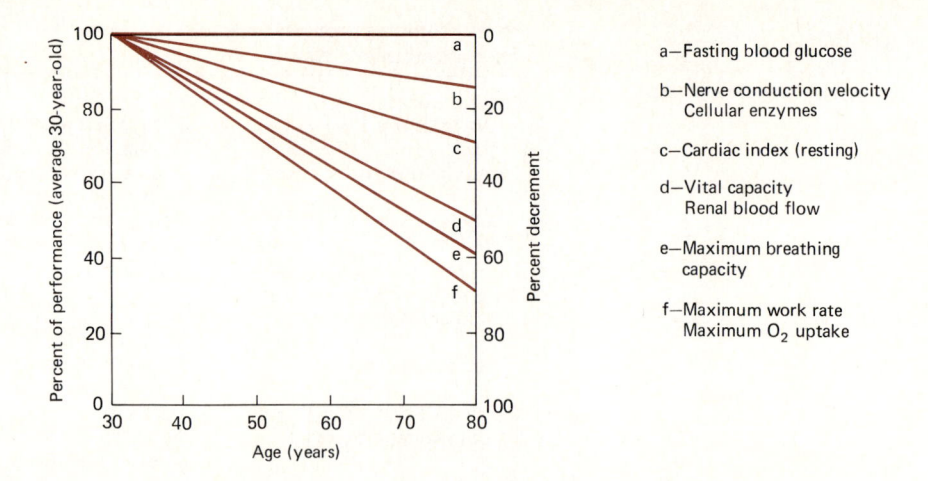

a—Fasting blood glucose
b—Nerve conduction velocity
  Cellular enzymes
c—Cardiac index (resting)
d—Vital capacity
  Renal blood flow
e—Maximum breathing capacity
f—Maximum work rate
  Maximum O$_2$ uptake

driving. These data show that while 57% of those aged 60 to 69 had optimal visual acuity (20–20), only 27% of those aged 70 to 79, and only 14% of those aged 80 and over functioned at this level. This study also found that *cataracts* (opacities of the lens that obstruct light waves) were present in 9% of those aged 60 to 69, 18% of those aged 70 to 79, and 36% of those aged 80 and over. What causes this increasing visual impairment?

The visual problems summarized above reflect the impact of two sets of age-related changes in the eye. The first set of structural changes becomes evident in the thirties and forties. These changes affect the *transmissiveness* (the amount of light reaching the eye) and *accommodative power* (the ability to focus and maintain an image on the retina) of the eye. Several factors, including decreased pupil size and increased clouding and yellowing of the lens, reduce the amount of light reaching the retina. As a result of these changes middle-aged and older adults require more illumination than that needed by younger adults to maintain the same degree of visual discrimi-

Figure 11.4
Shows the corrected best distance vision in the better eye for older adults. Visual acuity decreases significantly with increasing age. (Based on Anderson & Palmore, 1974)

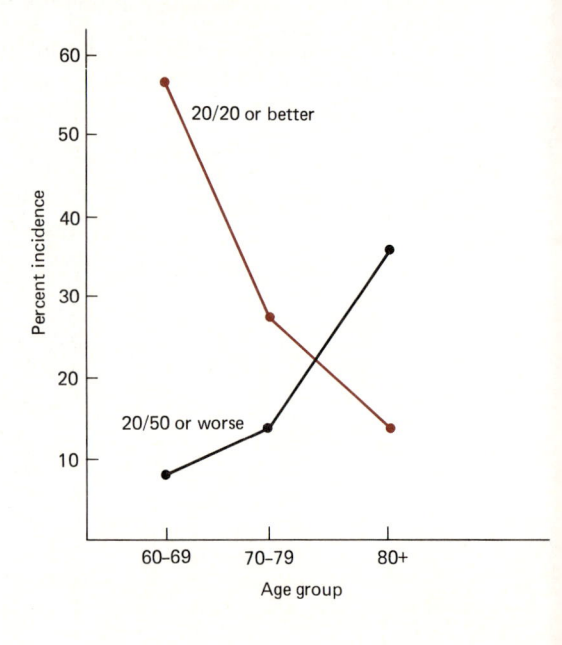

nation. They also result in less sensitivity to color and more susceptibility to glare. During the thirties and forties the lens also becomes thicker and less elastic. As a result, it cannot change shape as readily. This impairs the ability of the eye to focus and maintain an image on the retina. In particular, it becomes difficult for middle-aged and older adults to view close objects clearly *(presbyopia).* This can result in the need for bifocals. The second set of structural changes becomes evident in the fifties and sixties. These changes affect the retina itself. They appear to be primarily the result of reduced blood supply to the retina and, consequently, cell loss. As a consequence, the retina becomes less sensitive to low levels of illumination, and the size of the visual field decreases.

These structural changes in the eye have a significant impact on perception. For example, we noted that older adults are less sensitive to light at low levels of illumination. Many tasks, such as driving at twilight or night, require partial dark adaptation. This involves crossing over from rod to cone vision, and vice versa. Research suggests that under such conditions the decrease in acuity is much greater for older adults than for younger adults. Even at middle levels of illumination, older adults require more illumination than do younger adults. For example, a study by Hughes (reported in Fozard & Popkin, 1978) examined the effect of illumination level on the work performance of younger (19 to 27 years) and middle-aged (46 to 57 years) office workers. The task involved a search for 10 target numbers printed on sheets containing a total of 420 numbers. Each worker performed several searches under three levels of illumination. Increased levels of illumination resulted in greater efficiency for both younger and middle-aged workers. However, the middle-aged workers benefited more from the increase than did the younger workers.

Our brief review suggests that the structural changes which occur in the eye with increasing age have marked behavioral significance. The research also suggests that many of the visual problems of older adults may be eased by appropriate environmental design. For instance, increased local lighting

Some biological changes that occur in middle age directly influence our behavior—for example, the need to wear reading glasses. (Inger McCabe)

of work areas, steps, and ramps, and increased contrast in visual information displays, would compensate for many visual problems of the elderly.

Physical Exercise and Physiological Vigor. Research on the effects of physical exercise illustrates the influence of behavior on biological functioning. It is well known that a regular physical exercise regime produces significant improvements in the physiological functioning of young adults. The training effects of exercise include an increase in vital capacity (maximum amount of air that can be moved through the lungs during heightened activity) and muscle tone, and a decrease in heart rate, blood pressure, and body fat. However, to obtain such training effects, the exercise must be lengthy and strenuous enough to produce sufficient physiological stress. A short walk to the corner drugstore or a game of shuffleboard will not produce a training effect. Benefits come largely from regular *aerobic exercise,* which demands lots of oxygen, such as running, jogging, brisk walking, swimming, and bicycling.

The older adult has lost part of his or her capacity to respond to physiological stress as a result of both aging and disease. Consequently, until recently it was questioned whether middle-aged and older adults could benefit from physical exercise. Research during the last decade, however, has clearly demonstrated the beneficial effects of exercise well into old age. For example, deVries (1970) observed a significant training effect in men aged 51 to 87 who participated in a vigorous exercise program. The program consisted of calisthenics, running and walking, and either stretching exercises or swimming. The men were tested initially and after 6, 18, and 42 weeks of participation. The most significant findings were related to respiratory capacity. Various measures of the ability of the lungs to provide oxygen to the body increased by as much as 35%. Significant improvements in percentage of body fat, physical work capacity, and blood pressure were also observed. These effects were observed regardless of the participants' age or history of physical activity in young adulthood. Similar training effects have been observed in women aged 52 to 79 (Adams & deVries, 1973).

These studies suggest that physical exercise can significantly improve the physical vigor of middle-aged and older adults. Indeed, people who are physically active do tend to live longer than those who are not physically active. Unfortunately, such data are usually confounded by many other variables (e.g., physically active persons also smoke less). Nevertheless, the evidence relating physical exercise to longevity is suggestive, and the evidence relating it to increased functional capacity is clear.

The number of joggers along the road suggests that interest and participation in physical exercise is increasing. Strenuous physical exercise, however, should be undertaken cautiously, especially in middle and old age, since activity that overstresses the system is dangerous. Current research, therefore, has begun to focus on the question "How much is enough?" In this regard, data (deVries 1971) suggest that for all but highly conditioned elderly men, 30 to 60 minutes of vigorous walking which raises the heart rate to 100 to 120 beats per minute is sufficient to bring about some improvement in cardiovascular functioning. It has been consistently suggested, however, that an examination by a physician and an evaluation by an exercise physiologist precede any exercise program.

The Reproduction System and Sexual Behavior. Finally, we should note that certain biological changes with age shape behavior within the context

Men and women do not lose their capacity to enjoy sexual relations just because of age. (Frank Siteman/Stock Boston)

of past experience and expectations for activity. This point is illustrated by changes in the reproductive system and sexual functioning.

A woman's capacity to have children gradually declines from about age 45 and ceases altogether at about age 55. This period during which reproductive capacity diminishes is called the *climacteric*. One particular event in this process is *menopause* (the cessation of menstruation), which typically occurs during a 2-year period around age 47. The major biological change during the climacteric is the aging of the ovaries, resulting in a decline in the output of their two major products: eggs (ova) and hormones (*estrogens* and *progestogens*).

Several changes take place in sexual organs because of the decline in estrogens, including thinning of the vaginal epithelium, decreased vaginal lubrication, decreased vaginal size, increased incidence of vaginitis, and increased intensity of uterine contractions during orgasm. All of these changes may cause pain or discomfort during intercourse, and thus cause the woman to avoid sexual activity. However, the decline in estrogens does not change the female's sexual desire, interest, or ability to reach orgasm. Moreover, these changes seem to be related to the lack of sexual activity. According to Masters and Johnson (1966), women who maintained a pattern of regular intercourse once or twice a week did not complain of difficulties during intercourse when they were experiencing menopause. But those who had intercourse once a month or less, or who did not masturbate regularly reported difficulties. The continuation of sexual activity over the life span, therefore, depends in part on the frequency and regularity of past activity.

Although men do not experience menopause, their reproductive system does change with age. For example, sperm production gradually declines, although viable sperm are produced by the oldest of men. Similarly, hormone levels *(androgens)* gradually decrease; erection occurs more slowly; the amount of seminal fluid decreases; the force of the ejaculation decreases; erection is lost more rapidly after ejaculation; and it takes longer to achieve another erection after ejaculation. Any or all of these changes can cause a man to believe that he is losing his sexual abilities. Other factors which may contribute to a loss of sexual responsiveness in older men include career pressures, overindulgence in alcohol, general deterioration of health, and the perception that an older partner is boring or unattractive. As with women, older men who were sexually active earlier in life are more likely to continue to have and enjoy sexual relations.

Research shows that, in general, interest in and frequency of sexual intercourse decrease from middle age into old age. However, sex is still a significant activity for many older adults and is shared by even the very elderly. In a survey of adults aged 46 to 71, only 6% of the men and 33% of the women indicated that they were no longer interested in sex, and 12% of the men and 44% of the women indicated that they were no longer sexually active (Pfeiffer, Verwoerdt, & Davis, 1974). Much of this decline in sexual interest was not related to biological factors. For example, the overwhelming majority of women over age 60 who were sexually inactive said that they stopped having intercourse because their husbands lost interest in sex, became ill, or had died.

Research suggests, then, that multiple factors interact with biological changes in the reproductive system to affect sexual behavior during adulthood and aging. In particular, past sexual enjoyment and the availability of a socially sanctioned partner appear particularly crucial for continued sexual activity in later life. Certainly, men and women do not lose their capacity to enjoy sexual relations just because of age.

COGNITIVE FUNCTIONING

The perception that cognitive processes—learning, memory, intelligence—decline with increasing age is one of our most pervasive cultural stereotypes. The conclusion that there are age-related deficits in these processes is also reflected in the scientific community. For example, Arenberg and Robertson-Tchabo (1977) conclude that although age-related losses in learning and memory processes are not inevitable, they are widespread and substantial. These writers suggest that denying this pattern of decline is wishful thinking. Are age-related declines in cognitive processes characteristic of adults? Let us examine this quesiton.

The Slowing of Cognitive Behavior. Relatively clear evidence indicates that, with advancing age, people do respond more slowly when performing cognitive tasks. This is a gradual change, occurring across the entire life span. It is particularly evident on those so-called *speeded tasks* where errors would be unlikely if the person had an unlimited amount of time to do them. Typically, they involve relatively simple responses, such as pushing buttons, sorting items, and crossing out items. The objective, of course, is to complete the task as rapidly as possible.

For example, *reaction time* (RT) tasks involve a measure of the time elapsing between the appearance of a signal and the beginning of a responding movement. Reaction time is usually viewed as a measure of central nervous system processing. That is, it involves perceptual and decision-making processes. RT tasks vary in complexity. *Simple RT tasks* involve only one signal and one response (e.g., pushing a button when a light goes on). *Disjunctive RT tasks* involve multiple signals and/or responses (e.g., pushing the right-hand button when the red light goes on and the left-hand button when the green light goes on; pushing the button only when the red light goes on). Hodgkins (1962) examined simple RT performance (subject released a key when a signal light was lit) in over 400 females aged 6 to 84. Hodgkins found that mean speed increased with age until the late teens, remained constant until the mid-twenties, and then declined steadily for the rest of the age range. The degree of change in RT was 25% between the twenties and the sixties and 43% between the twenties and the seventies. The slowing seen with age in simple RT tasks is magnified for disjunctive RT tasks or those which require the subject to remember previous signals and responses.

The slowing of behavior with age appears in a wide range of tasks, including complex tasks such as copying materials or sorting playing cards as well as RT tasks. Indeed, it appears to be a general characteristic of older adults. That is, younger adults appear to be fast or slow, depending on the characteristics of the task and situation (e.g., familiarity, motivation, etc.). Older adults, however, seem to have a characteristic or general slowing of behavior independent of task and situational characteristics. This general slowing does not appear to be primarily a function of peripheral nervous system factors (e.g., sensory acuity, speed of peripheral nerve conduction, or speed of movement once a response is initiated). Rather, it appears to reflect a basic change in the speed with which the central nervous system processes information (Birren, 1974). In part, this may be related to diseases such as *atherosclerosis* (accumulation of fatty deposits in the arteries) which reduce blood flow, and thus oxygen, to the brain. However, behavioral variables are also important. For example, it has been demonstrated that older persons can increase their speed of response with practice (Hoyer, Labouvie, & Baltes,

1973), and that they can compensate for a loss of speed by increased accuracy (Rabbitt & Birren, 1967).

Memory. Recall from Chapter 7 that there are different types of memory. *Sensory memory* involves a brief literal copy of stimuli. *Short-term memory* is a temporary maintenance system for conscious processing. *Long-term memory* is a mechanism for retaining information permanently. What happens to these types of memory as people age?

Research on adult age differences in sensory memory is very limited. Although several studies have suggested the possibility of age-related declines in visual sensory memory, these appear of limited significance to overall age differences in memory performance (Craik, 1977).

There also appears to be little evidence that short-term memory capacity declines with age. One relatively pure measure of short-term memory is derived from the *free-recall* task. In free recall, a person is presented with a series of words during an input phase and is asked to recall as many of them as possible in any order during an output phase. Typically, one outcome of the free-recall procedure is that the last few items of the list are recalled first. This *recency effect* is considered to be a measure of short-term memory, and research has shown that it does not decline with age.

Short-term memory may also be assessed by immediate-memory-span tasks. The *immediate memory span* is defined as the longest string of items (digits, letters, words) that can be reproduced immediately in the order of presentation. If short-term memory does not decline with age, one would expect little decline in performance on immediate-memory-span tasks. This appears to be the case. Several studies have found no age-related losses on digit span tasks (e.g., Talland, 1968).

If sensory and short-term memory processes are related only minimally to age, observed age-related differences in performance should be in long-term memory. We noted in Chapter 7 that long-term memory requires a focus on the meaning of the material. For example, it has been suggested that memory depends on a person's perceptual and cognitive analysis of the

A person's store of information about the world tends to increase with age, and older adults may perform as well as younger adults on tasks that relate to such information. (George Bellerose/Stock Boston)

material: The more it is processed in terms of its semantic meaning, and the more elaborate this analysis, the better the acquisition and retention of the material (Craik & Lockhart, 1972). Compared to younger adults, older adults are deficient in terms of the deep and elaborative processing strategies of long-term memory (Craik, 1977). Older adults do not spontaneously use these strategies as extensively or effectively as younger adults. However, when various strategies are built into the situation, the performance of older adults improves significantly (Hultsch, 1971).

This point is illustrated by a study using Mandler's (1967) procedure summarized in Chapter 7, in which individuals are asked to categorize words to a criterion of two identical sorts prior to free recall. Individuals from three age groups performed the task. To determine the impact of organizational processes on recall, the opportunity to organize the words was manipulated experimentally. Half of those at each age level were instructed to sort the words into from two to seven categories. The other half were not allowed to sort the words physically into categories. These "nonsorting" persons inspected the words one at a time for the same number of trials as taken by a randomly assigned "sorting" partner to reach criterion. Thus the sorting and nonsorting conditions were designed to maximize and minimize the opportunity for a person to organize the material in ways that were meaningful, while equating the number of input trials prior to recall. The results of this study are summarized in Figure 11.5, which indicates that middle-aged and older people showed less of a recall deficit under conditions that maximized the possibility for meaningful organization.

Older adults also appear to be less efficient at retrieving information even after it has been encoded. This is illustrated by findings that age differences are typically minimal if people are asked to recognize the words (i.e., whether they were on the list studied or not) rather than to recall them. This is particularly true if care has been taken to "repair" encoding processes by providing people with effective encoding strategies.

In sum, older adults appear to have difficulty at both the encoding and retrieval stages of secondary memory. At both stages they appear to fail to engage in the type of deep and elaborate processing necessary for optimal memory performance. Such processing generally demands greater attention and mental effort. However, if deeper and more elaborate processing is made easier or more accessible, age differences in performance are reduced.

Recent studies have examined secondary memory performance by asking people to remember more familiar sorts of materials, such as sentences, sto-

Figure 11.5
Results of an experiment designed to show the impact of organizational strategies on recall in adulthood. Individuals either sorted a list of words into categories or inspected them one at a time before recalling them. Middle-aged and older people showed less of a recall deficit under the sorting condition, which maximized the possibility for meaningful organization, than under the nonsorting condition, which minimized it. (After Hultsch, 1971)

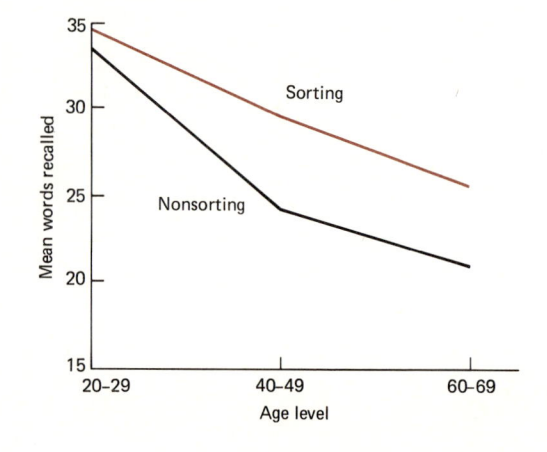

ries, and television programs. In these instances, the focus has been on remembering the meaning or gist of the material as opposed to its exact meaning. In general, it has been found that differences between younger and older people are not as large on such tasks compared to those requiring verbatim recall of lists of words (Hultsch & Dixon, 1984). In particular, few deficiencies are observed for people who are well educated and have superior verbal ability. For example, in a recent study, younger and older adults were asked to view a half-hour episode of a continuing TV series and then were asked to recall and recognize its content (Cavanaugh, 1983). Among people with relatively low verbal ability, younger adults outperformed older adults. However, there were no significant age differences in performance among people with relatively high verbal ability. Figure 11.6 shows the results for recall of statements central to the plot (e.g., main characters) and details relevant to the plot (e.g., subplots).

Another recent set of studies has focused on memory for knowledge which has been acquired through education and other real-world experience. This encompasses an enormous range of information, such as the location of the nearest gas station, the name of the starting quarterback of the Pittsburgh Steelers, and the importance of maintaining a balanced diet. Studies examining such memory have found either no age differences or age differences favoring older adults. For example, Lachman, Lachman, and Thronesbery (1979) asked young (19 to 22 years), middle-aged (44 to 53), and elderly (65 to 74 years) adults to respond to 190 questions covering such topics as famous people, news events, history, geography, the Bible, literature, sports, mythology, and general information (e.g., "What was the former name of Muhammad Ali?"; "What is the capital city of Canada?"). No evidence of age differences in retrieval of world knowledge was found. The elderly group actually answered more questions correctly than the younger groups, although the differences were not statistically significant.

The results of such recent work contrast with studies of list materials on

Figure 11.6
Shows the result of an experiment examining age differences in recall of the gist of familiar, meaningful material. People were asked to view a half-hour television episode and then to recall its content. In the case of both recall of information central to the plot and details relevant to the plot, no age differences were observed for people with good verbal abilities. However, for people with poorer verbal abilities, younger adults outperformed older adults. (Based on Cavanaugh, 1983)

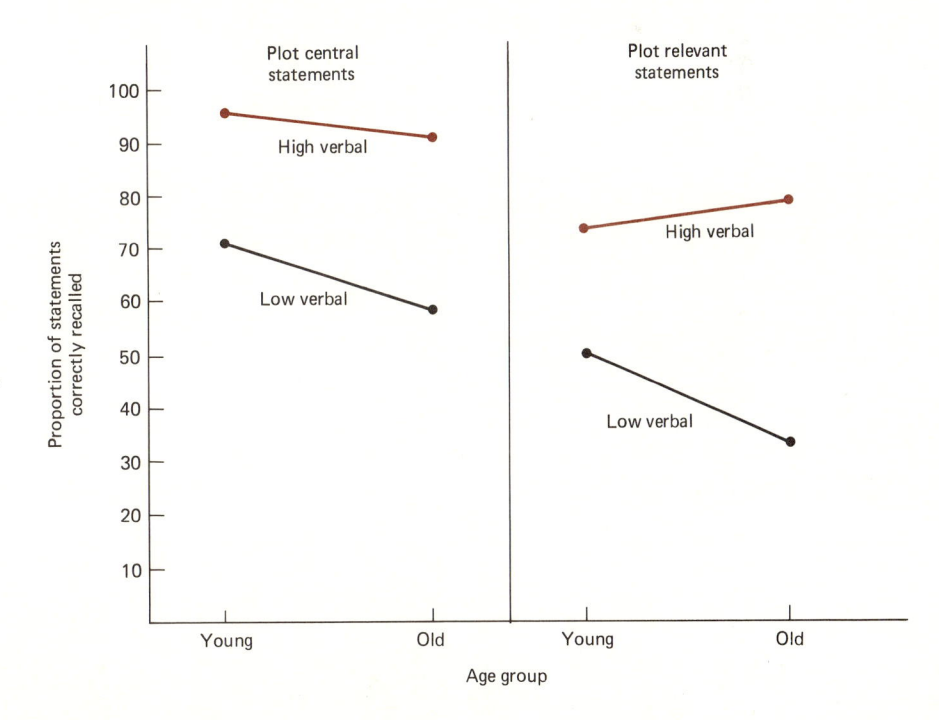

which even well-educated older adults typically perform more poorly than younger adults. One explanation of this discrepancy is that certain encoding and retrieval mechanisms actually do decline with age. However, the person's store of information about the world tends to increase with age. To the extent that a person has remained cognitively active and the task relates to such world knowledge, older adults may perform as well as younger adults despite less effective memory mechanisms.

Intelligence. Early theorists and researchers maintained that universal decline in intelligence during adulthood occurs as a result of intrinsic, biologically based aging processes. Wechsler (1958), for example, portrays a bleak picture, arguing that most *abilities* decline progressively after peaking between the ages of 18 and 25. But does *intelligence* decline with increasing age? Wechsler answered yes, but extensive research over 30 years has not provided a definitive answer. Rather, there has been increasing controversy over the timing, extent, and sources of intellectual change during adulthood. Thus, on the one hand, Baltes and Schaie (1974) have concluded that "general intellectual decline in old age is largely a myth" (p. 35), while, on the other hand, Botwinick (1977), has concluded that "decline in intellectual ability is clearly part of the aging picture" (p. 580). How do we resolve this discrepancy?

First, it is clear that there are multiple abilities and that these show different patterns of change with age. Recall, for example, Horn's distinction between fluid and crystallized intelligence described in Chapter 8. *Fluid intelligence* reflects the degree to which a person can perceive relationships and solve problems that are relatively free of culturally based content. *Crystallized intelligence*, on the other hand, reflects the degree to which a person has accumulated knowledge about the world.

As shown in Figure 11.7, Horn's theory postulates that fluid intelligence declines during adulthood after a peak in early adulthood, while crystallized intelligence increases throughout adulthood. Horn and Cattell (1966) examined age differences on tests reflecting fluid and crystallized intelligence. Their results are displayed in Figure 11.8. Fluid intelligence decreases steadily from adolescence through middle age, whereas crystallized intelligence increases.

Figure 11.7
Shows the pattern of change for fluid intelligence (degree to which the person can perceive relationships and solve problems that are relatively free of cultural content) and crystallized intelligence (degree to which the person has accumulated knowledge about the world) according to Horn's theory. Fluid abilities are hypothesized to peak in early adulthood and then to decline, whereas crystallized abilities are hypothesized to continue to increase throughout adulthood. (Based on Horn & Donaldson, 1980)

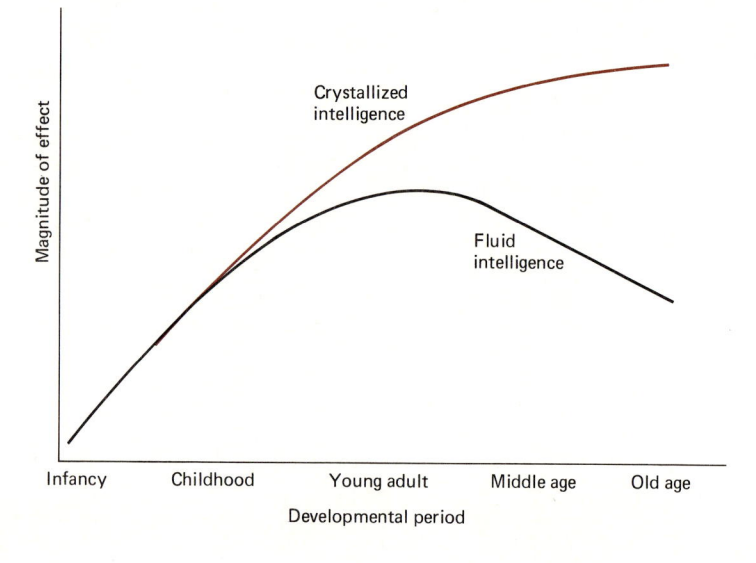

FOCUS ON THE PSYCHOLOGIST

Paul B. Baltes

PAUL B. BALTES, born in 1939 in Germany, is a developmental psychologist and gerontologist. After thirteen years as a professor in the United States (1968–1980), he returned to Germany to become Co-Director of the Berlin Max Planck Institute for Human Development and Education and Professor of Psychology at the Free University of Berlin. Baltes received his undergraduate and graduate training in psychology in Germany at the University of Saarbrücken. Paul Baltes' main research areas are longitudinal methodology, the study of adult and old-age intelligence, and research on the history and theory of life-span developmental psychology. Currently (1983–1987), he serves as President of the International Society for the Study of Behavioural Development.

Researchers who study life-span development are perhaps more prone than others to engage in a continuous dialogue with themselves as they compare their own life with their "scientific" knowledge of life-span development. Remembering one's past is as much a process of searching for what was, as it is a process of continuous reconstruction of the past in light of its aftermath. As a consequence, subjective stories about the past are often well organized and fitting. The objective "facts," however, may have been different.

My earliest personal memories about my interest in the idea of intelligence date back to an older brother who introduced psychology and competitive intelligence testing (in the form of the Raven Progressive Matrices) into our everyday family life. I realized then that psychology was emerging as a field of study that he wanted to pursue but for various accidental reasons beyond his control could not enter. Soon thereafter it was I, the younger brother, who set his course toward becoming a psychologist. I took with me the belief that the topic of intelligence was at the heart of psychology.

My commitment to the study of adult and old-age intelligence was subsequently enhanced by K. Warner Schaie, with whom I studied for a year (1963–1964) while on graduate student leave in the U.S. Throughout these years and even into the early 1970s, however, I remember myself being driven intellectually by statistical and methodological questions about the validity of age-comparative (cross-sectional, longitudinal) research. Indeed, my Ph.D. thesis on sequential strategies (1967) at Saarbrücken focused on these concerns. Luckily, this interest in developmental methodology did not proceed in a substantive vacuum. Rather, it turned out that my earlier studies on the topic of intelligence provided an empirically rich forum for demonstrating the relevance of the age/cohort methods discussed. One issue, in particular, became dominant: the search for the conditions and extent of plasticity or malleability of intelligence at various stages of the life course.

At that time, the view that aging is fairly fixed and synonymous with decline was pervasive. Aside from the question of empirical evidence on the matter, I confess that my personal ideologies played a strong role in not accepting this image of aging and in shaping my ensuing research and interpretive posture on plasticity. I see myself as someone who believes, as a matter of principle, in the self-regulatory power of individuals and also in the notion that much of psychological reality is the expression of "hidden" social conditions. These personal, "subjective" beliefs no doubt affected my view of the data on adult and old-age intelligence. Having observed large differences in the course of aging (between persons, generations, and subabilities of intelligence, for example), I came to believe that similar variability may also exist in individuals. I argued that, depending on their life conditions, people could display rather different trajectories of aging. This posture generated a new research program that dealt with the experimental study of intellectual plasticity and reserve capacity in old age. The results of this suggested more malleability of intellectual aging than assumed.

As I continue to study the course of adult and old-age intelligence, I am mindful of limits on performance and plasticity. We see intellectual aging as a dynamic interplay between growth and decline. Older persons have much reserve capacity and much potential for positive change. At the same time, they need special support to deal effectively with the biological losses that are also an intrinsic part of aging.

Figure 11.8
Shows age differences on measures reflecting fluid and crystallized intelligence. Fluid intelligence decreases steadily from adolescence through middle age, whereas crystallized intelligence increases. (Based on Horn & Cattell, 1966)

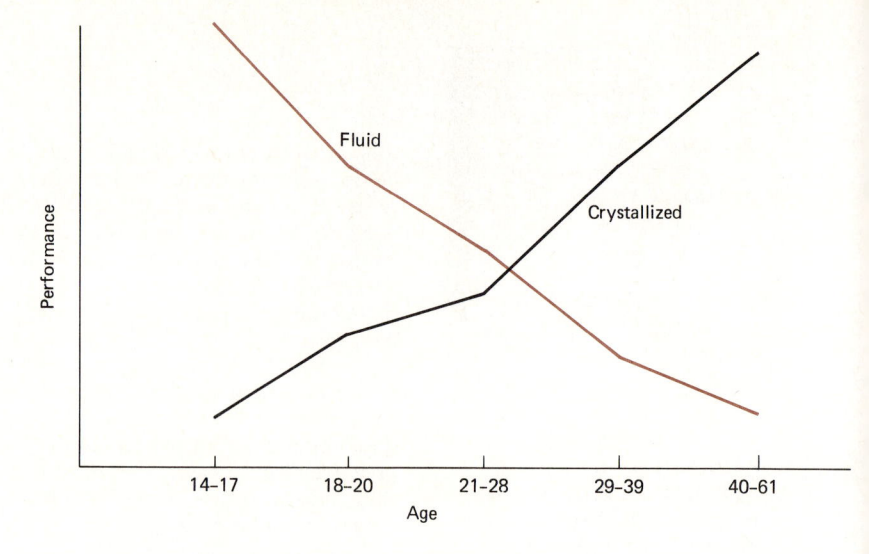

The research reviewed in the preceding section emphasizes both gains and losses in intellectual functioning during adulthood. Gains are seen in abilities which reflect measures of crystallized intelligence. Losses are seen in abilities which reflect measures of fluid intelligence. The latter abilities are thought to be particularly affected by the degeneration of physiological functioning with age. Thus it has been suggested that whereas some intellectual functions (e.g., crystallized) remain stable or increase, others (e.g., fluid) must be expected to decline as a logical consequence of the aging process.

In contrast, other researchers have argued that aging does not necessarily imply inevitable, irreversible, and universal loss—even for fluid abilities (e.g., Labouvie-Vief, 1977). Although these researchers do not deny the reality of loss in cognitive functioning in many elderly persons they do suggest that the former view of intellectual decline is too pessimistic.

At the heart of the disagreement over intellectual change is the issue of whether the observed differences reflect changes related to age or differences related to generational membership. The problem is that when we compare people at any one point in time, we are also comparing people who were born at different points in history. For example, in 1986, 60-year-olds are not only 40 years older than 20-year-olds, but they were also born in 1926 rather than 1966. More technically, they are members of different *birth cohorts* (those people born at a particular point in historical time). Of course, people born at different points in history have had very different experiences. Some of these, such as the nature of the schooling to which they have been exposed, may be very relevant for intellectual functioning. The question, then, is whether differences in intellectual performance are more a function of age changes or of cohort differences.

In fact, research has convincingly demonstrated the importance of historical change for intellectual functioning (e.g., Schaie, 1979). For the most part, differences between cohorts (people born at different points in history) are larger than age changes, particularly before age 65. For example, Figure 11.9 shows scores on measures of intelligence and educational aptitude for members of different cohorts (born at various points between 1899 and 1931), all of whom were 53 years of age at the time of testing. It is clear that people born later in history score better than people of the same age who were born earlier in history.

Figure 11.9
Shows scores on measures of intelligence and educational aptitude for members of different birth cohorts (born at various points between 1899 and 1931), all of whom were 53 years of age at the time of testing. People born later in history score better than people of the same age who were born earlier in history, thus showing the importance of historical change for intellectual functioning. (After Schaie & Labouvie-Vief, 1974)

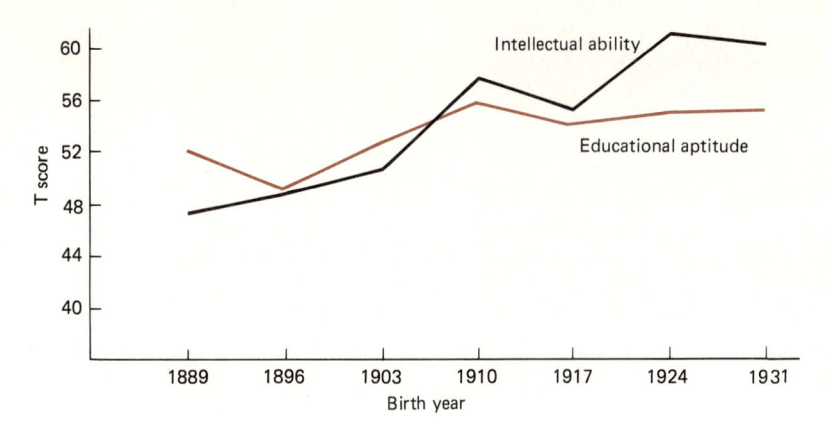

These data suggest that conclusions of an inevitable, universal, age-related decline are open to question. However, while intellectual decline may not be inevitable and universal, it does occur. In a now classical study, Birren, Butler, Greenhouse, Sokoloff, and Yarrow (1963) examined the relationship of health and psychological functioning in older men who were classified into two groups on the basis of their health. Group I consisted of "superhealthy" men with trivial health problems (e.g., varicose veins) or without any evidence of disease at all. Group II consisted of "less healthy" men with signs of potentially serious health problems (e.g., atherosclerosis). However, these men were not actually ill, and the incipient diseases were discovered only after rigorous medical tests. Nevertheless, the Group I men scored higher than the Group II men on a battery of 23 tests of cognitive functioning. In particular, the "superhealthy" men scored higher than the "less healthy" men on measures of verbal intelligence. Declines in intellectual functioning also appear to be related to cardiovascular disease, high blood pressure, and nearness to death.

Physical pathologies are not the only potential causes of intellectual deterioration late in life. Several writers have argued that the latter part of life, particularly the post retirement portions, is characterized by environmental conditions that discourage the development of social and intellectual competence. For example, youth and middle age have better defined roles and expectations than those of old age. If anything, the role of old age is to be "sick," and the expectations are for increasing dependence and incompetence. Langer (1981) calls this the *senility stereotype*. Such expectations are often accompanied by the withdrawal of appropriate reinforcers for competent behavior. As a result, decline becomes a self-fulfilling prophecy in which the older person expects to and actually does become less competent.

Thus intellectual decline in adulthood is not uniformly distributed in the population. Most of adulthood is characterized by stability or increases in intellectual performance. Decline, however, does occur late in life and is particularly associated with disease or reduced environmental stimulation.

PERSONALITY DEVELOPMENT

What happens during adulthood to those characteristics and behavioral tendencies typically labeled personality? The traditional position is that personality patterns are established during childhood and adolescence and then

Sixty-year-olds tend to see their environment as threatening and themselves as passive and accommodating. (Ray Ellis)

remain stable during adulthood. Is this the case? Are our personalities in adulthood, shaped by events early in life, essentially constant? Or do our personalities undergo major changes as we encounter new events and situations while growing older? Actually, several major cross-sectional and longitudinal studies have found evidence for both constancy and change in adult personality.

The Kansas City Studies. Neugarten and her colleagues at the University of Chicago (Neugarten, 1964) conducted a sequence of interrelated cross-sectional studies over 10 years. Relatively large samples of healthy adults between the ages of 40 and 80 residing in Kansas City during the 1950s participated in these studies. Generally, these studies found evidence for both continuity and change of adult personality. On the one hand, personality structure was stable. That is, the same "types" of people were observed at all ages. Similarly, characteristics associated with adapting to the world (e.g., goal-directed behavior, coping styles, life satisfaction) were not age-related. For example, Neugarten and her colleagues found no relationship between age and a measure of life satisfaction considered to reflect adaptive adjustment to aging.

On the other hand, Neugarten and her colleagues found marked age differences in the person's style of coping with the inner world of experience. For example, 40-year-olds felt in charge of their environment, saw themselves as a source of energy, and felt positive about taking risks. Sixty-year-olds, however, saw the environment as threatening and even dangerous and themselves as passive and accommodating. This change was described as a movement from *active mastery* to *passive mastery*. Gutmann (1977) found the same changes in men in four other societies: the Navajo of Arizona, the Lowland and Highland Mayans of Mexico, and the Druze of Israel.

Similarly, older adults appear to be more preoccupied with their inner life. They were more introspective and self-reflective than younger adults and showed a general movement from an outer-world toward an inner-world orientation. Older persons tend to withdraw emotional investments, become less assertive, and avoid challenges. This change was described as an increased *interiority* of the personality.

Along with the increase in passive mastery and interiority, Neugarten and her colleagues noted a sex difference among the older portion of their sample. On the one hand, older men seemed more receptive to their affiliative and nurturant impulses than younger men. On the other hand, older women seemed more receptive to their aggressive and egocentric impulses than younger women. This shift in sex-role perceptions occurred only for the older people in the sample. This perception may reflect the actual decreased authority older men experience with retirement and the increased authority older women experience with widowhood.

The Berkeley Studies. During the late 1920s and early 1930s, three longitudinal studies were begun at the University of California at Berkeley: the Berkeley Guidance Study, Berkeley Growth Study, and Oakland Growth Study. Each of these studies involved regular assessments during childhood and several follow-up assessments during adulthood.

Block (1971) combined data from the Berkeley Guidance Study and Oakland Growth Study to assess patterns of personality development from early adolescence to early adulthood. Data were available from the junior high school and high school periods, and Block collected follow-up data when the subjects were in their mid-thirties. Based on these data, Block identified five personality types for males and six personality types for females. He found evidence for substantial stability in these types over time. For example, the average correlation between personality types at senior high school and early adulthood was about .50. However, as new data on the same persons at middle age were analyzed focusing on personality traits rather than types, evidence of change as well as stability in personality change emerged. In particular, by middle age, people tended to become more candid, insightful, and comfortable with themselves and less guilty, less bothered by demands, and less defensive.

In addition, 142 parents of the Berkeley subjects were interviewed twice—initially when they were in their thirties and again when they were in their seventies (Maas & Kuypers, 1974). Several different patterns of life style and personality change emerged. For example, one group of younger women expressed dissatisfaction with their economic and marital situations, but found relief from these distresses as they aged. The relief was often associated with the loss of their spouses in their middle years. This event permitted the development of a new and gratifying life-style focused on their employment, independence, and new friends. However, perhaps the most interesting finding of this study was the suggestion that most peoples' lives did not follow a downhill course. Most of the elderly people interviewed were involved in diverse and rewarding activities. Most of them were coping well with growing older.

HIGHLIGHT 11.4
The Life Review

It is commonly observed that older persons spend much time reminiscing about the past. What is the significance of this activity? Butler (1963) proposed that the reminiscence of the aged reflects, in part, a universal process of life review which may have both positive and negative outcomes.

Reminiscence often is viewed as a nonpurposeful activity which, while filling the void of later life, reduces the person's contact with reality. In contrast, Butler suggested that the *life review* is a necessary examination of past experiences, particularly unresolved conflicts. In many respects, the life review appears to be a culmination of a life-long evaluative process that occurs prominently at various points in adulthood such as midlife. According to Butler, the life review is brought about by the realization of impending death. As a result, it is commonly observed in the aged, although it also occurs in younger persons who expect to die (e.g., the terminally ill).

The life review may be associated with negative feelings. Many experience feelings of mild regret and nostalgia. In extreme instances, the person may become obsessed with their past and experience severe anxiety or depression. Three groups appear to be particularly prone to such despair: those who always placed great emphasis on the future but disliked the present; those who are afflicted by real guilt because of attempts to injure others; and the highly narcissistic, for whom death is the ultimate threat. However, for many people the life review leads to the reorganization of past experience, expanded understanding, and personality growth. Such positive manifestations of the life review may help to account for the serenity and wisdom of some older adults.

STAGES OF ADULT DEVELOPMENT

Some theorists contend that adult personality cannot be understood in isolation. Rather they argue that the individual's personality must be seen in the larger social/cultural context. The demands of this context change during adulthood, thus imposing a changing set of developmental tasks which influence personality development. As a result, adult development may be understood as a sequence of stages, transitions, or transformations which reflect the emergence of qualitatively different characteristics at different points in the life span. Although people may differ in terms of specific behaviors and characteristics, the sequence of change defined by the various stages, transitions, or transformations is universal.

Erikson's Theory. According to Erikson (1959, 1963), personality is determined by an inner maturational "ground plan" and by the external demands of society. For Erikson, personality development involves a sequence of eight psychosocial stages. These stages are biologically based and constitute a fixed sequence that everyone experiences. Within each stage, however, a particular capability of the personality must be developed if people are to adapt to the demands placed on them by society at that point in their life. If the capability is not developed within the allotted time, that aspect of the personality will be impaired. Each stage, then, constitutes a crisis—between attaining and sensing the attainment of the appropriate capability. Erikson's last three stages concern young adulthood, adulthood, and maturity.

In young adulthood, the crisis is between developing a sense of intimacy versus a sense of isolation. During adolescence a person should achieve a sense of identity and know who he or she is. The society now requires the person to enter into an institution that will help the society to continue to exist. Accordingly, a new family unit must be formed—for example, through marriage. The young adult must form a relationship with another person which will allow such an institution to prosper. Erikson argues that to enter into and maintain such a relationship successfully requires persons to give of themselves totally. Such openness is not limited to sexual relations. Rather, Erikson argues that all facets of one person (e.g., feelings, ideas, goals, attitudes, values) must be unconditionally available to the other person. Moreover, the person must be unconditionally receptive to these same things from the partner. To the extent that one can attain such an interchange, one will feel a sense of *intimacy*. If people cannot share and be shared, they will feel a sense of *isolation*.

In adulthood the crisis is between developing a sense of generativity versus a sense of stagnation. *Generativity* requires that the person contribute to the maintenance and perpetuation of society. One can be generative by creating products associated with the maintenance of society (e.g., goods and services), or by producing, rearing, and/or socializing children to perpetuate society. If the person cannot create products for the maintenance or perpetuation of society, a sense of *stagnation* results.

In maturity, people realize that they are reaching the end of life. If they have successfully progressed through the previous stages of development, they will face old age with enthusiasm; they will feel that they have led a full and complete life. In Erikson's terms, they will either achieve a sense of *integrity* or feel *despair*—that life has been wasted.

Evidence relevant to Erikson's theory comes from data collected as part of the Grant study (Vaillant, 1977), in which 268 men were selected from the 1939–1941 and 1942–1944 classes of Harvard University, studied as

Adults are expected to be productive, contributing members of their societies by producing, rearing, and socializing children. (Stock Boston)

undergraduates, and followed regularly by mail after graduation. Vaillant interviewed a random sample of 94 men from the classes of 1942–1944 when they were in their forties and fifties.

Vaillant interprets his data as both supporting and expanding Erikson's theory. He notes that from age 20 to 30 the Grant study men focused on the crisis of intimacy versus isolation. Once the men won real autonomy from their parents and established their own independent identities, they sought to entrust themselves to others. Often, this change was represented by marriage. Failure to achieve intimacy was important for later development. For example, 28 of the 30 best-adjusted men at age 47 had achieved stable marriages before age 30 and had remained married until age 50. In contrast, 23 of the 30 worst-adjusted men had either married after age 30 or separated from their wives before age 50.

From age 25 to 35 the Grant study men focused on their careers and developing their nuclear family. The focus is on work rather than play, outer life rather than inner life. This emphasis on achievement often resulted in the sacrifice of adolescent idealism and openness to new experiences. Vaillant suggests that this stage of development is not reflected in Erikson's theory.

Finally, Vaillant argues that during the late thirties and the forties, the Grant study men underwent a "second adolescence;" in which they reassessed and reordered what had occurred in adolescence and young adulthood. This is often a time of change and turmoil. However, part of the outcome of this process may be a sense of generativity—a concern for future generations. For example, by age 50, 19 of the 44 men who had entered business had become their own bosses. In doing so, their career patterns had broadened. They assumed responsibility for others. In contrast, others failed to achieve generativity, continuing to worry about "making it" and not about the welfare of others.

Vaillant concludes that the lives of the Grant study men support both the basic stages outlined by Erikson and his assertion that a given stage of development can rarely be achieved until the previous one is mastered.

Levinson's Theory. Recently, Levinson (1978) and his colleagues have proposed a sequence of five eras and periods, shown in Figure 11.10, which span the male adult life cycle. The eras are (1) preadulthood, age 0 to 22; (2) early adulthood, age 17 to 45; (3) middle adulthood, age 40 to 65; (4) late adulthood, age 60 to 85; and (5) late late adulthood, age 80+. The evolution of these eras is structured by a series of developmental periods and transitions. The primary task of the stable period is to build a life structure. Building a life structure involves making certain crucial choices and striving to attain particular goals. Stable periods ordinarily last 6 to 8 years. the primary task of the transition periods is to terminate the existing life structure and initiate a new one. This involves reappraising the current structure, exploring new possibilities for change, and moving toward crucial choices that will provide the basis for a new life structure. Transition periods ordinarily last 4 to 5 years. To date, Levinson's (1978) research has focused on the periods within early and middle adulthood.

The *early adult transition* begins at age 17 to 18 and extends until age 22 to 23. It links preadulthood and early adulthood and involves two major tasks. The first is to terminate the adolescent life structure. This involves modifying relationships with the family and other persons, groups, and institutions significant to the preadult world. The second is to make a preliminary step into the adult world. This involves making initial explorations and choices for adult living. Major life events within this transition may include

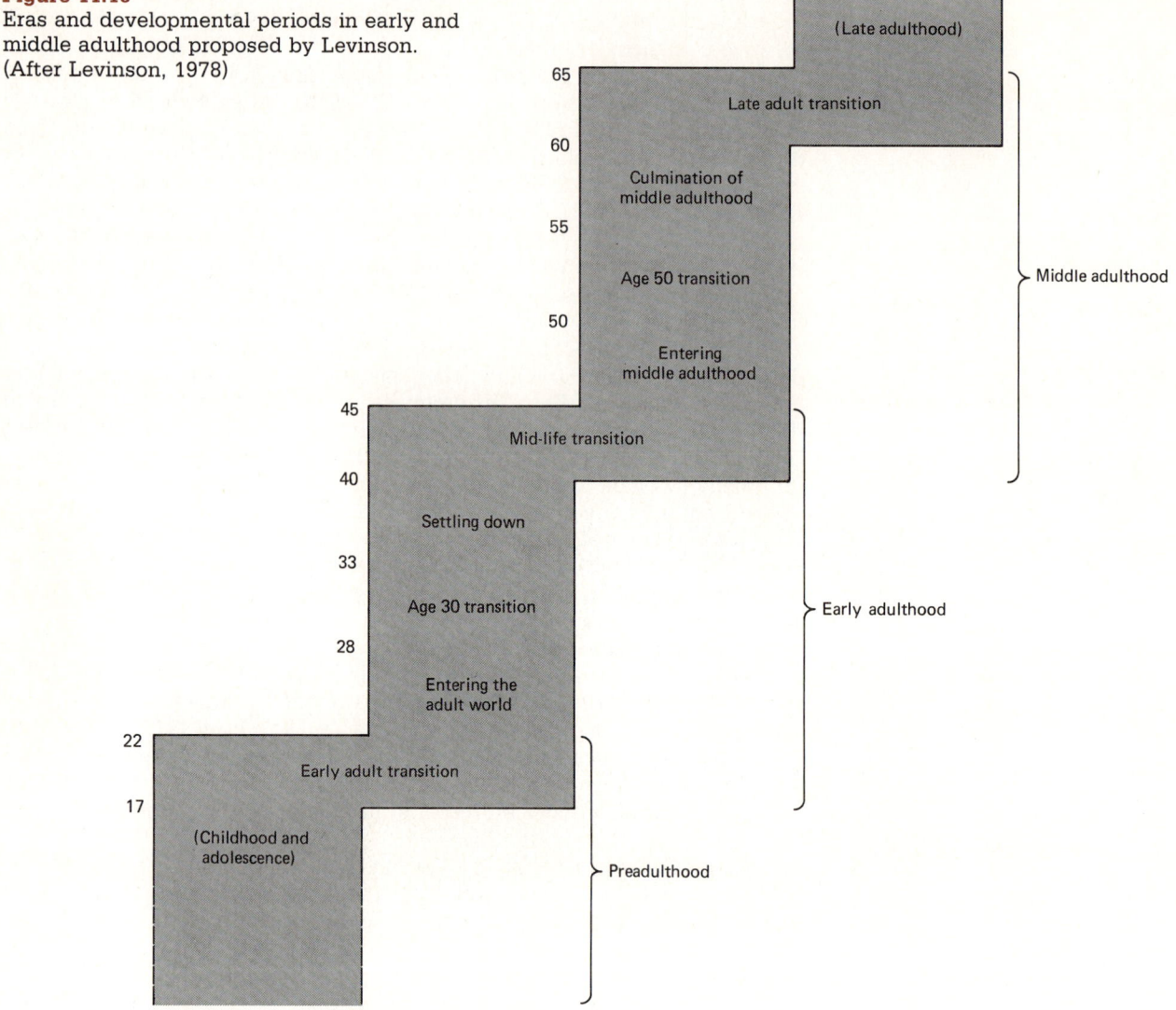

Figure 11.10
Eras and developmental periods in early and middle adulthood proposed by Levinson. (After Levinson, 1978)

graduating from high school, moving out of the family home, entering college, and graduating.

The next period *(entering the adult world)* runs from the early twenties to the late twenties. The focus is on exploration and provisional commitment to adult roles and responsibilities. The young adult faces two opposite tasks according to Levinson. On the one hand, he must explore alternative possibilities for adult living—keeping options open and avoiding strong commitments. On the other hand, he must create a stable life structure—becoming responsible and "making something" of himself. Examples of life events which are often crucial during this period include occupational choice, first job, marriage, and the birth of children.

The *age thirty transition* (28 to 33 years) provides an opportunity to modify the provisional adult life structure created earlier. Some men have a relatively smooth transition, building directly on the past. The focus is on adjustment and enrichment. However, Levinson notes that most men experience a moderate to severe crisis. Divorce and occupational change are frequent during this period.

The *settling down* period begins in the early thirties and extends until about age 40. As implied in the name, this period emphasizes stability and security. A man makes deeper commitments to occupation, family, or other significant enterprises. There is also an emphasis on what Levinson calls "making it." This involves long-range planning toward specific goals within the context of a timetable for their achievement. Until the early thirties, the young man has been a novice adult. During the settling down period, he must become a full-fledged adult.

The *mid-life transition* spans a period of from 4 to 6 years reaching a peak in the early forties. The midlife transition represents a developmental link between early adulthood and middle adulthood and is part of both eras. The transition may be relatively smooth, but is more likely to involve considerable turmoil. However, the outcome does not entirely depend on a man's previous success or failure in achieving goals. The creation of a life structure in early adulthood involved a commitment to some goals and a rejection of others. No one life structure can permit the expression of all aspects of the self. A task of the midlife transition is to work on and partially resolve this discrepancy between what is and what might be. According to Levinson, the midlife transition is not prompted by any one life event or series of events. Rather, multiple processes and events are involved, including the reality and experience of bodily decline, changing relations among the various generations, and the evolution of career and other enterprises.

As the midlife transition ends, there is a new period of stability *(entering middle adulthood)*. A new life structure emerges which provides the basis for moving into middle adulthood. This period begins at about age 45 and extends until about age 50. Sometimes the start of this new life structure is marked by a significant life event—a change in job or occupation, divorce or love affair, or a move to a new community. In other instances, the changes are more subtle. As was true after the age thirty transition, the life structure that emerges following the midlife transition is crucial for the person's adjustment.

Entering middle adulthood is the last specific period for which Levinson has data because of the current age of the men in his sample. However, he has projected a tentative view of subsequent periods during middle adulthood. An *age fifty transition*, analogous to the age thirty transition, is postulated to occur from age 50 to 55. In this period, a man can modify the life structure formed in the mid-forties. A stable period, analogous to settling down, is postulated to occur from age 55 to 60. This period is the culmination of middle adulthood. Finally, from age 60 to 65, a *late adult transition* is postulated to terminate middle adulthood and provide a basis for living in late adulthood. Also of great interest is whether women exhibit the same sequence of changes as men.

DYING, DEATH, AND GRIEF

The ultimate result of aging is death. What do you think of when you think about death? Do you visualize a hospital, a corpse, a funeral home, a religious service, or a cemetery? Do you believe that once you are dead you will

The ultimate result of aging is death, an inevitable, universal event that affects our developmental course even though we only experience it at the end of life. (Ray Ellis)

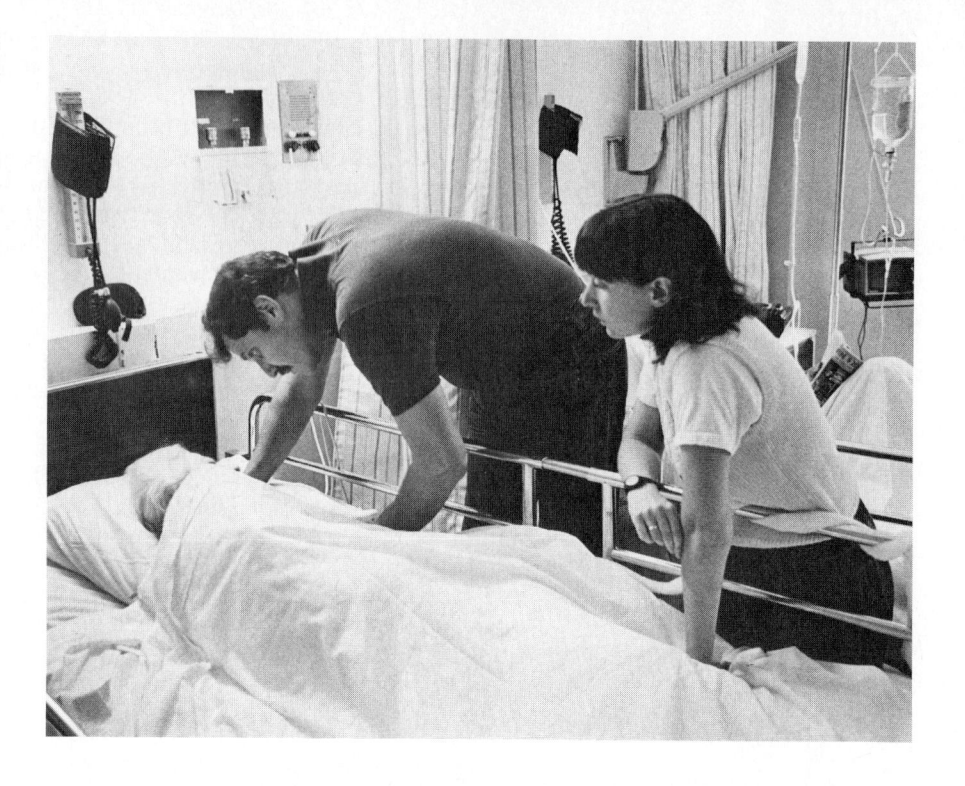

experience eternal life, a return to this world, a period of restful waiting, or nothing? Although death is an inevitable, universal event that occurs daily, our own death occurs only once. Death is a mysterious paradox, therefore, because it affects our developmental course even though we only experience it at the end of life. Becker (1973), for example, contends that the major concern of all ages is death and what it represents. If we did not have to face death, our lives probably would be transformed. We would have different views about the events we experience and the relevance of their timing.

Attitudes Toward Death. Older people talk more and think more about death than younger people. However, paradoxically they appear to be less frightened by it. Kalish (1976) proposes three reasons for this attitude. First, once people have lived to a certain age they may feel they have received the time they are entitled to. Second, the elderly recognize that real factors limit their continued enjoyment of life (e.g., health problems, role losses). Finally, older persons have generally had experience with death through the loss of friends and family members. As a result, much of its mystery is lost.

Many variables other than age affect how death is perceived. For example, people who are more religious have less anxiety about death than those who are less religious. More specifically, the very religious have the least fear of death, the most nonreligious have a moderate fear of death, and irregular religious worshippers have the highest fear of death (Kalish, 1976).

The Dying Process. Undoubtedly, the best known description of the dying process is that proposed by Kübler-Ross (1969). Based on a set of clinical experiences with dying patients, she proposed a series of five stages of dying: denial, anger, bargaining, depression, and acceptance.

Denial is the first stage. The person resists the reality of impending death and in essence says "No!" to death. Denial is displayed in various ways. For instance, some people seek a more favorable diagnosis, others forms of religious assurance, still others try "miracle cures."

Anger is the second stage. "Why me?" The dying feel hostility, resentment, and even envy. They hate the fact that they are to die, resent their situation, and envy all those who are not dying. These feelings may be directed at family, friends, the medical staff, aspects of the environment (e.g., a pen that won't work), or even God. The person feels frustrated by all that will remain unfinished.

Bargaining is the third and middle stage. Here the person decides to change his or her strategy. That is, rather than saying "No" and "Why me?", favors are asked to extend life or postpone death. Although such bargaining is often conducted between the person and God in a covert fashion, sometimes it is evidenced overtly in interactions with others. For example, a person might say: "If I rewrite my will and leave money to more people and charities rather than for a lavish funeral, then please let me live longer. I am a good person." Or "I will be a better person if I can have just a little more time."

Depression is the fourth stage. This occurs when the manifestations of the patient's terminal illness become too significant to ignore. Increasingly severe symptoms, hospitalization, and more surgery eventually lead to a realization that death cannot be avoided and to a sense of great loss.

Acceptance is the final stage. Actually, the person is resolute about death, although not happy. Tired and weak physically, the person "is almost void of feelings. It is as if the pain had gone, the struggle is over, and there comes a time for 'the final rest before the long journey' as one patient phrased it" (Kübler-Ross, 1969, p. 100).

Kübler-Ross (1974) cautions that not all people go through this stage sequence and that we could potentially harm dying patients by viewing this series of feelings as invariant and universal. Unfortunately, her stages have become a prescription for dealing with dying patients—a kind of "pop death." In fact, Küber-Ross has recently emphasized individual differences in the dying process and the importance of identifying and accepting a patient's response pattern. She stresses that the defenses of dying people should not be challenged or broken down by family, friends, or medical staff. For example, some persons may exhibit denial throughout the dying process and it is not productive to attempt to push them through the stages.

Grief and Bereavement. *Grief* is an emotional response to loss. Many researchers feel that there are phases of grief (Glick, Weiss, & Parkes, 1974). The initial phase begins when the death occurs and continues for a few weeks after the funeral. At first, people react with shock and disbelief. The bereaved often state that they feel dazed, numb, empty, and confused. This reaction lasts several days and then gives way to all-encompassing feelings of sorrow which often manifests itself in crying and weeping. With the passage of time, controlling emotions becomes associated with "doing well." Thus the bereaved person is encouraged to inhibit emotional responses. Some may turn to tranquilizers, sleeping pills, or alcohol, or they may report a variety of psychophysiological symptoms (e.g., shortness of breath, tightness in the throat, loss of appetite, irritability, muscular aches and pains, headaches, etc.). Typically, these symptoms are reduced after the first month of bereavement.

The intermediate phase of normal grief usually occupies the balance of the first year. Behavior in this phase consists of obsessional review, searching for an understanding of death, and searching for the presence of the deceased. The obsessional review is highlighted by dwelling on specific events associated with the death and berating one's self for not doing enough (e.g., "If I only called the ambulance sooner" or "If I had only been with him in the hospital"). Searching for answers to understand death often ends with: "It's God's will." Finally, searching for the deceased occurs in various ways. Many activities remind the bereaved of the person or result in thoughts about or memories of the person. These behaviors decrease during the first year. Glick et al. (1974) reported, for example, that 60% of the widows in their study were beginning to feel more like their old selves after a few months and felt they had done quite well by the end of the year.

The second year of bereavement is referred to as the recovery phase, because the bereaved evidence a positive attitude toward life. They are alive and have a life to live. Most state that they have pride in having coped with and survived a traumatic, potentially devastating event. Although professional treatment is available for those who are bereaved, the majority who experience bereavement do so with the support of family and friends.

SUMMARY

1. Adolescence is a period of transition between childhood and adulthood. Numerous characteristics undergo important changes during this period.

2. Adolescence is not generally a period of storm and stress. Available evidence indicates that adolescents and their parents do not have many *major* differences in attitudes and values. The influence of parents and of the peer group often is compatible.

3. The internal and external physical and physiological changes which occur in adolescence are associated with puberty, and are divisible into three phases: prepubescence, pubescence, and postpubescence. Adolescents differ in their rate of change through these phases. Early maturation in males is associated with many positive psychological and social characteristics; late maturation in males tends to be associated with negative psychological and social characteristics. In females, being either an early or a late maturer is associated with fewer favorable self-perceptions and evaluations by others than is the case with being "on time" in regard to rate of maturation.

4. Major change occurs in regard to the quality of adolescent thought. According to Piaget and others, this new ability involves thinking hypothetically, counterfactually, and in accordance with the structure of scientific reasoning.

5. Important socioemotional changes also occur in adolescence. Erikson's concept of identity crisis is useful since it helps us understand the emotional implications of the combination of all the changes undergone by adolescents, and the developments the adolescent must attain (a new definition of self, a role in society) to deal adequately with these changes.

6. Sexual intercourse is now experienced by most adolescents in the United States, although for many the event does not occur until late adolescence.

7. Biological changes in adulthood have a genetic base and affect all major organ systems of the body.

8. With age there is a loss of physiological vigor (respiratory capacity, muscle tone, etc.), but health-related behaviors such as physical exercise can result in significant improvements in vigor even in late life.

9. Both men and women show deterioration of the reproductive system with age. However, sexual activity in middle and old age appears to depend on past experience and other social factors.
10. The speed at which people can do cognitive tasks slows considerably in later life. This slowing is related to both disease processes and basic aging processes.
11. There is little age-related decline in sensory and short-term memory processes. However, older adults show substantially poorer performance than younger adults on some long-term memory tasks. This seems to be a result of their failure to engage in the type of deep and elaborate processing necessary for optimal memory.
12. When people have remained cognitively active during their lives, and the task relates to what they know, fewer age-related differences in memory are seen.
13. There are multiple types of intellectual ability, and these show different patterns of change with age.
14. Fluid intelligence declines after early adulthood. Crystallized intelligence increases throughout most of adulthood and old age.
15. Much of the difference between younger and older adults on intellectual ability measures is the result of having grown up in different historical eras.
16. Intellectual decline does occur in late life and is related to disease and reduced environmental stimulation.
17. Personality appears to show both constancy and change in adulthood. A person's "traits" seem to remain stable. But older people think about the environment differently, turning inward and viewing the environment as more threatening.
18. Some theorists have suggested there are many stages to adult life. Each of these constitutes a crisis or transition with its own unique tasks to be completed.
19. Death is the final event of life. Older people talk and think more about death but are less frightened by it.
20. Both people who are dying and those grieving over losing someone appear to experience multiple stages of adaptation.

KEY TERMS

Peer Group
Pubescence
Anorexia nervosa
Identity
Role
Average life expectancy
Maximum life span
Climacteric
Fluid intelligence
Crystallized intelligence
Birth cohort
Life review
Intimacy versus isolation
Generativity versus stagnation
Integrity versus despair
Grief

SUGGESTED READINGS

ADELSON, J. (Ed.). *Handbook of adolescent psychology*. New York: Wiley, 1980. This book is the first handbook specifically devoted to adolescence. It summarizes the major theoretical and empirical contributions to each of the several facets of adolescent development.

BIRREN, J. E., & SCHAIE, K. W. (Eds.). *Handbook of the psychology of aging* (1st and 2nd eds.). New York: Van Nostrand Reinhold, 1977, 1985. A comprehensive review of research on the psychological aspects of adulthood and aging.

BUTLER, R. N. *Why survive? Being old in America*. New York: Harper & Row, 1975. An examination of attitudes, stereotypes, and sociopolitical conditions affecting the elderly in our society.

ERIKSON, E. H. *Identity, youth, and crisis*. New York: Norton, 1968. Presents several essays by Erikson pertinent to his views of adolescence and of the key crisis of that period, that of identity.

HULTSCH, D. F., & DEUTSCH, F. *Adult development and aging: A life-span perspective.* New York: McGraw-Hill, 1981. A textbook survey of biological, cognitive, personality, and social changes in adulthood and aging.

LERNER, R. M., & SPANIER, G. B. *Adolescent development: A life-span perspective.* New York: McGraw-Hill, 1980. This is a scientifically sophisticated textbook about adolescent development. The authors pay particular attention to the relations between the adolescent and his or her social context. The childhood antecedents and adulthood consequences of adolescence are emphasized.

PART FIVE

Personality and Individuality

12

Tests and Measures

REQUIREMENTS OF TESTS
  Reliability
  Validity
MEASURES OF INTELLECTUAL
  ABILITY
  The Stanford-Binet
    Intelligence Scale
  The Wechsler Intelligence Tests
  Are Intelligence Tests Fair?
TESTS OF APTITUDE AND
  ACHIEVEMENT
MEASURES OF DEVIANT AND
  NORMAL PERSONALITY

  Objective Measures
  Projective Methods
BEHAVIORAL ASSESSMENT
  Naturalistic Observation
  Self-monitoring
  Analogue Assessments
THE GOAL OF
  PSYCHOLOGICAL
  MEASUREMENT
SUMMARY
KEY TERMS
SUGGESTED READINGS

Most of us do not spend much time worrying about the end of the world. We do not worry about our own death all that much, and we rarely worry about the deaths of unrelated persons in far-off regions. This sense of security can be quickly undermined, however, if one begins to consider the increasing number of nuclear warheads, nuclear power plants, the potential for destruction that is contained in just one nuclear mistake, and the vulnerability to which we are all subject if just one disturbed person has and abuses access to the nuclear controls.

    Although you probably were not worrying about the potential for the destruction of your entire community by nuclear catastrophe, bringing the topic to your attention may be all that is needed to start you wondering. For instance, you might ask: "Who is in control of these nuclear power plants?" The more you think about that question, the more likely you are to want to have these nuclear controllers checked out by a psychologist before they are given access to the controls. For that matter, you may want the controllers to be checked by psychologists several times a year for a "mental health checkup." One nuclear accident is so costly that added precaution is far from frivolous. What features of the nuclear controllers would the psychologist check? How would the psychologist proceed to assess the psychological factors selected?

You are watching a sports event on television and the score in the final seconds is very close. Your team is threatening to score, and if they do they will win. Your emotions are high—higher than at any other time in the game. A news bulletin cuts across the screen: "An unidentified man has attempted to assassinate the president of the United States." The bulletin is repeated twice more before the cameras are turned to a news team who begin to fill in the sketchy facts surrounding the attempted assassination.

You are angered that your game was interrupted. You jumped to your feet and shouted: "How could they do that?" In so doing you broke a glass and spilled a basket of chips. After a moment or two you realize that you are a concerned citizen, and you feel upset that the president's life was threatened. Your emotional state at this time is very complex. What caused you to jump and scream? Had you lost control? Would you or could you have caused more damage if, for example, a gun were available? The principles of psychological measurement could be applied to assess your current functioning.

Psychological measurements could also be used to assess the mental status of the culprit—the alleged attempted assassin. Is he seriously mentally disturbed? Did his psychological condition cause the illegal and destructive act?

Although these examples provide notable instances where psychological assessments can help to provide meaningful answers to difficult questions, there are many other instances, closer to home, where psychological assessments can be very useful. Who, among your classmates, has the highest IQ? Who is the most talented musically? Who is the most anxious? Who has suffered the most due to a deep-seated conflict between parental love and hate? Who behaves badly with friends most frequently? Answers to these questions, and others like them, require some form of psychological measurement. Indeed, tests of intelligences and musical skill, personality inventories, measures of intrapsychic conflict, and procedures of behavioral observation are methods of psychological measurement designed to address these very questions.

Assessment is the process of gathering information about a client or subject to understand the person better. Within this process, the psychologist selects the assessment method, conducts the assessment, organizes and makes sense of the resulting information, and draws the relevant conclusions. As we shall see in this chapter, the types of psychological measurements employed in assessment include a variety of tests and observations. The material presented in later chapters on personality, abnormal behavior, and various sections on theories of intelligence are related to the present chapter's emphasis on how to measure such concepts properly.

Assessments are conducted for both basic research and applied reasons. In basic research, psychological measurements are developed and used to test hypotheses about the relationships among psychological concepts and the causes of psychological conditions. A psychological concept must be operationalized before it can be scientifically examined, and psychological tests and measures provide operationalizations of important concepts. Because tests and measures play an important role in research in general, numerous basic studies focus directly on the tests and measures themselves: asking and attempting to answer questions about the consistency and accuracy of the tests and measures and devising and evaluating ways to improve them.

On the applied side, assessments are conducted to help the psychologist make informed decisions. Should Ned be placed in special education? How would you diagnose Mr. Rose's problem? Was the treatment provided for Ms. Quentin successful? Each of these questions deserves a knowledgeable

TESTS AND MEASURES 375

and reasoned response and psychologists use assessments to gather data to help them make one. Screening job candidates, diagnosing psychological maladjustment, and evaluating the effects of psychological therapy are three examples of applied psychological measurements.

For centuries, the Chinese used exams to select members of the civil service. In the early twentieth century, in France, tests were developed to identify those who were to be admitted to institutions for the retarded. Today, civil service exams and psychological tests of intelligence are still used for these and many other reasons. The actual measures, however, have been advanced and improved over the years. An extended history of psychological measurement would cover the wide-ranging influences that have affected the various types of assessment. Our brief history, however, will focus on what is perhaps the most influential process of assessment—the measurement of intellectual ability.

Some more specific instances of historically relevant assessments include Sir Francis Galton's work which began at the International Exposition in London in 1884 and continued thereafter at the South Kensington Museum. As part of his interest in studying the heredity of genius and other psychological processes, Galton measured the reaction time, head size, speed of movement, sensitivity to pain, and so on, of the persons who visited his booth at the exposition. To further his work, Galton pioneered the development of the correlation coefficient, which was later to be advanced by his student Pearson. Galton also pioneered the use of questionnaires and rating scales.

The term *mental test*, which later became a most influential concept, was first introduced in 1890 by James McKeen Cattell. Cattell was interested in assessing the intellectual level of his subjects and, like Galton, used tests of reaction time and sensory discrimination. The measuring of subjects' mental skills and perceptual processes continued to be an exciting topic of the time and Jastrow, at an exposition in Chicago in 1893, collected data on a sample of American subjects.

Measures of intelligence as we know them today, and as they are described later in this chapter, can be traced to the early work of Binet, who at the request of the French Minister of Public Instruction and in collaboration with Simon, developed a scale to determine admission standards for services for the retarded in France. Later, at Stanford University, Terman revised the Binet-Simon scales and the idea of the IQ (the ratio of mental to chronological age) was introduced. Group tests of intelligence were developed via the U.S. Army by a committee directed by Yerkes. This committee was charged with designing a psychological measure that would assess the intelligence of recruits. Two historically important tests of intelligence, the Army Alpha and Army Beta tests, were produced.

The measures of intelligence developed by David Wechsler are currently among those that enjoy widespread use. Wechsler scales are available for assessing the intelligence of adults, children, and preschoolers. Most recently, these tests have been revised to improve on their ability to provide accurate and predictive estimates of intellectual functioning. We will have more of these tests when we discuss specific measures of intelligence.

As we close this brief history, we would like to introduce you to the names of the tests that are most highly valued by practicing psychologists. To do this we draw on a survey published by Wade and Baker (1977). As part of their survey, the authors asked their respondents (members of APA's Division of Clinical Psychology) to list the tests that they would advise their students to learn. The results indicated that the full range of types of tests

Sir Francis Galton (1822–1911) was one of the first scientists to try to measure intellectual ability. (Bettmann Archive)

Alfred Binet (1857–1911) published the first test for assessing intelligence in 1905. (Bettmann Archive)

were recommended. The tests that were most often endorsed as tests that students should learn included objective measures of intelligence (e.g., Wechsler Adult Intelligence Scale, Wechsler Intelligence Scale for Children, Stanford-Binet Intelligence Scale), objectives tests of personality/psychopathology (e.g., Minnesota Multiphasic Personality Inventory), projective tests (e.g., Rorschach Inkblot Test, Thematic Apperception Test), and neuropsychological tests (e.g., Halsted-Reitan Neuropsychological Battery). Each of these tests, as well as the procedures for behavioral assessment, are discussed in this chapter.

REQUIREMENTS OF TESTS

We typically think of tests as demanding something of us—we have to take the tests and are expected to achieve high scores. But tests, too, have requirements and must also achieve high scores. If a test does not meet its requirements, it is of no value to its user. Anyone can make up a psychological test, as is occasionally done in popular magazines, but tests are useful and respected only when they meet scientific requirements. The basic scientific concepts that underlie the requirements of tests are *reliability* and *validity*.

RELIABILITY

Reliability is the degree to which a test (or a series of observations) is stable, dependable, and self-consistent. In a word, reliability estimates can be seen as estimates of "consistency." Although consistency can serve as a one-word reference for reliability, test consistency has many meanings, such as consistency over time, consistency across scorers, and consistency within itself. The three major types of test reliability have to do with these three types of consistency.

Test-retest reliability refers to consistency over time. When the same test is administered at two different times, the degree to which the scores on the first administration are correlated with scores from the second testing is the *retest* reliability. (See Appendix A for an explanation and discussion of correlations.) Assuming that we are measuring something that should not change during the intertest interval (e.g., musical aptitude over a 2-week interval without training), scores on the first and second test administration of a reliable test will be highly correlated. *Interscorer* reliability involves consistency across test scorers: the degree to which independent test scorers agree on their scoring. Multiple-choice tests, for example, have very high interscorer reliability, but more open-ended tests such as essays often have lower interscorer reliability. Objective tests fare better than subjective ones in terms of interscorer reliability.

Internal consistency (a test's consistency within itself) can be established by intercorrelating the items of the test using split-half, or odd-even correlations. For instance, if the test is intended to measure one concept, scores on the first half of the test should be highly correlated with scores on the second half (the same is true for the odd- and even-numbered questions). However,

TESTS AND MEASURES

when the test is designed to measure several concepts, internal consistency for the entire test is less important than the consistency of the separate sections that measure each concept.

The types of reliability are illustrated in the use of a ruler to measure the dimensions of your textbook. Use ruler A from Table 12.1. The ruler is a highly reliable instrument if (1) each time you use it, it produces the same measurement; (2) when different people use it, it produces the same measurement; and (3) any portion of the ruler can be used interchangeably. Almost all rulers that can be purchased at stores would qualify as reliable: An elastic ruler, however, would probably fare very poorly since it would produce different measurements depending on how tensely it were stretched.

TABLE 12.1
The ruler as illustration of reliability and validity

I. Two measurements by the same person using a wooden ruler

Subject	First Measurement	Second (retest) Measurement
1	9.75	9.70
2	9.65	9.65
3	9.60	9.50
4	9.45	9.45
5	9.35	9.40
6	9.20	9.35
7	9.10	9.30
8	9.05	9.25
9	9.00	9.20
10	8.85	9.20

II. Two measurements by two different people using an elastic ruler

Subject	Measurer 1	Measurer 2
1	9.60	9.75
2	9.45	9.70
3	9.30	9.55
4	9.00	9.50
5	8.70	9.05
6	8.60	8.80
7	8.60	8.55
8	8.05	8.35
9	7.85	7.80
10	7.05	7.05

III. Two rulers, only one of which has accurate calibrations. Although both could produce reliable results, only one would be valid.

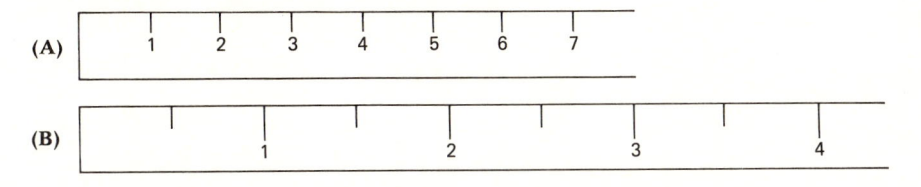

(A) ruler marked 1 2 3 4 5 6 7

(B) ruler marked 1 2 3 4

Note: These hypothetical measurements illustrate fairly high test-retest reliability (top section) and less than adequate interscorer reliability (second section). Taking the measurement on two different occasions would have little effect on your results, whereas having a different person take the measurements with an elastic ruler has a very large and unwanted effect on your results.

VALIDITY

Reliable results obtained from a reliable instrument may still not be valid. The second requirement of a test is *validity*, the degree to which a test actually measures what it is intended to measure. Check ruler A—are the inch markings accurately calibrated? What about ruler B? One of these rulers has inch markings that are incorrectly calibrated. Both rulers can produce reliable results, but only one will be valid. Only ruler B has the properly calibrated inch markings and only ruler B can be considered valid. Thus the reliable results produced by ruler A will not be valid results.

Evaluating the validity of a psychological measurement instrument is more difficult than evaluating a ruler—for the ruler we can identify an exact standard for inch markings (we know the criterion), but for many psychological measures an exact standard is often not available. Establishing the validity of a psychological measurement instrument is often a continuous process requiring a variety of methods. Each method provides more data to help answer the question: Does this test measure what it intends to measure?

According to APA test standards (American Psychological Association, 1974), there are three major types of validity: content validity, criterion related validity, and construct validity. *Content validity* is the most direct—does the test include a representative sample of questions from the universe of material relevant to the variable being measured? In concrete terms, does a math test have a representative sample of questions from the various types of mathematics problems? If the test does contain representative math questions, it is content valid, if there are questions about history, or religion, the test lacks content validity. The idea of *face validity* is related to content validity. Based on *prima facie* (Latin: on first appearance) evidence, the test seems valid. However, face validity as a method of examining a test is not alone sufficient for claims of validity.

Criterion-related validity is determined by calculating the correlation between the test score and an outside criterion. A test that is said to measure "intelligence" is not considered valid unless it shows a strong relationship to measures that we accept as criteria. For instance, strong correlations between a test and grades in high school or college might help establish the validity of the test as a measure of intelligence. The correlation between the test score and the criterion is referred to as a validity coefficient.

There are two types of criterion-related validity: *predictive* and *concurrent*. The difference between them is one of time—in predictive validity the criterion is gathered at a time after the test is given; in concurrent validity the test and the criterion are gathered at the same time. Criterion-related validity, of either type, is essential to determine the merits of the test. If a test does not evidence a strong relationship with an accepted criterion, it should not be said to be valid.

Although a strong relationship between a test and a criterion can establish some validity for the test, as with intelligence and school grades, single criteria are not always available. How can the validity of a test be established when there is no single accepted criterion? The problem is not an easy one to solve, but the approach of *construct validation* provided by Cronbach and Meehl (1955) has become an accepted course of action.

A construct is a concept that is "constructed" to explain and organize certain pieces of information. For example, anxiety is a construct that organizes the data on emotionality, muscle tension, cognitive uneasiness, and physiological activation, all of which seem to go together when a person is threatened. Construct validity is established not by one correlation, but by a set of relationships among behavioral manifestations. These relationships would include both meaningful correlations where expected and an absence of meaningful correlations where no relationship is expected.

Take, for example, a psychological measurement instrument that is intended to assess anxiety. To investigate construct validity, we would examine the relationship between the anxiety test scores and behavior when performing before an audience, when awaiting a dental appointment, how palms sweat before an important exam, nervous gesturing during a job interview, athletic ability, and body size. For most of these relationships, we would expect to find a meaningful positive correlation, such as between the anxiety test scores and nervous gesturing during an interview. But we also hope to document that the anxiety scores are not correlated with other measures where we do not expect a relationship: anxiety is not likely to be significantly related to athletic ability or body size. In construct validation, the investigator employs numerous correlation coefficients. An instrument is said to have construct validity when several studies are integrated and judged to support the idea that the underlying construct does help organize and explain the observed data.

MEASURES OF INTELLECTUAL ABILITY

The assessment of intellectual ability is one of the major areas of psychological measurement. In Chapter 8 we examined the concept of intelligence, including various theories of intelligence and studies of cognitive abilities. In this chapter we take a close look at the tests that are used to measure intellectual functioning. Tests that can be administered in groups are available, but we will examine the more-often-used individually administered tests. Perhaps it is a competitive drive in some of us or self-inquisitiveness in others, but interest in our own and others' mental abilities does seem almost universal.

Structured measurement instruments, such as those for assessing intelligence, try to reduce or eliminate the unwanted effects of extraneous variables. The goal is to produce a score that is as unaffected as possible by nontest factors. *Standardization* and *norms* help achieve this goal, and many tests, besides those for assessing intelligence, make use of standardization and norms. Most measures of intelligence are administered to subjects in a standard fashion. For example, the instructions, procedures, and time limits are identical for all those who take the test—whether today or a month or year from today. There certainly would be no standardization if each test administrator could decide how much time to allow for the test. Would you want your scores to be compared to someone who had 3 hours to take a test when you had only 1 hour? When your examiner gave no hints, but another provided clues? Standardization is an important cornerstone in all forms of assessment because it helps to ensure that all subjects are tested and treated equally.

Interpretation of test scores must also be equal for all subjects. Test *norms* are collected so that a person's score is evaluated by comparing it with the scores obtained by others. The "others" who compose the normative group should be representative of the entire population of potential takers of the test—be it an intelligence test or any other type of psychological test. The norms for intelligence tests, for example, are typically based on a sample of people with a range of ages, both males and females, both urban and rural backgrounds, differing occupational and educational backgrounds, and rep-

TABLE 12.2
The percentage of people at each level of intellectual functioning

Percentage	Level of Intellectual Functioning	IQ
2.2	Very superior	130 and over
6.7	Superior	120–129
16.1	High average (bright)	110–119
50.0	Average	90–109
16.1	Low average (dull)	80–89
6.7	Borderline	70–79
2.2	Mentally deficient	69 and below

resentation from different racial groups and different geographical regions. Thus the score that a subject obtains is interpreted in relation to the scores obtained by a representative sample on which the test was normed. When a representative sample of subjects is tested, a fairly well established distribution of scores is found, with few subjects scoring at the very high and the very low ends, and most scoring in the average range (see Table 12.2).

THE STANDFORD-BINET INTELLIGENCE SCALE

Binet and Simon published the original instrument for assessing intelligence in 1905. Since then the scale has undergone several revisions. The first revision was done by Terman at Stanford University in 1916 and is known as the Stanford-Binet. It broke new ground in its efforts to obtain a representative sample of the American population, to specify detailed instructions for test administration, and to provide specific criteria for scoring. A second revision, in 1937, resulted in two alternative forms of the test, both of which were expanded to include the many measures that could together be considered "intelligence." The third revision took place in 1960 and returned the test to one form. The single form of the 1960 Stanford-Binet combined the best items—those that were most highly correlated with meaningful criteria—from the two previous forms.

The 1960 version of the Stanford-Binet (Terman & Merrill, 1960) requires subjects to respond to test questions that are grouped according to age level (from age 2 to adult). The examiner selects, based on the subject's age and general mental status, the age level of questions that will be the starting point. If the subject does not answer all questions from this age level correctly, the examiner asks questions that are taken from a younger age level, and this continues until the subject answers all items at one age level correctly: This is called the *basal* age. If the subject answers all items at an age level correctly, the examiner proceeds until the subject gets to a level when he or she cannot answer any items. This is called the *ceiling* age.

The concept of *mental age* has been around since the original Binet-Simon scales. Mental age notions categorize test items according to age: the 8-year-old level contains test items that the majority of 8-year-olds in a normative sample could complete. However, the "mental age" unit turns out to be inconsistent across different ages—it shrinks with increasing age. Intellectual growth between ages 4 and 10 is much greater than between ages 40 and 46, even though 6 years pass in both cases. The *intelligence quotient* (IQ) was introduced to yield estimates of intelligence that are comparable across different ages. The ratio IQ was introduced by Stern in 1912. The formula for the ratio IQ is as follows:

TESTS AND MEASURES

A five-year-old boy taking the Stanford-Binet test. This version of the test, which has been used since 1960, requires subjects to respond to test questions that are grouped according to age level. (Nancy Hays/Monkmeyer)

$$IQ = 100 \times \frac{MA}{CA} \quad (MA = \text{mental age}, CA = \text{chronological age})$$

With this formula, average intellectual performance turns out to be an IQ of 100. For instance, an 18-year-old whose mental age is also 18 would receive an IQ of 100.

HIGHLIGHT 12.1
Tests Designed Just for You?

As anyone who has taken a test knows, some of the questions are too easy, whereas others seem impossible. Why is this? The answer is that the test developer has chosen items to assess, as accurately as possible, all persons at all levels of what the test is intended to measure. As a result, some questions on the test are designed for those less skilled and some for those more skilled than yourself.

Adaptive testing, or tailored testing, employs different sets of test questions for each person taking the test, with the specific questions being chosen depending on the person's skill level (Weiss, 1982). For example, the subject responds to one test item, and the tester selects other test items from the item pool based on the response. The items in the pool have known difficulty levels and known discriminative abilities, and the items selected take these data into account. Thus the items are adapted to each person taking the test.

Some of the major advantages of adaptive testing include improved efficiency and increased accuracy. Adaptive tests have been found to yield "measurements of comparable or superior quality to those of conventional tests with considerable fewer items administered to each individual" (Weiss, 1985). Thus, unlike most tests, which require all subjects to answer the same fixed number of questions, adaptive testing employs varying numbers of items as needed for optimal measurement.

A new idea?—no. A real advance?—yes. Adaptive testing is an advance, but the basic idea is not entirely new. The individually administered Binet intelligence test, developed in the early 1900s, employed an adaptive approach: a different starting point for each subject, items scored by the examiner during testing, successive items determined by prior responses, and testing terminated according to a predetermined criterion. Contemporary adaptive tests are often administered via computers, not unlike the microcomputer systems available for the home and office.

Items used in the Wechsler Intelligence Scale for Children (WISC-R) test. This test is used to measure the intelligence of children between the ages of six years and seventeen years. (Peter Vandermark/Stock Boston)

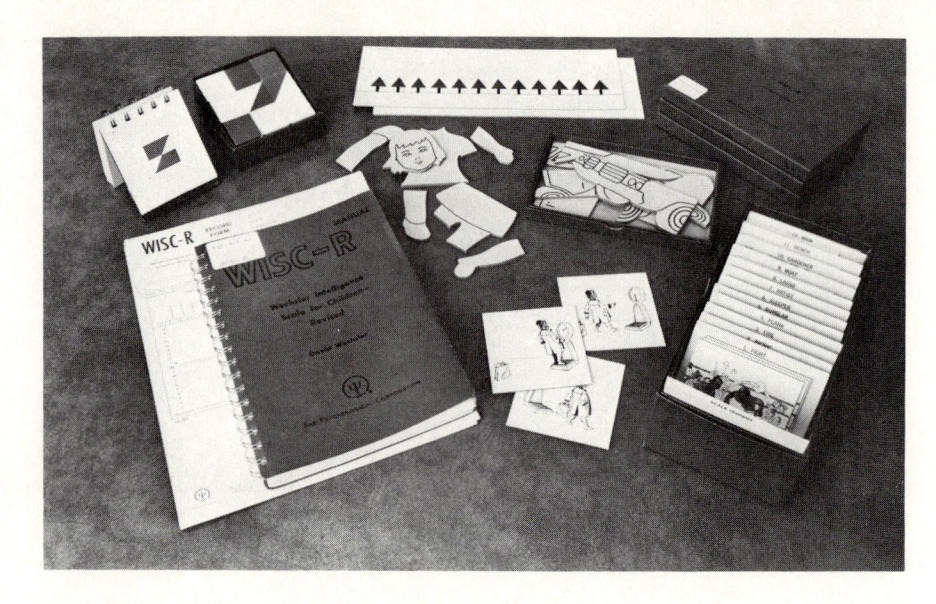

THE WECHSLER INTELLIGENCE TESTS

Advancing from the original scales published in the 1930s, Wechsler has produced three age-specific measures on intelligence that are currently among the most often used psychological tests. The adult test is called the Wechsler Adult Intelligence Scale (WAIS) and has recently been revised (WAIS-R, 1981), as has the children's version, the Wechsler Intelligence Scale for Children (WISC-R). The Wechsler Preschool and Primary Scale of Intelligence (WPPSI) is for preschool and primary subjects. The appropriate ages for the three tests are provided in Table 12.3.

Because Wechsler did not believe that intelligence can be represented by a single score, each of the Wechsler scales produces scores for individual subjects on separate verbal and performance sections of the tests. Correspondingly, the test provides a Full Scale IQ, a Verbal IQ, and a Performance IQ. The verbal section of the test includes measures of general information, comprehension, arithmetic, similarities, and vocabulary. The performance section includes the following subtests: Digit Symbol, Picture Completion, Block Design, Picture Arrangement, and Object Assembly. Sample items from several of the Verbal and Performance sections of the WAIS-R are presented in Tables 12.4 and 12.5.

The Wechsler scales are individually administered measures that require that the same procedures be followed for each subject and that these procedures parallel those used to collect the normative data. This standardized administration is essential. The items on each of the subtests are arranged in order of increasing difficulty, and after a certain number of errors the examiner discontinues the subtest. Thus, the test is designed to prevent a poorly performing subject from becoming frustrated or feeling a failure.

Intelligence tests make demands on us, and it seems only fair that we ask how well intelligence tests stack up in terms of the requirements of a good test. Taking the WAIS as an illustrative test, the reported reliabilities are high, often producing correlations between .90 and .97 for the Full IQ, and from .84 to .96 for the Verbal and Performance sections (Matarazzo, 1972). These data are solid indicators that the test has test-retest reliability. Interscorer

TABLE 12.3
Appropriate ages for the Wechsler Intelligence Tests

WAIS-R	16 years and older
WISC-R	6 years to 16 years 11 months 30 days
WPPSI	4 years to 6 years 6 months

TESTS AND MEASURES

TABLE 12.4
Sample questions resembling those on the verbal section of the WAIS-R

General Information:
1. What is steam made of?
2. What is pepper?

Comprehension:
1. Why do some people save sales receipts?
2. Why is copper often used in electrical wires?

Arithmetic:
1. If a pencil costs 15¢, what will be the cost of a half-dozen pencils?
2. Three children divided 21 pennies equally among themselves. How many pennies did each child receive?

Similarities:
1. In what way are a lion and a tiger alike?
2. In what way are a circle and a triangle alike?

Vocabulary:
1. What is the meaning of the word "tenant"?
2. What is the meaning of the word "culpable"?

reliability is also quite high, and the internal consistency of the subtests is acceptable.

But do the Wechsler scales really measure intelligence? The consensus of research supports the validity of the WAIS. For instance, IQ scores are typically predictive of college grades and of success in job training (Ghiselli, 1973). However, the predictive validity of IQ scores varies as a function of the criterion that is being predicted. Predictions of academic success provide more positive evidence of the validity of IQs than do predictions of marital satisfaction, athletic competence, or physical health. The IQ does not predict everything, only those aspects of behavior that have intellectual components.

The typical correlation between IQ and academic grades is about .50. However, the correlation is sometimes higher and sometimes lower. For instance, the correlation is higher when the criterion grades are gathered for elementary school children and lower when graduate students are used. The correlation range for the different levels of education, taken from Jensen (1980), are presented in Table 12.6. Note that the predictiveness of IQ scores decreases as you move up the educational ladder. Although there are many causes of the decline in prediction over the years, it is not due to inherent weaknesses of the tests. One major factor, for instance, is that the subjects

TABLE 12.5
Sample questions resembling those on the performance section of the WAIS-R

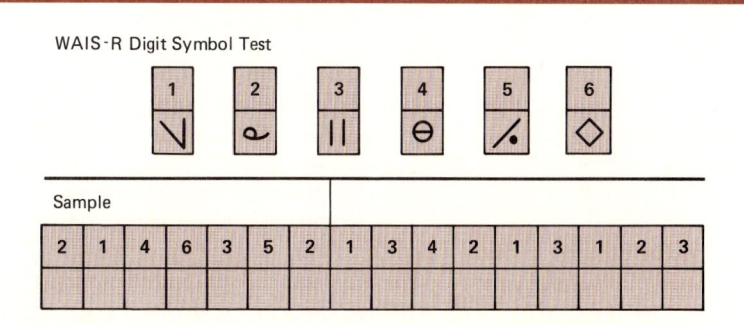

TABLE 12.6
Correlations between IQ scores and indices of academic achievement at four levels of education

Elementary school	.60–.70
High school	.50–.60
College	.40–.50
Graduate school	.30–.40

Source: Jensen (1980).

who are being tested as you go up the educational ladder become an increasingly more select group. With the increased restrictiveness of the sample comes the reduction in prediction. Whenever a restricted range of scores is employed in a correlation, the correlation is reduced from what it would otherwise be when the full range of scores is employed.

The growing interest in and apparent importance of information processing approaches to the study of human cognition suggests that an information processing view of intelligence may be enlightening. Sternberg (1981) described several procedures used for assessing human processing of information (such as the speed of recognition on a letter-matching task or accuracy of memory scanning), discussed some of the strengths and weaknesses of related measures, and detailed how such measures might affect the assessment of intelligence. For instance, standardized testing might be supplemented by computer-assisted measurement of the components of information processing.

It may be premature to say that scores on information processing tasks will be more accurate assessments of intelligent action. Indeed, the increased predictiveness of such tests over traditional ones has yet to be demonstrated. The more specific information available from information processing tasks may be more prescriptive for remedial training programs than are the scores provided by traditional tests, but again, more research is needed to evaluate such a notion.

One new theoretical focus that seems to hold promise is the study of cognitive flexibility, where high levels of intellectual functioning entail a flexible adaptation to, or changing of, the environment. Both automatic processing and adaptation to novelty are seen as important, where efficient automatic processing allows allocation of additional resources to other tasks and where effective adaptation allows automatization to occur more quickly (Sternberg, 1984).

ARE INTELLIGENCE TESTS FAIR?

Although you have seen only a few samples of the types of questions asked on tests of intelligence, you may nevertheless be concerned that the questions are unfair. You might question their cultural fairness—questions seem pertinent to white middle-class culture but not to other cultures. For example, reexamine the Comprehension subtest question (Table 12.4) that asked "Why do some people save sales receipts?" and think about whether this question would be fair in cultures which use barter rather than money. Questions which are clearly culturally unfair are rare, but the existence of even a few such questions has caused some concern among those developing and using intelligence tests.

One approach to solving the alleged cultural bias of test questions has been to devise a test that is free from all cultural components. Both Raven's Progressive Matrices (Raven, 1938) and Cattell's Culture Free Intelligence Test (R. B. Cattell, 1949) are designed to be culture free. A sample item from each of these tests is provided in Table 12.7.

Are the tests really culture free? The test items do not appear to reflect a cultural perspective, but some data does suggest that subjects from other cultures score considerable lower than North American norms.

Are the culture-free tests valid predictors? According to Anastasi (1968), correlations between the culture-free tests and other tests of intelligence are

TESTS AND MEASURES

TABLE 12.7
Sample items from "culture-free" tests of intelligence

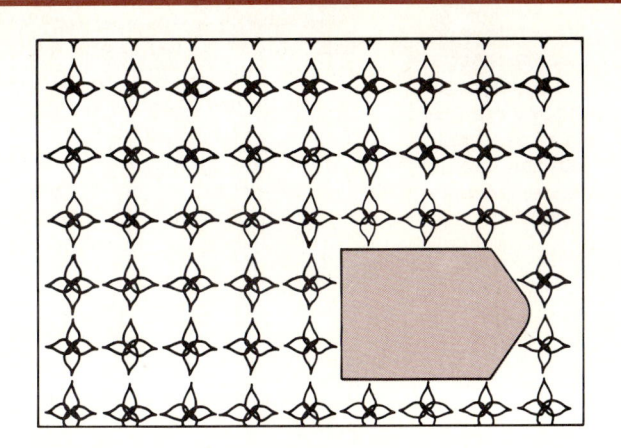

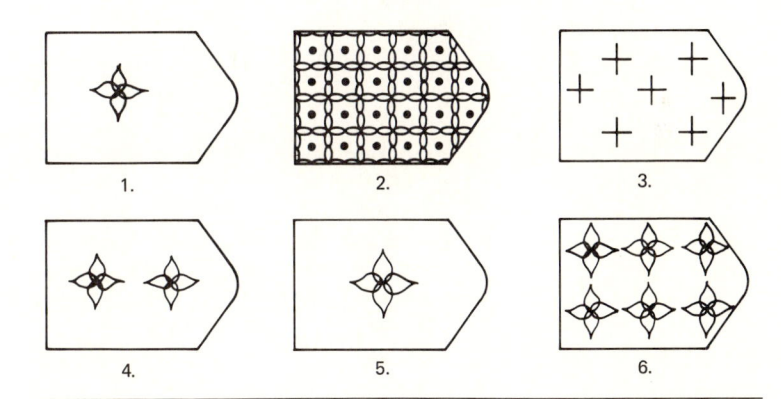

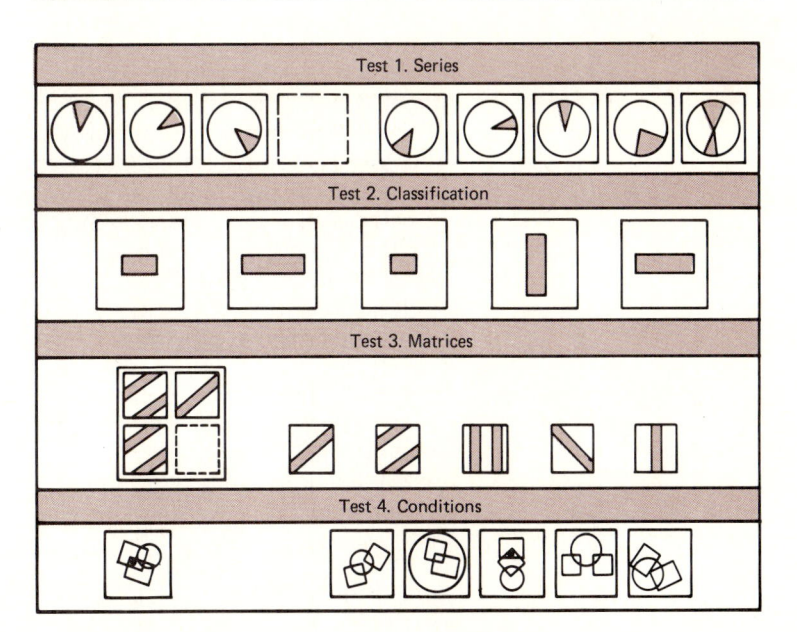

Culture-free tests were designed to remove white, middle-class value judgments from measures of intellectual functioning, but they are less valid predictions of academic performance than the usual tests of intelligence. (Michael Kagan/Monkmeyer)

moderate (.40 to .75), but predictions of academic performance are less accurate than the usual tests of intelligence. Culture-free tests were designed to remove white middle-class value judgments from measures of intellectual functioning. This goal is applauded, but the less accurate predictions that result from the culture-free test scores leave room for improvement. One further thought: Perhaps intelligence tests cannot or should not be culture free; after all, the questions that are asked are related to experiences in a particular culture and the behaviors that we are trying to predict occur in a particular culture.

Another way of considering the fairness of intelligence tests is to examine whether the test scores unfairly discriminate between groups. For instance, do members of certain minority groups score lower than members of the majority even though their true abilities do not differ? In California, a disproportionate number of minority children were found to have been tested and assigned to classes for the retarded or behaviorally disturbed. Such a placement can profoundly affect the children's long-range development, and in part because the tests were seen as unfair, California declared the use of intelligence tests for testing and placing minority students in special classes to be unconstitutional.

If tests of intelligence uncover real group differences, it seems reasonable to provide remedial programs. However, some have argued that the observed differences between groups represent genetic differences—differences that are inherited—and are mistakenly seen as evidence for racial prejudice.

Do intelligence tests have a built-in bias? Do they predict higher scores for one group over another when the actual performance of the two groups on the criterion would not differ? The position of one outspoken scientist, Arthur Jensen, is clear cut. The following quote is taken from his book *Bias in mental testing* (Jensen, 1980, p. 715).

Little, if any fault can be found with most psychological tests as far as their alleged cultural bias against minorities is concerned. When specific tests are carefully examined by a variety of psychometric methods for detecting bias of various kinds, almost invariably, in the case of current standardized tests, the alleged cultural bias is not statistically substantiated, or is so slight in magnitude or so inconsistent as to be practically negligible. More often than not, the bias goes in the direction that would *favor* minority applicants where the test scores are used for selection. In short, most standard tests, with rare exceptions, are psychometrically equivalent for minority and majority groups; the tests measure largely the same ability factors in minority and majority groups, with essentially the same reliability and validity, as these terms are traditionally defined in psychometrics.

Even if we accept that the tests are not unfair or biased, the use of the tests can be biased. For example, test interpreters can unfairly make more of the test score than is appropriate. Interpreting the IQ score as an innate ability that cannot be altered goes beyond the data and beyond the proper uses of the test.

The System of Multicultural Pluralistic Assessment (SOMPA) is a recent approach to the testing of children from minority or culturally deprived backgrounds (Mercer & Lewis, 1979). The SOMPA employs several tests and measures and compares the scores of individual children to the typical scores of children of the same sociocultural background. Instead of producing an IQ, the test results in an *estimated learning potential* (ELP). The SOMPA battery of tests includes the WISC-R, tests of perceptual functioning, tests of physical dexterity, a measure of overall health, and an interview (conducted in the child's preferred language) with the child's principal caretaker.

In contrast to the use of representative norms for comparing a person's scores with the scores of others, the SOMPA compares a person's scores with those of others who have the same background. Thus comments about functioning in the larger context may not be accurately provided. The true test of the SOMPA method, however, rests on its ability to demonstrate predictive criterion validity. Critics and supporters alike await the outcome of validational research.

TESTS OF APTITUDE AND ACHIEVEMENT

Tests of intelligence often contain relatively circumscribed subtests and/or verbal and performance sections, but they are generally devised to provide one global indication of level of intellective functioning. Because more specific information may be preferred or required, aptitude tests have been developed. "Aptitude tests" refer to "tests measuring relatively homogeneous and clearly defined segments of ability" (Anastasi, 1968, p. 14). For example, there are tests of mechanical, clerical, and musical aptitude. Although some testers have tried to interpret subtest scores of intelligence tests as indicators of special aptitudes, subtests contain too few items (and the items were selected for a different purpose) to provide a reliable index of a special aptitude.

Achievement tests are intended to assess the attainment of broad educational goals. According to Anastasi (1968), "achievement tests are designed to measure the effects of a specific program of instruction or training" (p. 390). Thus achievement tests represent a terminal evaluation at the completion of some form of training and can be useful to identify pupils needing remedial education. Examples of achievement tests include the Scholastic Achievement Tests (SAT), the Iowa Tests of Basic Skills, and the College Entrance Examination Board (CEEB) tests.

FOCUS ON THE PSYCHOLOGIST

Anne Anastasi

ANNE ANASTASI (Ph.D., Columbia University) taught psychology at Barnard College, Queens College (CUNY), and the Graduate School of Fordham University. She has been president of the American Psychological Association, the Eastern Psychological Association, and several divisions of the APA. Among her awards are the American Psychological Foundation Gold Medal, the APA Distinguished Scientific Award for the Applications of Psychology, and the American Educational Research Association Award for Distinguished Contributions to Research in Education. Her publications include *Psychological Testing, Differential Psychology,* and *Fields of Applied Psychology.*

My first love was mathematics; I had planned to major in it when I entered Barnard College in 1924. Two events in my sophomore year led me to change to psychology. First, I took a course with Harry L. Hollingworth, then Chair of the Psychology Department. He was a fascinating lecturer and a scientist to the core, who saw scientific questions in every nook and cranny of daily life. He was also very critical of slipshod procedures and loose reasoning, which were not too difficult to find in psychological writings of the 1920s.

The second event was my reading an article by the British psychologist, Charles Spearman, in which I learned not only about correlation coefficients but also about some further intriguing analyses that Spearman applied to such coefficients in his studies of the nature and composition of intelligence. This did it! I realized that mathematics had a place in psychology; I could thus enjoy the best of two possible worlds. I changed my major and was launched on a lifetime career.

Now for psychological testing. When I entered psychology, test construction offered the major opportunities for applying mathematical and statistical methodology. My choice was obvious. Although my Ph.D. was in general experimental psychology (the only psychology degree then available at Columbia), I obtained all the preparation available in statistics and testing. My doctoral dissertation was inspired directly by the work of Spearman, and it utilized techniques that were the precursors of modern factor analysis.

There was another influence that helped to shape my ultimate area of specialization. Although testing was even then beginning to be used for many purposes, I was particularly interested in its use in measuring individual differences in psychological traits. This was the burgeoning area of differential psychology in which I wrote my first book in 1937.

The 1920s and 1930s were a period of turmoil, controversy, and transition in differential psychology. The strongly hereditarian, traditional explanations of individual differences were being questioned by psychologists, anthropologists, and geneticists. I identified closely with these novel ideas, partly because the evidence for the hereditary interpretations was so vulnerable on methodological grounds. In fact, so weak were the supporting data that what prevailed were better described as hereditary assumptions, rather than explanations. Whatever could not be readily explained was dumped into the heredity box. Because so much less was known about heredity than is known today, this dumping was easy to do and tempting.

Today, testing has expanded into many areas of practical application and has great potential for social good. At the same time, I have long been concerned about misuses of tests and misinterpretations of test scores by inadequately qualified or irresponsible persons. In many cases, adverse side-effects of testing arise from a widespread demand for shortcuts and quick solutions. People are looking for magic; they expect tests to make decisions for them and thus spare them the necessity of exercising their own judgment. For many years, I have been combating such misuses of tests. The proper interpretation of test results requires psychological knowledge about the behavior domain assessed, as well as additional information about the person tested. Test scores provide only one kind of data that, in combination with other data, can be utilized in reaching wise decisions about oneself or others.

High-school students taking the Scholastic Achievement Tests (SATs). Many colleges use the results of the SATs to help decide which applicants they will accept for admission. (Stock Boston)

Aptitude tests may not assume a particular prior experience, whereas achievement tests measure the mastery of specific educational experiences. Pretend, for example, that you are employed in a computer company where your job is to select from all the novice job applicants those who have the greatest likelihood of becoming whiz-kid computer programmers. Since no specific background is assumed, you would use aptitude tests. However, if, as part of the same job, you were asked to determine which of a class of new programmer trainees benefited the most from the job training program, an achievement test would be appropriate.

MEASURES OF NORMAL AND DEVIANT PERSONALITY

We have thus far focused on measures that differentiate people based on their intellectual abilities. But as any thoughtful and careful observer knows, people show great variability in nonintellectual areas such as personality (see also Chapter 13). The reserved, somber, and cautious mathematician is markedly dissimilar to the gregarious, silly, and impulsive actor. How do psychologists assess these and other differences in personality through the two main approaches of objective assessment and projective assessment?

OBJECTIVE MEASURES

Objective assessment seeks to describe the characteristics or traits of a person scientifically as a means of predicting that person's behavior. Features of the objective approach to personality assessment include well-defined questions requiring limited answers (such as true-false) and comparing the person's responses to normative data (Butcher, 1971). Take a moment and read the sample items provided in Table 12.8. These items are clear cut and the required response is true or false. The items are from an objective measure.

HIGHLIGHT 12.2

The Interview

Can a psychologist gather the information necessary to make an informed decision about a person without ever meeting, talking to, or interacting with that person? The answer depends on the type of decision that is to be made. Decisions about acceptance into college based on general ability/aptitude tests might be reasonable without personal contact. The test scores are predictive of the desired criterion, and few if any personal features would prevent acceptance in college when the test scores are acceptable. However, a different scenario emerges when the decision pertains to certain types of job selection. Consider a candidate for a top-management position that requires interaction with both supervised staff and the company's board of directors. Besides these in-house responsibilities, the job requires representing the firm to outside agencies and some international travel. Would it be wise to select a person for this job based on test scores alone? Probably not, and accepted practice employs some form of interview to test how the candidate interacts with others.

Diverse professionals rely on the interview for assessment. When used by psychologists, the interview is often one of several methods of assessment that combine to produce predictive information. Because the interview is used so widely, it might be considered the most basic method of assessment.

Different types of interviews are designed to gain certain types of information. Some interviews are meant to stimulate the interviewee to produce more information about him or herself, while others focus solely on a specific decision. One of the main distinctions among styles of interviewing concerns the open-ended versus the structured interview.

The *open-ended interview* tries to gather as much information as possible and is not restricted to answering a single question or set of questions. The interviewer wants to keep the communication open and the atmosphere friendly. Some strategies for "keeping the channels open" include attentive silence, nonverbal expressions of interest, encouraging comments, and providing clarifications. Introducing new topics at slow moments and leaving unproductive topics can also facilitiate open discussion (Storrow, 1967). In a less open-ended situation, where the interviewer wants specific answers, direct questions, leading questions, and confrontations are helpful.

The *structured interview* stands in marked contrast to the open-ended interview. The structured interview seeks to gain more standardization, and the interviewer must ask a series of predetermined questions in a predetermined order. The exact nature of the structured interview depends on the reason for the interview, but the diagnostic interview is a good situation to select for further illustration. One version of a structured diagnostic interview is the SADS (Schedule for Affective Disorders and Schizophrenia; Spitzer & Endicott, 1978). The SADS contains a structured set of questions designed to help diagnose certain severe types of abnormal behavior. The specific questions are designed to gather information about the client's background, the psychological disturbance, and any specific instances of notably abnormal behavior. The SADS is arranged to permit the interviewer to proceed with the questions, and depending on certain answers, to branch to other questions and eventually make a diagnosis. Careful adherence to the questions is both required and helpful—the diagnostic decision emerges at the end of the sequence of questions and answers.

In an extreme case, the structured interview could be presented via computer. Although this would have very many positive features, such as accuracy, cost-effectiveness, and storage capacity, computer assessment would prevent the psychologist from meeting and interacting with the person interviewed. As we stated at the outset, this interaction can be an important component of many assessments.

Minnesota Multiphasic Personality Inventory (MMPI). The MMPI was developed by Hathaway and McKinley in 1942 (Hathaway & McKinley, 1942). The test consists of 550 items to which the subject responds by endorsing either "true" or "false." In various ways, the test items combine to provide scores on specific scales. These are referred to as clinical scales for the main scales that help identify abnormality, and as validity scales for the four scales that help identify whether the subject was presenting himself or herself accurately or in an evasive, defensive, or intentionally disturbed fashion. We will return later to the description of the MMPI scales.

TESTS AND MEASURES

TABLE 12.8
Sample items from the Minnesota Multiphasic Personality Inventory (MMPI)

1. I like mechanics magazines.		T	F
2. I have a good appetite.		T	F
3. I wake up fresh and rested most mornings		T	F
4. I think I would like the work of a librarian.		T	F
5. I am easily awakened by noise.		T	F

Consistent with the ideals of objective assessment, the clinical scales of the MMPI were devised by comparing the responses of known groups of disturbed persons with those of normal groups. At first, many test items were administered to both groups. Only those items that successfully discriminated between the two groups were kept—items that failed to distinguish the two groups were eliminated. The items were selected in this way separately for each of the clinical scales. Thus there were many selection and elimination studies. The end result is a set of test items that have been demonstrated to separate disturbed from nondisturbed respondents, and more important, the items help differentiate the different types of psychologically disturbed subjects.

Norms are further involved in the MMPI in that each subject's scale scores are converted into standardized scores (T scores). The T scores allow for comparisons of elevations and low points across the different MMPI scales. A T score of 50 is average for the general population; the standard deviation is 10: Thus most people (68.7%) will get T scores between 40 and 60. Clinical meaning (such as making a diagnosis) is often attached to T scores greater than 70 since such scores are obtained by less than 3% of the respondents. These high scores are rare and indicate that the subject deviated from the average in certain ways. Similarly, very low scores provide information. A T score below 30 is obtained by few subjects and may suggest that the person is quite different in this respect.

The main scales of the MMPI are identified in Table 12.9. As noted earlier, the validity scales help to identify the accuracy of the manner in which the person completed the inventory. These scale scores are important because the psychologist does not want to interpret an MMPI that is not valid. Once the MMPI is considered valid, meaningful interpretations are then made of the person's scores on the clinical scales. Although high and low scores on each scale carry a certain meaning, the profile of scores, as plotted on the MMPI profile sheet (see Figure 12.1), provides an overall description of the person.

A close look at the meaning of elevations on two of the clinical scales will illustrate the use of the MMPI. When scale 4, psychopathic deviant, is unusually high, the person can be described as antisocial, rebellious, unsocialized, and untrustworthy. A severely psychopathic person scores very high on this scale and is often in trouble with authorities and having difficulties with family and spouse. Scale 9, mania, reflects the degree to which a person is described on a continuum from outgoing, sociable, and optimistic, to excessively energetic, disoriented, and confused. When elevations are seen on scales 4 and 9 (elevations relative to the other scales and to the normative data represented by T scores), the pattern is said to indicate "antisocial personality." The person is likely to have problems with alcohol consumption, hostility, and home and work conflicts. Interestingly, these persons are also described as not particularly prone to experience anxiety or stress. Instead, problems are someone else's fault. Their attitude is one of not worrying, and can be encapsulated in the phrase "I don't give a damn."

The development of the MMPI took the *empirical* approach. The items that are included in each of the scales were determined empirically to differentiate normals from subjects with identified psychological disorders. This method has some initial validity built in—we know the items work; otherwise, they would not be part of the test. However, a novice reader of the test questions may ask: "Why ask whether or not I like mechanics magazines? What does that have to do with my being depressed?" In another case, the test-taker might ask: "What does having a good appetite and waking up

TABLE 12.9
Basic MMPI scales

Validity scales	
?	Cannot say
L	Lie scale
F	Fake bad
K	Subtle defensiveness

Clinical scales	
Hs	Hypochondriasis (1)
D	Depression (2)
Hy	Hysteria (3)
Pd	Psychopathic deviant (4)
Mf	Masculinity-femininity (5)
Pa	Paranoia (6)
Pt	Psychasthenia (7)
Sc	Schizophrenia (8)
Ma	Mania (9)
Si	Social introversion (0)

Figure 12.1
(A) A sample MMPI profile. See Table 12-9 for the full titles of the MMPI scales.

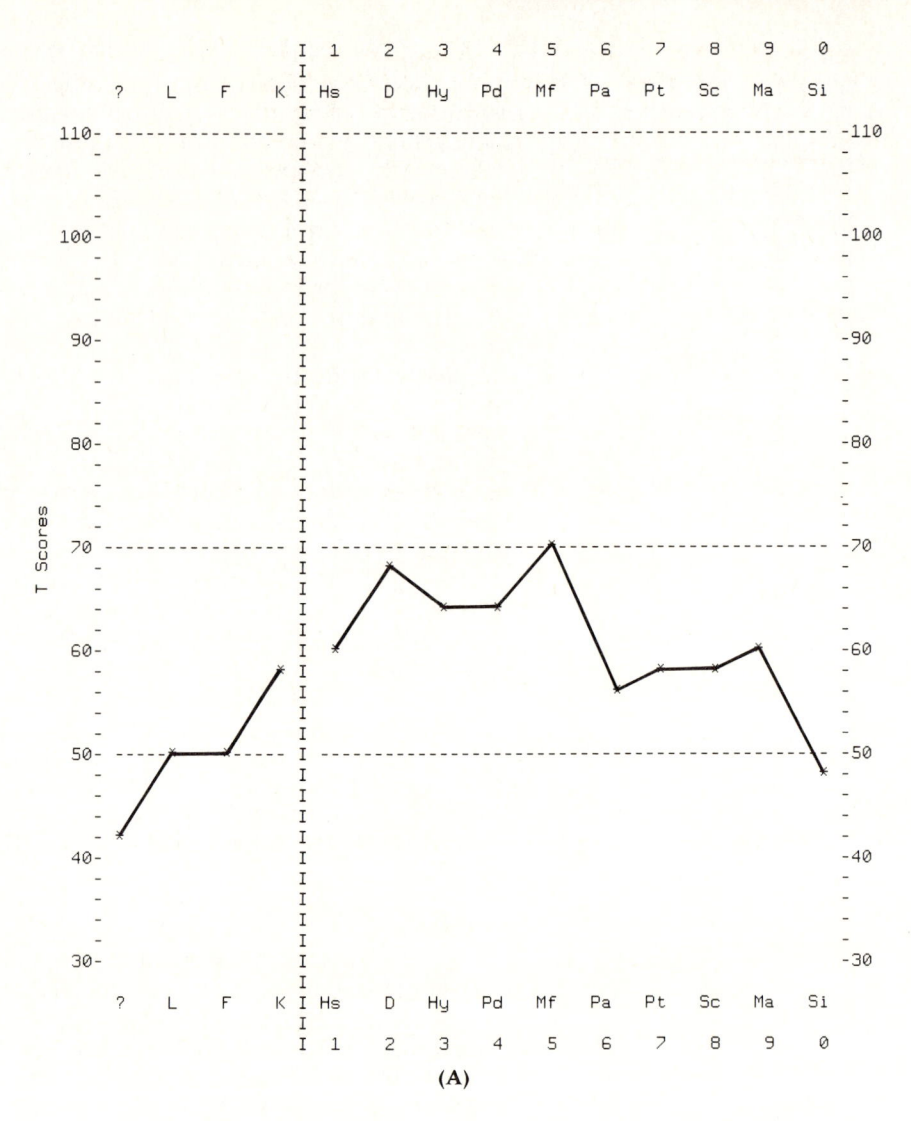

(A)

fresh and rested have to do with being crazy?" Each of these questions pertains to content validity. In other words, the questions do not appear to come from the universe of content that seems appropriate for a test of psychopathology and personality. However, content validity is not crucial. Indeed, even if the questions on *prima facie* evidence do not seem to belong on a psychological test (i.e., they lack face validity), they are very valuable if they reliably differentiate disturbed from nondisturbed subjects. The empirical accuracy of the items outweighs and overrides their appearance.

Objective Measures of Nondeviant Personality. The MMPI remains the most often used objective measure of deviant personality (psychopathology), but does the test best serve its user when the intent is to assess variations in normal personality? Some would say no, since the criterion groups were persons with psychopathology. The California Psychological Inventory (CPI) is an example of an objective measure designed specifically to describe normal

Figure 12.1 (*Continued*)
(B) An excerpt from a computer scoring/interpreting system (courtesy James Butcher).

THE MINNESOTA REPORT™*

for the Minnesota Multiphasic Personality Inventory™: Adult System

PROFILE VALIDITY

This client's approach to the MMPI was open and cooperative. The resulting MMPI profile is valid and probably a good indication of his present level of personality functioning. This suggests that he is able to follow instructions and to respond appropriately to the task, and may be viewed as a positive indication of his involvement with the evaluation.

SYMPTOMATIC PATTERN

The client has feelings of personal inadequacy and tends to view the future with some uncertainty and pessimism. He is somewhat moody, rather sensitive to criticism and may tend to blame himself for things that go wrong. He seems to worry excessively, have low energy, a slow personal tempo, and is somewhat dissatisfied with his life situation.

He has diverse interests that include aesthetic and cultural activities. He is usually somewhat passive and compliant in interpersonal relationships, is generally self-controlled, and dislikes confrontation. He may have difficulty in expressing anger directly and may resort to indirect means.

INTERPERSONAL RELATIONS

He tends to be hesitant and pessimistic about personal relationships. He is somewhat shy and introverted and feels rather inadequate in social situations.

BEHAVIORAL STABILITY

This profile may result from a high stress environment or a recent traumatic experience. The possibility of such circumstances should be evaluated.

DIAGNOSTIC CONSIDERATIONS

The tendency toward low moods should be evaluated. The MMPI profile does not provide sufficient information for formal diagnosis in this case.

There is some possibility that he is having difficulties of an addictive nature. He may be abusing or over-using addicting substances. Further evaluation of alcohol or drug usage is recommended.

TREATMENT CONSIDERATIONS

He may be motivated to obtain and respond to therapy because of his low mood and high level of distress, as well as his general willingness to discuss his problems of poor morale. Response to psychotherapy is usually good.

(B)

people. Less useful for making diagnoses, the CPI is useful for describing nondeviant personality.

The CPI consists of 480 items contributing to 18 scales (Gough, 1957). The CPI shares 178 items with the MMPI, but does not contain symptom-oriented questions. Most of the content of the CPI consists of reporting typical behavior patterns and customary feelings, opinions, and attitudes about social ethics and family matters (Megargee, 1972).

The scales of the CPI are categorized into four classes. A sample scale from each class illustrates the full range of characteristics assessed: Dominance (Do), Self-control (Sc), Achievement via Independence (Ai), and Psychological Mindedness (Py).

Single-Dimension Self-Report Inventories. If one were to judge from the inventories described thus far, it would be reasonable to conclude that all personality inventories assess the entire scope of personality. This is in fact not the case. Most objective personality inventories have been developed to measure one aspect of personality or psychopathology at a time.

Not all objective measures use the true/false format either. Rather, there is a great variety in the formats employed by objective inventories. To illustrate some of the different types of test formats and to provide a sample of inventories designed to measure a single dimension, we will look at Rotter's locus of control scale, the Beck Depression Inventory, and the State-Trait Anxiety Inventory.

Locus of control (Rotter, 1966) refers to a person's generalized expectancy for internal versus external control of reinforcement. A person with an internal locus of control perceives both positive and negative outcomes as depending on his or her own behavior. Persons with internal locus of control believe that what they do affects what happens to them. A person with external locus of control believes that outcomes are beyond his or her personal control—events are determined by luck, fate, and or others.

Persons who differ on this one dimension have been found to show many other behavioral differences (Phares, 1976). For instance, studies have demonstrated that the effectiveness of structured versus unstructured group therapy is associated with a participant's locus of control. Participants with internal locus of control responded better to a group with less structure, whereas those participants with an external locus of control gained more from groups where the leader provided a great deal of structure (Kilmann, Albert, & Sotile, 1975; Abramowitz, Abramowitz, Roback, & Jackson, 1974).

Rotter's Locus of Control Scale is a 29-item forced-choice test. Only 23 items are scored, since the other 6 are fillers (items to help disguise from the subject the dimension of personality that is being measured). Sample items, and a sample filler item, are shown in Table 12.10. In the forced-choice format, the subject is asked to indicate which of the two statements is *most* true.

TABLE 12.10
Sample items from the Rotter Locus of Control Scale

For each set of items, circle the letter of the one that you believe is *most* true. It may be that you feel neither is true, but circle the one you feel is *most* true. Please do not skip any.

1. a. Without the right breaks one cannot be an effective leader.
   b. Capable people who fail to become leaders have not taken advantage of their opportunities.
2. a. In my case getting what I want has little or nothing to do with luck.
   b. Many times we might just as well decide what to do by flipping a coin.
3. a. With enough effort we can wipe out political corruption.
   b. It is difficult for people to have much control over the things politicians do in office.
4. a. One should always be willing to admit mistakes.
   b. It is usually best to cover up one's mistakes.

Note: An external locus of control score includes answering numbers 1a, 2b, and 3b. Number 4 is not scored (buffer).

Since Freud's seminal writings, many psychological theories have involved the concept of anxiety. For Freud anxiety was an unpleasant *state*, similar to nervousness, that was a signal that the person was not fully ready to cope with present psychological conflicts. Many years later, psychologists began developing measurement instruments to assess a person's level of anxiety. One of the earlier scales to assess anxiety was the Taylor Manifest Anxiety Scale (TMAS) (Taylor, 1953), a 52-item inventory (questions were taken from the MMPI, but validated separately).

The TMAS measures *trait* anxiety—a feature of personality that is thought to be stable and characteristic. As researchers continued to study the concept of anxiety, an important distinction emerged: that between state anxiety and trait anxiety. State anxiety refers to a current condition—the degree to which a person is anxious at a particular time. In contrast, trait anxiety reflects the person's typical and characteristic pattern. Traits are seen as stable, whereas states are more sensitive to environmental fluctuations. The *State-Trait Anxiety Inventory* (STAI; Spielberger, Gorsuch, & Lushene, 1970) contains two separate scales to assess state and trait anxiety as distinct aspects of the individual's personality. Sample items from each portion of the scale are provided in Table 12.11. As you can see, this inventory asks subjects to make judgments on a 4-point scale. Some more recent measures of anxiety make another distinction—they are designed to assess different types of trait anxiety, anxiety traits for specific situations. For example, a measure developed by Endler and Okada (1975) assesses one's general tendency to feel anxious

TABLE 12.11
Sample items from the State-Trait Anxiety Inventory (Revised Form)

Instructions and sample items for the state anxiety scale.

Directions: A number of statements which people have used to describe themselves are given below. Read each statement and then blacken in the appropriate circle to the right of the statement to indicate how you *feel* right now, that is, *at this moment*. There are no right or wrong answers. Do not spend too much time on any one statement but give the answer which seems to describe your present feelings best.

	Not at All	Somewhat	Moderately So	Very Much So
1. I feel calm	1	2	3	4
2. I feel secure	1	2	3	4
3. I am tense	1	2	3	4
4. I feel strained	1	2	3	4

Instructions and sample items for the trait anxiety scale

Directions: A number of statements which people have used to describe themselves are given below. Read each statement and then blacken in the appropriate circle to the right of the statement to indicate how you *generally* feel. There are no right or wrong answers. Do not spend too much time on any one statement but give the answer which seems to describe how you generally feel.

	Almost Never	Sometimes	Often	Almost Always
21. I feel pleasant	1	2	3	4
22. I feel nervous and restless	1	2	3	4
23. I feel satisfied with myself	1	2	3	4
24. I wish I could be as happy as others seem to be	1	2	3	4

when in differing situations such as "situations where you are about to or may encounter physical danger" and "situations where you are being evaluated by other people." Some data suggest that we can make improved predictions about a person's state anxiety when we assess the level of his or her situation-specific trait anxiety (Kendall, 1978).

We are all familiar with depression. All of us, at some time, feel sad or unhappy. However, the psychological concept of depression refers to a syndrome of related symptoms that are more severe than the variations in mood that we typically experience. Syndrome depression includes, for example, sad mood, poor appetite, difficulties in sleeping, loss of interest or pleasure in usual activities, negative self-concept, and a loss of energy. The complete list is long, with many possible variations in the degree of depression—one person might feel somewhat dejected, while another reports repeated thoughts of suicide. One measure that has been used as a self-report indicant of depression is the *Beck Depression Inventory* (Beck, Ward, Mendelsohn, Mock, & Erbaugh, 1962). Sample items are provided in Table 12.12. For this inventory, the subject is asked to select from several choices the one that most accurately describes how he or she is feeling today. Thus the scale can be said to measure the state of depression.

PROJECTIVE METHODS

The projective methods of measuring personality developed from the psychodynamic theoretical perspective in which personality is viewed as the result of underlying psychodynamic features. The projective methods of assessment are therefore designed to tap these underlying features. Projective testing involves providing the subject with novel, ambiguous, and almost contentless forms to which the examiner asks for a response. Theoretically, the examiner assumes that if all the testing materials contain only a minimum of content or form, the subject's responses are solely a function of the subject's

TABLE 12.12
Sample items from the Beck Depression Inventory

Circle the one statement in each group that best describes the way you feel today. Some alternatives are worded in (a) and (b) forms. If you choose that alternative, circle only (a) or (b), whichever describes your feelings best.

1. 0 I do not feel sad.
   1 I feel blue or sad.
   2a I am blue or sad all the time and I can't snap out of it.
   2b I am so sad or unhappy that it is quite painful.
   3 I am so sad or unhappy that I can't stand it.

2. 0 I don't feel I am any worse than anybody else.
   1 I am critical of myself for my weaknesses or mistakes.
   2 I blame myself all the time for my faults.
   3 I blame myself for everything bad that happens.

3. 0 I don't feel disappointed in myself.
   1a I am disappointed in myself.
   1b I don't like myself.
   2 I am disgusted with myself.
   3 I hate myself.

Note: Items matched a and b are scored similarly. Some researcher have altered the instructions on the BDI from "how you feel today" to "how you felt over the last week, including today." This change was intended to convert the BDI from a state measure to somewhat of a trait measure.

HIGHLIGHT 12.3

Cognitive Assessment: "The Power of Nonnegative Thinking"

Perhaps you recall Norman Vincent Peale's *The Power of Positive Thinking* (1952), or perhaps you remember the children's story of the train that was struggling to reach the top of the mountain and was chanting "I think I can, I think I can." We are promised meaningful gains in our own lives if we follow the leaders of self-encouragement. But what are the data on positive thinking? As it turns out, several facets of adjustment are related *not* to positive thinking, but to the absence of negative thinking—the power of nonnegative thinking (Kendall, 1983; Kendall & Korgeski, 1979).

The methods used for cognitive assessment vary. Some researchers have developed self-report inventories where a series of thoughts are presented and the subject is asked to respond by indicating how often, during a specified time, he or she had each thought. Others have used a more open-ended approach, called thought listing, where the subject is instructed to list on a form the thoughts that he or she had during a particular time or during a specific interaction. Still others have videotaped the subject in a specific situation, and asked him or her to recall, while observing the replay, the thoughts that were going through his or her head. Despite the variations in the methods used to assess cognitions (see also Merluzzi, Glass, & Genest, 1981), the findings are relatively consistent in support of "the power of nonnegative thinking."

For example, Schwartz and Gottman (1976) studied subjects who differed in their level of assertiveness. High-assertive subjects as a group reported very few negative self-statements and many positive self-statements, while low-assertive subjects had a comparable amount of both positive and negative self-statements. The more assertive subjects had fewer negative self-statements. Cacioppo, Glass, and Merluzzi (1979) reported that whereas neither the number of positive nor the number of neutral self-statements was related to self-evaluation, the more negative self-statements, the lower the self-evaluations. Craighead, Kimball, and Rehak (1979) reported that of the mood changes, physiological responses, and self-statements recorded on subjects high and low on a measure of need for social approval, the groups differed significantly in the frequency of negative self-referent self-statements. Other studies report similar findings in terms of the distinction between positive and negative self-statements (e.g., M. A. Bruch, 1981; Galassi, Frierson, & Sharer, 1981).

In a study of the treatment of debilitating performance anxiety (Kendrick, Craig, Lawson, & Davidson, 1982), positive and negative self-talk was examined in relation to therapeutic changes. These authors reported that the gains produced by treatment were largely associated with reductions in negative self-statements.

What can we learn from the power of nonnegative thinking? First, simple self-encouragement is probably not enough. We can tell ourselves over and over that we want to achieve this or that, or improve ourselves in a select way—but we may not believe it ourselves. That is, we may follow prescribed self-encouragement with our own counterarguments. "I can do it if I really try" followed by "Yeah, but I've tried before . . . I just can't"!

Second, we may achieve more or be better at overcoming existing weaknesses if we focus on removing negative thinking. Identifying the types of negative and nonproductive thought that dominates a person's thinking, and subsequently working to reduce or modify these unwanted thoughts, promises to improve the gains made by other psychological treatments.

Third, we may be better able to understand the differences among people, the variations in what has been called personality, by taking a look at how people talk to themselves. A great challenge remains, of course, since the assessment of a person's thoughts is most difficult and can be undermined by subjects who are defensive and cautious, intentionally lying, or uncooperative.

---

personality. Stated differently, the more opportunity the subject has to respond freely and idiosyncratically, the more personal and meaningful will be the responses. Because the test materials are ambiguous, they are like screens onto which the subject "projects" his or her feelings, conflicts, and desires. Unlike the direct questions of objective assessment, where subjects' responses are said to reflect aspects of their personality of which they were already aware, projective tests seek to discover the unconscious side of personality.

Projective tests come in many different styles. For example, subjects might be asked to *associate* to inkblots, to *construct* a story based on a picture, to complete an incomplete sentence, to place a set of pictures in their proper *order*, or to *express* their personality in the form of drawings. Three types of projective tests, the Rorschach Inkblots, the Thematic Apperception Test, and the Draw-A-Person test, will be discussed to illustrate the association, construction, and expression forms of projective testing.

Rorschach Inkblots. The Rorschach Inkblots are 10 cards—5 are black and white and 5 have color. Subjects are shown one card at a time and are asked to tell what the card looks like or reminds them of. This portion of the testing is called *free association*, because the examiner simply shows each card and records the various perceptions (referred to as percepts) that the subjects describe. The examiner also records any comments or questions, the subjects latency to respond to the blots, and any marked mannerisms or gestures. Following complete administration of the 10 cards, the examiner then conducts an inquiry. The subject is then asked to tell what factors contributed to the different percepts.

Scoring the inkblot test involved ascertaining the *location* of the subject's percept, catergorizing the *content* of the percept, and recording the *determinants* of the percept. Although the test is clearly a projective device, objective scoring systems have been developed. These systems are typically based on location, content, and determinants.

Referring to Figure 12.2, let's assume that a subject gave the response "This part here looks like the head of some sort of, I don't know, animal or something." During the inquiry it is learned that the subject was referring to the lower middle part of the Rorshach blot. An "animal's head" is the content, but what is the determinant? The examiner asks the subject: "What made it look like an animal head to you?" The subject might respond "The shape" or "The way it is shaded." Shape, shading, and movement are possible percept determinants.

Interpretation of the Rorschach Inkblots is a more difficult task than either administering the test or scoring the subject's responses. The examiner must review the percepts, their scoring, and the information gathered about the subject during the testing, such as mannerisms, tone of voice, hesitation or reluctance, and interpersonal impact. Some interpreters rely heavily on the scores assigned to the percepts and to the ratios of type of percepts to one another. Others, however, prefer to rely on a more holistic view of the subject's percepts, how they were reported, and the general impression left by the person during the testing interaction.

Thousands of research studies for the Rorschach Inkblot test have been conducted. As a result of the diversity of approaches and the diversity of outcomes, no single statement can do justice to the research status of the test. However, it is possible to draw some conclusions regarding the reliability and validity of the test data. Zubin, Eron, and Schumer (1965) noted that much is to be desired before reliability can be claimed for the Rorschach. When validity is examined, Goldfried, Stricker, and Weiner (1972) concluded that the results are, at best, equivocal. Though some recent work seems to be producing advances (Exner, 1983), more research on the new approach is needed. For some reason, despite the limited research support, the Rorschach Inkblots remain one of the most often used psychological tests. Although the test responses may seem to help some practicing clinical psychologists diagnose and understand personality, their diagnoses and understandings may be based more on their own clinical skills than on the test responses.

Figure 12.2
A sample Rorschach inkblot.

Thematic Apperception Test. The Thematic Apperception Test (TAT) was designed by Morgan and Murray in 1935, and published in 1943 (Murray, 1943) after several years of development. The TAT has been used to assess the "needs" that were important in a person's life and in Murray's theory of personality. The TAT consists of a series of drawings portraying people in various situations (see the example in Figure 12.3). A sample of the pictures is selected (often 10 to 15) and the subject is asked to construct a story about each picture—telling what led up to the scene, who the characters are, what is presently going on, and what will happen in the future. The subject is instructed to include the thoughts and feelings of the characters in the story.

Interpretation of the TAT does not typically involve scoring systems, such as those that have been developed for the Rorschach test. The interpreter of the TAT wants to understand what caused the subject to tell those stories in that way. The interpreter often reads and rereads the stories to glean a general picture of the type of person who sees the world in the way described in the stories. Consistency across stories is considered important in developing hypotheses about the determinants of the subject's stories, but divergences from what might be expected can also be helpful. These divergences are particularly noteworthy when they are accompanied by signs of strong emotion or when stated in an unusually emphatic or intense fashion. In general, making sense of responses to the TAT involves identifying whom the subject sees as the "hero" of the story and the hero's needs and environmental pressures (forces pushing on the hero).

Scoring systems for the TAT have been limited to specific features of personality and no global objective scoring systems are currently in use. Of the specific features of personality that have been studied, need for achievement has a rather extensive literature (McClelland, Atkinson, Clark, & Lowell, 1953). Need for achievement (n. Ach) has been defined as competition with a standard of exellence. If the subject creates stories that describe a "hero" who is trying to strive for goals and accomplishments, such as earning an advanced degree, developing a special skill, or completing a challenging feat, the subject is said to be projecting his or her own needs for achievement.

Some of the early investigations of the achievement motive involved different experimental conditions which aroused different levels of achievement

Figure 12.3

A sample drawing from the Thematic Apperception Test (TAT).

The Thematic Apperception Test (TAT) consists of a series of drawings portraying people in different situations. Subjects are asked to construct a story about each picture. (Sepp Seitz)

motivation. When subjects were placed in conditions intended to measure their abilities (as opposed to neutral or relaxed conditions), the TAT stories contained more achievement motivation. Scoring TAT stories for achievement motivation involves tabulating the presence or absence of responses such as achievement imagery (reference to a goal involving competition with a standard of excellence), need (stated desire to reach an achievement goal), and instrumental activity (reference to activities which are instrumental to achieving the goal). The higher the "n Ach" score, the greater the subject's motivation for high achievement.

Draw-A-Person. Requiring a subject to draw a person is considered an expressive type of projective assessment of personality. Artistic ability is of no concern, and the subject should draw however he or she wishes. After drawing one person, the subject is asked to draw another, but this time a person of the opposite sex of the first drawing.

An understanding of the respondent's personality is sought through an interpretation of the formal characteristics of the figures that are drawn—such as size, thickness of the lines, placement of the drawing on the page, and symmetry. Unfortunately, figure drawings have not fared well in the evaluation literature. Swensen (1968) concluded that human figure drawings are doubtful measures of personality and too unreliable in making reasonable clinical judgments. As a research tool for assessing personality, very few contemporary psychologists would use human figure drawings. However, some psychologists use the human figure drawing method as part of a larger battery of psychological tests or as a method for assessing subjects with limited verbal skills—such as children.

Projective tests remain part of the practicing psychologists methods of assessment, despite the generally less than enthusiastic research outcomes to support their use. Perhaps for those seeking to assess unconscious processes there simply is nothing better. Also, the projective method is the major technique for psychodynamic assessment, and many psychologists hold a psychodynamic point of view. However, the science of psychology might best proceed by improving its assessment methods rather than continuing to use those with limited research credentials.

HIGHLIGHT 12.4
Neuropsychological Testing

Damage to the brain, from strokes, infections, tumors, trauma, nutritional deficiency, and the like, is associated with deviations in behavior. Damage to different sections of the brain, and to different regions within each section, is associated with different types of behavioral deviation. Neuropsychological testing involves measuring behavioral signs that reflect healthy or impaired brain functioning. Many tests are available to the clinical neuropsychologist (see Filskov & Locklear, 1982; Golden, 1977; Lezak, 1976; Reitan & Davidson, 1974). The tests are designed to measure all areas where behavioral functioning can reflect brain damage. The following is a sample of the measures from the areas taped by neuropsychological assessment.

Tests of facial recognition: One at a time, the subject views several pictures of faces, and after each must match the face with one of six similar faces. The task is made progressively more difficult by showing stimulus pictures with increasingly variant views—such as side views (Benton & Van Allen, 1973).

Tests of auditory perceptions: The Seashore Rhythm Test asks the subject to discriminate among 30 pairs of rhythmic beats that are sometimes the same and sometimes a little or very much different (Seashore, Lewis, & Soetvert, 1960).

Tests of tactile perception: The examiner traces a series of one-digit numbers on the fingertips of each hand and the subject must identify, with eyes closed, the correct number (Reitan & Davison, 1974).

Tests of motor coordination: The subject taps his or her index finger as fast as possible on a telegraph key for 10 seconds. The arm is restrained and the test is repeated several times with the preferred and nonpreferred hand (Reitan & Davison, 1974).

Tests of sensorimotor construction: In the Bender-Gestalt Test subjects are told to reproduce nine different, two-dimensional figures on a blank sheet of unlined paper. The examiner presents each figure one at a time (Bender, 1938; Hult, 1969).

Tests of memory: The Wechsler Memory Scale tests short- and long-term verbal and nonverbal memory (Wechsler, 1945).

Tests of verbal/language abilities: The Aphasia Screening Test, the Token Test, and the Neurosensory Center Comprehensive Examination for Aphasia measure verbal abilities affected by damage to the brain. In the Neurosensory Center Exam, subjects performed 20 separate subtests, each of which assesses a distinct language skill (Spreen & Benton, 1969).

Tests of conceptual reasoning: The Trial Making Test (Reitan & Davison, 1974) requires the subject to draw lines connecting a series of numbers and/or letters that are scattered on a sheet of paper. First, the subject connects the numbers, then the subject must connect the numbers and letters in sequence, alternating from number to letter.

These samples illustrate the types of measures used by clinical neuropsychologists to gather data about brain functioning. Based on our knowledge of the psychophysiology of the brain, we can determine the location of the brain damage by identifying the types of functioning that evidence deterioration. A great deal of information about brain functioning must be mastered by the practicing clinical neuropsychologist and an extensive armamentarium of tests are kept handy for making increasingly difficult discriminations.

It would be incorrect, however, to draw the conclusion that the tests are administered alone or in pairs. Rather, the standard practice is to administer an entire battery of neuropsychological tests. Comprehensive test batteries include the Halstead–Reitan and the Luria–Nebraska Neuropsychological Test Batteries.

The results of neuropsychological testing are used to make determinations about brain functioning. The following are some of the questions that might be asked and answered with neuropsychological assessments. Is the brain damage focal or diffuse? Is the damage progressive or nonprogressive? Is the damage acute or chronic? Is the dysfunction organic or functional? (Is the dysfunction due to a real underlying physical problem or is it the result of psychological problems?)

Let's take a look at one study, by Filskov and Goldstein (1974), which used the Halstead-Reitan Test Battery. These authors reported that the test data were equal or more accurate in both identifying and localizing brain damage than the more risky and invasive medical procedures such as angiograms and pneumoencephalograms, or the more expensive medical assessments from computerized axial tomography (CAT) scans, skull x-rays, or EEGs. Although the average accuracy is about 75% to 80%, the Halstead–Reitan had a 100% hit rate in this study for diagnosing the specific pathology—for example, trauma, neoplasms, degenerative disease, or arteriosclerotic cerebrovascular disease.

BEHAVIORAL ASSESSMENT

Behavioral assessment is a *situation-specific* approach to psychological measurement. Behavioral assessment seeks to measure actual behavior in the actual environment. The environmental situation is important to the behavioral assessor because behavior is said to be, in part, a function of the environment in which it takes place. That is, because behavior may vary from one situation to another, an accurate measurement of it must be made in each situation. Naturalistic observation, self-monitoring, and analogue observations are representative behavioral assessment methods (Barlow, 1981).

NATURALISTIC OBSERVATION

Natualistic observation involves watching and carefully recording a person's actual behavior in the natural environment. The target behaviors to be observed and recorded vary, so that there is no single "test" or "method" for naturalistic observations. Rather, general procedures are followed, and variations depend on the specific situation. In general, the steps that are followed in producing a system for naturalistic observation include selecting the behaviors to be observed; operationally defining them; choosing the observers and the type, schedule, and form the observations will take; training the observers; and establishing that the system and the observers are reliable.

Because the needs and specific interests of those involved directly affect what is observed and how the observations are gathered, many naturalistic observation systems, as opposed to a few standardized ones, are evident in the literature. One system for home observation, the Behavior Coding System, was developed by Patterson and colleagues (1977). This system contains 28 separate behaviors (categories) that the observer records as having occurred or not during sequential 6-second periods. Sample behaviors and their operational definitions, as well as a typical observational coding sheet, appear in Figure 12.4.

In general, observational systems are designed to produce frequency data on single target individuals. For instance, after employing an observational system in the home, the data might indicate that the mother spends considerable time giving commands and that the child is typically uninvolved. In contrast to this approach, Mash, Terdal, and Anderson (1973) have described the *response-class matrix* as a method of behavioral assessment that focuses more explicitly on the *interactions* among those who are observed. Observers record an observation every interval of time (e.g., 10 seconds), but rather than observing one person at a time, both parent and child behaviors are recorded by placing a single mark in one of the cells of the matrix. The matrix has child antecedent behaviors listed on one side and parent consequent behaviors listed on the other side (see Figure 12.5). When a behavior takes place and is observed, such as a child playing and the parent praising the child, one check mark is made in the appropriate cell of the matrix—in this case in the row for child play and under the column heading for parental praise. Thus the frequency of behavioral interactions, as opposed to the frequency of behaviors, is recorded.

Although we have described observational systems appropriate for the home, naturalistic observational systems have been designed for use in laboratory settings for research projects, and in classrooms and inpatient hospitals for assessing and evaluating clients' actions and the effects of interventions.

TESTS AND MEASURES

Figure 12.4
Sample behavior codes and their operational definitions, and a sample observational coding sheet.

Observer's Name _____
Person being observed _____
Setting _____
Date _____ Time _____

Place a check (✓) in the proper location, when a behavior is observed during that interval.

Command (CM)	An immediate and clearly stated request or command
Ignore (IG)	When person A has directed behavior at person B and person B appears to have recognized that the behavior was directed at him, but does not respond in an active fashion.
Compliance (CO)	A person immediately does what is asked of him.

Behavior	6 second intervals
CM	
IG	
CO	

As with all psychological measurements, naturalistic observation requires reliable and valid data. To assure reasonably sound assessments, certain cautions must be exercised. For instance, people who know that they are being observed may alter their actions and reactions because they are unnerved by the observer or because they are trying to put forth a false image of themselves. Behavioral assessors avoid this *reactivity* by having the observer enter the natural environment before the period when data will be collected, so that subjects will get used to the observer's presence.

Another potential dilemma is *observer bias*. When the observers are aware of the research hypothesis or the course of the psychological intervention, or when they hold their own assumptions about what behaviors "should" be occurring, the data may be biased.

SELF-MONITORING

Even a cursory overview of naturalistic observation indicates that the procedures are very time consuming and demanding. For numerous reasons, naturalistic observation is not always possible. *Self-monitoring*, when people serve as observers of their own actions and interactions, offers one approach to gathering behavioral frequency data in the natural environment without having difficulties associated with naturalistic observation (Ciminero, Nelson, & Lipinski, 1977).

Figure 12.5
Sample portion of a response-class matrix.

Child antecedent behaviors	Parents Consequent Behaviors			
	Command	Question	Praise	Negative
Compliance				
Ignore				
Play				

Research comparing self-monitoring with data from unobtrusive observers indicates that self-monitoring can be highly to moderately accurate when the behaviors being recorded are noninteractive. However, when the target for assessment is more interactive behavior patterns, self-monitoring results in questionable reliability. When simple and discrete behaviors are the target of assessment, devices such as wrist counters and pocket-sized data forms can be used for self-monitoring.

The issues of reactivity and bias also pertain to self-monitoring. Some data have indicated that the mere act of monitoring one's own behaviors can lead a person to initiate change in those behaviors. For instance, suppose that you were asked to count the frequency of "hellos" that you offer strangers as you pass them walking on campus. The mere fact that you are now paying attention to this behavior is likely to have a reactive effect—because saying hello has a positive value, the reactivity will cause the behavior to increase. In contrast, suppose that you were told by a friend that you make a nasty grimace when someone says hello to you. You initiate self-monitoring of the unwanted grimacing. Because the value of this behavior is negative, the reactivity will cause it to go down.

ANALOGUE ASSESSMENTS

The game "Monopoly" is an analogue for the world of finance and real estate. An *analogue* is a facsimile of reality, but a scaled-down version. In a simplified manner, an analogue presents a sample of certain characteristic features of reality. When naturalistic observation is deemed too time consuming or expensive, and when self-monitoring is considered too susceptible to unwanted effects, the behavioral assessor may employ an analogue assessment. These analogues can involve audio/videotapes, enactments, and role-plays.

The audio and videotapes provide the subject with many cues that make the behavior that is emitted similar to that which would be seen in the real situation. For example, Arkowitz, Lichtenstein, McGovern, and Hines (1975) assessed dating skills by having subjects listen to taped instructions and then respond.

In an enactment analogue, the subject is brought in direct contact with the relevant stimuli, but in a controlled fashion. For instance, behavioral avoidance tests require the subject, typically a phobic client, to approach the feared object as closely as possible. Observational data can then be collected.

If one wanted to assess a person's ability to perform a certain sales job, the assessor might play a role. Several confederates of the assessor could act as customers, and the sales candidate would have to demonstrate his or her skills in handling the prepared situations. Role playing can create a very real and challenging situation that is likely to produce behaviors that are helpful to the assessor.

THE GOAL OF PSCYHOLOGICAL MEASUREMENT

Our survey of psychological measurement instruments and procedures offers ample testimony to the breadth of the enterprise. The diversity of psychological measurements may have you wondering what holds the enterprise together. Clearly, responses to an inkblot, scores on a computer aptitude test, and the frequencies of specific behaviors appear unglued. However, one general goal provides continuity to the diversity of measurement efforts. Measurements are undertaken to provide data for improved understandings and enhanced predictions. Psychologists of all varieties employ measurements to help determine what sample of data, gathered in what fashion, on what subject, produces what information. All forms of assessment fit together when viewed in efforts to answer this question.

SUMMARY

1. Assessment is the process of gathering information about a client or subject to better understand the person and make more accurate predictions about him or her.

2. The basic scientific concepts that underlie the requirements of psychological tests are reliability and validity. Reliability is the degree to which a test (or series of observations) is stable, dependable, and self-consistent. Types of reliability include retest (test–retest), interscorer, and internal consistency. Validity refers to the degree to which a test actually measures what it is intended to measure. Types of validity include content validity, criterion-related validity (predictive and concurrent), and construct validity.

3. Psychological measures have been developed to assess intellectual ability, aptitude and achievement, deviant and normal personality, and the frequencies of specific behaviors.

4. By using standardized procedures of test administration and by interpreting an individual's test scores against those scores obtained by a representative sample of potential test takers (norms), psychological tests strive to reduce or eliminate unwanted, nonmeaningful influences on test scores.

5. Measures of intellectual ability include the Stanford–Binet Intelligence Scale and three age-related Wechsler intelligence scales (for adults, children, and preschoolers). The Stanford–Binet employs the concepts of basal age and ceiling age. Wechsler scales include subscales assessing verbal IQ and performance IQ.

6. The intelligence quotient (IQ) is calculated by dividing a person's mental age by his/her chronological age and multiplying the result by 100.

7. Adaptive testing is a strategy that uses different sets of test questions for each person taking the test, with specific questions being chosen based on the person's skill level.

8. Because there have been allegations about the bias or lack of fairness in tests of intelligence, some tests have sought to measure IQ using "culture-fair" questions. Bias in intelligence tests has also been examined in terms of whether or not the test scores discriminate unfairly between the cultural majority and minority groups.

9. Aptitude tests measure segments of ability (such as mechanical or musical), whereas achievement tests assess the attainment of broad educational goals.

10. Objective psychological measures provide well-defined questions requiring limited answers and comparisons with normative data. The Minnesota Multiphasic Personality Inventory (MMPI) and the California Psychological Inventory (CPI) are examples of objective measures of deviant and normal personality, respectively. In addition to these measures of the many facets of personality, there are many other measures of more singular dimensions such as locus of control, anxiety, and depression.

11. Projective measures provide the subject with ambiguous materials and provide an unbounded opportunity for responding. The Rorschach Inkblots, the Thematic Apperception Test (TAT), and the Draw-A-Person test are examples of projective measures.

12. Behavioral assessment seeks to assess behavior in the actual environment in which it takes palce. Naturalistic observation, self-monitoring, and analogue assessments are examples of the behavioral approach to psychological assessment.

13. The goal of psychological measurements is to provide data for improved understandings and enhanced predictions.

KEY TERMS

Assessment
Reliability
Validity
Retest reliability
Interscorer reliability
Internal consistency
Content validity
Face validity
Construct validity
Criterion-related validity
Predictive validity
Concurrent validity
Standardization
Norms
Stanford-Binet Intelligence Scale
Basal age
Ceiling age
Mental age
IQ
Wechsler Intelligence Tests
Adaptive testing
Objective assessment
Minnesota Multiphasic Personality Inventory
Locus of control
State
Trait
State-Trait Anxiety Inventory
Beck Depression Inventory
Nonnegative thinking
Projective assessment
Rorschach Inkblots
Thematic Apperception Test
Draw-A-Person
Neuropsychological testing
Behavioral assessment
Situational specificity
Naturalistic observation
Response-class matrix
Reactivity
Observer bias
Self-monitoring
Analogue assessments

SUGGESTED READINGS

American Psychological Association. *Standards for educational and psychological tests.* Washington, D.C.: American Psychological Association, 1974. This book presents the report of a special committee that examined psychological tests. The standards for tests, test manuals, the reliability and validity studies of tests, and the use of tests are presented.

ANASTASI, A. *Psychological testing* (3rd ed.). New York: Macmillan, 1968. This testing textbook provides the principles of test construction, knowledge about the behavior that is being measured, and a familiarity with the field of available psychological tests.

CRONBACH, L. J. *Essentials of psychological testing* (4th ed.). New York: Harper & Row, 1984. This textbook provides a comprehensive coverage of all the principles and procedures of psychological measurement.

13

Personality

THE STUDY OF PERSONALITY
FREUD'S PSYCHOANALYTIC
    THEORY OF PERSONALITY
  The Structures of Personality
  Stages of Psychosexual
    Development
  Neo-Freudians
TYPES AND TRAITS
  Sheldon's Constitutional
    Psychology
  Personality Traits and Factor
    Analysis
SELF-THEORIES
  Roger's Self-Theory
LEARNING AND SOCIAL
    LEARNING THEORIES
  Learning Theory and
    Personality
  Social Learning and
    Personality
THE COGNITIVE SIDE OF
    PERSONALITY
  Schemata
  Attributional Processes
THE SOURCE OF BEHAVIOR:
    PERSONALITY TRAITS
    VERSUS SITUATIONAL
    INFLUENCES
SUMMARY
KEY TERMS
SUGGESTED READINGS

THE STUDY OF PERSONALITY

The study of personality is the study of people's psychological and behavioral individuality, that is, of what characteristics make each person an individual; and psychologists have an array of ideas about just what makes each of us an individual. This range of ideas may be summarized by reference to an often-cited observation by Kluckhohn and Murray (1948, p. 35) that in certain respects every person is:

1. Like *all* other people.
2. Like *some* other people.
3. Like *no* other person.

Thus there are characteristics common to all people. For example, all people can adapt to their worlds, can do what is needed to survive. There are also characteristics that people share with only some other people. For example, our society and culture lead us to have certain values, attitudes, and beliefs which differ from those held by people who grow up in a different society

407

Each person is unique. But all persons also have many characteristics in common. (Owen Franken/Stock Boston)

and culture. Finally, there are characteristics that are each person's alone. For example, each of us has a unique genetic inheritance *and* a singular history of environmental experiences.

Given that *all* people share some characteristics with all others, with only some others, and with no others, a comprehensive study of personality would involve describing and explaining all three sets of features in people. Understandably, however, this complex task has not really been attempted. Instead, psychologists have tended to develop theories and research which focus on one of these emphases.

Personality psychologists (or "personologists") have, therefore, focused on either:

1. *The generic human being:* (meaning the "general case" of humanity) and have emphasized a *nomothetic* approach to personality, that is, one stressing *group laws*—principles that apply to all, or to large groups of human beings.
2. *Idiographic laws:* principles that may apply only to the individual.

Further information about these two approaches to personality is presented in Highlight 13.1. However, despite different *emphases*—on either nomothetic or idiographic principles—no approach to personality denies the point made by Kluckhohn and Murray (1948): Each person has characteristics which are common to all people, shared only by others in the person's group or groups, and specific to that person. As we review major approaches to personality, we shall see evidence of concern with all these facets of the person. Indeed this will be evident even in the psychoanalytic approach of Sigmund Freud, which most clearly exemplifies a stress on the generic or universal characteristics of personality.

FREUD'S PSYCHOANALYTIC THEORY OF PERSONALITY

Sigmund Freud was born in Freiberg, Moravia (today part of Czechoslovakia) in 1856 and died in London, England, in 1939, a refugee from the Nazis. He lived most of his life, however, in Vienna, where in 1881 he obtained his medical degree. Although working first in other branches of medicine, Freud began to practice psychiatry and to evolve a view of personality which he labeled as *psychoanalysis.* Freud proposed that the structures of personality are common to all people and that personality develops through a universal and unchanging series of stages.

Dominant by its sheer longevity, yet weakened by its lack of research support, the psychoanalytic view of personality remains influential (Freud, 1917/1943, 1940/1949). Art critics have used Freud's theoretical contributions to attempt to uncover the hidden meanings of artistic expressions and historians to help describe the evolution of nations. Freud's works have had such a far-reaching effect that marketing strategists, in the not-too-distant past, had a Freudian explanation of the successes of certain advertisements. Freud's approach has endured in part because it was the first major psychological theory of human behavior. Being first and having great generality, the theory attracted many followers and generated influences in fields outside psychology. Not withstanding certain reservations, psychoanalytic theory is still very influential.

HIGHLIGHT 13.1
Idiographic and Nomothetic Pursuits

How does a student of personality approach the topic: Should one study the features that make a single personality both integrated and unique, or should one pursue the investigation of general traits and how a variety of people differ on them? One of the classic distinctions in personality is the contrast of the two approaches.

The idiographic approach stresses the importance of individuals. Allport's theories (1961) pioneered the uniqueness of individuals and the fact that behavior was the result of each person's own combination of traits. Allport's idiographic approach seeks to gain an accurate and detailed understanding of each person's *individual traits*. Personality resides in the "psychological matrix" within a person (Allport, 1960).

The nomothetic approach tries to provide an understanding of people in general, not one person, in terms of their similarities and differences on many *common traits*. Instead of focusing on the unique features of one person, the focus is on how many people differ.

The behavioral model has not been specifically interested in personality; thus it might be surprising to realize that Skinner's operant conditioning approach (see Chapter 6) parallels the idiographic study of the individual. For example, a typical behavioral analysis is not concerned with the average subject, but with the functional analysis of the behavior of a single subject. Moreover, since each organism can have its own learning history, an idiographic analysis is needed if one is to identify the specific behaviors in a given opganism's repertoire. In short, although the laws of learning may be general to all organisms (see Chapter 6), the behavioral repertoire that results may be unique for each organism.

One of the most influential aspects of Freud's theory was his notion of the unconscious. Freud argued that people are not always aware of the purposes of their behavior and that unconscious forces are determining factors of personality. This concept is referred to as *unconscious motivation*. Freud compared the mind to an iceberg: the smaller part above the water's surface is consciousness, while the enormous mass underwater represents the unconsciousness. The unconscious contains the drives, needs, and repressed experiences that control a person's awareness and actions.

The principle of *psychic determinism* refers to the idea that all behavior is

Sigmund Freud (1851–1939) emphasized the primacy of sexual instincts and argued that unconscious forces are determining factors of personality. (Mary Evans/Sigmund Freud)

directed by the inner forces of the mind. Goal-directed behavior as well as unusual and even maladaptive behavior can be explained by examining these unconscious motivations. Slips of the tongue, called *Freudian slips*, illustrate this notion. Freud saw unconscious meaning when people say something that they did not mean to say. For example, a student who has just shaved his head asked another student in the cafeteria line for change of a dollar. The student fumbles in and out of her pockets looking for some coins and eventually locates change but drops a coin in the process. She then comments, "Sorry, I've had a really hairy morning." The choice of the adjective "hairy" might well have been motivated by the unconscious. In reference to more general features of personality, behavior is said to have psychic causes that after careful and extensive analysis, can be identified and understood.

THE STRUCTURES OF PERSONALITY

Psychoanalytic theory holds that personality is determined by the interaction of three mental structures: the id, ego, and superego. These structures are *not* physical entities—they cannot be observed directly like a bodily organ, but are inferred to exist based on recurrent patterns of behavior. Such structures are best thought of as constructs: concepts which are "constructed" to help organize and explain behavior but which do not have actual physical presence. Each construct has its own distinct features as well as its own style for interacting with the others. Personality reflects the nature of the interaction of these three constructs.

Instinctual needs and drives for sexual and aggressive gratification are represented by the *id*. The id is the original psychic structure, containing everything present at birth (e.g., instincts) and holding the psychic energy that operates the other structures. This human mental (or psychic) energy is termed *libido*.

The id operates according to the *pleasure principle*. It cannot tolerate tension, so it works to avoid pain and experience pleasure. One way the id obtains pleasure without tolerating pain is via the *primary process*. Primary processes of fantasy and imagination, rather than fact and logic, create an image of the desired object which reduces the tension of the id. Since fantasy is not reality, the organism is not truly satisfied. Nevertheless, the id is gratified by the wish-fulfilling mental images.

Since we cannot be nourished by an imaginary meal, the hungry person must find real sustenance. The *ego* exists to modulate the id's interactions with the objective world of reality. The ego helps the person strive to meet the challenges posed by the external environment and functions according to the *reality principle*. The reality principle controls the discharge of tension until the appropriate time. It holds the id back from immediate satisfaction. Unlike the id's concern with pain or pleasure, the ego and reality principle are concerned with whether something is real (has external existence). *Secondary process* thinking is realistic thinking. It is the secondary process thinking of the ego that fosters meaningful reality testing. The ego is the executive function which oversees the search in reality for the desired product.

The *superego* is the last construct to develop. It represents the internalized values and ideas of society as transmitted by the person's parents, often taking a moralistic approach to life. The superego epitomizes the ideal, not the real, and judges actions against this ideal. The superego contains the conscience and the ego-ideal. The conscience includes all that society and parents say is unacceptable, whereas the ego-ideal includes what the person knows to be

PERSONALITY

Figure 13.1
If the id, ego, and superego could talk.

ID: "I CAN HAVE WHATEVER I WANT RIGHT NOW."
EGO: "I HAVE TO STRIKE A REALISTIC BALANCE BETWEEN WHAT I WANT AND WHAT I CAN REALLY HAVE."
SUPEREGO: "I OUGHT TO BE A BETTER PERSON."

ID: "I WANT A STEAK. I IMAGINE IT AND I'M SATISFIED."
EGO: "LET'S SEE WHERE CAN I FIND SOME FOOD."
SUPEREGO: "EATING A STEAK ISN'T RIGHT."

approved and rewarded. The supergo checks the uninhibited desires of the id, and influences the ego to be morally right and to seek high quality (perfection). The three constructs (id, ego, and superego) interact and variations in personality emerge based on the quality of the interactions and the relative strengths of each construct (see Figure 13.1). For example, suppose that three youngsters are playing near a garden and one wants to steal some fruit, another points out that it isn't right; and the third tries to strike a balance between the two. This is a three-person illustration of the interchange of the three constructs that Freud believed existed within each person.

STAGES OF PSYCHOSEXUAL DEVELOPMENT

Freudian personality theory places enormous emphasis on the first 5 years of life. During these early and formative years, the child progresses through three of the five stages of psychosexual development (see Table 13.1). It is

TABLE 13.1
Psychosexual stages and the approximate years of age for each

Psychosexual Stage	Age
Oral	First year
Anal	Second year
Phallic	3 to 5 years old
Latency	5 years of age to puberty
Genital	Puberty and onward

the progress, or lack thereof, during these developmental stages that contributes to adult personality.

The term *psychosexual* refers to Freud's notion of the sexual instinct (with *sexual* meaning *pleasurable*). At each of the different stages, pleasure is focused on a particular zone of the body. The first stage, for instance, is the *oral stage*, and the principal source of pleasure involves the oral cavity: eating, swallowing, sucking, and other forms of oral stimulation. In the *anal stage*, energies are focused on the holding-in and eliminating functions. Parental attitudes about toilet training as imposed on the child are said to have potent consequences in later life. The third stage, the *phallic stage*, lasts to age 5. It is during the phallic stage that the child's pleasure is derived from his or her sexual organs, that masturbation is discovered, and that the famed Oedipus complex affects young boys and the Electra complex young girls. The Oedipus complex consists of sexual interest in the parent of the opposite sex (mother) and hostile feelings toward the parent of the same sex (father). The resolution of the Oedipus complex has implications for a person's later attitudes toward the opposite sex and toward people in authority. According to Freudian theory, a son will fear castration by his father for desiring his mother and for disliking his father. To reduce this unwanted castration anxiety, a son identifies with the father and tries to be like him. The Electra complex is the related situation dealing with young girls and their relationships with their parents. The names Oedipus and Electra come from characters in dramas by the ancient Greek dramatist Sophocles—characters who were involved in incest, and father–son and mother–daughter rivalries. It is through the Oedipus or Electra complex and its resolution, according to Freud, that behavior patterns for dealing with authority are established in the developing person.

The *latency* and *genital stages* refer to the periods after the phallic stage where, respectively, there is a reduction in overt sexuality (latency) followed by the genital stage of adult love and sexual satisfaction.

Development through the psychosexual stages is an important process for the Freudian theory of personality development. If development is arrested at one stage, a person will be unable to master later stages. The person is described as *fixated*. When anxiety prevents further development, the person can, relatively speaking, become fixated at an early stage of development.

Regression also affects the process of development. That may occur when the developing organism encounters a traumatic experience. Regression is a retreat to an earlier form of interacting. For example, a teenage boy who is not receiving attention may display a temper tantrum. He is regressing to an earlier form of behavior.

NEO-FREUDIANS

Freud's theory of the structure and development of personality had a strong impact on the emerging field of psychology as well as a wider influence on literature, politics, and marketing. Those theorists close in time to Freud, even though they each disagreed with some form of his theory (often the primacy of sexual instincts), are lumped together as neo-Freudian. This "one versus all the others" division reflects the strength of the impression made by Freud's theory.

Carl Jung, a one-time associate of Freud, disagreed with Freud's reliance on sexual instincts. Jung did not remove sexuality from his theory, but he did put it in perspective by arguing that the sexual instinct is only one of

Carl Jung (1875–1961) postulated a "collective unconscious," which contains an inherited foundation for personality. (Mary Evans Picture Library/Photo Researchers, Inc.)

PERSONALITY

Karen Horney (1885–1952) believed that social and familial factors—how a young child experiences and reacts to the world—are important determinants of personality. (Bettmann Archive)

many. For instance, Jung addressed goal-directed behavior and discussed how an understanding of not only the past, but also the future, was needed for a theory of personality. Jung emphasized dreams and symbolism, as did Freud, but Jung went further in postulating a *collective unconscious* which contains an inherited foundation for personality, a system of "archetypes" or "primordial images." God is an example of an archetypal image that is part of the collective unconscious (Jung, 1936/1959, 1960).

Adler (1927) also broke with Freudian theory because of Freud's overemphasis on sexual instincts. Adler believed that social and familial factors were equally important in the emergence of personality. He described several different family patterns and detailed how each would lead to distinctive personalities. He also addressed birth order as an important familial feature affecting adult patterns of behavior. Two of Adler's most popular concepts were the notion of an *inferiority complex* and that each person strives to overcome inferiority. According to Adler, the child lives in a world dominated by adults and others who possess superior abilities. The human motive that drives behavior is an effort to overcome inferiority.

Karen Horney's theory contained, as did Adler's, a social emphasis. Horney (1945) argued that the child experiences the world as a small and dependent being and tries to adjust by reacting in one of three ways to the social world: (1) moving toward others and becoming affection oriented; (2) moving against others and behaving aggressively; or (3) moving away from others and being withdrawn.

Erich Fromm also divided with Freud along the lines of social influence (1941, 1955). Fromm emphasized the compelling human need to belong. Our basic sense of value and identity is the result of our interactions with others as we try to gain a sense of belonging. Otherwise, a person experiences the anxiety of being alone.

Erik Erikson, the last of the neo-Freudians whom we shall discuss, believed that the stages of psychosexual development exist along with *psychosocial stages* that involve the development of the ego. At each stage of development, the ego faces a crisis in helping the person adjust to reality (Erikson, 1950, 1959). As shown in Table 13.2, each crisis involves developing toward a positive or a negative sense of self. The content of each of these crises differs across life because what the person must do to meet the demands of reality, of his or her world, also differ across life. Moreover, since the world places

Erik Erikson argues that personality develops in a series of psychosexual and psychosocial stages. (UPI/Bettmann Archive)

TABLE 13.2
The stages of psychosocial development proposed by Erik Erikson

Stage	Ego Development Crisis Is Between:	
	Developing a Sense of:	Developing a Sense of:
Oral, sensory	Trust	Mistrust
Anal, musculature	Autonomy	Shame and Doubt
Genital, locomotor	Initiative	Guilt
Latency	Industry	Inferiority
Adolescence	Identity	Identity diffusion
Young adulthood	Intimacy	Isolation
Adulthood	Generativity	Stagnation
Maturity	Ego integrity	Despair

demands on people throughout their life spans, Erikson sees psychosocial development continuing well beyond the time when psychosexual stage development is complete.

TYPES AND TRAITS

A major issue in the study of personality is whether (1) people can be categorized into specific general groups, or types, or (2) whether there exists a relatively large set of "characteristics of individuality," or *traits*, and each person possesses a specific combination of them. We may recognize this issue as one between those who approach personality by emphasizing that each person is like *some* other people versus those who study personality by stressing that each person is unique, and in essence, like no one else. Thus, while both type and trait theories assume that there are characteristics of people that produce behavior in a variety of contexts, type theorists arrange and categorize people into a few types. Trait theorists posit many traits and combinations of traits. In this section we consider both type and trait approaches to personality.

SHELDON'S CONSTITUTIONAL PSYCHOLOGY

A major instance of the type or *typological* approach to personality occurs in the field of *constitutional psychology*. Constitutional psychology may be defined as the study of the relation between, on the one hand, the structure of the body and, on the other hand, psychological and social functioning (e.g., Hall & Lindzey, 1978; Sheldon, 1940). The early work of Kretschmer (1921/1925) and the later research of Sheldon (1940, 1942) exemplify this approach to personality.

Sheldon, a psychologist who was also a physician, theorized that the relation between body types and personality and social behaviors of a person is largely genetically predetermined. Sheldon noted that the embryo, in an early stage of development, is divided into three layers of cells: the endoderm, the mesoderm, and the ectoderm. From the endoderm arises fat (adipose) tissue and the digestive (visceral) organs, from the mesoderm the muscles and bones of the body develop, and from the ectoderm the nervous system and the sensory organs of the body arise. Although every human body is thus necessarily influenced by all three layers, Sheldon (1940, 1942) believed that the layers might not contribute equally to the formation of a given person's body. Rather, distinct *somatotypes* (*soma* means *body*, and thus the term means *body types*) will develop.

If a person's body is composed of a major contribution from the endoderm, and minor ones from the mesoderm and the ectoderm, fat and viscera will predominate. Here the somatotype will be *endomorphic*. Because of the predominance of adipose and visceral tissue, the body type will appear chubby, round, and plump. If a person's body is composed of a major contribution from the mesoderm, and minor ones from the other two layers, muscles and strong bones will dominate the body. Sheldon believed that a *mesomorphic* somatotype would then occur. In turn, if a person's body is composed of a major contribution from the ectoderm, and minor ones from the other two layers, there will be neither fat nor muscles and bones to give the body girth

Figure 13.2
An illustration of a male endomorph, mesomorph, and ectomorph.

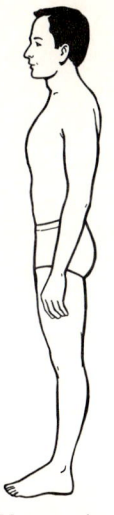

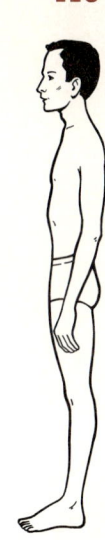

Endomorph　　Mesomorph　　Ectomorph

or mass. The *ectomorphic* somatotype that results is thin and frail-looking. Figure 13.2 presents an illustration of an endomorphic male, a mesomorphic male, and an ectomorphic male.

Sheldon (1940, 1942) believed that along with every somatotype there was a *temperament* type. In other words, he believed that a set of activity pattens was tied to what he considered genetically based body types. According to his notions, the endomorph was said to love to relax and to eat and was slow of movement. The mesomorph was athletic and liked exercise. The ectomorph was said to be unable to cushion himself or herself from stimulation because of the absence of fat or muscle, was withdrawing and introverted, and rather than being social, was dominated by thought (cerebral) functions. Table 13.3 presents a summary of the characteristics Sheldon (1942) believed to be associated with each somatotype.

To test his ideas about the necessary relation between body build and personality, Sheldon (1940, 1942) rated the physiques and temperaments of 4,000 Harvard male undergraduates. His method was criticized on the basis of researcher bias. He knew what he wanted to prove, he did all measurements himself, and indeed he found what he thought he would. Nevertheless, subsequent investigations have found some relations between body build and behavior (Walker, 1962). However, the relations have not been of the magnitude that Sheldon reported (e.g., correlations of +.2 to +.5 are found between body build and personality and social behavior).

The body has implications for one's personality, but what is the basis of

TABLE 13.3
Sheldon's somatotypes

Body Type	Physical Features	Personality, or Temperament, Type
Endomorph	Soft, round	A love of food and comfort, sociable, relaxed, dependent ("viscerotonia")
Mesomorph	Hard, muscled, strong	Powerful, driven, dominant, adventuresome, energetic, courageous ("somatotonia")
Ectomorph	Thin, delicate, sensitive nervous system	Self-conscious, private, heady, restrained ("cerebrotonia")

the relations? One answer suggested by some authors (e.g., R. M. Lerner, 1976) is that body build and behavior become linked through a *self-fulfilling prophecy*. If people have fixed attitudes *(stereotypes)* about what behavior is shown by endomorphs, mesomorphs, and ectomorphs, respectively, they may create social conditions which "fulfill" this "prophecy." For instance, they may encourage and push the mesomorph into leadership roles in sports, and thus give the person with this body type the opportunity to develop athletic skills. Although this interpretation is not well tested, social stereotypes do exist about behavior associated with endomorphy, mesomorphy, and ectomorphy, respectively (R. M. Lerner, 1969; Lerner & Korn, 1972). As shown in Table 13.4, which summarizes the behavior and personality expectations generally associated with each body type, the attitudes typically held toward the mesomorph are overwhelmingly positive and favorable; the appraisals of people having endomorphic body types are largely negative; and the attitudes shown toward those with ectomorphic physiques are predominantly negative.

PERSONALITY TRAITS AND FACTOR ANALYSIS

A personality "trait" is an interrelated cluster of mental and/or behavioral characteristics. For example, such behavioral characteristics as "bossy," "pugnacious," and "mean" may be interrelated and described by the trait "aggression."

Personality traits are often thought of as existing as *dimensions*, that is, as imaginary lines running between two endpoints. For example, "high aggression" and "low aggression" may characterize the two endpoints of the trait of "aggression." People may have any degree of aggression in between; for example, on a test of aggression having 10 possible points, some people may

TABLE 13.4
Typical stereotypes associated with the mesomorph, endomorph, and ectomorph

Mesomorph	Endomorph	Ectomorph
Healthy	Sad	Sick
Brave	Worst ballplayer	Afraid
Best ballplayer	Ugly	Weak
Has most muscles	Least wanted as a friend	Small
Good-looking	Not to be picked leader	Light
Be picked leader	Large	Has least muscles
Most want as a friend	Sloppy	Eats the least
Has many friends	Is left out of games	Thin
Happy	Has few friends	Doesn't fight
Others like him	Heavy	Quiet
Neat	Fat	
Clean	Eats the most	
Likes others	Slow	
Fast	Forgets	
Fights	Kind	
Remembers	Stupid	
Teases	Dirty	
Smart		
Nice		
Honest		
Helps others		

Source: Adapted from Lerner and Korn (1972).

PERSONALITY

score low (1 or 2), others intermediate (5 or 6), and others may score high (9 or 10). There may be numerous personality traits (dependency, assertiveness, ego strength, industriousness, etc.), and each person may have his or her own specific set of scores on these traits. Some people may be low on all traits, others may have high scores on all, and for others, probably for most people, scores would be mixed. One person may score high on dependency, intermediate on assertiveness, and low on aggression, while another person may score low, high, and intermediate on these three traits, respectively. Thus, rather than there being a few types of people, as theories such as that of Sheldon (1940, 1942) would suggest, trait-oriented psychologists believe that numerous subgroups of people may be formed on the basis of their scores on several traits.

Psychologists have been able to identify personality traits by applying sophisticated mathematical procedures (termed *factor analysis*, a means for grouping observations into interrelated sets) to large sets of descriptions of mental and/or behavioral characteristics. This procedure informs the researcher how various items are related and, through correlations, how much each item contributes to the factor. When hundreds of descriptions of hundreds of people are factor analyzed, the researcher can tell which descriptors go (cluster) together. Thus the main factors underlying personality can be extracted and identified. Both Hans Eysenck and Raymond B. Cattell have each proposed personality systems based on factor analytic research. Although both men used this methodology, Eysenck focused on a few personality traits, whereas Cattell studied a lengthy list of traits.

The main traits put forth by Eysenck (1953) are *introversion-extraversion* and *neuroticism*. These labels were applied to the factors which were produced by analyses of ratings and classifications of nearly 10,000 subjects. The major differences between introversion and extraversion, and between neuroticism and stability, are presented in Table 13.5.

Eysenck associated these main, or general, traits of personality with certain, more specific traits. Each trait, in turn, was related to habitual response patterns, and to an even more detailed degree, to specific behavior. It is this hierarchical structure that Eysenck proposed as the organization of personality (see Figure 13.3).

R. B. Cattell's theory of personality (1946, 1950, 1966) began with his factor analytic research of 4,500 of the 18,000 or so trait terms taken from the dictionary. After uncommon words and synonyms were deleted, 171 traits remained. Cattell's use of factor analysis sought to discover both *surface traits* and *source* traits. Surface traits are groupings of overt traits that seem to go together. Source traits are the factors that underlie surface variations

TABLE 13.5
Descriptive differences between features of personality of Eysenck's classification

Introversion	Extraversion
Introspective, quiet and retiring, reserved, likes books, mistrusts the impulse of the moment, well-ordered, under control, reliable, and seldom aggressive	Likes parties and friends, talks to people with pleasure; craves excitement, takes chances, willing to take chances, easygoing and optimistic, stays active, can be aggressive and loose tempered

Neuroticism	Stability
Moody, touchy, anxious, restless	Calm, carefree, reliable, easygoing, controlled

418   PERSONALITY AND INDIVIDUALITY

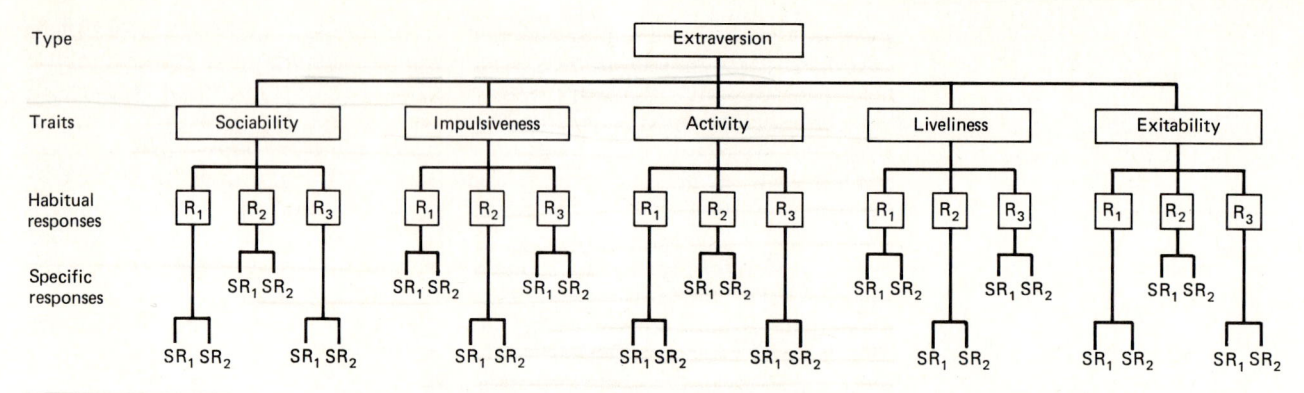

Figure 13.3 Eysenck's model of personality extroversion, including the traits of sociability, impulsiveness, activity, liveliness, and excitability. Habitual responses associated with each trait and the specific responses associated with habitual responses are also illustrated.

in behavior and were said to be the causes of the surface traits. Much of Cattell's work was directed toward the discovery of source traits and Cattell believes that 16 source traits (or factors) comprise the adult personality.

SELF-THEORIES

The self-theory of Carl Rogers postulates that personality is shaped not by situations themselves but by how a person perceives these situations. (D. Land)

Self-theories can also be referred to as *humanistic theories*. The theories share a concern with the *holistic view* of personality, that is, a view which respects personal experience and assumes a universal motivation for improvement and striving for self-actualization. Unlike both the trait and psychoanalytic approaches, self-theories emphasize how people perceive the world and strive for growth. Since such perception may be quite unique, psychologists working from this perspective often emphasize the core individuality of each person. A major illustration of this approach exists in the writings of Carl Rogers.

ROGERS' SELF-THEORY

Rogers' self-theory of personality gave special notice to a person's subjective experience and internal processes (1951, 1959, 1961). In Rogers' view, it is not the situations one is in, but how one experiences and perceives these situations that contributes to personality. With the individual as the center, Rogers spoke of the *phenomenal field*, which included the continually changing processes of personal experience. The phenomenal field is the person's world, and personality can be understood by knowing this phenomenal field.

A second assumption was that each person has an inborn tendency toward self-actualization. At the most basic level, *self-actualization* constitutes the satisfying of biological and social needs, but it also includes the drive toward independence and self-determination. The central motivational concept for Rogers' theory of personality is the drive for self-actualization. But how does one foster the development of self-actualization? Or, stated differently, how do we interfere with such development?

According to Rogers, personality can develop and self-actualization can

PERSONALITY

Eleanor Roosevelt (1884–1962) and Albert Einstein (1879–1955) could both be considered self-actualized personalities. Each have a broad enough concept of self to experience a rich and varied life. (Bettmann Archive)

be accomplished if one holds a broad definition of the self. Since one function of the self is to screen what behaviors, reactions, thoughts, and so on, are consistent with the self-concept, the broader the self-concept, the more that will be allowed into the person's experience and the richer and more varied will be the person's life.

Experiencing positive regard is also important for personality development. Positive regard refers to the satisfaction and happiness that comes with the respect and acceptance given by another person. But Rogers added another factor to positive regard—for personality to reach its height, positive regard should be unconditional. Unconditional positive regard means that there are no conditions of worth, no standard of conduct that a person must achieve to be accepted by another person. When another imposes few if any conditions of worth, the person is more able to recognize feelings, try diverse interests, and be open to a less constricted set of experiences. Rogers saw the human personality as a constellation around the self which would experience maximal growth with unconditional positive regard.

There are instances of self-theories of personalilty other than that of Rogers (1961). Highlight 13.2 discusses one approach that has attracted considerable attention.

LEARNING AND SOCIAL LEARNING THEORIES

A child in an arcade, fixed on the screen of a computer game, is racking up his highest score ever. Peers watch, the pressure mounts, and signs of tension become apparent. His last "man" breaks the high-score record, and he continues to add to the new record until an error produces the unwanted marker "Game Over." Congratulations come from a few friends; others just walk away. How did our supple-wristed whiz-kid develop his skill?

Another child is with his father and throws a temper tantrum on seeing an arcade. Jumping up and down and flailing his arms, the youngster cries out, "But I want to, I want to." The father gives in, and hands his son four quarters. How did our problem child acquire his skill?

HIGHLIGHT 13.2

Personal Construct Theory

Kelly's personal construct theory of personality (1955) is capturing the interest and inquiring energies of an increasing number of psychologists. Kelly's position is that each person strives, as we as psychologists do, to improve our understanding of the world and prediction of the future. In order to enhance understanding and prediction each of us tries to make sense out of our experiences by organizing the experiences according to their similarities and differences. Everyone has a unique set of experiences, so everyone develops his or her own constructs to organize the world. For example, assume that you were raised in a town where about half the townspeople worked for a large factory and that these people were more considerate and helpful than the community members who were independent of the factory. With this experience, you might develop a personal construct that you would use to understand and predict behavior. You could avoid unpleasant rejection by not asking the unaffiliated workers for assistance. This example is feigned, but it illustrates that we can and do organize our experiences and use this organization to improve our future experiences.

One of the reasons for the increased consideration afforded Kelly's theory is the current focus on cognition. In many areas of psychology, personality included, writers and researchers are taking seriously the importance of the individual's cognitive processing and its relation to behavior. Kelly's theory offers an approach where individual experiences lead to personal constructs, and this has appeal for current study.

Some psychologists see this question as falling within the study of personality. These psychologists typically apply either the associative learning and/or the cognitive learning principles discussed in Chapter 6 to the study of human personality. Some stress that observation of others leads to the acquisition of behavior, and as such, they are often labeled as social learning theorists. Moreover, because each person's learning history may be unique, theorists here feel comfortable with the view that each person may be like no other person. For instance, Skinner would maintain that while the laws of learning are common to all organisms, the specific behaviors acquired by any given organism may be unique.

Learning theorists and social learning theorists explain behavioral skills and skill deficits as a result of learning. Although the process is similar for learning skills that are adaptive and maladaptive, what is learned will be different. Behavior is influenced by the environment, and thus personality results from the environments in which the person finds himself or herself.

Although these features are common to learning and social learning theories, the two approaches assign different importance to cognitive and social features. As we shall see, *learning approaches* to personality are less cognitive and social than are the *social learning theories* (or social-cognitive learning theories).

LEARNING THEORY AND PERSONALITY

The outstanding advocates of a learning theory analysis of personality are Dollard and Miller (1950) and Skinner (1953).

Dollard and Miller's Perspective. According to Dollard and Miller, the four important elements of the learning process are drive, cue, response, and reinforcement. Drive is a motivational concept that is said to activate behavior; the stronger the drive, the more persistent the behavior. Drive reduction is reinforcing: An event that reduces the strength of a drive reinforces the associated response. Cues, be they auditory, visual, or other, are guiding stimuli. Thus Dollard and Miller's learning analysis essentially described how habits or behavior patterns are acquired through the reinforcing value of drive reduction.

But Dollard and Miller, in their integrative spirit, were also struggling to explain in learning theory terms Freudian concepts such as repression and conflict. Freudian repression was an unconscious process in which unwanted thoughts were kept from awareness. Dollard and Miller's learning analysis explained repression as an avoidance process whereby the response of not thinking about something was reinforcing because of its drive-reducing qualities. Instead of thinking about an exam and becoming anxious about it, the person who does not think about it reduces the unwanted drive/anxiety and thereby further reinforces not thinking about the exam. With this analysis, repression becomes less mysterious.

The Dollard and Miller analysis of conflict involved gradients of *approach* and *avoidance*. The gradient of approach increases as the person comes closer to the desired goal. In contrast, the gradient of avoidance decreases as the person comes closer to the unwanted condition. The gradient of avoidance is steeper than the gradient of approach. At any given point, approach or avoidance will occur depending on which response is stronger. Conflict arises around the resolution of competing approach and avoidance gradients (see Figure 13.4). For example, as a person with a strong avoidance drive moves closer to the feared condition (points A to B), the tendency to avoid increases

Figure 13.4
A graphic illustration of Dollard and Miller's analysis of conflict. The illustration shows conflict at two points: where strong approach and avoidance tendencies intersect, and where weak approach and avoidance tendencies intersect. As one approaches the feared condition, the avoidance gradient is steeper.

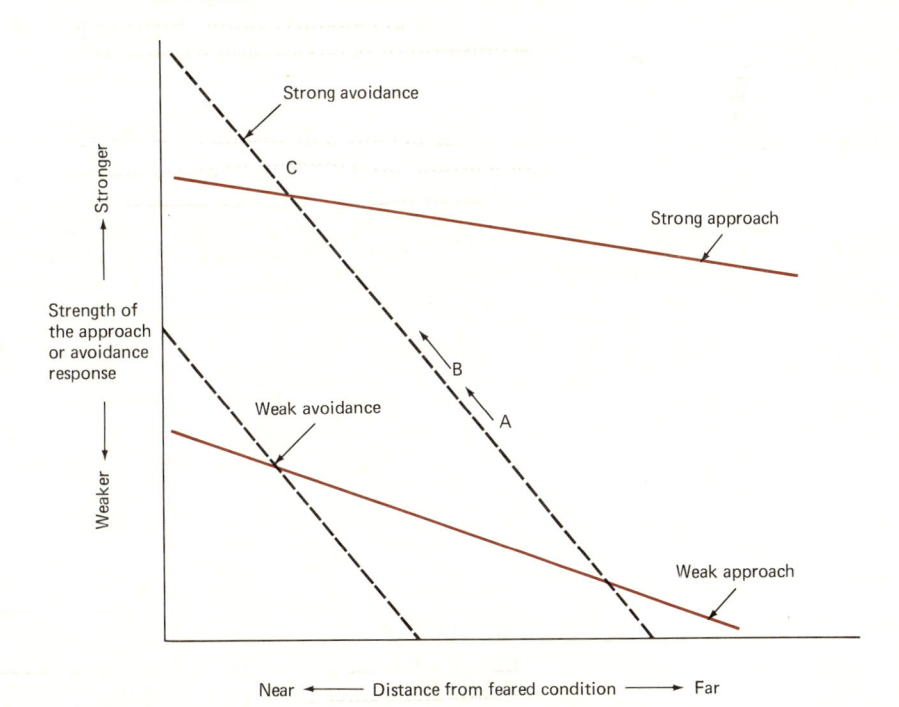

and, when it surpasses the approach gradient (point C), would eventually lead to fearful avoidance. Conflict occurs where approach and avoidance gradients intersect. Although the original research on this theory employed rats as subjects and hunger and fear as the respective approach and avoidance conflict, the analysis has often been extended to human beings.

For example, assume that you have just been asked to join some friends to go hang gliding off a cliff. They have extra equipment and they are experienced gliders. Initially, you are excited and eager and you approach the experience energetically, albeit with questions. However, as the day of the trip to the mountains nears, your tendency to avoid the situation increases. You experience the greatest conflict about "trying it" at the point where the approach and avoidance tendencies intersect.

The Skinnerian Approach. The approach to learning theory which employs the work of B. F. Skinner downplays the Freudian concepts in Dollard and Miller's analysis in favor of a singleminded focus on the law of effect. The law of effect refers to the strengthening or weakening of a response connection as a result of its consequences. As noted in Chapter 6, responses followed by satisfying and pleasing conditions will strengthen the connection, whereas displeasing, annoying, and unwanted consequences will weaken the response strength. Skinner did not concern himself with the unconscious and other mental processes and even argued that responses that are not observable are not necessary for a scientific understanding of behavior. Behavior is controlled, in the Skinnerian view (1938, 1953), by factors in the environment which either reward or punish.

Skinner rejected the need for a theory of personality, saying that we lack sufficient data. He also rejected personality theory in particular, as too involved with internal, mental characteristics. His work does, however, offer several concepts that can be helpful in understanding how personality develops. Skinner and his followers have provided data to specify how shaping, schedules of reinforcement, and principles of generalization and discrimination (see Chapter 6) contribute to the development of patterns of human behavior.

Skinner took his operant analysis to the limits in his book *Beyond Freedom and Dignity* (1971). Skinner argued that choice is an illusion and that what people see as choices are in fact determined by prior rewards and punishments. *Beyond Freedom and Dignity* generated much debate on a philosophical and moral level. If behavior is a function of its consequences, who will be in control? Who will control the reinforcers?

SOCIAL LEARNING AND PERSONALITY

Social learning theories emphasize the influence of cognitive, contextual, and generally social factors on learning. In other words, social learning theory brings the individual's cognitive functioning and the social environment to bear on learning theory.

The Theory of Rotter. One version of social learning theory, advanced by Julian Rotter in 1954, proposed that *expectancies* and *reward values* combine to produce potential behavior. Expectancies are subjective predictions about the consequences of different courses of action. Reward values, or reinforcement values, refer to the preference for certain rewards if all possible rewards were equally likely. Behavior potential refers to the likelihood of a behavior occurring in a particular situation. Rotter hypothesized that these variables hold meaningful relationships to each other, and he suggested the following formula:

$$BP = f(E + RV)$$

in which behavior potential (*BP*) is said to be a function (*f*) of expectancy (*E*) and reward value (*RV*). According to this model, for example, a person's choice to take illegal drugs would hinge on his or her expectations about probable outcomes (e.g., pleasant effects, social acceptance, health damage, being caught) and each outcome's subjective value (e.g., very positive, good, very negative).

Rotter also hypothesized that people are guided by *generalized expectancies* which develop as a result of many consistent lessons. When a person experiences such consistency, certain rules for understanding, dealing with, and predicting the world develop. Rotter's main generalized expectancy is *locus of control:* the belief that one is either controlled by external forces such as luck or powerful others (external locus of control) or that one is the master of one's own destiny (internal locus of control). The locus of control concept and its assessment are described in Chapter 12 (see Table 12.10).

The Theory of Bandura. As noted in Chapter 6, Albert Bandura's social learning theory (1969b, 1977b) highlights the importance of (1) learning through observation; and (2) the meaningfulness of different types of expectancies. According to this social learning theorist, observational learning, or modeling, is one of the prime methods by which behavior is acquired. Reinforcement for the observer may not be obvious, and the person need not practice the behavior. Assume that in your home all family members politely ask each other to pass the different dishes on the dinner table. Now imagine that one of your friends from college joins your family for dinner. His background is different. He reaches for what he wants and extends his reach with his fork. Moreover, his table manners consist of "showing his food" for laughs and drumming his utensils to express pleasure. Neither style is necessarily right or wrong, but you will be affected by watching his behavior. As an observer, and with your guest as a model, your behavior potential is being altered.

Perhaps out of politeness, your parents tolerate your guest and even reward him with surprising comments about his spontaneity and openness. These actions by your parents serve to reward your guest and demonstrate to you that such behavior is not only acceptable, but also appreciated. The likelihood of your table manners showing some dramatic changes has increased following this example of behavior.

Modeling effects can be disinhibiting, as in the preceding example, where the demonstrated behaviors were within your capability but you were inhibited from displaying them. Modeling can also help us to acquire new behaviors and erase old ones. Moreover, a behavior which leads to an emotional reaction (e.g., violence against people leading to compassion) may, after repeated demonstrations, no longer produce the same reaction. As an observer, you have been desensitized to the actions and no longer experience the same emotions (e.g., observing repeated television violence resulting in dispassionate viewers).

Albert Bandura. According to his social learning theory, observational learning, or modeling, is one of the prime methods by which behavior is acquired. (Albert Bandura)

Bandura views effective functioning not as the product solely of modeling, but of the continuous reciprocal interactions among (1) learning experiences, (2) the cognitive processes associated with learning, and (3) the person's behavior in the social environment. Thus Bandura's social learning theory endorses a reciprocal determinism, where cognition, behavior, and environment reciprocally affect each other. Bandura also considers rewards, punishments, and other principles of learning described in earlier learning theories important in understanding pesonality and the continued performance of specific actions.

The cognitive side of Bandura's theory is evident in his analysis of expectancies. Bandura distinguishes between *outcome expectancies,* one's expectancies that certain things will happen if certain actions are taken, and *efficacy expectations,* one's belief that one can perform the actions that need to be taken.

Bandura's concept of *self-efficacy* has been examined as a unifying theory of behavior change. Effective psychological therapies, even when their theoretical perspectives are not uniform, produce desired gains by affecting the client's self-efficacy. As Bandura (1977b) states: "Psychological procedures, whatever their form, serve as ways of creating and strengthening expectations of personal efficacy" (p. 5).

In a recent paper, Bandura (1982) argued that psychological theories have not devoted sufficient attention to the factors which determine people's life paths. Personality theories, including knowledge of a person's skills, can predict some behaviors that will occur later in life, but what role does *chance* play in each of our futures?

Take, for example, the initial meeting of two people. How did your parents first meet? How did you meet your closest friend? In each case, chance had an impact. The person you are closest to today affects your behavior: influencing your style of dress, the courses you take, where you socialize, and even your preference for dates. Isn't it surprising that someone influences you so greatly partly as a result of happenstance!

HIGHLIGHT 13.3

Determinism and Change

Many theories of personality are intent on providing an analysis of adult personality based on life experiences and developmental histories. For example, Freudians follow a proposed stage theory in which people proceed through an invariant succession of "stages," and behaviorists see prior learning as directly determining present pattens of behavior. These theories, and others like them, emphasize a deterministic analysis of current behavior.

According to social learning theorists, such as Bandura, people are affected by their environments, but can also create and select environments. Thus people can help regulate their own fate by determining the environments in which to place themselves. Reciprocal determinism does not see all behavior as determined by forces outside a person, although these effects are real. Reciprocal determinism gives the person credit for active participation in creating his or her own destiny.

Bandura (1982) includes a description of the features of a chance encounter which might predict its eventual impact. After all, we experience many chance events, but not all of them have a lasting effect. Both personal and social factors moderate the influence of chance. Among the personal factors said to influence the eventual impact of a chance experience, Bandura described persons' emotional ties, their values, and their personal standards. These features contribute to the potential influence of the chance event: Chance events will be more influential if the person has the skills (is prepared) to fit into the new experience, if the person becomes more emotionally tied to the new experience, and if the new experience is consistent with the person's values and standards. In a sense, if the chance encounter "fits," the person is more likely to "wear it."

Social factors also contribute to the lasting influence of chance encounters. To the extent that the chance experience reveals a new social environment which is rewarding, that time, resources, and physical limits do not restrict repeated access, and that the person's psychological needs are met, the chance encounter will be influential.

Chance, in the reciprocal determinism analysis, plays a role in determinism. But persons with greater personal agency (competent, self-directed) can make more of chance events than can those with fewer skills. Because life's influences can be unforeseeable, life paths may be difficult to predict. However, as Bandura (1982) notes: "Unforeseeability of determinants and determination of action by whatever events happen to occur are separate matters" (p. 749). "Fortuity of influence does not mean that behavior is undetermined" (p. 749).

In general, personality theories strive to provide a framework for understanding the similarities and differences among people. No single theoretical perspective has been able to account adequately for all variations in human behavior, yet each offers a valuable angle. One approach, the psychodynamic one, makes us aware of the potential meaningfulness of the inner mental world, whereas the trait and type approaches identify the major behavioral dimensions on which people differ. Self-theories call attention to our striving for personal growth, social learning theories examine the processes by which personality develops, and the cognitive side of personality considers the manner in which an individual processes information as a source of variation in behavior.

The diversity across theories of personality is striking, if not exciting. Nevertheless, while each theory has its strengths, each also has its weaknesses and sources of criticism. For instance, psychodynamic theory has been criticized for being too tied to the restricted sample of cases seen by Freud (women during the Elizabethan period in Vienna). Learning theory, prior to its recent entrance into the cognitive arena, was criticized for failing to take into account each person's unique mental appratus. Criticism aside, each theory of personality has merit in calling attention to at least one of the many facets of human behavioral functioning.

THE COGNITIVE SIDE OF PERSONALITY

Some of the theorists we have described thus far have offered cognitive views of personality. Kelly, Rotter, and Bandura, to varying degrees, propose cognitive factors which dramatically influence human behavior. In addition to these theoretical contributions, researchers have made advances in the cognitive science of personality. Two topics, schemata and attributional processes, are among those worthy of closer analysis.

SCHEMATA

As personality researchers investigated the cognitive aspects of human behavior, the topic of how cognition is organized took on new interest. As explained in Chapter 6, the notion of a cognitive schema is central in this area. A schema has been described as a cognitive set, or mental picture of a complex concept (Thorndyke & Hayes-Roth, 1979). Researchers have begun to examine the role of such schemata in personality, social interaction, and therapeutic behavior change. In general, they found that sets of information guide and flavor our perceptions, understandings, and recollections. For instance, a person's perceptions of an experience, what might be recalled from it, and what future stimuli will be attended to in similar experiences are affected by the person's cognitive schema.

The self-schema that each person holds about him or herself has been described as generalizations about the self, derived from past experience, that organize and guide the processing of information about one's own behavior (Markus, 1977). Current experiences and information about the self are attended to and incorporated (or not) based on reference to the self-schema. Markus (1977) had people rate themselves as independent, dependent, or neither. Various tasks and measures were then studied, including the content and latency of self-description, provision of behavioral evidence for self-descriptions, predictions of the likelihood of behavior, and interpretations of new information. As Markus reported, subjects with an independent self-schema used this schema to organize, summarize, and explain behavior.

For example, Landau (1980) found that people who were afraid of dogs overemphasized the importance of the size of a dog. Their schema for dogs produces an interpretation of the environment distorted by considerations of the size of the animal. Given that these people cognitively experience a dog in this manner, perhaps it is less surprising that they avoid dogs.

These studies of schemata illustrate that personality has a cognitive side and that each person's individual interpretations of events are flavored by the mental picture we have referred to as a schema.

ATTRIBUTIONAL PROCESSES

As noted above, "personality" suggests to many scientists (and to many nonscientists) that "traits" can describe a person and what that person's behavior is likely to be at different times and across various situations. When we say that "Harry is weird," we are making a trait statement—we expect Harry to be "weird" in different contexts. We expect traits to be *stable*, that is, to apply in different situations and at different times.

Jones and Nisbett (1971) theorized that those involved in an action and those observing it differ in their use of traits to explain behavior. They proposed that we have a strong tendency to explain our own actions in terms of context or situational variables, but that we explain others' behavior in terms of trait dispositions. For example, he (the other person) behaved violently because he is an aggressive person; I behaved violently because it was a provoking situation.

The theory states that this attributional tendency is at least partly due to our having more information about ourselves and our own behavior than we have about other people. Thus Jones and Nisbett feel that the trait assumption is generally incorrect and is employed only when the lack of information obscures the situational causes of behavior.

Research by Nisbett, Caputo, Legant, and Maracek (1973) supports this hypothesis. Each subject was asked to describe (1) why he chose his own girlfriend, (2) why he had chosen his college major, (3) why his best male friend had chosen his girlfriend, and (4) why his best friend had chosen his college major. In general, subjects attributed their own choices more to situational variables than to traits, but used trait explanations more often than situational variables to describe their best friends' choices.

However, other studies suggest that the Jones and Nisbett hypothesis may not be as pervasive as was originally thought. Monson and Snyder (1977) argue that Jones and Nisbett were both right and wrong. They were right when they argued that our self-explanations are based on more information—and are hence "more correct"—than our explanations of others' behavior; however, they erred when they argued that this "correct" explanation would necessarily be situational rather than in terms of traits. According to Monson and Snyder, we will sometimes "correctly" describe our behavior in terms of traits; at other times we will "correctly" describe it in terms of situational variables.

This point suggests that our personality is caused at times by traits which we possess, and at other times by situations within which we exist. But what *is* the source of our personality? Traits or situations?

THE SOURCE OF BEHAVIOR: PERSONALITY TRAITS VERSUS SITUATIONAL INFLUENCES

Perhaps the single most debated and researched topic within the field of personality studies is the question of the *major* influence on behavior—is it predisposing personality traits or variable situational influences? If traits were found to be the source of personality, then—given that most theorists believe in only a relatively few source traits (e.g., R. B. Cattell, 1966)—there would be at least some basis for believing that "all people are like some other people." However, if each situation we were in determined our behavior, it would not be people among whom similarity existed but, rather, situations. And as long as people were in different situations, they would be distinct.

The strongest argument for situational factors was put forth in 1968 by Walter Mischel. After reviewing a vast literature on trait consistency across situations he concluded that personality traits were not cross-situationally consistent, but that specificity prevailed—behaviors were more a function of the specific situation. Except for intelligence, Mischel (1968) argued, the idea of personality traits as broad predisposition was untenable. In contrast, personality theorists such as those described earlier in this chapter (e.g., R. B. Cattell, 1966) argue that personality traits exist, and that they are fairly stable sets of characteristics that determine a person's behavior in a variety of circumstances.

FOCUS ON THE PSYCHOLOGIST

Edward E. Jones

EDWARD E. JONES (Ph.D., Harvard University) is Stuart Professor of Psychology at Princeton University and a fellow of the American Academy of the Arts and Sciences. He has previously taught at Duke University and was the recipient of the Distinguished Scientific Contribution Award from the American Psychological Association. He is the author of *Ingratiation* and the co-author of *Foundations of Social Psychology, Attrition, and Social Stigma*.

In the summer of 1969, Professor Harold Kelley invited a few psychologists, including myself and Richard Nisbett, to Los Angeles to consider recent work dealing with how people perceive the causes of behavior. The group met daily for several weeks and gradually developed the outlines of a book dealing with what has come to be called *attribution theory*. Nisbett and I volunteered to write a chapter concerning some of the ways in which actors and observers appear to differ in perceiving the causes of the actor's behavior. Perhaps largely because of the simplicity of its message, the chapter received considerable attention. Let me say a few words about how my own interest in actor–observer differences evolved.

I was actually trained as a personality psychologist and was at least as inclined as anyone else to explain others' behavior in terms of their personal dispositions or traits. However, my own research on the perception of persons soon began to convince me that many of our actions are virtually controlled by the situations in which we find ourselves. Our results kept showing that perceivers generally underestimate the causal role of situations in shaping behavior and overestimate the role of the actor's personality dispositions.

Some of our experiments also began to provide clues that actors themselves are much more likely than observers to attribute their actions to the situation. Because the relevant evidence was slender, I was delighted to discover that Nisbett shared my intuition about probable actor–observer differences when we met at UCLA. It seemed to both of us that when you queried actors about why they acted in a particular way, they were more likely to say "because it was appropriate," or "it was the only available course," than to say "because that's the kind of guy I am."

And so we proposed in our chapter that actors tended to attribute their actions to situational requirements whereas observers tended to attribute the same actions to stable personal dispositions. We tried to present experimental data consistent with this proposition, and we examined some of the reasons why actors and observers might differ in their attributional tendencies. One important consideration that occurred to us is that, for observers, the action is perceptually linked with the actor, whereas the actor is focused outward, on the situation to which he must respond. Subsequently, this led to an important line of research into the causal role of perceptual salience. Many researchers were able to show how our causal explanations for interpersonal events tend to involve those who are for one reason or another salient, even though this salience may have nothing to do with actual behavior causation. Thus you may judge that the person across from you in a group discussion contributed more than her share to the discussion, simply because she was more often in your "line of sight" and therefore perceptually salient.

Some 15 years after our chapter was published, I think most psychologists generally accept some version of our proposed divergence between actors and observers. There is surely no reason for treating actor–observer differences as if they expressed a social psychological law, but I believe the principle at least deserves the status of an *actuarial summary:* By and large, more often than not, most of the time, actors are more likely to attribute their actions to the situation than observers.

Neither traits nor situations account solely for behavior. Features of personality and aspects of the situation are in constant interaction. (Paul J. Conklin/Monkmeyer)

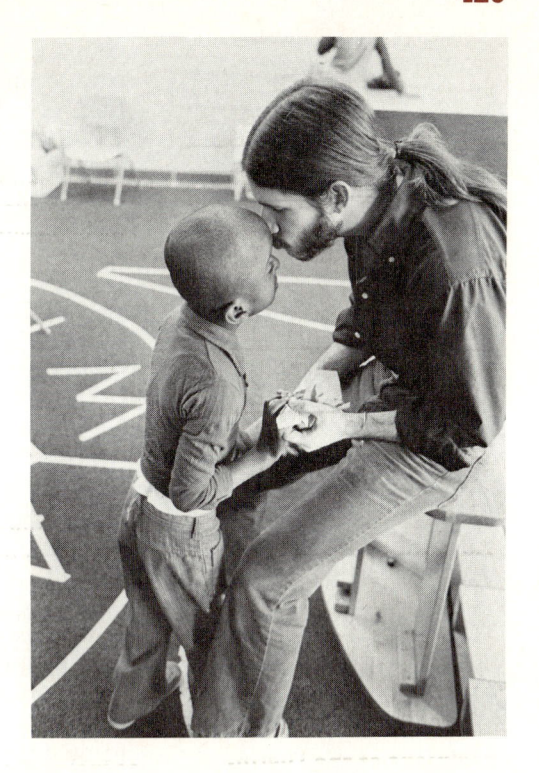

The oft-cited studies of deceit by Hartshorne and May (1928) offered fuel to the situationists' argument. In these studies, a large battery of deception tests and classroom, play, and home situations were used to test subjects' tendencies to lie. In the first of the five conclusions drawn by the authors, they state: "No one is honest or dishonest by 'nature'" (p. 412). Deception is a natural mode of adjustment, and deceitful children can be taught how to achieve goals in more honest ways. This conclusion had data to support it—a child who cheated in one situation would not necessarily lie in another. The not-often-cited statements from the same studies are that "Deception runs in families in about the same way as intelligence, eye color, or height" (p. 14) and that "Deception also goes by gangs and classrooms" (p. 15)—we are thus confronted with familial *and* contextual factors.

To discuss the traits versus situations issue, we will present some illustrative instances. For example, your introductory psychology instructor announces that he or she is going to randomly select someone from your class to come to the front of the room, and as part of a demonstration of the critical role of early childhood sexual experience, describe the first sexual experience that can be recalled. Someone is chosen, and as he begins to talk everyone in the class recognizes that the person is a nervous wreck. Anxiety has taken over. His voice is cracking, his speech is jumpy, and he is visibly nervous (e.g., hand wringing). Now, ask yourself: "Is this anxiety the result of the person's personality traits or the influences of the situation?" Save your answer while we look at another situation.

Your class instructor again announces that she will be randomly selecting someone at the end of class to collect the homework assignments (abstracts of a recent journal article). Class ends after the bell has sounded, and people begin to leave. Since no one was selected, you realize that the papers will not be collected until the next class. You then overhear someone in front of you say: "Gosh, was I glad she didn't call on me. I was really worried." Now, again, ask yourself: "Is this anxiety the result of the person's personality traits or the influences of the situation?"

Researchers have attempted to settle "traits versus situations" in several different ways, and we will examine an example of each type of effort in a moment. First, however, did you answer the questions posed in the two examples just described?

If you said that a personality trait determined behavior in both cases, you probably agree that traits produce consistency across situations. If you answered in favor of the situation, you would be comfortable in the situationist camp. However, the two examples contain different "pulls" for either the trait or the situation side of the debate. In the first example the situation is so strong that, one might argue, *anyone* would become anxious. In the second example, where most people would not become anxious, one is pulled toward a trait explanation—"That must be an anxious person!"

What we hope to have illustrated in these examples is that both traits and situations can contribute to the differences we observe among people. Even with a balanced view, one may still question which of the two explanations can account for more of the variations that are observed.

One approach to examining the traits versus situations question involves recognizing that situations are not totally different. Rather, there are *classes of situations that share certain similar features*. Using measures of anxiety that separately assess (1) the general trait of anxiety, and (2) anxiety traits that are specific to classes of situations, Kendall (1978) compared their ability to predict subjects' experienced level of anxiety in two stressful situations: (a) an evaluation threat, where an extremely difficult task was said to be an intelligence indicator; and (b) a physical danger, where subjects observed a car-crash film just before driving home. All the measures of trait anxiety were acquired well before the stressful situations were presented, whereas the measures of the subjects' anxiety states were taken immediately after each subjects' participation in each situation. The results indicated that subjects' anxiety reactions could be predicted from the trait measures that took into account classes of situations but not from the overall, nonsituational, trait measure. For instance, a measure of trait anxiety for the class of physical danger situations predicted subjects' anxiety levels in the physical danger stress better than the general trait measure did.

Another approach to the question of the consistency of behavior across situations was taken by Bem and Allen (1974). These researchers reasoned that people differ in their degree of consistency across situations, and that this variation was measurable. Bem and Allen sought to examine the behavior of those subjects who define themselves as cross-situationally consistent on a general trait dimension and those who do not. Conscientiousness and friendliness were chosen as the traits, and subjects completed a questionnaire to assess them (on a 7-point scale) and to indicate how consistent they are across situations as regards these traits. Subjects were described as variable or consistent according to whether they were above or below the median variability score. Outsider ratings of friendliness were obtained from the subjects' parents and friends, and behavioral observations were taken in a discussion with a stranger. The results of this study indicated, for example, that students who saw themselves as consistent in friendliness showed high agreement among the sources of friendliness data. That is, self-reported variability in friendliness was related to cross-situational consistency in friendliness. Similar reports were obtained for conscientiousness. These findings corroborate that for some people, the consistent ones, personality traits can be identified, but for others, the variable ones, traits seem less predictive of behavior across situations.

But even as researchers work to determine the predictive ability of traits and situations, rational arguments cause even the least reflective among us to give the question some additional thought. For instance, when situations seem to predict behavior more than traits, could this be because people choose the situations to be in—their personalities select the situations? Along these lines, others have argued that the situations studied in laboratory research are contrived and do not resemble reality where people choose their situations. Another comment concerns researchers' limited samples of behavior to be predicted. If predicting behavioral consistency is the goal, researchers will want to gather more data than is currently practiced and combine these many pieces of information. Recognizing that some features of personality are consistent, whereas others are not, and seeking to identify "which is which" are yet other facets of the efforts to answer our continuing questions about human behavior.

The trait versus situation debate continues with a trend toward the reacceptance of some degree of personality consistency across situations which cluster as similar. Neither traits nor situations account solely for behavior, and therefore neither can be ignored. Rather, features of personality and aspects of the situation are in constant interaction. In short, as we have emphasized throughout this chapter, some phenomena make us similar to other people *and* some make us distinct. As seen in the trait versus situation controversy, these phenomena are combined in all of us.

SUMMARY

1. The study of personality involves studying people's psychological and behavioral individuality.

2. There is no one definition of personality to which everyone adheres. However, many psychologists agree that there are some personality characteristics common to all people, some characteristics shared by some but not all people, and some characteristics that are particular to only a single person.

3. Unconscious motivation and psychic determinism play central roles in the theory of Sigmund Freud. Freud theorized that the personality was divided into three structures (id, ego, superego) and that people developed through stages of psychosexual development (oral, anal, phallic, latency, and genital).

4. A major instance of a typological approach to personality is the constitutional psychology theory of William Sheldon. Sheldon believed that one's body type (endomorph, mesomorph, or ectomorph) determined one's personality, or temperament.

5. Trait approaches to personality try to identify the key clusters of mental and/or behavioral characteristics (i.e., the main or "source traits" of human beings). A statistical technique termed factor analysis is often used to do this. Eysenck sees relatively few source traits as comprising adult personality. Cattell believes that there exist 16 source traits.

6. Self-theories, or humanistic theories, emphasize how people perceive the world and strive for growth. Carl Rogers' theory is illustrative. This theory emphasizes a person's subjective experience and internal processes.

7. Some psychologists apply associative learning and/or cognitive learning principles to the study of human personality. Cognitive learning-oriented personality theorists often stress that the observation of others leads to the acquisition of behavior, and such theorists are thus often termed social learning theorists or cognitive social learning theorists.

8. In Dollard and Miller's learning approach, the concepts of drive, cue, response, and reinforcement are stressed. In the approach taken to personality by Skinner and his followers, schedules of reinforcement are emphasized in the acquisition of a person's behavioral repertoire.

9. In the social learning theory of Julian Rotter, expectancies and reward values are seen as central in influencing behavior. In the theory of Albert Bandura, the role of expectancies is also stressed; in addition, observation of others is seen as central to personality development.

10. Like Bandura and Rotter, several other contemporary personality theorists stress the role of cognition in personality. Some of the current topics explored in the cognitive-personality area of research are (a) the role of "schemata" in moderating the impact of experiences on the person, and (b) the role of attribution processes in human behavior. Here a concern is with whether people correctly attribute the source of their behavior to traits or to the impact of the situation they are in.

11. A major controversy in the contemporary study of personality is, in fact, whether the source of personality lies in traits or in situations. Many psychologists believe that both traits and situations interrelate to influence personality.

KEY TERMS

Nomothetic
Idiographic
Unconscious motivation
Psychic determinism
Id
Ego
Pleasure principle
Primary process
Reality principle
Secondary process

Superego
Psychosexual stages
Psychosocial stages
Typologies
Traits
Constitutional psychology
Somatotypes
Factor analysis

Introversion-extroversion
Neuroticism
Self-theory
Expectancies
Reward values
Locus of control
Self-efficacy
Schemata
Attribution

SUGGESTED READINGS

ALLPORT, G. W. *Pattern and growth in personality*. New York: Holt, Rinehart and Winston, 1961. A classic statement about the need for an idiographic analysis of personality. Indicates the need to be concerned with the complexity and uniqueness of individual human behavior.

CATTELL, R. B. *The scientific analysis of personality*. Chicago: Aldine, 1966. This book details Cattell's trait approach to personality; it indicates the use of factor analysis in developing and testing this approach to personality.

FREUD, S. *An outline of psychoanalysis*. London: Hogarth Press, 1964. This is a short and quite readable introduction to Freud's theory written by Freud himself.

HALL, C. S., & LINDZEY, G. *Theories of personality* (3rd ed.). New York: Wiley, 1978. This book presents authoritative summaries of all major approaches to personality. It is the standard secondary source in the field.

ROGERS, C. R. *On becoming a person*. Boston: Houghton Mifflin, 1961. This book presents the key features of Rogers' self-theory of personality; it is written by Rogers himself.

PART SIX

Conflict, Adjustment, and Mental Health

14

Stress and Coping

THE NATURE OF STRESS
   The General Adaptation
      Syndrome
   Psychological Stress
SOURCES OF
    PSYCHOLOGICAL STRESS
   Harm
   Threat
   Conflict
   Overload and Underload
PSYCHOLOGICAL STRESS AND
   HEALTH

   From Life Events to Daily
      Hassles
   Causality and Process in the
      Stress-Health Relationship
APPRAISING STRESS
   Primary Appraisal
   Secondary Appraisal
COPING WITH STRESS
   Coping Resources
SUMMARY
KEY TERMS
SUGGESTED READINGS

A student is taking his final examination in statistics. Suddenly, his mind seems to go blank, he forgets formulas and procedures, and cannot seem to concentrate. His heart races and he begins to perspire. He fears that he will fail the test.

An executive has received a major promotion for which she has worked long and hard. It has been a great boost to her self-esteem, but occasionally she has doubts about whether she can handle the job. She also knows that there will be a lot of adjustments for her family to make as well—moving across the country, new schools, new friends.

A young woman has been married for 2 years. The relationship began very well, but things have deteriorated rapidly within the last 6 months. Her husband has become increasingly short-tempered and uncommunicative. No obvious events at home or at work appear to explain this change in his behavior. She has encouraged him to discuss what is bothering him with her or with a professional to no avail.

A middle-aged man has just learned that the steel mill he has worked in for 25 years will close in 6 months. He does not have any other salable skills, and in any event, job opportunities in the area are very limited. He does not know how he is going to tell his wife.

A young woman stands in the doorway of an airplane flying 3,000 ft above the ground. It is her first parachute jump. She is confident and apprehensive at the same time. She runs over the instructions she has received in her mind as her friends behind her urge her to "go for it."

All of these people are under some type of stress. Intuitively, we all have an idea what this means. There has been considerable discussion of stress in the popular media. We have all experienced events and circumstances that we would describe as stressful. But what exactly is stress? Is it a scientific construct? Can it help us to understand the behavioral development and functioning of people?

THE NATURE OF STRESS

Early investigators noted that when exposed to stressful stimuli, the body responds by going to a highly activated state. Heart and respiration rates increase, muscle tension increases, digestive functioning slows, and additional energy is released into the bloodstream. Cannon (1929) called these changes the "fight or flight" reaction because they prepared the organism to either attack or flee the source of threat. Thus the reaction was seen as adaptive for survival. Selye (1946) later noted that this reaction was not the entire response, but rather the initial stage of a sequence of physical changes that also involve a stage of resistance and a stage of exhaustion. Selye (1976) further argued that stress is the body's nonspecific response to *any* demand. Thus any stimulus, whether physical, psychological, or social, which requires the organism to adapt will produce stress. In other words, to be alive is to be under stress. Further, it has become apparent that the stress response can be a factor in both physical and psychological dysfunction. What is the evidence for these ideas?

THE GENERAL ADAPTATION SYNDROME

As noted above, Selye believes that stress is a unitary phenomenon. He has found evidence that all sorts of stressors, besides their specific effects (e.g., shivering when exposed to cold), also produce nonspecific effects characterized by a particular sequence of changes involving several systems of the body. This sequence has been labeled the *general adaptation syndrome* (GAS) and constitutes the organism's attempt to correct the deviation from homeostasis (state of equilibrium) produced by the stressor.

Stages of the GAS. As shown in Figure 14.1, the syndrome involves three stages: alarm, resistance, and exhaustion. The *alarm reaction* is seen as equivalent to Cannon's fight or flight response. This stage is elicited by sudden exposure to a stimulus to which the organism is not adapted. During the initial phase of this reaction, general resistance falls below normal. The organism exhibits various signs of injury such as loss of muscle tone and depressed temperature and blood pressure. This is the *shock phase*. During the next phase of this reaction, defensive forces are mobilized and general resistance rises above normal. Responses include the secretion of multiple hormones. This is the *countershock phase,* and it merges into the second defensive stage—the *stage of resistance*. This is marked by full mobilization of the organism's defenses. Homeostasis may be fully or partially restored and symptoms improve or disappear. However, the organism's capacity to adapt is finite. Thus if the stressor is severe enough, or is applied for long enough,

STRESS AND COPING

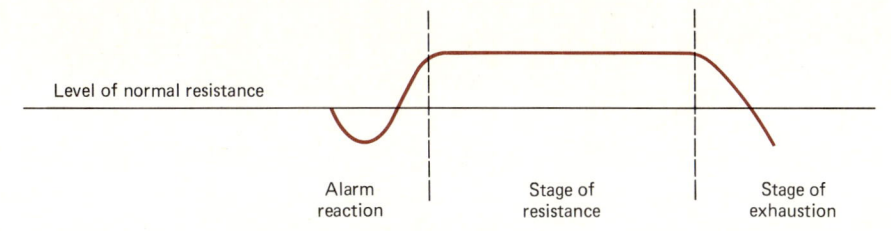

Figure 14.1 Diagram of level of general resistance during the various stages of the General Adaptation Syndrome. In the shock phase of the alarm reaction, general resistance to the stressor falls below normal. During the countershock phase of the alarm reaction and the stage of resistance, defenses are mobilized and general resistance rises above normal. Eventually, in the stage of exhaustion, resistance drops below normal again. (After Selye, 1974.)

exhaustion ensues. During this *stage of exhaustion,* the organism's general resistance falls below normal, and eventually it dies.

Mechanisms of the GAS. The organism's reaction to stressful stimuli is based on complex interrelations among multiple systems. It involves the control of vital functions such as heart rate, blood pressure, and metabolic activity, in concert with complex processes such as perception, reasoning, and emotion. Not all of these linkages are understood. However, one major mechanism involves the relationship between the brain and the endocrine system, particularly the adrenal glands. You will recall that the *endocrine system* consists of glands that secrete chemical messengers (hormones) into the bloodstream. These, in turn, have specific effects on various organs and tissues. The adrenal glands, in particular, are located on top of the kidneys and secrete a number of hormones that constitute the stress response. The basic sequence of events is outlined in Figure 14.2.

Selye notes that multiple symptoms of stress can be produced by injury to any part of the body as well as by psychosocial stimuli. Some way, then, must exist for this initial alarm reaction to be transmitted to the central nervous system. The nature of this "first mediator" is unknown, although it probably involves the nervous or vascular systems, since these are the only two systems that connect all parts of the body. In any event, the initial alarm signal, processed through the central nervous system, excites the hypothalamus. The *hypothalamus,* as you will recall, is a complex bundle of nerve cells and fibers that serves as a bridge between the brain and the endocrine system. Two pathways from the hypothalamus to the adrenal glands mediate the stress response.

First, in response to the excitation from the central nervous system, the hypothalamus releases a chemical messenger, *corticotrophic hormone-releasing factor* (CRF). This messenger stimulates the *pituitary* gland (located just under the brain over the roof of the mouth), causing discharge of *adrenocorticotrophic hormone* (ACTH) into the bloodstream. This hormone stimulates the cortex, or outer portion, of the adrenal glands. The *adrenal cortex,* stimulated by ACTH, releases *corticoids* such as *cortisol* and *cortisone* into the bloodstream. These hormones suppress inflammation and contribute to the release of stored energy necessary for adaptive reactions.

A second pathway from the hypothalamus to the adrenal glands is also involved. In this case, the hypothalamus stimulates the *autonomic nervous*

Figure 14.2
Diagram of the principal pathways mediating the physiological response to a stressor. (Based on Selye, 1976.)

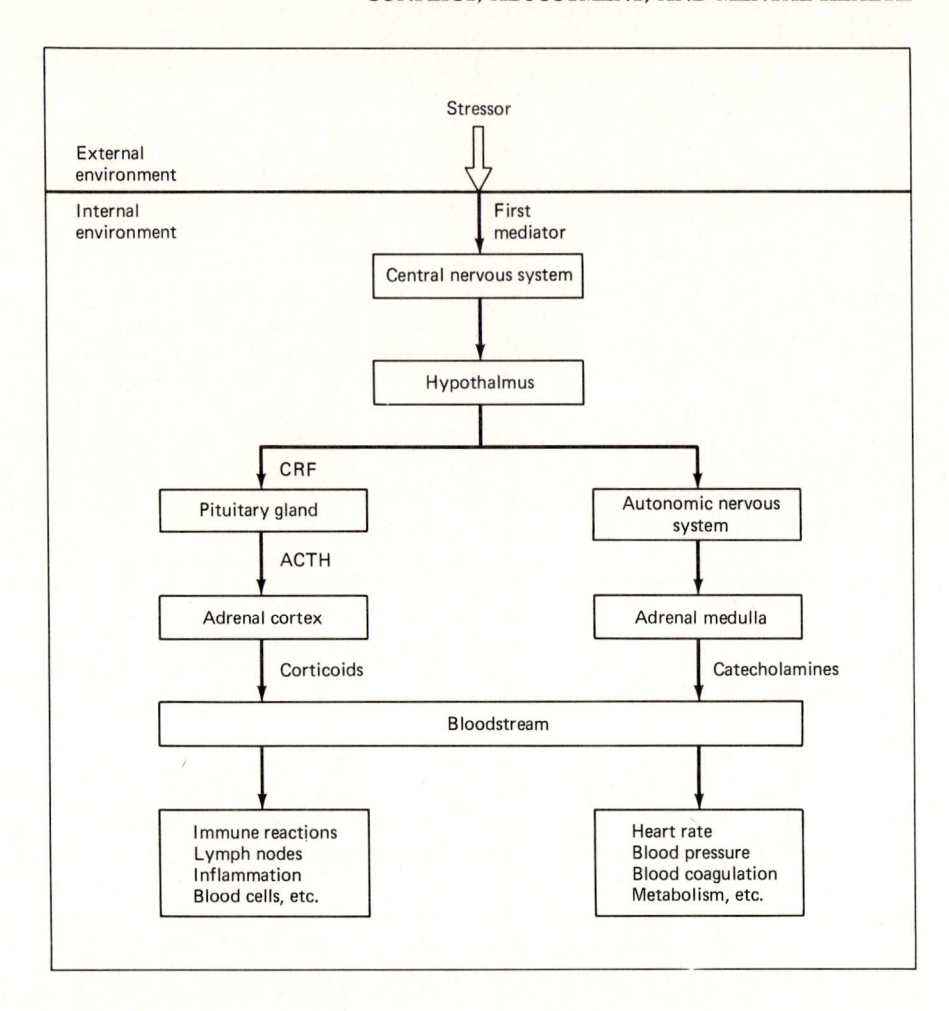

```
External environment         Stressor
                                ↓
─────────────────────────────────────────
Internal environment        First mediator
                                ↓
                      ┌──────────────────┐
                      │Central nervous system│
                      └──────────────────┘
                                ↓
                      ┌──────────────────┐
                      │   Hypothalamus   │
                      └──────────────────┘
                       CRF ↓         ↓
              ┌──────────────┐  ┌──────────────────┐
              │Pituitary gland│  │Autonomic nervous │
              └──────────────┘  │     system       │
                     ACTH ↓     └──────────────────┘
              ┌──────────────┐         ↓
              │Adrenal cortex│  ┌──────────────┐
              └──────────────┘  │Adrenal medulla│
                 Corticoids ↓   └──────────────┘
                                  Catecholamines ↓
              ┌─────────────────────────────────────┐
              │           Bloodstream               │
              └─────────────────────────────────────┘
                    ↓                      ↓
         ┌──────────────────┐   ┌──────────────────┐
         │Immune reactions   │   │Heart rate        │
         │Lymph nodes        │   │Blood pressure    │
         │Inflammation       │   │Blood coagulation │
         │Blood cells, etc.  │   │Metabolism, etc.  │
         └──────────────────┘   └──────────────────┘
```

system, which controls the internal visceral organs. In turn, the autonomic nervous system stimulates the *adrenal medulla*, or inner core, of the adrenal glands, resulting in the secretion of *catecholamines*, particularly epinepherine (adrenaline) and norepinepherine (noradrenaline). These hormones contribute to the mobilization of energy stores, accelerate blood coagulation, and increase heart rate and blood pressure, thus increasing the flow of blood to the muscles and stimulating the central nervous system.

The GAS and Health. The hormones secreted by the adrenal glands are necessary for healthy functioning. However, excessive or prolonged secretion of these hormones involved in the GAS may produce negative effects on the body. For example, an increase in corticosteroids can interfere with the body's ability to fight off infections. Similarly, an increase in catecholamines produces an increase in lipids in the blood. If these free fatty acids are not burned up by muscular activity, they may contribute to the development of atherosclerosis (a disease in which the arteries become increasingly blocked by fatty deposits). The catecholamines also lead to increases in blood pressure and blood coagulation, both factors contributing to cardiovascular disease.

Thus, although the GAS may have been quite adaptive for primitive peo-

In modern society, psychological stressors, such as those from work, not physical threats to our survival, are the main sources of our discomfort. (Arthur Tress)

ple living in a physically dangerous environment, it may be less adaptive for modern people living in a relatively safe, but psychosocially stressful environment.

PSYCHOLOGICAL STRESS

It is easy to recognize that certain life-threatening stressors such as a severe physical injury would result in the type of physiological response described above. However, in modern society, direct physical threats to our survival comprise only a minor amount of the stressors to which we are exposed. Rather, psychological stressors appear to be the main source of our discomfort. But what are *psychological stressors?* Lazarus (1980) suggests that they can be defined as circumstances that result in demands or conflicts that those involved perceive as taxing or exceeding their resources. This implies that a crucial difference between physical stress and psychological stress is the involvement of higher-order mental processes that give events their meaning. In other words, the stress is psychological because it is based on a person's cognitive appraisal of the situation. Whereas physical stressors, such as exposure to severe cold, are outside a person, psychological stressors, such as a job interview, require psychological processing to give them meaning. Nevertheless, considerable evidence indicates that such psychological stressors produce the same type of physiological reactions as physical stressors. Let us examine two examples involving work.

Rissler and Elgerot (1978, reported in Frankenhaeuser, 1980) examined the effect of an extended period of overtime on the stress responses of female employees of an insurance company. The extra time required was spread over 2 months, but most of it occurred during a 2-week period. The employees were free to schedule their overtime as they wished, and most chose to work on the weekends rather than lengthening the regular workday. Rissler and Elgerot anticipated that this increase in work load would call for adaptive efforts that would result in increased stress, not only during the overtime hours, but also during and after the regular workday. Their results supported this hypothesis. Figure 14.3 shows daytime and evening measures

Figure 14.3
The results of a study by Rissler and Elgerot showing daytime and evening measures of adrenaline secretion before, during, and after a period of overtime at work. The values during and after the overtime period are expressed as a percentage of the corresponding values before the overtime period. Adrenaline secretions increased during the overtime period, particularly during the evenings, which were spent at home "relaxing." (After Frankenhaeuser, 1980.)

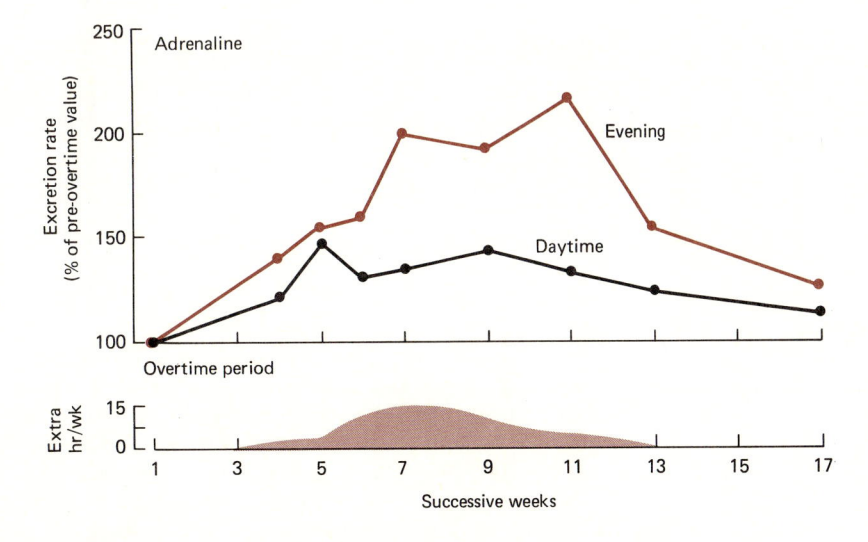

of adrenaline secretion before, during, and after the overtime period. The values during and after the overtime period are expressed as a percentage of the corresponding values before the overtime period. As you can see, adrenaline secretions increased during the overtime period. In fact, they increased more during the evenings which were spent at home "relaxing" than during the day when the subjects were at work. Note also that the highest adrenaline secretions occurred at the end of the period, when the amount of overtime had actually decreased.

In another effort to examine the impact of work-related stress, Kasl and his collegues studied a group of men who had lost their jobs because of a permanent plant shutdown (Kasl & Cobb, 1970; Kasl, Gore, & Cobb, 1975). The men were followed longitudinally over a 2-year period as they went through the stages of anticipating the loss of their current job, unemployment (for some), probationary reemployment, and stable reemployment. The men were seen at approximately 3- to 4-month intervals when multiple indicators of health were obtained. A comparison group of similar-aged men, continuously employed in comparable jobs, was measured in the same way. Kasl and his colleagues found that the loss of a job was associated with definite health-related consequences. For example, in the case of the laid-off men, diastolic blood pressure increased significantly during the anticipation phase until just before job loss, and then decreased significantly at later measurement points as the men were reemployed. The investigators also found that the observed drop in blood pressure was related to the severity of the unemployment experience. The shorter the period of unemployment, the greater the drop in blood pressure. Blood pressure values for the control men showed no such systematic changes over the same period.

In sum, strong evidence suggests that psychological events, including those that are relatively common to everyday life, produce the same physiological stress response as harmful physical stimuli. Let us examine these psychological stressors in more detail.

SOURCES OF PSYCHOLOGICAL STRESS

If psychological stress is considered to involve the appraisal that the environment taxes or exceeds one's resources, the number of potential psychological stressors is almost infinite. Social change, poverty, divorce, loss of a job, discrimination, examinations, relocation, only begin the list. However, rather than attempting to list all the potential sources of psychological stress, we may identify certain classes of situations thought to produce it. In particular, let us discuss four: harm, threat, conflict, and load.

HARM

People can be harmed by psychosocial events as well as by physical ones. One source of psychological harm is *frustration*. People become frustrated when an ongoing sequence of behavior or goal toward which they are striving is delayed or thwarted. Many events produce such interruptions and appear to produce stress or negative outcomes.

HIGHLIGHT 14.1
Post-Traumatic Stress Syndrome

Psychological stress reactions may occur well after the actual source of harm or threat has been removed. Post-traumatic stress syndrome (PTSS) is now a recognized psychiatric disorder (*Diagnostic and statistical manual of mental disorders,* American Psychiatric Association, 1980). It may occur after any unusually stressful event such as a fire, flood, hurricane, or airplane accident, but has received major attention because of its association with combat experiences during the Vietnam war. It is estimated that at least a half a million Vietnam veterans suffer from PTSS.

The symptoms of PTSS may begin soon after the event, but it is not unusual for them to occur days, months, or years later. The traumatic event may be reexperienced in a variety of ways. Frequently, these are recurrent dreams or nightmares during which the event is reexperienced. Also frequently, the person may recollect or think obsessively about the event. Less frequently, there are "flashbacks," lasting from a few minutes to several hours or even days, during which the event is relived, and the person behaves as though experiencing the event at that moment. Other symptoms include feelings of estrangement or detachment from others; diminished interest in previously significant activities; memory problems; hyperalertness or constantly being "on the lookout;" hostility, anger, or rage; guilt about having survived when others did not; and feelings of helplessness, apathy, and dejection. Post-trautmatic stress syndrome is association with a host of negative outcomes, including divorce, suicide, alcohol and drug abuse, and criminal activity.

Once PTSS was recognized, various treatment strategies began to be tested. Most of those working in this area suggest that group-treatment approaches are most effective. The group approach can provide the basis for relationships and a sense of comraderie that many of the veterans have not experienced since leaving Vietnam. Other techniques include relaxation training, thought stopping, modeling, and assertiveness training.

The psychological stress of poverty can produce the same physiological stress responses as harmful physical stimuli. (Owen Franken/Stock Boston)

Perhaps the most harmful psychosocial event is the death of a loved one (Holmes & Rahe, 1967). Major changes in a person's life follow from this event. It affects both social status (e.g., wife to widow) and daily activities. Many behavioral sequences and goals are terminated. The loss of a loved one produces complex emotional responses labeled grief. Distress is very evident, particularly just after the event, and generally lasts about a year.

The impact of this loss is seen in the mortality rates of those who have experienced the death of a spouse versus those who have not. For example, one study compared the death rates of nearly 4,500 widowers of different ages with the death rates of married men of the same ages (Young, Benjamin, & Wallis, 1963). As shown in Figure 14.4, the death rate for widowers of all ages (55 to 90+ years) was almost 40% greater during the first 6 months after the death of the spouse than that of married men. It then declined to similar levels. Similar results have been reported for widows (Cox & Ford, 1970). Thus, when one spouse dies, it increases the likelihood that the other spouse will die sooner than otherwise expected.

THREAT

Threat refers to harm that might occur. This anticipation of harm may involve either physical harm (e.g., concern over contracting cancer because of an unfavorable family history) or psychosocial harm (e.g., concern over poten-

Figure 14.4
Shows the percentage increase in death rate of widowers aged 55–90 years over that of married men of the same age. The death rate for widowers was almost 40 per cent greater than that of married men during the first six months following the death of the spouse. Following this, it declined to similar levels. (Based on Young, Benjamin, & Wallis, 1963.)

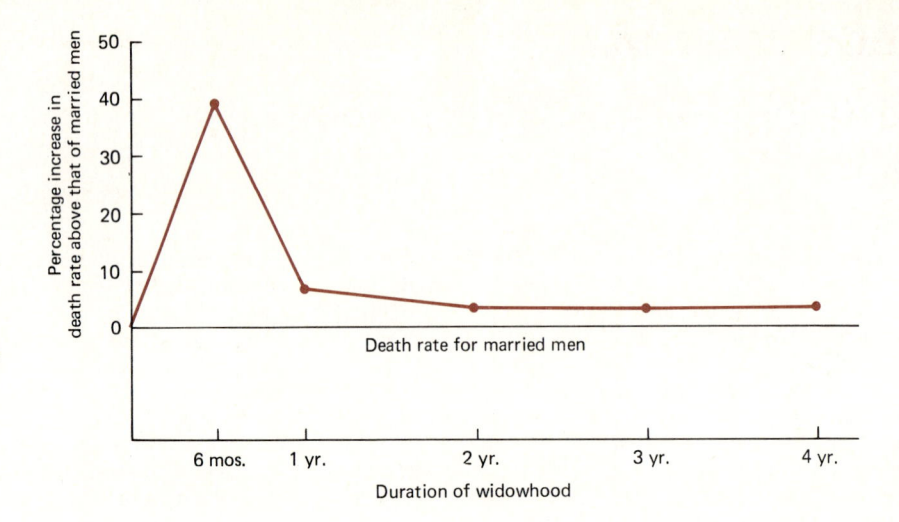

tial loss of social esteem because of failure to be promoted). Threat is clearly stress producing. Indeed, evidence suggests that the stress produced by anticipating a harmful event may exceed that experience when the event is finally confronted. This is illustrated by a study done in Lazarus's laboratory (Nomikos, Opton, Averill, & Lazarus, 1968).

To determine whether greater stress is produced by short or long anticipation intervals, these investigators showed two different groups of people two versions of the same film of three severe, injury-producing accidents. In one version of the film, approximately 20 to 30 seconds passed during which the viewer could anticipate that the accident would happen. In another version, the anticipatory scenes of two of the accidents were deleted. In these instances, then, only a few seconds of anticipation were permitted, barely enough to sense what was about to happen. The third accident kept the long anticipatory period. The results for one measure of stress, sweat gland activity as measured by the electrical conductivity of the skin, are shown in Figure 14.5. In accidents one and two, long anticipation produced far more stress than short anticipation, not only before the event but after it as well. The similarity of the curves for accident three suggests that the results are a function of the different anticipation intervals rather than differences in reactivity of the two groups. Similar results were found for a measure of heart rate. Thus the anticipation of harm can be stressful, and under some conditions, may produce more stress than the actual event itself.

CONFLICT

Conflict is the simultaneous presence of two or more incompatible response tendencies or goals. The initiation of one response tendency, or the satisfaction of one goal, countermands the others. No matter what you do, certain goals will be delayed or thwarted. Thus conflict produces frustration and may often be stressful.

For example, a parachute jump represents an acute approach-avoidance conflict for a novice sport parachutist. One the one hand is the desire to participate in an exciting recreational activity, while on the other is the fear of injury or death. Almost all novice jumpers express ambivalence about the jump and exhibit symptoms such as denial, anxiety, and cognitive and motor

STRESS AND COPING

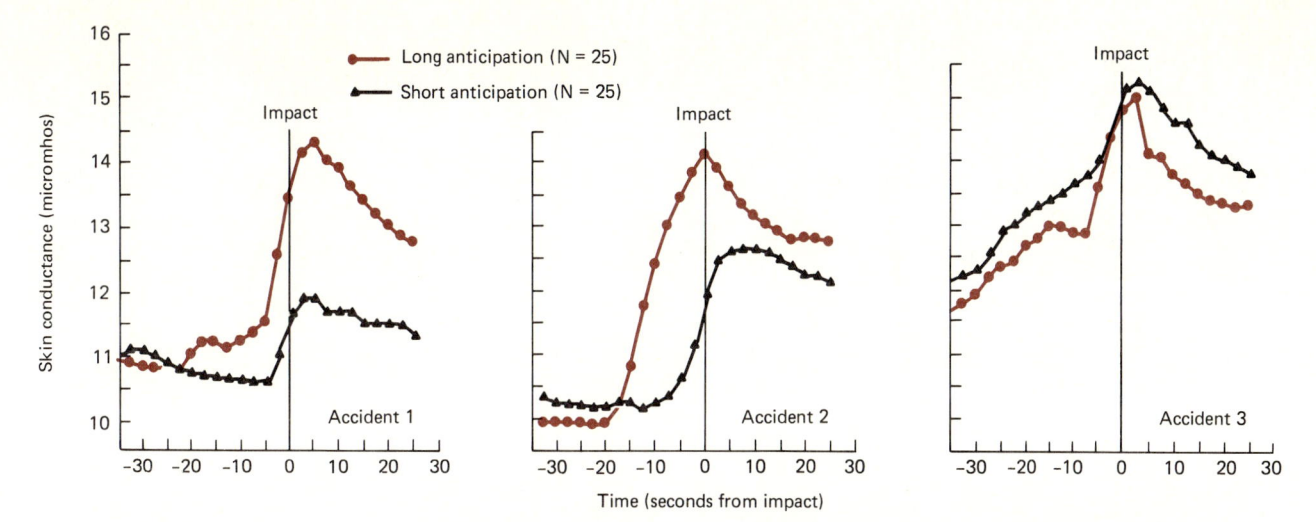

Figure 14.5 Results of an experiment done to determine whether greater stress is produced by long or short anticipation intervals. Two different groups of people saw two versions of the same film in which three severe injury-producing accidents occurred. In one of the versions, the people were able to anticipate that the accident would happen. In the other version, only a few seconds of anticipation were permitted for two of the accidents. The figure shows level of sweat gland activity as measured by the electrical conductivity of the skin. For accidents 1 and 2, the stress produced by long anticipation is far greater than that produced by short anticipation. (After Nomikos, Ofton, Averill, & Lazarus, 1968.)

disorganization. The pattern of conflict is illustrated by novice parachutists' ratings of approach and avoidance obtained at various points before, during, and after the jump, shown in Figure 14.6 (Epstein, 1962). As you can see, avoidance feelings increased until the ready-to-jump signal was given and then decreased. The most stressful point, then, appears to occur at the mo-

A parachute jump represents an acute approach-avoidance conflict for a novice parachutist. (Dave Waterman)

Figure 14.6
Ratings by novice parachutists showing feelings of approach and avoidance before, during, and after a parachute jump. The point of greatest conflict occurs just before the jump, at the moment of final commitment. (After Epstein, 1962.)

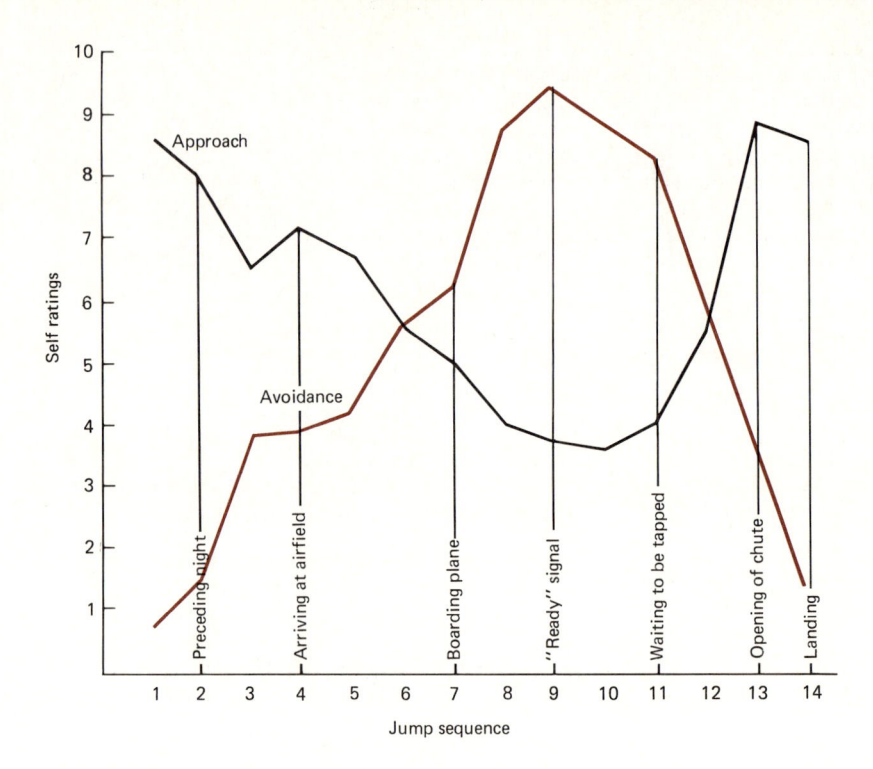

ment of final commitment to the jump. That is, it occurs at the moment of greatest conflict. Once the jump has actually occurred (the time of greatest objective danger), the threat has receded.

A second study that included physiological measures of stress confirmed this picture of the importance of conflict in the stress response (Fenz & Epstein, 1967). Figure 14.7 shows the changes in respiration rate at various points in the jump sequence for both novice and experienced parachutists. Note that in the case of the novice jumpers, this measure reaches its highest point at the last measurement just prior to the jump, followed by a sharp drop upon landing. Note also that experienced jumpers were much less aroused than novices, and appeared to resolve their approach-avoidance conflict more rapidly.

OVERLOAD AND UNDERLOAD

Psychologists have long postulated that the relationship between performance and level of emotional arousal may be represented by an inverted U-shaped curve (Duffy, 1962). In other words, it is proposed that the body's homeostatic mechanisms attempt to maintain an optimal level of arousal. *Overload* and *underload* refer to conditions that produce either too much or too little stimulation to maintain optimal arousal. Further, Frankenhaeuser (1980) has suggested that although they are opposites in terms of their physical characteristics, both overload and underload are perceived as stressful and produce stressful reactions.

Support for this assertion comes from a laboratory study examining the

STRESS AND COPING

Figure 14.7
The results of a study showing the importance of conflict in the stress response. The figure shows changes in respiration rate at various points in the jump sequence for novice and experienced parachutists. For novice parachutists, stress reaches its highest point at the last measurement prior to the jump. Experienced jumpers were much less aroused than novices and appeared to resolve their approach-avoidance conflict more rapidly. (After Fenz & Epstein, 1967.)

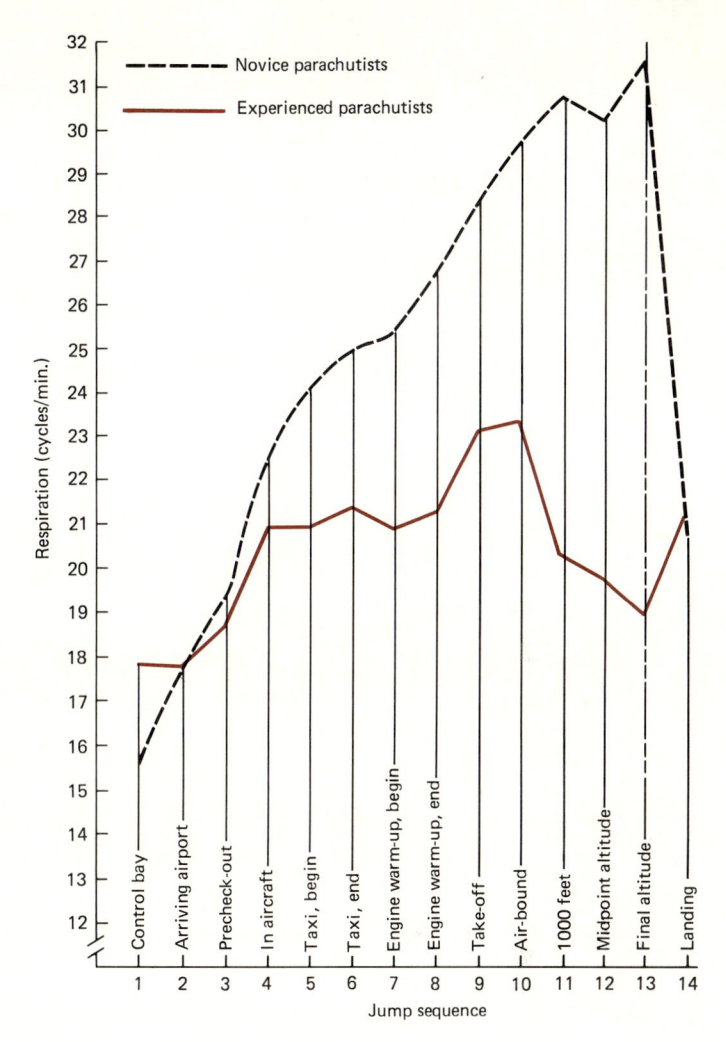

relationship of adrenaline secretions to various conditions of load (Frankenhaeuser, Nordheden, Myrsten, & Post, 1971). Underload was produced by asking the subjects to perform a monotonous, repetitive vigilance task (the people had to observe a visual signal that was lit for .75 second at 1.50-second intervals and report each increase in signal intensity by pushing a button). Overload was produced by asking subjects to perform a complex, audiovisual, choice-reaction time task. (The people had to observe multicolored visual signals and respond by pressing a similarly colored button as rapidly as possible. They also had to respond to a white signal appearing at irregular intervals to either side of the stimulus board by pressing a pedal with the right or left foot. Finally, they had to respond to high- or low-frequency auditory signals by pulling a right-hand or left-hand lever.) These conditions were compared with a control condition in which the subjects read magazines, and which served to provide baseline values for catecholamine secretion. Each subject performed all three tasks. As shown in Figure 14.8, both overload and underload produced greater excretion of adrenaline and noradrenaline than the control condition.

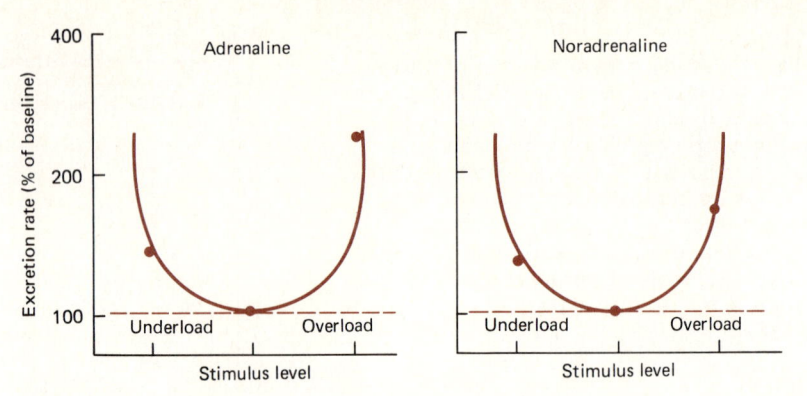

Figure 14.8 Results of an experiment showing the effects of overload and underload on the stress response. Subjects were exposed to a complex audio-visual-choice–reaction-time task (overload), a monotonous, repetitive, vigilance task (underload), or a control task. Both overload and underload produced greater excretion of adrenaline and noradrenaline than the control condition. (After Frankenhaeuser, Nordheden, Myrsten, & Post, 1971.)

Thus both overload and underload require effort and produce stress. However, the level of stress produced by overload appears to be somewhat greater than that produced by underload.

PSYCHOLOGICAL STRESS AND HEALTH

The research reviewed above indicates that psychological stress has specific physiological consequences. Multiple studies also suggest that it is associated with deleterious physical and psychological outcomes. Psychological stress has been associated with physical illnesses (e.g., cancer) psychiatric illnesses (e.g., schizophrenia), psychological symptomatology (e.g., depression), and morale, happiness, and life satisfaction.

FROM LIFE EVENTS TO DAILY HASSLES

Research relating psychological stress and dysfunctions received its major impetus with the development of the Social Readjustment Rating Scale (SRRS) by Holmes and Rahe (1967). This scale was designed to index the magnitude of change occurring in a person's life as a result of experiencing a number of significant life events (see Highlight 14.2). Since the development of the SRRS, many more life event lists have been introduced, some of which include well over 100 potential events. All of the research using such measures, however, has been based on two assumptions: that life changes require adaptation by a person and are therefore stressful; and that persons experiencing marked degrees of life change during the recent past are more susceptible to physical and psychological problems than those experiencing less marked degrees of life change. Results supporting the basic linkage between life change and dysfunctional outcomes have been obtained in hundreds of studies. Table 14.1 contains a partial listing of some of the outcomes for which a positive correlation with life event levels has been found. Let us look at some.

HIGHLIGHT 14.2
The Measurement of Life Events

How do life events differ from one another? Intuitively, we know that events such as the death of a spouse, changing schools, getting a promotion, and acquiring a pet are different in many ways. One major experimental approach to this problem has been to measure the amount of stress or behavioral change associated with different events (Dohrenwend, Krasnoff, Askenasy, & Dohrenwend, 1978; Holmes & Rahe, 1967). Generally, researchers have done this by asking people to rate lists of life events compiled by the investigator. The widely used Social Readjustment Rating Scale developed by Holmes and Rahe (1967) to measure the stress of life events illustrates this approach. In their procedure, a designated target stimulus is assigned a value, and judges are asked to rate the stimuli in relation to this target. Holmes and Rahe designated marriage as the target and assigned it a value of 500. People were then asked to judge the amount of readjustment required for each of the other events on the list in relation to marriage. The average rating (divided by 10) was then used to index the stressfulness of events reported by other people. The events on Holmes and Rahe's list and their average life change unit scores are shown below. How many of these events have you, or others you know, experienced recently? Would you rank the events in the same way?

Social Readjustment Rating Scale

Rank	Life Event	Mean Value	Rank	Life Event	Mean Value
1	Death of a spouse	100	23	Son or daughter leaving home	29
2	Divorce	73	24	Trouble with in-laws	29
3	Marital separation	65	25	Outstanding personal achievement	28
4	Jail term	63	26	Wife begins or stops work	26
5	Death of close family member	63	27	Begin or end school	26
6	Personal injury or illness	53	28	Change in living condition	25
7	Marriage	50	29	Revision of personal habits	24
8	Fired at work	47	30	Trouble with boss	23
9	Marital reconciliation	45	31	Change in work hours or conditions	20
10	Retirement	45	32	Change in residence	20
11	Change in health of family member	44	33	Change in schools	20
12	Pregnancy	40	34	Change in recreation	19
13	Sex difficulties	39	35	Change in church activities	19
14	Gain of new family member	39	36	Change in social activities	18
15	Business readjustment	39	37	Mortgage or loan less than $10,000	17
16	Change in financial state	38	38	Change in sleeping habits	16
17	Death of close friend	37	39	Change in number of family get-togethers	15
18	Change to different line of work	36	40	Change in eating habits	15
19	Change in number of arguments with spouse	35	41	Vacation	13
20	Mortgage over $10,000	31	42	Christmas	12
21	Foreclosure of mortgage or loan	30	43	Minor violations of the law	11
22	Change in responsibilities at work	29			

Source: Holmes & Rahe (1967).

Holmes and Masuda (1974) asked physicians to relate their life event experiences and major health changes for the last 10 years. They found that most health changes were associated with a clustering of life events whose value summed to at least 150 life change units (LCUs) (based on the SRRS)

TABLE 14.1
Partial list of problems for which a positive correlation with life event stress has been found

Physical Problem	Psychological Problem
Physical illness in general	Mental illness in general
Cancer	Schizophrenia
Hypertension	Suicide
Stroke	Depression
Myocardial infarction	Anger
Sudden cardiac death	Anxiety
Tuberculosis	Unhappiness
Influenza	Low morale
Pneumonia	Marital problems
Diabetes	Parental ineffectiveness
Multiple sclerosis	Poor academic performance
Ulcers	Poor job performance

per year. Further, the more severe the life crisis, the greater the associated risk of a health change. Of those experiencing a mild life crisis (150 to 199 LCU), 37% had an associated health change. This figure increased to 51% for moderate life crisis (200 to 299 LCU), and to 79% for major life crises (300+ LCU).

This study examined the relationship between life and health changes that had already occurred. Other studies have attempted to measure life event changes before the onset of illness episodes (Rahe, 1968; Rahe, Mahan, & Arthur, 1970). For example, Rahe and his colleagues studied approximately 2500 naval officers and enlisted men aged 17 to 30. Life events that occurred in the 6 months before shipboard tours of duty were compared with health-change data collected during a 6-month cruise. The upper 30% of the life change units were used to identify the high-risk group, whereas the lower 30% were used to identify the low-risk group. In the first month of the cruise, the high-risk group had nearly 90% more first illness than the low-risk group. The high-risk group also had more illnesses each month for the 6-month cruise period than the low-risk group. Finally, the high-risk group had more serious illnesses than the low-risk group.

These two studies report a relationship between life events and physical illness. Similar relationships have also been found for psychological problems.

Life changes such as moving require adaptation and are therefore stressful. (Jean-Claude Lejeune/Stock Boston)

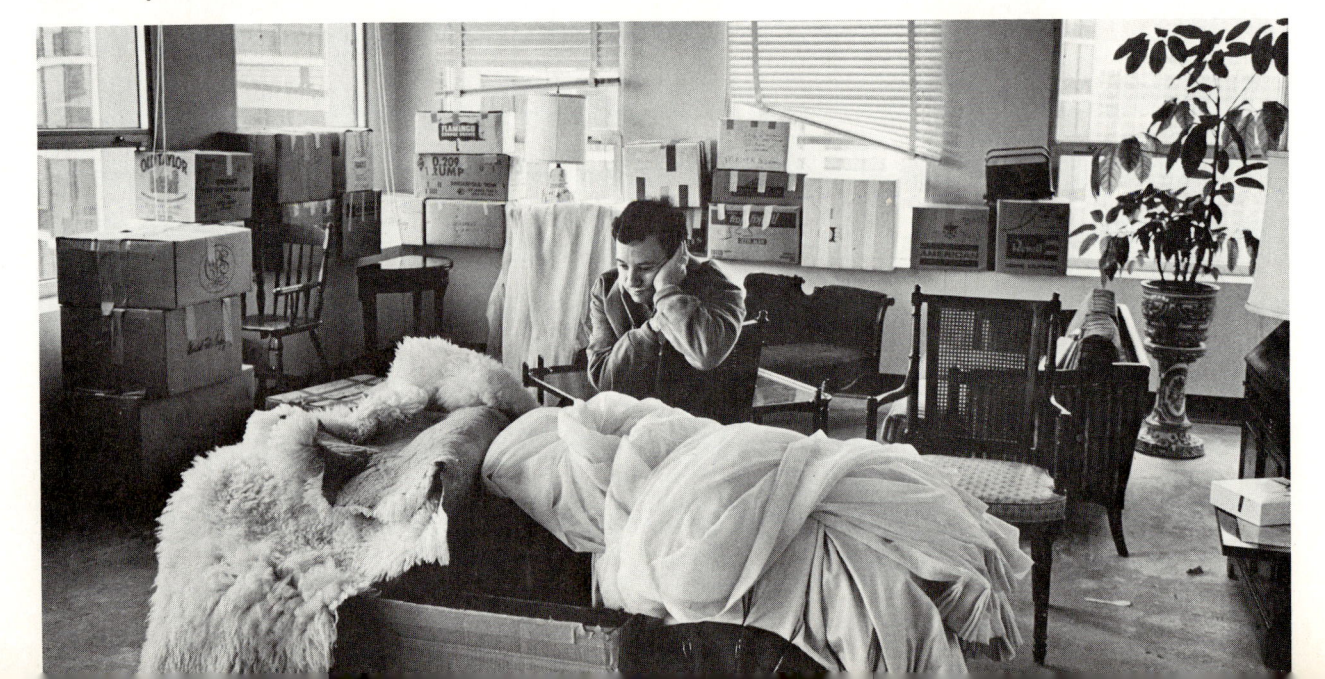

For example, Paykel (1974) compared the life event experiences of 185 depressed patients and 185 nondepressed control subjects matched on sex, age, race, marital status, and social class. The occurrence of the events was recorded for the 6-month period before the onset of depression for the depressed patients, and for the 6 months preceding the interview for the control subjects. Overall, the depressed patients were found to report about three times as many events as the controls. Events that significantly differentiated the groups included increased arguments with spouse, marital separation, changing to a new type of work or starting work, death of an immediate family member, serious illness of a family member, departure of family member from home, serious personal illness, and substantial change in work conditions.

As you may have noticed, many of the events noted above would be considered undesirable by most people. Are desirable *and* undesirable events associated with problems, or only undesirable events? Originally, Holmes and Rahe (1967) and others argued that only change or readjustment was the critical factor. Thus whether the event was perceived as desirable or undesirable was seen as irrelevant. However, recently, evidence suggests that undesirable events are the key factor in the relationship. With few exceptions, the correlations between physical and psychological problems and life event indices are stronger for undesirable events than for desirable ones. For the latter, the relationships are often not significant.

The studies mentioned above have emphasized the role of major life events, such as marriage, childbirth, divorce, job loss, and loss of a family member, in contributing to health problems. Recently, Lazarus and his colleagues have suggested that stress may be produced by relatively minor daily hassles as well as by major life events. Daily hassles are irritating, frustrating, and distressing demands that characterize our everyday interactions with the environment. Examples include having to wait for someone, misplacing or losing things, and being interrupted. Such hassles may be contrasted with uplifts, such as getting a good night's rest, hearing from a friend, and being complimented. Lazarus hypothesized that hassles may contribute to negative physical and psychological outcomes independent of more major life events. He and his colleagues examined the relationship between exposure to daily hassles, daily uplifts, and major life events and physical and psychological symptoms and self-rated happiness in 100 middle-aged men and women (DeLongis, Coyne, Dakof, Folkman, & Lazarus, 1981). They found significant correlations between the frequency of daily hassles and physical (.35) and psychological (.60) symptoms (i.e., those with more hassles had more symptoms). These relationships were higher than those indicating a link between uplifts and symptoms and life events and symptoms. Further analyses indicated that hassles contributed to symptoms independently of major life events. That is, the relationship was not simply due to the fact that major life events produced daily hassles which then correlated with symptoms. These studies suggest that even relatively minor occurrences in our daily lives may be stressful and produce negative outcomes.

The loss of a loved one is a major, undesirable life event and can cause serious physical and psychological problems. (Paul Conklin/Monkmeyer)

CAUSALITY AND PROCESS IN THE STRESS-HEALTH RELATIONSHIP

There is overwhelming evidence of a correlation between the incidence of event experiences and multiple dysfunctions of both a physical and psychological nature. But do daily hassles or critical life events actually contribute to the development of these problems? For example, do people who experience many stressful life events tend to become depressed? Or do people who are depressed tend to experience many stressful life events? Causality in life event research is very difficult to establish with human samples. To approach it, we must rely on natural "experiments" of the type described above. It is unethical to deliberately expose people to severe and prolonged stressful events of the type that occur in the natural environment in order to determine if they become ill or disturbed. However, although controversial, such studies have been done with animals.

In a recent study of this type, the investigators examined the relationship between social stress and the development of atherosclerosis in monkeys (Kaplan, Manuck, Clarkson, Lusso, Taub, & Miller, 1983). Thirty male monkeys were assigned at random to two groups. Within each larger group, the monkeys were further divided randomly into three- to five-member living groups. In the stressed condition, the membership of these living groups was periodically altered by redistributing the animals. In the unstressed condition, membership of the living groups remained constant throughout the experiment. Reorganization fosters a great deal of social instability among these animals, and hence is stressful. Throughout the study, the monkeys were fed a "prudent" diet containing almost no cholesterol and low amounts of saturated fats. The two groups exhibited significant behavioral differences. The stressed monkeys showed a higher percentage of both extreme aggression (biting, grabbing, slapping) and extreme submission (fleeing, cowering, grimacing), and spent less time huddling affiliatively (passive body contact) than did the unstressed monkeys. After 21 months, autopsies were done, and as shown in Figure 14.9, the stressed monkeys had more coronary artery damage than did the unstressed monkeys. Moreover, the differences in lesion size were not associated with group differences in serum lipids, serum glucose, or blood pressure.

Figure 14.9 Results of an experiment with monkeys to determine whether social stress produces vascular disease. Monkeys were assigned at random to two groups. In the stressed condition, the membership of living groups was periodically altered by redistributing the animals. In the unstressed condition, membership of the living groups remained constant throughout the experiment. The figure shows the area occupied by lesions in the coronary arteries of the two groups. Each bar represents an animal. Overall, the stressed monkeys showed greater evidence of atherosclerosis than the unstressed monkeys. (After Kaplan, Manuck, Clarkson, Lusso, Taub, & Miller, 1983.)

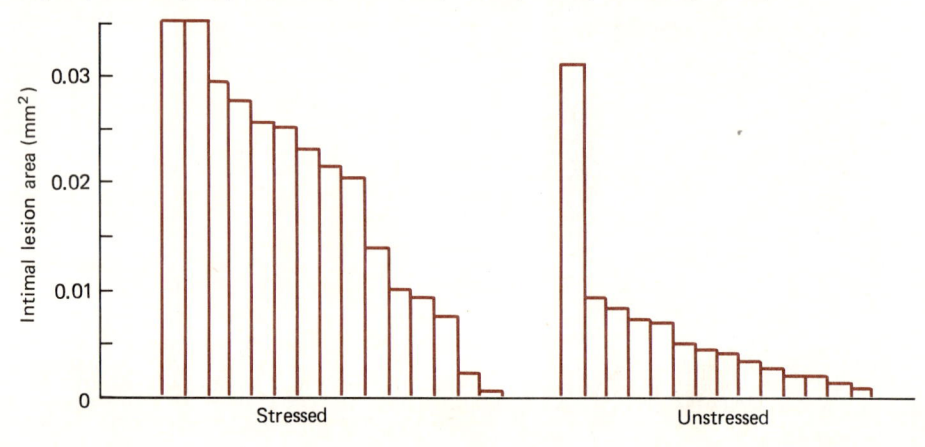

Experimental studies with animals, such as the one described above, suggest that stress actually does contribute to the onset of disease. How important is this relationship, however? The average correlation between the frequency or magnitude of life events and outcome measures is on the order of .20. Such results have directed researchers' attention to the issue of why the same events or similar amounts of change are associated with negative outcomes for some people but not others. A catastrophe for some people appears to be a challenge for others. This is evident in data collected from adults of different ages by Lowenthal, Thurnher, and Chiriboga (1975). They distinguished between exposure to stress (incidence of life events) and perceived stress (preoccupation with themes of loss and deprivation in a life-history interview). They identified four types of people. "Overwhelmed" people were exposed to frequent stress and perceived their lives as stressful. "Challenged" people, although also exposed to frequent stress, did not perceive their lives as stressful. The "lucky" were exposed to infrequent stress and perceived their lives as unstressful. Finally, the "self-defeating" were exposed to infrequent stress, but still perceived their lives as stressful. As shown in Table 14.2, substantial portions of the sample exhibited a "mismatch" between the objective and subjective indicators of stress. Note also that a greater percentage of men than women were challenged, whereas a greater percentage of women than men were self-defeating.

Observations such as this led investigators to conclude that the outcomes of stress cannot be predicted solely from the frequency or intensity of stress people experience. Instead, people confront events with a variety of perceptions, cognitions, behaviors, and circumstances that often alter the impact of the event. Clearly, stressful experiences influence behavior and health. But what makes an event stressful for one person and not for another? What do people do when confronted with a stressful event to cushion its effects?

APPRAISING STRESS

We have seen that multiple psychosocial situations may produce stress. However, even when exposed to such situations, people do not exhibit continual distress. Why not? Recall that the experience of psychological stress depends, in part, on cognitive processing. For example, Lazarus and colleagues (Lazarus, 1980; Lazarus & Launier, 1978) have argued that psychological stress is the product of a three-stage *appraisal process*. *Primary appraisal* involves evaluating the significance of a transaction between the self and the environment for one's well-being. *Secondary appraisal* involves evaluating the event in terms of the resources and strategies available to cope with it. Finally, both

TABLE 14.2
Percentage of men and women classified into four stress types

Exposure to Stress: Perception of Stress: Stress Type:	High High Overwhelmed	High Low Challenged	Low Low Lucky	Low High Self-defeating
Men	28	23	32	17
Women	34	14	26	26

Source: Based on Lowenthal, Thurnher, and Chiriboga (1975).

primary and secondary appraisal recur as the transaction unfolds and new information becomes available from changes in the internal and external environments. This is called *reappraisal*.

PRIMARY APPRAISAL

Primary appraisal essentially asks: "Am I okay or in trouble?" (Lazarus, 1980). Three types of primary appraisals are possible: the judgment that the transaction is (1) irrelevant, (2) benign-positive, or (3) stressful. Lazarus also suggests that stressful transactions may be classified into three subtypes: harm-loss, threat, and challenge. Harm-loss refers to transactions that the person perceives have already caused injury or damage. Threat refers to transactions in which the person anticipates that injury or damage will occur. Finally, challenge refers to transactions in which the person perceives the opportunity for mastery, growth, or gain.

SECONDARY APPRAISAL

Secondary appraisal, following naturally from primary appraisal, essentially asks: "If I am in trouble, what can I do about it?" (Lazarus, 1980). Secondary appraisal centers on the evaluation of resources and strategies for coping with the transaction. Lazarus argues that the fit between the person's coping strategies and resources and the demands of the situation determines whether the transaction will be experienced as stressful. For example, appraisals of harm-loss or threat are likely to occur if the person perceives the environment as dangerous and believes that he or she lacks the skills or resources to master it. In contrast, appraisals of challenge are likely to occur if the person perceives the environment as difficult but believes that he or she can cope with it.

It is important to note that the appraisal process determines the quality and intensity of the emotional response to the transaction. Benign-positive appraisals are likely to produce positively toned emotional reactions, such as joy, love, relief, and contentment. Stressful appraisals are likely to produce negatively toned emotions, such as fear, anger, anxiety, and depression. Each particular emotion has its own appraisal pattern. For example, fear is likely to be evoked by the perception of threat from an unambiguous source, whereas anxiety is likely to be evoked by the perception of threat from an ambiguous source. Anger is likely to occur when an external source is seen as responsible for harm and the person judges that he or she has sufficient power to overcome the provoking agent. Depression is likely to occur when the situation is perceived as hopeless and the person sees himself or herself as responsible for it.

It is also important to note that primary and secondary appraisals influence one another and change over time as the transaction unfolds. For example, to the extent that the implemented strategies identified by the secondary appraisal process appear to work, the original primary appraisal of threat may be changed. Similarly, to the extent that they do not work, appraisals of threat or harm-loss may be greatly increased.

The interaction of these two types of appraisals may be seen in the recent experience of a young colleague interviewing for her first academic position. Her primary appraisal of the event was stressful. It certainly was not irrelevant because its successful outcome was important for her career. It was also not

STRESS AND COPING

Anger is likely to occur when an external source is seen as responsible for harm, and the person has enough power to overcome the provoking agent. (Magnum)

perceived as benign-positive because she knew that 2 days of discussions with senior members of her field, together with a formal public presentation of her current research, would be taxing. Thus she perceived the encounter as involving elements of both threat and challenge. She had a history of superior performance in other evaluation situations, and she had prepared carefully for the task ahead. Yet she had never interviewed for a position before and knew that there would be stiff competition from other competent candidates. Her emotions fluctuated from hope to anxiety. She attempted to cope by telling herself that she was just going to do the best she should, and anyway, the faculty at the university weren't "out to get her." She also practiced her talk and sought advice at her own university. When the actual interview occurred and she began to interact with her potential new colleagues, things seemed to go very well. She perceived that they were interested in her and that she "fit in" to the department. Her talk seemed to be well received. Her appraisal of threat receded and that of challenge grew. By the time she was on her way home, she was almost positive that she would be offered the job. Two weeks later, she was.

In sum, psychological stress involves a complex, ongoing appraisal process. From this perspective, the stress of any event is in neither the event nor a person. Rather, stress involves a transaction between the environment and a person. It is a function of the balance between the demands of the environment and a person's resources for dealing with them.

COPING WITH STRESS

The two key questions of primary and secondary appraisal—"Am I in trouble" and "What can I do about it?"—begin the adaptation process. The next step is coping. This refers to what people actually *do* when confronted with a stressful transaction. It may be formally defined as cognitive and behavioral efforts to master, reduce, or tolerate internal and external demands, and conflicts among them, that tax or exceed the person's resources (Folkman & Lazarus, 1980). Within this context, it is important to distinguish between *coping resources* and *coping responses*. Resources refer to what people have available to them in developing their coping repertoires; responses refer to the use of particular strategies from the repertoires. Obviously, these two aspects of coping are closely interrelated.

COPING RESOURCES

Coping resources may refer to characteristics of the environment (e.g., money, family, friends, social agencies), or personal characteristics (e.g., health, problem-solving skills, personality, values, and beliefs). These resources are important for two reasons. First, they are part of the primary appraisal process. To the extent that the person perceives that the situation taxes or exceeds his or her resources, the transactions is likely to be appraised as stressful. Second, they provide the basis for coping responses designed to eliminate, reduce, or tolerate the stress the person is experiencing. Let us examine several categories of resources that appear to be important.

Utilitarian Resources. Money, tools, health and recreational facilities, and governmental programs are examples of utilitarian resources that are differentially available to people. The availability of such resources greatly affects the coping strategies available to the person. Contrast, for example, the options of an elderly couple living in a rural setting supported by income solely from social security with one living in an urban setting supported by income from pensions and investments as well as social security. If confronted with a stressful event such as the serious illness of one of the partners, the second couple will probably have more resources (availability of superior health care facilities and the ability to afford such care) than the first couple. Of course, utilitarian resources do not guarantee successful adaptation, but they probably facilitate positive outcomes for many life crises.

Physical and Cognitive Integrity. Adaptation requires a certan expenditure of energy dependent on physical health. Similarly, various cognitive abilities, such as the ability to attend to, encode, store, and retrieve information, and the ability to perceive relationships in novel situations, are probably required to appraise threat accurately and to select and implement coping strategies effectively. That these resources would be important is fairly obvious. However, physical and cognitive resources may set a floor, or lower limit, on adaptation. That is, they are necessary but not sufficient for adaptation. If they are insufficient, adaptation will be impaired. But beyond some level of sufficiency, they will not contribute significantly to improved adaptation. There is evidence for this, at least in some settings. Lieberman (1975), for instance, examined the adaptation of elderly adults to institutionalization. The results of these studies suggested that those who were physically or cognitively impaired could not adapt. In one study, for example, physical and cognitive characteristics accounted for 73% of the variance in predicting deterioration of the residents' conditions. However, although inadequate physical and cognitive resources predicted breakdown, the reverse was not true. Thus physical and cognitive resources appear to set lower limits. Below these limits, the basic resources necessary for successful adaptation cannot be mobilized. Above these limits, other psychological and social resources appear to be more important.

Personality. Dispositions to respond to the environment in certain ways appear to mediate the stress-health relationship. For example, of particular interest is the work of Rosenman and Friedman, who have described a behavior pattern associated with high coronary risk (Friedman & Rosenman, 1974; Rosenman, 1974). This has been labeled the *Type A behavior pattern* and is contrasted with the *Type B behavior pattern,* which is associated with low coronary risk. As described in Highlight 14.3, the Type A pattern is characterized by behavioral tendencies, including excessive competitiveness, acceleration of the pace of ordinary activities, impatience with the rate at which most events take place, thinking about or doing several things simultaneously, hostility, and feelings of struggling against time and the environment. The converse of the Type A pattern is characterized by the relative absence of these behavioral tendencies.

HIGHLIGHT 14.3

Are You Type A or Type B?

Although only 10% of their subjects were wholly one type or the other, Friedman and Rosenman (1974) defined these two patterns of behavior. Type A had far more tendency toward heart disease than did Type B. You are a Type A if:

1. You explosively accent key words when you speak and tend to speed up toward the end of your sentences.
2. You always move, talk, and eat rapidly.
3. You're often impatient with how slowly things happen. You try to hurry people through what they're saying. You're furious at cars on the road that hold you back, at having to wait in line. You fume at repetitive chores. You race through every book.
4. You do or think about two or more things at once. You worry about work on your day off and think about unrelated topics when someone else is talking.
5. You prefer to talk about what *you* want and only pretend to listen to other people's topics.

6. You feel vaguely guilty when you relax.
7. You don't see the most important, interesting, or lovely things with which you come into contact.
8. You're preoccupied with *getting* rather than *being.*
9. You always feel a sense of urgency.
10. You feel hostile and challenged by other Type As.
11. You have habitual gestures or tics—fist clenching, tooth grinding, etc.—that suggest an inner struggle.
12. You're afraid to stop hurrying because you think that's what makes you successful.

You're Type B If:

1. You're free of all the Type A habits and traits.
2. You feel no general sense of hostility or competitiveness.
3. You play to relax rather than to prove yourself.
4. You can relax without guilt and work calmly.

There have been numerous studies of the linkage between Type A behavior and coronary disease. A primary investigation, however, was a study of over 3,500 men aged 39 to 59 begun in 1960. These men were free from coronary disease when the initial measures of behavior pattern and physiological indices were obtained. Follow-up evaluations were completed after 2½, 4½, and 8½ years. The data indicated that coronary heart disease was much more prevalent among Type A men than among Type B men. The figures from the 4½-year follow-up show that 71.5% of the 39- to 49-year-old men who developed coronary heart disease were Type A, while only 28.5% were Type B. In cases where coronary heart disease was not present, 46.8% were Type A and 53.2% were Type B. The figures for the older age group are similar. Type A men also show chemical changes associated with coronary heart disease prior to the onset of clinical signs, including elevated serum cholesterol, accelerated blood coagulation, and increased daytime excretion of catecholamines.

Personality also appears to be an important mediator of psychological adaptation. For example, Costa and McCrae (1980) examined the relationship between personality traits and general adaptation in over 1,000 men aged 35 to 85. Personality was defined by two broad clusters of traits: neuroticism and extraversion. People high on the neuroticism scale are characterized as being anxious, hostile, impulsive, and emotional. People high on the extraversion scale are characterized as being vigorous, sociable, and assertive. General adaptation was measured by assessing the men's subjective sense of well-being (e.g., indicators of positive affect such as pleasure, excitement, pride, and indicators of negative affect such as depression, loneliness, boredom). Costa and McCrae found that positive affect was correlated with extraversion, whereas negative affect was correlated with neuroticism. However, the reverse was not true. Further, measures of extraversion and neuroticism made 10 years earlier predicted current positive and negative affect. These findings led Costa and McCrae to suggest that personality mediates the person's reaction to current situations. Extraverted traits appear to contribute to one's positive adaptation, whereas neurotic traits contribute to one's negative adaptation. In other words, there appear to be adjusted and unadjusted people, and these characteristics contribute to how they cope with new situations.

Beliefs About Control. Control refers to the ability to influence intended outcomes by selecting one's repsonses. *Perceived control* refers to beliefs about whether control is possible. Perceived control has two subcomponents (Bandura, 1977a). *Efficacy expectations* refer to the person's estimate of the probability that he or she can execute the behaviors required to produce a certain outcome. *Outcome expectations* refer to the person's estimate of the extent to which a given behavior, even if properly executed, will lead to a certain outcome. In general, research suggests that increased feelings of control have a positive impact on adaptation, whereas decreased feelings of control have a negative impact.

Laboratory studies have suggested that control over the stimulus situation reduces the stressfulness of demanding tasks. For example, Frankenhaeuser and her colleagues (1980) measured adrenal-cortical responses in an achievement situation designed to produce feelings of mastery and control. The subjects were asked to perform a choice-reaction time task. To induce feelings of mastery and control, they were given a preparatory period during which they could try out different stimulus presentation rates in order to arrive at an individually preferred pace. Sustained work only began when the person felt confident. Further, every 5 minutes, the person could modify the rate of presentation to maintain an optimum work pace. Under these conditions, cortisol secretions actually decreased from baseline levels. Confirming this reduction in stressfulness, the participants reported that the task was pleasant and stimulating.

The importance of perceived control is also illustrated in a field experiment conducted by Langer and Rodin (1976). They theorized that both objective helplessness and feelings of helplessness and hopelessness may contribute to psychological withdrawal, physical illness, and death late in life. To investigate this idea, they attempted to determine whether the deterioration that generally occurs when elderly adults are placed in nursing homes could be slowed or reversed by influencing the person's sense of choice and control.

Two groups of elderly adults residing on different floors of the nursing home participated in the study. The two groups did not differ in terms of age, sex, severity of illness, or length of stay in the home. One group received a communication from the hospital administrator which implied that they had responsibility for many of the decisions in their lives and should exercise this responsibility. He enumerated what they could do and where decisions could be made (e.g., what you want your rooms to look like; what nights you want to go to the movies). The other group received a communication from the hospital administrator that implied diminished responsibility in their lives. He told them that it was the staff's desire and responsibility to care for them; their job was to inform the staff of their needs. Both interventions were designed to affect perceptions of choice and control. The actual choices and opportunities to change the setting were already potentially available to both groups.

Langer and Rodin found that patients in the responsibility-induced group showed significant improvements over a 4-week period in alertness, self-rated happiness, and social interaction compared to the control group. Eighteen months later, Rodin and Langer (1977) reassessed the surviving participants. They found that the responsibility-induced group was still more alert and socially active than the control group. However, the most striking finding was the difference in mortality rates between the two groups. The average death rate for the entire nursing home during the 18-month period was 25%. Similarly, 13 of 44 people (30%) in the control group died. However, only 7 of 47 people (15%) in the responsibility-induced group died.

Social Support. Although other people can interfere with coping, research in general suggests that social support systems (e.g., family, friends) can be an extremely important coping resource (Cassel, 1976; Cobb, 1976). Indeed,

Social support systems can be an extremely important coping resource. (Sepp Seitz)

people with elaborate social networks appear to live longer than isolates. Berkman and Syme (1979), for example, examined the relationship between longevity and reported social contact in a random sample of almost 7,000 adults. They found that people without social and community contacts were over twice as likely to die during the 9-year follow-up period as those with well-developed social contacts. This finding could be a function of differences in social class or other variables. However, other more tightly controlled studies suggest that close relationships appear to facilitate good health and psychological well-being. In particular, studies have suggested that social support may buffer the negative effects of stressful life events. What is the evidence for this?

One frequently cited study examined the extent to which psychosocial assets, particularly social support, buffered the impact of stressful life events for pregnant women (Nuckolls, Cassel, & Kaplan, 1972). The outcome variable of interest was complications of pregnancy, such as difficult labor and low birth weight. Nuckolls and her colleagues found no significant relationship between stressful life change and complications. However, when they differentiated among those experiencing different levels of stress before and during pregnancy and with high and low levels of social support, a different picture emerged. As shown in Figure 14.10, women with high stress before and during pregnancy, and who also received little support, showed more complications than did those in all other groups. These data suggest that neither exposure to stressful situations, nor poor psychosocial assets alone, account for negative outcomes. Rather, as Lazarus and others have argued, it is the balance between the two that is crucial. High stress together with lack of social support appears to render the person particularly susceptible to dysfunction.

A similar conclusion is provided by Gore's (1978) analysis of data from a longitudinal study of men who lost their jobs because of a permanent plant

Figure 14.10
Shows the relationship between levels of stress, social support, and complications of pregnancy for a group of young women. Women with high stress prior to and during pregnancy, and who also received little social support, showed a marked elevation of complications compared to all other groups. (After Nuckolls, Cassell, & Kaplan, 1972.)

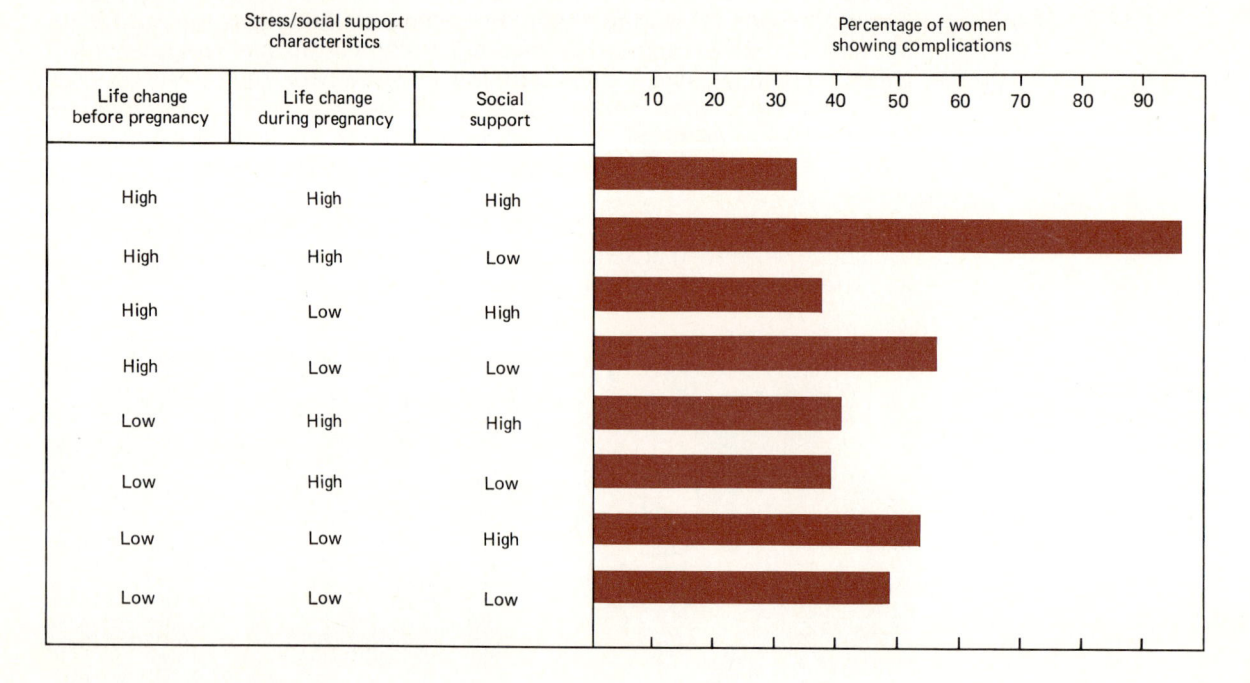

Life change before pregnancy	Life change during pregnancy	Social support	Percentage of women showing complications
High	High	High	~33
High	High	Low	~95
High	Low	High	~38
High	Low	Low	~55
Low	High	High	~42
Low	High	Low	~40
Low	Low	High	~53
Low	Low	Low	~48

STRESS AND COPING

TABLE 14.3
Mean serum cholesterol levels as a function of levels of stress and social support at different stages of job loss

Level of Stress and Support	Stage of Unemployment				
	Anticipation	Termination	Readjustment	1-year	2-year
Prompt reemployment supported and unsupported	230.1	226.5	215.3	217.5	207.4
Unemployed at stage 2					
Supported	221.2	220.9	197.7	182.2	198.0
Unsupported	222.6	247.5	224.2	218.0	219.9

Source: Adapted from Gore (1978).

shutdown. Recall from our earlier discussion of this study that the early stages of the job change experience were more stressful than the later stages. Gore also distinguished between those who found immediate reemployment and those who did not. Again, level of perceived social support from wives, friends, and relatives appeared to mediate the impact of stress. Tables 14.3 and 14.4 show the results for two health measures: serum cholesterol and number of illness symptoms. In both cases there were no significant differences between supported and unsupported men under low stress (those who found immediate reemployment). However, there were differences between those under high stress (unemployed after the plant shutdown) who were supported and those who were not. Unemployed and unsupported men had higher serum cholesterol levels than the other two groups at stages 2, 4, and 5. Unemployed and unsupported men had more illness symptoms than the other two groups at stages 1 and 2. Gore also found that for both the high- and low-stress groups, supported men were less depressed than unsupported men.

In sum, research has suggested that social support is a significant coping resource which can buffer stress. Recent research distinguishing between social network (number of relationships a person has) and perceived social support (perception of the supportive value of social interactions) suggests that the latter is most important (Schaefer, Coyne, & Lazarus, 1981). However, how social support works is less clear. Social support, for example, may involve tangible support (gifts, loans, services), informational support (feedback, advice), and emotional support (intimacy, attachment, reassurance). Schaefer and her colleagues found evidence to suggest that both tangible and emotional support are important for averting or reducing depression. Al-

TABLE 14.4
Mean number of illness episodes as a function of level of stress and social support at different stages of job loss

Level of Stress and Support	Stage of Unemployment				
	Anticipation	Termination	Readjustment	1-year	2-year
Prompt reemployment supported and unsupported	1.51	1.36	1.55	1.43	1.42
Unemployed at stage 2					
Supported	1.24	0.91	1.17	1.21	1.16
Unsupported	3.07	2.93	2.07	2.27	1.86

Source: Adapted from Gore (1978)

though it is clear that social support is an important coping resource, it is also becoming clear that its role is not a simple one.

COPING RESPONSES

When confronted with a stressful transaction, people generally implement a variety of coping responses. These are designed to permit them to eliminate, reduce, or tolerate stress. Broadly speaking, this can be done in two ways. The first is through problem solving, sometimes called *problem-focused coping*. That is, people can change the situation, either by modifying the threatening environment or by changing their own behavior. For example, confronted by the discovery of a toxic waste dump near your home, you might organize a campaign to force the offending party to remove the waste and detoxify the site. Alternatively, you may choose to move away from the area. The second approach to reducing stress is through regulation of emotional responses, sometimes called *emotion-focused coping* or *palliative* (or soothing) *coping*. That is, people can change how they think or feel about a situation. For example, you could tell yourself that the dump is too far away from your home to worry about, or that you have always been an alarmist and few of the things you worry about ever happen.

Coping Modes. Within the context of these broad functions of coping are a multitude of specific responses. The list is virtually limitless. However, they may be classified into several modes (Lazarus & Launier, 1978). Specifically, we may *seek information* (e.g., how to stop smoking, where to apply for unemployment compensation), take *dircrct action* (e.g., save for our retirement, look for a new job), *inhibit taking action* (e.g., not respond to a shove from an intoxicated patron in a bar, avoid commenting on our spouse's nasty remark), and *regulate our emotions* by our thoughts (tell yourself you are a nice person, tell yourself you are not hurt by the fact you were not invited to the party). Each of these modes can be oriented either toward the environment or the self; toward solving the problem or regulating emotions; and toward the past, present, or future.

But how do people employ these coping strategies in stressful encounters? Folkman and Lazarus (1980) attempted to answer this question by examining the responses of 100 middle-aged adults to stressful life events experienced over a year. The people were interviewed seven times at 4-week intervals about the stressful events they experienced during the past weeks. They also filled out a questionnaire detailing the problem- and emotion-focused coping responses they employed to deal with the most stressful event of the period. Folkman and Lazarus found that the people's coping responses exhibited several general characteristics.

First, both problem-focused and emotion-focused coping were used in almost every stressful episode. Of over 1,300 coping episodes, there were less than 2% in which only one type of coping was used. Second, for most people, the proportion of problem-focused and emotion-focused coping used to deal with different events varied greatly. That is, people often changed their coping responses to fit the situation. Related to this, different types of coping tended to be associated with different types of problems or stressful events. For example, work was associated with higher levels of problem-focused coping, while health problems were associated with higher levels of emotion-focused coping. Finally, there was little evidence of major differences in coping responses as a function of age or sex.

Social support may involve the intimacy, attachment, and reassurance that close friends provide. (Anestis Diakopoulous/Stock Boston)

FOCUS ON THE PSYCHOLOGIST

Richard S. Lazarus

RICHARD S. LAZARUS obtained his doctorate in 1948. He immediately was appointed as an Assistant Professor at the Johns Hopkins University. Later, as an Associate Professor at Clark University, he also directed the clinical training program. In 1957 he came to the University of California at Berkeley and in 1959 was made a full professor.

Although the words used to define problems of living have varied, including anxiety, frustration, stress, defense mechanism, and coping, I have never abandoned the conviction that stress and coping were the central processes to understand and that the emotional life was the best entry point for studying mental health and illness.

Nevertheless, a general conviction of this sort does not indicate how theoretical or research questions about the psychodynamics of emotion should be framed and examined. World War II stimulated the beginnings of stress and emotion research, illustrated by the writings of two research psychiatrists named Grinker and Spiegel, who wrote an influential book entitled *Men Under Stress*. They looked at air crews who had succumbed to stress with all sorts of symptoms of mental illness. After the war, the Air Force wanted psychologists to discover how to reduce stress where possible and how to train people to manage stress more successfully. In our early work on this problem, we found that these questions had to be reformulated because people were affected very differently by the same stressful conditions, and it appeared that these differences had to do with individual goals and ways of thinking and coping with stress.

In the 1950s and 1960s, we all believed that the best science was done with experiments in the laboratory, but it was difficult to create realistic stress in the laboratory or generate the full range of coping processes that people naturally use. So I hit upon an experimental approach that was more naturalistic, yet capitalized on the advantages of the laboratory—namely, generating stress with stressful motion picture films and measuring heart rate, skin conductance, and subjective distress while people watched.

In this research I became impressed by the capacity of thoughts to affect the stress reaction and by how people managed the stress through divergent ways of thinking about it. In our research we influenced such thought by using soundtracks and orienting statements before the film was played. Some of these statements encouraged subjects to deny or distance themselves from what was in the movie and thereby to experience less emotional distress.

After some years of doing this, I became convinced, however, that at our present state of knowledge about stress in living and the ways people cope with it, a better research strategy would be to study the stress process as it occurred naturally, that is, in field research rather than in the laboratory. So now my research involves looking at sources of stress, coping processes, and their effects on mental and physical health in ordinary people, mostly by having them talk to interviewers about daily stresses (hassles), major stressful events of the recent past, and about how they coped with these stresses in thought and act. In effect, just as is done in psychotherapy, we have people reconstruct their emotional experiences, so that we can study them and learn what brings them about. We assess subjects' values and goals, belief systems, sources of stress in daily life, how these are appraised—which is our jargon word for evaluating the significance of what is happening for their well-being—how they cope, the short-term emotions they experience in connection with stressful encounters, and long-term outcomes such as their sense of well-being, psychological symptoms, and symptoms of physical illness.

Our research aims are, of course, complex, but above all we want to know which appraisal and coping processes result in positive and which in negative outcomes.

461

HIGHLIGHT 14.4

Defense Mechanisms

The defense mechanisms have been called ego defense mechanisms, because they tie in with Freud's concept of the ego. That is, in reality testing, which is the job of the ego, the ego tries to master the conflicts that occur in everyday life. Something happens which is not desirable, and the ego is supposed to work to make everything come out as smoothly as possible. The ego sometimes resorts to using defense mechanisms to try to resolve anxiety and conflict. The following are examples of these defense mechanisms.

Repression can be described as forgetting. You do not want to think about something, so you simply keep it out of your mind. But remember, it is unconscious. A person who responds to anxiety or conflict by not remembering at an unconscious level is repressing. Excessive repression can leave a person "bound-up" inside with many unresolved experiences. *Suppression* is conscious forgetting. In that sense, it is really not a defense mechanism, as defense mechanisms are thought to be unconscious. If you work to forget on purpose, it is suppression.

Projection is a defense mechanism which can best be remembered as blaming others. The actual defense mechanism involves attributing to others a sense of what is unacceptable in ourselves. For instance, you are in the back of the room during an exam and you want to copy answers from your neighbor's paper. You may not be aware of it, but the anxiety created by the desire to cheat leads to projection: going up to the instructor and saying, "Hey, you better put empty seats between people in this exam—some kids are cheating." The unacceptable impulse is blamed on someone else.

Rationalization is a defense method that is easily remembered by thinking about making excuses. A rationalization is a constructed, socially acceptable explanation for some behavior that is socially unacceptable. You go to an X-rated movie, and when seen by someone you know, you explain that you are doing research for a class project.

Denial is essentially equivalent to falsifying reality. We say it does not exist when it in fact does. An overweight smoker with coronary heart disease is recovering from a stroke. A friend visits and asks, "How are you doing?" The patient responds, "Fine, no problem." Given that there *are* problems, this can be denial.

Displacement is easily remembered if you think about "kicking the cat." We do not recommend that you do this, but it is an interesting mnemonic device. Displacement is the reassigning of aggressive impulses or desires

---

Effectiveness of Coping Responses. Are some coping responses more effective or adaptive than others? This is a difficult question for which there is no clear answer. Traditionally, many theorists have argued that certain coping responses were more adaptive, and hence to be preferred, than others. Vaillant (1977), for example, orders the classic defense mechanisms described in Highlight 14.4 from primitive to mature, suggesting that denial, repression, and projection are less mature than identification, displacement, and sublimation. In general, it is argued that coping responses that distort reality are less adaptive than those that do not.

From this traditional perspective, then, direct action responses are likely to be more useful than palliative responses. Indeed, palliative responses may be maladaptive. For example, one of the most common responses to the discovery of symptoms of cancer (e.g., a lump in the breast) is a pattern of denial and avoidance. If the growth is malignant, the resulting delay in seeking medical attention may preclude successful treatment. On the other hand, palliative strategies sometimes appear to be effective. For example, it has been noted that denial may be effectively employed by weak and helpless victims of severe injuries (e.g., spinal cord injuries, severe burns) to deal with the early and most debilitating phases of the crisis (Hamburg & Adams, 1967). Then, when stronger, they can turn to more reality-based strategies.

onto an object that is not as threatening as the source of the discomfort. You substitute a different object against which to aggress. For instance, your boss or teacher creates a frustrating situation which leads you to be prone to aggression toward him or her. You cannot kick your boss or teacher, so you kick the cat.

Fantasy, or another word for fantasy—daydreaming—can be an effective way of coping with conflicts, anxieties, and frustrations. When we are trying to gratify frustrating experiences, it is very easy to sit back and fantasize.

In *reaction formation* the true motive, the true intended behavior, is unacceptable. Motives are reversed, and an unacceptable motive is converted into its opposite, or its reverse, so that it becomes acceptable. A parent who dislikes his or her children and sees them as bothersome and unwanted cannot accept this and, instead, is excessively fussy and caring in dealing with the children. The true motive is disguised.

In *sublimation* we have a socially approved outlet that is sought for a socially unapproved motive. It is unacceptable, in our society, to pry into others' personal affairs. However, private investigators are allowed to do so. Not all private investigators are sublimating, but the idea that an unacceptable motive can be experienced in an acceptable way illustrates sublimation.

In *compensation* the person tries to resolve conflicts and cope with frustration and anxiety by substituting goals. Failure in one activity is made up by success in another activity. One can compensate for one deficit by extreme success in another area.

Another defense mechanism is *identification*. How does one cope with frustration by identification? Well, you are in a position where you are trying to reduce anxiety about, let's say, your own identity. You can reduce that anxiety by identifying with someone who has the attributes you wish. So identification, associating yourself with people in a powerful position, does reduce the conflict or anxiety associated with not having the power yourself. A child who wanted to be a leader in an old neighborhood moves to a new one and makes friends with the leader of the new neighborhood.

In *regression* we are talking about acting childish. Regression is retreating to earlier forms of coping. You are, perhaps, an early maturing adult, you are in a situation in which there is some conflict, and you do not quite have the adult ways to cope with this conflict mastered as yet. Thus, you find yourself retreating to earlier ways of coping—acting childish. Temper tantrums in persons who are older than typical for tantrum behavior is regression.

Denial (when you falsify reality) and repression (unconscious forgetting) *block* anxiety. They do not allow the anxiety to be discharged, which is particularly problematic. Some of the other defense mechanisms are less problematic, because they allow the anxiety or discomfort to be discharged, perhaps onto other objects, by reversing the motives, or substituting an acceptable motive.

Defensive has a special meaning in the psychological context we are discussing. By defensive we mean the following: We try to avoid recognizing our own unwanted feelings. We try to avoid making ourselves look less desirable. We try to avoid being threatened or having our security undermined. When we are being defensive, we are doing things that make ourselves look better, that put ourselves in a better light, yet they may not be true to reality or true to another observer.

One major study that attempted to examine the issue of coping response effectiveness was conducted by Pearlin and Schooler (1978). They examined the responses of 2,300 people to the stresses created by strains in four major life roles: marriage, parenting, occupation, and household economics. Pearlin and Schooler identified 17 coping responses that fell into one of three major groupings: responses that changed the situation, responses that controlled the meaning of the situation after it occurred but before the emergence of stress, and responses that control thoughts and feelings after the emergence of stress. They found that the use of various coping responses actually did reduce stress in the various role areas. Stresses associated with marriage and parenting appeared more amenable to reduction than those associated with occupations. They also observed differences in the effectiveness of particular coping strategies across the different role domains. For occupational and household economic roles, the manipulation of goals and values was most effective in reducing stress. For example, in the occupational sphere, this might involve devaluing the intrinsic rewards of work, and limiting one's goals for advancement. In the household economic sphere, it might involve devaluing the importance of money, and deciding to abandon the goal of a new car or a larger house. However, strategies involving the modification of goals and values did not appear to be effective for reducing stress associated with the strains of marriage and parenting. Instead, in these areas, the most effective strategies were those that inhibited avoidance and withdrawal. In marriage, this might involve reflective probing of problems rather than emotional outbursts. In parenting, it might involve maintaining the conviction that one can influence one's children, rather than resigning oneself to feelings of helplessness. It is important to note, however, that like Folkman and Lazarus, Pearlin and Schooler found that multiple responses are used, and that the reduction of stress provided by any one response was small. Instead, the more coping responses people used the more stress appeared to be reduced. Stress associated with the strains of marriage and parenting appeared to be completely eliminated when people used as many as five or six responses.

Goodness of Fit. There is little evidence, then, that any one set of coping responses is inherently superior to another. What seems to be important is the *goodness of fit* between (1) the coping strategy and the task demands of the environment, and (2) the coping strategy and the goals, values, and commitments of the person (Folkman & Lazarus, 1980). When goodness of fit is optimal, the person can employ coping responses that meet the demands of the environment without conflicting with his or her personal agenda.

The concept of goodness of fit is illustrated by an experiment reported by S. M. Miller (1980). She distinguished between the coping strategies of monitoring and blunting. In *monitoring*, the person seeks out threat-relevant information, whereas in *blunting*, the person seeks to distract themselves from threat-relevant information. Consider what you would do if you needed surgery to correct a minor problem. Would you seek out information about the nature of the procedures to be used and the potential complications that might occur, or would you avoid such information and attempt to distract yourself from the upcoming event? The goodness-of-fit notion suggests that stress will be reduced if there is a match between a preferred strategy and the environment. In contrast, stress will remain high if there is a discrepancy between the person's preferred strategy and the environment.

This reasoning suggests that monitors will benefit from information, whereas blunters will not. Miller tested this hypothesis by studying patients about to undergo a relatively benign gynecological examination. Through a questionnaire, patients were differentiated according to whether they preferred to monitor or to blunt. Half of each group was then given a 20-minute communication designed to detail the procedures of the forthcoming examination and the sensations it would produce. The other half was given the usual minimal information. Figure 14.11 shows the patients' pulse rates before, during, and after the examination. There were initially no pulse-rate differences between the groups. Only blunters given low information showed a decrease in pulse rate before the examination. Monitors given high information showed a decrease in pulse rate by the end of the examination. Thus groups for whom there was a "fit" between preferred style and situation showed a reduction in stress. Groups for whom there was a lack of "fit" did not.

In sum, whether a coping response is adaptive or not depends on the fit between the strategy and the demands of the situation. In this context it is important to remember that stressful situations are not static affairs. They are transactions that change over time. Thus coping is an ongoing process, and what may be an effective strategy one time may be ineffective another time. Coping, then, is a complex process that cannot be understood simply by

Figure 14.11
Results of an experiment demonstrating the importance of goodness of fit of coping responses. A distinction was drawn between people who prefer to seek out threat-relevant information (monitors) and those who prefer to distract themselves from it (blunters). Prior to a surgical procedure, half of each group was given detailed information about the procedure, whereas the other half of each group was given minimal information. Groups for whom there was a "fit" between preferred style and the situation (monitors/high information; blunters/low information) showed a reduction in stress. Groups for whom there was a lack of fit did not. (After Miller, 1980.)

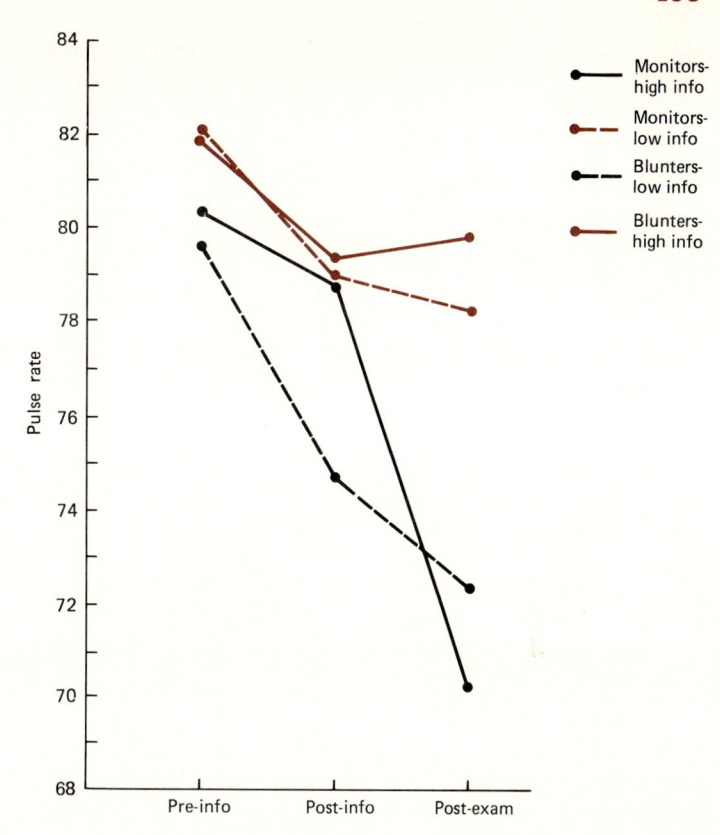

developing catalogs of "healthy" and "unhealthy" responses. Much more work will be required before we understand this fundamental psychological process.

SUMMARY

1. Stress may be defined as the nonspecific response of the body to any demand.
2. The stress response involves a sequence of stages labeled the general adaptation syndrome. The stages are the alarm reaction (initial shock and mobilization of defenses), stage of resistance (full mobilization of defenses), and stage of exhaustion (depletion of defenses).
3. The organism's physiological response to stress is based on the relationship between the brain and the endocrine system, particularly the adrenal glands. Two major pathways are involved: from the hypothalamus through the pituitary gland to the adrenal cortex; and from the hypothalamus via the autonomic nervous system to the adrenal medulla.
4. Excessive or prolonged secretion of the hormones involved in the general adaptation syndrome produces deleterious changes in the body.
5. Psychological stress may be defined as an unfavorable perception of the psychosocial environment.
6. Psychological stress produces the same physical stress responses as harmful physical stimuli.

7. The number of potential psychological stressors is almost infinite. In particular, psychological stress may be caused by situations that involve harm (delay or thwarting of response tendencies or goals), threat (the anticipation of harm), conflict (simultaneous presence of two or more incompatible response tendencies or goals), and overload or underload (too much or too little stimulation.)

8. Psychological stress has been associated with deleterious outcomes. It is related to both physical disease and psychological disorders.

9. In particular, undesirable major life events (e.g., divorce, loss of a job, death of a spouse) and annoying daily hassles (having to wait, losing things, bad weather) appear to contribute to the onset of difficulties. These effects appear to be cumulative. The more negative events experienced, the greater the likelihood of dysfunction.

10. The outcomes of stress, however, cannot be predicted solely from the frequency or intensity of the events to which people are exposed. People confront events with a variety of perceptions, cognitions, behaviors, and circumstances that often alter the impact of the event.

11. In particular, the way the person appraises the event appears to be important. Primary appraisal asks the question: "Am I okay or in trouble?" Secondary appraisal asks the question: "If I am in trouble, what can I do about it?"

12. Based on these processes of appraisal the event may be judged as irrelevant, benign-positive, or stressful (i.e., involving harm-loss, threat, or challenge).

13. Coping refers to cognitive and behavioral efforts to master, reduce, or tolerate internal and external demands and conflicts among them that tax or exceed the person's resources.

14. Coping involves two elements: coping resources and coping responses.

15. Coping resources refer to characteristics of the environment or person that provide the basis for coping responses. They include tangible resources such as money, personal resources such as health, cognitive abilities, and personality, and interpersonal resources such as a supportive social network.

16. Many coping resources such as a sense of personal control and perceived social support appear to buffer the effects of stressful events.

17. Coping responses may be classified into two broad types. Problem-focused coping involves changing the situation either by modifying the threatening environment or one's own behavior. Emotion-focused coping involves changing the way one thinks or feels about the situation.

18. People appear to use both problem-focused and emotion-focused coping. Also, different types of coping tend to be associated with different types of problems. There are few age or sex differences in coping responses.

19. There is little evidence that any one set of coping responses is inherently superior to another.

20. The effectiveness of coping responses seems to be determined by the goodness of fit between the coping strategy and (a) the task demands of the environment, and (b) the goals, values, and commitments of the person.

KEY TERMS

General adaptation syndrome
Harm
Frustration
Threat
Conflict
Overload
Underload
Primary appraisal
Secondary appraisal
Reappraisal
Coping resources
Coping responses
Problem-focused coping
Emotion-focused coping
Goodness of fit

SUGGESTED READINGS

Antonovsky, A. *Health, stress, and coping.* San Francisco: Jossey-Bass, 1980. An examination of the factors that enable people to manage stress and maintain health.

Dohrenwend, B. S., & Dohrenwend, B. P. (Eds.). *Stressful life events: Their nature and effects.* New York: Wiley, 1974. A collection of reports examining the relationship between stressful life events and physical and psychological dysfunctions.

Kutash, I. L., & Schlesinger, L. B. (Eds.). *Handbook on stress and anxiety.* San Francisco: Jossey-Bass, 1980. A collection of reports examining theoretical perspectives, research findings, and treatment approaches to stress and anxiety.

Lazarus, R. S., & Folkman, S. *Stress, appraisal, and coping.* New York: Springer, 1984. Presents a detailed theory of stress as a transaction between the person and the environment.

Selye, H. *The stress of life* (2nd ed.). New York: McGraw-Hill, 1976. The classic treatment of the issue by the "father" of modern stress research.

15

Abnormal Behavior

A BRIEF HISTORY OF THOUGHT ABOUT ABNORMAL BEHAVIOR
DEFINING ABNORMAL BEHAVIOR
MODELS OF ABNORMAL BEHAVIOR
   Learning Model
   Psychodynamic Model
   Systems Model
   Medical Model
CLASSIFYING ABNORMAL BEHAVIOR
   DSM III System
   Pros and Cons of Classification
SCHIZOPHRENIA
   Genetics and Schizophrenia
   Stress and Schizophrenia
   Subtypes of Schizophrenia
AFFECTIVE DISORDERS
   Bipolar Disorder
   Major Depression
   Cyclothymic Disorder
   Understanding the Causes of Depression

ANXIETY DISORDERS
   Generalized Anxiety Disorder
   Phobic Disorder
   Obsessive-Compulsive Disorder
SOMATOFORM DISORDERS
PERSONALITY DISORDERS
   Narcissistic Personality Disorder
   Dependent Personality Disorder
   Antisocial Personality Disorder
   Paranoid Personality Disorder
PSYCHOSEXUAL DISORDERS
   Sexual Dysfunctions
   Sexual Preferences
ADDICTIVE DISORDERS
ABNORMAL BEHAVIOR IN CHILDHOOD
   Attention Deficit Disorder
   Autism
SUMMARY
KEY TERMS
SUGGESTED READINGS

Ron was one of the most enjoyable clients seen at the outpatient mental health center. He was a young, sociable, and seemingly happy young man. Typically, he greeted the mental health center staff, told light and cute jokes, and referred to many of the professional staff by their first names. In some ways, Ron had come to feel quite at home in the setting of the mental health center.

   In the context of Ron's sessions with the mental health professionals, much more disturbing behavior was evident. For instance, Ron often whined like a spoiled child who was trying to get a forbidden toy from his mother. Chronic complaining and dissatisfaction with life was a recurring topic for discussion. But even more disturbed thinking became evident.

Ron was unemployed and living on a disability check from the military. After some effort, Ron took several civil service exams and scored sufficiently high to receive an offer of a job in a government office in the state capitol. He came to therapy complaining—now what was he going to do? He had a job offer, but he was worried. What follows illustrates Ron's thinking about the potential job.

"Well, I can't really take the job. It's too hot at the state capitol. And when it's hot I wear sunglasses . . . and I also wear a hat, you know, to help keep the sun out of my eyes. When I wear a hat, well, I get this tight feeling around my forehead, and it can give me a headache and make me lose my balance. If the hot sun gets in my eyes and I lose my balance, I know I'll be falling all over the place. When I fall, my sunglasses will break, and I'll get glass in my eyes. And that will be the end."

The mental health professional then commented, "What do you mean the end, the end of what?"

Ron replied, "The end of my sex life. If I get glass in my eyes and go blind, I'll never have a sex life."

The disturbance in Ron's thinking is evident in several places. For instance, he equates taking a job at the state capitol with a series of unlikely events that lead to blindness and the absence of a sex life. The logic and rationality of this thinking is questionable and the catastrophic conclusion is unwarranted. Ron was not joking around when he described his fear. Indeed, he had resorted to his whining childish style while he described it.

Ron's thinking had evidenced a disordered pattern. However, after leaving the session, Ron said goodbye to the secretary at the desk, said "hi" to a few other clients in the waiting area, and smiled as he left the building.

Bob's day began in a manner not unlike yours or mine. He awoke, showered, dressed, and proceeded to the kitchen for a cup of coffee, toast, and a piece of fruit. After eating a quick breakfast and skimming the headlines, Bob was off to work. Here is where the similarity to our lives ends.

On the rear lawn of Bob's estate awaited a helicopter that would transport him to his office. He was a chief executive officer in a major firm, and the heliport was on the roof of his firm's building in the heart of downtown. He used to look out of the helicopter window and reflect on his earlier days when he would be among the commuters snarled in traffic, but now bored with the view, his morning commute involves reading reports and preparing fiscal plans.

It is Friday afternoon, about 7:00 p.m., and Bob is returning home. The helicopter drops him on the rear lawn of his home and he walks toward the house. His sailboat is in the adjacent water, his cars are in the garage, and his family awaits his arrival in the home. Bob is a success.

On Saturday morning, Bob's wife found him dead on the floor in the recreation room, shot in the head with a revolver. The gun was beside him. There was no note.

Why, you might ask, did he commit suicide? Didn't he have everything that anyone could want, and more? Materially, yes. Bob did have an accomplished set of possessions. However, his psychological state was quite troubled.

Bob had been involved in two recent extramarital affairs. He no longer loved his wife, but she would not consider divorce. Both of his female friends were pushing for a closer relationship and the respectability of marriage.

Bob had made some unwise financial investments. His personal wealth was plummeting as several recent "remedies" did not provide the needed solution. In a related fashion, he had manipulated the company funds to provide personal financial assistance. The company bloodhound was on his trail.

Even with his $640,000 annual salary, plus bonuses and benefits, Bob was dissatisfied. There were three other executives who made a higher salary, and the person holding a comparable position at a competitive company made $750,000 a year. You can see that Bob was not satisfied.

In this chapter we will examine the various types of psychological disturbances that affect so many people. Before we do, however, we will take a brief look at some of the approaches to maladaptive behavior that have been dominant in history.

A BRIEF HISTORY OF ABNORMAL BEHAVIOR

It will be easy for the interpersonally sensitive reader to be less than pleased by our current knowledge and treatment procedures for individuals with maladaptive behavior problems. What facilities does society provide for the disturbed? How do the members of society treat their disturbed peers? The typical reaction from a student who visits even a most contemporary mental health facility for the severely disturbed is the gut-level statement, "Gee, is this the best we can do?" It is as though, without knowledge of the financial and social restraints, the human response is to want to do more than what is being done. That we, as human beings, are not yet satisfied with the way we treat our disturbed brethren speaks favorably of our human nature.

It may also be consoling for the student to realize the extent of the progress that has been made in the way that society and, in particular, its mental health professionals treat abnormality. The progress is most evident when one examines the past. Three forces can be identified as having had historically relevant impact upon the mentally disturbed: demons, diseases, and religion.

Often stated to be the earliest explanation of abnormality, demonic possession was for many years considered a reasonable way to understand seriously disturbed behavior. This Stone-Age explanation had an associated form of treatment: if you were possessed by evil spirits who were causing disturbing behavior, then the spirits must be released. According to anthropologists, the spirits were released by cutting holes in the disturbed person's head. The procedure was known as *trephining*.

A step forward from demonic possession was the idea that insanity was a disease, the result of natural bodily causes. The early disease notions followed the work of the Greek physician Hippocrates, who wrote detailed descriptions of the types of behaviors seen in his disturbed patients. Hippocrates also developed a "humoral theory" of psychopathology, which posited that there were four bodily humors or elements and that an imbalance among them resulted in mental (or any other) illness (see Table 15.1).

ABNORMAL BEHAVIOR 471

A trephined skull from the Stone Age, when it was believed that abnormal behavior could be cured by cutting a hole in the disturbed person's head to release evil spirits. (Bettmann Archive)

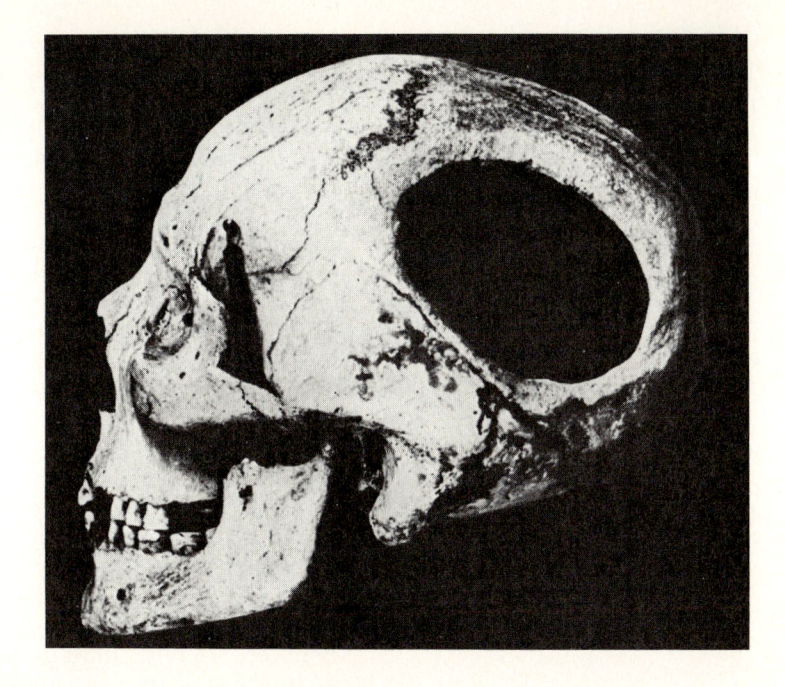

For having the vision to recognize that abnormality was not the result of demonic possession, and for turning toward natural causes, Hippocrates is often said to have turned the tide of the thinking about mental illness. Treatment of the disturbed according to the disease model was similar to the way physical disorders were treated and this involved the use of hospitals and physical therapy. Records indicate that patients were treated by *bloodletting*—draining quantities of blood from the patient to reduce behavioral abnormalities. Approximately 200 years ago, Benjamin Rush, considered the father of American psychiatry, treated patients by drawing blood. His belief was that insanity was the result of excess blood on the brain.

Religious beliefs have also influenced how society views its disturbed members. Religious thinking suggested that disturbed persons were being punished for their sins—that having sinned, the devil came to reside within them. Others contended that witches were sent to do the devil's work, and that the disturbed were witches. These beliefs about the causes of abnormal behavior had associated ideas about treatment. For instance, witches were put to death or subjected to extreme public punishment, while other deviants were subjected to *exorcisms*. An exorcism involved prayers, noisemaking, fantastic concoctions, and in some cases flogging and starvation.

TABLE 15.1
Hippocrates' "humoral" theory of mental disorders

Humors of the Body	Earthly Source	Humoral Problem	Temperament/Behavioral Problem
Blood	Heat	Excess	Sanguine: hopeful, confident
Black bile	Moisture	Excess	Melancholic: depressed
Yellow bile	Dryness of the earth	Excess	Choleric: irritable, excited, angry
Phlegm	Cold air	Excess	Phlegmatic: dull, sluggish, cold

DEFINING ABNORMAL BEHAVIOR

Fortunately, scientists have progressed well beyond the now-outdated magical explanations of abnormal behavior. More detailed and carefully studied theories are presently available to help us understand and treat psychopathology. But there are still debates about the most accurate and appropriate way to define what is and what is not "abnormal." One approach states that abnormal behavior is that which deviates from the norm. This may seem simple enough, but we must inquire further. Who sets the norm? How much deviation from the norm must be shown? Who determines what behaviors are deviations? As we will see, many perspectives must be considered in determining the abnormality of behavior.

The *cultural* perspective for defining abnormal behavior is based on the notion that appropriate behavior is that which is approved by the most people. If most people in a given culture accept certain behaviors, those behaviors fall within the normal limits. This definition has problems because the same behavior pattern may be considered normal in one culture, yet abnormal in another. There are so many cultures and subcultures that the definition becomes very blurred. Moreover, within a single culture a behavior may go from being normal to abnormal, or vice versa, as cultural standards change. Therefore, scientists must go beyond the cultural perspective when defining psychopathology.

When a person seeks the help of a mental health professional, he or she can be said to be using the *personal* definition of abnormality. That is, that person initiates the mental health contact and therefore defines himself or herself as suffering psychologically. This facet of the definition of psychopathology is important because no one else can describe the nature and degree of a person's suffering. However, personal definitions are insufficient for several reasons: The person may not know about the availability of mental health services; the person may incorrectly conclude that he or she does not need psychological services; and the person may recognize the need for treatment but be reluctant to make the contact for fear of being socially stigmatized.

A third approach to defining abnormal behavior employs *statistical* reasoning. Characteistics of the behavior in question, such as its incidence rate, can be determined and a distribution of the data can be drawn. The distributions of most behaviors often resemble the bell-shaped curve (see Appendix A). Using the fact that most people (95%) fall between ±2 standard deviations (see Figure 15.1), one can decide that if your behavior is less than or greater than 2 standard deviations from the mean, you are different from 95% of the people, and therefore one can conclude that you are abnormal. The statistical definition is based on real data about a person compared to real data about the population from which that person comes. The statistical

Figure 15.1
A display of a normal distribution of scores indicating the percentage of people falling between the standard deviation from the mean.

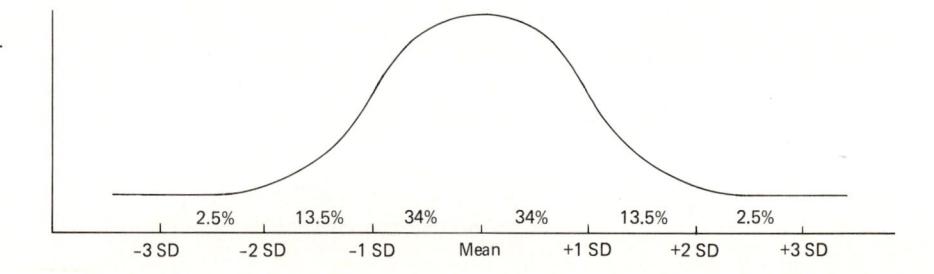

ABNORMAL BEHAVIOR

John Hinkley, who attempted to assassinate President Reagan in 1981, pleaded not guilty by virtue of insanity. *Insanity* is a legal term and refers to someone who lacks the insight or capacity to make responsible decisions. (AP)

approach to defining abnormality has the advantage of "hard" data, but being statistically different is not always the same as being psychologically maladaptive. Consider, for instance, the batting average of the best hitter in baseball or the IQ of the smartest person at your university—these scores are statistically beyond the limits we set (better hitting or smarter than 95% of the people), but they are not necessarily maladaptive.

The *clinical (professional)* definition of normality and abnormality is the most comprehensive because it includes an analysis of a person's current and past cultures, an examination of the person's own statements about his or her mental and behavioral health, and extensive comparisons of the person's data in relation to normative comparison groups. The clinical psychologist develops a careful understanding of social and cultural factors, and develops and uses psychological tests, interviews, and clinical experience to generate educated judgments about what is abnormal behavior. By including cultural, personal, and statistical factors, the clinical determination and definition of abnormality is superior to any one approach by itself.

You may have read or heard about someone who was considered to be "insane." It may surprise you, but insanity is a *legal* term, and sanity or insanity follows a legal, not a psychological definition. The legal concept of insanity refers to someone who is incompetent and may require commitment. *Incompetence* means that the person lacks sufficient insight or capacity to make responsible decisions. *Commitment* results when a person is considered dangerous to himself or herself or to others, or when the person cannot adjust to life in the community. *Insanity* has a legalistic definition that does not include much psychologically meaningful information. Knowing that someone is insane tells us little about specific psychological and behavior problems. Nevertheless, when courts of law seek to determine a person's sanity, they often call on clinical psychologists, as well as psychiatrists, to provide expert testimony and clinical opinion.

MODELS OF ABNORMAL BEHAVIOR

When we use the term "model," we refer to the psychologists' conceptual system or general orientation to the field. Models have "as if" qualities. For instance, a proponent of the medical model sees abnormal behavior as if it were an organic or disease process. Models can help guide our thinking and research and can provide the context for incorporating new information. However, models can be detrimental when we use them beyond their limits, as in assuming that because one behavior problem is related to a disease, all behavior problems are diseases, or when we forget that they are "as if" analogues and not exact explanations. Psychologists currently follow several models as conceptual frameworks for understanding and treating abnormal behavior: the learning model, the psychodynamic model, the systems model, and to a much lesser extent, the medical model.

LEARNING MODEL

In the learning model, abnormal behavior is seen as learned according to the same basic principles that govern the learning of normal behavior. That is, there is nothing inherently abnormal about the process of learning, only that some people learn maladaptive behavior. Developments in the basic study of classical conditioning, instrumental conditioning, and observational learning contribute to the increased understanding of the learning model of abnormal behavior.

Recall that in classical conditioning responses become so connected to stimuli that the stimuli automatically lead to certain responses. A child might learn a fear of the nighttime because of the association with unexplained noises that occur in dark places. Instrumental learning involves the strengthening of behavior as a result of the consequences that are attached to the behavior. A child might learn to have an upset stomach if each time she reports a tummy ache she is allowed to stay home from school. Observational learning might also contribute to abnormal behavior. A child can learn to be anxious in certain situations by observing the anxiety of adult models, such as parents. For example, if parents have an excessive fear of dogs, their son is also likely to behave fearfully when exposed to dogs.

Although the learning model recognizes the role of biological and physiological processes, it concentrates more on behavior itself than do any of the other models. By emphasizing behavior, this model can make efficient use of the scientific methods of investigation and can advance its theory without a heavy reliance on "assumptions." Behavior itself is the target of scientific inquiry, and the findings on the rate of the behavior guide the theory. Although this may seem simple, two features of the learning model make it at times preferable. First, the model and its explanatory system not only explain the development of abnormal behavior, but also describe the treatment of abnormal behavior. Second, contemporary followers of the social learning approach have incorporated cognitive factors (e.g., beliefs, expectations, self-talk) into their model. Thus the appearance of simplicity is simply an appearance—the model has begun to include more complicated cognitive (and emotional) factors in its analysis of abnormal behavior.

PSYCHODYNAMIC MODEL

Developing mainly from the writings of Freud, the psychodynamic model places great importance on the early years of a person's development and the degree to which certain age-related conflicts are resolved (see Chapter 13). When these conflicts are unresolved, psychological difficulties arise. Psychological disturbances are said to be the result of *fixations* at different states of psychosexual development. These fixations are considered to be a "stunting" or "freezing" of psychological growth. Childhood conflicts at particular stages of psychosexual development cause fixations, which, in turn, result in specific types of psychopathology. For instance, the person who is said to be fixated at the anal stage of psychosexual development may be considered an anal retentive personality and would be described as stingy, orderly, and meticulous.

The severity of the psychological disorder is said to be determined by the time of the fixation. Persons who suffer fixations at early stages of development, such as in early childhood before the ego is fully developed, would experience severe psychotic level problems. If the fixation occurs later in life and involves the development of the superego, the disorder will be of the less severe neurotic type. (See Highlight 15.4 for discussion of neurotic–psychotic distinction.)

In the psychodynamic model, unconscious processes play an integral role in determining normality and abnormality. The ego employs unconscious defense mechanisms to ward off anxiety. Although this can be said to be true for all of us, disturbed persons resort to an excessive dependence on certain defense mechanisms to protect them from anxiety. Descriptions of neurotic disorders often involve reference to dominant defense mechanisms.

The influence of the psychodynamic approach has been far-reaching. Viewed in relation to its period in history, it can be applauded for moving the explanations of abnormal behavior toward "psychological" analyses. Unfortunately, however, the model has several shortcomings, not the least of which is that the many assumptions of the psychodynamic position have either not been supported by experimental research or have not been put to the test.

SYSTEMS MODEL

In systems theory social networks, such as families or peer groups, are seen as producing repetitious patterns of behavior because they have a low tolerance for change. Any change, whether good or bad, affects the homeostatic function of the system, and the system seeks to maintain balance and order to maximize its chance of survival. For example, the family is a social system that seeks to maintain a certain status quo and changes in people are often frowned on.

Abnormal behavior patterns develop when people are forced to behave in psychologically painful ways in order to fit their social network. Anyone who has tried to engage in psychologically less painful behavior only to find the social system (e.g., family) nonsupportive will understand the basic position of the systems model. Abnormality can also result when people try to change the social system but cannot have any meaningful effects on it. They butt against forces greater than themselves, and maladaptive behavioral patterns result.

The true systems theorist downplays the role of physiological, cognitive, and learning factors in psychopathology, and instead emphasizes the role of complex patterns of interpersonal interaction. A person's social context is seen as defining deviance and causing abnormal behavior. Some current systems theorists are, however, incorporating the influences of physical, cognitive, and learning factors into their systems approach.

MEDICAL MODEL

The medical model sees abnormal behavior as the result of biological and/or biochemical maladies. This model has also been called the disease or organic model. The roots of the medical model are, as one would expect, within the field of medicine. The prototype for the medical model is *general paresis* (syphilitic infection of the brain), where an identifiable physical disease resulted in psychological deterioration. Other physical causes, such as viral infection, physical trauma, ingestion of poisons, and genetic factors, are also part of the medical model. Furthermore, advocates of the medical model are quick to point to the successful use of penicillin as a treatment. Thus the study of the psychological effects of brain disorders and the use of physical treatments have been part of the development of the medical model. Note, however, that there are many ways for the mind and the body to interact (see Highlight 15.1).

HIGHLIGHT 15.1

The Mind, the Body, and Abnormal Behavior: Three Instances of Interrelatedness

One of the recurring debates within psychology and other related disciplines concerns the mind-body question. Does the mind exist? Does it affect the body?

The behavioral movement within psychology has resulted in many advances, but it has also temporarily put aside interest in the "mind." Some contemporary psychologists are more willing to study mental processes, but they refer to these unobservable events as cognitive processes. Thus the long-standing question of the relation between the mind and the body has come to be termed the "cognitive-body debate."

Abnormal behavior patterns of several varieties are associated with the relations between cognitive processes and the physical body: for example, conversion, organic brain, and psychophysiological disorders.

1. In conversion disorders, the presenting problem appears to be physical (a body problem), but the actual dysfunction is entirely psychological (cognitive or mental).
2. In organic brain disorders, the pathological behavior is a direct result of brain dysfunction. The organic brain disorder causes the behavior problems.
3. In psychophysiological disorders, the person's behavior pattern makes the physical problem worse. A real physical difficulty may be present, but it is the maladaptive pattern of behavior that makes the physical problem more severe. Unlike conversion disorders, there are real physical problems in these cases.

Because the medical model views abnormal behavior as similar to physical illness, each of the abnormal behavior patterns is thought to have an organic cause that produces a set of symptoms, and once the symptoms are identified, the patient should be hospitalized for treatment. Contemporary mental health professionals recognize that a seriously disturbed person may require hospitalization, but persons with most abnormal behavior patterns are probably best treated without hospitalization. Nevertheless, advances continue to be made in the understanding of the biological causes of disturbed behavior and in the use of medications for treatment. For example, some recent evidence suggests that severe panic attacks can be treated with antianxiety drugs and that they can be provoked with injections of sodium lactate.

One of the leading critics of the medical model, psychiatrist Thomas Szasz, argues that assigning someone to the role of "sick" person and having him or her treated as sick would only encourage that person to continue to behave just that way. *The Myth of Mental Illness* (1961) presents Szasz's case that behavioral abnormality is a departure from social norms, not a disease.

"Models" are just that: ways to conceptualize and organize the data. No one model can explain all types of abnormal behavior, and rigid adherence to any one model will limit understanding. Some models fit certain types of behavior problems; other models fit other problem patterns somewhat better. Knowledge of the role of the principles of learning and internal cognitive factors, as well as social systems and physical factors, are necessary for a truly comprehensive account of abnormal behavior.

CLASSIFYING ABNORMAL BEHAVIOR

In the study of personality, classification encompasses all the variations in all types of behavior. In abnormal psychology, however, classification deals only with maladaptive behavior. The behavior and symptoms that are characteristic of each disorder are organized in patterns and arranged in a system.

An "official" publication of the classification of abnormal behavior did not appear until recently. The publication, called the *Diagnostic and Statistical Manual* (DSM), was the product of the American Psychiatric Association and included a listing of the various disorders. The DSM was revised in 1968 (DSM II) and again in 1980 (DSM III). *DSM III* offered the most comprehensive classification system to date (see Table 15.2) and currently enjoys the widest reception.

TABLE 15.2
DSM III summary table

DISORDERS USUALLY FIRST EVIDENT IN INFANCY, CHILDHOOD, OR ADOLESCENCE		
Mental retardation Mild mental retardation Moderate mental retardation Severe mental retardation Profound mental retardation Unspecified mental retardation *Attention deficit disorder,* with hyperactivity without hyperactivity residual type *Conduct disorder,* undersocialized, aggressive undersocialized, nonaggressive socialized, aggressive socialized nonaggressive atypical *Anxiety disorders of childhood or adolescence* Separation anxiety disorder Avoidant disorder of childhood or adolescence Overanxious disorder *Other disorders of infancy, childhood or adolescence* Reactive attachment disorder of infancy Schizoid disorder of childhood or adolescence Elective mutism Identity disorder	*Eating disorders* Anorexia nervosa Bulimia Pica Atypical eating disorder *Stereotyped movement disorders* Transient tic disorder Chronic motor tic disorder Tourette's disorder Atypical tic disorder Atypical stereotyped movement disorder *Other disorders with physical manifestations* Stuttering Functional enuresis Functional encopresis Sleepwalking disorder Sleep terror disorder *Pervasive developmental disorders* Infantile autism Childhood onset pervasive developmental disorder Atypical *Specific developmental disorders* Developmental reading disorder Developmental arithmetical disorder Developmental language disorder Developmental articulation disorder Mixed specific developmental disorder Atypical specific developmental disorder	ORGANIC MENTAL DISORDERS *Section 1. Organic mental disorders whose etiology or pathophysiological process is listed below* *Dementias arising in the senium and presenium* Primary degenerative dementia, senile onset with delirium with delusions with depression uncomplicated Primary degenerative dementia, presenile onset Multi-infarct dementia *Substance-induced* Alcohol intoxication idiosyncratic intoxication withdrawal withdrawal delirium hallucinosis amnestic disorder dementia associated with alcoholism Barbiturate or similarly acting sedative or hypnotic intoxication withdrawal withdrawal delirium amnestic disorder Opioid intoxication withdrawal

TABLE 15.2 *(Continued)*

Cocaine
  intoxication
Amphetamine or similarly acting
  sympathomimetic
    intoxication
    delirium
    delusional syndrome
    withdrawal
Phencyclidine (PCP) or similarly
  acting arylcyclohexylamine
    intoxication
    delirium
    mixed organic mental disorder
Hallucinogen
  hallucinosis
  delusional disorder
  affective disorder
Cannabis
  intoxication
  delusional disorder
Tobacco
  withdrawal
Caffeine
  intoxication
Other or unspecified substance

Section 2. Organic brain syndromes whose etiology and pathophysiological process are either noted as an additional diagnosis or is unknown

Delirium
Dementia
Amnestic syndrome
Organic delusional syndrome
Organic hallucinosis
Organic affective syndrome
Organic personality syndrome
Atypical or mixed organic brain syndrome

SUBSTANCE USE DISORDER

Alcohol abuse
Alcohol dependence (Alcoholism)
Barbiturate or similarly acting
  sedative or hypnotic abuse
Barbiturate or similarly acting
  sedative or hypnotic dependency
Opioid abuse
Opioid dependence
Cocaine abuse
Amphetamine or similarly acting
  sympathomimetic abuse
Amphetamine or similarly acting
  sympathomimetic dependence
Phencyclidine (PCP) or similarly
  acting arylcyclohexylamine abuse
Hallucinogen abuse
Cannabis abuse
Cannabis dependence
Tobacco dependence

SCHIZOPHRENIC DISORDERS

Schizophrenia
  disorganized
  catatonic
  paranoid
  undifferentiated
  residual

PARANOID DISORDERS

Paranoia
Shared paranoid disorder
Acute paranoid disorder
Atypical paranoid disorder

PSYCHOTIC DISORDERS NOT ELSEWHERE CLASSIFIED

Schizophreniform disorder
Brief reactive psychosis
Schizoaffective disorder
Atypical psychosis

AFFECTIVE DISORDERS

Major affective disorders

Bipolar disorder
  mixed
  manic
  depressed
Major depression
  single episode
  recurrent

Other specific affective disorders

Atypical affective disorders

Atypical bipolar disorder
Atypical depression

ANXIETY DISORDERS

Phobic disorders
  Agoraphobia with panic attacks
  Agoraphobia without panic attacks
  Social phobia
  Simple phobia
Anxiety states
  Panic disorder
  Generalized anxiety disorder
  Obsessive compulsive disorder
Post-traumatic stress disorder
  acute
  chronic or delayed
Atypical anxiety disorder

SOMATOFORM DISORDERS

Somatization disorder
Conversion disorder
Psychogenic pain disorder
Hypochondriasis
Atypical somatoform disorder

DISSOCIATIVE DISORDERS

Psychogenic amnesia
Psychogenic fugue
Multiple personality
Depersonalization disorder
Atypical dissociative disorder

PSYCHOSEXUAL DISORDERS

Gender identity disorders

Transsexualism
Gender identity disorder of childhood
Atypical gender identity disorder

Paraphilias

Fetishism
Transvestism
Zoophilia
Pedophilia
Exhibitionism
Voyeurism
Sexual masochism
Sexual sadism
Atypical paraphilia

Psychosexual dysfunctions

Inhibited sexual desire
Inhibited sexual excitement
Inhibited female orgasm
Inhibited male orgasm
Premature ejaculation
Functional dyspareunia
Functional vaginismus
Atypical psychosexual dysfunction

Other psychosexual disorders

Ego-dystonic homosexuality
Psychosexual disorder not elsewhere classified

DISORDERS OF IMPULSE CONTROL NOT ELSEWHERE CLASSIFIED

Pathological gambling
Kleptomania
Pyromania
Intermittent explosive disorder
Isolated explosive disorder
Atypical impulse control disorder

ADJUSTMENT DISORDER

  with depressed mood
  with anxious mood
  with mixed emotional features
  with disturbance of conduct
  with mixed disturbance of emotions and conduct
  with work (or academic) inhibition
  with withdrawal
  with atypical features

TABLE 15.2 (Continued)

PSYCHOLOGICAL FACTORS AFFECTING PHYSICAL CONDITION	Borderline Avoidant Dependent	Childhood or adolescent antisocial behavior Academic problem
Psychological factors affecting physical condition	Compulsive Passive-Aggressive Atypical, mixed or other personality disorder	Occupational problem Uncomplicated bereavement Noncompliance with medical treatment
PERSONALITY DISORDERS		Phase-of-life problem or other life-circumstance problem
Paranoid Schizoid Schizotypal Histrionic Narcissistic Antisocial	CONDITIONS NOT ATTRIBUTABLE TO A MENTAL DISORDER Malingering Borderline intellectual functioning Adult antisocial behavior	Marital problem Parent-child problem Other specified family circumstances Other interpersonal problem

Note: "Nervous breakdown" and "insanity" do not appear as categories—in fact, they do not appear in the system at all. These terms are not psychologically meaningful; the nerves do not break down, and sanity, as we have noted, is a legal term. The disorders that do appear in DSM III represent a comprehensive account of the various forms and subtypes of abnormal behavior.
Source: Adapted From American Psychiatric Association (1980), pp. 15–19.

Even a cursory overview of the DSM III categories shown in Table 15.2 will reveal the diversity of types of abnormal behavior. Table 15.3 documents the incidence of abnormal behavior in the general population.

TABLE 15.3
Sample estimated statistics on the incidence of abnormal behavior in the United States, 1978

Millions of Cases	Type of Abnormal Behavior
.2	Reported cases of child abuse[a]
.2	Reported suicide attempts[a]
1	Active cases of schizophrenia
2	Profound depression
6	Emotionally disturbed children and teenagers
7	Mentally retarded
10	Arrests for serious crimes
10	Alcohol problems
20	Neurotic disorders
53.5	Mild to moderate depression

[a] The actual rate may be higher than the reported rate; many cases of child abuse, for example, go unreported.
Source: These data were adapted from Coleman, Butcher, and Carson (1980).

THE DSM III SYSTEM

The text of DSM III contains lists of the essential features of each of the disorders, features that must be present for a diagnosis to be made. Features that are often related to the disorder are also described, and data about the age of onset, the likely course, and the prevalence are provided. Facts that are important for differentiating one disorder from another are also listed. More than any other classification system, DSM III offers specific, detailed statements about the features that define each category. For instance, instead of a paragraph or two describing the symptoms, DSM III provides definitional criteria: For the diagnosis of each disorder, it lists the specific features that must be present. Some scholars and practitioners have found fault with DSM III, but its effort to provide the criteria for each diagnosis is a step in the proper direction.

The DSM III diagnostic system is *multiaxial,* requiring five different diagnostic statements for each case. Previous diagnostic systems required only one—a statement about the type of disorder. You may be wondering what the other dimensions are—what else besides the type of disorder needs to be identified? As we shall learn, the others are intended to bring relevant information to bear on the handling of each case.

DSM III uses the first two axes for the classification of abnormal behavior. The first axis is reserved for the major disorders, such as schizophrenia; the second axis is for the less serious impairments, such as personality disorders. Each of these types of disorders are discussed in separate sections of the chapter. The third axis is for other information pertinent to nonmental *medical dysfunctions,* thus providing a place where disorders such as diabetes, which might have complications with some forms of medication treatment, can be recorded. Axes IV and V refer to psychological features that affect the disorder. Axis IV concerns the severity of the psychological and social stressors that contribute to the current abnormal behavior. This rating of environmental stress helps the mental health professional who treats the client to better understand the factors involved in the onset and maintenance of the problem. Axis V indicates the highest level of *adaptive* functioning that the client has exhibited during the last year. Using the multiaxial system will take more professional time, but it should improve the services that are provided. A knowledge of the client's degree of environmental stress (Axis IV) and personal positive resources (Axis V) should facilitate determining the most appropriate treatment and making accurate statements about the likelihood and magnitude of improvement.

PROS AND CONS OF CLASSIFICATION

Students, as well as the friends and family of those suffering from psychological problems, often inquire about the value of classification. First, isn't it degrading and insensitive to "label" people crazy? Second, doesn't pigeonholing persons into one category or another ignore some of the central facts about them as unique individuals with unique problems? Third, critics of labeling argue that once a diagnosis or label is attached to someone, that person's behavior becomes self-fulfilling. For example, after being diagnosed "depressed," someone will behave more like a depressed person than if the diagnosis had not been made. In other words, labeling leads one to play the role expected by the label.

A fourth criticism of classification is based on scientific questions. Is classification valuable if and when it is not reliable? Stated differently, do diagnostic classification procedures show too many disagreements from one diagnostician to another to be valuable to mental health professionals? In fact, earlier versions of DSM had serious problems with unreliability resulting from disagreements among diagnosticians. In a study of the earlier DSM by Beck and his colleagues (Beck, et al., 1962), the lack of specific criteria for making diagnoses was found to be the major factor resulting in low reliability. Specifically, diagnosticians attributed the lack of reliability of the system to inconsistencies on the part of the patient (5%), inconsistencies on the part of the diagnostician (32.5%), and inconsistencies in the diagnostic system (62.5%). Unclear criteria were the main source of unreliability, and DSM III, as we noted, has made a special effort to provide specific diagnostic criteria for each disorder.

Advocates of the classification of abnormal behavior point out that the use of a diagnostic term allows for efficient professional communication. The diagnostic label allows the professional to understand much about the client and the client's behavior without long-winded, detailed, and perhaps repetitious explanations. Using the diagnostic label is a form of professional shorthand. Pretend, for a moment, that I ask you for a ½-in. extended socket. If you do not know what that is, it will take you some time, without more information, to locate one. You may ask "What does it look like?" I might reply: "It is the shape and size of a stubby carrot, it has a cylindrical tip on one end with a hexagon-shaped opening, and at the other end there is a square-shaped plug. This piece fits into another tool to extend the reach of the tool." Using the label in this case, as in the classification of psychopathology, allows for easy communication among those knowledgeable about the specific meanings of each diagnosis. A label such as depression, schizophrenia, or autism has professional meaning.

Advocates of classification also point to the increased predictions that can be made when a diagnosis is available over predictions made without a diagnosis. There is sufficient similarity among clients receiving the same diagnosis that to ignore diagnostic information is to ignore the meaningful probability statements that are associated with the diagnosis (Meehl, 1959).

Research requires classification. Think about this statement in relation to the treatment of abnormal behavior. Do we want to treat all behavioral pathology the same? Physicians do not treat a broken ankle in the same way as a tumorous growth. Similarly, different behavioral disorders require different treatments, and to learn what treatment works best for each type of problem requires classifying clients. If we want to research the effects of treatments for depression, we would have to diagnose the participants as depressed. People with other psychological dysfunctions would have to be excluded from this study because their inclusion would hinder our ability to discover the most effective treatment for depression.

Although communication, prediction, and research are three very important reasons for classifying abnormal behavior patterns, the enterprise is worthwhile only if and when it is performed reliably and without known harm to those classified. Because perfect reliability has not yet been achieved, and natural variations in the human organism may prevent perfect classification, more research is required.

SCHIZOPHRENIA

One of the most serious and most puzzling of the psychological disorders is schizophrenia. The term *schizophrenia* literally means "split mind" and was introduced by Bleuler in 1911, when he characterized the disorder as a "splitting" of "mental" functions. Note that although schizophrenia means split mind, the disorder is *not* the same as split (multiple) personality. Multiple personality is a distinct type of psychopathology classified among the dissociative disorders (see Table 15.2).

The classic symptoms of schizophrenia are Bleuler's four "A's"—association, affect, ambivalence, and autism. Traditionally, disturbances in a person's thought processes reflected the *association* difficulties, problems with emotional control were associated with *affect*, defects in attitude evidenced the *ambivalence*, and the withdrawal from reality and social isolation documented the *autism*. Although the current classification of the various symptoms of schizophrenia is somewhat modified, further illustration of the four A's provides valuable perspectives on the disorder.

The schizophrenic is often said to have a loosening of associations. These loose associations are often seen in the person's speech. For instance, schizophrenic speech might include *neologisms*, newly created words that do not have meaning to the listener, and *clang associations*, words that are responses to the sound as opposed to the meaning of the stimulus word. A schizophrenic patient asked to sit at a desk might produce a neologism such as "this desk is a cramstile" (This desk cramps my style), or a clang association such as "Sit you wit, no time to flit." The failure of the schizophrenic to conform to the rules of verbal communication is not the result of low intellectual ability or educational deprivation, but symptoms of the underlying disorder. Moreover, schizophrenic language cannot always be decoded into meaningful communication. Meehl (1962) referred to the process of defective associations as "cognitive slippage."

Eugen Bleuler (1857–1939) introduced the term *schizophrenia*, which he associated with symptoms of association, affect, ambivalence, and autism. (New York Academy of Medicine Library)

The inappropriateness of the affect, or mood, of the schizophrenic is apparent in the extent to which the nature of the emotional reaction is not consistent with the evocative stimulus situation. Crying in response to a funny story and laughing in response to a tragedy are examples.

Ambivalence is seen in the extreme attitudes taken on the same position—"I hate my mother, the bitch, but I love her for feeding me." The antithetical attitudes vacillate back and forth, and the ambivalence is seen both in verbal and nonverbal behavior.

Being out of contact with reality for part of the waking day, the schizophrenic is apt to be preoccupied with his or her own inner world. The person withdraws from social contact, and his or her thinking becomes governed by internal reasoning that is not always consistent with reality.

Salzinger (1980) pointed to three additional A's that have been added to the description of schizophrenia in the last 20 or so years. The first of the new A's is *anhedonia*, the schizophrenic's inability to derive pleasure from the events and experiences that typically produce pleasure in others. The second A concerns *social aversion*. Schizophrenics dislike the social events that others find rewarding. *Attentional* difficulties refer to an inability to focus and concentrate, and the tendency to respond to different stimuli simutaneously.

The features of the schizophrenic disorder that we have described provide a sense of the severity of the disorder and of the devastating breadth of the related problems. Nevertheless, two additional symptomatic features of schizophrenia require our attention: delusions and hallucinations. *Delusions* are beliefs not supported by the facts. When a delusional person is confronted with reality, his or her beliefs do not change. For example, suppose that a woman who lives by herself and watches workmen with long hair and hard hats welding sewer pipes believes that these men are a cult of hippies putting electrons in the water system. The delusion develops over time until the woman will no longer drink tap water and has all of her water delivered in bottles. The delusional belief about electrons controls some of her behavior.

That reality does not alter the delusion is evident in the anecdote reported in Mahoney (1974). Here a patient stated that he was convinced he was dead. Many mental health workers told him that he wasn't dead, but the patient continued to believe he was. One day his therapist asked if dead people bleed, and the patient replied, "No, dead people don't bleed." The therapist then proceeded to prick the patient's finger and draw a drop of blood. "See there, you are bleeding," said the therapist, to which the patient merely replied, "Oh! Dead people do bleed!"

Hallucinations are reports of sensory stimulation when, in reality, no such stimulation is present. Hallucinations can occur in any of the sensory modalities: seeing, hearing, tasting, touching, and smelling. One example of a hallucination is seen in a client's report that he hears voices that tell him to kill young women in cars. The voices, he says, are coming from the dog in the yard of the house next door. Another example is the report that small insects, such as ants, are crawling all over the person's body. He wiggles and brushes himself as if to remove the insects, but none are there. The hallucinations that are a part of the diagnosis of schizophrenia are different from the occasional misperception or even rare hallucination among nondisturbed persons. Hallucinations by nondisturbed persons are typically the result of an out-of-the-ordinary condition, such as ingestion of a hallucinatory drug or extended sleep deprivation.

DSM III specifies several criteria for the diagnosis of schizophrenia. These criteria include deteriorated functioning in social, work, and self-care areas; the presence of delusions, hallucinations, or marked loosening of associations; a period of at least 6 months of symptoms like those described as the "A's"; and the absence of depression and/or organic mental disorder. DSM III also reports that the lifetime prevalence rate ranges from .2 to 1%, with slightly higher rates reported from studies done in the United States.

GENETICS AND SCHIZOPHRENIA

The classic methodology for studying the genetic contribution to a disorder is to examine the concordance rates of twins—that is, the similarity of twins as measured by the percentage who are alike on the dimension being studied. What are the concordance rates for schizophrenia? First, it depends on whether the twins are monozygotic (developed from a single fertilized egg; identical) or dizygotic (developed from different eggs; fraternal). The concordance rates for identical twins are greater than those for fraternal twins.

As can be seen from Table 15.4, monozygotic twins show a greater concordance rate than do dizygotic twins. When the data in Table 15.4 are placed with other data describing degrees of family relatedness, a meaningful relationship emerges: as one has more and more genetic similarity with an index case of schizophrenia, the greater the chances of being identified as schizophrenic.

However, schizophrenia is not solely a genetic disorder. If it were a genetically transmitted disorder, the concordance rate for monozygotic twins would be 100%—and it isn't. Because the concordance rate is closer to 50% than to 100%, we can conclude that a person may inherit a genetic predisposition to develop schizophrenia, but that the disposition alone is insufficient.

Another method of studying the genetic contributions to schizophrenia involves the study of adoptees. In this approach, children who were adopted away from their schizophrenic parents are examined, and the rate of schizophrenia in this group is compared to the rate seen in control groups. Heston (1966) reported that of the 47 offspring of schizophrenic mothers, 5 were themselves schizophrenic. None of the control group offspring was considered schizophrenic. It should be noted that the offspring of schizophrenic parents were also at greater risk than controls for other psychological disorders.

TABLE 15.4
Summary of concordance rates for monozygotic and dizygotic twins

Study Author(s) and Country of Investigation	Number of Twin Pairs (Monozygotic/Dizygotic)	Concordance Rates (%) Monozygotic	Dizygotic
Kallman, 1946 (United States)	174/517	69–86.2	10–14.5
Inouye, 1961 (Japan)	55/17	36–60	6–12
Gottesman & Shields, 1966 (England)	24/33	41	9.1
Kringlen, 1967 (Norway)	55/172	25–38	8–10
Fischer, 1968 (Denmark)	16/34	19–56	6–15

Source: Adapted from Rosenthal (1970).

Cross-fostering studies are yet another method for gathering information about the possible causal role of genetics in schizophrenia. Cross-fostering studies include a group of persons whose biological parents were normal but whose adopted parents were schizophrenic. In the sample reported by Wender, Rosenthal, Kety, Schulsinger, and Wilmer (1974), the rate of schizophrenia in the cross-fostered group was not greater than that of the controls. These data suggest that the childrearing practices of schizophrenic parents are not the sole cause of its disorder.

A Note on Biochemistry. Some of the earliest theories of the causes of schizophrenia reflected an acknowledgment of the importance of biochemistry. Today, although we no longer consider "poisons" to be *the* causal agent, researchers do look for excessive or defective neurotransmitters as potential keys to the puzzle of schizophrenia. For example, based on the biochemical actions of the drugs used to treat schizophrenia and the schizophreniclike effects of certain other drugs, researchers have speculated that excessive activity in the dopamine nerve tracks are etiologically involved in schizophrenia. Although there are data to support such biochemical theorizing, the evidence is not totally compelling. Continued biochemical research is warranted, but one must remember that an effective treatment does not validate a causal explanation: Aspirin reduces headache (as phenothiazines have been effective in reducing schizophrenic symptomatology), but that does not mean that headaches are caused by an absence of aspirin in the system. Thus biochemical research will have to go beyond drug effects to support biochemical causes.

STRESS AND SCHIZOPHRENIA

Stress means many things to many different people. One essential ingredient of all types of stress, however, is the perception of some threat and a sense of not being fully able to respond to it. When researchers have studied stress and schizophrenia, they have often looked at the role of the family and the effects of a demanding society.

Early studies of the family focused on the mother-child relationship and its role in schizophrenia (e.g., Lidz, Cornelison, & Fleck, 1965). Focusing more on the communication patterns of entire families, Bateson, Jackson, Haley, and Weckland (1956) believe that an important component in the development of schizophrenia concerns the person being raised in an environment where he or she experiences a "double bind" system. A double bind occurs when a person is exposed to contradictory messages and is not permitted to point out that this crazy system is in effect. An example of a contradictory message is as follows: At one level (basic content) the message is friendly ("How are you?"), but at another level the message is unfriendly (the tone of voice is aggressive, the face is rigid, and the interpersonal style is angry). Repeated exposure to incongruent communication, it is argued, results in the learning that communications in general are incongruent and that communications need not be congruent.

Although the double-bind hypothesis has received much attention, there are limited research outcomes to support it. For instance, Mishler and Waxler (1968) studied double-bind communications of parents with a disturbed child, but did not find that parents behaved that way all the time—they were congruent in their communication with a nondisturbed child. Others point to the problem associated with the fact that we do not know if such disturbed communication preceded the schizophrenia or is a consequence of it.

When considering the demands of society, researchers look for social class differences in the incidence of schizophrenia. As noted by Neale and Oltmanns (1980), the highest rates of schizophrenia are almost invariably found in the lowest social class. Numerous studies have confirmed this finding (e.g., Hollingshead & Redlich, 1958). But what is the reason for this? Could it be that the degrading treatment a person receives when a member of the lower class causes schizophrenia? Another, more likely hypothesis is referred to as the *social drift hypothesis*—the disproportionate number of schizophrenics in the lowest social class results from a downward social drift. The challenges of day-to-day life become increasingly difficult as the social withdrawal and cognitive distortion associated with schizophrenia take their toll. Some data are consistent with the notion of downward social drift, but this does not explain the cause of the disorder. One causal model which helps understand the role of genetics and stress is detailed in Highlight 15.2.

HIGHLIGHT 15.2

Diathesis-Stress Model: The Interaction of Predisposition and Environmental Factors

Predisposing factors seem to be involved in the development of schizophrenia, but they do not account for all the data. This is true because the development of abnormal behavior depends also on the person's current stresses. The diathesis-stress model takes both factors into account.

Diathesis here refers to predisposing factors, which include biological determinants, such as the person's genotype, and personality determinants, such as the person's characteristic ways of responding. *Stress* refers to the current environmental factors that can, but do not always, contribute to abnormal behavior, such as illness, work failures, loss of loved ones, accidents, and the simple taking on of too much responsibility.

One diathesis-stress explanation of schizophrenia, proposed by Meehl (1962), has been very highly regarded over the years. Meehl proposed three related concepts. He proposed that *schizotaxia* is the genetically inherited predisposition toward schizophrenia. Second, Meehl stated that the person's social learning history will determine whether or not schizotaxia will produce *schizotypy*. With environmental stress, the schizotype will show personality disorganization leading to *schizophrenia*. Thus only those persons with a certain genetic makeup can become schizophrenic, but they will become schizophrenic only if exposed to a detrimental learning environment and stressful life experience. In this way, the diathesis-stress approach to the causes of schizophrenia takes into account both predisposing and environmental factors.

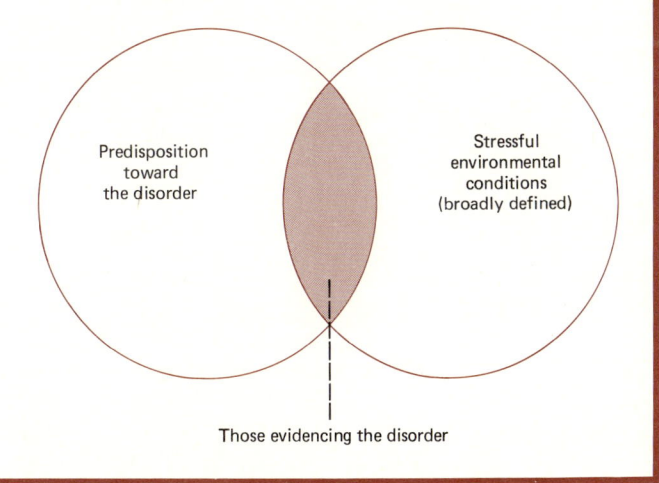

SUBTYPES OF SCHIZOPHRENIA

The wide range of dysfunctional behaviors and thought problems associated with schizophrenia has led researchers to propose subdivisions of the disorder. The subdivisions are designed to help create more homogeneous clusters, which in turn help research on cause and treatment. Over the years there have been nearly one dozen different terms to refer to different types of schizophrenia. Currently, however, DSM III includes five subtypes.

Disorganized Type. The disorganized subtype is marked by silly affect, incoherent speech, fragmentary (as opposed to systematic) delusions and hallucinations, and extreme social impairment. The disorder is said to have an early onset, insidious development, and a rather chronic course. This subtype was once referred to as hebephrenic schizophrenia, but the term "disorganized" has been adopted as a more descriptive label.

Catatonic Type. The main feature of catatonic schizophrenia concerns motor activity. The motor activity can be stuporous and rigid or extremely excited, or can switch from one extreme to the other. "Posturing" has been used to describe the catatonic's assumption of a certain bizarre body position and a rigid adherence to that position. A somewhat less rigid posturing might be called "waxy flexibility," where, like a warm candle, the schizophrenic body posture can be easily molded or shaped. During periods of catatonia, patients are not reactive to the environment and will require feeding and assistance with self-care needs. There are reports that catatonic schizophrenic patients are so unresponsive to the environment that they fail to respond to threats of electric shock.

Paranoid Type. The paranoid schizophrenic has delusions of grandiosity or persecution. Associated with this extremely elevated self-perception (you must be extremely important for others to be trying to persecute you!) are intense

Catatonic schizophrenics often maintain a bizarre body position. (Grunnitus/Monkmeyer)

FOCUS ON THE PSYCHOLOGIST

Paul E. Meehl

PAUL E. MEEHL received his doctorate in clinical psychology from the University of Minnesota in 1945, where he was department chairman from 1951–1957, and currently is Regents' Professor of Psychology, Professor of Psychiatry, and Professor in the Center for Philosophy of Science. In 1958 he received the Distinguished Scientific Contributor Award of the American Psychological Association and served as its President in 1962. In 1979 he received the Bruno Klopfer Distinguished Contribution Award of the Society for Personality Assessment. A practicing psychotherapist (psychoanalytic and RET), his current research interest is development of new taxometric methods in psychopathology, especially for testing genetic models.

Although I came to psychology via my teenage reading of Karl Menninger's *The Human Mind* plus a lot of Freud, I was largely free of the dogmatic environmentalism that prevailed among American psychoanalysts (and sociologists!) when I was a student (1938–1945). Minnesota's faculty included three strong "hereditarians," Donald G. Paterson (who taught the differential psychology course and believed that intelligence was 80 per cent heritable), William T. Heron (who taught comparative psychology and who did some of the earliest work on hereditary factors in rats' maze-learning ability, activity level, sexual drive, etc.), and my doctoral adviser, Starke R. Hathaway, inventor of the MMPI. Having such mentors, when I first read Kallmann's schizophrenia research in the early 1950s, I was fully prepared to accept it. (I had read Rosanoff's genetic studies of schizophrenia and manic-depression as a first-year graduate student in 1941.) My analyst and analytic supervisor, B. C. Glueck, M.D., was Rado-oriented, which led me to read Rado, unique among New York training analysts for his strong emphasis on heredity.

Meanwhile my own practice as a psychotherapist (first psychoanalytic, then increasingly RET) did not clash with the quantitative data, because the more I worked with patients, the clearer it seemed that neurotic and psychotic people had reacted much more pathologically than others to both their childhood experiences and current stress. I have not become a therapeutic pessimist because of understanding this, but I believe my helping goals are realistically conservative. I am in good company here, since that was Freud's view throughout his professional life. There is simply no contradiction between a sophisticated psychodynamics and strong genetic etiology of mental illness. Oversimplifying somewhat, a psychoanalytic session devoted to dream-interpretation is about learned *content* (needs, social objects, defenses, indirect expressions), whereas a genetic etiology ("Why did this person fall ill from such things and that one did not?") is a matter of *parameters* of the learning functions and affective states involved. For Freud, these included the strength and adhesiveness of the instincts, "somatic compliance," and so on.

In the framework of rational emotive therapy, both temperamental and cognitive ability factors of an inherited nature contribute to the development of irrational thinking and impair the client's ability to change inefficient mental habits. Behavior modification obviously involves quantitative properties of learning curves that are influenced by genes. Despite the considerable influence of Skinner (at Minnesota when I was a student), I could never discern any intimate connection between operant behaviorism and the environmentalist preference that one finds in most Skinnerians. So the marked shift in social science and medical acceptance of genetic factors from 1940 to the present time was for me quite painless, as it merely showed the profession finally accepting what I already knew as an undergraduate in the late 1930s.

487

interpersonal relations, anger, and argumentativeness. Unlike the disorganized type, paranoid schizophrenics do not show the gross deterioration of personality and behavior. An intriguing description of three paranoid schizophrenics, each of whom claimed to be Jesus Christ, is provided in Highlight 15.3.

HIGHLIGHT 15.3
The Three Christs of Ypsilanti

"I'm Jesus Christ." "No, I'm Jesus Christ." "Both of you are wrong, I'm Jesus Christ."

Although this brief dialogue is fictional, it might have occurred if three patients, each claiming to be Jesus Christ, were brought together for the first time. Have three people at once ever claimed to be Jesus Christ? Yes, and Milton Rokeach (1964, 1981) describes what happened when he arranged for three patients at Ypsilanti State Hospital to be brought together. Each of the patients had a delusional belief system surrounding his claim to be Jesus Christ.

Joseph was 58, of medium height and build. He was bald and was missing a few front teeth. He had been hospitalized for nearly 20 years. He stated that his name was Joseph Cassel, and that he was God. He had been born Josephine Cassel, but disliked his name intensely and changed it to Joseph. Neither parent was overly religious, but when his mother died his grandmother took him to live with her—she was inclined to appeal to God for personal help. Joseph was afraid of his father and left home to try to get a good job. He read more than most people and thought that he might someday be a writer. Until he married at age 34, he showed little interest in women. Joseph was described as lacking a sense of humor.

Joseph's wife was reported by Rokeach to think that Joseph's problem started after an automobile accident when he turned off the car ignition but did not avoid the other vehicle. Everyone in the car was badly hurt except Joseph. He quit his job, began suspecting that people were poisoning his food, and eventually was committed.

Clyde was 70, over 6 feet tall, toothless, and had been in mental institutions for 17 years. He introduced himself as Clyde Benson, but stated that he had other names, such as God and Jesus.

Clyde was the son of hardworking parents. His father was said to be severe, and his mother tended to be overprotective. Clyde married at 24 and, with his wife, lived with his parents until he could buy a farm for himself. His wife died of an abortion after 18 years of marriage, followed soon after by the death of his father, the death of his wife's father, and the death of his mother. Clyde had been drinking heavily. A second marriage ended because of the continued heavy drinking. He was jailed for alcohol-related offenses and became violent. He would pray and curse, later claiming to hear his first wife's voice and claiming to be God.

Leon was 38 and had been committed only 5 years earlier. He was tall, thin, dignified, and, as Rokeach noted, he looked the most like Christ. Leon declared that on his birth certificate he was Dr. Domino Dominorum et Rex Rexarum, Simplis Christianus Pueris Mentalis Doktor—the reincarnation of Jesus Christ of Nazareth.

Leon's parents did not stay together for very long and Leon's mother, Mary, who barely spoke English, had primary responsibility for raising him. She was a religious fanatic who reported hearing voices. Leon had attended a pre-seminary school but was expelled. He served in the military, tried college, but ended up with a poor work pattern on several jobs.

His mother thought that all his behavior was sinful—even buying a radio was unacceptable. His mother now thought that Leon was not good enough to be a priest. She began to cover the walls of the house with religious paraphernalia and to pray excessively.

For nearly a year before the commitment, Leon heard voices telling him he was Jesus—he said it was God telling him he was Jesus. One day Leon defaced all the religious materials in the house and became violent—he was then committed.

The actual encounter between these three men—all of whom were diagnosed schizophrenic, paranoid type—was described in detail by Rokeach. The following brief sample illustrates the conflict that three claims to the same identity can cause (Rokeach, 1981, pp. 7–8).

Undifferentiated Type. Classification is an imperfect effort, and the imperfections often result from individual cases that do not fit neatly into any one category. The undifferentiated type of schizophrenia is reserved for cases where the prominent psychotic symptoms cannot be classified in other categories or where the symptoms fit the criteria for more than one psychotic

---

"My belief is my belief and I don't want your belief, and I'm just stating what I believe," Leon said.

"I know who I am."

"I don't want to take it away from you," Leon said. "You can have it. I don't want it."

—Clyde, what do you think?—

"I represent the resurrection. Yeh! I'm the same as Jesus. To represent the resurrection . . . [mumbling and pausing] I am clear . . . as saint . . . convert . . . you ever see. The first standing took me ten years to make it. Ah, forty cars a month. I made forty Christs, forty trucks."

—What did you make them out of?—

"I think that means forty sermons, I think that that's what it means," Clyde answered.

—Well, now, I'm having a little trouble understanding you, Mr. Benson—

"Well, you would because you're probably Catholic and I'm Protestant up to a saint."

—Did you say you are God?—

"That's right. God, Christ, and the Holy Spirit."

"I don't know why the old man is saying that," Joseph interrupted. "He has it on his mind. He's trying to discharge his mind. It's all right, it's all right as far as I'm concerned. He's trying to take it out of his mind."

—Take what out of his mind?—

"What he just said. He made God and he said he was God and that he was Jesus Christ. He has made so many Jesus Christs."

Clyde yelled: "Don't try to pull that on me because I will prove it to you!"

"I'm telling you I'm God!" Joseph was yelling, too.

"You're not!" Clyde shouted.

"I'm God, Jesus Christ and the Holy Ghost! I know what I am and I'm going to be what I am!"

"You're going to stay and do just what I want you to do!" Clyde said.

"Oh, no! Oh, no!" Joseph insisted. "You and everybody else will not refrain me from being God because I'm God and I'm going to be God! I was the first in the world and I created the world. No one made me."

At the end of this session, Leon was quiet during an outburst between Joseph and Clyde. Clyde protested that the meeting was "mental torture" and announced that he was not going to come to any more meetings. The next day, Rokeach entered the ward where the men were living and informed them that it was time for another meeting. They all followed willingly.

The three men met fairly routinely for 25½ months. Many events transpired during that time: outbursts of emotion, including name-calling and physical pushing; the installation of a "rotating chairmanship," where the men took turns leading the meetings; reading and discussing correspondence; Leon claiming the Virgin Mary as his wife; changes in behavior resulting from outside positive authorities; changes in behavior from placebos; and even Leon's adoption of a new name.

One of the interesting findings reported by Rokeach is that while the three contradictory delusional systems created conflict in the beginning, such as violent arguments and outbursts, the three men soon began to overlook conflicting delusional material. When someone would mention delusional material that offended the identity of the others, the comment might be overlooked or a motion made to adjourn. One of the men (Leon) would typically respond with, "That's your belief, sir."

The three Christs did not recover their sanity as a result of the efforts to have them confront one another. Rather, Rokeach noted that two of the men engaged in denial—the other persons were not Christ because they did not exist. Clyde tried to make the problem go away by concluding that the others were really corpses with machines inside them to do the talking. Joseph stated that if the truth hurts, man should turn away from it (illustrating denial). When he saw a newspaper article about the three Christs, he found it interesting, but he did not know the three men described in the story.

Leon did not deny the facts, but he explained them in terms of an intricate and delusional system. He did not deny that the others were Christ, but he explained how they were different types of Christ.

From M. Rokeach *The three Christs of Ypsilanti.* New York: Columbia University Press, 1981.

disorder. Delusions, hallucinations, and gross distortions of reality and behavior must be present to ensure that the disorder is of the psychotic level.

Residual Type. Persons who have been identified as schizophrenic but are not now psychotic are candidates for the residual classification. DSM III does, however, require that there be continuing signs of the original episode, such as eccentricity, social isolation, emotional flatness, and illogical or loose thinking.

AFFECTIVE DISORDERS

The dominant disturbance in the affective disorders is mood. Individuals with disorders of affect are at the extremes of the mood continuum—either very low mood (depression), or extremely elated mood (mania). The terms used to refer to the several affective disorders include *bipolar affective disorder* (formerly referred to as manic-depression), *major depression,* and *cyclothymic disorder.*

BIPOLAR DISORDER

Bipolar (touching both poles of the extremes in mood) disorder is characterized by extreme changes in mood: The person shows elevated mood and a sense of greatness followed by a period of hopeless dejection. Persons showing extreme mania engage in constant conversation that lacks a coherent theme (flight of ideas), excessive motor activity that is relatively unproductive, and the general initiation of numerous and diverse activities, plans, and deals. Although appearing sociable, the manic is uninhibited, impatient, impulsive, and inconsistent. Capable of "talking" big deals, listeners may be mistakenly impressed by grandiose plans. The following brief excerpt of a case of bipolar disorder (adapted from Spitzer, Skodol, Gibbon, & Williams, 1983) provides a better sense of manic behavior.

Terry, a middle-aged civil service employee, was brought to the hospital by police. His hyperactive behavior and nonstop talking had alarmed his relations. Approximately a month before hospitalization, Terry bought an expensive car and a large number of cuckoo clocks. He planned to use the car to travel around and sell his clocks. His plan was, in his opinion, a sure shot at making money. When he was not selling clocks, he was continuously on the phone "wheeling and dealing." He rarely slept. He reported feeling "on the top of the world" but accumulated a large debt and had driven his family to exhaustion.

Persons having experienced a manic episode are classified as having bipolar disorder. Most cases of mania have had or will soon have an episode of severe depression. Mania alone is very rare.

Jamison reported (1984) that the severe emotional swings seen in manic-depression may simply be the price one has to pay for creative genius. Her conclusion was based on 47 prominent British artists and creative writers, of which Jamison found 18 to have had major mood disorders. This 38% mood-disordered rate is particularly telling since it is six times greater than in the normal population. Are creativity and manic-depression related? Think about the case of Handel, for example, who wrote "Messiah" in 25 days during a manic high.

HIGHLIGHT 15.4
Key Distinctions in Abnormal Behavior

ACUTE VERSUS CHRONIC

Acute disorders have a relatively quick onset. They are seen as reactive—they follow an identifiable environmental event and are seen as a reaction to it. Because acute disorders come on suddenly, the term "crisis" may be applied.

Chronic disorders are insidious in their onset. They have a long and gradual development and they tend to persist. This type of maladaptive behavior pattern has also been referred to as a *process disorder*.

NEUROTIC VERSUS PSYCHOTIC

Neurotic disorders were originally described as neurological problems (hence the term "neurotic"), but contemporary scholars recognize that neurotic behavior patterns are more the result of faulty learning. Neurotic disorders reflect a pattern that includes feelings of inadequacy, a lack of confidence, self-defeating and self-deprecating behavior, and a general predisposition to *avoid* rather than confront problems. Trying to cope by avoiding is an important feature. Equally important, neurotic behavior is concerned with *anxiety*. The neurotic person feels inadequate, becomes anxious, and avoids the situation to reduce the anxiety. The avoidance of anxiety is an essential feature of neurosis. Keep in mind, however, that the neurotic person may be relatively untroubled in other areas. Neurotic persons may be successfully holding jobs, maintaining marriages and families, and contributing to their communities and society.

Psychotic disorders stand in contrast to neurotic disorders in terms of severity—psychotic disorders are gross distortions of reality, including such symptoms as hallucinations, delusions, personality deterioration, and loss of social contact. To give an idea of the severity of psychotic disorders, a person who is psychotic might think that he or she is Jesus Christ or Napoleon. In other cases, the psychotic may see himself as a mandated murderer—the dog next door is telling me secretly to kill all young heretics. These gross distortions of reality are not always obvious, and the person may be living a routine life. Sometimes, neighbors and acquaintances are surprised when they learn of the psychotic features of the behavior of someone they saw as unbothered. However, psychotic disorders more often require hospitalization, and powerful medications are prescribed to help the psychotic person regain sensible thinking.

ORGANIC VERSUS FUNCTIONAL

Within the psychotic disorders is another distinction worth noting. *Organic psychotic disorders* result primarily from an underlying physical malady. Organic problems can be associated with brain tissue damage, genetic defects, chemical ingestion, or traumatic incidents.

Functional disorders are of psychological rather than organic origin. Psychotic disorders of thinking (e.g., schizophrenia) and mood (e.g., psychotic level depression) are considered functional disorders.

One should not be seduced into the positive side of the manic high which precedes the severe depression. Rather, for many of those who suffer with the disorder, the swings in mood can be frightening. Sufferers sometimes report a loss of control of their feelings and major changes in their behavior, relationships, eating habits, and so on. A brief news article written by a person with manic-depression evidenced a current state of tranquility but also documented anticipatory fears and pains about the down times. The invigorating and creative high that may be a part of the manic phase is, unfortunately, true for only a limited number of sufferers.

MAJOR DEPRESSION

Some degree of depression is probably not foreign to any of us. Following the loss of a family member, a loved friend, a close pet, or after a tragedy of health or weather, it is neither uncommon nor maladaptive to be depressed.

Having the occasional "blahs" or being annoyed by the interference of an unexpected winter storm are parts of life. Clinical depression, or syndrome depression, goes beyond the routine experience of being blue, however.

Major depression involves sleep and appetite disturbance, decreased energy, feelings of worthlessness, guilt, and a preoccupation with negative thinking. There is also a loss of interest or pleasure in activities that were once prized. When delusions are involved, they are consistent with the depression (mood congruent): such as a delusion about being the most worthless human being. Suicide is a real concern when caring for seriously depressed clients. The risk increases just after the person has emerged from the depths of his or her depression. The person may continue to despair and feel worthless, but he or she has regained some of the energy that was lost. The new energy provides a means to do something about the depression, and suicide is one course of action (Beck, 1967). In contrast to the bipolar disorder, major depression is called a unipolar disorder.

Major depression involves sleep and appetite disturbance, decreased energy, and feelings of worthlessness and guilt. (George Malave/Stock Boston)

CYCLOTHYMIC DISORDER

Cyclothymic disorder resembles the bipolar disorder, but the mood swings are less severe. Cyclothymia involves mood swings but without the presence of the extreme symptoms needed for diagnosing the other affective problems. No psychotic features are seen in cyclothymia, and the person often has periods of normal mood lasting as long as several months. The pattern must persist for 2 years before cyclothymic disorder can be diagnosed.

UNDERSTANDING THE CAUSES OF DEPRESSION

No single theoretical model or research paradigm can explain all aspects of the affective disorders. Some forms of affective disturbance seem to have a genetic and physiological cause, whereas other forms emerge more as an outcome of psychological factors.

Biological Views. The biological perspective includes analyses of the role of genetics and neural transmitters and seems to offer a meaningful model of the bipolar disorders. Examination of the genetic contribution parallels the research on schizophrenia—where the concordance rates for identical and fraternal twins are compared. The findings generally indicate a much higher concordance rate for identical twins than for fraternal twins, but while these data are supportive of a genetic contribution to the more severe forms of depression, such as bipolar disorder, the evidence is not the same for the moderate and mild forms of depression.

The catecholemine hypothesis about depression involves a defect in the supply of neurotransmitters. Catecholemines are neural transmitter substances that are associated with the emotions. When the brain experiences an over- or undersupply of catecholomines, the person experiences major changes in mood; an oversupply produces mania and an undersupply produces depression (Schildkraut, 1965). Although this hypothesis, and the genetic notion, are considered to be reasonably well supported, they cannot fully account for the development of the bipolar disorder. For example, Akiskal and McKinney (1973, 1975) proposed that biochemical causes combine with psychological factors to produce depression.

Psychodynamic View. Intrapsychic conflicts are seen as the cause of depression for those who hold psychodynamic viewpoints (Mendelson, 1974). One conflict consists of anger turned inward. Instead of expressing anger directly to others, the person punishes himself or herself. Another conflict leading to depression results from insufficient gratification as a child. If the person did not feel loved, cared for, and wanted as a child, the person will not develop a sense of being worthy of love as an adult. When persons with these types of background suffer loss of a love object, the result is serious depression.

Cognitive-Behavioral View. Several psychological explanations for depression take a cognitive-behavioral perspective. That is, behavioral theories of the role of reinforcement and conditioning, and cognitive theories of the role of thought processes are interrelated in clarifying the development of depression.

Response contingent reinforcement means that the person receives a desired outcome, such as a reward, when the response is made. One behavioral analysis of depression emphasizes the dulling effect of a low rate of response-contingent positive reinforcement. In other words, depression follows after a person performs behaviors that rarely lead to positive consequences. After a while, the person learns that behaviors go unrewarded, and his or her activity is reduced. The reduced activity further reduces the chances of being rewarded, and the depression worsens.

Lewinsohn and his colleagues suggest that more depressed people take part in fewer pleasant events and report having fewer pleasant experiences (Lewinsohn, 1974). The low rate of reinforcement and the lack of reported pleasure may occur for several reasons: The events may not be seen as rewarding, rewarding events may not be available, the depressed person may lack the skills necessary to achieve the rewards, or the depressed person's behavior may drive others away.

Another behavioral view of depression accentuates uncontrollable aversive experiences. Seligman (1975) draws a parallel between the behavior of research animals (dogs) and human beings. When dogs are placed in an apparatus where they have to jump from one side to another to escape an electric shock, they can learn the response. However, when the dogs are first given a series of unavoidable, uncontrollable shocks, they did not learn to jump to escape—they seemed to have given up, or to have *learned helplessness.*

In similar studies with human beings (e.g., Hiroto & Seligman, 1975; Klein & Seligman, 1976), subjects exposed to uncontrollable aversive experiences were impaired in their ability to solve simple problems. They, like the dogs, had learned, at least for the moment, that it did not pay to try—they had developed a sense of learned helplessness. Constant exposure to events which are out of one's control leads to a sense of impotence and the perceived inability to have an effect on the world around one, leading to further depression.

Yet another behavioral analysis of depression is based on the self-management system developed by Kanfer (1970). Rehm (1977) used Kanfer's model of self-management—self-monitoring, self-evaluation, and self-reinforcement behaviors—and postulated that depression results from a selective self-monitoring of negative events, setting too stringent criteria for self-evaluation, and engaging in low rates of self-reinforcement.

An interesting feature of several of the behavioral models is their implicit reliance on cognitive processes. For instance, Rehm's position places great importance on the cognitive processes of the self-system: self-monitoring, self-evaluation, and self-reinforcement. A more explicit reliance on cognitive processes has been proposed by Seligman and his colleagues. The learned helplessness model of depression has been revised, with an emphasis on *attributions*. To what cause does a person attribute negative events? Depressed persons, as a result of their learning history, are said to make attributions about failure that are internal, stable, and global. Specifically, this means that the depressed person sees himself or herself as responsible for negative events, and that this responsibility is chronic and pervasive. Experiencing a negative situation, when its cause is seen as a personal fault, is associated with depression.

The most clear-cut instance of a cognitive model of depression is proposed by Beck (1964). Beck describes a depressive "cognitive set" as the key aspect of depression. This cognitive set has three parts: a negative view of the self, the world, and the future. Most people find a certain event neither elating nor depressing, but seen through the depressive's "cognitive set," the same event is taken as further evidence of the person's limited self-worth and the bleakness of the future. Depressed persons cognitively perceive events in such a way as to encourage depression. As noted earlier, many of the current systems for understanding the cause and development of depression are cognitive-behavioral—they consider both the importance of reinforcement and response-contingent outcomes and the centrality of the type of thinking style possessed by the depressed person.

ANXIETY DISORDERS

You are alone in an unfamiliar setting and the weather turns cold and windy. Foreign noises are heard from near and far, and a loud crash causes you to jump. This scene, or any other "horror-movie" scenario will produce a reaction in even the most stable and rational among us. The reaction is *fear*, a reality-based response to frightening conditions.

You are being driven to the community center for the big concert. You have won a contest, and you and your guest will be seated in the best seats in the house. As you ride along you think about how the real "big shots" must feel, and how nice it would be to be a millionaire. The thought that dominates your thinking, however, is how much you are looking forward to the concert. Here you are *eager:* a positive anticipation.

Anxiety is different from both fear and eagerness. Anxiety is a sense of impending disaster or general threat. Something, out of your control and despite your best efforts, is going to happen. The anxious person displays behavioral signs, such as trying to go in many directions without a particular course, stuttering, or tremors; has physiological reactions such as an uneasy or upset stomach, perspiration, and dry mouth; and experiences the cognitive/emotional side of the problem as a lack of self-confidence, misperception of the demands of the environment, and feelings of tension and insecurity.

There are several types of anxiety disorders, and we will take a close look at three of them: generalized anxiety disorder, phobic disorder, and obsessive-compulsive disorder.

HIGHLIGHT 15.5

"Neuroses No Longer Psychological Problem"

The fictional headline above could have appeared in any newspaper across the country and, as DSM III went into effect, the title would have "technically" been accurate. At that time, the classification of disorders known for so long as "neuroses" was eliminated from the diagnostic classification system. Unfortunately, however, the disorders themselves were *not* eliminated. The new classification system describes similar disorders but employs a different nomenclature. Moreover, the traditional terms are still in common usage.

The major reason for discontinuing the term neurosis was to make the classification system as descriptive as possible. By *descriptive* we mean that the system discusses the different disorders by referring to the features that describe the disorder. This approach is in contrast to a system in which the disorders are classified by their causes.

The following table provides a brief description of the various types of disorders that had previously been called neurotic, and it also provides the proper current classification.

Neurosis	Brief Description	Current Classification
Anxiety neurosis	General excessive anxiety—said to be "free-floating" since it is not associated with specific situations	Generalized anxiety disorder
Phobic neurosis	Fear and avoidance of a specific object or situation	Phobic disorder
Obsessive-compulsive neurosis	Persistent and uncontrollable thoughts and compulsions to repeat actions	Obsessive-compulsive disorder
Hysterical neurosis: Conversion type	Physical problems without an organic cause	Conversion disorder
Hysterical neurosis: Dissociative type	Separation of mental processes, as in amnesia and multiple personality	Dissociative disorder
Hypochondriacal neurosis	Preoccupation with bodily functions and presumed illnesses	Hypochondriasis
Neurasthenic neurosis	Characteristic fatigue and exhaustion	Not a current diagnosis
Depressive neurosis	Extreme and/or extended sadness in reaction to a specific event	Dysthymic disorder

GENERALIZED ANXIETY DISORDER

As suggested by the terms used to identify this disorder, the essential features of it concern persistent feelings of diffuse anxiety, including muscle tension, cognitive apprehensiveness, and physiological reactivity. The anxiety is unfocused and not tied to any particular situation. A person suffering from a generalized anxiety disorder would not know what he or she is so afraid of; it is as if they are waiting for something dreadful to happen, but they do not know what it is. The person finds it difficult to concentrate, senses an aroused nervous system, and may even have muscle aches or twitches. An important aspect of identifying the generalized anxiety disorder is the elimination of the possibility of other disorders. For instance, the symptoms of the phobias, and obsessions and compulsions, should not be present.

PHOBIC DISORDERS

When a person suffers from extreme anxiety that is associated with a specific object, activity, or situation, the disorder is called a phobia. The person is aware of the anxiety and knows what triggers it. Moreover, the person knows that the degree of anxiety is out of proportion to any real threat.

An elevator phobic would display an irrational and excessive fear of elevators. Anyone who has ever worked in or even visited a tall building clearly recognizes that the elevator phobia will be disruptive to the person who has it. No one wants to walk up 5, 7, 10, or 20 flights of stairs! Do not be misled into thinking that facts will reduce the phobia—no amount of data and no number of arguments will be compelling. Even though no elevators have crashed in the entire state for over 3 years, even though the elevator has an emergency phone and exit and was recently inspected and found to be in tip-top shape, the phobic is still fearful.

Because of the phobia, the person *avoids* the feared situation: The elevator phobic avoids elevators. Avoidance learning is said to play an important role in the development of phobias. In avoidance learning the person makes a response which prevents an unwanted event or situation. By maintaining an elevator phobia the person may be able to avoid tall buildings and also, perhaps, having to take a stressful job. "I can't work here, I'm afraid of elevators"—the phobia assures the person that he or she can avoid working.

The study of phobic disorders often examines one of the most common phobias, fear of snakes. (Susan Rosenberg)

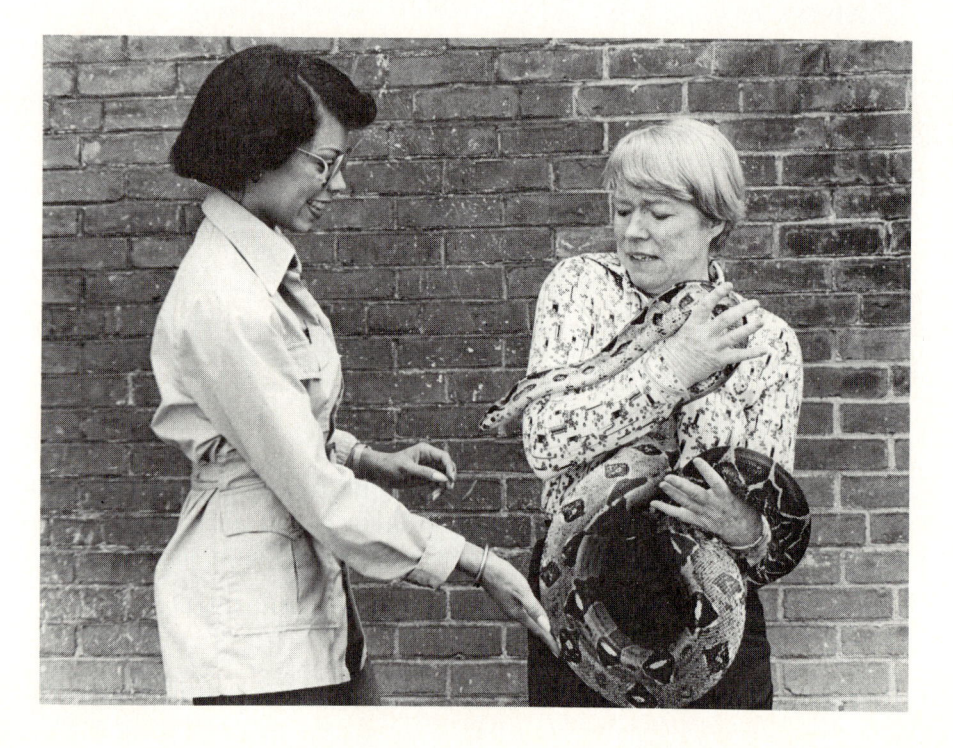

Examples of other phobias include claustrophobia, fear of closed places, and agoraphobia, fear of experiencing fear.

OBSESSIVE-COMPULSIVE DISORDER

Sometimes a tune may stay with us longer than we might prefer—an advertising jingle that we really do not like but keep humming. In a small way, this is like an obsession: *Obsessions* are persistent thoughts, ideas, or images that the person does not want and does not intentionally produce, but rather are perceived as invading the person's thinking. The recurring thoughts are unnecessary and troublesome, and the person tries to suppress them. Compulsions are ritualistic and repetitive behavior patterns. The behaviors are not ends in themselves, but are undertaken to prevent or postpone other actions. These two features are interrelated and often appear within one person.

Unlike a repeating jingle, a pathological obsession is very unwanted, recurs day to day, and typically involves some unacceptable action. A man, 50 years of age, was obsessed by an act performed at age 10, when he poured gasoline into a hole thought to house wild animals and ignited the fuel. He was obsessed with thoughts of having killed innocent animals.

Checking rituals illustrates compulsive action. People with a compulsive ritualistic checking interrupt routine activities to "check and make sure" that they have done something that they were supposed to do. Checking that the stove was turned off or that the doors were locked might take several hours out of each day to accomplish. People with cleaning compulsions might wash their hands excessively, as if to attempt to wash away something that is unwanted (some would suggest to cleanse the person from guilt, such as that resulting from excessive masturbation).

Our discussion of the anxiety disorders, because of space limitations, has not been exhaustive. The limited coverage should not, however, be taken as evidence of the restricted range of these disorders or of the number of people troubled by them. Problems with anxiety afflict many men and women (see Table 15.3).

Although there are several theories about the development of anxiety-related disorders, the psychodynamic (or psychoanalytic) and the learning (or behavioral) explanations are the most widely followed. Briefly, psychodynamic thinking posits that there are unconscious conflicts between our impulses and wishes and the rules and prohibitions of society. These conflicts lead to the anticipation of danger and the ego's attempt to protect the person, often by means of the defense mechanisms. Ineffective management of the anticipation of danger is evident in the symptoms of the neurotic person.

The learning model also emphasizes early experiences, but it is the acquisition of behaviors that is important, not the inferred internal processes. A traumatic experience that led to anxiety or the repeated experience of anxiety arousal in a certain situation or context results in anxiety being evoked by that situation and situations similar to those that created the original anxiety. By making a response, such as leaving the situation, the person reduces the anxiety. Soon the person makes the response before the anxiety, and thus prevents it from occurring. Persons with anxiety disorders often employ avoidance responses to prevent unwanted anxiety. The responses are maintained by the anxiety reduction that becomes associated with them. The elevator-phobic avoids elevators and feels less anxious by taking the stairs.

SOMATOFORM DISORDERS

Paradoxically, however, by continuing to avoid, the phobic makes it more and more difficult ever to confront the elevator.

Soma means "body," and *somatoform* refers to "bodylike" disorders. Thus somatoform disorders appear to be physical but are not. The symptoms presented by a person suggest that the problem is physical, such as the inability to move an arm, sudden blindness or deafness, becoming paralyzed, or losing bodily sensations, but there are no organic or physiological explanations for the problem. There is, however, strong evidence that the problem is related to psychological factors. The immobile arm is not a physical problem, but a behavioral sample of a psychological problem. Somatoform disorders are not under a person's voluntary control. The problem is neither physically caused nor a case of faking—the symptoms are the result of psychological processes that the person is unaware of. It is a rare, yet most interesting disorder (see Highlight 15.6).

HIGHLIGHT 15.6
Identifying a Case of Conversion Disorder

Conversion disorder involves a loss or alteration of physical functioning which suggests a physical difficulty but which is actually a direct expression of a psychological problem. Although this may be an acceptable definition, is it enough to identify such a disorder? Probably not. As we noted when we discussed DSM III, the *diagnostic criteria* are important aids in determining a diagnosis. Thus to identify a conversion disorder we must first examine the diagnostic criteria. DSM III (1980, p. 247) reads as follows:

A. The predominant disturbance is a loss or alteration of physical functioning suggesting a physical disorder.
B. Psychological factors are judged to be etiologically involved in the symptom, as evidenced by one of the following:
  1. There is a temporal relationship between an environmental stimulus that is apparently related to a psychological conflict or need and the initiation or exacerbation of the symptom.
  2. The symptom enables the individual to avoid some activity that is noxious to him or her.
  3. The symptom enables the individual to get support from the environment that otherwise might not be forthcoming.
C. It has been determined that the symptom is not under voluntary control.
D. The symptom cannot, after appropriate investigation, be explained by a known physical disorder or pathophysiological mechanism.
E. The symptom is not limited to pain or to a disturbance in sexual functioning.
F. Not due to somatization disorder or schizophrenia.

Now let's examine a real clinical case which may or may not be a conversion disorder. Milt was a 32-year-old serviceman. His job in the military was as a translator of the German language. He came from a very poor and uncomfortable background and was the only member of his family to graduate from high school and college. In

PERSONALITY DISORDERS

According to Millon(1981), a personality disorder consists of a combination of traits that produce an inflexible style, which in turn impairs psychological, social, and occupational functioning. DSM III has a similar view of personality disorders, that of deeply ingrained maladaptive patterns of relating that are severe enough to impair adaptive functioning or cause subjective distress. Although the severity must be sufficient to cause distress, personality disorders are not major psychological disorders. Indeed, DSM III uses Axis II for diagnoses of personality disorder. We will discuss four of the various personality disorders.

NARCISSISTIC PERSONALITY DISORDER

Greek myth held that Narcissus, a beautiful young man, fell in love with his own reflection and withered away gazing at it in a pool.

The narcissistic personality disorder is an ingrained pattern of responding that impairs interpersonal relationships. The narcissist has a grandiose sense

---

fact, his learning the German language and becoming a translator was his ticket out of his deprived home environment. The military gave him a uniform, three meals a day, and a place to live, and for this he was grateful. He was assigned to Germany, where translating for the upper-level officers as they discussed top-priority matters with the German government and military made him feel exceedingly successful.

Milt met a woman while stationed in Germany. His involvement with German officials and his interacting with German leaders eventually resulted in his meeting an elite woman. She was the daughter of an influential leader, and she and Milt were romantically swept away. The relationship developed rapidly, and soon the notion of marriage seemed a certainty. However, when Milt's woman friend asked to go back to the United States with him to meet his family, Milt began to suffer *aphonia* (an inability to speak above a whisper). Milt was seen by several expert physicians, but they were unable to find a physical problem. Milt was eventually returned to the States for further medical testing and subsequently was referred for a psychological assessment and opinion.

Was this a case of conversion disorder? Let's check back against the criteria provided earlier, A through F. A. Yes, the predominant disturbance suggests a physical disorder. B. Yes, psychological factors are involved in the etiology; the symptom got worse at the time of psychological conflict, and the symptom enabled Milt to avoid an unwanted situation. C. Yes, as part of the psychological testing, it was determined that Milt was not simply faking it. D. Yes, as part of the medical testing it was determined that Milt's aphonia was not a physical problem. E and F. Yes, the symptom was not related to sexual functioning, and the disorder was not somatization or schizophrenia.

Although conversion disorders are relatively rare, Milt's case seems to be a true case. The aphonia appeared just as a major conflict developed in Milt's life. By having aphonia, Milt was able to postpone and even prevent his girlfriend from seeing his "embarrassing" family and background. Perhaps Milt had even lied to his prospective wife about his family, and his new problem helped him not get caught in his fabricated stories.

Does all this seem too well organized? Do all the pieces seem to fall into place too easily? Perhaps so, but do not be misled by thinking that Milt planned the aphonia. If Milt had staged the aphonia as a way to escape his dilemma, it would not be a conversion disorder. Conversion problems are not known to the sufferer as psychological. Milt, in fact, was convinced that his problem was entirely physical, and he continued to request that additional, more qualified, medical experts check his throat and vocal system. Accordingly, the psychological treatment of aphonia takes a great deal of time and caution—one does *not* tell the sufferer "Oh, it's all in your head." Rather, the first portion of the treatment might involve the gradual resolution of the initial problem—Milt's relationship and his embarrassment about his family—with little emphasis on the aphonia.

of self-importance and fantasizes about unrealistic goals. There is also an exaggerated self-centeredness—when something happens in the workplace or the community, the narcissist's only concern is how that event will affect him or her. Narcissistic persons are overly concerned with managing how they impress others; appearance is more important than substance. Interestingly, while the narcissist has an overblown sense of importance, this self-esteem is very sensitive and there is an alarming need for attention and admiration. A person who characteristically interacts with the world in this way often finds limited acceptance. Most people do not become close and lasting friends with someone who expects special favors without being willing to reciprocate. The narcissistic personality disorder invariably involves difficulties with interpersonal relationships.

In Greek mythology, Narcissus fell in love with his own reflection in a pool and withered away gazing at it. (Bettmann Archive)

DEPENDENT PERSONALITY DISORDER

Many people, while not as independent as they would like, are not excessively dependent. Those few who are excessively dependent on others are considered dependent personalities. Associated with this disorder is the failure to assume responsibility for decisions, an unwillingness to make reasonable demands on others, and a lack of self-confidence. The dependent personality also finds it very discomforting to be alone for more than brief periods of time. The subordinate nature of the dependent style leaves the person nearly helpless in many situations unless a more dominant person is willing to take the lead.

ANTISOCIAL PERSONALITY DISORDER

A lack of ethical and moral standards and an inability to adhere to acceptable modes of behavior characterize the antisocial individual. Antisocial persons, sometimes referred to as *psychopaths* or *sociopaths,* are unsocialized, lack significant loyalties to other persons or groups, are unprincipled in business, nonempathic and nonanxious, and less sensitive than normals to threats of punishment. Because the antisocial person can put up and keep up a good front, they can, at first, seem impressive and they try to and do exploit others. Individuals with antisocial styles are more often found in jails than in volunteer community groups, are more in conflict with than in concert with authority figures, and have shallow and fleeting as opposed to stable and loving interpersonal relationships. As you may have sensed already, antisocial persons are not seen as "good friends." Indeed, they typically blame others, including "friends," for faults that are their own.

PARANOID PERSONALITY DISORDER

Occasionally, it is wise to be suspicious of others. The paranoid personality, however, is consistently suspicious: the mistrust is pervasive and is evident in unwarranted situations. Moreover, a person with a paranoid personality is not convinced by evidence that contradicts his or her suspicions and might even become suspicious of the evidence and of the person presenting it. Problems at work and with other people are likely to result from the paranoid's style. Interestingly, the person may be wise enough to recognize the merits of keeping the suspicions to himself or herself. Other people describe the paranoid personality as devious, scheming, secretive, and interpersonally cold. Persons with paranoid personality disorder are critical of others, but do not accept criticism well themselves.

Personality disorders are said to stem from immature, incomplete, or distorted personality development. They are associated with maladaptive interpersonal interactions, and they can affect overall adjustment. However, not all experts agree on how to classify personality disorders. Some see personality disorders as severe enough to warrant a major diagnosis, while other professionals hesitate to employ the diagnostic category of personality disorders. They argue that it is outside the realm of mental health to diagnose all the slight variations among people. Individual differences do not necessarily indicate abnormality. These critics also argue that personality disorders are based on the position that people have enduring "personalities," and they are quick to cite the evidence which suggests that personality is, in part, a function of the situation (Mischel, 1968).

PSYCHOSEXUAL DISORDERS

Discussions of sexuality were once taboo. Societal norms about sexuality have shown dramatic changes over the years, however, and one result has been the liberation of the study of human sexuality. The work of Masters and Johnson (1966; 1970) has helped to advance our knowledge as well as gain respect for the candid and scientific study of sexuality. One of their early and important contributions was the description of the cycle of sexual arousal (see Table 15.5), considered to be representative of normal sexual functioning. In keeping with the theme of this chapter, we consider some of the disorders associated with human sexuality: sexual dysfunctions and preferences.

SEXUAL DYSFUNCTION

Sexual dysfunction concerns both the inability to achieve sexual gratification and the absence of the desire for it. We are concerned less with physical ability than with the psychological aspects of sexuality. These dysfunctions can affect sexual desire, excitement, and orgasm.

TABLE 15.5
Phases of sexual arousal described by Masters and Johnson

Phase	Description
Excitement	Begins with sexual stimulation, of whatever type is stimulating for the person. With increased stimulation comes increased levels of sexual tension.
Plateau	The phase of increased sexual tension where the drive for sexual release must be strong enough to produce orgasm.
Orgasmic	When stimulation and excitement reach maximum intensity and the body shows an involuntary response.
Resolution	A lessening of sexual tension after orgasm. In males, restimulation during this period is impossible, whereas females are capable of repeated orgasms. The period in which restimulation is impossible is called the *refractory* period.

For males and females, dysfunctions of desire are rarely identified unless the lack of desire is marked and a source of distress for either the person or the person's partner. Dysfunctions of excitement are referred to as impotence for males and frigidity for females. *Impotence,* the inability to achieve or maintain an erection sufficient for sexual intercourse, is also called erectile insufficiency. *Frigidity,* often accompanied by an absence of sexual desire, is evident in the failure of the female to produce the lubricant that facilitates intercourse. Premature ejaculation, or ejaculation after an unsatisfactory brief period of sexual stimulation, is an orgasmic dysfunction in males. Functional vaginismus, involuntary muscle spasms when intercourse is imminent that prevent penetration, and functional dyspareunia, painful intercourse not due to physical problems, are rare disorders that affect satisfactory sexual intercourse for females.

SEXUAL PREFERENCES

Disorders of sexual preference are referred to as *paraphilias*. DSM III includes fetishism, transvestism, zoophilia, pedophilia, exhibitionism, voyeurism, and sexual sadism and masochism among the paraphilias. Generally, the diagnosis of a paraphilia requires that the deviant sexual preference be necessary for sexual excitement. An occasional or rare sense of excitation from an unusual stimulus would not qualify as a paraphilial disorder. However, the disorder can exist even if the person does not actually engage in observable sexual activity. As long as the person achieves sexual excitement and the deviant attraction is required for sexual excitement, the deviant sexual activity can take place solely in the imagination.

Having a sexual fetish for shoes, for example, seems odd enough, but does it hurt anyone? It seems to be a victimless problem. Unless the fetish interferes with other people, does the fetish require treatment? The need for treatment is much more readily visible when we consider pedophilia. Adults who act out or fantasize about sexual activity with prepubertal children as their preferred or exclusive method of sexual excitement are pedophiliae, and when they have sex with a child, they create a victim. Our society does not encourage adults taking advantage of children. Pedophilia requires psychological treatment, but the results of treatments, including hormone therapy and castration, are not entirely effective.

Other sexual preferences require treatment only when a person identifies them as a problem. For example, *homosexuality* is a behavioral pattern that involves an atypical sexual preference, but homosexuality by itself is not considered a psychological or psychiatric disorder. Early systems of classification had listed homosexuality as a sexual deviation, but in 1973 homosexuality was dropped from the official list of sexual disorders. Currently, only homosexual behavior that is *ego-dystonic* is considered a psychological disorder. Ego-dystonic homosexuality refers to homosexual arousal which distresses the person who experiences it, who wishes to be heterosexual.

ADDICTIVE DISORDERS

The immediate effects of alcohol, marijuana, cocaine, and the entire range of other drugs are often described as pleasant, and there are pressures from peers and advertisements to share in the pleasure. We are coaxed to think

The short-term effects of alcohol include a relaxed sense of warmth and conviviality. (Susan Rosenberg)

that a certain beer will make us more successful socially. Alcohol does result in a more relaxed state for most people. Although alcohol has certain physiological and expectational effects that produce relaxation, what are the long-term effects of involvement with alcohol and drugs? When the involvement goes beyond reasonable limits, *abuse* and *dependence* can result.

Substance abuse is different from the occasional, nonpathological use of a substance. In substance abuse the person shows a pattern of pathological and excessive use that results in physical and psychological deterioration and impairs social and work performance. DSM III requires that this pattern be evident for at least a month for a diagnosis of substance abuse.

Substance dependence is more severe than abuse and is said to require physiological dependence on the substance. Tolerance and withdrawal are used as evidence of the physiological dependence. *Tolerance* refers to the need for increased amounts of the substance to achieve a certain desired effect. Tolerance can also be seen in a diminished effect from the same dose. *Withdrawal* refers to the pattern of behavior that results from reducing or ending taking the substance.

Because the short-term effects of alcohol and drugs may be pleasant, one might speculate that the addictions result from too much of a good thing. But what do the data suggest are the best explanations for the development of addictive behavior?

Let's consider alcoholism. Familial, psychological, and social factors have been suggested as causal contributors to alcoholism. Although there does appear to be a greater chance that an offspring of an alcoholic will become alcoholic compared to the offspring of nonalcoholics, the data (Goodwin, 1976; 1979) are not entirely convincing. Not all children of alcoholics become alcoholic. Indeed, most do not develop alcohol problems. Thus, although there seem to be some familial features, a familial or genetic explanation is not sufficient by itself.

Psychological factors leading to problems with alcohol can be as varied as the types of people who have alcohol-related troubles. Of those that have received wide attention, the tension reduction cycle and its associated reinforcement are often subscribed to. The stress reduction cycle involves the taking of alcohol as a learned response to anxiety, tension, and general stress. As we know, alcohol does have certain relaxing qualities. It is argued that the person who turns to alcohol when tense experiences this reduction, which reinforces the use of alcohol in later stressful situations. The pattern is maintained by the immediate tension reduction. Thus alcoholism is seen as a learned, maladaptive response that is maintained by the short-term effects of tension reduction even in the face of the negative long-term effects.

Social influences have also been implicated in the development of alcohol problems. Peer pressure is one such influence. Most students in your class probably began to drink under peer influence. The same can be said of drugs and the role of the social group. Evidence for the impact of social factors on alcoholism comes from cross-cultural research. Some cultural groups that show restrained practices of alcohol use have low rates of alcoholism, whereas in other cultures, with an acceptance of the liberal ingestion of alcohol, the incidence is 10 times that of other populations.

HIGHLIGHT 15.7
Expectations and the Effects of Alcohol

Did you ever hear that alcohol affected sexuality? Do you think it does? Some people think that alcohol reduces sexual pleasure—after all, alcohol is a depressant. Others think that alcohol heightens it. Or is the effect one way or the other simply the result of what we expect?

Wilson and his colleagues (Wilson & Lawson, 1976; Abrams & Wilson, 1979) conducted a series of studies to determine the separate effects of having ingested *actual alcohol* and the effects of the *expectation* of having had an alcoholic drink. Men social drinkers were assigned to one of two groups. In one the subjects were led to believe that the beverage they were drinking was vodka and tonic. In the other condition, subjects were told that the drink was tonic only. For half of each group the drink was really alcohol. For the other half of each group, it was really only tonic. Thus the researchers could study the separate effects of alcohol and expectations.

Subjects were shown erotic films and sexual arousal was measured using several methods, such as a penile strain gauge. The results indicated that alcohol had *no* effect on sexual arousal. However, subjects who *believed* that they had consumed alcohol manifested greater sexual arousal than those believing they had consumed the tonic, regardless of the actual contents of their drinks!

In a study using women social drinkers, subjects were again either given or led to believe that they were given vodka and tonic or tonic only. Instead of the erotic films, subjects were instructed to interact with a confederate as part of a study of social anxiety. Women who *expected* that they had drunk alcohol evidenced elevations in physiological arousal and were noted by observers as more anxious. Subjects who believed that they had consumed alcohol, irrespective of the actual contents of their drinks, showed significant increases in the level of arousal.

Using men and the same social anxiety paradigm, Wilson and Abrams (1977) again found that expectations, not alcohol itself, affected arousal. For males, however, the expectational effects reduced arousal. Taken together, these data show the decisive influence of cognition (expectations) as opposed to physiological processes in determining the effects of alcohol.

ABNORMAL BEHAVIOR IN CHILDHOOD

As with adult disorders, there have been several systems proposed for the classification of childhood psychopathology. Within the DSM III system a separate section was set aside for disorders "usually arising in childhood or adolescence." Our coverage will take a closer look at two of them—attention deficit disorder and autism.

ATTENTION DEFICIT DISORDER

Hyperactivity, or attention deficit disorder with hyperactivity, is probably the most common of the childhood disorders. Barkley (1982) suggests that approximately 3 to 5% of the school-aged population show problems of this type. Various sources note that the disorder is seen more in boys than girls, at a ratio of about 10:1.

The main features of this problemmatic behavior pattern include distractibility, limited attention span, impulsiveness, restlessness, overactivity, and noncompliance. For DSM III, a duration of at least a year and onset before age 5 (Barkley, 1982) are required for the diagnosis.

Medication of hyperactive children with a psychostimulant seems to produce slowed and more focused behavior (Whalen, 1982). Medicated children do not necessarily improve in their schoolwork, nor do they learn "better," but they do seem to be less troublesome in class. It was once thought that this slowing effect produced by a psychostimulant medication was "paradoxical." However, hyperactive children and normal children seem to respond similarly to the drug (e.g., Rapaport, Buchsbaum, Weingarten, Zahn, Ludlow, & Mikkelson, 1980). These data speak to the need to be very careful when attempting to label someone as hyperactive simply because he or she showed the slowed behavior as a result of the stimulant medication. Although the drug has some short-term benefits, side effects, such as decreased appetite and sleep disturbances, and the absence of enduring benefits make a decision to use it quite difficult.

The exact causes of attention deficit disorders are not known. Current thinking would involve multiple causes, including learning history within the family and school, biological predispositions, cognitive deficits, and biological and brain dysfunctions. Similarly, current recommendations for treatment are varied, ranging from medications to behavioral (O'Leary, 1980) and cognitive-behavioral training (Kendall & Braswell, 1985).

AUTISM

One of the most serious disorders of childhood, autism, can often be recognized in the very early years of life and hence has been referred to as "early infantile autism." This disorder was first described by Kanner (1944) and later discussed by Rimland (1964). The disorder affects 1 in 2,000 to 3,000 births, and occurs more in boys than in girls.

Autism seems to know no bounds—autistic children can come from families of all backgrounds, races, or cultures. Scholars suggest that the disorder involves dysfunctional development affecting the brain. Unfortunately, this conclusion is based in part on the fact that other explanations are unsatis-

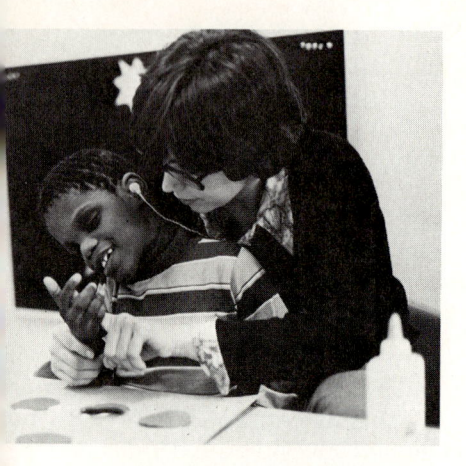

Autism, one of the most serious childhood disorders, affects 1 in 2000 to 3000 births and occurs more often in boys than girls. (David M. Grossman)

factory. For example, Hanson and Gottesman (1976) concluded that the disorder did not appear to be a genetic or inherited problem, and many others have long discounted the notion that autistic children are the result of cold and unloving parents.

The autistic child is reported to have been "noncuddly" as an infant and nonresponsive to others: for example not reaching out when being lifted and not smiling when being talked to or fed. Communication difficulties are apparent in the restricted use of speech seen in autistic children. *Echolalia*, the repeating back of words spoken by another person, is often present, as is reversal of pronouns and the use of noncommunicative verbalizations. Some of the behavioral peculiarities that have been reported include a preoccupation with sameness, an interest in fitting together small objects, attachments to odd objects, and repetitive gestures.

Rutter (1978) provided a comprehensive review of the literature on autism, and his criteria for a diagnosis represent the essential features of the disorder as seen by most contemporary professionals. Indeed, they parallel the features required by DSM III:

1. Onset prior to the age of 30 months
2. Pervasive lack of responsiveness to others
3. Delayed and deviant language development
4. Insistence on sameness and preoccupation with the unusual objects

Autistic children have been treated with many medical and psychological therapies, but no cure is currently available.

One important note: Early infantile autism is considered a separate disorder from childhood schizophrenia. Typically, children identified as schizophrenic have gone through a period of relatively normal development. The age of onset is older (closer to 10 years of age or adolescence), and the disorder occurs less frequently than autism.

SUMMARY

1. Attempts to define abnormality have included cultural, personal, statistical, and clinical approaches. From each perspective it seems clear that abnormal behavior is maladaptive behavior. Insanity is a legal term associated with incompetence and the need for commitment to an institution.

2. Explanations of abnormal behavior include learning, psychodynamic, systems, and medical models. The learning model proposes that abnormal behaviors are acquired by the same principles of learning that govern normal behavior. The psychodynamic perspective focuses on internal mentalistic concepts such as id, ego, superego and on the effects of stunted psychological growth. Social networks, such as families and peer groups, are seen as producing repetitious patterns of behavior, including abnormal behavior, and these forces are central to the systems theorist. The medical model views abnormal behavior as the result of disease (biological/biochemical maladies).

3. There are advantages and disadvantages associated with efforts to classify abnormal behavior. The major system for such classification is the third edition of the Diagnostic and Statistical Manual (DSM III).

4. Schizophrenia is a set of major disorders marked by dysfunctions in thinking, affect, and behavior. Symptoms include delusions, hallucinations, extreme social

withdrawal, and occasional bizarre behavior. Genetic and biochemical factors, as well as environmental factors, are associated with the etiology of schizophrenia. Subtypes of schizophrenia include disorganized, catatonic, paranoid, undifferentiated, and residual.

5. Affective disorders, including bipolar affective disorder, major depressive disorder, and cyclothymic disorder, have been explained by biological, psychodynamic and cognitive-behavioral theories.

6. Anxiety disorders concern an unwanted and irrational sense of threat and impending danger. Anxious persons avoid conflict and misperceive the demands of the environment. Samples of anxiety disorders include generalized anxiety disorders, phobic disorders, and obsessive-compulsive disorders.

7. Somatoform disorders are problems that appear to be physical but are related to psychological difficulties.

8. Personality disorders, such as the narcissistic, dependent, antisocial, and paranoid personality disorders, are not major psychological maladies, but they are ingrained maladaptive patterns that impair adaptive functioning.

9. Psychological factors are involved in sexual functioning and psychological causes are a part of many sexual dysfunctions.

10. Childhood psychopathology includes attention deficit disorder (perhaps the most prevalent problem among children) and a more rare but serious disorder, autism.

KEY TERMS

trephining
exorcism
cultural definition of abnormality
personal definition of abnormality
statistical definition of abnormality
clinical definition of abnormality
insanity
learning model
psychodynamic model
systems model
medical model
fixation
DSM III
multiaxial diagnosis
schizophrenia
neologisms
anhedonia
delusions
hallucinations
social drift hypothesis

diathesis-stress model
disorganized schizophrenia
catatonic schizophrenia
paranoid schizophrenia
undifferentiated schizophrenia
residual schizophrenia
bipolar disorder
acute disorder
chronic disorder
neurotic disorder
psychotic disorder
organic disorder
functional disorder
depression
cyclothymia
learned helplessness
attributions
anxiety
generalized anxiety disorder
phobic disorders

obsessive-compulsive disorder
somatoform disorder
conversion disorder
narcissistic personality disorder
dependent personality disorder
paranoid personality disorder
sexual dysfunction
impotence
frigidity
paraphilia
ego-dystonic homosexuality
substance abuse
substance dependence
tolerance
withdrawal
attention deficit disorder
autism
echolalia

SUGGESTED READINGS

American Psychiatric Association. *Diagnostic and statistical manual of mental disorders* (3rd ed.): *DSM III.* Washington, D.C.: American Psychiatric Association, 1980. The third edition of the diagnostic manual contains a wealth of information about all the disorders. As part of this comprehensive classificatory system, DSM III provides diagnostic criteria, the essential features of the disorder, and related information (e.g., age of onset, prevalence, sex ratio, differential diagnosis).

Coleman, J. C., Butcher, J. N., & Carson, C. R. *Abnormal psychology and modern life.* (7th ed.). Glenview, Ill.: Scott, Foresman, 1984. The textbook provides a comprehensive presentation of the psychology of abnormal behavior. The presentation includes a framework for understanding abnormal behavior, the details of the causes and treatments of abnormal behavior, and general issues related to assessment and prevention of abnormal behavior.

Neale, J. M., & Oltmanns, T. F. *Schizophrenia.* New York: Wiley, 1980. This book provides an in-depth look at the conceptualizations, causes, symptoms, and treatments for the various forms of schizophrenia.

16

Therapies for Behavior Problems

PSYCHOANALYTIC THERAPY:
   THE FREUDIAN
   APPROACH
  Psychoanalysis: Does It Work?
CLIENT-CENTERED THERAPY:
   THE ROGERIAN
   APPROACH
  The Effects of Client-Centered
   Therapy
BEHAVIOR THERAPY
  Systematic Densensitization
  Operant Procedures
  Modeling
COGNITIVE-BEHAVIORAL
   THERAPY
  Rational Emotive Therapy
  Cognitive-Behavioral
   Treatment of Depression
  Cognitive-Behavioral Therapy
   with Children
OTHER PSYCHOLOGICAL
   THERAPIES

  Reality Therapy
  Gestalt Therapy
  Transactional Analysis
  Existential Therapy
GROUP THERAPY
  Family Therapy
COMMUNITY INTERVENTIONS
THE EFFECTS OF
   PSYCHOLOGICAL
   THERAPY
  Negative Effects of Therapy
MEDICAL APPROACHES TO
   THE TREATMENT OF
   PSYCHOLOGICAL
   PROBLEMS
  Drugs
  Psychosurgery
  Electroconvulsive Therapy
SUMMARY
KEY TERMS
SUGGESTED READINGS

It is Sunday morning and you are going to treat yourself and a friend to brunch. As you stroll to the restaurant you pass a woman in her mid-thirties shaving her legs, shaving cream and all, right in front of a main shopping area. What is she doing?

   You are at the airport about to depart for a visit with old friends. A young man approaches and introduces himself. He says that he is very fearful of people and has difficulty talking to strangers. As he finishes the sentence, he seems to be lost for words. You try to fill in the dead time and reply with a quizzical "Oh, I didn't know." What was he doing?

Both instances are illustrations of homework assignments given by a therapist for a client. In each case, the therapist and client have worked together to identify the client's problem. The homework tasks are assigned to help the client work on and overcome the target problem. For example, our public shaver is a neurotic perfectionist. Not your average perfectionist, but one whose life is burdened by needs for perfection in everything. She would arrive at work at 7:55 every day. Just thinking about a different time of arrival made her extremely tense and anxious. At work, all reports had to be retyped if there was even one error. Our client would worry excessively about what others would think about her and about an error or typo. Each hair on her head was in place, every piece of clothing starched and pressed. Are you getting the picture? Our client was so overcontrolled and worried about what others thought that she could not allow herself a chance to live and enjoy life. Her homework assignment was designed to demonstrate to her that even after she does something "shameful" she is still an okay person.

The socially anxious male who approached you at the airport was also trying to overcome his problem. Because his concern was interpersonal and social, the homework task was to go out and say hello to some strangers. This assignment was given to the client after the client had had a chance to learn conversation skills in the therapist's office and after he had a chance to practice them in a role-play with the therapist. The homework is intended to help the client learn to behave differently outside the treatment sessions.

Nick had been diagnosed schizophrenic. He had been living alone, in an abandoned shack, taking handouts and part-time dishwashing jobs, and eking out an extremely basic life-style.

One afternoon Nick arrived at a mental health center. He was interviewed and again diagnosed as schizophrenic. To assist Nick in his personal and social functioning, he was assigned a therapist and scheduled for a standing weekly appointment. The therapist would provide support as well as seek to remediate some of Nick's maladaptive and bizarre thinking and behavior. Correspondingly, Nick was assigned a time for his medication clinic and given a prescription for a drug that would clear his thinking and help him to adjust. A social worker arranged to visit Nick's residence and sought to find him more stable living quarters and a consistent means of employment. It was decided that Nick did not need to be hospitalized, but that the outpatient multidisciplinary program would be tried first.

A wide range of psychological therapies is available for helping disturbed clients. Indeed, the bulk of this chapter describes the major therapeutic approaches used today. Some of these therapies emphasize enhancing self-knowledge, others emotional well-being, and still others behavioral skills.

Although therapists use a variety of techniques to achieve their goals, certain features are common to them all. First, therapists establish a genuine and caring relationship with their clients. Second, therapists and clients work together to improve the client's ability to overcome psychological problems. Third, therapists teach skills to clients to enhance their future functioning. Fourth, therapists apply principles derived from psychological theory and research.

Although therapy is a complicated and demanding endeavor, the basic definitions of different theoretical orientations have some remarkable similarities. For instance, all *therapy* emphasizes helping clients overcome personal problems and acquiring more self-determination—therapy is an educational process.

The present chapter will describe some of the major psychological therapies—major in the sense that they are most prominent (see data in Highlight

16.1) and/or most effective (see data on pages 536–538). Other psychological approaches will also be described, but in less detail. Medical approaches to therapy and the ethics of therapy will also be considered.

PSYCHOANALYTIC THERAPY: THE FREUDIAN APPROACH

Thirty-five years ago many nonprofessionals thought of Sigmund Freud's *psychoanalysis* as *the* sole form of psychological therapy. Professionals were aware of some other intervention strategies, but the public was still enamored with the lie-on-the-couch, tell-all-you-know form of treatment. Traditional psychoanalysis often involved several 1-hour sessions per week for 2 to 5 years or longer. Due to dissatisfactions with the length and cost of analytic treatment and concerns about the effectiveness of psychoanalysis, other forms of psychological therapy have developed and flourished in recent years. Nevertheless, psychoanalysis remains both an oft-used and historically important form of treatment.

The process of psychoanalysis involves the therapist's use of interpretations to help the client accept into conscious awareness certain feelings, thoughts, and needs that have been kept unconscious. That is, problems resulting from an overuse of the defense mechanisms to reduce anxiety. These defense mechanisms (see Chapter 14) lead the person to avoid rather than confront and resolve conflicts, and the conflcits, left unresolved, are banished to the unconscious. The psychoanalyst believes that the conflicts will never be fully resolved unless the client accepts them into consciousness and understands them. Current emotional problems are said to stem from unresolved childhood experiences, and by uncovering and resolving the childhood experiences, the therapist tries to resolve the current problems.

How are these unconscious conflicts brought into awareness? Psychoanalytic therapists believe that "insight," the conscious knowledge of one's

Sigmund Freud (1856–1939) in his study in 1936. (Mary Evans/Sigmund Freud)

conflicts, is essential to therapeutic success. Analysts help their clients gain insight first by aiding them to reveal their unconscious impulses and defenses, and then by offering interpretations designed to help the client understand and accept them. *Free association* is intended to help the client reveal unconscious conflicts. When asked to free associate, clients are being asked to express thoughts and feelings as they come into consciousness without censure. *Interpretations* are an important tool for communicating with the client. I. B. Weiner (1975) describes an interpretation as a statement that uses something the patient has said or done to identify features of the client's behavior of which he or she has not been fully aware. Thus the therapist interprets the client's free associations, dreams, silences, and slips of the tongue to bring repressed conflict into awareness.

Roadblocks are experienced as the therapist tries to drive unconscious material into consciousness. This *resistance* is said to be evident when the client is unwilling to express true feelings, to divulge actual thoughts, or to accept the interpretations of the therapist. There are other signs of resistance for some, such as the pauses in the client's speech and the blocking of ideas in thought. Because clients are at first unwilling to accept interpretations in general and interpretations of resistance in particular, the therapist may simply make notes. Later in treatment, however, the therapist will interpret slips of the tongue and/or hesitations as resistance.

The *transference* relationship is one of the main forces of resistance in psychoanalytic therapy. In the transference relationship, the client reexperiences the thoughts and feelings experienced in childhood when relating to an authority figure. With the therapist as the authority figure, the early and unresolved conflicts are reenacted. If the client aggressed toward authority, he or she will also aggress toward the therapist (see Transcript 1). The therapist's job is to help the client to understand these unconscious conditions, and having overcome them, relate to the therapist in a more meaningful fashion. This process is referred to as "working through." *Countertransference* refers to the feelings that the therapist has toward the client. These feelings must also be recognized and kept from interfering with treatment.

Transcript 1: Example of Psychoanalytic Features of Therapy

INTERPRETATIONS: *Because effective interpretations are often associated with their careful and cautious use, the following transcript illustrates how to proceed toward an interpretation.*

CLIENT: We had a salesmen's meeting, and a large group of us were cramped together in a small room, and they turned out the lights to show some slides, and I got so jumpy and anxious I couldn't stand it.

THERAPIST: So what happened? [Question]

CLIENT: I just couldn't stand it, I was sweating and shaking, so I got up and left, and I know I'll be called on the carpet for walking out.

THERAPIST: You became so anxious and upset that you couldn't stand being in the room, even though you knew that walking out would get you into trouble. [Clarification]

CLIENT: Yeah . . . What could have bothered me so much to make me do a dumb thing like that?

THERAPIST: You know, we've talked about other times in your life when you've become upset in close quarters with other men, once when you were in the army and again in your dormitory at college. [Confrontation]

CLIENT: That's right, and it was the same kind of thing again.

THERAPIST: And if I'm correct, this has never happened to you in a group of men and women together, no matter how closely you've been cramped together. [Further confrontation]

CLIENT: Uh . . . Yes, that's right.

THERAPIST: So it appears that something especially about being physically close to other men, and especially in the dark, makes you anxious, as if you're afraid something bad might happen in that kind of situation. [Interpretation]

CLIENT: (Pause) I think you're right about that . . . and I know I'm not physically afraid of other men. Do you think it might be sexual, that I might get worried about something homosexual taking place?

—from I. B. WEINER (1975), p. 142.

RESISTANCE: *When the client is slow or unwilling to express his or her true feelings, psychoanalysts refer to this as resistance. Consider the following example.*

CLIENT: I can see that there must be something more to my coming so late today, but I don't know what it could be.

THERAPIST: It's as if you don't want to talk much.

C: How do you mean?

T: The less time you're here, the less time there is for you to talk.

C: Okay, but that would seem to mean there's something I don't want to talk about. Could that be it?

T: You seemed to have some strong feelings during our last session.

C: Did I? Oh yes, I remember, I had just started to tell you about what I did with my husband before we were married—you know, sexually—and how guilty I feel about it, and . . . well, that must be it. I remember when I left I had the thought that I never wanted to come back if it meant I would have to talk more about that subject.

—from I. B. WEINER (1975), p. 198.

TRANSFERENCE: *The therapist's task is to know how the client's perceptions might differ from reality. The client may be unaware of the transference reations and they will require clarification. For instance:*

CLIENT: You seem in a sour mood today, like you're ready to bite my head off.

THERAPIST: What suggests that to you?

C: I don't know. I'm just not getting the right vibes, like you're not in a good mood or you're feeling down on me.

T: I'm not aware of being in a bad mood or feeling down on you. I wonder if there might be some reason why you're perceiving me in that way.

C: (Pauses, appears thoughtful) Well, I suppose maybe there is. I've got something I think I should tell you, and I don't know how you'll take it. (Pause) I've decided to move in with my boyfriend, and I have the feeling you may disapprove.

—from I. B. WEINER (1975), p. 235.

PSYCHOANALYSIS: DOES IT WORK?

Given that psychoanalysis has been a major influence in psychological therapy, it is exceedingly surprising that there are few, even reasonably well controlled studies of its effectiveness. The oft-described years of analytic treatment are as yet unevaluated experimentally, and the data that we do have typically refer to short or condensed versions of analysis (e.g., Sloane, Staples, Cristol, Yorkston, & Whipple, 1975). There are volumes and volumes on psychoanalytic procedures and case reports of outcomes, but most reports are lacking sufficient assessments and controls (and other types of methodological rigor). As readers, the theory and practical approach are interesting, if not exciting. However, as scientists, we must remain unconvinced of the efficacy of psychoanalytic treatment until evidence is presented.

CLIENT-CENTERED THERAPY: THE ROGERIAN APPROACH

Carl Rogers (1951), the originator and major proponent of client-centered therapy, argues that effective therapy results when certain identifiable "therapist conditions" are available and presented to the client. When these are present to a high degree, improvement will be greater than when the conditions are only minimally present. The specific therapist conditions that Rogers desires are *genuineness, accurate empathy,* and *unconditional positive regard.*

Genuineness, considered the most basic of the three therapist conditions, refers to the therapist's allowing his or her inner experiences and feelings to emerge honestly and openly within the therapy. With no room for facade, the therapist must be his or her true self and respond honestly.

Empathy refers to shared emotional responsiveness, involving both an understanding of the client's experience and the emotions associated with it. Accurate empathy involves the active emersion of the therapist in the experiences of the client. As part of this process, the therapist tries to understand the client's personal situation.

Unconditional positive regard means accepting the client as a decent human being without judgment or evaluation, and trusting the client's own abilities to improve.

One of the premises underlying the humanistic, client-centered approach is that for personal growth, people must take a careful and honest look at themselves. The therapist does not direct this self-examination but facilitates it, and by creating a climate with high levels of genuineness, empathy, and positive regard will best facilitate the client's own resolutions to his or her own problems. Indeed, one of the techniques of the client-centered therapy is reflecting, where the *therapist* helps the client to solve his or her own problems by restating and reflecting back to the client the client's own statements (see Transcript 2).

Carl Rogers, the originator of client-centered therapy. (Bettmann Archive)

Transcript 2: An Example of the Client-Centered Approach

CLIENT: I have the feeling it isn't guilt. (Pause; she weeps) Of course I mean, I can't verbalize it yet. (Then with a rush of emotion) It's just being terribly hurt!

THERAPIST: M-hm. It isn't guilt except in the sense of being very much wounded somehow.

C: (Weeping) It's—you know, often I've been guilty of it myself but in later years when I've heard parents say to their children, "stop crying," I've had a feeling, a hurt as though, well, why should they tell them to stop crying? They feel sorry for themselves, and who can feel more adequately sorry for himself than the child? Well, that is sort of what—I mean, as though I mean, I thought that they should let him cry. And—feel sorry for him too, maybe. In a rather objective kind of way. Well, that's—that's something of the kind of thing I've been experiencing. I mean, now—just right now. And in—in—

T: That catches a little more the flavor of the feelings that it's almost as if you're really weeping for yourself.

C: Yeah. And again you see there's conflict. Our culture is such that—I mean, one doesn't indulge in self-pity. But this isn't—I mean, I feel it doesn't quite have that connotation. It may have.

T: Sort of think that there is a cultural objection to feeling sorry about yourself. And yet you feel the feeling you're experiencing isn't quite what the culture objected to either.

C: And then of course, I've come to—to see and to feel that over this—see, I've covered it up. (Weeps) But I've covered it up with so much bitterness, which in turn I had to cover up. (Weeping) That's what I want to get rid of! I almost don't care if I hurt.

T (Softly, and with an empathic tenderness toward the hurt she is experiencing): You feel that here at the basis of it as you experience it is a feeling of real tears for yourself. But that you can't show, mustn't show, so that's been covered by bitterness that you don't like, that you'd like to be rid of. You almost feel you'd rather absorb the hurt than to—than to feel the bitterness. (Pause) And what you seem to be saying quite strongly is, I do hurt, and I've tried to cover it up.

C: I didn't know it.

T: M-hm. Like a new discovery really.

C (Speaking at the same time): I never really did now. But it's—you know, it's almost a physical thing. It's—it's sort of as though I were looking within myself at all kinds of—nerve endings and bits of things that have been sort of mashed. (Weeping)

T: As though some of the most delicate aspects of you physically almost have been crushed or hurt.

C: Yes. And you know, I do get the feeling, "Oh, you poor thing." (Pause)

T: Just can't help but feel very deeply sorry for the person that is you.

C: I don't think I feel sorry for the whole person; it's a certain aspect of the thing.

T: Sorry to see that hurt.

C: Yeah.

T: M-hm. M-hm.

C: And then of course there's this damn bitterness that I wanted to get rid of. It's—it gets me into trouble. It's because it's a tricky thing. It tricks me. (Pause)

T: Feel as though that bitterness is something you'd like to be rid of because it doesn't do right by you.

—*from* WEDDING AND CORSINI *(1979), pp. 86–87.*

THE EFFECTS OF CLIENT-CENTERED THERAPY

Although firmly based on a humanistic philosophy, the client-centered approach nevertheless recognizes the merits and uses the methods of science to study its effectiveness. Large-scale evaluations of treatment outcome as

In client-centered therapy, the therapist helps the client to solve his or her own problems by restating and reflecting back to the client the client's own statements. (George S. Zimbel/Monkmeyer)

well as more circumscribed investigations of specific features of the therapy have been published. For example, Truax, Wargo, Frank, Imber, Battle, Hoehn-Saric, Nash, and Stone (1966) reported that the clients who had received therapy with high levels of the three therapist conditions improved more than those whose therapists provided lesser degrees of the desired conditions.

Current debate on the effectiveness of client-centered therapy focuses on how the therapist conditions are measured. An outsider who listens to therapy tapes and rates the presence of the therapist conditions often rates the therapist conditions lower than a client does. That is, we are interested in the relationship between the *client's* perceptions of genuineness, empathy, and positive regard and the eventual outcome of the treatment. Gurman (1977) reported a positive relationship between the client's perceptions of the therapeutic conditions and positive outcomes. Critics may respond, however, that clients who perceive their therapist as genuine, empathic, and positive may be different from other clients before the therapy began, but current evidence suggests that the therapist features of genuineness, empathy, and unconditional positive regard may be important factors in effective psychotherapy.

BEHAVIOR THERAPY

Behavior therapy can be said to be the application of principles derived from experimental research on learning, cognition, and social and personality psychology to maladaptive behavior (Wilson, 1978). Most behavior therapists believe that maladaptive behavior is learned according to the same laws as normal behavior—the learning process is the same, but what is learned is different.

FOCUS ON THE PSYCHOLOGIST

G. Terence Wilson

G. TERENCE WILSON received B.A. (1965) and B.A. (Honours) (1966) degrees at the University of Witwatersrand, South Africa and a Ph.D. from the State University of New York at Stony Brook (1971). From 1971, except for two years spent at Stanford, he has been a faculty member at Rutgers University. He was a Fellow at the Center for Advanced Study in the Behavioral Sciences, at Stanford, (1976–77) and was appointed Oscar K. Buros Professor of Psychology at Rutgers University in 1985. In 1980 he was elected President of the Association for Advancement of Behavior Therapy.

I attended the University of Witwatersrand, South Africa. In my third year of studies I became interested in learning theory and behavior therapy. I decided to apply to a behavioral clinical Ph.D. program in the United States and, with good luck and the advice of Arnold Lazarus, chose the State University of New York at Stony Brook. The objectivity and rigor of behavior therapy appealed to me for several reasons. I came to view psychology as a scientific discipline. Behavior therapy seemed a logical extension of this scientific orientation. Although I was an avid reader of Freud, influenced by the writings of the philosopher Karl Popper and others, I felt that his theory was beyond the pale of scientific analysis. I was particularly influenced by my study of history. As an undergraduate I was fortunate to study history in the Oxford tutorial system, in which a small group of students met with their professor weekly. One of the group presented an essay, and the others had to critique it. We were taught to base our arguments and criticism on the "facts" of the matter. We were required always to document our position rather than engage in idle speculation. I credit this basic philosophical approach to scholarship as a key reason for my subsequent attraction to behavior therapy, based as it is on the same demand for logical and empirical justification of concepts and methods.

Last, but hardly least, personal influences helped to determine my decision to pursue a career in behavior therapy. My major mentor in Psychology at Wits was Alma Hannon, a staunch behaviorist from the Hullian tradition, who set standards of intellectual rigor to which I have always aspired. Peter Radloff, a remarkably well-read experimental psychologist, imbued me with a commitment to research. They, and the rest of the small Psychology Department, supported me when I was attacked, by the then and still dominant psychoanalytic hegemony in clinical psychology and psychiatry in South Africa, during my Honours year when a fellow student, Ian Evans, and I wrote papers critical of psychoanalysis. Although behavior therapy was very unpopular in South Africa, I was also sustained by the inspirational examples of three former South Africans, all with degrees from Wits, who, collectively, perhaps did more than anyone else to found the field of clinical behavior therapy, which was then (the mid-1960s) just emerging as a major force in Britain and the United States. I refer, of course, to Joseph Wolpe, Arnold Lazarus, and Stanley Rachman.

Originally, in going to the U.S., I had hoped to study with Wolpe and Lazarus, but they were not part of a doctoral program in psychology. Instead, Lazarus advised me to enroll at Stony Brook, where my mentor was Jerry Davison, a former student of Lazarus's at Stanford University. In Davison, and Harry Kalish, I found friends and teachers who cemented my commitment to a scientist-practitioner model of the clinical psychologist that is best exemplified by behavior therapy. While at Stony Brook, I frequently visited Lazarus in Philadelphia, where I received clinical instruction that helped to shape my view of therapy. From Davison, I received my introduction to Bandura's social learning theory and to cognitive psychology and how it could usefully expand the conditioning or learning theory foundations of behavior therapy.

Behavior therapy is also *performance based* (see Transcript 3). A performance-based intervention provides learning experiences for the client—experiences that involve attempts by the client to perform and practice new, to-be-learned behaviors. To maximize the effects, the therapist demonstrates the behaviors for the client, provides instructions and guidance, and offers feedback about the client's performance. In contrast to other therapeutic modalities, the behaviorist is less interested in early childhood experiences, in talking over the problems at length, or in an extensive examination of the client's life. The behaviorist is most interested in remedying the presenting problem by teaching new behavioral skills and evaluating the effects of the training via the scientific method.

Transcript 3: An Example of Behavior Therapy

Behavior therapy is performance-based. Here is an example of a role-play exercise. The client is a socially inadequate male.

THERAPIST: Let's take the situation where you see a woman standing in front of the bulletin board, and you go over to strike up a conversation. Ms. Phillips can play the part of the woman. [This situation involves being in the post office, which in no way resembles this consulting room. I'll have to spend some time setting the stage, so we can more realistically simulate the actual situation.] Tell me more about the physical setup. Where would the bulletin board be?

CLIENT: Right about here (pointing toward the wall).

T: What else?

C: Well, it would be in the post office, right near the window where they sell stamps.

T: And where would that be?

C: (Pointing) Right about here.

T: Where would you enter?

C: The corridor is down along here (pointing).

T: Do you have any questions before we begin?

C: No, I don't think so.

T: All right, then why don't you go down to the other end of the corridor, and come in.

C: (In role) Hello. My name is Bob. What's yours?

COTHERAPIST: (In role) Ann.

C: (Pause) Umm . . . what are you doing?

COTHERAPIST: Looking at this bulletin board.

T: [He's obviously having difficulty handling this situation. His social deficiency seems to be greater than I originally anticipated. I think I'll stop the interaction at this point, and let him hear himself on tape; I hope he'll be able to hear where he's having trouble.] (Rewinding tape recorder) Let's stop here and listen to it. (After reviewing tape) What do you think of it?

C: I sounded very awkward.

T: In what way?

C: I couldn't think of anything to say.

T: All right, let's discuss that for a moment. [Giving him feedback from the cotherapist would probably be helpful. It's unlikely that anyone in a real-life interaction would tell him what they thought of his comment.] (Turning to cotherapist) What was your reaction in that situation?

THERAPIES FOR BEHAVIOR PROBLEMS

COTHERAPIST: Well, I really didn't know how to take it when he came over to speak to me. I had never seen him before, and I thought it was strange that he should introduce himself so suddenly. I guess many other women would probably feel the same way in my situation.

T: [Time for some information on what might be a more socially appropriate alternative.] What do you think might be more appropriate to this particular situation?

COTHERAPIST: I guess if he came over and started reading the bulletin board, he might be able to make some comment about the notice itself.

T: (Turning to client) What's your reaction to that?

C: That probably would have been easier.

T: [Good. It's always helpful when the client seems receptive to your suggestion of a new way to respond. In light of the initial problems he had, though, I think it would be a good idea for me to model both the appropriate content and style of responding.] Let me be you for a moment, and go through this situation again. (In role, reading notice on bulletin board) They keep increasing the cost of stamps.

COTHERAPIST: (In role) I know. It's really outrageous.

T: (In role) I wonder why the cost keeps going up?

COTHERAPIST: Undoubtedly because of the incredible waste and inefficiency that goes on.

T: (Out of role) What did you notice in that situation?

C: (Smiling) It seemed to work better that time. You also seemed more sure of yourself.

T: [I feel flattered—a completely inappropriate reaction in this situation! Back to being a therapist. Let's see if he's able to identify some of the specific behavioral components associated with how I was interacting.] How could you tell?

C: Well, you started by saying something about what was on the bulletin board. Also, you didn't hesitate when you spoke, the way I did.

T: Okay. Why don't you go through that situation again, this time trying to react in much the same way as I did.

—*from* GOLDFRIED AND DAVISON *(1976), pp. 147–149.*

SYSTEMATIC DESENSITIZATION

Systematic desensitization (Wolpe, 1958) is based on counterconditioning. In *counterconditioning,* through repeated training a new incompatible response is substituted for an existing undesirable response. Where counterconditioning is applied to treat anxiety, for example, the client is gradually taught to replace an anxiety response with a relaxation response. Two features of systematic desensitization are worth elaboration: relaxation training and the anxiety hierarchy.

Since relaxation is the incompatible response that will replace the anxiety response, the client must first be taught how to relax. The first several sessions and homework assignments therefore teach relaxation. Cassette tapes are often provided to facilitate home learning. Once clients have learned to relax, they are instructed to relax deeply while imagining the anxiety-producing situation(s). To guarantee that relaxation will replace the anxiety response, the client imagines the anxiety "scenes" in a predetermined hierarchy. The therapist acquires detailed information about the client's anxiety, and after a thorough assessment, the anxiety-producing situations are ranked according to the degree of anxiety associated with each—the anxiety hierarchy. The least anxiety-provoking item on the hierarchy is presented first to the client, who is now relaxed. The anxiety associated with the hierarchy item should be weak enough to be inhibited by the state of relaxation. Gradually, more and more anxiety-producing stimuli are presented to the client, moving up the hierarchy, replacing anxiety with relaxation.

Besides imaginary desensitization scenes, the therapist can use the systematic desensitization procedures in the client's actual environment and in the presence of the feared stimulus (or situation). *Contact* or *in situ desensitization* is the name for these procedures by which the client engages in graduated exposure in the naturalistic setting. Paul (1966) reported on a study which focused on college students who were identified as being under high distress when speaking in public. Participants were assigned to one of four groups: systematic desensitization, insight-oriented psychotherapy, an attention-placebo control group, and a test-retest control group. Subjects in the desensitization condition were taught to relax and were then presented with a hierarchy of anxiety items that began with reading about a speech and culminated with delivering a speech before a large audience. The insight-oriented therapy used interpretive methods to pursue the reasons for the anxiety and to seek self-understanding by the client. The attention-placebo group received sessions where they performed a task and were administered a drug (placebo). The test-retest subjects constituted a no-treatment control.

The treatment lasted for five sessions distributed over 6 weeks. The results of this study indicated that, in general, systematic desensitization was superior to the other treatment conditions. Other studies (see Kazdin & Wilcoxon, 1976) have supported the therapeutic effectiveness of systematic desensitization. However, although we can be confident that it works with phobias, it is not necessarily effective with other disorders, and although it produces desired gains, it is currently being debated and tested to see whether the effects are truly due to counterconditioning.

OPERANT PROCEDURES

The application of the principles of positive and negative reinforcement, shaping by successive approximations, and discrimination/generalization training represent a widely used approach within behavior therapy. Such operant methods are at the heart of behavioral interventions, interventions based on the behavior change technologies of B. F. Skinner. Operant conditioning procedures are a part of many behavioral interventions, including assertiveness training, treatment of depression, biofeedback, hospital ward management programs (token economies), parent training programs, and classroom management strategies, to mention a few.

Behavior therapy for depression includes a treatment strategy that illustrates the application of positive reinforcement (e.g., Lewinsohn, Biglan, & Zeiss, 1976; McLean, 1976). Clients are aided in developing "menus" of "pleasant events" that can reinforce self-enhancing behaviors, such as maintaining social relationships, exercising, and working productively. Positive reinforcement contingencies increase the frequency of such mood-promoting actions. For instance, a depressed person might develop a plan to get up and work on a meaningful project each morning, rather than sleeping excessively.

THERAPIES FOR BEHAVIOR PROBLEMS

Biofeedback is one of many operant conditioning procedures developed from the behavior change technologies of B. F. Skinner. (Peter Menzel/Stock Boston)

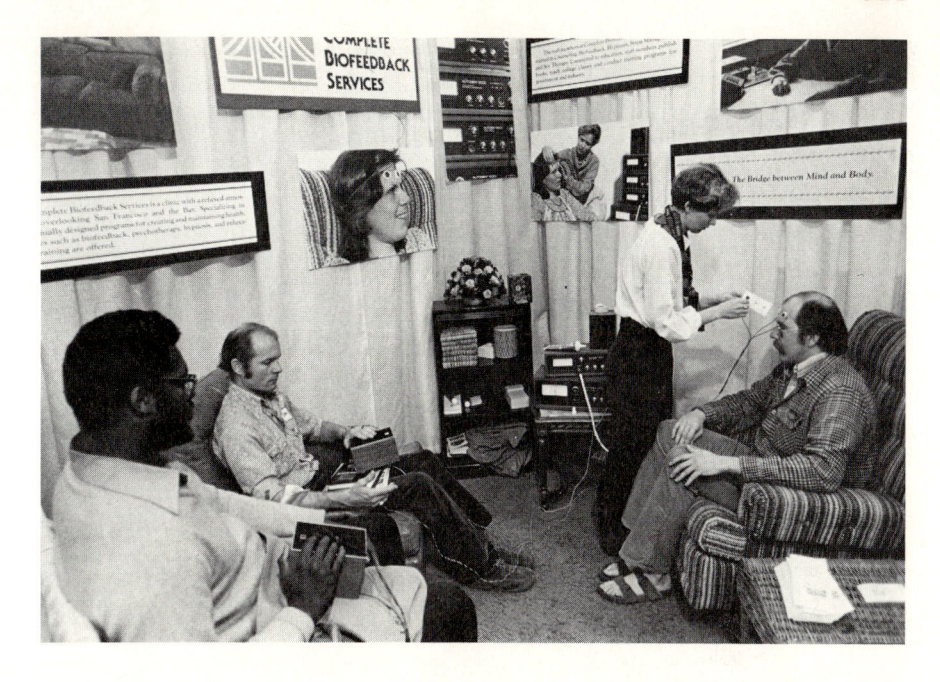

The enjoyment of the project serves as a positive reinforcer to sustain the renewing habit of rising each morning.

Shaping (by successive approximations) of behavior is often effective, especially when a complex skill, such as assertiveness (Rich & Schroeder, 1976), must be learned. People who experience difficulty standing up for their rights, expressing their opinions, or refusing unreasonable requests are referred to as unassertive. Assertion training encompasses several behavioral strategies, including shaping. Indeed, shaping by successive approximations is perhaps the fundamental method, involving the provision of positive reinforcement to clients as they gradually learn to perform more and more assertive behaviors. Similar to desensitization, a hierarchy of assertion skills is often constructed by the therapist and client, with each successive skill building on all previous ones. The client is usually rewarded by sincere praise from the therapist and by the satisfaction of seeing improvement for successively mastering each skill.

Probably the most systematic and illustrative example of applied operant conditioning is the token economy (Kazdin, 1977). A token economy is the use of a simulated economic system to establish systematic reinforcement contingencies (Atthowe & Krasner, 1968; Ayllon & Azrin, 1968). On a mental hospital ward, for example, this might take the form of (1) an explicit statement of the behaviors that can earn reinforcers, and (2) a simulated monetary currency that is used for actually distributing reinforcers. The desired behaviors might include actions relevant to personal hygiene (e.g., bathing, clean clothes), ward maintenance (e.g., chores such as washing floors), social interaction (e.g., conversation with another patient), and self-improvement (e.g., participation in educational or therapy groups). When the desired behavior is satisfactorily completed, the patient is credited with reinforcement points through the use of "tokens" (e.g., poker chips, point cards) that can later be exchanged for reinforcers such as snacks, day or weekend passes out of the hospital, special time for meetings with the ward psychologist, or advancement to a higher status in the ward program. Many token economies use "level systems." Patients are placed in one of several hierarchical levels depending on their earnings and performance in the token economy, with each level affording greater freedom and access to luxuries. The basic intention of the token economy is to teach clients that responsible behavior has a positive payoff.

For the token economy system to have the effects for which it was designed, it requires staff training, system monitoring, and the proper choice of "reinforcers." Staff training may be the key feature to a successful token economy. It is a serious drawback when staff fail to employ the program consistently; not only will clients learn that the system is flawed, but also that they can get away with inappropriate behavior (or have desired actions go unrewarded).

MODELING

In modeling, behavior is learned simply by observing another person perform the behavior. Modeling has produced beneficial effects in many areas: overcoming behavioral deficits, reducing excessive fears, and enhancing interpersonal behavior (Bandura, 1969; Rosenthal & Bandura, 1978).

When behavior therapists employ modeling procedures, they expose the client to a person or group who actually demonstrate the behaviors to be learned by the client. If a client lacks the ability to ask someone for a date, the model would demonstrate several versions of approach behavior. The client, literally, gets to see the behavior in action and its effects. Since words often cannot describe the necessary and appropriate features of behavior, demonstrations are very helpful for clients trying to learn new skills.

Role-playing involves having clients observe role models and then participate in a role-playing exercise in which they receive corrective feedback and reward for improved behavior. (Marion Faller/Monkmeyer)

Research has indicated that characteristics of the model can have significant effects on observational learning. If you were to observe a high-status person whom you perceived as similar to yourself in some ways, you would be more likely to acquire the modeled behavior. Furthermore, if the model has been associated with positive reinforcement, the behaviors that are modeled are more likely to be picked up by the observer. Similarly, if the model's behavior actually results in positive consequences, the observer is more likely to engage in that behavior than if the behavior was not rewarded or punished. Apparently, many of the principles of learning apply to observational learning, and behavior therapists use modeling techniques to help their clients learn the skills to live a more autonomous and satisfying life.

The therapeutic application of modeling can benefit greatly from attention to one further distinction: the difference between mastery and coping models. Let's examine this direction in terms of teaching a child who is afraid of the water how to swim. A *mastery model* would demonstrate fearless behavior: walking up to the pool, diving in, swimming a few laps crawl stroke, and perhaps another lap backstroke. The mastery model demonstrated fearless and competent swimming. But is this the most beneficial style for client? Is the model failing to take advantage of any possible similarities to the client? Research evidence (Kazdin, 1974; Meichenbaum, 1971; Sarason, 1975) documents that a *coping model* produces superior effects to a mastery model. A coping model initially demonstrates fear, includes a demonstration of overcoming the fear, and subsequently performs successfully. Our swimming model, as a coping model, would first approach the pool, but then back off, perhaps gradually dipping a foot, leg, and so on, into the water. Once half immersed, a head dip to get totally wet might follow after a minute of just getting comfortable in the water. Once in the pool and wet, the model would try a stroke or two, stop and recognize the success, and then proceed to swim further. The coping model has several features more similar to the client than the mastery model—for instance, a strategy for overcoming the fear of immersing oneself in water.

Including for the client access to the model's "thoughts" as he or she demonstrates as a coping model further enhances therapeutic effectiveness. But how do we gain such access? One method that has been shown to facilitate observational learning involves having the model "talk out loud" while serving as a coping model (Meichenbaum, 1971). A model who self-verbalizes out loud provides further strategy for overcoming the fear. For instance, our coping swimming model who self-verbalizes might approach the pool hesitantly and say, "I can't swim well, I'm not going in." After a moment or two, he or she could add, "Well, I'll just go in to get wet, it's like a big bath." After additional elapsed time, the model might state, "Hey, this isn't too bad, I think I may dunk my head. No, I don't want water up my nose—but I can pinch my nose, that will work. I'll do one quick dunk." As you can see, this self-dialogue helps model for the client (fearful swim student) several ways to overcome some of the fear.

Numerous behavioral therapies involve some form of modeling, and an equally large number of behavior therapists report using modeling procedures. Research has indicated that modeling can be beneficial and its widespread use seems justified. However, modeling techniques are typically not employed as the sole clinical treatment, but are included as a part of more comprehensive interventions. Indeed, although more circumscribed problems can be treated using a predominantly modeling approach, complicated problems justify a combination of intervention techniques.

HIGHLIGHT 16.1

Therapists' Self Identification: Therapists Answer the Question: "What Kind of Therapist Are You?

Many varieties of psychological therapy are described and discussed in this chapter. Some have a longer history than others, while some have a more sound research base than others. Also, some are more prominent among mental health practitioners than others. Knowing how therapists self-identify in terms of their school of therapy tells us about the distribution of different types of therapists.

Garfield and Kurtz (1976) surveyed 855 doctoral-level clinical psychologists and found that 54% identified themselves as holding an *eclectic* orientation. Eclecticism does not mean a poorly systematized approach, nor does it imply a lack of discipline. Rather, contemporary eclecticism refers to masterful integration, where the therapist is not blinded by a single set of theoretical assumptions or limited by a unitary approach to treatment.

Similarly, Smith (1982) surveyed clinical and counseling psychologists (members of the clinical and counseling divisions of APA). Again, the largest group of subjects identified themselves as eclectic (171 of 415): 41.2%. Other than eclectic, the two major theoretical orientations were psychoanalytic (10.84%) and cognitive-behavioral (10.36%). The figure illustrates the distribution of therapists by their self-identified orientation. The large unmarked area represents a collection of minor approaches.

The repeated finding that eclecticism is a dominant perspective among therapy-oriented psychologists is consistent with the current trend toward rapproachment among schools of therapy. For instance, formerly antagonistic approaches have been written about as potentially cooperative in Wachtel's (1977) book entitled *Psychoanalysis and Behavior Therapy,* and Goldfried (1980) has described the climate of "convergence." Although there remain many ardent followers of single schools of thought, integration is clearly a dominant trend in the psychological therapies. Cognitive-behaviorism is an example (Kendall, 1982).

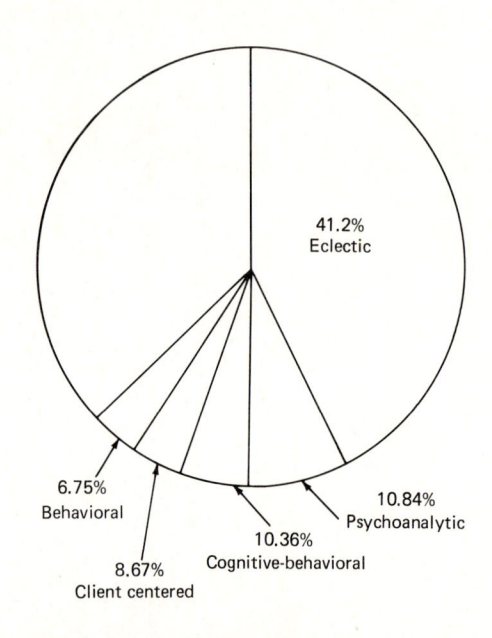

- 41.2% Eclectic
- 10.84% Psychoanalytic
- 10.36% Cognitive-behavioral
- 8.67% Client centered
- 6.75% Behavioral

COGNITIVE-BEHAVIORAL THERAPY

The cognitive-behavioral therapies are a rational amalgam of behavioral treatment procedures and features of cognitive therapy and intervention. The resulting strategies are performance based, often employ learning enhancing techniques, but also pay close attention to the client's mental operations. For instance, a client observes a model and then participates in a role-play exercise which includes rewards for desired performance. Besides these behavioral strategies, cognitive-behavioral treatment would address the client's expectations about future behavior, attributions about prior successes/failures, accuracy of self-monitoring and self-evaluation, and perhaps even the rationality of the client's life philosophy. Thus cognitive-behavioral interventionists are concerned with the thought and action of psychotherapy (Kendall & Bemis, 1983).

RATIONAL EMOTIVE THERAPY

Rational emotive therapy (RET) was developed by Albert Ellis (1962) and focuses on changing *irrational beliefs.* Ellis's treatment helps clients become aware of these self-defeating, irrational beliefs and adopt a more rational personal philosophy. According to RET, not the environment but how a person interprets it produces either psychological maladjustment or well-being.

The essence of RET can be summarized by a consideration of Ellis's "ABC" model. "A" refers to the activating event, the situation that the client is exposed to, and "C" stands for the consequences (both emotional and behavioral) that the client reports resulted from A. The central factor is "B," the beliefs that the client holds about the situation in question. It is the existence of and self-reflection on these irrational beliefs, in the form of irrational self-talk, that produce the emotional consequences experienced at point C. A does not cause C; C is the result of the mediating beliefs. For example, suppose that you want to ask someone for a date. You locate the person and make your approach. Suddenly, you are exceedingly nervous; you feel tense, your palms are sweaty, and your voice actually cracks as you begin to talk. Did asking for a date cause the anxiety? No. The activating event did not itself cause the emotional and behavioral consequences. Rather, the unnecessary emotional reaction resulted from irrational thinking. That is, for simply asking for a date to cause so much anxiety, you must have been thinking that the person *must* say yes, or *else* you would see yourself as a completely worthless human being. If you do not get this date, you will never get a date—no one will ever go out with you. Such thinking is, of course, incorrect. Most people have been rejected by someone at some point. The irrational belief causes the unwanted anxiety. Thus emotional and behavioral consequences are mediated by the rationality or irrationality of the person's thinking.

The ABC model can be expanded to include treatment—"D," the process whereby the therapist disputes the client's irrationality. RET seeks to alter the client's problematic behavior by actively attacking the person's beliefs that are seen as producing the maladaptive consequences. The therapist challenges the client, requires explanations for all sorts of assumptions, and expresses disbelief and disapproval when the client describes irrational beliefs. However, the attack is directed at the irrational beliefs, not at the client personally. In fact, RET prescribes full acceptance and tolerance of the client as an individual. The client's beliefs, however, are directly challenged and actively dismantled by the therapist (see Transcript 4).

**Transcripts 4: An Example
of Rational Emotive Therapy**

CLIENT: I guess I'm afraid, perhaps, of what I'm going to find out—about me.
THERAPIST: Well, so let's suppose you find out something dreadful about

you—that you're thinking foolishly, or something. Now why would that be awful?

C: Because I, I guess I'm the most important thing to me at the moment.

T: No, I don't think that's the answer. It's, I believe, the opposite! You're really the least important thing to you. You are prepared to beat yourself over the head if I tell you that you're acting foolishly. If you were not a self-blamer, then you wouldn't care what I said. It would be important to you—but you'd just go around correcting it. But if I tell you something really negative about you, you're going to beat yourself mercilessly. Aren't you?

C: Yes, I generally do.

T: All right. So perhaps that's what you're really afraid of. You're not afraid of me. You're afraid of your own self-criticism.

C: All right.

T: So why do you have to criticize yourself? Suppose I find you're the worst person I ever met? Let's just suppose that. All right, now why would you have to criticize yourself?

C: (Pause) I'd have to. I don't know any other behavior pattern, I guess, in this point of time. I always do. I guess I think I'm just a shit.

T: Yeah. But that, that isn't so. If you don't know how to ski or swim, you could learn. You can also learn not to condemn yourself, no matter what you do.

C: I don't know.

T: Well, the answer is: You don't know how.

C: Perhaps.

T: I get the impression you're saying, "I have to berate myself if I do something wrong." Because isn't that where your depression comes from?

C: Yes, I guess so. (Silence for a while)

T: Now, what are you mainly putting yourself down for right now?

C: I don't seem quite able, in this point of time, to break it down very neatly. The form gave me a great deal of trouble. Because my tendency is to say everything. I want to change everything; I'm depressed about everything; et cetera.

T: Give me a couple of things, for example.

C: What I'm depressed about? I, uh, don't know that I have any purpose in life. I don't know what I—what I am. And I don't know in what direction I'm going.

T: Yeah. But that's—so you're saying, "I'm ignorant!" (Client nods) Well, what's so awful about being ignorant? It's too bad you're ignorant. It would be nicer if you weren't—if you had a purpose and knew where you were going. But just let's suppose the worst: For the rest of your life you didn't have a purpose, and you stayed this way. Let's suppose that. Now why would you be so bad?

C: Because everyone should have a purpose!

T: Where did you get the should?

C: 'Cause it's what I believe in. (Silence for a while)

T: I know. But think about it for a minute. You're obviously a bright woman; now, where did that *should* come from?

C: I don't know! I'm not thinking clearly at the moment. I'm too nervous! I'm sorry.

T: Well, but you can think clearly. Are you now saying, "Oh, it's hopeless! I can't think clearly. What a shit I am for not thinking clearly!" You see: you're blaming yourself for that.

C: (Visibly upset; can't seem to say anything; then nods)
T: Now, you're perfectly able to think.
C: Not at the moment! (Chokes up)
T: Yes you are! Want to bet?
C: (Begins to sob)
T: What are you crying about now?
C: Because I feel so stupid! And I'm afraid!
T: Yeah. But "stupid" means "I'm putting myself down for acting stupidly."
C: All right! I didn't expect to be put on so fast. I expected a moment to catch my breath and see who you were; and to establish some different kind of rapport.
T: Yeah. And that would be nice and easier; but we would really waste our time.
C: Yes. I guess we would.
T: But you're really upset because you're not giving the right answers—and isn't that awful!
C: Yes. And I don't think that anybody likes to be made a, a fool, a fool of!
T: You can't be made a fool of!
C: (Chokes a little)
T: You see, that's the point: that's impossible. Now, why can't you be made a fool of?
C: (Angry outburst) Why don't you stop asking me!
T: (Interrupting) No! You'll never get better unless you think. And you're saying, "Can't we do something magical to get me better?" And the answer is: "No!"
C: (Angrily interrupting) Well, maybe I would have liked just a moment to relax when I walked in here! All right: why do I think I should? Uh, uh "everyone should have a purpose." (Restatement of her original statement) Because I can't imagine existing, uh, or that there would be any reason for existing without a purpose!
T: No, but the vast majority of human beings don't have much purpose.
C: (Angrily) All right, then. I should not feel bad about it.
T: No, no, no! Wait a minute, now. You just jumped. (Laughs) You jumped from one extreme to another! You see, you said a sane sentence and an insane sentence. Now, if we could get you to separate the two—which you're perfectly able to do—you would solve the problem. What you really mean is: "It would be better if I had a purpose. Because I'd be happier." Right?
C: Yes.
T: But then you jump magically to: "Therefore I should!" Now do you see the difference between, "It would be better if I had a purpose," and "I should, I must, I've got to"?

—*from* CORSINI *(1973), pp. 185–186.*

Behavioral principles are also evident in some of the current practice of RET. Role-playing particular scenes and regulating homework assignments are two often-used behavioral strategies. The "emotive" part of RET concerns not only the therapist's focus on emotionality, but also the use of techniques, such as overemphasis, to point out to the client how unrealistic certain beliefs are.

RET is not the most systematically investigated approach to treatment, but the influx of research-oriented behavioral psychologists has added to the research focus of the rational emotive approach. Goldfried and Sobocinski (1975), for instance, tested whether the tendency to hold irrational beliefs was related to emotional arousal. Subjects were asked to imagine themselves in various scenes—some were neutral; others involved an instance where the subject might experience rejection. Subjects scoring "irrational" on the portion of a measure of irrational beliefs that deals with social rejection reported greater emotional arousal following the scenes with potential rejection. There were no differences, however, in the emotional arousal following the neutral scenes.

Research on the therapeutic effectiveness of RET has been somewhat slow to appear, especially considering the impact of the RET perspective on practicing psychologists. Nevertheless, two studies are worth noting. Trexler and Karst (1972) compared the effectiveness of RET to relaxation training and a control group in the treatment of speech anxious college students. RET was reported to be superior to the control condition and, to a lesser extent, to the relaxation training. Lipsky, Kassinove, and Miller (1980) studied the effects of RET with an actual sample of clinical cases. On several measures of outcome, the authors reported that the RET interventions were superior to both an alternative treatment and a no-contact group. Testing the effects of RET with clinic patients is to be encouraged and applauded but, unfortunately, the Lipsky et al. project relied entirely on subject self-report as measures of outcome. RET has been an influential model of emotional maladjustment and clearly deserves more detailed research evaluations.

COGNITIVE-BEHAVIORAL TREATMENT OF DEPRESSION

Not unlike Ellis's emphasis on irrational beliefs as the mediators of psychopathology, Aaron T. Beck hypothesized that depression results from how people have come to think *illogically*: There are self-defeating thoughts and cognitive distortions that characterize the depressed person. The typical negative thoughts of depressed clients fit into one of the following three categories described by Beck: negative ideas about the world, negative thoughts about the self, and negative perceptions of the future. These three areas of concern are often referred to as the *negative triad*. They include negative self-evaluations brought about by comparisons with more successful others, self-criticism and blame resulting from an overemphasis on personal shortcomings, inaccurate negative evaluations of even the simplest event, and a sense of being overwhelmed by typical responsibilities to the point of helplessness (Beck, 1972). Rather than a global set of beliefs that are said to pertain to a global set of abnormal behavior patterns, Beck's position focuses on depression and the depressed person's tendency to misinterpret events in a way to confirm his or her negative self-image.

Following a careful assessment of the negative thoughts that are influencing the client, the therapist guides the client to replace the negative thinking with more accurate and positive thoughts. The strategy employed by the therapist has been called *collaborative empiricism:* the client and therapist together identify problems and gather data to test the logic and rationality of the client's thinking. Self-monitoring is an important skill that is taught to the client—important because it is the client's self-monitored mood, activities, and thoughts that are examined collaboratively by the therapist and client (see Transcript 5).

Transcript 5: Examples of Cognitive-Behavioral Therapy

Cognitive-behavioral therapy for depression includes demonstrating with the data how the client is generalizing from negative cues and disqualifying positive experiences.

Generalizing from the Negative

CLIENT: I don't have any self-control at all.
THERAPIST: On what basis do you say that?
C: Somebody offered me candy and I couldn't refuse it.
T: Were you eating candy every day?
C: No, I just ate it this once.
T: Did you do anything constructive during the past week to adhere to your diet?
C: Well, I didn't give in to the temptation to buy candy every time I saw it at the store.... Also, I did not eat any candy except that one time when it was offered to me and I felt I couldn't refuse it.
T: If you counted up the number of times you controlled yourself versus the number of times you gave in, what ratio would you get?
C: About 100 to 1.
T: So if you controlled yourself 100 times and did not control yourself just once, would that be a sign that you are weak through and through?
C: I guess not—not through and through (smiles).

Discounting the Positive

CLIENT: I really haven't made any progress in therapy.
THERAPIST: Didn't you have to improve in order to leave the hospital and go back to college?
C: What's the big deal about going to college every day?
T: Why do you say that?
C: It's easy to attend these classes because all the people are healthy.
T: How about when you were in group therapy in the hospital? What did you feel then?
C: I guess I thought then that it was easy to be with the other people because they were all as crazy as I was.
T: Is it possible that whenever you accomplish you tend to discredit?

—From BECK, RUSH, SHAW, *and* EMERY *(1979), pp. 68–69.*

Besides self-monitoring, the therapist assists the client to enjoy him or herself. Often, depressed clients have withdrawn from activities and brood over their lack of interests. Via *activity scheduling,* the therapist helps the client plan and participate in potentially enjoyable events. Depressed clients also often fail to engage in or complete routine tasks. Here, the therapist and client work together to set up tasks that are broken down into small steps—*graded task assignments.*

Several studies support the effectiveness of the cognitive-behavioral treatment of depression. For example, Rush, Beck, Kovacs, and Hollon (1977) compared Beck's therapy to the use of imipramine, an antidepressant drug that is often prescribed for outpatients with depressive symptomatology. The cognitive-behavioral therapy involved a maximum of 20 sessions over 12 weeks. Results showed more improvements for the cognitive-behavioral therapy. Other studies support this type of therapy (e.g., Fuchs & Rehm, 1977; McLean & Hakstian, 1979; B. F. Shaw, 1977; Taylor & Marshall, 1977; Zeiss, Lewinsohn, & Monoz, 1979).

COGNITIVE-BEHAVIORAL THERAPY WITH CHILDREN

Meichenbaum (1977) has emphasized that the therapist's ability to change what clients say to themselves is crucial. Self-instructional training for children involves not talking at or with the child client, but modeling the thinking strategy that will effectively solve a problem. The therapist thinks out loud, saying specific steps which guide thinking toward a solution: "What am I supposed to do," "Focus in," "Make a plan," and upon successful completion, "I did a good job." Thus the child is exposed to a therapist who shares his or her thinking strategy, including self-reward for good work.

As part of a cognitive-behavioral treatment for children with self-control problems (Kendall & Braswell, 1985), self-instructional training takes place together with behavioral contingencies (i.e., a response-cost and reward program), role-playing, and homework assignments. The self-instructional training component is considered important in teaching self-control because children who lack such skills are often described as acting without thinking—behaving impulsively. Self-instructions teach the child to take a more systematic look at problems, to think about solutions, and to inhibit misguided actions. The child is not taught *what* to think, but is taught *how* to think. In this manner, the trained child uses new skills as needed in situations that require careful forethought.

Cognitive-behavioral procedures have been employed in an effort to remedy several different types of childhood problems (Meyers, & Craighead, 1984). However, most research has focused on producing impulse control or self-control. Hyperactive children, acting-out children, and impulsive children are just a few of the target samples. In each case, the problem is seen as one where the child is lacking in guiding self-talk and the training is intended to teach these skills.

Research results have been encouraging. For instance, Kendall and Braswell (1982) compared the cognitive-behavioral program to a solely behavioral program and to a control condition. The 12 one-hour sessions lasted 7 weeks. Although both treatments produced positive gains, the gains resulting from the cognitive-behavioral training were superior. Like the cognitive-behavioral treatments described for adults, teaching children self-control involves a combination of behavioral procedures that focus on changing cognitive processes.

OTHER PSYCHOLOGICAL THERAPIES

You should now have a reasonable understanding of the major approaches to the remedying of psychological dysfunctions. There are, however, many alternative theories that are employed to help clients overcome their difficulties and live fuller lives. Although the best way to learn about these might be through advanced course work in abnormal and clinical psychology, the following section contains a sample of some of the additional strategies used by psychotherapists.

REALITY THERAPY

In reality therapy it is first assumed that the basic problem is the client's inability to fulfill their present needs in realistic ways. Fulfilling needs such as the need to love and be loved is a present concern, and Glasser (1965) argues that therapy need not be concerned with the patient's past history.

Glasser describes three features of reality therapy: (1) involvement; (2) rejection of the client's unrealistic behavior, but still accepting the client as a good person; and (3) teaching better ways to fulfill needs. Involvement refers to the therapist's becoming so involved with the client that the client will begin to see that certain behaviors are unrealistic. A conventional therapist (Glasser was referring to psychoanalysts) might be impersonal and objective; the reality therapist becomes involved. The therapist challenges unrealistic behavior: "What are you doing that for?" The person is not attacked, just his or her behavior, which must be changed because it will never satisfy his or her needs. Once the unrealistic behavior is rejected, the therapist must teach the patient better ways to fulfill basic needs within the confines of reality. Thus Glasser views patient problems as interpersonal and social and sees treatment as a form of reeducating clients about how to fulfill basic interpersonal needs.

A session of gestalt therapy. The client is attempting to understand how she communicates with others by working through an imaginary dialogue with an absent partner represented by the empty chair. (Susan Rosenberg)

GESTALT THERAPY

Gestalt means organized whole, and the Gestalt therapist tries to teach awareness so that clients will be fully integrated whole persons. Gestalt therapy, introduced by F. Perls, seeks to promote individual growth and fulfill human potential. Perls (1969) speaks of becoming "real," of taking a stand, and of understanding the reason for being.

The basic tenet of the Gestalt approach is that the clients need to be taught to be more aware. Clients' awareness of their feelings, thoughts, needs, and behaviors will help them overcome the self-defeating features of their existence. The concept of awareness is tied to the term "Gestalt therapy." When an experience in life is incomplete, it demands the full attention of the person. There is no need for the therapist to remember important topics for continued discussion; the client will return to important themes because these themes represent "unfinished business."

Gestalt therapy focuses on the "here and now." Awareness is viewed as an understanding of all that is felt, sensed, and thought within a person, and this awareness can only be achieved at the present time—the here and now. The therapist's task is to coach the client to realize the whats and whys of their current behavior. The therapist serves as an aware model for the clients.

Gestalt therapists also strive to have their clients be fully integrated. Integration includes making every aspect of how you communicate with others consistent with your feelings. For example, saying you are sad and smiling would be inconsistent.

TRANSACTIONAL ANALYSIS

Transactional analysis involves an intensive examination of the "transactions" that people enact with other persons and within themselves (Berne, 1970). Like the psychoanalytic concepts of id, ego, and superego, which must be kept in balance for the person to experience psychological adjustment, transactional analysis (TA) posits three separate mental agencies: the child, the adult, and the parent. The child is similar to the id, wanting satisfaction promptly and being relatively unsocialized, but Berne places more emphasis on the playfulness of children. The adult is like the ego, being a reality oriented and needs–versus–rules balancing agent. Like the superego, the parent is the controlling and potentially guilt inducing mental concept. Using these concepts, the analysis focuses on the client's transactions with others.

Faulty interpersonal transactions are seen in "the games people play," and the scripts they use and reuse. Games are described as the repeated and often destructive interactions that people have with one another. The interactions are so routine that there is no genuine contact. Scripts are also repetitive and unfulfilling. A script is a narrow and self-defeating strategy—rather than coping effectively, the person engages in the same old inflexible behavior. The analysis in TA focuses on the nature of personal and interpersonal relationships.

EXISTENTIAL THERAPY

Existential therapy is nonacademic, nonscientific, nontheoretical, and not interested in specific therapeutic techniques. Instead, the therapist is most interested in achieving an understanding of the client's mode of existence. What is the client's psychological experience and human condition? The therapist interacts with the client to try to understand these aspects of the client's life. In other words, the therapist seeks to understand the "being," inner nature, or uniqueness of the client's human existence.

Existential therapists do not try to change clients—clients are responsible for changing themselves. The client grows from the therapeutic interactions with the therapist and learns about his or her existence, and this growth leads the client to change.

Each of these other psychological approaches to treatment has attracted considerable support, both among practitioners and clients, and many practitioners continue to employ several select components of each. Unfortunately, research evaluations are rare and cannot serve as the source of the data for selecting which features to continue to employ and which ones to let slip away. Proponents of these therapies point to many selected successful cases and to their own personal history of what was effective and therefore worth continuing. Some supporters agree that research is needed, while others argue that treatment is so individualistic that research is not possible. Since methods for evaluating individual therapeutic cases are available (Kazdin, 1982; Mintz & Kiesler, 1982), the latter argument is not valid. From the scientific perspective on psychotherapy, these forms of treatment could be enhanced by systematic evaluation.

GROUP THERAPY

When people get together they create an interpersonal situation. Since many of the problems that lead people to seek psychological therapy are interpersonal, the group is a valuable context for education, change, and growth. Group members can learn much about themselves by watching and listening to one another, as well as to the feedback provided by the therapist.

HIGHLIGHT 16.2
Self-Help

What is the first thing that you do when you realize that you are under excessive stress? When you feel depressed? Or when you are mourning the loss of a close friend? Many people pick up a self-treatment or self-help book. Self-help programs do not require professional consultation.

The self-help book promises to fulfill, in an easy and enjoyable way, your desire to change. Simply buy the book and follow the instructions. Unfortunately, although some self-help books can be helpful, selling the book seems to be the main objective. Establishing and reevaluating the effectiveness of the program contained in it are at best secondary.

The most popular self-help books deal with weight loss, health enhancement, helping you stop smoking and/or drinking, and sensual sex. Increasing your assertiveness, learning to relax, and improving your skills as a parent are also popular.

Self-help manuals can provide helpful information to more people than would be possible if each reader had to seek professional help on an individual basis. It is humane to disseminate information that will help as many people for as little cost as possible.

However, there are at least three arguments against self-help programs. First, an overabundance of cure-yourself manuals may decrease the public's faith in the necessity for professional help—why seek and pay for professional help when you can get it in a book? Second, the quality of the help provided by self-help books may be less than satisfactory. Clients are not best served, especially when their problems are complex, by a book that cannot respond or advise beyond its printed words. People may be demoralized if they try a self-help program that does not work. Where do they turn then? Given that the people who buy these books are seeking to change, they will very likely need some guidance. Feelings of helplessness and a loss of self-respect can result from the unsuccessful self-help effort. These can reduce a person's efforts to change.

The third reason for caution emerges from the scientific concerns of clinicians and researchers who specialize in evaluating treatment outcome. Their concern is that self-help books often cannot document that their program works, although supportive data for some books has been reported. Nevertheless, most self-help books do not report, and often do not have, scientifically acceptable evidence of positive results. In some cases the treatment described in the book was indeed effective, but was provided in a one-to-one or group format with a professional therapist, not in a book. Most self-help books cannot document their effectiveness when administered through the printed format in which they are marketed.

One way to conduct therapy is to organize previously unacquainted persons into a group. This new collection of people will establish rules and standards of interaction, and the therapist can help the clients learn about how each person contributes to these group rules and how each person deals with other people by examining the interaction process within the group.

Groups of clients have been organized for psychological therapy for nearly a century, but group interventions flourished in the 1960s and 1970s when training groups, or *T-groups*, were introduced. T-groups were developed to help people learn to communicate more effectively with others and emphasized engaging all members in honest and open dialogue. The T-group model has been widely disseminated as valuable for personal education, and clinical interventions with groups of disturbed clients are common as well.

A second type of group consists of people who are already involved with one another. Perhaps a couple or an entire family will become involved in therapy. Here the group is also the one in which the clients live, and the psychologist seeks to help the client by altering the group system. Family therapy is a prime example of this type of group treatment.

CONFLICT, ADJUSTMENT, AND MENTAL HEALTH

FAMILY THERAPY

The central interpersonal system in almost everyone's life is the family. Reasonably well adjusted persons must give some credit to the family that raised them, and children with some types of psychological dysfunctions may derive their problems from unresolved problems in their family. The family therapy perspective seeks to remedy individual or group problems by intervening with the entire family.

Family therapists employ several methods to work with the members of the family: In *conjoint therapy* all relevant persons are seen in a single group; in *concurrent therapy* family members are seen separately. Because the family must deal with the therapy process as a unit as well as try to work together for change, conjoint family therapy has the advantage over concurrent therapy.

One focus of therapy that is specific to the treatment of families is the systems/communication approach. In the systems/communication model family members' well-being hinges on the nature and quality of the patterns of interaction that define the family system (e.g., Haley, 1976; Satir, 1964). As part of the therapeutic effort, systems/communication therapists teach families new ways to conceptualize their individual problems as a *family* responsibility. The therapist *reframes* psychological dysfunctions to help family members feel better about themselves and the family. Reframing includes reinterpreting negative actions as reflecting more positive concerns. For example, an adolescent who sees his mother's job as a sign that she does not care for him can have his perception reframed as his mother's indirect way of caring—the added income can provide the children with more opportunities.

More direct strategies are also employed to assist dysfunctional families to improve the manner of their interactions. For instance, family members are asked to speak only for themselves as individuals (rather than speaking

In family therapy, the psychologist seeks to help the client by changing the group system. (Hanna W. Schreiber)

for other members) and/or to talk directly to one another rather than to the therapist. Clients may be asked to use structured communication patterns such as "I" statements. "I" statements require that the speaker take the responsibility for what is said and not blame someone else.

COMMUNITY INTERVENTIONS

Psychologists can work to improve the lives of many people when programs are introduced at the level of an entire community. Community interventions involve the development of new educational and therapeutic service and support networks. For example, establishing a community-based center for teenage alcohol problems, or lobbying for the rerouting of a planned highway, so that a neighborhood would not be divided and destroyed, are community oriented interventions. Rather than helping individuals, the focus of community interventions is on changing environments for the betterment of many people.

One way to modify the environment is to create new settings. For example, Fairweather, Sanders, and Tornatzky (1974) described the creation of a community-based "lodge" for assisting mental patients. Patients from a problem-solving program in the hospital were placed in a house in the community where they received training in handling basic responsibilities—cooking, cleaning, recreation, and managing a self-supporting business (a janitorial service). Since the patients did not have families in the community, the lodge provided an opportunity for a successful reintegration into nonhospital life.

Another version of community interventions involves creating special programs to address community problems. The growing concern about deficiencies in standards for environmental conservation has led to several community projects. Programs for increasing bus ridership (e.g., Everett, Hayward, & Meyers, 1974), litter cleanup (e.g., Chapman & Risley, 1974), and energy conservation (e.g., Hayes & Cone, 1977) are three examples. In each of these programs, rewards were provided to foster the desired behavior. For instance, bus riders *earned* rewards (chips) that could be redeemed by local merchants, and participants who reduced their use of electricity were given varying monetary *payments*, depending on how much energy was conserved.

Diversion programs are our final example of community psychology in action. A diversion program is designed to reduce the burden on the courts and prisons, to provide low-risk persons with a chance to avoid a prison term, and to prevent further illegal acts. Diversion programs involve the use of assessments to identify low-risk persons who can be diverted from the courts and perhaps returned to the community. One such program was described by Seidman, Rappaport, and Davidson (1976). In their program, trained college students served as advocates for the troubled adolescents and worked with them, the community, and their families to establish more positive environments and to reduce future court involvements. The authors reported that the diversion program significantly reduced the number of police contacts, the seriousness of the police contacts, and the number of court hearings. These gains were not seen in the control groups.

HIGHLIGHT 16.3
Ethics Guiding Psychotherapy

Assuming responsibility for the care of the psychological well-being of another person carries with it important ethical directives. By the very nature of the relationship—close, revealing, sensitive, and the fact that one person is a professional—certain ethical guidelines must be followed to protect the client's health and welfare.

Confidentiality is perhaps the single most important ethical issue. Can an employer, family member, or government official gain access to a client's files? Is the clinician required by law to reveal information acquired during the therapeutic relationship? The answers, in general, are no. According to the guidelines of the American Psychological Association, a client's right of privacy is to be protected at all times. Only when multiple professionals are involved in providing service, or when the client gives written permission, can information be discussed or released to others.

There is one limit on confidentiality: When a client threatens to harm, or reports having already harmed, either himself or herself or someone else. In such cases, when careful reasoning and sound judgment suggests, the clinician must report the threat or incident to the proper authorities.

Confidentiality also pertains to participation in research. Subjects who provide personal information—an actual sample of their behavior or simply completing a questionnaire—supply these data with the researcher's guarantee that the data will not be open to the public. The current practice to assure confidentiality is to assign each subject a number and to use only the number as identification.

"Trespassers will be experimented upon" read the sign at the foot of an ominous castle. This suggests a mad scientist who, in Frankenstein fashion, uses human beings as subjects against their will. This does not happen in psychology. Psychologists endorse the principle that before subjects are allowed to participate in research, they must be informed about the experience that they are likely to have. The idea of "informed consent" is designed to protect human subjects by allowing them to decide whether to participate. Subjects should be told of the features of a study that might affect their interest and/or willingness to participate. Subjects do not, however, have to be told every detail of the study.

In evaluations of the effects of psychological therapies participating clients must also have an opportunity to give their consent. However, consent requires a competent person who is free to give or withhold it and who has knowledge of the treatment(s) or alternative treatment(s) that might be provided. Although the provision of knowledge about the treatments is typically not a problem, some clients may be seriously disturbed and not considered competent, while others may be confined and may therefore not feel free to choose. Special cautions must be exercised for these special cases.

THE EFFECTS OF PSYCHOLOGICAL THERAPY

In a now classic yet controversial paper, Eysenck (1952) reviewed the limited evidence that was available at the time and concluded that the data failed to prove that psychotherapy facilitates the recovery of clients considered to be neurotic. Instead, Eysenck argued, *spontaneous remission* accounted for equal improvement in neurotic symptoms. He stated that two out of three neurotic clients will improve within 2 years whether or not they receive psychotherapy.

Eysenck's concern with the amount of change that occurs "naturally" was reasonable, and his paper spurred many scientifically controlled evaluations of therapy. Today, there are literally hundreds of studies that go beyond Eysenck's contention and provide evidence of the effectiveness of psychological therapy. We have described some of the important studies of each of the types of therapy in their respective sections, but how do all the treatments compare? If you could read all the separate studies, what could you reasonably conclude about effectiveness? About relative effectiveness? About degree of change?

Two types of cumulative answers have appeared: the "box-score tally" and "meta-analysis." In the box-score approach, studies are reviewed and the results are categorized as signifying that interventions are either "better," "tied," or "worse" than comparison treatments in each study. The Luborsky, Singer, and Luborsky (1975) cumulative analysis suggested that therapy *is* effective but that no one therapy approach is consistently superior to all others. Luborsky concluded that all have won, and all deserve prizes. This conclusion has been criticized as excessively general.

Using meta-analysis, Smith and Glass (1977) conducted another comprehensive analysis of the outcomes of therapy. Meta-analysis involves statistical operations on the results of many studies—nearly 400 were in Smith and Glass's review. "Effect sizes" were calculated for each dependent variable reported in the study. An *effect size* indicates how much the treated group improved with respect to the control group. Since there are typically several measures of outcome in each therapy study, Smith and Glass produced and examined 875 effect-size scores. These scores were then analyzed to determine how much change results on different types of dependent measures, or from different types of treatment.

Different dependent measures produced different effect sizes. For instance, effect sizes were large for measures of fear or anxiety, moderate for measures of general adjustment, and rather low for measures of school or work achievement. These findings suggest that either our therapies have greater effects on anxiety than on achievement, that anxiety is easier to change than achievement, or some combination of these two ideas.

HIGHLIGHT 16.4

What Accounts for Therapeutic Change?

This circle (pie diagram) represents the total amount of change produced by psychological therapy. How much of the circle is the result of client characteristics? of the features of the therapist? of the therapeutic technique? To what extent are changes the result of "placebo" (a nonactive treatment but one that engenders high expectations or beliefs that change will occur). The lines that are drawn in the illustration are only speculation. Now, assuming that you assign parts of the whole to each of these factors, you still must acknowledge that some change results from spontaneous improvement (but how much?) and from some other features (e.g., expectations, credibility of the therapy). To date, we have only modest evidence about the "active" features of the different forms of therapy. Future research will provide more data, and more confidence, for the dividing of the pie.

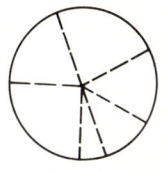

100% of change

Which goes where?

—client features
—therapist characteristics
—therapy techniques
—spontaneous change
—placebo effects
—other factors

Perhaps the most exciting results were related to the comparisons of different types of therapy. These results show that systematic desensitization, rational emotive therapy, and behavior modification produced the largest effect sizes. When therapies were classified as behavioral or nonbehavioral, the combined behavioral treatments produced the larger effect size. However, Smith and Glass's meta-analysis was criticized for failing to eliminate studies that were methodologically weak.

In a more recent meta-analysis, Shapiro and Shapiro (1982) selected studies based on the type of comparison conducted: comparisons between two or more treatments and a control group. The overall effect size further documented that therapy works. Shapiro's analyses produced the largest effect sizes for behavioral and cognitive treatments.

Early negative reactions to meta-analytic studies were justified (e.g., Kazdin & Wilson, 1978)—the process is not a statistical cure-all. However, the methods have been modified and continue to be improved. As the claims for meta-analysis become tempered, as the specificity of the questions asked is advanced, and as the quality of individual studies is improved, refinements and advances in our understanding of the effectiveness of psychotherapy are forthcoming.

NEGATIVE EFFECTS OF THERAPY

Can psychotherapy also produce negative effects? Can therapy cause more conflicts for clients? Can it increase the symptoms that led to treatment instead of reducing them? Although these are important questions, negative effects can also be concerned with the client's misuse or abuse of therapy and/or the client's mistrust of the therapy process. Misuse and abuse may be the client's fault, while distrust may result from the therapist's behavior. Most effects of therapy are positive, but we must be attentive to potential negative effects.

A client who becomes overly dependent on therapy and who uses it as an excuse for failing to be active in other life pursuits is misusing it. Consider a case where the client is excessively anxious about interpersonal interactions and where dating is a rare occurrence. One of the therapist's goals will no doubt focus on increasing self-confidence and practicing the skills for interacting with others, but what if the client, even when progressing toward treatment goals, does not become more interpersonally involved? The client might be using therapy as an excuse—"No one wants to be involved with me 'cause I'm in therapy"; or "Therapy isn't over yet, so I'm not really ready to start interacting." Even more seriously, negative effects would be evident if the client does not apply for a job, discontinues participating in athletics, or stops social involvement as a consequence of the therapy experience. Therapists have to be cautious not to allow the few clients who may misuse therapy to detract from the otherwise desirable effects of treatment.

Some negative effects are due to the therapist. Therapists can foster dependency in their clients, employ deficient assessments, misapply therapeutic procedures, or simply take advantage of the client-therapist relationship.

One study of the outcome of group therapy offers an interesting illustration of negative as well as positive effects of therapy. Lieberman, Yalom, and Miles (1973) compared 10 different types of group therapy. The subjects, 200 undergraduates, were randomly assigned to the alternative treatments. Among the findings were some observed relationships between the leadership styles of the group leaders and positive and negative outcomes. Leaders who fo-

HIGHLIGHT 16.5

Ideal and Unwanted Clients

Therapist factors, features of the client, and aspects of the therapy process are variables that separately or together influence and determine the outcome of therapy (Kiesler, 1966). Regarding client features, numerous studies have been conducted and several reviews have been written (e.g., Garfield, 1978). This line of research seeks to identify features of the client that are predictors of successful or unsuccessful therapy. To date, the findings are mixed. For example, client socioeconomic status, motivation, and expectancy of gain have received mixed but generally positive support as predictors of outcome. Client sex, marital status, and race have either not been sufficiently researched or have been shown to be poor predictors. As a result, the clinical psychologist cannot, as yet, turn to any single client variable and make confident predictions about the outcome of therapy.

There are certain client characteristics that therapists describe as part of the "ideal client." The desired client features are captured in the phrase *YAVIS*—YAVIS clients are young, attractive, verbal, intelligent, and successful.

Add to this according to Schofield (1964), psychologists, psychiatrists, and social workers preferred young, educated, and married females as clients. Unfortunately, both for therapists and clients, not all psychologically distressed persons are YAVIS. Clinical services and related research for older, less attractive, less verbal and intelligent, and less successful clients are equally required by society.

Practicing therapists also have least liked clients. For instance, clients who lie, fail to comply with therapy assignments, and are disrespectful of schedules and/or the therapist's personal life are not favored.

Therapists also liked the easy clients and disliked the difficult ones. Clients perceived as most difficult had higher degrees of pathology; the easy clients were less disturbed (Merbaum & Butcher, 1982). Therapists establish preferences for clients, and these attachments may be associated with the effectiveness of the treatment. However, since therapists like the easy clients more, the easy clients may show the greatest gain simply because they were easier.

---

cused on emotional stimulation, interpretive statements about measuring behavior, and their own executive function were *least* likely to promote positive changes in group members and were *most* likely to have group members whose test data indicated some deterioration. Eight percent of subjects, for example, were worse on the assessment measures at 6-month follow-up. In contrast, leaders who focused on communicating caring, especially when added to an equal emphasis on meaning interpretations, were more uniformly and highly successful.

MEDICAL APPROACHES TO THE TREATMENT OF PSYCHOLOGICAL PROBLEMS

In keeping with the title of this chapter, our main focus has been on the psychological approaches to therapy for psychological problems. Many psychologists and other helping professionals subscribe to a psychological model of treatment. However, other mental health practitioners hold a more biologically oriented view, and still others, such as psychiatrists (medical doctors working with mentally disordered clients), are trained almost entirely in the medical/biological perspective. Also, some forms of psychological disturbance may not be as responsive to psychological treatment as to medications, especially during the crisis periods.

TABLE 16.1
Drugs used for treating abnormal behavior

Disorder	Drug Treatment
Anxiety	Minor tranquilizers (e.g., Valium)
Depression	Tricyclics (e.g., imipramine)
Manic-depression	Lithium carbonate
Psychosis	Phenothiazines (e.g., Thorazine, Stellazine) Major tranquilizers

Note: This list is simply a sample of the drug treatments used.

DRUGS

Drug treatment is by far the most common form of medical treatment, although it is often not the sole form of intervention used. Many psychiatrists see the merits of combining medications with psychological therapy. Medications are prescribed for less severe disorders involving anxiety, more severe problems such as depression, and the truly severe disturbances such as schizophrenia (see Table 16.1).

The antianxiety drugs are typically referred to as tranquilizers. Tranquilizers reduce anxiety and tension through their effect on the central nervous system. Since the 1950s, tranquilizers have enjoyed a remarkable economic success with one of the tranquilizers, Valium, being one of the most widely prescribed drugs in the world. This widespread success is not surprising when one recognizes that stress, pressure, and anxiety are common symptoms in many contemporary cultures. The success is an enigma, however, when one realizes that there are side effects, such as fatigue, that excessive use can lead to addiction, that heavy use with alcohol can result in death, and that once the drug use is discontinued the original problem often still remains.

A separate class of drugs are considered appropriate for the control of depression. Antidepressants include the tricyclics and MAO (monoamine oxidase) inhibitors. These drugs are reported to have the desired effect of "mood elevation" by increasing the presence of neuronal transmitter substances (norepinephrine and serotonin) in the brain. Along with an improved mood comes a better outlook on life and a greater capacity to engage in life's daily routines. The exact mechanism underlying the mood-elevating effect of the antidepressant drugs is not yet known. This state may be in part due to the fact that the elevating effect was discovered by accident! It was during the study of the effects of a drug for treating tuberculosis that patients reported an improved mood—a mood elevation. Some of the unwanted side effects reported by clients include dry mouth, restlessness, vision problems, and some weight gain.

Specific to the treatment of one of the more severe depressive disorders, manic-depression, lithium carbonate has received increased usage in recent times. Manic-depressive disorder involves extreme variations in mood—experiences of manic elation and grandiosity transposed with episodes of deep depression and hopelessness. Lithium reduces the extremes of mood swing and returns the patient to a state of relative emotional equilibrium. On the positive side, researchers and practitioners have hailed lithium for its successful management of manic-depressive disorder. On the negative side, there are certain attendant difficulties, such as the requirement of careful and frequent assessment of the amount of lithium in the bloodstream. If the lithium level gets too high, serious complications, even coma and death, can occur.

Perhaps the most supportive reaction displayed by the mental health professions to any of the new drugs was in response to the antipsychotic medications. "Back-ward" cases, as the near hopeless patients of secluded mental hospitals were referred, experienced marked reductions in their symptoms following the application of the antipsychotic drugs, phenothiazines. Thorazine and Stelazine are two of the more often prescribed phenothiazines. Often used with cases identified as schizophrenic, the phenothiazines (also called major tranquilizers) reduce aggressive behavior and the unwanted agitation that often accompanies active psychotic behavior. The drugs also have a positive effect on the disturbed thinking that is seen in schizophrenia—

reducing bizarre thinking and decreasing delusional preoccupations. As a result, the psychotic behavior of hospitalized schizophrenics is markedly reduced and overall behavioral control is enhanced. From the physical restraints and straightjackets of the recent past to the extensive use of medications in practice today, patients in mental hospitals are freer to move about but no less burdened by the "medication" controls we impose on their abnormal behavior.

The fact that the phenothiazines are used extensively in this country and elsewhere, and the fact that the drugs do have observable effects on bizarre behavior are contrasted markedly with the little that we know about why the drugs are effective. Although different theories abound, we do not know the exact mechanism of the drug effects.

Serious side effects are associated with long term use of some medications. For instance, *tardive dyskinesia* is a disturbance of motor control, believed to be irreversible, that results from an extended use of antipsychotic medications. Involuntary thrusting of the tongue or smacking of the lips are tardive dyskinesias. Other side effects include problems with muscle coordination (Stellazine is said to cause a characteristic walk, or strut, with stiffened leg muscles), possible seizures, dryness of the mouth, and low blood pressure.

Drugs have documented effects on the behaviors that they are prescribed to treat, and the effects are quick and cost-efficient. Are the drugs cures? Clearly not. Indeed, when the drugs are discontinued the client may still experience unwanted anxiety or depression because the problem that caused the negative emotional states has not been resolved. Similarly with the antipsychotic medications, the symptoms tend to reappear when the patient quits taking the drug. When these concerns are combined with the issue of side effects, it becomes clear that while drugs have a place in the treatment of some behavioral disorders, they are not sufficiently effective to rule out other forms of intervention. Quite the contrary is true; drug treatment is only one form of treatment that achieves its maximal effectiveness when used cautiously and when combined with psychological treatments that teach new skills for effective living.

PSYCHOSURGERY

Recall that one of the primitive methods of treatment was trephining; opening the skull to rid the person of the demons that caused the "crazy" behavior. A more recent parallel is evident in the operations referred to as either a lobotomy (severing the connectedness of brain tissue) or a lobectomy (removal of brain tissue). Lobotomies were popular during the 1950s and 1960s, but are almost extinct in current practice.

The scientific basis for the widespread performance of lobotomies was abysmally weak. According to Davison and Neale (1982), it was a Portuguese psychiatrist, Moniz, who heard of brain surgery performed on monkeys and learned that the surgery turned violent and emotionally volatile animals into calm and indifferent ones. Based on the single report using two chimpanzees, Moniz later performed brain surgery, with his colleague Lima, on human beings.

Lobotomies received a great deal of attention in the United States beginning in the early 1950s. Today, however, the use of brain surgery to control behavior is not often recommended, and when it is, it is overseen with great caution.

One fact about the lobotomy story is most educational. Moniz, for his work on lobotomies, shared a Nobel Prize in 1949. In most people's opinions, the Nobel Prize is the most influential and important prize within the sciences. Correspondingly, we have faith that the award signifies a true breakthrough or marked advance in our knowledge and understanding. The lifespan of the highly prized procedure, the lobotomy, was appropriately short: it simply is not the solution it was once thought to be. The lesson we can all learn from this is that we must be cautious in our claims for the effects of procedures to treat abnormality—especially when the treatments may have serious and irreparable complications.

ELECTROCONVULSIVE THERAPY

The initial hypothesis stimulating the development of electroconvulsive therapy (ECT), or shock therapy, was that the seizures experienced by epileptics might help reduce schizophrenia among them. Thus, inducing seizures might help in the treatment of schizophrenia. Convulsions were first produced using massive injections of insulin, but insulin has been replaced by electric shock as the preferred method.

In current practice, ECT is used for severe depression, and rarely, if at all, for schizophrenia. Although no one knows exactly how or why shock treatments work, and they are reported to be effective for the severely depressed, they involve placing electrodes on each side of the patient's forehead and passing an electrical current between them for a few seconds. In some cases the electrodes are placed on one side of the head, above the right hemisphere. The electric shocks are often between 90 and 150 V and are administered two to three times a week for several weeks. Because patients might hurt themselves during the convulsions that occur, they are first given barbiturates to relax their muscles. While relaxed, they are far less likely to harm themselves.

When used for severe depression, where all else has failed, ECT has proved effective (Klerman, 1972). However, temporary memory loss, confusion, and

Electroconvulsive therapy (ECT) is reported to be effective for the severely depressed. (Will McIntyre)

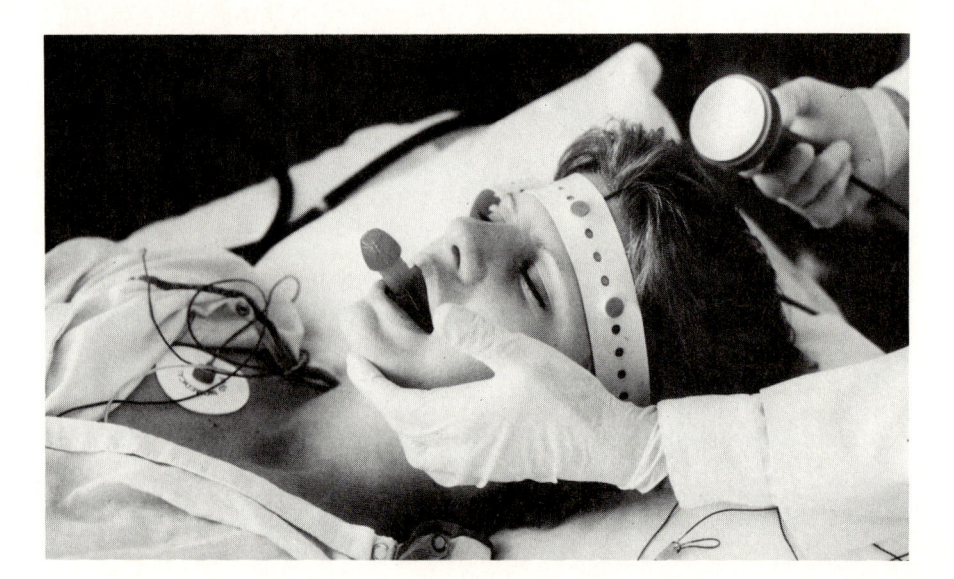

disorientation are often reported, the positive effects may be short-lived, and there are instances of serious problems with amnesia following ECT. Because drugs, surgery, and ECT are more biological forms of treatment, you may be misled into thinking that we therefore have a clearer understanding of how they work. Unfortunately, this is not true. We know much about the human organism, its anatomy and biology, but we are still far from understanding all the details of the brain-behavior relationships. This is especially true when we are addressing abnormal behavior among human beings.

SUMMARY

1. Psychoanalytic therapy, developed from the work of Sigmund Freud, employs free association and interpretations in an effort to assist the client in gaining insight. Understanding the client's transference relationship is also important. While there are many published case reports, there are few published reports of the scientific evaluation of psychoanalysis. Nevertheless, it remains a major approach to the treatment of psychological disorders.

2. Therapeutic benefits are said to accrue when the therapist conditions of genuineness, accurate empathy, and unconditional positive regard are present. These concepts, introduced by Carl Rogers, are basic to client-centered therapy.

3. Behavior therapy is performance-based, focusing on providing learning experiences for the client. Practice and homework are involved. Systematic desensitization involves the exposure of anxious/fearful clients to the feared situations/stimuli in a graduated manner. Operant learning procedures and modeling procedures are other examples of behavioral strategies for treating behavior disorders. A great deal of research has been conducted evaluating behavioral therapy.

4. Maintaining performance-based procedures while including the client's cognitive activities as part of the treatment, cognitive-behavioral procedures include specific strategies for anxiety, depression, and impulsive children. Rational-emotive therapy focuses on changing the client's irrational beliefs and cognitive-behavioral treatments for depression emphasize collaborative empiricism. Work with children has emphasized self-instructional training.

5. Alternative approaches to the treatment of psychological dysfunctions include reality therapy, gestalt therapy, transactional analysis, and existential therapy. In addition, there are many self-help approaches for psychological problems.

6. Group therapy approaches bring an interpersonal context to the treatment situation. Family therapy involves the primary interpersonal system, as in conjoint family therapy where parents and children are seen together and their interpersonal behaviors are the target for the therapist.

7. Community interventions involve educational and therapeutic services for the betterment of many people. Psychologically based programs to solve community problems are examples.

8. Research supports the effectiveness of several of the varieties of psychotherapy, but therapy researchers have yet to determine the exact causes of therapeutic change. Therapy researchers follow careful methods and abide by ethical considerations in their studies of behavior change.

9. Meta-analysis, a data analytic method applied to many studies on a selected topic, suggests that therapy works and that therapies with some behavioral components produce the largest effects.

CONFLICT, ADJUSTMENT, AND MENTAL HEALTH

10. Medical approaches to treatment are medications, psychosurgery, and electroconvulsive therapy. Tricyclics are medications used for depression, phenothiazines for psychotic disorders, and tranquilizers for anxiety. Lobotomies, once but not currently popular, involve severing brain tissue connections. In electroconvulsive therapy (ECT), or shock therapy, electrical current is passed through the patient's brain. ECT has been used to treat severe depression.

KEY TERMS

Therapy
Psychoanalysis
Free association
Interpretation
Resistance
Transference
Countertransference
Client-centered therapy
Genuineness
Accurate empathy
Unconditional positive regard
Behavior therapy
Performance based
Systematic desensitization
Operant procedures
Token economy
Modeling
Mastery model

Coping model
Eclecticism
Cognitive-behavior therapy
Rational emotive therapy
Irrational beliefs
Cognitive-behavioral treatment of depression
Negative triad
Collaborative empiricism
Activity scheduling
Cognitive-behavioral therapy with children
Reality therapy
Gestalt therapy
Transactional analysis
Existential therapy

Self-help
Group therapy
Family therapy
Conjoint therapy
Concurrent therapy
Community interventions
Spontaneous remission
Confidentiality
Effect size
YAVIS
Valium
Tricyclic
Lithium carbonate
Phenothiazines
Tardive dyskinesia
Lobotomy
Electroconvulsive therapy

SUGGESTED READINGS

CORSINI, R. J. (Ed.) *Current psychotherapies* (2nd ed.). Itasca, Ill.: Peacock, 1979. This edited book contains descriptions of many of the types of psychological therapy. Each contribution is written by a recognized authority, with experience providing the specific type of therapy.

GARFIELD, S. L., & BERGIN, A. E. (Eds.). *Handbook of psychotherapy and behavior change* (2nd ed.). New York: Wiley, 1978. A comprehensive research summary of the studies pertinent to psychotherapy. The book does not describe how to perform therapy, but it does provide an extensive review of the research literature.

GOLDFRIED, M. R., & DAVISON, G. C. *Clinical behavior therapy.* New York: Holt, Rinehart and Winston, 1976. The authors describe the procedures used in providing the behavioral approach to therapy. The book includes sample transcripts and other material to help implement behavior therapy.

KENDALL, P. C., & NORTON-FORD, J. *Clinical psychology: Scientific and professional dimensions.* New York: Wiley, 1982. Five chapters deal specifically with clinical psychological interventions. The guiding theories, intervention procedures, and outcome evaluations are described and discussed. Issues related to psychological therapy, such as ethics, crises, negative effects, and spontaneous change, are examined. The full range of types of therapy are presented.

PART SEVEN

Social Behavior

17

Attitudes and Social Perception

ATTITUDES
   The Nature of Attitudes
   Attitude Formation
   Attitude Change
   Attitudes and Behavior
   Attraction: The Case of
     Interpersonal Attitudes
SOCIAL PERCEPTION
   Inferring Emotions
   Inferring Personality Traits

Biases in Social Perception
   Implicit Theories of Personality
   The Survival of False Beliefs
SELF-PERCEPTION
   Perceiving Our Emotions
   Inferring Our Attitudes
SUMMARY
KEY TERMS
SUGGESTED READINGS

The next two chapters are about *social psychology*. This area of psychology is concerned with how people (or groups of people) affect others and are, in turn, affected by them. One major theme of social psychology is that people's social behavior is greatly influenced by their perceptions, feelings, and thoughts. A second major theme is that people's social behavior is greatly influenced by other people. The first theme is the topic of Chapter 17, and the second, Chapter 18.

By the time you read this chapter, we can predict that two things will have happened: (1) you will have formed an attitude toward the discipline of psychology, and (2) you will have formed an impression of your psychology professor. How did your attitude toward psychology develop? How did your impression of your professor develop? And how have your attitude and impression influenced your behavior? The question of how our feelings, beliefs, and perceptions both shape and are shaped by our social experience has fascinated social psychologists for decades. The areas of *social attitudes* and *social perception* are especially concerned with this issue.

ATTITUDES

THE NATURE OF ATTITUDES

Whether considering people's reactions to the issue of capital punishment, various brands of ice cream, politicians, or virtually any aspect of our world, we encounter great diversity. Psychologists use the term *attitude* to refer to the reactions people have to the objects and concepts in their environment. Attitudes are generally assumed to have three components: (1) *affect* (feelings), (2) *cognition* (beliefs), and (3) *behavior* (readiness to act). Generally, we assume some logical relationship among these components. For example, a person who *believes* that a particular ethnic group is aggressive may *feel* dislike for such people and therefore may tend to *act* in a discriminatory manner.

The importance of attitudes seems self-evident. Central to the acquaintanceship process, for instance, is the discovery of one another's attitudes. To "know" someone well means, among other things, having an intimate knowledge of the person's attitudes. Attitudes are also presumed to be important because most people believe that changes in behavior occur through changes in attitudes.

ATTITUDE FORMATION

Psychologists generally agree that our attitudes toward environmental protection, television commercials, Kiwi fruit, country music, or any other object or concept are not innate but are acquired (Rajecki, 1982). Two determinants of attitude acquisition are exposure and learning.

Mere Exposure. Every recording artist acknowledges the value of getting his or her recording played on the air. The more air time a record receives, the more popular it is likely to become, according to the conventional wisdom of the recording industry. The social psychologist Robert Zajonc (1965) believes this wisdom is, in fact, correct. According to Zajonc, one's liking of any object, idea, or person will increase simply through repeated exposure to it. Zajonc (1968) demonstrated this principle by showing that the more frequently the names of various cities and countries occurred in print, the more positively people evaluated them. Even meaningless stimuli become better liked with more exposure. It is unlikely that you have strong attitudes—positive or negative—to the Turkish words *Nansoma, Saricik, afworbu, ikitaf* and *kadirya*. But Zajonc (1968) has demonstrated that it is even possible

Attitudes toward any object or concept are not innate but acquired through exposure or learning. This is illustrated by the rapid rise in the 1980s of the number of those protesting nuclear weapons after many years in which those arms were largely ignored or taken for granted. (Marc Anderson)

ATTITUDES AND SOCIAL PERCEPTION

to produce increasingly positive attitudes toward incomprehensible foreign words such as these through repeated exposure.

The Learning of Attitudes. Attitudes, like other responses, are acquired through various mechanisms of learning. As we saw in Chapter 6, a behavior that is followed by a reinforcing stimulus will tend to be repeated (i.e., it will be learned). Attitudes can be acquired in the same way. Consider the formation of attitudes about gender differences. Sexist attitudes may develop in children because they are exposed to information that promotes sexism or because they are reinforced for expressing such attitudes. For example, if a child is greeted with smiles and nods every time that she or he says something sexist, such statements will become more frequent. They will be adopted by the child because they have been instrumental in obtaining outcomes the child values.

Insko (1965) conducted an interesting study which showed how subtly attitudes can be instrumentally conditioned. He called students at the University of Hawaii by telephone and asked them to indicate whether they agreed with a set of statements about a campus issue. For half the students, the interviewer said "good" (positive reinforcement) whenever the statements favored the pro side of the issue. For the other half, the experimenter said "good" whenever their statements favored the con side of the issue. A week later, an instructor handed out an attitude survey in class. Some of the items on the survey were identical with those that had been reinforced with a "good" on the telephone a week earlier. The students did not realize that the survey was related to those phone calls. The results indicated that even in a different context, and after a week's delay, students continued to endorse the attitude statements that had been reinforced over the phone.

The pairing of words with attitude objects may also contribute to attitude formation. To say that a Jew is "cheap" or "shrewd," or that blacks are "shiftless" or "lazy," not only conveys false information but pairs an ethnic name with a word which has previously been conditioned to evoke a negative emotion. One effect of this pairing is to bring about a negative feeling every time Jews or blacks are considered. Attitudes acquired in this way are difficult to change even when they are contradicted by further information. The negative feeling will often remain attached to the social categories even after the label that generated this feeling is seen not to apply.

ATTITUDE CHANGE

Once formed, attitudes do not remain fixed; they can and do change. Most of us have little difficulty identifying a variety of issues, ranging from political questions to consumer goods, on which we have changed our attitudes. Attitude change is often brought about by the same mechanisms that contributed to the formation of the original attitude: experience and learning. A person's attitude toward "big-city" living, for instance, may change as he or she spends more time in one. Another mechanism of attitude change that has fascinated psychologists is *persuasion.* Often, we change our attitudes because of what others tell us. Psychologists became especially interested in persuasion after observing the tremendous influence that propaganda had during World War II. Most research on persuasion focuses on the factors that facilitate it (Hovland, Janis, & Kelley, 1953). Two of the most important factors in this regard are the communicator and the communication.

Koala bears evoke positive feelings in most people because the labels attached to them—cute, cuddly, furry—evoke positive feelings. (Ted Burmiller/Monkmeyer)

Communicator Characteristics. One important determinant of what information we believe is whom we hear it from. The person who is associated with an attempt to influence us is critically important to its success. This fact is clearly demonstrated in the people whom advertisers select to "sell" their products on televison. For most of the 1970s and well into the 1980s the person most sought after by television advertisers was the news anchorman Walter Cronkite. The reason was simple enough. Cronkite was the most "trusted" person in America. Perceived *trustworthiness* is one of the most important characteristics of an effective or credible source. Perceived *expertise* is another. The more knowledgeable people are perceived to be about what they are discussing, the more credible they will seem to us and the more influenced we will be by their appeals. Expertise can take the form of either personal experience or technical knowledge. For example, proponents of nuclear disarmament may try to increase the credibility of their message by seeking the endorsement of a victim of a nuclear explosion (such as a survivor of Hiroshima) or a Nobel-prize-winning nuclear physicist. Similarly, advertisers may try to promote laundry detergent by selecting a spokesperson who has technical expertise in this area (e.g., a chemist who tells you of the product's uniquely effective chemical makeup) or one with obvious practical experience (e.g., a woman with nine exceptionally dirt-prone children).

Another characteristic of a communicator that affects persuasive power is his or her *attractiveness*. Chaiken (1979) found that physically attractive communicators were more successful in changing people's beliefs. The prevalence

HIGHLIGHT 17.1
Television and Attitude Change

Various individuals and institutions (parents, peers, teachers, governments) act as important agents of attitude formation. They control the information we are exposed to and shape the nature of our social experience. One of the most powerful agents of attitude formation and change is television.

Television is so central to our lives that it is difficult to imagine what they would be like without it. Indeed, it has been estimated that by the time the average American youth finishes high school, he or she will have spent as many hours watching television as in school (Comstock, Chaffee, Katzman, McCombs & Roberts, 1978).

The influence of the medium on the process of attitude formation and change is difficult to estimate. The most obvious type of persuasion that occurs on television is advertising. Manufacturers of every conceivable product attempt to influence our attitudes and behavior through a series of carefully designed 30-second commercials. The fact that advertisers pay hundreds of thousands of dollars for a few seconds of prime viewing time should indicate just how influential this strategy can be.

Evidence of the effectiveness of TV advertising is easy to find. For example, not too many years ago, A & W root beer boosted its share of the market from 15% to 50% after only 6 months of television advertising. And why do you think that while the Consumer Union says that "an aspirin is an aspirin is an aspirin," some aspirin costs five times as much as others? You've got it—advertising. The power of television to "sell" products is well known by politicians, who spend an increasing proportion of their campaign funds on TV advertising. Joseph Grush (1980) analyzed candidate expenditures in all the 1976 Democratic presidential primaries and found that those who spent the most money on TV advertising usually got the most votes.

Perhaps the most serious (and subtle) persuasive effect of the medium is its influence on our attitudes toward social categories. Television, in its depiction of people be-of young, beautiful actresses and actors in television commercials suggests that advertising agencies believe in the power of attractiveness to persuade. Likability also affects communicator effectiveness, as a study by Eagly and Chaiken (1975) demonstrates. A communicator who expressed positive attitudes toward students (the likable communicator) produced more change in students' attitudes toward health issues than did a communicator who expressed negative attitudes (the unlikable communicator).

Communication Characteristics. The nature of the communication also determines how successful an attempt to influence will be. Many factors pertaining to communication form and content have been studied (e.g., complexity, novelty, and organization). The research suggests that in devising persuasive communications, such as advertisements or political speeches, many factors need to be taken into account. One that should be addressed is whether to present both sides of an issue or only one side. For example, if someone wished to convince an audience that the development of nuclear energy is undesirable, should he or she acknowledge that nuclear energy has some benefits, or only dwell on its disadvantages? Arguments that present both sides of an issue are generally more persuasive than arguments merely advocating the communicator's view. Hovland, Lumsdaine, and Sheffield (1949) found that two-sided arguments were especially effective with better educated people who were initially opposed to the communicator's view but were willing to listen to it.

longing to various social groups, can greatly affect general attitudes toward these groups. Gerbner (1980), for example, contends that mental patients suffer an unjustifiably negative image because they are portrayed on television as unpredictable, dangerous, and evil. He finds that while 40% of all prime-time "normal" male characters are shown to be violent, 73% of mentally ill males are depicted as violent; and while only 29% of prime-time "normal" female characters are violent, 71% of females portrayed as mentally disordered are violent. Gerbner believes that these portrayals can lead to unreasonable fear, degradation, and ostracism of those who have been afflicted with mental illness. To support his charge, he cites one study which asked respondents in 413 households to describe *criminally insane* people without defining the term. All those described by the respondents were murderers, and many were mass murderers. In fact, Gerbner asserts, only 14% of people diagnosed as criminally insane are even accused of murder.

But television can also produce positive shifts in attitudes. Wuthrow (1982) comments on a study conducted by the American Jewish Committee following the television drama "Holocaust," a 9-hour mini-series, first broadcast in 1978. Forty percent of the viewers of this program said that their feelings about Jews had been changed by the program, and virtually all changes were positive. Furthermore, those who watched the program were more in favor of American support for Israel after watching the program than before.

Television can affect virtually all our conceptions of the world. One misconception it appears to promote concerns crime. Gerbner and Gross (1976) have found that television both inflates people's estimates of the likelihood that they will be victimized by crime, and increases the amount of fear they experience about crime. As Haney and Manzolati (1984) indicate, this misconception may lead people to advocate more punitive solutions to crime than they otherwise would.

The power of television has recently been directed toward changing undesirable beliefs. During 1978–1979 a public television series, "Freestyle," was designed to alter children's sex-role stereotypes. It attempted to convince them, for example, that it is all right for females to do mechanical, scientific, and athletic things and for males to be nurturant and do housework. Johnson, Ettema, and Davidson (1980) studied over 7,000 children, some of whom had not seen the programs, some of whom had seen them, and some of whom had seen them and discussed them with their teacher. The program was a qualified success. Simply viewing the program produced a slight change in attitudes. However, when children both viewed the program and discussed it with their teacher, the change in attitudes was considerable.

Another question that someone devising a persuasive communication must address concerns the emotionality of the appeal. Is a communication likely to be more or less effective if it arouses fear in its audience? A lively controversy has developed over the effectiveness of *fear appeals*. Early studies indicated that low-fear appeals were more persuasive than high-fear appeals (Janis & Feshbach, 1953), perhaps because the tension associated with high-fear levels led the audience to block out the message. However, more recent studies have found that high-fear appeals are more influential in changing attitudes toward such things as the advisability of taking injections for tetanus (Dabbs & Leventhal, 1966), adhering to safe driving recommendations (Leventhal & Niles, 1965), and improving dental hygiene practices (Evans, Rozelle, Lasater, Dembroski, & Allen, 1970). It appears that fear arousal does increase attitude change as long as it is not too extreme, and is accompanied by reassurances that the feared outcome (e.g., cancer, gum disease, nuclear destruction) can be avoided.

ATTITUDES AND BEHAVIOR

Attitudes in and of themselves do not have much relevance to society. Attitudes do not kill people, elect politicians, or make television advertisers rich. It is people's action (or inaction), not their attitudes, that alters the world. But don't people's attitudes influence their actions? Most psychologists believe so. Psychologists have been dismayed, however (as you probably are), to find that research on this question has often failed to find a strong link between attitudes and behavior (Wicker, 1969). In other words, it is often impossible to use people's attitudes to predict their behavior, and knowledge of behavior does not necessarily enable you to deduce attitudes. The alarm caused by these early findings has diminished as we have come to realize the complexities involved in the relationship between attitudes and behaviors.

For one thing, we now know that if you wish to predict a specific behavior, it is necessary to assess a correspondingly specific attitude (Ajzen & Fishbein, 1980). For example, if you wish to predict how often people brush their teeth, you should ask them for their attitude toward toothbrushing rather than toward a more general concept such as "personal hygiene." If you wish to change people's behavior, such as their health practices, you must change their attitude toward particular practices (e.g., jogging) rather than toward the general concept of "health fitness" (Olson & Zanna, 1983).

Another reason our attitudes do not always predict our behavior is that we are not always mindful of them. We often act simply without taking much thought. Snyder and Swann (1976) asked 120 male students for their attitudes toward affirmative-action employment policies. Two weeks later the students were invited to act as mock jurors in a sex-discrimination court case. Some of them were first asked to take "a few minutes to organize your thoughts and views on affirmative action" before giving their verdict; others were not. The results indicated that a correspondence between attitudes and verdicts occurred only for those students asked to reflect on their attitudes.

The Theory of Cognitive Dissonance. Some years ago, a sample of smokers and nonsmokers were surveyed about their beliefs on the link between smoking and cancer (Kassarjan & Cohen, 1965). Only 10% of the nonsmokers disagreed with the proposition that a strong link had been established between smoking and cancer. However, over 40% of the smokers disagreed with this proposition. How are we to explain the difference in the beliefs of smokers and nonsmokers? Are people who believe that smoking is not dangerous more likely to smoke, or does the experience of smoking lead people to believe that it is not dangerous?

Leon Festinger (1957), in his highly influential theory of *cognitive dissonance,* contends that while attitudes may often precede actions, actions (e.g., smoking) can often precede the development of beliefs (e.g., smoking is not dangerous to your health). Dissonance theory focuses primarily on the discrepancies between actions and beliefs. People like to be consistent—we like our attitudes to be consistent with our behavior. Whenever we experience inconsistency in our cognitions (the knowledge of our feelings, beliefs, and actions), we also experience an unpleasant state known as *dissonance.* One way to reduce dissonance, according to Festinger, is to bring our attitudes more in line with our actions.

To illustrate how this works, let us return to the example about smoking. The cognition "I smoke" is inconsistent (dissonant) with the cognition "Smoking is dangerous to my health." A person who simultaneously holds these cognitions is likely to experience some psychological discomfort (i.e., dissonance). How does the person escape this discomfort? The most obvious solution would be to quit smoking. The cognition "I do not smoke" is consonant (not dissonant) with the cognition "Smoking is dangerous to my health." But if you have ever tried to quit smoking, you realize that it is not easy. If quitting is too difficult, the smoker could change her attitude about its dangers instead. If she can convince herself that "smoking hasn't really been proven to be dangerous," the inconsistency in her cognitions will be eliminated and her dissonance reduced. It is through just such a process of self-justification that dissonance theory predicts how our actions can influence our attitudes.

Fear arousal increases attitude change toward such things as quitting smoking as long as it is not too extreme and is accompanied by reassurances that the feared outcome—in this case, cancer—can be avoided. (American Cancer Society)

Dissonance theory has generated more research than any other theory of attitude change because it is so counterintuitive. To say that actions can influence attitudes seems to be equivalent to saying that effects can come before causes. It has also led to many surprising findings. One of the best known is that the *less* justification people are provided with for behaving in a manner inconsistent with their attitude, the *more* likely they are to change their attitude toward their behavior. This effect was first demonstrated in a classic experiment conducted by Festinger and Carlsmith (1959). Subjects were asked to perform an exceedingly boring task: either repeatedly shifting each of the pegs in a pegboard a quarter-turn, or lining up spools in a tray, dumping them out, and lining them up again and again. When subjects were finished they were offered either a small reward ($1) or a large one ($20—it was 1959) for telling the next subject that the tasks they had just performed were really quite interesting (a blatant lie). All the subjects voluntarily complied with this request. After engaging in this attitude-discrepant (deceitful) behavior, subjects were asked to indicate their own liking for the tasks. Those who had been paid $20 for telling the lie found the tasks boring, as did a control group of people who were not asked to talk to the next subjects. But those who had been paid only $1 for telling the same lie reported a more positive attitude toward the tasks (see Figure 17.1).

How are we to explain this *less-leads-to-more effect?* Apparently, if our attitude-discrepant behavior can be situationally justified (as it was for subjects paid a lucrative $20), there is no need to change our attitudes. Presumably, subjects in this condition believed that anyone would tell a "white lie" in the same circumstances. On the other hand, if our attitude-discrepant behavior cannot be situationally justified (as it appears not to have been for the subjects paid a mere $1), dissonance will appear and give rise to self-justification. Self-justification generally takes the form of attitude change.

ATTRACTION: THE CASE OF INTERPERSONAL ATTITUDES

Attitudes toward other people are among the most significant of all social attitudes. Few of us could agree with Will Rogers, who said that he had never met a man he didn't like. Probably even *he* liked some people more than others. Most of us have wondered both why we like some people more than

Figure 17.1
Dissonance and Attitude Change. Average rating of task enjoyment. Dull tasks were rated as somewhat more enjoyable when a small monetary incentive, one dollar, was given, but students who were paid twenty dollars for lying rated the tasks as dull as did those in a control group. (Adapted from Festinger & Carlsmith, 1959).

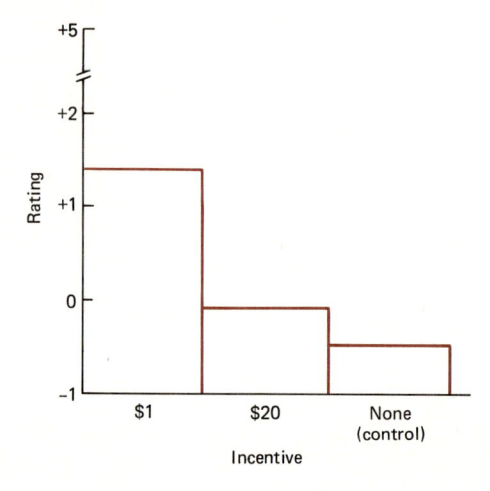

ATTITUDES AND SOCIAL PERCEPTION

others and how we might make ourselves more likable. Social psychologists have found that two factors exert considerable influence on the liking process: familiarity and similarity.

Familiarity. People, like songs, often "grow on us." Consistent with the mere exposure hypothesis we discussed earlier, studies have shown that familiarity, rather than leading to contempt, generally leads to increased liking for people (Moreland & Zajonc, 1982). Zajonc (1968) showed subjects photographs of people. Some pictures were shown often, others were shown infrequently. Later, subjects were asked how much they liked the people depicted in the photographs. People whose pictures were seen frequently were rated as more likable than people whose pictures were only seen once or twice. In the real world as well, we generally like most the people with whom we are most familiar. A study of 44 Maryland State Police trainees (Segal, 1974) illustrates this point nicely. As is common in police training, the trainees in this study were assigned to classroom seats and to living quarters according to the alphabetical order of their last names. Thus the trainees near one another in the alphabet also had the most experience with each other during the training period. When their friendship choices were examined at the end of the training session, familiarity proved to be the major determinant of liking. The Ardvarks and Bakers preferred each other to the Youngs and Zowzers.

Similarity. According to one proverb, "birds of a feather flock together," but another tells us that "opposites attract." Which is true: Is similarity or dissimilarity more likely to lead to attraction? By and large, research agrees with the first proverb. Whether considering physical characteristics, such as height, age, and physical attractiveness, or psychological characteristics, such as attitudes and personalities, we appear to like similar others more than dissimilar others (Berscheid, 1985). Are all types of similarity equally important, however? Not according to a study conducted by Touhey (1972), who used a computer dating service to investigate attraction. Some couples in this study were purposely matched according to religious or sexual atti-

Similarity of looks, attitudes, and personalities is more likeable than dissimilarity. (Baron Wolman, Freda Feinwand/Monkmeyer, Judy S. Gelles)

tudes; others were *mis*matched in these areas. After the couples had their date, their attraction for each other was measured. Pairs with similar attitudes were found to be more attracted to each other than were mismatched pairs. Even more interesting, the results showed that although males were most attracted to females with similar *sexual* attitudes and least attracted to females with dissimilar sexual attitudes, females were most attracted to men with similar *religious* attitudes and least attracted to men with dissimilar religious attitudes.

HIGHLIGHT 17.2
Love

Most of us have wondered about the nature of love. People are especially likely to consider this question when they are trying to decide whether they reallly *love* someone or just *like* them a lot. What is the difference between liking and loving someone? Do the two types of feeling differ only in degree, or also in quality? You may be surprised to know that psychologists have only addressed this issue in the last 10 or 15 years. Rubin (1973) defined love as consisting of three components:

1. *Caring:* the feeling that another person's satisfactions are as important to you as your own.
2. *Attachment:* the need or desire to be with the other, to make physical contact, to be approved of and cared for.
3. *Intimacy:* the bond or link between two people. It is manifested by close and confidential communication between them.

On the basis of his definition of love, Rubin set out to devise a questionnaire that could measure this emotion. He wrote items that were thought to measure each of the three elements of love:

1. *Caring:* (for example, "If ____ were feeling badly, my first duty would be to cheer him (her) up.")
2. *Attachment:* (for example, "If I were lonely, my first thought would be to seek ____ out.")
3. *Intimacy:* (for example, "I feel that I can confide in ____ about virtually everything.")

Besides creating a *love* scale, Rubin also created a *liking* scale that assessed the feelings of liking and respect, the basis of the type of interpersonal attraction investigated in most attraction studies. Examples:

1. "I think that ____ is unusually well adjusted."
2. "I have great confidence in ____'s good judgment."
3. "____ is the sort of person whom I myself would like to be."

Rubin gave his love and liking scales to 182 dating couples. Alone and confidentially, each member of the couple filled out the scales with their partner as the object of the questions. Later they were asked to complete the scales a second time with a same-sex friend as the object of the questions. Several interesting results emerged from this research. First, friends and lovers were both well liked, but friends did not score highly on the love scale. This was as expected. More surprising were the differences that emerged between males and females. Contrary to the popular belief that women are more romantic than men, no differences were found between males and females in the degree of love expressed for their partner. Moreover, subsequent research (Rubin, Peplau, & Hill, 1981) has shown that men fall in love more easily than women and that women fall out of love more easily than men. However, females expressed more love for their same-sex friends. This result supports the view that female same-sex friendships are closer and more intimate than male friendships. Males usually express love feelings only in opposite-sex relationships. There also appear to be different types of love. Hatfield and Walster (1981) have emphasized the distinction between passionate and companionate love. *Passionate love* is an intense emotional experience that we feel in our bodies. As Hatfield and Walster say, it is characterized by "a confusion of feelings: tenderness and sexuality, elation and pain, anxiety and relief, altruism and jealousy." *Companionate love,* on the other hand, is lower key. It is a deep, affectionate attachment that involves intimacy and respect. As Baron and Byrne (1984) observe, it is difficult to write a catchy song about companionate love, but it is this variety that helps couples reach that elusive interpersonal goal of a lasting relationship.

FOCUS ON THE PSYCHOLOGIST

Ellen S. Berscheid

ELLEN S. BERSCHEID (Ph.D., University of Minnesota), is professor of psychology at the University of Minnesota, and editor of *Contemporary Psychology*. She is the former President of the Society of Personality and Social Psychology, and a former fellow of the American Psychological Association, from which she received the award for Distinguished Research in Social Psychology. She recently co-authored *Close Relationships*, and her current research focuses on interpersonal attraction.

I am always a bit disconcerted when students ask, "What originally interested you in the physical attractiveness variable?" The fact of the matter is that I didn't choose physical attractiveness as a research area—it chose me, or so it has often seemed.

For I was, and am, fascinated with questions of interpersonal attraction: Why one person likes another, but the other does not reciprocate; why feelings of love toward another can be so strong that family, friends, and honor—indeed, even a kingdom—will be forsaken for that love; why the loss of a close companion often initiates the most severe and prolonged anguish that we humans, along with many other creatures in the animal kingdom, ever experience. All of human life—*all* of it, from beginning to end, from conception through the final death rattle—is shot through and through with the causes and consequences of interpersonal attraction. And this is true for every person, whether misanthropic hermit or social butterfly. Since sentiment for others is the theme of human life, it is obvious why the study of interpersonal attraction is both interesting and important.

The physical attractiveness factor, it turns out, comes with this territory. That physical attractiveness was a factor to be reckoned with in social attraction was first demonstrated by my colleague at the University of Minnesota, Elaine Walster (Hatfield). At that time, however, we thought it probably was important only among adolescents and in the dating and mating context.

We *had* been a bit curious about whether the tentacles of the physical attractiveness factor reached farther, especially into younger age groups, but we hadn't received much encouragement for this speculation. We'd asked elementary school teachers, for example, whether they had observed a relationship between a child's popularity and his or her physical attractiveness. Virtually all told us that our question was absurd! "All children are beautiful" was their inevitable reply, "They don't differ among themselves in how attractive they are." Their answer made good sense to us. After all, the young of any species tend to be attractive—even little wart hogs are cute!

But then Karen Dion, a graduate student in our lab at Minnesota, discovered data that would allow us rather easily to investigate the physical-attractiveness–popularity hypothesis. And since this would be a very different textbook if psychologists always believed everything people told us about themselves and human behavior, we went ahead with the study even though we didn't expect to find anything. We *did* find something, of course; there *was* an association between a child's attractiveness as judged by adults and how he or she was evaluated and perceived by other children in the nursery school class.

It was then that we knew that, like it or not, the influence of physical attractiveness was surely much stronger and more widespread than anyone had previously thought. And, whether one was interested in it or not, the physical attractiveness factor could no longer be ignored by those seeking to understand social attraction. It has not been. Over the years, many researchers in social psychology and in other of the social and behavioral sciences have developed a robust literature outlining the correlates and effects of physical attractiveness and demonstrating its potency for social attraction in almost all contexts and for persons of all ages and backgrounds. Today, applied professionals in many areas—physicians, plastic and oral surgeons, dentists, lawyers, mental health professionals, and the like—make good use of that information.

SOCIAL PERCEPTION

Except ourselves, nothing is more important to us than other people. People influence virtually every aspect of our life. It is not surprising, therefore, that we are so interested in understanding them. The process by which we learn about the moods, motivations, and personality traits of other people is called *social perception*.

INFERRING EMOTIONS

In our interactions with people, it is generally desirable, and sometimes critical, to know their emotional state. Are they upset that we were late? Glad to see us? Depressed over the break up of a love affair? Nervous about starting school? Happy with their math grade? Securing accurate knowledge about the emotional state of others may not be difficult if we ask them directly *and* if they answer truthfully. But often we are inhibited, or it is inconvenient to ask. Even when we do ask, we may suspect that others are not admitting their true feelings, to us or to themselves. As a result, we often rely on another source of information about feelings: a person's *nonverbal behavior*. Nonverbal behaviors that inform us of another's mood, feelings, or physical states include facial expressions, gestures, and body movements (Argyle, 1982). Without a doubt, the most informative nonverbal cue to our emotional state is our facial expression. As Cicero, the Roman orator, observed over 2,000 years ago, "The face is the image of the soul." Can you tell what emotions the people in Figure 17.2 are experiencing?

If you judged that person A is disgusted, person B is happy, and person C is angry, you agree with most other people. Certain facial expressions are widely believed to be linked to certain emotions (see Chapter 9). In fact, researchers have identified six emotions (happiness, sadness, fear, surprise, contempt/disgust, anger) that human beings from a diverse range of cultures reliably associate with particular facial expressions (Ekman & Friesen, 1975).

The face is not the only nonverbal cue to a person's internal state, however. Posture, for instance, will often tell us whether a person is bored or tense. Another particularly informative cue is body movement. Excessive body movement—especially when one part of the body is touching another (e.g., hair or chin stroking)—suggests emotional arousal. The more people engage in such behaviors, the higher their level of arousal or nervousness is assumed to be (Knapp, 1978).

How others feel about us is often of great interest, but we are not likely to ask about it directly. Fortunately, feelings of liking or hostility are often evident in nonverbal cues. Among the actions that suggest liking are: sitting face to face, leaning in the other's direction, and nodding in agreement to what is said. In contrast, we interpret sitting to avoid facing us directly, looking at the ceiling (or elsewhere) while we are speaking, and headshaking in response to our remarks as signs of negative feelings. (Clore, Wiggins, & Itkin, 1975).

Not all people are skilled at reading nonverbal cues. Research has shown that children become more nonverbally sensitive as they grow older, and that nonverbally sensitive people tend to be both better adjusted and more interpersonally skillful than those lacking nonverbal sensitivity (Rosenthal, Hall, Archer, Di Matteo & Rogers, 1979; Zuckerman, DeFrank, Spiegel & Larrance, 1982). The belief in "female intuition" may also be justified. Women have

ATTITUDES AND SOCIAL PERCEPTION   559

Figure 17.2
When asked to identify the emotions revealed in faces like these, individuals from several different countries showed considerable agreement. (Based on Ekman & Friesen, 1975.)

		\multicolumn{6}{c	}{Percent of subjects who correctly identified the emotion shown in each photo}
		United States	Brazil	Chile	Argentina	Japan	New Guinea
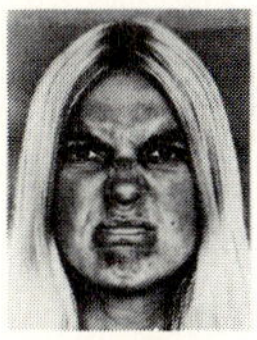	Disgust	92%	97%	92%	92%	90%	44%
	Happiness	97%	95%	95%	98%	100%	82%
	Anger	67%	90%	94%	90%	90%	50%

been consistently found to interpret voice cues as well as facial and body cues of emotions more accurately than men (J. A. Hall, 1978). Whether this difference reflects innate or learned abilities is not currently known.

INFERRING PERSONALITY TRAITS

Knowing another's emotional states or moods is not generally enough for us. Moods and emotional states change from situation to situation. To feel that we know other people and can confidently anticipate their actions, we must also know something about their personalities. What are their enduring characteristics or dispositions? Despite the common belief that it takes a long time to get to know anyone, social psychologists have found that we often make judgments about the personalities of others quite quickly and with remarkably little information.

Attribution Theory. If asked where our knowledge of other people's personality characteristics come from, most of us would indicate people's behavior or actions. It is not surprising, therefore, that a favorite topic of social psychologists in recent years is the complex process by which we go from observing behavior to inferring personality characteristics (Ross & Fletcher, 1985). For example, what would you assume about the personalities of the following people: a person who quit college in midsemester and took a job; a person who showed up late for an appointment; a student who complimented a professor on her lecture? Obviously, this is not easy to do without

Body posture will often tell us whether a person is relaxed or tense. (Peter Vandermark)

more information. Before we can make confident judgments about what a given act says about a person's personality, we must know the circumstances behind the act. Circumstances shed light on motivation: Why did he or she act that way? *Attribution theory* is concerned with this question of causal explanation.

The basic task confronting a person trying to interpret another's action is deciding whether the action reveals more about the person or about the situation in which the act occurs. Attributions to characteristics of the person are called *internal* attributions; attributions to characteristics of the situation are called *external* attributions. Many factors guide our search for the cause of another's behavior. To illustrate some of the basic principles of attribution theory, imagine that you overhear a student telling a group of people that her psychology course is "wonderful." How would you explain this student's enthusiasm for the course? Would you assume it revealed more about her or about the course? In the language of attribution theory, would you make an internal attribution (e.g., she's an extremely people-oriented person) or would you make an external attribution (e.g., it was an exceptionally well taught course)? Attribution theory (Kelley, 1967) says that in searching for a causal explanation, three types of information will be important to you:

1. How do other people respond to the same situation? If everyone raves about this particular psychology course, the student's behavior will be seen as having *high consensus,* and you will lean toward an external attribution. On the other hand, if no one else feels enthusiastic about the course, her behavior will be seen to have *low consensus,* and you will lean toward an internal attribution.
2. How does the person respond to similar situations? If the student raves about all her psychology courses, her behavior will be perceived to have *high consistency,* and you will lean toward an internal attribution. On the other hand, if the student does not like her other psychology courses, her behavior will be perceived to have *low consistency,* and you will lean toward an external attribution.
3. How does the person respond to dissimilar situations? If the student raves about all her psychology courses but none of her other courses, her behavior will be seen to have *high distinctiveness,* and you will lean toward an internal attribution. On the other hand, if she raves about all her courses (people-oriented and non-people-oriented courses alike), her behavior will be seen to have *low distinctiveness,* and you will be reluctant to make an internal attribution.

It is not difficult to think of occasions when we consider the factors of *consistency, consensus,* and *distinctiveness* in our search for causal understanding. It is also easy, however, to think of occasions when we do not know enough to assess the presence of these factors and yet still make an attribution. What principles do we follow in making an attribution when we do not have consensus, distinctiveness, or consistency information? The theory of *correspondent inferences* proposed by Jones and Davis (1965) offers one suggestion. These psychologists were interested in the following question: When do we assume that a particular act (e.g., an aggressive or friendly act) reflects a corresponding personality disposition (e.g., an aggressive or friendly nature). Jones and Davis addressed this question because it seemed obvious to them that some acts are much more revealing of underlying dispositions than are others. They identify two conditions that lead people to make *correspondent inferences* (inferences about disposition that correspond to the observed acts). First, the act must be done freely. If a person is told by a superior to be friendly to us, we will not assume that the person's friendliness reflects a friendly personality. Second, actions that are highly predictable or socially desirable are not as likely to lead to correspondent inferences as are unpredictable or undesirable acts. For example, rudeness in a waiter is more likely to lead to a correspondent inference than is courtesy. We expect courtesy from a waiter, not rudeness.

BIASES IN SOCIAL PERCEPTION

On the basis of attribution theory, it might appear that we are quite rational, even scientific, in our search for causal explanation. But are we? Psychologists have identified several attributional biases and errors that occur in social perception.

The Fundamental Attribution Error. One error we make repeatedly, so often in fact that it has been called the *fundamental attribution error* (Ross, 1977), is to infer more about people's personality from their behavior than is warranted. Even when their behavior is entirely explicable by the social constraints present in a situation, we still tend to believe that it is at least somewhat revealing of their personalities. Napolitan and Goethals (1979) had college students talk with a person, allegedly a clinical psychology graduate student, who acted either warm and friendly, or aloof and critical. Half the students were told beforehand that her behavior would be spontaneous. The other half were told that she had been instructed to pretend to be friendly (or unfriendly). The students' evaluations of the graduate student's behavior were startling. Whether they were told it was spontaneous or feigned made no difference in how they evaluated her character. When she *behaved* in an unfriendly manner, she was perceived to have an unfriendly personality, and when she *behaved* in a friendly manner, she was seen as having a friendly personality.

The fundamental attribution error is a problem for everyone, but especially for those whose job requires them to behave in ways inconsistent with their personality. Actors and actresses, for example, are frequently frustrated by the common belief that they actually have the characteristics of the parts they play. Leonard Nimoy, who played Spock on *Star Trek,* suffered so much from this bias that he even wrote a book entitled *I Am Not Spock* (Myers, 1983). Most of us do not go to the lengths of writing a book, but such common expressions as "I'm only doing my job," "It was only an act," or "I'm not myself today" indicate that we are all aware of the fundamental attribution error and often try hard to avoid being victimized by it.

The Just-World Effect. The fundamental attribution error has many negative consequences. Among the most devastating is the tendency to derogate victims of misfortune. People prefer to attribute a victim's misfortune to his or her character or actions rather than to circumstances or bad luck (Lerner & Miller, 1978). For example, research by M. J. Lerner (1980) indicates that merely observing another person being innocently victimized is enough to make the victim seem less worthy. Lerner (1980) suggests that this results from our need to believe that the world is a just place in which people get what they deserve and deserve what they get. From early childhood, Lerner argues, we are taught that good is rewarded and evil punished. From this it is but a short leap to assuming that those who are rewarded must be good and those who suffer must deserve their fate. Knowing that others blame them for their misfortune is a large part of the burden experienced by rape victims, the terminally ill, and many others (Wortman, 1983).

The Self-serving Attribution Bias. Suppose that you had taken an exam on which you obtained a very high score. How would you explain this outcome? Would you attribute it to external factors (e.g., the test was easy, good luck)? We doubt it. Wouldn't you be more likely to attribute it to internal factors (e.g., your high level of intelligence, the long hours of study). Now imagine that you obtained a very low score on the same test. Wouldn't you be inclined to attribute this result to external factors, such as the unfairness of the test, bad luck, or the incompetence of the instructor?

This tendency to take credit for success and deny responsibility for failure has been termed the *self-serving attributional bias* (Miller & Ross 1975), and has been demonstrated in many situations (Tetlock & Levi, 1982). Examples of the self-serving bias abound in everyday life. Have you ever heard a team cite bad officiating as a reason for their *winning* a game, or heard an unsuccessful politician credit the intelligence of the electorate?

HIGHLIGHT 17.3

The Divergent Perceptions of Actors and Observers

Arabs and Israelis have fought five wars with each other in the last 40 years, yet they each see themselves as basically a "peace-loving" people (R. K. White, 1977). How is this possible? If we look at how each side explains these wars, we gain some insight into this paradox. Both Arabs and Israelis attribute the military activities of the other group to their "aggressive, expansionistic" nature. Their own military activities, on the other hand, are seen as primarily "defensive" and dictated by the nature of the enemy. The same behavior of self and others is thus explained quite differently. Consistent with the fundamental attribution error, each side explains the other side's behavior in dispositional terms, while interpreting their own in situational terms.

The divergence in perceptions of self and other is not unique to Arabs and Israelis. For example, I will be inclined to see my vote in the last election as determined by the qualities of the candidates, while an observer might be more inclined to see my political ideology as playing the determining role. The tendency for those performing an action to explain their own behavior more situationally than observers is a widely demonstrated phenomenon (Jones & Nisbett, 1971).

The *actor-observer* effect, as it is called, can lead to many misconceptions and is a frequent source of interpersonal conflict. To study the consequences of attributional disagreements, Orvis, Kelley, and Butler (1976) asked each member of a group of young heterosexual couples to describe major disagreements in their relationship. The incidents frequently involved criticism, teasing, or fighting. They were also asked to explain their own behavior in these incidents and to indicate how their behavior would be explained by their partner. Not surprisingly, people explained their own behavior in terms of external and unstable factors, such as other people and their physical or psychological state at the time. However, their partners tended to blame the actors' behavior on the latter's general characteristics, such as his or her selfishness or negative attitude toward the partner. Interpersonal conflict arises not only from what people do but apparently also from how people explain what they do.

The motivation behind the self-serving attribution bias appears to be the protection or bolstering of our own self-esteem. We are more likely to engage in self-serving attributions, for instance, when doing well on the task is important to us than when it is not (D. T. Miller, 1976). Moreover, people who explain their successes and failures with the most self-serving bias also tend to score *highly* on tests of self-esteem (Ickes, 1985). On the other hand, people who do not exhibit a self-serving bias tend toward depression (Miller & Moretti, 1985). Studies assessing the accuracy of self-attributions made by depressed and nondepressed people reveal that depressives are generally more accurate than their nondepressed counterparts (Alloy and Abramson, 1979). This finding suggests that depressed people may suffer because they see reality more accurately than do nondepressed people. They are, in effect, sadder but wiser.

IMPLICIT THEORIES OF PERSONALITY

Assume that you have inferred from Karen's behavior that she is a cold person. What else would you think you knew about Karen? Let's see. Would you infer that she was trustworthy or untrustworthy, generous or stingy, imaginative or unimaginative, happy or unhappy? Probably, you would say that she was also untrustworthy, stingy, unimaginative, and unhappy. Right? Why were you inclined, on the basis of one trait (coldness), to assume the presence of other traits (e.g., stinginess, unimaginativeness, and unhappiness)? Apparently, we believe that various traits are related to one another. These *implicit* (unverbalized) *theories* of *personality* enable us to take one trait (e.g., coldness) and make inferences about what other traits are also likely to be present. In the same way that our theory of combustion leads us to infer that "Where there's smoke, there's fire," our implicit theory of personality leads us to infer that where there is coldness there is unhappiness, stinginess, and so on.

Asch's Warm-Cold Study. Early evidence for implicit theories of personality was discovered by Asch (1946) in what has become a classic study in social psychology. Asch's experiment was simple and elegant. He presented subjects with one of two lists of trait adjectives that described a particular person. Subjects receiving the first list were told that the person was "intelligent, skillful, industrious, warm, determined, practical, and cautious," while subjects receiving the second list were told that the person was "intelligent, skillful, industrious, cold, determined, practical, and cautious." Note that the lists are identical except for the word "warm" in the first list and "cold" in the second.

Despite the high degree of similarity between the two lists, subjects in the two groups formed radically different impressions (see Table 17.1). While over 90% of those exposed to the "warm" target thought that the person would also be generous, happy, and sociable, less than 40% thought that the "cold" target would have these qualities. Asch's study not only demonstrated that we have theories about how various traits are related to one another, but also that when we are given pieces of information about a person, we integrate them into coherent and unified impressions. Even though six of the seven pieces of information about the two targets were identical, the overall impressions formed were quite different.

TABLE 17.1
Percent of subjects endorsing each adjective in the warm-cold conditions

Judged Adjective	"Extra" Adjective Warm	"Extra" Adjective Cold
Generous	91	8
Happy	90	34
Sociable	91	38
Imaginative	51	19
Humorous	75	10
Reliable	94	99

Source: Adapted from S. Asch. Forming impressions of personality. *Journal of Abnormal and Social Psychology*, 1946, 41, 258–290.

We infer people's characters on the basis of their appearance, because we associate certain personality traits with various levels of physical attractiveness. (John Running/Stock Boston)

Stereotypes. Imagine that you had observed that Karen was attractive, instead of cold. What else would you think you knew about her? Quite possibly you are inclined to say you wouldn't know much about her. After all, beauty is only skin deep, and so on. But think a little harder. Would you guess that she is friendly or unfriendly; truthful or deceitful; intelligent or unintelligent? If you are like most people, you probably guessed that she is more likely to be friendly than unfriendly, truthful than deceitful, and intelligent than unintelligent (Berscheid & Walster, 1978). Why do people make inferences about a person's character on the basis of his or her physical appearance alone? Apparently, we not only have theories about which personality traits go with what other personality traits, but also about which personality traits go with different levels of physical attractiveness. Children are taught these assumptions at an early age. Snow White and Cinderella are beautiful and kind; the witch and the stepsisters are ugly and wicked.

We also have theories, it turns out, about the personality characteristics associated with various specific physical characteristics, such as baldness, beardedness, and obesity. However, the implicit theories we hold about particular physical characteristics are often not very elaborate—knowing that a man has a beard may suggest to you that he is intelligent and psychologically strong but not much more (Roll & Verinis, 1971). Theories about social categories, such as gender, race, occupation, and nationality, will often be much more elaborate. Theories about the relationship between personality and physical or social characteristics are termed *stereotypes*. Stereotypes, like implicit theories of personality, operate as probabilistic statements: If a woman is warm, we assume that she is probably happy, generous, and kind; if a person is elderly, we assume that he is probably poor, sexually inactive, and lonely (Kogan, 1979).

THE SURVIVAL OF FALSE BELIEFS

Theories about people, or anything else, offer us several advantages. It is convenient to be able to know a book by its cover. Ultimately, however, theories about people are useful only if they are correct—if personality traits really do relate to physical and social characteristics as we believe they do. The problem, most social psychologists feel, is that our theories are often wrong, and therefore lead us to erroneous inferences about people. But if our theories about people are incorrect, how do they survive when confronted with reality?

Imagine that it is the first day of classes. You attend your psychology course and discover that the professor has red hair. You are happy because your stereotype of people with red hair is that they are warm and friendly. How might this affect your experience with your new professor?

Let us consider the effects of stereotypes on three processes: selective attention, selective interpretation, and self-fulfilling prophecies.

Selective Attention. We cannot attend to all aspects of reality; the complexity of our physical and social world forces us to be selective. One of the guides to selective processing of our social world is our beliefs or expectations (whether or not they are true). We are more likely to notice things if they are consistent with our preconceptions than if they are not (Zadny & Gerard, 1974). In fact, we are so strongly constrained by our preconceptions that the familiar expression "If I didn't see it, I wouldn't have believed it" could be modified to say, "If I didn't believe it, I wouldn't have seen it." If you expect the professor to be warm, for instance, you will be especially likely to notice signs of warmth, such as smiles, jokes, and eye contact. You will pay less attention to aspects of her behavior that suggest coldness, such as frowns, sternness, or sarcasm.

Our stereotypes also affect what we remember from a behavioral episode. Darley and Gross (1983) showed college students a videotape of a fourth-grade girl, Hannah, in which she was either in a depressed urban neighborhood, supposedly the child of lower-class parents, or in an affluent suburban setting, the child of professionals. On a second videotape all subjects observed Hannah taking an oral achievement test, on which she got some questions right and some wrong. The observers were then asked what they could remember of Hannah's performance. The results were dramatic. Those who had previously been introduced to "upper-class" Hannah recalled her getting most questions right; those who had met "lower-class" Hannah recalled her missing almost half the questions. Even though the performance of the "two" Hannahs was identical, the stereotype the observers had about social class made them see this "reality" quite differently.

Selective Interpretation. Stereotypes also influence how we interpret what we do notice. If you expect your professor to be warm, her voice will probably seem warm to you, as will her features, style of dress, and so on. Consider how the widespread belief that the physically attractive are more honest than the physically unattractive affects our perceptions. In one well-known study, Dion (1972) found that people viewed the minor transgressions of attractive children as less "naughty" than the same actions when performed by unattractive children. That physically attractive defendants receive shorter sentences in criminal trials than unattractive defendants (Stewart, 1980) further demonstrates how stereotypes can be perpetuated by interpretive distortion.

Ethnic stereotypes also greatly influence how people explain or interpret behavior. In a study conducted by Duncan (1976), white subjects watched a videotape that showed either a black or white man shove another person. When the subjects later reported their reactions to the incident, they said the act was more violent when it was performed by a black than by a white. When asked to explain the cause of the shove, subjects pointed to the situation when the perpetrator was white, but blamed the perpetrator himself when he was black.

Self-fulfilling Prophecies. As you are selectively attending to and intepreting your "warm" professor's behavior, you will not be passive. You will probably be laughing at her jokes, nodding at her statement of the course's objectives, and responding to her questions. In short, you will be responding warmly to her. Your warmth, in turn, may elicit warmth from her. Stereotypes or false beliefs can perpetuate themselves because their influence on our behavior can subsequently influence the behavior of others. The term *self-fulfilling prophecy* describes that phenomenon in which initially false expectancies (prophecies) become confirmed (fulfilled) because of their effect on the interaction sequence.

Let's see how the self-fulfilling prophecy can work with the physical attractiveness stereotype. Snyder, Tanke and Berscheid (1977) showed male subjects a picture of a woman with whom they believed they were going to have a telephone conversation. Half the subjects were shown a very attractive woman and half an unattractive one. The women they actually talked with were of average attractiveness. Snyder and his colleagues wanted to see how the beliefs of the males would affect the way women responded during the telephone conversations. Analysis of the women's comments during the conversations revealed that the women who were presumed attractive did, in fact, speak in a more warm, likable way than the women who were presumed unattractive. The men's erroneous beliefs had become a self-fulfilling prophecy, leading them to influence the women to fulfill the stereotype that attractive people are also desirable people.

SELF-PERCEPTION

How much did you enjoy the last party you attended? How helpful a person are you? What is your attitude toward energy conservation? In thinking about these questions, what information did you consider? We know that if you were answering these questions about someone else, a major source of information would be that person's behavior: How did they act at the party? Do they often help other people? Do they help only when it is convenient or even when it isn't? Do they own a fuel-efficient car? How do they heat their house? But surely we do not have to infer our own feelings, traits, and attitudes from our behavior. Don't we have inside information about ourselves that we do not have about others? According to *self-perception theory* (Bem, 1972), we do not have "privileged" information abour our own emotional states, attitudes, and traits. We have more information than others, to be sure, but only because we have had more opportunity to *observe* ourselves.

PERCEIVING OUR EMOTIONS

Just as we observe others, we also draw inferences about ourselves on the basis of behavior and the context in which it occurs. You may be surprised to learn that it is very difficult to find physiological differences between people who are angry and ones who are sexually aroused (Fehr & Stern, 1970). We have all experienced anger and sexual arousal, and the two emotions would certainly seem to be quite distinct. But if our physiological reactions are so similar in the two states, why do we see the emotions as being so distinct? According to self-perception theory, we distinguish between the two emotions because the situational contexts in which we experience them are generally so distinct.

As we saw in Chapter 9, Schachter and Singer (1962) proposed that the experience of emotions requires two things: (1) a state of undifferentiated physiological arousal, which tells the person that he or she is agitated; and (2) a cognitive inference, based on situational cues, which tells the person what the agitation means.

We are particularly likely to misattribute our arousal, and think we are feeling something which we are not, when situational cues are ambiguous. The Roman poet Ovid recognized this over 2,000 years ago. In his book *The Handbook of Romantic Conquest* (a precursor to *Sex and the Single Male*), he recommended to men that a good time to arouse passion in a woman was while she was observing gladiators fight. The arousal produced by observing men kill each other was apparently often misattributed by the women, at least in part, to the charms of their dates.

Zillmann and his colleagues (Zillmann, Johnson, & Day 1974) found that people who were shown erotic material after they had been aroused through physical exercise reported being more sexually aroused than did those who

A person working for a political candidate can be motivated by either intrinsic interest (the desire to see the candidate elected) or extrinsic interest (a job, influence, etc.) (Paul Conklin/Monkmeyer)

had not exercised. In a second experiment (Zillmann, Katcher & Milavsky, 1972), people who had been aroused through physical exercise expressed more anger at someone who had frustrated them than did those who had not exercised. In both of these experiments, the subjects probably knew that at least some of their arousal was due to physical exercise, but they did not appear to think that the exercise could account for all of their arousal.

INFERRING OUR ATTITUDES

When Alice in Wonderland said, "How do I know what I think till I hear what I say?", she was speaking like a self-perception theorist. According to self-perception theory, just as we infer the attitudes of others from their words and actions, we also infer our own attitudes from our words and actions. Consider a person who engages in an activity for which he or she is rewarded lavishly. Would you assume that the person's motivation for engaging in the activity was intrinsic interest (for the task's own sake) or extrinsic interest (for the reward)? Obviously, it could be either. But what if the person had not received any reward for engaging in the activity? Wouldn't you now be more confident in assuming that the person was motivated by intrinsic interest? The presence of a reward, therefore, reduces the likelihood that we will assume that another is intrinsically motivated. Self-perception theory asks whether the presence of rewards affects our self-perceptions in a similar fashion. That is, do we assume that we have less intrinsic interest in activities for which we are rewarded?

Lepper, Greene, and Nisbett (1973) asked nursery school children to draw with attractive, new Magic Markers. Some of the children were told that they were drawing to obtain a Good Player award, which included a certificate with colored ribbons. Two other groups of children were offered no extrinsic reward for playing with the equipment, although one of the groups did receive the award (unexpectedly) after the activity. Several days later, the children from all groups were allowed to play with any toys they wanted. Children who had originally anticipated and received an external reward for playing with the drawing material played with it only about half as much as the children from the other groups (see Figure 17.3). It appeared that their

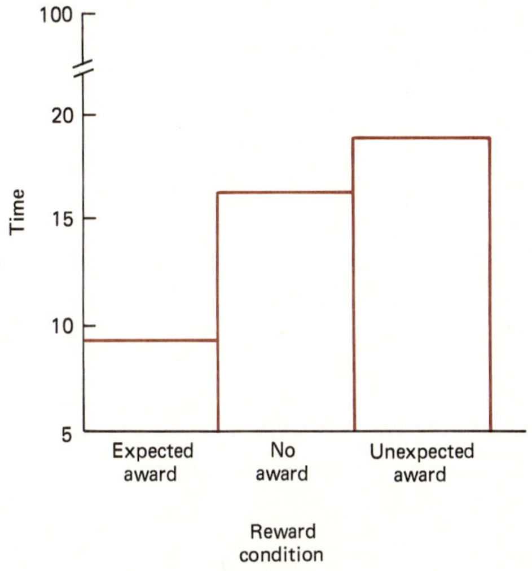

Figure 17.3
Overjustification and self-perception. The average percentage of free response time that children spent drawing in each of the reward conditions. (Adapted from Lepper et al., 1973.)

interest in the art activity had been diminished by the offer of the Good Player award.

The research on the *overjustification effect* does not suggest that we should never reward people. If people do not like particular activities, it may be of little danger to use incentives to coax the desired behavior (Boggiano & Ruble, 1981). On the other hand, if the interest is initially high, oversufficient justification may actually undermine it (Deci, Nezlek, & Sheinman, 1981).

SUMMARY

1. Social psychology is concerned with the ways in which people (or groups of people) affect others and are, in turn, affected by them. Two important determinants of social behavior are social perception and attitudes.

2. Attitudes are generally assumed to have an affective (feeling) component, a cognitive (belief) component, and a behavioral (action) component.

3. We develop attitudes through mere exposure to objects and through various mechanisms of learning. Television has a major influence on the development of social attitudes.

4. Attitudes can be changed through experience and learning as well as persuasion. Both communicator and communication characteristics influence the effectiveness of persuasion attempts.

5. Various characteristics of the communicator increase attitude change, for example expertise, trustworthiness, and attractiveness.

6. Communications that present two sides of an issue, and ones that arouse fear, are generally more persuasive than ones that present only one side of an issue and are emotionally neutral.

7. Attitudes and behavior are not always closely related. One reason that people's attitudes do not predict their behavior is that they do not always think of their attitudes when they act.

8. The theory of cognitive dissonance proposes that attitudes can be effects of behavior as well as causes. We tend to bring our attitudes in line with our behavior whenever there is a discrepancy between them that is not justified by some aspect of the situation.

9. Among our most significant social attitudes are those directed toward other people. Two factors that influence our attitudes toward other people are our familiarity with them and our similarity to them.

10. In judging the emotional states of others, we rely heavily on facial expression and other forms of nonverbal behavior, such as gesture, posture, and body movement.

11. Attribution theory is concerned with how people explain behavior. It attempts to specify those conditions under which they explain behavior by reference to internal characteristics of the actor, and those under which they make reference to external characteristics of the situation.

12. Our causal explanations are sometimes biased or in error. The tendency to underestimate systematically the effect that situations have on people's behavior is termed the fundamental attribution error. The tendency to take more personal responsibility for successful than unsuccessful outcomes is termed the self-serving attribution bias.

ATTITUDES AND SOCIAL PERCEPTION

13. People hold beliefs about how traits or characteristics are related to one another. Beliefs about which personality traits go together are termed implicit theories of personality. Beliefs about which traits go with various social categories are called stereotypes.

14. Self-perception theory contends that inferences about our own emotional states and attitudes are drawn in much the same way as are inferences about others.

KEY TERMS

Attitude
Cognitive dissonance theory
Nonverbal behavior
Attribution theory
Correspondence inference
Fundamental attribution error
The just-world effect
Actor-observer effect
Self-serving attribution bias
Implicit theories of personality
Stereotypes
Self-fulfilling prophecy
Overjustification effect

SUGGESTED READINGS

Buck, R. *Nonverbal behavior and the communication of affect.* New York: Guilford Press, 1983. A comprehensive, up-to-date discussion of many key aspects of nonverbal communication.

Duck, S. & Gilmour, R. *Personal relationships.* London: Academic Press, 1982. This volume provides an extensive review of research on the way in which interpersonal relationships develop.

Fiske, S. T., & Taylor, S. E. *Social cognition.* Reading, Mass.: Addison-Wesley, 1983. An entertaining and illuminating discussion of many aspects of social perception.

Rajecki, D. W. *Attitudes: Themes and advances.* Sunderland, Mass.: Sinauer Associates, 1982. A very thorough survey of current knowledge concerning attitudes and their effects.

18

Social Influence and Group Behavior

SOCIAL INFLUENCE
   Social Comparison
   Conformity
   Compliance
GROUP DYNAMICS
   Group Influence and
      Individual Performance

Group Problem Solving
   Social Roles
   Crowding and Personal Space
SUMMARY
KEY TERMS
SUGGESTED READINGS

We are social animals. Most of our daily life is spent interacting with other people. We tend to live in family units, work in groups, and play in the company of others. The acts, beliefs, and feelings of those with whom we interact greatly influence us. Consider four examples of social influence.

1. A group of social psychologists conducted a large study of American troops during World War II. These investigators found that men in the Army Air Corps were much less satisfied with opportunities for promotion than were men in the Military Police. What is surprising is that promotions in the Air Corps were extremely fast, while promotions in the Military Police were very slow. Why should the Air Corps troops have been unhappy with objectively better outcomes?
2. Steve and Sandy jog separately every Tuesday and Thursday, and together on Sunday. Both of them find that they run their 7-mile route 1- to 2-minutes faster when they jog together. Why should being together make them jog faster?
3. In the movie *Twelve Angry Men*, 12 jurors are locked in a bare, unpleasant room on an oppressively hot summer afternoon. Their task is to decide the fate of a young man accused of murdering his father. On the first vote, 11 of the jurors vote guilty; 1 votes not guilty. As the afternoon wears on, the arguments become more heated, but gradually the lone juror who originally voted for acquittal convinces the others that there is a reasonable doubt about the defendant's guilt. How was one person able to change the opinion of the majority?

SOCIAL INFLUENCE AND GROUP BEHAVIOR

We tend to live, work, and play in the company of others. (Marc Anderson)

4. Before capital punishment was abolished in most states, prisons often found it difficult to hire executioners. Then it was found that electrocutions could be performed with less personal anguish if each of three executioners pressed a button simultaneously. Although only one button would complete the electrical circuit, none of the three knew who had pushed the fatal button. A similar method has been used by military firing squads, where some rifles have been loaded with blanks and others with real bullets. Why are people more willing to harm others when their identity is concealed?

These examples illustrate four fascinating forms of social influence: relative deprivation, social facilitation, minority influence, and deindividuation. In this chapter we discuss these and other forms of social influence.

SOCIAL INFLUENCE

People influence one another in many ways. We begin with a discussion of how others influence the way we think about ourselves and our world.

SOCIAL COMPARISON

Curiosity is a powerful motivator of human behavior. Learning about ourselves and our world is important to all of us. Knowledge of this type can be acquired in different ways. Consider the following two sets of questions:

"Can you run 10 miles in less than an hour?" "What was your grade on your last psychology exam?" "How much did you give to charity last year?" and

"Are you a good runner?" "Are you smart?" "Are you a generous person?"

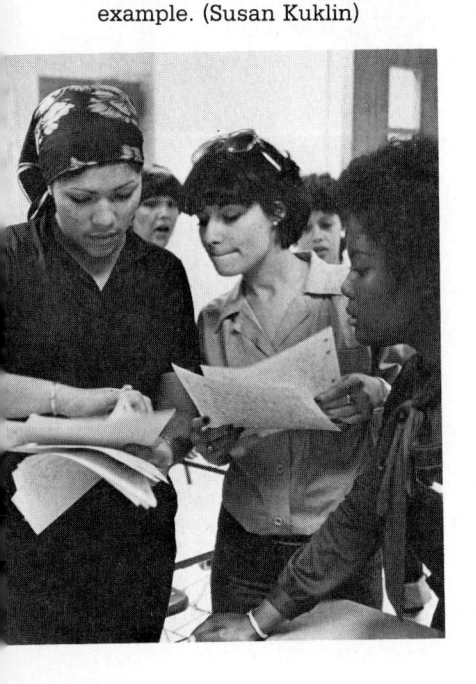

There are two clear differences between these sets of questions. First, knowing the answers to the second set is probably more important to you than knowing the answers to the first set. Second, while you can answer the first questions without reference to other people, you must compare yourself with others to answer the second set. The process of *social comparison* is an important part of social life. Without other people to compare ourselves to, we could not evaluate many things of great importance to us. We could not know whether our abilities were superior or inferior, whether our attitudes were liberal or conservative, or whether our fate was fair or unfair.

One implication of the social comparison process is that the particular people to whom we compare ourselves can greatly influence how we see ourselves. For example, whether we see ourselves as a "big fish" or "little fish" will depend on the size of the pond we are in as well as on the other fish in it. Davis (1966) reported that the best predictor of high school students' educational aspirational levels was not grades, SAT scores, or any other objective criterion of their intellectual ability, but the students' relative rank in their class. The higher students ranked, the more likely they were to aspire to college and postgraduate training. Students' perceptions of their intelligence, then, depended primarily on how intelligent they were *relative* to their classmates.

Social psychologists interested in social comparison processes have noted that we are not equally interested in comparing ourselves to all other people (Festinger, 1954). Some people are judged to provide more useful information about ourselves than others. For example, a person who has been playing tennis for 6 months might be very interested in evaluating his or her level of skill, but will probably not wish to compare him or herself with John McEnroe or Chris Evert Lloyd. Comparisons with players of similar experience and ability would be more useful. Many studies indicate that we value comparisons with those similar to us more than ones with those dissimilar to us when we are trying to evaluate our abilities, behaviors, and attitudes (Suls & Miller, 1977). To test this proposition, recall the last time you read the results of a survey on sexual attitudes or behavior. Didn't you first consult the data about people your own age? Surveys on topics such as sex are so popular because they provide people with information (otherwise hard to get) that helps them put their own attitudes and behavior in perspective.

Affiliating with Others. Imagine that your professor asked you not to talk about your next psychology lecture with your classmates after class. Would this be hard to do? Not likely. But what if your professor asked you not to talk about your next exam after it was over? Wouldn't this be much more of an imposition? This example illustrates an important point about social comparison processes: We do not depend equally on others for information in all situations. More specifically, we are most interested in comparing our actions and thoughts with those of others when we are anxious, uncertain, or confused (such as after an exam). If we depend more on social comparison information when we are anxious or uncertain, we should especially want to be with people when our level of anxiety is high.

In a classic series of studies Stanley Schachter (1959) studied the link between anxiety and the desire to affiliate. In the first of these experiments, college women who were strangers to one another were divided into two groups. Subjects in both groups entered a room where they found a serious-looking man wearing a white laboratory coat. He introduced himself as "Dr. Gregor Zilstein of the Medical School's Department of Neurology and Psychiatry." This "Dr. Zilstein" went on to explain that the subjects were par-

We are most interested in comparing our actions and thoughts with those of others when we are anxious or uncertain, as after an exam, for example. (Susan Kuklin)

ticipating in an experiment dealing with the effects of electric shock. (These students had originally signed up for the experiment to earn a course credit.) For subjects in the "high-anxiety" group Zilstein continued: "Now, I feel I must be completely honest with you and tell you exactly what you are in for. These shocks will hurt, they will be painful . . . but, of course, there will be no permanent damage." Subjects in the "low-anxiety" group, on the other hand, were told by Zilstein not to be disturbed by the word "shock" and were assured "that what you feel will not in any way be painful. It will resemble more a tickle or a tingle than anything unpleasant."

All subjects were told that they would have to wait outside for 10 minutes while the equipment was being set up. Subjects could wait alone or with others. After the subjects had indicated their preferences, the experiment was discontinued and the subjects were told its real purpose. The results confirmed Schachter's hypothesis. Approximately 66% of subjects in the "high-anxiety" group preferred to wait with other subjects, while only about 33% of the subjects in the "low-anxiety" group chose to wait with others.

The results of Schachter's first experiment support the proposition that anxiety leads people to want to be with others, but it does not tell us why. Remember, social comparison theory contends that people want to affiliate when they are anxious because anxiety increases dependency on information from others. In a second experiment, Schachter exposed all subjects to the "high-anxiety" instructions of the first experiment. Again, some subjects were given the choice of waiting alone or together with other students participating in the same experiment. However, another group of subjects was given the choice of waiting alone or with students who were waiting to talk to their academic advisors. The choice, then, for the first group was between waiting alone or together with similar others (i.e., others in the same boat as they were), and for the second group, between waiting alone or together with dissimilar people. On the basis of the earlier discussion you can guess what the first group did (over 60% chose to wait with others), but what do you think people in the second group did? Schachter predicted that since students waiting to talk to their advisors could provide little relevant information, the anxious subjects would not be interested in affiliating with them. Indeed, none of the subjects in the second group expressed a desire to wait with the other students. These results led Schachter to modify the proverb "misery loves company." In Schachter's words, "Misery doesn't just love any kind of company, it loves only miserable company" (Schachter, 1959, p. 24).

Fairness Is Relative. In response to a question about the fairness of the legendary football coach, Vince Lombardi, one of his players is alleged to have said: "Sure, he's fair, he treats us all like dogs." As well as being humorous, this statement provides an important insight into the psychology of justice. Generally, we decide whether our fate is fair by comparing ourselves with others (Crosby, 1982). When our fate is similar to that of others with whom we compare ourselves (however positive or negative it might be), we feel that we have been treated fairly; when it is different, we feel that we have been treated unfairly. It is a sense of *relative deprivation* rather than *absolute deprivation*, therefore, that causes the strongest resentment. As with other comparisons, the outcomes of our *reference group* (those people we consider similar to ourselves) will affect us most strongly. This is probably why the men in the Air Corps (described in the first example) experienced more dissatisfaction with their opportunities for promotion than men in the Military Police, whose chances for promotion were objectively worse. The reference group for the men in the Military Police was other men in the

Military Police, compared to whom they were doing quite well. The reference group for the men in the Air Corps did not include less fortunate units such as the Military Police, but rather other Air Corps members. That many of their own reference group were promoted faster than themselves prompted Air Corps members to feel dissatisfied with their opportunities.

Our satisfaction with our fate often changes when our reference group changes. The women's movement provides an interesting example. Many social observers have been puzzled that while women as a group appear to be better off than they were a few decades ago, their dissatisfaction with their lot appears to be increasing. How are we to explain this? Walster, Walster, and Berscheid (1978) suggest that while women traditionally have tended to compare their outcomes (such as wages and social prestige) only to those of other women, women today increasingly compare their outcomes to those of men. The women's movement, therefore, by changing the reference group of many women, has also increased their sense of injustice and resentment.

CONFORMITY

In addition to influencing how we think and feel about ourselves, other people influence our actions. Psychologists have identified several forms of behavioral influence. One common variety is *conformity*. Conformity occurs when the attitudes or behavior of a person or group is adopted by a second person or group. Conformity can occur without any intention to influence. Each of us has conformed to others on numerous occasions; but we have also resisted the pressure to conform on many other occasions. What determines when we conform and when we do not? Psychologists believe that we are especially likely to "go along" with others when we fear being seen or treated as a deviant. You do not always conform, therefore, because you are convinced that what you are saying or doing is correct. You may simply believe that others prefer, or even demand, that you do so.

The Asch Experiment. Imagine that you are participating in your first psychology experiment, which the experimenter tells you is concerned with "visual perception." You are a little nervous, but the task seems simple enough. You and five other subjects are seated at a circular table and shown a card with a vertical line (see Figure 18.1). With this line still in view, all the group members look at another card, which has three vertical lines of different lengths. One of these lines is the same length as the line on the first card;

There is great pressure to conform to the judgment of our peers on such things as taste in clothes and hair styles. (Donald Dietz/Stock Boston)

SOCIAL INFLUENCE AND GROUP BEHAVIOR

Figure 18.1
One of Asch's conformity experiments. The real subject, second from the right, experiences conflict and tension after hearing the five persons before him respond incorrectly. (Photo by William Vandivert, 65 Crescent St., Plympton, MA 62367, with permission of *Scientific American*.)

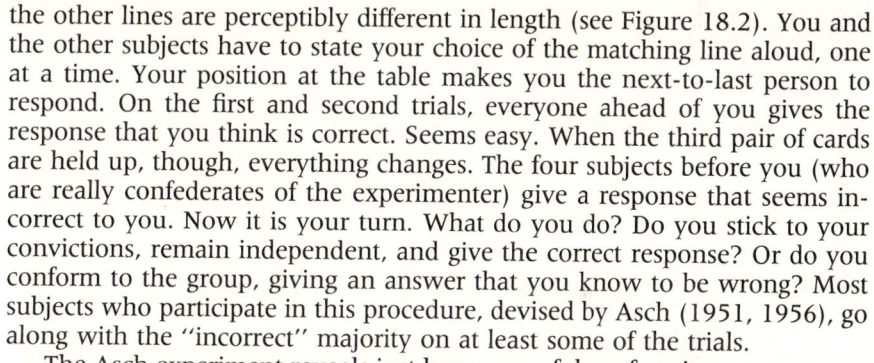

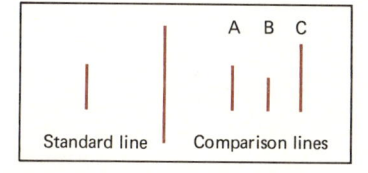

Figure 18.2
An example of the problems used by Asch in his studies of conformity. The subjects' task was that of indicating which of the three comparison lines (A, B, or C) matched the standard line in length.

the other lines are perceptibly different in length (see Figure 18.2). You and the other subjects have to state your choice of the matching line aloud, one at a time. Your position at the table makes you the next-to-last person to respond. On the first and second trials, everyone ahead of you gives the response that you think is correct. Seems easy. When the third pair of cards are held up, though, everything changes. The four subjects before you (who are really confederates of the experimenter) give a response that seems incorrect to you. Now it is your turn. What do you do? Do you stick to your convictions, remain independent, and give the correct response? Or do you conform to the group, giving an answer that you know to be wrong? Most subjects who participate in this procedure, devised by Asch (1951, 1956), go along with the "incorrect" majority on at least some of the trials.

The Asch experiment reveals just how powerful conformity pressures can be. First, the other people in this situation were strangers to the subjects, not people who could punish or reward the subjects to any great extent. The pressure to conform can be expected to be even greater when the others are friends or peers. Second, the judgment underlying the critical behavior in the Asch situation is an objective one—the perceived length of a line. Think how much greater the pressure to conform would be when the judgment is primarily subjective—having to do, for instance, with tastes in food, dress, or music.

Minority Influence. There is strong pressure on the minority to conform to the majority. This does not mean that the minority will always yield to the majority, however. For example, Asch (1951) found that a single confederate who breaks the majority's unanimity and gives the correct answer reduces the subject's conformity to less than 10%. A minority can sometimes even influence a majority. Moses, Jesus, Mohammed, St. Joan, Buddha, Galileo, and Gandhi are all examples of people who resisted pressure to conform and ultimately held sway over the majority.

Moscovici (1976) and his colleagues have explored factors that might lead a minority member to affect the majority. Especially important is the *behavioral style* of the deviant member, the way in which the person behaves in presenting and supporting a divergent position to others. A majority is most likely to be influenced by a deviant when he or she maintains a consistent and undeviating position, suggesting certainty and an unswerving dedication to a given point of view.

COMPLIANCE

People can often induce conformity in others without any intention of doing so. The term *compliance* refers to direct and intentional behavioral influence. Three techniques or strategies for inducing compliance are (1) the foot-in-the-door technique, (2) the door-in-the-face technique, and (3) low balling (Cialdini, 1984).

The Foot-in-the Door Technique. Door-to-door salespeople often start their "pitches" by asking potential customers to accept a free sample or a brochure describing their products. Having gotten their "foot-in-the-door," they then try for the big sell. This technique of first inducing people to comply with a small request before asking them to comply with a larger one has been shown to be effective in a wide variety of situations. In one of the most impressive demonstrations (Freedman & Fraser, 1966), suburban homemakers were called

---

HIGHLIGHT 18.1
Bystander Behavior in Emergencies

In 1963, a young woman, Kitty Genovese, was brutally murdered outside her apartment home in New York City. Although there were over 20 witnesses, no one intervened to help her until it was too late. The case of Kitty Genovese received enormous media attention both because it was so tragic and because it was identified by many social critics as an increasingly common phenomenon. The explanations for the failure of bystanders to intervene ranged from the dehumanizing consequences of urban life to the inherent sadism of Americans.

Two social psychologists, Bibb Latané and John Darley, were so intrigued by the phenomenon of bystander behavior in emergency situations that they conducted several studies. They wanted to know how the number of bystanders witnessing an event affected the likelihood of anyone intervening. The general finding in what is now over 200 studies on this question is that as the number of bystanders *increases*, the likelihood that anyone will intervene *decreases* (Latané & Nida, 1981). This may puzzle you. You might reasonably expect that as the number of bystanders increases, the likelihood of at least someone helping would increase. There appear to be two major reasons why we are less likely to intervene in emergencies when others are present: (1) the presence of others reduces the likelihood that we will correctly define the situation as an emergency, and (2) the presence of others reduces the responsibility we feel to intervene.

DEFINING THE SITUATION AS AN EMERGENCY

Many emergency situations are ambiguous. (Is that a fight, or are they just "horsing" around? Is that person ill, or is he just drunk?) Distinguishing emergencies from other situations is not always easy, especially since most of us have very little experience with emergencies. If we are confronted by a possible emergency while we are alone,

on the phone by a male experimenter who identified himself as a member of a consumer's group. He asked the women to answer a few simple questions about the soap they used at home. A week or so later, the same man called again with a much larger request. This time he asked if his organization could send a five- or six-man crew to the woman's home to conduct a thorough inventory of all the products she had on hand. This inventory was described as requiring over 2 hours and necessitating a complete search of all closets, cabinets, and drawers in the house. Clearly, this was no small request. Nevertheless, over 52% of those homemakers who had been first approached with the small request complied. This compliance rate was more than twice as great as that found in another group of homemakers who were called only once and presented with the second, larger request. Similar increases in compliance through the foot-in-the-door technique have been found in requests to sign a petition (Baron, 1973), participate in an experiment (Wagner & Laird, 1980), contribute to charity (Pliner, Hart, Kohl, & Saari, 1974), and place a giant sign on one's front lawn (Freedman & Fraser, 1966). The most widely accepted explanation of the foot-in-the-door effect relates to self-perception theory discussed in Chapter 17. The initial compliance with the small request leads people to infer that they are the type of person who "does that sort of thing"—who helps people requesting it. This perception, in turn, makes them more willing to comply with a larger, subsequent request.

we must rely on our own judgment. When other bystanders are present, however, we can observe their reactions before defining the situation. This appears to be when the problem starts. Since other people probably find the situation as ambiguous as we do, they will be trying to gauge our reaction and those of other bystanders. As they do this, however, they will be attempting to keep "cool" and poised. To overact or to be an alarmist in our society is considered undesirable, and most of us are very skilled at appearing calm and unconcerned when we are beset with fear and doubts. The problem, of course, occurs when puzzled and concerned bystanders look to other detached and unconcerned-looking bystanders and conclude that the situation is not really an emergency after all. If it were, surely these other people wouldn't appear so calm. Furthermore, the more calm-looking bystanders there are, the more likely we will be to define the situation as a nonemergency. In emergencies, therefore, the human tendency to check one's own view of reality with the views of others can have very adverse effects—especially for the victim.

DIFFUSION OF RESPONSIBILITY

Failure to define the situation as an emergency is not the only consequence of being one of a group of bystanders; ambiguity also exists as to the responsibility of any one person to intervene. Even if a bystander does define a situation as an emergency that requires intervention, he may be unsure of his *personal* responsibility to intervene. The more bystanders present, the less personal responsibility any one bystander will experience, and consequently the lower the likelihood that anyone will intervene. Darley and Latané (1968) tested this *diffusion of responsibility* explanation for the bystander inhibition effect. In this experiment, subjects overheard a young man (presumably in the next room) discuss the fact that he frequently had seizures similar to grand mal epilepsy. Shortly thereafter, subjects heard from the young man (actually a prerecorded tape) the following: "I-er-um-I think I-I need-er-if-if-could-er somebody er-er-er-er-er give me a little-er give me a little-er give me a little help here because I-er I'm . . ." (chokes, then quiet) (p. 379). The experimenter sat outside the room and recorded how long it took before the subject sought assistance for the victim. The results strongly supported the diffusion of responsibility hypothesis. About 85% of the subjects who were "alone" rushed to the victim's assistance. However, only 62% of the subjects in pairs, and 31% of those in five-person groups offered help.

HIGHLIGHT 18.2
Jonestown: A Case Study of Social Influence

In 1974, the followers of Jim Jones heeded his call to build a Christian, socialist commune in the wilds of Guyana. They planted their crops and built substantial, if plain, housing. They established medical facilities that were advanced by Guyanese standards. There was little racial friction. Children seemed especially happy.... Then... life at Jonestown began to change. Meat, served twice a day at first, was served once, then not at all. The workday increased from eight hours to eleven. The commune's security forces began to impose harsher discipline. Jones himself seemed to deteriorate physically.... In Jonestown's final months, [meetings] became a nightly ritual that often lasted from 7:30 until 3 a.m. Jones would ramble on for hours.... To [him], everyone—including the cult members themselves—was a potential enemy.... Announcing that the commune was on the verge of being destroyed, Jones ordered his medical team to bring out "the potion," a battered tub of strawberry Flavor-aide, laced with tranquillizers and cyanide. "Everyone has to die," said Jones. "If you love me as much as I love you, we must all die or be destroyed from the outside.... Bring the babies first," he commanded.

At the fringe of the huge crowd, armed guards fingered guns and bows and arrows. Some families edged forward voluntarily. Others held their ground. The guards moved in, grabbing babies from recalcitrant mothers holding them up to let "nurses" spray the poison down their throats with hypodermics.... "It's time to die with dignity," said Jones on the loudspeaker.... The apocalyptic end of Reverend Jones and his People's Temple left more than 900 people dead (*Newsweek*, 1978).

Inducing people to take their own life is the ultimate social influence. How was this accomplished? Should we look to the personalities of the cult members to explain their behavior, or can it be explained by social psychological processes that influence all of us? It would be simplistic to say that a few psychological principles can account for all aspects of Jonestown, but we think they can

The ultimate social influence: Jim Jones induced 900 people to commit suicide or murder in Jonestown, Guyana in 1978. (AP)

help make the phenomenon somewhat more comprehensible. Remember, although something like Jonestown does not happen every day, it is not unique. As Bayee Rensberger observed in the *New York Times* (November 26, 1978), "the birth and death of the People's Temple fit a pattern repeated many times in many cultures." Three of the social psychological phenomena we have discussed are particularly relevant to the case of the People's Temple: (1) the foot-in-the-door technique, (2) self-justification, and (3) social comparison processes.

The Door-in-the-Face Technique. Not only is the strategy of approaching people with a small request before a large one effective, but so is the opposite strategy. A number of studies have demonstrated that approaching a person with a large, unreasonable request (which the person invariably refuses) increases the likelihood that the person will comply with a second, smaller and more reasonable request. For example, Cialdini, Vincent, Lewis, Catalan, Wheeler, and Danby (1975) stopped college students on the street and asked

THE FOOT-IN-THE-DOOR TECHNIQUE

As we saw earlier, it is easier to induce people to comply with a large request if they have first complied with a smaller request. Jim Jones was an expert in this technique. The request to take lethal poison had been preceded by a long and carefully planned series of much smaller requests. For many of the victims of Jonestown, the requests began as early as 10 years before, with *voluntary* church meetings that involved only a few hours of commitment a week. Contributions at the beginning were also voluntary. In small increments, however, Jones began to increase the demands he made on the members. For instance, he first moved from a voluntary contribution to a 10% tithe, then to 25%, and finally he demanded that they turn over to him all their worldly possessions. The same was true of emotional and physical investments. Gradually, he demanded that members devote more of their time and energy to the People's Temple, until he finally required that they actually leave their homes and jobs and move to Guyana. One ex-member describes Jones' use of the foot-in-the-door technique this way.

> Nothing was ever done drastically. That's how Jim Jones got away with so much. You slowly gave up things and slowly had to put up with more, but it was always done very gradually. It was amazing, because you would sit up sometimes and say, Wow, I really have given up a lot. I really am putting up with a lot. But he did it so slowly that you figured, I've made it this far, what the hell is the difference? (Conway & Sigelman, 1979, p. 236)

THE PROCESS OF SELF-JUSTIFICATION

As we saw in Chapter 17, people induced to make extreme sacrifices or engage in behavior that is discrepant with their true beliefs or values will often attempt to justify these actions to themselves to reduce the dissonance the acts produce. Jones may never have heard of cognitive dissonance theory, but he had a diabolical ability to put it to work. He induced dissonance and self-justification in his followers and, consequently, increased their commitment to himself and to the People's Temple. We have already noted the material sacrifices his followers were expected to make. Jones also knew that inducing people to engage in various abnormal behaviors would similarly produce increased commitment to the group. For example, Jones gradually induced parents to separate from their children, ultimately demanding that the parents sign a document which assigned the "custody rights" of the child to Jones and the People's Temple. Also, Jones forced spouses to have extramarital sexual relations which were often humiliating or homosexual. These practices, and the demands that the members publically repudiate former friends and family and sign self-incriminating statements before entering church service, must have induced considerable dissonance in the members. Rather than tolerate this dissonance, many cult members ended up convincing themselves that it had all been worth it.

CONSTRUCTING SOCIAL REALITY

As we noted, when people are uncertain, disoriented, and anxious, they depend more on others to understand reality. Jones appeared to have an intuitive grasp of this social psychological principle. First, it is important to note that Jones and his message began to gain popularity in the late 1960s, a time of widespread discontent, turmoil, and disillusionment. The People's Temple appeared to offer its members hope, comradeship, peace, and purpose. It sounded like Utopia to many people at that time. People are particularly likely to be drawn to simple, uncomplicated, and sometimes dogmatic ideas when they are faced by threats or uncertainty (Sales, 1972). Once people joined the People's Temple, Jones did everything he could to control the information to which members would be exposed. He isolated them from their past and from all external contacts. The physical and social isolation of Guyana made the cultists especially dependent on Jones for their view of reality. Demanding that members refer to him as "Dad" gave Jones even more power to construct their world view. The fear and sense of imminent threat that Jones continually whipped up about "enemies" in and outside the group also increased the members' receptivity to his preaching. (The latter two practices were used even more diabolically by Adolf Hitler.) Jones also seemed to know that people are more easily influenced when they are deindividuated. All members had to renounce their former identity, a process called *mortification* by Kanter (1972), and were forced to submerge themselves into the group and its activities. It was especially difficult for them to maintain a sense of identity when the group moved to Guyana, where separations between husbands and wives, and parents and children, were enforced.

them whether they would agree to serve as nonpaid counselors for juvenile delinquents 2 hours a week over the next 2 years (certainly a large request). Unsurprisingly, none said yes. However, when the experimenters then scaled down their request to a much smaller one—taking a group of delinquents on a 2-hour trip to the zoo—50% agreed. This compliance rate was approximately three times as great as that produced by the same request when it was presented alone—without the first, larger request.

FOCUS ON THE PSYCHOLOGIST

Robert B. Cialdini

DR. ROBERT B. CIALDINI, professor of Psychology at Arizona State University, received his undergraduate, graduate, and postgraduate training at the University of Wisconsin, University of North Carolina, and Columbia University, respectively. He has held visiting appointments at Ohio State University and the University of California—San Diego. Dr. Cialdini has been named Arizona State University Distinguished Research Professor. His primary research interest is in social influence techniques, with special emphasis on persuasion and compliance. He is the author of the recently published book, *Influence: The New Psychology of Modern Persuasion*.

All my life I had been a pushover for the appeals of salespeople and fundraisers. More often than I would like, I found myself saying yes to requests to purchase products I didn't need or to contribute to causes I hardly recognized. Although this was a frustrating experience, it was also fascinating, as I recognized that there must be a psychology to the process of getting a person to say yes to such requests. So, I decided that, as a university-based researcher, I would examine what makes one person comply with the requests of another.

The general research strategy I ultimately came to favor combined two approaches. The first has involved systematic observation in the natural environment. I sought to locate the most powerful and reliable tactics in current use by the compliance professionals of our society—those whose business it is to get others to comply (salespeople, recruiters, advertisers, fundraisers, lobbyists, con artists, etc.). Often this process of intensive observation involved going undercover to infiltrate the training or recruitment programs of the compliance "pros." Without question, the time I spent as a kind of anthropologist in the culture of compliance within our society provided a set of insights I could not have gained elsewhere. I learned which were the procedures and principles used in common by compliance agents of all sorts.

Whenever I observed that a particular tactic was employed by different practitioners over a wide range of compliance settings and professions, my research approach changed from systematic observation to controlled experimentation. I could turn my attention to the question of why, psychologically, these procedures worked; the answer to that question is best provided by controlled experimental research, in which the ability of theoretical accounts to explain the phenomenon under study can be tested.

This sequence of systematic natural observation coupled with follow-up experimentation has served my research purposes very well. That is so because each component of the sequence lacks a critical piece of information for which the other nicely compensates. The intensive examination of the actions of an array of compliance professionals can tell us what works forcefully and regularly in our culture to produce a yes response, but not why. Rigorous experimentation, on the other hand, can tell us why a tactic works, but not whether it is strong enough to be effective in the natural environment. By coupling the two research approaches, we get a shot at the jackpot—an understanding of why the genuinely *effective* procedures around us work as they do.

Why should refusing to comply with a large request, in effect slamming the door in the requester's face, increase a person's willingness to comply with a subsequent smaller request? A popular explanation (Pendleton & Batson, 1979) is that the act of refusal raises doubts for the refuser about his or her self-image ("Maybe I'm just not a nice, helpful person"), which, in turn, disposes the person to seize the opportunity to comply with the smaller request to dispel these doubts ("I really am a helpful person as long as the request is not unreasonable").

The Low-Ball Technique. Every shrewd salesperson knows the importance of getting potential buyers to commit themselves to making a purchase—on whatever terms. Unscrupulous salespeople may actually use a strategy called the low-ball technique to capitalize on the impact of commitment. The first step in the low-ball technique (the term is derived from a type of poker game) is to make potential customers an extremely attractive offer (e.g., a used car for much less money than previously advertised). If the customer accepts the offer (the low ball), the salesperson reveals a complication that makes the deal much less attractive (e.g., an expensive option that the person thought was included is now described as *not* part of the offer). The last step in the sequence involves the salesperson trying to interest the customer in the second, less attractive offer. The frequency with which this strategy is used in the business world suggests that throwing people a low-ball may very well increase their willingness to accept the usually unacceptable.

People appear to be more likely to go along with something if you withhold the "bad news" from them until after they have committed themselves. One study which supports this logic was conducted by Cialdini, Cacioppo, Bassett, and Miller (1978). This study involved two groups of students. One group of students was asked to participate in a study that they were told would start at 7:00 a.m. It may not surprise you that only 25% of them agreed to the request and showed up on time. What may surprise you is that 50% of another group of students, who were not told of the starting time until after they had agreed to participate in the experiment, also showed up. The road to commitment seems a slippery one, and once we start down it, it is difficult to stop, however less attractive the destination may become.

GROUP DYNAMICS

GROUP INFLUENCE AND INDIVIDUAL PERFORMANCE

Social Facilitation. The behavior and characteristics of others can greatly affect us, but so can their mere presence. Simply knowing that we are being observed can affect our behavior. When and why the presence of others affects our behavior fascinates psychologists. Zajonc (1965) argues that the mere presence of others—either as passive spectators or as coactors—is arousing. Moreover, this arousal facilitates simple, well-learned responses and impairs the performance of unpracticed or poorly learned responses.

To illustrate this phenomenon, think of the difference between professional tennis players and weekend players, performing before a large crowd. The professionals, for whom the mechanics of tennis are well learned and highly practiced, will probably benefit from the added arousal produced by the audience and will therefore perform better. The weekend players, for whom the mechanics of tennis are neither well learned nor highly practiced, will probably play less well than they would without the arousal caused by the audience.

Some psychologists have challenged Zajonc's contention that the "mere presence" of others produces arousal. Instead, it has been proposed that the added arousal resulting from the presence of others is produced by the performer's concern that the others will be evaluting his or her performance (Geen, 1980). In other words, the increase in arousal is generated by "evaluation apprehension."

People do frequently experience evaluation apprehension in the presence of others, and this experience contributes to both arousal and *social facilitation.* Nevertheless, it appears that Zajonc's proposal that the "mere presence" of others is arousing is also true. Markus (1978), for example, asked subjects for a response that was clearly not subject to evaluation: dressing themselves. Dressing, at least for most of us, is a natural, highly routinized, well-learned response, not likely to invoke evaluation apprehension. This response was performed under both "alone" and "audience" conditions.

In Markus's experiment, the subject had to (1) take off his own shoes, (2) put on shoes and socks provided by the experimenter, (3) put on a lab coat, (4) take off the lab coat, (5) take off the experimental shoes, and (6) put on his own shoes. Note that, while all of these responses appear simple, responses 1 and 6 are more well learned and routinized for the subject than are responses 2, 3, 4, and 5. Consistent with the hypothesis that the "mere presence" of others is arousing, subjects performed the simple and familiar tasks (1 and 6) faster and the more complex and less familiar tasks (2, 3, 4, 5) slower in the presence of others than when alone.

Social Loafing. Social facilitation effects occur in those situations where people are working toward individual goals and where individual performance can be measured. A different situation exists when a group of people are working toward a common goal, and individual performance is not easily measured.

Many tasks require collaboration. It is very diffcult for one person to lift a piano, climb Mt. Everest, or organize a political campaign. It is impossible for one person to sing a quartet, play baseball, or constitute a jury. Many other activities, however, can be done alone or with others (e.g., writing a textbook). In these situations we can ask whether individual effort is increased or decreased in group activities. Considerable research suggests that people decrease their effort when they are part of a group (Latané, 1981). Whether the activity is rope pulling, bicycling, shouting, hand clapping, or swimming, people "loaf" when they are part of a group. For example, the noise produced by six people instructed to shout or clap "as loud as you can" was less than three times that produced by one person alone (Latané, Williams, & Harkins, 1979). The major variable underlying the *social loafing* response appears to be anonymity. When people combine their outputs in a group, each individual becomes unidentified with his or her output, allowing each to slack off unobtrusively (Williams, Harkins, & Latané, 1981). Evidence of social loafing, or free riding as it has sometimes been called, has even been identified in creative enterprises such as songwriting. Two psychologists, and Beatles fans, Jackson and Padgett (1982), demonstrated, for example, that songs written individually by John Lennon and Paul McCartney were of higher quality (at least they sold more records) than were the songs on which they collaborated. The finding that people respond with less effort when they are part of a group gives new and less inspirational meaning to the old saying that "many hands make light work."

Contrary to appearances, people decrease their effort when they are part of a group because they do not identify with their own output. (Stock Boston)

GROUP PROBLEM SOLVING

Who is better at solving problems—groups or individuals? Cultural wisdom is unclear on this point. The proverb "Two heads are better than one" suggests that groups have the advantage. The proverb "Too many cooks spoil the broth" implies that groups may not always produce better solutions than individuals. Psychologists have discovered that both proverbs have some validity.

Working Alone or Together. When the problem to be solved has a single answer which can be clearly recognized once it is discovered, groups do seem to be more proficient than individuals (G. W. Hill, 1982). Student scores on multiple-choice exams, for example, would almost certainly be higher if they could work in groups. Every time one member of the group knew the correct answer, the whole group would get it right. The superiority of groups on what are often called "Eureka" (Greek for "I found it") problems was demonstrated in an early study by M. Shaw (1932), in which individuals and groups faced problems such as the following:

On one side of a river are three wives and three husbands. All of the men but none of the women can row. Get them all across the river by means of a boat carrying only three at a time. No man will allow his wife to be in the presence of another man unless he is also there.

Shaw found that 60% of the groups and only 14% of the individuals who worked alone solved this problem.

Often, however, the problems we tackle have no correct answers, only better or worse ones. Consider questions such as "How would you increase tourism in your hometown?" or "How might the arms race be contained?" The solutions to problems such as these are not as clear cut as those to multiple-choice questions. When there is no clear-cut solution to the problem, groups rarely produce solutions that are superior to those of the average individual in the group, and almost never ones that are superior to those of the most competent individual in the group (G. W. Hill, 1982).

Brainstorming. About 30 years ago, an advertising executive named Osborn (1957) began to advocate a technique for generating potential solutions to problems. The technique, which he called brainstorming, requires group members to come up with as many different ideas for solving a problem as quickly as possible. The ground rules for brainstorming sessions are as follows:

1. All group members are encouraged to express whatever solutions and ideas come to mind, and "the wilder the better."
2. All ideas are recorded.
3. All criticism or analysis of suggestions is withheld until the end of a session.
4. The elaboration of previous suggestions by different members is encouraged.

Osborn (1957) claimed that "the average person can think up twice as many ideas when working with a group than when working alone." Contrary to Osborn's prediction, however, research indicates that people brainstorming in groups produce fewer (not more) ideas than the same number of individuals brainstorming alone (Lamm & Trommsdorf, 1973).

Groupthink. Most of the studies investigating group problem solving and decision making have involved newly formed groups that lack strong feelings of solidarity. You might expect that when groups are composed of individuals with strong allegiances to one another and a common commitment to success, their decision-making ability would improve. In fact, decision making often deteriorates under these conditions. Janis (1972) called this phenomenon *groupthink*. It occurs when group members become so concerned over keeping a high degree of consensus and cohesiveness that they suspend their reality-testing powers and fail to exercise their ability to evaluate ideas critically. Janis has argued that groupthink is responsible for some disastrous political decisions, including (1) the decision not to heed warnings of the Japanese attack on Pearl Harbor in 1941, (2) the decision of the Kennedy Administration to endorse the ill-fated Bay of Pigs invasion of Cuba in 1961, (3) the Johnson Administration's decision to escalate U.S. involvement in Vietnam in the mid-1960s, and (4) the decision of the Nixon administration to attempt to cover up the Watergate break-in in the early 1970s.

Janis has identified several symptoms of groups who suffer from groupthink. Among the most serious are:

1. *The illusion of invulnerability:* the belief that the group cannot fail whatever the apparent risks.
2. *Rationalization:* the tendency to justify the group's actions and discredit any evidence that is inconsistent with its plans.
3. *The illusion of unanimity:* the tendency for each member of the group to assume that the other members hold the same opinion, thereby eliminating the need for group discussion.
4. *Mind guards:* the tendency of one or more persons in the group to protect the group leader from dissenting opinion by suppressing the expression of deviant opinions.

To reduce the likelihood that group decision making will suffer from groupthink, Janis (1982) offers a number of prescriptions, including:

1. Tell group members about groupthink, its causes and consequences.
2. The leader should instruct everyone to evaluate ideas critically, encouraging objections and doubts.
3. One or more members should be assigned the role of "devil's advocate."
4. After a preliminary decision, a "second-chance" meeting should be called at which each member is asked to express remaining doubts.
5. Several independent groups should work simultaneously on the same question.

SOCIAL ROLES

A *role* is a set of norms that defines how people in a given position ought to behave. The role a person occupies can greatly influence his or her behavior.

Leaders and Followers. If you were ever "left in charge" by an adult when you were a child, you probably had early evidence of the influence that social roles can exert on behavior. Most people, even young children, become more confident and assertive when they assume the *role* of leader—arrogant and bossy may be how subordinates see it.

A study conducted by Bell and French (1950) on leadership behavior in new Navy recruits provides an impressive demonstration of how leaders can be created. The major finding of this study was that people who had been *randomly* selected from squads of recruits to serve as "acting petty officers" came to be seen by their fellow recruits as having special leadership qualities. By simply discharging their role responsibilities, such as lining men up for roll call and leading them to mess hall, the appointed leaders became leaders. It may also be true that being a follower in a group for a prolonged period will make it especially difficult to move into a leadership position. During World War II, when the casualty rate for commissioned officers in the infantry was quite high, the U.S. Army found it necessary to appoint enlisted men to "field commissions," suddenly appointing them to officer status. Experience soon indicated that the new recruits had to be transferred to other units to assume command, for they were having difficulty leading their former buddies (Raven and Rubin 1983).

The role of follower appears no less powerful than that of leader, as a study by Langer and Benevento (1978) demonstrates. In the experiment, pairs of women first solved some arithmetic problems working individually. They then solved anagrams, with one of the women serving as "boss" and the other as a subservient "assistant." Finally, the women individually worked on more arithmetic problems exactly as they had in the first task. Whether they had played the "boss" or the "assistant" when solving the anagrams greatly affected how the subjects performed in the second set of arithmetic problems. The women who acted as "bosses" actually solved more problems than they had initially. The subservient "assistants," on the other hand, apparently developed a false sense of incompetence, for they solved *fewer* problems the second time around. A demeaning role had demeaned the people who played it (Myers, 1983).

The Stanford Prison Study. Sometimes, a role can have a surprising impact on behavior. Most people who become parents, for example, are surprised (and sometimes distressed) to see how their behavior resembles that of other parents, including their own. The power of social roles to make us behave in surprising ways was demonstrated convincingly in a study conducted by

Zimbardo, Haney, Banks, and Jaffe (1973). To investigate the impact that two particular roles—prisoner and prison guard—exert on social behavior, these researchers created a "mock prison" and randomly assigned students the role of "prisoner" or "prison guard." The mock prison was created in the basement of the Stanford University Psychology building. The prison included three-man cells, with only matresses, sheets, and pillows; a yard for exercise and recreation; and an unlit closet for solitary confinement. From 75 male volunteers, they selected the 21 students who appeared most mature and stable, and least involved in antisocial behavior, and assigned them randomly to be guards or prisoners. To enhance the realism of the situation, they secured the cooperation of the Palo Alto Police Department, who, with sirens wailing, drove to the prisoners homes, charged them with armed robbery or burglary, "arrested" them, and delivered them to the station for fingerprinting and preparation of identification files. The prisoners were next taken to the mock prison, where they were stripped, sprayed for lice, and forced to stand naked and alone in the prison yard. They were then issued shapeless smocks to be worn as uniforms, placed in their cells, and ordered to remain silent. After this, the prisoners stayed in their prison 24 hours a day. Their schedule included exercise, meals, and free time. The guards, on the other hand, worked in three 8-hour shifts and went home when off duty. Physical violence toward prisoners was strictly forbidden, but guards could set up most of their own rules for running the prison. Guards, like prisoners, were dressed impersonally.

The project was scheduled to run for 2 weeks. During this time, the experimenters maintained constant observation of the situation, using both audio and video tape equipment, and administered a series of questionnaires. However, the intended 2-week simulation had to be abruptly terminated after 6 days. During the first 5 days, 4 of the 10 prisoners had to be released as a result of fits of rage, crying, and acute anxiety. A fifth was released because he developed a rash on large portions of his body. Guards increasingly enjoyed their power. They stretched the 10-minute line-up periods that had been established for counting prisoners into 2-hour interrogation sessions that featured verbal insult and abuse. They also issued arbitrary commands to do push-ups and refused requests to go to the toilet. None of the investi-

The power of social roles to make us behave was demonstrated in the Stanford Prison study when student "guards" began to abuse student "prisoners." (Philip G. Zimbardo)

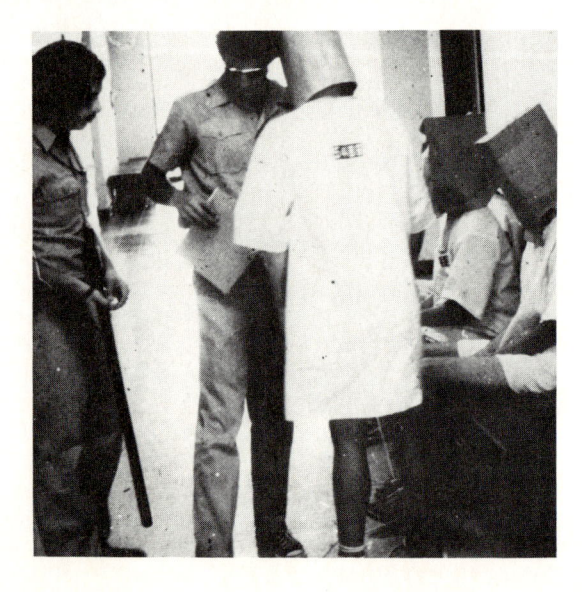

gators foresaw how easily the well-adjusted subjects would fall into these roles, nor how traumatic and destructive these temporary roles would be.

Obedience to Authority. If a person came up to you on the street and asked you to perform some antisocial act (kick a dog, say), you would probably think the request preposterous and show no inclination to obey. But what if you were in the military and your commanding officer told you to commit an atrocity; would you do it? Perhaps not, but we are more disposed to obey when obeying is part of our role requirements. The extent to which people will obey those in roles of authority is demonstrated in a famous series of studies conducted by Stanley Milgram (1963; 1965).

In the guise of a verbal learning experiment, Stanley Milgram (1963) asked his subjects to administer shocks to another person. The "learner" was seated in the next room, and whenever the "learner" made an error, the subject, playing the role of "teacher," had to push a lever on the "shock machine." After each error, the "teacher" was also asked to increase the intensity of the shocks, which were labeled from "mild " to "extreme danger-xx."

In reality, the "learner" was not receiving electric shocks, but was a confederate of the experimenter, who activated a tape recorder that played a standardized sequence of screams and pleadings over an intercom. The experiment actually tested how far the "teacher" would go in shocking the "learner" in obedience to the experimenter's orders.

To the surprise of both psychologists and the general public, Milgram found that 65% of his subjects obeyed the experimenter's commands to deliver increasingly severe shocks to a man in an adjoining room whom they believed was a fellow student. They did this even though the man pounded on the wall, begged the subject to stop, and eventually fell completely silent. No physical efforts were made to prevent subjects from leaving if they got up or refused to push the shock buttons. The experimenter limited his promptings to verbal commands that they continue.

The "learner's" indications of pain were somewhat effective, as 9 of the 40 participants stopped after hearing the pounding on the wall. But for most subjects, the experimenter's insistence overcame any misgivings they had about what they were doing. Twenty-six of 40 subjects continued until they had pressed the switch that administered the most intense shocks. Even so, they were clearly uneasy about the situation. Profuse sweating, trembling, groaning, and nervous laughter were common. Many requested permission to stop and many expressed fear for the "learner's" health. Nevertheless, the authority represented by the experimenter was sufficiently compelling to overcome any inhibitions the subjects had against harming another human being. Milgram (1974) extended his research program to study some of the situational factors that may lead subjects to obey or refuse to obey when the experimenter tells them to hurt another person. One finding was that the closer the victim was to the subject, the more likely it was for subjects to refuse to obey the experimenter. Thus when the victim was 1½ feet away, only a third of the subjects were willing to deliver the maximum shock level. Milgram also found that obedience was less frequent when the experimenter presented his commands by telephone or tape recorder rather than face to face.

Deindividuation. Why should social roles so alter people's behavior? One consequence of being in a role is that we are depersonalized or *deindividuated* (Diener, 1979). Symptoms of deindividuation include loss of identity, aimlessness, and feelings of isolation. Zimbardo (1970) has argued that among the factors that produce deindividuation are anonymity, sensory overload, and physical involvement in a group activity. These conditions are believed to reduce a person's concern about both self-evaluation and the evaluations of others. The result of deindividuation is uninhibited behavior, freedom from normal self-controls, impulsiveness, and emotionalism. As Zimbardo (1970) described the experience of the Stanford Prison study, there was "a growing confusion between reality and illusion, between role playing and self-identity. . . . This prison which we had created . . . was absorbing us as creatures of its own reality." A similar observation was made by a New York City policeman cited by Maslach and Jackson (1979): "You change when you become a cop—you become tough and hard and cynical. You have to condition yourself that way in order to survive. . . ."

Simply altering a person's physical appearance may produce a deindividuated state. R. I. Watson (1973), for example, studied warfare in over 200 cultures. He found a greater tendency to torture captives in cultures whose warriors deindividuated themselves by wearing masks and paint than in cultures whose warriors were not deindividuated. In an experiment conducted by Zimbardo (1970), college women were deindividuated by shrouding them in hoods, placing them in groups of four in a dark room, and giving them an opportunity to shock a female victim. Other women were "individuated" by wearing large prominent name tags and taking part in the experiment in a bright room. Zimbardo found that the deindividuated women delivered longer shocks and failed to discriminate between deserving and undeserving victims. In contrast, the individuated women administered shorter shocks and were more lenient toward the undeserving victims than the deserving victims.

Johnson and Downing (1979) found that the deindividuated state produced by clothing need not always lead to increased antisocial behavior. Their study was very similar to Zimbardo's except that instead of wearing Klan-like outfits, a group of women put on nurse's uniforms before deciding how much shock someone should receive. The shocks they delivered in this state were much less severe than those they delivered out of uniform when their names and personal identities were stressed. The uniform of the nurse appeared to make them think of the nurse's role rather than their own personal inclinations.

CROWDING AND PERSONAL SPACE

We tend to treat the area immediately around our bodies as though it was an integral part of ourselves. Each of us protects this region as our *personal space*. How much personal space we will attempt to maintain depends on a variety of factors. One is culture: For example, very close interactions are common in Central America, France, Greece, and the Middle East, while more distant interpersonal spacing is preferred in Great Britain, Sweden, Switzerland, and the United States (E. T. Hall, 1966; Sommer, 1969). Even within the same culture, personal space varies considerably across different situations. Some years ago, E. T. Hall (1963) observed that Americans interact at one of four distances, depending on who the other people are and what behavior is taking place. One study of such behaviors (known as proxemics) indicates that from 0 to 1½ feet is an *intimate distance* appropriate for such acts as lovemaking or fighting; 1½ to 4 feet is a *personal distance* used by friends in conversation; 4 to 12 feet is the *social distance* we maintain in conducting impersonal business transactions, and over 12 feet is the public distance used between a speaker and his or her audience.

Violations of Personal Space. When another person occupies our personal space, we tend to have a strong, negative emotional reaction (Ashton & Shaw, 1980). You may have been standing quietly by yourself on a street corner waiting for the light to change, when a stranger stepped up and stood next to you. Konečni, Libuser, Morton and Ebbesen (1975) observed people's responses to such an occurrence and found that the closer a confederate stood to the subject, the faster the subject crossed the street. To find out how such an invader is perceived, Smith and Knowles (1979) repeated the sidewalk study, but had an experimenter on the other side of the street ready to interview each subject after he or she crossed over. As you might expect, the invader was described as unpleasant, rude, hostile, and aggressive.

An interesting difference in personal space preferences has been discovered between violent and nonviolent people (Kinzel, 1970). Using video tapes to assess prisoner reactions to various approach distances, Gilmour and Walkey (1981) found a clear difference between violent and nonviolent offenders in their tolerance for interpersonal closeness. To feel comfortable, violent prisoners are found to require nearly three times as much area around them as nonviolent prisoners do. This result suggests that spatial preferences may unwittingly trigger some acts of violence.

Crowding. In our society it is increasingly difficult to avoid other people. Studies have documented the negative consequences that result from crowded conditions existing in our daily lives. As density increases in preschools, for instance, so does aggression and verbal abuse (Loo, 1979). As the number

We define the area immediately around our bodies as our *personal space* and tend to treat it as part of ourselves. (Marc Anderson)

Crowding affects us negatively because it reduces our sense of personal control and increases our feelings of helplessness. (Charles Gatewood/Stock Boston)

of prisoners in an institution increases, inmates have more disciplinary problems, report more illnesses, and are more likely to commit suicide (Cox, Paulus, & McCain, 1984). Kelley (1982) in a recent study of 175 cities in the United States found that the number of murders, rapes, robberies, and car thefts per person increased with community size. There also appears to be a general tendency for task performance to suffer as density increases (Langer & Saegert, 1977). Finally, people are less well liked when they are encountered in crowded conditions than in noncrowded conditions (Zuckerman, Schmitz, & Yosha, 1977).

We should not assume, however, that every time people find themselves in a densely populated area, they will experience adverse effects. For one thing, the perception of being crowded is often not closely related to the objective physical state of crowding (Paulus, 1979). A packed football stadium, for example, may not seem as "crowded" as an equally densely packed bus.

Why should crowding affect us negatively? One popular explanation is that high density often reduces our sense of personal control and increases our feelings of helplessness (Epstein, 1981). The relationship between perceived control and population density was demonstrated in an interesting field experiment conducted by Rodin, Solomon, and Metcalf (1978). In a densely packed elevator, subjects who were standing by the control panel indicated that they felt less crowded and actually thought the elevator was larger than did those standing away from the panel.

SUMMARY

1. Many forms of self-knowledge depend on comparisons with others. It is through this process of social comparison that we evaluate our opinions, abilities, and outcomes.

2. People are especially dependent on information from others when they are fearful or uncertain. The desire to affiliate with similar others is therefore increased in such situations.

3. Asch studied conformity to social pressure by using a simple perceptual task with an obvious correct answer. He found that incorrect responses by the group placed strong pressure on the minority to agree with the majority's decision.

4. Although it is more likely for a majority to influence a minority than vice versa, the latter can happen. Minority group influence is most likely to occur when the minority maintains a consistent and undeviating position.

5. People's willingness to comply with a request is greater if they have previously complied with a smaller request of a similar type. This strategy of compliance induction is called the foot-in-the-door technique.

6. People's willingness to comply with a request is also greater if they have previously refused to comply with a larger request. Concern over tarnishing one's self-image is presumed to underly the success of this strategy, which is referred to as the door-in-the-face technique.

7. Social facilitation occurs when we are in the presence of others. The arousal produced by the mere presence of others facilitates performance on easy tasks and interferes with it on difficult or poorly learned tasks.

8. Groups are better than individuals at solving problems that have a single correct answer. When there is no clear-cut answer, however, individuals produce higher-quality solutions than do groups.

9. A role is a set of norms that defines how people in a given position ought to behave. The role a person occupies can greatly influence his or her behavior. Examples of social roles are leader, subordinate, prisoner, and guard.

10. One consequence of occupying a social role is deindividuation. Symptoms of deindividuation include loss of identity, aimlessness, and feelings of anonymity.

11. People tend to treat the area immediately around their body as personal space. When another person enters our personal space, we tend to have a strong, negative emotional reaction.

12. Crowding has a variety of negative effects on social behavior. One reason for these effects is that crowded conditions often reduce our sense of personal control.

KEY TERMS

Social comparison
Relative deprivation
Reference group
Social facilitation
Foot-in-the-door technique

Door-in-the-face technique
Low-ball technique
Social loafing
Brainstorming

Groupthink
Social role
Deindividuation
Personal space

SUGGESTED READINGS

CIALDINI, R. B. *Influence*. New York: Morrow, 1984. A very readable account of various influence techniques.

HOLAHAN, C. J. *Environmental psychology*. New York: Random House, 1982. A comprehensive discussion of the topics of crowding and personal space.

JANIS, I. L. *Victims of groupthink: A psychological study of foreign-policy decisions and fiascos* (rev. ed.). Boston: Houghton Mifflin, 1982. A fascinating social psychological analysis of decisions made by groups in such situations as the Bay of Pigs invasion, the escalation of the Vietnam war, and the Watergate cover-up.

SHAW, M. E. *Group dynamics: The psychology of small group behavior*. New York: McGraw-Hill, 1976. A comprehensive discussion of group influence and group problem solving.

WHEELER, L., DECI, E., REIS, H., and ZUCKERMAN, J. *Interpersonal influence* (2nd ed.). Boston: Allyn and Bacon, 1978. A brief, interesting discussion of many aspects of social influence.

19

Psychology and Contemporary Society

SOCIAL POLICY AND SCIENCE
   Social Problems:
      Understanding,
      Remediation, Prevention,
      and Enhancement
   Conclusion: The Role of
      Psychology in Social Policy
FEATURES OF
   CONTEMPORARY
   SOCIETY
THE FAMILY IN
   CONTEMPORARY
   CONTEXT
   Divorce
   Maternal Employment
   Child Abuse
PSYCHOLOGY AND THE LAW
   The Jury
   Judges Versus Juries
PSYCHOLOGY AND MEDICINE:
   I. THE SAMPLE CASE OF
   BEHAVIORAL MEDICINE
   Life-Style Change
   Medical Compliance
PSYCHOLOGY AND MEDICINE:
   II. THE SAMPLE CASE OF
   COGNITIVE PSYCHOLOGY
   AND THE DIAGNOSIS
   AND TREATMENT OF
   ALZHEIMER'S DISEASE
SUMMARY
KEY TERMS
SUGGESTED READINGS

The world within which we live changes rapidly and in numerous ways. All one has to do to learn of this complexity is to read a local newspaper or listen to the evening news report. There are changes in political leaders and alliances; in the availability of natural resources (e.g., oil); in the geographic distribution of populations, for example, from the northeast portion of the United States to the Sunbelt; in values and mores regarding accepted standards of behavior (e.g., see the discussion in Chapter 11 about changes in adolescent sexuality); in the nature and availability of technology (e.g., consider the "explosion" in recent years in the availability of personal computers); in the nature of the economy (e.g., regarding inflation, budget deficits, unemployment, and balance of trade inequalities); in the age distribution of society (e.g., the median age of American citizens will be greater than 40 years well before the turn of this century; Bouvier, 1980; Population Reference Bureau,

1982); and in the occurrence of weather patterns (e.g., unexpectedly heavy and prolonged rainy or snowy seasons), or in the occurrence of natural disasters (e.g., earthquakes).

Changes in these and other domains of human existence make our world even more complex than it is already. It seems that as soon as we have adjusted to our current state of affairs we are confronted with a new set of circumstances. In a sense, the "future" comes earlier than we expected it. Toffler (1970) labeled this experience "future shock."

How do we contend with a changing society? In one sense, our society is constructed to deal with change. We have political institutions which can change laws, restate administrative policies, or act in emergencies.

But how do our governmental leaders decide what new laws should be enacted or what new policies should be followed? Obivously, political pressures from constituents and lobbyists influence such decisions. But there are other sources of influence as well.

SOCIAL POLICY AND SCIENCE

The fact that the average citizen is getting older raises many social questions for the future. (David M. Grossman)

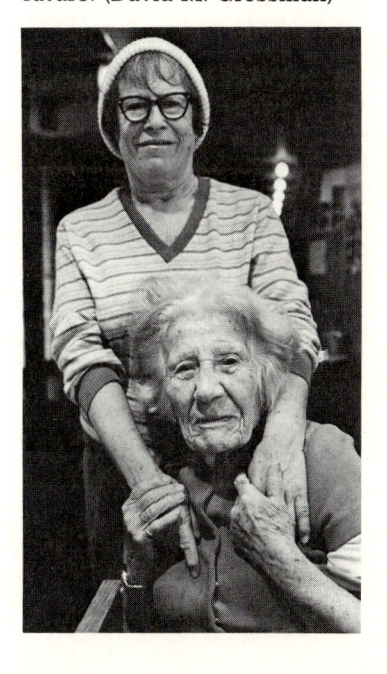

Political science has as one of its goals the understanding of the variables that influence governmental leaders' decisions. Thus political scientists would often study how the voters in a Senator's state, or a lobbyist for a special interest group, might affect the legislator's views or votes. But as we have said, such political "pressures" are not the only basis of a governmental leader's formulation of a policy that will affect society. Political scientists may not only study how political decisions are made, they may also help to set social policy.

For instance, what does it mean for society that the average citizen is getting older (Population Reference Bureau, 1982)? Do we need to change our retirement laws or our social security system to deal with more aged people in our society? Do we need to redesign our parks and other recreational settings to more readily accommodate aged people, whose leisure-time interests may be different from those of young people? Indeed, what are the leisure-time interests of the young and the old? Furthermore, will there be special problems for our medical and health systems since more and more patients will be aged? Will there be problems of mental health and adjustment for aged people, who because their life expectancies are greater than in previous generations, can expect to live as a retired person for far longer than was previously the case? Will the youth of society face an adjustment problem as a consequence of being a "minority group?" That is, youth will be in an age group that is not the predominant one (in terms of size) in the population.

Answers to these questions require the assistance of economists, sociologists, physicians, political scientists, and quite clearly, psychologists. For instance, the leisure-time interests of different age groups and the possible adjustment problems of the aged or youth could best be addressed by psychological research. To devise a useful *general philosophy or specific plan to deal with an issue facing society,* that is, a *social policy,* a governmental leader will need to attend to the knowledge of scientists. Often, this knowledge will be based on both basic and applied research pertinent to the issue or problem toward which the social policy is directed. Such research is typically intended to address at least one of several aspects of a social problem.

SOCIAL PROBLEMS: UNDERSTANDING, REMEDIATION, PREVENTION, AND ENHANCEMENT

Scientists can help formulate social policy by contributing information to at least four aspects of a social problem.

Understanding the Problem. "Don't fix it if it ain't broken" is a well-known American political adage. Simply put, we do not want to formulate and then implement a policy to redress a problem which does not exist. For instance, although our population is aging, does this mean necessarily that there will be problems? No. Thus scientists can contribute to the formulation of social policy by going on a scientific "fact-finding mission." They can do exploratory research to discover what problems, if any, may arise as a consequence of the changing age of the population. For instance, they may discover the percentage of the federal government's budget used to deal with the social security benefits of the current population of aged. Then, by estimating both (1) the projected increase in the aged proportion of the population in a future year, and (2) the projected governmental revenue for that year, scientists could estimate the economic pressures that might exist for the federal budget given the increased aged proportion of the population.

The example above is drawn from economics. However, similar types of psychological "projections" can be made. What, for example, are the problems of adjustment for today's aged? Why do these adjustment problems exist? For instance, one source of adjustment problems for today's aged arises as a consequence of having to retire at age 65 and having to "face" an average of 14 or so years of post-retirement longevity with "nothing to do" (Botwinick, 1978; Reichard, Livson, & Peterson, 1962). If the expected life span increases add, say, another 5 or 10 years to this longevity, a psychologist might predict an increase in adjustment problems (Maddox, 1966; Sauer & Warland, 1982). Thus, by understanding the nature and bases of a problem, scientists may contribute useful knowledge to a social policy issue.

Remediation. Once a problem and its source have been identified, a scientist may help formulate plans or policies useful for *diminishing the effects of a problem*, that is, plans useful for *remediating* a problem. For instance, a psychologist may suggest that funds be made available for skill training programs for the retired, so that they could learn to engage in socially useful tasks for which there may be no paid employment available but for which there is a need (e.g., they could be taught job counseling skills). Similarly, because more families have both parents working outside the home, more children are being left in day care. Retired people could be trained as child-care specialists, and subsequently employed in "foster grandparent" programs. Thus, since having "nothing to do" is one basis of a retiree's adjustment problems (e.g., Botwinick, 1978; Sauer & Warland, 1982), entrance into such a program might diminish or eliminate these negative effects.

Prevention. If the course of a problem is known a scientist may be able to suggest steps to take to *avoid the ocurrence of a problem*. Such avoidance is termed *prevention*. For instance, to prevent adjustment problems subsequent to retirement, problems caused by having "nothing to do," a psychologist might suggest that policies be instituted before retirement. By assessing the person's interests, attitudes, and motivations, the psychologist might then be able to best match the pre-retirement training with potential post-retirement activities. Thus the person expecting and trained for a post-retirement "job" might never experience any adjustment problems due to having a post-retirement period devoid of activity. In general, then, we engage in prevention when the person is "at risk" to encounter some difficulty, and we want to prevent the risk from becoming an actuality.

Enhancement. When a person's functioning is *enhanced,* his or her behavior is *changed for the better.* Much of what we have already said is relevant to enhancement. By recommending plans which will remediate a problem and/or prevent a problem, a scientist is contributing information which will enhance human functioning. In other words, when we engage in enhancement, a person is not "at risk" (as is the case in prevention). Here, instead, the person is merely seeking to better his or her life.

CONCLUSION: THE ROLE OF PSYCHOLOGY IN SOCIAL POLICY

Science may contribute information that shapes social policy. Psychology may be particularly useful here because of its central concern with the nature and bases of a person's mental and behavioral functioning. The psychological study of human personality, abilities, intelligence, motivation, emotion, physiology-behavior relations, development across life, and social functioning can present a broad and deep array of information useful to those responsible for the formulation and implementation of social policy.

In the following sections of this chapter, we illustrate how psychological theory and research can help understand, remediate, or prevent numerous problems confronting contemporary society. By making these contributions psychology plays a central role in enhancing the human condition.

FEATURES OF CONTEMPORARY SOCIETY

At the beginning of this chapter we discussed some of the infinite number of ways that society may change. Similarly, the features of contemporary society are infinitely varied. However, to indicate how psychology contributes to understanding, remediating, and preventing problems confronting society, we need not, of course, discuss each of the features of our current context. Instead, we will focus on some of the important problems to which psychological theory and research is making central contributions.

First, we discuss how psychology contributes to dealing with several problems confronting the contemporary American family. Second, we discuss the relation between psychology and the law. Third, we discuss the relation between psychology and medicine, and in so doing, present some of the features of the area of medical specialization termed "behavioral medicine."

THE FAMILY IN CONTEMPORARY CONTEXT

The family is the basic institution of our society. Yet it is a changing institution (Belsky, Lerner, & Spanier, 1984). For instance, today people often delay marriage until well beyond their early twenties and even after marriage they often delay having children until in their late twenties or early thirties. More than ever before, the American family is a dual-career household, and mothers—even of preschool children—more often than ever before place the child in day care and return to full-time work outside the home. In turn, because the divorce rate is rising, there are more single-parent homes than ever before, and the children of these homes are also likely to be placed in day care when the parent is working. Thus children today are more likely than were children of previous historical periods to experience in their early years considerable caregiving by adults other than their parents. Finally, due to such factors as increased financial stress and unemployment, the incidence of family violence appears to be on the rise; thus there seems to be an increase in the abuse of children within the family.

Three issues come to the fore as a consequence of these changes in the contemporary family: divorce, maternal employment, and child abuse. Let us now consider the problems associated with each of these issues and the contributions made by psychology in dealing with them.

DIVORCE

The divorce rate reached an all-time high by the end of the 1970s (National Center for Health Statistics, 1980). In the United States there are now more than 1,150,000 divorces each year, involving more than 2,300,000 adults and more than 1,100,000 children. About two of every five divorcing couples have at least one child. An average of about two children are involved in each divorce in which there are any children under the age of 18 (Spanier & Glick, 1980).

During the 15-year period from 1960 to 1975, the number of children under 18 whose parents divorced increased by 143%, while the number of divorces increased by 164%. This increase in marital disruption has resulted in a significant increase in the number of children living with only one parent. From 1970 to 1978, for example, there was a 43% increase in the number of children under 18 living with their mothers only and a 32% increase in the number of children living with their fathers only. But what are some of the effects of divorce on the parent-child relation?

Effects of Divorce. Hetherington (1979) notes that most children experience the transition from living in an intact family to one wherein a divorce has occurred as painful. Initial reactions to divorce are anger, fear, depression, and guilt. More than a year goes by after a divorce before most children's tensions are reduced and more positive feelings begin to occur (Hetherington, 1979).

However, there is no one pattern of reaction to divorce characteristic of all children. Boys may be more vulnerble to the adverse effects of divorce than girls, although the reasons for this difference are not clear (Hetherington, 1979). Extrafamilial factors are also related to how children respond to divorce. The stress created within a family by a divorce can be increased or decreased by support (or lack of it) from other social institutions, from the family's social network of friends and relatives, by the quality of the family's housing and their neighborhood, by the availability of child care, and by the economic status of the single-parent family (Colletta, 1978; Hetherington, 1979).

Whether a child adjusts successfully to a divorce is related to his or her level of cognitive and social development. Hetherington (1979) and others

FOCUS ON THE PSYCHOLOGIST

E. Mavis Hetherington

E. MAVIS HETHERINGTON received her Ph.D. in psychology from Berkeley. One of the leading authorities on the effects of divorce on children, she has been president of the Society for Research in Child Development and is currently James M. Page Professor of Psychology at the University of Virginia.

My work in the past twenty years has made it increasingly clear that the loss of a father through separation, divorce, or death triggers a series of life changes and alterations in family roles and relationships that mediate changes in child development. Although divorce is a stressful experience for most parents and children, they can usually readjust to their new situation within about three years if the adverse effects of conflict and separation from the noncustodial parent are not compounded by additional continuing stresses. However, for many families divorce triggers a series of stressful life experiences. Poverty; multiple changes in homes, neighborhoods, and schools; continued interparental acrimony; greatly diminished contact or loss of contact with the noncustodial parent; and inept parenting by both parents all may ensue following divorce.

Boys seem to have more intense and enduring negative responses to divorce and life in a mother-custody home than do girls. Boys are more vulnerable to the effects of family conflict and are more likely to get involved in destructive cycles of coercive behavior with their divorced mothers.

Although girls in preschool and elementary school show fewer problems following their parents' divorce than do boys, some studies have suggested that there may be delayed effects for girls that appear in adolescence, particularly in heterosexual relations, and take the form of anxiety and problems in relationships with males and earlier dating and sexual behavior.

When we talk about the differences in response to divorce of boys and girls, it should be remembered that 90 per cent of children are in mother-custody homes following divorce and that most of the research has involved such families. However, recent research suggests that boys may do better in father-custody homes and girls in mother-custody homes. Although we have been saying that we cannot conceive of the outcomes of divorce as a simple effect of father absence, contact with the same-sex parent does seem to be important for children. If divorced parents can resolve their conflict and come to some agreement on child-rearing issues, and if the noncustodial parent is a reasonably stable and responsible person, continued involvement of the noncustodial parent can serve as major support and have positive outcomes for both the child and the custodial parent.

However, if the effects of divorce are compounded by multiple continued stresses and few support systems or resources, the results can be harmful for both parents and children. Children show fewer problems in a well-functioning, supportive one-parent household than they do in a conflict-ridden, two-parent household. Many divorced parents and their children have close cohesive relationships, and children in these families often are unusually mature and self-sufficient after having coped with the stress of divorce and assumed responsibility in helping the one-parent household function.

Divorce is a good example of the importance of viewing the impact of life events from a developmental, ecological perspective. There is no simple answer to the question of how divorce affects children. It depends on the age, sex, and personal attributes of the child, the stresses encountered, and the supports and resources available in the family and in the larger social ecology.

(e.g., Tessman, 1978) note that younger children are more likely to be dependent on parents than are older children; the former are less able to appraise accurately all the aspects of the divorce situation and of the parents' feelings. Indeed, because of their greater egocentrism, younger children may be more inclined to view the divorce as a result of their actions rather than as a consequence of marital difficulties.

Processes of Influence. Popular reports in the news media of the effects of divorce often leave the impression that there is something automatic about marital separation disrupting child development. Serious consideration of the social interactional process by which divorce affects the child suggests that not only is this not the case but that when certain conditions are met, the separation of parents need *not* impair the children's social, emotional, and cognitive functioning. In fact, under certain circumstances, the dissolution of a marriage may be in the child's best interests. This is especially true in cases of extreme marital discord, since abundant evidence indicates that marital discord itself is associated with impaired development.

Indeed, one common finding is that children from maritally conflicted homes are likely to engage in aggressive and antisocial behavior (Gibson, 1969). Johnson and Lobitz (1974), for example, discerned a consistent negative relationship between marital satisfaction and levels of observed child deviance. Similarly, Rutter (1971) reported that 10-year-olds from families characterized by severe marital discord showed an increased rate of both behavioral deviance in school and psychiatric disorders. Hetherington, Cox, and Cox (1978) found that it was not divorce per se that negatively affected children, but rather marital and post-divorce relations between parents that determined the influence of parental separation. When divorced parents maintained reasonably friendly relations, mothers with custody of their preschoolers tended to be more involved and supportive of their children than when continued strife characterized the relationship between two separated parents. It was primarily when the quality of parenting was compromised by such stressful relations that Hetherington and her colleagues found that the quality of children's academic performance, peer relations, and sense of self suffered.

Indeed, Hetherington et al. discovered that if divorce led to an *improvement* in relations between parents, children benefited since their parents' caregiving was not undermined by the marital stress. Unfortunately, these investigators also found that when marriages marked by conflict remained intact, parenting and child development tended to be negatively affected. Children from such families differed little from those raised by divorced parents still in conflict with their former spouses.

MATERNAL EMPLOYMENT

Fifty-one percent of all married women aged 18 to 34 were in the labor force in 1978. The proportion was 43% for those with at least one child. Moreover, in 1978, one-third of the married women who had given birth within the past year were currently in the labor force (U.S. Bureau of the Census, 1979). In addition, more than 40% of married mothers with a preschool child (2 to 4 years old) are employed (U.S. Bureau of the Census, 1979), and throughout the last decade, over 50% of married mothers with school-aged children have been employed (Hoffman, 1979). All these rates are higher for mothers in

Psychologists have found that it is more the quality of the parenting given to children that affects their academic performance, peer relations, and sense of self than the quantity of parenting. (Marc Anderson)

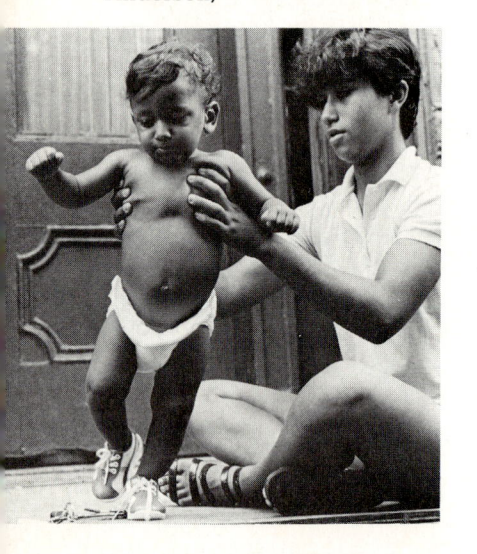

single-parent families. Therefore, employment outside the home is now, and is likely to continue to be, part of a woman's role for most American mothers. Such a trend requires some rethinking of the idea that a woman quits work after the birth of her first child.

The increase in working mothers indicates the desire of many women to establish careers in life. It may also indicate a willingness to enhance a family's standard of living by having two incomes. While many couples see this as a worthwhile sacrifice, many women value work because of the rewards it brings. In a national sample of working women studied in 1976, 76% said they would continue to work even if they did not have to (Dubnoff, Veroff, & Kulka, 1978). This percentage represents a considerable increase over the percentage of working women responding similarly to the same question asked in a 1957 survey (Hoffman, 1979). The increasing percentage of working women who claim they would continue their employment even if they did not have to suggests that many women find the world of work particularly satisfying. Highlight 19.1 discusses this issue.

HIGHLIGHT 19.1
Are Working Women More Satisfied?

There appears to be a sharp discrepancy in the literature examining the meaning of work for men and women (Wright, 1978). When the focus is on working men, work is generally pictured as degrading, alienating, and unsatisfying. In contrast, when the focus is on working women, work is generally pictured as enriching, liberating, and satisfying in spite of the fact that women are more likely to be found in less desirable occupations. The positive aspects of work for women are often contrasted with the role of the full-time housewife; the latter role is generally viewed as lonely, boring, and demeaning.

Who does lead the more satisfying life—women with jobs outside the home or full-time housewives? Many studies find little difference in overall satisfaction between the two roles (Blood & Wolfe, 1960; Wright, 1978). For example, in an analysis of national survey data collected between 1971 and 1976, Wright (1978) found no significant differences between working women and housewives in satisfaction with their lives in general or components thereof (e.g., their work, marriages, or families). Similarly, in a study of 142 middle-class women, Baruch and Barnett (1980) found no differences between working women and women at home in their role satisfaction or self-esteem. Thus in spite of the fact that some studies have found working women to be happier than nonworking women (Ferree, 1976), the bulk of the studies suggest that involvement in the multiple roles of wife, mother, and worker neither enhances nor diminishes general satisfaction with life.

Yet perhaps this is not the most important issue. For example, Baruch and Barnett (1980) found that the sources of satisfaction and self-esteem varied for employed and nonemployed women. Specifically, the well-being of nonemployed women was highly dependent on their husband's approval of their activities. In contrast, the well-being of the employed women was significantly affected by their satisfaction with their jobs and careers as well as their interactions with their husbands. As Baruch and Barnett (1980) point out, these work-related variables are likely to constitute a more stable base for well-being since they are more directly under the woman's own control. Given the high rate of divorce in our contemporry society, building one's life on the approval of one's spouse can be a risky strategy. Baruch and Barnett (1980) conclude that the development of women is likely to be facilitated by the acquisition of occupational competence and the capacity for economic independence.

The growing proportion of women in the work force demands that we recognize that ever-increasing numbers of children are being cared for by persons other than their parents. This care comes in a variety of forms: in-home care by relatives or babysitters, family day care in which small groups of children are cared for in the homes of others, and center-based day care in which larger groups of children are cared for in church basements, school facilities, or other formal establishments designed to provide care for the young (Belsky, Steinberg, & Walker, 1982). The rise in utilization of day-care services in the past decade, which is expected to increase into the 1980s, represents a social adaptation to the changing nature of the American family (Belsky et al., 1982). How do such changes influence child development?

Effects on Children. The effect of maternal employment and/or day-care rearing need not be negative. Most preschool children of working mothers are cared for in their own homes and not in day-care centers (U.S. Department of Labor, 1977), and thus one need not fear that most face any effects of "institutionalization" (Hoffman, 1979). This is not to say that day-care placement is equivalent to institutionalization. Indeed, studies thus far have *not* demonstrated adverse effects of *good-quality* day care for infants and young children (Belsky & Steinberg, 1978; Belsky et al., 1982). Some data also indicate that there is no difference in the amount of one-to-one mother-child contact occurring between working and nonworking mothers and their preschool children (Goldberg, 1977).

Effects of maternal employment on the child have been documented best in regard to the child's own vocational aspirations and expectations, and these effects are most pronounced in regard to the daughters of "working mothers." As summarized by Huston-Stein and Higgins-Trenk (1978, pp. 279–280):

The most consistent and well-documented correlate of career orientation and departure from traditional feminine roles is maternal employment during childhood and adolescence. Daughters of employed mothers (i.e., mothers who were employed during some period of the daughter's childhood or adolescence) more often aspire to a career outside the home (Almquist & Angrist, 1971; Hoffman, 1974; Stein, 1973), get better grades in college (Nichols & Schauffer, 1975), and aspire to more advanced education (Hoffman, 1974; Stein, 1973). College women who have chosen a traditionally masculine occupation more often had employed mothers than those preparing for feminine occupations (Almquist, 1974; Tangri, 1972).

Moreover, when females are raised within a family in which their mother is employed, it has also been shown that (1) they have less stereotyped views of female roles than do daughters of nonworking mothers; (2) they have a broader definition of the female role, often including attributes that are traditionally male ones; and (3) they are more likely to emulate their mothers; that is, they more often name their mothers as the person they aspire to be than is the case with daughters of nonworking mothers (Huston-Stein & Higgins-Trenk, 1978).

These effects of developing in a family wherein the mother is employed outside the home can be identified in early childhood. Bacon and Lerner (1975) found that second-, fourth-, and sixth-grade females whose mothers were employed outside the home had societal vocational role perceptions that were more egalitarian than were the perceptions of grade-mate daughters of nonworking mothers. Gold and Andres (1978) found that the sex-role concepts of both female *and* male nursery school children were more egalitarian if their mothers were employed. These children's perceptions of their mothers, along a negative-positive dimension, were not related to maternal employment status. However, fathers were perceived more negatively by their sons if the mothers were employed. In summary, data suggest that interaction in family settings having particular characteristics may promote the development of vocational role orientations and behaviors that are nontraditional.

CHILD ABUSE

Child abuse is "any nonaccidental injury sustained by a child under 18 years of age resulting from acts of commission or omission by a parent, guardian, or caretaker" (Burgess, 1979, p. 1). Because of legal and moral sanctions, as well as lack of clarity about when appropriate physical punishment ends and *abuse* or *neglect* begins, it is difficult to know precisely how many children are abused in their families each year. For example, in 1973 estimates ranged from 41,000 (Light, 1973) to 1,500,000 (Fontana, 1973). More recent estimates continue to be within this wide range (Starr, 1979). Most experts agree, however, that whatever the exact number, the problem is large and serious (Garbarino, 1976, 1977; Parke & Collmer, 1975).

The Etiology of Child Abuse. There are several explanations for child maltreatment. Probably the most common, and the most popular explanation directs attention to the psychological disturbances of the parents, since parents who are abusers are often impulsive, immature, self-centered, and hypersensitive (Parke & Collmer, 1975). Frodi and Lamb (1980), however, offer provocative evidence that besides these factors, child-abusing parents may have different physiological reactions to children than do non-child-abusing parents. Frodi and Lamb had 14 child-abusers and a matched group of nonabusers watch videotapes of crying and smiling infants. Their psychological responses were monitored throughout the session. After each videotape, the subjects described their emotional responses on a mood-adjective checklist. The crying infant elicited heart-rate acceleration and increases in skin electrical activity from both groups, although the abusers experienced greater increases in heart rate and reported more aversion and less sympathy. The nonabusers responded to the smiling infant with either no change in or with a decline in physiological activation. The abusers, however, responded similarly to the smile and cry stimuli.

That many parents who mistreat their children were themselves mistreated during their own childhood suggests further that abusive and neglectful parenting may have learned patterns of functioning (Belsky, 1980; Parke & Collmer, 1975). Indeed, abusive parents may simply be modeling the parenting they received, or they simply have not learned how to nurture and care for others because of years of insensitive care. They lack the ability to take the point of view of their children and sometimes even expect their children to care for them.

Burgess (1979, p. 11) has noted that some characteristics of the child are associated with his or her abuse. Working from an evolutionary perspective, he suggests these attributes for the abused child:

usually involve either low reproductive potential for those children later in life, e.g., retardation and Down's Syndrome (Martin, Beezley, Conway, & Kempe, 1974; Sandgrund, Gaines, & Green, 1974) or they require effortful and costly care. For instance, Johnson and Morse (1968) reported that 70 percent of their child abuse

HIGHLIGHT 19.2

Family Interaction in Abusive, Neglectful, and Normal Families

Are there particular types or patterns of behavior that occur in child-abusing families? Burgess and Conger (1978) attempted to discover if there were distinct patterns of day-to-day behavioral interactions that distinguished families that had a history of child abuse, a history of child neglect, or no known history of abusing or neglecting their children.

There were 17 abusive families studied; in such families there were authenticated occurrences of nonaccidental physical injury (abuse) to one or more children by a caretaker. There were 17 neglectful families studied as well; in these families there were one or more children who experienced a lack of parental attention (neglect) so severe that it reached the attention of legal authorities. Finally, there were 19 comparison (or "control") families studied; these families had no official record of abuse or neglect, but they were similar to the first two types on a number of dimensions, such as age of parents and of children, number of children, and income and education levels of parents. All families had an average income of less than $9,000 a year, and parents averaged between 10 and 11 years of formal schooling. The mean number of children per family was just over three.

Each of the three family types selected for study was observed in their homes. Two raters recorded verbal and physical interactions of all family members during four observation sessions. During each of these sessions the families were involved in three tasks (of about 15 to 20 minutes' duration each): (1) a construction task (e.g., involving use of a building block set or tinker toys), (2) a skill task (e.g., a game involving tossing rings over a wooden post), and (3) a discussion task (e.g., involving discussing

cases showed some form of developmental problem ranging from poor speech to physical deformities and handicaps. Moreover, even the child welfare workers who dealt with these children found them hard to handle, fussy, demanding, stubborn, negativistic, and unsmiling.

Thus the role of the parent and the role of the child appear important in the occurrence of child abuse, and this suggests that a reciprocal, interactive process is responsible for the mistreatment of children. Highlight 19.2 describes a study comparing interactions in abusive and neglectful families and in nondisturbed families.

It is important to recognize that factors beyond the internal workings of families also play a role in child maltreatment. Especially important are sociological characteristics of families, such as unemployment (Light, 1973), frequent family moves (Gil, 1970), and social isolation from formal and informal support systems (e.g., friends, church). Indeed, evidence indicates that child abuse is correlated with social class (Burgess, 1979; Starr, 1979). Gil (1970) reported that child abuse is more likely in families having a lower socioeconomic status; he noted that more than 48% of abusive families had annual incomes less than $5,000 (the national percentage of families within this income was 25% at the time of Gil's 1970 report). Similarly, Burgess (1979) reviews data indicating that parents whose annual income is less than $6,000 report abusing their children at a rate 62% higher than other parents; and in data reported by the American Humane Association (1978), insufficient income has been cited as a factor in almost 50% of child-abuse and child-neglect cases.

Finally, we must point out that cultural belief systems and values contribute to the child-abuse problem. America's exposure to violence (tele-

such issues as "What would your family like to do for a vacation?").

At various times during these sessions different family members were the focus of observation. The observers recorded whether the family member of focus spoke or touched another family member (scored as a "verbal give" or a "physical give," respectively) or was spoken to or touched by another family member (a "verbal receive" or a "physical receive," respectively). In addition, the observers recorded the emotional affect associated with each interaction (neutral, positive, or negative), who interacted with the focal family member, and whether a common person was involved in the interaction. Each family member was the focus of such observation for at least 3 minutes during each task with each session.

Burgess and Conger found that parents in the abusive families interacted less frequently on both verbal and physical dimensions than did parents in the comparison families. Parents in the abuse group interacted physically with their children at a rate 23% lower than that for the control parents and were also less positive than the controls. Neglectful parents were extremely negative, and in addition, had a low rate of positive interactions. They were only half as likely to emit a positive response as were the control parents and were twice as likely to behave in a negative fashion.

Burgess and Conger found also that it is the mothers in the abusive families who are most different from their control counterparts. They show lower rates of verbal behavior overall and lower rates of verbal and positive contacts with their children. Neglectful mothers, on the other hand, stand out for their extremely negative behavior and their low rates of positive interactions.

Finally, however, Burgess and Conger note that there was little evidence to suggest that *children* in abusive families behave in a manner very different from children in the comparison families. They did show lower rates of verbal and physical interaction with their mothers, but this may result from (1) maternal neglect as much as from their own behavioral atypicalities, or (2) a reciprocal influence between maternal and child characteristics which leads to increasing withdrawal between mother and child. Since the present study provided only descriptive information about patterns of covariation in behaviors within families, these two interpretations cannot be resolved. Burgess and Conger note that experimental analyses are needed to determine the extent to which certain behavior patterns functionally are related to specific others. Such analyses will allow for a determination of what maintains such dysfunctional patterns of interaction, and may provide insight into how such behaviors initially develop.

Poverty and unemployment tend to adversely affect parents' relations with their children. (Sybil Shelton/Monkmeyer)

vision, sports) and its widespread acceptance of physical punishment as an appropriate means of disciplining children illustrate the role that the wider social context can play in creating environments in which child abuse can thrive. The denigration of the role of parent and the popular belief that children belong to parents, to be handled as the family chooses, also contribute to the incidence of child maltreatment (Belsky, 1980).

PSYCHOLOGY AND THE LAW

Our legal system is one of the most important institutions in our society. Many aspects of the U.S. legal system are older than the country itself, having been imported bodily from the British system of common law. Although the legal system stresses previous precedents and is highly resistant to change, the work of psychologists is having an increasing impact on it.

A review of the many applications of psychological and social science research in U.S. courts has been published by Collins (1978). It begins in 1908 with a famous brief by Louis Brandeis, which used research findings about public opinion to convince the Supreme Court that the workday for women employed in laundries should be limited to 10 hours. Some of the other applications include the reliability of eyewitness testimony (see Chapter 7) and lie detectors (see Chapter 5), regulations on bail and pretention, the psychological consequences of desegregation, and findings of public opinion regarding trademarks, tracking of students in the schools, use of standardized testing for employment, and arguments for and against the death penalty.

For those brought up in the United States, Canada, or England, the jury is probably the major symbol of justice and fairness. The jury system is not without its critics, however, and much of the contemporary debate on it is being informed by the research of psychologists.

THE JURY

Psychologists interested in the law have focused a great deal of attention on the jury because it is a highly visible and important aspect of the legal system and also because it is one of the most controversial. Three topics pertaining to the jury have generated particular attention from psychologists: (1) jury prejudice, (2) jury decision making, and (3) jury competence.

One of the first applications of psychology to the law in the United States occurred in 1908 when psychological findings helped convince the Supreme Court that the workday for laundresses should be limited to ten hours. (Bettmann Archive)

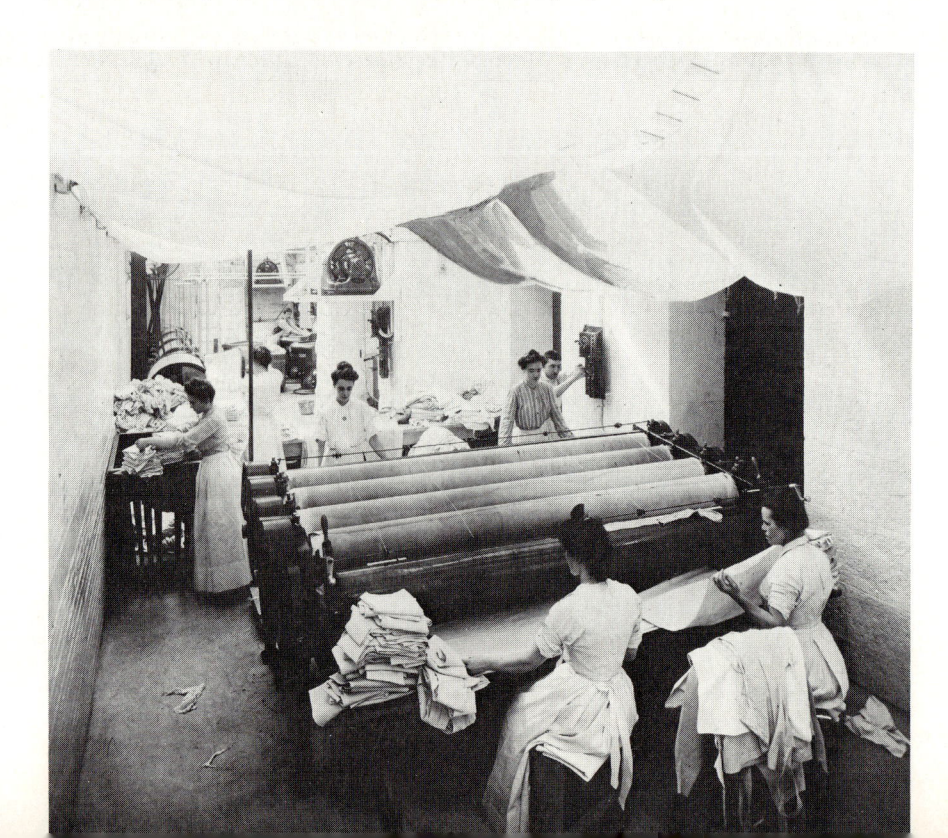

Jury Competence. Critics of the jury system charge that juries are incompetent, unreliable, prejudiced, and tend to disregard the law. Supporters of the jury system argue that the collective wisdom of 12 citizens is greater than that of one trained judge—the most likely alternative to the jury. Psychologists have examined many aspects of jury competence, incuding a jury's ability to (1) apply the presumption of innocence principle, and (2) follow the judge's instructions.

We have all heard the phrase "innocent until proven guilty." It is an assumption of U.S. law that jurors must presume the defendant's innocence at the start of the trial. However, the available evidence suggests that jurors' presumptions are not always the same as those prescribed by law. Some surveys of actual jurors, for example, have found that many of them presume *guilt* rather than innocence (Buckhout & Baker, 1977).

Kerr, Atkin, Stasser, Meek, Holt & Davis (1976) were interested in whether variations in the requirements of proof actually affected verdicts. They presented a simulated jury with three definitions of reasonable doubt: a lax criterion ("you need not be absolutely sure that the defendant is guilty to find him guilty"), a stringent criterion ("if you are not sure and certain of his guilt you must find him not guilty"), and a condition where reasonable doubt was not defined. The mock jurors in this study recommended more guilty verdicts when the lax criterion was emphasized than when either of the other criteria were used. One change in court procedures that might help facilitate the jury's use of the presumption of innocence principle is the point at which it is drawn to the jury's attention. Although instructions about the presumption of innocence and the beyond-a-reasonable-doubt standard of proof are traditionally given after the trial, research by Kassin and Wrightsman (1979) found that these instructions were most effective if given before the trial.

Often evidence is introduced into testimony that the judge considers inadmissible or prejudicial. The judge then instructs the jurors to disregard this evidence. But do they? One type of inadmissible evidence that can emerge in criminal court testimony concerns the defendant's criminal record. The law contends that evidence of a defendant's prior crimes should not be used as proof of guilt of the crime he or she is being tried for. In other words, the defendant should not be convicted on the basis of past misconduct. Research on this point is mixed. Some research indicates that judicial instructions to ignore the defendant's criminal record are effective (Wolf & Montgomery, 1977); other research (Doob & Kirschenbaum, 1973) indicates that such instructions are not wholly effective (i.e., higher conviction rates occur when such information is introduced). The inconsistency of findings on this question has led psychologists to find ways to make a judge's instructions more understandable and effective (Charrow & Charrow, 1979; Severance & Loftus, 1982).

Jury Prejudice. Prejudice is one of the ugliest factors that enters into and sometimes distorts the jury process. People express prejudice against all kinds of things—race, gender, religion, appearance, and so on—and all jurors cannot be expected to be free of prejudice. Many studies have examined how potential targets of prejudice influence jury decision making. Dane and Wrightsman (1982) have reviewed the research and summarized it as follows:

1. *Gender:* Effects seem to differ depending on crime, but more research is still needed.

2. *Socioeconomic status:* No consistent influence has been found.
3. *Moral character:* Prior offenses seem to increase the likelihood of a conviction; the more repentant a defendant appears, the less likely is a conviction.
4. *Physical attractiveness:* Attractive defendants are more leniently treated, except when the attractiveness was used to facilitate the crime.
5. *Race:* Defendants of the same race as jurors are less likely to be convicted.
6. *Attitude similarity:* Jurors seem to be more lenient toward defendants with attitudes similar to their own.

The research clearly indicates that jury prejudice exists, but that its effect is probably not very strong. The facts of the case usually exert the greatest influence, as they should.

Jury Decision Making. The modern criminal jury system was first used in sixteenth-century England, and until now juries have been made up of 12 persons—although no one knows why that number was chosen. In recent years, however, several U.S. states have reduced the size of juries to six people. It is argued that the smaller size is administratively more efficient and cheaper. The change in size from 12 to 6 is also justified by the contention that this change does not affect the jury's ability to render justice. The question of how jury size influences decision making is a natural one for social psychologists to tackle, and there is now considerable research on it. The general thrust of this research seems to be that jury size can affect verdicts and that courts need to consider more carefully the effects of jury size "on such things as the accuracy of evidence recall and the quality of deliberations" (Roper, 1980).

Psychological research may eventually have implications for another aspect of jury functioning. Historically, juries have been required to reach a unanimous verdict, but several state jurisdictions have allowed juries to return verdicts based on a majority decision of as few as 8 of the 12 members. However, arguments similar to those used regarding changes in jury size can be mustered against the use of majority-decision rules. Group discussion, for example, may not be as thorough under a majority rule. If only one or two members express doubts about the majority view, their objections need not be considered.

Simulation experiments comparing juries operating under majority and unanimity decision rules tend to support the merits of the unanimity rule (Hans, 1977; Nemeth, 1976; Saks, 1977). Findings such as these could be useful to legislative bodies and courts considering changes in the unanimity rules under which juries have traditionally operated.

JUDGES VERSUS JURIES

One test of the effectiveness of the jury is to compare verdicts reached by juries with those made by judges. In a monumental study, Kalven and Zeisel (1966) asked presiding judges whether they agreed or disagreed with the jury's verdict in more than 3,500 criminal jury trials. They found that the judge and jury agreed in 78% of the cases. In those cases in which the jury turned in a verdict contrary to what the judge's verdict would have been, it was overwhelmingly in favor of the defendant. It seems that jurors decide cases more according to the spirit than to the letter of the law and that this accounts for the disagreement between jurors and judges. Advocates of the jury system cite this bias toward the spirit of the law as a strong point in its favor.

PSYCHOLOGY AND MEDICINE:
I. THE SAMPLE CASE OF BEHAVIORAL MEDICINE

At 11:30 each morning, a 38-year-old department manager for a large accounting firm closes the door to her office, takes off her shoes, loosens her collar, and sits down in her chair, letting her hands fall comfortably into her lap. She closes her eyes and begins to imagine herself walking on a warm, secluded California beach. She can feel the hot, white sand become damp and cool as she approaches the rolling surf. She feels the icy water wash up and around her ankles and then recede. She concentrates on the smell of the salt air and the crashing waves. Immersed in her pleasant image, for 15 relaxing minutes the stresses of a breakneck work schedule are washed out with the tide.

A 14-year-old boy sits on the edge of his bed staring pensively at his thigh, and holding the syringe with his allergy medication in his right hand. When he was younger, he went to his doctor twice a week for an injection; now he is giving them to himself. Although he has done it many times before, it doesn't seem to get any easier. "I'm scared. I don't want to do this," he whispers under his breath. Then he remembers the skill his uncle the psychologist taught him: Talk to yourself. The boy tries the phrases he rehearsed in his uncle's office: "Just relax and take a deep breath. I know I can do this, I've done it before. It's only a little pinprick. Even if it hurts, it's only for a second. Go ahead and get it over with. The long-range benefits outweigh the brief discomfort." The boy raises the syringe and brings the needle down. He injects the medicine, pulls the needle out, wipes his skin with cotton, and then tells himself: "Good job. I knew I could handle it."

Teaching people to relax is a strategy of behavioral medicine designed to help prevent illness by changing potentially unhealthy lifestyles. (Paul Conklin/Monkmeyer)

These stories illustrate techniques used in behavioral medicine, a broad field of interdisciplinary study that focuses on the relationship between health and behavior. It represents the overlapping interests not only of psychologists and medical personnel, but also of sociologists, epidemiologists, physiologists, and others. As a particular field of study, it is a relative newcomer, dating back to the mid-1970s, but the concept of a relationship between health and behavior goes back to antiquity. Because behavioral medicine is so new there is still disagreement about its definition, but the one most widely cited comes from a conference held in 1978:

Behavioral medicine is the field concerned with the development of behavioral science knowledge and techniques relevant to the understanding of physical health and the application of this knowledge and these techiques to prevention, diagnosis, treatment, and rehabilitation. Psychosis, neurosis, and substance abuse are only included insofar as they contribute to physical disorders as the endpoint. (Schwartz & Weiss, 1978, p. 6)

In simplest terms, we might think of behavioral medicine as having two related goals: (1) getting people to do things that are good for their health, and (2) getting people to stop doing things that are bad for their health. Of course, to know what is good and bad the field must involve basic research as well as clinical practice. Let us consider some instances of the application of behavioral medicine.

LIFE-STYLE CHANGE

Unlike 100 years ago, when America's leading causes of death were infectious diseases, today's top killers are more chronic and more closely associated with controllable unhealthy behaviors. One need not be a researcher to know that smoking greatly increases one's risk of heart attack, cancer, and stroke, by far the nation's leading causes of death. A poor diet also contributes to the top three, as well as other potentially fatal disorders such as diabetes. Excessive alcohol consumption plays a major role in the number four killer, accidents, as does the failure to use seat belts. Poor exercise and a host of other behaviors may also contribute to premature death. There are other disabling but nonfatal consequences of unhealthful behaviors, including permanent disability, reduced occupational functioning, chronic fatigue, costly medical treatment, and interpersonal withdrawal, all of which detract from the quality of life.

Traditionally, public health programs have attempted to alter such behaviors through education, particularly through preventive efforts with school-aged children. Although such programs have been useful, the prevalence of these problems suggests that more is needed. For instance, a smoker may know that she should quit, but may lack the skills to do so, or an obese man may "know" that statistically he is at greater risk than others for heart attack, but not believe that the statistics apply to him. In these cases, not only is education needed, but also a behavioral intervention. Behavioral medicine, then, attempts to modify unhealthy behavior at several levels, both before and after prevention. Before prevention, researchers attempt to understand the etiology of unhealthy life-styles in terms of both environmental demands (e.g., socially and physically reinforcing properties of the behavior) and individual personality factors (e.g., learning history, genetic factors). Following prevention, practitioners attempt to assess and provide patients with strategies for change (e.g., skills training, relaxation). In patients with irreversible damage, intervention may focus on rehabilitation (i.e., learning to live with disability).

MEDICAL COMPLIANCE

Medical compliance is an example of how life-style and pattern of behavior interact with an important specific situation: adherence to a medical treatment program. Some examples of noncompliance would include a high school student who takes fewer antibiotics than directed, for fear of getting "hooked"; a business executive who refuses to slow down after a heart attack; an elderly widow who ingests too many sleeping pills, because through the course of the night she forgets how many she has taken; and a diabetic who occasionally forgets to inject himself with insulin. Obviously, medical directions and prescriptions do little good if they are improperly followed, and the potential for harm is great and perhaps fatal.

There are many reasons why a person might not adhere to a medical regimen: The patient may not have understood directions; he or she may be lazy or forgetful, or intentionally uncooperative; he or she may be denying his or her illness; he or she may not believe the treatment will help, even if he or she complies; or he or she may refuse to undergo a treatment because it is too painful or otherwise aversive. It is important to realize that noncompliance may be due to aspects of the patient's personality, the nature and presentation of the treatment, or both.

The resistance of some cancer patients to follow through with their chemotherapy treatment is a good illustration of how serious noncompliance can be. It has been estimated that 7 to 33% of all patients undergoing chemotherapy either miss appointments or discontinue treatment (Penta, Poster, & Bruno, 1983). This occurs even though for many patients chemotherapy is a potential cure with a high success rate. Typically, such noncompliance has been combated with a heavy dose of persuasion, reasoning with the patient about the importance of treatment. Some investigators, however, have taken a different tack. Recognizing that chemotherapy side effects are extremely aversive, and probably contribute to the patient's unwillingness to take treatment, these investigators have attempted to apply behavioral principles to reduce these side effects. In one study (Burish & Lyles, 1981), for example, the researchers hypothesized that the nausea and vomiting which often precedes chemotherapy are a result of respondent conditioning, taught patients to relax, and dramatically reduced these side effects.

Returning to the two goals of behavioral medicine (getting people to do things that are good for their health, and getting people to stop engaging in unhealthy behaviors), it should be clear from our examples that simply educating people is often not enough. Implementing change is often complicated and requires many intervention techniques and a broad base of theory and research upon which the techniques can rest.

Behavioral medicine cuts across many disciplines, as well as issues of etiology, prevention, assessment, treatment, and rehabilitation. It has been applied to a broad range of conditions and disorders, including obesity, smoking, hypertension, insomnia, asthma, arthritis, diabetes, headache, chronic and acute pain, and cancer. The range of interventions is as great and includes such techniques as systematic desensitization, relaxation training, hypnosis, contingency management, self-instruction, community education, biofeedback, behavioral contracting, self-monitoring, and stress inoculation. Behavioral medicine, however, is less a unique set or combination of techniques, disciplines, and problem areas than a way of looking at health and behavior. Despite specific differences, specialists in behavioral medicine share a common view which emphasizes a reciprocal relationship between health and behavior. This perspective has grown in popularity, not only among scientists and practitioners, but also among those responsible for administrating health care, since behavioral approaches often prove a practical alternative when weighed against the costs of traditional medical care. For patients, behavioral medicine also represents a move toward greater patient responsibility and participation in maintaining their own health. Behavioral medicine, it then appears, holds great promise for both the providers and receivers of health care.

PSYCHOLOGY AND MEDICINE: II. THE SAMPLE CASE OF COGNITIVE PSYCHOLOGY AND THE DIAGNOSIS AND TREATMENT OF ALZHEIMER'S DISEASE

Mrs. L. is 75 years old and lives with her daughter and her family. Recently, she put some water on the stove to boil to make tea, and then, becoming engrossed in a television program, forgot about it. The tea kettle boiled dry and was ruined, and more extensive damage to the house was narrowly averted. This incident causes her daughter to recall several other incidents in which her mother forgot to do something, misremembered some event, or mislaid something. Now she is worried that her mother is getting "senile."

What is "senility?" First, it is important to point out that senility is a lay person's term with no precise meaning. It is loosely linked to certain symptoms if they occur in later life. These include forgetfulness, confusion, and certain other changes in personality and behavior. Contrary to popular opinion, such symptoms are not the inevitable result of growing older. Nor are slight confusion or minor memory lapses, such as forgetting to turn off the stove, necessarily a sign of serious illness. Such problems occur throughout life and may only reflect information overload or preoccupation with current concerns. However, some older adults exhibit significant signs of global mental impairment. Such global decline of cognitive functioning from some previously attained level is called *dementia*. Thus the term *senile dementia* refers to global cognitive decline that occurs late in life. Estimates are that about 10% of persons over 65 years of age exhibit mild to moderate levels of cognitive impairment, while another 4 to 5% suffer from severe dementia.

However, dementia may be produced by many causes. It may be the result of psychological disturbances such as depression, or organic conditions such as brain disorders. More important, some of these problems may be treated and cured, whereas others, at this time, can only be treated. Without a precise identification of the problem, the typically observed symptoms of dementia may provoke the wrong treatment.

Two of the most important incurable forms of cognitive impairment in old age are Alzheimer's (pronounced "ALTZ-hi-merz") disease and multi-infarct dementia. These are estimated to account for approximately 80% of the dementia in old age.

Some 50 to 60% of elderly adults with dementia suffer from *Alzheimer's disease*, making it the most common cause of dementia. It is characterized by slow and progressive deterioration. Early symptoms are a loss of attentiveness and initiative—the person may appear vaguely different to family and friends. Additional changes include gradual memory loss, especially for recent events, deterioration of judgment, and a lessened ability to plan. Depression, hallucinations, and delusions may also occur. Ultimately, the person cannot deal with the environment and generally requires institutional care. The life expectancy of persons suffering from Alzheimer's disease is less than one-third that of normal-age peers. At autopsy, the brains of Alzheimer's patients show certain characteristic changes, including loss of neurons and enzymes important for neurological functioning. However, the actual cause or causes of these changes are unknown.

Multi-infarct dementia is less common than Alzheimer's disease, but accounts for approximately 15 to 20% of dementia cases. It is caused by multiple blockages of small cerebral arteries in widely distributed areas of the brain (many small strokes). The symptom are similar to Alzheimer's disease, but the dementia progresses in a stepwise rather than steady fashion, and is usually patchy rather than uniform.

Although Alzheimer's disease and multi-infarct dementia account for most dementias in old age, over 100 reversible conditions may mimic these disorders. An estimated 10 to 20% of those with dementia in later life have such reversible conditions. Symptoms similar to those of Alzheimer's disease and multi-infarct dementia may be produced by such diverse conditions as depression, nutritional deficiencies, drug intoxications, infections, tumors, or heart disease. For example, in one case, a woman admitted to a nursing home for dementia was found to be suffering from the effects of several drugs that had been prescribed by different physicians for various conditions. Once the toxic effect produced by this combination of drugs was eliminated, she was able to return home.

How can "normal" aging and reversible problems such as depression be differentiated from irreversible conditions such as Alzheimer's disease? Diagnosis must be based on a thorough and multifaceted examination, including a detailed history, comprehensive medical examination, specific tests such as a brain scan, and psychological evaluation. Cognitive tests can play a crucial role in this diagnostic procedure. Such tests can indicate the level and pattern of impairment. Some of the types of items frequently used in such diagnostic procedures are shown in Table 19.1. Research has demonstrated that careful interpretation of such items can be used to make relatively precise discriminations between unimpaired and impaired persons or among those suffering from different types of impairment. For example, in a recent study, Storandt and her colleagues were able to discriminate successfully between healthy older adults and patients with mild dementia of the Alzheimer's type, using a battery of four psychological tests. Only 2 persons out of 84 (one patient and one normal control) were misclassified (Storandt, Botwinick, Danziger, Berg, & Hughes, 1984). Similarly, Montgomery and Costa (1983) found that psychological tests were effective in discriminating senile dementia from other types of organic and psychogenic disorders.

Even if a person has an irreversible disease, much can be done to help

TABLE 19.1
Sample items from cognitive tests used to diagnose senile dementia

1. Patient is asked to demonstrate orientation as to place, time, and person.
   e.g., "What month is it?"
2. Patient is asked to respond to successive commands.
   e.g., "Open your mouth and close your eyes."
3. Patient is asked to make alternating movements.
4. Patient is asked to copy single and complex figure.
   e.g., "Copy this."

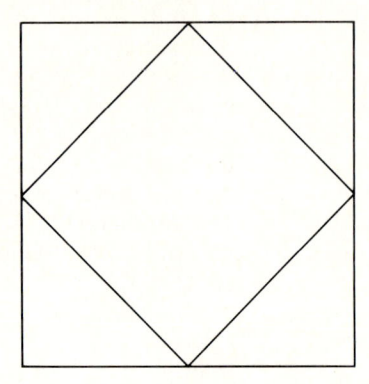

5. Patient is asked about similarities and differences among objects.
   e.g., "I am going to name three things. You tell me which one doesn't belong with the others. Which one is different?" (fish, car, train)
6. Patient is asked to read a sentence and recall it later.
   e.g., "The boy has a brown dog."
7. Patient is asked to judge and match designs.
   e.g., "Which of these designs (point to designs at bottom) looks like this one?" (Point to design at top.)

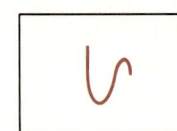

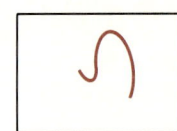

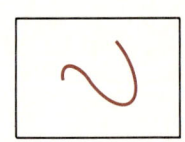

Source: Mattis (1976).

the patient and to help the family cope with the problem. Again, multiple therapies are important, including proper nutrition, careful use of drugs, and prompt treatment of even minor illnesses. Psychologically based interventions are also particularly important. Providing simple memory aids can assist people in maintaining their capacity to engage in daily activities. Such aids might include items such as a calendar, list of daily activities, posted notes about simple safety measures, and labels and directions for commonly used items. Similarly, structuring the environment to provide salient cues may help the person from becoming disoriented. The use of color coding to identify locations in nursing homes is an example of this technique. Finally, the occurrence of irreversible dementia constitutes a significant source of stress for unafflicted family members. The institutionalization and ultimately the death of a spouse or relative are often a direct result of the disease. Thus psychological intervention must focus on assisting the family in coping with these events.

SUMMARY

1. Psychology may contribute to the formulation of social policy and to redressing the problems of contemporary society. It may do this by contributing knowledge which will aid in understanding a societal problem, in remediating a problem, in preventing a problem, or in enhancing human functioning.

2. The incidence of divorce has increased markedly in recent years. The effects of divorce on the child depend in part on the child's age and sex.

3. Maternal employment is now a common feature of contemporary American families. Some of the major effects identified relate to daughters career aspirations and role changes.

4. Child abuse appears to have increased in recent years. Family characteristics contributing to abuse include parent unemployment and family social isolation. Negatively perceived child characteristics may also contribute to abuse.

5. Psychology has implications for the practice of law. Psychologists have, for instance, studied the jury system. Here jury behavior and the bases of verdicts are studied. The differences between the decisions of juries and of judges have been studied; it has been found that jurors, more so than judges, decide cases more according to the spirit than to the letter of the law.

6. Behavioral medicine uses behavioral science knowledge and techniques to understand physical health and to prevent, diagnose, treat, and rehabilitate health problems.

7. Cognitive psychology may be used to diagnose and treat Alzheimer's disease, a cognitive impairment associated typically with old age. For instance, there exist several types of cognitive tests which can be used to detect this disorder and to indicate its degree of severity.

KEY TERMS

Social policy
Remediation
Prevention
Enhancement
Child abuse

Jury competence
Jury prejudice
Behavioral medicine
Medical compliance
Dementia

Senile dementia
Alzheimer's disease
Multi-infarct dementia

SUGGESTED READINGS

BELSKY, J., LERNER, R. M., & SPANIER, G. B. *The child in the family*. Reading, Mass.: Addison-Wesley, 1984. Describes the nature of the contemporary family and discusses the problems that may occur in child-family relations. An emphasis is placed on reciprocal relations within the family and between the family and the broader context.

GATCHEL, R. J., & BAUM, A. *An introduction to health psychology*. Reading, Mass.: Addison-Wesley, 1983. Presents a thorough introduction to the general field of activity in which psychological knowledge and medical science converge: health psychology.

LOFTUS, E. F. *Eyewitness testimony.* Cambridge, Mass.: Harvard University Press, 1979. Describes the role of human memory processes in the testimony given at trials by eyewitnesses to crimes, accidents, and so on. The book represents a major instance of the role of psychological knowledge in the study of law and in the functioning of our legal system.

TURK, D. C., MEICHENBAUM, D., & GENEST, M. *Pain and behavioral medicine: A cognitive-behavioral perspective.* New York: Guilford Press, 1983. Presents the role of cognitive-behavioral psychology within a behavioral medicine approach to the treatment of pain.

APPENDIX A
Descriptive and Inferential Statistics

DESCRIPTIVE STATISTICS
   Frequency Distributions
   Measures of Central Tendency
   Measures of Variability
   The Normal Frequency
      Distribution
   Correlation

INFERENTIAL STATISTICS
   Populations and Samples
   The Significance of a
      Difference
SUMMARY
KEY TERMS
SUGGESTED READINGS

Measurement is a pervasive aspect of everyday experience. A college lecture, for instance, can be measured using several dimensions, including its length (long versus short), interest value (interesting versus boring), and its difficulty level (simple versus complicated). Often measurement is reflected in numbers rather than descriptive adjectives. Time, weight, and distance are variables typically represented by numbers. Many of our own attributes are measured in numbers: Our intelligence is measured by an IQ score, our knowledge of introductory psychology by a percentage score, and our physical attractiveness by a number between 1 and 10. Because numbers are more precise measures than adjectives, science relies almost exclusively on numerical measurement.

    Psychologists measure characteristics or performances by assigning numbers to them according to an orderly system or scale of measurement. Statistical methods, the focus of this appendix, are used to interpret the numbers used by psychologists and to make valid generalizations about them. There are two general types of statistics: descriptive statistics and inferential statistics.

DESCRIPTIVE STATISTICS

    To study behavior psychologists must be able to describe it. Describing behavior, especially the behavior of large groups of people, is not easy. If we are concerned with only a few persons, it may be meaningful simply to report

TABLE A.1
Exam scores for 21 students

79	66	74
76	68	74
65	74	86
50	86	82
92	74	93
55	81	74
64	77	83

the scores or responses of every person. For example, in describing how your friends Rita, Harry, and Carlos did on their psychology exam, you could simply say that Rita got 86%, Harry got 72%, and Carlos got 82%. However, the enumeration of individual scores becomes less informative when you wish to describe the scores of the entire class (see Table A.1). It is difficult to comprehend the pattern of scores when they are simply listed as in Table A.1. Something more concise is desirable.

FREQUENCY DISTRIBUTIONS

One way to represent a distribution of scores more concisely is to group them in a *frequency distribution*. To group individual scores, we must first divide the scale on which they are measured into intervals and then count the number of scores falling into each interval. An interval into which scores are grouped is called a *class interval*. To decide into how many intervals the scores should be grouped, we consider both the range of values in our scores and the number of scores we have to group. The frequency distribution shown in Table A.2 presents the scores from Table A.1 using class intervals of 10.

The frequency distribution can be expressed graphically. A common means for doing this is the *histogram* (see Figure A.1). Histograms (also called bar graphs) are constructed by drawing bars. The bases of the bars reflect class intervals, and their heights the corresponding class frequencies.

MEASURES OF CENTRAL TENDENCY

Although a frequency distribution is a more concise description of a group of responses than the list of individual scores, we may often want a description that is even more concise. Summarizing a distribution of scores with a single number is as concise as we can be. One such number is called a *measure of central tendency*. Three measures of central tendency are in common use: the *mean,* the *median,* and the *mode*.

Mean. The *mean* is the number you arrive at when you add up all the scores and divide by the number of scores. It is the arithmetic average. The mean of the distribution of scores presented in Table A.1 is 75. We arrive at this number by dividing 1573 (the sum of the individual scores) by 21 (the number of scores).

TABLE A.2
Frequency distribution of scores from Table A.1

Class Interval	Frequency of Persons in Class Interval
50–59	2
60–69	5
70–79	7
80–89	5
90–99	2

Figure A.1
A frequency histogram of the scores reported in Table A.1.

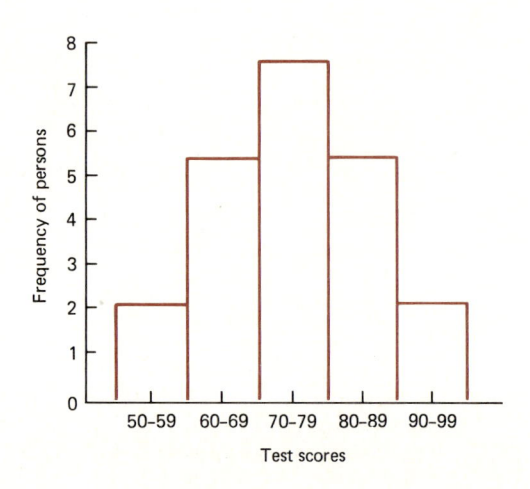

DESCRIPTIVE AND INFERENTIAL STATISTICS

Figure A.2
A normal distribution curve.

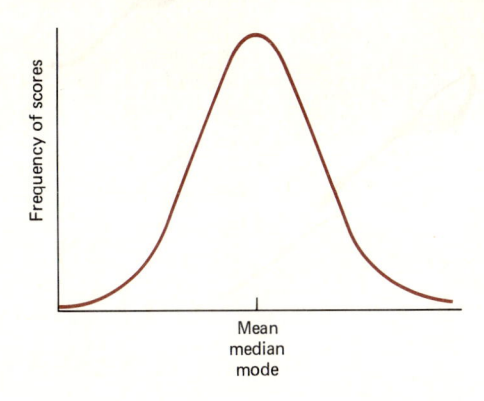

Median. The *median* is the point that divides the distribution into two equal halves. To find the median of the distribution of scores, we first must arrange the scores in increasing order. Next, we find the score that has the equal number of scores above and below it. This score is the median of the distribution. In Table A.1 the median is 74. When there are an equal number of scores, the median is simply the average of the two scores on either side of the middle. When there are an odd number of scores, as in our example, this problem does not arise.

Mode. The *mode* is the score that occurs most frequently. In Table A.1 the most common score is 74. Any distribution of scores can have only one mean and one median, but it can have more than one mode. When a distribution has two modes it is called a *bimodal* distribution.

When the distribution of scores is symmetrical and takes the form of a bell (see Figure A.2), the mean, median, and mode are all represented by the same score. But not all distributions are so regular in shape (see Figure A.3). The term used to describe the slanted distributions represented in Figure A.3 is *skewness*. A distribution is said to be *negatively* skewed when the tail of the distribution slants left and *positively* skewed when the tail of the distribution slants right. In a skewed distribution, the mean, median, and mode will generally be different. The median is often considered the best measure of central tendency in such cases.

Table A.3 shows the distribution of annual income in a company where nine employees earn between $8,000 and $12,000 and a tenth person (the boss) earns $200,000. This distribution is positively skewed. The mean income of the group is $19,000; the median income is $11,000. Clearly, $11,000 is a more representative measure of the employee's incomes than is $19,000. When a distribution has one or two extreme scores in it, the median is a more appropriate measure of central tendency.

Figure A.3
Examples of skewed distributions.

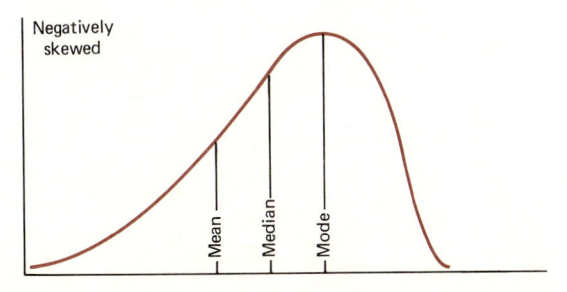

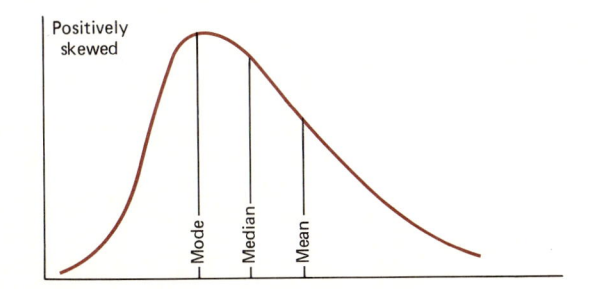

TABLE A.3
The income distribution of 10 employees

Employee Number		Annual Salary
1		$ 8,000
2		8,000
3		10,000
4		10,000
5		10,000
6	Median →	12,000
7	$11,000	12,000
8		12,000
9		12,000
10		200,000

MEASURES OF VARIABILITY

A single measure of central tendency is a very concise way to represent a distribution of scores, but it does not give the complete picture. Consider the differences in the two distributions shown in Figure A.4. Note that while the means, modes, and medians of the two distributions are identical (they all equal 70), the distributions themselves are not. Each distribution has a different spread of scores around its center. In the top distribution all the scores are relatively close to the center, whereas in the bottom one the spread of scores is relatively great. A measure of the spread of scores around the mean is called a *measure of variability*. The greater the spread, the greater the variability.

Range. Two measures of variability commonly used by psychologists are the *range* and the *standard deviation*. Let us illustrate the differences between these two measures by considering the number of children per household on each of two residential blocks.

Block A: 1,1,4,4,7,7
Block B: 2,4,4,4,5,5

For each of these blocks the mean number of children per household is 4, but the variability in the distribution of children across the two blocks is quite different. The range is the easiest measure of variability to compute, and is defined as the highest score minus the lowest score. For Block A the range is 6 (7 - 1); for Block B the range is 3 (5 - 2). While the range is easy to compute, it reflects very little about the distribution. It is based on only two scores, and, indeed, the two most unusual scores.

Standard Deviation. A better and more commonly used measure of variability is the *standard deviation* (SD). The *standard deviation* incorporates every score in the distribution, not just the extreme scores. To compute the SD we first take each score (X) and subtract the mean $\overline{X}$ from it, as we have done in Table A.4. You might think that the next step is to sum the resulting difference (d) scores, but the sum of the difference scores will always add up to zero. That is, every score above the mean is canceled by a score below the mean. To avoid this problem, we *square* each difference score, as we have done in Table A.4, and thus are left with only positive numbers. If we sum the squared difference scores (d^2) and take their mean, we are left with a statistic called the *variance*, which is generally represented by the lowercase Greek letter sigma squared (σ^2). The variance is a good measure of variability.

Figure A.4
Two distributions of scores with different amounts of variability.

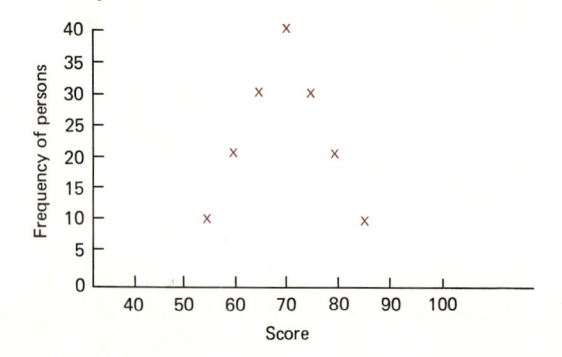

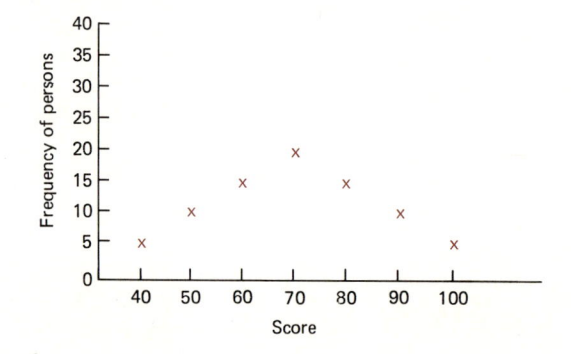

DESCRIPTIVE AND INFERENTIAL STATISTICS

TABLE A.4
Computation of the variance and standard deviation for two sets of scores

Distribution of Children per Household

Block A			Block B		
$X - \bar{X}$	d	d^2	$X - \bar{X}$	d	d^2
1 − 4	−3	9	2 − 4	−2	4
1 − 4	−3	9	4 − 4	0	0
4 − 4	0	0	4 − 4	0	0
4 − 4	0	0	4 − 4	0	0
7 − 4	+3	9	5 − 4	+1	1
7 − 4	+3	9	5 − 4	+1	1
Sum of X = 24	Sum of d = 0		Sum of X = 24	Sum of d = 0	
$\bar{X}$ = 4	Sum of d^2 = 36		$\bar{X}$ = 4	Sum of d^2 = 6	

$$\text{variance} = \sigma^2 = \frac{\text{Sum of } d^2}{\text{Number of cases}} = \frac{36}{6} = 6$$

$$\text{standard deviation} = \sqrt{\sigma^2} = \sqrt{6} = 2.45$$

$$\text{variance} = \sigma^2 = \frac{\text{Sum of } d^2}{\text{Number of cases}} = \frac{6}{6} = 1$$

$$\text{standard deviation} = \sqrt{\sigma^2} = \sqrt{1} = 1.00$$

It is generally more convenient, however, to use the square root of the variance. We squared the difference scores before we added them up, so now we take the square root of the variance to get back to the original scale of measurement. The square root of the variance is the standard deviation (represented by σ). By comparing the standard deviations of the two sets of scores (2.45 versus 1.00), we can see that the variability in the first set of scores is much greater than that in the second.

THE NORMAL FREQUENCY DISTRIBUTION

Frequency distributions that are symmetrical (bell shaped) are said to be *normal distributions* (see Figure A.2). Most of the scores in a normal distribution are near the mean, and frequency drops off smoothly toward the ends of the distribution. Many variables of psychological interest have normal distributions; for example, IQ, height, weight, and scholastic aptitude test (SAT) scores.

If we know that a variable is normally distributed *and* know its mean and standard deviation, we can construct the distribution of the variable. We can do this because of theoretical properties of the normal distribution. In any normal distribution the SD can be used to divide the distribution into sections containing fixed percentages of the cases. Roughly two-thirds of the cases (68%) in a normal distribution will fall between plus or minus 1 SD from the mean. Ninety-five percent of the cases will fall within plus or minus 2 SDs of the mean and virtually all (99.7%) within plus or minus 3 SDs.

The regularities of the normal distribution can be seen in the distribution of IQ scores. IQ, as we said, is normally distributed (see Figure A.5). Its distribution has a mean of 100 and a standard deviation of 16. Based on our knowledge of the properties of the normal curve, we can infer from these two measures that 68% of IQ scores will tend to fall between ±1 standard deviations from the mean (84 to 116), 95% of IQ scores within ±2 standard deviations (68 to 132), and virtually all IQ scores within ±3 standard deviations (52 to 148).

DESCRIPTIVE AND INFERENTIAL STATISTICS

variables. Correlation coefficients measure the degree to which two sets of scores vary similarly, or covary.

Scores can covary in one of two ways. First, scores can be *positively correlated*, in which case high scores on one variable (e.g., psychology) tend to be associated with high scores on the other variable (e.g., math) and, correspondingly, low scores tend to be associated with low scores. Second, scores can be *negatively correlated*, in which case high scores on one variable (e.g., psychology) tend to be associated with low scores on the other variable (e.g., mathematics), and vice versa. Two variables that are positively correlated are height and weight. Generally, the more people weigh, the taller they are. Two variables that are negatively correlated are alcohol consumption and the ability to drive a car. The more alcohol people have consumed, the less able they are to drive.

Correlational data are often displayed in a *scatter plot*, in which values of one variable are shown on the horizontal axis and values of the other variables on the vertical axis. Figure A.6 shows three possible relationships between the scores of seven people on two tests. In the top scatter plot you can see that the seven points all fall on a straight line. This means that the correlation is perfect. You can also see that the line slopes upward to the right. This means that the correlation is positive—as your score increases on one test, it also goes up on the other. In the middle scatter plot, the seven points also all fall on a straight line, but here the line slopes downward to the right.

Figure A.6
Correlational patterns.

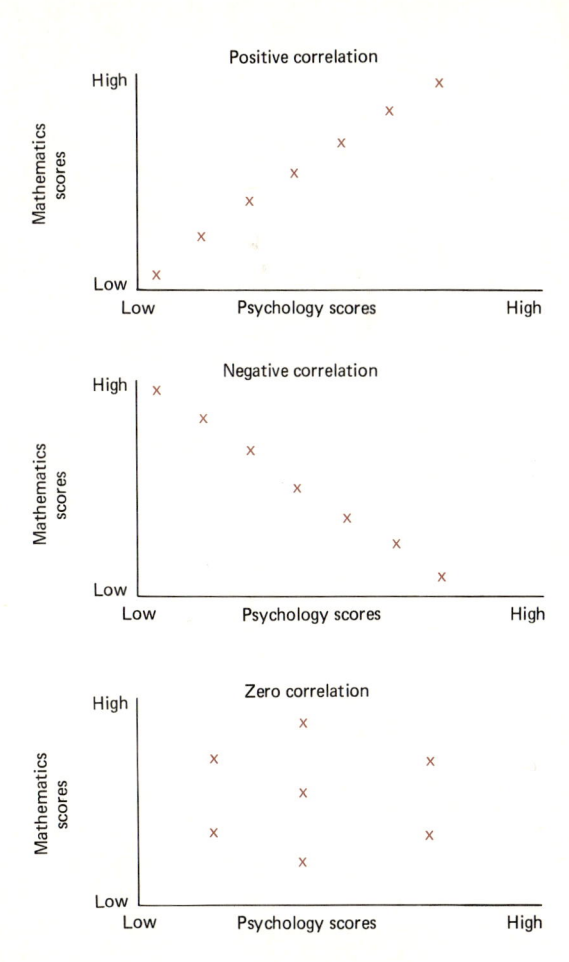

The straight line indicates that here, too, we have a perfect correlation, but the direction of the slope indicates that the correlation is negative—as your score goes up on one test, it goes down on the other. In the bottom scatter plot, the points do not fit a straight line. When they are scattered in this manner, the correlation tends to be low, approaching zero. Two variables have a zero correlation when a person's score on one variable is not at all related to the person's score on the other variable.

Correlations are rarely perfect. Generally, the points are scattered all over the graph—hence the term "scatter plot." It is helpful to draw a straight line through the plot which comes as close as possible to all of the various points. This line is called a *line of best fit* and it indicates the general trend of the relation between the two variables.

While the relation between two variables can be estimated roughly by plotting them on a scatter plot, the degree of correlation is more precisely measured by a correlation coefficient.

Correlation Coefficient. The most frequently used method of determining the coefficient of correlation is the *Pearson product-moment method*, which yields the measure conventionally designated r. The product-moment coefficient r varies between $+1.00$ and -1.00. For positive correlations r is positive; for negative correlations, it is negative; and for variables which are completely uncorrelated, $r = 0$. The largest positive value r can have is $+1.00$, which represents a perfect correlation (see the top panel in Figure A.6); the largest possible negative value is -1.00, which is also a perfect correlation (see the middle panel in Figure A.6). Note that the sign of the correlation (positive or negative) reveals nothing about the degree of the correlation, but only indicates the direction. Thus a correlation of $-.85$ is just as strong as a correlation of $.85$. The closer the points in a scatter plot come to falling on the line of best fit, the nearer r will be to $+1.00$ or -1.00, and the more confidently we can predict scores on one variable from scores on the other.

The calculation formula for r is presented in Table A.5. To illustrate the calculation of a correlation coefficient, Table A.5 presents the scores of subjects on both a test-anxiety scale and an exam. In the formula, X refers to a subject's score on variable X, and Y is a subject's score on variable Y. N is

TABLE A.5
Calculating the Pearson product-moment correlation coefficient

Name	Text Anxiety, X	X^2	Exam Score, Y	Y^2	XY (X Times Y)
Susan	3	9	10	100	30
Mary	5	25	6	36	30
Harry	7	49	7	49	49
George	10	100	3	9	30
$N = 4$	$\Sigma X = 25$	$\Sigma X^2 = 183$	$\Sigma Y = 26$	$\Sigma Y^2 = 194$	$\Sigma XY = 139$

$$r = \frac{N \Sigma XY - (\Sigma X)(\Sigma Y)}{\sqrt{[N \Sigma X^2 - (\Sigma X)^2][N \Sigma Y^2 - (\Sigma Y)^2]}}$$

$$= \frac{(4)(139) - (25)(26)}{\sqrt{[(4)(183) - (25)^2][(4)(194) - (26)^2}} = \frac{556 - 650}{\sqrt{(732 - 625)(776 - 676)}}$$

$$= \frac{-94}{\sqrt{(107)(100)}} = \frac{-94}{\sqrt{10,700}} = \frac{-94}{\sqrt{103.44}} = -.91$$

the number of paired observations (i.e., the number of subjects measured on both variables). The calculation of r involves a number of arithmetic operations on the X and Y scores. ΣX is simply the sum of the scores on the variable X. ΣX^2 is the sum of the squared scores on X (each score is first squared and then the sum of the squared scores is obtained). The quantity $(\Sigma X)^2$ is the square of the sum of the scores; the total of the X scores (ΣX) is first calculated and then this total is squared. It is important not to confuse the quantities ΣX^2 and $(\Sigma X)^2$. The same calculations are made using Y scores, to obtain ΣY, ΣY^2, and $(\Sigma Y)^2$. To find XY, each subject's X score is multiplied by his or her score on Y; these values are then summed for all subjects. Once these calculations have been made, r is computed by using the formula in Table A.5.

Interpreting Correlations. The existence of a correlation between two variables informs us that a person's score on one variable can be predicted (with greater or lesser precision depending on the magnitude of the correlation) from the person's score on the other variable. For example, if test anxiety is negatively correlated with exam performance, we can predict that a student who has high test anxiety (relative to other students) will probably do relatively poorly on exams, and that a student who has low test anxiety (relative to other students) will probably do relatively well on exams. The existence of a negative correlation between test anxiety and exam performance also enables us to predict anxiety from performance. We would predict that a person who does well on exams will tend to be low in test anxiety, and vice versa. Prediction is an important goal of science, and correlation coefficients are very useful in this regard.

Correlation coefficients are not as useful in pursuing the interpretation of cause-effect relationships. This limitation of correlation coefficients is important and frequently overlooked. For example, when we hear that there is a positive correlation between time spent viewing violent television shows and viewer aggressiveness, we may be tempted to believe that this constitutes evidence that the viewing of violent television makes viewers aggressive. This belief may be correct, but it is not justified on the basis of the correlation coefficient. A correlation between two variables does not imply that one variable causes or influences the other. Correlation coefficients are ambiguous with respect to cause-effect links. Thus a positive correlation between amount of time spent viewing violent television and viewer aggressiveness is not only consistent with the hypothesis that the viewing of violent television makes people more aggressive, but also with the hypothesis that aggressive people tend to be attracted to violent television programs. To complicate the issue further, the existence of the correlation between the two variables may not reflect causal influence in *either* direction. For example, a third variable, such as parental aggressiveness, may lead people both to become aggressive and to watch violent television. A correlation between two variables A and B, therefore, could occur because A influences B, because B influences A, or because both are influenced by a third variable, C.

INFERENTIAL STATISTICS

A second type of statistic used by psychologists is inferential in nature. Besides describing data, psychologists also wish to draw inferences about their meaning. Two inferences commonly made by researchers concern the representativeness of a mean and the significance of a difference between two groups of scores.

POPULATIONS AND SAMPLES

Whenever psychologists measure a group of people, they have one of two reasons for choosing them. First, they may be interested in some aspect of the people themselves (e.g., the IQs of current freshmen at a particular college). Much more often, however, their real concern is with a larger group of people, of which the ones they measure are only a subgroup (e.g., all freshmen in the country). In this case the group of people measured is called a *sample*, and the larger group, to which the psychologists wish to generalize, is called a *population*.

Most psychological research involves studying samples of much larger populations. For example, survey researchers, who ask a few thousand people their attitudes toward nuclear disarmament, political candidates, or television shows, are concerned with making inferences not only about the few thousand people they interview, but also about the entire American population. Similarly, a researcher who studied the relation between anxiety and performance in a group of college students would probably be interested not only in this sample but also in the population of university students, and even in the entire human race. But how can we be confident that our sample mean provides an accurate estimate of the population mean? There are a number of factors to consider in this regard.

Representativeness. First, we must ensure that our sample is representative of the population. This is usually accomplished by *random sampling*. Random sampling means that however large or small your sample is, every member of the population of interest has an equal chance of being included. Nonrandom sampling can lead to seriously inaccurate inferences about the population. For instance, it is highly unlikely that we could accurately estimate the sexual attitudes of the American population if we restricted our sample to subscribers of either *Penthouse* or *Reader's Digest*.

Sample Size. A second factor is the size of the sample. The larger the sample, the more likely the mean is to be representative of the population. If we attempted to estimate the national popularity of a politician by randomly measuring the attitudes of only one person, we would run a high risk of making an inaccurate inference about the nation's attitude. On the other hand, if our sample included all but one member of the population, we would obviously have a very representative estimate of the population mean; indeed, it would be virtually identical. One interesting thing about sampling is that although the larger the sample the better, it is possible to get a very accurate idea of the population with even a relatively small sample. Thus a sample of 100 or so Americans, if properly drawn, will provide a fairly accurate picture of the entire American population. Techniques exist to help you calculate how big a sample you need for a given level of accuracy.

THE SIGNIFICANCE OF A DIFFERENCE

Most psychological research involves a comparison between groups of subjects. This is done to test a hypothesis. A hypothesis is a statement about the effect of one variable on another. Actually, every experiment tests two hypotheses: the *experimental hypothesis*, which contends that there is a difference between the experimental groups, and the *null hypothesis*, which contends that there is no difference.

Hypothesis Testing. To illustrate the difference between the two types of hypotheses, let us assume we are conducting an experiment to determine if a new drug, Braingro, increases people's IQ. To answer this question, we decide to compare two randomly selected groups. Group 1 receives a small dosage of Braingro every day for 6 months, and group 2 receives a small dosage of a placebo drug (an inert substance) every day for the same period. The experimental hypothesis is that after the 6 months the subjects randomly assigned to the Braingro group will have higher IQs than the subjects randomly assigned to the placebo group. The null hypothesis is that the IQs of the two groups will not differ. The results of the experiment can support only one of these hypotheses. Let us assume that after 6 months we find that the mean IQ of the Placebo group is 100, while the mean of the Braingro group is 110. How should we interpret the mean difference of 10 IQ points between the two groups? Does such a difference justify a rejection of the null hypothesis or the experimental hypothesis?

To answer this question, let us review the logic of our experiment. In effect, we are claiming that if we administered Braingro to the human population, it would increase the average IQ. To test this proposition, we conduct an experiment using a *sample* of the human population. We hope to show in our experiment that a sample of the human population which ingests Braingro will develop higher IQs than a sample which does not ingest Braingro. Since we expect that those who ingest Braingro will become a different population than those who do not, we assume that IQ differences between our two groups exist because they are samples from two different populations—those who have taken Braingro and those who have not. The null hypothesis, on the other hand, contends that Braingro will not produce two different populations and thus the two groups of scores in our experiment are simply two samples from the same population. The null hypothesis does not specify that the scores will be identical, of course, since chance variation will often produce differences between two samples from the same population. We would not assume, for instance, that just because flipping two coins 10 times produced nonidentical distributions of heads and tails that these two coins came from different populations (e.g., head-prone versus tail-prone coins). To determine whether a mean difference of 10 IQ points reflects the presence of two populations of IQ scores, we use inferential statistics.

Comparing Sample Means. Inferential statistics provide us with a precise way of evaluating mean differences. To test a mean difference statistically, we must know not only the means of the two samples but also their standard deviations. Whether a difference is statistically significant depends on its size and on the size and variability of the samples on which it is based. Remember that the null hypothesis contends that the two sets of scores are, in fact, just two samples of the same population (i.e., giving people Braingro does not make them different). One clue as to whether we are dealing with samples from separate populations of scores or just samples from the same population is the magnitude of the mean difference. The greater the difference, the greater the likelihood that the difference is reliable (i.e., there is a significant difference between the two groups). But the magnitude of the mean difference alone is not sufficient to establish a significant difference. The variability in the scores is also important.

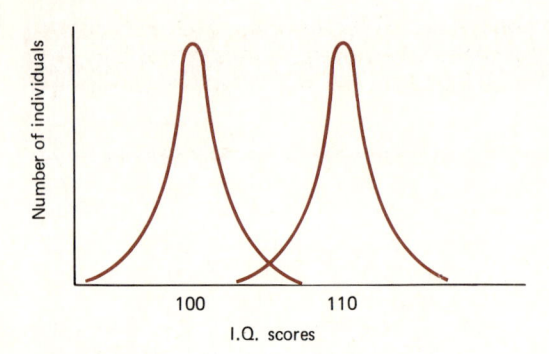

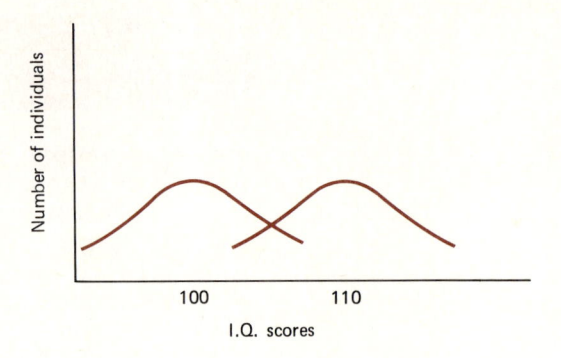

Figure A.7
The hypothetical IQ scores of two groups of subjects. The overlap in the scores is much greater in the right panel than in the left panel.

To understand this point, look at the two panels in Figure A.7. In each panel we see a hypothetical frequency distribution of IQ scores for two groups of subjects. The mean difference between the two groups in each panel is identical (mean difference = 10), but the variability of the scores in the two panels is quite different. In the top panel there is no overlap between the scores of the two groups; all consumers of Braingro score higher than all consumers of the placebo drug. The scores of consumers of Braingro bunch closely around 110 and the scores of placebo consumers bunch around 100. In the bottom panel, however, the distribution of scores is quite different: there is considerable overlap between the two distributions, with the scores in each being widely distributed around the means of 100 and 110, respectively. Which pattern of results is more suggestive of a significant difference? Specifically, in which of the two panels are you more certain that you are seeing two samples of scores from two distinctive populations (rather than two samples from the same population)? Clearly, you are more certain about the pattern in the top panel. Thus both the mean difference and the variability influence the reliability of differences between groups.

Statistical Tests. The objective way of deciding whether the null hypothesis can be rejected is to perform a statistical test. A common statistical test for hypothesis testing is the t test. (The formulas for the t test and many other tests of significance can be found in elementary statistics books.) Statistical tests of significance, such as the t test, take both the mean difference and the variability of the groups into account. These tests basically compute a ratio, with the mean difference constituting the numerator and an estimator of the variability constituting the denominator. The ratio for the comparison represented in the top panel of Figure A.7 will be greater than that in the lower panel because the estimate of variability (the denominator) will be greater in the bottom panel. But how do we interpret a ratio of this type? More specifically, at what point does a t ratio become significant? By convention, psychologists consider any ratio that could occur by chance fewer than 5 times in 100 to be significant. In other words, psychologists wish to be 95% certain that a difference is real before they reject the null hypothesis. The probabilities associated with various t ratios are found in statistical tables.

The point to remember is that virtually every time two experimental groups are compared, there will be a difference. Inferential statistics, such as t tests, allow you to decide whether or not to reject the null hypothesis by telling you the likelihood that the difference could have occurred by chance. When a difference could only have occurred by chance 5 or fewer times out of 100, it is probable that the two means represent different populations, and we

DESCRIPTIVE AND INFERENTIAL STATISTICS

reject the null hypothesis and assume that the difference is significant. When differences could have occurred by chance *more* than 5 times out of 100, we reject the experimental hypothesis and assume that the difference is not significant.

SUMMARY

1. Statistics serve two functions. Descriptive statistics are used to summarize and describe a large number of scores or responses. Inferential statistics are used to generalize from a sample to a population and to determine the significance of a difference between groups.

2. Measures of central tendency for a distribution of scores represent one class of descriptive statistics. They include the mean (the arithmetical average), the median (the middle score), and the mode (the most common score).

3. Measures of variability are a second type of descriptive statistics. The range and the standard deviation are the most common of these. The range simply represents the difference between the largest and smallest scores. The standard deviation is both a more useful and more complex measure of variability.

4. Correlations are a third type of descriptive statistic. They measure the degree of association between two variables. Correlation coefficients can range from +1.00 to −1.00. The more it deviates from 0, the greater the degree of association between the variables. The sign of the correlation (+, −) reflects not the degree but rather the direction of the association.

5. There is an important distinction between sample and population. The population is the entire group about which the researcher wishes to draw conclusions. The sample is the small subset of that population which is actually measured or studied. Generalizations from sample to population are possible only if the one is representative of the other. Selecting samples randomly is the most common way to ensure representativeness.

6. Every experiment involves a null hypothesis and an experimental hypothesis. The null hypothesis states that there are no systematic differences between the scores of the experimental groups, and that they are actually just different samples from the same population. The experimental hypothesis states that there is a difference between the groups and that they are samples from different populations.

7. Statistical tests are used to determine whether to reject the null or the experimental hypothesis. The null hypothesis is rejected if there is less than a 5% chance of the scores from the different groups coming from the same population. If the chance is greater than 5%, the experimental hypothesis is rejected.

KEY TERMS

Descriptive statistics
Inferential statistics
Frequency distribution
Measure of central tendency
Mean
Median
Mode
Skewness
Measure of variability
Range
Standard deviation
Normal distribution
Standard score
Correlation coefficient
Scatter plot
Line of best fit
Sample
Population
Experimental hypothesis
Null hypothesis

SUGGESTED READINGS

Huff, D. *How to lie with statistics*. New York: Norton, 1984. This is an entertaining and informative book about the misuses of statistics.

Kimble, G. *How to use (and misuse) statistics*. Englewood Cliffs, N.J.: Spectrum Books, 1978. This book illustrates how statistics are used in various practical tasks.

APPENDIX B
The Psychology Journal Article

SCIENTIFIC COMMUNICATION
THE RESEARCH REPORT
  Title
  Author and Institution
  Abstract
  Introduction
  Method
  Results
  Discussion
  References
PSYCHOLOGY JOURNALS

SCIENTIFIC COMMUNICATION

Mastering the techniques of scientific communication is a difficult task, yet it is an essential one if you are considering going on in any of the many branches of psychology. To keep up with an ever-changing and expanding field, you must be able to read and understand the results of psychological experiments as they are published in scientific journals. Therefore, this section is aimed at helping you to learn what to look for when you read a psychology journal article and to help you write your first reports.

At first you might be somewhat puzzled by the style of writing that you see in scientific journals. The articles seem to be filled with many long words and complex phrases that appear to be specifically designed to confuse the reader and inflate the self-importance of the author. On closer examination, however, you may see that most of these large words are used to convey precise shades of meaning. Without this precision, much of the value of the article would be lost. This is not to say that there is any virtue at all in the indiscriminate use of jargon. There isn't. But careful expression makes it necessary for a scientist to use just the right word in the appropriate context. For example, you might say that the observers in an experiment were "disinterested" (meaning impartial), but you would not want to say that they were "uninterested observers" (unless they were). The scientific writer must not say "a lot of the subjects answered most of the questions correctly." Rather, the writer of a scientific paper must tell exactly how many subjects there were and convey precisely just how many questions were answered correctly.

Precision is the very essence of scientific writing. The reader must be able to find out such things as exactly how the observations were conducted, what measures were taken, what types of subjects were employed, and how they responded. The data must be presented in a fashion that is complete, unambiguous, and yet compact and readable. All this is not easy to accomplish.

Probably the best source of information about the preparation of psychology journal articles is the *Publication Manual of the American Psychological Association,* Third Edition. It should be available in your campus bookstore, but if not, copies may be ordered from

> Order Department
> American Psychological Association
> 1200 Seventeenth Street, N.W.
> Washington, D.C. 20036

You should write for information about the current price. This excellent style guide contains information about all phases of manuscript preparation and is useful for many other disciplines besides psychology. Much of the material in the following sections is based on information contained in the Publication Manual, so you should be able to go directly to it if you need more information.

THE RESEARCH REPORT

Standard psychology research articles have several major parts. We shall discuss each of these parts and through this discussion you should learn what to expect to find in each section of a journal article. Also, you should learn something about putting together a well-written manuscript of your own.

TITLE

In as few words as possible, the title should capture the main ideas of the paper. A good title should state the major independent and dependent variables studied in the research or the important theoretical issues that were discussed. Either too few or too many words in a title can cause problems. For example, "Impaired discrimination learning in rats following hippocampal lesions" is a much better title than "Brain damage and learning." Or if one is reporting a clinical study of child development, a title such as "The effects of forced delay on impulsive 8- to 12-year-old children" is much more useful to a reader than a title such as "Delaying responses in children." A good title should give the reader enough information so that he or she will know whether or not the article deals with topics on which they want further information.

AUTHOR AND INSTITUTION

Providing your name and affiliation (and that of any coauthors) is probably the only simple part of writing a journal article. Even though it is simple, it is still very important that the information be absolutely correct, for authorship is the only way that people can receive recognition and credit for their contributions. When there are several authors of an article, it is usually the first author who is thought of as having made the principal contribution to the work.

ABSTRACT

Most psychology journal articles have an abstract and it is usually found at the beginning of the article, although in some journals it is found at the end, just before the list of references. The abstract is a brief summary of why the research was performed and what was found. It allows the reader to survey the article quickly to determine whether or not it is of interest and worth reading in its entirety. An abstract is usually about 100 to 150 words in length, although major articles in some journals not published by the American Psychological Association, especially large review articles, will have abstracts that are somewhat longer.

When writing an abstract for a college term paper or for a journal article, you should make sure that the topic is clearly defined, that the methods and subjects are briefly but unambiguously described, that the major findings are stated, and that the most important conclusions are summarized. Even experienced authors find abstracts difficult to write, because so much information must be compressed into so very few words.

INTRODUCTION

Although not set off with its own heading, the introduction nevertheless has an important purpose. It tells the reader why the experiment was done or why a particular topic was investigated. Often, this section contains a short historical review of earlier research relevant to the topic. This review should not be exhaustive and should cite only those studies that bear directly on the specific issues investigated in the paper. The literature review in the introductory section should emphasize the major conclusions and controversies resulting from earlier research. The introduction should set the stage for the experiment and explain the logic behind it.

In any review of scientific literature, references to other articles and books will have to be cited, just as your authors have done in this textbook. Citations are made in a manuscript by placing in parentheses the names of the authors of the article or book followed by the year of publication. For example, (Kelley, 1973) is the appropriate citation for a journal article with a single author, while (Bandura & McDonald, 1963) cites an article with more than one author. The citation (Thompson, 1967, pp. 285–293) is a book, and books are cited in the body of the paper in the same manner as journal articles. The only difference is that page numbers are sometimes included in the citation when books are being referenced.

METHOD

The purpose of the Method section of an article is to tell the reader how the experiment was conducted. This section must include sufficient detail so that another researcher could repeat the experiment to check the reliability of the findings or to extend them. It is very important that no critical details be omitted in the Method section. To aid in organization and clarity, the Method section is usually divided into several subsections.

Subjects. This subsection identifies the participants in the research. If the subjects were animals, they should be identified by species and strain. Also, other important information that will aid other researchers in understanding and reproducing the experiment, such as age and sex of the subjects, should be included. If the subjects were human beings, this section should report how they were selected, and also describe their ages, sex, and other relevant demographic information.

Apparatus/Measures. This part of the Method section should include a brief description of the equipment and materials used in the experiment. Special equipment should be described in enough detail so that the experimental conditions could be duplicated in another laboratory. Commercially obtained apparatus should be identified using the manufacturer's name and model number, but usual or common items of laboratory equipment such as stopwatches or test tubes need not be described in detail.

In studies in which assessments of human performance are made, the researcher will want to describe the tests (measures) that were used. For instance, if the researcher measured the intelligence of the subjects using the Wechsler Adult Intelligence Scale, this test would be described under "measures."

Procedure. This section is where exactly what was done is described. Each step in the experiment should be summarized. If the subjects were animals, there should be a description of how they were trained and what other manipulations were performed. If the participants in the study were human subjects, the instructions given to them should be described. If the instructions form an essential part of the experimental manipulation, they should be written out verbatim. Standard testing procedures need not be described in detail, but the reader should be referred to a journal article which does describe these procedures, and that article should be cited together with the other references.

RESULTS

This section of a journal article tells what was observed when the experiment was conducted. Usually, this section does not contain all the raw data that were gathered, but rather a summary of the findings together with whatever statistical tests were used to analyze the data. Experienced writers usually summarize the important findings first and then support these statements with a more detailed explanation of the data later.

Often, writers of journal articles will include several tables or graphs that summarize their findings. A graph can clearly convey a great deal of information, but it is important that it be carefully labeled. Both the abscissa and the ordinate should have labels that tell what measure is being plotted and what units of measurement are being used. Further, each graph or figure should have a caption that explains it; otherwise, a reader can easily become confused.

The Results section is usually not the appropriate place to discuss the implications of the findings. A good Results section simply presents the findings and places them in statistical perspective—no more and no less. Interpretation of the findings is usually reserved for the Discussion section.

DISCUSSION

In this section the outcome of the research is interpreted and placed in context with other research and theoretical positions. It is often a good idea to begin this section with a summary of the ways that the findings support (or do not support) the hypotheses presented in the introduction. This draws the reader's attention to some of the theoretical implications of the research.

The Discussion section is the place to point out the practical value of the research and to discuss future studies that ought to be performed. Knowledgeable authors avoid long, rambling speculation about the meaning of their findings and concentrate on a few central issues. A good Discussion section tells the reader how the study answered the original problem, suggests some conclusions that can be drawn from the data, and emphasizes the more important implications of the findings.

REFERENCES

Each article should contain a complete list of all references that were cited in the text. There is a standard procedure for citing references that is used by most psychologists, and once you become accustomed to it, you will find it easy to use and very helpful.

The following examples provide models of the most common types of references. For the less common types of references, you should check the *Publication Manual of the American Psychological Association*.

1. A journal article with one author:
   Kelley, H. H. (1973). The processes of causal attribution. *American Psychologist, 28,* 107–128.
2. A journal article with multiple authors:
   Bandura, A., & McDonald, F. J. (1963). Influence of social reinforcement and the behavior of models in shaping children's moral judgments. *Journal of Abnormal and Social Psychology, 67,* 274–281.

References are alphabetized by the last name of the first author of each article. The year of publication is placed in parentheses and it follows the names of the authors. Notice that only the first word of the title of each journal article is capitalized. The title of the journal in which the article appeared should be written out in full and underlined to indicate that it should be typeset in italics. Journal titles should not be abbreviated, as the use of abbreviations often results in confusion when some of the lesser known journals are cited. The volume number of the journal (underlined) and the page numbers of the article follow.

3. An article in a popular magazine:
   Alper J. (1985, March). The roots of morality. *Science 85,* pp. 70–76.
4. A book with one author:
   Hilgard, E. R. (1977). *Divided consciousness: Multiple controls in human thought and action.* New York: Wiley-Interscience.

In the case of books, the name of the author is given first, the date of publication follows, and the book title is underlined. The city of publication is given next, followed by a colon, and then the book publisher is identified. Chapters in edited books are treated in the following way.

5. An article with multiple authors in an edited book:
   Jensen, R. A., Messing, R. B., Martinez, J. L., Jr., Vasquez, B. J., & McGaugh, J. L. (1980). Opiate modulation of learning and memory in the rat. In L. W. Poon (Ed.), *Aging in the 1980s: Psychological Issues* (pp. 191–200). Washington, DC: American Psychological Association.

PSYCHOLOGY JOURNALS

Listed here are a few of the hundreds of journals that publish the results of research in psychology. This list is not exhaustive in any way, but it does list some of the major journals and indicates the types of articles that they publish. These journals should be found in most college and university libraries. Back issues are usually bound in volumes in the library stacks, while the more current issues are usually found in a special area devoted to new arrivals.

The American Psychologist: The official journal of the American Psychological Association. It publishes articles on current issues in psychology, as well as empirical, theoretical, and practical articles dealing with broad aspects of psychology. Lists of meetings and conventions, as well as a variety of announcements and official papers, can be found here.

Animal Learning and Behavior: Publishes theoretical and experimental articles on animal learning, conditioning, motivation, emotion, and comparative aspects of behavior of animals other than human beings.

Behavior Research Methods, Instruments, and Computers: Articles in the area of the methods, techniques, and instrumentation in experimental psychology. The journal emphasizes the use of computers in psychological research.

Behavior Therapy: Publishes articles dealing with the behavioral modification of maladaptive behavior. Includes group research, case studies, and literature reviews.

Behavioral Neuroscience: Research papers covering the broad field of the biological basis of behavior. Topics covered include anatomy, neurochemistry, physiology, endocrinology, and pharmacology, as well as genetic, evolutionary, and developmental studies.

Behavioral and Neural Biology: Publishes research papers concerned with the relationships between biological factors and behavior. Topics include the neurobiological basis of learning and memory, modulation of behavior, psychopharmacology, motivation, and behavior genetics.

Bulletin of the Psychonomic Society: Short research articles in all areas of experimental psychology. These articles are not refereed but are published quite rapidly following submission to the journal.

Cognitive Psychology: Articles dealing with memory, language processing, perception, problem solving, and thinking. Articles in this journal emphasize research on human cognition.

Cognitive Therapy and Research: Contains research focusing on assessment, etiology, and treatment of maladjustment from a cognitive and a cognitive-behavioral perspective.

Contemporary Psychology: Contains critical reviews of books, films, tapes, and other media relevant to psychology.

Developmental Psychobiology: Basic research and theoretical articles about biological factors and environmental influences that control and modulate the development of the behavior of animals other than human beings.

Developmental Psychology: Publishes articles dealing with factors that influence human development across the life span from infancy to aging.

Journal of Abnormal Child Psychology: Research focusing on child psychopathology, including articles about abnormal development, and assessment and treatment of childhood disorders.

Journal of Abnormal Psychology: Covers abnormal behavior, its determinants and correlates. Also presented are articles dealing with psychopathology, normal processes in abnormal persons, experimental studies, and research dealing with social and group effects on abnormal behavior.

Journal of Applied Psychology: Research and theoretical articles dealing with topics related to business, industry, and government, as well as the legal, health, military, and educational systems.

Journal of Comparative Psychology: Laboratory and field studies of the behavioral patterns of various animal species as they relate to evolution, development, and ecology.

Journal of Consulting and Clinical Psychology: Experimental and theoretical articles dealing with techniques of diagnosis and treatment for psychological problems. There are also studies of populations of clinical interest, such as hospital, prison, and geriatric groups, as well as cross-cultural studies and research dealing with personality.

Journal of Counseling Psychology: Theoretical, research, and practical articles of interest to counselors in schools, colleges, governmental agencies, business, and military settings.

Journal of Educational Psychology: Studies of learning and cognition related to measurement of psychological development, the assessment of different methods of instruction, and the adjustment of students to the school environment.

Journal of Experimental Psychology: Animal Behavior Processes: Experimental studies on aspects of learning, memory, perception, motivation, and performance in nonhuman animals.

Journal of Experimental Psychology: General: Long, scholarly, integrative articles dealing with all areas of experimental psychology.

Journal of Experimental Psychology: Human Perception and Performance: Studies of perception, verbal or motor performance, and related information processing and cognitive processes.

Journal of Experimental Psychology: Memory, Learning, and Cognition: Articles on fundamental encoding, transfer, memory, and cognitive processes in human beings.

Journal of Mathematical Psychology: Theoretical articles in many fields of psychology which can use mathematical models. Articles deal with mathematical theories of models of topics such as problem solving, language processing, perception, and computer simulations.

Journal of Personality and Social Psychology: This journal is divided into three parts. The first deals with aspects of attitudes and social cognition; the second with interpersonal relations and group processes; the third with personality processes and individual differences.

Journal of the Experimental Analysis of Behavior: Studies of how environmental factors affect the behavior of animals. Articles focus on the principles of reinforcement and punishment, often in operant situations.

Memory and Cognition: Studies of learning, memory, conceptual processes, psycholinguistics, decision making, and skilled performance.

Perception and Psychophysics: Theoretical and research articles dealing with sensory processes, psychophysics, and perception in human beings.

Physiological Psychology: Research articles in all fields of neuroscience that relate directly to behavior and experience. Topics covered include biology, pharmacology, anatomy, electrophysiology, and neuroendocrinology.

Psychological Abstracts: Publishes abstracts and summaries of all articles in the field of psychology and related subject areas.

Psychological Bulletin: Evaluative and integrative reviews and discussions of issues in scientific psychology that highlight major research developments and bridge specialized fields.

Psychological Review: Theoretical and evaluative articles in any area of scientific psychology.

Glossary

Accommodation. The process by which the lens of the eye changes shape so that the image of near or far objects can be brought into focus on the retina. The lens becomes flattened when focusing on distant objects and more rounded when focusing on nearer objects.

Accurate empathy. *See* Empathy.

Acquisition. The period in learning during which a new response is learned and gradually strengthened.

Action potential. The brief electrochemical impulse that provides the basis for the conduction of information along the length of the axon of a neuron. The action potential results from a change in the permeability of the axon membrane to sodium and potassium ions.

Active mastery. Being in charge of one's environment; viewing the self as a source of energy.

Active sleep. Sometimes known as rapid-eye-movement (REM) sleep, this stage of sleep is characterized by EEG activity similar to that seen during waking and by an almost complete relaxation of skeletal muscles. Dreaming is associated with this stage of sleep.

Activity scheduling. As part of the treatment of depression, the therapist guides the client in planning and participating in potentially enjoyable events.

Acute disorder. Used to describe a disorder of sudden onset and relatively short duration.

Adaptive testing. Or tailored testing; employs different sets of test questions for each person taking the test. Specific questions are determined by the person's skill level.

Adequate stimulus. A type of stimulus that is appropriate for a particular sensory receptor. For example, light is an adequate stimulus for the rod receptors of the eye, while molecules of a certain shape provide adequate stimuli for the olfactory system.

Adipsia. Inability to drink.

Adolescence. The period within the life span when most of a person's characteristics are changing from those typical of children to those typical of adults.

Adrenal cortex. The outer portion of the adrenal glands, responsible for the release of corticoid hormones into the bloodstream.

Adrenal medulla. The inner core of the adrenal glands, responsible for the release of norepinephrine and epinephrine (adrenalin) into the bloodstream.

Adrenocorticotrophic hormone (ACTH). A pituitary hormone that stimulates the cortex, or outer portion of the adrenal glands, to release corticoid hormones into the bloodstream.

Aerobic exercise. Exercise that demands oxygen, such as jogging, swimming, and bicycling.

Alarm reaction. The first stage of the general adaptation syndrome. Elicited by sudden exposure to a stressful stimulus to which the organism is not adapted. Involves an initial shock reaction and a mobilization of defensive forces to deal with the stressor.

Alleles. Two genes, one from the male germ cell (sperm) and one from the female germ cell (ovum), which form a pair and together influence an inherited characteristic. Alleles may be the same or different; *see* Homozygotic and Heterozygotic.

All-or-none law. A principle which states that once an action potential is initiated in an axon, it continues without decrease in signal strength to the end of the axon.

Alpha rhythm. Activity seen in an EEG record that is fairly regular and occurs at a frequency of between 8 and 12 Hz. Alpha waves are associated with a calm, relaxed, but awake state. Alpha rhythm is best observed when the subject's eyes are closed.

Alzheimer's disease. An incurable cognitive impairment generally in old age, with early symptoms of decreased attentiveness and initiative. This form of dementia is a slow and progressive deterioration which affects a person's memory and judgment; the cause is unknown.

Amniotic sac. A membrane which covers the developing fetus and acts as a cushion against shocks. This sac develops and fills with fluid during the embryonic period.

Amphetamines. A class of drugs which generally has stimulating effects on the central nervous system. Amphetamines can cause strong psychological dependence and have a high potential for abuse.

Analogue assessments. Creating a situation which is like

637

the real situation in order to simulate the context for the subject's behavior. Behavioral observations are made in the analogue context when the real situation is not accessible.

Androgen. A male sex hormone secreted by the testes. Testosterone is the principal androgen.

Anhedonia. The inability to experience pleasure from events that are pleasurable to others.

Anorexia nervosa. A dangerous condition of self-imposed starvation characterized by behavior directed toward losing weight, by peculiar patterns of food handling, by weight loss, by an intense fear of gaining weight, by a disturbance in body image, and by other medical and psychological problems.

Anxiety. A general feeling of fear and apprehension; more specifically, a sense of impending danger or threat.

Apgar score. A score representing the physical and behavioral conditions of the newborn in the perinatal period.

Aphagia. Inability to eat. *See also* Hyperphagia.

Assessment. The process of gathering information about a client or subject to better understand the person.

Associative shifting. Another term used to describe classical conditioning.

Atherosclerosis. The development of arterial lesions accompanied by the accumulation of fat, cholesterol, and collagen at the lesion site.

Attention deficit disorder. A disorder of childhood (with or without hyperactivity) characterized by distractibility, limited attention span, impulsiveness, and overactivity. An inability to maintain attention on a single activity or goal.

Attitude. A specific and consistent way of reacting to people, things, and concepts. Most attitudes are learned and have an affective, cognitive behavioral component.

Attribution theory. A theory concerned with the principles people use to infer the causes of other people's behavior.

Autism. A disorder which emerges in early childhood and dramatically affects the child's ability to form interpersonal relationships and build a self-concept. Autism, as an absorption in fantasy, is also a primary symptom of schizophrenia.

Autonomic nervous system. The division of the peripheral nervous system that modulates the actions of the body's internal organs. It consists of two parts: the sympathetic division, which mediates those bodily functions occurring during states of arousal, and the parasympathetic division, which mediates those functions occurring during periods of relaxation.

Average life expectancy. The average length of life.

Axon. A long, thin portion of a neuron capable of transmitting action potentials along its length, thus carrying messages toward its synaptic terminals.

Axon hillock. The region of a neuron where the axon joins the cell body. Action potentials are initiated in this region.

Barbiturates. Drugs derived from barbituric acid; typically used as sedatives or hypnotics.

Basal age. The age level at which a subject correctly answers all test items.

Basal ganglia. Large collections of cell bodies and synapses in the core of each cerebral hemisphere. The basal ganglia consist primarily of the caudate nucleus and the putamen and are involved in the initiation and control of movement.

Beck Depression Inventory (BDI). A self-report test that assesses a person's level of depression.

Behavior. The observable activities of an organism.

Behavioral assessment. A situation-specific approach to assessment. This method seeks to assess actual behavior in the environment (situation) in which it occurs.

Behavioral medicine. A field of interdisciplinary study that focuses on the relationship between health and behavior.

Behaviorism. An approach to psychology founded by John B. Watson which focuses on behavior; a response (R) to an objectively definable stimulus (S).

Behavior therapy. Initially a form of therapy based on the application of the principles of learning (classical and instrumental), behavior therapy is currently viewed more broadly as the application of principles derived from experimental research on a variety of topics, including learning, cognition, and social psychology. A common feature of behavior therapy is the emphasis on performance-based interventions.

Benzodiazepines. A class of drugs used primarily as antianxiety agents and hypnotics.

Binaural cues. Stimuli involving the use of both ears.

Biopsychology. The study of the biological and physiological aspects of mental and behavioral functioning.

Bipolar disorder. A disorder characterized by severe mood swings, also referred to as manic-depression. The sufferer experiences very elevated states of mania and very low states of depression, often in a cyclical fashion.

Birth cohort. That group consisting of persons born in a given year.

Blind spot. The region of the retina where the axons of ganglion cells converge to form the optic nerve and pass through the retina. There are no sensory receptors in this region of the retina, often called the optic disk.

Brain stem. The region of the brain connecting the forebrain structures and the spinal cord; composed of the pons and the medulla. Inside the brain stem are many important groups of cell bodies that are involved in the control of bodily processes, as well as a number of pathways carrying information to and from the brain.

Broca's aphasia. A speech disorder resulting from damage to Broca's area in the frontal cortex; characterized by extreme difficulty in enunciation, extremely slow speech, and the loss of many small connective words in speech.

Broca's area. A region of the frontal cortex vital for normal speech production. It is almost always located in the left hemisphere just above the lateral fissure and in front of the central sulcus. Damage to this area results in a disorder known as Broca's aphasia.

Caffeine. A central nervous system stimulant found in

GLOSSARY

coffee, tea, chocolate, and many soft drinks. Its use is socially accepted in most cultures, and a large proportion of the world's population is mildly dependent on this drug.

Calcarine sulcus. The major sulcus of the occipital lobe. Those regions of the cortex which process visual information surround this sulcus.

Cataplexy. A sudden loss in muscle tone often associated with an attack of sleepiness in people suffering from narcolepsy.

Cataracts. Opacities of the lens that obstruct light waves.

Catatonic schizophrenia. A subtype of schizophrenia marked by disturbances in motor activity, either stuporous and rigid or extremely excited.

Catecholamines. (dopamine; epinephrine/adrenaline; norepinephrine/noradrenaline). These substances serve as neurotransmitters in the brain and as hormones released by the adrenal medulla. Peripherally, they contribute to the mobilization of energy stores and increase heart rate and blood pressure.

Ceiling age. The age level at which a subject cannot answer any test items correctly.

Cell body. Often called the soma, it contains the cell nucleus and various other components which carry out the basic life-support functions of the cell.

Cell nucleus. Found in the soma of cells, this spherical structure contains the chromosomes which carry the genetic information of the cell.

Central nervous sytem (CNS). A system composed of two parts in vertebrates: the brain and spinal cord.

Central sulcus. Sometimes called the fissure of Rolondo, it is an infolding of the cerebral cortex that forms the boundary between the frontal lobe and the parietal lobe. Anterior to the central sulcus are brain regions that are predominantly involved in motor control, while posterior to it are brain regions that are involved in the perception of bodily senses.

Cerebellum. A deeply grooved structure which lies on top of the pons and medulla and looks something like a small "sub-brain." This structure is important for the coordination of muscle movements and some conditioned reflexes.

Cerebral cortex. A six-layered arrangement of cell bodies and synaptic connections which covers the cerebral hemispheres of the human brain. It is thought that functions such as information processing, complex thought, and language are carried out in the cortex.

Cerebral hemispheres. Two large groups of neurons and nerve pathways which constitute the major portion of the brain in human beings and other higher animals. The hemispheres are separated by a deep fissure and are mirror images of one another. They are connected by several bands of axons, the largest of which is the corpus callosum.

Chemotherapy. The use of chemical agents to prevent or treat disease (e.g., cancer).

Child abuse. Any nonaccidental injury sustained by a child under 18 years of age resulting from acts of commission or omission by a parent, guardian, or caretaker.

Chromosomes. The genetic structures carrying a person's genes.

Chronic disorder. A disorder with a relatively permanent maladaptive pattern.

Chunking (organization). A strategy involving grouping or relating items to promote memory.

Circadian rhythms. The rhythmic biological and behavioral cycles that repeat approximately every 24 hours. Sleeping and waking, body temperature, hormone release, alertness, and mood all follow these cycles.

Classical conditioning. An unconditioned stimulus (UCS) which elicits an unconditioned response (UCR) is paired repeatedly with a neutral conditioned stimulus (CS). Through repeated pairings the CS will come to elicit a conditioned response (CR) which is similar to the original UCR.

Client-centered therapy. Also called Rogerian therapy, after its founder Carl Rogers, this form of intervention does not involve interpretations or active advice giving. Rather, the therapist creates a nondirective and facilitative environment where the client can work to solve his or her own problems.

Climacteric. The period of declining reproductive capacity in men and women; known as menopause for women.

Clinical definition of abnormality. A comprehensive definition, including consideration of the person's state, cultural background, scores on tests, and a professional judgment.

Clinical psychology. The branch of psychology concerned with assessing, researching, and treating—modifying and/or eliminating—undesired behavioral, cognitive, or emotional problems.

Cocaine. A drug that inhibits synaptic reuptake of catecholamines, especially dopamine. It produces feelings of euphoria and well-being, and reduces fatigue. The psychological dependence produced by regular use of cocaine can be very debilitating.

Cochlea. A small snail-shaped structure embedded in the bones of the skull just behind the ear. The cochlea contains the receptors that transduce sound energy into patterns of neural activity.

Cognitive-behavior therapy. A rational amalgam of behavioral, performance-based treatments, and the features of cognitive therapy. This system of therapy concerns both the thought and action necessary for behavior change.

Cognitive-behavior treatment of depression. Also referred to as cognition therapy of depression, this form of treatment was developed by Aaron T. Beck and involves teaming with the client to identify problems and gather data to check the logic of the client's thinking. Other features of the treatment include activity scheduling and mood monitoring.

Cognitive dissonance. The condition in which one has beliefs or knowledge that disagree with each other or with behavioral actions. When such cognitive dissonance is aroused, the person is motivated to reduce the dissonance through changes in behavior or cognition.

Cognitive learning. Learning processes which involve knowledge.

Cognitive map. A cognitive image of the organization of an area or a territory in which a person lives.

Collaborative empiricism. A feature of Beck's cognitive-behavioral therapy for depression in which the therapist and client team up to identify problems and gather data to test the logic of the client's thinking.

Color blindness. A defect in the ability to discriminate accurately between different wavelengths of light.

Community interventions. Working at the level of an entire community, community efforts are designed to help improve the lives of many people even if they are not in direct contact with the therapist.

Complex cortical cells. A cell in the visual cortex that responds maximally to a bar of light positioned at a particular angle which can be projected on a wide area of the visual field. *See also* Simple cortical cells.

Comprehension. The understanding of languge.

Concept. An abstraction from particular instances.

Conception. The instant when the reproductive or germ cell (the sperm) of the father fertilizes the germ cell of the mother (the ovum).

Concurrent therapy. A variation of family therapy in which family members are seen separately by the therapist.

Concurrent validity. A criterion-related validity where the test data and the criterion are gathered at the same time.

Conditioned emotional response (CER). An involuntary emotional response to a conditioned stimulus (CS).

Conditioned response (CR). The response which is elicited from a conditioned stimulus (CS) which did not originally evoke the CR.

Conditioned stimulus (CS). A stimulus to which a subject responds after repeated pairings with an unconditioned stimulus (US).

Cone receptor cells. Receptor cells that respond to light, located at the back of the retina and concentrated in the fovea. The cone receptors are specialized for color vision and mediate photopic vision. *See also* Rod receptor cells.

Conservation. The ability to know that one aspect of a stimulus array has remained unchanged, although other aspects have changed.

Confidentiality. A guideline guaranteeing the client's right to have his or her privacy protected.

Conflict. The simultaneous presence of two or more incompatible response tendencies or goals. A source of psychological stress.

Conformity. Behavior that goes along with group behavior or opinions.

Conjoint therapy. A variation of family therapy in which all relevant persons are seen in a single group.

Constructive hypothesis. The view that people use knowledge to construct meaning beyond the information actually presented, and that this information is stored in memory together with what is actually presented.

Construct validity. Established by a set of relationships, construct validity involves the presence of meaningful relationships where they should be found and the absence of relationships where there should be none. The data from several studies are examined to determine construct validity.

Content validity. Pertains to whether a test includes a representative sample of questions from the universe of material relevant to the variable being measured.

Continuous reinforcement. (CRF). A system of reinforcement wherein one response is associated with one reinforcement.

Control process. Memory strategies that people apply voluntarily, such as altering the format of the information, organizing it, and rehearsing it.

Controlled observation. A scientific method of observation wherein the researcher controls the situation in which the behavior will take place but does not directly manipulate the behavior.

Conversion disorder. A loss of alteration in physical functioning which suggests a physical disorder but instead is primarily a reflection of a psychological problem.

Coping model. A form of behavior change, a coping model initially demonstrates fear, and then demonstrates a strategy for overcoming the fear and subsequently performs successfully.

Coping resources. Characteristics of the environment (e.g., money, family, friends, social agencies) or personal characteristics (e.g., health problem-solving skills, personality) that provide the basis for primary appraisal and coping responses.

Coping responses. Particular behaviors implemented by people to eliminate, reduce, or tolerate stress.

Corpus callosum. A large bridge of myelinated axons connecting the two cerebral hemispheres and permitting them to communicate with one another.

Correlation. A relationship or association between two variables.

Correlation coefficient. A measure indicating the strength of association between two sets of variables. The most common measure is the Pearson product-moment coefficient, designated by r.

Correspondent inference. The inference that there is a match between an action and the personal disposition of the person engaging in the action.

Corticoids (e.g., cortisol, cortisone). Hormones released into the bloodstream by the adrenal cortex. They suppress inflammation and contribute to the release of stored energy.

Corticotropic hormone-releasing factor (CRF). A chemical messenger secreted by cells in the hypothalamus that stimulates the pituitary gland to release adrenocorticotrophic hormone (ACTH) into the bloodstream.

Counseling psychology. A branch of psychology with emphases on vocational issues and helping basically healthy people to find ways to enhance their lives.

Countershock phase. The second phase of alarm reaction of the general adaptation syndrome. During this phase, defense forces are mobilized and general resistance to the stressor begins to rise.

GLOSSARY

Countertransference. The psychoanalytic therapist's feelings for his or her client that actually emerge from the therapist's own emotional conflicts.

Covert. Not openly shown or engaged in.

Criterion-related validity. Validity determined by the correlation between a test score and an outside criterion.

Cross adaptation. As a result of a sensory system becoming adapted, or less sensitive, to one kind of stimulus, it often becomes less sensitive to other similar stimuli.

Crowding. The psychological state of feeling surrounded and intruded on by the people around you; occurs in situations where there are too many people or too many activities for a person to attend to comfortably.

Crystallized intelligence. General cognitive capacity reflecting the degree to which a person has incorporated the knowledge and skills of the culture into thinking and actions; postulated to increase with age.

Cue. A secondary stimulus that guides behavior.

Cultural definition of abnormality. The notion that normal behavior is that which is approved by the majority of people within the culture.

Cyclothymia. A style or personality evidencing mood swings (from elation to mild depression) beyond normal limits but not as severe as bipolar disorder.

Decibel. A unit used to measure the intensity of sound. The decibel scale of sound intensities is logarithmic.

Deductive reasoning. Moving cognitively from the general to the more specific.

Deep processing. Operations that code the semantic aspects of information. Produces memory traces that are long-lived.

Deindividuation. A psychological state in which persons feel that they have lost their personal identities. This state often leads to aggressive and impulsive behavior.

Delta waves. Activity seen in the EEG record of a deeply sleeping subject. Characteristic of stage 3 and 4 sleep, delta waves are high amplitude irregular waves ranging in frequency from 0.5 to 4 Hz.

Delusions. Beliefs not supported by facts in reality. These nonnormal perceptions may have private meaning and may, on the surface, seem real.

Dementia. A global decline of cognitive functioning from some previously attained level.

Dendrites. Treelike processes attached to the cell body of neurons which receive information from synaptic connections made by other neurons.

Dendritic spines. Small projections on the surface of some dendrites that receive synaptic inputs from other neurons.

Deoxyribonucleic acid (DNA). Large molecules found in the nucleus of every cell that encode genetic information.

Dependence. The physiological and psychological need for a psychoactive drug that develops following repeated administrations. A drug-dependent person must continue to take the drug to prevent withdrawal symptoms and to function normally.

Dependent personality disorder. An ingrained behavior pattern that impairs interpersonal relationships. This pattern involves a failure to accept responsibility, a lack of self-confidence, and an unwillingness to make demands of others.

Dependent variables. The variable in an experiment which is assessed for change as a function of the manipulation of the independent variable.

Depression. An emotional condition, which is, when severe, marked by a sense of hopelessness, negative thinking, feelings of worthlessness, and some sleep and eating disturbances.

Despair. In Erikson's theory, the negative pole of the crisis of old age; characterized by a rejection of one's life as meaningless and wasted.

Development. Refers to systematic changes in a person across his or her life.

Diathesis-stress model. A model of psychopathology that emphasizes the interaction of biological predispositions with stressful life events and social learning histories.

Diethylstilbestrol (DES). A drug, used by women in the 1950s and 1960s to prevent miscarriage, related to a higher-than-average probability of developing cancer of the cervix in daughters.

Differential approach. An approach to studying intelligence which attempts to identify the structure of abilities by examining relationships among individual differences or multiple ability tests.

Diffusion of responsibility. The tendency for persons in a group situation to share responsibility for taking action, thereby reducing the likelihood of anyone taking action; a factor that inhibits bystanders from intervening in emergency situations.

Discriminative stimulus. A stimulus that is a cue to an operant response.

Disjunctive reaction time. The length of time before a person makes a response to a task involving multiple signals and/or responses.

Disorganized schizophrenia. A subtype of schizophrenia marked by silly affect, incoherent speech, social impairment, and unsystematic delusions. Formerly called hebephrenic schizophrenia.

Display rules. Cultural norms pertaining to when and where various emotions can be expressed.

Doctrine of specific nerve energies. The concept that perceived differences in the quality of stimuli arise not from differences in the stimuli themselves but from the fact that they activate different neural structures.

Dorsal roots. Nerve pathways on the back or top side of the spinal cord. All sensory information enters the spinal cord through the dorsal roots.

Draw-A-Person. The use of a subject's drawings of people to make assessments of personality; a projective method of assessment.

Drive. The state of arousal or unlearned motivation that occurs when a need is not met. Drives motivate goal-directed behavior.

Drug. Any substance which, when taken into the body, alters physiological or psychological functions.

Drug abuse. The use of a drug to the extent that it interferes with a person's physical, economic, social, or psychological well-being.

Drug tolerance. A group of physiological and psychological processes that cause a progressively smaller response to the drug with each repeated administration. When one becomes drug tolerant, a larger dose is required to obtain the effect previously caused by a smaller dose.

DSM III. The third edition of the *Diagnostic and Statistical Manual*. This comprehensive system classifies abnormal behavior.

Echoic memory. Auditory sensory memory.

Echolalia. The repeating back of words spoken by another person (the communication is nonmeaningful).

Eclecticism. A term referring to the absence of a single guiding theory. An eclectic therapist is guided by various theoretical systems, and thereby not restricted by a single set of theoretical assumptions.

Ectoderm. A layer of embryonic cells from which the nervous system and sensory organs arise.

Ectomorph. A body type characterized by a sensitive nervous system and by a thin, frail-looking appearance.

Effect size. A numerical indicator of the degree to which treated clients improved with respect to control (e.g., untreated) clients.

Efficacy expectations. A person's estimate of the probability that he or she can execute the behaviors required to produce a certain outcome.

Ego. According to Freud, the hypothetical mental structure which interacts with the objective world of reality and functions according to the reality principle.

Ego-dystonic homosexuality. Homosexual arousal which distresses the person experiencing it (*homosexuality* refers to sexual preference for members of one's own sex).

Elaboration. The extensiveness or richness of operations performed on incoming information regardless of the depth involved.

Elaborative rehearsal. A memory strategy involving repetition that relates information to other information and improves long-term memory.

Electroconvulsive therapy (ECT). A form of medical treatment in which electric current is passed through the client's brain. Used and said to be effective in some cases of depression; also seen as causing side effects such as memory loss.

Electroencephalogram. The recording of small electrical currents produced by synaptic activity in the brain using electrodes placed on the surface of the skull. Often abbreviated EEG, this recording technique is used to study naturally occurring events such as sleep and to diagnose pathology or disturbances in brain function such as epilepsy.

Electromagnetic spectrum. The range of electromagnetic energy. These radiations vary in wavelength from many miles to small fractions of a nanometer (a billionth of a meter). Visible light is a portion of the electromagnetic spectrum with wavelengths ranging in wavelength from about 750 nanometers to about 400 nanometers.

Emotion. A complex reaction consisting of both physiological change and a subjective experience of feeling.

Emotional response. A strong, relatively uncontrollable feeling that is accompanied by physiological changes.

Emotion-focused (palliative) coping. Coping responses intended to change the way one thinks or feels about a situation.

Empathy. The experience of a shared emotional response; the understanding or experience of another's personal situation.

Encoding. The process of modifying information in memory by representing it in coded form (e.g., via sounds, images, semantic meanings, etc.).

Encoding specificity hypothesis. The hypothesis that a retrieval cue is likely to be effective only if it reinstates the conditions of encoding.

Encoding strategies. The process by which information is stored in memory.

Endoderm. A layer of cells in the embryo from which one's fat (adipose) tissue and one's digestive (visceral) organs originate and develop.

Endomorph. A body type characterized by a predominance of adipose and visceral tissue; hence the body type will appear round and plump.

Endoplasmic reticulum. A component of the interior of most cells; a structure that provides a location for the synthesis and distribution of proteins.

Episodic memory. Memory for specific events in specific contexts.

Estrogen. A female sex hormone produced by the ovaries.

Ethical. Conforming to accepted standards of personal and/or professional conduct.

Ethyl alcohol. A psychoactive agent usually produced as a product of fermentation. It is typically consumed as an intoxicant and it has a high potential for producing psychological and physiological dependence.

Excitatory postsynaptic potential (EPSP). A change in voltage in a neuron which occurs as a result of synaptic activity which depolarizes a postsynaptic cell and increases the likelihood that it will generate an action potential.

Existential therapy. A treatment in which the therapist tries to gain an understanding of the client's mode of existence. The therapist does not try to change the client, but tries to better understand the client as the client changes for himself or herself.

Exorcism. An outdated method of treating mental illness involving prayers, noisemaking, fantastic concoctions, and in some cases, flogging and starvation.

Expansion. A strategy used by parents to shape a child's language involving inserting missing words into the child's utterance and repeating it.

Expectancies. Subjective predictions about the consequences of different causes of action.

Experiment. A scientific method of observation in which the investigator manipulates an independent variable and observes changes in a dependent variable.

Extinction. A decrease in response strength by repeated nonreinforcements.

Factor analysis. A statistical means for grouping observations (or other forms of data) into interrelated sets.

Family therapy. A form of group therapy in which the collection of involved persons consists of the client and

GLOSSARY

his or her family. The intervention typically involves the entire family.

Fertilization. *See* Conception.

Fixations. From the psychodynamic model of abnormality, fixations are shuntings or freezings of psychological growth.

Fluid intelligence. General cognitive capacity reflecting the degree to which the person has developed unique qualities of thinking independent of culturally based content; postulated to peak in early adulthood.

Fovea. The region near the center of the human retina containing the highest concentration of cone receptors. The fovea mediates our greatest visual acuity and detailed color vision.

Free association. A psychoanalytic technique intended to help the client reveal unconscious conflicts. In free association, the client is asked to express, without censure, the feelings and thoughts that come into awareness.

Free-recall task. A task in which a series of items is presented to a person, who is then asked to recall as many of the items as possible in any order.

Frequency distribution. The number of occurrences of various values (scores) in a set of values (scores).

Frequency theory of hearing. A theory suggesting that the rate of generation of action potentials in the auditory nerve mirrors the frequency of the sound stimulating the auditory system. *See also* Place theory of hearing.

Frigidity. Inability to experience sexual pleasure or orgasm; evident in the female's failure to produce the lubricant that facilitates intercourse.

Frustration. The delay or thwarting of an ongoing sequence of behavior or goal toward which a person is striving. A source of psychological stress.

Frustration-aggression hypothesis. The hypothesis that frustration of a person's goal-directed efforts induces an aggressive drive, which, in turn, motivates aggressive behavior.

Functional. A perspective that maladaptive behaviors are of psychological rather than organic origin.

Functional fixedness. A perceptual set in which a person fails to see the potential use of some object because it is currently serving another function.

Functionalism. An approach to psychology that emphasizes the function of behavior and thought.

Fundamental attribution error. The tendency to underestimate situational causes and overestimate the dispositional causes of behaviors of others.

Ganglion cells. Cells of the retina whose axons form the optic nerve.

General adaptation syndrome (GAS). The body's nonspecific response to stressors; consists of a sequence of changes involving several systems of the body.

Generalized anxiety disorder. Persistent feelings of anxiety without specific focus.

Generalized expectancies. Rules for understanding, dealing with, and predicting the world.

Generativity. In Erikson's theory, the positive pole of the crisis of middle age; a deep concern for and contribution to the maintenance and perpetuation of society.

Genes. Heredity factors constituted by DNA; units of transmission of hereditary characteristics.

Genotype. The set of genes inherited from our parents.

Genuineness. In client-oriented therapy, this refers to the therapist's ability to allow his or her own inner experiences to emerge honestly and openly within therapy.

Germ cells. The reproductive cells (i.e., sperm of the male and ovum of the female).

Gestalt psychology. An approach to psychology that emphasizes the holistic study of the mind.

Gestalt therapy. Developed by Fritz Perls, this form of therapy promotes personal growth and the fulfillment of human potential by focusing on the here and now to help increase clients' awareness of their thoughts, feelings, and behaviors.

Golgi apparatus. A component of the interior of secretory cells that prepares the products of cellular metabolism for release out of the cell.

Goodness of fit. The degree of fit or match between (1) a person's coping strategy and the demands of the environment, and (2) a person's coping strategy and his or her goals, values, and commitments.

Gray matter. Contains the cell bodies of neurons, their dendrites, and axon terminals. It is the region where interactions between neurons occur. These regions of the nervous system appear to be gray in color because they contain only a few axons covered with fatty white myelin sheaths.

Grief. An emotional response to loss characterized by somatic distress and feelings of sadness, guilt, anger, and depression.

Group therapy. The use of collections of persons, often with a single therapist, as a method of treating disordered behavior.

Groupthink. A decision-making situation where a group suspends objectivity and careful analysis in an effort to preserve group cohesiveness.

Gyrus. A ridge between the grooves (sulci) of the cerebral cortex. Each gyrus contains an inner core of white matter, which is made up of the myelinated axons of cells entering and leaving the cortex.

Hallucinations. The perception of stimuli that do not physically exist.

Heritability. The degree to which differences among people on some characteristic are associated with genetic differences among them.

Heroin. A synthetic opiate that has a high potential for abuse because it crosses easily from the bloodstream into the central nervous system. At present there are no medically approved uses for heroin in the United States, although it is used as an analgesic in terminally ill patients in some countries.

Hertz (Hz). The rate of repetition of a regularly occurring event, usually in reference to sound vibrations or vibrations in the electromagnetic spectrum.

Heterozygotic. Different alleles from each parent.

Higher-order concepts. A type of cognitive learning which involves the acquisition of knowledge about the principles or abstract relations involved in a problem.

Histogram. A bar graph indicating a frequency distribution.

Homeostasis. The physiological tendency to maintain an internal, bodily state of balance in terms of food, water, air, sleep, and temperature.

Homozygotic. Same alleles from both parents.

Hypercomplex cortical cells. Cells of the visual cortex that respond maximally to visual stimulation of a specific kind, such as lines of light meeting at a particular angle, or bars of light of a particular length and orientation. These cortical cells are often thought of as cells which respond to particular features in the visual field.

Hyperphagia. Pathological overeating. *See also* Aphagia.

Hypersomnia. A disorder characterized by excessive sleep and daytime sleepiness not associated with disturbed sleep at night.

Hypnosis. An altered state of awareness characterized by deep relaxation and suggestibility.

Hypnotic drug. A drug that is used to induce or promote sleep.

Hypothalamus. A region of the brain located below the thalamus (*hypo* = beneath or below). The hypothalamus regulates vital bodily functions through the control of the release of hormones and by controlling internal organs through direct neural messages.

Hypothesis. A statement about the relationship between two or more variables. Inferential statistics are used to test hypotheses. *See also* Null hypothesis.

Iconic memory. Visual sensory memory.

Id. According to Freud, the hypothetical mental structure containing instincts and psychic energy or libido.

Idiographic laws. Principles that apply only to the individual.

Imagery. A memory strategy involving the development of a mental image of information.

Imitation. Acquisition of knowledge and behavior by watching other people act and then doing the same thing.

Imitative learning. Learning by imitation.

Immediate-memory-span task. A task involving both primary and secondary memory components which assesses the longest string of items that can be immediately reproduced in the order of presentation.

Implicit theories of personality. One's private theories of how various personality traits are related to one another; used to fill in gaps in our impression of others.

Impotence. Also referred to as erectile insufficiency, impotence is the inability to achieve or maintain an erection sufficient for sexual intercourse.

Incentive. Objects or events in the environment that motivate an organism in the absence of any known physiological need state.

Incidental learning task. A memory task in which people are asked to process information in some way but are not told that they will be asked to remember it later.

Independent variable. A condition or event that the psychologist varies in order to observe the effects of this change on the subject's behavior.

Inductive reasoning. Moving cognitively from the specific to the more general.

Infancy. The first 2 years of life.

Inferior colliculi. A group of neurons that are arranged in the shape of a small hill or mound in the midbrain. These neurons are involved in auditory perception and the localization of sound sources in three-dimensional space.

Information processing. A general term for presumed cognitive operations by which stimuli impinging on the senses are modified (e.g., perceived, remembered, etc.).

Inhibitory postsynaptic potential (IPSP). A change in voltage of a neuron as a result of synaptic action which hyperpolarizes the postsynaptic cell and makes it less likely that an action potential will be generated.

Insanity. A legal term (with limited diagnostic meaning) referring to someone who is incompetent and in need of commitment to an institution.

Insight. A rapid perception of the relationship among objects involved in a problem.

Insomnia. A chronic inability to obtain an adequate amount of sleep resulting in excessive daytime sleepiness.

Instrumental learning. *See* Operant conditioning.

Integrity. In Erikson's theory, the positive pole of the crisis of old age; an inner sense of peace and order which allows one to view one's personal life as meaningful and worthwhile.

Intelligence. Knowledge or knowing; cognition; mental abilities.

Interiority. The tendency to respond to inner rather than outer stimuli.

Intermittent reinforcement. A situation in which several responses are produced before reinforcement is given.

Internal consistency. A test of consistency within a measure, established by correlating odd-numbered and even-numbered items (or correlating the first and second half of the test).

Interpretation. Used in psychoanalytic therapy, an interpretation is a statement made by the therapist to help the client identify features of his or her behavior that he or she was not aware of.

Interscorer reliability. The degree to which independent test scorers agree on their scoring of a test or measure.

Interval schedule. A schedule of reinforcement in which reinforcement occurs only after a specific period of time has elapsed.

Intimacy. In Erikson's theory, the positive pole of the crisis of young adulthood; the quality of affection and rapport found in deep, personal relationships.

Introspection. A report of one's subjective events on conscious mental experience.

In vitro. An artificial environment.

In vivo. Within living tissue.

Involuntary musculature. Bodily organs (e.g., the heart, blood vessels, and smooth muscles) which receive their motor innervation from the parasympathetic and sympathetic systems.

Involuntary nervous system. *See* Autonomic nervous system.

IQ. The subject's mental age divided by his or her chronological age and multiplied by 100.

Iris. Composed of two circular rings of muscle, the iris regulates the amount of light reaching the retina by reflexively opening and closing.

Irrational beliefs. Self-defeating assumptions that are said to be the root of disordered behavior according to rational emotive therapists.

Isolation. In Erikson's theory, the negative pole of the crisis of young adulthood, characterized by the inability to achieve a close personal relationship with another person.

James-Lange theory. A theory of emotion which states that physiological arousal, followed by awareness and labeling of that arousal, is what we experience as emotion.

Jury competence. The ability of the jury to (1) apply the presumption of the innocence principle, and (2) follow the judge's instructions.

Jury prejudice. The preconceived judgment of persons in a jury toward or against the defendant's gender, socioeconomic status, moral character, physical attractiveness, race, or attitude similarity.

Just world effect. The tendency of people to believe that the fates of others reflect their characters. It often results in innocent victims being blamed for their misfortune.

Latent learning. Learning that is covert or not demonstrated in behavior and involves expectancies that one object or event will follow another.

Lateral geniculate nucleus. Part of the thalamus which receives visual information from the neurons of the optic tract. Lateral geniculate cells relay this information to visual cortex in the occipital lobe via the optic radiations.

Lateral hypothalamus (LH). An area of the hypothalamus important in the regulation of food intake.

Lateral inhibition. A phenomenon produced by interconnected networks of neurons. When some neural elements are activated, they inhibit the actions of neighboring neurons, thus producing enhanced contrast at the edges of a stimulus.

Lateralization of function. The idea that the two hemispheres are specialized to carry out different functions. For example, speech is lateralized to the left hemisphere in most people.

Law of effect. The strengthening or weakening of a response as a result of its consequences.

Learned helplessness. A condition said to resemble depression which results from an organism's experience with unavoidable punishment.

Learning. The acquisition of a behavior or the potential to behave which occurs by either associative learning or cognitive learning.

Learning model. A model which maintains that abnormal behavior is the result of faulty learning. There is nothing inherently wrong with the process of learning; abnormal behavior is simply learned as is normal behavior.

Levels of processing. A model of memory which maintains that memory is determined by operations performed on incoming information. Perceptual operations produce memory traces that are short-lived, while conceptual operations produce memory traces that are long-lived.

Libido. According to Freud, mental and psychic energy.

Life review. The process of reviewing one's life as the result of a realization of impending death.

Limbic system. A group of brain structures that includes the amygdala, some medial areas of the cortex, the hippocampus, the hypothalamus, and the septal area. The limbic system is important in regulating internal bodily functions, emotional behavior, and some forms of learning and memory.

Lobotomy. A brain operation involving the severing of nerve pathways in the frontal lobes. The goal of this now outdated medical treatment was to foster the production of new pathways and produce desired behavior change.

Locus of control. The belief that one is either controlled by external forces (external locus of control) or that one is the master of one's own destiny (internal locus of control).

Long-term memory. The retention of information no longer in consciousness. The capacity of long-term memory is essentially unlimited and its duration is lengthy if not permanent.

Loudness. The dimension of intensity of sounds. The greater the difference in the relative pressure of the compressions and rarefactions of a sound wave, the greater the perceived loudness of the sound.

Lysergic acid diethylamide (LSD). A hallucinogenic drug which induces vivid visual hallucinations and distortions of thought processes.

Lysosome. A component of most cells. Lysosomes contain high concentrations of enzymes that break down waste products of cellular metabolism.

Maintenance rehearsal. A memory strategy involving simple repetition of information in order to hold it in short-term memory; does not improve long-term memory.

Marijuana. A psychoactive drug derived from the hemp plant *Cannabis sativa*. Its behavioral effects appear to depend on personal and social factors. It has little or no potential for producing physical dependence.

Mastery model. Used in therapy, a mastery model demonstrates successful behavior.

Maximum life span. The extreme upper limit of length of life.

Mean. The arithmetical average value (score) of a distribution.

Mean length of utterance (MLU). An index of language development measured in terms of morphemes.

Measure of central tendency. A value (score) representative of a frequency distribution, around which other values (score) are dispersed. *See also* Mean, Medium, and Mode.

Measure of variation. A measure of the dispersion or spread of scores in a frequency distribution, such as the range or standard deviation. *See also* Standard deviation.

Median. The "middle" value (score) in a distribution (as many values above it as below it).

Medical compliance. Adherence to a medical treatment program.

Medical model. A model which maintains that maladaptive behavior is the result of biological and/or biochemical maladies; also referred to as the disease or organic model.

Meditation. The concentration of attention and thought on a single word, idea, or source of stimulation for a substantial period of time. Meditation appears to help some people achieve feelings of tranquility and relaxation as well as enhance the perception of certain experiences.

Medulla. Sometimes called the medulla oblongata or myelencephalon, this brain region forms the junction with the spinal cord. The medulla has many neural pathways running through it as well as regions important in controlling vital functions such as breathing and swallowing.

Memory trace. An enduring record presumably left in the nervous system when information is processed.

Menarche. The first menstrual cycle.

Menopause. The cessation of menstruation, typically occurring during a 2-year period at an average age of 47.

Mental age. A measure of intelligence expressed in years and months. Mental age is based on the age at which average children make a certain score on the test.

Mesoderm. A layer of embryonic tissue from which the muscles and bones of the body develop.

Mesomorph. A body type characterized by muscles and strong bones.

Midbrain. Sometimes called the mesencephalon, the midbrain is located between the thalamus and the pons, and contains the inferior and superior colliculi as well as a number of other cell groups including the substantia nigra.

Minnesota Multiphasic Personality Inventory (MMPI). An objective test that measures the degree to which persons evidence various types of psychological pathology.

Mitochondria. Important components of all cells. These tiny structures produce much of the energy used by cells.

Mnemonic techniques. Strategies for facilitating memory.

Mode. The most frequently occurring value (score) in a distribution.

Modeling. A process whereby behavior is learned by observing another person perform the behavior.

Monozygotic twins. Twins which develop from one fertilized egg cell which splits and each half develops as a separate individual.

Morpheme. The smallest significant unit of meaning in a language (e.g., the word *cats* has two morphemes: *cat* + *s*).

Motivation. A general term used to describe an internal state which arouses, maintains, and directs a person's or animal's behavior toward a goal.

Motive. A force that provokes or impels an animal to behave; the reason for behavior.

Motor homunculus. A schematic representation of the regions of the motor cortex that send information to various parts of the body. This representation, except for the face, is essentially upside down. Regions of the body capable of making rapid and precise movements are greatly magnified in the motor homunculus because there is more cortex devoted to them.

Multiaxial diagnosis. A diagnostic system, such as DSM III, which employs several axes on which diagnostic judgments can be made. DSM III has a five-axis system.

Multi-infarct dementia. A form of dementia caused by many small strokes which progresses in a stepwise fashion; the symptoms are similar to those of Alzheimer's disease.

Multistore models of memory. Theories suggesting that memory consists of structurally separate memory stores (sensory, short-term, long-term). Information is said to flow through the separate stores in serial order and to be encoded, maintained, and lost different ways.

Muscle spindles. Sensory receptors found in most skeletal muscles that respond to changes in the length of the muscle.

Narcissistic personality disorder. An ingrained behavior pattern that impairs interpersonal relationships, and includes a sense of grandiosity, self-importance, and fantasies of unrealistic goals.

Narcolepsy. A disorder characterized by frequent and irresistible attacks of sleepiness.

Naturalistic observation. A scientific method of observation in which behavior is studied in the natural setting within which it occurs.

Natural selection. A principle of the theory of evolution first proposed by Charles Darwin. It holds that those animals which have physical and behavioral characteristics that allow them to meet the demands of the environment—to fit their natural settings—will survive and reproduce.

Negative identity. A social role which involves delinquent or antisocial behavior.

Negative triad. Negative thoughts of depressed persons typically involving negative ideas about the self, the world, and the future.

Neologisms. New words (created by disordered persons) that do not have meaning to the listener.

Neonate. A newborn (from birth to 7 to 10 days old).

Neuropsychological testing. The measurement of behavioral signs that reflect healthy or impaired brain functioning.

Neurotic disorder. A nonpsychotic condition based primarily on anxiety and avoidance. Neurotic persons misperceive the demands of the environment and avoid rather than cope with stress.

Neurotransmitter substance. Chemicals released by presynaptic nerve terminals which influence the actions of target cells.

Neutral stimulus. A stimulus in the environment which does not interact in the UCS → UCR relationship of classical conditioning.

Nicotine. The primary active agent in tobacco products. Nicotine stimulates acetylcholine systems and produces tolerance and dependence.

Node of Ranvier. The gap between adjacent segments of

GLOSSARY

the myelin sheath where the axon membrane is exposed. This region contains a high concentration of sodium- and potassium-ion channels. In myelinated axons action potentials occur only in this region.

Nomothetic. Group laws, or principles, that apply to all people.

Nonnegative thinking. The relative absence of negative thinking that seems to characterize nondistressed persons as compared to distressed persons.

Normal distribution. The standard symmetrical (bell-shaped) frequency distribution; its properties are commonly used in making statistical inferences.

Norms. The results based on measurement of a large group of people. Norms are used as a comparison against which to judge the performance of people relative to the population.

Null hypothesis. A statistical hypothesis that any difference observed among treating conditions occurs by chance and does not reflect a true difference. Rejection of the null hypothesis means that we believe the experimental treatment is actually having an effect.

Obesity. In human beings, defined as being more than 15% over the weight appropriate for a person of a given age and height.

Objective. Relating to the use of facts and expressing the nature of reality without distention by personal feelings and subjectivity.

Objective assessment. Using structured tests to gather data on the characteristics or traits of a person to predict the person's behavior.

Object permanence. A child's ability to understand that an object still exists even when it is not in his or her field of vision.

Observational learning. A type of learning which occurs through exposure to the behaviors of others. This learning occurs without external reinforcement or without performing the behavior observed.

Observer bias. An unwanted effect, due to behavioral observers being aware of the research hypothesis or having other interfering assumptions, that undermines the validity of the observations.

Obsessive-compulsive disorder. An anxiety disorder characterized by intrusion of unwanted thoughts, and by impulses to perform specific ritualistic acts.

Occipital lobe. The most posterior region of the cortex. It contains regions where much processing of visual information occurs.

Ohm's acoustical law. A principle which states that the auditory system has the capacity to separate complex sounds into several simple components.

Operant conditioning. A form of associative learning which involves emitting a response (R) in the presence of an appropriate discriminative stimulus (S^D), which is followed by a reinforcing stimulus (S^R).

Operant procedures. Used in behavior therapy, these procedures help the client to acquire or eliminate a response by manipulating the environmental contingencies surrounding reward and punishment.

Opiates. Natural and synthetic drugs that have effects similar to those of morphine. Opiates relieve pain, produce feelings of euphoria, control cough and diarrhea, and produce drug tolerance and dependence.

Opium. The natural extract obtained from the sap of the opium poppy seed pod. Morphine and codeine can be extracted from opium.

Opponent-process theory of color vision. A theory of color vision which suggests that there are three antagonistic pairs of colors: red-green, blue-yellow, and black-white. When one member of a pair is excited, the other is inhibited.

Optic chiasm. The region of the visual pathway where the axons extending from the nasal half of each retina cross over to the opposite hemisphere of the brain.

Optic nerve. The portion of the visual pathway extending from the retina to the optic chiasm.

Optic radiations. The portion of the visual pathway extending from the lateral geniculate nucleus of the thalamus to the visual cortex in the occipital lobe.

Optic tract. The portion of the visual pathway extending from the optic chiasm to the lateral geniculate nucleus of the thalamus.

Organic. A perspective on abnormal behavior that holds that disorders have a biological (organic) cause.

Organization (chunking). A memory strategy involving grouping or relating items. Organization promotes memory.

Osmoreceptors. Receptors in the hypothalamus that are sensitive to the amount of fluid inside the body's cells. They play a role in regulating drinking. *See also* Volumetric receptors.

Ossicles. The three small bones of the middle ear which transmit sound vibrations from the eardrum to the cochlea. They are called the malleus, incus, and stapes.

Outcome expectancies. Expectancies that certain things will happen if certain actions are taken.

Overjustification effect. The reduction of intrinsic interest in an activity that a person experiences when he or she receives extrinsic reward for engaging in the activity.

Overload. Conditions that produce too much stimulation to maintain optimal arousal. A source of psychological stress.

Overt. Manifest, open to view.

Paranoid personality disorder. An ingrained pattern of behavior (featuring consistent suspiciousness and pervasive mistrust) that impairs interpersonal relationships.

Paranoid schizophrenia. A subtype of schizophrenia in which delusions of grandiosity and persecution are prominent.

Paraphilia. Disorders of sexual preference, where the deviant sexual preference is required for sexual excitement (e.g., fetishism, pedophilia, exhibitionism).

Passive mastery. Perception of the environment as threatening and dangerous, and the self as passive and accommodating.

Pavlovian conditioning. *See* Classical conditioning.

Pediatricians. A physician who specializes in the branch of medicine which deals with the growth and development of the child through his or her adolescence.

Peer group. A social group defined as all people who are social equals or who have similar characteristics.

Perceived control. Beliefs about whether control over one's environment and its related events is possible.

Perceptual set. In problem solving, the tendency to perceive a problem from only one perspective.

Performance based. This is a central feature of behavior therapy involving the provision of learning experiences where the client can perform and practice the newly acquired behaviors.

Perinatal period. The brief period surrounding birth.

Peripheral nervous sytem (PNS). Those parts of the nervous system other than the brain and spinal cord. The peripheral nervous system is often thought of as being divided into the skeletal motor system and the autonomic system.

Personal definition of abnormality. When a person seeks the help of a mental health professional, the person is defining himself or herself as suffering psychologically.

Personal space. That area around a person over which he or she feels ownership or control.

Phenomenal field. In Rogers' self-theory, the phenomenal field is the person's world, which includes the continually changing processes of personal experience.

Phenotype. The outcome of a particular interaction between genotype and experience.

Pheromones. Substances of a particular odor released by some animals to cause particular reactions in others of the same species. Pheromones are often used as attractants.

Phobia. An irrational fear associated with a specific object, activity, or situation.

Phoneme. The smallest significant unit of sound in a language (e.g., the words *cat, rat, mat,* and *sat* differ by a single phoneme).

Phonological encoding. Encoding based on how information sounds.

Photopic vision. Visual processes that operate at moderate to high levels of light. Photopic vision is mediated by cone receptors and has the capacity to perceive colors. *See also* Scotopic vision.

Placenta. The organ on the wall of the uterus to which the umbilical cord attaches.

Place theory of hearing. A theory of frequency discrimination which suggests that the place of maximal displacement of the basilar membrane determines the pitch of the sound that is heard. *See also* Frequency theory of hearing.

Political science. A social science concerned chiefly with the description and analysis of political and governmental institutions and processes.

Polygraph. An instrument that simultaneously records several physiological responses. Measures such as brain activity, heart rate, respiration, blood pressure, and the galvanic skin response are typically recorded using a polygraph. When used to measure emotional responses in investigative situations, the polygraph is sometimes referred to as a "lie detector."

Pons. A region of the brain stem that lies between the medulla and the midbrain. In addition to a number of important brain structures, it contains many neural pathways which carry information to and from the periphery. It also is the region where the cerebellum is connected to the brain stem.

Population. The total universe (set) of possible cases from which samples of cases may be drawn. *See also* Sample.

Positive regard. The satisfaction and happiness that comes with respect and acceptance by another person.

Posthypnotic amnesia. A loss of memory for events that occurred during a hypnotic state. This amnesia usually occurs in response to suggestions from the hypnotist.

Posthypnotic suggestion. A request or suggestion to perform a particular act given to a person while hypnotized. Typically, this act is to be carried out in response to a specified signal some time after the hypnotic state has ended.

Postpubescence. A phase of bodily changes in adolescence during which most of the bodily changes have already occurred.

Predictive validity. A criterion-related validity where the outside criterion is gathered at a time after the test is given.

Prepubescence. A phase of bodily changes in adolescence marked by beginnings of change in height, weight, fat, muscle distribution, glandular secretions, and/or sexual characteristics.

Presbyopia. A defect in vision, often associated with aging, characterized by recession of the near point of vision so that objects very near the eyes cannot be seen clearly.

Prevention. A problem-solving tool in which one suggests steps to take to avoid the occurrence of a problem.

Primacy effect. The finding that people recall the items presented at the beginning of a list better than those presented in the middle of the list, although not as well as those presented at the end of the list.

Primary appraisal. Evaluation of the significance of a transaction between the self and the environment for one's well-being. The transaction may be seen as irrelevant, benign-positive, or stressful. Stressful transactions may be appraised as involving harm, threat, or challenge.

Primary sexual characteristics. Sexual characteristics present at birth.

Proactive interference. Previously learned information interferes with one's ability to remember new information.

Problem-focused coping. Coping responses intended to change the situation either by modifying the environment or one's own behavior.

Problem solving. A process of overcoming obstacles to achieve a goal. This may be accomplished through trial and error or insight.

Production. The generation of language.

Projection neurons. Cells with axons which convey information between different regions of the nervous system.

Projective assessment. Assessments using ambiguous

GLOSSARY

materials, such as inkblots, to identify aspects of the personality of which the subject is said to be unaware.

Psychedelic. Mind revealing or mind manifesting; often used to refer to drugs that induce hallucinations or distortions of perception.

Psychiatry. The medical specialty that deals with the origins, diagnosis, prevention, and treatment of mental and emotional disorders.

Psychic determinism. The principle that all behavior is directed by the inner forces of the mind.

Psychoactive drug. Any substance that affects the operation of the central nervous system. Substances such as alcohol, opiates, tranquilizers, caffeine, and barbiturates are all psychoactive drugs. Psychoactive drugs are the primary drugs of abuse.

Psychoanalysis. A theory of personality formulated by S. Freud proposing that structures of personality are common to all people and that personality develops through a universal series of stages; a method of individual psychotherapy.

Psychodynamic model. A model of abnormal behavior that places great emphasis on the early years of life and the unresolved conflicts that affect unconscious processes.

Psychological motive. A motive that is primarily learned rather than based on biological needs.

Psychological stress. The appraisal that the environment taxes or exceeds one's resources.

Psychological stressors. Circumstances that result in demands or conflicts perceived by people as taxing or exceeding their resources.

Psychology. The scientific study of mental and behavioral functioning.

Psychometricians. Those people who study and measure mental intelligence and behavioral characteristics.

Psychotic disorder. A severe psychological disorder involving gross distortions of reality and sometimes requiring hospitalization.

Puberty. The point during the pubescent phase when the person reaches an adult level of reproductive maturity and can reproduce.

Pubescence. A period of growth and bodily changes in adolescence characterized by initiation of change in height, weight, fat, muscle distribution, glandular secretions, and sexual characteristics.

Quiet sleep. Stages 2 through 4 of sleep in which there is progressively less cortical arousal. In quiet sleep there are no rapid eye movements and therefore it is sometimes called non-REM sleep.

Rapid Eye Movement (REM) **sleep.** A stage of sleep in which lateral eye movement occurs. Dreaming is often associated with this stage of sleep.

Rational emotive therapy. A form of psychotherapy (consistent with cognitive-behavioral therapy) that places the source of disordered behavior in the irrational thinking of the client. The irrationality is seen in the ways people talk to themselves and the therapy seeks to remediate the client's crooked thinking. Albert Ellis is the founder of rational emotive therapy.

Ratio schedule. A schedule of reinforcement in which reinforcement occurs only after a specific number of responses have been emitted.

Reaction time (RT). The length of time between the appearance of a signal and the beginning of a responding movement.

Reactivity. People who know they are being observed may alter their actions or reactions because of the observer's presence or to present a certain image of themselves. This effect of the observer's presence is referred to as reactivity.

Reality therapy. Introduced by W. Glasser, this form of therapy seeks to help clients fulfill their needs in realistic ways.

Reappraisal. Changing the primary and secondary appraisal of events as changes in the self and the environment occur.

Recall clustering. A phenomenon reflecting the process of organization. People tend to recall words from the same conceptual categories together even though they were presented in random order.

Recency effect. The finding that people recall the items presented at the end of a list better than those presented at any other point in the list. Considered to indicate the contents of working memory.

Receptive field. That region which, when stimulated, alters the activity of some neuron or neural system. Usually, this term is applied to studies of the visual system in which a region of the retina is stimulated and cell activity is monitored.

Reconstructive hypothesis. The view that people remember the gist or general outline of information that was presented and then reconstruct the event on the basis of their general knowledge and what they are able to retrieve about the event.

Reference group. Those people with whom we compare ourselves. It is through comparison with members of our reference group that we evaluate our abilities, attitudes, and resources.

Reflex. A simple, unlearned, and stereotyped muscle response or glandular secretion produced in response to a particular stimulus (e.g., salivation in response to the presence of food in the mouth).

Reflexive responses. Automatic responses that require no conscious effort.

Regression. In psychoanalytic theory, a person's retreat to an earlier term of behavior.

Rehabilitation. The restoration of maximum independence to a disabled individual, commensurate with his or her limitations, by developing his or her residual capacities.

Rehearsal. A memory strategy involving the repetition of information either overtly or covertly.

Reinforcement. A stimulus which produces or maintains behavior; a stimulus which makes behavior more probable.

Reliability. The degree to which a test, or series of observations, is stable, dependable, and self-consistent. Reliability estimates are estimates of consistency.

Remediation A problem-solving technique in which one

formulates plans or policies useful for diminishing the effects of a problem.

Resistance. In psychoanalytic therapy, this refers to the client's roadblocks that are experienced as the therapist tries to drive unconscious material into consciousness.

Respondent conditioning. See Classical conditioning.

Response (R). The behavioral result of stimulation in the form of movement or glandular secretion. This can also include responses such as images.

Response-class matrix. A form of behavioral assessment in which observers record the interactions among those who are observed.

Response set. In problem solving, the continued use of a solution that has worked in the past, but that is inefficient or ineffective in the current situation.

Resting potential. The electrical potential (or voltage difference) across the cell membrane of neurons or muscles during an inactive period. This potential, in which the inside of the cell is negatively charged relative to the outside by about 70 mV in most neurons, is the result of the passive diffusion of positively charged potassium ions out of the cell.

Retest reliability. The relationship between scores on a test that is given on two occasions.

Reticular formation. A network of neural tissue (on the interior of the brain stem) which extends from the medulla to the thalamus and is involved in modulating arousal.

Retina. A layered structure at the back of the eye which contains the visual receptors and neurons for processing and transmitting visual information.

Retrieval. A stage of the memory process involving recovery of information at some time following its acquisition.

Retrieval cue. A stimulus that facilitates the recovery of information from memory.

Retroactive interference. Recently learned information interferes with one's ability to remember previously learned information.

Reward. Any stimulus which increases the likelihood of a response.

Ribonucleic acid (RNA). The messenger protein that carries the "code" contained in the DNA to the cytoplasm.

Rigidity. The tendency to fixate on one aspect of a problem and ignore others that are relevant for success.

Rod receptor cells. Receptor cells in the retina that respond to low intensities of light and mediate scotopic vision. They do not respond differently to light of different wavelengths and therefore do not generate the sensation of color. See also Cone receptor cells.

Rorschach inkblots. A form of projective testing that seeks to assess aspects of a person's personality about which he or she may be unaware.

Rubella. A virus-caused disease which, when contracted early in pregnancy by mothers, can result in heart defects, deafness, cataracts, blindness, or mental retardation in the developing fetus.

Sample. A selection of scores from a total set of scores known on the "population." See also Population.

Scatter plot. A simple graphic device picturing the relation between two sets of values (scores).

Schachter-Singer theory. A theory of emotion which states that physiological arousal, and the interpretation of the source of that arousal, determine the nature of the emotional response. See also James-Lange theory.

Schedules of reinforcement. A role that determines how often a response is reinforced.

Schemata (Schema). Mental pictures of images, places, events, or objects that organize our knowledge and allow us to retrieve information from our memory.

Schemes. In Piaget's theory, organized sensorimotor action sequences.

Schizophrenia. A set of disorders marked by dysfunctions in thinking, affect, and behavior. Dominant symptoms include delusions, hallucinations, extreme social withdrawal, and occasional bizarre motor behavior. See also specific types of schizophrenia.

Scientific method. Techniques of systematical and purposeful observation.

Scotopic vision. A visual process that operates at low levels of light and is mediated by rod receptors. Colors are not seen in scotopic vision.

Secondary appraisal. Evaluation of an event in terms of the resources and strategies available to cope with it.

Secondary reinforcement (S'). An initially neutral stimulus that acquires reinforcing properties through pairing with another stimulus that is already reinforcing.

Secondary sexual characteristics. Sexual characteristics which emerge during the prepubescent through postpubescent phases of adolescence.

Sedative drug. A substance that tends to reduce excitability and induce calmness.

Self-actualization. The final phase of Maslow's need hierarchy; a person's fundamental tendency toward maximal realization of his or her potentials.

Self-efficacy theory. A theory that considers the significance of people's expectation that they have the power to take control of situations and influence events in a positive way.

Self-fulfilling prophecy. The condition in which people cause others to act in accordance with the expectations they have about them.

Self-help. A form of treatment that uses either a book or a collection of people, and does not directly involve professionals.

Self-monitoring. People serving as observers of their own actions and reactions; often used when observation by others would be very difficult.

Self-perception theory. The theory that one's attitudes and beliefs are influenced by observations of one's own behavior.

Self-schema. The schema that each person holds about himself or herself.

Self-serving attributional bias. The tendency of people to attribute their successes to their personal qualities and their failures to external forces.

Self-theories. A group of personality theories which share a concern with the holistic view of personality.

GLOSSARY

Semantic encoding. Encoding on the basis of the information's linguistic or psychological meaning.

Semantic memory. A person's knowledge of symbols, words, concepts, and rules for manipulating them. Semantic memory is not related to a specific time or place.

Semicircular canals. Three fluid-filled curved tubes set at right angles to one another. They are part of the vestibular system and they detect head movements.

Senile dementia. A global cognitive decline that occurs late in life in some individuals.

Senility. A nontechnical term used to signify symptoms, occurring later in life, such as forgetfulness and confusion.

Sensory homunculus. A schematic representation of the regions of the cortex that receive information from sensory receptors in various parts of the body. This representation, except for the face, is essentially upside down. Those body regions capable of making fine sensory discriminations are greatly magnified in the sensory homunculus, a finding that reflects the fact that the cortex analyzes features and interprets bodily sensory events.

Sensory memory. The momentary retention of an unprocessed copy of a stimulus. The duration of sensory memory is very brief.

Serial position curve. A summary of the percentage of items people recall from each of the positions of a list of items they have been asked to remember.

Sexual dysfunction. Both the inability to achieve sexual satisfaction and the absence of the desire for it. These disorders are concerned less with physical ability and more with psychological aspects of sexuality.

Shallow processing. Operations that code the sensory aspects of information; produce memory traces that are short-lived.

Shaping. An instrumental conditioning technique in which closer and closer approximations to a desired response are reinforced.

Shock phase. The first phase of alarm reaction of the general adaptation syndrome. During this phase, general resistance to stressor falls below normal and the organism exhibits loss of homeostasis.

Short-term memory (working memory). The conscious retention of information that has just been presented or retrieved from long-term memory. The capacity of short-term memory is limited and its duration is short, unless the material is manipulated consciously.

Simple cortical cells. Cells of the visual system that respond maximally to a bar of light or straight edge oriented at a particular angle and projected onto a particular region of the retina. *See also* Complex cortical cells.

Simple reaction time. The length of time required by a person to make a single response to a single signaling stimulus.

Situational specificity. The feature of behavioral assessment that posits that behavior is a function of the environment in which it takes place. Therefore, behavior is situationally specific, occurring at a certain rate because of the environmental conditions present at that time.

Skewness. Deviation of the shape of a frequency distribution from a normal distribution. A skewed distribution either has more cases on the right of the mean than on the left, or vice versa; in a skewed distribution the mean, median, and mode are not identical.

Sleep spindles. Short bursts of regular 14- to 18-Hz activity that persists for only 1 or 2 seconds (seen in the EEG records of sleeping subjects). They are characteristic of stage 2 and stage 3 sleep.

Social comparison theory. The theory that people come to know and evaluate their attitudes and abilities by comparing themselves with others.

Social drift hypothesis. A suggested explanation for the disproportionate number of schizophrenics in the lowest social class.

Social facilitation. The condition where the presence of an audience or coactors improves the quality of a person's performance. The presence of others can interfere with behavioral performance if the behavior is not well learned.

Social learning. *See* Observational learning and Imitative learning.

Social loafing. The tendency of people to contribute less energy the more others there are participating in the activity.

Social milieu. One's social setting.

Social network. The persons or groups with whom a person maintains contact and has some form of social bond.

Social policy. A general philosophy or specific plan to deal with an issue facing society.

Social referencing. The use of social information (usually provided by the mother) by an infant in determining his/her own emotion reactions.

Social role. A set of norms and expectations that defines how a person in a particular position must act. Roles greatly influence social behavior.

Sociobiology. The study of the biological basis of social behavior in human beings and animals.

Soma. The cell body.

Somatoform disorders. A group of disorders (e.g., psychogenic pain, somatization disorder, conversion disorder) which appear to suggest physical maladies but which are seen as the result of psychological causes. Underlying organic causes are not found.

Somatosensory system. Those parts of the nervous system that carry and interpret information about bodily sensations such as touch, pain, and temperature.

Somatotypes. Body types.

Source traits. The factors that underlie surface variations in behavior; the causes of surface traits.

Spatial frequency filter model. A hypothesis of visual pattern analysis emphasizing the reduction of complex visual stimuli into several simple components.

Speeded task. A simple assessment task in which the object is to complete the task as rapidly as possible.

Spinal cord. A long, thin cylinder of neural tissue that extends from the medulla, down the central core of the spinal column, to the level of the upper lumbar vertebral segments. The spinal cord receives sensory input from the periphery which it transmits to the brain. The spinal cord also transmits information from the brain to lower bodily regions, provides motor output to skeletal muscles and to the autonomic system, and generates many different reflexes.

Spontaneous recovery. An increase in the tendency to perform an extinguished response after a time interval in which neither CS or UCS are presented.

Spontaneous remission. The notion that many clients improve their disordered behavior over time without psychological therapy.

Spreading activation model. A model of how semantic memory is organized and accessed. Knowledge is depicted as a network of interconnected concepts. Activation of a concept results in activation of adjacent concepts.

Stage of exhaustion. The final stage of the general adaptation syndrome, produced by a stressor to which an organism is unable to adapt. The organism's general resistance falls below normal and, eventually, death occurs.

Stage of resistance. The second stage of the general adaptation syndrome, involving full mobilization of the organism's defenses to cope with a stressor. Homeostasis may be fully or partially restored.

Stagnation. In Erikson's theory, the negative pole of the crisis of middle age; characterized by self-indulgence and a sense of impoverishment.

Standard deviation. The square root of the average squared deviation from the mean of a distribution (a measure of variability).

Standardization. The administration of tests and measures with instructions, procedures, and time limits identical for all those who take the test.

Standard score (Z score). The number of standard deviations between a score (X) and the mean ($\overline{X}$) of the distribution of scores.

Stanford-Binet Intelligence scale. One of the earliest measures of intelligence. This test is often used with children, and has been revised on several occasions. The test is based on age norms, and employs basal and ceiling age performances to estimate intellectual functioning.

State. A current emotional condition; a person's psychological condition at a given time.

State-Trait Anxiety Inventory (STAI). A two-part self-report scale that assesses a person's current state of anxiety as well as the person's characteristic, or trait, of anxiety.

Statistical definition of abnormality. Abnormality is defined by the person's place on a statistical distribution of scores on a measure of the type of psychological problem in question.

Statistical significance. The trustworthiness of an obtained statistical measure as a statement about reality. A pattern of data is statistically significant when the likelihood of it occurring by chance is less than 5%.

Stereochemical theory of odor. A theory of olfaction which suggests that the perception of a particular odor is determined by the three-dimensional shape of the molecules stimulating receptors of the olfactory system.

Stereotypes. A generally false belief held by an individual concerning the characteristics of people belonging to a specific social category.

Still birth. The birth of a dead child.

Stimulus. Anything in the environment to which the organism can perceive and respond.

Stimulus substitution. *See* Classical conditioning.

Storage. A stage of the memory process involving retention of information for later use.

Structuralism. An approach to psychology which analyzes the component elements of the mind into images, feelings, and sensations.

Subjective. Relating to or determined by the mind; a view dependent on the person.

Subjective organization. A phenomenon reflecting the process of organization, in which people tend to recall clusters of "unrelated" words together even though they were presented in random order.

Substance abuse. Pathological and excessive use of a substance that results in psychological and physical deterioration and impairs work and social performance.

Substance dependence. More severe than substance abuse, dependence requires a physiological dependence on the substance. Tolerance and withdrawal are used as evidence of the physiological dependence.

Sulcus. A groove in the surface of the cerebral cortex.

Superego. According to Freud, the hypothetical mental structure composed of the conscious and the ego-ideal.

Superior colliculi. Small hill or mound-shaped collections of neurons on the top part of the midbrain. The superior colliculi coordinate eye movements so that one can react appropriately to different visual stimuli.

Surface traits. A group of overt mental and/or behavioral characteristics.

Synapse. The connection between two neurons. Synapses are composed of a presynaptic (axon) terminal, a postsynaptic (usually a dendrite or cell body) membrane, and a small gap or cleft between them. The postsynaptic membrane contains receptors that respond to the presence of chemical messengers which are released from the presynaptic terminal and travel across the synaptic cleft.

Synaptic vesicles. Small spherical structures found in presynaptic terminals which contain neurotransmitter substances.

Syntax. Rules of a language for combining morphemes and words into phrases and sentences.

Systematic desensitization. A form of behavior therapy in which specific fears are weakened through a process of counterconditioning.

Systems model. A model which claims that abnormality emerges from faulty social systems, such as families or peer groups, where maladaptive patterns of behavior are forced on persons by constricted rules.

Tardive dyskinesia. A disturbance in motor control, believed to be irreversible, that results from an extended use of antipsychotic medications.

GLOSSARY

Taste buds. Receptors for the sense of taste which are located on the surface of the tongue.

Taste potentiation. The phenomenon observed when exposure to one taste enhances sensitivity to a different taste.

Tectum. The top part or "roof" of the midbrain. It contains the superior colliculi and the inferior colliculi.

Tegmentum. The bottom part or "floor" of the midbrain. It contains a number of important brain structures that control or modulate muscle movements.

Teratogens. Harmful chemicals delivered to the fetus through the umbilical cord.

Test. A device used to measure a specific characteristic of functioning.

Thalamus. A large egg-shaped group of neurons that lies near the center of the cerebral hemispheres. All sensory information except olfaction travels through the thalamus before it goes to the cerebral cortex.

Thalidomide. A tranquilizing drug, used by women in the 1950s and 1960s, which produces gross anatomical defects in the limbs of infants.

Thanatos. Freud's term for the death instinct.

Thematic Apperception Test (TAT). A projective test which asks subjects to tell a story about a stimulus picture in order to gain a better understanding of the person.

Therapy. Helping clients overcome personal problems and acquire more satisfying lives through an educative process.

Threat. A perception of harm that might occur; a source of psychological stress.

Threshold. A degree of depolarization, usually produced by the release of neurotransmitter substances, which is just strong enough to trigger the generation of an action potential at the axon hillock of a neuron.

Token economy. A behavior therapy procedure based on operant procedures. Clients can earn rewards for appropriate behavior, often in the form of chips, tokens, or scrips, and exchange the tokens for desired items or privileges.

Tolerance. The need for increased amounts of a substance to achieve a desired effect following repeated use (the diminished effect produced by the same dose of a substance).

Trait. An interrelated cluster of mental and/or behavioral characteristics.

Transactional analysis (TA). A psychological therapy that involves an intense examination of the transactions among people. According to TA, adjustment is seen as a balance of three agencies within each of us: the child, the adult, and the parent.

Transcendental meditation. A form of meditation that involves focusing attention on a single word or phrase.

Transduction. The process of converting some physical event or stimulus in the external world into neural messages.

Transference. The relationship with the therapist (as part of psychoanalytic therapy) in which the client reexperiences the thoughts and feelings that were experienced in childhood when relating to an authority.

Transitions. Periods wherein a person undergoes major physical, cognitive, and/or social changes.

Transmissiveness. The amount of light reaching the eye.

Trepanning. An outdated method of treating mental disorder that involved cutting holes into the disturbed person's head to release evil spirits.

Trichromatic theory of color vision. A theory suggesting that there are three different kinds of cone receptors in the retina, each maximally stimulated by a light of a different wavelength.

Type A behavior pattern. A behavior pattern characterized by a number of behavioral tendencies including excessive competitiveness, acceleration of the pace of ordinary activities, hostility, and feelings of struggling against the environment. This pattern is associated with an increased incidence of coronary disease in middle age.

Type B behavior pattern. A behavioral pattern characterized by the relative absence of Type A behavior pattern characteristics.

Umbilical cord. An organ connecting the embryo to the placenta on the uterine wall.

Unconditional positive regard. In client-centered therapy, this refers to an acceptance of the client as a decent human being without judgment or evaluation and a trust that the client can improve.

Unconditional stimulus (UCS). A stimulus which elicits the unconditioned response (UCR).

Underload. Conditions that produce too little stimulation to maintain optimal arousal; a source of psychological stress.

Undifferentiated schizophrenia. A subtype of schizophrenia used when the prominent psychotic symptoms cannot be classified into other categories.

Universal characteristics. Characteristics which are common to all human beings.

Validity. The ability of an observation or measurement to accurately reflect or measure what it is supposed to measure.

Variable. Any condition or event that changes or varies.

Variance. The square of a standard deviation; a useful measure of the amount of dispersion around the mean of a distribution.

Ventral roots. Neural pathways on the front or bottom of the spinal cord. All motor information leaving the spinal cord does so via the ventral roots.

Ventricles. Open spaces or chambers in the brain which are filled with cerebrospinal fluid.

Ventromedial hypothalamus (VMH). The area of the hypothalamus believed to have a role in satiation or inhibition of eating.

Verbal self-instructions. A form of therapy, often used with impulsive children, whereby the therapist teaches the client to talk to himself or herself in a cautious and problem-solving fashion.

Vestibular sacs. Two small chambers which are part of the vestibular system. They contain small crystals that stimulate hair cells inside the sacs. As the head moves, the crystals move to stay at the bottom of the sacs, thus stimulating different hair cells and generating a sense of head position.

Vestibular system. A set of receptors embedded in the bones of the skull that provide information about head position and head movements.

Visual encoding. Encoding on the basis of how information looks.

Volumetric receptors. Receptors that regulate water intake by responding to the volume of blood and body fluids. Renin, a substance secreted by the kidneys into the bloodstream, may be one volumetric receptor. *See also* Osmoreceptors.

Voluntary musculature. Skeletal muscles which are controlled by the central system.

Wechsler Intelligence Tests. A set of intelligence tests for adults, children, and preschoolers developed by David Wechsler. The tests use performance and verbal estimates of intelligence.

Wernicke's aphasia. An impairment in language which is characterized by speech with little meaning and difficulties in the comprehension of language.

Wernicke's area. A cortical region usually found in the left temporal lobe of human beings which is important in the comprehension of language and the production of meaningful speech.

White matter. Regions of the central nervous system composed of axons whose cell bodies are found in gray matter. These axons are sheathed in myelin, a white, fatty substance that facilitates nerve conduction. Information is transmitted from one place to another in the nervous system through white matter.

Withdrawal symptoms. A wide range of physiological symptoms exhibited by a person when a substance on which he or she is dependent is not available.

Working memory (short-term memory). The conscious retention of information that has just been presented or retrieved from long-term memory. The capacity of short-term memory is limited and its duration is short unless the material is manipulated consciously.

YAVIS. Features of the "desired" client: young, attractive, verbal, intelligent, and successful.

Zygote. The fertilized cell formed after conception. *See also* Conception.

References

ABRAMOWITZ, C. V., ABRAMOWITZ, S. I., ROBACK, H. B., & JACKSON, C. (1974). Differential effectiveness of directive and nondirective therapies as a client internal-external control. *Journal of Consulting and Clinical Psychology, 42,* 849–853.

ABRAMS, D. B., & WILSON, G. T. (1979). Effects of alcohol on social anxiety in women: Cognitive versus physiological processes. *Journal of Abnormal Psychology, 88,* 161–173.

ABRAMSON, L. Y., SELIGMAN, M. E. P., & TEASDALE, J. (1978). Learned helplessness in humans: Critique and reformulation. *Journal of Abnormal Psychology, 87,* 49–74.

ADAMS, G. M., & DEVRIES, H. A. (1973). Physiological effects of an exercise training regimen upon women aged 52 to 79. *Journal of Gerontology, 28,* 50–55.

ADAMS, G. R., & GULLOTTA, T. (1983). *Adolescent life experiences.* Monterey, Calif.: Brooks/Cole.

ADELSON, J. (Ed.) (1980). *Handbook of adolescent psychology.* New York: Wiley.

ADELSON, J., & DOEHRMAN, M. J. (1980). The psychodynamic approach to adolescence. In J. Adelson (Ed.), *Handbook of adolescent psychology.* New York: Wiley.

ADLER, A. (1927). *The practice and theory of individual psychology.* New York: Harcourt Brace.

AINSWORTH, M. D. S. (1973). The development of infant-mother attachment. In B. M. Caldwell & H. N. Ricciuti (Eds.), *Review of child development research* (Vol. 3). Chicago: University of Chicago Press.

AJZEN, I., & FISHBEIN, M. (1980). *Understanding attitudes and predicting social behavior.* Englewood Cliffs, N.J.: Prentice-Hall.

AKISKAL, H. S., & MCKINNEY, W. T. (1973). Depressive disorders: Toward a unified hypothesis. *Science, 182,* 20–29.

AKISKAL, H. S., & MCKINNEY, W. T. (1975). Overview of recent research in depression: Integration of ten conceptual models into a comprehensive clinical frame. *Archives of General Psychiatry, 32,* 285–305.

ALLOY, L. B., & ABRAMSON, L. Y. (1979). Judgment of contingency in depressed and nondepressed students: Sadder but wiser? *Journal of Experimental Psychology: General, 108,* 441–485.

ALLPORT, G. W. (1960). *Personality and social encounter: Selected essays.* Boston: Beacon Press.

ALLPORT, G. W. (1961). *Pattern and growth in personality.* New York: Holt, Rinehart and Winston.

ALMQUIST, E. M. (1974). Sex stereotype in occupational choice: The case for college women. *Journal of Vocational Behavior, 5,* 13–21.

ALMQUIST, E. M., & ANGRIST, S. S. (1971). Role-model influences on college women's career aspirations. *Merrill-Palmer Quarterly, 17,* 263–279.

American Humane Association (1978). *National analysis of official child neglect and abuse reporting.* Englewood, Colo.: American Humane Association.

American Psychiatric Association (1980). *Diagnostic and statistical manual of mental disorders* (3rd ed.): *DSM III.* Washington, D.C.: American Psychiatric Association.

American Psychological Association (1973). *Ethical principles in the conduct of research with human participants.* Washington, D.C.: American Psychological Association.

American Psychological Association (1974). *Standards of educational and psychological tests.* Washington, D.C.: American Psychological Association.

American Psychological Association (1981). Ethical principles of psychologists. *American Psychologist, 36,* 633–638.

AMOORE, J. E., JOHNSTON, JR., J. W., & RUBIN, M. (1964). The stereochemical theory of odor. *Scientific American, 210,* 42–49.

ANASTASI, A. (1958). Heredity, environment, and the question "how?" *Psychological Review, 65,* 197–208.

ANASTASI, A. (1968). *Psychological testing* (3rd ed.). New York: Macmillan.

ANDERSEN, A. E. (1977). Atypical anorexia nervosa. In R. A. Vigersky (Ed.), *Anorexia nervosa.* New York: Raven Press.

ANDERSON, B., JR., & PALMORE, E. (1974). Longitudinal evaluation of ocular function. In E. Palmore (Ed.), *Normal aging II: Reports from the Duke longitudinal studies, 1970–1973.* Durham, N.C.: Duke University Press.

ANDERSON, J. E. (1939). The limitations of infant and preschool tests in the measurement of intelligence. *Journal of Psychology, 8,* 351–379.

ANDERSON, J. R. (1976). *Language, memory, and thought.* Hillsdale, N.J.: Lawrence Erlbaum.

ANDREW, S. (1970). Recovery from surgery, with and with-

out preparatory instruction, for three coping styles. *Journal of Personality and Social Psychology, 15,* 223–226.
ANGEVINE, J. B., JR., & COTMAN, C. W. (1981). *Principles of neuroanatomy.* New York: Oxford University Press.
ANTHONY, E. J. (1969). The reaction of adults to adolescents and their behavior. In G. Caplan & S. Lebovici (Eds.), *Adolescence.* New York: Basic Books.
ARENBERG, D., & ROBERTSON-TCHABO, E. A. (1977). Learning and aging. In J. E. Birren & K. W. Schaie (Eds.), *Handbook of the psychology of aging.* New York: Van Nostrand Reinhold.
ARGYLE, M. (1982). The social skills of intercultural interaction. In S. Bochmer (Ed.), *Cross-cultural interaction.* Oxford: Pergamon.
ARKOWITZ, H., LICHTENSTEIN, E., MCGOVERN, K., & HINES, P. (1975). The behavioral assessment of social competence in males. *Behavior Therapy, 6,* 3–13.
ASCH, S. E. (1946). Forming impressions of personality. *Journal of Abnormal and Social Psychology, 41,* 258–290.
ASCH, S. E. (1951). Effects of group pressure upon the modification and distortion of judgment. In H. Guetzkow (Ed.), *Groups, leadership, and men.* Pittsburgh, Pa.: Carnegie Press.
ASCH, S. E. (1956). Studies of independence and conformity: A minority of one against a unanimous majority. *Psychological Monographs, 9* (Whole No. 416).
ASERINSKY, E., & KLEITMAN, N. (1953). Regularly occurring periods of eye motility, and concomitant phenomena, during sleep. *Science, 118,* 273–274.
ASERINSKY, E., & KLEITMAN, N. (1955). Two types of ocular motility occurring in sleep. *Journal of Applied Physiology, 8,* 1–10.
ASHTON, N. L., & SHAW, M. E. (1980). Empirical investigations of a reconceptualized personal space. *Bulletin of the Psychonomic Society, 15,* 309–312.
ATKINSON, R. C., & JUOLA, J. F. (1974). Search and decision processes in recognition memory. In D. H. Krantz, R. C. Atkinson, R. D. Luce, & P. Suppes (Eds.), *Contemporary developments in mathematical psychology.* San Francisco: W. H. Freeman.
ATKINSON, R. C., & SHIFFRIN, R. M. (1968). Human memory: A proposed system and its control processes. In K. W. Spence & J. T. Spence (Eds.), *The psychology of learning and motivation* (Vol. 2). New York: Academic Press.
ATTHOWE, J. M., & KRASNER, L. (1968). Preliminary report on the application of contingent reinforcement procedures (token economy) on a "chronic" psychiatric ward. *Journal of Abnormal Psychology, 73,* 37–43.
AVERILL, J. R. (1975). A semantic atlas of emotional concepts. J.S.A.S. *Catalogue of Selected Documents in Psychology, 5,* 330 (Ms. No. 421).
AVERILL, J. R. (1980). The emotions. In E. Staub (Ed.), *Personality, basic aspects and current research* (pp. 133–200). New York: Prentice-Hall.
AYLLON, T., & AZRIN, N. (1968). *The token economy.* New York: Appleton-Century-Crofts.
BACON, C., & LERNER, R. M. (1975). Effects of maternal employment status on the development of vocational-role perception in females. *Journal of Genetic Psychology, 126,* 187–193.
BAIRD, J. C., & NOMA, E. (1978). *Fundamentals of scaling and psychophysics.* New York: Wiley.
BALDESSARINI, R. J. (1980). Drugs and the treatment of psychiatric disorders. In A. G. Gilman, L. S. Goodman, & A. Gilman (Eds.), *The pharmacological basis of therapeutics* (6th ed.) (pp. 391–447). New York: Macmillan.
BALTES, P. B., & SCHAIE, K. W. (1974). The myth of the twilight years. *Psychology Today,* March, pp. 35–38.
BANDLER, R., GRINDER, J., & SATIR, V. (1977). *Changing with families.* Palo Alto, Calif.: Science & Behavior Books.
BANDURA, A. (1964). The stormy decade: Fact or fiction? *Psychology in the Schools, 1,* 224–231.
BANDURA, A. (1965). Influence of models' reinforcement contingencies on the acquisition of imitative responses. *Journal of Personality and Social Psychology, 1,* 589–595.
BANDURA, A. (1969a). *Principles of behavior modification.* New York: Holt, Rinehart and Winston.
BANDURA, A. (1969b). Social-learning theory of identificatory processes. In D. A. Goslin (Ed.), *Handbook of socialization theory and research* (pp. 213–262). Chicago: Rand McNally.
BANDURA, A. (1971). *Social learning theory.* Morristown, N.J.: General Learning Press.
BANDURA, A. (1977a). Self-efficacy: Toward a unifying theory of behavioral change. *Psychological Review, 84,* 191–215.
BANDURA, A. (1977b). *Social learning theory.* Englewood Cliffs, N.J.: Prentice-Hall.
BANDURA, A. (1978). The self system in reciprocal determinism. *American Psychologist, 33,* 344–358.
BANDURA, A. (1980a). The self and mechanisms of agency. In J. Suls (Ed.), *Social psychological perspectives on the self.* Hillsdale, N.J.: Lawrence Erlbaum.
BANDURA, A. (1980b). Self-referent thought: A developmental analysis of self efficacy. In T. H. Flavell & L. D. Ross (Eds.), *Cognitive social development: Frontiers and possible futures.* New York: Cambridge University Press.
BANDURA, A. (1982). Self-efficacy mechanisms in human agency. *American Psychologist, 37,* 122–147.
BANDURA, A. (1983). Psychological mechanisms of aggression. In R. Geen & E. Donnerstein (Eds.), *Aggression: Theoretical and empirical reviews* (Vol. 1). New York: Academic Press.
BARASH, D. P. (1982). *Sociobiology and behavior* (rev. ed.). New York: Elsevier.
BARBER, T. X. (1979). Suggested ("hypnotic") behavior: The trance paradigm versus an alternative paradigm. In E. Fromm & R. E. Shor (Eds.), *Hypnosis: Developments in research and new perspectives* (pp. 217–271). Hawthorne, N.Y.: Aldine.
BARKLEY, R. (1982). Guidelines for defining hyperactivity in children: Attention deficit disorder with hyperactivity. In B. B. Lahey & A. E. Kazdin (Eds.), *Advances in clinical child psychology* (Vol. 5). New York: Plenum Press.
BARLOW, D. (Ed.). (1981). *Behavioral assessment of adult disorders.* New York: Guilford Press.

REFERENCES

Baron, R. A. (1973). The "foot-in-the-door" phenomenon: Mediating effects of size of first request and sex of requester. *Bulletin of the Psychonomic Society, 2,* 113–114.

Baron, R. A., & Byrne, D. (1984). *Social psychology: Understanding human interaction,* Boston, MA: Allyn and Bacon.

Barron, F. (1969). *Creative person and creative process.* New York: Holt, Rinehart and Winston.

Barron, F., & Harrington, D. M. (1981). Creativity, intelligence, and personality. *Annual Review of Psychology, 32,* 439–476.

Bartlett, F. C. (1932). *Remembering.* Cambridge: Cambridge University Press.

Baruch, G. K., & Barnett, R. C. (1980). On the well-being of adult women. In L. A. Bond & J. C. Rosen (Eds.), *Competence and coping during adulthood.* Hanover, N.H.: University Press of New England.

Bateson, G., Jackson, D., Haley, J., & Weckland, J. (1956). Toward a theory of schizophrenia. *Behavioral Science, 1,* 251–264.

Baumrind, D. (1967). Child care practices anteceding three patterns of the preschool behavior. *Genetic Psychology Monographs, 75,* 43–88.

Baumrind, D. (1968). Authoritarian vs. authoritative parental control. *Adolescence, 3,* 255–272.

Baumrind, D. (1971). Current patterns of parental authority. *Developmental Psychology Monographs, 4,* 99–103.

Baumrind, D. (1972). Some thoughts about child rearing. In U. Bronfenbrenner (Ed.), *Influences on human development.* Hinsdale, Ill.: Dryden Press.

Bayley, N. (1935). The development of motor abilities during the first three years. *Monographs of the Society for Research in Child Development,* No. 1.

Baley, N. (1949). Consistency and variability in the growth of intelligence from birth to eighteen years. *Journal of Genetic Psychology, 75,* 165–196.

Bayley, N. (1956). Individual patterns of development. *Child Development, 27,* 45–74.

Bayley, N. (1968). Behavioral correlates of mental growth: Birth to thirty-six years. *American Psychologist, 23,* 1–17.

Beck, A. T. (1964). Thinking and depression: II. Theory and therapy. *Archives of General Psychiatry, 10,* 561–571.

Beck, A. T. (1967). *Depression: Clinical, experimental, and theoretical aspects.* New York: Harper & Row.

Beck, A. T. (1972). *Depression: Causes and treatment.* Philadelphia: University of Pennsylvania Press.

Beck, A. T., Rush, A. J., Shaw, B. F., & Emery, G. (1979). *Cognitive therapy of depression.* New York: Guilford Press.

Beck, A. T., Ward, C. H., Mendelson, M., Mock, J. E., & Erbaugh, J. K. (1961). An inventory for measuring depression. *Archives of General Psychiatry, 4,* 561–571.

Beck, A. T., Ward, C. H., Mendelson, M., Mock, J. E., & Erbaugh, J. K. (1962). Reliability of psychiatric diagnosis: I. A study of consistency of clinical judgments and ratings. *American Journal of Psychiatry, 119,* 351–357.

Becker, E. (1973). *The denial of death.* New York: Free Press.

Békésy, G. von (1957). The ear. *Scientific American, 197,* 66–78.

Békésy, G. von (1960). *Experiments in hearing.* New York: McGraw-Hill.

Bell, G. B., & French, R. L. (1950). Consistency of individual leadership position in small groups of varying memberships. *Journal of Abnormal and Social Psychology, 45,* 764–767.

Bell, R. Q. (1974). Contributions of human infants to caregiving and social interaction. In M. Lewis & L. A. Rosenblum (Eds.), *The effect of the infant on its caregiver.* New York: Wiley.

Belsky, J. (1980). Child maltreatment: An ecological integration. *American Psychologist, 35,* 320–335.

Belsky, J., Lerner, R. M., & Spanier, G. B. (1984). *The child in the family.* Reading, Mass.: Addison-Wesley.

Belsky, J., & Steinberg, L. D. (1978). The effects of day care: A critical review. *Child Development, 49,* 920–949.

Belsky, J., Steinberg, L. D., & Walker, A. (1982). The ecology of day care. In M. E. Lamb (Ed.), *Childrearing in nontraditional families.* Hillsdale, N.J.: Lawrence Erlbaum.

Bem, D. J. (1972). Self-perception theory. In L. Berkowitz (Ed.), *Advances in experimental social psychology* (Vol. 6). New York: Academic Press.

Bem, D. J., & Allen, A. (1974). On predicting some of the people some of the time: The search for cross-situational consistencies in behavior. *Psychological Review, 81,* 506–520.

Bender, L. (1938). *A visual-motor gesalt test and its clinical use.* New York: American Orthopsychiatric Association.

Bennett, M. V. L. (1977). Electrical transmission: A functional analysis and comparison to chemical transmission. In E. R. Kandel (Ed.), *Handbook of physiology, section 1: The nervous system* (pp. 357–416). Bethesda, Md.: American Physiological Society.

Benton, A. L., & Van Allen, M. W. (1973). *Test of facial recognition manual* (Neurosurgery Center Publication No. 287). University of Iowa.

Berkman, L. F., & Syme, S. L. (1979). Social networks, host resistance, and mortality: A nine-year follow-up study of Alameda County residents. *American Journal of Epidemiology, 109,* 186–204.

Berkowitz, L. (1968). Impulse, aggression and the gun. *Psychology Today, 2,* 18–22.

Berkowitz, L. (1980). *A survey of social psychology,* 2nd edition. New York: Holt, Rinehart & Winston.

Berne, E. (1970). *Games people play.* New York: Grove Press.

Berscheid, E. (1985). Interpersonal attraction. In G. Lindzey & E. Aronson (Eds.), *Handbook of social psychology* (3rd Edition). New York: Random House.

Berscheid, E., & Walster, E. (1978). *Interpersonal attraction* (2nd ed.). Reading, Mass.: Addison-Wesley.

Bhaskar, R., & Simon, H. A. (1977). Problem solving in semantically rich domains: An example from engineering thermodynamics. *Cognitive Science, 1,* 193–215.

Bijou, S. W. (1976). *Child development: The basic stage of early childhood.* Englewood Cliffs, N.J.: Prentice-Hall.

Bijou, S. W., & Baer, D. M. (1961). *Child development, Vol.*

1: A systematic and empirical theory. New York: Appleton-Century-Crofts.

BINET, A., & SIMON, T. (1905a). Application des méthodes nouvelles pour le diagnostic de niveau intellectuel chez des infants normaux et anormaux d'hospice et d'école primaire. *L'Année Psychologique, 11,* 245–336.

BINET, A., & SIMON, T. (1905b). Méthodes nouvelles pour le diagnostic du niveau intellectuel des anormaux. *L'Année Psychologique, 11,* 191–244.

BINET, A., & SIMON, T. (1905c). Sur la necessité d'établir un diagnostic scientifique des états inférieurs de l'intelligence. *L'Année Psychologique, 11,* 162–190.

BIRREN, J. E. (1974). Transitions in gerontology—from lab to life: Psychophysiology and speed of response. *American Psychologist, 29,* 808–815.

BIRREN, J. E., BUTLER, R. N., GREENHOUSE, S. W., SOKOLOFF, L., & YARROW, M. R. (Eds.) (1963). *Human aging: A biological and behavioral study.* Washington, D.C.: U.S. Government Printing Office.

BLEULER, E. (1950). *Dementia praecox or the group of schizophrenics.* New York: International Press. (English translation of 1911 work.)

BLOCK, J. (1971). *Lives through time.* Berkeley, Calif.: Bancroft.

BLOOD, R. O., & WOLFE, D. M. (1960). *Husbands and wives.* New York: Free Press.

BLOOM, B. S. (1964). *Stability and change in human characteristics.* New York: Wiley.

BLOOM, L., HOOD, L., & LIGHTBOW, P. (1974). Imitation in language development—If, when, and why. *Cognitive Psychology, 6,* 380–420.

BOGGIANO, A. K., & RUBLE, D. N. (1981). *Self-perception vs. cued expectancy: Analyses of the effects of reward on task interest.* Paper presented at the American Psychological Association Annual Convention, Los Angeles.

BORING, E. G. (1950). *A history of experimental psychology* (2nd ed.). New York: Appleton-Century-Crofts.

BORNSTEIN, M. H., KESSEN, W., & WEISKOPF, S. (1976). Color-vision and hue categorization in young infants. *Journal of Experimental Psychology, 2,* 115–129.

BOTWINICK, J. (1977). Intellectual abilities. In J. E. Birren & K. W. Schaie (Eds.), *Handbook of the psychology of aging.* New York: Van Nostrand Reinhold.

BOTWINICK, J. (1978). *Aging and behavior.* New York: Springer.

BOUCHARD, T., & McGUE, M. (1981). Familial studies of intelligence: A review. *Science, 212,* 1055–1057.

BOURNE, L. E. (1970). Knowing and using concepts. *Psychological Review, 77,* 546–556.

BOUSFIELD, W. A. (1953). The occurrence of clustering in the recall of randomly arranged associates. *Journal of General Psychology, 49,* 229–240.

BOUVIER, L. F. (1980). America's baby boom generation: The fateful bulge. *Population Bulletin, 35,* (1). Washington, D.C.: Population Reference Bureau.

BOWER, G. H. (1970). Organizational factors in memory. *Cognitive Psychology, 1,* 18–46.

BOWER, G. H. (1972). Mental imagery and associative learning. In L. W. Gregg (Ed.), *Cognition in learning and memory.* New York: Wiley.

BOWER, G. H., CLARK, M. C., LESGOLD, A. M., & WINZENZ, D. (1969). Hierarchical retrieval schemes in recall of categorized word lists. *Journal of Verbal Learning and Verbal Behavior, 8,* 323–343.

BOWER, G. H., MONTEIRO, K. P., & GILLIGAN, S. G. (1978). Emotional mood as a context for learning and recall. *Journal of Verbal Learning and Verbal Behavior, 17,* 563–587.

BOWER, T. G. R., & PATERSON, J. G. (1973). Separation of place, movement, and object in the world of the infant. *Journal of Experimental Child Psychology, 15,* 161–168.

BRACKBILL, Y. (1970). Continuous stimulation and arousal level in infants: Additive effects. *Proceedings, 78th Annual Convention, American Psychological Association, 5,* 271–272.

BRANSFORD, J. D., & FRANKS, J. J. (1971). The abstraction of linguistic ideas. *Cognitive Psychology, 2,* 331–350.

BRANSFORD, J. D., & FRANKS, J. J. (1972). The abstraction of linguistic ideas: A review. *Cognition: International Journal of Cognitive Psychology, 1,* 211–249.

BRAZELTON, T. B. (1970). Effect of prenatal drugs on the behavior of the neonate. *American Journal of Psychiatry, 126,* 1261–1266.

BRAZELTON, T. B. (1973). *Neonatal behavioral assessment scale.* London: Heinemann.

BRELAND, K., & BRELAND, M. (1961). The misbehavior of organisms. *American Psychologist, 16,* 681–684.

BRICKMAN, P., RABINOWITZ, V. C., KARUZA, J., COATES, D., COHN, E., & KIDDER, L. (1982). Models of helping and coping. *American Psychologist, 37,* 368–384.

BROADBENT, D. E. (1958). *Perception and communication.* Oxford: Pergamon Press.

BRODY, E. B., & BRODY, N. (1976). *Intelligence: Nature, determinants, and consequences.* New York: Academic Press.

BROWN, J. W. (1972). *Aphasia, apraxia, and agnosia.* Springfield, Ill.: Charles C Thomas.

BROWN, L. T. (1983). Some more misconceptions about psychology among introductory psychology students. *Teaching of Psychology, 10,* 207–210.

BROWN, P. L., & JENKINS, H. M. (1968). Auto-shaping of the pigeon's key-peck. *Journal of the Experimental Analysis of Behavior, 11,* 1–8.

BROWN, R. (1973). *A first language: The early stages.* Cambridge, Mass.: Harvard University Press.

BROWN, R., & BELLUGI, U. (1964). Three processes in the child's acquisition of syntax. In E. H. Lenneberg (Ed.), *New directions in the study of language.* Cambridge, Mass.: MIT Press.

BRUCH, H. (1973). *Eating disorders: Obesity, anorexia nervosa, and the person within.* New York: Basic Books.

BRUCH, H. (1977). Psychological antecedents of anorexia nervosa. In R. A. Vigersky (Ed.), *Anorexia nervosa.* New York: Raven Press.

BRUCH, M. A. (1981). A task analysis of assertive behavior revisited: Replication and extension. *Behavioral Therapy, 12,* 217–230.

BUCK, R. (1983). *Human motivation and emotion.* (2nd ed.). New York: Wiley.

BUCKOUT, R., & BAKER, E. (1977). Surveying the attitudes of seated jurors. *Social Action and the Law, 4,*(6) 98–101.

REFERENCES

BULL, N. (1951). The attitude theory of emotion. *Nervous and Mental Diseases Monographs* (No. 81). New York: Collidge Foundation.

BULLOCK, T. H. (1973). Seeing the world through a new sense: Electroreception in fish. *American Scientist, 61,* 316–325.

BUNDY, R. S. (1980). Discrimination of sound localization cues in young infants. *Child Development, 51,* 292–294.

BURGER, J. M., & PETTY, R. E. (1981). The low-ball technique: Task or personal commitment? *Journal of Personality and Social Psychology, 40,* 492–500.

BURGESS, R. L. (1979). Child abuse: A social interactional analysis. In B. B. Lahey & A. E. Kazdin (Eds.), *Advances in clinical child psychology.* New York: Plenum Press.

BURGESS, R. L., & CONGER, R. D. (1978). Family interaction in abusive, neglectful, and normal families. *Child Development, 49,* 1163–1173.

BURISH, T. G., & LYLES, J. N. (1981). Effectiveness of relaxation training in reducing adverse reactions to cancer chemotherapy. *Journal of Behavioral Medicine, 4,* 64–78.

BURT, C. (1955). The evidence for the concept of intelligence. *British Journal of Educational Psychology, 25,* 159–177.

BURT, C. (1958). The inheritance of mental ability. *American Psychologist, 13,* 1–15.

BURT, C. (1966). The genetic determination of differences in intelligence: A study of monozygotic twins reared together and apart. *British Journal of Psychology, 57,* 137–153.

BUSS, A. H. (1961). *The psychology of aggression.* New York: Wiley.

BUTCHER, J. N. (1971). *Objective personality assessment.* New York: General Learning Press.

BUTLER, R. N. (1963). The life review: An interpretation of reminiscence in the aged. *Psychiatry, 26,* 65–76.

CACIOPPO, J. T., GLASS, C. R., & MERLUZZI, T. V. (1979). Self-statements and self-evaluations: A cognitive response analysis of heterosexual social anxiety. *Cognitive Therapy and Research, 3,* 249–262.

CALVIN, W. H., & OJEMANN, G. A. (1980). *Inside the brain.* New York: New American Library.

CAMPBELL, F. W., & ROBSON, J. G. (1968). Application of Fourier analysis to the visibility of gratings. *Journal of Physiology* (London), *197,* 551–556.

CAMPOS, J. J. (1980–81). Human emotions: Their new importance and their role in social referencing. *Annual Report for the Research and Clinical Center for Child Development.* Sapporo, Japan: Hokkaido University, Faculty of Education.

CAMPOS, J. J., & STENBERG, C. R. (1981). Perception, appraisal, and emotion: The onset of social referencing. In M. E. Lamb & L. R. Sherrod (Eds.), *Infant social cognition.* Hillsdale, N.J.: Lawrence Erlbaum.

CANNON, W. B. (1927). The James-Lange theory of emotions: A critical examination and an alternative theory. *American Journal of Psychology, 39,* 106–124.

CANNON, W. B. (1929). *Bodily changes in pain, hunger, fear, and rage: An account of recent researchers into the function of emotional excitement* (2nd ed.). New York: Appleton-Century-Crofts.

CARLSON, N. R. (1981). *Physiology of behavior* (2nd ed.). Boston: Allyn and Bacon.

CARPENTER, M. B. (1976). *Human neuroanatomy* (7th ed.). Baltimore: Williams & Wilkins.

CARROLL, J. B. (1978). How shall we study individual differences in cognitive abilities? Methodological and theoretical perspectives. *Intelligence, 2,* 87–115.

CARSKADON, M. A., MITLER, M. M., & DEMENT, W. C. (1974). A comparison of insomniacs and normals: Total sleep time and sleep latency. *Sleep Research, 3,* 130.

CARTWRIGHT, D. C. (1975). The nature of gangs. In D. S. Cartwright, B. Tomson, & H. Schwartz (Eds.), *Gang delinquency.* Monterey, CA: Brooks/Cole.

CASSEL, J. (1976). The contribution of the social environment to host resistance. *American Journal of Epidemiology, 104,* 107–123.

CATTELL, P. (1947). *The measurement of intelligence of infants and young children.* New York: The Psychological Corporation.

CATTELL, R. B. (1946). *Description and measurement of personality.* New York: World Book.

CATTELL, R. B. (1949). *Culture fair intelligence test.* Institute for Personality and Ability Testing, Inc.

CATTELL, R. B. (1950). *Personality: A systematic, theoretical, and factual study.* New York: McGraw-Hill.

CATTELL, R. B. (1966). Psychological theory and scientific method. In R. B. Cattell (Ed.), *Handbook of multivariate experimental psychology.* Chicago: Rand McNally.

CATTELL, R. B. (1971). *Abilities: Their structure, growth, and action.* Boston: Houghton Mifflin.

CATTELL, R. B. (1973). *Personality and mood by questionnaire.* San Francisco: Jossey-Bass.

CAVANAUGH, J. C. (1983). Comprehension and retention of television programs by 20- and 60-year-olds. *Journal of Gerontology, 38,* 190–196.

CHAIKEN, S. (1979). Communicator physical attractiveness and persuasion. *Journal of Personality and Social Psychology, 37,* 1387–1397.

CHAMOVE, A. S. (1978). Therapy of isolate rhesus: Different partners and social behavior. *Child Development, 49,* 43–50.

CHAPMAN, C., & RISLEY, T. R. (1974). Anti-litter procedures in an urban high-density area. *Journal of Applied Behavior Analysis, 7,* 377–383.

CHARROW, R. P., & CHARROW, V. (1979). Making legal language understandable: A psycholinguistic study of jury instructions. *Columbia Law Review, 79,* 1306–1374.

CHI, M. T. H. (1978). Knowledge structures and memory development. In R. Siegler (Ed.), *Children's thinking: What develops?* Hillsdale, N.J.: Lawrence Erlbaum.

CHI, M. T. H., & KOESKE, R. D. (1983). Network representation of a child's dinosaur knowledge. *Developmental Psychology, 19,* 29–39.

CHOATE, R. (1975). *Testimony Before the House Subcommittee on Communications.* Washington, D.C.: United States House of Representatives, Council on Children, Media and Merchandising.

CHOMSKY, N. (1957). *Syntactic structures.* The Hague: Mouton.

CHOMSKY, N. (1968). *Language and mind.* New York: Harcourt Brace & World.

CIALDINI, R. B. (1983). *Influence.* New York: Morrow.

CIALDINI, R. B., CACIOPPO, J. T., BASSETT, R., & MILLER, J. A. (1978). Low-ball procedure for producing compliance: Commitment then cost. *Journal of Personality and Social Psychology, 36,* 463–476.

CIALDINI, R. B., VINCENT, J. E., LEWIS, S. K., CATALAN, J., WHEELER, D., & DANBY, B. L. (1975). Reciprocal concessions procedure for inducing compliance: The door-in-the-face technique. *Journal of Personality and Social Psychology, 31,* 206–215.

CIMINERO, A. R., NELSON, R. O., & LIPINSKI, D. (1977). Self-monitoring procedures. In A. R. Ciminero, K. S. Calhoun, & T. H. Adams (Eds.), *Handbook of behavioral assessment.* New York: Wiley.

CLAPMAN, L. J., & CHAPMAN, J. P. (1973). *Disordered thought in schizophrenia.* New York: Appleton-Century-Crofts.

CLARK, E. V., & HECHT, B. F. (1983). Comprehension, production, and language acquisition. *Annual Review of Psychology, 34,* 325–349.

CLARK, H. H., & CLARK, E. V. (1977). *Psychology and language.* New York: Harcourt Brace Jovanovich.

CLARKE, A. M., & CLARKE, A. D. B. (Eds.) (1976). *Early experience: Myth and evidence.* New York: Free Press.

CLORE, G. L., WIGGINS, N. H., & ITKIN, G. (1975). Gain and loss in attraction: Attributions from nonverbal behavior. *Journal of Personality and Social Psychology, 31,* 706–712.

COATES, B., PUSSER, H. E., & GOODMAN, I. (1976). Influence of Sesame Street and Mister Rogers Neighborhood on children's social behavior in preschool. *Child Development, 47,* 138–144.

COBB, S. (1976). Social support as a moderator of life stress. *Psychosomatic Medicine, 38,* 300–314.

COLEMAN, J. C., BUTCHER, J. N., & CARSON, R. C. (1980). *Abnormal psychology and modern life* (6th ed.). Glenview, Ill.: Scott, Foresman.

COLLETTA, N. D. (1978). *Divorced mothers at two income levels: Stress, support, and child-rearing practices.* Unpublished thesis, Cornell University.

COLLINS, A. M., & LOFTUS, E. F. (1975). A spreading-activation theory of semantic processing. *Psychological Review, 82,* 407–428.

COLLINS, A. M., & QUILLIAN, M. R. (1969). Retrieval time from semantic memory. *Journal of Verbal Learning and Verbal Behavior, 8,* 240–247.

COLLINS, S. M. (1978). The use of social research in the courts. In L. E. Lynn, Jr. (Ed.), *Knowledge and policy: The uncertain connection* (Study Project in Social Research and Development, Vol. 5). Washington, DC: National Academy of Sciences.

COMSTOCK, G., CHAFFEE, S., KATZMAN, N., MCCOMBS, M., & ROBERTS, D. (1978). *Television and human behavior.* New York: Columbia University Press.

CONRAD, R. (1964). Acoustic confusions in immediate memory. *British Journal of Psychology, 55,* 75–84.

CONRAD, R. (1965). The role of the nature of the material in verbal learning. *Acta Psychologia, 24,* 244–252.

CONRAD, R. (1971). The chronology of the development of covert speech in children. *Developmental Psychology, 5,* 398–405.

CONWAY, F., & SIEGELMAN, J. (1979). *Snapping: America's epidemic of sudden personality change.* New York: Delta Books.

COOPER, L. A., & SHEPARD, R. N. (1973). Chromometric studies of the rotation of mental images. In W. G. Chase (Ed.), *Visual information processing.* New York: Academic Press.

COREN, S., PORAC, C., & WARD, L. M. (1984). *Sensation and perception* (2nd ed.). Orlando, Fla.: Academic Press.

CORNSWEET, T. N. (1970). *Visual perception.* New York: Academic Press.

CORSINI, R. (Ed.) (1973). *Current psychotherapies.* Itasca, Ill.: Peacock.

COSTA, P. T., & MCCRAE, R. R. (1980). Influence of extraversion and neuroticism on subjective well-being. Happy and unhappy people. *Journal of Personality and Social Psychology, 38,* 668–678.

COTE, L. (1981). Basal ganglia, the extrapyramidal motor system, and diseases of transmitter metabolism. In E. R. Kandel & J. H. Schwartz (Eds.), *Principles of neural science* (pp. 347–357). New York: Elsevier/North-Holland.

COX, P. R., & FORD, J. R. (1970). The mortality of widows shortly after widowhood. In T. Ford & G. F. DeJong (Eds.), *Social demography.* Englewood Cliffs, N.J.: Prentice-Hall.

COX, V. C., PAULUS, P. B., & MCCAIN, G. (1984). Prison crowding research: The relevance for prison housing standards and a general approach regarding crowding phenomena. *American Psychologist, 39,* 1148–1159.

CRAIGHEAD, W. E., KIMBALL, W. H., & REHAK, P. J. (1979). Mood changes, physiological responses, and self-statements during social rejection imagery. *Journal of Consulting and Clinical Psychology, 47,* 385–396.

CRAIGHEAD, W. E., WILCOXON-CRAIGHEAD, L., & MEYERS, A. W. (1978). New directions in behavior modification with children. In M. Hersen, R. Eisler, & P. Miller (Eds.), *Progress in behavior modification* (Vol. 6). New York: Academic Press.

CRAIK, F. I. M. (1977). Age differences in human memory. In J. E. Birren & K. W. Schaie (Eds.), *Handbook of the psychology of aging.* New York: Van Nostrand Reinhold.

CRAIK, F. I. M. (1981). Encoding and retrieval effects in human memory: A partial review. In J. B. Long & A. B. Baddeley (Eds.), *Attention and performance.* Hillsdale, N.J.: Lawrence Erlbaum.

CRAIK, F. I. M., & LOCKHART, R. S. (1972). Levels of processing: A framework for memory research. *Journal of Verbal Learning and Verbal Behavior, 11,* 671–684.

CRAIK, F. I. M., & TULVING, E. (1975). Depth of processing and the retention of words in episodic memory. *Journal of Experimental Psychology: General, 104,* 268–294.

CRAIK, F. I. M., & WATKINS, M. J. (1973). The role of rehearsal in short-term memory. *Journal of Verbal Learning and Verbal Behavior, 12,* 599–607.

CRAVIOTO, J., & DELICARDIE, E. (1975). Longitudinal study of language development in severely malnourished children. In G. Serban (Ed.), *Nutrition and mental functions.* New York: Plenum Press.

REFERENCES

CRISP, A. H. (1970). Premorbid factors in adult disorders of weight, with particular references to primary anorexia nervosa (weight phobia). *Journal of Psychosomatic Medicine, 14,* 1–22.

CRISP, A. H. (1974). Primary anorexia nervosa or adolescent weight phobia. *Practitioner, 212,* 525–535.

CRONBACH, L. J. (1984). *Essentials of psychological testing* (4th ed.). New York: Harper & Row.

CRONBACH, L. J., & MEEHL, P. E. (1955). Construct validity in psychological tests. *Psychological Bulletin, 52,* 281–302.

CROSBY, F. J. (1982). *Relative deprivation and working women.* New York: Oxford University Press.

CURRAN, J. P., & CATTELL, R. B. (1975). *Manual for the eight state questionnaire.* Champaign, IL: Institute for Personality and Ability Testing.

DABBS, J. M., JR., & LEVENTHAL, H. (1966). Effects of varying the recommendations in a fear-arousing communication. *Journal of Personality and Social Psychology, 4,* 525–531.

DANE, F., & WRIGHTSMAN, L. (1982). Effects of defendants' and victims' characteristics on jurors' verdicts. In N. Kerr & R. Bray (Eds.), *The psychology of the courtroom.* New York: Academic Press.

DANKS, J. H., & GLUCKSBURG, S. (1980). Experimental psycholinguistics. *Annual Review of Psychology, 31,* 391–417.

DARLEY, J. M., & GROSS, P. H. (1983). A hypothesis-confirming bias in labeling effects. *Journal of Personality and Social Psychology, 44,* 20–33.

DARLEY, J. M., & LATANÉ, B. (1968). Bystander intervention in emergencies: Diffusion of responsibility. *Journal of Personality and Social Psychology, 8,* 377–383.

DARWIN, C. (1859). *On the origin of species.* London: J. Murray.

DARWIN, C. (1872). *The expression of emotions in man and animals.* London: Murray.

DAVIDSON, W. S., II. (1974). Studies of aversive conditioning for alcoholics: A critical review of theory and research methodology. *Psychological Bulletin, 81,* 571–581.

DAVIS, J. A. (1966). The campus as a frog pond: An application of the theory of relative deprivation to career decisions of college men. *American Journal of Sociology, 72,* 17–31.

DAVIS, R., BUCHANAN, B. G., & SHORTLIFFE, E. H. (1977). Production rules as a representation for a knowledge-based consultation program. *Artificial Intelligence, 8,* 15–46.

DAVISON, G. C., & NEALE, J. M. (1982). *Abnormal psychology: An experimental clinical approach.* (3rd ed.). New York: Wiley.

DAWKINS, R. (1982). *The extended phenotypes.* San Francisco: W. H. Freeman.

DEARDEN, R. F. (1967). The concept of play. In R. S. Peter (Ed.), *The concept of education.* London: Routledge.

DECI, E. L., NEZLEK, J., & SHEIMMAN, L. (1981). Characteristics of the rewarder and intrinsics of motivation of the rewardee. *Journal of Personality and Social Psychology, 40,* 1–10.

DEGROOT, A. D. (1965). *Thought and choice in chess.* The Hague: Mouton.

DELONGIS, A., COYNE, J. C., DAKOF, G., FOLKMAN, S., & LAZARUS, R. S. (1982). Relationship of daily hassles, uplifts, and major life events to health status. *Health Psychology, 1,* 119–136.

DEMENT, W. C. (1978). *Some must watch while some must sleep.* New York: W. W. Norton.

DEMENT, W. C., GUILLEMINAULT, C., & ZARCONE, V. (1975). The pathologies of sleep: A case series approach. In D. B. Tower (Ed.), *The nervous system, Vol. 2: The clinical neurosciences* (pp. 501–518). New York: Raven Press.

DEMENT, W. C., HOLMAN, R. B., & GUILLEMINAULT, C. (1976). Neurochemical and neuropharmacological foundations of the sleep disorders. *Psychopharmacology Communications, 2,* 77–90.

DEMENT, W. C., & KLEITMAN, N. (1957). Cyclic variations in EEG during sleep and their relation to eye movements, body mobility and dreaming. *Electroencephalography and Clinical Neurophysiology, 9,* 673–690.

DEMENT, W. C., & WOLPERT, E. A. (1958). The relation of eye movements, body motility, and external stimuli to dream content. *Journal of Experimental Psychology, 55,* 543–553.

DEPUE, R. A., & MONROE, S. M. (1978). The unipolar-bipolar distinction in the depressive disorders. *Psychological Bulletin, 85,* 1001–1029.

DESPRES, M. A. (1937). Favorable and unfavorable attitudes toward pregnancy in primaparae. *Journal of Genetic Psychology, 51,* 241–254.

DEVALOIS, R. L., & DEVALOIS, K. K. (1975). Neural coding of color. In E. C. Carterette & M. P. Friedman (Eds.), *Handbook of perception* Vol. 5: *Seeing.* New York: Academic Press.

DEVALOIS, R. L., & DEVALOIS, K. K. (1980). Spatial vision. *Annual Review of Psychology, 31,* 309–341.

deVILLIERS, J. G., & deVILLIERS, P. A. (1974). Competence and performance in child language: Are children really competent to judge? *Journal of Child Language, 1,* 11–22.

deVRIES, H. A. (1970). Physiological effects of an exercise training regimen upon men aged 52 to 88. *Journal of Gerontology, 25,* 325–336.

deVRIES, H. A. (1971). Prescription of exercise for older men from telemetered exercise heart rate data. *Geriatrics, 26,* 102–111.

DICKSTEIN, L. S. (1976). Differential difficulty of categorical syllogisms. *Bulletin of the Psychonomic Society, 8,* 330–332.

DIENER, E. (1979). Deindividuation, self-awareness, and disinhibition. *Journal of Personality and Social Psychology, 37,* 1160–1171.

DION, K. K. (1972). Physical attractiveness and evaluation of children's transgressions. *Journal of Personality and Social Psychology, 24,* 285–290.

DOHRENWEND, B. S., KRANSNOFF, L., ASKENASY, A. R., & DOHRENWEND, B. P. (1978). Exemplification of a method for scaling life events: The PERI life events scale. *Journal of Health and Social Behavior, 19,* 205–229.

DOLLARD, J., & MILLER, N. E. (1950). *Personality and psychotherapy.* New York: McGraw-Hill.

DOLLARD, J., DOOB, L., MILLER, N. E., MOWRER, O. H., & SEARS, R. F. (1939). *Frustration and aggression.* New Haven: Yale University Press.

DONNERSTEIN, E. (1980). Aggressive erotica and violence

against women. *Journal of Personality and Social Psychology, 39,* 269–277.

DOOB, A., & KIRSCHENBAUM, H. M. (1972). Some empirical evidence on the effect of S.12 of the Canadian Evidence Act upon the accused. *Criminal Law Quarterly, 15,* 88–96.

DOUGLAS, V. I. (1972). Stop, look, and listen: The problem of sustained attention and impulse control in hyperactive and normal children. *Canadian Journal of Behavioral Science, 4,* 259–282.

DOUVAN, E., & ADELSON, J. (1966). *The adolescent experience.* New York: Wiley.

DOWLING, J. E., & BOYCOTT, B. B. (1966). Organization of the primate retina: Electron microscopy. *Proceedings of the Royal Society* (London), Series B, *166,* 80–111.

DUBNOFF, S. J., VEROFF, J., & KULKA, R. A. (1978). *Adjustment to work: 1956–1976.* Paper presented at the American Psychological Assoiciation Annual Convention, Toronto, August.

DUFFY, E. (1962). *Activation of behavior.* New York: Wiley.

DUNCAN, S. L. (1976). Differential social perception and attribution of intergroup violence. Testing the lower limits of stereotyping of blacks. *Journal of Personality and Social Psychology, 34,* 590–598.

DUNCKER, K. (1945). On problem solving. *Psychological Monographs, 58* (Whole No. 270).

EAGLY, A. H., & CHAIKEN, S. (1975). An attribution analysis of the effect of communicator characteristics on opinion change: The case of communicator attractiveness. *Journal of Personality and Social Psychology, 32,* 136–144.

EBBINGHAUS, H. (1964). *Memory: A contribution to experimental psychology* (H. A. Roger & C. E. Bussenius, trans.). New York: Dover.

ECCLES, J. C. (1966). *Brain and conscious experience.* Heidelberg: Springer-Verlag.

EGAN, J. P. (1975). *Signal detection theory and ROC analysis.* New York: Academic Press.

EKMAN, P., & FRIESEN, W. V. (1975). *Unmasking the face: A guide to recognizing emotions from facial clues.* Englewood Cliffs, N.J.: Prentice-Hall.

EKSTROM, R. B., FRENCH, J. W., HARMAN, H. H., & DERMEN, D. (1976). *Manual for kit of factor-referenced cognitive tests.* Princeton, N.J.: Educational Testing Service.

ELKIND, D. (1967). Egocentrism in adolescence. *Child Development, 38,* 1025–1034.

ELLIS, A. (1962). *Reason and emotion in psychotherapy.* New York: Lyle Stuart.

ELLIS, H. C., & HUNT, R. R. (1983). *Fundamentals of human memory and cognition* (3rd ed.). Dubuque, Iowa: W. C. Brown.

EMDE, R., GAENSBAUER, T., & HARMON, R. (1976). Emotional expression in infancy: A biobehavioral study. *Psychological Issues, 10*(37). New York: International Universities Press.

ENDLER, N. S., & OKADA, M. (1975). A multidimensional measure of trait anxiety: The S-R Inventory of General Trait Anxiousness. *Journal of Consulting and Clinical Psychology, 43,* 319–329.

ENGEN, T., LIPSITT, L. P., & PECK, M. B. (1974). Ability of newborn-infants to discriminate sapid substances. *Developmental Psychology, 10,* 741–744.

EPSTEIN, R. (1981). On pigeons and people: A preliminary look at the Columbian simulation project. *The Behavior Analyst, 4,* 43–55.

EPSTEIN, S. (1962). The measurement of drive and conflict in humans: Theory and experiment. In M. R. Jones (Ed.), *Nebraska symposium on motivation.* Lincoln: University of Nebraska Press.

ERICKSON, J. R., & JONES, M. R. (1978). Thinking. *Annual Review of Psychology, 29,* 61–90.

ERIKSON, E. H. (1950). *Childhood and society.* New York: Norton.

ERIKSON, E. H. (1959). Identity and the life cycle: Selected papers. *Psychological Issues, 1,* 50–100.

ERIKSON, E. H. (1963). *Childhood and society.* New York: Norton.

ERIKSON, E. H. (1968). *Identity, youth, and crisis.* New York: Norton.

ERON, L. D. (1982). Parent-child interaction, television violence, and aggression of children. *American Psychologist, 37,* 197–211.

ERON, L. D., LEFKOWITZ, M. M., HUESMANN, L. R., & WALDER, L. O. (1972). Does television violence cause aggression? *American Psychologist, 27,* 253–263.

ERSEN-MÖLLER, E. (1941). Psychiatrische Untersuchungen an einer Serie von Zwillingen. *Acta Psychiatrica et Neurological Scandinavica,* Supplement 23.

EVANS, R. I., ROZELLE, R. M., LASATER, T. M., DEMBROSKI, T. M., & ALLEN, B. P. (1970). Fear arousal, persuasion and actual vs. implied behavioral change: New perspective utilizing a real-life dental hygiene program. *Journal of Personality and Social Psychology, 16,* 220–227.

EVERETT, P. B., HAYWARD, S. C., & MEYERS, A. W. (1974). The effects of a token reinforcement procedure on bus ridership. *Journal of Applied Behavior Analysis, 7,* 1–9.

EXNER, J. E., Jr. (1983). Rorschach assessment. In I. B. Weiner (Ed.), *Clinical methods in psychology* (2nd ed.). New York: Wiley.

EYSENCK, H. J. (1952). The effects of psychotherapy: An evaluation. *Journal of Consulting Psychology, 16,* 319–324.

EYSENCK, H. J. (1953). *The structure of human personality.* New York: Wiley.

EYSENCK, H. J. (1967). *The biological basis of personality.* Springfield, Ill.: Charles C Thomas.

FAGAN, F. J. (1974). Infant color-perception. *Science, 183,* 973–975.

FAIRWEATHER, G. W., SANDERS, D., & TORNATZKY, L. (1974). *Creating change in mental health organizations.* Elmsford, N.Y.: Pergamon Press.

FANTZ, R. L. (1961). The origin of form perception. *Scientific American, 204,* 66–72.

FANTZ, R. L., ORDY, J. M., & UDELF, M. S. (1962). Maturation of pattern vision in infants during the first six months. *Journal of Comparative and Physiological Psychology, 55,* 907–917.

FARRAN, D. C., & RAMEY, C. T. (1980). Social class differences in dyadic involvement during infancy. *Child Development, 51,* 254–257.

REFERENCES

Fehr, R. S., & Stern, J. A. (1970). Peripheral physiological variables and emotion: The James-Lange theory revisited. *Psychological Bulletin, 74,* 411–424.

Feinman, S., & Lewis, M. (1983). Social referencing at ten months: A second-order effect on infants' responses to strangers. *Child Development, 54,* 878–887.

Fenz, W. D., & Epstein, S. (1967). Gradients of physiological arousal in parachutists as a function of an approaching jump. *Psychosomatic Medicine, 29,* 33–51.

Ferree, M. (1976). Working class jobs: Housework and paid work as sources of satisfaction. *Social Problems, 23,* 431–441.

Ferreira, A. (1969). *Prenatal environment.* Springfield, Ill.: Charles C Thomas.

Ferster, C. B., & Skinner, B. F. (1957). *Schedules of reinforcement.* New York: Appleton-Century-Crofts.

Festinger, L. (1954). A theory of social comparison processes. *Human Relations, 7,* 117–140.

Festinger, L. (1957). *A theory of cognitive dissonance.* Stanford, Calif.: Stanford University Press.

Festinger, L., & Carlsmith, J. M. (1959). Cognitive sequences of forced compliance. *Journal of Abnormal and Social Psychology, 58,* 203–210.

Field, J., Muir, D., Pilon, R., Sinclair, M., & Dodwell, P. (1980). Infants' orientation to lateral sounds from birth to three months. *Child Development, 51,* 295–298.

Filskov, S. B., & Locklear, E. (1982). A multidimensional perspective on clinical neuropsychological research. In P. C. Kendall & J. N. Butcher (Eds.), *Handbook of research methods in clinical psychology.* New York: Wiley.

Folkman, S., & Lazarus, R. S. (1980). An analysis of coping in a middle-aged sample. *Journal of Health and Social Behavior, 21,* 219–239.

Folkman, S., Schaefer, C., & Lazarus, R. S. (1979). Cognitive processes as mediators of stress and coping. In V. Hamilton & D. M. Warburton (Eds.), *Human stress and cognition.* New York: Wiley.

Fontana, V. J. (1973). Further reflections on maltreatment of children. *Pediatrics, 51,* 780–782.

Fowles, B. (1975). *Testimony Before the House Subcommittee on Communications.* Washington, D.C.: U.S. Government Printing Office.

Fox, C. A., Hillman, D. E., Siegesmund, K. A., & Dutta, C. R. (1967). The primate cerebellar cortex: A Golgi and electron microscope study. In C. A. Fox & R. S. Snyder (Eds.), *The cerebellum: Progress in brain research* (Vol. 25). Amsterdam: Elsevier.

Fozard, J. L., & Popkin, S. J. (1978). Optimizing adult development: Ends and means of an applied psychology of aging. *American Psychologist, 33,* 975–989.

Frankenhaeuser, M. (1980). Psychoneuroendocrine approaches to the study of stressful person-environment transaction. In H. Selye (Ed.), *Selye's guide to stress research* (Vol. 1). New York: Van Nostrand Reinhold.

Frankenhaeuser, M., Nordheden, B., Myrsten, A. L., & Post, B. (1971). Psychophysiological reactions to understimulation and overstimulation. *Acta Psychologica, 35,* 298–308.

Frazier, T. M., Davis, G. H., Goldstein, H., & Goldberg, I. D. (1961). Cigarette smoking and prematurity: A prospective study. *Journal of Obstetrics and Gynecology, 81,* 988–996.

Freedman, D. X. (1969). The psychopharmacology of hallucinogenic agents. *Annual Review of Medicine, 20,* 409–418.

Freedman, J. L., & Fraser, S. G. (1966). Compliance without pressure: The foot-in-the-door technique. *Journal of Personality and Social Psychology, 4,* 195–202.

Freemon, F. R. (1972). *Sleep research: A critical review.* Springfield, Ill: Charles C Thomas.

French, J. W., Ekstrom, R. B., & Price, L. A. (1963). Kit of reference tests for cognitive factors. Princeton, N.J.: Educational Testing Service.

Freud, S. (1943). *A general introduction to psychoanalysis.* Garden City, N.Y.: Garden City Publishing Co. (First German edition, 1917.)

Freud, S. (1949). *An outline of psychoanalysis.* New York: Norton. (First German edition, 1940.)

Freud, S. (1963). Introductory lectures on psychoanalysis. In *Standard edition* (Vols. 15 and 16). London: Hogarth Press. (First German edition, 1917.)

Freud, S. (1964). An outline of psychoanalysis. In *Standard edition* (Vol. 23). London: Hogarth Press. (First German edition, 1940.)

Friedman, M., & Rosenman, R. H. (1959). Association of specific overt behavior pattern with blood and cardiovascular findings. *Journal of the American Medical Association, 169,* 1289–1296.

Friedman, M., & Rosenman, R. H. (1974). *Type A behavior and your heart.* New York: Knopf.

Frodi, A. M., & Lamb, M. E. (1980). Child abusers' responses to infant smiles and cries. *Child Development, 51,* 238–241.

Fromm, E. (1941). *Escape from freedom.* New York: Rinehart.

Fromm, E. (1955). *The sane society.* New York: Rinehart.

Fuchs, C. Z., & Rehm, L. P. (1977). A self-control behavior therapy program for depression. *Journal of Consulting and Clinical Psychology, 45,* 206–215.

Fuller, J. L., & Clark, L. D. (1966a). Effects of rearing with specific stimuli upon post-isolation syndrome in dogs. *Journal of Comparative and Physiological Psychology, 61,* 258–263.

Fuller, J. L., & Clark, L. D. (1966b). Genetic and treatment factors modifying the post-isolation syndrome in dogs. *Journal of Comparative and Physiological Psychology, 61,* 251–257.

Furman, W., & Masters, J. C. (1980). Peer interactions, sociometric status, and resistance to deviation in young children. *Developmental Psychology, 16,* 229–236.

Furman, W., Rahe, D. F., & Hartup, W. W. (1979). Rehabilitation of socially withdrawn preschool children through mixed-aged and same-aged socialization. *Child Development, 50,* 915–922.

Galanter, E. (1962). Contemporary psychophysics. In R. Brown, E. Galanter, E. Hess, & G. Mandler (Eds.), *New directions in psychology.* New York: Holt, Rinehart and Winston.

Galassi, J. P., Frierson, H. T., & Sharer, R. (1981). Behavior of high, moderate, and low test anxious students during an actual test situation. *Journal of Consulting and Clinical Psychology, 49,* 51–62.

GARBARINO, J. (1976). A preliminary study of some ecological correlates of child abuse: The impact of socioeconomic stress on mothers. *Child Development, 47,* 178–185.

GARBARINO, J. (1977). The human ecology of child maltreatment: A conceptual model for research. *Journal of Marriage and the Family, 39,* 721–736.

GARCIA, J., ERVIN, F. E., & KOELLING, R. A. (1966). Learning with prolonged delay of reinforcement. *Psychonomic Science, 5,* 121–122.

GARDNER, H. (1978). *Developmental psychology.* Boston: Little, Brown.

GARDNER, R. A., & GARDNER, B. T. (1969). Teaching sign language to a chimpanzee. *Science, 165,* 664–672.

GARDNER, R. A., & GARDNER, B. T. (1975). Early signs of language in child and chimpanzee, *Science, 187,* 752–754.

GARDNER, R. M., & HUND, R. M. (1983). Misconceptions of psychology among academicians. *Teaching of Psychology, 10,* 20–22.

GARFIELD, S. L. (1978). Research on client variables in psychotherapy. In S. L. Garfield & A. E. Bergin (Eds.), *Handbook of psychotherapy and behavior change* (2nd ed.). New York: Wiley.

GARFIELD, S. L., & KURTZ, R. (1976). Clinical psychologists in the 1970s. *American Psychologist, 31,* 1–9.

GEEN, R. G. (1980). The effects of being observed on performance. In P. B. Paulus (Ed.), *Psychology of group influence.* Hillsdale, N.J.: Lawrence Erlbaum.

GERBNER, G. (1980). Stigma: Social functions of the portrayal of mental illness in the mass media. In J. G. Rabkin, L. Gelb, & J. B. Lazar (Eds.), *Attitudes toward the mentally ill: Research perspectives.* Report of an NIMH Workshop, January 24–25. Department of Health and Human Services Publication No. (ADM) 80-1031. Washington, D.C.: U.S. Government Printing Office.

GERBNER, G., & GROSS, L. (1976, April). The scary world of TV's heavy viewer. *Psychology Today, 89,* 41–46.

GERBNER, G., GROSS, L., SIGNORELLI, N., & MORGAN, M. (1980). Television, violence, victimization, and power. *American Behavioral Scientist, 23,* 705–716.

GESCHWIND, N. (1979). Specializations of the human brain. *Scientific American, 241,* 180–199.

GESELL, A. L., & AMATRUDA, C. S. (1941). *Developmental diagnosis: Normal and abnormal child development.* New York: Hoeber.

GESELL, A. L., & AMATRUDA, C. S. (1947). *Developmental diagnosis* (2nd ed.). New York: Hoeber/Harper.

GEWIRTZ, H. B., & GEWIRTZ, J. L. (1968). Caretaking settings, background events and behavior differences in four Israeli child-rearing environments: Some preliminary friends. In B. M. Foss (Ed.), *Determinants of infant behavior* (Vol. 4) pp. 229–252). London: Methuen.

GEWIRTZ, J. L. (1965). The course of smiling by groups of Israeli infants in the first eighteen months of life. *Scripta Hieroslymitana, 16,* 9–58. Jerusalem: Magnes Press.

GHISELLI, E. E. (1973). The validity of aptitude tests in personnel selection. *Personnel Psychology, 26,* 461–477.

GIBSON, H. (1969). Early delinquency in relation to broken homes. *Journal of Abnormal Psychology, 74,* 33–41.

GIBSON, J. J. (1968). What gives rise to the perception of motion? *Psychological Review, 75,* 335–346.

GIL, D. C. (1970). *Violence against children: Physical abuse in the United States.* Cambridge, Mass.: Harvard University Press.

GILLIE, O. (1976). Crucial data was faked by eminent psychologist. *The Sunday Times,* London, October 24, pp. 1–2.

GILMOUR, D. R., & WALKEY, F. H. (1981). Identifying violent offenders using a video measure of interpersonal distance. *Journal of Consulting and Clinical Psychology, 49,* 287–291.

GINSBURG, A. P., & CAMBPELL, F. W. (1977). Optical transforms and the "pincushion grid" illusion? *Science, 198,* 961–962.

GLANZER, M., & CUNITZ, A. R. (1966). Two storage mechanisms in free recall. *Journal of Verbal Learning and Verbal Behavior, 5,* 351–360.

GLASGOW, R. E., & ROSEN, G. M. (1978). Behavioral bibliotherapy: A review of self-help behavior therapy manuals. *Psychological Bulletin, 85,* 1–23.

GLASSER, W. (1965). *Reality therapy: A new approach to psychiatry.* New York: Harper & Row.

GLICK, I. O., WEISS, R. S., & PARKES, C. M. (1974). *The first year of bereavement.* New York: Wiley.

GODDEN, D. R., & BADDELEY, A. D. (1975). Context-dependent memory in two natural environments: On land and under water. *British Journal of Psychology, 66,* 325–331.

GOLD, D., & ANDRES, D. (1978). Developmental comparisons between ten-year-old children with employed and nonemployed mothers. *Child Development, 49,* 75–84.

GOLDBERG, R. J. (1977). *Maternal time use and preschool performance.* Paper presented at the biennial meeting of the Society for Research in Child Development, New Orleans, March.

GOLDBERGER, A. S. (1979). Heritability. *Economica, 46,* 327–347.

GOLDEN, C. J. (1977). Validity of the Mainstead-Retain Neuropsychological Battery in a mixed psychiatric and brain-injured population. *Journal of Consulting and Clinical Psychology, 45,* 1043–1051.

GOLDFARB, W. (1945). Psychological privation in infancy and subsequent adjustment. *American Journal of Orthopsychiatry, 15,* 244–257.

GOLDFARB, W. (1947). Variations in adolescent adjustment to institutionally reared children. *Journal of Orthopsychiatry, 17,* 449–457.

GOLDFRIED, M. R. (1980). Toward the delineation of therapeutic change principles. *American Psychologist, 35,* 991–999.

GOLDFRIED, M. R., & DAVISON, G. C. (1976). *Clinical behavior therapy.* New York: Holt, Rinehart and Winston.

GOLDFRIED, M. R., & ROBINS, C. (1983). Self-schema, cognitive bias, and the processing of therapeutic experiences. In P. C. Kendall (Ed.), *Advances in cognitive-behavioral research and therapy* (Vol. 2). New York: Academic Press.

REFERENCES

GOLDFRIED, M. R., & SOBOCINSKI, D. (1975). Effect of irrational beliefs on emotional arousal. *Journal of Consulting and Clinical Psychology, 43,* 504–510.

GOLDFRIED, M. R., STRICKER, G., & WEINER, I. B. (1972). *Rorschach handbook of clinical and research applications.* Englewood Cliffs, N.J.: Prentice-Hall.

GOLDIN-MEADOW, S., SELIGMAN, M. E. P., & GELMAN, R. (1976). Language in the two-year-old. *Cognition, 4,* 189–202.

GOLDSTEIN, A. G., & CHANCE, J. E. (1971). Visual recognition memory for complex configurations. *Perception and Psychophysics, 9,* 237–241.

GOODWIN, D. W. (1976). *Is alcoholism hereditary?* New York: Oxford University Press.

GOODWIN, D. W. (1979). Alcoholism and heredity. *Archives of General Psychiatry, 36,* 57–61.

GORE, S. (1978). The effect of social support in moderating the health consequences of unemployment. *Journal of Health and Social Behavior, 19,* 157–165.

GOTTESMAN, I. I., & SHIELDS, J. (1966). Contributions of twin studies to perspectives on schizophrenia. In B. A. Maher (Ed.), *Progress in experimental personality research* (Vol. 3). New York: Academic Press.

GOUGH, H. G. (1957). *Manual for the California Psychological Inventory.* Palo Alto, Calif.: Consulting Psychologists Press.

GRANIT, R. (1977). *The purposive brain.* Cambridge, Mass.: MIT Press.

GRANT, D. A., HAKE, H. W., & HORNSETH, J. P. (1951). Acquisition and extinction of a verbal conditioned response with differing percentages of reinforcement. *Journal of Experimental Psychology, 42,* 1–5.

GRAY, S. W., & KLAUS, R. A. (1965). An experimental preschool program for culturally deprived children. *Child Development, 36,* 887–898.

GRAY, S. W., RAMSEY, B. K., & KLAUS, R. A. (1979). *The early training project in cognitudinal perspective.* Paper presented at the biennial meeting of the Society for Research in Child Development, San Francisco, March.

GREEN, D. M., & SWETS, J. A. (1966). *Signal detection theory and psychophysics* (reprint, 1974). New York: Krieger.

GREEN, R. G. (1983). Aggression and television violence. In R. G. Green & E. I. Donnerstein (Eds.), *Aggression: Theoretical and empirical reviews* (Vol. 2). New York: Academic Press.

GREEN, R. S., & CLIFF, N. (1975). Multidimensional comparison of structures of vocally and facially expressed emotions. *Perception and Psychophysics, 17,* 429–438.

GREENBERG, J. H. (1980). Sleep and the cerebral circulation. In J. Orem & C. D. Barnes (Eds.), *Physiology in sleep* (pp. 57–95). New York: Academic Press.

GREENO, J. G. (1975). Hobbits and orcs: Acquisition of a sequential concept. *Cognitive Psychology, 6,* 270–292.

GREGORY, R. L. (1978). *Eye and brain* (3rd ed.). New York: World University Library.

GREULICH, W. W. (1957). A comparison of the physical growth and development of American-born and native Japanese children. *American Journal of Physical Anthropology, 15,* 489–515.

GRUSH, J. E. (1980). Impact of candidate expenditures, regionality, and prior outcomes on the 1976 Democratic presidential primaries. *Journal of Personality and Social Psychology, 38,* 337–347.

GUILFORD, J. P. (1950). Creativity. *American Psychologist, 14,* 469–479.

GUILFORD, J. P. (1954). *Psychometric methods.* New York: McGraw-Hill.

GUILFORD, J. P. (1967). *The nature of human intelligence.* New York: McGraw-Hill.

GUILFORD, J. P., & CHRISTENSEN, P. R. (1973). The one-way relation between creative potential and IQ. *Journal of Creative Behavior, 7,* 247–252.

GURMAN, A. E., & KNISKERN, D. (1978). Research on marital and family therapy: Progress, perspective, and prospect. In S. L. Garfield & A. E. Bergin (Eds.), *Handbook of psychotherapy and behavior change* (2nd ed). New York: Wiley.

GURMAN, A. S. (1977). The patient's perception of the therapeutic relationship. In A. S. Gurman & A. M. Razin (Eds.), *The effective therapist: A handbook.* Elmsford, N.Y.: Pergamon Press.

GUTMANN, D. L. (1977). The cross-cultural perspective: Notes toward a comparative psychology of aging. In J. E. Birren & K. W. Schaie (Eds.), *Handbook of the psychology of aging.* New York: Van Nostrand Reinhold.

HADLEY, S. W., & STRUPP, H. H. (1976). Contemporary views of negative effects in psychotherapy: An integrated account. *Archives of General Psychiatry, 33,* 1291–1301.

HAIGLER, H. J., & AGHAJANIAN, G. K. (1977). Serotonin receptors in the brain. *Federation Proceedings, 36,* 2159–2164.

HAINLINE, L. (1978). Developmental changes in visual scanning of face and non-face patterns by infants. *Journal of Experimental Child Psychology, 25,* 90–115.

HALEY, J. (1976). *Problem solving therapy.* San Francisco: Jossey-Bass.

HALL, C. S., & LINDZEY, G. (1978). *Theories of personality* (3rd ed.). New York: Wiley.

HALL, E. T. (1963). A system for the notation of proxemic behavior. *American Anthropologist, 65,* 1003–1026.

HALL, E. T. (1966). *The hidden dimension.* New York: Anchor Books.

HALL, J. A. (1978). Gender effects in decoding nonverbal cues. *Psychological Bulletin, 85,* 845–857.

HAMBURG, D. A., & ADMAS, J. E. (1967). A perspective on coping behavior: Seeking and utilizing information in major transitions. *Archives of General Psychiatry, 27,* 277–284.

HANEY, C., & MANZOLATI, J. (1984). Television criminology: Network illusions of criminal justice realities. In E. Aronson (Ed.), *Readings about the social animal* (4th ed., pp. 120–132). San Francisco: W. H. Freeman.

HANS, V. (1977, March). *The unanimity requirement: Issues and evidence.* Report prepared for the Law Reform Commission of Canada.

HANSEL, C. E. M. (1980). *ESP and parapsychology: A critical reevaluation.* Buffalo, N.Y.: Prometheus Books.

HANSON, D. R., & GOTTESMAN, I. I. (1976). The genetics, if any, of infantile autism and childhood schizophrenia. *Journal of Autism and Childhood Schizophrenia, 6,* 209–234.

HARLOW, H. F. (1959). Learning set and error factory theory. In S. Koch (Ed.), *Psychology: A study of science* (Vol. 2). New York: McGraw-Hill.

HARLOW, H. F., & HARLOW, M. K. (1962). Social deprivation in monkeys. *Scientific American, 207*, 137–146.

HARLOW, H. F., & HARLOW, M. K. (1966). Learning to love. *American Scientist, 54*, 244–272.

HARLOW, H. F., & HARLOW, M. K. (1970). The young monkeys. In P. Cramer (Ed.), *Readings in developmental psychology today*. Del Mar, Calif.: CRM Books.

HARLOW, H. F., & ZIMMERMAN, R. R. (1959). Affectional responses in the infant monkey. *Science, 130*, 421–432.

HARRISON, G. A., WEINER, J. S., TANNER, J. M., & BARNICOT, N. A. (1977). *Human biology* (2nd ed.). London: Oxford University Press.

HARTMANN, E. L. (1973). *The functions of sleep*. New Haven, Conn.: Yale University Press.

HARTMANN, E. L. (1978). *The sleeping pill*. New Haven, Conn.: Yale University Press.

HARTSHORNE, M., & MAY, M. A. (1928). *Studies in the nature of character*, Vol. 1: *Studies in deceit*. New York: Macmillan.

HARTUP, W. W. (1979). The social worlds of childhood. *American Psychologist, 34*, 944–950.

HARVEY, S. C. (1980). Hypnotics and sedatives. In A. G. Gilman, L. S. Goodman, & A. Gilman (Eds.), *The pharmacological basis of therapeutics* (6th ed.) (pp. 339–375). New York: Macmillan.

HATFIELD, E., & WALSTER, G. W. (1981). *A new look at love*. Reading, MA: Addison-Wesley.

HATHAWAY, S. R., & McKINLEY, J. C. (1942). *Minnesota multiphasic personality inventory*. Minneapolis: University of Minnesota Press.

HAYES, C. (1951). *The ape in our house*. New York: Harper & Row.

HAYES, J. R., & SIMON, H. A. (1976). Understanding complex task instructions. In D. Klahr (Ed.), *Cognition and instructions*. Hillsdale, N.J.: Lawrence Erlbaum.

HAYES, S. C., & CONE, J. D. (1977). Reducing residential energy use: Payments, information, and feedback. *Journal of Applied Behavior Analysis, 10*, 425–435.

HAYFLICK, L. (1965). The limited in vitrol lifetime of human diploid cell strains. *Experimental Cell Research, 37*, 614–636.

HEARNSHAW, L. S. (1979). *Cyril Burt, psychologist*, Ithaca, N.Y.: Cornell University Press.

HEBB, D. O. (1970). A reply to Jensen and his social critics. *American Psychologist, 25*, 568.

HELD, R., & HEIN, A. (1963). Movement-produced stimulation in the development of visually guided behavior. *Journal of Comparative and Physiological Psychology, 56*, 872–876.

HELLER, H. C., CRANSHAW, L. I., & HAMMEL, H. T. (1978). The thermostat of vertebrate animals. *Scientific American, 239*, 102–113.

HELSON, H. (1964). *Adaptational-level theory*. New York: Harper & Row.

HERING, E. (1964). *Outlines of a theory of the light sense* (Hurvich, L. M., & Jameson, D., trans.). Cambridge, Mass.: Harvard University Press. (Originally published, 1878.)

HERMAN, C. P., & POLIVY, J. (1980). Restrained eating. In A. J. Stunkard (Ed.), *Obesity*. Philadelphia: Saunders.

HERMAN, J. H., ELLMAN, S. J., & ROFFWARG, H. P. (1978). The problem of NREM dream recall re-examined. In A. M. Arkin, J. S. Antrobus, & S. J. Ellman (Eds.), *The mind in sleep: Psychology and psychophysiology* (pp. 59–92). Hillsdale, N.J.: Lawrence Erlbaum.

HESTON, L. L. (1966). Psychiatric disorders in foster home reared children of schizophrenic mothers. *British Journal of Psychiatry, 112*, 819–825.

HETHERINGTON, E. M. (1979). Divorce: A child's perspective. *American Psychologist, 34*, 851–858.

HETHERINGTON, E. M., COX, M., & COX, R. (1978). The development of children in mother headed families. In H. Hoffman & D. Reiss (Eds.), *The American family: Dying or developing*. New York: Plenum Press.

HETHERINGTON, E. M., & PARKE, R. D. (1975). *Child psychology*. New York: McGraw-Hill.

HETHERINGTON, E. M., & PARKE, R. D. (1979). *Child psychology: A contemporary viewpoint*. New York: McGraw-Hill.

HILGARD, E. R. (1965). *Hypnotic susceptibility*. New York: Harcourt Brace & World.

HILGARD, E. R. (1968). *The experience of hypnosis*. New York: Harcourt Brace & World.

HILGARD, E. R. (1979). *Personality and hypnosis* (2nd ed.). Chicago: University of Chicago Press.

HILL, G. W. (1982). Group versus individual performance: Are $N + 1$ heads better than 1? *Psychologial Bulletin, 91*, 517–539.

HILL, J. P. (in press). Early adolescence: A research agenda. *Journal of Early Adolescence*.

HIROTO, D. S., & SELIGMAN, M. E. P. (1975). Generality of learned helplessness in man. *Journal of Personality and Social Psychology, 31*, 311–327.

HIRSCH, J. (1970). Behavior-genetic analysis and its biosocial consequences. *Seminars in Psychiatry, 2*, 89–105.

HODGKIN, A. L. (1964). *The conduction of the nervous impulse*. Springfield, Ill.: Charles C Thomas.

HODGKINS, J. (1962). Influence of age on the speed of reaction and movement in females. *Journal of Gerontology, 17*, 385–389.

HOFFMAN, L. W. (1974). The effects of maternal employment on the child—A review of research. *Developmental Psychology, 10*, 204–228.

HOFFMAN, L. W. (1979). Maternal employment: 1979. *American Psychologist, 34*, 859–865.

HOLLINGSHEAD, A. B., & REDLICH, F. C. (1958). *Social class and mental illness: A community study*. New York: Wiley.

HOLLON, S. D., & BECK, A. T. (1979). Cognitive-behavioral intervention for depression. In P. C. Kendall & S. D. Hollon (Eds.), *Cognitive-behavioral interventions: Theory, research, and procedures*. New York: Academic Press.

HOLMES, T. H., & MASUDA, M. (1974). Life change and illness susceptibility. In B. S. Dohrenwend & B. P. Dohrenwend (Eds.), *Stressful life events: Their nature and effects*. New York: Wiley.

HOLMES, T. H., & RAHE, R. H. (1967). The social readjustment rating scale. *Journal of Psychosomatic Research, 11*, 213–218.

HOLT, E. L., JR. (1972). Energy requirements. In H. L. Bar-

REFERENCES

nett & A. H. Ernhorn (Eds.), *Pediatrics* (15th ed.). New York: Appleton-Century-Crofts.

HORN, J. L. (1970). Organization of data on life-span development of human abilities. In L. R. Goulet & P. B. Baltes (Eds.), *Life-span development psychology: Research and theory*. New York: Academic Press.

HORN, J. L. (1978). Human ability systems. In P. B. Baltes (Ed.), *Life-span development and behavior* (Vol. 1). New York: Academic Press.

HORN, J. L., & CATTELL, R. B. (1966). Age differences in primary mental ability factors. *Journal of Gerontology, 21,* 210–220.

HORN, J. L., & DONALDSON, G. (1980). Cognitive development. II. Adulthood development of human abilities. In O. G. Brim, Jr., & J. Kagan (Eds.), *Constancy and change in human development: A volume of review essays.* Cambridge, Mass.: Harvard University Press.

HORNEY, K. (1945). *Our inner conflicts.* New York: Norton.

HORTON, D. L., & MILLS, C. B. (1984). Human learning and memory. *Annual Review of Psychology, 35,* 361–394.

HOVLAND, C. I., JANIS, I. L., & KELLEY, H. H. (1953). *Communication and persuasion.* New Haven, Conn.: Yale University Press.

HOVLAND, C. I., LUMSDAINE, A. A., & SHEFFIELD, F. D. (1949). *Experiments on mass communication.* Princeton, N.J.: Princeton University Press.

HOWARD, D. V. (1983). *Cognitive psychology: Memory, language, and thought.* New York: Macmillan.

HOYER, W. J., LABOUVIE, G. V., & BALTES, P. B. (1973). Modification of response speed deficits and intellectual performance in the elderly. *Human Development, 16,* 233–242.

HOYLE, G. (1983). *Muscles and their neural control.* New York: Wiley.

HUBEL, D. H., & WIESEL, T. N. (1962). Receptive fields, binocular interaction and functional architecture in the cat's visual cortex. *Journal of Physiology* (London), *160,* 106–154.

HUBEL, D. H., & WIESEL, T. N. (1965). Receptive fields and functional architecture in two nonstriate visual areas (18 and 19) of the cat. *Journal of Neurophysiology, 28,* 229–289.

HUBEL, D. H., & WIESEL, T. N. (1979). Brain mechanisms of vision. *Scientific American, 82,* 84–97.

HULL, C. L. (1932). The goal gradient hypothesis and maze learning. *Psychological Review, 39,* 25–43.

HULTSCH, D. F. (1971). Adult age differences in free classification and free recall. *Developmental Psychology, 4,* 338–342.

HULTSCH, D. F., & DIXON, R. A. (1984). Memory for text materials in adulthood. In P. B. Baltes & O. G. Brim, Jr. (Eds.), *Life-span development and behavior* (Vol. 6, pp. 77–108). New York: Academic Press.

HUMPHREYS, L. G. (1939). The effect of random alternation of reinforcement on the acquisition and extinction of conditioned eyelid reactions. *Journal of Experimental Psychology, 25,* 141–158.

HURVICH, L. M. (1981). *Color vision.* Sunderland, Mass.: Sinauer Associates.

HURVICH, L. M., & JAMESON, D. (1974). Opponent processes as a model of neural organization. *American Psychologist, 29,* 88–102.

HUSTON-STEIN, A., & HIGGINS-TRENK, A. (1978). Development of females from childhood through adulthood: Career and feminine orientations. In P. B. Baltes (Ed.), *Life-span development and behavior* (Vol. 1). New York: Academic Press.

HUTT, M. (1969). *The Hutt adaptation of the Bender-Gestalt Test* (2nd ed.). New York: Grune & Stratton.

ICKES, W. (1985). Attributional styles and self-conceptions: Implications for mental health and mental illness. In L. Abramson (Ed.), *Social-personal influence in clinical psychology.* New York: Guilford Press.

ILLINGWORTH, R. S. (1975). *The development of the infant and young child: Normal and abnormal.* Edinburgh: Churchill Livingstone.

INHELDER, B., & PIAGET, J. (1958). *The growth of logical thinking from childhood to adolescence.* New York: Basic Books.

INOUYE, E. (19610. Similarity and dissimilarity of schizophrenia in twins. Proceedings of the Third World Congress of Psychiatry (Vol. 1). Toronto: University of Toronto Press.

INSKO, C. A. (1965). Verbal reinforcement of attitude. *Journal of Personality and Social Psychology, 2,* 621–623.

IZARD, C. E. (1977). *Human emotions.* New York: Plenum Press.

IZARD, C., HUEBNER, R. R., RISSER, D., MCGINNES, G. C., & DOUGHTERTY, L. M. (1980). The young infant's ability to produce discrete emotional expressions. *Developmental Psychology, 16,* 132–140.

JACKSON, C. M. (1929). Some aspects of form and growth. In W. J. Robbins, S. Brody, A. F. Hogan, C. M. Jackson, & C. W. Green (Eds.), *Growth.* New Haven, Conn.: Yale University Press.

JACKSON, J. M., & PADGETT, V. R. (1982). With a little help from my friend: Social loafing and the Lennon-McCartney songs. *Personality and Social Psychology Bulletin, 8,* 672–677.

JACOBY, L. L., & CRAIK, F. I. M. (1979). Effects of elaboration of processing at encoding and retrieval: Trace distinctiveness and recovery of initial context. In L. S. Cermak & F. I. M. Craik (Eds.), *Levels of processing in human memory.* Hillsdale, N.J.: Lawrence Erlbaum.

JAFFE, J. H. (1980). Drug addiction and drug abuse. In A. G. Gilman, L. S. Goodman, & A. Gilman (Eds.), *The pharmacological basis of therapeutics* (6th ed.) (pp. 535–584). New York: Macmillan.

JAMES, W. (1980). *The principles of psychology.* New York: Holt.

JAMISON, K. R., GERNER, R. H., HAMMEN, C., & PADESKY, C. (1980). Clouds and silver linings: Experiences associated with primary affective disorders. *American Journal of Psychiatry, 137,* 198–202.

JANIS, I. L. (1972). *Victims of group think.* Boston: Houghton Mifflin.

JANIS, I. L. (1982). *Victims of group think: A psychological study of foreign-policy decisions and fiascos* (rev. ed.). Boston: Houghton Mifflin.

JANIS, I. L., & FESHBACK, S. (1953). Effects of fear-arousing communications. *Journal of Abnormal and Social Psychology, 48,* 78–92.

JARVIK, M. E. (1979). Tolerance to the effects of tobacco. In N. A. Krasnegor (Ed.), *Cigarette smoking as a dependence process.* National Institute on Drug Abuse, Department of Health, Education and Welfare, Publication No. (ADM) 79-800.

JAVAID, J. I., FISCHMAN, M. W., SCHUSTER, C. R., DEKIRMENJIAN, H., & DAVIS, J. M. (1978). Cocaine plasma concentration: Relation to physiological and subjective effects in humans. *Science, 202,* 227–228.

JENKINS, J. J. (1974). Remember that old theory of memory? Well forget it. *American Psychologist, 29,* 785–795.

JENKINS, J. G., & DALLENBACH, K. H. (1924). Oblivescence during sleep and waking. *American Journal of Psychology, 35,* 605–612.

JENSEN, A. R. (1969). How much can we boost IQ and scholastic achievement? *Harvard Educational Review, 39,* 1–123.

JENSEN, A. R. (1973). *Educability and group differences.* New York: Harper & Row.

JENSEN, A. R. (1980). *Bias in mental testing.* New York: Free Press.

JESSOR, R., COSTA, F., JESSOR, L., & DONOVAN, J. E. (1983). The time of first intercourse: A prospective study. *Journal of Personality and Social Psychology, 44,* 608–626.

JOFFE, J. M. (1969). *Prenatal determinants of behavior.* Oxford: Pergamon Press.

JOHNSON, B., & MORSE, H. A. (1968). Injured children and their parents. *Children, 15,* 147–152.

JOHNSON, J., ETTEMA, J., & DAVIDSON, T. (1980). An evaluation of *FREESTYLE:* A television series to reduce sex-role stereotypes. Ann Arbor: Institute for Social Research, University of Michigan.

JOHNSON, M. K., BRANSFORD, J. D., & SOLOMON, S. K. (1973). Memory for tactic implications of sentences. *Journal of Experimental Psychology, 98,* 203–205.

JOHNSON, N. (1965). The psychological reality of phase structure rules. *Journal of Verbal Learning and Verbal Behavior, 4,* 469–475.

JOHNSON, R. D., & DOWNING, L. T. (1979). Deindividuation and valence of cues: Effects of prosocial and antisocial behavior. *Journal of Personality and Social Psychology, 37,* 1532–1538.

JOHNSON, S., & LOBITZ, G. (1974). The personal and marital adjustment of parents as related to observed child deviance and parenting behaviors. *Journal of Abnormal Child Psychology, 2,* 193–207.

JONES, E. E., & DAVIS, K. E. (1965). From acts to dispositions: The attribution process in person perception. In L. Berkowitz (Ed.), *Advances in experimental social psychology* (Vol. 2). New York: Academic Press.

JONES, E. E., & NISBETT, R. E. (1971). *The actor and the observer: Divergent perceptions of the causes of behavior. Attributions: Perceiving the causes of behavior.* Morristown, N.J.: General Learning Press.

JONES, M. C., & BAYLEY, N. (1950). Physical maturing among boys as related to behavior. *Journal of Educational Psychology, 41,* 129–148.

JULIEN, R. M. (1981). *A primer of drug action* (3rd ed.). San Francisco: W. H. Freeman.

JUNG, C. G. (1959). The archetypes and the collective unconscious. In *Collected Works* (Vol. 9, Part I). Princeton, N.J.: Princeton University Press. (First German edition, 1936–1955.)

JUNG, C. G. (1960). *Collected works.* H. Read, M. Fordham, & G. Adler (Eds.). Princeton, N.J.: Princeton University Press.

KAGAN, J. (1969). Inadequate evidence and illogical conclusions. *Harvard Educational Review, 39,* 274–277.

KAGAN, J., & KLEIN, R. E. (1973). Cross-cultural perspectives on early development. *American Psychologist, 28,* 947–961.

KALISH, R. A. (1976). Death and dying in a social context. In R. H. Binstock & E. Shanas (Eds.), *Handbook of aging and the social sciences.* New York: Van Nostrand Reinhold.

KALLMANN, F. J. (1946). The genetic theory of schizophrenia: An analysis of 691 schizophrenic twin index families. *American Journal of Psychiatry, 103,* 309–322.

KALVEN, H. G., JR., & ZEISEL. H. (1966). *The American jury.* Boston: Little Brown.

KAMIN, L. (1974). *The science and politics of I.Q.* Hillsdale, N.J.: Lawrence Erlbaum.

KANDEL, D. B., & LESSER, G. S. (1969). Paternal and peer influences on educational plans of adolescents. *American Sociological Review, 34,* 213–223.

KANDEL, E. R. (1981). Nerve cells and behavior. In E. R. Kandel & J. H. Schwartz (Eds.), *Principles of neural science* (pp. 14–23). New York: Elsevier/North-Holland.

KANFER, F. H. (1970). Self-regulation: Research issues and speculations. In C. Neuringer & J. L. Michael (Eds.), *Behavior modification in clinical psychology.* New York: Appleton-Century-Crofts.

KANNER, A. D., COYNE, J. C., SCHAEFER, C., & LAZARUS, R. S. (1981). Comparison of two modes of stress management: Daily hassles and uplifts versus major life events. *Journal of Behavioral Medicine, 4,* 1–39.

KANNER, L. (1944). Early infantile autism. *Journal of Pediatrics, 25,* 211–217.

KANTER, R. M. (1972). Commitment and internal organization of millenial movements. *American Behavioral Scientist, 16*(2), 219–243.

KAPLAN, J. R., MANUCK, S. B., CLARKSON, T. B., LUSSO, F. M., TAUB, D. M., & MILLER, E. W. (1983). Social stress and atherosclerosis in normocholesterolemic monkeys. *Science, 220,* 733–735.

KARMILOFF-SMITH, A. (1977). More about the same: Children's understanding of post-articles. *Journal of Child Language 4,* 377–394.

KASL, S. V., & COBB, S. (1970). Blood pressure changes in men undergoing job loss: A preliminary report. *Psychosomatic Medicine, 32,* 19–38.

KASL, S. V., GORE, S., & COBB, S. (1975). The experience of losing a job: Reported changes in health, symptoms, and illness behavior. *Psychosomatic Medicine, 37,* 106–122.

KASSARJAN, H., & COHEN, J. (1965). Cognitive dissonance and consumer behavior. *California Management Review, 8,* 55–64.

REFERENCES

Kassin, S. M., & Wrightsman, L. S. (1979). On the requirements of proof: The timing of judicial instruction and mock juror verdicts. *Journal of Personality and Social Psychology, 37,* 1877–1887.

Katchadourian, H. (1977). *The biology of adolescence.* San Francisco: W. H. Freeman.

Kaufman, L., & Rock, I. (1962). The moon illusion. *Scientific American, 207,* 120–130.

Kaufmann, H. (1968). *Introduction to the study of human behavior.* Philadelphia: Saunders.

Kazdin, A. E. (1974). Covert modeling, model similarity, and reduction of avoidance behavior. *Behavior Therapy, 5,* 325–340.

Kazdin, A. E. (1977). *The token economy: A review and evaluation.* New York: Plenum press.

Kazdin, A. E. (1979). Imagery elaboration and self-efficacy in the covert modeling treatment of unassertive behavior. *Journal of Consulting and Clinical Psychology, 47,* 725–733.

Kazdin, A. E. (1982). Single-case experimental designs. In P. C. Kendall & J. N. Butcher (Eds.), *Handbook of research methods in clinical psychology.* New York: Wiley.

Kazdin, A. E., & Wilcoxon, L. A. (1976). Systematic desensitization and nonspecific treatment effects: A methodological evaluation. *Psychological Bulletin, 83,* 729–758.

Kazdin, A. E., & Wilson, G. T. (1978). *Evaluation of behavior therapy: Issues, evidence, and research strategies.* Cambridge, Mass.: Ballinger.

Kelley, H. H. (1967). Attribution theory in social psychology. In D. Levine (Ed.), *Nebraska symposium on motivation.* Lincoln: University of Nebraska Press.

Kelley, K. (1982). Population size or density effects on eight social indices. Unpublished manuscript, State University of New York at Albany.

Kellogg, W. N., & Kellogg, L. A. (1933). *The ape and the child.* New York: McGraw-Hill.

Kendall, P. C. (1978). Anxiety: States, traits, situations? *Journal of Consulting and Clinical Psychology, 46,* 280–287.

Kendall, P. C. (1981). Cognitive-behavioral interventions with children. In B. Lahey & A. E. Kazdin (Eds.), *Advances in child clinical psychology* (Vol. 4). New York: Plenum.

Kendall, P. C. (1982). Integration: Behavior therapy and other schools of thought. *Behavior Therapy, 13,* 559–571.

Kendall, P. C. (1983). Methodology and cognitive-behavioral assessment. *Behavioural Psychotherapy, 11,* 63–74.

Kendall, P. C., & Bemis, K. M. (1983). Thought and action in psychotherapy: Cognitive-behavioral approaches. In M. Hersen, A. E. Kazdin, & A. S. Bellack (Eds.), *The clinical psychology handbook.* Elmsford, N.Y.: Pergamon Press.

Kendall, P. C., & Braswell, L. (1982). Cognitive-behavioral self-control therapy for children: A components analysis. *Journal of Consulting and Clinical Psychology, 50,* 672–689.

Kendall, P. C., & Braswell, L. (1985). *Cognitive-behavioral therapy for impulsive children.* New York: Guilford Press.

Kendall, P. C., & Korgeski, G. P. (1979). Assessment and cognitive-behavioral interventions. *Cognitive Therapy and Research, 3,* 1–21.

Kendler, H. H., & Kendler, T. S. (1962). Vertical and horizontal processes in problem solving. *Psychological Review, 69,* 1–16.

Kendrick, M. J., Craig, K. D., Lawson, D. M., & Davidson, P. O. (1982). Cognitive and behavioral therapy for musical-performance anxiety. *Journal of Consulting and Clinical Psychology, 50,* 353–362.

Kerr, N. L., Atkin, R. S., Stasser, G., Meek, D., Holt, R. W., & Davis, J. H. (1976). Guilt beyond a reasonable doubt: Effects of concept definition and assigned decision rule on judgments of mock jurors. *Journal of Personality and Social Psychology, 34,* 282–294.

Keynes, R. D. (1979). Ion channels in the nerve-cell membrane. *Scientific American, 240,* 126–135.

Kiesler, D. J. (1966). Some myths of psychotherapy research and the search for a paradigm. *Psychological Bulletin, 65,* 110–136.

Kilmann, P. R., Albert, B. M., & Satile, W. M. (1975). The relationship between locus of control, structure of therapy, and outcome. *Journal of Consulting and Clinical Psychology, 43,* 588.

Kimble, G. A. (1961). *Hilgand and Marquis' conditioning and learning.* New York: Appleton-Century-Crofts.

Kimble, G. A., Mann, L. I., & Dufort, R. H. (1955). Classical and instrumental eyelid conditioning. *Journal of Experimental Psychology, 49,* 407–417.

Kinsey, A. C., Pomeroy, W. B., & Martin, C. E. (1948). *Sexual behavior in the human male.* Philadelphia: Saunders.

Kinsey, A. C., Pomeroy, W. B., Martin, C. E., & Beghard, P. H. (1953). *Sexual behavior in the human female.* Philadelphia: Saunders.

Kintsch, W. (1974). *The representation of meaning in memory.* Hillsdale, N.J.: Lawrence Erlbaum.

Kintsch, W. (1978). On comprehending stories. In M. A. Just & P. A. Carpenter (Eds.), *Cognitive processes in comprehension.* Hillsdale, N.J.: Lawrence Erlbaum.

Kinzel, A. S. (1970). Body-buffer zone in violent prisoners. *American Journal of Psychiatry, 127,* 59–64.

Klaus, R. A., & Gray, S. W. (1968). The early training project for disadvantaged children: A report after five years. *Monographs of the Society for Research in Child Development, 33* (Serial No. 120).

Klein, D., & Seligman, M. E. P. (1976). Reversal of performance deficits in learned helplessness and depression. *Journal of Abnormal Psychology, 85,* 11–26.

Klein, K. E., Wegmann, H. M., & Hunt, B. I. (1972). Desynchronization of body temperature and performance circadian rhythm as a result of outgoing and home-going transmeridian flights. *Aerospace Medicine, 43,* 119–132.

Klein, P. S., Forbes, G. B., & Nader, P. R. (1975). Effects of starvation in infancy (pyloric-stenosis) or subsequent learning abilities. *Journal of Pediatrics, 87,* 8–15.

Kleitman, N. (1963). *Sleep and wakefulness* (2nd ed.). Chicago: University of Chicago Press.

Kleitman, N., & Englemann, T. G. (1953). Sleep characteristics of infants. *Journal of Applied Physiology, 6,* 269–282.

KLERMAN, G. L. (1972). Drug therapy of clinical depressions. *Journal of Psychological Research, 9,* 253–270.

KLINGER, E. (1975). Consequences of commitment to and disengagement from incentives. *Psychological Review, 82,* 1–25.

KLUCKHOHN, C., & MURRAY, H. (1948). Personality information: The determinants. In C. Kluckhohn & H. Murray (Eds.), *Personality in nature, society, and culture.* New York: Knopf.

KNAPP, M. L. (1978). *Nonverbal communication in human interaction* (2nd ed). New York: Holt, Rinehart & Winston.

KOESTER, J. (1981). Resting membrane potential. In. E. R. Kandel & J. H. Schwartz (Eds.), *Principles of neural science* (pp. 27–35). New York: Elsevier/North-Holland.

KOFFKA, K. (1935). *Principles of Gestalt psychology.* New York: Harcourt Brace.

KOGAN, N. (1979). Beliefs, attitudes and stereotypes about old people: A new look at some old issues. *Research on Aging, 1,* 11–36.

KÖHLER, W. (1925). *The mentality of apes.* New York: Harcourt Brace.

KÖHLER, W. (1959). Gestalt psychology today. *American Psychologist, 14,* 727–737.

KONEČNI, V. J., LIBUSER, L., MORTON, H., & EBBESEN, E. B. (1975). Effects of a violation of personal space on escape and helping responses. *Journal of Experimental Social Psychology, 11,* 288–299.

KOTOVSKY, K., & SIMON, H. A. (1973). Empirical tests of a theory of human acquisition of concepts for sequential patterns. *Cognitive Psychology, 3,* 399–424.

KRAMER, J. C., FISCHMAN, V. S., & LITTLEFIELD, D. C. (1967). Amphetamine abuse. *Journal of the American Medical Association, 201,* 305–309.

KRASNER, L. (1971). Behavior therapy. *Annual Review of Psychology, 22,* 483–532.

KRETSCHMER, E. (1925). *Physique and character.* New York: Harcourt Brace. (Translated by W. J. H. Spnaff from *Korperbau und Charakter.* Berlin: Springer, 1921.)

KRINGLER, E. (1967). Heredity and social factors in schizophrenic twins: An epidemiological-clinical study. In J. Romano (Ed.), *The origins of schizophrenia.* New York: Excerpta Medica Foundation.

KÜBLER-ROSS, E. (1969). *On death and dying.* New York: Macmillan.

KÜBLER-ROSS, E. (1974). *Questions and answers on death and dying.* New York: Macmillan.

KULIK, J. A., & BROWN, R. (1979). Frustration, attribution of blame, and aggression. *Journal of Experimental Social Psychology, 15,* 183–194.

LABOUVIE-VIEF, G. (1977). Adult cognitive development: In search of alternative interpretations. *Merrill-Palmer Quarterly, 23,* 227–263.

LACHMAN, J. L., LACHMAN, R., & THRONESBERY, C. (1979). Metamemory through the adult life span. *Developmental Psychology, 15,* 503–551.

LAIRD, J. D. (1974). Self-attribution of emotion: The effects of expressive behavior on the quality of emotional experience. *Journal of Personality and Social Psychology, 29,* 475–486.

LAMM, H., & TROMMSDORF, G. (1973). Group versus individual performance on tasks requiring ideational proficiency (brainstorming): A review. *European Journal of Social Psychology, 3,* 361–388.

LANDAU, B. (1980). *Will the real grandmother please stand up: The psychological reality of multiple meaning representations.* Unpublished manuscript, University of Pennsylvania.

LANDESMAN-DWYER, S., KELLER, S. L., & STREISSGUTH, A. P. (1977). *Naturalistic observations of newborns: Effects of maternal alcohol intake.* Paper presented at the American Psychological Association Annual Convention, San Francisco.

LANDMAN, J. T., & DAWES, R. M. (1982). Psychotherapy outcome: Smith and Glass' conclusions stand up under scrutiny. *American Psychologist, 37,* 504–516.

LANGER, E. J. (1981). Old age: An artifact? In J. McGaugh, J. G. March, & S. B. Kiesler (Eds.), *Aging: Biology and behavior* (pp. 255–282). New York: Academic Press.

LANGER, E. J., & BENEVENTO, A. (1978). Self-induced dependence. *Journal of Personality and Social Psychology, 36,* 886–893.

LANGER, E. J., & RODIN, J. (1976). The effects of choice and enhanced personal responsibility for the aged: A field experiment in an institutional setting. *Journal of Personality and Social Psychology, 34,* 191–198.

LANGER, E. J. & SAEGERT, S. (1977). Crowding and cognitive control. *Journal of Personality and Social Psychology, 35,* 175–182.

LATANÉ, B. (1981). The psychology of social impact. *American Psychologist, 36,* 343–356.

LATANÉ, B., & NIDA, S. (1981). Ten years of research on group size and helping. *Psychological Bulletin, 89,* 308–324.

LATANÉ, B., WILLIAMS, K., & HARKINS, S. (1979). Many hands make light the work: The causes and consequences of social loafing. *Journal of Personality and Social Psychology, 37,* 822–832.

LAYZER, D. (1974). Heritability analyses of IQ scores: Science or numerology. *Science, 1983,* 1259–1266.

LAZARUS, R. S. (1980). The stress and coping paradigm. In L. A. Bond & J. C. Rosen (Eds.), *Competence and coping during adulthood.* Hanover, N.H.: University Press of New England.

LAZARUS. R. S., & FOLKMAN, S. (1984). *Stress, appraisal, and coping.* New York: Springer.

LAZARUS, R. S., & LAUNIER, R. (1978). Stress-related transactions between person and environment. In L. A. Pervin & N. Lewis (Eds.), *Perspectives in interactional psychology.* New York: Plenum Press.

LEHFELDT, H. (1971). Psychology of contraceptive failure. *Medical Aspects of Human Sexuality, 5,* 68–77.

LEHRMAN, D. S. (1970). Semantic and conceptual issues in the nature-nurture problem. In L. R. Aronson, E. Tobach, D. S. Lehrman, & J. S. Rosenblatt (Eds.), *Development and evolution of behavior: Essays in memory of T. C. Schneirla.* San Francisco: W. H. Freeman.

LENNEBERG, E. H. (1967). *Biological functions of language.* New York: Wiley.

LEONARD, L. B., SCHWARTZ, R. G., FOLGER, M. K., NEWHOFF,

REFERENCES

M., & WILCOX, M. J. (1979). Children's imitation of lexical items. *Child Development, 50,* 19–27.

LEPPER, M. R., GREENE, D., & NISBETT, R. E. (1973). Undermining children's intrinsic interest with extrinsic rewards: A test of the "overjustification" hypothesis. *Journal of Personality and Social Psychology, 28,* 129–137.

LERNER, M. J. (1980). *The belief in a just world: A fundamental delusion.* New York: Plenum Press.

LERNER, M. J., & MILLER, D. T. (1978). Just world research and the attribution process: Looking back and ahead. *Psychological Bulletin, 85,* 1030–1051.

LERNER, R. M. (1969). The development of stereotyped expectancies of body-build behavior relation. *Child Development, 40,* 137–141.

LERNER, R. M. (1976). *Concepts and theories of human development.* Reading, Mass.: Addison-Wesley.

LERNER, R. M. (1981). Adolescent development: Scientific study in the 1980s. *Youth and Society, 12,* 251–275.

LERNER, R. M. (1982). Children and adolescents as producers of their own development. *Developmental Review, 2,* 342–370.

LERNER, R. M., & HULTSCH, D. F. (1983). *Human development: A life-span perspective.* New York: McGraw-Hill.

LERNER, R. M., & KORN, S. J. (1972). The development of body build stereotypes in males. *Child Development, 43,* 912–920.

LERNER, R. M., & SPANIER, G. B. (1980). *Adolescent development: A life-span perspective.* New York: McGraw-Hill.

LESTER, B. M. (1975). Cardiac habituation of the orienting response to an auditory signal in infants of varying nutritional status. *Developmental Psychology, 11,* 432–442.

LEVENTHAL, H., & NILES, P. (1965). Persistence of influence for varying duration of response to threat stimuli. *Psychological Reports, 16,* 223–233.

LEVINSON, D. J. (1978). *The seasons of a man's life.* New York: Knopf.

LEWINSOHN, P. M. (1974). A behavioral approach to depression. In R. J. Friedman & M. M. Katz (Eds.), *The psychology of depression: Contemporary theory and research.* Washington, D.C.: Winston.

LEWINSOHN, P. M., BIGLAN, A., & ZEISS, A. M. (1976). Behavioral treatment of depression. In P. O. Davidson (Ed.), *The behavioral management of anxiety, depression, and pain.* New York: Brunner/Mazel.

LEWIS, M., & BROOKS, J. (1974). Self, other and fear: Infants' reactions to people. In M. Lewis & L. Rosenblum (Eds.), *The origins of fear.* New York: Wiley.

LEWIS, M., & BROOKS-GUNN, J. (1979). Toward a theory of social cognition: The development of self. *New Directions for Child Development, 4,* 1–20.

LEWIS, M., & MCGURK, H. (1972). Evaluation of infant intelligence. *Science, 178,* 1174–1177.

LEWIS, M., & ROSENBLUM, L. A. (Eds.) (1974). *The effect of the infant on its caregiver.* New York: Wiley.

LEZAK, M. D. (1976). *Neuropsychological assessment.* New York: Oxford University Press.

LIDZ, T., CORNELISON, A., & FLECK, S. (1965). *Schizophrenia and the family.* New York: International Universities Press.

LIEBERMAN, M. A. (1975). Adaptive processes in late life. In N. Datan & L. H. Ginsberg (Eds.), *Life-span developmental psychology: Normative life crises.* New York: Academic Press.

LIEBERMAN, M. A., YALOM, I. D., & MILES, M. B. (1973). *Encounter groups: First facts.* New York: Basic Books.

LIEBERT, R. M., & WICKS-NELSON, R. (1981). *Developmental psychology.* Englewood Cliffs, N.J.: Prentice-Hall.

LIGHT, R. (1973). Abuse and neglected children in America: A study of alternative policies. *Harvard Educational Review, 43,* 556–598.

LINDE, S. M., & SAVARY, L. M. (1974). *The joy of sleep.* New York: Harper & Row.

LINDSAY, P. H., & NORMAN, D. A. (1977). *Human information processing.* New York: Academic Press.

LIPSKY, M. J., KASSINOVE, H., & MILLER, N. J. (1980). Effects of rational-emotive therapy, rational role reversal, and rational-emotive imagery on the emotional adjustment of community mental health center patients. *Journal of Consulting and Clinical Psychology, 48,* 366–374.

LISKA, K. (1981). *Drugs and the human body.* New York: Macmillan.

LLOYD-STILL, J. D., HURWITZ, I., WOLFF, P. H., & SCHWACHMORE, H. (1974). Intellectual development after severe malnutrition in infancy. *Pediatrics, 54,* 306–311.

LOFTUS, E. F. (1975). Leading questions and the eyewitness report. *Cognitive Psychology, 7,* 560–572.

LOFTUS, E. T. (1979). *Eyewitness testimony.* Cambridge, MA: Harvard University Press.

LOFTUS, E. T., & PALMER, J. C. (1974). Reconstruction of automobile destruction: An example of the interaction between language and memory. *Journal of Verbal Learning and Verbal Behavior, 13,* 585–589.

LOO, C. M. (1979). A factor analytic approach to the study of spatial density effects on preschoolers. *Journal of Population, 2,* 47–68.

LORENZ, K. (1966). *On aggression.* New York: Harcourt, Brace, & World.

LOVAAS, O. I., & KOEGEL, R. L. (1973). Behavior therapy with autistic children. In C. E. Thoresen (Ed.), *Behavior modification in education.* Chicago: University of Chicago Press.

LOWENTHAL, M. F., THURNHER, M., & CHIRIBOGA, D. (1975). *Four stages of life.* San Francisco: Jossey-Bass.

LUBCHENCO, L. O. (1976). *The high risk infant.* Philadelphia: Saunders.

LUBORSKY, L., SINGER, B., & LUBORSKY, L. (1975). Comparative studies of psychotherapies: Is it true that "Everyone has won and all must have prizes?" *Archives of General Psychiatry, 32,* 995–1008.

LUCHINS, A. S. (1942). Mechanization in problem solving. *Psychological Monographs, 54* (Whole No. 248).

LURIA, A. (1968). *The mind of a mnemonist* (L. Solotaroff, trans.). New York: Basic Books.

LURIA, A. R. (1970). The functional organization of the brain. *Scientific American, 222,* 66–79.

LYLE, J., & HOFFMAN, H. (1972). Children's use of television and other media. In E. A. Rubinstein, G. A. Comstock, & J. P. Murray (Eds.), *Television and social behavior,* Vol. 4: *Television in day-to-day life: Patterns of use.* Washington, D.C.: U.S. Government Printing Office.

MAAS, H. S., & KUYPERS, J. A. (1974). *From thirty to seventy.* San Francisco: Jossey-Bass.

MADDOX, G. L. (1966). Retirement as a social event in the United States. Abridged from J. C. McKinney & F. T. deVyuer (Eds.), *Aging and social policy* (pp. 119–135). New York: Appleton-Century-Crofts.

MAHONEY, M. J. (1974). *Cognition and behavior modification.* Cambridge, Mass.: Ballinger.

MALAMUTH, N., & CHECK, J. V. P. (1980). Penile tumescence and perceptual responses to rape as a function of victim's perceived reactions. *Journal of Applied Social Psychology, 10,* 528–547.

MALAMUTH, N. M., & CHECK, J. V. P. (1981). The effects of mass media exposure on acceptance of violence against women: A field experiment. *Journal of Research in Personality, 15,* 436–446.

MALAMUTH, N. M., & DONNERSTEIN, E. (1983). *Pornography and sexual aggression.* New York: Academic Press.

MALAMUTH, N. M., & SPINNER, B. (1980). A longitudinal content analysis of sexual violence in the best-selling erotic magazines. *The Journal of Sex Research, 16,* 226–237.

MANDLER, G. (1967). Organization and memory. In D. W. Spence & J. T. Spence (Eds.), *The psychology of learning and motivation* (Vol. 1). New York: Academic Press.

MANDLER, G. (1975). *Mind and emotion.* New York: Wiley.

MANGOLD, R., SOKOLOFF, L., CONNER, E., KLEINERMAN, J., THERMAN, P. O. G., & KETY, S. S. (1955). The effects of sleep and lack of sleep on the cerebral circulation and metabolism of normal young men. *Journal of Clinical Investigation, 34,* 1092–1100.

MANSON, T. C., & SNYDER, M. (1977). Actors, observers and the attribution process: Toward a reconceptualization. *Journal of Experimental Social Psychology, 13,* 89–111.

MARAÑON, G. (1924). Contribution á etude de l'action emotive de l'adrenaline. *Revue Française Endocrinologie, 2,* 301–315.

MARKS, D., & KAMMANN, R. (1980). *The psychology of the psychic.* Buffalo, N.Y.: Prometheus Books.

MARKUS, H. (1978). The effect of mere presence on social facilitation: An unobtrusive test. *Journal of Experimental Social Psychology, 14,* 389–397.

MARSHALL, G. O., & ZIMBARDO, P. G. (1979). Affective consequences of inadequately explained physiological arousal. *Journal of Personality Social Psychology, 37,* 970–988.

MARTIN, A. R. (1977). Junctional transmission. II. Presynaptic mechanisms. In E. R. Kandel (Ed.), *Handbook of physiology,* Sec. 1: *The nervous system* (pp. 329–355). Bethesda, Md.: American Physiological Society.

MARTIN, H. P., BEEZLEY, P., CONWAY, E. F., & KEMPE, C. H. (1974). The development of abused children. Part I. A review of the literature. Part II. Physical, neurologic, and intellectual outcome. *Advances in Pediatrics, 21,* 15–73.

MASH, E. J., TERDAL, L., & ANDERSON, K. (1973). The response-class matrix: A procedure for recording parent-child interactions. *Journal of Consulting and Clinical Psychology, 40,* 163–184.

MASLACH, C. (1979). The emotional consequences of arousal without reason. In C. E. Izard (Ed.), *Emotion in personality and psychopathology.* New York: Plenum Press.

MASLACH, C., & JACKSON, S. E. (1979). Burned-out cops and their families. *Psychology Today,* May, pp. 59–62.

MASLOW, A. H. (1968). *Toward a psychology of being* (2nd ed.). New York: Van Nostrand.

MASLOW, A. H. (1970). *Motivation and personality* (rev. ed.). New York: Harper & Row.

MASTERS, W. H., & JOHNSON, V. E. (1966). *Human sexual response.* Boston: Little, Brown.

MASTERS, W. H., & JOHNSON, V. E. (1970). *Human sexual inadequacy.* Boston: Little, Brown.

MATARAZZO, J. D. (1972). *Wechsler's measurement and appraisal of adult intelligence.* Baltimore, Williams & Wilkins.

MATAS, L., AREND, R. A., & SROUFE, L. A. (1978). Continuity of adaptation in the second year: The relationship between quality of attachment and later competence. *Child Development, 49,* 547–556.

MATTIS, S. (1976). Mental status examination for organic mental syndromes in the elderly patient. In L. Bellak & T. E. Karasu (Eds.), *Geriatric psychology.* New York: Grune & Stratton.

MCCLANE, T. K., & MARTIN, W. R. (1976). Subjective and physiologic effects of morphine, pentobarbital, and meprobamate. *Clinical Pharmacology and Therapeutics, 20,* 192–198.

MCCLELLAND, D. C., ATKINSON, J. W., CLARK, R. W., & LOWELL, E. L. (1953). *The achievement motive.* New York: Appleton-Century-Crofts.

MCDOUGALL, W. (1926). *An introduction to social psychology* (Rev. ed.). Boston: Luce.

MCEWEN, B. S. (1976). Interactions between hormones and nerve tissue. *Scientific American, 235,* 48–58.

MCKENZIE, B. E., & DAY, R. H. (1976). Infants' attention to stationary and moving objects at different distances. *Australian Journal of Psychology, 28,* 45–51.

MCLEAN, P. D. (1976). Therapeutic decision-making in the behavioral treatment of depression. In P. O. Davidson (Ed.), *The behavioral management of anxiety, depression, and pain.* New York: Brunner/Mazel.

MCLEAN, P. D., & HAKSTIAN, A. R. (1979). Clinical depression: Comparative efficacy of outpatient treatments. *Journal of Consulting and Clinical Psychology, 47,* 818–836.

MEDDIS, R. (1979). The evolution and function of sleep. In D. A. Oakley & H. C. Plotkin (Eds.), *Brain, behavior, and evolution.* London: Methuen.

MEDVEDEV, Z. A. (1974). Caucasus and Altay longevity: A biological or social problem? *The Gerontologist, 14,* 381–387.

MEDVEDEV, Z. A. (1975). Aging and longevity: New approaches and new perspectives. *The Gerontologist, 15,* 196–201.

MEEHL, P. E. (1959). Some ruminations on the validation of clinical procedures. *Canadian Journal of Psychology, 13,* 103–128.

MEEHL, P. E. (1962). Schizotaxia, schizotypy, schizophrenia. *American Psychologist, 17,* 827–838.

MEGARGEE, E. I. (1972). *The California psychological inventory handbook.* San Francisco: Jossey-Bass.

MEICHENBAUM, D. (1971). Examination of model characteristics in reducing avoidance behavior. *Journal of Personality and Social Psychology, 17,* 298–307.

MEICHENBAUM, D. (1977). *Cognitive-behavior modification: An integrative approach.* New York: Plenum Press.

MENDELSON, M. (1974). *Psychoanalytic concepts of depression* (2nd ed.). New York: Spectrum Publications.

MERBAUM, M., & BUTCHER, J. N. (1982). Therapists' liking their psychotherapy patients: Some issues related to severity of disorder and treatability. *Psychotherapy: Theory, Research, and Practice, 19,* 69–76.

MERCER, J. R., & LEWIS, J. F. (1979). *SOMPA: For the meaningful assessment of culturally different children.* New York: The Psychological Corporation.

MERLUZZI, T. V., GLASS, C. R., & GENEST, M. (Eds.). (1981). *Cognitive assessment.* New York: Guilford.

MERVIS, C. B., & ROSCH, E. (1981). Categorization of natural objects. *Annual Review of Psychology, 32,* 89–115.

MEYERS, A., & CRAIGHEAD, W. E. (EDS.). (1984). *Cognitive behavior therapy with children.* N.Y.: Plenum.

MILGRAM, S. (1963). Behavioral study of obedience. *Journal of Abnormal and Social Psychology, 67,* 371–378.

MILGRAM, S. (1965). Some conditions of obedience and disobedience to authority. *Human Relations, 18,* 57–76.

MILGRAM, S. (1974). *Obedience to authority.* New York: Harper & Row.

MILLER, D. T. (1976). Ego involvement and attributions for success and failure. *Journal of Personality and Social Psychology, 34,* 901–906.

MILLER, D. T., & MORETTI, M. M. (1985). The causal attributions of depressives: Self-serving or self-disserving? In L. Alloy (Ed.), *Cognitive processes in depression.* New York: Guilford Press.

MILLER, D. T., & ROSS, M. (1975). Self-serving biases in attribution of causality: Fact or fiction? *Psychological Bulletin, 82,* 213–225.

MILLER, G. A. (1956). The magical number seven plus or minus two: Some limits on our capacity for processing information. *Psychological Review, 63,* 81–97.

MILLER, G. A., & TAYLOR, W. G. (1948). The perception of repeated bursts of noise. *Journal of Acoustical Society of America, 20,* 171–182.

MILLER, N. E. (1941). The frustration-aggression hypothesis. *Psychological Review, 48,* 155–178.

MILLER, S. M. (1980). When is a little information a dangerous thing? Coping with stressful events by monitoring versus blunting. In S. Levine & H. Ursin (Eds.), *Coping and health.* New York: Plenum Press.

MILLON, T. (1981). *Disorders of personality.* New York: Wiley.

MILNER, B. (1966). Amnesia following operation on the temporal lobes. In C. W. M. Whitty & O. L. Zangwill (Eds.), *Amnesia.* London: Butterworth.

MINTZ, J., & KIESLER, D. J. (1982). Individualized measures of psychotherapy outcome. In P. C. Kendall & J. N. Butcher (Eds.), *Handbook of research methods in clinical psychology.* New York: Wiley.

MISCHEL, W. (1968). *Personality and assessment.* New York: Wiley.

MISCHEL, W. (1973). Toward a cognitive social learning reconceptualization of personality. *Psychological Review, 80,* 252–283.

MISHLER, E. G., & WAXLER, N. E. (1968). *Interaction in families: An experimental study of the family.* New York: Wiley.

MONTGOMERY, K., & COSTA, L. (1983). Concurrent validity of the Mattis Dementia Rating Scale. Paper presented at the Eleventh Annual Meeting of the International Neuropsychological Society, Lisbon, June.

MORELAND, R. L., & ZAJONC, R. B. (1980). Is stimulus recognition a necessary condition for the occurrence of exposure effects? *Science, 207,* 557–558.

MORELAND, R. L., & ZAJONC, R. B. (1982). Exposure effects in person perception: Familiarity, similarity, and attraction. *Journal of Experimental Social Psychology, 18,* 395–415.

MORGAN, C. D., & MURRAY, H. A. (1935). A method for investigating fantasies: The Thematic Apperception Test. *Archives of Neurology and Psychiatry, 34,* 289–306.

MORROW, W. R., & WILSON, R. C. (1961). Family relations of bright high-achieving and under-achieving high school boys. *Child Development, 32,* 501–510.

MOSCOVICI, S. (1976). *Social influence and social change.* New York: Academic Press.

MUIR, D., & FIELD, J. (1979). Newborn infants orient to sounds. *Child Development, 50,* 431–436.

MURDOCK, B. (1962). The serial position effect of free recall. *Journal of Experimental Psychology, 64,* 482–488.

MURRAY, H. A. (1943). *Thematic Apperception Test.* Pictures and manual. Cambridge, Mass.: Harvard University Press.

MUSSEN, P. H., CONGER, J. J., & KAGAN, J. (1979). *Child development and personality* (5th ed.). New York: Harper & Row.

MUSSEN, P. H., CONGER, J. J., KAGAN, J., & GEIWITZ, J. (1979). *Psychological development: A life-span approach.* New York: Harper & Row.

MUSSEN, P. H., & JONES, M. C. (1957). Self-conceptions, motivations, and interpersonal attitudes of late- and early-maturing boys. *Child Development, 28,* 249–256.

MYERS, D. G. (1983). *Social psychology.* New York: McGraw-Hill.

MYERS, F. H., JAWETZ, E., & GOLDFEIN, A. (1972). *Review of medical pharmacology* (3rd ed.) (p. 280). Los Altos, Calif.: Lange.

NAGASAKI, H., KITAHAMA, K., VALATX, J. L., & JOUVET, M. (1980). Sleep-promoting effect of the sleep-promoting substance (SPS) and delta sleep-inducing peptide (DSIP) in the mouse. *Brain Research, 192,* 276–280.

NAPOLITAN, D. A., & GOETHALS, G. R. (1979). The attribution of friendliness. *Journal of Experimental Social Psychology, 15,* 105–113.

National Center for Health Statistics (1980). *Monthly vital statistics report, provisional statistics.* U.S. Department of Health, Education and Welfare.

National Institute on Alcohol Abuse and Alcoholism (1980). *Facts about alcohol and alcoholism.* Department of Health and Human Services Publication No. (ADM) 80–31.

NAUS, M. J., GLUCKSBURG, S., & ORNSTEIN, P. A. (1972). Taxonomic word categories and memory search. *Cognitive Psychology, 3,* 643–654.

NEALE, J. M., & OLTMANNS, T. F. (1980). *Schizophrenia.* New York: Wiley.

NEISSER, U. (1976). *Cognition and reality.* San Francisco: W. H. Freeman.

NELSON, K. (1973). Structure and strategy in learning to talk. *Monographs of the Society for Research in Child Development, 38* (No. 149).

NELSON, T. O., & ROTHBART, R. (1972). Acoustic saving for items forgotten from long-term memory. *Journal of Experimental Psychology, 93,* 357–360.

NEMETH, C. (1976). Rules governing jury deliberations: A consideration of recent changes. In G. Bermant, C. Nemeth, & N. Vidmar (Eds.), *Psychology and the law.* Toronto: D. C. Heath.

NEUGARTEN, B. L. (1964). *Personality in middle and late life.* New York: Academic Press.

NEWBY, H. A. (1979) *Audiology* (4th ed.). Englewood Cliffs: Prentice Hall.

NEWELL, A. (1973). Artificial intelligence and the concept of mind. In R. C. Schank & K. M. Colby (Eds.), *Computer models of thought and language.* San Francisco: W. H. Freeman.

NEWELL, A., & SIMON, H. A. (1962). Computer simulation of human thinking. *Science, 134,* 2011–2017.

Newsweek. (1978, December 18). The cult of death.

NICHOLS, I. A., & SCHAUFFER, C. B. (1975). *Self-concept as a predictor of performance in college women.* Paper presented at the 83rd American Psychological Association Annual Convention, Chicago.

NIELSEN, Co., A. C. (1982, August 2). 1981 data cited by *U. S. News & World Report,* p. 29.

NISBETT, R. E., CAPUTO, C., LEGANT, P., & MARACEK, J. (1973). Behavior as seen by the actor and as seen by the observer. *Journal of Personality and Social Psychology, 27,* 154–164.

NOMIKOS, M. S., OPTON, E., JR., AVERILL, J. R., & LAZARUS, R. S. (1968). Surprise versus suspense in the production of stress reaction. *Journal of Personality and Social Psychology, 8,* 204–208.

NOWLIS, G. H., & KESSEN, W. (1976). Human newborns differentiate differing concentrations of sucrose and glucose. *Science, 191,* 865–866.

NOWLIS, V. (1965). Research with the Mood Adjective Check List. In S. S. Tomkins & C. E. Izard (Eds.), *Affect, cognition and personality.* New York: Springer.

NUCKOLLS, K. B., CASSEL, J., & KAPLAN, B. H. (1972). Psychosocial assets, life crisis, and the prognosis of pregnancy. *American Journal of Epidemiology, 95,* 431–441.

O'CONNELL, D. N., SHOR, R. E., & ORNE, M. T. (1970). Hypnotic age regression: An empirical and methodological analysis. *Journal of Abnormal Psychology* (Monograph Supplement No. 3), 1–32.

OFFER, D. (1969). *The psychological world of the teenager.* New York: Basic Books.

OKADA, S., & O'BRIEN, J. S. (1969). Tay-Sachs disease: Generalized absence of a beta-D-N-acetylhexosaminidase component. *Science, 165,* 698–700.

O'LEARY, K. D. (1980). Pills or skills for hyperactive children. *Journal of Applied Behavior Analysis, 13,* 191–204.

OLSON, J. M., & ZANNA, M. (1983). Attitudes and beliefs. In D. Perman & P. C. Cozby (Eds.), *Social psychology.* New York: Holt, Rinehart & Winston.

ORNE, M. T. (1975). Hypnosis. In G. Lindzey, C. Hall, & R. F. Thompson (Eds.), *Psychology* (pp. 150–154). New York: Worth.

ORVIS, B. R., KELLEY, H. H., & BUTLER, D. (1976). Attributional conflict in young couples. In J. Harvey, W. J. Ickes, & R. E. Kidd (Eds.), *New directions in attribution research* (Vol. 2). Hillsdale, NJ: Erlbaum.

OSBORN, A. F. (1957). *Applied imagination* (rev. ed.). New York: Scribner's.

PALAY, S. L., & CHAN-PALAY, V. (1977). General morphology of neurons and neuroglia. In E. R. Kandel (Ed.), *Handbook of physiology,* Sect. 1: *The nervous system* (pp. 5–37). Bethesda, Md.: American Physiological Society.

PALMER, F. H. (1977). *The effects of early childhood education intervention on school performance.* Unpublished manuscript, July.

PAPPENHEIMER, J. R., MILLER, T. B., & GOODRICH, C. A. (1967). Sleep-promoting effects of cerebrospinal fluid from sleep-deprived goats. *Proceedings of the National Academy of Sciences* (U.S.A.), *58,* 513–517.

PARKE, F., & SAWIN, D. (1975). *Infant characteristics and behavior as elicitors of maternal and paternal responsibility in the newborn period.* Paper presented at the biennial meeting of the Society for Research in Child Development, Denver, April.

PARKE, R. D., & COLLMER, C. (1975). Child abuse: An interdisciplinary review. In E. M. Hetherington (Ed.), *Review of child development research* (Vol. 5). Chicago: University of Chicago Press.

PARTEN, M., & NEWHALL, S. W. (1943). Social behavior of preschool children. In R. G. Barker, J. S. Kounin, & H. F. Wright (Eds.), *Child behavior and development.* New York: McGraw-Hill.

PATTERSON, F. G. (1978). The gestures of a gorilla: Language acquisition in another pongid. *Brain and Language, 5,* 72–97.

PATTERSON, G. R. (1977). Naturalistic observation in clinical assessment. *Journal of Abnormal Child Psychology, 5,* 309–322.

PATTERSON, G. R., & REID, J. B. (1970). Reciprocity and coercion: Two facets of social systems. In C. Neuringer & J. L. Michaels (Eds.), *Behavior modification in clinical psychology* (pp. 133–177). New York: Appleton.

PAUL, G. L. (1966). *Insight vs. desensitization in psychotherapy.* Stanford, Calif.: Stanford University Press.

PAULUS, P. B. (1979). Crowding. In P. B. Paulus (Ed.), *Psychology of group influence.* Hillsdale, N.J.: Lawrence Erlbaum.

PAVIO, A. (1971). *Imagery and verbal processes.* New York: Holt, Rinehart and Winston.

PAVLOV, I. P. (1927). *Conditioned reflexes.* London: Oxford University Press.

PAYKEL, E. S. (1974). Life stress and psychiatric disorder: Applications of the clinical approach. In B. S. Dohrenwend & B. P. Dohrenwend (Eds.), *Stressful life events: Their nature and effects.* New York: Wiley.

REFERENCES

Peale, N. V. (1952). *The power of positive thinking.* New York: Prentice-Hall.

Pearlin, L. I., & Schooler, C. (1978). The structure of coping. *Journal of Health and Social Behavior, 19,* 2–21.

Pendleton, M., & Batson, C. D. (1979). Self-presentation and the door-in-the-face technique for including compliance. *Personality and Social Psychology Bulletin, 5,* 77–81.

Penta, J., Poster, D., & Bruno, S. (1983). The pharmacologic treatment of nausea and vomiting caused by cancer chemotherapy: A review. In J. Laszlo (Ed.), *Antiemetics and cancer chemotherapy.* Baltimore: Williams & Wilkins.

Perls, F. S. (1969). *Gestalt therapy verbatim.* Lafayette, Calif.: Real People Press.

Petersen, A. C. (1983). Menarche: Meaning of measures and measures of meaning. In S. Golub (Ed.), *Menarche: An interdisciplinary view.* New York: Heath.

Peterson, L. R., & Peterson, M. J. (1959). Short-term retention of individual verbal items. *Journal of Experimental Psychology, 58,* 193–198.

Pfeiffer, E., Verwoerdt, A., & Davis, G. C. (1974). Sexual behavior in middle life. In E. Palmore (Ed.). *Normal aging II: Reports from the Duke longitudinal studies, 1970–1973.* Durham, N.C.: Duke University Press.

Phares, E. J. (1976). *Locus of control and personality.* Morristown, N.J.: General Learning Press.

Piaget, J. (1950). *The psychology of intelligence.* London: Routledge & Kegan Paul.

Piaget, J. (1970). Piaget's theory. In P. H. Mussen (Ed.), *Carmichael's manual of child psychology* (Vol. 1). New York: Wiley.

Piaget, J. (1972). Intellectual evolution from adolescence to adulthood. *Human Development, 15,* 1–12.

Pichert, J. W., & Anderson, R. C. (1977). Taking different perspectives in a story. *Journal of Educational Psychology, 69,* 309–315.

Pliner, P., Hart, H., Kohl, J., & Saari, D. (1974). Compliance without pressure: Some further data on the foot-in-the-door technique. *Journal of Personality and Social Psychology, 10,* 17–22.

Plutchik, R. (1980). *Emotion: A psychoevolutionary synthesis.* New York: Harper Row.

Popper, K. R., & Eccles, J. C. (1977). *The self and its brain.* Heidelberg: Springer-Verlag.

Population Reference Bureau (1982). U.S. population: Where we are, where we're going, *Population Bulletin 35*(2). Washington, D.C.: Population Reference Bureau.

Posner, M. I., & McLeod, P. (1982). Information processing models—In search of elementary operations. *Annual Review of Psychology, 33,* 477–514.

Pratt, J. G., & Blom, J. G. (1964). A confirmatory experiment with a "borrowed" outstanding ESP subject. *Journal of Personality and Social Psychology, 17,* 381–389.

Provence, S., & Lipton, R. C. (1962). *Infants in institutions.* New York: International Universities Press.

Rabbitt, P., & Birren, J. E. (1967). Age and responses to sequences of repetitive and interruptive signals. *Journal of Gerontology, 22,* 143–150.

Rachman, S. (1980). *Obsessions and compulsions.* Englewood Cliffs, N.J.: Prentice-Hall.

Rahe, R. H. (1968). Life-change measurement as a prediction of illness. *Proceedings of the Royal Society of Medicine, 61,* 1124–1126.

Rahe, R. H., Mahan, J. L., & Arthur, R. J. (1970). Prediction of near-future health change from subjects' preceding life changes. *Journal of Psychosomatic Research, 14,* 401–406.

Rajecki, D. W. (1982). *Attitudes: Themes and advances.* Sunderland, Mass.: Sinauer Associates.

Rall, T. W. (1980). Central nervous system stimulants. In A. G. Gilman, L. S. Goodman, & A. Gilman (Eds.), *The pharmacological basis of therapeutics* (6th ed.) (pp. 592–607). New York: Macmillan.

Rapoport, J. L., Buchsbaum, M. S., Zahn, T. P., Weingarten, H., Ludlow, C., & Mikkelson, E. J. (1978). Dextroamphetamine: Cognitive and behavioral effects in normal prepubertal boys. *Science, 199,* 560–563.

Raven, B. H., & Rubin, J. Z. (1983). *Social psychology* (2nd ed.). Wiley.

Raven, J. C. (1938). *Progressive matrix: A perceptual test of intelligence, individual form.* London: H. K. Lewis.

Rehberg, R. A., & Westby, D. L. (1967). Parental encouragement, occupation, education, and family size: Artifactual or independent determinants of adolescent educational expectations? *Social Forces, 45,* 362–374.

Rehm, L. P. (1977). A self-control model of depression. *Behavior Therapy, 8,* 787–804.

Reichard, S., Livson, F., & Peterson, P. G. (1962). Adjustment to retirement. Reprinted from S. Reichard, F. Livson, & P. G. Peterson, *Aging and personality* (pp. 170–172). New York: Wiley.

Reitan, R. M., & Davison, L. A. (Eds.) (1974). *Clinical neuropsychology: Current states and applications.* Washington, D.C.: Winston.

Rensberger, B. (1978, November 26). *New York Times.*

Rescorla, R. A., & Holland, P. C. (1976). Some behavioral approaches to the study of learning. In M. R. Rosenzweig & E. L. Bennett (Eds.), *Neuromechanisms of learning and memory.* Cambridge, Mass.: MIT Press.

Rescorla, R. A., & Holland, P. C. (1982). Behavioral studies of associative learning in animals. *Annual Review of Psychology, 33,* 265–308.

Rescorla, R. A., & Wagner, A. R. (1972). A theory of Pavlovian conditioning: Variations in the effectiveness of reinforcement and non-reinforcement. In A. H. Black & W. F. Prokasy (Eds.), *Classical conditioning II.* New York: Appleton-Century-Crofts.

Rhine, J. B. (1942). Evidence of precognition in the covariation of salience ratios. *Journal of Parapsychology, 6,* 111–143.

Rich, A. R., & Schroeder, H. E. (1976). Research issues in assertiveness training. *Psychological Bulletin, 83,* 1081–1096.

Riddell, W. I. (1979). Cerebral indices and behavioral differences. In M. E. Hahn, C. Jensen, & B. C. Dudek (Eds.), *Development and evolution of brain size.* New York: Academic Press.

Riegel, K. F. (1975). Toward a dialectical theory of development. *Human Development, 18,* 50–64.

RIGSBY, L. C., & MCDILL, E. L. (1972). Adolescent peer influence processes: Conceptualization and measurement. *Social Science Research, 37,* 189–207.

RIMLAND, B. (1964). *Infantile autism: The syndrome and its implications for a neural theory of behavior.* New York: Appleton-Century-Crofts.

RINGLER, N., TRAUSE, W. A., KLAUS, M., & KENNELL, J. (1978). The effects of extra postpartum contact and maternal speech, and language comprehension at five. *Child Development, 49,* 862–865.

RITCHIE, J. M. (1980). The aliphatic alcohols. In A. G. Gilman, L. S. Goodman, & A. Gilman (Eds.), *The pharmacological basis of therapeutics* (6th ed.) pp. 376–390). New York: Macmillan.

RODIN, J. (1981). Current status of the internal-external hypothesis of obesity: What went wrong? *American Psychologist, 36,* 361–372.

RODIN, J., & LANGER, E. J. (1977). Long-term effects of a control-relevant intervention with the institutionalized aged. *Journal of Personality and Social Psychology, 35,* 897–902.

RODIN, J., SOLOMON, S. K., & METCALF, J. (1978). Role of control in mediating perceptions of density. *Journal of Personality and Social Psychology, 36,* 988–999.

ROFF, M. F., SELLS, S. B., & GOLDEN, M. M. (1972). *Social adjustment and personality development in children.* Minneapolis: University of Minnesota Press.

ROFFWARG, H. P., MUZIO, J. N., & DEMENT, W. C. (1966). Ontogenetic development of human sleep-dream cycle. *Science, 152,* 604–619.

ROGERS, C. R. (1951). *Client-centered therapy: Its current practice, implications, and theory.* Boston: Houghton Mifflin.

ROGERS, C. R. (1959). A theory of therapy, personality, and interpersonal relationships, as developed in the client-centered framework. In S. Kock (Ed.), *Psychology: A study of a science* (Vol. 3). New York: McGraw-Hill.

ROGERS, C. R. (1961). *On becoming a person.* Boston: Houghton Mifflin.

ROKEACH, M. (1964). *The three Christs of Ypsilanti.* New York: Knopf.

ROKEACH, M. (1981). *The three Christs of Ypsilanti.* New York: Columbia University Press.

ROLL, S., & VERNIS, J. S. (1971). Stereotypes of scalp and facial hair as measured by the semantic differential. *Psychological Reports, 28,* 975–980.

ROPER, R. T. (1980). Jury size and verdict consistency: A line has to be drawn somewhere. *Law and Society Review, 14*(4), 977–995.

ROSCH, E. (1973). On the internal structure of perceptual and semantic categories. In T. E. Moore (Ed.), *Cognitive development and the acquisition of language.* New York: Academic Press.

ROSCH, E., MERVIS, C. B., GRAY, W. D., JOHNSON, D. M., & BOYES-BRAEM, P. (1976). Basic objects in natural categories. *Cognitive Psychology, 8,* 382–439.

ROSEN, C. E. (1974). The effects of socio-dramatic play on problem solving behavior among culturally disadvantaged preschool children. *Child Development, 45,* 920–927.

ROSEN, G. M. (1976). The development and use of non-prescription behavior therapy. *American Psychologist, 31,* 139–141.

ROSENMAN, R. H. (1974). The role of behavior patterns and neurogenic factors in the pathogenesis of coronary heart disease. In R. S. Eliot (Ed.), *Stress and the Heart.* Mt. Kisco, N.Y.: Futura.

ROSENTHAL, D. (1970). *Genetic theory and abnormal behavior.* New York: McGraw-Hill.

ROSENTHAL, R., HALL, J. A., ARCHER, D., DIMATTEO, M. R., & ROGERS, P. L. (1979). The PONS test: Measuring sensitivity in nonverbal cues. In S. Weitz (Ed.), *Nonverbal communication* (2nd ed.). New York: Oxford University Press.

ROSENTHAL, T., & BANDURA, A. (1978). Psychological modeling: Theory and practice. In S. L. Garfield & A. E. Bergin (Eds.), *Handbook of psychotherapy and behavior change* (2nd ed.). New York: Wiley.

ROSENZWEIG, M. R. (1979). Responsiveness of brain size to individual experience: Behavioral and evolutionary implications. In E. Hahn, C. Jensen, & B. C. Dudek (Eds.), *Development and evolution of brain size.* New York: Academic Press.

ROSS, L. (1977). The intuitive psychologist and his shortcomings: Distortions in the attribution process. In L. Berkowitz (Ed.), *Advances in experimental social psychology* (Vol. 10). New York: Academic Press.

ROSS, M., & FLETCHER, G. (1985). Attribution and social perception. In G. Lindzey & E. Aronson (Eds.), *Handbook of social psychology* (3rd edition, Vol. 2). New York: Random House.

ROTTER, J. B. (1954). *Social learning and clinical psychology.* Englewood Cliffs, N.J.: Prentice-Hall.

ROTTER, J. B. (1966). Generalized expectancies for internal versus external control of reinforcement. *Psychological Monographs, 80* (Whole No. 609), 1–28.

RUBIN, K. H., & MAIONI, T. L. (1975). Play preference and its relationship to egocentrism, popularity, and classification skills in preschoolers. *Merrill-Palmer Quarterly, 21,* 171–179.

RUBIN, Z. (1973). *Liking and loving: An invitation to social psychology.* New York: Holt, Rinehart and Winston.

RUBIN, Z., PEPLAU, L. A., & HILL, C. T. (1981). Loving and leaving: Sex differences in romantic attachments. *Sex Roles, 7,* 821–835.

RUMELHART, D. E., & ORTONY, A. (1977). The representation of knowledge in memory. In R. C. Anderson, R. J. Spiro, & W. E. Montague (Eds.), *Schooling and the acquisition of knowledge.* Hillsdale, N.J.: Lawrence Erlbaum.

RUNDUS, D., & ATKINSON, R. C. (1970). Rehearsal procedures in free recall: A procedure for direct observation. *Journal of Verbal Learning and Verbal Behavior, 9,* 99–105.

RUSH, A. J., BECK, A. T., KOVACS, M., & HOLLON, S. D. (1977). Comparative efficacy of cognitive therapy and pharmacotherapy in the treatment of depressed outpatients. *Cognitive Therapy and Research, 1,* 17–38.

RUSHTON, J. P. (1979). Effects of prosocial television and film material on the behavior of viewers. In L. Berkowitz (Ed.), *Advances in experimental social psychology* (Vol. 12). New York: Academic Press.

REFERENCES

Russell, J. A. (1980). A circumplex model of affect. *Journal of Personality and Social Psychology, 39,* 1161–1178.

Rutter, M. (1971). Parent-child separation: Psychological effects on the children. *Journal of Child Psychology and Psychiatry, 12,* 233–260.

Rutter, M. (1978). Diagnosis and definition of childhood autism. *Journal of Autism and Childhood Schizophrenia, 8,* 139–161.

Sachs, J. S. (1967). Recognition memory for syntactic and semantic aspects of connected discourse. *Perception and Psychophysics, 2,* 437–442.

Sachs, J. S., & Devlin, J. (1976). Young children's use of age appropriate speech styles in social interaction and role playing. *Journal of Child Language, 3,* 81–98.

Saks, M. (1977). *Jury verdicts.* Lexington, MA: D. C. Heath.

Sales, S. M. (1972). Economic threat as a determinant of conversion rates in authoritarian and nonauthoritarian churches. *Journal of Personality and Social Psychology, 23,* 420–428.

Salzinger, K. (1980). Schizophrenia. In A. E. Kazdin, A. S. Bellack, & M. Hersen (Eds.), *New perspectives in abnormal psychology.* NY: Oxford University Press.

Sandberg, E. C., & Jacobs, R. I. (1972). Psychology of the misuse and rejection of contraception. *Medical Aspects of Human Sexuality, 6,* 34–70.

Sandgrund, A., Gaines, R. W., & Green, A. H. (1974). Child abuse and mental retardation: A problem of cause and effect. *American Journal of Mental Deficiency, 79,* 327–330.

Sarason, E. G. (1975). Test anxiety and the self-disclosing model. *Journal of Consulting and Clinical Psychology, 43,* 148–153.

Satir, V. (1964). *Conjoint family therapy.* Palo Alto, Calif.: Science & Behavior Books.

Sauer, W. J., & Warland, R. (1982). Morale and life satisfaction. In D. J. Mangen & W. A. Peterson (Eds.), *Research instruments in social gerontology.* Vol. 1: *Clinical and social psychology.* Minneapolis: University of Minnesota Press.

Scales, P., & Beckstein, D. (1982). From macho to mutuality: Helping young men make effective decisions about sex, contraception, and pregnancy. In I. R. Stuart & C. F. Wells (Eds.), *Pregnancy in adolescence: Needs, problems, and management.* New York: Van Nostrand Reinhold.

Scarr-Salapatek, S. (1971). Unknowns in the IQ equation. *Science, 174,* 1223–1228.

Schachter, F. F., Shore, E., Hodapp, R., Chalfin, S., & Bundy, C. (1978). Do girls talk earlier? Mean length of utterance in toddlers. *Developmental Psychology, 14,* 388–392.

Schachter, S. (1964). The interaction of cognitive and physiological determinants of emotional state. In L. Berkowitz (Ed.), *Advances in experimental social psychology.* New York: Academic Press.

Schachter, S. (1978). Pharmacological and psychological determinants of smoking. *Annals of Internal Medicine, 88,* 104–114.

Schachter, S. (1975). *The psychology of affiliation.* Stanford, Calif.: Stanford University Press.

Schachter, S., & Singer, J. E. (1962). Cognitive, social, and physiological determinants of emotional state. *Psychological Review, 69,* 379–399.

Schaefer, C., Coyne, J. C., & Lazarus, R. S. (1981). The health-related functions of social support. *Journal of Behavioral Medicine, 4,* 381–406.

Schaie, K. W. (1979). The primary mental abilities in adulthood: An exploration in the development of psychometric intelligence. In P. B. Baltes & O. G. Brim, Jr. (Eds.), *Life-span development and behavior* (Vol. 2). New York: Academic Press.

Schaie, K. W., & Labouvie-Vief, G. (1974). Generational versus ontogenic components of change in adult cognitive behavior: A fourteen-year cross-sequential study. *Developmental Psychology, 10,* 305–320.

Schank, R. C., & Abelson, R. (1977). *Scripts, plans, goals, and understanding.* Hillsdale, N.J.: Lawrence Erlbaum.

Schiffman, H. R. (1976). *Sensation and perception: An integrated approach.* New York: Wiley.

Schildkraut, J. J. (1965). The catecholamine hypothesis of affective disorders: A review of supporting evidence. *American Journal of Psychiatry, 122,* 509–522.

Schlosberg, H. (1954). Three dimensions of emotion. *Psychological Review, 61,* 81–88.

Schmidt, H. (1969). Precognition of a quantum process. *Journal of Parapsychology, 33,* 99–108.

Schoenenberger, G. A., & Monnier, M. (1977). Characterization of a delta-electroencephalogram (sleep)-inducing peptide. *Proceedings of the National Academy of Sciences* (U.S.A.), *74,* 1282–1286.

Schofield, W. (1964). *Psychotherapy: The purchase of friendship.* Englewood Cliffs, N.J.: Prentice-Hall.

Schonfeld, W. A. (1969). The body and the body image in adolescents. In G. Caplan & S. Lebovici (Eds.), *Adolescence: Psychosocial perspectives.* New York: Basic Books.

Schwartz, G. E., & Weiss, S. M. (1978). Yale conference on behavioral medicine: A proposed definition and statement of goals. *Journal of Behavioral Medicine, 1,* 3–12.

Schwartz, J. H. (1981). Chemical bias of synaptic transmission. In E. R. Kandel & J. H. Schwartz (Eds.), *Principles of neural science* (pp. 106–120). New York: Elsevier/North Holland.

Schwartz, R. M., & Gottman, J. M. (1976). Toward a task analysis of assertive behavior. *Journal of Consulting and Clinical Psychology, 44,* 910–920.

Scribner, S. (1975). Recall of classical syllogisms: A cross-cultural investigation of error on logical problems. In R. J. Falmagne (Ed.), *Reasoning: Representation and process.* Hillsdale, N.J.: Lawrence Erlbaum.

Sears, R. R. (1977). Sources of life satisfactions of the Terman gifted men. *American Psychologist, 32,* 119–128.

Seashore, C. E., Lewis, D., & Soetvert, D. L. (1960). *Seashore measure of musical talents* (rev. ed.). New York: The Psychological Corporation.

Segal, M. W. (1974). Alphabet and attraction: An unobtrusive measure of the effect of propinquity in a field setting. *Journal of Personality and Social Psychology, 30,* 654–657.

Seidman, E., Rappaport, J., & Davidson, W. S. (1976). *Adolescents in legal jeopardy: Initial success and replication of an alternative to the criminal justice system.* Invited address at the American Psychological Association Annual Convention, Washington, D.C.

SELIGMAN, M. E. P. (1975). *Helplessness: On depression, development, and death.* San Francisco: W. H. Freeman.

SELIGMAN, M. E. P., & MAIER, S. F. (1967). Failure to escape traumatic shock. *Journal of Experimental Psychology, 74,* 1–9.

SELIGMAN, M. E. P., MAIER, S. F., & SOLOMON, R. L. (1971). Unpredictable and uncontrollable aversive events. In F. R. Brush (Ed.), *Aversive conditioning and learning.* New York: Academic Press.

SELYE, H. (1946). The General Adaptation Syndrome and diseases of adaptation. *Journal of Clinical Endocrinology, 6,* 117–230.

SELYE, H. (1974). *Stress without distress.* Philadelphia: Lippincott.

SELYE, H. (1976). *The stress of life* (2nd ed.). New York: McGraw-Hill.

SEVERANCE, L., & LOFTUS, E. (1982). Improving the ability of jurors to comprehend and apply criminal jury instructions. *Law & Society Review, 17,* 153–198.

SEWELL, W. H., & SHAH, V. P. (1968a). Parents' education and children's educational aspirations and achievements. *American Sociological Review, 33,* 191–209.

SEWELL, W. H., & SHAH, V. P. (1968b). Social class, parental encouragement, and educational aspirations. *American Journal of Sociology, 73,* 559–572.

SHAFFER, D. R. (1979). *Social and personality development.* Monterey, Calif.: Brooks/Cole.

SHAH, F., ZELNIK, M., & KANTNER, J. F. (1975). Unprotected intercourse among unwed teenagers. *Family Planning Perspectives, 7,* 39–44.

SHAPIRO, D. A., & SHAPIRO, D. (1982). Meta-analysis comparative therapy outcome studies: A replication and refinement. *Psychological Bulletin, 92,* 581–604.

SHAW, B. F. (1977). Comparison of cognitive therapy in the treatment of depression. *Journal of Consulting and Clinical Psychology, 45,* 543–551.

SHAW, M. (1932). A comparison of individuals and small groups in the rational solution of complex problems. *American Journal of Psychology, 44,* 491–504.

SHAW, M. E., & WHITE, D. L. (1965). The relationship between child-parent identification and academic underachievement. *Journal of Clinical Psychology, 21,* 10–13.

SHEA, J. A. (1984). Adolescent sexuality. In R. M. Lerner & N. L. Galambos (Eds.), *Experiencing adolescents.* New York: Garland Press.

SHELDON, W. H. (1940). *The varieties of human physique.* New York: Harper & Row.

SHELDON, W. H. (1942). *The varieties of temperament: A psychology of constitutional differences.* New York: Harper.

SHEPARD, R. N. (1978). The mental image. *American Psychologist, 33,* 125–137.

SHIRLEY, M. M. (1933). *The first two years.* Minneapolis: University of Minnesota Press.

SHOCK, N. W. (1972). Energy metabolism, caloric intake and physical activity of the aging. In L. A. Carlson (Ed.), *Nutrition in old age (10th symposium of the Swedish Nutrition Foundation).* Uppsala, Sweden: Almqvist & Wiksell.

SHOCK, N. W. (1977). Biological theories of aging. In J. E. Birren & K. W. Schaie (Eds.), *Handbook of the psychology of aging.* New York: Van Nostrand Reinhold.

SHOR, R. E. (1979). The fundamental problem in hypnosis research as viewed from historic perspectives. In E. Fromm & R. E. Shor (Eds.), *Hypnosis: Developments in research and new perspectives* (pp. 15–41). Hawthorne, N.Y.: Aldine.

SHULMAN, H. G. (1970). Encoding and retention of semantic and phonemic information in short-term memory. *Journal of Verbal Learning and Verbal Behavior, 9,* 499–508.

SHULMAN, H. G. (1972). Semantic confusion errors in short-term memory. *Journal of Verbal Learning and Verbal Behavior, 11,* 221–227.

SIMON, H. A. (1975). The functional equivalence of problem solving skills. *Cognitive Psychology, 7,* 268–288.

SIMON, H. A. (1979). Information processing models of cognition. *Annual Review of Psychology, 30,* 363–396.

SKEELS, H. (1966). Adult status of children with contrasting early life experiences. *Monographs of the Society for Research in Child Development, 31* (Serial No. 3).

SKINNER, B. F. (1938). *The behavior of organisms.* New York: Appleton-Century-Crofts.

SKINNER, B. F. (1953). *Science and human behavior.* New York: Macmillan.

SKINNER, B. F. (1957). *Verbal behavior.* New York: Appleton-Century-Crofts.

SKINNER, B. F. (1971). *Beyond freedom and dignity.* New York: Knopf.

SLOANE, R. B., STAPLES, F. R., CRISTOL, A. H., YORKSTON, N. J., & WHIPPLE, K. (1975). *Psychotherapy versus behavior therapy.* Cambridge, Mass.: Harvard University Press.

SMITH, D. (1982). Trends in counseling and psychotherapy. *American Psychologist, 37,* 802–809.

SMITH, M. L., & GLASS, G. V. (1977). Meta-analysis of psychotherapy outcome studies. *American Psychologist, 32,* 752–760.

SMITH, R. J., & KNOWLES, E. S. (1979). Affective and cognitive mediators of reactions to spatial invariance. *Journal of Experimental Social Psychology, 15,* 437–452.

SNOW, C. E., & HOEFNAGEL-HOHLE, M. (1978). The critical period for language acquisition: Evidence from second language learning. *Child Development, 49,* 1114–1128.

SNYDER, M., & SWANN, W. B., JR. (1976). When actions reflect attitudes: The politics of impression management. *Journal of Personality and Social Psychology, 34,* 1034–1042.

SNYDER, M., TANKE, E. D., & BERSCHEID, E. (1977). Social perception and interpersonal behavior; on the self-fulfilling nature of social stereotypes. *Journal of Personality and Social Psychology, 35,* 656–666.

SNYDER, S. H., & CHILDERS, W. R. (1979). Opiate receptors and opioid peptides. In W. M. Cowan, Z. W. Hall, & E. R. Kandel (Eds.), *Annual Review of Neuroscience,* Vol. 2, Palo Alto: Annual Reviews.

SOAL, S. G., & BATEMAN, F. (1954). *Modern experiments in telepathy.* New Haven, Conn.: Yale University Press.

SOLOMON, F., WHITE, C. C., PARRON, D. L., & MENDELSON, W. B. (1979). Sleeping pills, insomnia, and medical practice. *New England Journal of Medicine, 300,* 803–808.

REFERENCES

Sommer, R. (1969). *Personal space: The behavioral basis of design.* Englewood Cliffs, N.J.: Prentice-Hall.

Sontag, L. W. (1941). The significance of fetal environment differences. *American Journal of Obstetrics and Gynecology, 42,* 996–1003.

Sours, J. A. (1969). Anorexia nervosa: Nosology, diagnosis, developmental patterns, and power-control dynamics. In G. Caplan & S. Lebovici (Eds.), *Adolescence: Psychosocial perspectives.* New York: Basic Books.

Spanier, G. B. (1976). Perceived sex knowledge, exposure to eroticism and premarital sexual behavior: The impact of dating. *Sociological Quarterly, 17,* 247–261.

Spanier, G. B., & Glick, P. C. (1980). The life cycle of American families: An expanded analysis. *Journal of Family History, 5,* 97–111.

Spearman, C. (1927). *The abilities of man.* New York: Macmillan.

Sperling, G. (1960). The information available in brief visual presentations. *Psychological Monographs, 74* (No. 498).

Sperry, R. W. (1982). Some effects of disconnecting the cerebral hemispheres. *Science, 217,* 1223–1226.

Spielberger, C. D., Gorsuch, R. C., & Lushene, R. E. (1970). *Manual for the State-Trait Anxiety Inventory.* Palo Alto, Calif.: Consulting Psychologists Press.

Spiro, R. J. (1977). Constructing a theory of reconstructive memory: The state of schema approach. In R. C. Anderson, R. J. Spiro, & W. E. Montague (Eds.), *Schooling and the acquisition of knowledge.* Hillsdale, N.J.: Lawrence Erlbaum.

Spitz, R. A. (1945). Hospitalism: An inquiry into the genesis of psychiatric conditions in early childhood. In A. Freud et al. (Eds.), *The Psychoanalytic Study of the Child,* (Vol. 1). New York: International Universities Press.

Spitz, R. A. (1946). Hospitalism: A follow-up investigation. In A. Freud et al. (Eds.), *The Psychoanalytic Study of the Child* (Vol. 2). New York: International Universities Press.

Spitz, R. A. (1949). The role of ecological factors in emotional development in infancy. *Child Development, 20,* 145–155.

Spitz, R. A., & Wolff, K. M. (1946). Anaclitic depression: An inquiry into the genesis of psychiatric conditions in early childhood. In A. Freud et al. (Eds.), *The psychoanalytic study of the child* (Vol. 2). New York: International Universities Press.

Spitzer, R. L., & Endicott, J. (1978). *Schedule for affective disorders and schizophrenia—Life-time version.* New York: New York State Psychiatric Institute, Biometric Research.

Spitzer, R. L., Skodol, A. E., Gibbon, M., & Williams, J. B. W. (1983). *Psychopathology: A case book.* New York: McGraw-Hill.

Spreen, O., & Benton, A. L. (1969). *Neurosensory Center Comprehensive Examination for Aphasia.* Victoria, B.C.: University of Victoria, Department of Psychology, Neuropsychology Laboratory.

Sroufe, L. A. (1978). Attachment and the roots of competence. *Human Nature,* October, pp. 50–59.

Sroufe, L. A. (1979). The coherence of individual development. *American Psychologist, 34*(10), 834–841.

Standing, L. (1973). Learning 10,000 pictures. *Quarterly Journal of Experimental Psychology, 25,* 207–222.

Stanton, M., Mintz, J., & Franklin, R. M. (1976). Drug flashbacks. *International Journal of Addictions, 11,* 53–59.

Starr, R. H., Jr. (1979). Child abuse. *American Psychologist, 34,* 872–879.

St. Clair, K. L. (1978). Neonatal assessment procedures: A historical review. *Child Development, 49,* 280–292.

Stein, A. H. (1973). The effects of maternal employment and educational attainment on the sex-typed attributes of college females. *Social Behavior and Personality, 1,* 111–114.

Stein, A. H., & Friedrich, L. K. (1975). Impact of television on children and youth. In E. M. Hetherington (Ed.), *Review of child development research* (Vol. 5). Chicago: University of Chicago Press.

Sternberg, R. J. (1979). The nature of mental abilities. *American Psychologist, 34,* 214–230.

Sternberg, R. J. (1981). Testing and cognitive psychology. *American Psychologist, 36,* 1181–1189.

Sternberg, R. J. (1984). Toward a triarchic theory of human intelligence. *The Behavioral and Brain Sciences, 7,* 269–315.

Sternberg, S. (1966). High speed scanning in human memory. *Science, 153,* 652–654.

Stevens, C. F. (1979). The neuron. *Scientific American, 241,* 54–65.

Stevens, S. S. (1975). *Psychophysics: Introduction to its perceptual, neural, and social prospects.* New York: Wiley.

Stewart, J. E., II. (1980). Defendant's attractiveness as a factor in the outcome of criminal trials: An observational study. *Journal of Applied Social Psychology, 10,* 348–361.

Storandt, M., Botwinick, J., Danziger, W. L., Berg, L., & Hughes, C. P. (1984). Psychometric differentiation of mild senile dementia of the Alzheimer's type. *Archives of Neurology, 41,* 497–499.

Storrow, H. A. (1967). *Introduction of scientific psychiatry.* Des Moines, Iowa: Meredith.

Strauss, M. A., & Gelles, R. J. (1980). *Behind closed doors: Violence in the American family.* New York: Anchor/Doubleday.

Strauss, M., Lessen-Firestone, J., Starr, R., & Ostrea, E. (1973). Behavior of narcotics-addicted newborns. *Child Development, 46,* 887–893.

Stunkard, A. J. (Ed.) (1980). *Obesity.* Philadelphia: Saunders.

Suls, J. M., & Miller, R. L. (Eds.) (1977). *Social comparison processes.* Washington, D.C.: Hemisphere.

Suomi, S. J., & Harlow, H. F. (1972). Social rehabilitation of isolate-reared monkeys. *Developmental Psychology, 6,* 487–496.

Swenson, C. H. (1968). Empirical evaluations of human figure drawings: 1957–1966. *Psychological Bulletin, 70,* 20–44.

Swets, J. A. (1961). Is there a sensory threshold? *Science, 134,* 168–177.

Swift, D. F. (1967). Family environment and 11+ success: Some basic predictions. *British Journal of Educational Psychology, 37,* 10–21.

Szasz, T. F. (1961). *The myth of mental illness.* New York: Harper & Row.

TALLAND, G. A. (1968). Age and the immediate memory span. In G. A. Talland (Ed.), *Human aging and behavior*. New York: Academic Press.

TANGRI, S. S. (1972). Determinants of occupational role innovation in college women. *Journal of Social Issues, 28*, 177–199.

TANNER, J. M. (1973). Growing up. *Scientific American, 299*, 34–43.

TAYLOR, F. G., & MARSHALL, W. L. (1977). Experimental analysis of a cognitive-behavioral therapy for depression. *Cognitive Therapy and Research, 1*, 59–72.

TAYLOR, J. A. (1953). A personality scale of manifest anxiety. *Journal of Abnormal and Social Psychology, 48*, 285–290.

TERENIUS, L. (1978). Significance of endorphins in endogenous nociception. In E. Costa & M. Trabuchi (Eds.), *The Endorphins: Advances in Biochemical Pharmacology*, Vol. 18. New York: Raven.

TERMAN, L. M., & MERRILL, M. A. (1960). *Stanford-Binet Intelligence Scale: Manual for the third revision, Form L-M*. Boston: Houghton Mifflin.

TERMAN, L. M., & ODEN, M. H. (1947). *Genetic studies of genius: IV. The gifted child grows up*. Stanford, Calif.: Stanford University Press.

TERMAN, L. M., & ODEN, M. H. (1959). *Genetic studies of genius: V. The gifted group at mid-life*. Stanford, Calif.: Stanford University Press.

TESSMAN, L. H. (1978). *Children of parting parents*. New York: Aronson.

TETLOCK, P. E., & LEVI, A. (1982). Attribution bias: On the inconclusiveness of the cognitive-motivation debate. *Journal of Experimental Social Psychology, 18*, 68–88.

THOMPSON, L., & SPANIER, G. B. (1978). Influence of parents, peers, and partners on the contraceptive behavior of college men and women. *Journal of Marriage and the Family, 40*, 481–492.

THORNDIKE, E. L. (1898). Animal intelligence: An experimental study of the associative processes in animals. *Psychological Monographs, 2* (No. 8).

THORNDIKE, E. L. (1911). *Animal intelligence*. New York: Macmillan.

THORNDYKE, P. W., & HAYES-ROTH, B. (1979). The use of schemata in the acquisition and transfer of knowledge. *Cognitive Psychology, 11*, 82–106.

THURSTONE, L. L., & THURSTONE, T. G. (1941). *Factorial studies of intelligence* (Psychometric Monograph No. 2). Chicago: University of Chicago Press.

TOCH, H. (1969). *Violent men*. Chicago: Aldine.

TOCH, H. (1980). *Violent men*. (rev. ed.). Cambridge, MA: Schenkman.

TOFFLER, A. (1970). *Future shock*. New York: Random House.

TOLMAN, E. C. (1932). *Purposive behavior in animals and men*. New York: Appleton-Century-Crofts.

TOLMAN, E. C., & HONZIK, C. H. (1930). Introduction and removal of reward, and maze performance in rats. *University of California Publication Psychology, 4*, 257–275.

TOMPKINS, W. T. (1948). The clinical significance of nutritional deficiencies in pregnancy. *Bulletin of the New York Academy of Medicine, 24*, 376–388.

TOUHEY, J. C. (1972). Comparison of two dimensions of attitude similarity on heterosexual attraction. *Journal of Personality and Social Psychology, 23*, 8–10.

TREXLER, L. D., & KARST, T. O. (1972). Rational-emotive therapy, placebo, and nontreatment effects on public-speaking anxiety. *Journal of Abnormal Psychology, 79*, 60–67.

TRUAX, C. B., WARGO, D. G., FRANK, J. D., IMBER, S. D., BATTLE, C. C., HOEHN-SARIC, R., NASH, E. H., & STONE, A. R. (1966). Therapist empathy, genuineness, and warmth and patient therapeutic outcome. *Journal of Consulting Psychology, 30*, 395–401.

TULVING, E. (1972). Episodic and semantic memory. In E. Tulving & W. Donaldson (Eds.), *Organization of memory*. New York: Academic Press.

TULVING, E. (1974). Cue-dependent forgetting. *American Scientist, 62*, 74–82.

TULVING, E., & PEARLSTONE, Z. (1966). Availability versus accessibility of information in memory for words. *Journal of Verbal Learning and Verbal Behavior, 5*, 381–391.

TULVING, E., & PSOTKA, J. (1971). Retroactive inhibition in free recall: Inaccessibility of information available in the memory store. *Journal of Experimental Psychology, 87*, 1–8.

TULVING, E., & THOMPSON, D. M. (1973). Encoding specificity and retrieval processes in episodic memory. *Psychological Review, 80*, 352–373.

TV Guide, January 26, 1977, pp. 5–10.

U.S. Bureau of the Census. (1978). *Characteristics of American Children and youth: 1976*. Current Population Reports, Series P-23, No. 66. Washington, D.C.: U.S. Government Printing Office.

U.S. Bureau of the Census (1979). Unpublished data analyzed by Graham Spanier and Paul Glick.

U.S. Bureau of the Census (1980). *Statistical abstract of the United States*. Washington, D.C.: U.S. Government Printing Office.

U.S. Commission on Obscenity and Pornography. (1970). The report of the Commission on Obscenity and Pornography. Washington, D.C.: Government Printing Office.

U.S. Department of Health, Education and Welfare (1978). *Vital statistics of the United States, 1976*. Hyattsville, Md.: National Center for Health Statistics.

U.S. Department of Labor, Women's Bureau (1977). *Working mothers and their children*. Washington, D.C.: U.S. Government Printing Office.

VAILLANT, G. (1977). *Adaptation to life*. Boston: Little, Brown.

VAUGHAN, K. B., & LANZETTA, J. T. (1981). The effect of modification of expressive displays on vicarious emotional arousal. *Journal of Experimental Social Psychology, 17*, 16–30.

VIGERSKY, R. A. (Ed.) (1977). *Anorexia nervosa*. New York: Raven Press.

VON FRISCH, K. (1967). Honeybees: Do they use direction and distance information provided by their dancers? *Science, 158*, 1072–1076.

WACHTEL, P. L. (1977). *Psychoanalysis and behavior therapy*. New York: Basic Books.

WADE, T. C., & BAKER, T. B. (1977). Opinions and use of psychological tests: A survey of clinical psychologists. *American Psychologist, 33*, 874–882.

REFERENCES

Wagner, J. J., & Laird, J. D. (1980). The experimenter's foot-in-the-door: Self-perception, body weight, and volunteering. *Personality and Social Psychology Bulletin, 6,* 441–446.

Wahler, R. G. (1969). Infant social development: Some experimental analyses of an infant-mother interaction during the first year of life. *Journal of Experimental Child Psychology, 7,* 101–113.

Walk, R. D., Shepherd, J. D., & Miller, D. R. (1978). Attention as an alternative to self-induced motion for perceptual behavior of kittens. *Society for Neuroscience Abstracts, 4,* 129.

Walker, R. N. (1962). Body build and behavior in young children: I. Body build and nursery school teachers' ratings. *Monographs of the Society for Research in Child Development, 27* (Serial No. 3).

Wallach, M. A., & Kogan, N. (1965). *Modes of thinking in young children.* New York: Holt, Rinehart and Winston.

Wallgren, H., & Berry, H., III (1970). *Actions of alcohol* (Vol. 1). New York: American Elsevier.

Walster, E., & Walster, G. W. (1978). *A new look at love.* Reading, Mass.: Addison-Wesley.

Walster, E., Walster, G. W., & Berscheid, E. (1978). *Equity: Theory and research.* Boston: Allyn and Bacon.

Walters, J. (1975). Birth defects and adolescent pregnancies. *Journal of Home Economics, 67,* 23–27.

Wason, P. C., & Johnson-Laird, P. N. (1972). *Psychology of reasoning.* Cambridge, Mass.: Harvard University Press.

Waters, E., Wippman, J., & Sroufe, A. L. (1979). Attachment, positive affect, and competence in peer group: Two studies in construct validation. *Child Development, 50,* 821–829.

Watson, J. B. (1913). Psychology as the behaviorist views it. *Psychological Review, 20,* 158–177.

Watson, J. B. (1918). *Psychology from the standpoint of a behaviorist.* Philadelphia: Lippincott.

Watson, R. I., Jr. (1973). Investigation into deindividuation using a cross-cultural survey technique. *Journal of Personality and Social Psychology, 25,* 342–345.

Webb, W. B. (1975). *Sleep: The gentle tyrant.* Englewood Cliffs, N.J.: Prentice-Hall.

Webb, W. B., Agnew, H. W., Jr., & Williams, R. L. (1971). Effect on sleep of a sleep period time displacement. *Aerospace Medicine, 42,* 152–155.

Webb, W. B., & Cartwright, R. D. (1978). Sleep and dreams. *Annual Review of Psychology, 29,* 223–252.

Wechsler, D. (1945). A standardized memory scale for clinical use. *Journal of Psychology, 19,* 87–95.

Wechsler, D. (1958). *The measurement and appraisal of adult intelligence.* (4th ed.). Baltimore: Williams & Wilkins.

Wechsler, D. (1974). *Wechsler Intelligence Scale for Children—Revised manual.* New York: The Psychological Corporation.

Wechsler, D. (1978). *Wechsler Intelligence Scale—Revised.* New York: The Psychological Corporation.

Wedding, D., & Corsini, R. J. (Eds.) (1979). *Great cases in psychotherapy.* Itasca, Ill.: Peacock.

Weil, A., & Rosen, W. (1983). *Chocolate to morphine: Understanding mind-active drugs.* Boston: Houghton Mifflin.

Weiner, B. (1980). *Human motivation.* New York: Holt, Rinehart and Winston.

Weiner, I. B. (1975). *Principles of psychotherapy.* New York: Wiley.

Weiss, D. J. (1982). Improving measurement quality and efficiency with adapt testing. *Applied Psychological Measurement, 6,* 473–492.

Weiss, D. J. (1985). Adaptive testing. *International Encyclopedia of Education,* Elmsford, N.Y.: Pergamon Press.

Wender, P. H., Rosenthal, D., Kety, S. S., Schulsinger, F., & Wilmer, J. (1973). Social class and psychopathology in adoptees: A natural experimental method for separating the roles of genetic and experiential factors. *Archives of General Psychiatry, 28,* 318–325.

Wender, P. H., Rosenthal, D., Kety, S. S., Schulsinger, F., & Wilmer, J. (1974). Crossfostering: A research strategy for clarifying the role of genetic and experiential factors in the etiology of schizophrenia. *Archives of General Psychiatry, 30,* 121–128.

Wener, N. (1980). Norepinephrine, epinephrine, and the sympathomimetic amines. In A. G. Gilman, L. S. Goodman, & A. Gilman (Eds.), *The pharmacological basis of therapeutics* (6th ed.) (pp. 138–175). New York: Macmillan.

Werblin, F. S. (1973). The control of sensitivity in the retina. *Scientific American, 228,* 70–79.

Wertheimer, M. (1959). *Productive thinking* (English ed.). New York: Harper & Row.

Wesson, D. R., & Smith, D. E. (1977). Cocaine: Its use for central nervous system stimulation including recreational and medical uses. In R. C. Petersen & R. C. Stillman (Eds.), *Cocaine* (pp. 137–150). National Institute on Drug Abuse Research Monograph No. 13.

Wever, E. G. (1970). *Theory of hearing.* New York: Wiley.

Whalen, C. K. (1982). Hyperactivity and psychostimulant treatment. In J. R. Lackenmeyer & M. S. Gibbs (Eds.), *Psychopathology in childhood.* New York: Gardner Press.

White, R. K. (1977). Misperception in the Arab-Israeli conflict. *Journal of Social Issues, 33*(1), 190–221.

White, S. H. (1968). The learning-maturation controversy: Hall to Hull. *Merrill-Palmer Quarterly, 14,* 187–196.

Wicker, A. W. (1969). Attitudes versus actions: The relationship of verbal and overt behavioral responses to attitude objects. *Journal of Social Issues, 25,* 41–78.

Williams, D. R., & Williams, H. (1969). Auto-maintenance in the pigeon: Sustained pecking despite contingent nonreinforcement. *Journal of Experimental Analysis of Behavior, 12,* 511–520.

Williams, K. D., Harkins, S., & Latane, B. (1981). Identifiability as a deterrent to social loafing: Two cheering experiments. *Journal of Personality and Social Psychology, 40,* 303–311.

Williams, P. L., & Warwick, R. (1975). *Functional neuroanatomy of man.* Philadelphia: Saunders.

Wilson, E. O. (1978). *On human nature.* Cambridge, MA: Harvard University Press.

Wilson, G. T. (1978). On the much discussed nature of the term "behavior therapy." *Behavior Therapy, 9,* 89–98.

WILSON, G. T., & ABRAMS, D. B. (1977). Effects of alcohol on social anxiety and physiological arousal: Cognitive versus pharmacological processes. *Cognitive Therapy and Research, 1,* 195–210.

WILSON, G. T., & LAWSON, D. M. (1976). Expectancies, alcohol, and sexual arousal in male social drinkers. *Journal of Abnormal Psychology, 85,* 587–594.

WINICK, M., KARNIG, K. M., & HARRIS, R. C. (1975). Malnutrition and environmental enrichment by early adaptation. *Science, 190,* 1173–1175.

WITTGENSTEIN, L. (1953). *Philosophical investigations.* New York: Macmillan.

WOLF, R. M. (1964). *The identification and measurement of environmental process-variables related to intelligence.* Unpublished doctoral dissertation, University of Chicago.

WOLF, S., & MONTGOMERY, D. A. (1977). Effects of inadmissable evidence and level of judicial admonishment to disregard on the judgments of mock jurors. *Journal of Applied Social Psychology, 7,* 205–219.

WOLPE, J. (1958). *Psychotherapy by reciprocal inhibition.* Stanford, Calif.: Stanford University Press.

WOLPE, J. (1962). The experimental foundations of some new psychotherapeutic methods. In A. J. Bachrach (Ed.), *Experimental foundations of clinical psychology.* New York: Basic Books.

WOLPE, J. (1973). *The practice of behavior therapy* (2nd ed.). Elmsford, N.Y.: Pergamon Press.

WORTMAN, C. B. (1983). Coping with victimization: Conclusions and implications for future research. *Journal of Social Issues, 39,* 195–222.

WRIGHT, J. D. (1978). Are working women really more satisfied? Evidence from several national surveys. *Journal of Marriage and the Family, 40,* 301–313.

WUTHROW, R. (1982). Anti-semitism and stereotyping. In A. Miller (Ed.), *In the eye of the beholder.* New York: Praeger.

YARROW, L. J. (1979). Emotional development. *American Psychologist, 34,* 951–957.

YOUNG, M., BENJAMIN, B., & WALLIS, C. (1963). The mortality of widowers. *The Lancet, 2,* 454–456.

ZADNY, J., & GERARD, H. B. (1974). Attributed intentions and informational selectivity. *Journal of Experimental Social Psychology, 10,* 34–52.

ZAJONC, R. B. (1965). Social facilitation. *Science, 149,* 269–274.

ZAJONC, R. B. (1968). Attributional effects of mere exposure. *Journal of Personality and Social Psychology, Monograph Supplement, 9,* 1–27.

ZARCONE, V. (1973). Narcolepsy. *New England Journal of Medicine, 288,* 1156–1166.

ZEISS, A. M., LEWINSOHN, P. M., & MUNOZ, R. F. (1979). Nonspecific improvement effects in depression using interpersonal skills training, pleasant activity schedules, and cognitive training. *Journal of Consulting and Clinical Psychology, 47,* 427–439.

ZELNIK, M., & KANTNER, J. F. (1977). Sexual and contraceptive experience of young unmarried women in the United States, 1976 and 1971. *Family Planning Perspective, 9,* 55–71.

ZILLMANN, D. (1983). Transfer of excitation in emotional behavior, In J. T. Cacioppo & R. E. Petty (Eds.), *Social psychophysiology.* New York: Guilford Press.

ZILLMANN, D., JOHNSON, R. C., & DAY, K. D. (1974). Attribution of apparent arousal and proficiency of recovery from sympathetic activation affecting excitation transfer to aggressive behavior. *Journal of Experimental Social Psychology, 10,* 503–515.

ZILLMANN, D., KATCHER, A. H., & MILAVSKY, B. (1972). Excitation transfer from physical exercise to subsequent behavior. *Journal of Experimental and Social Psychology, 8,* 247–259.

ZIMBARDO, P. G. (1970). The human choice: Individuation, reason, and order versus deindividuation—impulse and chaos. In W. J. Arnold & D. Levine (Eds.), *Nebraska symposium on motivation.* 1969, Lincoln, Nebraska: University of Nebraska Press.

ZIMBARDO, P. G. (1972). Pathology of imprisonment. *Transactional Society,* April, pp. 4–8.

ZIMBARDO, P. G., HANEY, C., BANKS, W. C., & JAFFE, D. A. (1973). A Pirandellian prison. *The New York Times Magazine,* April 8, pp. 38–60.

ZUBIN, J., ERON, L. D., & SCHUMER, F. (1965). *An experimental approach to projective techniques.* New York: Wiley.

ZUCKERMAN, M., DEFRANK, R. S., SPIEGEL, N. H., & LARRANCE, D. T. (1982). Masculinity-femininity and encoding of nonverbal cues. *Journal of Personality Social Psychology, 42,* 548–556.

ZUCKERMAN, M., SCHMITZ, M., & YOSHA, A. (1977). Effects of crowding in a student environment. *Journal of Applied Social Psychology, 7,* 67–72.

Name Index

Ableson, R., 242
Abramowitz, C. V., 394
Abramowitz, S. I., 394
Abramson, L. Y., 563
Adams, G. M., 350
Adams, G. R., 344
Adams, J. E., 462
Adelson, J., 337
Adler, A., 413
Aghajanian, G. K., 169
Agnew, H. W., 138
Ainsworth, M. D. S., 322–323
Ajzen, I., 552
Akiskal, H. S., 492
Albert, B. M., 394
Allen, A., 430
Allen, B. P., 552
Alloy, L. B., 563
Allport, G. W., 409
Almquist, E. M., 600
Amatruda, C. S., 315, 318
American Psychological Association, 18–19, 378
Anastasi, A., 307, 384, 386, 387, 390
Andersen, A. E., 341
Anderson, B., Jr., 348
Anderson, J. A., 264
Anderson, J. E., 326
Anderson, K., 402
Anderson, M. P., 122
Anderson, R. C., 242–243
Andres, D., 600
Angevine, J. B., 28, 35
Angrist, S. S., 600
Anthony, E. J., 343
Apgar, V., 313
Arenberg, D., 352
Arend, R. A., 323
Argyle, M., 558
Arkowitz, H., 404
Aristotle, 26, 209
Arthur, R. J., 448
Asch, S. E., 563, 575
Aserinsky, E., 139, 142
Ashton, N. L., 589
Askenasy, A. R., 447
Atkin, R. S., 605
Atkinson, J. W., 399

Atkinson, R. C., 223, 231, 233–234
Atthowe, J. M., 521
Averill, J. R., 295, 299, 442, 443
Ayllon, T., 521
Azrin, N., 521

Bacon, C., 600
Baddeley, A. D., 228
Baer, D. M., 194
Baird, J. C., 106
Baker, E., 605
Baker, T. B., 375
Baldessarini, R. J., 160
Baltes, P. B., 352–353, 356–357
Bandura, A., 204, 205, 289, 293, 294, 337, 338, 423, 425, 456, 522
Banks, W. C., 586
Barasch, D. P., 289
Barber, T. X., 155
Barkley, R., 505
Barlow, D., 402
Barnett, R. C., 599
Barnicot, N. A., 308
Baron, R. A., 556
Barron, F., 270, 271
Bartlett, F., Sir, 237
Baruch, G. K., 599
Bassett, R., 581
Bateman, F., 132
Bateson, G., 484
Batson, C. D., 581
Battle, C. C., 516
Baumrind, D., 328–329
Bayley, N., 314, 315, 318, 325
Beck, A. T., 195, 396, 480, 492, 494, 528, 529
Becker, E., 366
Beckstein, D., 344
Beezley, P., 601
Bell, A. G., 89
Bell, G. B., 585
Bell, R. Q., 316
Bellugi, U., 328
Belsky, J., 595, 600, 601, 603
Bem, D. J., 430, 566
Bender, L., 401
Benevento, A., 585

Benjamin, B., 442
Bennett, M. V. L., 45
Benson, H., 173
Benton, A. L., 401
Berg, L., 611
Berkeley, G., 209
Berkman, L. F., 458
Berkowitz, L., 292
Berne, E., 531
Bernstein, G. G., 282
Berscheid, E. S., 555, 557, 564, 565, 574
Bhasker, R., 260
Biglan, A., 520
Bijou, S. W., 194, 253
Binet, A., 375, 380
Birren, J. E., 352, 353
Blakemore, C., 120
Blass, E. M., 288
Bleuler, E., 481
Block, J., 360–361
Blom, J. G., 133
Blood, R. O., 599
Bloom, B. S., 317, 326
Bloom, L., 254
Boggiano, A. K., 568
Bornstein, M. H., 315
Botwinick, J., 356, 594, 611
Bouchard, T., 273
Bourne, L. E., 262
Bousfield, W. A., 224
Bouvier, L. F., 592
Bower, G. H., 225–226, 228
Bower, T. G. R., 315
Boycott, B. B., 71
Boyes-Braem, P., 263
Brandeis, L., 604
Bransford, J. D., 219, 235–236
Braswell, L., 505, 530
Brazelton, T. B., 311, 318
Brickman, P., 290
Broadbent, D. E., 211, 222
Brody, E. B., 309
Brody, N., 309
Brooks, J., 317
Brown, J. W., 59
Brown, L. T., 4
Brown, R., 107, 256, 294, 327, 328
Bruch, H., 341

683

NAME INDEX

Bruch, M. A., 397
Bruno, S., 609
Buchanan, B. G., 260
Buchsbaum, M. S., 505
Buck, R., 299
Buckhout, R., 605
Bull, N., 297
Bullock, T. H., 44
Bundy, C., 327
Bundy, R. S., 315
Burgess, R. L., 601–602
Burish, T. G., 609
Burt, C., 273
Buss, A. H., 293
Butcher, J. N., 389, 479, 539
Butler, D., 562
Butler, R. N., 361
Byrne, D., 556

Cacioppo, J. T., 397, 581
Calvin, W. H., 69
Campbell, C., 282
Campbell, F. W., 81, 84
Campos, J. J., 316, 317
Cannon, W. B., 296, 436
Caputo, C., 427
Carlsmith, J. M., 554
Carlson, N. R., 38
Carpenter, M. B., 36, 44, 55
Carroll, J. B., 269
Carskadon, M. A., 149
Carson, R. C., 479
Cartwright, D. C., 293
Cartwright, R. D., 146
Cassel, J., 457, 458
Catalan, J., 578–579
Cattell, P., 318
Cattell, R. B., 17, 267, 268, 356, 358, 384, 385, 417, 427
Cavanaugh, J. C., 355
Chaffee, S., 550
Chaiken, S., 550, 551
Chalfin, S., 327
Chance, J. E., 219
Chan-Palay, V., 33
Chapman, C., 535
Charrow, R. P., 605
Charrow, V., 605
Check, J. V. P., 294
Cherryh, C. J., 209
Chi, M. T. H., 238
Childers, W. R., 167
Chiriboga, D., 451
Choate, R., 331
Chomsky, N., 211, 249, 251, 254
Christensen, P. R., 271
Cialdini, R. B., 578–579, 580, 581
Cicero, 558
Ciminero, A. R., 403
Clark, E. V., 252, 253
Clark, L. D., 323
Clark, M. C., 225–226
Clark, R. W., 399
Clarke, A. D. B., 325
Clarke, A. M., 325

Clarkson, T. B., 450
Cliff, N., 300
Clore, G. L., 558
Coates, B., 332
Coates, D., 290
Cobb, S., 440, 457
Cohen, J., 552
Cohn, E., 290
Coleman, J. C., 479
Colletta, N. D., 596
Collins, A. M., 240–241
Collins, S. M., 604
Collmer, C., 601
Comstock, G., 550
Cone, J. D., 535
Conger, J. J., 273, 311
Conger, R. D., 602
Conner, E., 138
Conrad, R., 215, 216
Conway, E. F., 601
Conway, F., 579
Cooper, L. A., 216
Coren, S., 76, 77, 85, 89, 113, 122
Cornelison, A., 484
Cornsweet, T. N., 76, 77
Corsini, R. J., 514–515, 525–527
Costa, F., 344
Costa, L., 611
Costa, P. T., 456
Cote, L., 57
Cotman, C. W., 28, 29, 35
Cox, P. R., 441
Cox, V. C., 590
Coyne, J. C., 449, 459
Craig, K. D., 397
Craighead, W. E., 397, 530
Craik, F. I. M., 220–221, 222, 223, 234, 354
Cranshaw, L. I., 31
Cravioto, J., 308
Crisp, A. H., 341
Cristol, A. H., 514
Cronbach, L. J., 326, 378
Cronkite, W., 550
Crosby, F. J., 573
Cunitz, A. R., 232
Cureton, K. J., 282

Dabbs, J. M., Jr., 552
Dakof, G., 449
Dallenbach, K. H., 229
Danby, B. L., 578–579
Dane, F., 605–606
Danks, J. H., 253
Danziger, W. L., 611
Darley, J. M., 565, 576–577
Darwin, C., 8, 9, 289, 298–299
Davidson, L. A., 401
Davidson, P. O., 397
Davidson, T., 551
Davidson, W. S., 535
Davis, G. C., 351
Davis, G. H., 311
Davis, J., 282
Davis, J. A., 572

Davis, J. H., 605
Davis, J. M., 165
Davis, K. E., 560
Davis, R., 260
Davison, G. C., 518–519, 541
Davison, J., 517
Dawkins, R., 292
Day, K. D., 566
Dearden, R. F., 330
Deci, E. L., 568
deGroot, A. D., 259–260
Dekirmenjian, H., 165
DeLicardie, E., 308
DeLongis, A., 449
Dembroski, T. M., 552
Dement, W. C., 140, 143, 145, 147, 149, 150, 152, 153
DeQuincey, T., 168
Dermen, D., 270
Despres, M. A., 313
Deutsch, J. A., 282
DeValois, K. K., 83, 84, 86
DeValois, R. L., 83, 84, 86
deVilliers, J. G., 328
deVilliers, P. A., 328
Devlin, J., 256
deVries, H. A., 350
Dickstein, L. S. 264
Diener, E., 587
Dion, K., 557, 565
Dixon, R. A., 355
Dodwell, P., 315
Doehrman, M. J., 338
Dohrenwend, B. P., 447
Dohrenwend, B. S., 447
Dollard, J., 292, 420–422
Donaldson, G., 267, 356
Donnerstein, E., 294
Donovan, J.E., 344
Doob, A., 605
Doob, L., 292
Dougherty, L. M., 299
Douvan, E., 337
Dowling, J. E., 71
Downing, L. T., 588
Dubnoff, S. J., 599
duBois-Reymond, E., 39
Duffy, E., 444
Dufort, R. H., 182
Duncan, S. L., 565
Duncker, K., 259
Duta, C. R., 37

Eagly, A. H., 551
Ebbesen, E. B., 589
Ebbinghaus, H., 210
Eccles, J. C., 33, 43
Egan, J. P., 110
Einstein, A., 419
Ekman, P., 299, 558, 559
Ekstom, R. B., 270
Elkind, D., 319, 320, 321, 341
Ellis, A., 525
Ellis, H. C., 262
Emde, R., 316

NAME INDEX

Emery, G., 529
Endicott, J., 390
Endler, N. S., 395–396
Engen, T., 315
Englemann, T. G., 143
Epstein, R., 200, 590
Epstein, S., 443, 444
Erbaugh, J. K., 396
Erickson, J. R., 257, 260
Erikson, E. H., 8, 337, 343, 362, 413–414
Eron, L. D., 293, 331, 398
Escher, M. C., 104
Ettema, J., 551
Evans, R. I., 552
Everett, P. B., 535
Exner, J., 398
Eysenck, H., 417, 536

Fairweather, G. W., 535
Fantz, R. L., 315
Farran, D. C., 322
Fechner, G. T., 111, 112
Fehr, R. S., 296, 566
Feinman, S., 317
Fenz, W. D., 444
Ferree, M., 599
Ferreira, A., 313
Ferster, C. B., 194, 196
Feshbach, S., 552
Festinger, L., 553, 554, 572
Field, J., 315
Filskov, S. B., 401
Fischman, M. W., 165
Fischman, V. S., 164
Fishbein, M., 552
Fleck, S., 484
Fletcher, G., 290, 559
Folger, M. K., 254
Folkman, S., 449, 454, 460, 464
Fontana, V. J., 601
Forbes, G. B., 308
Ford, J. R., 441
Fowles, B., 331
Fox, C. A., 37
Fozard, J. L., 349
Frank, J. D., 516
Frankenhaeuser, M., 439, 444–445, 456
Franklin, R. M., 170
Franks, J. J., 219, 235
Fraser, S. G., 576, 577
Frazier, T. M., 311
Freedman, D. X., 169
Freedman, J. L., 576, 577
Freemon, F. R., 145
French, J. W., 270
French, R. L., 585
Freud, S., 8, 291, 292, 395, 408–412, 474, 487, 511
Friedman, M., 455
Friedman, M. I., 281
Friedrich, L. K., 331
Frierson, H. T., 397
Friesen, W. V., 299, 558, 559
Frodi, A. M., 601

Fromm, E., 413
Fuchs, C. Z., 529
Fuller, J. L., 323
Fuortes, M. G. F., 82
Furman, W., 329–330

Gaensbauer, T., 316
Gaines, R. W., 601
Galanter, E., 107
Galassi, J. P., 397
Galton, F., 375
Galvani, L., 38–39
Garbarino, J., 601
Garcia, J., 282
Gardner, B. T., 254
Gardner, R. A., 254
Gardner, R. M., 4
Garfield, S. L., 524, 539
Geen, R. G., 293, 582
Geiwitz, J., 273
Genest, M., 397
Gerard, H. B., 564
Gerbner, G., 551
Geschwind, N., 58
Gerwirtz, H. B., 316
Gewirtz, J. L., 316
Gelles, R. J., 293
Gelman, R., 252
Gerbner, G., 293
Gesell, A. L., 315, 318
Ghiselli, E. E., 383
Gibbon, M., 490
Gibson, H., 598
Gibson, J. J., 117
Gil, D. C., 602
Gillie, O., 273
Gilligan, S. G., 228
Gilmour, D. R., 589
Ginsburg, A. P., 85
Glanzer, M., 232
Glass, C. R., 397
Glass, G. V., 537, 538
Glasser, W., 531
Glick, I. O., 367, 368
Glick, P. C., 596
Glucksburg, S., 218, 253
Glueck, B. C., 487
Godden, D. R., 228
Goethals, G. R., 561
Gold, D., 600
Goldberg, D., 311
Goldberg, R. J., 600
Goldberger, A. S., 272, 273
Golden, C. J., 401
Golden, M. M., 329
Goldfarb, W., 325
Goldfein, A., 164
Goldfried, M. R., 398, 518–519, 524, 528
Goldin-Meadow, S., 252
Goldstein, A. G., 219
Goldstein, H., 311
Goldstein, R., 140
Goodman, I., 332
Goodrich, C. A., 139
Goodwin, D. W., 503

Gore, S., 440, 458
Gorsuch, R. C., 395
Gottesman, I. I., 506
Gottman, J. M., 397
Gough, H. G., 393
Granit, R., 32
Grant, D. A., 194
Gray, S. W., 274
Gray, W. D., 263
Green, A. H., 601
Green, D. M., 107, 108
Green, R. S., 300
Greenberg, J. H., 138
Greene, D., 567
Greeno, J. G., 260
Gregory, R. L., 71
Greulich, W. W., 309
Grinker, R. R., 284, 461
Gross, L., 293, 551
Gross, P. H., 565
Grush, J., 550
Guilford, J. P., 106, 267, 271
Guilleminault, C., 152
Gullotta, T., 344
Gurin, G., 284
Gurman, A. S., 516
Gutmann, D. L., 360

Haigler, H. J., 169
Hainline, L., 315
Hake, H. W., 194
Hakstian, A. R., 529
Haley, J., 484, 534
Hall, C. S., 414
Hall, E. T., 588
Hall, G. S., 8, 9
Hall, J. A., 559
Hall, W. G., 288
Hamburg, D. A., 462
Hammel, H. T., 31
Hammond, S., 268
Hammurabi, 157
Haney, C., 551, 586
Hannan, A., 517
Hans, V., 606
Hansel, C. E. M., 133
Hanson, D. R., 506
Harkins, S., 582
Harlow, H. F., 201–202, 323–324
Harman, H. H., 270
Harmon, R., 316
Harrington, D. M., 270, 271
Harris, R. C., 309
Harrison, G. A., 308
Hart, H., 577
Hartmann, E. L., 138, 142, 143, 145
Hartshorne, M., 429
Hartup, W. W., 329–330
Harvey, S. C., 159
Hatfield, E., 556
Hathaway, S. R., 390, 487
Hayes, C., 255
Hayes, J. R., 260
Hayes, S. C., 535
Hayes-Roth, B., 426

685

Hayflick, L., 345
Hayward, S. C., 535
Hearnshaw, L. S., 273
Hebb, D. O., 273
Hecht, B. F., 252, 253
Hein, A., 130
Held, R., 130
Heller, H. C., 31
Helmholtz, H. L., 93
Helson, H., 112
Henson, C., 82
Herbart, J. F., 106
Hering, E., 86
Heron, W. T., 487
Hess, E. H., 107
Heston, L. L., 483
Hetherington, E. M., 308, 310, 311, 313, 329, 330, 596–597
Higgins-Trenk, A., 600
Hilgard, E. R., 154, 156
Hill, C. T., 556
Hill, G. W., 583, 584
Hill, J. P., 338
Hillman, D. E., 37
Hines, P., 404
Hippocrates, 26
Hirsch, J., 307
Hodapp, R., 327
Hodgkin, A. L., 42
Hodgkins, J., 352
Hoefnagel-Hohle, M., 254
Hoehn-Saric, R., 516
Hoffman, H., 330
Hoffman, L. W., 599, 600
Hoffman, A., 170
Holland, P. C., 184
Hollingshead, A. B., 485
Hollon, S. D., 529
Holman, R. B., 152
Holmes, T. H., 441, 446, 447, 449
Holt, E. L., Jr., 308
Holt, R., 605
Homer, 157
Honzik, C. H., 180, 200, 204
Hood, L., 254
Horn, J. L., 267, 268, 269, 356, 358
Horney, K., 413
Hornseth, J. P., 194
Horton, D. L., 198
Houland, C. I., 549, 551
Howard, D. V., 258
Hoyer, W. J., 352–353
Hoyle, G., 35
Hubel, O. H., 78, 81, 82, 120
Huebmer, R. R., 299
Huesmann, L. R., 331
Hughes, C. P., 611
Hughes, J. R., 349
Hull, C. L., 187
Hultsch, D. F., 197, 354, 355
Hume, D., 209
Humphreys, L. G., 194
Hund, R. M., 4
Hunt, B. I., 138
Hunt, R. R., 262
Hurvich, L. M., 86

Hurwitz, I., 309
Huston-Stein, A., 600

Ickes, W., 563
Illingworth, R. S., 313
Imber, S. D., 516
Inhelder, B., 341
Insko, C. A., 549
Itkin, G., 558
Izard, C. E., 299

Jackson, C. M., 314, 394
Jackson, D., 484
Jackson, J. M., 582
Jackson, S. E., 588
Jacobs, R. I., 344
Jacoby, L. L., 234
Jaffe, D. A., 586
Jaffe, J. H., 165, 169, 172
James, W., 8, 19, 296
Jameson, D., 86
Jamison, K. R., 490
Janis, I. L., 584
Jarvie, G. J., 282
Jarvik, M. E., 166
Jasper, H., 82
Javaid, J. I., 165
Jawetz, E., 164
Jenkins, J. G., 229
Jenkins, J. J., 235
Jensen, A. R., 272, 273, 383, 384, 386
Jessor, R., 344
Joffe, J. M., 313
Johnson, B., 601–602
Johnson, D. M., 263
Johnson, M. K., 235–236
Johnson, N., 251
Johnson, R. D., 588
Johnson, S., 598
Johnson, V. E., 351, 501
Johnson-Laud, P. N., 265
Jones, E. E., 426–427, 428, 562
Jones, J., 578
Jones, M. C., 340
Jones, M. R., 257, 260
Jouvet, M., 139
Julien, R., 157–158, 164
Jung, C., 412–413
Juola, J. F., 233–234

Kagan, J., 272, 273, 311, 312, 325
Kales, A., 141, 142
Kales, J., 142
Kalish, H., 517
Kalish, R. A., 366
Kallmann, F. J., 487
Kalven, H. G., Jr., 606
Kamin, L., 272, 273
Kammann, R., 133
Kandel, D. B., 339
Kandel, E. R., 33
Kanfer, F. H., 493
Kanner, L., 505

Kant, I., 66
Kanter, R. M., 579
Kantner, J. F., 343, 344
Kaplan, B. H., 458
Kaplan, J. R., 450
Karmiloff-Smith, A., 252
Karnig, K. M., 309
Karst, T. O., 528
Karuza, J., 290
Kasl, S. V., 440
Kassarjan, H., 552
Kassin, S. M., 605
Kassinove, H., 528
Katchadourian, H., 308, 338
Katcher, A. H., 295, 567
Katzman, N., 550
Kaufman, L., 124
Kaufmann, H., 5
Kazdin, A. E., 520, 521, 523, 532, 538
Kearsley, R., 312
Keller, S. L., 311
Kelley, H. H., 428, 549, 560, 562
Kelley, K., 590
Kellogg, L. A., 255
Kellogg, W. N., 255
Kelly, G. A., 420, 425
Kempe, C. H., 601
Kendall, P. C., 197, 396, 397, 430, 505, 524, 530
Kendler, H. H., 202–204
Kendler, T. S., 202–204
Kendrick, M. J., 397
Kennell, J., 256
Kenshalo, D. R., 96
Kerr, N. L., 605
Kessen, W., 315
Kety, S. S., 138, 484
Keynes, R. D., 40
Kidder, L., 290
Kiesler, D. J., 532, 539
Kilmann, P. R., 394
Kimball, W. H., 397
Kimble, G. A., 182, 183, 194
Kinsey, A. C., 340
Kintsch, W., 235, 242
Kinzel, A. S., 589
Kirschenbaum, H. M., 605
Kitahama, K., 139
Klaus, M., 256
Klaus, R. A., 274
Klein, K. E., 138
Klein, P. S., 308
Klein, R. E., 325
Kleinerman, J., 138
Kleitman, N., 137, 138, 139, 142, 143
Klerman, G. L., 542
Kluckhohn, C., 407, 408
Knapp, M. L., 558
Knowles, E. S., 589
Koeske, R. D., 238
Koester, J., 40
Koffka, K., 10, 115
Kogan, N., 271, 564
Kohl, J., 577
Köhler, W., 10, 115, 199
Konečni, V. J., 589

NAME INDEX

Korgeski, G. P., 397
Korn, S. J., 416
Kotovsky, K., 264
Kovacs, M., 529
Kraepelin, E., 106
Kramer, J. C., 164
Krasner, L., 521
Krasnoff, L., 447
Krayer, O., 82
Kretschmer, E., 414
Kübler-Ross, E., 366–367
Kuffer, S., 82
Kuffler, S., 79, 83
Kulik, J. A., 294
Kulka, R. A., 599
Kurtz, R., 524
Kuypers, J. A., 361

Labouvie-Vief, G. V., 352–353, 359
Lachman, J. L., 355
Lachman, R., 355
Laird, J. D., 296, 577
Lakey, D. B., 282
Lamb, M. E., 601
Lamm, H., 584
Landau, B., 426
Landesman-Dwyer, S., 311
Langer, E. J., 457, 595, 590
Lanzetta, J. T., 296
Lasater, T. M., 552
Latané, B., 576–577, 582
Launier, R., 451, 460
Lawson, D. M., 397, 504
Layzer, D., 272
Lazarus, A., 517
Lazarus, R. S., 439, 442, 443, 449, 451, 452, 454, 458, 459, 460, 464
Lefkowitz, M. M., 331
Legant, P., 427
Lehfeldt, H., 344
Lehrman, D. S., 273
Leiman, A. L., 41
Lenneberg, E. H., 246, 254, 326
Leonard, L. B., 254
Lepper, M. R., 567
Lerner, M. J., 561
Lerner, R. M., 190, 197, 322, 338, 343, 416, 595, 600
Lesgold, A. M., 225–226
Lessen-Fireston, J., 311
Lesser, G. S., 339
Lester, B. M., 309
Leventhal, H., 552
Levi, A., 562
Levinson, D. J., 363–365
Lewin, K., 10
Lewinsohn, P. M., 443, 520, 529
Lewis, D., 401
Lewis, M., 317, 329
Lewis, S. K., 578–579
Lezak, M. D., 401
Libuser, L., 589
Lichtenstein, E., 404
Lidz, T., 484
Lieberman, M. A., 454, 538–539

Liebert, R. M., 204
Light, R., 601, 602
Lightbow, P., 254
Linde, S. M., 147
Lindsay, P. H., 95
Lindzey, G., 414
Lipinski, D., 403
Lipsitt, L. P., 315
Lipsky, M. J., 528
Lipton, R. C., 324
Liska, K., 158, 160, 161, 170
Littlefield, D. C., 164
Livson, F., 594
Lloyd-Still, J. D., 309
Lobitz, G., 598
Locke, J., 65, 209
Lockhart, R. S., 222, 234, 354
Locklear, E., 401
Loftus, E. F., 236–237, 240–241, 605
Loo, C. M., 589
Lorenz, K., 291
Lowell, E. L., 399
Lowenthal, M. F., 451
Lubchenco, L. O., 313
Luborsky, L., 537
Ludlow, C., 505
Lumsdaine, A. A., 551
Luria, A., 59, 226
Lushene, R. E., 395
Lusso, F., 450
Lyle, J., 330
Lyles, J. N., 609

Mass, H. S., 361
McCain, G., 590
McClane, T. K., 159
McClelland, D. C., 399
McCombs, M. M., 550
McCrae, R. R., 456
McDill, E. L. 339
McDougall, W., 288
McGaugh, J. L., 144
McGinnes, G. C., 299
McGovern, K., 404
McGue, M., 273
McGurk, H., 317
McKinley, J. C., 390
McKinney, W. T., 492
McLean, P. D., 520, 529
McLeod, P., 257
Maddox, G. L., 594
Mahan, J. L., 448
Mahoney, M. J., 482
Maier, S. F., 193, 195
Malamuth, N. M., 294
Mandler, G., 107, 224–225, 354
Mangold, R., 138
Mann, L. I., 182
Manuck, S. B., 450
Manzolati, J., 551
Maracek, J., 427
Maranon, G., 297
Marks, D., 133
Markus, H., 426, 582
Marshall, G. O., 298

Marshall, W. L., 529
Martin, A. R., 46
Martin, C. E., 340
Martin, H. P., 601
Martin, W. R., 159
Mash, E. J., 402
Maslach, C., 298, 588
Masters, J. C., 329
Masters, W. H., 351, 501
Matarazzo, J. D., 382
Matas, L., 323
Mattis, S., 612
Maxwell, J. C., 69
May, M. A., 429
Meddis, R., 145
Medvedev, Z. A., 345
Meehl, P. E., 378, 481, 485, 487
Meek, D., 605
Megargee, E. I., 393
Meichenbaum, D., 523, 530
Mendelsohn, M., 396, 493
Mendelson, W. B., 150
Menninger, K., 487
Merbaum, M., 539
Merluzzi, T. V., 397
Merrill, M. A., 380
Mervis, C. B., 262, 263
Metcalf, J., 590
Meyers, A., 530
Meyers, A. W., 535
Milavsky, B., 295, 567
Miles, M. B., 538–539
Milgram, S., 587
Miller, D. R., 130, 131
Miller, D. T., 253, 561, 562, 563
Miller, E. W., 450
Miller, G. A., 93, 217
Miller, J. A., 581
Miller, N. E., 292, 420–422
Miller, N. J., 528
Miller, R. L., 572
Miller, S. M., 464, 465
Miller, T. B., 139
Millon, T., 499
Mills, C. B., 198
Milner, B., 233
Minty, J., 170, 532
Mischel, W., 427, 501
Mishler, E. G., 484
Misiak, H., 20
Mitler, M. M., 149
Mock, J. E., 396
Monnier, M., 139
Monoz, R. F., 529
Monteiro, K. P., 228
Montgomery, D. A., 605
Montgomery, K., 611
Moreland, R. L., 555
Moretti, M. M., 563
Morgan, C. D., 399
Morgan, M., 293
Morrow, W. R., 339
Morse, H. A., 601–602
Morton, H., 589
Moscovici, S., 575–576
Mowrer, O. H., 292

NAME INDEX

Mueller, J., 67–68
Muir, D., 315
Munsterberg, H., 8
Murdock, B., 232
Murray, H. A., 399, 407, 408
Mussen, P. H., 273, 311, 340
Muzio, J. N., 143
Myers, D. G., 561, 585
Myers, F. H., 164
Myrsten, A. L., 445

Nader, P. R., 308
Nagasaki, H., 139
Napolitan, D. A., 561
Nash, E. H., 516
National Commission on Marijuana and Drug Use, 171–172
National Institute on Alcohol Abuse and Alcoholism, 163
Naus, M. J., 218
Neale, J. M., 485, 541
Nelson, K., 255
Nelson, R. O., 403
Nelson, T. O., 218–219
Nemeth, C., 606
Neugarten, B. L., 360
Newby, H. A., 88
Newell, A., 211, 257
Newhall, S. W., 330
Newhoff, M., 254
Newton, I., 68–69
Nezlek, J., 568
Nicholls, J. G., 79, 83
Nida, S., 576
Niles, P., 552
Nimoy, L., 561
Nisbett, R. E., 287, 426–427, 428, 562, 567
Noma, E., 106
Nomikos, M. S., 442, 443
Nordheden, B., 445
Norman, D. A., 95
Nowliss, G. H., 315
Nuckolls, K. B., 458

O'Brien, J. S., 37
O'Connell, D. N., 154
Offer, D., 338
Ohm, G. S., 89
Ojemann, G. A., 69
Okada, M., 395–396
Okada, S., 37
O'Leary, K. D., 505
Olson, J. M., 552
Oltmanns, T. F., 485
Opton, E., Jr., 442, 443
Ordy, J. M., 315
Orne, M. T., 154
Ornstein, P. A., 218
Ortony, A., 237
Orvis, B. R., 562
Osborn, A. F., 584
Ostrea, E., 311
Overmier, B., 195
Ovid, 566

Padgett, V. R., 582
Palay, S. L., 33
Palmer, F. H., 274
Palmer, J. C., 236–237
Palmore, E., 348
Pappenheimer, J. R., 139
Parke, F., 329
Parke, R. D., 308, 310, 311, 313, 329, 330, 601
Parkes, C. M., 367
Parron, D. L., 150
Parten, M., 330
Paterson, D. G., 487
Paterson, J. G., 315
Paterson, F. G., 255
Patterson, G. R., 293, 402
Paul, G. L., 520
Paulus, P. B., 590
Pavio, A., 226
Pavlov, I. P., 181, 182, 183, 312
Paykel, E. S., 449
Peole, N. V., 397
Pearlin, L. I., 463, 464
Pearlstone, Z., 227
Peck, M. B., 315
Pendleton, M., 581
Penta, J., 609
Peplau, L. A., 556
Perls, F., 531
Petersen, A. C., 340
Peterson, L. R., 216
Peterson, M. J., 216
Peterson, P. G., 594
Pfeiffer, E., 351
Phares, E. J., 394
Penfield, W., 57
Piaget, J., 317–322, 341
Pichert, J. W., 242–243
Pilon, R., 315
Pliner, P., 577
Plutchik, R., 300
Pomeroy, W. B., 340
Popkin, S. J., 349
Popper, K. R., 33, 517
Porac, C., 76, 77, 85, 89, 113, 122
Posner, M. I., 257
Post, B., 445
Poster, D., 609
Pratt, J. G., 133
Presidential Commission on Obscenity and Pornography, 294
Provence, S., 324
Psotka, J., 229
Pusser, H. E., 332
Pythagoras, 138

Quinllan, M. R., 240

Rabbitt, P., 353
Rabinowitz, V. C., 290
Rachman, S., 517
Radloff, P., 517
Rahe, D. F., 329–330

Rahe, R. H., 441, 446, 447, 448, 449
Rajecki, D. W., 548
Rall, T. W., 166
Ramey, C. T., 322
Ramsey, B. K., 274
Rapaport, J. L., 505, 535
Rasmussen, T., 57
Raven, B. H., 585
Raven, J. C., 384, 385
Rechtschaffen, A., 141
Redlich, F. C., 485
Rehberg, R. A., 339
Rehlak, P. J., 397
Rehm, L. P. 493, 494, 529
Reichard, S., 594
Reid, J. B., 293
Reitan, R. M., 401
Rensberger, B., 578
Rescorla, R. A., 184
Rhine, J. B., 132
Rich, A. R., 521
Riddell, W. I., 53
Rigsby, L. C., 339
Rimland, B., 505
Ringler, N., 256
Risley, T. R., 535
Risser, D., 299
Rissler, A., 439
Roback, H. B., 394
Roberts, D., 550
Robertson-Tchabo, E. A., 352
Robinson, D. N., 42
Robson, J. G., 81
Rock, I., 124
Rodin, J., 286, 287, 457, 590
Roff, M. F., 329
Roffwarg, H. P., 143
Rogers, C., 418, 514–516
Rokeach, M., 488–489
Roll, S., 564
Roosevelt, E., 419
Roper, R. T., 606
Rosch, E., 240, 262, 263
Rosen, C. E., 330
Rosen, W., 157
Rosenblum, L. A., 329
Rosenman, R. H., 455
Rosenthal, D., 483, 484
Rosenthal, T., 522
Rosenszweig, M. R., 41, 53
Ross, L., 561
Ross, M., 290, 559, 562
Rothbart, R., 218–219
Rotter, J. B., 394, 422
Rozelle, R. M., 522
Rubin, J. Z., 585
Rubin, Z., 556
Ruble, D. N., 568
Rumelhart, D. E., 237
Rundus, D., 223
Rush, A. J., 529
Rush, B., 471
Rushton, J. P., 332
Russek, M., 282
Russell, J. A., 300
Rutter, M., 506, 598

NAME INDEX

Saari, D., 577
Sachs, J. S., 251, 256
Saegert, S., 590
Saks, M., 606
Sales, S. M., 579
Salzinger, K., 482
Sandberg, E. C., 344
Sanders, D., 535
Sandgrund, A., 601
Sarason, E. G., 523
Satir, V., 534
Savary, L. M., 147
Sauer, W. J., 594
Sawin, D., 329
Scales, P., 344
Scarr-Salapatek, S., 272
Schacter, F. F., 327
Schacter, S., 166, 286, 297, 566, 572
Schaefer, C., 459
Schaie, K. W., 356, 357, 359
Schank, R. C., 242
Schiffman, H. R., 112
Schildkraut, J. J., 492
Schlosberg, H., 300
Schmidt, H., 132
Schmitz, M., 590
Schoenenberger, G. A., 139
Schofield, W., 539
Schonfeld, W. A., 339
Schosler, C., 463, 464
Schroeder, H. E., 521
Schulsinger, F., 484
Schumer, F., 398
Schuster, C. R., 165
Schuyler, D., 195
Schwachmore, H., 309
Schwartz, G. E., 608
Schwartz, J. H., 38
Schwartz, R. G., 254
Schwartz, R. M., 397
Scribner, S., 264, 265
Sears, R. F., 292
Seashore, C. E., 401
Segal, M. W., 555
Seidman, E., 535
Seligman, M. E. P., 193, 195, 252, 493, 494
Sells, S. B., 329
Selye, H., 436, 438
Severance, L., 605
Sewell, W. H., 339
Sexton, V. S., 20
Shaffer, D. F., 205
Shah, F., 344
Shah, V. P., 339
Shakespeare, W., 305
Shapiro, D., 538
Shapiro, D. A., 538
Sharer, R., 397
Shaw, B. F., 529
Shaw, D. L., 339
Shaw, M., 583
Shaw, M. E., 589
Sheffield, F. D., 551
Sheinman, L., 568
Sheldon, W. H., 414–415, 417

Shepard, R. N., 216, 219
Sheperd, J. D., 130, 131
Shiffrin, R. M., 231
Shirley, M. M., 315
Shock, N. W., 345, 346, 348
Shor, R. E., 153, 154
Shore, E., 327
Shortliffe, E. H., 260
Shulman, H. G., 233
Siegesmund, K. A., 37
Sigelman, J., 579
Signorelli, N., 293
Simon, H. A., 211, 257, 259, 260, 264
Simon, T., 380
Sinclair, M., 315
Singer, B., 537
Singer, J. E., 297, 566
Skeels, H., 274, 325
Skinner, B. F., 187, 194, 196, 197, 253, 420, 422, 487, 520, 521
Skodol, A. E., 490
Sloane, R. B., 514
Smith, D., 524
Smith, D. E., 165
Smith, M. L., 537, 538
Smith, R. J., 589
Snow, C. E., 254
Snyder, M., 552, 565
Snyder, S. H., 167
Soal, S. G., 132
Sobocinski, D., 528
Soetvert, D. L., 401
Sokoloff, L., 138
Solomon, F., 150, 151
Solomon, R. L., 193, 195
Solomon, S. K., 235–236, 590
Sommer, R., 588
Sontag, L. W., 313
Sotile, W. M., 394
Sours, J. A., 341
Spanier, G. B., 343, 344, 395, 596
Spearman, C., 266
Sperling, G., 214–215
Sperry, R. W., 60
Spiegel, J. P., 461
Spielberger, C. D., 395
Spinner, B., 294
Spiro, R. J., 237
Spitz, R. A., 324
Spitzer, R. L., 390, 490
Spreen, O., 401
Sroufe, L. A., 316, 317, 323
Standing, L., 219
Stanton, M., 170
Staples, F. R., 514
Starr, R., 311
Starr, R. H., Jr., 601, 602
Stasser, G., 605
St. Clair, K. L., 318
Stein, A. H., 331, 600
Steinberg, L. D., 600
Stemberg, R. J., 269
Stenberg, C. R., 317
Stern, J. A., 566
Sternberg, R. J., 384
Sternberg, S., 217

Stevens, C. F., 39
Stevens, S. S., 112
Stewart, J. E. H., 565
Stone, A. R., 516
Storandt, M., 611
Storrow, H. A., 390
Stratton, G., 130–131
Straus, M. A., 293, 296
Strauss, M., 311
Streissguth, A. P., 311
Stricker, G., 398
Stunkard, A. J., 195, 284
Suls, J. M., 572
Suomi, S. J., 323–324
Swann, W. B., Jr., 552
Swensen, C. H., 400
Swets, J. A., 107, 108
Swift, D. F., 339
Syme, S. L., 458
Szasz, T., 476

Talland, G. A., 353
Tangri, S. S., 600
Tanke, E. D., 565
Tanner, J. M., 308, 340
Taub, D. M., 450
Taylor, F. G., 529
Taylor, W. G., 93
Terdal, L., 402
Terenius, L., 167
Terman, L. M., 375, 380
Tessman, L. H., 598
Tetlock, P. E., 563
Therman, P. O. G., 138
Thompson, D. M., 228
Thompson, J. K., 285
Thompson, L., 344
Thorndike, E. L., 185–186
Thorndyke, P. W., 426
Thronesbery, C., 355
Thurnher, M., 451
Thurstone, L. L., 267
Thurstone, T. G., 267
Tichener, E. B., 8
Toch, H., 293
Toffler, A., 593
Tolman, E. C., 180, 200, 204
Tomkins, W. T., 311
Tornatzky, L., 535
Toukey, J. C., 555
Trabasso, T., 265
Trause, W. A., 256
Treisman, A., 222
Trexler, L. D., 528
Trommsdorf, G., 584
Truax, C. B., 516
Tulving, E., 220–221, 222, 227–228, 229, 239

Udelf, M. S., 315

Vaillant, G., 362, 462
Valatx, J. L., 139

NAME INDEX

Van Allen, M. W., 401
Vandivert, W., 121
Vaughan, K. B., 296
Verinis, J. S., 564
Veroff, J., 599
Verwoerdt, A., 351
Vigersky, R. A., 341
Vincent, J. E., 578–579
Vital-Durand, F., 120
Von Baeyer, A., 158
von Békésy, G., 92
von Frisch, K., 255

Wachtel, P. L., 524
Wade, T. C., 375
Wagner, A. R., 184
Wagner, J. J., 577
Wahler, R. G., 254
Walder, L. O., 331
Walk, R. D., 130, 131
Walker, A., 600
Walker, R. N., 415
Walkey, F. H., 589
Wallach, M. A., 271
Wallis, C., 442
Walster, E., 557, 564, 574
Walster, G. W., 556, 574
Walters, J., 313
Ward, C. H., 396
Ward, L. M., 85, 89, 113
Wargo, D. G., 516
Warland, R., 594
Warwick, R., 55
Wason, P. C., 265
Waters, E., 323
Watkins, M. J., 221, 223
Watson, J. B., 8, 9
Watson, R. I., 588
Waxler, N. E., 484

Webb, W. B., 138, 139, 146
Weber, E. H., 111–112
Wechsler, D., 356, 375, 401
Weckland, J., 484
Wedding, D., 514–515
Wegmann, H. M., 138
Weil, A., 157
Weiner, B., 164, 290
Weiner, I. B., 398, 512, 513
Weiner, J. S., 308
Weingarten, H., 505
Weinstein, S., 96
Weisel, T. N., 78, 81, 82, 120
Weiskopf, S., 315
Weiss, D. J., 380
Weiss, R. S., 367
Weiss, S. M., 608
Welford, A., 222
Wender, P. H., 484
Werblin, F. S., 77
Wertheimer, M., 10, 115
Wesson, D. R., 165
Westby, D. L., 339
Wever, E. G., 94
Whalen, C. K., 505
Wheeler, D., 578–579
Whipple, K., 514
White, C. C., 150
White, M. E., 339
White, R. K., 562
Wicker, A. W., 552
Wicks-Nelson, R., 204
Wiggins, N. H., 558
Wilcox, M. J., 254
Wilcoxon, L. A., 520
Williams, J. B., 490
Williams, K. D., 582
Williams, P. L., 55
Williams, R. L., 138
Wilmer, J., 484
Wilson, E. O., 289, 292

Wilson, G. T., 504, 517, 538
Wilson, R. C., 339
Winick, M., 309
Winzenz, D., 225–226
Wippman, J., 323
Wittgenstein, L., 252
Wolf, R. M., 339
Wolf, S., 605
Wolfe, D. M., 599
Wolff, K. M., 324
Wolff, P. H., 309
Wolpe, J., 197, 517, 519
Wolpert, E. A., 147
Wortman, C. B., 562
Wright, J. D., 599
Wrightsman, L. S., 605–606
Wundt, W., 8
Wuthrow, R., 551

Yalom, I. D., 538–539
Yarrow, L. J., 317
Yogi, Mahesh, Maharishi, 173
Yorkston, N. J., 514
Yosha, A., 590
Young, M., 442

Zadney, J., 564
Zahn, T. P., 505
Zajonc, R., 548, 555, 581, 582
Zanna, M., 552
Zarcone, V., 151
Zeisel, H., 606
Zelazo, P., 312
Zelnick, M., 343, 344
Zillmann, D., 294, 295, 298, 557, 566
Zimbardo, P. G., 298, 586, 588
Zimmerman, R. R., 323
Zubin, J., 398
Zuckerman, M., 590

Subject Index

ABC model, in rational emotive therapy, 525
Abnormal behavior, 468–506
  acute versus chronic, 491
  addictive disorders, 502–504
  affective disorders, 490–494
  antisocial personality behavior, 500
  anxiety disorders, 494–498
  attention deficit disorder, 505
  autism, 505–506
  bipolar disorders, 490–491, 492
  in childhood, 505–506
  classifying, 477–481
  conversion disorder, 476, 498–499
  definition, 472–473
  dependent personality disorder, 500
  depression, 491–494
  generalized anxiety disorder, 495–496
  history of, 470–471
  insanity and, 473
  models of, 473–475
    learning, 473–474
    medical, 475–476
    psychodynamic, 474–475
    systems, 475
  narcissistic personality disorder, 499–500
  obsessive-compulsive disorders, 497
  organic versus functional, 491
  paranoid personalilty disorder, 500–501
  personality disorders, 499–501
  phobic disorders, 496–497
  psychosexual, 501–502
  schizophrenia, 483–490
  sexual dysfunction, 501–502
  somatoform disorders, 498
  see also Behavior problems, therapy for
Absolute deprivation, 573
Absolute thresholds, 106–107
Abstract, of psychology journal articles, 631
Academic achievement, IQ scores and, 383, 384
Acceptance, as stage of dying, 367
Accommodation
  cognitive development and, 318
  eye and, 71
Accommodative power, aging and, 348
Accumulation theory, of aging, 347
Accurate empathy, in client centered therapy, 514

Acetylcholine, 38, 49
Achievement tests, 387–388
Achromatic colors, 126
Acoustical encoding, in short-term memory, 215–216
Acquisition
  associative learning and, 189–190
  memory and, 211
  stimulus-response (S-R) bonds and, 210
Acting-out children, cognitive-behavioral program for, 530
Action, of a production, 260
Action potential
  of neuron, 40–44
  reflexes and, 48–49
  synaptic transmission and, 45–46, 47
Active mastery, personality in adulthood and, 360
Active sleep. *See* Rapid-eye movement sleep
Activity scheduling, cognitive-behavioral treatment of depression and, 528–529, 529
Actor-observer effect, 562
Acute disorders, 491
  see also Abnormal behavior
Adaptation
  learning as, 179–180
  personality and, 456
  of sensory systems, 98, 112–113
Adaptive testing, 381
Addictive disorders, 502–504
  see also Psychoactive drugs
Additive color mixtures, 128
Adequate stimulus, for sensation, 66–67
Adipsia, lateral hypothalamus lesions causing, 284
Adolescence, 335–345
  cognitive changes in, 341–342
  definition, 336–337
  education in, 339
  identity development in, 337, 342–343
  peer group in, 337, 338, 339
  personality in, 362
  physical and physiological changes of, 338–340, 341
  pregnancy and, 313, 344–345
  sexuality in, 343–345
  storm and stress in, 336, 337–338
Adrenal glands, stress and, 437, 438
Adrenalin. *See* Epinephrine
Adrenocorticotrophic hormone (ACTH)
  memory retention and, 144

691

Adrenocorticotrophic hormone (ACTH) (cont.)
  stress and, 437
Adult, in transactional analysis, 531–532
Adulthood and aging, 345–368
  biological changes in, 345–351
  cognitive functioning in, 352–359, see also Intelligence tests
  cognitive impairments in, 610–613
  death and dying and, 365–368
  life review in, 361
  personality in, 359–365
  sleep patterns in, 143
  stages of development in, 362–365
Advertising on television, attitude change and, 550
Aerobic exercise, aging and, 350
Affect. See Emotions
Affective disorders, 490–494
Age fifty transition, in personality development, 365
Age regression, under hypnosis, 155
Age thirty transition, in personality development, 364–365
Aggression
  child abuse and, 601–603
  children from maritally conflicted homes and, 598
  crowding and, 589–590
  motivational factors in, 291–295
  spatial preferences and, 589
  television and, 331
Aggressive cue, stimulus as, 293
Aging. See Adulthood and aging
Agnosias, 59
Alarm reaction, in general adaptation syndrome, 436, 437
Alcohol and alcoholism, 150, 156, 157, 160–163, 197, 503–504
  prenatal development and, 311
Alcohol dependence syndrome, 163
All-or-none law, 42–43
Alleles, 307
Alpha rhythm, sleep and, 140
Altruism, 289
Alzheimer's disease, 144, 611
Amacrine cells, 72, 75–76
American Psychiatric Association, *Diagnostic and Statistical Manual* of, 477–480
American Psychological Association (APA), 6, 8
  ethical principles of, 18–19
American Sign Language (Ameslam), 255
Ames room, 121
Amnesia, anterograde, 233
Amphetamines, 163–165
Amplitude, of sound, 88
Ampulla, 97
Anal stage, in psychosexual development, 411, 412
Analogue observations, as behavioral assessment methods, 404
Androgens, aging and, 351
Anger, as stage of dying, 367
Anhedonia, schizophrenia and, 482
Anorexia, lateral hypothalamus lesions causing, 284
Anorexia nervosa, 339, 340
Anterograde amnesia, 233
Antianxiety agents, 159–160, 540
Anticipated consequences, motivation and, 290
Antidepressants, 540
Antisocial behavior, children from maritally conflicted homes and, 598
Antisocial personality disorder, 500
Anxiety, 494
  affiliating with others and, 572–573
  antianxiety agents and, 159–160, 540

measures of, 430
  tests of, 395–396
  see also Stress
Anxiety disorders, 494–498
Anxiety hierarchy, in systematic desensitization, 520
Apes
  language taught to, 255
  visual system of, 120
Apgar score, 313–314
Aphagia, lateral hypothalamus lesions causing, 284
Aphasia Screening Test, 400
Aphonia, 499
Apparatus/measures, in method section of psychology journal article, 632
Apparent movement, 118
Approach, conflict analysis involving, 421–422
Aptitude tests, 387–388
Army Alpha test, 375
Army Beta test, 375
Asch experiment, conformity and, 574–575
Assertion training, 521
Assessments, 374–375
  see also Tests
Assimilation, cognitive development in, 318
Associations
  memory and, 209–210
  schizophrenia and, 481
Associative learning, 180–181, 189–197, 198
  acquisition and, 189–190
  applications of, 197
  discrimination and, 191
  extinction and, 190
  generalization and, 191
  limits of, 198
  reinforcement and
    negative, 192–194
    positive, 192–194
    primary, 191–192
    schedules of, 194, 196–197
    secondary, 192
  spontaneous recovery and, 190
  see also Classical conditioning; Operant conditioning
Assumptions, in scientific method, 5
Atherosclerosis, 352, 438
Attachment, in infancy, 322–325
Attention
  schizophrenia and difficulties with, 482
  selective, 564–565
Attention deficit disorder, 164, 505
Attitudes, 547–557
  behavior and, 552–554
  change in, 549–552
  formation of, 548–549
  inferring, 567
  interpersonal, 554–557
  learning and, 549
  see also Social perception
Attribution theory, inferring personality characteristics and, 559–561
Attributional processes, personality and, 426–427, 428
Attributions, major depression and, 494
Auditory area, of cerebral cortex, 55
Auditory nerve, 50
Auditory perception, tests of, 401
Auditory projection area, of cerebral cortex, 55
Auditory sensory memory, 215

SUBJECT INDEX

Auditory space, perception of, 94–95
Auditory system, 65, 87–95
  auditory space perception and, 94–95
  hearing
    frequency theory of, 93, 94
    place theory of, 92–93
    valley theory of, 93–94
  in infancy, 315
  sound, 87–89
    transduction of, 90–94
Author and institution, in psychology journal article, 630
Authoritarian parent, 328, 329
Authority, obedience to, 587
Autism, 505–506
Autonomic nervous system (ANS). *See* Nervous system
Autonomy vs. shame and doubt, 413
Average life expectancy, 346
Aversive experiences, major depression and, 493
Avoidance, in learning process, 421
Avoidance learning, 193
  phobias and, 496
Awareness, Gestalt therapy and, 531
Axon, 33–34, 37–38, 39, 44, 45, 47
Axon hillock, 37, 38, 47

Babbling, as vocalization stage, 326
Backward conditioning, classic conditioning and, 182
Barbiturates, 150, 158–159
Bargaining, as stage of dying, 367
Basal ganglia, 53, 56–57
  Parkinson's disease and, 52
Basic level categories, concept formation and, 263
Basilar membrane, 90, 91, 92
Bayley Scales of Mental and Motor Development, 318
Beck Depression Inventory, 396
Behavior, 5, 8
  assessment of, 402–404
  attitudes and, 548, 553–554
  changes in. *See* Learning
  nervous system directing, 32
  see also Personality
Behavior Coding System, 402, 403
Behavior problems, therapy for, 516–543
  behavior therapy, 516–523
    for depression, 520–521
    modeling, 522–523
    operant procedures, 520–522
    as performance-based, 518–519
    systematic desensitization, 519–520
  children from maritally conflicted homes and, 598
  client characteristics and, 539
  cognitive-behavioral therapy, 524–530
    with children, 530
    for depression, 528–529
    rational emotive therapy, 525–528
  community interventions, 535
  eclecticism in, 524, *see also* cognitive-behavioral therapy, *above*
  effects of, 538–540
  existential therapy, 532
  Gestalt therapy, 531
  group therapy, 532–535, 538–539
    family therapy, 533–535
  medical approaches, 539–543
    drugs, 540–541
    electroconvulsive therapy, 542–543

    psychosurgery, 541–542
  operant conditioning and, 197
  reality therapy, 530–531
  self-help, 533
  transactional analysis, 531–532
  see also Abnormal behavior
Behavior therapy. *See* Behavior problems, therapy for
Behavioral medicine. *See* Medicine, psychology and
Behavioral plasticity, 29
Behavioral stimulants. *See* Psychoactive drugs
Behavioral theories, major depression and, 493–494
Behaviorism, 8
Bender-Gestalt Test, 401
Benzodiazepines, 144, 150, 160
Bereavement, death and dying and, 367–368
Berkley Studies, 360–361
Beta activity, sleep and, 140
Beyond Freedom and Dignity (Skinner), 422
Bimodal distribution, 617
Binet-Simon scales, 375
Binocular disparity, 119
Binocular vision, 119, 120, 121
Biochemistry, schizophrenia and, 484
Biological theories
  of aggression, 291–292
  of aging, 345–347
  of behavior, 289
  of motivation, 288–289, *see also* Motivation
Biopsychologists, 6
Bipolar affective disorder, 490–491
Bipolar cell, of retina, 71, 72, 73, 78, 80
Bipolar factors, of emotion, 300
Birth, 313–314
Birth control. *See* Contraception
Bitter, as taste, 98
Blind spot, of eye, 73, 75
Blood loss, drinking motivated by, 288
Blunting, as coping strategy, 464
Bodily rhythms, 136–138
Body temperature, nervous system controlling, 31
Bouton, 45, 47
Box-score tally, on effects of psychological therapy, 537
Brain, 27
  aging and, 610–613
  brain stem, 50–51
  cerebellum, 27, 50, 51
  cerebral cortex, 27, 51, 53–59
    feature detectors in, 81, 83–84
    motor areas, 56–57
    sensory projection areas of, 54–56, 57
    visual pathways from eye to, 78, 80–81
  cerebral hemispheres, 27, 53–54, *see also* cerebral cortex; lobes, *herein*
    lateralization and, 59–61
    subcortical brain regions in, 53
  early ideas about, 26
  hormones and, 30
  lateralization in, 59–61
  lobes of, 53
    frontal, 50, 53, 54, 57–58
    occipital, 53, 55, 57, 80
    parietal, 53, 54, 55, 59
    temporal, 50, 53, 54, 58–59
  malfunctions of, 33
  medulla, 50, 51
  midbrain, 51–52

SUBJECT INDEX

Brain (cont.)
   neurons in, 33, 40, *see also* Nervous system
   pons, 50–51
   synaptic plasticity, 29
   thalamus, 51, 53, 55, 80
   see also Hypothalamus; Nervous system
Brain stem, 50–51
Brain surgery, for behavior problems, 541–542
Brainstorming, in groups, 584
Brazelton Neonatal Behavioral Assessment Scale, 318
Brightness, color and, 126–127
British associationists, 210
British Empiricists, knowledge and, 65–66
Broca's aphasia, 58
Broca's area, 57–58, 58
Bystander, in emergencies, 576–577

Caffeine, 165–166
Calcarine sulcus, 54, 55, 56, 80
Calcium, reflexes and, 49
Calcium ions, synaptic transmission and, 46
California Psychological Inventory (CPI), 392–394
Camera, eye compared to, 69–71
Cannabis sativa, 171
Caregiving practices, 328–329
Cataplexy, 151
Catatonic schizophrenia, 486
Catecholamines
   major depression and, 492
   stress and, 438
Categorization, concept formation and, 262–263
Cattell Infant Intelligence Scale, 318
Cattell's Culture Free Intelligence Test, 384, 385
Causal explanation, motivation and, 290
Ceiling age, 380
Cell body, of neuron, 33, 34, 36, 37
Cell membranes, of neuron, 36, 39
Cellular error theory, of aging, 347
Central axon, 34
Central branch, of neuron, 34
Central nervous system. *See* Nervous system
Central sulcus, 54, 55, 56
Cerebellum, 50, 51
Cerebral cortex. *See* Brain
Cerebral hemispheres. *See* Brain
Chance, personality and, 424–425
Channel capacity, 211
Child, in transactional analysis, 531
Child abuse, 601–603
Childbirth, 313–314
Childhood, 325–331
   abnormal behavior in, 505–506
   cognitive development in, 320
   intelligence in, 325–326, *see also* Intelligence tests
   language development in, 326–328
   nutrition and, 308–309
   play and, 330–331
   social development in, 328–331
   television and, 331–332
Choroid, 70
Chromatic colors, 126
Chromosomes, 306–307
Chronic disorders, 491
   see also Abnormal behavior

Chunking
   long-term memory and, 224
   short-term memory and, 217
Cigarettes. *See* Nicotine
Ciliary body, 70
Ciliary stalk, of rod and cone, 74
Cingulate gyrus, 54
Circadian rhythms, 137–138
   see also Sleep
Clairvoyance, 132
Clang associations, schizophrenia and, 481
Class interval, 616
Classical conditioning, 181–184
   aggression and, 292
   application of, 197
   see also Associative learning
Client-centered therapy, 514–516
Climacteric, 351
Clinical psychologists, 7
Closure, perceptual organization and, 115–116
Clustering, long-term memory and, 224
Cocaine, 165
Cochlea, 90–92, 97
Cochlear duct, 91
Cochlear fluid, 90, 92
Cochlear nerve, 90
Coding, in auditory nerve neurons, 94
Cognition, 6
   in attitudes, 548
Cognitive assessment, 397
   see also Intelligence tests
Cognitive-behavior therapy. *See* Behavior problems, therapy for
Cognitive-body debate, abnormal behavior and, 476
Cognitive development, 317–322
Cognitive dissonance, 552–554
Cognitive impairment, aging and, 610–613
Cognitive learning, 197–205
   cognitive maps and, 200–201
   higher-order concepts and, 201–204
   insight and, 199–200
   latent learning and, 200–201
   observational learning and, 204–205, *see also* Imitation; Modeling
Cognitive maps, 200–201
Cognitive processes
   in adolescence, 341–342
   aggression and, 294–295
   aging and, 352–361
   in infancy, 317–320, 322
   personality and, 425–427
   see also Intelligence; Language; Learning; Memory; Thought
Cognitive psychology, 6, 209, 211
   cognitive impairments in old age and, 610–613
Cognitive theories
   of major depression, 493, 494
   of motivation, 290
Collaborative empiricism, cognitive-behavioral treatment of depression and, 528–529
Collective unconscious, 413
College Entrance Examination Board (CEEB), 387
Colliculi, 51
Color, perception of, 126–128
Color blindness, 86–87
Color circle, 127
Color constancy, 105
Color solid, 127

SUBJECT INDEX

Color vision, 84–87
   aging and, 349
   in infancy, 315
Commitment, to institution, 473
Communication, persuasion and, 550–552
Communication science, memory and, 211
Community interventions, therapy based on, 535
Companionate love, 556
Comparative psychologists, 6
Compensation, as defense mechanism, 463
Competence, language and, 251–252
Complex cortical cells, 81
Complex protein molecules, of cell membrane of neuron, 36
Compliance. *See* Group influence
Comprehension, of language, 252–253
Compression, sound and, 88, 89
Computer-assisted learning, 197
Computer science, memory and, 211
Concept formation, 260–263
Conception, 306
Concepts, tests of, 401
Conceptual hierarchies, effect of organization on recall studied with, 225–226
Concrete operational stage, of cognitive development, 321, 322
Concurrent therapy, 534
Concurrent validity, 378
Condition, of a production, 260
Conditional reasoning, 265
Conditioned emotional response (CER), 184
Conditioned response (CR), classic conditioning and, 182–183
Conditional stimulus (CS), classic conditioning and, 182–184
Conditioning. *See* Classical conditioning; Operant conditioning
Conduction velocity, along on axon, 44
Cone receptor cells, 71, 72, 73, 74
Cone receptors, 84–85
Conflict, stress due to, 442–444, 445
Conflict analysis, approach and avoidance strategies for, 421–422
Conformity, 574–576
Conjoint therapy, 534
Consciousness, 35
   see also Bodily rhythms; Hypnosis; Meditation; Psychoactive drugs; Sleep
Consensus, in attribution, 560
Consequences, anticipation and aggression and, 294
Conservation, cognitive development and, 320–321
Conservative focusing, concept formation and, 261
Consistency, in attribution, 560
Constancies, perceptual, 104–106
Constitutional psychology, 414–416
Construct validity, 378–379
Constructive hypothesis, memory and, 235–236
Contact desensitization, in systematic desensitization, 520
Content, of intelligence, 268–271
Content validity, 378
Contingency, classical conditioning and, 184
Continuity, perceptual organization and, 116
Continuous growth, in adolescent period, 338
Continuous reinforcement schedule, 194
Contraception, adolescents' use of, 344–345
Control, as coping resource, 456–457
Control processes, memory and, 212
Controlled experiment, 12–15
Controlled observation, 12
Conversion disorder, 476, 498–499
Cooperative play, 330
Coping. *See* Stress

Coping model, in behavior therapy, 523
Cornea, 70
Coronary disease, Type A behavior and, 456
Corpus callosum, 51, 53–54, 54
   severing, 60, 61
Correctional mechanism, in regulatory system, 279
Correlation, 17
   descriptive statistics and, 620–623
   IQ scores studied with, 325
Correlation coefficient, 17, 620–623
Correspondent inferences, theory of, 560–561
Cortex, cerebral. *See* Brain
Corticoids, stress and, 437
Corticosteroids, stress and, 438
Corticotrophic hormone-releasing factor (CRF), stress and, 437
Cortisol, stress and, 437
Cortisone, stress and, 437
Counseling psychologists, 7
Counterconditioning, systematic desensitization based on, 519
Countershock phase, in general adaptation syndrome, 436, 437
Creativity
   intelligence and, 271
   manic-depression and, 490
   nervous system producing, 32
Criterion-related validity, 378
Critical period, of language, 254
Cross adaptation, 113
   taste and, 98
Cross-fostering studies, schizophrenia studied with, 484
Cross-linkage theory, of aging, 347
Crowding, 589–590
Crying, language development and, 326
Crystallized intelligence, 267, 269, 270–271
   aging and, 356, 358
Cue, in learning process, 421
Culture-free, intelligence tests as, 384–387
Cyclothymic disorder, 492
Cytoplasm, 307

Dark adaptation, 74
Day-care, 600
Daydreaming, as defense mechanism, 463
Death and dying, 365–368
   grief, 441
   stress from, 441, 442
Death instinct, aggression and, 291
Decibels (dB), 89
Deductive reasoning, 264–265
Deep structure, of a sentence, 249, 250, 251
Defense mechanisms, 462–463, 511
Defensive, being, 463
Dehydration, drinking motivated by, 288
Deindividuation, roles and, 587–588
Delayed imitation, in preoperational stage, 320
Delta-9-tetrahydrocannabinol (THC), 171–172
   see also Marijuana
Delusions, schizophrenia and, 482
Dementia, 610
   Alzheimer's disease and, 611
   multi-infarct, 611
Dendrites, 33, 34, 37, 47
Dendritic spines, 37, 45
Denial
   as defense mechanism, 462, 463
   as stage of dying, 367

Deoxyribonucleic acid (DNA), 307
  aging and damage theory of, 347
  of cell nucleus of neuron, 36
Dependent personality disorder, 500
Dependent variable, 13–15
Depolarization, synaptic transmission and, 46
Depolarizing stimuli, neural conduction and, 41
Depressants (sedative-hypnotic drugs). *See* Psychoactive drugs
Depression
  behavior therapy for, 520–521
  cognitive-behavioral treatment of, 528–529
  drug treatment for, 540
  electroconvulsive therapy for, 542
  imipramine for, 529
  major, 491–494
  as stage of dying, 367
  tests of, 396
Deprivation
  early, 323–324
  relative vs. absolute, 573
Depth perception, 118–123
Descriptive statistics. *See* Statistics
Despair, personality of aging and, 362
Determinism, personality and, 424–425
Development, 305–307
  genes and, 307
  heredity-environment interaction and, 307–308
  psychosexual, 411–412
  see also Adolescence; Adulthood and aging; Childhood; Cognitive development; Infancy; Prenatal development
Developmental psychologists, 6
Diabetes, 281
Diagnostic and Statistical Manual (DSM), 477–480
Diathesis-stress model, schizophrenia and, 485
Diazepam, 150
Diethylstilbestrol (DES), prenatal development and, 311
Difference thresholds, 111–112
Differential approach, to intelligence, 266
Differentiated crying, as vocalization stage, 326
Dimensions, personality traits as, 416–417
Discrimination, associative learning and, 191
Discussion, of psychology journal articles, 632–633
Disjunctive tasks, aging and, 352
Displacement, as defense mechanism, 462–463
Display rules, of a culture, 299
Dissonance theory. *See* Cognitive dissonance
Distance, size constancy and, 105
Distinctiveness, in attribution, 560
Distribution, normal, 619–620
Diversion programs, in community psychology, 535
Divorce, 596–598
DNA. *See* Deoxyribonucleic acid
Doctrine of specific nerve energies, 67–68
Door-in-the-face technique, 578–579, 581
Dopamine, 38, 164
  cocaine and, 165
  Parkinson's disease and, 52
Dorsal root ganglion, 48
Dorsal roots, 28, 48, 49
Double-bind hypothesis, schizophrenia and, 484–485
Downers, barbiturates as, 159
Dramatic play, 330
Dreams. *See* Sleep
Drinking, (thirst) as maturation, 287–288
Drive, in learning process, 421
  see also Motivation

Drug
  definition, 156
  prenatal development and, 311
  see also Psychoactive drugs
Drug abuse, 502–504
Drug tolerance, 157
  see also Psychoactive drugs
Dura mater, 28
Dying, death and, 365–368

Ear, 90–92
  see also Auditory system
Ear canal, 90
Eardrum, 90
Early adult transition, in personality development, 363–364
Early infantile autism, 505, 506
Early Training Project, Peabody College, 274
Eating behavior
  anorexia nervosa, 339, 340
  hunger as motive and, 279–287
  in infancy, 316
Echoic memory, 215
Echolalia
  autistic children and, 506
  as vocalization stage, 326
Eclecticism. *See* Behavior problems, therapy for
Ectoderm, 310
Ectomorph, 340, 415–416
Education
  adolescents' attitude toward, 339
  associative learning principles and, 197
Educational psychologists, 7
Effect sizes, on effect of psychological therapy, 537–538
Efficacy expectations
  as coping resource, 456
  personality and, 424
Ego, 410, 411
Ego-dystonic homosexuality, 502
Ego integrity vs. despair, 413
Egocentric, infant as, 319
Ejaculation
  in adolescence, 340
  aging and, 351
  premature, 502
Elaboration, memory and, 234
Elaborative rehearsal, long-term memory and, 223, 224
Electra complex, 412
Electrical synapses, 45
Electroconvulsive therapy (ECT), for behavior problems, 542–543
Electroencephalogram (EEG), sleep research and, 139–140
Electromagnetic spectrum, 68–69
Embryo, 310
Emotion-focused coping, 460
Emotional states, retrieval in long-term memory, 228–229
Emotions, 295–300
  affective disorders and, 490–494
  aggression and, 294–295
  attitude and, 548
  classical conditioning and, 184
  coping based on, 460
  expression of, 298–299
  facial-feedback hypothesis of, 296–297
  in infancy, 316–317
  inferring, 558–559
  innate basis to expression of, 298–299
  James-Lange theory of, 296

SUBJECT INDEX

697

learned component of expression of, 299
    nature of, 295–296
    perceiving, 566–567
    prenatal development and, 313
    Schachter-Singer theory of, 297–298
    structure of, 300
Empathy, in client-centered therapy, 514
Empiricists, knowledge and, 65–66
Employment, of married mothers, 598–601
Encoding. *See* Memory
Encoding specificity hypothesis, 227–228
Endocrine system, stress and, 437
Endoderm, 310
Endomorph, 340, 414–416
Endoplasmic reticulum, of neuron, 36, 37
Endorphins, opiates and, 167
Enhancement, psychology assisting in, 595
Enkephalins, opiates and, 167
Entering the adult world, in personality development, 364
Entering middle adulthood, in personality development, 365
Environment
    development and, 307–308
    intelligence and, 272–273
    retrieval in long-term memory and, 228
    schizophrenia and, 485
    therapy based on changing, 535
Epilepsy
    amphetamines and, 164
    corpus callosum severing and, 60, 61
    phenobarbital and, 159
Epinephrine, 163
    memory retention and, 144
    nicotine and, 166
    stress and, 438
Episodic memory, 239
Equilibration, Piaget on, 319
Escape learning, 193
Estrogens, aging and, 351
Ethics, of psychological research, 17–19
Ethyl alcohol. *See* Alcohol and alcoholism
Eustachian tube, 90
Evolution, behavior and, 289
Excitement, as phase of sexual arousal, 501
Exercise
    aging and, 350
    weight-loss and, 285
Existential therapy, 532
Exorcism, disturbed persons subjected to, 471
Expansion, in language acquisition, 256
Expectations
    alcohol and, 504
    as coping resource, 456
    perception influenced by, 103, 104
    personality and, 422–423
Experimental hypothesis, 625
Experimental observation, 12–15
Expert knowledge, problem solving and, 259–260
External attributions, 560
Extinction, associative learning and, 190
Extracellular fluid, 287
Extrasensory perception (ESP), 131–133
Extraversion, as personality trait, 417, 418
Eye movements
    dreams and, 146–147
    in infancy, 316
Eyes. *See* Visual system

Face validity, 378
Facial expressions, emotions indicated by, 298–299
Facial-feedback hypothesis, of emotions, 296–297
Facial recognition, tests of, 401
Factor analysis, 266
    personality traits identified by, 417
Faded Sun, The (Cherryh), 209
False beliefs, survival of, 564–566
Familiarity, liking process and, 555
Family, 595–603
    child abuse, 601–603
    divorce, 596–598
    maternal employment, 598–601
    see also Parent-child relationship
Family therapy, 533–535
Fantasy, as defense mechanism, 463
Father of American psychology, James as, 8
Fats, hunger and, 281
Fear appeals, effectiveness of, 552
Feature detectors, in cortex, 81, 83–84
Feelings. *See* Emotions
Fetal Alcohol Syndrome (FAS), 311
Fetus, 310
Figure-ground relationships, in perceptual system, 114, 115
Fixations, psychological disturbances based on, 474
Fixed interval (FI) schedule, of reinforcement,, 196
Fixed ratio (FR) schedule, of reinforcement, 196
Flashbacks, LSD and, 170
Fluid-crystallized theory, of intelligence, 267, 269
Fluid intelligence, 267, 269, 270
    aging and, 356, 358
Flurazepam, 150
Follower, role of, 585
Foot-in-the-door, compliance induced by technique of, 576–577, 579
Forgetting, 210
    see also Memory
Formal operational stage, of cognitive development, 321–322
Forward pairing, classic conditioning and, 182
Fourier analysis, 83
Fovea, 73
Frame of reference, movement perception and, 118
Free association, 512
    Rorschach Inkblots and, 398
Free-radical theory, of aging, 347
Free recall tasks
    distinction between short- and long-term memory and, 231
    short-term memory measured by, 353
Frequency distributions, 616
Frequency theory, of hearing, 93, 94
Freudian slips, 410
Frigidity, 502
Frontal lobe, 50, 53, 54, 57–58
Frustration, as source of psychological harm, 440
Frustration-aggression hypothesis, 292
Functional disorders, 491
Functional dyspareunia, 502
Functional fixedness, problem solving and, 259
Functional vaginismus, 502
Functionalism, 8
Fundamental attribution error, 561, 562
"Future shock," 593

Games, in transactional analysis, 532
Ganglion, 28

Ganglion cells, 71, 72, 73, 78, 80
General adaptation syndrome (GAS), 436–439
General intelligence, 266
General paresis, 475
Generalization
　associative learning and, 191
　higher-order concepts and, 201–204
Generalized anxiety disorder, 495–496
Generalized expectancies, personality and, 423
Generativity, personality in young adulthood and, 362
Generativity vs. stagnation, 413
Generic human being, personality psychologists studying, 408, 409
Genes, 307
　see also Heredity
Genetic inheritance, 306–307
Genetics. See Heredity
Genital stage, in psychosexual develpment, 412
Genotype, 307
Genuineness, in client-centered therapy, 514
Gesell Developmental Schedules, 318
Gestalt, 10
Gestalt psychology, perceptual organization and, 115
Gestalt therapy, 531
Giant axon, of the squid, 39
Giant boutons, 47
Glucoreceptors, hunger and, 281, 282–283
Glucose levels, hunger and, 281
Goal-directed behavior, eating involving, 280
Golgi apparatus, of neuron, 36, 37
Goodness of fit, coping responses and, 464–465
Grammar, in language development, 327–328
Grammatical morphemes, in language development, 327–328
Grant study, 362–363
Gray matter, 28, 48, 50
Grief, 441
　death and dying and, 367–368
Ground, figure separated from, 114, 115
Group dynamics, 581–590
　crowding and, 589–590
　deindividuation and, 587–588
　leaders and followers and, 585
　obedience to authority and, 587
　personal space and, 588–589
　problem solving and, 583–585
　social facilitation and, 581–582
　social loafing and, 582
　social roles and, 585–588
Group influence, compliance and, 576–581
　door-in-the-face technique, 578–579, 580
　foot-in-the-door technique, 576–577, 579
　low balling, 580
　see also Group dynamics, Social influence
Group laws, personality psychologists studying, 408, 409
Group therapy, 532–535, 538–539
Groupthink, group problem solving and, 584–585
Growth
　in adolescence, 338–340, 341
　in infancy, 314
Gyri, 53, 54

Hair cells, of cochlea, 91, 92
Hallucinations, 169
　schizophrenia and, 482
　serotonin and, 38

Hallucinogens, 158, 169–172
Halsted-Reitan Neuropsychological Battery, 376, 401
Harm, stress due to, 440–441, 442
Harrison Narcotics Act of 1914, 168
Hashish, 171
　see also Marijuana
Hearing. See Auditory system
Hearing threshold, method of limits determining, 107
Heart rate, on Apgar scores, 313
Hebephrenic schizophrenia, 486
Helplessness. See Learned helplessness
Hemispheres, cerebral. See Brain
Here and now, Gestalt therapy and, 531
Heredity
　aging and, 345–347
　development and, 306–308
　intelligence and, 272–273
　major depression and, 492
　schizophrenia and, 483–484
Heroin, 168–169
　prenatal development and, 311
Hertz (HZ), 88
Heterozygotic, 307
Hierarchical model, of memory, 239–240
Higher-order concepts, learning of, 201–204
Histogram, 616
Holistic view, of personality, 418
Homeostasis, motivation and, 278–279
Homosexuality, 502
Homozygotic, 307
Homonuclus, 55, 57
Horizontal cells, 72, 75, 75–76
Hormones, 30
　memory retention and, 144
Hue, color and, 126
Human participants, ethical principles in conduct of research with, 18–19
Humanistic philosophy, client-centered therapy as, 515
Humanistic theories, of personality, 418–419, 420
Humoral theory, mental disorders and, 471
Hunger, as motive, 279–287
Hyperactive children, 505
　cognitive-behavioral program for, 530
Hypercomplex cortical cells, 81
Hyperkinesis. See Attention deficit disorder
Hyperpolarizing stimuli, neural conduction and, 41
Hypersomnia, 149
　narcolepsy and, 151–152
Hypnosis, 153–156, 173
　retrieval in long-term memory and, 228–229
Hypnotic, 158
　sedative-hypnotic drugs as. See Psychoactive drugs
Hypnotic regression, 155
Hypothalamus, 51, 52
　eating behavior and, 283–284
　stress and, 437–438
Hypothesis testing, inferential statistics and, 625–627
Hypovolemic thirst, 288

Iconic memory, 214–215
Id, 410, 411
Identification, as defense mechanism, 463
Identity, adolescence and, 337, 342–343
Identity crisis, 337, 343
Identity vs. identity diffusion, 413

SUBJECT INDEX

Idiographic laws, personality psychologists studying, 408, 409
Illusions, 123–125
Imagery, long-term memory and, 226
Imipramine, for depressive symptomotology, 529
Imitation, 204
   delayed, 320
   language acquisition and, 253, 254, 326
Imitative learning, 204
Immediate memory span, short-term memory measured by, 353
Immunological theory, of aging, 347
Implicit theories of personality, 563–564
Impotence, 502
Impulsive children, cognitive-behavioral program for, 530
In situ desensitization, in systematic desensitization, 520
Incidental learning task, 220–221
Incompetence, legal concept of, 473
Incubation, problem solving and, 259
Incus, 90
Independent variable, 13, 14
Individualization of instruction, 197
Inductive reasoning, 263–264
Industrial/organizational psychologists, 7
Industry vs. inferiority, 413
Infancy, 314–325
   cognitive changes in, 317–320, 322
   eating behavior in, 316
   emotions in, 316–317
   motor development in, 315
   nutrition and, 308–309
   parent-child interactions in, 322–325
   physical growth in, 314
   reflexes in, 315
   sensory and perceptual changes in, 315
   sleep patterns in, 143, 316
   social development in, 322–325
   toileting behaviors in, 316
Inferential statistics. *See* Statistics
Inferior colliculi, 51
Inferiority complex, 413
Information coding, by nervous system, 43–44
Information processing, memory and, 210–212
Information processing approach
   to cognition, 257, *see also* Thought
   to intelligence, 384
Information theory, memory and, 211
Infrared radiation, 69
Initiative vs. guilt, 413
Inner ear, 90, 91
Inner segment, of rod and cone, 74
Insanity, 470
   legal concept of, 473
   see also Abnormal behavior
Insight
   cognitive learning and, 199–200
   problem solving and, 259
Insomnia, 149–150
Instinct theories, of motivation, 288–289
Instrumental conditioning, attitude formation and, 549
Instrumental learning, 184–189
   aggression and, 293
   law of effect and, 186–187
   shaping and, 188–189
   Thorndike and, 185–186
   see also Operant conditioning
Integrity, personality of aging and, 362
Intelligence, 266–276

   aging and, 356–359
   in childhood, 325–326
   content of, 269–271
   creativity and, 271
   fluid-crystallized theory of, 267, 269, 270–271
   general, 266
   heredity and environment and, 272–273
   improving, 273–274
   of infant, 317, 318
   information processing approach to, 384
   malnutrition and, 308–309
   primary mental abilities and, 267
   structure of, 266–267, 269
   see also Intelligence tests
Intelligence quotient (IQ), 375–376, 379–387
   see also Intelligence tests
Intelligence tests, 375, 376, 379–387
   cultural fairness of, 384–387
   historical background, 375
   in infancy, 317
   norms for, 379–380
   scores
      in childhood, 325–326
      normal distribution and, 619–620
   Stanford-Binet Intelligence Scale, 380
   Wechsler scales, 382–384
      Wechsler Adult Intelligence Scale, 376, 382
      Wechsler Adult Intelligence Scale-Revised, 382, 383
      Wechsler Intelligence Scale for Children, 376
      Wechsler Intelligence Scale for Children-Revised, 382
      Wechsler Memory Scale, 401
      Wechsler Preschool and Primary Scale of Intelligence, 382
Intentionality, inference of and aggression, 294
Interactionism, language acquisition and, 255–256
Interactive imagery, memory improved with, 230
Intercourse
   adolescence and, 344–345
   aging and, 351
   painful, 502
   see also Sexuality
Interference, retrieval in long-term memory and, 229–231
Intermittent reinforcement schedule, 194, 196
Internal attributions, 560
Internal consistency, of test, 376–377
Interpersonal attraction, 555–557
Interpretations, in psychoanalysis, 512
Interscorer reliability, 376
Intervention, intelligence improved by early, 273–274
Interviews, 15–17
   assessment, 390
Intimacy, personality in young adulthood and, 362
Intimacy vs. isolation, 413
Introduction, of psychology journal articles, 631
Introspection, memory and, 210
Introversion-extraversion, as personality trait, 417
Invalid syllogism, 264
Iodopsin, 75
Ions, neuron membrane and, 39–42
Iowa Test of Basic Skills, 387
IQ. *See* Intelligence quotient
Iris, 70, 71
Irrational beliefs, rational emotive therapy and, 525, 528
Isolation. *See* Social isolation

James-Lange theory, of emotion, 296
Jet lag, 137–138

Job loss, social support as coping resource in, 458–459
Jonestown massacre, 578–579
Journals. *See* Psychology journals
Judges, versus juries, 606–607
Jury, psychology and, 604–606
Just noticeable difference (JND), 111
Just-world effect, 561–562

Kansas City Studies, 360
Kinesthetic system, 95–96
Knee-jerk reflex, 48–49
Knowledge, 65–66
Koans, 173

L-dopa, 52
Lallation, as vocalization stage, 326
Language, 245–256
   acquisition of, 253–256, 326–328
     linguistic speech stages in, 327–328
     vocalization stage in, 326–327
   apes learning, 255
   competence vs. performance and, 251–252
   comprehension and production of, 252–253
   frontal lobe and, 58
   schizophrenia and, 481
   structure of, 246–250
     morphemes, 246, 247–248, 327
     phonemes, 246–247
     phrases and sentences, 247, 248–250
     syntax, 248
   temporal lobe and, 59
   tests of, 401
Late adult transition, in personality development, 365
Latency stage, in psychosexual development, 412
Latent learning, 180, 200–201
Lateral geniculate nucleus, 56, 80
Lateral hypothalamus (LH), eating suppression and, 284
Lateral inhibition, in retina, 77
Lateral sulcus, 54, 55
Lateralization, brain function and, 59–61
Law, psychology and, 604–607
Law of effect, 186–187
Learned helplessness, 193, 195
   major depression and, 493, 494
Learning, 179–181
   attitude formation and, 549
   drinking (thirst) and, 288
   eating behavior and, 281–282
   emotional expression and, 299
   latent, 180
   nervous system and, 31–32
   see also Associative learning; Classical conditioning; Cognitive learning; Memory; Operant conditioning; Perception
Learning model
   of abnormal behavior, 473–474
   of anxiety-related disorders, 497
Learning-performance distinction, 180
Learning psychologists, 6
Learning sets, learning of principles and, 201–202
Learning theories, of motivation, 289
Lens, 70
Levels of processing, memory as different, 234
Libido, 410
Librium, 160
Life change units, stress and, 446–449

Life cycle, sleep patterns in, 143
   see also Development
Life events, stress and, 446–449
Life review, 361
Life span, 345, 346
Lifestyle change, as application of behavioral medicine, 608–609
Light, visible, 68–69
   see also Visual system
Liking process, 555–557
   familiarity and similarity, 555–556
   love and, 556
Limbic system, 53
Line of best fit, 622
Linguistic speech, as stage in language development, 327–328
Linguistics, memory and, 211
Lipids, hunger and, 281
Lithium carbonate, for manic-depressive disorder, 540
Liver factors, eating behavior regulated by, 282–283
Load, stress due to, 444–446
Lobectomy, 541
Lobes. *See* Brain
Lobotomy, 541–542
Local-circuit neurons, 35
Location constancy, 105
Locus of control, personality and, 423
Locus of Control Scale, 394
Long-term memory. *See* Memory
Loudness, of sound, 88
Love, nature of, 556
LSD, 169–172
Luria-Nebraska Neuropsychological Test Battery, 401
Lysergic acid diethylamide. *See* LSD
Lysosomes, of neuron, 36–37

Mach bands, 76
Maintenance rehearsal, long-term memory and, 223, 224
Major depression, 491–494
Major tranquilizers, for psychoses, 540–541
Majority, minority influencing, 575–576
Malleus, 90
Malnutrition, development and, 308–309, 311
Mania, as bipolar disorder, 490–491
Manic-depression, 450, 490–491
Mantra, 173
MAO (monoamine oxidase), for depression, 540
Marijuana, 171–172
Marriage, 595
   see also Family
Mastery model, in behavior therapy, 523
Masturbation, 412
Maternal age, prenatal development and, 313
Maternal employment, 598–601
Maximum life span, 346
Mean, 616
Meaning, in long-term memory, 220
Means, sample, 625–626
Means-ends relationship, problem solving and, 259
Measurement psychologists, 7
Measurements. *See* Tests
Measures of central tendency, 616–617
Measures of variability, 618–619
Median, 617
Medical compliance, as application of behavioral medicine, 609–610
Medical management of behavior problems. *See* Behavior problems, therapy for

SUBJECT INDEX

Medical model, of abnormal behavior, 475–476
Medicine, psychology and, 607–613
   behavioral medicine and, 607–610
      lifestyle change and, 608–609
      medical compliance and, 609–610
   cognitive psychology and cognitive impairments in old age and, 610–613
Meditation, 172–173
Medulla (medulla oblongata), 50, 51
Membranous duct of cochlea, 97
Memory, 208–243
   aging and, 353–356
      senile dementia and, 610–613
   constructive, 235–236
   as different levels of processing, 234
   of dreams, 147
   early ideas about, 209–210
   encoding, 215
      aging and, 354
      long-term memory and, 218–221, 226
      short-term memory and, 215–216
   episodic, 239
   hierarchical model of, 239–240
   improving, 230
   information processing approach to, 210–212
   long-term, 213, 218–231
      aging and, 353–356
      encoding in, 218–220
      meaning in, 220–221, 223–226
      multistore models and, 231–234
      problem solving and, 260
      storage and retrieval in, 227–231
   malnutrition and, 308
   multistore models of, 231–234
   narcolepsy and, 152
   nervous system and, 31–32
   network models of, 239–241
   organization of knowledge and, 238, 239–242
   prior knowledge and, 234–238
   research on, 144
   retrieval, 211
      long-term memory and, 227–231
      short-term memory and, 217–218
   schema theory of, 242–243
   schemata and, 198–199
   semantic, 239, 240–241
   sensory, 213–215, 353
   short-term, 213, 215–218
      aging and, 353
      multistore models and, 231–234
   spreading activation model of, 241
   stages of, 211
   storage, 211
      long-term memory and, 227–231
      short-term memory and, 216–217
   structure of language and, 251
   tests of, 401
Memory trace, memory and, 211
Men Under Stress (Grinker and Spiegel), 461
Menarche, 340
Menopause, 351
Menstrual cycle
   anorexia nervosa and, 341
   menarche, 340
   menopause and, 351
Mental age, 380

Mental philosophy, psychology as, 5
Mental process, of learning, 204
Mental test, 375
Meprobamate, 160
Mesoderm, 310
Mesomorph, 340, 414–416
Meta-analysis, on effects of psychological therapy, 537
Methaqualone, 159
Method, of psychology journal articles, 631–632
Method of constant stimuli, absolute threshold determined by, 106
Method of limits, absolute threshold determined by, 106, 107
Method of loci
   long-term memory and, 226
   memory improved with, 230
Method of successive approximations, instrumental learning and, 188–189
Microns, neurons and, 36
Mid-life transition, in personality development, 365
Midbrain, 51–52
Mind, introspection and, 8
   see also Brain
Mind-body question, abnormal behavior and, 476
Minnesota Multiphasic Personality Inventory (MMPI), 376, 390–392, 393
Minor tranquilizers, antianxiety agents as, 159–160
Minority, influence of on majority, 575–576
Minority groups, intelligence tests for, 384–387
"Mister Rogers' Neighborhood," 332
Mitochondria, of neuron, 36, 37, 45
Mnemonic techniques, memory improved with, 230
Mode, 617
Modeling, 204
   as behavior therapy, 522–523
   in cognitive-behavioral therapy with children, 530
   personality and, 423
Models, 473
   see also Abnormal behavior
Monitor, in regulatory system, 279
Monitoring, as coping strategy, 464
Monocular depth cues, 121–122
Monozygotic twins, 307
Mood, affective disorders and, 490–494
   see also Emotions
Moon illusion, 124
Morphemes, 246, 247–248
   mean length of utterance measured by, 327
Morphine, 167, 168
   prenatal development and, 311
Mortality rates, 345
Mortification, Jonestown massacre and, 579
Mother-child relationship. *See* Parent-child relationship
Mothers, employment of, 598–601
Motivation, 277–295
   aggression and, 291–295
   definition, 277
   drive, 278–279
   homeostasis and, 278–279
   hunger, 279–287
   regulatory systems and, 279
   thirst, 287–288
   unconscious, 409
Motivational psychologists, 6
Motives, biological and psychological, 288
   see also Motivation
Motor control, cerebral cortex and, 56–57

Motor coordination, tests of, 401
Motor development, in infancy, 315
Motor homunculus, 56, 57
Motor neuron, 35, 48, 49
Movement
    apparent, 118
    perception of, 117
    stroboscopic, 118
Müller-Lyer illusion, 125
Multi-infarct dementia, 611
Multiple personality, 481
Muscle spindle, 48
Muscle tone, on Apgar scores, 313
Myelin, 38
Myelin sheath, 44, 47
Myth of Mental Illness, The (Szasz), 476

Narcissistic personality disorder, 499–500
Narcolepsy, 151–152
    amphetamines used in, 164
Narcotics. *See* Psychoactive drugs
Narrative chaining, memory improved with, 230
Nasal half, of retina, 80
Nativism. *See* Performationism
Natural categories, concept formation and, 263
Natural selection, 8
Naturalistic observation, 10–12
    as behavioral assessment method, 402–403
Nature-nurture, intelligence and, 272–273
Needs, Thematic Apperception Test assessing, 399–400
Negative correlation, 621–622
Negative identity, in adolescence, 343
Negative reinforcement, associative learning and, 192–194
Negative triad, cognitive-behavioral treatment of depression and, 528
Negatively skewed, distribution as, 617
Neo-Freudians, 412–413
Neologisms, schizophrenia and, 481
Neonate, 313
Nervous breakdown, 479
Nervous system, 26–64
    autonomic, 30
        eating behavior and, 283–284
        stress and, 437–438
    central, 26, 27–28, *see also* Brain; Psychoactive drugs
        neurons of, 35
        spinal cord, 27–28, 31, 48–50
    coding of information in, 43–44
    functions, 30–33
        behavior, 32
        bodily maintenance, 31
        creativity, 32
        learning and memory, 31–32
        monitoring outside world, 30–31
        personality, 32–33
        thinking, 32
    neuroendocrine system and, 30
    neurons, 33–47
        action potential of, 40–44, 45–46, 47, 48–49
        all-or-none law, 42–43
        axons of, 33–34, 36, 37–38, 39, 44, 45, 47
        cell body of, 33, 36–37
        cell membrane of, 36, 39
        of central nervous system, 35
        conduction velocity, 44
    dendrites of, 33, 34, 37, 47
    information coding and, 43–44
    local-circuit, 35
    motor, 35, 48, 49
    neural conduction, 40–44
    of peripheral nervous system, 35
    projection, 34, 35
    resting potential of, 38–40
    sensory, 35, 48
    signaling by, 38–48
    synaptic terminals, 38
    synaptic transmission, 37, 44–47
    peripheral, 26, 27, 28, 30
        neurons of, 35
    reflex and, 48–49
    somatic, 28
    stress and, 437–438
Network models, of memory, 239–240
Neuroendocrine system, 30
Neuroendocrine theory, of aging, 347
Neuron. *See* Nervous system
Neuronal conduction, 40–44
Neuropsychological assessment, 401
Neurosensory Center Comprehensive Examination for Aphasia, 401
Neuroses, 417, 495
Neurotic disorders, 491, 495
    see also Abnormal behavior
Neurotransmitter substances, 38
Neurotransmitters, 45
    amphetamines and, 164, 165
    major depression and, 492
    reflex and, 49
    synaptic transmission, 46–47
Neurotrophic factors, 29
Newborns, 315
    see also Infancy
Nicotine, 156, 166–167
    see also Tobacco
Nightmares, 148–149
Node of Ranvier, 44
Noise, 89
    signal-detection theory and, 108
Nomothetic approach, to personality, 408
Nonbarbiturate sedative-hypnotic drugs, 159
Nonequivalence of category members, concept formation and, 263
Nongenetic theories, of aging, 347
Nonnegative thinking, power of, 397
Nonreversal shifts, learning and, 202–204
Nonsense syllables, memory of, 210
Nonverbal behavior, 558–559
Norepinephrine, 163
    amphetamines and, 164
    cocaine and, 165
    stress and, 438
Norm of reaction, 307
Normal frequency distribution, 619–620
Normative information, controlled observation providing, 12
Norms, 12
    in intelligence tests, 379–380
Nucleus, of cell, 307
Nutrition, infant and child development and, 308–309, 311

Obesity, 284–287

SUBJECT INDEX

amphetamines used in, 164
    tumors of the hypothalamus and, 283–284
Object permanency, infants' lack of, 320
Observation
    aggression and, 293
    controlled, 12
    experimental, 12–15
    naturalistic, 10–12, 402–404
    in scientific method, 5
Observational learning, 204—205
    personality and, 423
    see also Imitation; Modeling
Observer bias, in naturalistic observation, 403
Obsessive-compulsive disorder, 497
Occipital lobe, 50, 53, 54, 55, 80
Off-center cells, 78
Ohm's acoustical law, 89
Olfactory bulb, 50
Olfactory epithelium, 98
Olfactory system
    absolute thresholds for, 107
    adaptation of, 113
    perception of odors by, 97–99
Oligodendroglial cell body, 44
On-center cells, 78
Open-ended interview, 388
Operant conditioning, 184, 188–189
    behavior problems and, 197
    see also Associative learning; Instrumental learning
Operant procedures, in behavior therapy, 520–522
Operational structures, of cognitive development, 321
Opiates. See Psychoactive drugs
Opium, 167–168
Opponent-process theory, of color vision, 86
Optic chiasm, 50, 56, 61, 80
Optic nerve, 50, 51, 56, 70, 71, 72, 75, 78, 80
Optic radiations, 56, 80
Optic tract, 56, 80
Ora serrata, 70
Oral stage, in psychosexual development, 411, 412
Organ of Corti, 91
Organelles, of neuron, 36
Organic brain disorders, 476
Organic psychotic disorders, 491
Organization, long-term memory and, 224–226
Orgasmic, as phase of sexual arousal, 501
Orienting reflex, classic conditioning and, 182
Osmoreceptors, thirst and, 288
Ossicles, 90
Outcome expectancies
    as coping resource, 456
    personality and, 424
Outer ear, 90
Outer segment, of rod and cone, 74
Oval window, 90, 92, 97
Overgeneralization, in language development, 327
Overjustification effect, 567–568
Overload, stress due to, 444–446
Overregularization, in language development, 327
Ovum, 309

Palliative coping, 460
Paradoxical sleep, 142
Parahippocampal gyrus, 54
Parallel play, 330

Paralysis, acetylcholine lack and, 38
Paranoid personality disorder, 500
Paranoid schizophrenia, 486, 488–489
Paraphilias, 502
Parapsychology, 132
Parent, in transactional analysis, 531, 532
Parent-child relationship
    in adolescence, 339
    in childhood, 328–329
    divorce and, 596–598
    in infancy, 322–325
    language acquisition and, 256
    schizophrenia and, 484
    see also Family
Parietal lobe, 53, 54, 55, 59
Parieto-occipital sulcus, 54
Parkinson's disease, 52
Partial-reinforcement effect, 194, 196
Partial reinforcement schedule, 194
Passionate love, 556
Passive mastery, personality in adulthood and, 360
Past performance accomplishments, motivation and, 289
Pearson product-moment method, 622–623
Pedophilia, 502
Peer groups
    in adolescence, 327, 328, 329
    child development and, 329–330
Penile erections, REM sleep and, 148
Perceived control, as coping resource, 456, 457
Perception, 102–135, 349, 562
    of color, 126–128
    constancies in, 104–106
    depth, 118–123, 130
    development and modification of, 128–131
    extrasensory, 131–133
    illusions, 123–125
    in infancy, 315
    of movement, 117–118
    perceptual organization and, 115–117
    self, 566–568
    sensation and, 102–104
    sensory thresholds, 106–113
        absolute thresholds, 106–107
        adaptation of sensory systems and, 112–113
        difference thresholds, 111–112
        signal-detection theory and, 107–111
    see also Sensation; Social perception; Visual perception
Perceptual organization, 115–117
Perceptual psychologists, 6
Perceptual set, problem solving and, 259
Perfect correlation, 622
Performance, language and, 251–252
Performance-based, behavior therapy as, 518–519, see also Behavior problems, therapy for
Performationism, language acquisition and, 254, 255
Perinatal period, 313
Peripheral axon, 34
Peripheral branch, of neuron, 34
Peripheral nervous system. See Nervous system
Permissive parent, 328–329
Personal construct theory, of personality, 420
Personal space, 588–589
Personality, 389, 407–431, 561, 562
    adolescence and, 362
    adulthood and aging and, 359–365
    cognitive views of, 425–427

Personality (*cont.*)
   as coping resource, 455–456
   disorders of, 499–501
   fundamental attribution error, 561
   idiographic approach to, 408, 409
   implicit theories of, 563–564
   nervous system generating, 32
   nomotheic approach to, 408, 409
   psychoanalytic approach to, 408–414
      Freudian, 408–412
      neo-Freudians, 412–414
   self-theories of, 418–419, 420
      learning theory, 420–422
      social learning theories, 420, 422–425
   sleep and, 145
   stereotypes and, 564
   study of, 407–408, 409
   traits, 416–418, 426–427
      inferring, 559–561
      situational influences versus, 427–430
   Type A, 455–456
   Type B, 455–456
   typological approach and constitutional psychology, 414–416
   see also under Behavior; Personality tests
Personality psychologists, 6
Personality tests, 389–400
   objective measures, 389, 391–396
      California Psychological Inventory (CPI), 392–394
      Minnesota Multiphasic Personality Inventory, 389, 391–392, 393
      single-dimension self-report inventories, 394–396
   projective measures, 396–400
      Draw-A-Person test, 400
      Rorschach Inkblots, 376, 398
      Thematic Apperception Test, 399–400
Perspective cue, for depth perception, 121
Persuasion, attitude change and, 549–552
Petit mal epilepsy, amphetamines used in, 164
Phallic stage, psychosexual development and, 411, 412
Phenobarbital, 159
Phenomenal field, Rogers on, 418
Phenothiazines, for psychoses, 540–541
Phenotype, 308
Pheromones, 99
Phi phenomenon, 118
Phobic disorders, 496–497
Phonemes, 246–247
Phonological encoding, long-term memory and, 219–220
Photons, 69
Photopic vision, 74
Photopigment, of rod and cone, 74
Phrases, 247, 248–250
Physical attractiveness, interpersonal attraction and, 557
Physical dependence, 157
   see also Psychoactive drugs
Physical exercise. *See* Exercise
Physical growth. *See* Growth
Pigment, 74
Pigment epithelium, 72, 73
Pitch, of sound, 88
Pituitary gland, 51
   stress and, 437
Place theory of hearing, 92–93
Placenta, 310
Plasticity, mature brain and, 29
Plateau, as phase of sexual arousal, 501

Play
   attachment in infancy and, 323
   child development and, 330–331
   symbolic, 320
Pleasure principle, id and, 410
Polygraph, in sleep research, 140
Pons, 50–51
Ponzo illusion, 123
Populations, inferential statistics and, 624
Pornography, aggression and, 294
Position senses, 95–97
Positive correlation, 621, 622
Positive reinforcement
   associative learning and, 192–194
   in therapy for depression, 520–521
Positively skewed, distribution as, 617
Post-traumatic stress syndrome (PTSS), 441
Posthypnotic amnesia, 155
Posthypnotic suggestion, hypnosis and, 155
Postpubescent stage, 340
Postsynaptic cell, 47
Postsynaptic element, 45, 46
Postsynaptic membrane, 46, 47
Postsynaptic motor neuron, reflex and, 49
Posture
   catatonic schizophrenia and, 486
   emotion and, 297
Potassium ions
   resting potential and, 39–40, 42
   synaptic transmission and, 46
Precognition, 132
Predictive validity, 378
Pregnancy
   adolescents and, 314, 344–345
   psychoactive drugs and, 166
   social support as coping resource in, 458
   see also Prenatal development
Prejudice, of jury, 605–606
Prelinguistic period, of language development, 326–327
Premarital intercourse, adoelscents and, 344–345
Premature ejaculation, 502
Prenatal development, 309–314
   birth, 313–314
   embryo, 310
   fetus, 310–311
   influences on, 311, 313
   ovum, 309
   see also Pregnancy
Preoperational stage, of cognitive development, 320–321, 322
Prepubescent phase, 339, 340
Presbyopia, aging and, 349
Preschool intervention, intelligence improved by, 273–274
Presynaptic element, 45
Presynaptic membrane, 46
Presynaptic terminals, reflex and, 49
Primary appraisal, of stress, 451, 452–453
Primary effect, distinction between short- and long-term memory and, 231, 232
Primary mental abilities, 267
Primary process, id and, 410
Primary reinforcement, associative learning and, 191–192
Primary sexual characteristics, 340
Primates
   language taught to, 255
   visual system of, 120
Principles, learning of, 201–202

SUBJECT INDEX

Principles of Psychology, The (James), 8
Proactive interference, retrieval in long-term memory and, 229
Problem-focused coping, 460
Problem solving, 257–267
   attachment in infancy and, 322
   coping based on, 460
   group dynamics and, 583–585
   learning behavior for, 202–204
Procedure, in method section of psychology journal article, 632
Process disorder, 491
   see also Abnormal behavior
Product-moment coefficient, 622–623
Production
   of language, 252–253
   problem solving and, 260
Programmed instruction, 197
Programmed texts, 197
Projection, as defense mechanism, 462
Projection neurons, 34, 35
Projective measures. *See* Personality tests
Prosocial behavior, television fostering, 332
Proximity, perceptual organization and, 116
Psychedelics, 158, 169–172
Psychic determinism, 409–410
Psychoactive drugs, 156–173
   for behavioral problems, 540–541
   behavioral stimulants, 158, 163–167
      amphetamines, 163–165
      caffeine, 165–166
      cocaine, 156, 165
      nicotine, 166–167
   definition, 157
   opiates and narcotics, 158, 167–169
      heroin, 168–169
      opium, 167–168
   physical dependence on, 157
   pregnancy and, 166
   psychedelics and hallucinogens, 158, 169–172
      LSD, 169–171
   sedative-hypnotic drugs, 158–163
      alcohol, 150, 156, 157, 160–163, 197, 311, 503–504
      antianxiety agents, 159–160
      barbiturates, 150, 158–159
      nonbarbiturates, 159
   synergistic effect and, 159
   tolerance to, 157
Psychoanalysis, 8, 511–514
   Freudian, 408–412
   neo-Freudian, 412–414
   psychodynamic model of abnormal behavior and, 474–475
Psychodynamics
   abnormal behavior and, 474–475
   anxiety-related disorders and, 497
   major depression and, 493
Psychological dependence, on caffeine, 166
Psychological disturbances. *See* Abnormal behavior
Psychological laboratory, James and, 8
Psychological motives, 288
   see also Motivation
Psychological stress. *See* Stress
Psychological therapies. *See* Behavior problems, therapy for
Psychologists, 5, 10
   types of, 6–7
Psychology, 610
   definition, 4
   ethical considerations in, 17–19
   history of, 5, 8–10
   as science, 5, *see also* Scientific method
   subject matter of, 5
Psychology journals
   listing of, 634–635
   writing article for, 629–633
Psychometricians, 7, 10
Psychopaths, 500
Psychoses, 491
   drug treatment for, 540
Psychosexual development, 411–412
Psychosexual disorders, 501–502
Psychosocial development, 413–414
Psychosurgery, for behavior problems, 541–542
Puberty, 339–340
   see also Adolescence
Pubescent phase, 339
Publication Manual of the American Psychological Association, 630, 633
Punishment, associative learning and, 193–194
Pupil (of eye), 70

Questionnaires, 15–17

Race, intelligence and, 272–273
Random sampling, inferential statistics and, 624
Range, 618
Rapid-eye movement (REM) sleep, 142–143, 146–148
Rarefaction, sound and, 88, 89
Rational emotive therapy (RET), 525–528
Rationalization, as defense mechanism, 462
Raven's Progressive Matrices, 384, 385
Reaction formation, as defense mechanism, 463
Reaction time (RT)
   aging and, 352–353
   retrieval from short-term memory and, 217, 218
Reality principle, ego and, 410
Reality therapy, 530–531
Reasoning, 263–266
   tests of, 401
Recall clustering, long-term memory and, 224
Receiver operating characteristic curve (ROC), 109–110
Recency effect
   distinction between short- and long-term memory and, 231, 232
   short-term memory measured by, 353
Receptive field, in visual system, 77–78, 79
Receptor cells, of retina, 70, 72–74, 78
Reciprocal determinism, personality and, 424–425
Reconstructive hypothesis, of memory, 236–238
Red-green color blindness, 86–87
Reference group, 573–574
Reference, of psychology journal articles, 633
Reflex irritability, on Apgar scores, 313
Reflexes, 27, 28, 48–49
   in infancy, 315
Reframing, in family therapy, 534
Regression
   as defense mechanism, 463
   hypnotic, 155
   psychosexual development and, 412
Rehearsal
   in long-term memory, 221, 223, 224
   memory improved with, 230

Reinforcement
  aggression and, 293
  classical conditioning and, 184
  instrumental learning and, 187
  language acquisition and, 253, 254
  in learning process, 421
  positive, 192–194, 520–521
  response contingent positive, 493
  schedules of, 194, 196–197
  token economy and, 521–522
  see also Associative learning
Relative deprivation, 573
Relative size, for depth perception, 121
Relaxation training
  rational emotive therapy versus, 528
  in systematic desensitization, 519–520
Reliability of tests, 376–377
  correlation and, 620–623
Remembering, 210
  see also Memory
Representational ability, in preoperational stage, 320
Repression, as defense mechanism, 462, 463
Research report. *See* Psychology journals
Residual schizophrenia, 490
Resistance, in psychoanalysis, 512
Resistance stage, in general adaptation syndrome, 436, 437
Resolution, as stage of sexual arousal, 501
Respiratory effort, on Apgar scores, 313
Response (R), 8
  instrumental learning and, 185
  learning and, 210, 421
Response acquisition, associative learning and, 189–190
Response bias, signal detection and, 108
Response-class matrix, for behavioral assessment, 402, 403
Response contingent reinforcement, major depression and, 493
Response set, problem solving and, 258–259
Resting potential, of neurons, 38–40
Results, of psychology journal articles, 632
Retest reliability, 376
  correlation and, 620–623
Retina. *See* Visual system
Retrieval. *See* Memory
Retrieval cues, in long-term memory, 227
Retroactive interference, retrieval in long-term memory and, 229
Retrograde amnesia, 144
Reversal shifts, learning and, 202–204
Reversible figures, 124, 125
Reward values, personality and, 422–423
Rhodopsin, 74
Rhyming, memory improved with, 230
Ribonucleic acid (RNA), 307
Rigidity, problem solving and, 258–259
Rod receptor cells, 71, 72, 73, 74
Role
  adolescence and, 342–343
  social, 585–588
Role playing
  behavior assessed with, 404
  in behavior therapy, 518–519
  in cognitive-behavioral therapies, 524
Role-taking, play fostering, 330
Rooting reflex, 315
Rorschach Inkblot Test, 376, 398
Round window, 90, 97
Rubella, prenatal development and, 313
Rule learning, concept formation and, 261–262

Saccule, 97
SADS (Schedule for Affective Disorders and Schizophrenia), 388
Salty, as taste, 98
Sample means, comparing, 625–626
Sample size, inferential statistics and, 624
Samples, inferential statistics and, 624
Satiety, signals for, 282–283
Saturation, color and, 126, 127
Scatter plot, 621–622
Schachter-Singer theory, of emotion, 297–298
Schedules of reinforcement, 194, 196–197
Schema theory, of memory, 242–243
Schemata, 198–199
  personality and, 426
  Piaget on, 319
Schizophrenia, 481–490
  dopamine lack and, 38
  phenothiazines for, 540–541
Schizotaxia, 485
Schizotypy, 485
Scholastic Achievement Tests (SAT), 387
Science
  psychology as, 5, *see also* Scientific method
  social policy and, 593–595
Scientific communication. *See* Psychology journals
Scientific method, 5
  controlled observation, 12
  experimental observation, 12–15
  naturalistic observation, 10–12
  questionnaires and/or interviews, 15–17
Scientific psychology, 8
Sclera, 70
Scopolomine, 144
Scotopic vision, 74
Scripts, in transactional analysis, 532
Seashore Rhythm Test, 401
Second language, acquisition of, 254
Second order factors, for fluid and crystallized intelligence, 269, 270
Secondary appraisal, of stress, 451–453
Secondary process, ego and, 410
Secondary reinforcement, associative learning and, 192
Secondary sexual characteristics, 340
Sedative-hypnotic drugs. *See* Psychoactive drugs
Selective attention, stereotypes and, 564–565
Selective interpretation, stereotypes and, 565
Selectively permeable, neuron membrane as, 39–40
Self-actualization, 418–419
Self-concept, development of, 317
Self-efficacy
  motivation and, 289
  personality and, 424
Self-fulfilling prophecies
  body build and behavior, 416
  stereotypes and, 565–566
Self-help, as therapy, 533
Self-instructional training, in cognitive-behavioral therapy with children, 530
Self-justification, Jonestown massacre and, 579
Self-management system, major depression and, 493–494
Self-monitoring
  as behavioral assessment method, 403–404
  cognitive-behavioral treatment of depression and, 528–529
Self-perception, 566–568
Self-perception theory, foot-in-the-door effect and, 577
Self-schema, personality and, 426

SUBJECT INDEX

Self-serving attribution bias, 562–563
Self-theories, of personality, 418–419, 420
Semantic encoding, in long-term memory, 219–220
Semantic memory, 239, 240–241
Semantically rich domains, problem solving and, 260
Semicircular canals, 97
Senile dementia, 610–613
Sensation, 65–68
    adequate stimulus for, 66–67
    cerebral cortex and, 55
    doctrine of specific nerve energies and, 67–68
    in infancy, 315
    memory and, 213–215
    perception and, 102–104
    stimulus and sensory response and, 67
    see also Auditory system; Olfactory system; Perception; Taste; Touch; Visual system
Senses. *See* Sensation
Sensorimotor construction, tests of, 401
Sensorimotor stage
    Piaget on, 319–320, 322
    test of in infant, 317, 318
Sensory homunculus, 55, 57
Sensory memory, 213–215, 353
Sensory neuron, 35, 48
Sensory psychologists, 6
Sensory registers, 213–215
Sensory systems. *See* Perception; Sensation
Sensory thresholds. *See* Perception
Sentences, in language development, 247, 248–250, 327–328
Serial position curve, distinction between short- and long-term memory and, 231–232
"Sesame Street," 332
Set point
    for body weight, 280, 284, 285
    in regulatory system, 279
Settling down, in personality development, 365
Sex, determination of, 306–307
Sex chromosomes, 306–307
Sex differences
    in adulthood, 360
    in language development, 327
Sexual dysfunction, 501–502
Sexual preference, disorders of, 502
Sexuality
    in adolescence, 343–345
    aging and, 350–351
    arousal phases, 501
    dysfunctions, 501–502
    preferences, 502
    psychosexual development and, 411–412
    see also Intercourse
Shape constancy, 104–105
Shaping
    for assertion training, 521
    instrumental learning and, 188–189
Shock phase, in general adaptation syndrome, 436, 437
Shock therapy. *See* Electroconvulsive therapy
Short-term memory. *See* Memory
Sight. *See* Visual system
Signal-detection theory, 107–111
Significance of a difference, inferential statistics and, 624–627
Similarity
    liking process and, 555–556
    perceptual organization and, 116–117
Simple cortical cells, 81

Simple reflex. *See* Reflexes
Simple RT tasks, aging and, 352
Simultaneous pairing, classic conditioning and, 182
Single-dimension self-inventories, of personality, 394–396
Situation-specific approach, behavioral assessment as, 402
Situational influences, on personality, 427–430
Size constancy, 105
Skewness, slanted distribution ad, 617
Skinner Box, 188–189
Sleep, 138–153
    caffeine and, 166
    dreaming and, 145–149
        eye movements and, 146–147
        memory of, 147
        nightmares, 148–149
    in infancy, 316
    memory retention and, 144
    pathologies of, 149–153
        insomnia, 149–150
        narcolepsy, 151–152, 164
        sleeping pills, 150–151
        sleepwalking, 153
    patterns of, 143, 145
    reasons for, 138–139
    REM (active), 142–143, 146–148
    research techniques for, 139–140
    sedative-hypnotic drugs and. *See* Psychoactive drugs
    stages of, 139, 140–142
Sleep spindles, 141
Sleeping pills, 150–151
    barbiturates, 158–159
Sleepwalking, 153
Smell. *See* Olfactory system
Smoking. *See* Nicotine
Social attitudes. *See* Attitudes
Social aversion, schizophrenia and, 482
Social comparison theory, 572, 573
Social deprivation. *See* Deprivation
Social development
    in childhood, 328–331
    in infancy, 322–325
    see also Parent-child relationship; Peer group; Play
Social drift hypothesis, schizophrenia and, 485
Social facilitation, 581–582
Social influence, 571–581
    bystander behavior in emergencies and, 576–577
    conformity and, 574–576
    Jonestown massacre and, 578
    minority influence and, 575–576
    reference groups and, 573–574
    social comparison and, 572, 573
Social isolation
    child abuse and, 602
    deprivation and, 322–325
    personality in young adulthood and, 362
Social learning, 204, 205
    aggression and, 293
    schizotypy and, 485
Social learning theory, of personality, 420, 422–425
Social loafing, 582
Social perception, 558–566
    biases in, 561–563
    emotions inferred in, 558–559
    implicit theories of personality and, 563–564
    personality traits inferred in, 559–561
    survival of false beliefs and, 564–566

Social policy, role of psychology in, 593–595
Social problems, social policy on, 594–595
Social psychology, 6–7, 547
   see also Attitudes; Group dynamics; Social influence; Social perception
Social Readjustment Rating Scale (SRRS), 446, 447
Social referencing, by infant, 317
Social roles, 585–588
Social support, as coping resource, 457–460
Sociobiology
   aggression and, 291–292
   motivation and, 289
Sociodramatic play, 330
Socioeconomic status
   child abuse and, 602
   schizophrenia and, 485
Sociopaths, 500
Sodium ions, synaptic transmission and, 45–46
Sodium-potassium pump mechanism, 42
Solitary play, 330
Somatic mutation theory, of aging, 347
Somatic system, 28
Somatoform disorders, 498
Somatosensory areas, 55
Somatosensory system, 55–56, 57
Somatotypes, personality based on, 414–416
Somnambulism, 153
Sound, 87–89
   localization of, 94–95
   see also Auditory system
Sour, as taste, 98
Source traits, of personality, 417–418
Space. See Personal space
Spatial frequency filter, of visual perception, 81, 83–84, 85
Specific nerve energies, doctrine of, 67–68
Spectral sensitivity curves, 84, 85
Speech. See Language
Speeded tasks, aging and, 352–353
Spinal cord, 27–28, 31, 49–50
   reflex and, 48–49
   see also Nervous system
Spinal nerve, 28
Split-brain research, 60–61
Spontaneous recovery, associative learning and, 190
Spreading activation model, of memory, 241
Squid, giant axons of, 39
Stability, as personality trait, 417
Stage 1 sleep, 140–141
Stage 2 sleep, 141, 142
Stage 3 sleep, 141, 142
Stage 4 sleep, 141, 142
Stage theory of development, 317
   Piaget on, 317–322
Stagnation, personality in adulthood and, 362
Standard deviation (SD), 618–619
Standard score, 620
Standardization, in intelligence tests, 379
Stanford Binet Intelligence Scale, 376, 380–381
Stanford Prison study, 585–587
Stapes, 90, 92
State-Trait Anxiety Inventory (STAI), 395–396
Statistical tests, hypotheses tested with, 626–627
Statistics, 17, 615–627
   descriptive, 615–623
      correlation, 620–623
      frequency distributions, 616
      measures of central tendency, 616–617
      measures of variability, 618–619
      normal frequency distribution, 619–620
   inferential, 623–627
      hypothesis testing and, 625–627
      population, 624
      sample means comparison and, 625–626
      samples, 624
      statistical tests and, 626–627
Stellazine, 541
Stereoscopic vision, 118–123
Stereotypes
   of personality, 564
   of somatotypes, 416
   survival of false beliefs and, 564–566
Stimulants, behavioral. See Psychoactive drugs
Stimulus (S), 8
   adequate, 66–67
   classical conditioning and, 181–184
   instrumental learning and, 185, 186
   learning and, 210
Stimulus generalizaton gradient, 191
Stimulus-response (S-R) connections, 8, 10
Stomach factors, eating behavior regulated by, 281, 282
Storage. See Memory
Stress, 435–465
   appraising, 451–453
      primary appraisal, 451, 452–453
      secondary appraisal, 451–453
   coping resources and, 454–460
      beliefs about, 456–457
      personality, 455–456
      physical and cognitive, 454–455
      social support, 457–460
      utilitarian, 454
   coping responses and, 454, 460–465
      defense mechanisms, 462–463
      effectiveness of, 462–464
      goodness of fit and, 464–465
   general adaptation syndrome and, 436–439
   health and, 446–454
      causality and process and, 449–450
      life events and, 446–449
   hormonal release and, 31
   nature of, 436–440
   schizophrenia and, 484–485
   sources of
      conflict, 442–444, 445
      harm, 440–441, 442
      load, 444–446
      threat, 441–442, 443
Stroboscopic movement, 118
Structuralism, 8
Structure, of intelligence, 266–267, 269
Structured interview, 388
Strychnine, 159
Subcortical brain regions, 53
Subjective organization, long-term memory and, 224–225
Subjects, in method section of psychology journal article, 631–632
Sublimation, as defense mechanism, 463
Substance abuse, 503
   see also Psychoactive drugs
Substance dependence, 503
Substantia nigra, 52
Subtractive color mixture, 128

SUBJECT INDEX

Suggestibility, hypnosis and, 154–155
Suicide, major depression and, 492
Sulci(us), 53, 54, 55
Superego, 410–411
Superior colliculi, 51, 56
Suppression, as defense mechanism, 462
Surface structure, of a sentence, 249, 250, 251
Surface traits, of personality, 417–418
Surgent growth, in adolescent period, 338
Survival of the fittest, 8
Sweet, as taste, 98
Syllogisms, 264–265
Symbolic play, in preoperational stage, 320
Sympathetic chain, 28
Synapse, 45
Synaptic cleft, 45, 47
Synaptic plasticity, 29
Synaptic terminal, 38, 46, 47
Synaptic transmission, 37, 44–47
Synaptic vesicles, 45, 46
Synergistic effect, drugs and, 159
Syntax, 248
System of Multicultural Pluralistic Assessment (SOMPA), 387
System variable, in regulatory system, 279
Systematic desensitization, 519–520
Systems/communication approach, in family therapy, 534

T-groups, 533
t test, 626
Tabula rasa, 66
Tactile perception. *See* Touch
Tailored testing. *See* Adaptive testing
Tapetum, 73
Tardive dyskinesia, 541
Taste, sense of, 97–99
   absolute thresholds for, 107
   in infancy, 315
Taste-aversion learning, 282
Taste buds, 98
Taste potentiation, 98
Tay-Sachs disease, 37
Taylor Manifest Anxiety Scale (TMAS), 395
Teaching machines, associative learning and, 197
Tectorial membrane, 91, 92
Tectum, 51
Tegmentum, 51, 52
Telegraphic sentences, 327
Telepathy, 132
Television
   aggression and, 293, 331
   attitude change and, 500–551
   child development and, 331–332
   prosocial behavior and, 332
Temperature, adaptation to, 113
Temperment, somatotype with, 415
Temporal, half, of retina, 80
Temporal lobe, 50, 53, 54, 55, 58–59
Teratogens, prenatal development and, 311
Test-retest reliability, 376
Tests, 373–404
   adaptive, 381
   of aptitude and achievement, 387–388
   of behavior, 402–404
   cognitive assessment, 397
   goal of, 404–405

   history of, 375
   interview and, 388
   neuropsychological, 401
   of psychometricians, 7
   reliability of, 376–377
   validity of, 377, 378
   see also Intelligence tests; Personality tests
Texture gradients, as monocular depth cue, 121–122
Thalamus, 51, 53, 55
   lateral geniculate nucleus of, 80
Thalidomide, prenatal development and, 311
Thanatos, aggression and, 291
Thematic Apperception Test (TAT), 376, 399–400
Theory of odor, 98
Therapies for behavior problems. *See* Behavior problems, therapy for
Thiopental, 159
Thirst, 287–288
Thought, 256–265
   cognitive development and, 317–322
   concept formation and, 260–263
   problem solving and, 257–260
   reasoning and, 263–266
Threat, stress due to, 441–442, 443
Three-dimensional space, perception of, 118–123
Thresholds
   absolute, 106–107
   difference, 111–112
   neural conduction and, 40, 41, 42
   sensory. *See* Perception
Timbre of a sound, 89
Title, of psychology journal article, 630
Tobacco, prenatal development and, 311
   see also Nicotine
Toileting, in infancy, 316
Token economy, 197, 521–522
Token Test, 401
Tolerance, substance dependence and, 503
Tongue, taste buds on, 98
Touch
   absolute thresholds for, 107
   adaptation to, 113
   sense of, 95, 96
   tests of, 401
"Tower of Hanoi" puzzle, 259
Toxemia, prenatal development and, 313
Trait anxiety
   measures of, 430
   tests of, 395–396
Traits. *See* Personality
Tranquilizers, for anxiety, 540
Transactional analysis (TA), 531–532
Transcendental meditation, 173
Transduction
   in retina, 71, 74–78
   of sound, 90–94
Transference, in psychoanalysis, 512
Transformation, problem solving and, 259
Transitive inferences, 265
Transmissiveness, aging and, 348
Traveling wave, 92
Trephining, 470
Trial Making Test, 401
Trichromatic theory, of color vision, 86
Tricyclics, for depression, 540
Trust vs. mistrust, 413

SUBJECT INDEX

Tumultuous growth, in adolescent period, 338
Two-point threshold, 95, 96
Tympanic canal, 91
Type A behavior pattern, 455–456
Type B behavior pattern, 455–456
Typological approach, to personality, 414–416

Ultraviolet light, 69
Umbilical cord, 310
Unconditional positive regard, in client-centered therapy, 514
Unconditional response (UCR), classic conditioning and, 182–183
Unconditional stimulus (UCS), classic conditioning and, 181–184
Unconscious
  collective, 413
  psychoanalysis involving, 511
  in psychodynamic model of abnormal behavior, 474–475
Unconscious motivation, 409
Underload, stress due to, 444–446
Undifferentiated crying, as vocalization stage, 326
Undifferentiated schizophrenia, 489–490
Unemployment, social support as coping resource in, 458–459
Unipolar factors, of emotion, 300
Unique colors, 126, 127
Utilitarian resources, as coping resource, 454
Utricle, 97

Valid syllogism, 264–265
Validity, of tests, 377, 378
Valium, 160, 540
Variable
  dependent, 13–15
  independent, 13, 14
Variable ratio (VR) schedule, of reinforcement, 196
Variance, 618–619
Ventral root, 28, 48, 50
Ventromedial hypothalamus (VMH), obesity and lesion of, 283
Verbal persuasion, motivation and, 289
Vertebra, 28
Vestibular canal, 91
Vestibular nerve, 90
Vestibular sacs, 96
Vestibular system, 96–97
Vestibule, 90
Viable, fetus as, 310
Vicarious learning
  aggression and, 293
  motivation and, 289
Violence, spatial preferences and, 589
  see also Aggression
Visible light, 68–69
Vision. See Visual system
Visual cliff apparatus, 129
Visual cortex, 56, 80

Visual encoding
  in long-term memory, 219
  in short-term memory, 216
Visual perception, 114–117
  development of, 128–130
  modification of, 130–131
Visual pigment, 74
Visual sensory memory, 214–215
Visual system, 68–87
  absolute thresholds for vision and, 107
  aging and, 347–350
  blind spot, 73, 75
  camera/eye comparison, 69–71
  cerebral cortex and, 55, 56
  electromagnetic spectrum and visible light and, 68–69
  eye structure, 69–71, see also retina, below
  in infancy, 315
  of primate, 120
  receptive field of, 77–78, 79
  retina, 70, 71–78
    color vision and, 84–87
    receptor cells of, 70, 72–74, 78
    transduction and, 71, 74–78
    visual pathway to cortex from, 78, 80
  spatial frequency filter model and, 81, 83–84, 85
  vestibular system and, 97
  visual pathways from eye to cortex, 78, 80–81
  see also Perception
Vitreous body, 70
Vitreous humor, 71
Vocalization, in language development, 326–327
Vocational psychologists, 7
Volley theory, of hearing, 93–94
Volumetric receptors, blood volume detected by, 288

Warm-cold study, implicit theories of personality and, 563
Wear and tear theory, of aging, 347
Weber fraction, 111–112
Weber's law, 111–112
Wechsler scales of intelligence. See Intelligence
Weight control, amphetamines used in, 164
Wernicke's aphasia, 59
Wernicke's area, 58
Withdrawal, substance dependence and, 503
Women, employment of married, 598–601
Working (short-term) memory. See Memory

YAVIS, in psychological therapy, 539

Z score, 620
Zen meditation, 173
Zero correlation, 622
Zygote, 309